CORPORATE FINANCE

THEORY AND PRACTICE

CORPORATE FINANCE

THEORY AND PRACTICE

ASWATH DAMODARAN

STERN SCHOOL OF BUSINESS
NEW YORK UNIVERSITY

 JOHN WILEY & SONS, INC.
NEW YORK CHICHESTER BRISBANE TORONTO SINGAPORE WEINHEIM

ACQUISITIONS EDITOR   Whitney Blake
DEVELOPMENTAL EDITOR   Rachel Nelson
MARKETING MANAGER   Wendy Goldner
SENIOR PRODUCTION EDITOR   Jeanine Furino
SENIOR DESIGNER   Ann Marie Renzi
ASSISTANT MANUFACTURING MANAGER   Mark Cirillo
ILLUSTRATION EDITOR   Sigmund Malinowski
EDITORIAL ASSISTANCE   Pui Szeto, Jeri-Lynn Caliendo

COVER   Designer: David Levy
         Photograph: Deborah Davis/Tony Stone Images, New York, Inc.

This book was set in Times Ten Roman by Carlisle Communication and printed and bound by R. R. Donnelley & Sons. The cover was printed by Phoenix Color Corp.

Library of Congress Cataloging in Publication Data:
Author's name entry.
Brief title entry: Subtitle, if any
L.C. Call no.   Dewey Classification No.   L.C. Card No.
ISBN 0-471-07680-5
Printed in the United States of America
10 9 8 7 6 5 4 3 2 1

DEDICATION

This book is dedicated to Michele,
whose patience and support made it possible,
and to Ryan, Brendan, and Kendra,
who helped in their own way.

ABOUT THE AUTHOR

Aswath Damodaran received his MBA and Ph.D. from the University of California at Los Angeles. His research interests include the examination of market efficiency, the effects of information and market structure characteristics, equity valuation, and issues in real estate investing. He has published in the *Journal of Financial and Quantitative Analysis,* the *Journal of Finance* and the *Review of Financial Studies* and has written two widely used books on valuation—*Damodaran on Valuation* and *Investment Valuation*—both published by John Wiley and Sons.

Dr. Damodaran was a visiting lecturer at the University of California, Berkeley, from 1984 to 1986, where he received the Earl Cheit Outstanding Teaching Award in 1985. He has been at New York University since 1986, where he received the Stern School of Business Excellence in Teaching Award (awarded by the graduating class) in 1988, 1991, and 1992, and was the youngest winner of the university-wide Distinguished Teaching Award, in 1990. He was profiled in *BusinessWeek* as one of the top twelve business school professors in the United States in 1994.

PREFACE

Corporate finance covers any decisions made by firms which have financial implications. Thus, there is a corporate financial aspect to almost every action taken by a firm, no matter which functional area claims responsibility for it. There are three basic questions that corporate finance attempts to answer:

1. How should the firm's scarce resources be allocated? (*Investment Decisions*)
2. How should these investments be financed? In particular, should the owners use their own funds (equity) or should they borrow money (debt)? (*Financing Decisions*)
3. How much, if any, of the cash flows generated by these investments should be returned to the owners and how much should be reinvested? (*Dividend Decisions*)

The value of the firm reflects its success in each of these three areas. Firms that allocate resources to "good" projects, finance them with the "appropriate mix" of debt and equity, and reinvest the "right amount" back into operations will have higher value than firms that fail on any or all of these criteria. Notice that there is nothing in this description that presupposes that firms are large or publicly traded or that financial markets function efficiently. While these characteristics may simplify corporate financial analysis, the fundamental principles of corporate finance apply to all firms—small and large, private and public, domestic and foreign.

There is only one way to learn corporate finance well, and that is by analyzing real companies with real problems. Consequently, throughout this book we use extended applications involving two companies—the Home Depot and Boeing—to illustrate principles. We also use other companies selectively through the book to illustrate specific problems. The applications developed here are not mere addendum to models but are an integral part of explaining and developing them.

Intended Audience and Purpose

In keeping with the encompassing definition of corporate finance given above, this book is designed for a wide audience. First and foremost, it is written for an introductory course in corporate finance at the MBA level. It may also be appropriate for use in more rigorous undergraduate programs at the junior or senior level. Obviously, it will be most useful for those who plan to make a living in corporate finance, whether in corporations, investment banks, or management consulting firms. At the same time, those in other areas of business—be it marketing, production, or organizational behavior—should find the tools and principles developed here of use in their chosen fields. Finally, there are several parts of this book that would be useful to small business owners and entrepreneurs looking for ways to improve their understanding of the financial aspects of their businesses.

A wide range of books on corporate finance are currently available. First, there are the "nuts and bolts" books, which essentially focus on working through problems and exercises. They do not raise provocative questions or provide closure on complicated questions. Next, there are the "big picture" books that provide readers with the state of the art in corporate finance and a tantalizing vision of things to come. Finally, there are the "practitioner" books that focus on corporate financial tools and techniques and pay little attention to the underlying theory. This book is my attempt to find common ground between theory, applications, and examples, and to provide a guide for those who not only want to practice corporate finance but to understand it well enough to develop their own models as they do so.

I believe that this book's primary strength is its focus on applying complex theory to real firms, while minimizing the compromises that inevitably have to be made in the process. I have also tried to maintain a balance between immersing readers in the details of corporate financial analysis—the tools and techniques that are used on a day to day basis—and the big picture of corporate finance that allows them to see how these tools and techniques fit together and what the common principles are that apply across all of them.

Organization

This book is organized into six parts. The first part provides an *introduction* to corporate finance, starting with the description of corporate finance in Chapter 1 and extending to a discussion in Chapter 2 of the objective of maximizing stockholder wealth, which provides the basis for much of modern corporate finance. The next four chapters provide the basic tools of corporate finance—present value principles and formulae in Chapter 3, basic accounting principles and financial statement analysis in Chapter 4, and models for measuring and rewarding risk in Chapters 5 and 6.

The second part of the book looks at the *investment decision*. In Chapter 7 we introduce the basic decision rules available—some based on accounting income and some on cash flows—and examine their strengths and weaknesses. In Chapter 8 we consider the process of estimating cash flows in a project. In Chapter 9 we examine the effects of having limited access to capital on project choice, as well as ways of choosing among mutually exclusive projects. In Chapters 10 and 11 we present ways of dealing with uncertainty in investment analysis, and in Chapter 12 we explore the capital budgeting process itself by looking at what makes a project a good project and ways of following up on projects after they have been chosen. In Chapter 13 we consider a special category of investment analysis—leasing—and examine the issues that are specific to it. Finally, in Chapter 14 we consider an important aspect of investment analysis by looking at investments in working capital.

The third section of the book examines the *financing decision*. In Chapter 15 we consider the financing choices firms have to make in raising funds in both private and public markets. In Chapter 16 we evaluate some lessons that can be learned from studies of market efficiency by firms considering which types of financing to use and when to use them. In Chapter 17 we establish the basic tradeoff on the use of debt—the tax benefits and discipline that debt creates, on the one hand, against the bankruptcy risk and loss of flexibility that may result from using too much debt on the other. We also examine the specific conditions under which debt is irrelevant. In Chapter 18 we introduce several practical approaches that can be used to determine the optimal debt ratio for a firm and consider their limitations. In Chapter 19 we provide a framework for determining the right kind of financing for a firm—short term versus long term, fixed rate versus floating rate—based upon its asset mix.

The fourth section of the book examines *how much cash to return to the owners of the business and the best way to do so*. In Chapter 20 we examine the most common approach for returning cash to stockholders—cash dividends—and the issues that have to be weighed in deciding how much to pay in dividends. In Chapter 21 we develop a framework for analyzing a firm's cash flows and coming up with the appropriate amount to return to its stockholders. Finally, in Chapter 22 we expand our discussion to examine whether the cash should be returned in the form of dividends, equity repurchases, or forward contracts to buy back stock.

The fifth section of the book links the investment, financing, and dividend decisions to the *value of the firm*. Chapter 23 provides an introduction to discounted cash flow models for value and relative valuation models (such as multiples) and the reasons for the differences between the two approaches. Chapter 24 extends this discussion to look at corporate restructuring effects on value and value enhancement strategies being adopted by many firms. Chapter 25 discusses the special issues relating to valuing mergers, including the value of control and synergy.

The final section looks at a diverse set of topics. Chapter 26 examines additional issues, such as currency and political risk, that arise as a consequence of investing in foreign markets. Chapters 27 and 28 develop the basics of option pricing and applications of option pricing models in corporate finance, including the options to expand and delay projects in investment analysis and the value of flexibility in financing decisions. Chapter 29 examines whether and how firms should manage risk, and Chapter 30 expands on the use of corporate financial models for small and private companies.

Pedagogical Features

Each chapter begins with a bulleted overview that describes the issues that will be examined in the chapter and goes on to develop the theory before moving on to *In Practice applications* of a few companies that are used repeatedly throughout the book (Home Depot and Boeing, among others). To aid retention, *important concepts, principles,* and *equations* are highlighted, and key terms are defined in a *running glossary* throughout the book. *Concept checks* appear after each new topic is introduced, inviting the student to consider an applicable question and test his or her understanding of the concept before moving on. Each chapter ends with a *conclusion* that summarizes the key lessons from the chapter. In keeping with the view that corporate finance can be learned only by doing, exercises are included at the end of each chapter, ranging from short concept *questions* to extended *problems*. The solutions to the odd-numbered questions and problems are provided at the end of the book.

Supplements Package

It is my hope that the extended examples in this book will induce readers to try out the theory on other companies. By doing so, they will not only increase their understanding of the limitations of the theory but also learn how to adapt it for use in the real world. To make this process easier, a diskette containing spreadsheets that were used to generate the applications in this book is available. Readers can use these spreadsheets to analyze a project, examine the optimal debt ratio for a firm, estimate how much cash it has available to pay out to stockholders, and value the firm. Additional supplements to accompany *Corporate Finance: Theory and Practice* include the following.

The *Instructor's Resource Guide* with Solutions was prepared by John Shao of Oklahoma City University. It contains sample syllabi, teaching notes, additional resources, and complete solutions to all end-of-chapter text material.

The *Test Bank*, authored by Troy Adair of Hofstra University and George Kutner of Marquette University, contains over 1000 questions, including problems, true/false, multiple-choice, and essay questions. A full-featured computerized test bank is also available in IBM format.

A set of full-color *transparency acetates* of key text figures is available. In addition, there is a *PowerPoint Lecture Presentation* package, which includes key text figures, as well as a comprehensive outline for each chapter. This package was developed by Troy Adair and Lorinda P. Adair of Hofstra University.

For the student, there is a complete *Study Guide and Problems Manual*, developed by John Shao. This includes study tips, chapter summaries, and an extensive set of self-tests for each chapter.

ACKNOWLEDGMENTS

The genesis for this book lay in the classroom, and it has been shaped by the reactions and responses of students to examples that I have used in my own lectures. Ideas for the text and its accompanying supplements package were also tested out on instructors in focus groups to examine whether they worked for others and to fill in gaps in the material that were viewed as important. In particular, I would like to thank the following instructors for participating in these focus groups.

Troy Adair
Hofstra University

Charles Cox
Southern Methodist University

Thomas Eyssel
University of Missouri, St. Louis

E. Bruce Fredrikson
Syracuse University

George Hempel
Southern Methodist University

Ken Nunn
University of Connecticut

Ajay Patel
Wake Forest University

Tavy Ronen
Rutgers University

Emery Trahan
Northeastern University

Many people at John Wiley & Sons worked together to make this book a reality. First and foremost, I would like to thank Whitney Blake, who encouraged me to write this book, and Rachel Nelson, who edited the book, checked my grammar and was an invaluable source of good advice. I would also like to thank all of the production, editorial, and marketing staff who allowed it to become a final product: Jeanine Furino (Senior Production Editor), Ann Renzi (Senior Designer), Sigmund Malinowski (Illustration Editor), Wendy Goldner (Associate Marketing Manager), Andrea Bryant (Supplements Editor), Mark Cirillo (Assistant Manufacturing Manager), Jeri-Lynn Caliendo (Senior Editorial Assistant), and Pui Szeto (Program Assistant).

Concerns about the first edition of any book arose during focus groups and market research. In response, we hired graduate students and academics to work through every example, question, and problem in the book, in both the manuscript and later stages of production. For this invaluable service, I express my gratitude to John Shao of Oklahoma City University, and Kathleen Petrie of Indiana University, Bloomington. I also thank John Shao and Troy Adair of Hofstra University for the additional questions and problems they contributed to the end of each chapter.

Several others were involved in the development of the supplementary materials that accompany this text. John Shao of Oklahoma City University prepared the *Instructor's Resource Guide*. Troy Adair of Hofstra University and George Kutner of Marquette University authored the *Test Bank*. John Shao developed the *Study Guide and Problems*. I thank them all for their contributions.

Finally, I would like to thank all of those involved in reviewing the book, whose comments were critical in improving and completing the text.

V. T. Alaganar
Hofstra University

Jay Choi
Temple University

Phillip Daves
University of Tennessee

John Ellis
Colorado State University

Edwin Elton
New York University

Thomas Eyssell
University of Missouri, St. Louis

Martin Gruber
New York University

Ronnie Karanjia
Fordham University

George Kutner
Marquette University

Kenneth Martin
University of Iowa

Sam Mensah
University of Michigan

Michael Muoghalu
Pittsburg State University

James Seward
Dartmouth College

John Shao
Oklahoma City University

Emery Trahan
Northeastern University

Aswath Damodaran
Stern School of Business
New York University

Brief Table of Contents

CONTENTS

PART ONE

AN INTRODUCTION TO CORPORATE FINANCE

Corporate finance is the study of any decisions made by firms that have financial implications. We categorize these decisions into three areas—those relating to resource allocation (the investment decision), those covering the financing of these investments (the capital structure decision) and those determining how much cash gets reinvested and taken out) of the business (the dividend decision). In Chapter 1 we provide an introduction to the "big picture" of corporate finance, and the interrelationships between these decisions. In Chapter 2 we examine the objective of stockholder wealth maximization which underlies much of modern corporate finance and its implications for decision making. In Chapter 3 we illustrate the principles of present value which are drawn upon repeatedly through the rest of the book. In Chapter 4 we examine the basic accounting principles and statements that provide the raw material for financial analysis. In Chapters 5 and 6 we introduce the notion of risk and develop models for measuring risk and using them in the context of decision making.

The Objective Function

Maximize the value of the firm

Basic Corporate Financial Decisions

1. How do you allocate scarce resources across competing uses?
2. How do you raise funds to finance these projects?
3. How much do you reinvest back into the business and how much do you return to your stockholders?

The Corporate Financial Toolbox

| Accounting Statements and Ratios | Present Value | Risk and Return Models | Option Pricing Models |

CHAPTER 1

INTRODUCTION TO CORPORATE FINANCE

There is a financial aspect to almost every decision a business makes—from deciding where to invest to strategic decisions to marketing decisions—bringing it under the purview of corporate finance. In this chapter, we provide an introduction to corporate finance and the topics that will be covered in this book. In the process, we hope to answer the following questions:

- What is corporate finance?
- What are the basic questions that corporate finance tries to address, and how are they related to one another?
- What does the "big picture" of corporate finance look like?

WHAT IS CORPORATE FINANCE?

In our view, corporate finance is often defined much too narrowly as relating to decisions made by financial officers at businesses. Although these decisions may form the core of corporate finance, *we define corporate finance much more broadly to include any decisions made by a business that affect its finances.* Defined as such, strategic, production, and marketing decisions all possess a significant corporate financial component. In the most general terms, corporate financial decisions can be categorized into three groups: investment decisions, financing decisions, and dividend decisions.

Investment Decisions
Firms have scarce resources that must be allocated among competing uses. The first and foremost function of corporate finance as a theory is to provide a framework for firms to make these decisions wisely. Accordingly, we define *investment decisions* to include not only those that create revenues and profits (such as introducing a new product line), but also those that save money (such as building a new and more efficient distribution system). Furthermore, we argue that decisions about how much and what inventory to maintain and whether and how much credit to grant to customers, which are traditionally categorized as working capital decisions, are ultimately investment decisions as well. At the other end of the spectrum, broad strategic decisions regarding which markets to enter and acquisitions of other companies can also be considered investment decisions.

Hurdle Rate: A hurdle rate is a minimum acceptable rate of return for investing resources in a project.

At the risk of giving away the punch line, corporate finance attempts to measure the return on a proposed investment decision and compare it to a **hurdle rate,** which is set taking into account the riskiness of the project, in order to decide whether or not the project is acceptable.

We consider the investment decision in a series of chapters starting with Chapter 7, which describes alternative investment decision rules and their relative strengths and weaknesses, continuing with Chapter 8, where we consider how to estimate the relevant cash flows for projects, and concluding in Chapter 9, where we consider special issues in capital budgeting, including capital rationing and the effects of inflation. In Chapter 10, we examine how best to organize the investment decision as well as how to follow up and evaluate investments once they have been taken. We examine leasing as a special category of investment decision in Chapter 11, and we conclude with a discussion of the effects of uncertainty on investment decisions in Chapters 12 and 13. Working capital investments and choices are examined in Chapter 14.

Financing Decisions

As firms make decisions concerning where to invest their resources, they also have to decide how they should raise *additional* resources. In the broadest terms, a business can either raise funds from its owners as equity, or it can borrow money. The key distinction between the two sources of financing lies in the fixed commitments created by borrowing to pay interest and principal. As we will see later in this book, a myriad of choices exist not only *within* each of these categories but also between them. The question of whether there is an optimal mix of debt and equity to finance investment needs—and, if so, what that optimal mix is—cannot be addressed without considering the costs and benefits of borrowing.

In general, the benefits of borrowing are the tax advantages that accrue from the fact that interest payments are tax deductible, and the increased discipline these payments impose on managers to take good projects. The downside of borrowing is that it increases the expected cost of bankruptcy and may create conflicts between the borrowers, who are usually the equity investors in the firm, and the lenders. In the balance, debt is beneficial as long as the marginal benefits of borrowing exceed the marginal costs.

Corporate finance not only helps firms decide whether or not to borrow money in the first place, but it also provides insight into what *types* of financing—long term or short term, fixed rate or floating rate, straight or convertible—a company should issue. Starting with the fundamental proposition that the characteristics of the financing should closely match the characteristics of the assets being financed, and adding on considerations relating to taxes and external monitors (equity research analysts and ratings agencies), we arrive at surprisingly strong conclusions about the design of the financing.

We introduce the financing decision by first discussing the alternative financing vehicles that are available to both private and public firms in Chapter 15, and the lessons that empirical studies of market efficiency provide in Chapter 16. The tradeoffs of taking on debt are introduced in Chapter 17, where we discuss both the benefits and the costs of borrowing. These tradeoffs are then converted into tools that can be used to help a firm decide on its optimal financing mix in Chapters 18 and 19.

Dividend Decisions

The third and final question corporate finance attempts to address is the dividend decision; *dividends* are defined broadly as any cash returned by a business to its owners. All businesses, from the largest corporations to the smallest private businesses, have to decide how much of the cash they generate from operations should be reinvested back into the business and how much should be taken out in the form of dividends and return on capital. Again, the tradeoff should appeal to common sense. On the one hand, paying out more to the owners may help them meet their personal cash needs; on the other hand, doing so has tax implications, and a business that reinvests less will grow slower and be worth less. The "foregone growth" will be much greater for firms with great investment opportunities, some of which may not be taken, as a consequence of the failure to reinvest.

The tradeoffs on dividend policy are introduced in Chapter 20; the process by which a firm can decide on the right amount to return to its stockholders is examined in Chapter 21. In Chapter 22, we expand the discussion of dividend policy to include other ways of returning cash to stockholders, including stock repurchases, and we discuss how to choose between these options.

THE OBJECTIVE FUNCTION OF THE FIRM

No discipline can develop cohesively over time without a unifying objective function. The growth of corporate financial theory can be traced to its choice of a single objective function and its development of models built around this function. *The objective in conventional corporate financial theory is to maximize firm value.* Consequently, any decision (investment, financial, or dividend) that increases firm value is considered a "good" one, whereas one that reduces firm value is considered a "poor" one. Although the choice of this objective function has provided corporate finance with a unifying theme and internal consistency, it has come at a cost. To the degree that one buys into this objective function, much of what corporate financial theory suggests makes sense. To the degree that this objective function is flawed, however, it can be argued that the theory on which it is built is flawed as well. Many of the disagreements between corporate financial theorists and others (academics as well as practitioners) can be traced to fundamentally different views about the correct objective function for the firm. For instance, there are those who argue that firms should have multiple objectives by which a variety of interests (stockholders, labor, customers) are met, whereas others would have firms focus on what they view as simpler and more direct objectives, such as market share or profitability.

Given the significance of this objective function for both the development and the applicability of corporate financial theory, it is important that we examine it much more carefully and address some of the very real concerns and criticisms it has garnered: it assumes that what stockholders do in their own self-interest is also in the best interests of the firm; it requires the existence of efficient markets; and it is blind to the social costs associated with value maximization. In the next chapter, we consider these and other issues and compare firm value maximization to alternative objective functions.

CORPORATE FINANCIAL DECISIONS, FIRM VALUE, AND EQUITY VALUE

If the objective function in corporate finance is to maximize firm value, it follows that firm value must be linked to the three corporate finance decisions we have outlined: investment, financing, and dividend decisions. The link between these decisions and firm value can be made by recognizing that *the value of a firm is the present value of its expected cash flows, discounted back at a rate that reflects both the riskiness of the project and the financing mix used to finance it.* Investors form expectations about future cash flows based on observed current cash flows and expected future growth, which, in turn, depend on the quality of the firm's projects (its investment decisions) and the amount of its earnings it reinvests (its dividend decision). The financing decisions affect the value of a firm through both the discount rate and, potentially, the expected cash flows.

This neat formulation of value is put to the test by the interactions among the investment, financing, and dividend decisions, and the conflicts of interest that arise between stockholders and bondholders, on the one hand, and stockholders and managers, on the other.

We introduce the basic models available to value a firm in Chapter 23 and relate them back to management decisions in Chapter 24. In the process, we examine the determinants of value and the best ways firms can increase their value. Finally, the effects of mergers and acquisitions on value are described in Chapter 25.

THE NECESSARY TOOLS OF CORPORATE FINANCE

In the process of developing the models that can be used to make sensible investment, financing, and dividend decisions, we will employ a number of tools that apply across all these decisions. Many of these rules are developed early in the book and are used throughout nearly all the chapters.

Present Value

One of the simplest, yet most powerful, rules in corporate finance is *the present value rule,* which states that the value of any asset is the present value of its expected cash flows. Two pieces of information are needed to calculate present value—expected cash flows and a discount rate(s) to apply to these cash flows. The process of calculating present value is often simplified by drawing on present value tables or formulas that can be used to calculate the present value of a number of different kinds of cash flows. These cash flows range from *annuities* (constant cash flows at regular intervals for a specified period of time) to *growing annuities* (cash flows growing at a constant rate during each interval for a specified period) to *perpetuities* (constant cash flows forever) to *growing perpetuities* (cash flows growing at a constant rate forever). Corporate finance also relies on a simple principle in economics, known as the *separation principle*. This concept states that investors will agree on a discount rate, even if they have very different risk-aversion characteristics, as long as there are active capital markets, in which they can invest, lend, or borrow at the prevailing market rate. This principle is introduced and explained in Chapter 3.

Financial Statement Analysis

The numbers used in corporate financial analysis come primarily from financial statements. In particular, it is important that we understand the difference between *operating and capital expenses* and why some expenses are set off against current revenues to arrive at net income, whereas others are "capitalized" on balance sheets and depreciated over time. It is also critical that we understand many of the financial ratios used by analysts following the firm and by rating agencies.

We make a number of fundamental points relating to financial statements in the coming chapters. First, the proverbial bottom line frequently used to describe firms—the net income in the income statement—is not always a good measure of the returns earned by a firm. Thus, one firm may be profitable on paper but have a significant cash deficit, and another may be reporting losses while generating large positive cash flows. This is largely a consequence of noncash charges like depreciation, which have to be added back to net income to get to the cash flow, as well as nonoperating cash expenditures, such as capital expenditures and working capital increases, which reduce cash flows. Second, the focus of financial statements on accounting book value is misplaced; in contrast, we argue that market values should be used whenever they are available. Third, unlike financial statements, which focus primarily on reporting past events, the objective in financial analyses is to make sensible decisions for the future.

The generally accepted accounting principles that underlie the standard financial statements—income statement, balance sheet, and statement of cash flows—are introduced in Chapter 4. In addition, Chapter 4 defines and explains the most widely used financial ratios.

Risk and Return

Underlying much of the discussion in the chapters to come is the notion that investors and firms taking higher risk should be compensated with a higher expected return. This, of course, begs the question of how risk should be measured and how high the return should be for a given level of risk. To answer these questions, we need a model that defines risk, specifies that portion of risk that will be rewarded, and converts that risk measure into an expected return. In this book, we consider two models which argue that only that portion of the risk in an investment that cannot be eliminated by a diversified investor will be rewarded—the *capital asset pricing model* and the *arbitrage pricing model*. In discussing these models, we note their strengths and their weaknesses and discuss the practical issues of measuring and using risk parameters in corporate financial decisions.

We introduce the basics of risk and return and present the alternative risk and return models in Chapter 5. The issues that arise in applying and using these models are described more fully in Chapter 6.

Option Pricing

Many people associate *option pricing theory* with investments and financial markets rather than corporate finance. There are a wide range of applications in corporate finance, however, for which option pricing theory is not only useful but critical. In investment analysis, firms are faced with options to delay, expand, or abandon projects; option pricing theory provides useful insights into the determinants of the values of these options. In financing decisions, option pricing theory is useful in designing and valuing securities with embedded options, such as warrants, convertible securities, and callable bonds. Finally, option pricing theory provides useful insights into the determinants of value.

The basics of option pricing and the determinants of the value of an option are examined in Chapter 27. The applications of option pricing in corporate finance are explored in Chapter 28.

THE BIG PICTURE OF CORPORATE FINANCE

One of the basic propositions of this book is that there is a "big picture" of corporate finance in which all of the decisions and tools we have talked about thus far come together. Figure 1.1 provides the big picture, as we see it, of corporate finance. Note that the investment, financing, and dividend decisions are under the control of the decision makers of the firm, subject to the constraints of the marketplace. These decisions affect the value of the firm, but only after they are viewed through the prism of investor expectations. We return to this big picture repeatedly as we move through this book.

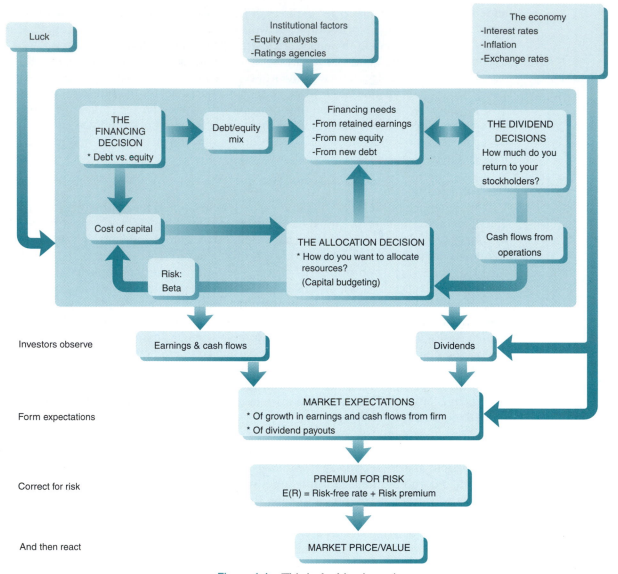

Figure 1.1   This is the big picture!

SOME FUNDAMENTAL PROPOSITIONS ABOUT CORPORATE FINANCE

The basic arguments we make repeatedly throughout this book are as follows.

1. Corporate finance has an internal consistency that flows from its choice of maximizing firm value as the only objective function and its dependence on a few bedrock principles: risk has to be rewarded; cash flows matter more than accounting income measures; markets are not easily fooled; and every decision a firm makes has an effect on its value.

2. Corporate finance must be viewed as an integrated whole rather than as a collection of decisions. Investment decisions generally affect financing decisions, and vice versa; financing decisions generally affect dividend decisions, and vice versa. Although these decisions may be independent of each other, this is seldom the case. Accordingly, firms that deal with their problems on a piecemeal basis will likely never resolve these problems. For instance, a firm that believes that it has a dividend problem and just cuts dividends may experience consequences for its financing and investment decisions.

3. Corporate finance matters to everybody. Almost every decision made by a business has a corporate financial aspect. Although not everyone will find a use for all the components of corporate finance, everyone will find a use for at least some *part* of it.

4. Corporate finance is fun. This may seem to be the tallest claim of all. After all, most people associate corporate finance with numbers and accounting statements and hard-headed analyses. Corporate finance is quantitative in its focus, but a significant component of creative thinking is involved in coming up with solutions to the financial problems businesses may encounter. It is no coincidence that financial markets remain the breeding grounds for innovation and change.

5. The best way to learn corporate finance is to apply its models and theories. Although the theory that has been developed over the last few decades is impressive, the ultimate test of any theory is in applications. As we show in this book, much, if not all, of the theory can be applied to real companies and not just to abstract examples, although we have to compromise and make assumptions in the process.

CONCLUSION

This chapter provides both an overview and a philosophical basis for what is to come in this book. We defined corporate finance as all decisions made by businesses that affect their finances; we categorized them broadly into investment, financing, and dividend decisions. We also noted that corporate finance has only one objective: to maximize the value of the firm. Finally, we presented the big picture of corporate finance, complete with the interactions among different corporate financial decisions and the effect on value.

CHAPTER 2

THE OBJECTIVE FUNCTION IN CORPORATE FINANCE

Corporate financial theory attempts to answer three basic questions: (1) How do you pick projects? (2) How do you decide on the optimal financing mix for these projects? (3) How much of the cash flows on these projects should be returned to stockholders? In developing a framework for answering these questions, *the objective in decision making is assumed to be the maximization of stockholder wealth.*

Much of the theory and most of the models developed in corporate finance are based on this premise of maximizing stockholder wealth. Therefore, it is critical that we spend some time examining the strengths and weaknesses of this objective function and comparing it to alternatives. In doing so, this chapter attempts to answer the following questions:

- What are the assumptions that we need to make to justify the focus on maximizing stockholder wealth?
- What are some of the conflicts and costs associated with each of these assumptions?
- What are the alternatives to maximizing stockholder wealth, and what are the strengths and weaknesses of each?
- How can we reduce the side costs associated with stockholder wealth maximization?

THE NEED FOR AN OBJECTIVE FUNCTION

Let us start with a description of what an objective function is and the purpose it serves in developing theory. An *objective function* specifies what the decision maker is trying to accomplish and, by so doing, provides a framework for analyzing different decision rules. In most cases, the objective function is stated in terms of maximizing some function or variable (profits, size, value, social welfare) or minimizing some function or variable (risk, costs).

To those unfamiliar with the controversy about the "right" objective function to use in corporate finance, this may seem like a tempest in a teapot. After all, why have an objective function at all? And if you have to have an objective function, why not have multiple objectives and satisfy all sides of the debate? Although splitting the difference between the competing objective functions may seem to be an attractive option, it is not a viable one for the following reasons.

1. If an objective function is not chosen, there is no way to pick between alternative decision rules. The consensus in corporate finance, for instance, that the net present value rule is the best approach to picking projects is conditioned on the objective function of maximizing stockholder wealth. Without an objective function, there would be a menu of approaches for picking projects, ranging from reasonable ones, like maximizing return on investment, to obscure ones, like maximizing size, and no statements could be made about their relative value.

2. If multiple objectives are chosen, we are faced with a different problem. A theory developed around multiple objective functions of equal weight is like a man who serves several masters: in trying to meet its multiple objectives, it ends up meeting none of them. And even if objective functions are prioritized, we are faced with the same stark choices as in the case of a single objective function. Should the top priority be the maximization of stockholder wealth or market share? Thus since there is no gain from having multiple objective functions, and developing theory becomes much more difficult, we would argue that there should be only one objective function.

THE CHARACTERISTICS OF THE "RIGHT" OBJECTIVE FUNCTION

The costs of choosing the wrong objective function can be catastrophic. In some sense, the collapse of government-run enterprises in Eastern Europe, the former Soviet Union, and Asia can be traced to a failure to enunciate a clear objective function for managers in these firms in some cases and to use of the wrong objective function in others.[1] For instance, if the manager of a firm believes that the firm's sole objective is to maximize size, he will pick larger projects over smaller ones, even if they are less profitable. In the long term, the firm will pay a price and may even go out of business.

So how will we know whether the objective function that we have chosen is the "right" one? A good objective function has the following characteristics.

(1)   It is clear and unambiguous. An ambiguous objective function will lead to decision rules that vary from case to case and from decision maker to decision maker.

(2)   It comes with a clear and timely measure that can be used to evaluate the success or failure of decisions. Objective functions that offer noble platitudes but do not come with a measurement mechanism are likely to fail. For instance, if we define our objective to be maximizing social welfare, it is not at all clear what comprises "social welfare" and how this objective function will translate into decisions.

(3)   It does not create side costs that erase firm-specific benefits and leave society worse off overall.

(4)   It is consistent with maximizing the firm's long-term health and value.

These characteristics can be used to screen alternative objective functions.

THE CLASSICAL OBJECTIVE FUNCTION

There is general agreement, at least among corporate finance theorists, that *the objective of the firm is to maximize wealth.* There is some disagreement, however, as to whether the objective is to maximize the wealth of *stockholders* or the wealth of *the*

---

[1]It is difficult to separate fact from fiction in accounts of public-sector firms in the erstwhile socialist countries. Stories abound of factories that churned out substandard products that were not wanted by the general public but were still considered successful because they employed thousands of people and had high output (measured in terms of production).

firm, which includes other financial claimholders (debtholders, preferred stockholders, etc.) in addition to stockholders. Furthermore, even those who argue for stockholder wealth maximization debate whether or not this actually translates into maximizing the stock price.

These objective functions vary in terms of the assumptions that are needed to justify them. The least restrictive of the objectives is to maximize the firm value; the most restrictive is to maximize the stock price.

☐ Concept
Check

> Managers and analysts often talk about maximizing firm value, value of equity, and the stock price as if they were interchangeable. When are they in fact interchangeable? When might maximizing one *not* lead to maximizing another? Think of a couple of examples.

Organizational Structure and Classical Theory

The classical objective of maximizing wealth (stockholder or firm) seems uncontroversial until we take into account the size and complexity of modern corporations in which *owners* (stockholders) hire *managers* to make decisions for them and borrow money from *lenders* who cannot monitor perfectly how their money is being used. The incentives and objectives of even these three primary stakeholders in the firm are often very different, resulting in conflicts among them. Managers might want to make decisions that are in their best interests, while not serving stockholder interests; when they do make decisions in the stockholders' interests, they may make lenders unhappy.

These problems are further accentuated if we consider three additional stakeholders in the firm. The *employees* of the organization often have no or only a secondary interest in maximizing stockholder wealth; they have a much larger interest in seeing their job security enhanced and benefits/wages increased. The *customers* of the organization may want to have the best possible product at the lowest feasible price, an objective that may conflict with the desire of stockholders to maximize wealth. Finally, the overall interests of *society* may conflict with those of the stockholders of the firm.

☐ Concept
Check

> Corporate financial theory has been accused of being "insensitive" to the needs of employees, customers, and society because of its focus on stockholder wealth. Is this criticism merited? If not, how would you counter it?

Potential Side Costs of Wealth Maximization

If the only objective in decision making is to maximize firm or stockholder wealth, the potential side costs to society may drown out the benefits from wealth maximization. To the extent that these costs are large relative to the wealth created by the firm, the objective function may have to be modified. To be fair, however, this problem is likely to persist even if an alternative objective function is used.

The objective of wealth maximization may also face obstacles when ownership and management are separate, as they are in most large public corporations. When managers act as agents for the owners (stockholders), there is the potential for a conflict of interest between stockholder and managerial interests. This conflict of interest can, in turn, lead to decision rules that maximize managerial utility but not stockholder or firm wealth.

When the objective function is stated in terms of stockholder wealth, the conflicting interests of stockholders and bondholders have to be reconciled. Because stockholders are the decision makers, and bondholders are not completely protected, one way of maximizing stockholder wealth is to take actions that expropriate wealth from the bondholders, even though such actions may reduce the wealth of the firm.

Finally, when the objective function is narrowed further to one of maximizing stock price, inefficiencies in the financial markets may lead to misallocation of resources and bad decisions. For instance, if stock prices do not reflect the long-term consequences of decisions but respond, as some critics maintain, to short-term earnings effects, a decision that increases stockholder wealth may reduce the stock price. Conversely, a decision that reduces stockholder wealth but creates earnings increases in the near term may increase the stock price.

☐ Concept Check

> If you were analyzing a private company, in which the owner is also the manager, would your potential side costs from maximizing equity value be smaller or larger than those associated with maximizing equity value in a large publicly traded company? Why?

Underlying Assumptions

The assumptions needed to justify the objective function of maximizing wealth are driven by the potential for the side costs listed above. These assumptions can be classified into four groups:

(1)   Assumptions relating to the relationship between stockholders and managers: The underlying assumption in classical theory is that stockholders, by virtue of their capacity to hire and fire managers and to design their compensation contracts, exercise control over managers. In return, managers consider wealth maximization to be their primary objective function in making decisions, even if it conflicts with their self-interest.

(2)   Assumptions relating to the relationship between stockholders and bondholders: To prevent the zero or negative sum games that can result from actions stockholders take to expropriate wealth from bondholders, we assume that bondholders are fully protected. This protection can be in the form of covenants, which explicitly put constraints on actions that can expropriate wealth, such as investment and dividend decisions. It can also arise from the desire of firms to maintain good reputations in bond markets, for they might have to return to these markets to raise more funds in the future.

(3)   Assumptions relating to the relationship between managers and financial markets: If the objective function is stated in terms of maximizing stock price, we have to assume the existence of a financial market that efficiently impounds information into prices. The information itself should be conveyed to markets in a truthful and timely manner, either by the managers of the firm or by analysts following the firm. The notion of market efficiency does not assume that the market price is always equal to the true value, but that it is an "unbiased" estimate, albeit one with error, of the true value.

Social Cost: A social cost is a cost created by a firm in the process of doing business, which cannot or is not traced back and charged to the firm.

(4)   Assumptions relating to the relationship between firms and society: In the broadest terms, we assume that when we maximize firm or stockholder wealth the **social costs** created can either be traced and charged to the firm like any other cost item, or they are trivial relative to the value created in the process of wealth maximization.

Figure 2.1   The classical objective function

The least restrictive objective of firm wealth maximization does not require the assumptions of market efficiency or bondholder protection. Stockholder wealth maximization as an objective adds on the assumption of bondholder protection, and the most restrictive objective of stock price maximization is based on the assumption that financial markets are efficient.

The assumptions needed for the classical objective function are summarized in Figure 2.1.

SOME REAL-WORLD PROBLEMS

The assumptions underlying the classical objective function are subject to debate, and it is not obvious that they will hold under all scenarios. Do managers put stockholder interests above their own? Can bondholders assume that they are protected from stockholder attempts to expropriate wealth? Can we assume that information flows freely to financial markets and that markets respond appropriately to such information? Are social costs trivial and, therefore, can they be ignored? The answer to all these questions is: Not always, and not as a rule.

Stockholders and Managers

The assumption that stockholders can hire and fire managers is grounded in the corporate charter, with two institutions designed to provide power to stockholders. The first is the *annual meeting,* at which stockholders can voice their displeasure with incumbent management and remove it if necessary. The other is the *board of directors,* whose fiduciary duty it is to ensure that managers serve the stockholders. Although the legal justification is obvious, the practical power of these institutions to enforce stockholder control is debatable.

The annual meeting   The power of stockholders to exercise control by voting at annual meetings is diluted by two factors. For most small stockholders, the cost of going to a meeting exceeds the benefit, resulting in a large proportion of absentees. They do have a choice of exercising their power with proxies,[2] but in the absence of a **proxy fight**, incumbent management starts off with a clear advantage.[3] Many stockholders do not bother to fill out their proxies, and even among those who do, voting for incumbent management is often the default option. When larger stockholders with significant holdings in a large number of securities are dissatisfied with incumbent management, their easiest option is to "vote with their feet"—that is, sell their stock and move on. An activist posture on the part of these stockholders would go a long way toward making managers more responsive to their interests. In fact, recent trends have been toward more activism, which are documented later in this chapter.

Proxy Fight: In a proxy fight, an investor or a group of investors contests incumbent management by appealing to stockholders for their proxy votes.

The board of directors   The capacity of the board of directors to discipline management and keep them responsive to stockholders is also diluted by a number of factors.

1.   Most individuals who serve as directors cannot spend much time on their fiduciary duties, partly because of other commitments and partly because many of them serve on the boards of several corporations. One study of directorial compensation and time spent by directors on their work by Korn-Ferry, an executive recruiter, illustrates this very clearly.[4] The average director spent 92 hours *a year* on board meetings and preparation in 1992, down from 108 hours in 1988, and was paid $32,352, up from $19,544 in 1988.[5]

2.   Even those directors who spend time trying to understand the internal workings of a firm are stymied by their lack of expertise on many issues, especially those relating to accounting rules and tender offers, and rely instead on outside experts.

3.   Although most directors are outsiders, they are not independent, insofar as the company's chief executive officer (CEO) has a major say in who serves on the board. Korn-Ferry's annual surveys of boards also found that 74% of the 426 companies surveyed relied on recommendations by the CEO to come up with new directors, whereas only 16% used a search firm.

4.   The CEOs of other companies are the favored choice for directors, leading to a potential conflict of interest when CEOs sit on each others' boards.

5.   Most directors hold only small or token stakes in the equity of their corporations, making it difficult for them to empathize with the plight of shareholders when stock prices go down. The consulting firm Institutional Shareholder Services found that 27 directors at 275 of the largest corporations in the United States owned *no* shares at all, and about 5% of all directors owned fewer than five shares.

[2]A *proxy* enables stockholders to vote in absentia for boards of directors and for resolutions that will be coming to a vote at the meeting. It does not allow them to ask open-ended questions of management, however.

[3]This advantage is magnified if the corporate charter allows incumbent management to vote proxies that were never sent back to the firm. This is the equivalent of an election in which the incumbent gets the votes of anybody who does not show up at the voting booth.

[4]Korn-Ferry surveys the boards of large corporations and provides insights into their composition.

[5]This amount actually understates the true benefits received by the average director in a firm, because it does not count benefits and perquisites, insurance and pension benefits being the largest component. Hewitt Associates, an executive search firm, reports that 67% of 100 firms surveyed offer retirement plans for their directors.

The net effect of all these factors is that the board of directors often fails in its assigned role, which is to protect the interests of stockholders. The CEO sets the agenda, chairs the meeting, and controls the information, and the search for consensus generally overwhelms any attempts at confrontation. Although there is an impetus toward reform, these revolts have been sparked not by board members, but by large institutional investors.

The board of directors' failure to protect stockholders can be illustrated with numerous examples from the United States, but this should not blind us to more troubling fact. Stockholders exercise more power over management in the United States than in any other financial market. If the annual meeting and the board of directors are, for the most part, ineffective in the United States at exercising control over management, they are even more powerless in Europe and Asia as institutions that protect stockholders. Students of the German and Japanese systems of corporate governance will argue that these systems have other ways of keeping errant management in line, but such a claim is difficult to back up with evidence.

Greenmail: Greenmail refers to the purchase by the target firm of a potential hostile acquirer's stake at a premium over the price paid for that stake.

So what's next? When the cat is idle, the mice will play... If the two institutions of corporate governance—annual meetings and the board of directors—fail to keep management responsive to stockholders, as argued in the previous section, we cannot expect managers to maximize stockholder wealth, especially when their interests conflict with those of stockholders. There are several examples where, arguably, managers put their interests over those of stockholders. The managers of some firms that were targeted by acquirers (raiders) for hostile takeovers in the 1980s were able to avoid being acquired by buying out the raider's existing stake, generally at a price much greater than the price paid by the raider. This process, called **greenmail**, has negative consequences for stock prices, but it does protect the jobs of incumbent managers. Another widely used anti-takeover device is a **golden parachute**, a provision in an employment contract that allows for the payment of a lump-sum or cash flows over a period, if the manager covered by the contract loses his or her job in a takeover. Some economists have justified the payment of golden parachutes as a way of reducing the conflict between stockholders and managers, yet it is unseemly that managers should need large side-payments to do the job they were hired to do—maximize stockholder wealth. Finally, firms sometimes create securities called **poison pills**, the rights or cash flows on which are triggered by hostile takeovers. The objective is to make it difficult and costly to acquire control. Greenmail, golden parachutes, and poison pills do not require stockholder approval and are usually adopted by compliant boards of directors.

Golden Parachute: A golden parachute refers to a contractual clause in a management contract that allows the manager to be paid a specified sum of money in the event control of the firm changes, usually in the context of a hostile takeover.

Poison Pill: A poison pill is a security or provision that is triggered by the hostile acquisition of the firm, resulting in a large cost to the acquirer.

Anti-takeover amendments have the same objective as greenmail and poison pills—that is, to dissuade hostile takeovers—but they differ on one very important count. They require the assent of stockholders to be instituted. Several types of anti-takeover amendments exist—all designed to reduce the likelihood of a hostile takeover. Among them are *super majority requirements* (whereby the acquirer has to acquire more than a bare majority to acquire the firm), *fair-price amendments* (whereby the offer price has to exceed a price specified relative to earnings) and *staggered elections to boards of directors* (which prevent acquirers from getting control for several years). They do increase the bargaining power of managers and prevent two-tier takeovers.[6] For these explanations to be credible, however, managers should be viewed as acting in the best interests of stockholders, and that remains a stretch.

☐ Concept
Check

> As a stockholder in a company, would you vote for an anti-takeover amendment? If you would, what factors would you consider in making your decision?

Managers can make their stockholders worse off in many ways—by taking bad projects, by taking on too much or too little debt, and by adopting defensive mechanisms against potentially value-increasing takeovers. The quickest, and perhaps most decisive, way to impoverish stockholders is to overpay on a takeover, for the amounts paid on takeovers tend to dwarf those involved in the other decisions listed above. Of course, the managers of the firms doing the acquiring will argue that they never overpay on takeovers,[7] and that the high premiums paid in acquisitions can be justified using any number of reasons: there is **synergy** between the firms; there are strategic considerations; the target firm is undervalued and badly managed; and so on. The stockholders in acquiring firms do not seem to share the enthusiasm for mergers and acquisitions that their managers have, since the stock prices of bidding firms decline on the takeover announcements a significant proportion of the time.[8]

Synergy: Synergy is the additional value created by bringing together two entities and pooling their strengths. In the context of a merger, synergy is the difference between the value of the merged firm, and the sum of the values of the firms operating independently.

What are the consequences of overpaying on a takeover? It transfers wealth from the stockholders of the acquiring firm to those of the acquired firm, and the amounts involved can be staggering in some cases. Consider, for instance, the takeover of Sterling Drugs by Eastman Kodak in 1988. After a hotly contested battle with Hoffman La Roche, Eastman Kodak won the bidding war and acquired Sterling Drugs on January 22, 1988, at $90.90 per share (which worked out to $5.1 billion for the equity in the firm).[9] The market value of equity for Sterling Drugs had been $3 billion,

---

[6]In a two-tier takeover, the raider offers a higher price for the first 51% who tender their shares and a lower price for those who tender afterward.

[7]One explanation given for the phenomenon of overpaying on takeovers is that it is managerial hubris (pride) that drives the process.

[8]Jarrell, Brickley, and Netter (1988), in an extensive study of returns to bidder firms, note that excess returns on these firms' stocks around the announcement of takeovers declined from an average of 4.95% in the 1960s to 2% in the 1970s to –1% in the 1980s. You, Caves, Smith and Henry (1986) examined 133 mergers between 1976 and 1984 and found that the stock prices of bidding firms declined in 53% of the cases.

[9]The term *won* is actually a misnomer here. A "winner's curse" might well apply, a term used to describe the winner of a bidding war at an auction. The winner bids the highest price; therefore, everybody else at the auction thinks that he or she paid too much.

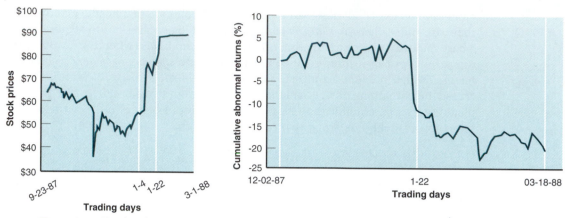

Figure 2.2   Stock price reaction to take over: Sterling Drug (left) and Eastman Kodak (right)

30 days prior to acquisition. On the announcement of the takeover on January 22, the stock price of Eastman Kodak dropped 15%, a decline in the market value of equity of approximately $2.2 billion. Although it is dangerous to draw strong conclusions from stock price reactions alone, the drop in Kodak's value is strikingly close to the market premium paid by it of $2.1 billion. Figure 2.2 charts the divergent paths of stockholders' wealth in Sterling Drugs and Eastman Kodak around the time of the acquisition.

These illustrations are meant not to imply that managers are venal and selfish, which would be an ufair charge, but to indicate a much more fundamental problem: when there is conflict of interest between stockholders and managers, stockholder wealth maximization is likely to take second place to management objectives.

❏ Concept
Check

Managers involved in acquistions often argue that they cannot take over other firms without paying substantial premiums, and that they are therefore unavoidable. Do you agree?

Stockholders and Bondholders

In a world devoid of conflicts of interest between stockholders and bondholders, the bondholders might not have to worry about protecting themselves from expropriation. In the real world, however, bondholders who do not protect themselves may be taken advantage of by stockholders increasing leverage, paying more dividends, or undercutting the security on which the loans were based.

The source of the conflict   The source of the conflict of interest between stockholders and bondholders lies in the differences in the nature of the cash-flow claims of the two groups. Bondholders generally have first claim on cash flows but receive fixed amounts, assuming that the firm makes enough income to meet its debt obligations. Equity investors have a claim on the residual cash flows but have the option of declaring bankruptcy if the firm has insufficient cash flows to meet its financial obligations. Consequently, bondholders tend to view the risk in project choice and other decisions much more negatively than do stockholders, since they do not get to participate on the upside if the projects succeed and could bear a significant portion of the cost if they fail. Stockholders and bondholders are likely to disagree on many issues, two of which are examined in the following section.

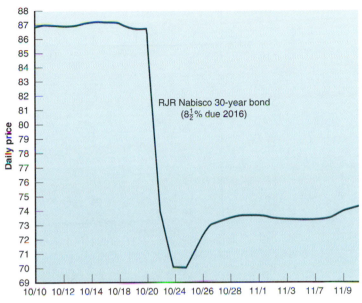

Figure 2.3   RJR Nabisco's bonds sink following announcement of the leveraged buyout

Increases in financial leverage   Existing bondholders can be made worse off by increases in leverage, especially if these increases are large and affect the default risk of the firm and the bondholders are unprotected (the stockholders' wealth increases concurrently). This effect is dramatically illustrated in the case of leveraged buyouts, whereby the debt ratio increases and the bond rating drops significantly. The prices of existing bonds fall to reflect the higher default risk.

One of the more publicized examples of bondholder wealth expropriation occurred in the case of RJR Nabisco. On October 20, 1988, RJR Nabisco's CEO announced plans to take the company private in a $17.6 billion leveraged buyout. Existing bondholders in Nabisco saw the prices of their bonds drop as much as 20%, as the expected default risk increased dramatically with the higher leverage foreseen in the LBO. The price of a Nabisco 30-year bond around the buyout announcement is graphed in Figure 2.3. This loss of wealth is unfair to existing bondholders, because they had no say in whether Nabisco would do the leveraged buyout in the first place. At the same time, their failure to protect themselves exposed them to this considerable loss. In their defense, the bond issues for most large, highly rated industrial firms at the time of this LBO had few or no covenants against such actions. Bondholders assumed that since these firms made repeated forays into financial market to borrow money, the fear of losing credibility and reputation would keep them honest. They also assumed that these firms were too big to be acquired in leveraged transactions. Unfortunately, they assumed incorrectly with RJR Nabisco and paid a price for it.

Increases in dividends   Dividend policy is another potential source of conflict of interest between stockholders and bondholders. The effect of higher dividends on stock prices can be debated in theory, with differing opinions as to whether it should increase or decrease prices, but the empirical evidence is clear: Increases in dividends, on average, lead to higher stock prices, whereas decreases in dividends lead to lower stock prices. Bond prices, on the other hand, react negatively to dividend increases and positively to dividend cuts, as illustrated in Figure 2.4. These price changes may seem

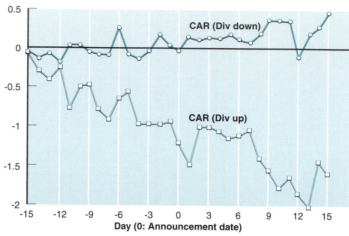

Figure 2.4   Excess returns on straight bonds around dividend changes

trivial, but there have been extreme cases of stockholders expropriating wealth from bondholders using large one-time dividends.

Cumulative Abnormal Returns (CARs):   The abnormal or excess return is the difference between the actual return on an asset and the return it should have made, given the market return and its risk. The *cumulative abnormal return* is the aggregate abnormal return made over the entire period.

Consequences of stockholder-bondholder conflicts   As these two illustrations indicate, stockholders and bondholders have different objective functions, and some decisions can transfer wealth from one group (usually bondholders) to the other (usually stockholders). An objective function that focuses on maximizing stockholder wealth may result in stockholders taking perverse actions that harm the overall firm but increase their personal wealth at the expense of bondholders.

Covenants: Covenants are restrictions built into contractual agreements. The most common reference in corporate finance to covenants is in bond agreements; they represent restrictions placed by lenders on the firm's investment, financing, and dividend decisions.

It is possible that we are making too much of the expropriation possibility, for a couple of reasons. Bondholders are aware of the potential of stockholders to take actions that are inimical to their interests and generally protect themselves, either by writing in **covenants** or restrictions on what stockholders can do, or by taking an equity interest in the firm. Furthermore, the need to return to the bond markets to raise additional funds in the future will keep many firms honest, for the gains from any one-time wealth transfer are likely to be outweighed by the loss of reputation associated with such actions. These issues are considered in more detail in the next section.

☐ Concept
  Check

It has been argued that convertible bonds (bonds that are convertible into stock at the option of the bondholders) provide one form of protection against expropriation by stockholders. What is the basis of this argument?

The Firm and Financial Markets

There is an advantage to maintaining an objective function that focuses on stockholder or firm wealth rather than stock prices or the market value of the firm: stockholder or firm wealth does not require any assumptions about the efficiency or otherwise of financial markets. The downside, however, is that stockholder or firm wealth is not easily measurable, making it difficult to establish clear standards for success and failure. It is true that there are valuation models, some of which we will examine in this book, that attempt to measure equity and firm value, but they are based on a large number of essentially subjective inputs. Because an essential characteristic of a good objective function is that it comes with a clear and unambiguous measurement mechanism, the advantages of shifting to an objective function that focuses on market prices are obvious. The measure of success or failure is there for all to see. A successful manager raises his or her firm's stock price, and an unsuccessful one reduces his or hers.

The trouble with market prices, of course, is that they are set by financial markets. To the extent that financial markets are efficient and use the information that is available to make measured and unbiased estimates of future cash flows and risk, market prices will reflect true value. In such markets, both the measurers and the measured will accept the market price as the appropriate mechanism for judging success and failure. There are two potential barriers to this acceptance, however. The first is that information is the lubricant that enables markets to be efficient. To the extent that this information is hidden, delayed, or misleading, market prices will deviate from true value, even in an otherwise efficient market. The second problem is that many people argue that markets are *not* efficient, even when information is freely available. In both cases, decisions that maximize stock prices may not be consistent with long-term value maximization.

The information problem   Market prices are based on **public and private information**. In the world of classical theory, information is revealed promptly and truthfully to financial markets. In the real world, firms sometimes suppress or delay information, especially when it contains bad news; in some cases, misleading or fraudulent information is released to markets. The extent of the problem clearly varies from market to market and even from firm to firm.

Public and Private Information: Public information refers to any information that is available to the investing public, whereas private information is restricted to insiders or a few investors in the firm.

Suppressed information   Anecdotal evidence indicates that firms do indeed sometimes suppress bad news about their performance and future prospects from financial markets. The extent of the problem is likely to vary widely among firms, and smaller firms are much more likely to get away with it than are larger firms. Given the number of analysts following larger firms, it becomes much more difficult and dangerous to withhold information from markets.

If the problem is sizable in U.S. financial markets—and it is—it is further accentuated in other markets, where firms often are the sole providers of information, and the information that has to be provided to investors is sparse. In emerging markets, for instance, in which foreign investors may know little or nothing about most of the firms in which they are investing, the problem of suppressed information is likely to be acute.

Delayed information   It is human nature to try to control how and when bad news is revealed to others. Managers try to control how and when information about their firms reaches financial markets for two reasons. First, some, if not all, managers believe that

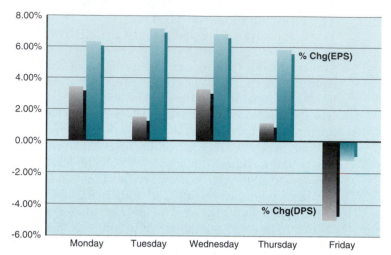

Figure 2.5   Do managers delay bad news? EPS and DPS changes by weekday

financial markets cannot be trusted to react appropriately to new information and that panic trading may cause prices to change more than they should. Second, there is the hope that if bad news is delayed long enough, it will either go away or can be paired with some good news about the firm.

Substantial empirical evidence indicates that managers do in fact delay bad news. One study reports, for instance, that earnings and dividend reports on Fridays contain significantly more bad news than do earnings and dividend reports on any other day of the week, as shown in Figure 2.5. Penman (1987) finds that earnings reports that are delayed relative to their expected report date are much more likely to contain bad news than are earnings reports that are made early or are on time.

It is not clear that delayed information, by itself, will cause prices to deviate dramatically from value. The length of the delays is small for most companies—a matter of days rather than weeks or months—and may not really matter for investors who measure success or failure using longer time intervals. Furthermore, markets react to delays by assuming the worst and marking down prices.[10] Finally, all the planning by managers may come to naught if analysts following the firm dig up the information and reveal it to financial markets themselves.

Misleading information   In their zeal to keep investors happy and raise market prices, some firms release intentionally misleading information about the firm's current conditions and future prospects to financial markets. These misrepresentations can cause stock prices to deviate significantly from value. Consider the example of Leslie Fay, a leading women's apparel manufacturer that found favor on Wall Street and saw its stock price rise largely on the strength of its earnings reports. In January 1993, the CEO of Leslie Fay admitted that the books had been cooked and that earnings in 1992 were not in fact $23.9 million as reported, but that the firm actually *lost* $14 million! Investors were shocked and rushed to sell their stock, causing the price to drop to $3.50 from $30.

The implications of such fraudulent behavior can be profound, for managers are often evaluated on the basis of stock price performance. Thus, managers at Leslie Fay would have been richly rewarded between 1989 and 1992 as the stock price rose, largely as a consequence of their manipulation of information.

---

[10]Some larger firms are so concerned about this that they actually choose to go to markets early with bad news rather than allow investors to respond to rumors and exaggerations.

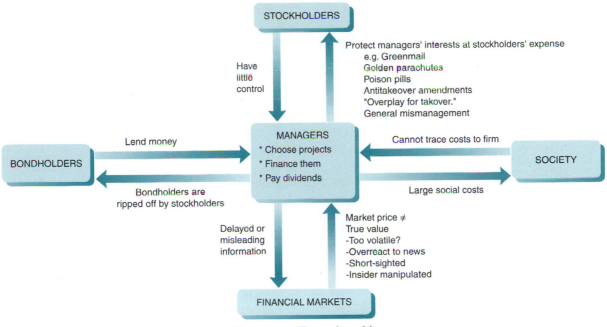

Figure 2.6   The real world

☐ **Concept Check**

Some companies need to access capital markets repeatedly to raise money, in the form of either debt or equity, whereas other companies do so very infrequently. Which of these two groups will be less inclined to mislead financial markets and why?

Are markets inefficient?   Even if information were to flow freely and with no distortion to financial markets, there is no guarantee that what emerges as the market price will be an unbiased estimate of true value. In fact, many analysts argue that the fault lies deeper and that investors are much too irrational and unreliable to come up with a good estimate of the true value. Some of the criticisms that have been mounted against financial markets are legitimate, some are overblown, and some are flat out wrong, but they all deserve to be considered seriously.

Financial markets are too volatile   Anyone who has ever observed the working of a financial market during the course of a trading day knows that markets are *volatile* and that prices often move dramatically, not only based on information but sometimes in the absence of it. Are markets too volatile? One school of thought argues unquestionably that they are, that this **volatility** is caused by the shifting moods and perceptions of irrational investors, and that short-term price movements have little to do with information. This is a popular belief with a large number of adherents in financial markets, ranging from technicians, who use chart patterns to decipher changes in moods, to fundamentalists, who look for bargains in the fundamentals of firms. At the other extreme are the theorists who argue that market movements can be explained entirely by information, especially if allowance is made for the fact that the very act of trading reveals some information to others.

Volatility: The volatility of an asset is measured by the variability in its prices over time—that is, the variance or standard deviation in prices.

The prudent course may be to stand the middle ground. Most large movements in market prices can be explained by the arrival of information, but market mood swings can cause sudden and dramatic fluctuation in prices, especially during short time periods. Although it would be dangerous to evaluate management performance using stock prices on a weekly or monthly basis, the "excess volatility" in prices becomes less of an issue when measurement is made on an annual basis, or longer.

Financial markets overreact to information   When markets are confronted with new information, they have to react instantaneously. Some analysts argue that markets tend to *overreact* to information, however. For example, DeBondt and Thaler (1985) created portfolios of stocks based on earnings surprises after the initial report and tracked them for the following three years. They found that the portfolio of stocks with the most negative earnings surprises outperformed both the overall market and the portfolio of stocks with the most positive surprises by a wide margin. On a more general level, there is evidence of return reversals in stocks, especially in the long term (one to five years).[11]

Financial markets are short term   The most damning indictment against financial markets, in particular, and corporate financial theories, in general, is that they promote a focus on short-term results. The reasoning goes as follows. Stock prices are determined by traders, short-term investors, and analysts, all of whom hold the stock for short periods and spend their time trying to forecast the next quarter's earnings. Managers who concentrate on creating long-term value, rather than short-term results, will be penalized by markets.

The evidence presented by those who present this viewpoint, and there are many, is primarily anecdotal. There can be no denying some of the facts that they raise, although their conclusions do not necessarily follow. Analysts do spend a considerable amount of time forecasting next quarter's earnings, but that is because changes in earnings that cannot be explained by one-time occurrences (like accounting changes) or pure luck provide good signals of shifts in future prospects. And many investors hold their stock for short periods of time, but that is still entirely consistent with a market that focuses on long-term results.

Since this issue has become so controversial, and positions are often etched in stone, the only way to resolve it is with empirical evidence, most of which is consistent with a market that looks at long-term potential. It is not consistent with the arguments made by those who believe that markets are short term:

1.   Hundreds of firms, especially small and start-up firms, do not have any current earnings and cash flows and do not expect to have any in the near future, but are still able to raise substantial amounts of money on the basis of expectations of success in the future. If markets were in fact as short term as the critics suggest, these firms should be unable to raise funds in the first place.

2.   If the evidence suggests anything, it is that markets do not value current earnings and cash flows enough and they value future earnings and cash flows too much. Studies

----

[11]Stocks that have done well during a period underperform the market in the following period, and stocks that have done badly during a period outperform the market in the following period.

indicate that stocks with low price earnings ratios (i.e., high current earnings) have generally been underpriced relative to stocks with high price earnings ratios.

3.   The market response to research and development and investment expenditure is not uniformly negative, as the "short-term" critics would lead you to believe. Instead, the response is tempered, with stock prices, on average, rising on the announcement of R&D and capital expenditures.

None of this evidence proves that financial market participants consider the long-term consequences of decisions, but it is consistent with a market that values long-term performance. It is also worth noting that many of the managers who criticize markets for being short term work for firms whose stock prices have gone down significantly. Therefore, they may have a slightly vested interest in getting investors to buy into their arguments.

Concept Check

> If you are convinced that financial markets are not efficient, do you have to abandon the objective of value maximization? Why or why not?

The bottom line: To believe in markets, or not...   The information that flows into financial markets is often delayed, incorrect, and misleading, and the prices that flow out are very noisy estimates of the true value. But this fact does not take away from the central contribution of financial markets: they assimilate and aggregate a remarkable amount of information on current conditions and future prospects into one measure—the stock price. No competing measure comes close to providing as timely or as comprehensive a measure of a firm's standing.

The value of market prices is best illustrated when working with a private firm as opposed to a public firm. Although managers of the public firm may resent the second-guessing of analysts and investors, there is a great deal of value to knowing how investors perceive the actions the firm takes.

The Firm and Society

Most management decisions have social consequences, and the question of how to deal with these consequences is not easily answered. An objective function of maximizing firm or stockholder wealth implicitly assumes that the social side costs are either trivial enough that they can be ignored or can be priced and charged to the firm. In many cases, these assumptions may not be justifiable.

Sometimes the social costs are considerable but cannot be traced to the firm. In these cases, the decision makers, though aware of the costs, may choose to ignore the costs and maximize firm wealth. The ethical and moral dilemmas of forcing a manager to choose between his or her survival (which may require stockholder wealth maximization) and the broader interests of society can be debated, but there is no simple solution that can be offered in this book.

When substantial social costs exist, and firms are aware of these costs, ethicists might argue that wealth maximization has to be sublimated to the broader interests of society. But what about those cases in which firms create substantial social costs without being aware of these costs? In the 1950s and 1960s, for example, John Manville Corporation produced asbestos with the intention of making a profit and was unaware of the carcinogenic potential of the product. Thirty years later, the lawsuits from those afflicted with asbestos-related cancers have driven the firm to bankruptcy.

To be fair, conflicts between the interests of the firm and the interests of society are not restricted to the objective function of maximizing stockholder wealth. They may in fact be endemic to a system of private enterprise, and there may never be a solution to satisfy the purists who would like to see a complete congruence between the social and firm interests.

❏ Concept
   Check

> Societies attempt to keep private interests in line by legislating against behavior that might create social costs (such as pollution). If the legislation is comprehensive enough, does the problem of social costs cease to exist? Why or why not?

The Real World—A Pictorial Representation

We have spent the last few pages chronicling the problems with each of the linkages—managers and stockholders, stockholders and bondholders, firms and financial markets, and firms and society. Figure 2.6 graphically summarizes the problems with each linkage. Given these problems, there are two possible alternative courses of action. The first is to keep the objective function of maximizing stockholder wealth and minimize its limitations. The second is to drop this objective function altogether and adopt an alternative instead.

MAXIMIZE STOCKHOLDER WEALTH, SUBJECT TO . . .

There can be no complete solution to the problems discussed in the previous section, but some of the problems can be alleviated. The objective is to reduce the conflicts of interest between stockholders, bondholders, and managers, and to reduce deviations between price and value.

Stockholders and Managers

Clearly, conflicts of interests exist between stockholders and managers, and the traditional mechanisms for stockholder control—annual meetings and boards of directors—often fail in their role of discipline management. This does not mean that the chasm between the two groups is too wide to be bridged, however, either by closing the gap between the parties' interests or by increasing stockholder power over managers.

Making managers think more like stockholders As long as managers have interests different from those of the stockholders they serve, there is potential for conflict. One way to reduce this conflict is to provide managers with an equity stake in the firms they manage, by providing them with either stock or **warrants** on the stock. In doing so, the benefits that accrue to management from higher stock prices may provide an inducement to maximize stock prices.

Warrants: A warrant is a security issued by a company that provides the holder with the right to buy a share of stock in the company at a fixed price during the life of the warrant.

There is a downside to this approach, however. While providing managers with an equity stake in the firm reduces the conflict of interest between stockholders and managers, it may exacerbate the other conflicts of interest highlighted in the prior section. That is, it may increase both the potential for expropriation of wealth from bondholders and the probability that misleading information may be conveyed to financial markets.

❑ Concept
Check

Many of the leveraged buyouts in the 1980s involved managers borrowing money and buying firms back from stockholders. If these buyouts were motivated, in part, by the desire to eliminate the separation of ownership and management, what types of firms (in terms of size, profitability, and performance) would have been the best candidates for these leveraged buyouts?

Increasing stockholder power   There are many ways to increase stockholder power over management. The first is to provide stockholders with better and more updated information so that they can make better judgments on how well the management is doing. The second is to appoint a large stockholder with a large holding to be part of incumbent management. This person would have a direct role in the firm's decision-making. Examples include Warren Buffett's role in the resuscitation of Salomon Brothers and Larry Tisch's stint as CEO of CBS Inc. In both cases, companies, that were in serious trouble with declining stock prices were rescued by stockholders with large holdings who reformulated policy to preserve and increase stockholder wealth.[12] The third way to increase stockholder power is to have more "activist" institutional stockholders, who play a larger role in issues such as the composition of the board of directors, the question of whether to pass anti-takeover amendments, and overall management policy. In recent years, institutional investors have used their considerable power to pressure managers into becoming more responsive to their needs. Among the most aggressive of these investors has been the California Public Employees Retirement System (CALPERS), one of the largest institutional investors in the country. Table 2.1 summarizes some of the changes that firms have made in response to institutional investors.

❑ Concept
Check

The interests of institutional investors and individual investors may sometimes diverge. Can you think of a scenario in which the two groups might have conflicting interests?

Table 2.1   **INSTITUTIONAL INVESTORS VERSUS MANAGERS**

Company	Agreement	Investors' Groups
K Mart	Phase out poison pill provision.	Wisconsin Inv. Board
Avon	Meet regularly with stockholders.	Calpers
Boise Cascade	Count only submitted proxy ballots.	Calpers
Boise Cascade	Require vote on golden parachutes.	United Shareholders Assn.
Baxter International	Make all proxy votes confidential.	United Shareholders Assn.
Consolidated Freight	Phase out golden parachutes.	United Shareholders Assn.
General Motors	Require a majority of outside directors.	Calpers
General Signal	Make all proxy votes confidential.	United Shareholders Assn.
W.R. Grace	Seat outside directors on pay committee.	Calpers
Unisys	Make all proxy votes confidential.	United Shareholders Assn.
Weyerhauser	Make all proxy votes confidential.	United Shareholders Assn.

[12]In the interest of the truth, it should be pointed out that neither was entirely successful in doing so.

The threat of a takeover   The perceived excesses of many takeovers in the 1980s drew attention to the negative consequences of such actions. In movies and books, the raiders who were involved in these takeovers were portrayed as "barbarians," while the firms being taken over were viewed as hapless victims. Although this may have been true in some cases, the reality was that, in most cases, companies that were taken over deserved to be taken over. A study by Bhide, for instance, found that target firms in hostile takeovers in 1985 and 1986 were generally much less profitable than were their competitors. These firms had provided sub-par returns to their stockholders, and their managers had significantly lower holdings of the equity. In short, badly managed firms were much more likely to become targets of hostile takeover bids, as shown in Figure 2.7.

One implication of this finding is that takeovers operate as a disciplinary mechanism, keeping managers in check by introducing a cost to bad management. Often, the very threat of a takeover is sufficient to force firms to restructure their assets and respond to stockholder concerns. It is not surprising, therefore, that legal attempts to regulate and restrict takeovers have had negative consequences for stock prices. One example was the anti-takeover law devised by the Pennsylvania legislature to protect companies incorporated in the state against hostile takeovers. The law was initiated in 1989, with much support from the state's chambers of commerce. Karpoff and Malatesta (1990) examined the consequences of this law for stock prices of Pennsylvania firms and found that they dropped (after adjusting for market movements), on average, 1.58% on October 13, 1989, the first day the law was mentioned in the news. Over the whole period, from the first news story to the introduction of the bill into the Pennsylvania legislature, these firms had a cumulative market-adjusted return of −6.90%.

The story of the Pennsylvania anti-takeover law would not be complete without documenting stockholder reactions. Institutional investors in the firms that would have been covered by the law chose to fight it. They expressed their displeasure to managers and threatened to sell their stock in these firms. Their threats worked, as most firms chose to opt out of the law, thereby illustrating the power stockholders can have if they choose to exercise it.

❑ Concept
  Check

One of the arguments made for having legislation restricting hostile takeovers is that unscrupulous speculators may take over well-run firms and destroy them for personal gain. Allowing for this possibility, do you think that this is sensible? Why or why not?

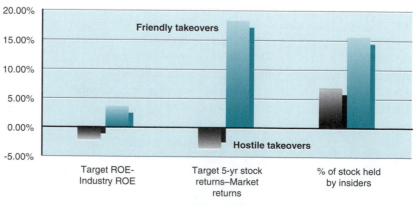

Figure 2.7   Target characteristics—hostile vs. friendly takeovers

The consequences of stockholder power   As stockholders exercise their newfound power, managers are becoming more responsive to their interests. This helps alleviate, if not eliminate, the problems associated with the separation of ownership and management.

Stockholders and Bondholders

The conflict of interest between stockholders and bondholders can lead to actions that transfer wealth from the bondholders to the stockholders, such as taking risky projects, paying more dividends, and increasing leverage, without compensating bondholders for the loss of wealth associated with these actions. There are ways bondholders can obtain at least partial protection against some of these actions, however.

The effect of covenants   The most direct way for bondholders to protect themselves is to write in covenants in their bond agreements specifically prohibiting or restricting actions that may be wealth expropriating. Many bond agreements have covenants that do the following:

1.   Restrict the firm's investment policy. Taking on projects riskier than anticipated can result in a transfer of wealth from stockholders to bondholders. Some bond agreements restrict where firms can invest and how much risk they can take on in their new investments in order to provide bondholders with the power to veto actions that are not in their best interests.

2.   Restrict dividend policy. In general, increases in dividends increase stock prices and decrease bond prices because they transfer wealth from bondholders to stockholders. Many bond agreements restrict dividend policy by tying dividend payments to earnings.

3.   Restrict additional leverage. Some bond agreements require firms to get the consent of existing bondholders before issuing new secured debt. This is done to protect the interests of existing secured bondholders.

Covenants can help protect bondholders against some abuses, but they come with a price tag. In particular, firms may find themselves having to turn down profitable opportunities because of bondholder-imposed constraints and having to pay (indirectly) for the legal and monitoring costs associated with the constraints.

Protective puts   The Nabisco illustration in the previous section provided an example of an "extreme" action (a leveraged buyout) that transferred wealth from existing bondholders to the equity investors in the firm. One way in which bondholders can protect themselves against such actions is to attach **protective puts** to their bonds, giving them the right to sell their bonds back to the firm at face value in the event of such actions.[13] In some cases, the right to exercise these puts is triggered by a change of control.

Protective Puts: A protective put in a bond allows a bondholder to return the bonds to the issuer before maturity and receive the face value, under a series of conditions that are enumerated in the bond covenants; for instance, the put may be triggered by an increase in the leverage.

---

[13]Harris Corporation and Northwest Pipeline, a subsidiary of Williams Companies, made a bond issue whereby bondholders would have had the right to put the bonds back to the firm at face value if the issue was downgraded below investment grade and one of a series of "designated events" occurred (including a merger, a major dividend payment, or a major stock repurchase).

Taking an equity stake   Since the primary cause of the conflict of interest between stockholders and bondholders lies in the nature of their claims, another way that bondholders can reduce the conflict of interest is by owning an equity stake in the firm. This can be done by buying stock in the firm at the same time as bonds or by attaching warrants to the debt or making bonds convertible into stock. In either case, bondholders who feel that equity investors have enriched themselves at their expense can become stockholders and share in the spoils.

Firms and Financial Markets

The information that firms convey to financial markets is noisy and sometimes misleading. The market price that emerges from financial markets is often wrong, partly because of inefficiencies in markets and partly because of errors in the information. There are no easy or quick-fix solutions to these problems. In the long term, however, certain actions will improve information quality and reduce deviations between price and value.

Improving the quality of information   Although regulatory bodies like the Securities and Exchange Commission can require firms to reveal additional information and penalize firms that provide misleading and fraudulent information, the quality of information cannot be improved with information disclosure laws alone. In particular, firms will always have a vested interest in when and what information they reveal to markets. To provide balance, therefore, there must be an active market for information, whereby analysts, who are not hired or fired by the firms they follow, collect and disseminate information. Analysts are just as likely to make mistakes but they have a greater incentive to unearth negative information about the firm and to disseminate that information to their clients.

Improving market efficiency   Just as better information cannot be legislated into existence, markets cannot be made more efficient by edict. In fact, there is widespread disagreement on what is required to make markets more efficient. At the minimum, the following conditions are necessary (though not sufficient) for more efficient markets:

1.   Trading should be both inexpensive and easy. The higher transactions costs are, and the more difficult it is to execute a trade, the more likely it is that markets will be inefficient.
2.   At least some investors in this market should have access to information about the stocks being traded as well as the resources to trade on the information.

Restrictions imposed on trading, though well intentioned, often lead to market inefficiencies. For instance, restricting short sales may seem good public policy, but it can create a scenario whereby negative information about stocks cannot be reflected adequately in prices.

❑ Concept
   Check

> Many emerging financial markets are characterized by the absence of good information about firms, thin trading, and extreme volatility. What are the consequences for value maximization in these markets? What about stock price maximization?

Firms and Society

Social costs will always be associated with actions taken by firms operating in their own best interests. The basic conundrum is as follows: social costs cannot be ignored in making decisions, but they are also too nebulous to be factored in explicitly into analyses.

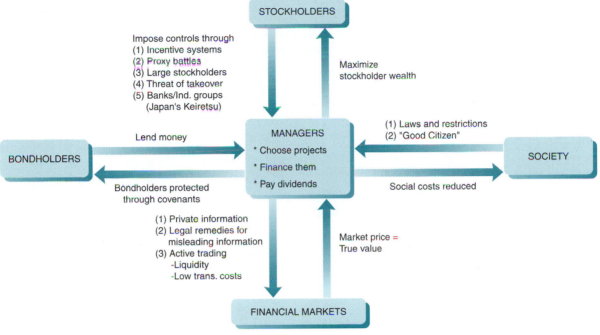

Figure 2.8   A partial solution

One solution is for firms to maximize firm or stockholder value, subject to a "good citizen" constraint, whereby attempts are made to minimize or alleviate social costs, even though the firm may not be under any legal obligation to do so. The problem with this approach, of course, is that the definition of a "good citizen" is likely to vary from firm to firm and from manager to manager. Some companies, however, have established reputations for being good corporate citizens and have managed to use it to their benefit. Exhibit 2.1 looks at how Levi Strauss views its social responsibilities.

Clearly, problems are associated with wealth maximization, but some of these problems can be reduced by making changes in how managers are hired and fired, in how they are compensated, in bondholder agreements, and in financial markets. Figure 2.8 summarizes some of these changes.

CHOOSING AN ALTERNATIVE OBJECTIVE FUNCTION

Given its limitations, the easy answer may be to cast aside wealth maximization as an objective function. The tough part is replacing it with another one. It is not that there are no alternatives but that the alternatives come with their own sets of problems. Whether there is a benefit to switching is not at all obvious, especially when the alternative objective is evaluated on the basis of the four criteria used to evaluate the wealth maximization objective: (1) Is the objective function clear and unambiguous? (2) Does it come with a measure that can be used to evaluate success and failure easily and promptly? (3) Does it create side costs that may exceed the overall benefits? (4) Is it consistent with maximizing the firm's long-term health and value?

The alternatives to the wealth maximization objective function can be categorized into four groups: intermediate, profit maximization, size/revenue, and social welfare objective functions.

Exhibit 2.1   L<small>EVI</small> S<small>TRAUSS</small> A<small>SPIRES TO</small>

NEW BEHAVIORS

Management must exemplify "directness, openness to influence, commitment to the success of others, and willingness to acknowledge our own contributions to problems."

DIVERSITY

Levi's "values a diverse workforce (age, sex, ethnic group, etc.) at all levels of the organization. . . . Differing points of view will be sought; diversity will be valued and honestly rewarded, not suppressed."

RECOGNITION

Levi's will "provide greater recognition—both financial and psychic—for individuals and teams that contribute to our success . . . those who create and innovate and those who continually support day-to-day business requirements."

ETHICAL MANAGEMENT PRACTICES

Management should epitomize "the stated standards of ethical behavior. We must provide clarity about our expectations and must enforce these standards throughout the corporation."

COMMUNICATIONS

Management must be "clear about company, unit, and individual goals and performance. People must know what is expected of them and receive timely, honest feedback. . . ."

EMPOWERMENT

Management must "increase the authority and responsibility of those closest to our products and customers. By actively pushing the responsibility, trust, and recognition into the organization, we can harness and release the capabilities of all our people."

Intermediate Objective Functions

Intermediate objective functions focus on variables that are believed to be strongly related to the firm's long-term health and value but are easier to measure than wealth maximization. For instance, maximizing market share can be viewed as an intermediate objective function, because underlying it is the belief that higher market share will mean higher profits and value in the long term. The rationale for adopting these intermediate objectives is that long-term value is too difficult to measure, whereas these intermediate variables are easily observable and measurable. The problem with these objective functions is that they are based on faith that there is—and will continue to be—a strong relationship between the intermediate variable and long-term value. If the link is broken, the firm may find itself in serious trouble. Consider American Airlines, which decided in the early 1980s to maximize market share in the U.S. airline industry, under the mistaken belief that this would mean higher ticket prices and profits in the long term. In 1993, Robert Crandall, the CEO of American Airlines, admitted that the strategy had been a failure and promised to focus on profitability instead.

Corporate strategists have been fond of using Japanese companies as counterexamples to illustrate what they believe is wrong with American firms. These strategists have pointed to the focus on market share as evidence that Japanese firms think long term, and attribute this vision to their success. The recent difficulties that many of these firms have experienced, especially in the electronics industry, however, illustrates the downside of market share maximization.

❏ **Concept
Check**
     Having a "customer focus" is undoubtedly an important part of any successful business. What would you think of a firm that made its objective function maximizing customer satisfaction?

Profit Maximization Objective Functions

Some objective functions focus on profitability rather than value. The rationale is that profits can be measured more easily than value and that higher profits translate into higher value in the long term. There are several problems with these objective functions, however. First, the emphasis on current profitability may result in short-term decisions that maximize profits now at the expense of long-term profits and value. Second, the notion that profits can be measured more easily than value may be incorrect, given the leeway that accountants have to shift profitability across periods.

Size/Revenue Objective Functions

There are a whole set of objective functions that have little to do with stockholder wealth but focus instead on size. Empire building may no longer be in vogue, but undeniably some corporations have made decisions that increase their size and perceived power at the expense of stockholder wealth and profitability. These objective functions are clearly the result of the stockholders' failure to have or to exercise much power over their managers.

Social Welfare Objective Functions

Some firms, especially government-owned firms, concentrate on social welfare objective functions. For instance, a firm that is directed to maximize the employment that it provides in the area in which it operates will make decisions accordingly, even though this may be fatal for its long-term health. A less extreme case would be a not-for-profit firm, say a hospital, whose mission might be to provide reasonable health care at an affordable cost. The meaning of "reasonable" and "affordable" in this context is not clear, especially when scarce resources have to be allocated among competing uses.

❑ Concept
   Check

> Assume that you have been hired to run a not-for-profit organization. Do you still need an objective function? How would you come up with an objective function and put it into practice in decision making in the organization?

Many firms use one or another of these objective functions instead of maximizing stockholder or firm wealth. It is not clear that they are gaining by doing so, however.

A POSTSCRIPT—THE LIMITS OF CORPORATE FINANCE

Corporate finance has come under more than its fair share of criticism in the last decade. Many analysts argue that the failures of corporate America can be traced to its dependence on corporate finance. Some of the criticism is justified and based on the limitations of a single-minded pursuit of stockholder wealth. Some of it, however, is based on a misunderstanding of what corporate finance is all about. Most of the criticism exaggerates the role corporate finance plays in significant decisions made by firms.

The Corporate Strategists' Critique of Corporate Finance

Michael Porter, a leading thinker on corporate strategy, has argued that U.S. firms are crippled by the fact that investors are short term and demand quick returns. He contrasts them with Japanese firms, which, he maintains can afford to adopt strategies that make sense in the long term, even though it might not maximize profits in the short term. Porter suggests that investors form long-term relationships with firms and work with them to devise long-term strategies.[14] His view of the world is not unique and is shared by many corporate executives, even in the United States.

The problem with this reasoning is that it might be based on the wrong premise. Although many stockholders in the United States do have short time horizons, that does not necessarily imply that they focus solely on profits in the near term. There is substantial evidence, in fact, that whereas stockholders react to earnings announcements, they look beyond these earnings in setting prices. It is also a mistake to assume that the absence of pressure from stockholders results in decisions that are in the best long-term interests of the firm, since managers may have objectives that conflict with those of the firm.

The notion that investors should work with the management of the firm in devising strategy and making decisions seems to be in the best traditions of cooperation. It draws strongly from the German and Japanese systems of corporate governance, whereby firms own stakes in other firms and often make decisions that are in the best interests of the industrial group to which they belong rather than their own best interests. Although this approach may protect the system against the waste that is a byproduct of stockholder activism and inefficient markets, it has its own disadvantages. Industrial groups are inherently more conservative than investors in allocating resources, and thus are much less likely to finance high-risk and venture capital investments by upstarts who do not belong to the group. Another problem is that entire groups can be dragged down by individual firms that have run into trouble. This alternative may have its advantages, but it is not a panacea for the problems outlined in the previous section.

The Efficient Market Critics

The trust that corporate finance places in well-functioning financial markets exposes it to a different group of critics who argue, with some justification, that markets are not efficient. These critics go too far, however, when they contend, on this basis, that corporate financial theory has no basis. Much of corporate financial theory is built on the objective of stockholder wealth maximization, and that theory holds whether or not markets are efficient. It is only if stock prices are used as a measure of success or failure that assumptions about market efficiency are made.

Still another group of critics disagrees with some of the models around which corporate finance is built, especially the capital asset pricing model. Again, although the criticism may be valid, it does not make sense to cast out an entire body of theory just because a model, no matter how important it is to the theory, is incorrect.

The Moralist Critique and the Role of Ethics

Economics was once branded the gospel of Mammon because of its emphasis on money and finances. The descendants of those critics have labeled corporate finance as unethical because of its emphasis on the "bottom line" and market prices, even if it means that workers lose their jobs and take cuts in pay. In cases like restructuring and liquidations, it is true that value maximization for stockholders may mean that other stakeholders, such as customers and employees, lose out. In most cases, however, decisions that increase market value also benefit customers and employees. Furthermore, if the firm is really in trouble, either because it is being undersold by competitors or because its prod-

---

[14]There is some movement toward "relationship investing" in the United States, where funds such as Allied Partners (run by Dillon Read), Corporate Partners (run by Lazard Freres), and Lens (run by activist Robert Monks) have attempted to create long-term relationships with managements of firms.

ucts are technologically obsolete, the choice is not between liquidation and survival but between a speedy resolution—which is what corporate financial theory would recommend—and a slow death, where the firm declines over time, and costs society considerably more in the process.

The conflict between wealth maximization for the firm and social welfare is the genesis for the attention paid to ethics in business schools. There will never be an objective function, and, therefore, decision rules that perfectly factor in societal concerns, simply because many of these concerns are difficult to quantify and are subjective. Thus, corporate financial theory, in some sense, assumes that decision makers will not make decisions that create large social costs, even if their models suggest otherwise. This assumption that decision makers are, for the most part, ethical and will not create unreasonable costs for society or for other stakeholders, is unstated but underlies corporate financial theory. When it is violated, it exposes corporate financial theory to ethical and moral criticism, although it may be better directed at the violators.

CONCLUSION

Corporate financial theory is built around the objective function of maximizing either stockholder or firm wealth. This objective function has the potential to create significant side costs, in the form of conflicts between stockholders and managers, stockholders and bondholders, and firms and society. These side costs can be reduced by adopting strategies that reduce the likelihood of these conflicts—by increasing stockholder power over managers, by providing protection for bondholders, and by developing "good citizen" constraints. This may be the optimal strategy to adopt, since alternative objective functions come with their own set of baggage. Finally, much of the criticism of corporate finance can be traced to disagreements critics have with the value maximization objective function, although their prescriptions do not necessarily provide improvement.

QUESTIONS AND PROBLEMS

1. The objective of decision making in corporate finance is
   a. To maximize earnings
   b. To maximize cash flows
   c. To maximize the size of the firm
   d. To maximize market share
   e. To maximize firm value/stock prices

2. For maximization of stock prices to be the sole objective in decision making, and to be socially desirable, the following assumptions have to hold true:
   a. Managers act in the best interests of stockholders.
   b. There is no conflict of interest between stockholders and bondholders.
   c. Financial markets are efficient.
   d. There are no costs that are created by the firm

that cannot be traced back and charged to the firm.
   e. All of the above.

3. There is a conflict of interest between stockholders and managers. In theory, stockholders are expected to exercise control over managers through the annual meeting or the board of directors. In practice, why might these disciplinary mechanisms not work?

4. Stockholders can transfer wealth from bondholders through a variety of actions. How would the following actions by stockholders transfer wealth from bondholders?
   a. an increase in dividends
   b. a leveraged buyout
   c. acquiring a risky business

How would bondholders protect themselves against these actions?

5. Financial market prices are much too volatile for financial markets to be efficient. Comment.

6. Maximizing stock prices does not make sense because investors focus on short-term results and not on long-term consequences. Comment.

7. Some corporate strategists have suggested that firms focus on maximizing market share rather than market prices. When might this strategy work, and when might it fail?

8. Anti-takeover amendments can be in the best interests of stockholders. Under what conditions is this likely to be true?

CHAPTER 3

PRESENT VALUE

The notion that a dollar today is preferable to a dollar some time in the future is intuitive enough for most people to grasp without the use of models and mathematics. The principles of present value provide more backing for this statement, however, and enable us to calculate exactly how much a dollar some time in the future is worth in today's dollars and to compare cash flow across time. The principles of present value also underlie most of what we do in corporate finance, from analyzing projects to valuing companies, and a great deal of what we do in our personal finances. In this chapter, we examine the following issues:

- What is the intuitive basis for present value? What are the determinants of the effect of timing on the value of cash flows?
- What are the different types of cash flows, and how can we estimate the present value of each of these types?
- What are the potential applications for present value rules in day-to-day living?
- What is the "separation theorem," and why does it matter?

TIME LINES AND NOTATION

The simplest tools in finance are often the most powerful. *Present value* is a concept that is intuitively appealing, simple to compute, and has a wide range of applications. It is useful in decision making, ranging from simple personal decisions—buying a house, saving for a child's education, estimating income in retirement—to more complex corporate financial decisions—picking projects in which to invest as well as the right financing mix for these projects.

Dealing with cash flows that are at different points in time is made easier using a *time line* that shows both the timing and the amount of each cash flow in a stream. Thus, a cash-flow stream of $100 at the end of each of the next four years can be depicted on a time line like the one depicted in Figure 3.1.

In the figure, 0 refers to right now. A cash flow that occurs at time 0 is therefore already in present value terms and does not need to be adjusted for time value. A distinction must be made here between a *period of time* and a *point in time*. The portion of the time line between 0 and 1 refers to *period* 1, which, in this example, is the first year. The cash flow that occurs at the *point* in time "1" refers to the cash flow that occurs at the end of period 1. Finally, the discount rate, which is 10% in this example, is specified for each period on the time line and may be different for each period. Had the cash flows been at the beginning of each year instead of at the end of each year, the time line would have been redrawn as it appears in Figure 3.2.

Figure 3.1 A time line for cash flows: end of each period

Figure 3.2 A time line for cash flows: beginning of each period

Note that, in present value terms, a cash flow that occurs at the beginning of year 2 is the equivalent of a cash flow that occurs at the end of year 1.

Cash flows can be either positive or negative; positive cash flows are called *cash inflows,* and negative cash flows are called *cash outflows.* For notational purposes, we will assume the following for the chapter that follows:

Notation	Stands for
PV	Present value
FV	Future value
Cf_t	Cash flow at the end of period *t*
A	Annuity—Constant cash flows over several periods
r	Discount rate
g	Expected growth rate in cash flows
n	Number of periods over which cash flows are received or paid

THE INTUITIVE BASIS FOR PRESENT VALUE

A cash flow in the future is worth less than a similar cash flow today because

1. Individuals *prefer present consumption to future consumption*. People would have to be offered more in the future to give up present consumption.

2. When there is *monetary inflation,* the value of currency decreases over time. The greater the inflation, the greater the difference in value between a dollar today and a dollar in the future.

3. Any *uncertainty (risk)* associated with the cash flow in the future reduces the value of the cash flow.

The process by which future cash flows are adjusted to reflect these factors is called *discounting,* and the magnitude of these factors is reflected in the **discount rate**.

Discount Rate: The discount rate is a rate at which present and future cash flows are traded off. It incorporates

1. The preference for current consumption (greater preference . . . higher discount rate).

2. Expected inflation (higher inflation . . .   higher discount rate).

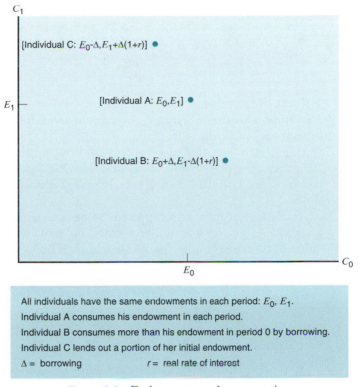

All individuals have the same endowments in each period: E_0, E_1.

Individual A consumes his endowment in each period.

Individual B consumes more than his endowment in period 0 by borrowing.

Individual C lends out a portion of her initial endowment.

Δ = borrowing r = real rate of interest

Figure 3.3   Endowments and consumption

3. The uncertainty in the future cash flows (higher risk. . .higher discount rate).

A higher discount rate will lead to a lower present value for future cash flows.

Tradeoff in Real Consumption Across Time

Although individuals prefer present consumption to future consumption, the degree of this preference varies across individuals. This tradeoff between present consumption (C_0) and future consumption (C_1) is presented in Figure 3.3. In the simple world described in this graph, individuals are endowed with wealth in each period and can either consume it or save it and lend it out.[1] Individual A chooses to consume all of his endowment in each period and neither saves nor borrows in either period. Individual B consumes Δ units more than his endowment in the current period by borrowing against his next-period endowment; accordingly, he has to pay it back in the next period with interest [$\Delta(1+r)$]. Individual C consumes less than her endowment in the current period and lends out the balance, enabling her to consume more than her endowment in the next period.

As noted earlier, when the preference for current consumption is strong, individuals will have to be offered much more in terms of future consumption to give up current consumption. This tradeoff is captured by a high "real" rate of return or discount rate. Conversely, when the preference for current consumption is weaker, individuals will settle for much less in terms of future consumption and, by extension, a low real rate of return or discount rate.

---

[1]The implicit assumption here is that any wealth that is saved will be lent out because it can then earn a return for the saver.

☐ Concept
Check

> The low savings rate in the United States has been contrasted with the higher savings rates in Japan to explain a variety of U.S. economic problems, from the budget to the trade deficit. What implications does the low savings rate have for discount rates?

Effects of Inflation

In addition to the preference for current over future consumption, another factor emerges when we move from real consumption to cash flows. A clear rationale for preferring a cash flow now to a similar cash flow in the future is inflation, which reduces the purchasing power of future cash flows. Other things being equal, the discount rate will increase with the inflation rate, thereby reducing the present value of future cash flows.

The effect of inflation on present value is evident when future cash flows are adjusted for expected inflation and stated in "real" terms. This adjustment reduces the value of future cash flows, but these real cash flows will have to be reduced further to reflect real returns (i.e., the tradeoff between current and future consumption) and any uncertainty associated with the cash flows to arrive at the present value. Thus, an investor who expects to make 10.5 million Mexican pesos a year from now will have to reduce this expected cash flow to reflect the expected inflation rate in Mexico. If that inflation rate is expected to be 35%, for instance, the real cash flow will be only 7.77 million Mexican pesos.

Effects of Risk

Although both the preference for current consumption, and expected inflation affect the present value of all cash flows, not all cash flows are equally predictable. A promised cash flow might not be delivered for a number of reasons: the promisor might default on the payment; the promisee might not be around to receive payment; or some other contingency might intervene to prevent the promised payment or to reduce it. The greater the uncertainty associated with a cash flow in the future, the higher the discount rate used to calculate the present value of this cash flow will be, and, consequently, the lower the present value of that cash flow will be.

The fact that higher uncertainty leads to higher discount rates is intuitively obvious, and models to measure this uncertainty and capture it in the discount rate are examined in Chapters 5 and 6.

THE MECHANICS OF PRESENT VALUE

The process of discounting future cash flows converts them into cash flows in present value terms. Conversely, the process of compounding converts present cash flows into future cash flows.

> **Present Value Principle 1:** Cash flows at different points in time cannot be compared and aggregated. All cash flows have to be brought to the same point in time before comparisons and aggregations can be made.

There are five types of cash flows—simple cash flows, annuities, growing annuities, perpetuities, and growing perpetuities.

Simple Cash Flows

A *simple cash flow* is a single cash flow in a specified future time period; it can be depicted on a time line:

where CF_t = the cash flow at time t.

This cash flow can be discounted back to the present using a discount rate that reflects the uncertainty of the cash flow. Concurrently, cash flows in the present can be compounded to arrive at an expected future cash flow.

Discounting: This is the process of moving a cash flow that is expected to occur in the future back to today's terms.

Discounting a simple cash flow   Discounting a cash flow converts it into present value dollars and enables the user to do several things. First, once cash flows are converted into present value dollars, they can be aggregated and compared. Second, if present values are estimated correctly, the user should be indifferent between the future cash flow and the present value of that cash flow. The present value of a cash flow can be written as follows:

$$\text{Present Value of Simple Cash Flow} = \frac{CF_t}{(1 + r)^t}$$

where

$$CF_t = \text{Cash Flow at the end of time period } t$$
$$r = \text{Discount Rate}$$

Other things remaining equal, the present value of a cash flow will decrease as the discount rate increases and continue to decrease the further into the future the cash flow occurs.

To illustrate, assume that you run a private retailing business, leasing the land under the store, and expect to make a lump-sum payment of $500,000 to the owner of the land 10 years from now. Assume that an appropriate discount rate for this cash flow is 10%. The present value of this cash flow can then be estimated:

$$\text{Present Value of Payment} = \frac{\$500,000}{(1.10)^{10}} = \$192,772$$

This present value is a decreasing function of the discount rate, as illustrated in Figure 3.4.

Compounding a cash flow   Current cash flows can be moved to the future by **compounding** the cash flow at the appropriate discount rate:

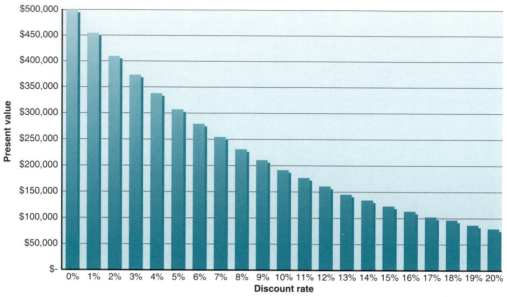

Figure 3.4 Present value of $500,000 in 10 years

$$\text{Future Value of Simple Cash Flow} = CF_0\,(1+r)^t$$

where

$$CF_0 = \text{Cash Flow now}$$
$$r = \text{Discount Rate}$$

Again, the compounding effect increases with both the discount rate and the compounding period.

Compounding: Compounding is the process by which cash flows are converted from present value to future value dollars.

As the length of the holding period is extended, small differences in discount rates can lead to large differences in future value. In a study of returns on stocks and bonds between 1926 and 1992, Ibbotson and Sinquefield found that stocks on the average made 12.4%, Treasury bonds made 5.2%, and Treasury bills 3.6%. Assuming that these returns continue into the future, Table 3.1 provides the future values of $100 invested in each category at the end of a number of holding periods—1 year, 5 years, 10 years, 20 years, 30 years, and 40 years.

The differences in future value from investing at these different rates of return are small for short compounding periods (such as one year) but become larger as the compounding period is extended. For instance, with a 40-year time horizon, the future value of investing in stocks, at an average return of 12.4%, is more than 12 times larger than the future value of investing in Treasury bonds at an average return of 5.2% and more than 25 times the future value of investing in Treasury bills at an average return of 3.6%.

Table 3.1: **FUTURE VALUES OF INVESTMENTS—ASSET CLASSES**

Holding Period	Stocks	T. Bonds	T. Bills
1	$112.40	$105.20	$103.60
5	179.40	128.85	119.34
10	321.86	166.02	142.43
20	1,035.92	275.62	202.86
30	3,334.18	457.59	288.93
40	10,731.30	759.68	411.52

❑ Concept
Check

Most pension plans allow individuals to decide where their pensions funds will be invested—stocks, bonds, or money market accounts. Where would you choose to invest your pension fund? Do you think your allocation should change as you get older? Why?

The Rule of 72—A Short Cut to Estimating the Compounding Effect   In a pinch, the rule of 72 provides an approximate answer the question "How quickly will this amount double in value?" by dividing 72 by the discount or interest rate used in the analysis. Thus, a cash flow growing at 6% a year will double in value in approximately 12 years, while a cash flow growing at 9% will double in value in approximately 8 years.

Effective Interest Rate: This is the true rate of interest, taking into account the compounding effects of more frequent interest payments.

The frequency of discounting and compounding   The frequency of compounding affects both the future and present values of cash flows. In the examples above, the cash flows were assumed to be discounted and compounded annually—that is, interest payments and income were computed at the end of each year, based on the balance at the beginning of the year. In some cases, however, the interest may be computed more frequently, such as on a monthly or semiannual basis. In these cases, the present and future values may be very different from those computed on an annual basis; the stated interest rate, on an annual basis, can deviate significantly from the effective or true interest rate. The **effective interest rate** can be computed as follows:

$$\text{Effective Interest Rate} = \left(1 + \frac{\text{Stated Annual Interest Rate}}{n}\right)^n - 1$$

where

n = number of compounding periods during the year (2=semiannual; 12=monthly)

For instance, a 10% annual interest rate, if there is semiannual compounding, works out to an effective interest rate of

$$\text{Effective Interest Rate} = 1.05^2 - 1 = .10125 \text{ or } 10.25\%$$

As compounding becomes continuous, the effective interest rate can be computed as follows:

$$\text{Effective Interest Rate} = \exp^r - 1$$

where

$$\exp = \text{exponential function}$$
$$r = \text{stated annual interest rate}$$

Table 3.2 provides the effective rates as a function of the compounding frequency.

Table 3.2   EFFECT OF COMPOUNDING FREQUENCY ON EFFECTIVE INTEREST RATES

Frequency	Rate (%)	t	Formula	Effective Annual Rate (%)
Annual	10	1	$.10$	10
Semiannual	10	2	$(1+.10/2)^2-1$	10.25
Monthly	10	12	$(1+.10/12)^{12}-1$	10.47
Daily	10	365	$(1+.10/365)^{365}-1$	10.5156
Continuous	10		$e^{.10}-1$	10.5171

As you can see, as compounding becomes more frequent, the effective rate increases, and the present value of future cash flows decreases.

To illustrate, most home mortgage loans in the United States require monthly payments and, consequently, have monthly compounding. Thus, the annual interest rates quoted on loans can be deceptive because they are actually too low. A loan with an annual interest rate of 8.00%, for example, when adjusted for the monthly compounding, will have an effective interest rate of:

$$\text{Effective Interest Rate} = \left(1 + \frac{.08}{12}\right)^{12} - 1 = 8.3\%$$

APR legislation   In 1968, Congress passed a law called the Truth-in-Lending Act, requiring that more information be provided on the true cost of borrowing to enable consumers to compare interest rates on loans. Under this law, which has been amended several times since its passage, financial institutions must provide an *annual percentage rate (APR)* in conjunction with any offer they might be making. The annual percentage rate is computed by multiplying the periodic rate by the number of periods per year. Thus, a monthly rate of 1% will result in an annual percentage rate of 12%. Because this does not allow for the compounding effect, some lenders may get higher effective annual interest rates by changing the compounding periods on their loans. The APR should also include an amortization of any fixed charges that have to be paid up front for the initiation of the loan. For instance, on a mortgage loan, these fixed charges would include the closing costs that are normally paid at the time at which the loan is taken.

Annuity: An annuity is a constant cash flow occurring at regular intervals of time.

Annuities

An **annuity** is a constant cash flow that occurs at regular intervals for a fixed period of time. Defining A to be the annuity, the time line for an annuity may be drawn as follows:

An annuity can occur at the end of each period, as in this time line, or at the beginning of each period.

Present value of an end-of-the-period annuity   The present value of an annuity can be calculated by taking each cash flow and discounting it back to the present and then adding up the present values. Alternatively, a formula can be used in the calculation. In the case of annuities that occur at the end of each period, this formula can be written as

$$PV \text{ of an Annuity} = PV\,(A,r,n) = A \left[\dfrac{1 - \dfrac{1}{(1+r)^n}}{r} \right]$$

where

$$A = \text{Annuity}$$
$$r = \text{Discount Rate}$$
$$n = \text{Number of Years}$$

Accordingly, the notation we will use in the rest of this book for the present value of an annuity will be $PV(A,r,n)$.

Suppose you run an advertising agency and you have a choice of buying a copier for $10,000 cash down or paying $3,000 a year for five years for the same copier. If the opportunity cost is 12%, which would you rather do?

$$PV \text{ of \$3,000 each year for next five years} = \$3,000 \left[\dfrac{1 - \dfrac{1}{(1.12)^5}}{.12} \right] = \$10,814$$

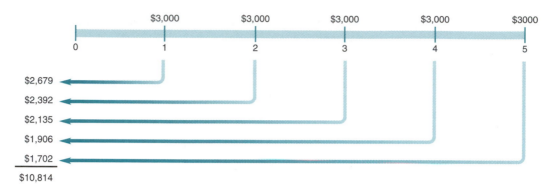

Figure 3.5   A time line for cash flows

The present value of the installment payments exceeds the cash-down price; therefore, you would want to pay the $10,000 in cash now.

Alternatively, the present value could have been estimated by discounting each of the cash flows back to the present and aggregating the present values, as illustrated in Figure 3.5.

 Concept Check

Often, you have the choice of buying an asset, such as a car, or leasing it. Is it appropriate to compare the present value of just your lease payments to your purchase price? Why or why not?

 IN PRACTICE   MAKING SENSE OF SPORTS CONTRACTS

Sports contracts for big-name players often involve mind-boggling amounts of money. Although the contracts are undoubtedly large, the use of nominal dollars in estimating the size of these contracts is misleading because the contracts are generally multiyear contracts.

- Consider, for instance, the $69 million contract signed by Derrick Coleman to play basketball for the New Jersey Nets in 1993. This contract required the payment of approximately $6.9 million a year for 10 years. Allowing for a discount rate of 10%, the present value of this contract can be calculated as follows:[2]

$$PV \text{ of } \$6.9 \text{ m each year for next 10 years} = \$6.9 \text{ m} \left[\frac{1 - \frac{1}{(1.10)^{10}}}{.10} \right] = \$42.39 \text{ mil}$$

[2]The contract was guaranteed, but it was contingent on Derrick Coleman remaining healthy. To the extent that there is a risk that he could be injured in the process of playing professional basketball, a rate higher than a risk-free rate is used as the discount rate.

• The use of nominal values for contracts serves a useful purpose. Both the player and the team signing him can declare victory in terms of getting the best deal. The player's ego is catered to by the size of the nominal contract, while the team's financial pain can be minimized by spreading the payments over more time, thus reducing the present value of the contract.

Concept Check

> Assume that you are negotiating a contract with your team's star player. You can afford to pay him only $1.5 million a year over three years (the remaining life of his contract). His agent insists that the player will not accept a contract with a nominal value less than $5 million. Can you meet his demand without relaxing your financial constraint on how much you can afford to pay him?

IN PRACTICE   HOW DO THEY DO THAT? LOTTERY PRIZES

State-run lotteries are usually created with some kind of noble mission to justify the state sponsorship of gambling. The New York State lottery, for instance, was expected to generate a considerable financial windfall for education—50% of the revenue generated from the lottery was supposed to go toward education. It is therefore surprising sometimes to see lottery prizes balloon way beyond the revenues from ticket sales. How, for instance, can a lottery pay out $40 million in prizes on ticket sales of $35 million and still claim to generate revenues for education? The answer lies in the fact that, while the sales are in current dollars, the prizes are paid out as annuities over very long time periods, resulting in a present value that is much lower than the announced prize.

Concept Check

> Assume that you run the lottery and you want to ensure that 50% of ticket revenues go toward education, while preserving the nominal prizes at $40 million. How much can you afford to pay out each year over 30 years, assuming a discount rate of 10%?

Amortization factors—annuities given present values   In some cases, the present value of the cash flows is known and the annuity needs to be estimated. This is often the case with home and automobile loans, for example, whereby the borrower receives the loan today and pays it back in equal monthly installments over an extended period of time. This process of finding an annuity when the present value is known is examined below:

$$\text{Annuity given Present Value} = A\ (PV, r, n) = PV \left[\frac{r}{1 - \dfrac{1}{(1 + r)^n}} \right]$$

To illustrate, suppose you are trying to borrow $200,000 to buy a house on a conventional 30-year mortgage with monthly payments. The annual percentage rate on the loan is 8%. The monthly payments on this loan can be estimated using the annuity due formula:

$$\text{Monthly Interest Rate on Loan} = \text{APR}/12 = 0.08/12 = 0.0067$$

$$\text{Monthly Payment on Mortgage} = \$200,000\left[\dfrac{0.0067}{1 - \dfrac{1}{(1.0067)^{360}}}\right] = \$1,473.11$$

This monthly payment is an increasing function of interest rates. When interest rates drop, homeowners usually have a choice of refinancing, though there is an up-front cost to doing so. We examine the question of whether or not to refinance later in this chapter.

Now suppose you are trying to buy a new car that has a sticker price of $15,000. The dealer offers you two deals:

- You can borrow $15,000 at a special financing annual percentage rate of 3%, for 36 months, or

- You can get $1,000 off the sticker price and borrow $14,000 at the normal financing rate of 12% per annum, for 36 months.

To examine which is the better deal, you must calculate the monthly payments on each one:

$$\text{Monthly Rate of Interest} = 3\%/12 = 0.25\%$$

$$\text{Monthly Payment on Special Financing Deal} = \$15,000\left[\dfrac{0.0025}{1 - \dfrac{1}{(1.0025)^{36}}}\right] = \$436.22$$

$$\text{Monthly Rate of Interest} = 12\%/12 = 1\%$$

$$\text{Monthly Payment on Discount Deal} = \$14,000\left[\dfrac{0.01}{1 - \dfrac{1}{(1.01)^{36}}}\right] = 1\ \$465.00$$

The monthly payments are lower on the special financing deal, making it the better one. Another way of looking at these choices is to compare the present value of the savings you get from the lower rate against the dollar value of the discount. In this case, for instance, the monthly payment on a $15,000 loan at an annual rate of 3% is $436.22, whereas the monthly payment on the same loan at an annual rate of 12% is $498.21. The monthly savings is $61.99, yielding a present value of savings of

$$\text{Present Value of Monthly Savings} = \$61.99\left[\dfrac{1 - \dfrac{1}{(1.01)^{36}}}{.01}\right] = \$1,866.34$$

The present value of the savings is greater than the price discount of $1,000. The dealer would therefore have to offer a much larger discount (>$1,866.34) for you to take the second deal.

Future value of end-of-the-period annuities   In some cases, an individual may plan to set aside a fixed annuity each period for a number of periods and will want to know how much he or she will have at the end of the period. The future value of an end-of-the-period annuity can be calculated as follows.

$$FV \text{ of an Annuity} = FV\,(A,r,n) = A\left[\frac{(1+r)^n - 1}{r}\right]$$

Thus, the notation we will use throughout this book for the future value of an annuity will be $FV(A,r,n)$.

Consider individual retirement accounts (IRAs), which allow some taxpayers to set aside $2,000 a year for retirement and exempts the income earned on these accounts from taxation. If an individual starts setting aside money in an IRA early in her working life, the value at retirement can be substantially higher than the nominal amount actually put in. For instance, assume that this individual sets aside $2,000 at the end of every year, starting when she is 25 years old, for an expected retirement at the age of 65, and that she expects to make 8% a year on her investments. The expected value of the account on her retirement date can be estimated as follows:

$$\text{Expected Value of IRA set aside at 65} = \$2,000\left[\frac{(1.08)^{40} - 1}{.08}\right] = \$518,113$$

The tax exemption adds substantially to the value because it allows the investor to keep the pretax return of 8% made on the IRA investment. If the income had been taxed at say 40%, the after-tax return would have dropped to 4.8%, resulting in a much lower expected value:

$$\text{Expected Value of IRA set aside at 65 is taxed} = \$2,000\left[\frac{(1.048)^{40} - 1}{.048}\right] = \$230,127$$

As you can see, the available funds at retirement drop by more than 55% as a consequence of the loss of the tax exemption.

Annuity given future value   Individuals or businesses who have a fixed obligation or a target to meet (in terms of savings) some time in the future need to know how much they should set aside each period to reach this target. If you are given the future value and are looking for an annuity—$A(FV,r,n)$ in terms of notation:

$$\text{Annuity given Future Value} = A(FV,r,n) = FV\left[\frac{r}{(1 + r)^n - 1}\right]$$

Balloon Payment Loan: A balloon payment loan refers to a loan on which only interest is paid for the life of the loan, and the entire principal is paid at the end of the loan's life.

To illustrate, in any **balloon payment loan,** only interest payments are made during the life of the loan, while the principal is paid at the end of the period. Companies that borrow money using balloon payment loans or conventional bonds (which share the same features) often set aside money in **sinking funds** during the life of the loan to ensure that they have enough at maturity to pay the principal on the loan or the face value of the bonds. Thus, a company with bonds that have a face value of $100 million coming due in 10 years would need to set aside the following amount each year (assuming an interest rate of 8%):

$$\text{Sinking Fund Provision each year} = \$10,000,000\left[\frac{.08}{(1.08)^{10} - 1}\right] = \$690,295$$

The company would need to set aside $690,295 at the end of each year to ensure that there would be enough funds ($10 million) to retire the bonds at maturity.

Concept Check

The size of the sinking fund provision is based on the level of interest rates. How would you recalculate the provision if one year into the 10-year process interest rates have dropped to 7%?

Sinking Fund: A sinking fund is a fund to which firms make annual contributions in order to have enough funds to meet a large financial liability in the future.

Effect of annuities at the beginning of each year   The annuities considered thus far in this chapter are end-of-the-period cash flows. Both the present and future values are affected if the cash flows occur at the beginning of each period instead of the end. To illustrate this effect, consider an annuity of $100 at the end of each year for the next four years, with a discount rate of 10%:

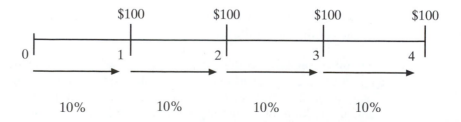

Contrast this with an annuity of $100 at the *beginning* of each year for the next four years, with the same discount rate:

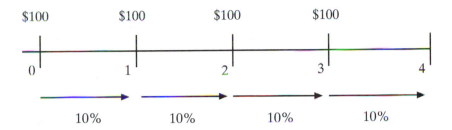

Because the first of these annuities occurs right now, and the remaining cash flows take the form of an end-of-the-period annuity over three years, the present value of this annuity can be written as follows:

$$PV \text{ of } \$100 \text{ at beginning of each of next four years} = \$100 + \$100 \left[\frac{1 - \dfrac{1}{(1.10)^3}}{.10} \right]$$

In general, the present value of a beginning-of-the-period annuity over n years can be written as follows:

$$PV \text{ of Beginning of Period Annuities over } n \text{ years} = A + A \left[\frac{1 - \dfrac{1}{(1 + r)^{n-1}}}{r} \right]$$

This present value will be higher than the present value of an equivalent annuity at the end of each period.

The future value of a beginning-of-the-period annuity typically can be estimated by allowing for one additional period of compounding for each cash flow:

$$FV \text{ of a Beginning-of-the-Period Annuity} = A\,(1+r) \left[\frac{(1 + r)^n - 1}{r} \right]$$

This future value will be higher than the future value of an equivalent annuity at the end of each period.

Consider again the example of an individual who sets aside $2,000 at the end of each year for the next 40 years in an IRA account at 8%. The future value of these deposits amounted to $518,113 at the end of year 40. If the deposits had been made at the *beginning* of each year instead of the end, the future value would have been higher:

$$\text{Expected Value of IRA (beginning of year)} = \$2,000\,(1.08)\left[\frac{(1.08)^{40}-1}{.08}\right] = \$559,562$$

As you can see, the gains from making deposits at the beginning of each period can be substantial.

Growing Annuity: A growing annuity is a cash flow growing at a constant rate and paid at regular intervals of time.

Growing Annuities

A **growing annuity** is a cash flow that grows at a constant rate for a specified period of time. If A is the current cash flow, and g is the expected growth rate, the time line for a growing annuity appears as follows:

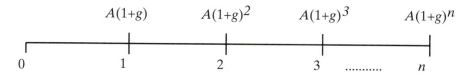

Note that, to qualify as a growing annuity, the growth rate in each period has to be the same as the growth rate in the prior period.

The process of discounting   The present value of a growing annuity can usually be estimated by using the following formula:

$$PV \text{ of a Growing Annuity} = A(1+g)\left[\frac{1-\dfrac{(1+g)^{n}}{(1+r)^{n}}}{r-g}\right]$$

The present value of a growing annuity can be estimated in all cases but one—if the growth rate is equal to the discount rate. In that case, the present value is equal to the nominal sums of the annuities over the period, without the growth effect.

$$PV \text{ of a Growing Annuity for } n \text{ years (when } r{=}g) = n\,A$$

Note also that the expanded formulation works even when the growth rate is greater than the discount rate.[3]
   To illustrate, suppose you have the rights to a gold mine for the next 20 years, over which period you plan to extract 5,000 ounces of gold every year. The current price per ounce is $300, but it is expected to increase 3% a year. The appropriate discount rate is

---

[3]Both the denominator and the numerator in the formula will be negative, yielding a positive present value.

10%. The present value of the gold that will be extracted from this mine can be estimated as follows.

$$PV \text{ of extracted gold} = \$300 * 5,000 * (1.03) \left[\frac{1 - \frac{(1.03)^{20}}{(1.10)^{20}}}{.10 - .03} \right] = \$16,145,980$$

The present value of the gold expected to be extracted from this mine is $16.146 million; it is an increasing function of the expected growth rate in gold prices. Figure 3.6 illustrates the present value as a function of the expected growth rate.

☐ Concept
    Check

If both the growth rate and the discount rate increase by 1%, will the present value of the gold to be extracted from this mine increase or decrease? Explain.

Perpetuity: A perpetuity is a constant cash flow paid (or received) at regular time intervals forever.

Perpetuities

A **perpetuity** is a constant cash flow at regular intervals *forever*. The present value of a perpetuity can be written as

$$PV \text{ of Perpetuity} = \frac{A}{r}$$

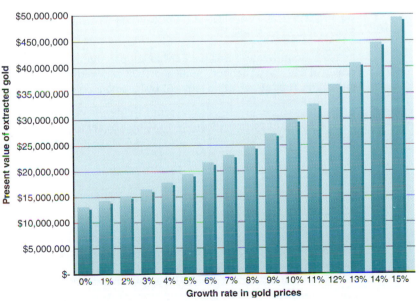

Figure 3.6   Present value of extracted gold as a function of growth rate

where A is the perpetuity. The future value of a perpetuity is infinite.

A *console bond* is a bond that has no maturity and pays a fixed coupon. Assume that you have a 6% coupon console bond. The value of this bond, if the interest rate is 9%, is as follows.

$$\text{Value of Console Bond} = \$60 \,/\, .09 = \$667$$

The value of a console bond will be equal to its face value only if the coupon rate is equal to the interest rate.

Growing Perpetuities

A **growing perpetuity** is a cash flow that is expected to grow at a *constant rate* forever. The present value of a growing perpetuity can be written as

$$PV \text{ of Growing Perpetuity} = \frac{CF_1}{(r-g)}$$

where CF_1 is the expected cash flow next year, g is the constant growth rate, and r is the discount rate.

 Growing Perpetuity: A growing perpetuity is a constant cash flow, growing at a constant rate, and paid at regular time intervals forever.

Although a growing perpetuity and a growing annuity share several features, the fact that a growing perpetuity lasts forever puts constraints on the growth rate. It has to be less than the discount rate for this formula to work.

IN PRACTICE VALUING A STOCK WITH STABLE GROWTH IN DIVIDENDS—SOUTHWESTERN BELL

In 1992, Southwestern Bell paid dividends per share of $2.73. Its earnings and dividends had grown at 6% a year between 1988 and 1992 and were expected to grow at the same rate in the long term. The rate of return required by investors on stocks of equivalent risk was 12.23%.

Current Dividends per share = $2.73
Expected Growth Rate in Earnings and Dividends = 6%
Discount Rate = 12.23%

$$\text{Value of Stock} = \$2.73 * 1.06 \,/\, (.1223 - .06) = \$46.45$$

As an interesting aside, the stock was actually trading at $70 per share. This price could be justified by using a higher growth rate. The value of the stock is graphed in Figure 3.7 as a function of the expected growth rate.

The growth rate would have to be approximately 8% to justify a price of $70. This growth rate is often referred to as an *implied growth rate*.

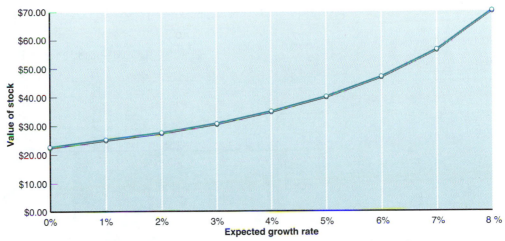

Figure 3.7   Southwestern Bell Value versus expected growth

Combinations and Uneven Cash Flows

In the real world, a number of different types of cash flows are combined including annuities, simple cash flows, and sometimes perpetuities.

* A conventional bond pays a fixed coupon every period for the lifetime of the bond and the face value of the bond at maturity. In terms of a time line:

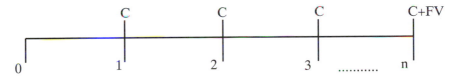

C: Annual Coupon on Straight Bond
FV: Face Value of Straight Bond
n: Maturity of the Straight Bond

Because coupons are fixed and paid at regular intervals, they represent an annuity, whereas the face value of the bond is a single cash flow that has to be discounted separately. The value of a straight bond can then be written as follows:

Value of Straight Bond = Coupon (*PV* of an Annuity for the life of the bond)
+ Face Value (*PV* of a Single Cash Flow)

The value of a straight bond   Suppose you are trying to value a straight bond with a 15-year maturity and a 10.75% coupon rate. The current interest rate on bonds of this risk level is 8.5%.

$$PV \text{ of cash flows on bond} = 107.50* PV(A,8.5\%,15 \text{ years}) + 1{,}000/1.085^{15}$$
$$= \$1{,}186.85$$

If interest rates rise to 10%,

$$PV \text{ of cash flows on bond} = 107.50* PV(A,10\%,15 \text{ years}) + 1{,}000/1.10^{15} = \$1{,}057.05$$

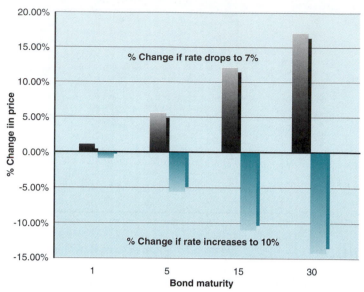

Figure 3.8   Price changes as a function of bond maturities

$$\text{Percentage change in price} = (\$1{,}057.05 - \$1{,}186.85)/\$1{,}186.85 = -10.94\%$$

If interest rate fall to 7%,

$$PV \text{ of cash flows on bond} = 107.50 * PV(A,7\%,15 \text{ years}) + 1{,}000/1.07^{15} = \$1{,}341.55$$
$$\text{Percentage change in price} = (\$1{,}341.55 - \$1{,}186.85)/\$1{,}186.85 = +13.03\%$$

This asymmetric response to interest rate changes is called *convexity*.

Contrasting short-term versus long-term bonds   Now say you are valuing four bonds with different maturities—1 year, 5 years, 15 years, and 30 years—with the same coupon rate of 10.75%. Figure 3.8 contrasts the price changes on these three bonds as a function of interest rate changes. Longer term bonds are more sensitive to interest rate changes than shorter term bonds.

> **Bond Pricing Proposition 1:**   The longer the maturity of a bond, the more sensitive it is to changes in interest rates.

Contrasting low-coupon and high-coupon bonds   Suppose you are valuing four different bonds, all with the same maturity—15 years, but different coupon rates—0%, 5%, 10.75%, and 12%. Figure 3.9 contrasts the effects of changing interest rates on each of these bonds.

> **Bond Pricing Proposition 2:**   The lower the coupon rate on the bond, the more sensitive it is to changes in interest rates.

- In the case of the stock of a company that expects high growth in the near future and lower and more stable growth forever after that, the expected dividends take the following form:

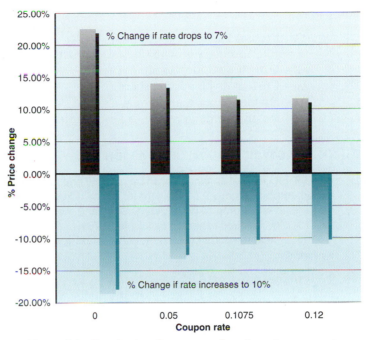

Figure 3.9   Bond price changes as a function of coupon rates

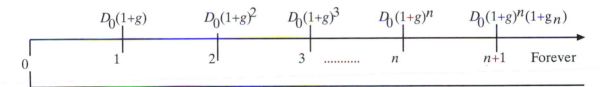

High-Growth Period   Stable-Growth Period

D_0 = Dividends per share currently
g = Expected growth rate in high-growth period (n years)
g_n = Expected growth rate after high-growth period

The dividends over the high-growth period represent a growing annuity, whereas the dividends after that satisfy the conditions of a growing perpetuity. The value of the stock can thus be written as the sum of the two present values:

$$P_0 = \frac{D_0*(1+g)*\left(1 - \dfrac{(1+g)^n}{(1+r)^n}\right)}{r-g} + \frac{D_{n+1}}{(r-g_n)(1+r)^n}$$

Growing Annuity   Growing Perpetuity - discounted back

where

P_0 = Present Value of expected dividends
g = Extraordinary growth rate for the first n years (n = high-growth period)
g_n = Growth rate forever after year n
D_0 = Current dividends per share
D_t = Dividends per share in year t
r = Required rate of return → Discount Rate

 IN PRACTICE THE VALUE OF A HIGH-GROWTH STOCK—ELI LILLY

In 1992, Eli Lilly had earnings per share of $4.50 and paid dividends per share of $2.00. Analysts expected both to grow 9.81% a year for the next five years. After the fifth year, the growth rate was expected to drop to 6% a year forever, and the payout ratio was expected to increase to 67.44%. The required return on Eli Lilly is 12.78%.

The price at the end of the high-growth period can be estimated using the growing perpetuity formula:

$$
\begin{aligned}
\text{Terminal price} \quad &= DPS_6 / (r - g_n) \\
&= EPS_6 * \text{Payout Ratio in Stable Growth} / (r - g_n) \\
&= EPS_0 (1 + g)^5 (1 + g_n) / (r - g_n) \\
&= \$4.50 * 1.0981^5 * 1.06 * 0.6744 / (.1278 - .06) = \$75.76
\end{aligned}
$$

The present value of dividends and the terminal price can then be calculated as follows.

$$
P_0 = \frac{\$2.00 * (1.0981) * \left(1 - \dfrac{(1.0981)^5}{(1.1278)^5}\right)}{.1278 - .0981} + \frac{\$75.76}{(1.1278)^5} = \$50.76
$$

The value of Eli Lilly stock, based on the expected growth rates and discount rate, is $50.76.

One annuity may follow another. In this case, the present value will be the sum of the present values of the two (or more) annuities. A time line for two annuities can be drawn as follows:

A1: First Annuity
A2: Second Annuity

The present value of these two annuities can be calculated separately and cumulated to arrive at the total present value. The present value of the second annuity has to be discounted back to the present.

To illustrate, suppose you are the pension fund consultant to MetTech, a small high-technology company that needs to know the present value of its expected obligations, which amount in nominal terms to the following:

Years	Annual Cash Flow
1–5	$2 million
6–10	$3 million
11–20	$4 million

If the discount rate is 10%, the present value of these three annuities can be estimated as follows.

$$\text{Present Value of first annuity} = \$2 \text{ million} * PV\,(A,10\%,5) = \$7.58 \text{ million}$$
$$\text{Present Value of second annuity} = \$3 \text{ million} * PV\,(A,10\%,5) / 1.10^5 = \$7.06 \text{ million}$$
$$\text{Present Value of third annuity} = \$4 \text{ million} * PV\,(A,10\%,10) / 1.10^{10} = \$9.48 \text{ million}$$

The present values of the second and third annuities can be estimated in two steps. First, the standard present value of the annuity is computed over the period that the annuity is paid. Second, that present value is brought back to the present. Thus, for the second annuity, the present value of $3 million each year for five years is computed to be $11.37 million; this present value is really as of the end of the fifth year.[4] It is discounted back five more years to arrive at today's present value, which is $7.06 million.

$$\text{Cumulated Present Value} = \$7.58 \text{ million} + \$7.06 \text{ million} + \$9.48 \text{ million}$$
$$= \$24.12 \text{ million}$$

WHOSE DISCOUNT RATE DO WE USE? THE SEPARATION THEOREM

Although present value is undoubtedly a valuable tool for dealing with cash flows that are distributed over time, different individuals may come up with different discount rates for the same set of cash flows, for a number of reasons:

1. The preference for current consumption over future consumption, which determines the real rate of return, may vary across individuals. Those with a stronger preference for current consumption will demand higher rates of return and, therefore, higher discount rates.

2. Expectations about inflation, which determine the nominal discount rates, may vary across individuals as well.

3. The degree of risk aversion may vary across individuals, resulting in differing premiums attached to the uncertainty associated with the cash flows.

If all present value analyses were done at the level of the individual getting the cash flows, and the discount rate could be adjusted to reflect that individual's preferences, this variability would not seem to be a problem. There is a problem, however, when a decision maker has to analyze the present value on investments made by a *group* of individuals, each of whom may have a different discount rate. This is the case, for example, when a manager in a publicly traded company with thousands of stockholders has to decide on the discount rate to use in project analyses. How can the manager pick a discount rate that will satisfy all, or at least most, of these stockholders? The introduc-

[4]A common error is to assume that since the first payment in this annuity is at the end of the sixth year, the present value is also at that point. The process of computing the present value, however, moves the cash flows back one year prior to the first cash flow, which, in this case, is to the end of the fifth year.

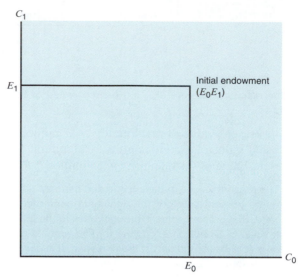

Figure 3.10 Robinson Crusoe World

tion of a market in which investors can lend and borrow, in addition to taking real projects, provides the solution. When such a market exists, the decision of which discount rate to use in real projects can be separated at least from individual preferences for current and future consumption. This is called the **separation theorem.**

Separation Theorem: The separation theorem argues that in the presence of capital markets, the risk of a project or an investment can be evaluated independently of the risk-aversion characteristics of the investors in that project or investment.

A Robinson Crusoe World

To derive the separation theorem, consider again a simple two-period world, in which individuals are provided with an endowment of consumable goods in each period. Also assume that there are no productive investments and that no trading is allowed between individuals. In this society, which is referred to as a *Robinson Crusoe World,* all individuals will have to consume their endowments, even if their preferences lie elsewhere, as illustrated in Figure 3.10.

Capital Markets—Individuals Can Lend and Borrow

Consider now the introduction of capital markets, in which individuals can either lend out a portion of their current endowment or borrow on the next period's endowment. The rate at which these endowments are lent out (and borrowed) is called a *market interest rate*. Preferences for current and future consumption will be captured through each individual's indifference curves, which trace out combinations of current and future consumption over which that individual is indifferent. Figure 3.11 traces the indifference curves of two individuals and derives their preferred consumption in the current and future periods.

The existence of capital markets now allows both individuals to choose consumption patterns that fit their preferences. Individual A will consume less than his endowment in the initial period and lend out the balance to individual B. Individual B will consume more than her endowment in the current period but will have to pay back the borrowed endowment with interest in the following period.

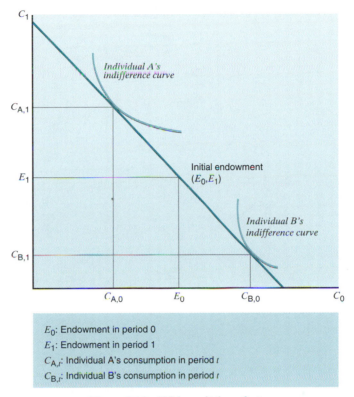

E_0: Endowment in period 0
E_1: Endowment in period 1
$C_{A,t}$: Individual A's consumption in period t
$C_{B,t}$: Individual B's consumption in period t

Figure 3.11   With capital markets

Productive Opportunities—Individuals Can Make Real Investments

As an alternative to capital markets, consider a society in which individuals can invest a portion of their current endowment in real projects; assume also that the marginal returns on these projects decreases with each additional investment. (This is captured in Figure 3.12; the marginal returns are measured by the slope of the productive opportunity set, which decreases as more and more projects are taken.) In this society, individual A invests a great deal of his initial endowment in real projects; he takes more projects and thus can be viewed as having a lower discount rate. Individual B, by contrast, invests far less of her initial endowment in real projects; she takes fewer projects and can be viewed as having a much higher discount rate.

Capital Markets and Productive Opportunities

Finally, consider the introduction of both capital markets and productive opportunities. In this case, individuals have the option of either investing in real projects or lending their endowment out on capital markets, at the market interest rate (see Figure 3.13). Individual A, who invested heavily in productive opportunities in the prior analysis, will continue to do so, but only as long as the returns on the real project exceed the market interest rate (which becomes the discount rate). Once he reaches the point at which the marginal returns on real projects is less than the market interest rate, he will lend his endowment out rather than invest it. Individual B will invest the same amount as individual A (i.e., until the marginal return on the project is equal to the market interest rate). However, having done that, she will now borrow on capital markets, based on the expected returns on her projects, for current consumption.

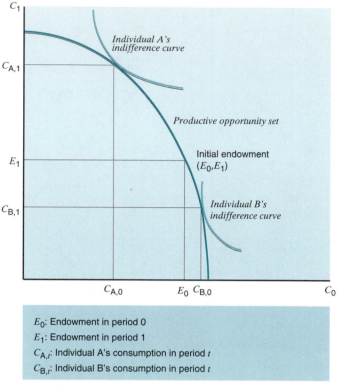

E_0: Endowment in period 0
E_1: Endowment in period 1
$C_{A,t}$: Individual A's consumption in period t
$C_{B,t}$: Individual B's consumption in period t

Figure 3.12   With productive opportunities

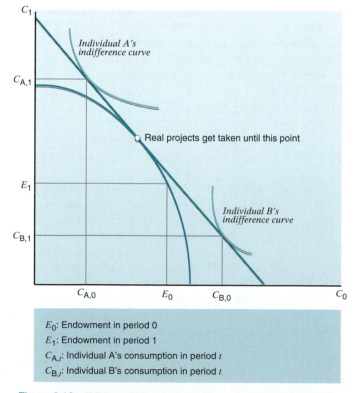

E_0: Endowment in period 0
E_1: Endowment in period 1
$C_{A,t}$: Individual A's consumption in period t
$C_{B,t}$: Individual B's consumption in period t

Figure 3.13   With capital markets and productive opportunities

Thus, the existence of capital markets in conjunction with productive opportunities creates a consensus between individuals who prefer current consumption less (Individual A) and those who prefer it more (Individual B) about which projects should be taken. Capital markets enable both individuals to adjust their consumption patterns to meet their preferences.

CONCLUSION

Present value remains one of the simplest and most powerful techniques in finance, providing a wide range of applications in both personal and business decisions. Cash flows can be moved back to present value terms by discounting and moved forward by compounding. The discount rate at which the discounting and compounding are done reflect three factors: (1) the preference for current consumption, (2) expected inflation, and (3) the uncertainty associated with the cash flows being discounted.

In this chapter, we explored approaches to estimating the present value of five types of cash flows: simple cash flows, annuities, growing annuities, perpetuities, and growing perpetuities.

QUESTIONS AND PROBLEMS

1. You have an expected liability (cash outflow) of $500,000 in 10 years, and you use a discount rate of 10%.

   a. How much would you need right now as savings to cover the expected liability?

   b. How much would you need to set aside at the end of each year for the next 10 years to cover the expected liability?

2. You are examining whether your savings will be adequate to meet your retirement needs. You saved $1,500 last year, and you expect your annual savings to grow 5% a year for the next 15 years. If you can invest your money at 8%, how much would you expect to have at the end of the fifteenth year?

3. You have just taken a 30-year mortgage loan for $200,000. The annual percentage rate on the loan is 8%, and payments will be made monthly. Estimate your monthly payments.

4. You are planning to buy a car worth $20,000. Which of the two deals described below would you choose:

   • The dealer offers to take 10% off the price and lend you the balance for 5 years at the regular financing rate (which is an annual percentage rate of 9%).

   • The dealer offers to lend you $20,000 (with no discount) for 5 years at a special financing rate of 3%.

5. A company is planning to set aside money to repay $100 million in bonds that will be coming due in 10 years. If the appropriate discount rate is 9%

   a. How much money would the company need to set aside at the end of each year for the

next 10 years to be able to repay the bonds when they come due?

   b. How would your answer change if the money were set aside at the beginning of each year?

6. What is the value of 15-year corporate bonds, with a coupon rate of 9%, if current interest rates on similar bonds is 8%? How much would the value change if interest rates increased to 10%? Under what conditions will this bond trade at par (face value)?

7. What is the value of stock in a company that currently pays out $1.50 per share in dividends and expects these dividends to grow 6% a year forever? (You can assume that investors require a 13% return on stocks of equivalent risk.)

8. What is the value of stock in a company that currently pays out $1.00 per share in dividends and expects these dividends to grow 15% a year for the next five years and 6% a year forever after that? (You can assume that investors require a 12.5% return on stocks of equivalent risk and that the dividend payout ratio will double after the fifth year.)

9. You buy a 10-year zero-coupon bond, with a face value of $1,000, for $300. What is the rate of return you expect to make on this bond?

10. You are reviewing an advertisement by a finance company offering loans at an annual percentage rate of 9%. If the interest is compounded weekly, what is the effective annualized interest rate on this loan?

11. You have a relative who has accumulated savings of $250,000 over his working lifetime and now plans to retire. Assuming that he wishes to withdraw equal installments from these savings for the next 25 years of this life, how much will each installment amount to, if he is earning 5% on his savings?

12. You are offered a special set of annuities by your insurance company, whereby you will receive $20,000 a year for the next 10 years and $30,000 a year for the following 10 years. How much would you be willing to pay for these annuities if your discount rate is 9% and the annuities are paid at the end of each year? How much would you be willing to pay if they were at the beginning of each year?

13. A bill that is designed to reduce the nation's budget deficit passes both houses of the legislature. Congress tells us that the bill will reduce the deficit by $500 billion over 10 years. What it does not tell us is the timing of the reductions.

Year	Deficit Reduction
1	$25 billion
2	$30 billion
3	$35 billion
4	$40 billion
5	$45 billion
6	$55 billion
7	$60 billion
8	$65 billion
9	$70 billion
10	$75 billion

If the federal government can borrow at 8%, what is the true deficit reduction in the bill?

14. New York State has a pension fund liability of $25 billion, due in 10 years. Each year the legislature is supposed to set aside an annuity to arrive at this future value. This annuity is based on what the legislature believes it can earn on this money.

    a. Estimate the annuity needed each year for the next 10 years, assuming that the interest rate that can be earned on the money is 6%.

    b. The legislature changes the investment rate to 8% and recalculates the annuity needed to arrive at the future value. It claims the difference as budget savings this year. Do you agree?

15. Poor Bobby Bonilla! The newspapers claim that he is making $5.7 million a year. He claims that this is not true in a present value sense and that he will really be making the following amounts for the next five years:

Year	Amount
0 (now)	$5.5 million (sign-up bonus)
1	$4 million
2	$4 million
3	$4 million
4	$4 million
5	$7 million

    a. Assuming that Bonilla can make 7% on his investments, what is the present value of his contract?

    b. If you wanted to raise the nominal value of his contract to $30 million, while preserving the present value, how would you do it? (You can adjust only the sign-up bonus and the final year's cash flow.)

16. You are comparing houses in two towns in New Jersey. You have $100,000 for a down payment, and 30-year mortgage rates are at 8%.

	Chatham	South Orange
Price of the house	$400,000	$300,000
Annual property tax	$6,000	$12,000

The houses are roughly equivalent.

    a. Estimate the total payments (mortgage and property taxes) you would have on each house. Which one is less expensive?

    b. Are mortgage payments and property taxes directly comparable? Why or why not?

    c. If property taxes are expected to grow 3% a year forever, which house is less expensive?

17. You bought a house a year ago for $250,000, borrowing $200,000 at 10% on a 30-year term loan (with monthly payments). Interest rates have since come down to 9%. You can refinance your mortgage at this rate, with a closing cost that will be 3% of the loan. Your opportunity cost is 8%. Ignore tax effects.

    a. How much are your monthly payments on your current loan (at 10%)?

    b. How much would your monthly payments be if you could refinance your mortgage at 9% (with a 30-year term loan)?

    c. You plan to stay in this house for the next five years. Given the refinancing cost (3% of the loan), would you refinance this loan?

    d. How much would interest rates have to go down before it would make sense to refinance this loan (assuming that you are going to stay in the house for five years)?

18. You are 35 years old today and are considering your retirement needs. You expect to retire at age 65, and your actuarial tables suggest that you will

live to be 100. You want to move to the Bahamas when you retire. You estimate that it will cost you $300,000 to make the move (on your sixty-fifth birthday) and that your living expenses will be $30,000 a year (starting at the end of year 66 and continuing through the end of year 100) after that. You expect to earn 8% on your money

a. How much will you need to have saved by your retirement date to be able to afford this course of action?

b. You already have $50,000 in savings. How much would you need to save each year for the next 30 years to be able to afford this retirement plan?

c. If you did not have any current savings and do not expect to be able to start saving money for the next five years, how much would you have to set aside each year after that to be able to afford this retirement plan?

19. You have been hired to run a pension fund for TelDet, Inc., a small manufacturing firm. The firm currently has $5 million in the fund and expects to have cash inflows of $2 million a year for the first five years followed by cash outflows of $3 million a year for the next five years. Assume that interest rates are at 8%.

a. How much money will be left in the fund at the end of the tenth year?

b. If you were required to pay a perpetuity after the tenth year (starting in year 11 and going through infinity) out of the balance left in the pension fund, how much could you afford to pay?

20. You are an investment advisor who has been approached by a client for help on his financial strategy. He has $250,000 in savings in the bank. He is 55 years old and expects to work for 10 more years, making $100,000 a year. (He expects to make a return of 5% on his investments for the foreseeable future. You can ignore taxes.)

a. Once he retires 10 years from now, he would like to be able to withdraw $80,000 a year for the following 25 years. (His actuary tells him he will live to be 90 years old.) How much would he need in the bank 10 years from now to be able to do this?

b. How much of his income would he need to save each year for the next 10 years to be able to afford these planned withdrawals ($80,000 a year) after the tenth year?

c. Assume that interest rates decline to 4%, ten years from now. By how much, if any, would your client have to *lower his annual withdrawal,* assuming that he still plans to withdraw cash each year for the next 25 years?

21. You have been asked to estimate the value of a 10-year bond with a coupon that will be low initially but is expected to grow later in the bond's life. The coupon is expected to be 5% of the face value of the bond (which is $1,000) for the first five years and will increase by 1% every year for the next five years—the coupon rate will be 6% in year 6, 7% in year 7, 8% in year 8, 9% in year 9, and 10% in year 10. Estimate the value of this bond if the market interest rate is 8%.

22. You are trying to assess the value of a small retail store that is for sale. The store generated a cash flow to its owner of $100,000 in the most profitable year of operation and is expected to have growth of about 5% a year in perpetuity.

• If the rate of return required on this store is 10%, what is your assessment of the value of the store?

• What would the growth rate need to be to justify a price of $2.5 million for this store?

CHAPTER 4

UNDERSTANDING FINANCIAL STATEMENTS

Much of the information that is used in valuation and corporate finance comes from financial statements. An understanding of the basic financial statements and some of the financial ratios that are used in analysis is therefore a necessary first step for either pursuit. This chapter examines the following questions:

- How are the financial statements—income statements, balance sheets, and statements of cash flows—constructed?

- What are the generally accepted accounting principles, and how do they influence the preparation of financial statements?

- What are some of the most widely used financial ratios, and what do they attempt to measure?

- What are some of the differences in accounting standards around the world, and what are the implications for corporate finance?

PRINCIPAL FINANCIAL STATEMENTS

The three basic financial statements are the *income statement,* which measures the revenues and expenses of the firm; the *balance sheet,* which reports on the assets and liabilities of the firm; and the *statement of cash flows,* which examines the sources and the uses of cash.

Income Statement

An *income statement* provides information about a firm's operating activities over a specific time period. The net income of a company is equal to its revenues minus expenses; revenues arise from selling goods or services, and expenses measure the costs associated with generating these revenues.

Generally Accepted Accounting Principles (GAAP): These are the principles that govern the construction of financial statements and help determine accounting rules.

Since income can be generated from a number of different sources, **generally accepted accounting principles (GAAP)** require that income statements be classified into four sections: (1) income from continuing operations; (2) income from discontinued operations; (3) extraordinary gains or losses; and (4) adjustments for changes in accounting principles. A typical income statement starts with revenues and adjusts for the cost of the goods sold, depreciation on assets used to produce the revenues, and any selling or administrative expenses to arrive at an operating profit. The operating profit, when reduced by interest expenses, yields the taxable income, which, when reduced by taxes, yields net income.

INCOME STATEMENT

Revenues
- − Cost of Goods Sold
- − Depreciation
- − Selling Expenses
- − Administrative Expenses
- = Earnings before interest and taxes (EBIT)
- − Interest Expenses
- = Earnings before taxes
- − Taxes
- = Net Income before extraordinary items
- + Gains (Losses) from discontinued operations
- + Extraordinary gains (losses)
- + Net Income Changes caused by changes in accounting methods
- = Net Income after extraordinary items
- − Preferred Dividends
- = Profit to Common Stockholders

IN PRACTICE EXAMPLES OF INCOME STATEMENTS: GENERAL MOTORS AND THE HOME DEPOT

Table 4.1 summarizes income statements for fiscal year 1993 for General Motors Corporation and the Home Depot.

Accrual versus cash-based income statements Firms often expend resources to acquire materials or manufacture goods in one period but do not sell the goods until the following period. Alternatively, they often provide services in one period but do not get paid for these services until the following period. In *accrual-based accounting,* the revenue from selling a good or service is recognized in the period in which the good is sold or the service is performed (in whole or substantially). A corresponding effort is made on the expense side to match expenses to revenues.[1] Under a *cash-based system* of accounting, revenues are recognized when payment is received, while expenses are recorded when paid. Because there is no matching of revenues and expenses, GAAP requires that firms use accrual-based accounting in income statements.

 Concept Check

> Under what conditions will switching from a cash-based to an accrual-based accounting statement increase or decrease income? Why?

---

[1]If a cost (such as an administrative cost) cannot be easily linked with a particular revenue, it is usually recognized as an expense in the period in which it is consumed.

Table 4.1 INCOME STATEMENTS FOR GENERAL MOTORS & THE HOME DEPOT

	(in millions) General Motors	(in millions) The Home Depot
Revenues	$138,220	$9,238
− Cost of Goods Sold	108,996	6,596
− Depreciation	9,442	90
− Selling Expenses	6,132	1624
− Administrative Expenses	5,400	220
= Earnings before interest and taxes (EBIT)	8,250	708
+ Interest Income	—	61
− Interest Expenses	5,637	31
= Earnings before taxes	2,613	738
− Taxes	110	280
= Net Income before extraordinary items	2,503	458
= Gains (Losses) from discontinued operations	—	—
+ Extraordinary Gains (Losses)	—	—
+ Income changes from changes in accounting methods	—	—
Net Income after extraordinary items	2,503	458
− Preferred Dividends	357	—
= Profit to Common Stockholders	2,146	458

GAAP—recognizing income Generally accepted accounting principles require the recognition of revenues when the service for which the firm is getting paid has been performed in full or substantially and has received in return either cash or a receivable that is both observable and measurable. Expenses that are directly linked to the production of revenues (like labor and materials), are recognized in the same period in which revenues are recognized. Any expenses that are not directly linked to the production of revenues are recognized in the period in which the firm consumes the services.

Although accrual accounting is straightforward in firms that produce and sell goods, in some cases accrual accounting can be complicated by the nature of the product or service being offered:

- *Long-term contracts:* Long-term contracts span several accounting periods, and customers often make periodic payments as the contract progresses. An example is home or commercial building. When a long-term contractor has a contract with a buyer with an agreed-upon price, revenue during the period of construction is recognized on the basis of the percentage of the contract that is completed. As the revenue is recognized on a percentage-of-completion basis, a corresponding proportion of the expense is also recognized. An alternative is to wait until the contract is completed and recognize the total revenue and expense upon completion. Because this approach delays the payment of income taxes, it is not permitted under the Internal Revenue Code for tax purposes.

- *Uncertainty about cash collections:* When there is considerable uncertainty about the capacity of the buyer of a good or service to pay for a service, the firm providing the good or service may recognize the income only when it collects portions of the selling price under the installment method. Although this is similar to revenue recognition in the cash method, the expenses under the installment method are recognized only when the cash is collected, even though payment may be made in the period of the initial sale. An alternative to this approach is the *cost-recovery-first method*, whereby cash receipts and expenses are matched dollar for dollar (thus generating no profits) until all the expenses are covered, after which any additional revenues are reported as profits.

Balance Sheet

Unlike the income statement, which measures flows over a period of time, the *balance sheet* provides a summary of what the firm owns in terms of assets and what it owes to both its lenders and its equity investors. The balance sheet is built around the equality:

$$\text{Assets} = \text{Liabilities} + \text{Shareholders' Equity}$$

Assets and liabilities can be further broken down into current and noncurrent portions as in Table 4.2.

Table 4.2 ASSETS AND LIABILITIES	
Assets	**Liabilities and Equity**
Current Assets	Current Liabilities
Cash and Marketable Securities	Accounts Payable
Accounts Receivable	Short-term Borrowing
Inventories	Other Current Liabilities
Other Current Assets	Long-term Debt
Investments	Other Noncurrent Liabilities
Property, Plant, and Equipment (Fixed Assets)	Stockholders' Equity
Intangible Assets	Preferred Stock
	Common Stock
	Retained Earnings
	Treasury Stock

Assets   An *asset* is any resource that has the potential either to generate future cash inflows or reduce future cash outflows. For a resource to be an asset, therefore, a firm has to have acquired it in a prior transaction and be able to quantify future benefits with reasonable precision. Assets can be classified on several bases—into fixed and current assets; into monetary assets (like cash and notes receivable) and nonmonetary assets—and the GAAP principles on valuation vary from asset to asset.

Fixed assets   Generally accepted accounting principles in almost all countries require the valuation of fixed assets at historical costs, adjusted for any depreciation charges on these assets. The rationale that is often provided for this practice is as follows:

- Book value is easier to obtain than market value for most assets, because an active secondary market does not exist for most assets.
- Book value can be more objectively valued than market value and is less likely to be manipulated by firms to suit their purposes.
- Book value is a more conservative estimate of true value than market value.

All these arguments are open to challenge, and it is quite clear that the book value of many fixed assets bears little resemblance to the market value.

Because fixed assets are valued at book value and are adjusted for depreciation provisions, the value of a fixed asset is strongly influenced by both its depreciable life and the depreciation method used. Since firms estimate the depreciable life, and lengthening the depreciable life can increase reported earnings,[2] this approach provides an opportunity for firms to manage reported earnings. Firms are also offered an opportunity to manage earnings through the choice of a depreciation method, since GAAP allows firms to use either *straight-line depreciation* (depreciation is spread evenly over the life of the asset) or *accelerated depreciation* methods (more depreciation is taken in the initial years, and less later on). Most U.S. firms use straight-line depreciation for financial reporting but accelerated depreciation for tax purposes, because firms can report better earnings with straight-line depreciation at least in the years immediately after the asset is acquired. In contrast, Japanese and German firms often use accelerated depreciation for both tax and financial reporting purposes, resulting in income that is understated relative to that of their U.S. counterparts.

☐ Concept Check

What factors might cause the market value of an asset to deviate dramatically from its book value? Which is more reliable—book value or market value? Why do accountants use book value rather than market value to value most fixed assets?

Inventory GAAP allows three basic approaches to valuing inventory—first-in, first-out (FIFO), last-in, first-out (LIFO), and weighted average.

1. *First-in, First-out (FIFO):* Under FIFO, the cost of goods sold is based on the cost of material bought earliest in the period, whereas the cost of inventory is based on the cost of material bought later in the year. As a result, inventory is valued close to current replacement cost. During periods of inflation, among the three approaches, the use of FIFO will result in the lowest estimate of cost of goods sold and the highest net income.

2. *Last-in, First-out (LIFO):* Under LIFO, the cost of goods sold is based on the cost of material bought toward the end of the period, resulting in costs that closely approximate current costs. The inventory, however, is valued on the basis of the cost of materials bought earlier in the year. During periods of inflation, among the three approaches, the use of LIFO will result in the highest estimate of cost of goods sold and the lowest net income.

3. *Weighted Average:* Under the weighted average approach, both inventory and the cost of goods sold are based on the average cost of all units bought during the period. When inventory turns over rapidly, this approach will more closely resemble FIFO than LIFO.

Firms often adopt the LIFO approach for the tax benefits it offers during periods of high inflation. Studies indicate that firms with the following characteristics are more likely to adopt LIFO: large firms and firms experiencing rising prices for raw materials and labor, more variable inventory growth, and an absence of other tax loss carry-forwards. When firms switch from FIFO to LIFO in valuing inventory, they are likely to experience a drop in net income and a concurrent increase in cash flows (because of the tax savings). The reverse will apply when firms switch from LIFO to FIFO.

[2]It has the opposite effect on cash flows, for lengthening the depreciable life reduces depreciation and increases both taxable income and taxes.

Given the income and cash-flow effects of inventory valuation methods, it is often difficult to compare firms that use different methods. There is, however, one way of adjusting for these differences. Firms that choose to use the LIFO approach to value inventories have to specify in a footnote the difference in inventory valuation between FIFO and LIFO; this difference is termed the *LIFO reserve*. The LIFO reserve can be used to adjust the beginning and ending inventories, and, consequently, the cost of goods sold, and to restate income based on FIFO valuation.

Intangible Assets: Intangible assets are those assets that do not have a physical presence and include patents and goodwill.

Intangible assets: **Intangible assets** include a wide array of assets, ranging from patents and trademarks to goodwill. GAAP require that intangible assets be accounted for in the following way.

1.   The costs incurred in developing the intangible asset are expensed in that period, even though the asset might have a life of several accounting periods. Thus, the research and development expenditure that creates the patent (the intangible asset) is expensed in the period in which it is incurred.

2.   When an intangible asset is acquired from an external party, the expenditure is treated as an asset, in contrast to the treatment of expenditures incurred in internally developing the same asset.

3.   Intangible assets have to be amortized over their expected lives, with a maximum amortization period of 40 years. The standard practice is to use straight-line amortization. For tax purposes, however, firms are not allowed to amortize goodwill and other intangible assets with no specific lifetime.

Intangible assets are often byproducts of acquisitions. When a firm acquires another firm, the purchase price is first allocated over tangible assets, and the excess price is then allocated to any intangible assets, such as patents or trade names. Any residual becomes goodwill. Although accounting principles suggest that goodwill captures the value of any intangibles that are not specifically identifiable, it is really a reflection of the difference between the book value of assets and their market value.

Liabilities   For an obligation to be recognized as a *liability,* it must meet three requirements—it must be expected to lead to a future cash outflow or the loss of a future cash inflow at some specified or determinable date; the firm cannot avoid the obligation; and the transaction giving rise to the obligation must have already happened.

Degree of certitude   Liabilities vary in the degree to which they create a future obligation. At one extreme, a straight bond creates an obligation to make fixed payments on fixed dates and results in a very specific and certain obligation. At the other extreme, an option contract entered into by the firm creates a contingent obligation, whereby the amount and timing of the obligation are unclear. Along the continuum, GAAP recognizes as accounting liabilities those obligations that create future payments that can be both quantified and timed, even if the firm has to estimate the amount and the timing. It does not recognize purchase or employment commitments or contingent contracts as accounting liabilities.

As firms enter into more and more complex arrangements to manage their financial and operating risk, a number of gray areas are emerging in which generally accepted accounting principles do not provide sufficient guidance on the right path to take. One example is the use of hybrid securities by firms. These securities possess some of the properties of debt and some of equity, making a classification into liabilities or stockholders' equity very difficult. Another is the use of off-balance sheet financing by firms, whereby a liability is created but not recognized. The evolving attitude toward this phenomenon is that firms must disclose information about the off-balance sheet risk of any financial instruments or agreements into which they have entered.[3]

Dealing with leases   Firms often choose to lease long-term assets rather than buy them, for a variety of reasons. First, the tax benefits are greater to the lessor (the owner) than the lessees. Second, leases offer more flexibility in terms of adjusting to changes in technology and capacity needs. Lease payments create the same kind of obligation created by interest payments on debt and have to be viewed in a similar light. If a firm is allowed to lease a significant portion of its assets and keep it off its financial statements, a perusal of the statements will give a very misleading view of the company's financial strength. Consequently, accounting rules have been devised to force firms to reveal the extent of their lease obligations on their books.

There are two ways of accounting for leases. In an *operating lease,* the lessor transfers only the right to use the property to the lessee. At the end of the lease period, the lessee returns the property to the lessor. Since the lessee does not assume the risk of ownership, the lease expense is treated as an operating expense in the income statement and the lease does not affect the balance sheet. In a *capital lease,* the lessee assumes some of the risks of ownership and enjoys some of the benefits. Consequently, the lease, when signed, is recognized as both an asset and a liability (for the lease payments) on the balance sheet. The firm gets to claim depreciation on the asset each year and to deduct the interest expense component of the lease payment each year. In general, capital leases recognize expenses sooner than do equivalent operating leases.

Since firms prefer to keep leases off the books, and sometimes prefer to defer expenses, they have a strong incentive to report all leases as operating leases. Consequently, the Financial Accounting Standards Board (FASB) has ruled that a lease should be treated as an operating lease if it meets any one of the following four conditions:

1. If the lease life exceeds 75% of the life of the asset.
2. If ownership transfers to the lessee at the end of the lease term.
3. If there is an option to purchase the asset at a "bargain price" at the end of the lease term.
4. If the present value of the lease payments, discounted at an appropriate discount rate, exceeds 90% of the fair market value of the asset.

The lessor uses the same criteria to determine whether the lease is a capital or an operating lease and accounts for it accordingly. If it is a capital lease, the lessor records the present value of future cash flows as revenue and recognizes expenses. The lease receivable is also shown as an asset on the balance sheet, and the interest revenue is recognized over the term of the lease, as paid.

From a tax standpoint, the lessor can claim the tax benefits of the leased asset only if it is an operating lease, although the revenue code uses slightly different criteria for making this determination.[4]

---

[3]The Financial Accounting Standards Board (FASB) statement (105) requires that the following be disclosed—the face value or notional principal amount; the terms of the instrument and the credit and market risk involved; and the accounting loss the firm will incur if any party to the agreement does not perform.

[4]The requirements for an operating lease in the revenue code are as follows: (1) the property can be used by someone other than the lessee at the end of the lease term; (2) the lessee cannot buy the asset using a bargain purchase option; (3) the lessor has at least 20% of his or her capital at risk; (4) the lessor has a positive cash flow from the lease, independent of tax benefits; and (5) the lessee does not have an investment in the lease.

Employee benefits   Employers often provide pension and health-care benefits to their employees. In many cases, the obligations created by these benefits are extensive, and the firm's failure to fund these obligations adequately needs to be revealed in financial statements.

Pension Plans   In a pension plan, the firm agrees to provide certain benefits to its employees, either by specifying a "defined contribution" (whereby a fixed contribution is made to the plan each year by the employer, without any promises about the benefits that will be delivered in the plan) or a "defined benefit" (whereby the employer promises to pay a certain benefit to the employee). Under the latter option, the employer has to put sufficient money into the plan each period, so that the amounts with reinvestment are sufficient to meet the defined benefits.

Under a defined contribution plan, the firm meets its obligation once it has made the prespecified contribution to the plan. Under a defined-benefit plan, the firm's obligations are much more difficult to estimate, because they will be determined by a number of variables, including the benefits to which employees are entitled, which will change as their salaries and employment status changes, the prior contributions made by the employer and the returns they have earned, and the rate of return the employer expects to make on current contributions. As these variables change, the value of the pension fund assets can be greater than, less than, or equal to pension fund liabilities (which include the present value of promised benefits). A pension fund whose assets exceed its liabilities is an *overfunded plan,* whereas one whose assets are less than its liabilities is an *underfunded plan;* disclosures to that effect have to be included in financial statements, generally in the footnotes.

When a pension fund is overfunded, the firm has several options. It can withdraw the excess assets from the fund, it can discontinue contributions to the plan, or it can continue to make contributions on the assumption that the overfunding is a transitory phenomenon that could well disappear by the next period. When a fund is underfunded, the firm has a liability, although FASB requires that firms reveal only the excess of accumulated pension fund liabilities over pension fund assets on the balance sheet.[5]

Health-Care Benefits   A firm can provide health-care benefits in one of two ways: (1) by making a fixed contribution to a health-care plan, without promising specific benefits (analogous to a defined contribution plan), or (2) by promising specific health benefits and setting aside the funds to provide these benefits (analogous to a defined-benefit plan). The accounting for health-care benefits is very similar to the accounting for pension obligations. The key difference is that firms do not have to report the excess of their health-care obligations over the health-care fund assets as a liability on the balance sheet, although a footnote to that effect has to be added to the financial statement.[6]

Income taxes   Firms often use different methods of accounting for tax and financial reporting purposes, leading to a question of how tax liabilities should be reported. Because the use of accelerated depreciation and favorable inventory valuation methods for tax accounting purposes leads to a deferral of taxes, the taxes on the income reported in the financial statements will be much greater than the actual tax paid. The same principles of matching expenses to income that underlie accrual accounting suggest that the "deferred income tax" be recognized in the financial statements. Thus, a

---

[5]The accumulated pension fund liability does not take into account the projected benefit obligation, where actuarial estimates of future beneifts are made. Consequently, it is much smaller than the total pension liabilities.

[6]While companies might not *have to* report the excess of their health-care obligations over assets as a liability, some firms choose to do so anyway. In 1993, for instance, Boeing reported an accrued retiree health-care obligation of $2.158 billion as a liability.

company that pays $55,000 on its taxable income based on its tax accounting, and that would have paid $75,000 on the income reported in its financial statements, will be forced to recognize the difference ($20,000) as deferred taxes. Because the deferred taxes will be paid in later years, they will be recognized as paid.

The question of whether the deferred tax liability is really a liability at all is an interesting one. Firms do not owe the amount categorized as deferred taxes to any entity, and treating it as a liability makes the firm look more risky than it really is.

Reserves in financial statements Reserves can appear in financial statements as a deduction from an asset, as a liability or as a reduction of stockholders' equity. Although reserves have to be created for specific purposes in the United States, firms in Germany and Japan are allowed to create general reserves to equalize income across time periods. Reserve accounts are created for several different reasons.

1. *To match expenses with benefits:* A firm can create a reserve for an expense that is expected to arise from an activity from the current period and reduce the income in the current period by the expense. When the expense actually occurs, the reserve is reduced by the amount, and the net income in the future period is not affected by the expense. Thus, a bank that expects 1% of its loans to go uncollected may create a reserve for bad debts in the period in which the loan is made and charge income in that period with a charge transferring funds to the reserve. Any subsequent loan defaults will be charged to the reserve.

2. *To keep expenses out of income statements:* Firms can keep some expenses out of the income statement by directly reducing the stockholders' equity through a reserve created to meet the expense. Although the net effect on stockholders' equity is the same as if the expense had been shown in the income statement, it results in an overstatement of net income for that period.

The varied uses to which reserves are put, and the wide diversity of accounting standards relating to reserves in different countries, suggest that analysts should be careful about how they factor in reserves when comparing the profitability of companies in different countries using different accounting standards.

Statement of Cash Flows

The statement of cash flows is based on a reformulation of the basic equation relating assets to liabilities:

$$\text{Assets} = \text{Liabilities} + \text{Stockholders' Equity}$$

If each of these variables is measured in terms of changes (Δ), this equation can be rewritten as follows:

$$\Delta \text{ Assets} = \Delta \text{ Liabilities} + \Delta \text{ Stockholders' Equity}$$

If assets are broken down into cash and noncash assets, this works out to

$$\Delta \text{ Cash} + \Delta \text{ Noncash Assets} = \Delta \text{ Liabilities} + \Delta \text{ Stockholders' Equity}$$

Rearranging terms:

$$\Delta \text{ Cash} = \Delta \text{ Liabilities} + \Delta \text{ Stockholders' Equity} - \Delta \text{ Noncash Assets}$$

Changes in cash flows can be traced to the following:

- An increase in noncash assets will decrease cash flows; increases in current assets (such as inventory and accounts receivable), financial assets (through the purchase of securities), and fixed assets (through capital expenditures) will result in a drain on cash flows.

- Net profit will increase cash flows; this cash flow will be increased further if there are any noncash charges (such as depreciation and amortization).
- Any payment of dividends or stock repurchases will decrease cash flows, as will the principal payment on debt; an issue of stock or debt will increase cash flows.

A statement of changes in cash flows classifies all changes into one of three categories—operating, investing, or financing activities. The final step in preparing a statement of changes in cash flows is to classify changes in liabilities, stockholders' equity, and non-cash assets into one of these three categories, although some items will not fit easily into one or another. Once categorized, the statement of cash flows provides a breakdown of the changes in the cash balance over the period.

 IN PRACTICE   STATEMENT OF CASH FLOWS: THE HOME DEPOT

Table 4.3 summarizes the statement of cash flows at the Home Depot in 1993.

Table 4.3 **HOME DEPOT'S STATEMENT OF CASH FLOWS**	
Cash Provided from Operations (in '000s)	
Net Earnings	$457,401
Reconciling Net Earnings to Net Operating Cash	
Depreciation and Amortization	*89,839*
Deferred Income Tax Expense	12,578
Increase in Receivables	(36,658)
Increase in Merchandise Inventory	(353,653)
Increase in Accounts Payable and Accrued Expenses	200,977
Increase in Income Taxes Payable	36,143
Other	(10,120)
Total	(60,894)
Net Cash Provided by Operations	$396,507
Cash Flows from Investing	
Capital Expenditures	$(864,158)
Proceeds from Sale of Property and Equipment	35,070
Sale of Short-Term Investments	14,903
Purchase of Long-term Investments	(840,361)
Proceeds from Maturities of Long-term Investments	269,988
Proceeds from Sale of Long-term Investments	935,279
Net Cash Used in Investing Activities	(449,279)
Cash Flows from Financing	
Proceeds from Long-term Borrowing	—
Repayments of Notes Receivables from ESOP	6,585
Principal Repayments of Long-Term Debt	(2,006)
Proceeds from Sale of Common Stock	76,789
Cash Dividends Paid to Stockholders	(50,343)
Net Cash Provided by Financing Activities	$31,025
Increase (Decrease) in Cash and Equivalents	(21,747)
Cash and Equivalents at beginning of year	121,744
Cash and Equivalents at end of the year	99,997

☐ Concept
Check

> Companies that have high growth in earnings often end up with significant cash deficits prior to cash flows from financing activities. Why does this happen? How would you reconcile high earnings growth and cash-flow shortfalls?

FINANCIAL RATIOS

Financial ratios are a useful byproduct of financial statements and provide standardized measures of a firm's profitability and riskiness. In this section, we consider a number of financial ratios and provide a framework for categorizing and understanding them.

Profitability Ratios

The profitability of an enterprise can be measured in a number of ways. One is to examine the profitability relative to the capital employed to get a rate of return on investment. This can be done either from the viewpoint of just the equity investors or by looking at the entire firm. Another approach is to examine profitability relative to sales by estimating a profit margin.

Return on assets (ROA)   The *return on assets* (ROA) of a firm measures its operating efficiency in generating profits from its assets, prior to the effects of financing.

> Return on Assets = Earnings before interest and taxes (1 − tax rate) / Total Assets

Alternatively, the return on assets can be written as

> Return on Assets = (Net Income + Interest Expenses (1 − tax rate) / Total Assets

By separating the financing effects from the operating effects, this measure provides a cleaner measure of the true profitability of these assets.

This measure can also be computed on a pretax basis, with no loss of generality, by using the earnings before interest and taxes, and not adjusting for taxes:

> Pretax ROA = Earnings before interest and taxes / Total Assets

This measure is useful if the firm or division is being evaluated for purchase by an acquirer with a different tax rate.

Finally, this measure can be computed using the book value of debt and equity in the denominator instead of total assets. When a substantial portion of the liabilities are either current (such as accounts payable) or noninterest bearing, this approach may provide a better measure of the true return earned on capital employed in the business.

$$\text{Modified ROA} = \text{EBIT}\,(1-t) / (BV \text{ of Debt} + BV \text{ of Equity})$$

Concept Check

There are a number of different definitions of return on assets. One measure divides the net income by the total assets. What are the problems with this measure, and which firms are likely to have low returns on assets using this measure?

IN PRACTICE   ESTIMATING PRETAX AND AFTER-TAX ROA FOR GENERAL ELECTRIC

In 1993, General Electric (not including GE Capital Services) reported earnings before interest and taxes of $4,452 million on total assets of $251,506 million. The tax rate applicable for 1993 was 36%. The accompanying table summarizes the pretax and after-tax return on assets for GE for 1992 and 1993.

	1993	1992
(in millions)		
EBT	$3,927	$4,238
+ Interest Expenses	$525	$768
EBIT	$4,452	$5,006
Tax Rate	36%	36%
EBIT(1-t)	$2,849	$3,204
Total Assets	$51,134	$48,075
Pretax ROA	8.71%	10.41%
ROA	5.57%	6.66%

Comparisons of ROA   Once computed, the return on assets can be used to compare different firms in the same business in order to evaluate operating efficiency. In making these comparisons, care has to be taken to account for significant differences in accounting standards across the companies. The return on assets can also be compared to the cost of capital of the firm to get a measure of realized returns on projects. Although the ROA is based on the book value of assets, a firm that picks good projects (with positive net present values) should have a return on assets that exceeds its cost of capital. Note that both the ROA and the cost of capital are concepts that measure returns to the firm rather than just to equity investors.

Determinants of ROA   The return on assets of a firm can be written as a function of the operating profit margin the firm has on its sales, and its asset turnover ratio.

$$\begin{aligned} \text{ROA} &= \text{EBIT}\,(1-t)\,/\,\text{Total Assets} \\ &= \text{EBIT}(1-t)/\text{Sales} * \text{Sales}\,/\text{Total Assets} \\ &= \text{After-tax Operating Margin} * \text{Asset Turnover Ratio} \end{aligned}$$

$$\text{After-tax Operating Margin} = \text{EBIT}\,/\,\text{Sales}$$

Thus, a firm can arrive at a high ROA either by increasing its profit margin or by more efficiently utilizing its assets to increase sales. There are likely to be competitive and technological constraints on the firm, but firms still have some freedom within these constraints to choose the mix of profit margin and asset turnover that maximizes their ROA.

The advantage of this decomposition of ROA is that it helps explain why some businesses have high ROA while others have low ROA. It also helps relate the return on assets to strategic decisions the firm makes as to whether it wants to be a low-margin, high-volume producer or a high-margin, low-volume competitor.

 IN PRACTICE   DECOMPOSITION OF ROA—GENERAL ELECTRIC

General Electric had revenues of $29,533 million in 1993. Incorporating this information with the numbers provided on page 000 for earnings and total assets, we see that the pretax return on assets in 1993 can be decomposed into profit margin and asset turnover components:

$$\text{Profit margin, 1993} = \text{Earnings before interest and taxes / Revenues}$$
$$= \$4{,}452/\$29{,}533$$
$$= 15.07\%$$

$$\text{Asset Turnover, 1993} = \text{Revenues / Total Assets}$$
$$= \$29{,}533 / \$51{,}134$$
$$= 57.76\%$$

$$\text{After-tax Return on Assets, 1993} = .1507 * .5776 = .0871 \text{ or } 8.71\%$$

Comparing ROA across industries   The return on assets varies widely across firms in different businesses, largely as a consequence of differences in profit margins and asset turnover ratios. Table 4.4 provides return on assets for major industry groups in 1994. Note that differences in ROA across industries exist for two reasons—differences in risk, which are likely to persist over time, and differences in competitive pressure, which are likely to encourage new firms to enter businesses with high profit margins and ROA and existing firms to leave businesses with low profit margins and ROA.

Changes in ROA over time   A firm's return on assets can change for a number of reasons. Because ROA is largely a function of the operating profit, any factors that affect operating profit, positively or negatively, will also affect ROA.

Changes in Sales   As sales increase or decrease, in response to economic cycles and the firm's own actions, the after-tax operating profit is likely to change, leading to changes in the return on assets. The **operating leverage** measures the sensitivity of operating profit to changes in sales.

> Operating Leverage = % Change in Operating Profit / % Change in Sales

A firm's operating leverage will be determined, in large part, by its cost structure. On the one hand, the operating income of firms with high fixed costs and low variable costs per unit is likely to be much more sensitive to changes in sales. On the other hand, a firm with high variable costs per unit and small fixed costs will have operating income that is not as sensitive to changes in sales.

Table 4.4   INDUSTRY AVERAGES—ROA, ROE, AND DEBT RATIOS, END OF 1994 (PERCENTAGE)

Industry	ROE	ROA	Debt Ratio
Agricultural products	15.28	11.78	37.67
Mining	11.07	9.03	40.21
Petroleum production and refining	13.35	10.08	44.43
Building contractors and related areas	11.84	10.09	30.04
Food production	17.31	13.03	37.87
Beverages	17.55	12.80	41.14
Tobacco	32.65	19.22	50.39
Textile and clothing manufacturers	13.45	11.41	27.42
Furniture	14.73	12.52	25.34
Paper and plastic production	15.48	11.41	42.96
Publishing	17.34	13.44	34.41
Chemicals	18.64	13.89	37.61
Pharmaceuticals	28.40	20.82	33.83
Consumer products	28.81	18.60	44.78
Autos and related	18.12	13.31	39.69
Miscellaneous manufacturing	16.42	12.72	35.51
Equipment manufacturing	13.89	11.01	36.47
Computers and office equipment	14.84	12.14	30.49
Consumer electronics	15.00	12.60	26.65
Other consumer durables	17.51	14.15	29.18
Transportation	12.79	9.51	48.29
Telephone utilities	16.10	11.38	46.70
Entertainment (TV and movies)	23.00	14.64	49.20
Electric and gas utilities	11.41	8.25	58.35
Wholesalers	16.50	12.82	35.01
Retailers	14.04	11.38	33.12
Restaurants and eating places	17.51	13.83	31.94
Banks and financial service	17.09	13.83	29.37
Insurance	23.62	18.22	30.66
Real estate	19.69	14.43	38.44
Other services	18.11	13.34	39.39
Computer software and services	20.66	19.31	9.18
Health services	14.33	12.02	27.78
Average	15.44	11.63	40.35

 IN PRACTICE   OPERATING LEVERAGE: THE HOME DEPOT AND TOYS'R'US

The Home Depot reported an increase of 28.6% in operating income from 1992 to 1993, while revenues increased by 29.2% over the same period. The operating leverage, based on 1992–1993 data, is as follows:

$$\text{Operating Leverage, Home Depot} = 28.6\% \,/\, 29.2\% = 0.98$$

In contrast, Toys'R'Us reported an increase of 27.15% in operating income, while revenues increased by only 17.06% from 1992 to 1993. The operating leverage, based on 1992–1993 data, is

Operating Leverage, Toys'R'Us = 27.15%/17.06% = 1.59

Based only on 1992–1993 data, it can be argued that Toys'R'Us has much higher operating leverage than the Home Depot.

ROA of a firm versus divisional ROA   A firm's return on assets can be further disaggregated by division, and each division's ROA can be estimated separately:

$$\text{Divisional ROA} = \text{EBIT of division } (1\text{-}t) \text{ / Total Assets of Division}$$

If the earnings and the assets of each division are clearly delineated, this statistic is easy to estimate. If assets are used by more than one division, and earnings are generated by multiple divisions, the analyst has to allocate the assets and earnings to the divisions before computing the ROA.

The advantage of computing ROA by division is that it can then be compared to the cost of capital for that division (the cost of capital can be different for different divisions because of risk and financing mix differences) to arrive at a conclusion about where the firm is creating wealth (those divisions where ROA exceeds cost of capital) and where it is losing wealth (those divisions where ROA is less than the cost of capital). It can also provide a basis for restructuring the firm by focusing attention on those divisions that need change the most.

IN PRACTICE   ROA BY DIVISION—GENERAL ELECTRIC

In 1993, General Electric reported operating profit, by segment, for its different operations. The accompanying table below provides ROA estimates for the different segments.

Operating Segment	Operating Income (in millions)	Total Assets (in millions)	ROA (%)
Aircraft engines	$798	$8,294	9.62
Appliances	372	7,002	5.31
Broadcasting	264	3,910	6.75
Industrial	782	9,301	8.41
Materials	834	6,355	13.12
Power systems	1,143	8,435	13.55
Technical products	706	5,261	13.42

Although General Electric did not provide a breakdown of total assets by division, the total assets were assumed to be in proportion to the revenues of the divisions.

❑ Concept
Check

When a company has different divisions with different returns on assets, does it necessarily follow that it should invest only in the high ROA divisions and divest itself of its low ROA divisions? Why or why not?

Return on equity (ROE)   Whereas the return on assets measures the profitability of the overall firm, the *return on equity* (ROE) examines profitability from the perspective of the equity investor, by relating profits to the equity investor (net profit after taxes and interest expenses) to the book value of the equity investment.

> Return on Equity = Net Income (after Preferred Dividends)
> / Book Value of Common Equity

Since preferred stockholders have a different type of claim on the firm than do common stockholders, the return on equity should be cleansed of the effects of preferred stock. This can be accomplished by using net income after preferred dividends in the numerator, and the book value of common equity in the denominator.

Comparisons of ROE   Because the ROE is computed from the viewpoint of common stockholders, the comparison made should be to the cost from the same viewpoint (i.e., the cost of equity). Generally speaking, a firm that takes good projects should have an ROE that exceeds its cost of equity. However, this is based on the presumption that the book value of equity is a good approximation of the market value of equity in existing assets, and that the realized returns during the period being examined are a good measure of the returns that the projects will make over their lifetime.[7] Because the return on equity can vary widely from year to year, analysts often look at an average ROE over a longer time period and compare this average to the cost of equity.

Determinants of ROE   Inasmuch as the ROE is based on earnings after interest payments, it is affected by the financing mix the firm uses to fund its projects. In general, a firm that borrows money to finance projects and earns an ROA on those projects that exceeds the after-tax interest rate it pays on its debt will be able to increase its ROE by borrowing. The ROE can be written as follows:[8]

$$ROE = ROA + D/E \left(ROA - i \left(1 - t\right)\right)$$

where

$$ROA = EBIT \left(1 - t\right) / \left(BV \text{ of Debt} + BV \text{ of Equity}\right)$$
$$D/E = BV \text{ of Debt} / BV \text{ of Equity}$$
$$i = \text{Interest Expense on Debt} / BV \text{ of Debt}$$
$$t = \text{Tax rate on ordinary income}$$

The second term captures the benefit of financial leverage.

Increased leverage also increases the cost of equity, and so the ROE will have to increase by more than the cost of equity for higher leverage to be in the best interests of the firm.[9]

❑ Concept Check

> Two firms in the same business can arrive at similar returns on equity, one by taking great projects (high ROA) and the other by taking high leverage on average projects. Is there a qualitative difference between the two firms? Which ROE is of higher quality? Why?

---

[7]The market value of equity includes the market value of equity both in assets in place and anticipated future growth. The book value of equity reflects the book value of assets in place, and the ROE measures returns on those assets.

[8]$ROA + D/E \left(ROA - i \left(1 - t\right)\right) = \left(NI + Int \left(1 - t\right)\right)/\left(D+E\right) + D/E \{ NI + Int \left(1 - t\right))/\left(D+E\right) - Int \left(1 - t\right)/D\}$
$$= \{\left(NI + Int \left(1 - t\right)\right)/\left(D+E\right)\} \left(1 + D/E\right) - Int \left(1 - t\right)/E$$
$$= NI/E + Int \left(1 - t\right)/E - Int \left(1 - t\right)/E = NI/E = ROE$$

[9]The relationship between financial leverage and betas is explored in the chapter on risk and return (Chapter 6). As the leverage increases, the beta increases, leading to a higher cost of equity.

IN PRACTICE   ROE AND LEVERAGE: BOEING

In 1993, Boeing had a book value of equity of $8,983 million and a book value of debt of $2,630 million. It had interest expenses of $140 million in 1993, and the company faced a tax rate of 31.69%. Boeing reported earnings before interest and taxes of $1,821 million that year. Based on these numbers:

$$\text{Return on Assets} = (\$1,821(1-0.3169)) / (8,983 + 2,630) = 10.71\%$$
$$\text{Debt/Equity Ratio} = \$2,630/\$8,983 = 29.28\%$$
$$\text{Interest rate on debt} = \$140 / \$2,630 = 5.32\%$$
$$\text{Return on Equity} = 10.71\% + 0.2928 (10.71\% - 5.32\% (1-0.3169)) = 12.78\%$$

This can be confirmed by dividing the net income ($1,148 million) in 1993 by the book value of equity:

$$\text{Return on Equity} = 1,148/8,983 = 12.78\%$$

Financial Ratios Measuring Risk

Firms face significant risk in their operations from a variety of sources, some of which are specific to the industry in which the firm operates and others of which are market-wide. A number of financial ratios measure a firm's exposure to risk, both from short-term liquidity pressures and long-term solvency needs.

Short-term liquidity risk   Short-term liquidity risk arises primarily from the need to finance current operations. To the extent that the firm has to make payments to its suppliers before it is paid for the goods and services it provides, a cash shortfall has to be met, usually through short-term borrowing. Although this financing of working capital needs is routinely done in most firms, financial ratios have been devised to keep track of the extent of the firm's exposure to the risk that it will not be able to meet its short-term obligations.

Current ratio   The *current ratio* is the ratio of current assets (cash, inventory, accounts receivable) to its current liabilities (obligations coming due within the next period).

$$\text{Current Ratio} = \text{Current Assets} / \text{Current Liabilities}$$

A current ratio below one, for instance, would indicate that the firm has more obligations coming due in the next year than it has assets that it can expect to turn to cash. This would be an indication of liquidity risk.

Although traditional analysis suggests that firms maintain a current ratio of 2 or greater, there is a tradeoff here between minimizing liquidity risk and tying up more and more cash in net working capital (Net Working Capital = Current Assets − Current Liabilities). In fact, it can be reasonably argued that a very high current ratio is indicative of an unhealthy firm that is having problems reducing its inventory. In recent years, firms have worked at reducing their current ratios and managing their net working capital better.

The use of current ratios has to be tempered by a number of concerns. First, the ratio can be easily manipulated by firms toward financial reporting dates to give the illusion of safety. Second, current assets and current liabilities can change by an equal amount, but the effect on the current ratio will depend on its level before the change.[10]

---

[10]If the current assets and current liabilities increase by an equal amount, the current ratio will go down if it was greater than one before the increase, and go up if it was less than one.

Quick ratio   The quick, or acid test, ratio is a variant of the current ratio. It distinguishes between current assets that can be converted quickly into cash (cash, marketable securities) from those that cannot (inventory, accounts receivable).

$$\text{Quick Ratio} = (\text{Cash} + \text{Marketable Securities}) / \text{Current Liabilities}$$

The exclusion of accounts receivable and inventory is not a hard-and-fast rule. If there is evidence that either can be converted into cash quickly, it can be included as part of the quick ratio.

Working capital turnover ratios   The management of working capital is often a key component of the management of cash and liquidity risk. One measure of the efficiency of working capital is the magnitude of inventory and accounts receivable, relative to annual cost of goods sold and sales.

$$\text{Accounts Receivable Turnover} = \text{Sales} / \text{Average Accounts Receivable}$$
$$\text{Inventory Turnover} = \text{Cost of Goods Sold} / \text{Average Inventory}$$

These statistics can be interpreted as measuring the speed with which the firm turns accounts receivable into cash or inventory into sales. These ratios are often expressed in terms of the number of days outstanding.

$$\text{Days Receivable Outstanding} = 365 / \text{Receivable Turnover}$$
$$\text{Days Inventory Held} = 365 / \text{Inventory Turnover}$$

A similar pair of statistics can be computed for accounts payable, relative to purchases.

$$\text{Accounts Payable Turnover} = \text{Purchases} / \text{Average Accounts Payable}$$
$$\text{Days Accounts Payable Outstanding} = 365 / \text{Accounts Payable Turnover}$$

Because accounts receivable and inventory are assets, and accounts payable is a liability, these three statistics (standardized in terms of days outstanding) can be combined to provide an estimate of how much financing the firm needs to raise to fund working capital needs.

$$\text{Required Financing Period} = \text{Days Receivable Outstanding} + \text{Days Inventory Held} - \text{Days Accounts Payable Outstanding}$$

The greater the financing period for a firm, the greater its short-term liquidity risk.

 IN PRACTICE WORKING CAPITAL TURNOVER RATIOS–GENERAL ELECTRIC AND THE HOME DEPOT

Table 4.5 provides a computation of working capital ratios for General Electric and the Home Depot.

Item	GE (in millions)	Home Depot (in millions)
Current Assets	$13,921	$1,966
Current Liabilities	$14,359	$972
Current Ratio	**0.97**	**2.02**
Cash and Marketable Securities	$1,536	$100
Current Liabilities	$14,359	$972
Quick Ratio	**0.11**	**0.10**
Sales	$29,533	$9,238
Accounts Receivable	$8,561	$198
Receivable Turnover	**3.45**	**46.66**
Days Receivable	**105.81 days**	**7.82 days**
Cost of Goods Sold	$22,630	$6,685
Average Inventory	$3,824	$1,293
Inventory Turnover	**5.92**	**5.17**
Days Inventory Held	**61.68 days**	**70.60 days**

Table 4.5 WORKING CAPITAL RATIOS: GE AND THE HOME DEPOT

The differences between the two firms reflect the different businesses in which they operate. The Home Depot sells few items on credit and, hence, has a much lower accounts receivable, relative to GE.

Long-term solvency and default risk Measures of **long-term solvency** attempt to examine a firm's capacity to meet interest and principal payments in the long term. Clearly, the profitability ratios discussed earlier in the section are a critical component of this analysis. The ratios specifically designed to measure long-term solvency try to relate profitability to the level of debt payments to see the degree of comfort with which the firm can meet these payments.

Interest coverage ratios The **interest coverage ratio** measures the firm's capacity to meet interest payments from predebt, pretax earnings.

Interest Coverage Ratio = Earnings before interest and taxes / Interest Expenses

The higher the interest coverage ratio, the more secure the firm's capacity to make interest payments from earnings. This argument has to be tempered, however, by the recognition that earnings before interest and taxes are volatile and can drop significantly if the economy enters a recession. Consequently, two firms can have the same interest coverage ratio but can be viewed very differently in terms of risk.

The denominator in the interest coverage ratio can be easily extended to cover other fixed obligations, such as lease payments. If this is done, the ratio is called a *fixed charges coverage ratio.*

Fixed Charges Coverage Ratio = Earnings before interest and taxes + Fixed Charges / Fixed Charges

Finally, this ratio, though stated in terms of earnings, can be restated in terms of cash flows, by using earnings before interest, taxes, and depreciation (EBITDA) in the numerator and cash fixed charges in the denominator.

Cash Fixed Charges Coverage Ratio = EBITDA / Cash Fixed Charges

Both interest coverage and fixed charge ratios are open to the criticism that they do not consider capital expenditures a cash flow that may be discretionary in the very short term, but not in the long term, if the firm wants to maintain growth. One way of capturing the extent of this cash flow, relative to operating cash flows, is to compute a ratio of the two.

Operating Cash Flow to CapEx = Cash Flows from Operations / Capital Expenditures

Although there are a number of different definitions of cash flow from operations, the most reasonable way to define it is to measure the cash flows from continuing operations, before interest but after taxes, and after meeting working capital needs.

Cash Flow from operations = EBIT (1 - tax rate) - Δ Working Capital

Debt ratios Interest coverage ratios measure the firm's capacity to meet interest payments, but they do not examine whether it can pay back the principal on outstanding debt. Debt ratios attempt to do this by relating debt to total capital or to equity. The two most widely used debt ratios are:

Debt to Capital Ratio = Debt / (Debt + Equity)
Debt to Equity Ratio = Debt / Equity

The first ratio measures debt as a proportion of the total capital of the firm and cannot exceed 100%. The second measures debt as a proportion of the book value of equity in the firm and can be derived easily from the first:

$$\text{Debt/Equity Ratio} = (\text{Debt/Capital Ratio})/(1 - \text{Debt/Capital Ratio})$$

Although these ratios presume that capital is raised from only debt and equity, they can be easily adapted to include other sources of financing, such as preferred stock. Preferred stock is sometimes combined with common stock under the "equity" label, but it is better to keep the two sources of financing separate and to compute the ratio of preferred stock to capital (which will include debt, equity, and preferred stock).

Variants on debt ratios   There are two close variants of these ratios. In the first, only long-term debt is used, rather than total debt, based on the rationale that short-term debt is transitory and will not affect the long-term solvency of the firm.

$$\text{Long-term Debt to Capital Ratio} = \text{Long-term Debt} / (\text{Debt} + \text{Equity})$$
$$\text{Long-term Debt to Equity Ratio} = \text{Long-term Debt} / \text{Equity}$$

Given the ease with which firms can roll over short-term debt, and the willingness of many firms to use short-term financing to fund long-term projects, these variants can provide a misleading picture of the firm's financial leverage risk.

The second variant of these ratios uses market value instead of book value, primarily to reflect the fact that some firms have a significantly greater capacity to borrow than their book values indicate.

$$\text{Market Value: Debt to Capital Ratio} = \text{MV of Debt} / (\text{MV of Debt} + \text{MV of Equity})$$
$$\text{MV Debt to Equity Ratio} = \text{MV of Debt} / \text{MV of Equity}$$

Many analysts disavow the use of market value in their calculations, contending that market values, in addition to being difficult to get for debt, are volatile and, hence, unreliable. These contentions are open to debate. Although the market value of debt is difficult to obtain for firms that do not have publicly traded bonds, the market value of *equity* is not only easy to obtain, but also constantly updated to reflect marketwide and firm-specific changes. Furthermore, using the book value of debt as a proxy for market value in those cases in which bonds are not traded does not significantly shift most market-value-based debt ratios.[11]

☐ Concept Check

A standard approach to analyzing the debt ratio of a firm is to compare it to the debt ratios of firms in its peer group, using book value debt ratios. Using this approach, which firms are likely to underutilize their debt capacities and why? Which are likely to overutilize debt and why?

[11]Deviations in the market value of equity from book value are likely to be much larger than deviations for debt and are likely to dominate in most debt ratio calculations.

IN PRACTICE   DEBT RATIOS AND VARIANTS—BOEING

In 1993, Boeing reported a book value of equity of $8,983 million and a book value of debt of $2,630 million (all long term). The market price per share at the end of 1993 was $42, and there were 349 million shares outstanding. The market value of the outstanding debt was $2,750 million:

$$\text{Market Value of Equity} = 349 \text{ million shares} * \$42 = \$14,658 \text{ million}$$
$$\text{Book Value of Equity} = \$8,983 \text{ million}$$
$$\text{Book Value of Debt} = \$2,630 \text{ million}$$
$$\text{Market Value of Debt} = \$2,750 \text{ million}$$
$$\text{Book Value - Debt/Capital Ratio} = \$2,630 / (\$8,983 + \$2,630) = 22.65\%$$
$$\text{Market Value - Debt/Capital Ratio} = \$2,750 / (\$14,658 + \$2,750) = 15.80\%$$
$$\text{Book Value - Debt/Equity Ratio} = \$2,630 / \$8,983 = 29.28\%$$
$$\text{Market Value - Debt/Equity Ratio} = \$2,750 / \$14,658 = 18.76\%$$

What to Include in Debt   A number of recent trends in financing have made estimating the debt to include in debt ratios much more difficult.

1. Hybrid securities: The first is the use of hybrid securities—part debt and part equity, like convertible bonds and preferred stock. The standard practice in calculating debt ratios has been all or nothing; a security is classified as debt if it has more debt characteristics than equity characteristics, which is itself a subjective judgment. This approach leads to large shifts in debt ratios, depending on whether or not a security is included in debt, and sudden changes in years in which a security is converted into equity. A more sensible way of dealing with hybrid securities is to estimate the debt and equity components separately for hybrid securities and add these components to their respective sides.

2. Off-balance sheet commitments: The second is the classification of off-balance sheet commitments, such as contingent liabilities. The general rule is to ignore contingent liabilities that hedge against risk, because the obligations on the contingent claim will be offset by benefits elsewhere.[12] In recent periods, however, the significant losses borne by firms from supposedly hedged derivatives positions have led to FASB requirements that these derivatives be disclosed as well.

3. Leases: The third area of debate is the treatment of leases. Although capitalized leases are now shown as part of debt, operating leases are not. Since a fine line separates the two, the conservative approach to estimating debt ratios will capitalize operating leases and show them as part of debt.

4. Pensions: Firms generally include in their debt the excess of accumulated benefit obligation over the pension fund assets. Here, again, a conservative estimate of the debt ratio will consider projected benefit obligation over pension fund assets.

5. Debt of nonconsolidated entities: Firms generally do not have to show as a liability that debt that is owed by their nonconsolidated subsidiaries, even though they may have guaranteed and stand liable for that borrowing. The conservative approach to estimating debt ratios is to add this debt on to the firm's total debt and compute the debt ratio on that basis.

A Note of Caution on Financial Ratios

Financial ratios are easy to compute and often useful in evaluating a firm's health and profitability and in comparing firms in the same business. Financial ratios are also used

---

[12]This assumes that the hedge is set up competently. It is entirely possible that a hedge, if set up sloppily, can end up costing the firm money.

widely as intermediate statistics to compute other measures, such as the Altman Z score, and in estimating levered betas. Like all financial statistics, they have to be used with caution, however, because firms can, and do, manipulate them to suit their needs. They are also often based on the financial statements of one period and do not reflect the variability in the underlying numbers.

OTHER ISSUES IN ANALYZING FINANCIAL STATEMENTS

Two additional issues bear our consideration before we conclude this section on financial statements. The first relates to differences in accounting standards and practices and how these differences may color comparisons across companies. The second relates to accounting for acquisitions and how this can affect both the acquisition method and price.

Differences in Accounting Standards and Practices

Differences in accounting standards across countries may affect the measurement of earnings. These differences, however, are not as great as they are made out to be and cannot be used to explain away radical departures from fundamental principles of valuation.[13] In a survey of accounting standards across developed markets, Choi and Levich note that most countries subscribe to basic accounting notions of consistency, realization, and historical cost principles in preparing accounting statements.

The two countries that offer the strongest contrast to the United States are Germany and Japan. First, companies in the United States generally maintain separate tax and financial reporting books, which, in turn, generates items like deferred taxes to cover differences between the two books, and different depreciation methods—straight line in the financial reports and accelerated in the tax reports. Companies in Germany and Japan do not maintain separate books. Consequently, depreciation methods in financial reports are much more likely to be accelerated and, hence, reduce stated income. Second, the requirement that leases be capitalized and shown as a liability is much more tightly enforced in the United States. In Japan, leases are generally treated as operating leases and do not show up as liabilities in the balance sheet. In Germany, firms can capitalize leases, but they have more leeway in classifying leases as operating and capital leases than do U.S. companies. Third, once created, goodwill can be amortized over 40 years in the United States and over much shorter time periods in Germany and Japan, again depressing stated income. Fourth, reserves in the United States can be created only for specific purposes, whereas German and Japanese companies can use general reserves to equalize income across periods; as a result, income may be understated during good years and overstated during bad years.

Most of these differences can be accounted and adjusted for when comparisons are made of U.S. companies and companies in other financial markets. Statistics such as price/earnings ratios, which use stated and unadjusted earnings, can be misleading when accounting standards vary widely across the companies being compared.

---

[13]At the peak of the Japanese market, many investors explained away the price earnings multiples of 60 and greater in the market by noting that Japanese firms were conservative in measuring earnings. Even after taking into account the general provisions and excess depreciation used by many of these firms to depress current earnings, however, the price earnings multiples were greater than 50 for many firms, suggesting either extraordinary expected growth in the future or overvaluation.

Accounting for Acquisitions

The two basic approaches of accounting for acquisitions are the purchase and pooling of interest methods. In the *purchase method,* the acquiring firm records the assets and liabilities of the acquired firm at market value, and goodwill is used to capture the difference between market value and the value of the assets acquired. This goodwill is then amortized, although the amortization is not tax deductible. If a firm pays cash on an acquisition, it has to use the purchase method to record the transaction.

In a *pooling of interest,* the book values of the assets and liabilities of the merging firms are added up to arrive at the values for the combined firm. Because the market value of the transaction is not recognized, goodwill is neither created nor amortized. This approach is allowed only if the acquiring firm exchanges its common stock for common stock of the acquired firm. With earnings not affected by the amortization of goodwill, the reported earnings per share under this approach will be greater than the reported earnings per share in the purchase approach.

CONCLUSION

Financial statements remain the primary source of information for most investors and analysts. Although an understanding of every detail and FASB rule may not be necessary, it is important to understand the basics. This chapter attempts to explain the basics of financial statements and the generally accepted accounting principles that underlie their construction, as well as the various financial ratios that often accompany financial analyses. As long as there is a recognition that financial statements and financial ratios are a means to an end—which is understanding and valuing the firm—they are useful.

QUESTIONS AND PROBLEMS

1. Your company anticipates having the following items on its income statement:

Revenues:	$15,000,000
Cost of goods sold	50% of Revenues
Depreciation	1,500,000
Other operating expenses	1,000,000
Tax rate	35%
Number of shares outstanding	1,300,000

If the earnings per share is expected to be $2, how much would be the total interest expenses for the year?

2. Companies often translate amount-based income statements into percentage-based income statements in order to analyze the cost structure. A particular company has gathered the following data for the year 1994 for both the company itself and the industry.

Items	Company (in millions)	Industry (in millions)
Revenues:	2,500	10,000
Cost of goods sold	1,000	5,000

Items	Company (in millions)	Industry (in millions)
Depreciation	500	1,500
Other operating expenses	200	1,500
Interest expenses	300	1,000
Tax rate	35%	30%

a. Construct percentage-based income statements for both the company and the industry.

b. Compare the cost structure of the company to that of the industry and comment on why the company is more profitable than the industry.

3. Since the 1980s, corporate restructuring has often meant reduction of costs through massive layoffs and other attrition of workers and midlevel managers. This approach is used to increase corporate profits when it is difficult to increase sales and revenues due to worldwide competition. This argument can be illustrated by analyzing the percentage change for each item in an income statement.

Items	1992	1993
Revenues	10,000	10,100
Costs of direct labor	4,000	2,500
Costs of materials	2,000	2,010
Depreciation	1,000	1,300
Other operating expenses	500	450
Interest expenses	500	520
Tax rate	35%	38%
Number of shares outstanding	1,500	1,500

a. Construct income statements for both 1992 and 1993.

b. Calculate the percentage change for each item of the income statement from 1992 to 1993.

c. What is the growth rate in earnings per share, and what is the dominating factor driving this growth rate?

4. The Bearings Specialty Company has total assets of $15 million, current liabilities of $5 million, and equity of $7 million. What is the total long-term debt of this company?

5. Your company has the following items on the balance sheet (all in millions):

Current liabilities	$20
Long-term debt	10
Common stock and retained earnings	20
Fixed assets	25
Cash and marketable securities	10
Accounts receivable	5

What is the total inventory of your company?

6. A company has net income of $1.5 million in 1995 and pays dividends in the amount of $1 per share in the year. The total number of shares outstanding remains at the level of 500,000 at the end of 1995. If the total common equity in the 1994 balance sheet was $10 million, what would be the total equity in the 1995 balance sheet? What is the percentage increase in equity from 1994 to 1995? Assume that the company did not issue any new issues of common stock and did not repurchase any shares in the year 1995.

7. Find the cash position for a company in 1995 based on the following data:

Cash in 1994	$10 million
Change in marketable securities	−2 million
Change in inventories	3 million
Change in accounts receivable	0.5 million
Change in fixed assets	2 million
Change in total assets	10 million

8. Some companies may grow rapidly in revenues and net earnings but run into trouble in cash flows. Suppose that a company's sales and revenues grew by 50% in 1994, resulting in net earnings of $30 million, an increase of 100% over the previous year. The following items on the balance sheet have changed in the year (those changes are necessary to support the high growth in revenues):

Depreciation	$2 million
Increase in accounts receivable	10 million
Increase in inventories	20 million
Capital expenditures	15 million

Even if the company does not pay dividends, how much financing will be needed to keep the cash at the same level as in the previous year?

9. A mature company may generate a lot of cash when it lacks new profitable investment opportunities. Suppose that a company has a net cash inflow of $40 million from its operations. The cash flows from investing and financing is zero. How much cash is available for paying dividends without resulting in a change in the cash level of the company? If the situation continues for another four years and the company only pays out $10 million in dividends per year, what would be the net accumulation of cash over these five years?

10. A company's return on assets is 20% with net income of $25 million. Its total debt amounts to $100 million and carries an average coupon rate of 10%. If common stock and retained earnings is $42.5 million, what is the effective tax rate on the earnings of this company?

11. Your company's Du Pont ROI was 25% last year, and the net profit margin was 10%. What are the total revenues for the year if the total assets are $100 million?

12. A company's operating leverage was 4.0, and its sales had increased by 3.5% in 1995. What were the operating profits in 1995 if the operating profits in 1994 were $20.5 million?

13. Your company expects to have ROA of 10%. The average interest rate on its debt is 7%, and the tax rate is 40%. What is the D/E ratio if the targeted ROE is 20%?

14. A company has a current ratio of 1.5 and a quick ratio of 1.0. If the current assets minus cash and marketable securities amount to $2.5 million, what are the current assets and current liabilities for this company?

15. Fill out the missing items on the following balance sheet based on the ratios given below:

Cash and marketable securities	200	Current liabilities	?
Accounts receivable	?		
Inventory	?	Long-term debt	?
Fixed Assets	?	Equity	?
Total Assets	2,200	Total liabilities and Equity	?

Current ratio	1.2
Quick ratio	0.6
Total asset turnover	0.7272
Account Receivable turnover	4.0
Debt equity ratio	2.143

16. What are the Days Payables Outstanding if we know the following:

Days Receivable Outstanding	35
Days Inventory Held	25
Required Financing Period	40

17. What are the fixed charges if we know the following:

Fixed charges coverage ratio	5
EBIT	$20 million

18. If a company has short-term sebt in the amount of $4,200,000, its book-value debt-capital ratio is 40%, and the long-term book value debt/equity ratio is 50%, what is its total long-term debt and total equity?

19. What is the company's inventory turnover based on the following data:

Accounts receivable turnover	5.6
Average Accounts receivable	$25 million
Cost of Goods Sold	50% of revenues
Average Inventory	$50 million

20. What is the company's total debt based on the following data:

Interest coverage ratio	10
EBIT	$400,000
Average Book interest rate	8.0%

CHAPTER 5

RISK AND RETURN—THEORY

Risk, in traditional terms, is viewed as a "negative." Webster's dictionary, for instance, defines risk as "exposing to danger or hazard." The Chinese symbols for risk give a much better description of risk:

The first symbol is the symbol for "danger," and the second is the symbol for "opportunity," making risk a mix of danger and opportunity. It is the opportunity component that encourages investors and companies to take on risk, but the danger component requires that they be rewarded for taking this risk. In this chapter, we examine the following questions:

- What are some of the different measures of risk, and what are their limitations?

- Why is some risk rewarded while other risk is not? What types of risk are most likely to be rewarded?

- What are the benefits of diversification, and what are the implications for models of risk and return?

- What are the basic assumptions made by alternative models for risk, and what are their conclusions?

- What is the empirical evidence on how well (or badly) the different models for risk and return work? What are the implications for their users?

INGREDIENTS FOR A GOOD RISK AND RETURN MODEL

As a prelude to examining different models for risk and return, it is worth exploring the ingredients that make a model a good one. A good risk and return model should do the following:

1. *Come up with a universal measure for risk.* To be useful, a risk measure has to apply to all investments, whether stocks or bonds or real estate, because they all compete for

the same investment dollar. A good risk and return model will come up with one measure of risk that applies to *all* investments, financial as well as real.

2. *Specify what types of risk are rewarded and what types are not.* It is an accepted part of investments that not all risks are rewarded. A good model should be able to distinguish between risk that is rewarded and risk that is not and provide an intuitive rationale for the distinction.

3. *Standardize risk measures, to allow for analysis and comparison.* While risk is always relative, a good risk measure should be standardized in such a way that an investor, when looking at the measure of risk for any one investment, should be able to come to a conclusion about the riskiness of that investment relative to others.

4. *Translate the risk measure into an expected return.* One of the objectives in measuring risk is to come up with an estimate of an expected return for an investment. This expected return then becomes the benchmark that determines whether the investment is a "good" or "bad" one. It is not sufficient for a model to say that higher risk investments should yield higher expected returns without providing a specific estimate of the risk premium.

5. *Work.* The ultimate test of a good model is that it works; that is, it provides a measure of risk which, at least in the long term and across the cross section of investments, is positively correlated with returns. A stronger test would be to examine whether the actual returns, again in the long term, match the expected returns derived from the model.

GENERAL MODELS FOR RISK AND RETURN

The awareness that risk matters is not new. Until recently, however, models for risk and return were largely subjective and varied widely among investors. Starting in the 1950s, with the development of modern portfolio theory, risk and return models have been formulated which, in addition to being more quantitative and specific in their predictions, have also been more widely accepted. As the ensuing discussion will make clear, however, the debate has not ended, and the search for a consensus—however elusive—continues.

The Capital Asset Pricing Model (CAPM)

The *capital asset pricing model (CAPM)* is the standard against which other risk and return models are measured. Given its wide use on Wall Street and in corporate policy making, the CAPM has also become a magnet for criticism, some warranted and some not. The advantages of the model are that it is simple and intuitive and provides some very strong and testable implications.

Variance in Returns: This is a measure of the squared difference between the actual and expected returns on an investment.

The capital asset pricing model is built on the premise that the **variance in returns** is the appropriate measure of risk but that only that portion of variance that is not diversifiable is rewarded. The model measures the nondiversifiable variance and relates expected returns to this measure of risk.

Measuring risk   In the capital asset pricing model, investments are measured on two dimensions: (1) the "expected return" on the investment comprises the reward; and (2) the variance in anticipated returns comprises the risk on the investment. The variance on any investment measures the disparity between actual and expected returns. In statistical terms, the variance can be captured in the return distribution. Figure 5.1 illustrates the return distributions on two investments. In the CAPM world, variance is the only measure of risk. Given a choice between two investments with the same standard deviation but different expected returns, investors will always pick the one with the higher expected return. In Figure 5.2, both investments have the same standard deviation, but investment A has much higher expected return.

Although the concept that investors choose on the basis of expected return and variance may seem intuitive, it is not as straightforward as it seems. In the real world, investors often consider other dimensions of risk and return beyond just the mean and the variance in making their decisions. For instance, an investor may accept a higher variance investment (over a lower variance investment with the same expected returns) because it offers a higher probability of extraordinary payoffs. In statistical terms, this probability of a high payoff is measured by the "skewness" of returns, and there is some evidence that investors like positively skewed distributions.[1]

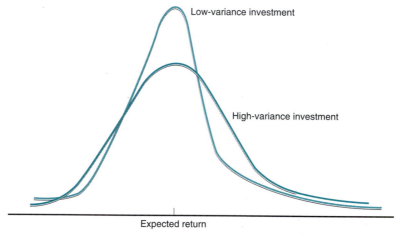

Figure 5.1   Return distributions on investment

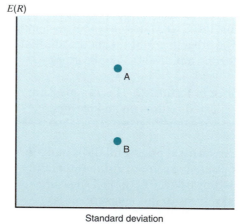

Figure 5.2   Comparing investments

---

[1]One rationale that has been advanced to explain why people play the lottery or indulge in other "negative-sum" games, in which the expected returns are negative and the variance in returns is high, is the individual's preference for skewness.

The assumptions about risk and return made by the capital asset pricing model are central to its derivation and have been defended by its proponents on two levels. On a theoretical level, the assumption that expected return is traded off against variance can be justified if investors possess utility functions where nothing else matters.[2] This is more an assumption of convenience than one that can be defended on empirical grounds, however, for there is no evidence that investors have such utility functions. The other way in which the expected return/variance tradeoff can be justified is by assuming that returns follow a normal distribution, in which case the entire distribution can be described in terms of the first two moments—the expected return and the variance. This assumption is also difficult to justify on empirical grounds because the investors' limited liability will result in return distributions that are positively skewed.

The other defense provided for the assumption that variance is the appropriate measure of risk is more believable because it is based on the empirical evidence relating average returns and variances on classes of assets over long time periods. For instance, an examination of returns on different classes of assets between 1926 and 1992 provides the following results:

Series	Average Annual Return (%)	Standard Deviation (%)
Common stocks	12.40	20.60
Small stocks	17.60	35.00
Long-term corporate bonds	5.80	8.50
Long-term government bonds	5.20	8.60
U.S. Treasury bills	3.60	3.30
Inflation	3.20	4.70

There is clear evidence here of a positive relationship between the variance in returns and the average returns on investment classes. For instance, the investment class with the highest average returns (small stocks) had the highest standard deviation, whereas the investment class with the lowest average returns (Treasury bill) had the lowest standard deviation. A leap in logic is still required, however, to arrive at the CAPM assumption that variance is the only measure of risk that matters.

Many analytical services also use the standard deviation to measure risk. For instance, Figure 5.3 shows the standard deviations for a wide variety of investment classes and mutual funds, used by Lipper Analytical Services as a measure of risk.

Figure 5.3   The Best Measure? A fund with a wide range of performance has a high standard deviation, meaning it has a great potential for volatility. A ruler could show volatility of fund categories and specific funds using standard deviation. By this measure, the T. Rowe Price International Bond fund comes in on the low side.

Source: The Lipper Risk Categorization

[2]A utility function is a way of summarizing investor preferences into a generic term called *utility* on the basis of some choice variables. In this case, for instance, investors' utility or satisfaction is stated as a function of wealth. By doing so, we can answer questions such as: Will an investor be twice as happy if he has twice as much wealth? Does each marginal increase in wealth lead to less additional utility than the prior marginal increase? In one specific form of this function, the quadratic utility function, the entire utility of an investor can be compressed into the expected wealth measure and the standard deviation in that wealth, which provides a justification for the use of CAPM.

☐ **Concept Check**

The variance used in these tables is the variance in historical (past) returns. Is this the variance that is the measure of risk in the CAPM? If not, what are we assuming?

IN PRACTICE   CALCULATION OF EXPECTED RETURNS/STANDARD DEVIATION USING HISTORICAL RETURNS

In the following example, the average returns and standard deviations in historical returns are calculated for two stocks—General Electric and the Home Depot. For purposes of brevity, the annual returns are calculated from 1990 to 1994, using the stock prices at the end of each year and the dividends paid during the course of the year (Table 5.1)

Table 5.1

	GE			Home Depot		
Year	Price at End of Year	Dividends During Year	Returns (%)	Price at End of Year	Dividends During Year	Returns (%)
1989	$32.25			$8.13		
1990	28.66	$0.95	−8.19	12.88	$0.04	58.92
1991	38.25	1.00	36.95	33.66	0.05	161.72
1992	42.75	1.00	14.38	50.63	0.07	50.62
1993	52.42	1.00	24.96	39.50	0.11	−21.77
1994	51.00	1.00	−0.80	46.00	0.15	16.84
Average			13.46			53.26
Standard deviation			18.42			68.48

Based on the annual returns, the standard deviation in returns for GE between 1990 and 1994 was 18.42%, whereas the standard deviation in returns for the Home Depot, over the same period, was 68.48%. While investing in the Home Depot was riskier, on the basis of the standard deviation, it also yielded much higher average returns—53.26%, versus average returns of 13.46% for stock held in General Electric.

Which of these stocks would dominate under the CAPM? The answer would depend on an investor's risk preferences. Those investors who are willing to take on more risk would prefer investing in the Home Depot, with its higher average returns, whereas those who had a greater aversion for risk would invest in GE, with its lower return variance.

☐ **Concept Check**

Although the Home Depot exhibited higher variance in returns, much of the variance seems to come from the stock price going up dramatically between 1989 and 1992. Why is this "upside" considered risk? Should risk not be defined purely in terms of "downside" potential (negative returns)? Explain.

What portion of the risk is rewarded?   Although the capital asset pricing model defines variance as risk, not all variance is rewarded by financial markets with higher returns. The CAPM is built on the tenet that some of the risk in any individual asset can be eliminated through **diversification** across large numbers and classes of assets, such as stocks, bonds, real estate, and other real assets. Because prices on these different asset classes do not always move together, investing in them should result in substantial savings in risk while not reducing expected returns substantially. The notion that diversification can reduce risk can be backed up on both intuitive and statistical grounds.

Diversification: This is the process of holding multiple investments in a portfolio, either across the same asset class (stocks) or across asset classes.

On an intuitive level, the risk in any asset comes from two sources—*firm-specific actions* that affect primarily the prices of that asset, and *marketwide movements* that affect the prices of all assets. The effects of firm-specific and marketwide actions can be either positive or negative. There is a key difference between the two effects, however: the effects of **firm-specific risk** on the prices of individual assets in a portfolio can be either positive or negative for any period. Thus, in large portfolios, it can be reasonably argued that this risk will average out to be zero and thus not impact the overall value of the portfolio. The effects of marketwide movements are likely to be in the same direction for all investments in a portfolio, although some assets may be affected more than others. For instance, other things being equal, an increase in interest rates will lower the values of most assets in a portfolio. Being more diversified does not eliminate this risk, although holding assets in different classes may reduce the impact.

Firm-Specific Risk: This is risk that affects only one asset or a small group of similar assets. In the case of a stock, it is risk that is specific to the company issuing the stock or to the industry in which the company operates.

The argument that diversification reduces risk is incontestable, but the assumption that CAPM makes—that diversifiable risk does not matter—is debatable. This argument is based on the presumption that the marginal investor in the market, who sets prices and therefore determines how risk is viewed, is well diversified and expects to be rewarded only for the nondiverisfiable risk. If the marginal investor is not well diversified, however, diversifiable risk may affect prices and expected returns.

More on diversifiable and nondiversifiable risk   A number of examples of actions can be cited that affect the returns of the firm taking those actions and, hence, create firm-specific risk. Some of these actions may have positive consequences: a consumer product company may profit because management introduced a successful product or revamped its marketing strategy, or an oil company may gain because it finds new oil reserves. Some actions may have negative consequences: a company's products may carry a defect that causes unexpected costs for the company, or the natural resource used by the company to manufacture its products may become more expensive. The risk associated with these actions should be diversifiable (i.e., become negligible as the portfolio includes more and more investments).

This definition can even be extended to actions that affect the returns of one specific sector of the economy. For instance, as a consequence of actions taken by the U.S. government to restrict the import of Japanese cars into the United States, all U.S. automobile companies may gain in terms of profitability. Alternatively, pollution laws directed primarily at auto emissions may make these same firms much less profitable. For a diversified investor who holds stocks across a wide variety of sectors and industries, this is still diversifiable risk.

Risk that is nondiversifiable affects all investments, although the degree of impact may vary across investments. One example would be an announcement by the Federal Reserve that it plans to raise interest rates. If, as a result of this announcement, market interest rates go up, all investments are affected, though to varying extents. Holding a diversified portfolio is not going to provide protection against this type of risk.

☐ Concept
   Check

> From the viewpoint of investors, is a company with a good management team less risky than a company with a poor management team? Explain.

A statistical analysis of diversification-reducing risk   The effects of diversification on risk can be illustrated by examining the effects of increasing the number of assets in a portfolio on variance. The variance in a portfolio is determined by the variances of the individual assets in the portfolio and the covariances between pairs of assets in that portfolio. It is the **covariance** term, which captures how asset prices move together, that provides an insight into why and by how much diversification will reduce risk. The chapter appendix provides a description of means, variances, and covariances.

Covariance: This is a measure of how two assets or investments move together. A *positive covariance* suggests that their prices move in the same direction most of the time, whereas a *negative covariance* suggests that their prices move in opposite directions.

Variance of a two-asset portfolio   Consider a portfolio of two assets. Asset A has an expected return of μ_A and a variance in returns of σ^2_A, whereas asset B has an expected return of μ_B and a variance in returns of σ^2_B.. The correlation in returns between the two assets is ρ_{AB}.. The expected returns and variance of a two-asset portfolio can be written as a function of these inputs and the proportion of the portfolio going to each asset.

$$\mu_{portfolio} = w_A \, \mu_A + (1 - w_A) \, \mu_B$$
$$\sigma^2_{portfolio} = w_A^2 \, \sigma^2_A + (1 - w_A)^2 \, \sigma^2_B + 2 \, w_A \, (1 - w_A) \, \rho_{AB} \, \sigma_A \, \sigma_B$$

where

$$w_A = \text{Proportion of the portfolio in asset A}$$

The last term in the variance formulation is sometimes written in terms of the covariance in returns between the two assets:

$$\sigma_{AB} = \rho_{AB} \, \sigma_A \, \sigma_B$$

The savings that accrue from diversification are a function of the correlation coefficient. Other things being equal, the higher the correlation in returns between the two assets, the smaller are the potential benefits from diversification.

IN PRACTICE   EXTENDING THE TWO-ASSET CASE—GENERAL ELECTRIC AND THE HOME DEPOT

Earlier in the chapter, we computed the average returns and standard deviation in returns for GE and the Home Depot. The effects of combining the two investments in a portfolio are examined in the following analysis.

Step 1:   *Use historical data to estimate average returns and standard deviations in returns for the two investments.* This has already been done on page 96. The following are the summary statistics for the two investments:

Stock	Average Return (1990–1994)	Standard Deviation (1990–1994)
General Electric	13.46%	18.42%
The Home Depot	53.26%	68.68%

Step 2:   *Estimate the correlation and covariance in returns between the two investments using historical data:*

Year	Returns on GE(R_{GE})	Returns on the Home Depot (R_H)	$[R_n - \text{Avge}(R_{GE})]$	$[R_H - \text{Avge}(R_H)]$	$(R_{Ge} - \text{Avge}(R_{GE}))$ $(R_H - \text{Avge}(R_H))$
1990	−8.19%	58.92%	0.04686	0.00320	(0.01225)
1991	36.95%	161.72%	0.05518	1.17636	0.25477
1992	14.38%	50.62%	0.00008	0.00071	(0.00024)
1993	24.96%	−21.77%	0.01322	0.56295	(0.08628)
1994	−0.80%	16.84%	0.02034	0.13265	0.05194
Total			0.13568	1.87696	0.20794

Covariance between GE and the Home Depot Returns = 0.20794/3 = 0.06931
Correlation between GE and the Home Depot Returns = $r_{GH} = \sigma_{GH}/\sigma_G\sigma_H$
= 0.06931/(0.1842 * 0.6848) = 0.5495

Step 3:   *Compute the expected returns and variances of portfolios of the two securities using the statistical parameters estimates above.* Consider, for instance, a portfolio composed of 50% in GE and 50% in the Home Depot:

Average Return of Portfolio = 0.5 (13.46%) + 0.5 (53.26%) = 33.36%
Variance of Portfolio = $(0.5)^2 (0.1842)^2 + (0.5)^2 (0.6848)^2 + 2 (0.5) (0.5) (0.5495)$
(0.1842) (0.6848) = 0.1605 = 1605%
Standard Deviation of Portfolio = 40.06%

Figure 5.4 summarizes the average returns and variances of a number of combinations of GE and the Home Depot.

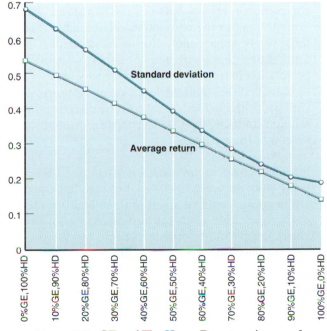

Figure 5.4   GE and The Home Depot: variances of portfolios.

Note that the gains to diversification seem smaller here because of the divergence in standard deviations between GE and the Home Depot. Nevertheless, the standard deviation decreases faster than the average return, which is indicative of the gains from diversification.

A minimum variance portfolio   There is a set of weights at which the variance of the portfolio of two assets is minimized. A more precise estimate of the weights on the two assets needed to minimize variance can be obtained from the variance equation for the two-asset portfolio:

$$\sigma^2_{portfolio} = w_A^2 \sigma^2_A + (1 - w_A)^2 \sigma^2_B + 2w_A(1-w_A)\rho_{AB}\sigma_A\sigma_B$$
$$\delta\sigma^2_{portfolio}/\delta w_A = 2w_A\sigma^2_A + (2w_A - 2)\sigma^2_B + 2\rho_{AB}\sigma_A\sigma_B - 4w_A\rho_{AB}\sigma_A\sigma_B = 0$$

Solving for w^*_A, the weight on asset A, which minimizes the variance of the portfolio,

$$w^*_A = (\sigma^2_B - \rho_{AB}\sigma_A\sigma_B)/(\sigma^2_A + \sigma^2_B - 2\rho_{AB}\sigma_A\sigma_B)$$

For a hypothetical portfolio where $\sigma_A = 30\%$, $\sigma_B = 40\%$ and $\rho_{AB} = .25$, this can be written as:

$$w^*_A = (40^2 - (0.25)(30)(40))/(30^2 + 40^2 - 2(0.25)(30)(40))$$
$$= 1300/(900 + 1600 - 600) = 1300/1900 = 68.42\%$$

Thus, a portfolio with 68.42% invested in asset A and 31.58% invested in asset B will minimize the variance of the portfolio.

☐ Concept
    Check

Is the minimum variance portfolio the best portfolio to hold for all investors? Why or why not?

Correlation coefficients and portfolio variance   The variance of the two-asset portfolio is clearly a function of the correlation in returns between the two assets. The greater the correlation in returns between the two assets, the smaller the benefit from diversification. As long as the correlation is less than 1 (the assets move in perfect proportion), there will be some benefit from diversification.[3] Figure 5.5 shows the variance of a portfolio of two assets, with half of the portfolio invested in each asset, as a function of the correlation in returns between the two assets.

Note that the standard deviation of the portfolio is halfway between the standard deviations of the individual assets (i.e., there is no gain from diversifying) when the correlation coefficient is 1. As the correlation coefficient declines, so does the standard deviation of the portfolio.

From two assets to three assets to n assets   If there is in fact a diversification benefit of going from one asset to two, as the preceding discussion illustrates, there must be a benefit in going from two assets to three and from three to more assets. The variance of a portfolio of three assets can be written as a function of the variances of each of the three assets, the portfolio weights on each, and the correlations between pairs of the assets. The variance can be written as follows:

$$\sigma_p^2 = w_A^2\sigma^2_A + w_B^2\sigma^2_B + w_c\sigma^2_c + 2w_Aw_B\rho_{AB}\sigma_A\sigma_B + 2w_Aw_C\rho_{AC}\sigma_A\sigma_C +$$
$$2w_Bw_C\rho_{BC}\sigma_B\sigma_C$$

---

[3]Thus, if stock A and B are perfectly correlated, when A moves up by 10%, B moves up by 15%; when A moves down by 5%, B moves down by 7.5%. As long as B moves exactly one and a half times as much as A in each direction, the two are perfectly correlated.

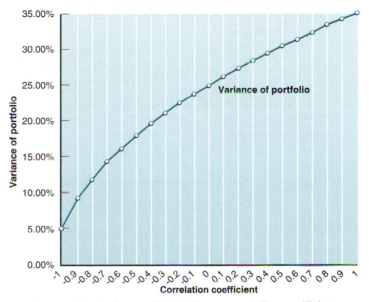

Figure 5.5   Variance of portfolio vs. correlation coefficient

where

w_A, w_B, w_C = Portfolio weights on assets
$\sigma^2_A, \sigma^2_B, \sigma^2_C$ = Variances of assets A, B, and C
$\rho_{AB}, \rho_{AC}, \rho_{BC}$ = Correlation in returns between pairs of assets (A&B, A&C, B&C)

Note that the number of covariance terms in the variance formulation has increased from one to three. This formulation can be extended to the more general case of a portfolio of n assets:

$$\sigma^2_p = \sum_{i=1}^{i=n} \sum_{j=1}^{j=n} w_i \, w_j \, \rho_{ij} \, \sigma_i \, \sigma_j$$

Note that the covariance of an asset with itself is the variance of that asset. The number of terms in this formulation increases exponentially with the number of assets in the portfolio, largely because of the number of covariance terms that have to be considered. In general, the number of covariance terms can be written as a function of the number of assets:

Number of covariance terms = $n \, (n - 1) \, / 2$

where n is the number of assets in the portfolio:

Number of Assets	Number of Covariance Terms
2	1
5	10
10	45
20	190
100	4,950
1,000	499,500

This formulation can be used to estimate the variance of a portfolio and the effects of diversification on that variance. For simplicity, assume that the average asset has a standard deviation in returns of σ and that the average covariance in returns between any pair of assets is σ_{ij}. Furthermore, assume that the portfolio is always equally weighted across the assets in that portfolio. The variance of a portfolio of *n* assets can then be written as

$$\sigma_p^2 = n \left(\frac{1}{n}\right)^2 \overline{\sigma}^2 + \frac{(n-1)}{n}\overline{\sigma}_{ij}$$

To illustrate, assume that the average asset has a variance in returns of 50% and that the average covariance in returns between any two assets is 10%. The variance of a portfolio of five assets can then be written as

$$\sigma^2_p = (1/5)\,(50\%) + (4/5)\,(10\%) = 18\%$$

The variance of a portfolio of 10 assets can be written as

$$\sigma^2_p = (1/10)\,(50\%) + (9/10)\,(10\%) = 14\%$$

Note that as the number of assets in the portfolio increases, the variance of the portfolio approaches the average covariance, and the first term in the equation (which is the firm-specific component of risk) approaches zero. The marginal gains from diversification are illustrated in Figure 5.6, where variance is shown as a function of the number of assets in the portfolio.

The marginal benefits of diversification decrease with the addition of each new asset to the portfolio. The variance of the portfolio drops from 50% to 11.60% as the number of assets increases from 1 to 25. Increasing the number of assets further provides only a small additional benefit, for the variance can drop to 10% at the minimum (with an infinite number of assets). Given that diversification can be costly, in terms of transactions and information costs, this provides a rationale for why most investors do not carry diversification to its logical limit and hold as many assets as there are available.

❑ Concept
Check

The marginal benefits of diversification calculated in the example above are based on random choices to the portfolio. If you followed a more deliberate strategy, such as picking stocks with low price/earnings ratios, would you need more or fewer stocks to get an equivalent amount of diversification?

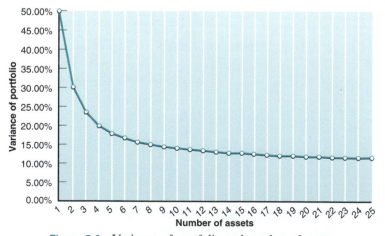

Figure 5.6   Variance of portfolio and number of assets

Markowitz Portfolio: This is the portfolio that yields the highest expected return for a specified level of risk or the minimum standard deviation for a specified expected return.

Return optimization—Markowitz portfolios The fact that variances can be estimated for portfolios made up of a large number of assets suggests an approach to optimizing portfolio construction in the mean/variance framework on which the CAPM is devised. If an investor can specify the maximum amount of risk he is willing to take on (in terms of variance), the task of portfolio optimization becomes the maximization of expected returns subject to this level of risk. Alternatively, if an investor specifies her desired level of return, the optimum portfolio is the one that minimizes the variance subject to this level of return. These optimization algorithms can be written as follows:

Return Maximization	**Risk Minimization**
Maximize expected return	Minimize return variance

$$E(R_p) = \sum_{i=1}^{i=n} w_i\, E(R_i) \qquad\qquad \sigma_p^2 = \sum_{i=1}^{i=n}\sum_{j=1}^{j=n} w_i w_j \sigma_{ij}$$

subject to

$$\sigma_p^2 = \sum_{i=1}^{i=n}\sum_{j=1}^{j=n} w_i w_j \sigma_{ij} \le \sigma^2 \qquad\qquad E(R_p) = \sum_{i=1}^{i=n} w_i\, E(R_i) \ge E(\hat{R})$$

where

$$\sigma^2 = \text{Investor's desired level of variance}$$
$$E(R) = \text{Investor's desired expected returns}$$

The portfolios that emerge from this process are called **Markowitz portfolios**. These portfolios are considered efficient because they maximize expected returns given the standard deviation; the entire set of portfolios is referred to as the *efficient frontier*. These portfolios are shown on the expected return/standard deviation dimensions in Figure 5.7.

The Markowitz approach to portfolio optimization, though intuitively appealing, suffers from two major problems. The first is that it requires a very large number of inputs, since the covariances between pairs of assets are required to estimate the variances of portfolios. This may be manageable for small numbers of assets, but it becomes less so when the entire universe of stocks or all investments are considered. The second problem is that the Markowitz approach ignores a very important asset choice that most

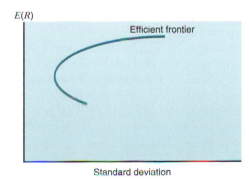

Figure 5.7 Markowitz portfolios

investors have—the choice of investing their money risklessly in default-free government securities—in coming up with optimum portfolios. The CAPM addresses these limitations and comes up with a far simpler approach to constructing optimal portfolios, while considering the riskless asset simultaneously.

Both the CAPM and Markowitz portfolio optimization make one assumption that exposes them to some criticism: they both assume that there are no transactions or information costs associated with diversification.[4]

Optimum portfolios with the riskless asset   Most investors have the choice of investing some or all of their money in a **riskless asset**, as a way of managing risk. By itself, the addition of one asset to the universe may seem trivial, but the riskless asset has some special characteristics that affect optimal portfolio choice for all investors.

Riskless Asset: A riskless asset is one for which the actual return is equal to the expected return.

1.   The riskless asset, by definition, has an expected return that will always be equal to the actual return (there is no return variance). For example, consider an investment in a short-term government security. The investment has no default risk and provides a guaranteed cash flow (at least in nominal terms) at the end of its maturity. The expected return is known when the investment is made, and the actual return should be equal to this, if the investor holds until maturity.

2.   While returns on risky assets vary, the absence of variance in the riskless asset makes it uncorrelated with returns on any of these risky assets. Consequently, combinations of any risky asset or portfolio with the riskless asset will yield linear results for the standard deviation. To prove this, assume that the variance of the risky portfolio is σ_r^2 and that w_r is the proportion of the overall portfolio invested to these risky assets. The balance is invested in a riskless asset, which has no variance, and is uncorrelated with the risky asset. The variance of the overall portfolio can be written as

$$\sigma^2_{\text{portfolio}} = w_r^2 \, \sigma^2_r$$
$$\sigma_{\text{portfolio}} = w_r \, \sigma_r$$

Note that the other two terms drop out and that the standard deviation of the overall portfolio is linearly related to the proportion of the portfolio invested in the risky portfolio.

The significance of this result can be illustrated by returning to Figure 5.8 and adding the riskless asset to the choices available to the investor. The effect of this addition is explored in Figure 5.8.

Consider investor A, whose desired risk level is σ_A. This investor, instead of choosing portfolio A, the Markowitz portfolio, will choose to invest in a combination of the riskless asset and a much riskier portfolio, because he will be able to make a much higher return for the same level of risk. Note, however, that the expected return does not necessarily increase as the riskiness of the risky portfolio increases, and it is maximized for combinations of the riskless asset and the risky portfolio (M), which is tangential to the riskless asset. Thus, investor A will maximize expected returns if he puts

[4]Transactions and information costs can be built into the Markowitz optimization algorithms explicitly. Both conceptual and practical problems are associated with doing so, however, since these costs are likely to vary from asset to asset, from investor to investor, and for different investment time horizons.

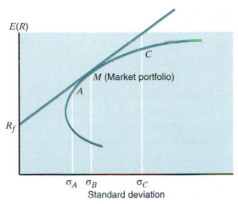

Figure 5.8   Introducing a riskless asset

some of his portfolio in the riskless asset and the balance in portfolio M. Investor B, whose desired risk level is σ_B, which happens to be equal to the standard deviation of the portfolio M, will choose to invest her entire portfolio in that portfolio. Investor C, whose desired risk level is σ_C, which exceeds the standard deviation of portfolio M, will borrow money at the riskless rate and invest in portfolio M.

The central role that the risky portfolio M plays in this process raises the question of how this portfolio is constructed and what assets are incorporated in it. Because all investors in the CAPM universe are assumed to have the same information and they all hold the same portfolio, it has to include all traded assets, in proportion to their market values. In other words, any asset that is *not* in this portfolio will be held by no investors and have no value. The fact that this portfolio includes all traded assets in the market is the reason why it is called the **market portfolio**. This should not be surprising, given the benefits of diversification and the absence of transactions costs in the capital asset pricing model. If diversification is good, and no costs are associated with adding more assets to the portfolio, the logical limit to diversification is to hold a small proportion of every traded asset in the economy.

Market Portfolio: This is the portfolio of all risky assets, held in proportion to their market value.

If this seems abstract, consider M to be an extremely well-diversified mutual fund that holds both financial and real assets, and Treasury bills to be the riskless asset. In the CAPM, all investors will hold combinations of Treasury bills and the same mutual fund and adjust for risk through their allocation decisions. They will put more of their money in the mutual fund if they want to take risk, and less into it if they want to decrease their risk exposure. At the limit, if they feel that putting all their money in the mutual fund does not expose them to enough risk, they can borrow money and invest it in the mutual fund.

These results are predicated on two assumptions. First, there exists a riskless asset, with the characteristics described earlier. Second, investors can lend and borrow at this riskless rate to arrive at their optimal allocations. Some variations of the CAPM allow these assumptions to be relaxed and still permit conclusions consistent with the CAPM.

Adding the riskless asset to the risky portfolios, developed using the Markowitz optimization techniques, yields very strong implications for optimal investment strategy. All investors will hold combinations of the riskless asset and the market portfolio. The only difference across investors is in the allocation decision; more risk-averse investors will invest more in the riskless asset, and less risk-averse investors will invest more in the market portfolio. Note in Figure 5.8 that all the optimal port-folios lie on a straight line, emanating from the risk-free asset. This is the **capital market line**, and it contains all possible combinations of the risk-free asset and the market portfolio.

Capital Market Line: This is the line that plots the expected return on an efficient portfolio as a function of the standard deviation of that portfolio. The efficient portfolios are all combinations of the riskless asset and the market portfolio.

☐ Concept
   Check

> The CAPM implies that the most efficient way to take risk is to borrow money and invest it in the market portfolio. Why is this more efficient than just investing in a portfolio of the "riskiest stocks" in the market?

Defenders of the capital asset pricing model should undoubtedly be troubled by the fact that investors in the real world hold a wide variety of portfolios and do not hold just the market portfolio. Some of these variations can be ascribed to the presence of transactions costs and others to differences in the information available to investors and to expectations about future returns. The question that remains, however, is whether these deviations from the predictions of the CAPM are serious enough to call into question its conclusions about how risk is measured. This empirical question is addressed later in this chapter.

Measuring nondiversifiable risk with the market portfolio as the standard   In a world in which investors hold a combination of only two assets—the riskless asset and the market portfolio—the risk of any individual asset will be measured relative to the market portfolio. In particular, the risk of any asset will be the risk it adds on to the market portfolio. To arrive at the appropriate measure of this added risk, assume that σ^2_m is the variance of the market portfolio prior to the addition of the new asset, and that the variance of the individual asset being added to this portfolio is σ^2_i. The market value portfolio weight on this asset is w_i, and the covariance in returns between the individual asset and the market portfolio is σ_{im}. The variance of the market portfolio prior to and after the addition of the individual asset can then be written as

$$\text{Variance prior to asset } i \text{ being added} = \sigma^2_m$$
$$\text{Variance after asset } i \text{ is added} = \sigma^2_{m'} = w_i^2 \, \sigma^2_i + (1 - w_i)^2 \, \sigma^2_m + 2 \, w_i \, (1 - w_i) \, \text{Cov}_{im}$$

The market value weight on any individual asset in the market portfolio should be small since the market portfolio includes all traded assets in the economy. Consequently, the first term in the equation should approach zero, and the second term should approach σ^2_m, leaving the third term (Cov_{im}, the covariance) as the measure of the risk added by asset i.

To illustrate, assume that the market portfolio includes 1,000 assets, a total market value of $1,000 billion, and a standard deviation of 20%. A new asset is added on, with a market value of $1 billion, a standard deviation of 80%, and a correlation of 0.5 with the market portfolio. To examine the marginal impact of adding this asset to the portfolio, the variance of the market portfolio has to be computed both before and after adding the asset:

Market Value weight of the new asset = 1/1001
Variance of market portfolio before addition = $(.20)^2 = .04$
Variance of market portfolio after addition = $\sigma^2_{m'}$
$= (1/1001)^2 (.80)^2 + (1000/1001)^2 (.20)^2 + 2 (1/1001)(1000/1001)(.5) (.80)(.20)$
$= 0 + .04 + (2/1001) (.08)$

Thus, the risk added by the new asset is proportional to its covariance with the market portfolio.

Concept Check

How would your conclusions change if the individual asset that you were examining was a significant proportion of the market portfolio (say, 10%)?

Beta: The beta of any investment in CAPM is a standardized measure of the risk it adds to the market portfolio.

Standardizing covariances   Since the covariance of the market portfolio with itself is the market variance, the covariances of individual assets with the market portfolio can be standardized by dividing by the market variance. This standardized measure of non-diversifiable risk is the **beta of the asset**.

$$\text{Beta of an asset } i = \text{Cov}_{im}/\sigma^2 m$$

The beta of the market portfolio is 1 (since $\text{Cov}_{mm} = \sigma^2_m$); assets that are riskier than average (using this measure of risk) will have betas that exceed 1, and assets that are safer than average will have betas that are lower than 1. The riskless asset will have a beta of zero.

The expected return on an asset is linearly related to the beta of the asset. This follows from Figure 5.8, where we saw that all the optimal portfolios lay on the capital market line. In particular, the expected return on an asset can be written as a function of the risk-free rate and the beta of that asset:

Expected Return on asset i

$= $ Risk-free rate + Beta of asset i * (Risk premium on market portfolio)
$= R_f + \beta_i [E(R_m) - R_f]$

where

$E(R_i)$ = Expected Return on asset i
R_f = Risk-free Rate
$E(R_m)$ = Expected Return on market portfolio
β_i = Beta of investment i

The relationship between betas and expected returns is illustrated in Figure 5.9.
If the CAPM is correct, all assets should fall on the security market line, which provides the expected return for any given beta.

Concept Check

Can an investment have a negative beta? What does this mean in terms of market risk? What kind of return would you expect to make on this investment in the long term (relative to the riskless rate)?

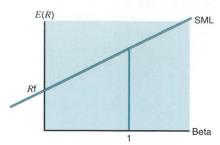

Figure 5.9 Expected returns and betas

Implications of the CAPM The capital asset pricing model does make some strong assumptions, but it provides equally strong and testable implications.

1. All investors will allocate their wealth across two assets—the riskless asset and a market portfolio of all risky assets, held in proportion to their market value.
2. The risk of any asset will be measured by how much risk it adds on to the market portfolio; this added risk can be estimated using the covariance between the returns on the asset and the returns on the market portfolio. This covariance can be standardized by dividing by the market variance to arrive at a beta for the asset.
3. The expected return on any asset is linearly related to its beta (i.e., the higher the beta, the higher the expected return).

$$E(R_i) = R_f + \beta_i[E(R_m) - R_f]$$

where

$$E(R_i) = \text{Expected Return on asset } i$$
$$R_f = \text{Risk-free Rate}$$
$$E(R_m) = \text{Expected Return on market portfolio}$$
$$\beta i = \text{Beta of investment } i$$

Testing the CAPM Does the CAPM work? Is beta a good proxy for risk, and is it correlated with expected returns? The answers to these questions have been debated widely in the last two decades. The first tests of the model suggested that betas and returns were positively related, although other measures of risk (such as variance) continued to explain differences in actual returns. This discrepancy was attributed to limitations in the testing techniques. In 1977, Roll, in a seminal critique of the model's tests, suggested that since the market portfolio could never be observed, the CAPM could never be tested. Therefore, all tests of the CAPM were joint tests of both the model and the market portfolio used in the tests (i.e., any test of the CAPM could only show that the model worked—or did not work—given the proxy used for the market portfolio). It could therefore be argued that in any empirical test that claimed to reject the CAPM, the rejection could be of the proxy used for the market portfolio rather than of the model itself. Roll noted that there was no way to prove that CAPM worked and, thus, no empirical basis for using the model.

Book-to-Market Ratio: This is the ratio of the book value of equity to the market value of equity.

In a damning indictment, Fama and French (1992) examined the relationship between betas and returns between 1963 and 1990 and concluded that there was no relationship

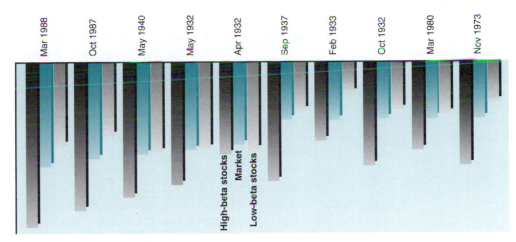

Figure 5.10   Returns and betas: ten worst months between 1926 and 1991

between the two. They also noted that two other variables—**size** and **book-to-market ratio**—explain differences in returns across firms much better than does beta and may in fact be better proxies for risk. These results have been contested on two fronts. First, Amihud, Christensen, and Mendelson, using the same data, performed different statistical tests and showed that betas did, in fact, explain returns during the time period. Second, Chan and Lakonishok examined a much longer time series of returns from 1926 to 1991 and found that the positive relationship between betas and returns broke down only in the period after 1982. They attribute this breakdown to indexing, which they argue has allowed the larger, lower-beta stocks in the S&P 500 to outperform smaller, higher-beta stocks. They also find that betas are a useful guide to risk in extreme market conditions, with the riskiest firms (the 10% with highest betas) performing far worse than the market as a whole, in the 10 worst months for the market between 1926 and 1991 (see Figure 5.10).

The Arbitrage Pricing Model

The failure of the capital asset pricing model to explain adequately differences in returns across assets using betas opened the door for other asset pricing models. The leading candidate for an alternative model is the *arbitrage pricing model* (APM). The logic behind the APM is much the same as that behind the capital asset pricing model: investors are rewarded for taking on nondiversifiable risk. In the capital asset pricing model, one factor (the sensitivity to the market portfolio) captures this nondiversifiable risk. In contrast, the measure of this nondiversifiable risk in the APM can come from multiple factors. The number and identity of the factors are determined by the data on historical returns.

The arbitrage pricing model is built on the simple premise that investors take advantage of arbitrage opportunities. In other words, if two portfolios have the same exposure to risk but offer different expected returns, investors will buy the portfolio that has the higher expected returns and, in the process, adjust the expected returns to equilibrium.

Decomposing returns into anticipated and unanticipated components   The return on any asset can be decomposed into two parts—a normal, or expected, return component that is predictable, and an unanticipated component that is not:

$$R = E(R) + U$$

where $E(R)$ is the expected component and U is the unexpected component of returns. It is the *unanticipated* component that creates the risk in investments.

The source of unanticipated returns—firm-specific and marketwide risk   The "surprise" in returns comes from two sources. The first is firm-specific and covers information that primarily affects the firm. The second is marketwide and affects most or all investments and includes unanticipated changes in a number of economic variables, including gross national product, inflation, and interest rates. Incorporating this into the return model above

$$R = E(R) + m + \varepsilon$$

where m is the marketwide component of unanticipated risk and ε is the firm-specific component. Note that this distinction is very similar to the distinction between firm-specific and market risk made in the capital asset pricing model.

The sources of marketwide risk   Although both the capital asset pricing model and the arbitrage pricing model make a distinction between firm-specific and marketwide risk, they part ways when it comes to measuring the market risk. The CAPM assumes that the market risk is captured in the market portfolio, whereas the arbitrage pricing model sticks with economic fundamentals allowing for multiple sources of marketwide risk, such as unanticipated changes in gross national product, interest rates, and inflation, and measures the sensitivity of investments to these changes with factor betas. In general, the market component of unanticipated returns can be decomposed into economic factors:

$$R = R + m + \varepsilon$$
$$= E[R] + (\beta_1 F_1 + \beta_2 F_2 + \ldots + \beta_n F_n) + \varepsilon$$

where

β_j = Sensitivity of investment to unanticipated changes in factor j
F_j = Unanticipated changes in factor j

Suppose that investment j is expected to have a return of 7% next year. There are four economic factors that drive returns, and the betas of investment j to each factor are given below:

Beta relative to factor 1 = 2.5
Beta relative to factor 2 = 0.5
Beta relative to factor 3 = −1.0
Beta relative to factor 4 = 0.8

The expected values for each of the factors are as follows:

Expected value for factor 1 = 4%
Expected value for factor 2 = 6%
Expected value for factor 3 = 0%
Expected value for factor 4 = 1.5%

Assume that the actual values for each of the factors are as follows:

Actual value for factor 1 = 6%
Actual value for factor 2 = 7%
Actual value for factor 3 = 1%
Actual value for factor 4 = 2%

The marketwide component for unanticipated returns will be as follows:

$$m = 2.5 \ (6\% - 4\%) + 0.5 \ (7\% - 6\%) - 1.0 \ (1\% - 0\%) + 0.8 \ (2\% - 1.5\%) = 4.9\%$$

If the firm-specific component for unanticipated returns is 3%, the total return for investment j is as follows:

$$R = 7\% + 4.9\% + 3\% = 14.9\%$$

Concept Check

> Can the number of factors that determine returns change over time? What might cause these changes?

The effects of diversification   The benefits of diversification have been discussed extensively in our treatment of the capital asset pricing model. The primary point of that discussion was that diversification of investments into portfolios eliminates firm-specific risk. The arbitrage pricing model makes the same point and concludes that the return on a portfolio will not have a firm-specific component of unanticipated returns. The return on a portfolio can be written as the sum of two weighted averages—that of the anticipated returns in the portfolio, and that of the factor betas:

$$R_p = (w_1R_1 + w_2R_2 + \ldots + w_nR_n) + (w_1\beta_{1,1} + w_2\beta_{1,2} + \ldots + w_n\beta_1, n) \ F_1 + (w_1\beta_{2,1} + w_2\beta_{2,2} + \ldots + w_n\beta_{2,n}) \ F_2 \ldots .$$

where

$$w_j = \text{Portfolio weight on asset } j$$
$$R_j = \text{Expected return on asset } j$$
$$\beta i,_j = \text{Beta on factor } i \text{ for asset } j$$

Arbitrage: An investment opportunity that requires no investment and has no risk and still yields a positive return is called an arbitrage opportunity.

Expected returns and betas   Based on the fact that the beta of a portfolio is the weighted average of the betas of the assets in the portfolio, in conjunction with the absence of arbitrage, we can conclude that expected returns should be linearly related to betas. To see why, assume that there is only one factor and that there are three portfolios. Portfolio A has a beta of 2.0 and an expected return on 20%; portfolio B has a beta of 1.0 and an expected return of 12%; and portfolio C has a beta of 1.5 and an expected return on 14%. Note that the investor can put half of his wealth in portfolio A and half in portfolio B and end up with a portfolio that has a beta of 1.5 and an expected return of 16%. Consequently, no investor will choose to hold portfolio C until the prices of assets in that portfolio drop and the expected return increases to 16%. By the same rationale, the expected returns on every portfolio should be a linear function of the beta, or there will be an opportunity for **arbitrage**. This argument can be extended to multiple factors, with the same results. Therefore, the expected return on an asset can be written as

$$E(R) = R_f + \beta_1 \ [E(R_1) - R_f] + \beta_2 \ [E(R_2) - R_f] \ldots + \beta_n \ [E(R_n) - R_f]$$

where

$$R_f = \text{Expected return on a zero-beta portfolio}$$
$$E(R_j) = \text{Expected return on a portfolio with a factor beta of 1 for factor } j \text{ and zero for all other factors}$$

The terms in the brackets can be considered risk premiums for each of the factors in the model.

Note that the capital asset pricing model can be considered a special case of the arbitrage pricing model, in which there is only one economic factor driving marketwide returns and the market portfolio is the factor:

$$E(R) = R_f + \beta_m (E(R_m) - R_f)$$

☐ Concept
Check

> If your task were to explain past returns on stocks, which model (the CAPM or the APM) would work better? Would your answer be different if you were forecasting expected returns? Why or why not?

Multifactor Models for Risk and Return

The arbitrage pricing model's failure to identify specifically the factors in the model may be a strength from a statistical standpoint, but it is a clear weakness from an intuitive standpoint. The solution seems simple: replace the unidentified statistical factors with specific economic factors, and the resultant model should be intuitive while still retaining much of the strength of the arbitrage pricing model. That is precisely what multifactor models do.

Multifactor models generally are not based on an extensive economic rationale but are driven by the data instead. Once the number of factors has been identified in the arbitrage pricing model, the behavior of the factors over time can be extracted from the data. These factor time series can then be compared to the time series of macroeconomic variables to determine whether any of the variables is correlated, over time, with the identified factors.

Unanticipated Inflation: This is the difference between actual inflation and expected inflation.

For instance, Chen, Roll, and Ross (1986) suggest that the following macroeconomic variables are highly correlated with the factors that come out of factor analysis: industrial production, changes in default premium, shifts in the term structure, **unanticipated inflation**, and changes in the real rate of return. These variables can then be correlated with returns to come up with a model of expected returns, with firm-specific betas calculated relative to each variable:

$$E(R) = R_f + \beta_{GNP} (E(R_{GNP}) - R_f) + \beta_i (E(R_i) - R_f) \ldots + \beta_\delta (E(R_\delta) - R_f)$$

where

β_{GNP} = Beta relative to changes in industrial production
$E(R_{GNP})$ = Expected return on a portfolio with a beta of one on the industrial production factor and zero on all other factors
β_i = Beta relative to changes in inflation
$E(R_i)$ = Expected return on a portfolio with a beta of one on the inflation factor, and zero on all other factors

The costs of going from the arbitrage pricing model to a macroeconomic multifactor model can be traced directly to the errors that can be made in identifying the factors. The economic factors in the model can change over time, as will the risk premia associated with each one. For instance, oil price changes were a significant economic factor driving expected returns in the 1970s but are not as significant in other time periods.

Using the wrong factor(s) or missing a significant factor in a multifactor model can lead to inferior estimates of cost of equity.

Another approach to developing multifactor models was developed by Fama and French, who note that actual returns over long time periods have been much more highly correlated with price/book value ratios and size. They suggest that these measures and similar ones developed from the data be used as proxies for risk and that the regression coefficients be used to estimate expected returns for investments. For instance, Fama and French report the following regression for monthly returns on stocks on the New York Stock Exchange, using data from 1963 to 1990:

$$R_t = 1.77\% - 0.11 \ln (MV) + 0.35 \ln (BV/MV)$$

where

$$MV = \text{Market Value of Equity}$$
$$BV/MV = \text{Book Value of Equity / Market Value of Equity}$$

The values for market value of equity and book-price ratios for individual firms, when plugged into this regression, should yield expected monthly returns. The reliability of the prediction is open to question, however, for the regression coefficients change significantly from period to period and the variables themselves may explain returns in some periods and not in others.

Concept Check

Is it possible for a "factor" in a multifactor model to be significant in some periods and not in others? What effect would this have on whether and how you construct and use a multifactor model in predicting expected returns?

A COMPARATIVE ANALYSIS OF RISK AND RETURN MODELS

All the risk and return models developed in this chapter have common ingredients. They all assume that only marketwide risk is rewarded, and they derive the expected return as a function of measures of this risk. The capital asset pricing model makes the greatest number of assumptions but arrives at the simplest model, with only one factor driving risk and requiring estimation. The arbitrage pricing model makes fewer assumptions but arrives at a more complicated model, at least in terms of the parameters that require estimation. The capital asset pricing model can be considered a specialized case of the arbitrage pricing model, in which there is only one underlying factor and it is completely measured by the market index. In general, the CAPM has the advantage of being a simpler model to estimate and to use, but it will underperform the richer APM when the company is sensitive to economic factors that are not well represented in the market index. For instance, oil companies, which derive most of their risk from oil price movements, tend to have low CAPM betas. Using an arbitrage pricing model, where one of the factors may be capturing oil and other commodity price movements, will yield a better estimate of risk and higher cost of equity for these firms.[5]

The biggest intuitive block in using the arbitrage pricing model is its failure to identify specifically the factors driving expected returns. Although this may preserve the flexibility of the model and reduce statistical problems in testing, it does make it difficult to understand what the APM beta coefficients for a firm mean and how they will change as the firm changes (or restructures).

[5]Weston and Copeland used both approaches to estimate the cost of equity for oil companies in 1989 and came up with 14.4% with the CAPM and 19.1% using the APM.

As noted earlier, the CAPM does not do very well in explaining differences in returns across firms, although predictions of its demise are premature. Multifactor models indeed do better than the CAPM in explaining past returns, but the comparison is a little unfair to the CAPM: the CAPM constrains itself to explaining differences in returns using only one factor, whereas the other models allow themselves the freedom of more than one factor. With regard to making predictions of expected returns in the future, the comparison provides a more ambiguous result, for the gains that can be made by having multiple factors can be offset by the errors associated with estimating both the factor loadings and the factor betas, especially for individual companies. The continued use of the capital asset pricing model attests to both its intuitive appeal and its simplicity.

MODELS OF DEFAULT RISK

When an investor lends to an individual or a firm, there is the possibility that the borrower may default on interest and principal payments on the borrowing. This possibility of default is called the *default risk*. Generally speaking, borrowers with higher default risk should pay higher interest rates on their borrowing than should those with lower default risk. This section examines the measurement of default risk and the relationship of default risk to interest rates on borrowing.

In contrast to the general risk and return models described above, which focus on market risk, models of default risk examine the consequences of firm-specific default risk on expected returns. Although the rationale for diversification can be used to explain why firm-specific risk will not be priced into expected returns, the same rationale does not apply for securities that have limited upside potential and much greater downside potential from firm-specific events. For instance, corporate bonds benefit only marginally from firm-specific events that increase the value of the firm and make it safer, while they bear the risk of any firm-specific events that lower the value of the firm and increase the probability of default. Consequently, the expected return on a corporate bond is likely to reflect the firm-specific default risk of the firm issuing the bond.

A General Model of Default Risk

The default risk of a firm is a broad function of two variables—the firm's capacity to generate cash flows from operations, and its financial obligations—including interest and principal payments.[6] All else equal:

* Firms that generate high cash flows relative to their financial obligations have lower default risk than do firms that generate low cash flows relative to obligations. Thus, firms with significant assets in place, which generate high cash flows, will have lower default risk than will firms that do not.
* The more stability there is in cash flows, the lower the default risk in the firm. Firms that operate in predictable and stable businesses will have lower default risk than will otherwise similar firms that operate in cyclical or volatile businesses.

---

[6]"Financial obligation" refers to any payment the firm has legally obligated itself to make, such as interest and principal payments. It does not include discretionary cash flows, such as dividend payments or new capital expenditures, which can be deferred or delayed, without legal consequences, although there may be economic consequences.

Most models of default risk use financial ratios to measure the cash-flow coverage (i.e., the magnitude of cash flows relative to obligations) and to control for industry effects in order to capture the variability in cash flows.

Bond Ratings and Interest Rates

The most widely used measure of a firm's default risk is its bond rating, which is generally assigned by an independent ratings agency, using a mix of private and public information.

The ratings process   The process of rating a bond starts when the issuing company requests a rating from the ratings agency. The ratings agency then collects information from both publicly available sources, such as financial statements, and the company itself, and makes a decision on the rating. If it disagrees with the rating, the company is given the opportunity to present additional information. This process is presented schematically for the Standard and Poor's ratings process in Figure 5.11.

Description of bond ratings   The two major agencies rating corporate bonds are Standard and Poor's (S&P) and Moody's. The ratings they assign are fairly similar, but there are some differences. Table 5.2 describes the bond ratings assigned by the two agencies.

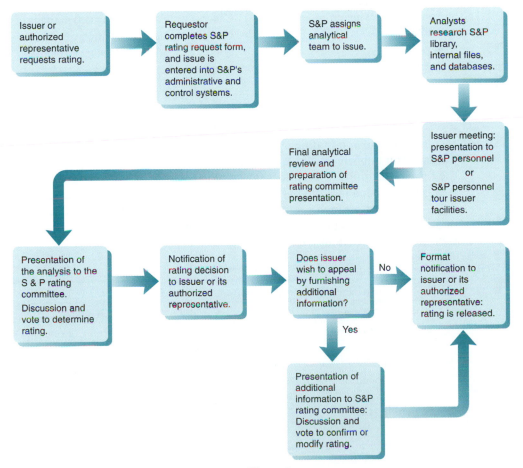

Figure 5.11   The ratings process

Table 5.2   **INDEX OF BOND RATINGS**

Standard and Poor's		Moody's	
AAA	The highest debt rating assigned. The borrower's capacity to repay debt is extremely strong.	Aaa	Judged to be of the best quality with a small degree of risk.
AA	Capacity to repay is strong and differs from the highest quality by only by a small amount.	Aa	High quality but rated lower than Aaa because margin of protection may not be as large or because there may be other elements of long-term risk.
A	Has strong capacity to repay; Borrower is susceptible to adverse effects of changes in circumstances and economic conditions.	A	Bonds possess favorable investment attributes but may be susceptible to risk in the future.
BBB	Has adequate capacity to repay, but adverse economic conditions or circumstances are more likely to lead to risk.	Baa	Neither highly protected nor poorly secured; adequate payment capacity.
BB,B, CCC, CC	Regarded as predominantly speculative, BB being the least speculative and CC the most.	Ba	Judged to have some speculative risk.
		B	Generally lacking characteristics of a desirable investment; probability of payment small.
D	The borrower is in default or has payments in arrears.	Caa	Poor standing and perhaps in default.
		Ca	Very speculative; often in default.
		C	Highly speculative; in default.

In financial markets, bonds with ratings of BBB or higher (Standard and Poor's) are considered "investment grade."

Determinants of bond ratings   The bond ratings assigned by ratings agencies are based primarily on publicly available information, although private information conveyed by the firm to the rating agency does play a role. The rating that is assigned to a company's bonds will depend in large part on financial ratios that measure the company's capacity to meet debt payments and generate stable and predictable cash flows. Although a multitude of financial ratios exist, Table 5.3 summarizes some of the key ratios that are used to measure default risk.

Table 5.3   **FINANCIAL RATIOS USED TO MEASURE DEFAULT RISK**

Ratio	Description
Pretax Interest Coverage	= (Pretax Income from Continuing Operations + Interest Expense)/Gross Interest Expense
EBITDA Interest Coverage	= EBITDA/Gross Interest Expense
Funds from Operations/Total Debt	=(Net Income from Continuing Operations + Depreciation)/Total Debt
Free Operating Cash Flow/Total Debt	= (Funds from Operations − Capital Expenditures − Change in Working Capital) / Total Debt

(continues)

(Table 5.3 continued.) Ratio	Description
Pretax Return on Permanent Capital	= (Pretax Income from Continuing Operations + Interest Expense) / (Average of Beginning of the year and End of the year of long- and short-term debt, minority interest and Shareholders' Equity)
Operating Income/Sales (%)	= (Sales − COGS (before depreciation) − Selling Expenses − Administrative Expenses − R&D Expenses) / Sales
Long-Term Debt/Capital	= Long-Term Debt / (Long-Term Debt + Equity)
Total Debt/Capitalization	= Total Debt / (Total Debt + Equity)

There is a strong relationship between the bond rating a company receives and its performance on these financial ratios. Table 5.4 provides a summary of the median ratios from 1990 to 1992 for different S&P ratings classes for manufacturing firms.

Table 5.4   FINANCIAL RATIOS BY BOND RATING: 1990–1992

	AAA	AA	A	BBB	BB	B	CCC
Pretax Interest Coverage	17.65	7.62	4.14	2.49	1.50	0.92	0.68
EBITDA Interest Coverage	21.03	10.52	6.17	4.24	2.60	1.87	1.16
Funds from Operations / Total Debt (%)	120.1	65.3	37.0	26.3	15.5	9.8	5.5
Free Operating Cash Flow/Total Debt (%)	42.3	28.0	13.6	6.1	3.2	1.6	0.80
Pretax Return on Permanent Capital (%)	31.9	20.6	15.6	10.9	10.9	6.9	4.6
Operating Income/Sales (%)	22.2	16.3	15.1	12.6	12.7	11.9	12.1
Long-Term Debt/Capital	12.5	23.3	34.7	43.8	59.3	59.9	69.3
Total Debt/Capitalization	21.9	32.7	40.3	48.8	66.2	71.5	71.2

Note that the pretax interest coverage ratio and the EBITDA interest coverage ratio are stated in terms of times interest earned, whereas the rest of the ratios are stated in percentage terms.

Not surprisingly, firms that generate income and cash flows that are significantly higher than debt payments and that have low debt ratios are more likely to be highly rated than are firms that do not have these characteristics. There will be individual firms whose ratings are not consistent with their financial ratios, however, because the ratings agency does bring subjective judgments into the final mix. Thus, a firm that performs poorly on financial ratios but is expected to improve its performance dramatically over the next period may receive a higher rating than that justified by its current financials. For most firms, however, the financial ratios should provide a reasonable basis for estimating at the bond rating.

Concept Check

Ratings agencies use primarily public information to come up with bond ratings. What implications does this have for how bond prices react to ratings changes?

Bond ratings and interest rates   The yield on a corporate bond should be a function of its default risk, which is measured by its rating. If the rating is a good measure of the default risk, higher rated bonds should be priced to yield lower interest rates than would lower rated bonds. This "default spread" will vary by maturity of the bond and can also change from period to period, depending on economic conditions.

CONCLUSION

The notion that risk is a "negative" and needs to be rewarded is not contestable, but the precise model for estimating risk and reward remains a subject of debate. For equity investments, all the models of risk and return that are widely used measure risk in terms of nondiversifiable risk. However, the capital asset pricing model measures it with just one "market" factor, whereas the arbitrage pricing and multifactor models use several factors. For debt investments, in which the holders have limited upside potential and significant downside risk, models of default risk are used to obtain estimates of appropriate returns.

This chapter provides background into the intuition behind and the assumptions underlying models of risk. The next chapter looks at the practical issues of how to estimate and use these models and how decisions made by firms affect their risk parameters.

APPENDIX: MEANS, VARIANCES, COVARIANCES, AND REGRESSIONS

Large amounts of data are often compressed and summarized to provide the user with a sense of the content, without overwhelming him or her with too many numbers. Data can be presented in many ways. One approach is to break the numbers down into individual values (or ranges of values) and provide probabilities for each range. This is called a *distribution*. Another approach is to estimate "summary statistics" for the data. For a data series, $X_1, X_2, X_3, \ldots X_n$, where n is the number of observations in the series, the most widely used summary statistics are as follows:

- The *mean* (μ), which is the average of all of the observations in the data series.

$$\text{Mean} = \mu_X = \frac{\sum_{j=1}^{j=n} X_j}{n}$$

- The *median*, which is the midpoint of the series; half the data in the series are higher than the median and half are lower.

- The *variance*, which is a measure of the spread in the distribution around the mean, and is calculated by first summing up the squared deviations from the mean and then dividing by either the number of observations (if the data represent the entire population) or by this number, reduced by one (if the data represent a sample).

$$\text{Variance} = \sigma^2_X = \frac{\sum_{j=1}^{j=n} (X_j - \mu)^2}{n-1}$$

When there are two series of data, several statistical measures can be used to capture how the two series move together over time. The two most widely used are the correlation and the covariance. For two data series, X (X_1, X_2,.) and $Y(Y_1, Y_2. . .)$, the *covariance* provides a nonstandardized measure of the degree to which they move together, and is estimated by taking the product of the deviations from the mean for each variable in each period.

$$\text{Covariance} = \sigma_{XY} = \frac{\sum_{j=1}^{j=n}(X_j - \mu_x)(Y_j - \mu_Y)}{n-2}$$

The sign on the covariance indicates the type of relationship the two variables have. A positive sign indicates that they move together; a negative sign indicates that they move in opposite directions. Although the covariance increases with the strength of the relationship, it is still relatively difficult to make judgments on the strength of the relationship between two variables by looking at the covariance, since it is not standardized.

The *correlation* is the standardized measure of the relationship between two variables. It can be computed from the covariance:

$$\text{Correlation} = \rho_{XY} = \sigma_{XY}/\sigma_X\sigma_Y = \frac{\sum_{j=1}^{j=n}(X_j - \mu_X)(Y_j - \mu_Y)}{\sqrt{\sum_{j=1}^{j=n}(X_j - \mu_X)^2}\sqrt{\sum_{j=1}^{j=n}(Y_j - \mu_Y)^2}}$$

The correlation can never be greater than 1 or less than minus 1. A correlation close to zero indicates that the two variables are unrelated. A positive correlation indicates that the two variables move together, and the relationship is stronger the closer the correlation gets to one. A negative correlation indicates that the two variables move in opposite directions, and that relationship gets stronger the closer the correlation gets to minus 1. Two variables that are perfectly positively correlated ($\rho = 1$) essentially move in perfect proportion in the same direction, whereas two assets that are perfectly negatively correlated move in perfect proportion in opposite directions.

A *simple regression* is an extension of the correlation/covariance concept. It attempts to explain one variable, which is called the *dependent variable*, using the other variable, called the *independent variable*. Keeping with statistical tradition, let Y be the dependent variable and X be the independent variable. If the two variables are plotted against each other on a scatter plot, with Y on the vertical axis and X on the horizontal axis, the regression attempts to fit a straight line through the points in such a way as to minimize the sum of the squared deviations of the points from the line. Consequently, it is called *ordinary least squares (OLS) regression*. When such a line is fit, two parameters emerge. One is the point at which the line cuts through the Y-axis, called the intercept of the regression, and the other is the slope of the regression line:

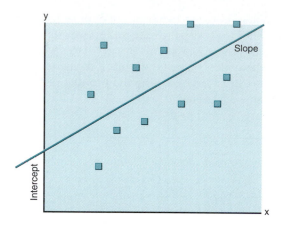

$$\text{OLS Regression: } Y = a + bX$$

The slope (b) of the regression measures both the direction and the magnitude of the relation. When the two variables are positively correlated, the slope will also be positive, whereas when the two variables are negatively correlated, the slope will be negative. The magnitude of the slope of the regression can be read as follows: for every unit increase in the independent variable (X), the dependent variable will change by b (slope). The close linkage between the slope of the regression and the correlation/covariance should not be surprising since the slope is estimated using the covariance:

$$\text{Slope of the Regression} = b = \frac{\text{Covariance}_{YX}}{\text{Variance of } X} = \frac{\sigma_{YX}}{\sigma_X^2}$$

The intercept (a) of the regression can be read in a number of ways. One interpretation is that it is the value that Y will have when X is zero. Another is more straightforward and is based on how it is calculated: it is the difference between the average value of Y and the slope-adjusted expected value of X.

$$\text{Intercept of the Regression} = a = \mu_Y - b*(\mu_X)$$

Regression parameters are always estimated with some noise, partly because the data are measured with error and partly because we estimate them from samples of data. This noise is captured in a couple of statistics. One is the R-squared of the regression, which measures the proportion of the variability in Y that is explained by X. It is a direct function of the correlation between the variables:

$$\text{R-squared of the Regression} = \text{Correlation}^2_{YX} = \rho_{YX}^2 = \frac{b^2 \sigma_X^2}{\sigma_Y^2}$$

An R-squared value closer to one indicates a strong relationship between the two variables, although the relationship may be either positive or negative. Another measure of noise in a regression is the standard error, which measures the "spread" around each of the two parameters estimated—the intercept and the slope. Each parameter has an associated standard error, which is calculated from the data:

$$\text{Standard Error of Intercept} = SE_a = \sqrt{\frac{\left(\sum_{j=1}^{j=n} X^2_j\right)\left[\dfrac{\left(\sum_{j=1}^{j=n}(Y_j - bX_j)^2\right)}{n-1}\right]}{n\sum_{j=1}^{j=n}(X_j - \mu_X)^2}}$$

$$\text{Standard Error of Slope} = SE_b = \sqrt{\frac{\left[\dfrac{\left(\sum_{j=1}^{j=n}(y_j - bx_j)^2\right)}{n-1}\right]}{\sum_{j=1}^{j=n}(X_j - \mu_X)^2}}$$

If we make the additional assumption that the intercept and slope estimates are normally distributed, the parameter estimate and the standard error can be combined to get a *t statistic*, which measures whether or not the relationship is statistically significant.

$$t \text{ statistic for intercept} = a/SE_a$$

$$t \text{ statistic from slope} = b/SE_b$$

For samples with more than 120 observations, a *t* statistic greater than 1.66 indicates that the variable is significantly different from zero with 95% certainty, whereas a statistic greater than 2.36 indicates the same with 99% certainty. For smaller samples, the *t* statistic has to be larger to have statistical significance.[7]

The regression that measures the relationship between two variables becomes a multiple regression when it is extended to include more than one independent variable ($X1, X2, X3, X4 \ldots$) in trying to explain the dependent variable Y. Although the graphical presentation becomes more difficult, the multiple regression yields a form that is an extension of the simple regression.

$$Y = a + b\,X1 + c\,X2 + dX3 + eX4$$

---

[7]The actual values that *t* statistics need to take on can be found in a table for the *t* distribution, which is reproduced at the end of this book as an appendix.

The R-squared still measures the strength of the relationship, but an additional R-squared statistic, called the *adjusted R-squared,* is computed to counter the bias that will induce the R-squared to keep increasing as more independent variables are added to the regression. If there are k independent variables in the regression, the adjusted R-squared is computed as follows:

$$\text{R-squared} = R^2 = \frac{\left(\sum_{j=1}^{j=n}(Y_j - bX_j)^2\right)}{n - k - 1}$$

$$\text{Adjusted R-squared} = R^2 - \left[\frac{k - 1}{n - k}\right]R^2$$

QUESTIONS AND PROBLEMS

1. Suppose that we have three securities, A, B, and C, with the following parameters:

Parameter	A	B	C
Expected return	12%	10%	8%
Standard deviation	30%	40%	35%

Which security would you prefer and why?

2. The following historical returns data for the last 10 years have been gathered for stock X:

Year	Annual Return
1995	42.1%
1994	−10.9%
1993	20.4%
1992	12.5%
1991	10.3%
1990	45.8%
1989	−30.5%
1988	11.4%
1987	10.2%
1986	−2.2%

a. Estimate the average annual return and the standard deviation for the stock.

b. If the company pays no dividends for the last 10 years and the stock price was $25.6 at the end of 1985, what would be the stock price at the end of 1995?

c. What would be the annual compounding growth rate on the stock price over this 10-year period? Is it the same as the average annual return found in (a)?

3. You are interested in forming a portfolio based on two securities with the following characteristics:

Parameter	A	B
Expected return	12%	18%
Standard deviation	25%	40%
Correlation coefficient between A and B		0.8

a. Calculate the expected return and the standard deviation for the equally weighted portfolio (equal amounts are invested in A and B).

b. Would you choose to invest in this portfolio or invest in a single security (either A or B) and why?

4. There are two securities with the following parameters:

Parameter	A	B
Expected return	12%	15%
Standard deviation	25%	45%
Correlation coefficient between A and B		−1.0

a. How can you construct a portfolio so that the portfolio will be risk-free?

b. What will be the expected return of this particular risk-free portfolio?

c. If you could get the same lending and borrowing interest rate of 8% from your local bank, how could you create a machine to reap arbitrage profits?

5. There are two securities with the following parameters:

Parameter	A	B
Expected return	15%	5%
Standard deviation	40%	0%

a. What would be the correlation coefficient between A and B?

b. If you constructed a portfolio with a standard deviation of 20%, what would be the weight in A and in B?

c. What would be the expected return of this particular portfolio?

6. Three securities have the following parameters:

Parameter	A	B	C
Expected return	15%	20%	35%
Standard deviation	20%	40%	70%
Correlation coefficient between A and B		0.5	
Correlation coefficient between A and C		0.7	
Correlation coefficient between B and C		0.9	

If you invest 30% of the investment capital in A, 40% in B, and 30% in C, what will be the expected return and the standard deviation of this portfolio?

7. What would be the expected risk premium for a stock with a beta of 1.5, if the expected market risk premium were 10%?

8. What would be the expected return for a stock with a beta of 0.9 if the historical average return of stock market were 12.5% and the Treasury bills have an average yield of 5%?

9. Analysts have a consensus estimate of expected return on the stock market for the next year that is 20% higher than the historical average return. What would be the percentage increase in the expected return of this stock from the answer in Question 5.8?

10. A company's stock has an expected return of 15%, and the stock market has an expected return of 12%. What is the beta of the stock if the risk-free return is 5%?

11. The CAPM is often used to evaluate the performance of professional money management. Suppose that a mutual fund has a 10-year average annual return of 14%, whereas the beta is 1.4. The S&P 500 Index grew by 12% per year over the same period, and the average Treasury bill yield was 5%. The manager of this mutual fund would probably claim that it had beaten the market index by a margin of 2% per year. Do you really believe that the mutual fund outperforms the market if the CAPM is valid to represent the risk-return relationship?

12. The market's expected return is 12%, whereas the risk-free return is considered to be 5%. We construct a portfolio in the following fashion:

	A	B	C
Beta	1.2	0.9	1.8
Investment weight	0.4	0.3	0.3

What is the beta of this portfolio, and what is its expected return?

13. Investing only in an S&P 500 Index mutual fund that should have a beta of 1.0 and risk-free assets such as Treasury bills is probably the simplest asset allocation strategy. Assume that the expected return of the S&P 500 Index is 12%, while the expected return on the Treasury bills is 5%.

a. If you want to get an expected return of 10% per year on your investment, what would be the weight on the S&P 500 Index and the weight on the Treasury bills?

b. What would be the beta of this portfolio?

14. A typical diversified stock mutual fund invests in hundreds of stocks because it is not allowed to invest more than 5% of its total assets in any single security by law.

a. What would you expect the beta of a mutual fund to be?

b. What would you expect the average annual return before expenses to be for a typical mutual fund, if the S&P 500 Index had a historical average annual return of 12%?

c. Would you be surprised to learn that about 80% of professional money managers underperform S&P 500 Index after they deduct annual expenses of about 1% to 3% of total assets under management?

15. Assume that a four-factor APT holds, and you have estimated the parameters for a particular company as the following:

R_f	5%		
β_1	1.2	$E(R_1)$	6.5%
β_2	0.5	$E(R_2)$	4.3%
β_3	0.8	$E(R_3)$	8.0%
β_4	1.6	$E(R_4)$	7.5%

a. What would be the expected return of this stock?

b. If the actual parameters turn out to be

$$R_1 = 7.2\%$$
$$R_2 = 5.2\%$$
$$R_3 = 6.3\%$$
$$R_4 = 10\%$$

What will be the "surprise" on the stock's return?

16. You might want to apply Fama and French's estimated equation of $Rt = 1.77\% - 0.11 \ln(MV) + 0.35 \ln(BV/MV)$ in your portfolio decisions. You divide your securities into two groups based on the ratio BV/MV. The first group has an BV/MV of 0.3, while the other group has 1.2 as its BV/MV.

What is the expected difference on the average monthly return between these two groups of stocks?

CHAPTER 6

RISK AND RETURN IN PRACTICE: ESTIMATION OF DISCOUNT RATES

The models of risk and return developed in the prior chapter are useful only if the risk parameters needed for the models can be estimated with relative ease and if these parameters can then be used to predict expected returns. This chapter examines issues relating to the use of these models in corporate finance. In particular, it attempts to answer the following questions:

- How do we estimate the parameters for risk and return models? In particular, what are the best estimates for the risk-free rate and the risk premium? How will these estimates vary across countries?

- How can we estimate the model parameters for private firms?

- What is the difference between the cost of equity and the cost of capital? How are they estimated? When would you use one or the other as the discount rate?

COST OF EQUITY

The *cost of equity* is the rate of return that investors require to make an equity investment in a firm. There are two approaches to estimating the cost of equity: the first is to use a risk and return model; the second is to apply a **dividend growth model.**

Dividend Growth Model: This is a model in which the value of a stock is estimated to be the present value of the dividends on the stock, growing at a constant rate.

Using the Capital Asset Pricing Model

As the discussion in Chapter 5 makes clear, the capital asset pricing model (CAPM) measures risk in terms of nondiversifiable variance and relates expected returns to this risk measure. The nondiversifiable risk for any asset is measured by its beta, which can be used to yield an expected return.

$$\text{Expected Return} = R_f + \text{ Equity Beta}*[E(R_m) - R_f]$$

where

$$R_f = \text{Risk-free rate}$$
$$E(R_m) = \text{Expected Return on the Market Index}$$

The return that investors expect to make on an equity investment, given its risk, becomes the cost of equity to managers in that firm.

125

The following inputs are required to use the CAPM: the current risk-free rate; the expected return on the market index; and the beta of the asset being analyzed. Two practical issues are involved in using CAPM. First, how do we measure the risk premium to be used in calculating the expected return on the market index? Second, what is the correct risk-free rate to use in the model?

Measurement of the risk premium   The risk premium used in CAPM is generally based on historical data. The premium is defined as the difference between average returns on stocks and average returns on risk-free securities over the measurement period. Two measurement questions remain. First, how long should the measurement period be? Second, should arithmetic or geometric averages be used to compute the risk premium? In answer to the first question, whereas measurement periods ranging from 10 years to longer (some go back to 1926[1]) are used in practice, the use of the longest possible historical period seems justified absent any trend in premiums over time. In much of the analysis in this book, the average premiums based on data from 1926 to 1990 will be used for U.S. stocks.

Geometric Mean: The geometric mean of a series is the average of the series, taking into account the effect of compounding on the data.

There is just as much disagreement among practitioners over the usage of the arithmetic versus geometric means. The *arithmetic mean* is the average of the annual returns for the period under consideration, whereas the **geometric mean** is the compounded annual return over the same period. The contrast between the two measures can be illustrated with a simple example containing two years of returns:

Year	Price	Return
0	50	
1	100	100%
2	60	−40%

The arithmetic average return over the two years is 30%, whereas the geometric average is only 9.54% ($1.2^{0.5}-1=1.0954$). Those who use the arithmetic mean argue that it is much more consistent with the mean-variance framework of the CAPM and a better predictor of the premium in the next period. The geometric mean is justified on the grounds that it takes into account compounding and that it is a better predictor of the average premium in the long term. There can be dramatic differences in premiums based on the choices made at this stage, as illustrated in Table 6.1 (see Appendix 1 for historical data).

Table 6.1 MAGNITUDE OF THE RISK PREMIUM				
Historical Period	**Stocks–Treasury Bills**		**Stocks–Treasury Bonds**	
	Arithmetic	**Geometric**	**Arithmetic**	**Geometric**
1926–1990	8.41%	6.41%	7.24%	5.50%
1962–1990	4.10%	2.95%	3.92%	3.25%
1981–1990	6.05%	5.38%	0.13%	0.19%

[1]The most widely used compendium of returns is put together by Ibbotson and Sinquefield and updated on an annual basis. Their return series, which includes stocks, bonds, and Treasury bills, goes back to 1926.

The geometric mean generally yields lower premium estimates than does the arithmetic mean. In the context of corporate finance, where expected returns are compounded over long time periods, the geometric mean provides a better estimate of the risk premium. Thus, the premium of 5.50% (the geometric mean of the premium over Treasury bonds) is used throughout this book for calculating expected returns for U.S. stocks.

Historical data on stock returns are easily available and accessible in the United States; for other countries reliable historical data are not available for as long a time period as is available for the United States, Table 6.2 summarized premiums from 1970 to 1990.

Table 6.2 **RISK PREMIUMS ACROSS THE WORLD 1970–1990**			
Country	Stocks (%)	Govt. Bonds (%)	Risk Premium (%)
Australia	9.60	7.35	2.25
Canada	10.50	7.41	3.09
France	11.90	7.68	4.22
Germany	7.40	6.81	0.59
Italy	9.40	9.06	0.34
Japan	13.70	6.96	6.74
Netherlands	11.20	6.87	4.33
Switzerland	5.30	4.10	1.20
U.K.	14.70	8.45	6.25
United States	10.00	6.18	3.82

The premium earned by stocks over Treasury bonds has typically been much lower in the European markets (not counting Britain) than in either the United States or Japan. Three fundamental principles determine the size of this premium:

1. *Variance in the underlying economy:* Risk premiums will be larger in economies that have more volatility associated with them. Thus, the premiums for emerging markets, with their higher-growth, higher-risk economies, will be larger than the premiums for developed markets. The higher uncertainty associated with future economic growth in China, for instance, would lead us to use a larger premium in the Chinese market than we would in the Singapore market, where there is much less uncertainty about future economic growth.

2. *Political risk:* Risk premiums will be larger in those markets where there is potential for political instability, which translates into economic instability. Although concrete measures of political risk remain difficult to come by, *The Economist,* for instance, provides measures of political risk for many countries on a regular basis. In early 1995, its measure of political risk, which goes from zero (least risk) to 100 (most risk) placed Iraq at the top (most risky) and Singapore at the bottom (least risky) of the nations surveyed. Ratings agencies, like Standard and Poor's, take an alternative approach; they assign bond ratings to countries that capture, among other factors, the political risk in these countries.

3. *Structure of the market:* In some markets, the risk premium for investing in stocks will be lower because the companies that are listed on the exchange are large, diversified, and stable. (Germany and Switzerland would be good examples.) In general, as smaller and riskier companies are listed on the market, as is the case in the United States and the United Kingdom, the average risk premium for investing in stocks will increase.

Using the U.S. premium for stocks over bonds of 5.50% as the benchmark, we see that these fundamentals point toward a larger premium for markets that are riskier than those of the United States on any or all of these counts and a smaller premium for less risky markets. The premiums used in this book for various markets are listed in Table 6.3.

Table 6.3 FINANCIAL MARKET CHARACTERISTICS AND RISK PREMIUMS

Financial Market Characteristics	Examples	Premium over the Government Bond Rate (%)
Emerging market, with political risk	South American markets, China, Russia	7.5–9.5
Emerging markets with limited political risk	Singapore, Malaysia, Thailand, India, some East European markets	7.5
Developed markets with wide stock listings	United States, Japan, U.K., France, Italy	5.5
Developed markets with limited listings and stable economies	Germany, Switzerland	3.5–4.5

 Concept Check

Risk premiums are usually estimated using historical data on stock and government bond returns. What are you assuming when you use the historical premium as your measure of future risk premiums? What factors would you consider in modifying this historical premium?

Variants on the Risk-free Rate

Variant 1   A short-term government security rate is used as the risk-free rate, and the historical premium earned by a broad equity market index over and above this security rate is used to estimate the expected return on the market. The cost of equity, thus obtained, is then used as the discount rate for each year's cash flows.

 IN PRACTICE   USING THE CAPM—CURRENT TREASURY BILL RATE: PEPSI COLA

In March 1995, Pepsi Cola Corporation had a beta of 1.06.[2] The Treasury bill rate at that time was 5.80%. The expected return can then be calculated as follows:

$$\text{Cost of Equity} = 5.80\% + 1.06(8.41\%) = 14.71\%$$

The market premium of 8.41% was based on historical data and is the premium earned by stocks, on average (arithmetic mean), over Treasury bills.[3]

The expected return has different implications for different groups. For investors in Pepsi Cola stock, it is a measure of *what they need to make* on the stock over the next period (year) to justify the risk they are taking on. Thus, if after researching the stock, they conclude that they would

---

[2]The beta was obtained from Value Line. It was based on a five-year regression of weekly returns on PepisCo against the NYSE Composite.

[3]With short-term rates, the arithmetic mean premium is used because the holding period is assumed to be only one period. With long-term rates, the geometric mean premium is used because of the compounding that occurs over multiple periods.

make only 13% over the next year, they would choose not to buy the stock. For managers, the required return becomes the cost of equity they then use as a hurdle rate in analyzing the returns to equity investors from taking on projects in the company. Thus, generally speaking, a project that is expected to return 17% to equity investors in the company would be considered a good project, whereas one that returned 10% would be considered a bad project.[4]

Variant 2   The current long-term government bond rate (with the **bond duration** matched up to the duration of the project or asset being analyzed) is used as the risk-free rate, and the historical premium earned by a broad market index above this long-term government security rate is used to estimate the expected return on the market. The cost of equity, calculated using these inputs, is used as the discount rate for each year's cash flows.

 Bond Duration: This is a measure of the sensitivity of bond prices to interest rates and is a function of both the maturity of the bond and its coupon rate.

 IN PRACTICE   USING THE CAPM—CURRENT TREASURY BOND RATE: PEPSI COLA

In March 1995, the 30-year bond rate was 7.5%. The premium that should be used here to calculate the expected return on the market is the one earned by stocks over Treasury bonds, not Treasury bills. Between 1926 and 1990, this premium was 5.5%. The cost of equity for Pepsi Cola Corporation, with a beta of 1.06, can be written as follows:

$$\text{Cost of Equity} = 7.5\% + 1.06\,(5.5\%) = 13.33\%$$

The cost of equity using the long-term bond rate is slightly lower than the cost of equity estimated using the Treasury bill rate.

In practical terms, this cost of equity has much the same meaning as that ascribed to the cost of equity calculated using the Treasury bill rate. It is different only insofar as it allows for a longer time horizon. A long-term investor looking at PepsiCo and expecting to hold the stock for five or ten years may view this as a better benchmark against which she can then compare the returns she thinks she can make in the long term. Managers looking at long-term projects may feel more comfortable using this as the hurdle rate, rather than the one based on a short-term government security rate.

 Concept Check

> Will the cost of equity estimated using a long-term bond rate always be lower than that estimated using the short-term Treasury bill rate? Why or why not?

Most analyses done in this book use the second variant, employing the long-term bond rate as the riskless rate and the historical premium between stocks and Treasury bonds as the risk premium.

Standard Procedures for Estimating CAPM Parameters—Betas and Alphas

The standard procedure for estimating betas is to regress stock returns (R_j) against market returns (R_m)[5]:

$$R_j = a + bR_m$$

---

[4]This statement assumes that the project the company is considering has about the same risk as the firm itself. When project risk deviates from firm risk, different hurdle rates will have to be estimated.

[5]The appendix to this chapter provides a brief overview of ordinary least squares regressions.

where

$$a = \text{Intercept from the regression}$$
$$b = \text{Slope of the regression} = \text{Covariance}(R_j, R_m)/\sigma^2_m$$

The *slope* of the regression corresponds to the beta of the stock and measures the riskiness of the stock.

The *intercept* of the regression provides a simple measure of performance during the period of the regression, relative to the capital asset pricing model.

$$R_j = R_f + \beta(R_m - R_f)$$
$$= R_f(1 - \beta) + R_m \quad \text{..........} \quad \text{Capital asset pricing model}$$
$$R_{j = a + bR_m} \quad \text{..........} \quad \text{Regression equation}$$

Thus, a comparison of the intercept (a) to $R_f(1 - \beta)$ should provide a measure of the stock's performance, at least relative to the capital asset pricing model.[6]

If $a > R_f(1 - \beta)$ .... stock did better than expected during regression period
$a = R_f(1 - \beta)$ .... stock did as well as expected during regression period
$a < R_f(1 - \beta)$ .... stock did worse than expected during regression period

The difference between a and $R_f(1 - \beta)$ is called **Jensen's alpha** and provides a measure of whether the asset in question under- or outperformed the market, after adjusting for risk, during the period of the regression.

Jensen's Alpha: This is the difference between the actual returns on an asset and the return expected from it during a past period, given what the market did, and the asset's beta.

The final statistic that emerges from the regression is the **R-squared** (R^2) of the regression. Although the statistical explanation of the R-squared is that it provides a measure of the goodness of fit of the regression, the financial rationale for the R-squared is that it provides an estimate of the proportion of the risk (variance) of a firm that can be attributed to market risk. The balance $(1 - R^2)$ can then be attributed to firm-specific risk.

R-Squared: The R-squared measures the proportion of the variability of a dependent variable that is explained by an independent variable or variables.

 IN PRACTICE   ESTIMATING CAPM RISK PARAMETERS FOR INTEL

Intel Corporation is one of the world's leading manufacturers of integrated circuits primarily for personal computers. In assessing risk parameters for Intel, the returns on the stock and the market index are computed as follows:

1. The returns to a stockholder in Intel are computed month by month from February 1989 to January 1994. These returns include both dividends and price appreciation and are defined as follows:

$$\text{Stock Return}_{\text{intel}, j} = (\text{Price}_{\text{Intel}, j} - \text{Price}_{\text{Intel}, j-1} + \text{Dividends}_j) / \text{Price}_{\text{Intel}, j-1}$$

---

[6]The regression can be run using returns in excess of the risk-free rate, for both the stock and the market. In that case, the intercept of the regression should be zero if the actual returns equal the expected returns from CAPM, greater than zero if the stock does better than expected, and less than zero if it does worse than expected.

where

$$\text{Stock Return}_{\text{Intel},j} = \text{Returns to a stockholder in Intel in month } j$$
$$\text{Price}_{\text{Intel},j} = \text{Price of Intel stock at the end of month } j$$
$$\text{Dividends}_j = \text{Dividends on Intel stock in month } j$$

Dividends are added to the returns of the month in which the stock went ex-dividend.[7] If there was a stock split[8] during the month, the returns have to take into account the split factor, for stock prices will be affected. For instance, in a two-for-one stock split, the stock price will drop by roughly 50% and, if not factored in, will result in very negative returns in that month. Splits can be accounted for as follows:

$$\text{Return}_{\text{intel},j} = (\text{Factor}_j * \text{Price}_{\text{Intel},j} - \text{Price}_{\text{Intel},j-1} + \text{Factor} * \text{Dividends}_j) / \text{Price}_{\text{Intel},j-1}$$

where, to illustrate, the factor is set equal to 2 for a two-for-one split and to 1.5 for a three-for-two split.

2. The returns on a market index are computed for each month of the period, using the level of the index at the end of each month, and the monthly dividend yield on stocks in the index:

$$\text{Market Return}_{\text{intel},j} = (\text{Index}_{\text{Intel},j} - \text{Index}_{\text{Intel},j-1}) / \text{Index}_{\text{Intel},j-1} + \text{Dividend Yield}_j$$

where Index_j is the level of the index at the end of month j and Dividend Yield_j is the dividend yield on the index in month j. Although the S&P 500 and the NYSE Composite are the most widely used indices for U.S. stocks and the local indices for stocks listed on overseas exchanges, they are at best imperfect proxies for the market portfolio in CAPM, which is supposed to include all assets.

Figure 6.1 graphs monthly returns on Intel against returns on the S&P 500 index from January 1989 to December 1993.

The regression statistics for Intel are as shown on the following page:[9]

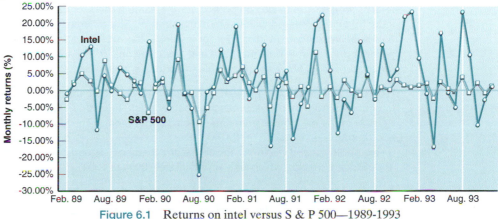

Figure 6.1   Returns on intel versus S & P 500—1989-1993

---

[7]The *ex-dividend day* is the day by which the stock has to be bought in order for an investor to be entitled to the dividends on the stock.

[8]A split changes the number of shares outstanding in a company without affecting any of its fundamentals. Thus, in a three-for-two split, there will be 50% more shares outstanding after the split. Because the overall value of equity has not changed, the stock price will drop by an equivalent amount (1 - 100/150 = 33.33%).

[9]The regression statistics are computed in the conventional way. The appendix explains the process in more detail.

Slope of the regression = 1.39   This is Intel's beta, based on returns from 1989 to 1993. Using a different time period for the regression or different return intervals (weekly or daily) for the same period can result in a different beta. Building on the beta, the expected return for Intel could have been computed in February 1994, based on a Treasury bond rate of 8% and a risk premium of 5.5%:

$$\text{Expected Return on Intel} = 8\% + 1.39\,(5.5\%) = 15.65\%$$

As the discussion earlier in this chapter indicates, this would be used by investors in Intel as a benchmark in deciding whether or not to invest in the stock, and by managers as a cost of equity.

☐ Concept
Check

> A regression provides a snapshot of a company over a specific time period, and estimates from a regression, such as the beta, are calculated with "noise." How would you develop a reasonable range for the beta instead of a point estimate ?

Intercept of the regression = 2.09%   This is a measure of Intel's performance, when it is compared with $R_f\,(1 - \beta)$. The monthly risk-free rate (since the returns used in the regression are monthly returns) between 1989 and 1993 averaged 0.4%, resulting in the following estimate for the performance:

$$R_f(1 - \beta) = 0.4\%\,(1 - 1.39) = -0.16\%$$
$$\text{Intercept} - R_f(1 - \beta) = 2.09\% - (-0.16\%) = 2.25\%$$

This analysis suggests that Intel performed 2.25% better than expected, when expectations were based on CAPM, on a monthly basis between January 1989 and December 1993. This results in an annualized excess return of approximately 30.6%:

$$\text{Annualized Excess Return} = (1 + \text{Monthly Excess Return})^{12} - 1$$
$$= 1.0225^{12} - 1 = 1.306 - 1 = 0.306$$

By this measure of performance, Intel clearly did much better than expected during the period of the regression. Note, however, that this does not imply that Intel would be a great investment for the future. It also does not indicate how much of this excess return can be attributed to "industrywide" effects and how much is specific to the firm. To make that breakdown, the excess returns would have to be computed over the same period for other firms in the semiconductor industry and compared with Intel's excess return. The difference would then be attributable to firm-specific actions. In this case, for instance, the average annualized excess return on other semiconductor firms between 1989 and 1993 was only 5.1%, suggesting that the remaining excess return of 25.5% was attributable to actions specific to Intel.

R-squared of the regression = 22.90%   This statistic suggests that 22.90% of the risk (variance) in Intel comes from market sources (interest rate risk, inflation risk, etc.), and that the balance of 77.10% of the risk comes from firm-specific components. The latter risk should be diversifiable, and therefore unrewarded, in CAPM.

Intel's R-squared was much lower than the median R-squared of companies listed on the New York Stock Exhange, which was approximately 30% in 1994

☐ Concept
Check

> Is a high R-squared good? Why or why not? If you were advising an investor with limited funds, and the capacity to buy only a few stocks, would you suggest high R-squared value stocks or low ones?

Estimation issues   The analyst must make four decisions in setting up the regression described in the preceding section. The first concerns the *length of the estimation period*. Most estimates of betas, including those by Value Line and Standard and Poor's, use five years of data, while Bloomberg uses two years of data. The tradeoff is simple: a longer estimation period provides more data, but the firm itself might have changed in its risk characteristics over the time period. For instance, using data from 1985 to 1994 to estimate betas for Microsoft might increase the amount of data available, but it will lead to a beta estimate that is much higher than the true beta, since Microsoft was a smaller and riskier firm in 1985 than it was in 1994.

The second estimation decision relates to the *return interval.* Returns on stocks are available on an annual, monthly, weekly, daily, and even intraday basis. Using daily or intraday returns will increase the number of observations in the regression, but it exposes the estimation process to a significant bias in beta estimates related to nontrading.[10] For instance, the betas estimated for small firms, which are more likely to suffer from nontrading, are biased downward when daily returns are used. Using weekly or monthly returns can reduce the nontrading bias significantly.[11] For example, the beta for America Online, the online service provider, was 1.20 using daily returns from 1990 and 1994, while it was 1.80 using monthly returns. The 1.80 figure is a much more reliable estimate of the firm's beta.

The third estimation issue relates to the choice of a *market index* to be used in the regression. The standard practice used by most beta estimation services is to estimate the betas of a company relative to the index of the market in which its stock trades. Thus, the betas of German stocks are estimated relative to the Frankfurt DAX, British stocks relative to the FTSE, Japanese stocks relative to the Nikkei, and U.S. stocks relative to the NYSE composite. Although this practice may yield an estimate that is a reasonable measure of risk for the parochial investor, it may not be the best approach for an international or cross-border investor, who would be better served with a beta estimated relative to an international index.

The fourth estimation issue relates to whether the betas obtained from regressions should be *adjusted* to reflect the likelihood of estimation errors and the tendency of betas to regress toward the average (of either the industry or the overall market). Most published betas use variants of a statistical technique that shrinks betas toward 1, based on the standard error of the regression beta estimate—the larger the error, the greater the shrinkage. The gains from using these techniques are large when daily returns are used to estimate betas, but they become smaller as longer return intervals are used.

> **Concept Check**
>
> When the betas of stocks listed on overseas markets are estimated against the New York Stock Exchange composite instead of their local indices, are the betas likely to increase or decrease? Which beta would you use and why?

Determinants of betas   The beta of a firm is determined by three variables: (1) the type of business(es) the firm is in; (2) the degree of operating leverage in the firm; and (3) the firm's financial leverage.

Cyclical nature of the business   Since betas measure the risk of a firm relative to a market index, the more sensitive a business is to market conditions, the higher its beta. Thus, other things remaining equal, **cyclical firms** can be expected to have higher betas than noncyclical firms. For example, companies involved in housing and automobiles, two sectors of the economy that are very sensitive to economic conditions, will have higher betas than companies that are in food processing and tobacco, which are relatively insensitive to business cycles.

[10]The nontrading bias arises because the returns in nontrading periods is zero (even though the market may have moved up or down significantly in those periods). Using these nontrading period returns in the regression will reduce the correlation between stock returns and market returns and the beta of the stock.

[11]The bias can also be reduced using statistical techniques suggested by Dimson and Scholes-Williams.

■ **Cyclical Firm:**   A cyclical firm has revenues and operating income that tend to move strongly with the economy—up when the economy is doing well and down during recessions.

Building on this point, we would also argue that the degree to which a product's purchase is discretionary will affect the beta of the firm manufacturing the product. Thus, the betas of food processing firms, such as General Foods and Kellogg's, should be lower than the betas of specialty retailers, since consumers can defer the purchase of the latter's products during bad economic times.

Degree of operating leverage   The degree of operating leverage is a function of the cost structure of a firm and is usually defined in terms of the relationship between fixed costs and total costs. A firm that has high operating leverage (i.e., high fixed costs relative to total costs) will also have higher variability in earnings before interest and taxes (EBIT) than would a firm producing a similar product with low operating leverage. Other things remaining equal, the higher variance in operating income will lead to a higher beta for the firm with high operating leverage.

This relationship between beta and operating leverage has consequences for a firm's major strategic decisions regarding future direction. Although much good comes from updating plants and getting the latest technology, there might also be a hidden cost. By reducing the firm's flexibility to respond to economic downturns, it may make the firm riskier.

Although operating leverage affects betas, it is difficult to measure the operating leverage of a firm, at least from the outside, since fixed and variable costs are often aggregated in income statements. It is possible to obtain an approximate measure of the firm's operating leverage, however, by looking at changes in operating income as a function of changes in sales.

Degree of Operating leverage = % Change in Operating Profit /
% Change in Sales

For firms with high operating leverage, operating income should change more than proportionately when sales change.

 IN PRACTICE   MEASURING OPERATING LEVERAGE OF SPECIALTY RETAILERS

In Table 6.4, we estimate the degree of operating leverage for the Gap, a specialty retailer, from 1985 to 1996.

The degree of operating leverage changes dramatically from year to year because of annual swings in operating income. Two important observations can be made about the Gap over the period. First, the operating leverage from 1985 to 1991 is slightly higher than the operating leverage from 1992 to 1996, but the difference is not significant. Generally, as firms get larger, operating leverage decreases. Second, the average operating leverage of 0.97 over the period is lower than the average operating leverage for specialty retailing firms overall, which is 1.08. This would provide a basis for arguing that, other things remaining equal, the Gap should be assigned a lower beta than the average specialty retailing firm.

Degree of financial leverage   Other things remaining equal, an increase in financial leverage will increase the equity beta of a firm. Intuitively, the obligated payments on

Table 6.4   THE GAP'S OPERATING LEVERAGE, 1985–1996

Year	Sales	% Change in Sales	Operating Income	% Change in Oper. Income	DOL
1985	$ 647		$ 250		
1986	848	31.07	369	47.60	1.53
1987	1,062	25.24	407	10.30	0.41
1988	1,252	17.89	437	7.37	0.41
1989	1,587	26.76	581	32.95	1.23
1990	1,934	21.87	754	29.78	1.36
1991	2,519	30.25	1,033	37.00	1.22
1992	2,960	17.51	1,119	8.33	0.48
1993	3,296	11.35	1,315	17.54	1.54
1994	3,723	12.96	1,541	17.19	1.33
1995	4,330	16.30	1,719	11.55	0.71
1996	5,025	16.05	1,985	15.47	0.96
1985–1996		20.66		21.35	0.97

Concept Check

European companies have long operated under much stricter labor law requirements than U.S. companies, making it more difficult for them to lay off employees during economic downturns. What effect should this have on their betas?

debt increase the variance in net income, with higher leverage increasing income during good times and decreasing income during economic downturns. If all of the firm's risk are borne by the stockholders (i.e., the beta of debt is zero),[12] and debt has a tax benefit to the firm, then,

$$\beta_L = \beta_u(1 + (1 - t)(D/E))$$

where

$$\beta_L = \text{Levered beta for equity in the firm}$$
$$\beta_u = \text{Unlevered beta of the firm (i.e., the beta of the firm without any debt)}$$
$$t = \text{Corporate tax rate}$$
$$D/E = \text{Debt/Equity ratio}$$

The unlevered beta of a firm is determined by the type of business in which it operates and its operating leverage. Thus, a company's equity beta is determined both by the riskiness of the business in which it operates and by the amount of financial leverage risk it has taken on.

 IN PRACTICE   EFFECTS OF LEVERAGE ON BETAS: BOEING

In 1990, Boeing had a beta of 0.95 and a debt/equity ratio of 1.71%, and it faced a tax rate of 34%.

---

[12]If debt has market risk (i.e., its beta is greater than zero), this formula can be modified. If the beta of debt is β_D, the beta of equity can be written as: $\beta_L = B_u[1 + (1 - t)(D/E)] - \beta_D(D/E)$

$$\text{Unlevered beta} = \text{Current beta} / (1 + (1 - \text{tax rate}) (\text{Current Debt/Equity}))$$
$$= 0.95 / (1 + (1 - 0.34) (0.0171)) = 0.94$$

The levered beta at different levels of debt can then be estimated:

$$\text{Levered beta} = \text{Unlevered beta} * [1 + (1 - \text{tax rate}) (\text{Debt/Equity})]$$

For instance, if Boeing were to increase its debt equity ratio to 10%, its equity beta would be

$$\text{Levered beta (@10\% D/E)} = 0.94 * (1 + (1 - 0.34) (0.10)) = 1.00$$

If the debt/equity ratio were raised to 25%, the equity beta would be

$$\text{Levered beta (@25\% D/E)} = 0.94 * (1 + (1 - 0.34) (0.25)) = 1.10$$

Table 6.5 summarizes the beta estimates for different levels of financial leverage, ranging from 0 to 90% debt. The costs of equity are also estimated, using the prevailing Treasury bond rate in 1990 of 9% and a risk premium of 5.5%.

	Table 6.5 FINANCIAL LEVERAGE AND BETAS		
D/(D+E) (%)	*D/E* (%)	**Beta**	**Cost of Equity (%)**
0	0.00	0.94	14.17
10	11.11	1.01	14.55
20	25.00	1.10	15.02
30	42.86	1.21	15.63
40	66.67	1.35	16.44
50	100.00	1.56	17.58
60	150.00	1.87	19.29
70	233.33	2.39	22.13
80	400.00	3.42	27.82
90	900.00	6.52	44.88

As Boeing's financial leverage increases, the beta increases concurrently, leading to higher costs of equity.

More on business risk and financial leverage   Financial leverage multiplies the underlying business risk, and so it stands to reason that firms that have high business risk should be reluctant to take on financial leverage. It also stands to reason that firms that operate in relatively stable businesses should be much more willing to take on financial leverage. Utilities, for instance, have historically had high debt ratios but have not had high betas, mostly because their underlying businesses have been stable and fairly predictable.

Breaking risk down into business and financial leverage components also provides some insight into why companies have high betas, since they can arrive at these betas in one of two ways—they can operate in a risky business, or they can use very high financial leverage in a relatively stable business. In 1994, for instance, both Novell and RJR Nabisco had high equity betas—1.50 for Novell and 1.80 for RJR Nabisco. When these betas were decomposed into business and financial leverage components, some key differences emerged between these companies:

Company	Debt/Equity Ratio	Unlevered Beta	Leverage Effect	Total Beta
Novell	0.00%	1.50	0	1.50
RJR Nabisco	140.00%	0.74	1.06	1.80

Nabisco's high beta can be attributed mostly to high financial leverage, whereas Novell's high beta is due entirely to the risky business in which it operates.

Table 6.6 summarizes betas in different industries in the United States in March 1995 and estimates unlevered betas in each industry.

Concept Check

As an investor in a stock, would you care whether the beta was high due to business risk or to financial leverage? Why or why not?

Table 6.6   INDUSTRY AVERAGES: BETAS AND UNLEVERED BETAS—1995

Industry	Debt Ratio (%)	Beta	Unlevered Beta
Electric and gas utilities	58.35	0.58	0.31
Petroleum production & refining	44.43	0.59	0.39
Mining	40.21	0.64	0.45
Real estate	38.44	0.69	0.49
Agricultural products	37.67	0.74	0.53
Food production	37.87	0.85	0.61
Beverages	41.14	0.95	0.66
Insurance	30.66	0.85	0.66
Tobacco	50.39	1.11	0.67
Transportation	48.29	1.10	0.69
Paper and plastic production	42.96	1.03	0.69
Autos and related	39.69	0.99	0.70
Consumer products	44.78	1.06	0.70
Publishing	34.41	0.99	0.74
Other services	39.39	1.05	0.74
Equipment manufacturing	36.47	1.02	0.75
Furniture	25.34	0.93	0.76
Telephone utilities	46.70	1.20	0.77
Entertainment (TV and Movies)	49.20	1.25	0.77
Textile & clothing manufacturers	27.42	0.98	0.79
Miscellaneous manufacturing	35.51	1.07	0.79
Wholesalers	35.01	1.08	0.80
Building contractors and related areas	30.04	1.08	0.85
Other consumer durables	29.18	1.08	0.85
Retailers	33.12	1.19	0.90
Restaurants & eating places	31.94	1.20	0.92
Chemicals	37.61	1.34	0.97
Banks and financial service	29.37	1.23	0.97
Computers and office equipment	30.49	1.27	0.99
Consumer electronics	26.65	1.26	1.02
Pharmaceuticals	33.83	1.36	1.02
Health services	27.78	1.32	1.06
Computer software and services	9.18	1.33	1.25
AVERAGE	36.47	1.04	0.77

Firm betas as weighted averages When a firm operates in more than one business area, its beta will be the weighted average of the betas of each of its different business lines, with the weights based on the market value of each. The market values used will vary depending on the betas being analyzed, with equity market values used for weighting levered betas (equity betas) and firm market values used for weighting unlevered betas (firm betas). There are two direct applications for this concept—one is to estimate the beta of a company after an acquisition of another business, and the other is to decompose the beta of a firm into division-level betas.

IN PRACTICE   BETA OF A FIRM AFTER AN ACQUISITION: DISNEY / CAPITAL CITIES

In 1995, Walt Disney Inc. announced that it was acquiring Capital Cities, the owner of the ABC television and radio network, for approximately $120 per share, and that it would finance the acquisition partly through the issue of $10 billion in debt. At the time of the acquisition, Disney had a market value of equity of $31.1 billion, debt outstanding of $3.186 billion, and a beta of 1.15. Capital Cities, based on the $120 offering price, had a market value of equity of $18.5 billion, debt outstanding of $615 million, and a beta of 0.95. (Corporate tax rate was 36%)

In order to evaluate the effects of the acquisition on Disney's beta, we can do the analysis in two parts. First, we examine the effects of the merger on the business risk of the combined firm, by estimating the unlevered betas of the two companies and calculating the combined firm's unlevered beta:

$$\text{Disney's unlevered beta} = 1.15/(1+0.64*[3186/31,100]) = 1.08$$
$$\text{Capital Cities unlevered beta} = 0.95/(1+0.64*[615/18,500]) = 0.93$$

The unlevered beta for the combined firm can be calculated as the weighted average of the two unlevered betas, with the weights based on the market values of the two firms.

$$\text{Market Value of Disney} = 31,100 + 3186 = 34,286$$
$$\text{Market Value of Capital Cities} = 18,500 + 615 = 19,115$$
$$\text{Unlevered beta for combined firm} = 1.08\,(34286/53401) + 0.93\,(19,115/53,401)$$
$$= 1.026$$

We then examine the effects of the financing of the merger on the betas by calculating the debt/equity ratio for the combined firm after the acquisition, assuming that $10 billion is borrowed to finance the acquisition:

$$\text{Debt} = \text{Capital Cities Old Debt} + \text{Disney's Old Debt} + \text{New Debt}$$
$$= \$615 + \$3,186 + \$10,000 = \$13,801 \text{ million}$$
$$\text{Equity} = \text{Disney's Old Equity} + \text{New Equity used for Acquisition}$$
$$= \$31,100 + \$8,500 = \$39,600 \text{ million}$$

where

$$\text{New Equity} = \text{Total Cost of Acquisition} - \text{New Debt Issued}$$
$$= \$18,500 - \$10,000 - \$8,500 \text{ million}$$

The debt/equity ratio can then be computed as follows:

$$\text{D/E Ratio} = 13,801/39600 = 34.82\%$$

This debt/equity ratio, in conjunction with the new unlevered beta for the combined firm, yields a new beta of

$$\text{New beta} = 1.026\,(1 + 0.64\,(.3482)) = 1.25$$

Concept Check

What would the beta be, if this acquisition were financed entirely with equity?

IN PRACTICE   DECOMPOSITION OF THE BETA FOR GENERAL ELECTRIC

As noted earlier, General Electric is a company with several divisions, each with different risk characteristics. Table 6.7 summarizes the divisions, including the market values of equity invested in each division and the divisional equity betas. Neither variable is easily accessible, because divisions do not trade their own stock, and the regression approach used to estimate betas earlier in this chapter cannot be used here. Thus, divisional betas are estimated using "comparable" firms for each division. For instance, the beta of the aircraft division is estimated by looking at comparable firms in aerospace, whereas the beta for the financial services arm is estimated by looking at similar financial service companies. The divisional market values are estimated based on the earnings of each division and the relevant multiple from comparable firms.

Table 6.7   **DIVISIONAL BETAS AND COSTS OF EQUITY**

Division	Market Value of Equity (billion)	MV Weight (%)	Beta	Cost of Equity (%)
Financial services	$20	25.00	0.80	11.90
Power systems	10	12.50	0.75	11.63
Aircraft engines	8	10.00	1.25	14.38
Industrial	10	12.50	1.10	13.55
Engineered plastics	12	15.00	1.00	13.00
Technical products	8	10.00	2.00	18.50
Appliances	4	5.00	1.00	13.00
Broadcasting	8	10.00	1.50	15.75
Company	*$80.00*	*100.00*	*1.13*	*13.73*

The costs of equity are computed using a Treasury bond rate of 7.5% and a risk premium of 5.5%. For instance, the cost of equity for the broadcasting division = 7.5% + 1.5 (5.5%) = 15.75%.

The betas and costs of equity vary widely across divisions, and suggest that they are in very different risk classes. A manager in the aircraft engines division should use a cost of equity of 14.38% in assessing whether or not to take projects within that division. In contrast, a manager in the financial services division should use a cost of equity of 11.50% in assessing projects within that division. Thus, within the same firm, riskier divisions should be forced to clear much higher hurdles before taking projects than should safer divisions, and that is appropriate.

Concept Check

What would happen to a firm that insisted on using the same cost of equity for all its divisions, even though they might have different risk characteristics? Which divisions would benefit? Which would lose?

This analysis also has value when firms are being restructured. Any division that has a return to its equity investors which is much lower than its cost of equity is draining value from the company and is a candidate for restructuring or divestiture. We will return to this issue later in the chapter on valuation and restructuring.

❑ Concept
Check

From this analysis, the weighted average of the divisional betas should be equal, in theory, to the beta from the regression, but it generally will not be. Why is that? How would you reconcile the two? Which beta is more reliable?

Other approaches to estimating betas   The standard approach for estimating betas requires market prices on an asset, which makes it difficult to apply for nontraded assets (or firms) or for assets that have only been traded for a short time period.

Using comparable firms   An alternative approach to estimating a beta for a nontraded firm is to use the betas of publicly traded firms that are comparable in terms of business risk and operating leverage. The relationship between betas and leverage, elucidated above, can be used to correct for differences in financial leverage between the firm being analyzed and the **comparable firms.**

Comparable Firm: A comparable firm is one that is similar to the firm being analyzed in terms of underlying business risk.

To illustrate, assume that you are trying to estimate the beta for a private firm that disposes of environmental and medical waste for other firms. The firm has a debt/equity ratio of 0.30 and a tax rate of 40%.[13] The betas of publicly traded firms involved in environmental waste disposal are as follows (they face an average tax rate of 40%):

Firm	Beta	Debt/Equity
Allwaste Inc.	1.25	0.33
Browning Ferris	1.20	0.24
Chemical Waste Mgmt.	1.20	0.20
Rollins Environmental	1.35	0.02
Waste Management	1.10	0.22
Average	1.22	0.20

Unlevered beta of environmental firms = Average beta / [1 + (1 − tax rate) (Debt/Equity)]
= 1.22 /[1 + (1-0.4) (0.20)] = 1.09
Beta for private firm involved in waste disposal = Unlevered beta [1+ (1 − tax rate) (Debt/Equity)]
= 1.09 [1 + (1-0.4) (0.3)] = 1.29

This analysis suggests that the private firm should use a beta of 1.29 in coming up with a cost of equity for use in capital budgeting and in valuation.

❑ Concept
Check

Assume that you have been asked to estimate the beta of a business with no publicly traded comparable firms. How would you come up with a group of publicly traded firms to use as comparables? (For instance, what if you had been responsible for arriving at a beta estimate for the Boston Celtics in 1986, the year they went public?)

[13]Since private firms do not have market values for debt and equity, the book value ratio is used. This creates an inconsistency in the valuation, which can be resolved by doing a series of iterations until the value used in the debt/equity ratio converges on the value from the valuation.

Using the Arbitrage Pricing Model

Like CAPM, the arbitrage pricing model defines risk to be nondiversifiable risk. Unlike the CAPM, however, APM permits multiple economic factors in measuring this risk. Although the process of estimation of risk parameters is different for the arbitrage pricing model, many of the issues raised relating to the determinants of risk in the CAPM continue to have relevance for the arbitrage pricing model.

The parameters of the arbitrage pricing model are estimated from a **factor analysis** on historical stock returns, which yields the number of common economic factors determining these returns, the risk premium for each factor, and the factor-specific betas for each firm.

Factor Analysis: This is a statistical technique, whereby past data are analyzed with the intent of extracting common factors that might have affected the data.

Once the factor-specific betas are estimated for each firm, and the factor premiums are measured, the arbitrage pricing model can be used to estimate expected returns on a stock.

$$\text{Cost of Equity} = R_f + \sum_{j=1}^{j=k} \beta_j (E(R_j) - R_f)$$

where

R_f = Risk-free rate
β_j = Beta specific to factor j
$E(R_j) - R_f$ = Risk premium per unit of factor j risk
k = Number of factors

To illustrate, assume that the parameters for the arbitrage pricing model have been estimated, and that there are three factors:
Risk-free rate = 5.80%

$E(R_1) - R_f = 3\%$ Risk Premium for factor 1
$E(R_2) - R_f = 4\%$ Risk Premium for factor 2
$E(R_3) - R_f = 1.5\%$ Risk Premium for factor 3

Assume that the betas specific to each of these factors are estimated for Pepsi Cola in 1994 and that the estimates are as follows:

$\beta_1 = 1.20$
$\beta_2 = 0.90$
$\beta_3 = 1.10$

Substituting into the APM

Cost of Equity = 5.80% + 1.20 (3%) + 0.90 (4%) + 1.1 (1.5%) = 14.65%

This can be contrasted with the cost of equity estimated for Pepsi Cola using CAPM. This cost of equity will then be used both in capital budgeting, as a hurdle rate, and in valuing the equity in the company. One simple way to judge the quality of a project or a division is to compare the returns that equity investors will be making from that project or division to the cost of equity—if the return to equity exceeds the cost of equity, it is a good project; if not, it should be rejected.

Determinants of risk parameters in APM   The determinants of risk parameters in the arbitrage pricing model are the same as the determinants of risk in CAPM—namely, the type of business in which the firm operates, the degree of operating leverage it uses to generate earnings, and the amount of financial leverage it has taken on.

Type of business   Because factor betas in the arbitrage pricing model measure the risk of an investment relative to specific economic factors, the type of business in which a firm operates will, in large part, determine its exposure to factor risk. Thus, if one of the economic factors in the model is unanticipated changes in inflation, natural resource companies whose revenues and profits are much more directly linked up with changes in inflation are likely to have higher betas relative to this factor. As an example, Exxon's earnings and cash flows are highly correlated with oil prices (and overall inflation), resulting in a high inflation beta for the company.

Just as the beta of a company is the market-value weighted average of the betas of its different divisions, the factor betas of a company are market-value weighted averages of the factor betas of divisions that are in different business lines.

Degree of operating leverage: By increasing the volatility of earnings, higher operating leverage increases the betas of companies in the capital asset pricing model. By the same rationale, operating leverage will also make firms more sensitive to specific economic conditions and increase factor betas in the arbitrage pricing model.

Degree of financial leverage   The linear relationship between betas and the debt/equity ratio laid out in the section on CAPM continues to hold for each factor beta in the arbitrage pricing model.

$$\beta_{jL} = \beta_{ju}[1 + (1 - t)(D/E)]$$

where

β_{jL} = Levered beta relative to factor j ($j = 1,2,3, ..n$ factors)
β_{ju} = Unlevered beta relative to factor j ($j = 1,2,3, ...n$ factors)

Thus, as a firm increases its financial leverage, the betas of the firm will increase, and the equity in the firm will become riskier.

WEIGHTED AVERAGE COST OF CAPITAL (WACC)

Intuitively, the cost of capital is the weighted average of the costs of the different components of financing—including debt, equity, and hybrid securities—used by a firm to fund its financial requirements. This section explores the estimation of the cost of capital in more detail.

The weighted average cost of capital (WACC) is defined as the weighted average of the costs of the different components of financing used by a firm:

$$\text{WACC} = k_e(E/(D + E + PS)) + k_d(D/(D + E + PS)) + k_{ps}(PS/(D + E + PS))$$

where

$$\text{WACC} = \text{Weighted Average Cost of Capital}$$
$$k_e = \text{Cost of Equity}$$
$$k_d = \text{After-tax Cost of Debt}$$
$$k_{ps} = \text{Cost of Preferred Stock}$$
$$E/(E + D + PS) = \text{Market Value proportion of Equity in Funding Mix}$$

$D/(E + D + PS)$ = Market Value proportion of Debt in Funding Mix
$PS/(E + D + PS)$ = Market Value proportion of Preferred Stock in Funding Mix

 IN PRACTICE   CALCULATING THE COST OF CAPITAL: PEPSI COLA

In March 1995, Pepsi Cola Corporation had a cost of equity of 13.33% and an after-tax cost of debt of 5.34%. Of the total financing for the firm, equity comprised roughly 80% (in market value terms) of the funding mix, and debt made up the remaining 20%. The cost of capital for PepsiCo can then be calculated as follows:

$$\text{WACC} = 13.33\% \ (0.80) + 5.34\% \ (0.20) = 11.73\%$$

The estimation of the cost of equity has been described in detail in the preceding section. A short description of the estimation of the cost of debt, preferred stock, and hybrid securities follows.

Where is the cost of capital used and how is it different from the cost of equity? Although this question may seem confusing, the cost of capital is also used in capital budgeting and valuation. It is, however, used in conjunction with or in comparison to returns or cash flows to all investors in the firm, not just the equity investors. Thus, PepsiCo can compare the return on capital, which is a return to both stockholders and bondholders in the firm, on a project or division to its cost of capital of 11.73% to make a judgment on whether that project or division is adding value to the company.

 Concept Check

As interest rates in the economy go up, what will happen to the cost of debt, the cost of equity, and the cost of capital?

Calculating the Cost of Debt

The *cost of debt* measures the current cost to the firm of borrowing funds to finance projects. In general terms, it is determined by the following variables:

1. *The current level of interest rates:* As the level of interest rates increases, the cost of debt for firms will also increase.

2. *The default risk of the company:* As the **default risk** of a firm increases, the cost of borrowing money will also increase. One way of measuring default risk is to use the bond rating for the firm; higher ratings lead to lower interest rates, and lower ratings lead to higher interest rates. If bond ratings are not available, as is the case in many markets outside the United States, the rates paid most recently by the firm on its borrowings may provide a measure of the default risk of the firm.

Default Risk: This is the risk that a firm will fail to make obligated debt payments, such as interest expenses or principal payments.

3. *The tax advantage associated with debt:* Since interest is tax deductible, the after-tax cost of debt is a function of the tax rate. The tax benefit that accrues from paying interest makes the after-tax cost of debt lower than the pretax cost. Furthermore, this benefit increases as the tax rate increases:

$$\text{After-tax cost of debt} = \text{Pretax cost of debt } (1 - \text{tax rate})$$

 Concept Check

Can the after-tax cost of debt ever be greater than the firm's cost of equity? What about the pretax cost of debt?

IN PRACTICE CALCULATING THE AFTER-TAX COST OF DEBT: SIEMENS AG (GERMANY)

Siemens AG had 4.244 billion deutsche marks (DM) of debt outstanding in July 1993. Because of its low leverage and substantial cash balances, its default risk is minimal, and it can borrow at 6.72%. The marginal tax rate it faces on income is 38%. The after-tax cost of debt for Siemens can then be estimated as follows:

$$\text{After-tax cost of debt} = 6.72\% \ (1-0.38) = 4.17\%$$

What the cost of debt is not . . . When firms borrow money, they often do so at fixed rates. When they issue bonds to investors, this rate that is fixed at the time of the issue is called the *coupon rate*. The cost of debt is not the coupon rate on bonds that the company has outstanding, nor is it the rate at which the company was able to borrow at in the past. Although these factors may help determine the dollar interest cost the company will have to pay in the current year, they do not determine the after-tax cost of debt. Thus, a company that has debt on the books, which it took on when interest rates were low, cannot contend that it has a low cost of debt if the overall level of interest rates or its risk of default has increased in the meantime.

Calculating the Cost of Preferred Stock

Preferred stock shares some of the characteristics of debt—the preferred dividend is prespecified at the time of the issue and is paid out before common dividend—and some of the characteristics of equity—the payments of preferred dividend are not tax deductible. If preferred stock is viewed as perpetual, the cost of preferred stock can be written as follows:

$$k_{ps} = \text{Preferred Dividend per share/ Market Price per preferred share}$$

This approach assumes that the dividend is constant in dollar terms forever and that the preferred stock has no special features (convertibility, callability, etc.). If such special features exist, they will have to be valued separately to come up with a good estimate of the cost of preferred stock. In terms of risk, preferred stock is safer than common equity but riskier than debt. Consequently, it should, on a pretax basis, command a higher cost than debt and a lower cost than equity.

 Concept Check

Preferred stock creates many of the same obligations as debt (fixed payments in the form of preferred dividends, another claimholder with prior claims on assets), without the tax advantage. Why do some companies continue to issue preferred stock rather than debt?

 IN PRACTICE CALCULATING THE COST OF PREFERRED STOCK: GENERAL MOTORS

In March 1995, General Motors had preferred stock that paid a dividend of $2.28 annually and traded at $26.38 per share. The cost of preferred stock can be estimated as follows:

$$\text{Cost of Preferred Stock} = \text{Preferred Dividend per share / Preferred Stock Price}$$
$$= \$2.28 \ / \ \$26.38 = 8.64\%$$

At the same time, GM's cost of equity, using the CAPM, was 13%, its pretax cost of debt was 8.25%, and its after-tax cost of debt was 5.28%. Not surprisingly, its preferred stock was less expensive than equity but much more expensive than debt.

Calculating the Cost of Other Hybrid Securities

 Convertible Debt: This is debt that can be converted into stock at a specified rate, called the *conversion ratio*.

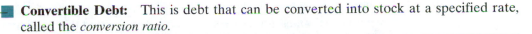

In general terms, *hybrid securities* share some of the characteristics of debt and some of the characteristics of equity. A good example is a convertible bond, which can be viewed as a combination of a straight bond (debt) and a conversion option (equity). Instead of trying to calculate the cost of these hybrid securities individually, they can be broken down into their debt and equity components and treated separately.

IN PRACTICE BREAKING DOWN A CONVERTIBLE BOND INTO DEBT AND EQUITY COMPONENTS: UNISYS CORPORATION

At the end of 1992, Unisys had an 8.25% convertible bond, coming due in the year 2000, which was trading at $1,400. It also had straight bonds, with the same maturity, trading in December 1992 at a yield of 8.4%. The convertible bond can then be broken down into straight bond and conversion option components.

$$\text{Straight Bond component} = \text{Value of a straight 8.25\% coupon bond due}$$
$$\text{in 2000 at a yield of 8.40\%.}$$
$$= \$991.50$$
$$\text{Conversion Option} = \$1,400 - \$991.50 = \$408.50$$

The straight-bond component of $991.50 is treated as debt, and the conversion option of $408.50 is treated as equity.

 Concept Check

As the stock price rises, the value of convertible bonds generally increases. What will happen to the proportion of value that can be attributed to debt?

Calculating the Weights of Debt and Equity Components

Market value versus book value weights   The weights assigned to equity and debt in calculating the weighted average cost of capital have to be based on market value, not book value. This rationale rests on the fact that the cost of capital measures the cost of issuing securities—stocks as well as bonds—to finance projects, and that these securities are issued at market value, not at book value.

There are three standard arguments against using market value, and none of them is convincing. First, it is argued that book value is more reliable than market value because it is not as volatile. Although it is true that book value does not change as much as market value, this is more a reflection of weakness than of strength, since the true value of the firm changes over time as both firm-specific and marketwide information is revealed. We maintain that market value, with its volatility, is a much better reflection of true value than is book value.[14] Second, it is suggested that using book value rather than market value is a more conservative approach to estimating debt ratios. This assumes that market value debt ratios are always lower than book value debt

[14]Some analysts argue that stock prices are much more volatile than the underlying true value. Even if this argument is justified (and it has not conclusively been shown to be so), the difference between market value and true value is likely to be much smaller than the difference between book value and true value.

ratios, an assumption not based on fact. Furthermore, even if the market value debt ratios are lower than the book value ratios, the cost of capital calculated using book value ratios will be lower than those calculated using market value ratios, making them less conservative estimates, not more so.[15] Third, it is claimed that lenders will not lend on the basis of market value, but this claim again seems to be based more upon perception than on fact.[16]

 IN PRACTICE DIFFERENCE BETWEEN MARKET VALUE AND BOOK VALUE DEBT RATIOS: PEPSI COLA

At the end of 1994, PepsiCo had a market value of equity of $32 billion and a book value of equity of $7.05 billion. The book value of debt at the same time was $9.75 billion, whereas the market value of debt was approximately $10 billion.[17] The debt ratios calculated on the basis of book and market value are as follows:

$$\text{Book Value Debt Ratio} = \$9,750 / (\$9,750 + \$7,050) = 58.04\%$$
$$\text{Market Value Debt Ratio} = \$10,000/(\$10,000 + \$32,000) = 23.81\%$$

The market value debt ratio is significantly lower than the book value ratio, and it clearly is much more representative of PepsiCo's financial strength.

A COMPREHENSIVE ANALYSIS OF RISK, RETURN, AND COSTS OF FINANCING— BOEING AND THE HOME DEPOT

In the following illustration, we apply the techniques developed in this chapter to two companies—Boeing and the Home Depot—to do the following:

- Estimate CAPM parameters—betas, alphas, and R-squared; we use these parameters to analyze the risk and performance characteristics of these firms and to link them up with the cost of equity.

- Estimate the cost of capital and contrast it with the cost of equity.

- Examine the risk differences within each company of different divisional areas.

Measuring Risk

We begin by collecting monthly returns for both companies from 1990 to 1994 and the returns on the S&P 500 over the same period. These returns are presented in Figure 6.2. A regression of stock returns against market returns yields the following results for the two companies:

---

[15]To illustrate this point, assume that the market value debt ratio is 10%, whereas the book value debt ratio is 30% for a firm with a cost of equity of 15% and an after-tax cost of debt of 5%. The cost of capital can be calculated

With market value debt ratios: 15% (.9) + 5% (.1) = 14%
With book value debt ratios: 15% (.7) + 5% (.3) = 12%

[16]Any homeowner who has taken a second mortgage on a house that has appreciated in value knows that lenders do lend on the basis of market value. It is true, however, that the greater the perceived volatility in the market value of an asset, the lower the borrowing potential on that asset.

[17]Not all of PepsiCo debt is traded. An approximate valuation of debt was made based on coupon rates and market interest rates.

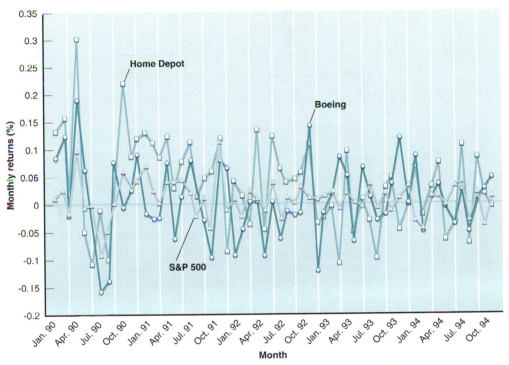

Figure 6.2   Monthly returns: Boeing, Home Depot, and S & P 500

Beta estimates

- Based on the regression, Boeing has a beta of 0.94, whereas the Home Depot has a beta of 1.38. This would suggest that the Home Depot is riskier than the average stock in the market and Boeing is slightly less risky.

- The regression parameters are estimated with noise. One way of quantifying this noise is to estimate a standard error for each of the beta estimates and to develop a range of estimates for each company:

Company	Beta	Standard Error	Range
Boeing	0.94	0.23	0.71–1.17
The Home Depot	1.38	0.26	1.12–1.64

These ranges are estimated using one standard error and suggest that, even with the standard errors, our conclusions hold. The Home Depot is a much riskier stock than the average stock in the market, whereas Boeing is close to or slightly below average risk.

- The beta estimates from the regression were different from the betas reported by a number of estimation services. Value Line, for instance, reported a beta of 1.00 for Boeing and 1.30 for the Home Depot. The differences can be attributed to at least a couple of factors. First, Value Line uses weekly rather than monthly returns to estimate betas. Second, Value Line adjusts betas toward 1 to reflect the long-term tendency of betas to converge toward one.

- In January 1995, the 30-year Treasury bond rate was 7.50%. Using the historical risk premium of 5.5% for stocks over long-term bonds and the beta estimates, we can estimate the required returns for both companies. For Boeing, the estimate of required return is

---

Expected Return for Boeing = 7.50% + 0.94 (5.5%) = 12.67%

For the Home Depot, the estimate of required return is

Expected Return for the Home Depot = 7.50% + 1.38 (5.5%) = 15.09%

- The required return has important implications for two groups. A prospective investor in Boeing (the Home Depot) would need to make 12.67% (15.09%) on his investment to justify the risk he is taking. If after analyzing Boeing (the Home Depot) he concluded that he would make only 10%, he would not make the investment. Alternatively, if he concluded that he could make more than the required return, he would make the investment. For managers in these two companies, these required returns provide estimates of their costs of equity.

- A simple approach to measuring performance is to compare the return on equity made by companies overall to the cost of equity. If one assumes that the book value of equity is a good measure of the market value of projects already taken, this comparison provides a measure of how good the past project choice has been. Between 1990 and 1994, for instance, this comparison would have yielded the following results for Boeing and the Home Depot:

Company	Cost of Equity	Average Return on Equity (1990–1994)
Boeing	12.67%	15.90%
The Home Depot	15.08%	17.62%

Based on these averages, both firms, on average at least, can argue that they have chosen good projects. Averages can be deceptive, however, Boeing's average return on equity was high because it had high returns between 1990 and 1992. In 1993 and 1994, the returns on equity were in the single digits. Although this may be because of industry-specific downturns in those years, it may also be the beginning of a longer term trend in returns that would be devastating for an investor in Boeing.

Measuring Performance

The regression also provides some insight into the performance of investments in both Boeing and the Home Depot between 1990 and 1994.

- The intercepts of the regression yield 2.19% for the Home Depot and -0.11% for Boeing. Using an average risk-free rate of 6.50% for the 1990-1994 period, we can convert these intercepts into measures of performance:

Company	Intercept	$R_f(1 - \beta)$	Intercept $- R_f(1 - \beta)$
Boeing	−0.11%	0.03%	−0.14%
The Home Depot	2.19%	−0.20%	2.39%

[The risk-free rate is first computed in monthly terms $(1.065^{1/12}-1)$, since the regression is based on monthly returns.]

- This measure of performance is the Jensen's alpha and can be confirmed using a more conventional approach. During the 1990–1994 period, the average monthly return on the S&P 500, including dividends, was 0.88%, whereas the average monthly risk-free rate (based on an annual risk-free rate of 6.5%) was 0.53%. The expected monthly returns on Boeing and the Home Depot, given the estimated betas, would have been

> E(Return) on Boeing: 1990–1994 = 0.53% + 0.94(0.88% − 0.53%) = 0.86%
> E(Return) on the Home Depot: 1990–1994 = 0.53% + 1.38
> (0.88% − 0.53%) = 1.01%

The actual average monthly return was 0.72% on Boeing and 3.40% on the Home Depot over the same period. The excess returns can then be estimated:

> Excess Monthly Return on Boeing = 0.71% − 0.86% = − 0.15%
> Excess Monthly Return on the Home Depot = 3.40% − 1.01% = 2.39%

The Home Depot was a much better investment, yielding a monthly excess return of 2.39% and an annual excess return of 32.82% between 1990 and 1994. Boeing did slightly worse than the market, after adjusting for risk, yielding negative excess return of <0.14%> and an annual negative excess return of <1.62%>.

- The performance of Boeing and the Home Depot as investments can be disaggregated into industrywide and firm-specific performance by calculating the average Jensen's alpha [Intercept − $R_f(1 − \beta)$] for firms in their peer group for the 1990-1994 period:

Company	Company Intercept − $R_f(1 − \beta)$]	Industry Intercept − $R_f(1 − \beta)$]	Difference
Boeing	−0.14%	0.11%	−0.25%
The Home Depot	2.39%	−0.02%	2.41%

This analysis suggests that the Home Depot's superior performance is due entirely to firm-specific factors (increasing sales and earnings; rapid growth), whereas Boeing's performance becomes even more negative when adjusted for the generally positive performance of stocks in the peer group.

- As a general rule, companies that report low returns on equity also have stocks that perform badly, whereas stocks in companies that report higher returns on equity are usually good investments. Trends in the return on equity also matter. Boeing, as an investment, did much more poorly in 1993 and 1994, relative to the market, and the lower returns on equity reported by the company during those years may share some of the blame.

- Finally, it is possible that what gets reported as "superior" or "inferior" performance may be attributable to a mismeasurement of the beta. Boeing, in the above analysis, would have had no excess returns if its beta had been 0.55. The Home

Depot, on the other hand, would have needed to have a beta of 8.22 to have no excess returns. Because these betas are significantly different from the estimated betas, misestimation of betas alone cannot explain the excess returns.

Analyzing Risk—Firm-Specific and Market Risk

The R-squared of the regression measures the proportion of the firm's risk that comes from market sources.

- The R-squared for Boeing was 22.77%, while the R-squared for the Home Depot was 33.76%. This would suggest that only 22.76% of the risk at Boeing comes from market sources, while the remaining 77.24% comes from firm-specific factors. At the Home Depot, 33.76% of the risk comes from market sources, and the remaining 66.24% comes from firm-specific factors.

- There may be a number of reasons for this difference. The Home Depot has more exposure to market risk than Boeing for at least two reasons. First, its business was concentrated in the United States during the 1990–1994 time period and it was therefore more exposed to cyclical movements in the U.S. economy. Boeing, on the other hand, gets almost half of its revenues from overseas, making it much less exposed to the U.S. economic cycles. Second, the Home Depot's business is home improvement, which is more likely to suffer during economic recessions than is aerospace, where acquirers often place orders for planes several years before they actually need them.

Determinants of Risk

The betas estimated from the regression can be traced to both financial and investment decisions made by Boeing and the Home Depot.

- The portion of the betas that can be attributed to financial leverage can be estimated by unlevering the betas, using the average debt/equity ratios that these firms had during the 1990–1994 period. Boeing had an average debt/equity ratio of 12%, whereas the Home Depot had an average debt/equity ratio of 4%. Using a tax rate of 34%, we can estimate the unlevered betas as follows.

Company	Beta	Average D/E	Unlevered Beta
Boeing	0.94	12.00%	0.87
The Home Depot	1.38	4.00%	1.34

- The bulk of both firms' betas can be attributed to their business risk and not to financial leverage. If these firms did in fact increase financial leverage now, this would cause their betas to increase dramatically. Figure 6.3 illustrates this effect.

- The business risk in each of these firms, represented by the unlevered beta, can be disaggregated further by looking at the different business lines in which each company operates. The Home Depot was a homogeneous company in January 1995, with all its business coming from its home improvement stores. As it gets larger and looks for opportunities in new areas, this will change. Boeing, on the other hand, has two distinct business lines—commercial aerospace and defense—with different risk characteristics. The accompanying table breaks down Boeing into these two groups, based on 1994 operating earnings from each group.

Business Group	Unlevered Beta	Market Value of Assets	Market Value Weight
Commercial aerospace	0.98	$16.0 billion	72.73%
Defense	0.80	$6.0 billion	27.27%

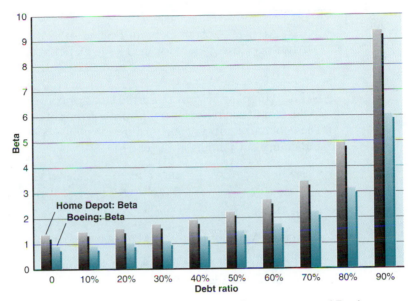

Figure 6.3   Betas and debt ratios: the Home Depot and Boeing

The unlevered betas for each business group were estimated using comparable firms, and the value of the assets was estimated from operating earnings of each division.

> Unlevered Beta for Boeing based on divisional betas
> = 0.98(.7273) + 0.80(.2727) = 0.93

This is slightly higher than the unlevered beta estimated from the regression (0.87), but it may actually be a more reliable estimate because it is based on averages of betas across a number of comparable firms.

- These unlevered betas, arising from business risk, will change in a predictable way if either of these firms embarks on a strategy of making acquisitions.

From Cost of Equity to Cost of Capital

The cost of equity, estimated from the betas, can be used in conjunction with an after-tax cost of debt to arrive at a cost of capital.

- Boeing has a rating of AA- from Standard and Poor's, leading to a pretax cost of debt of 8.25%. This pretax cost of debt is based upon the long term government bond rate of 7.50% and a default premium for AA- bonds of 0.75%. The Home Depot is not rated, but its latest borrowings were at a rate of 1% above the government bond rate, leading to a current pretax cost of debt of 8.50%. These pretax costs of debt are used to estimate after-tax costs of debt, assuming a marginal tax rate of 34%.[18]

---

[18]The corporate tax rate in 1994 was assumed to be the marginal tax rate. The tax rates reported on the income statements are skewed because of accounting differences.

> After-tax Cost of Debt for Boeing = 8.25% $(1-0.34)$ = 5.45%
> After-tax Cost of Debt for the Home Depot = 8.50% $(1-0.34)$ = 5.61%

- Neither company has any preferred stock or convertible debt outstanding, leading to the cost of capital based on the proportions of debt and equity in each company. The debt and equity proportions are calculated based on the market values of debt and equity outstanding at the end of 1994:

Company	Debt	Market Value of Equity	D/(D+E)
Boeing	$2,609	$18,073	12.61%
The Home Depot	$900	$20,815	4.14%

[Market Value of Equity = Market price per share * Number of Shares]

- The costs of capital are calculated based on the costs and proportions of each source of financing:

Company	D/(D+E)	Cost of Debt	E/(D+E)	Cost of Equity	Cost of Capital
Boeing	12.61%	5.45%	87.39%	12.67%	11.76%
Home Depot	4.14%	5.61%	95.86%	15.09%	14.70%

- The cost of capital is the appropriate benchmark to use to analyze projects on a predebt basis. The return on capital, which is computed based on the after-tax operating earnings, can be compared to the cost of capital to make a judgment on the performance of these companies. In 1994, for instance, this comparison would have yielded the following results:

Company	Return on Capital	Cost of Capital	Difference
Boeing	8.03%	11.76%	−3.73%
The Home Depot	18.36%	14.70%	3.66%

- Based on this comparison, we would conclude that, in 1994 at least, Boeing's projects did not measure up to the benchmark, whereas the Home Depot's projects yielded returns greater than the benchmark. This comparison is equivalent to the comparison made in the earlier section of return on equity to the cost of equity.

CONCLUSION

This chapter explains the process of estimating discount rates by relating them to the risk and return models described in the previous chapter.

- The cost of equity can be estimated using risk and return models—the capital asset pricing model, whereby risk is measured relative to a single market factor; the arbitrage pricing model, whereby the cost of equity is determined by the sensitivity to multiple unspecified economic factors, or a multiple factor model, whereby sensitivity to macroeconomic variables is used to measure risk.
- In both the CAPM and APM models, the key inputs are the risk-free rate, the risk premiums, and the beta (in the CAPM) or betas (in the APM). The last of these inputs is usually estimated using historical data on prices; in the case of private firms, they might have to be estimated using comparable publicly traded firms.

- Although the betas are estimated using historical data, they are determined by the fundamental decisions a firm makes on its business mix, its operating and financial leverage.

- The cost of capital is a weighted average of the costs of the different components of financing, with the weights based on the market values of each component. The cost of debt is the market rate at which the firm can borrow, adjusted for any tax advantages of borrowing. The cost of preferred stock, on the other hand, is the preferred dividend.

- Both the cost of equity and the cost of capital can be used to examine the quality of a firm's investment decisions, for they can be compared to the returns made on equity and capital, respectively. This comparison can be augmented by looking at the stock price performance of companies, after adjusting for market performance and risk.

QUESTIONS AND PROBLEMS

1. In December 1995, Boise Cascade's stock had a beta of 0.95. The Treasury bill rate at the time was 5.8%, and the Treasury bond rate was 6.4%.

   a. Estimate the expected return on the stock for a short-term investor in the company.

   b. Estimate the expected return on the stock for a long-term investor in the company.

   c. Estimate the cost of equity for the company.

2. Boise Cascade also had debt outstanding of $1.7 billion and a market value of equity of $1.5 billion; the corporate marginal tax rate was 36%.

   a. Assuming that the current beta of 0.95 for the stock is a reasonable one, estimate the unlevered beta for the company.

   b. How much of the risk in the company can be attributed to business risk and how much to financial leverage risk?

3. A biotechnology firm, Biogen Inc., had a beta of 1.70 in 1995. It had no debt outstanding at the end of that year.

   a. Estimate the cost of equity for Biogen, if the Treasury bond rate is 6.4%.

   b. What effect will an increase in long-term bond rates to 7.5% have on Biogen's cost of equity?

   c. How much of Biogen's risk can be attributed to business risk?

4. Genting Berhad is a Malaysian conglomerate, with holdings in plantations and tourist resorts. The beta estimated for the firm, relative to the Malaysian stock exchange, is 1.15, and the long-term government borrowing rate in Malaysia is 11.5%.

   a. Estimate the expected return on the stock.

   b. If you were an international investor, what concerns, if any, would you have about using the beta estimated relative to the Malaysian Index? If you have concerns, how would you modify the beta?

5. You have just done a regression of monthly stock returns of HeavyTech Inc., a manufacturer of heavy machinery, on monthly market returns over the last five years and come up with the following regression:

$$R_{HeavyTech} = 0.5\% + 1.2\,R_M$$

The variance of the stock is 50%, and the variance of the market is 20%. The current Treasury bill rate is 3% (it was 5% one year ago). The stock is currently selling for $50, down $4 over the last year, and it has paid a dividend of $2 during the last year and expects to pay a dividend of $2.50 over the next year. The NYSE composite has gone down 8% over the last year, with a dividend yield of 3%. HeavyTech Inc. has a tax rate of 40%.

   a. What is the expected return on HeavyTech over the next year?

   b. What would you expect HeavyTech's price to be one year from today?

   c. What would you have expected HeavyTech's stock returns to be over the last year?

   d. What were the actual returns on HeavyTech over the last year?

   e. HeavyTech has $100 million in equity and $50 million in debt. It plans to issue $50 million in new equity and to retire $50 million in debt. Estimate the new beta.

6. Safecorp, which owns and operates grocery stores across the United States, currently has $50 million in debt and $100 million in equity outstanding. Its stock has a beta of 1.2. It is planning a leveraged buyout

(LBO) whereby it will increase its debt/equity ratio to 8. If the tax rate is 40%, what will the beta of the equity in the firm be after the LBO?

7. Novell, which had a market value of equity of $2 billion and a beta of 1.50, announced that it was acquiring WordPerfect, which had a market value of equity of $1 billion, and a beta of 1.30. Neither firm had any debt in its financial structure at the time of the acquisition, and the corporate tax rate was 40%.

   a. Estimate the beta for Novell after the acquisition, assuming that the entire acquisition was financed with equity.

   b. Assume that Novell had to borrow the $1 billion to acquire WordPerfect. Estimate the beta after the acquisition.

8. You are analyzing the beta for Hewlett-Packard and have broken down the company into four broad business groups, with market values and betas for each group. (Corporate tax rate is 36%)

Business Group	Market Value of Equity	Beta
Mainframes	$2 billion	1.10
Personal Computers	2 billion	1.50
Software	1 billion	2.00
Printers	3 billion	1.00

   a. Estimate the beta for Hewlett-Packard as a company. Is this beta going to be equal to the beta estimated by regressing past returns on HP stock against a market index. Why or why not?

   b. If the Treasury bond rate is 7.5%, estimate the cost of equity for Hewlett-Packard. Estimate the cost of equity for each division. Which cost of equity would you use to value the printer division?

   c. Assume that HP divests itself of the mainframe business and pays the cash out as a dividend. Estimate the beta for HP after the divestiture. (HP had $1 billion in debt outstanding.)

9. The accompanying table summarizes the percentage changes in operating income, percentage changes in revenue, and betas for four pharmaceutical firms.

Firm	% Change in Revenue	% Change in Operating Income	Beta
PharmaCorp	27	25	1.00
SynerCorp	25	32	1.15
BioMed	23	36	1.30
Safemed	21	40	1.40

   a. Calculate the degree of operating leverage for each of these firms.

   b. Use the operating leverage to explain why these firms have different betas.

10. A prominent beta estimation service reports the beta of Comcast Corporation, a major cable TV operator, to be 1.45. The service claims to use weekly returns on the stock over the prior five years and the NYSE composite as the market index to estimate betas. You replicate the regression using weekly returns over the same period and arrive at a beta estimate of 1.60. How would you reconcile the two estimates?

11. Battle Mountain is a mining company, that mines gold, silver, and copper in mines in South America, Africa, and Australia. The beta for the stock is estimated to be 0.30. Given the volatility in commodity prices, how would you explain the low beta?

12. You have collected returns on AnaDone Corporation (AD Corp.), a large diversified manufacturing firm, and the NYSE index for five years:

Year	AD Corp	NYSE
1981	10%	5%
1982	5%	15%
1983	-5%	8%
1984	20%	12%
1985	-5%	-5%

   a. Estimate the intercept (alpha) and slope (beta) of the regression.

   b. If you bought stock in AD Corp. today, how much would you expect to make as a return over the next year? [The six-month Treasury bill rate is 6%.]

   c. Looking back over the last five years, how would you evaluate AD's performance relative to the market? (The average risk-free rate during the period was 5%.)

   d. Assume now that you are an undiversified investor and that you have all of your money invested in AD Corporation. What would be a good measure of the risk that you are taking on? How much of this risk would you be able to eliminate if you *diversify*?

   e. AD is planning to sell off one of its divisions. The division under consideration has assets that comprise half of the book value of AD Corporation, and 20% of the market value. Its beta is twice the average beta for AD Corp (before divestment). What will the beta of AD Corporation be after divesting this division?

13. You run a regression of monthly returns of Mapco Inc, an oil and gas producing firm, on the S&P 500 index and come up with the following output for the period 1991 to 1995:

Intercept of the regression = 0.06%
X-coefficient of the regression = 0.46
Standard error of X-coefficient = 0.20
R-squared = 5%

There are 20 million shares outstanding, and the current market price is $2. The firm has $20 million in debt outstanding. (The firm has a tax rate of 36%.)

a. What would an investor in Mapco's stock require as a return, if the Treasury bond rate is 6%?

b. What proportion of this firm's risk is diversifiable?

c. Assume now that Mapco has three division of equal size (in market value terms). It plans to divest itself of one of the divisions for $20 million in cash and acquire another for $50 million (it will borrow $30 million to complete this acquisition). The division it is divesting is in a business line in which the average unlevered beta is 0.20, and the division it is acquiring is in a business line in which the average unlevered beta is 0.80. What will the beta of Mapco be after this acquisition?

14. You have just run a regression of monthly returns of American Airlines (AMR) against the S&P 500 over the last five years. You have misplaced some of the output and are trying to derive it from what you have.

   a. You know the R-squared of the regression is 0.36 and that your stock has a variance of 67%. The market variance is 12%. What is the beta of AMR?

   b. You also remember that AMR was not a very good investment during the period of the regression and that it did worse than expected (after adjusting for risk) by 0.39% a month for the five years of the regression. During this period, the average risk-free rate was 4.84%. What was the intercept on the regression?

   c. You are comparing AMR Inc. to another firm that also has an R-squared of 0.36. Will the two firms have the same beta? If not, why not?

15. You have run a regression of *monthly* returns on Amgen, a large biotechnology firm, against *monthly* returns on the S&P 500 index, and come up with the following output:

$$R_{stock} = 3.28\% + 1.65\ R_{Market} \quad R^2 = 0.20$$

The current one-year Treasury bill rate is 4.8%, and the current 30-year bond rate is 6.4%. The firm has 265 million shares outstanding, selling for $30 per share.

a. What is the expected return on this stock over the next year?

b. Would your expected return estimate change if the purpose was to get a discount rate to analyze a 30-year capital budgeting project?

c. An analyst has estimated, correctly, that the stock did 51.10% better than expected, annually, during the period of the regression. Can you estimate the annualized risk-free rate that she used for her estimate?

d. The firm has a debt/equity ratio of 3% and faces a tax rate of 40%. It is planning to issue $2 billion in new debt and to acquire a new business for that amount, with the same risk level as the firm's existing business. What will the beta be after the acquisition?

16. You have just run a regression of monthly returns on MAD Inc., a newspaper and magazine publisher, against returns on the S&P 500 and arrived at the following result:

$$R_{MAD} = -0.05\% + 1.20\ R_{S\&P}$$

The regression has an R-squared of 22%. The current Treasury bill rate is 5.5%, and the current Treasury bond rate is 6.5%. The risk-free rate during the period of the regression was 6%. Answer the following questions relating to the regression.

a. Based on the intercept, you can conclude that the stock did

   0.05% worse than expected on a monthly basis during the regression.

   0.05% better than expected on a monthly basis during the period of the regression

   1.25% better than expected on a monthly basis during the period of the regression.

   1.25% worse than expected on a monthly basis during the period of the regression.

   None of the above.

b. You now realize that MAD Inc. went through a major restructuring at the end of last month (which was the last month of your regression) and made the following changes:

   • The firm sold off its magazine division, which had an unlevered beta of 0.6, for $20 million.

   • It borrowed an additional $20 million and bought back stock worth $40 million.

After the sale of the division and the share repurchase, MAD Inc. had $40 million in debt and $120 million in equity outstanding.

If the firm's tax rate is 40%, reestimate the beta, after these changes.

17. Time Warner Inc., the entertainment conglomerate, has a beta of 1.61. Part of the reason for the high beta is the debt left over from the leveraged buyout of Time by Warner in 1989, which amounted to $10 billion in 1995. The market value of equity at Time Warner in 1995 was also $10 billion. The marginal tax rate was 40%.

a. Estimate the unlevered beta for Time Warner.

b. Estimate the effect of reducing the debt ratio by 10% each year for the next two years on the beta of the stock.

18. Chrysler, the automotive manufacturer, had a beta of 1.05 in 1995. It had $13 billion in debt outstanding in that year, and 355 million shares trading at $50 per share. The firm had a cash balance of $8 billion at the end of 1995. The marginal tax rate was 36%.

a. Estimate the unlevered beta of the firm.

b. Estimate the effect of paying out a special dividend of $5 billion on this unlevered beta.

c. Estimate the beta for Chrysler after the special dividend.

19. You are trying to estimate the beta of a private firm that manufactures home appliances. You have managed to obtain betas for publicly traded firms that also manufacture home appliances.

Firm	Beta	Debt	MV of Equity
Black & Decker	1.40	$2,500	$3,000
Fedders Corp.	1.20	5	200
Maytag Corp.	1.20	540	2,250
National Presto	0.70	8	300
Whirlpool	1.50	2,900	4,000

The private firm has a debt equity ratio of 25% and faces a tax rate of 40%. The publicly traded firms all have marginal tax rates of 40% as well.

a. Estimate the beta for the private firm.

b. What concerns, if any, would you have about using betas of comparable firms?

20. As the result of stockholder pressure, RJR Nabisco is considering spinning off its food division. You have been asked to estimate the beta for the division, and decide to do so by obtaining the beta of comparable publicly traded firms. The average beta of comparable publicly traded firms is 0.95, and the average debt/equity ratio of these firms is 35%. The division is expected to have a debt equity ratio of 25%. The marginal corporate tax rate is 36%.

a. What is the beta for the division?

b. Would it make any difference if you knew that RJR Nabisco had a much higher fixed cost structure than the comparable firms used here?

21. Southwestern Bell, a phone company, is considering expanding its operations into the media business. The beta for the company at the end of 1995 was 0.90, and the debt/equity ratio was 1. The media business is expected to be 30% of the overall firm value in 1999, and the average beta of comparable media firms is 1.20; the average debt/equity ratio for these firms is 50%. The marginal corporate tax rate is 36%.

a. Estimate the beta for Southwestern Bell in 1999, assuming that it maintains its current debt/equity ratio.

b. Estimate the beta for Southwestern Bell in 1999, assuming that it decides to finance its media operations with a debt/equity ratio of 50%.

22. The chief financial officer of Adobe Systems, a growing software manufacturing firm, has approached you for some advice regarding the beta of his company. He subscribes to a service that estimates Adobe System's beta each year, and he has noticed that the beta estimates have gone down every year since 1991—2.35 in 1991 to 1.40 in 1995. He would like the answers to the following questions:

a. Is this decline in beta unusual for a growing firm?

b. Why would the beta decline over time?

c. Is the beta likely to keep decreasing over time?

23. You are analyzing Tiffany's, an upscale retailer, and find that the regression estimate of the firm's beta is 0.75; the standard error for the beta estimate is 0.50. You also note that the average unlevered beta of comparable specialty retailing firms is 1.15.

a. If Tiffany's has a debt/equity ratio of 20%, estimate the beta for the company based on comparable firms. (The tax rate is 40%.)

b. Estimate a range for the beta from the regression.

c. How would you reconcile the two estimates? Which one would you use in your analysis?

APPENDIX: HISTORICAL RETURNS ON STOCKS, TREASURY BILLS, (percentage distribution) AND TREASURY BONDS 1926–1992

Year	Stocks	Treasury Bills	Treasury Bond
1926	11.62	3.27	7.77
1927	37.49	3.12	8.93
1928	43.61	3.24	0.10
1929	−8.42	4.75	3.42
1930	−24.90	2.41	4.66
1931	−43.34	1.07	−5.31
1932	−8.19	0.96	16.84
1933	53.99	0.30	−0.08
1934	−1.44	0.16	10.02
1935	47.67	0.17	4.98
1936	33.92	0.18	7.51
1937	−35.03	0.31	0.23
1938	31.12	−0.02	5.53
1939	−0.41	0.02	5.94
1940	−9.78	0.00	6.09
1941	−11.59	0.06	0.93
1942	20.34	0.27	3.22
1943	25.90	0.35	2.08
1944	19.75	0.33	2.81
1945	36.44	0.33	10.73
1946	−8.07	0.35	−0.10
1947	5.71	0.50	−2.63
1948	5.50	0.81	3.40
1949	18.79	1.10	6.45
1950	31.71	1.20	0.06
1951	24.02	1.49	−3.94
1952	18.37	1.66	1.16
1953	−0.99	1.82	3.63
1954	52.62	0.86	7.19
1955	31.56	1.57	−1.30
1956	6.56	2.46	−5.59
1957	−10.78	3.14	7.45
1958	43.36	1.54	−6.10
1959	11.96	2.95	−2.26
1960	−0.47	2.66	13.78
1961	26.89	2.13	0.97
1962	−8.73	2.73	6.89
1963	22.80	3.12	1.21
1964	16.48	3.54	3.51
1965	12.45	3.93	0.71
1966	−10.06	4.76	3.65
1967	23.98	4.21	−9.19

(Continues)

(*Table continued*) Year	Stocks	Treasury Bills	Treasury Bond
1968	11.06	5.21	-0.26
1969	-8.50	6.58	-5.08
1970	4.01	6.53	12.10
1971	14.31	4.39	13.23
1972	18.98	3.84	5.68
1973	-14.66	6.93	-1.11
1974	-26.47	8.00	4.35
1975	37.20	5.80	9.19
1976	23.84	5.08	16.75
1977	-7.18	5.12	-0.67
1978	6.56	7.18	-1.16
1979	18.44	10.38	-1.22
1980	32.42	11.24	-3.95
1981	-4.91	14.71	1.85
1982	21.41	10.54	40.35
1983	22.51	8.80	0.68
1984	6.27	9.85	15.43
1985	32.16	7.72	30.97
1986	18.47	6.16	24.44
1987	5.23	5.47	-2.69
1988	16.81	6.35	9.67
1989	31.49	8.37	18.11
1990	-3.17	7.81	6.18
1991	30.55	5.60	19.30
1992	7.67	3.51	8.05
1926–1992	*Stocks*	*Treasury Bills*	*Treasury Bonds*
Arithmetic	12.40	3.60	5.20
Geometric	10.30	3.70	4.80
1962-1992			
Arithmetic	10.80	6.70	6.88
Geometric	9.62	6.67	6.36
1981-1992			
Arithmetic	14.63	8.58	14.50
Geometric	13.93	8.55	13.74

PART TWO

INVESTMENT ANALYSIS

Every business has three basic decisions to make: (1) which projects to take (*investment decisions*); (2) how to finance these projects (*financing decisions*); and (3) how much to return to investors (*dividend decisions*). While these decisions, for the most part, are not independent, it can be argued that the process starts, if not with the investment decision per se, at least with the recognition that a good investment opportunity exists. In the next few chapters we examine different facets of the investment decision-making process. In Chapter 7, we introduce the basic decision rules available, some based on accounting income and some on cash flows, and examine their strengths and weaknesses. In Chapter 8, we consider the process of estimating cash flows in a project. In Chapter 9, we examine the effects of having limited access to capital on project choice, as well as ways of choosing among mutually exclusive projects. In Chapters 10 and 11, we present ways of dealing with uncertainty in investment analysis, and in Chapter 12, we explore the capital budgeting process itself by looking at what gives projects positive net present values and ways of following up on projects after they have been chosen. In Chapter 13, we consider a special category of investment analysis—leasing—and examine the issues that are specific to it. Finally, in Chapters 14 and 15, we consider an important aspect of investment analysis by looking at investments in working capital.

CHAPTER 7

CAPITAL BUDGETING DECISION RULES

Allocating scarce resources among competing uses requires a mechanism or decision rule that separates those investments that are worth making from those that are not. The decision rule chosen to evaluate projects is significant for many reasons, the primary one being that it is a reflection of the objective function chosen by the firm's decision makers and is often influenced by the way they are rewarded. Over the last three decades, the dominant decision rules for investment making have shifted from those based on accounting income to those based on cash flows and stockholder wealth, reflecting the increased power of individual and institutional stockholders.

This chapter provides an introduction to the capital budgeting decision by examining its place in the big picture of corporate finance (Figure 7.1) and by defining both the scope and the types of investment decisions involved. It also defines and analyzes a variety of decision rules that can be used to evaluate projects to decide whether they should be accepted or rejected.

In this chapter, we examine a series of questions relating to alternative investment decision rules:

- What is a project? In particular, how general is the definition of an investment, and what are the different types of investment decisions that firms have to make?

- What is the difference between an "equity approach" and a "firm approach" to investment analysis?

- What are the basic accounting decision rules and their biases and limitations?

- Why are cash flows different from accounting income? What are the simplest cash-flow-based decision rules and their biases and limitations?

- What are the basic discounted cash-flow approaches? What are the differences between the approaches? When do they yield the same results, and when do they provide different conclusions and why?

- What approaches do firms actually use to make investment decisions and why?

WHAT IS A PROJECT?

Investment analysis concerns which projects to accept and which to reject; accordingly, the question of what comprises a "project" is central to this and the following chapters. The conventional project analyzed in capital budgeting has three criteria: (1) a large up-front cost; (2) cash flows for a specific time period; and (3) a **salvage value** at the end, which captures the value of the assets of the project when the project ends.

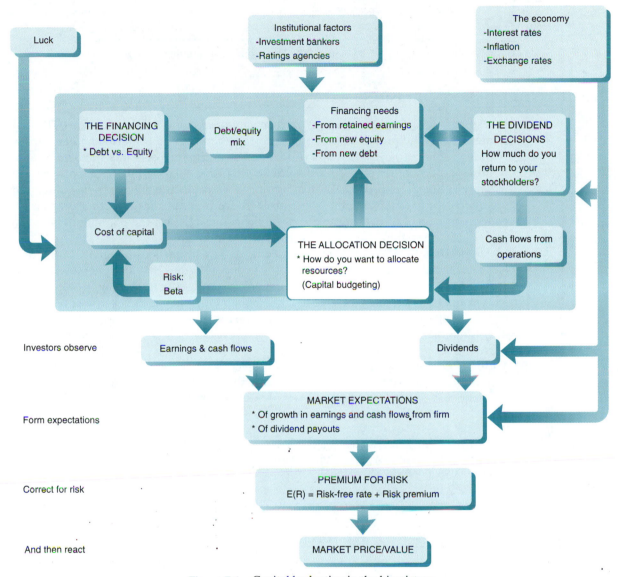

Figure 7.1   Capital budgeting in the big picture

Although such projects undoubtedly form a significant proportion of investment decisions, especially for manufacturing firms, it would be a mistake to assume that investment decision analysis stops there. We can define a project more broadly to include any decision that results in using the scarce resources of a business. Defined as such, a project would cover strategic decisions (new markets, acquisitions), business decisions (building a plant, opening a store), management and tactical decisions, and service decisions.

Salvage Value: This is the estimated liquidation value of the assets invested in a project at the end of the project life.

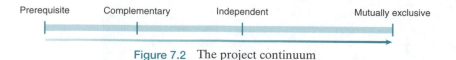

Figure 7.2   The project continuum

TYPES OF INVESTMENT DECISIONS

Investment decisions can be categorized on a number of different dimensions. The first relates to how the project affects other projects the firm is considering and analyzing. Although some projects are not dependent on any other projects, and thus can be analyzed separately, other projects are **mutually exclusive**—that is, taking one project will mean rejecting other projects; in this case, all of the projects will have to be considered together. At the other extreme, some projects are prerequisites for other projects. In general, projects can be categorized as falling somewhere on the continuum between prerequisites and mutually exclusive, as depicted in Figure 7.2.

The second dimension that can be used to classify projects is the ability of the project to generate revenues or reduce costs. The decision rules that analyze revenue-generating projects attempt to evaluate whether the earnings or cash flows from the projects justify the investment needed to implement them. When it comes to cost-reduction projects, the decision rules examine whether the reduction in costs justifies the up-front investment needed for the projects.

Mutually Exclusive Project: A group of projects is said to be mutually exclusive, when acceptance of one of the projects implies that the rest have to be rejected.

☐ Concept Check

How would your analysis of a project that is a prerequisite for another project be different from your analysis of a project that is independent? Can you think of an example of a project that is a prerequisite for another project?

APPROACHES TO INVESTMENT DECISION MAKING

There are two basic approaches to investment decision making. The first is the **equity approach.** It focuses on the equity investor in the project and asks the question: Are the returns to equity investors high enough to justify taking this project? The second approach is the **firm approach**. It expands the analysis to include all investors in the firm—equity investors, lenders, and preferred stockholders. This approach asks a broader question: Are the total returns made by this project for all the investor groups high enough to justify taking it on?

Equity Approach: This is an analysis done purely from the perspective of the equity investors in a firm.

Firm Approach: This is an analysis done from the perspective of all investors in the firm.

Implicit in these approaches is the notion of a benchmark—that is, a *hurdle rate* a project has to cross for it to be deemed acceptable. The hurdle rate in the equity approach is the rate of return equity investors demand on their investment—that is, the cost of equity. This rate typically depends on the perceived risk of the investment and is higher for riskier projects and lower for safer projects. In the firm approach, the hurdle rate is the rate of return demanded collectively by all investors in the firm—that is, the cost of capital. This rate depends not only on the perceived risk of the project but on the mix of debt and equity used to finance it as well.

Implicit in these two approaches is the *measurement of the return* on the project. Some investment decision rules measure returns on projects by estimating the expected accounting operating income they will have, whereas others focus on the cash-flow contribution the projects will make to the business that takes them. Thus, the return to equity can be calculated using the net income or the cash flows that are expected to these investors, after meeting all debt obligations. The return to the firm, in turn, can be calculated by looking at operating income, after taxes, or the cash flows that are expected to accrue to all investors in the firm—debt as well as equity.

 Concept
Check

Is it fair to demand that different projects meet different hurdle rates to qualify as good investments? Under what conditions is it appropriate for a firm to use the same hurdle rate for all projects with which it is faced?

INVESTMENT DECISION RULES

Firms utilize a number of investment decision rules in analyzing projects. Some are based on accounting net income, whereas others are based on cash flows; some are scaled for the size of the project, whereas others are not. All of these rules attempt to allocate the firm's resources in the most efficient way possible, although they sometimes disagree on the right choices to make.

The business world is partly made up of hundreds of successful businesses that have grown over time without any formal investment decision rules, depending largely on the intuitive feel of their founders for investment opportunities. In every successful business, however, the need to adopt a uniform investment decision rule increases for a number of reasons. First, as businesses get larger and decision making becomes less centralized, different decision-making units adopt a range of decision rules; as a result, similar projects come to be treated differently within the same organization. By contrast, adopting one decision rule results in standardization and a common language across the decision-making units. Second, the decision rules used in investment analysis are linked to the overall objectives of the firm. When different units adopt different rules, they may end up working at cross purposes, and the firm's overall objectives may not be met. Third, the reward and punishment mechanisms within the business for individuals making decisions will be arbitrary and difficult to enforce if each individual is allowed to adopt his or her own decision rules.

Many small and successful businesses are therefore faced with a moment of choice as they reach this stage in their expansion. In some cases, the owners of these businesses refuse to change their management styles and fight the need for formal decision rules. As a result, many end up paying a substantial price—either their businesses fail, or they are forced out ignominiously from their positions of power.[1]

---

[1] Howard Head provides a classic example of an extraordinary entrepreneur who had great ideas, founded and built up very successful small companies, and then was forced out of his position in each of these organizations once they reached a certain size. Stephen Jobs and Stephen Wozniak, the co-founders of Apple Computer, were both ejected from power at the organization for the same reasons.

Concept
Check

> A large number of businesses have managed to succeed without a formal investment analysis process or investment decision rule. Therefore, it is not particularly important what decision rule a firm adopts. Comment.

CATEGORIES OF DECISION RULES

Investment decision rules can be classified broadly into three groups. The first set of rules is based on accounting income and includes a number of the profitability measures, such as return on equity and return on assets, described in Chapter 4. The second set of measures is based on cash flows and reflects the differences that often arise between accounting income and cash flows. The final set of measures is based on discounted cash flows and factor in both the time value of money and the uncertainty associated with the cash flows.

Accounting Income-Based Decision Rules

Many of the oldest and most established investment decision rules have been drawn from the accounting statements and, in particular, from accounting measures of income. Some of these rules are based on income to equity investors (i.e., net income), whereas others are based on pre-debt operating income.

Return on capital   The expected *return on capital* on a project is a function of both the total investment required on the project and its capacity to generate operating income. Defined generally:

$$\text{Return on Capital (Pretax)} = \frac{\text{Earnings before interest and taxes}}{\text{Average Book Value of Total Investment in Project}}$$

$$\text{Return on Capital (After-tax)} = \frac{\text{Earnings before interest and taxes } (1 - \text{tax rate})}{\text{Average Book Value of Total Investment in Project}}$$

To illustrate, consider a one-year project, with an initial investment of $1 million, and earnings before interest and taxes of $300,000. Assume that the project has a salvage value at the end of the year of $800,000, and that the tax rate is 40 percent. In terms of a time line, the project has the following parameters:

Earnings before interest and taxes = $300,000

Book Value = $1,000,000   Salvage Value = $800,000

Average Book Value of Assets = $(1,000,000+$800,000)/2 = $900,000

The pre-tax and after-tax returns on capital can be estimated as follows:

$$\text{Return on Capital (Pretax)} = \frac{\$300,000}{\$900,000} = 33.33\%$$

$$\text{Return on Capital (After-tax)} = \frac{\$300,000\ (1 - 0.40)}{\$900,000} = 20\%$$

Although this calculation is rather straightforward for a one-year project, it becomes more involved for multiyear projects, where both the operating income and the book value of the investment change over time. In these cases, the return on capital can either be estimated each year and then averaged over time, or the average operating income over the life of the project can be used in conjunction with the average investment during the period to estimate the average return on capital.

Consider, for instance, a four-year project requiring an initial investment of $1,500, which will have the following operating income over time:

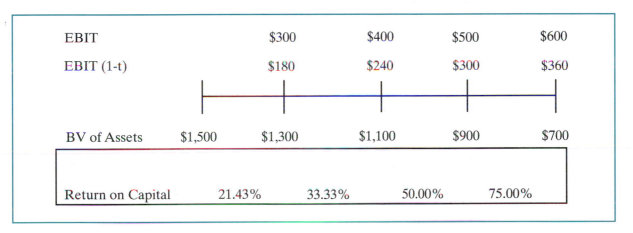

The book value of the assets decreases over time, as the assets are depreciated down to a salvage value of $700. The return on capital can be estimated each year and then averaged over time, as depicted in Table 7.1.

	Table 7.1	**EBIT on Four-Year Project**		
Year	**1**	**2**	**3**	**4**
EBIT	$300	$400	$500	$600
Average BV of Assets	$1,400	$1,200	$1,000	$800
Pretax ROC	21.43%	33.33%	50.00%	75.00%
After-tax ROC	12.86%	20.00%	30.00%	45.00%

The average (based on arithmetic averages) pretax return on capital over the four years is 44.94%, while the after-tax return on capital is 26.96%. The geometric averages are 43.58% for the pretax return on capital and 26.40% for the after-tax return on capital.

The return on capital can also be estimated from the average operating income and the average book value of assets over time:

Average EBIT = $450
Average after-tax EBIT = $450 (1 − .4) = $270
Average Book Value of Investment = ($1,500 + $700)/2 = $1,100
Return on Capital = $450/$1,100 = 40.91%
After-tax Return on Capital = $270 / $1,100 = 24.55%

The differences between the two approaches will widen as more **accelerated depreciation** methods are used, with the first approach providing higher estimates of return on capital.

Accelerated Depreciation: This is a depreciation method that yields higher depreciation in the early years, and less in the later years.

The after-tax return on capital on a project has to be compared to a hurdle rate that is defined consistently. Most firms use the cost of capital as the hurdle rate, since the return on capital is a return to the firm rather than to equity investors.

Decision Rule for Return on Capital for Independent Projects

If the after-tax return on capital > Cost of Capital ⟶ Accept the project
If the after-tax return on capital < Cost of Capital ⟶ Reject the project

---

When choosing between mutually exclusive projects of equivalent risk, the project with the higher return on capital will be viewed as the better project.

✈ IN PRACTICE   USING RETURN ON CAPITAL IN DECISION MAKING—BOEING

Table 7.2 is an investment analysis done for the Boeing 777, the next generation of the Boeing passenger jets, using return on capital as the decision-making tool. At the time of this analysis, in 1989, Boeing had already spent $2 billion in research and development costs on the new plane and anticipated spending $4 billion more in new investments. Both costs are lumped together and capitalized. Based on the anticipated sales of the plane, Boeing projected operating income (EBIT) and depreciation over a 15-year life for the project as indicated in Table 7.2. (The tax rate is 36% and the cost of capital is 12%)

The average after-tax return on capital anticipated on the project was 26.86%, which was well above the cost of capital of 12%.

Biases, limitations, and caveats   Although the return on capital is a simple and intuitive measure of the profitability of a project, its adherence to accounting measures of income and investment expose it to some serious problems:

Table 7.2 **OPERATING INCOME ON BOEING 777 PROJECT**

Year	BV of Assets	Capital Expenditure	Depreciation	Operating Income	Pre-tax (%) ROC	After-tax (%) ROC
0	$6,000					
1	$5,918		$82	$1,452	24.37%	15.59%
2	5,846		72	2,603	44.25	28.32
3	5,779		67	2,278	39.19	25.08
4	5,717		62	2,523	43.89	28.09
5	5,656		61	2,531	44.51	28.48
6	5,595		61	2,354	41.84	26.78
7	5,534		61	2,574	46.25	29.60
8	5,963	$489	61	3,003	52.24	33.43
9	5,861		102	2,590	43.81	28.04
10	5,763		98	1,440	24.78	15.86
11	5,673		90	2,684	46.94	30.04
12	5,595		78	2,967	52.66	33.70
13	6,020	500	75	2,562	44.11	28.23
14	5,947		73	1,831	30.60	19.58
15	5,896		52	2,961	50.00	32.00
Average	**$5,798**			**2,424**	**41.96**	**26.86**

Return on Capital$_t$ = Operating Income*2 / (BV of Assets$_{t-1}$ + BV of Assets$_t$)
After-tax Return on Capital = Return on Capital (1 − tax rate)

- The measure works better for projects that fit the conventional pattern (i.e., have a large up-front investment and generate income over time). For projects that do not require a significant initial investment, the return on capital has less meaning. For instance, a retail firm that leases space for a new store will not have a significant initial investment and may have a very high return on capital as a consequence.

- The focus on operating income rather than cash flows exposes this measure to potential problems when the operating income either lags or is very different from the cash flows generated by the project. Furthermore, changing depreciation methods and inventory costing may lead to changes in operating income and the return on capital, even though the underlying cash flows might be unaffected.

- The book value of the assets may not be a very good measure of the investment in the project, especially over time. Because depreciation reduces the book value of investments, the return on capital will generally increase over time, as it did in the Boeing above.

- Finally, the average return on capital does not differentiate between profits made in the early years of a project and profits made in later years. Thus, $100 in operating income in year 1 is counted more than $100 in operating income in year 4.

Note that all of the limitations of the return on capital measure are visible in the Boeing example. First, Boeing does not differentiate between money already spent and money still to be spent; rather, it is lumped together in the initial investment of $6 billion. Second, as the book value of the assets decreases over time, largely as a consequence of depreciation, the operating income rises, leading to an increase in the return on capital. Third, the average return on capital is taken over 15 years, even though the income made in year 15 is worth much less than an equivalent amount made in year 1. These problems are accentuated when service firms, which have smaller up-front investments, use return on capital to analyze projects.

IN PRACTICE ESTIMATING RETURN ON CAPITAL FOR A RETAIL FIRM—THE HOME DEPOT

A strategy employed by the Home Depot, which was one of the great success stories of the late 1980s and early 1990s, is to open huge home improvement stores, often in excess of 100,000 square feet. The initial cost to build and furbish such a store is estimated to be $12.5 million; in turn, the store is expected to generate sales of about $25 million for the company. Table 7.3 summarizes the operating income on one such store, over a 10-year lifetime.

Table 7.3   OPERATING INCOME ON THE HOME DEPOT STORE

Year	BV of Assets	Depreciation	Pretax Operating Income	Pre-tax Return on Capital (%)	After-tax Return on Capital (%)
0	$12,500,000				
1	11,000,000	$1,500,000	$793,578	6.75%	4.32%
2	9,800,000	1,200,000	1,208,257	11.62	7.44
3	8,840,000	960,000	1,568,670	16.83	10.77
4	8,072,000	768,000	1,887,103	22.32	14.28
5	7,457,600	614,400	2,173,458	27.99	17.91
6	6,966,080	491,520	2,435,731	33.77	21.62
7	6,572,864	393,216	2,680,398	39.60	25.34
8	6,258,291	314,573	2,912,722	45.40	29.06
9	6,006,633	251,658	3,137,001	51.15	32.74
10	5,805,306	201,327	3,356,766	56.84	36.38
Average	8,116,252			31.23	19.99

Here, as a result of the effects of the declining book value of the store, in conjunction with the rising operating income (which is itself driven by the declining depreciation), the return on capital increases dramatically over time. The average return on capital of 19.99% is significantly higher than the Home Depot's cost of capital (12.50%), suggesting that this is a good investment. Note, however, that the average is pushed up primarily by the high returns on capital that accrue in later years as the book value of the investment is written down.

 Concept Check

Given that the average return on capital weights returns on capital in each year equally, can you specify some of the problems that may arise with this approach? Is there a simple way you could modify the return on capital to reflect time value?

Return on equity The *return on equity* looks at the return to equity investors, using the accounting net income as a measure of this return. Again, defined generally:

$$\text{Return on Equity} = \frac{\text{Net Income}}{\text{Average Book Value of Equity Investment in Project}}$$

To illustrate, consider a four-year project with an initial equity investment of $800, and the following estimates of net income in each of the four years:

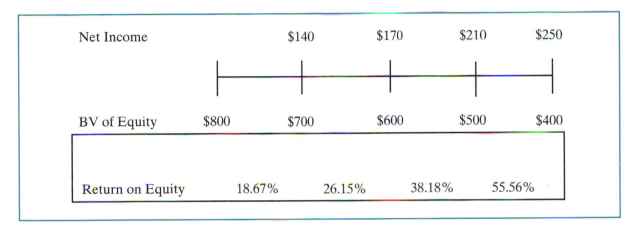

Net Income		$140	$170	$210	$250
BV of Equity	$800	$700	$600	$500	$400
Return on Equity		18.67%	26.15%	38.18%	55.56%

Like the return on capital, the return on equity tends to increase over the life of the project, as the book value of equity in the project is depreciated.

Just as the appropriate comparison for the return on capital is the cost of capital, the appropriate comparison for the return on equity is the *cost of equity,* which is the rate of return equity investors demand.

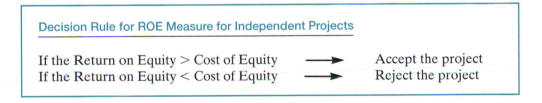

Decision Rule for ROE Measure for Independent Projects

If the Return on Equity > Cost of Equity   ⟶   Accept the project
If the Return on Equity < Cost of Equity   ⟶   Reject the project

The cost of equity should reflect the riskiness of the project being considered and the financial leverage taken on by the firm. When choosing between mutually exclusive projects of similar risk, the project with the higher return on equity will be viewed as the better project.

 IN PRACTICE ESTIMATING RETURN ON EQUITY—THE HOME DEPOT STORE

Consider again the Home Depot analysis for a new store requiring an initial investment of $12.5 million. If $5 million of this initial investment comes from borrowing, the book value of equity and the anticipated net income on the store are estimated as shown in Table 7.4. The increase in the return on equity over time mirrors the increase in the return on capital over the same period but is even more noticeable.

The average return on equity of 61.75% on the Home Depot project is compared to the cost of equity, which is 15%. These figures suggest that this store is a very good investment for the company.

Biases, limitations, and caveats The return on equity measure suffers from many of the same biases and limitations that plague the return on capital measure. First, it is much too dependent on accounting measures of income and investment and, accordingly, is susceptible to changes in accounting methods. Second, it tends to increase over time, as the book value is depreciated, and to provide unrealistically high values when

		Table 7.4 **RETURN ON EQUITY IN THE HOME DEPOT STORE**		
Year	**BV of Equity**	**Depreciation**	**Net Income**	**Return on Equity (%)**
0	$7,500,000			
1	6,000,000	$1,500,000	$(250,000)	−3.70
2	4,800,000	1,200,000	112,500	2.08
3	3,840,000	960,000	418,125	9.68
4	3,072,000	768,000	679,031	19.65
5	2,457,600	614,400	904,983	32.73
6	1,966,080	491,520	1,103,832	49.91
7	1,572,864	393,216	1,281,904	72.45
8	1,258,291	314,573	1,444,303	102.03
9	1,006,633	251,658	1,595,161	140.86
10	805,306	201,327	1,737,834	191.82
Average	3,116,252		902,767	61.75

the project does not require a significant initial investment. Finally, the gap between net income and cash flow may be large on many projects, which can cause significant problems for the company.

Other Accounting Return Measures The return on capital and return on equity are the two most conventional measures of accounting return, but variants of these two measures exist. Some of these measures are clearly inappropriate, however, because they match income to equity investors against total investment on a project and provide a return that is neither to equity investors nor to the firm. One such measure is the famed Du Pont return on investment, which divides net income by the total investment in the project.

Cash Flow-Based Decision Rules

The accounting income on a project may be very different from the cash flows generated by that project, for many reasons. First, a number of noncash expenses, such as depreciation and amortization, reduce net income but not cash flow. Second, an income statement contains significant cash outflows that are not expenses, such as capital expenditures and working capital needs. In particular, increases in working capital (such as inventory and accounts receivable) are cash outflows that are not reflected in the net income. The cash flows estimated on a project can be to either all investors in the firm or to just the equity investors.

Cash flow to the firm The **cash flow to the firm** measures the cash flows generated for all investors in the firm. It is a predebt, but after-tax, cash flow, and it can be estimated from the after-tax operating income as follows:

▬ **Free Cash Flow to Firm (FCFF):** This is the cash flow available to all investors in a firm, after paying taxes and meeting any net investment needs.

$$
\begin{aligned}
\text{Free Cash Flow to Firm} = \ & \text{EBIT } (1 - \text{tax rate}) \\
& + \text{Depreciation and Noncash Charges} \\
& - \text{Capital Expenditures} \\
& - \text{Change in Noncash Working Capital}
\end{aligned}
$$

On individual projects, the capital expenditures after the initial investment will take the form of capital maintenance expenditures or new investments needed to keep the project going. The changes in working capital can be either increases—in which case there is a cash outflow—or decreases—in which case there is a cash inflow.

☐ Concept
    Check

> Will the cash flow to the firm always be greater than the accounting income? Why or why not?

 IN PRACTICE ESTIMATING CASH FLOWS TO FIRM—BOEING

Table 7.5 estimates the free cash flow to the firm from the expected after-tax operating income for the Boeing 777 project described earlier from years 1 to 15.

Table 7.5 CASH FLOWS TO FIRM ON BOEING 777 PROJECT (IN MILLIONS)

Year	After-tax Operating Income	Capital Expenditures	Depreciation	Change in WC	FCFF
0		4,000			$(4,000)
1	$929		$82	$1,722	(711)
2	1,666		72	(17)	1,755
3	1,458		67	(343)	1,868
4	1,615		62	51	1,626
5	1,620		61	(91)	1,772
6	1,507		61	102	1,466
7	1,647		61	42	1,666
8	1,922	489	61	247	1,247
9	1,658		102	(212)	1,972
10	922		98	431	588
11	1,718		90	376	1,432
12	1,899		78	137	1,840
13	1,640	500	75	389	826
14	1,172		73	604	641
15	1,895		52	119	5,385

The cash flow to the firm in the final year (year 15) also includes salvage of working capital and the book value of the investment at the end of the year 15. In contrast with the accounting income approach, the $2 billion already spent on the project is viewed as a sunk cost; only the remaining $4 billion still to be spent is considered the initial investment.

Cash flow to equity The cash flow to equity investors can be similarly estimated from the net income by adjusting for the equity investment needed for net capital expenditures (capital expenditures − depreciation) and working capital changes. The general definition of **free cash flow to equity** therefore considers any new debt financing that creates cash inflows, and any debt repayments that creates cash outflows:

Free Cash-flow to Equity (FCFE): This is the cash-flow left over for equity investors after debt payments, taxes, and meeting net investment needs.

Free Cash flow to Equity = Net Income
+ Depreciation and Amortization
− Capital Expenditures
− Change in Working Capital
− Principal Repayments
+ Proceeds from New Debt Issues

If the debt ratio used to finance net capital expenditures and working capital needs is stable, the free cash flow to equity can be simplified:

Free Cash Flow to Equity = Net Income
− (Capital Expenditures − Depreciation) (1 − Debt Ratio)
− Change in Working Capital (1 − Debt Ratio)

In most projects, the cash flow to equity will be different from the net income and will be affected by the debt-financing mix used by the firm.

 Concept Check

Will the cash flow to equity always be smaller than the cash flow to the firm, since it is after cash flows associated with borrowing? Why or why not?

 IN PRACTICE ESTIMATING FREE CASH FLOW TO EQUITY—THE HOME DEPOT

Earlier, we estimated the net income for the Home Depot store. It is expected that 40% of net capital expenditures and working capital needs will be financed with debt. The free cash flows to equity are estimated in Table 7.6.

Table 7.6 **FREE CASH FLOWS TO EQUITY ON THE HOME DEPOT STORE**

Year	Net Income	Equity Capital Investment	Depreciation	Δ WC (1−Debt Ratio)	ATCF to Equity
1	$(250,000)		$1,500,000	$125,000	$1,125,000
2	112,500		1,200,000	131,250	1,181,250
3	418,125		960,000	137,813	1,240,313
4	679,031		768,000	144,703	1,302,328
5	904,983	$720,000	614,400	151,938	647,445
6	1,103,832		491,520	159,535	1,435,817
7	1,281,904		393,216	167,512	1,507,608
8	1,444,303		314,573	175,888	1,582,988
9	1,595,161		251,658	184,682	1,662,137
10	1,737,834		201,327	193,916	4,122,787

Again, the cash flows to equity in year 10 include the salvage value of working capital and the book value of equity in the investment.

Earnings versus cash flows When earnings and cash flows are different, as they are for many projects, we must examine which one provides a more reliable measure of performance. We would argue that accounting earnings, especially at the equity level (net income), can be manipulated at least for individual periods, through the use of creative accounting techniques and strategic allocations. In a book entitled *Accounting for Growth,* which won national headlines in the United Kingdom, Terry Smith, an analyst at UBS Phillips & Drew, examined 12 legal accounting techniques commonly used to mislead investors about the profitability of individual firms. To show how creative accounting techniques can increase reported profits, Smith highlighted such companies as Maxwell Communications and Polly Peck, both of which eventually succumbed to bankruptcy.

The contrast between earnings and cash flows was also starkly drawn in a controversy relating to the movie *Forrest Gump,* released by Paramount Pictures in 1994. Winston Groom, the author of the book on which the movie is based, was promised 2% of the net income on the movie. Understandably, Groom believed that one of the top grossing movies of all time, with worldwide revenues in excess of $650 million must have made *some* net income for Paramount. But he was shocked to find that Paramount was reporting a $62 million loss on the movie, largely as a consequence of a 32% commission the studio charged the movie to cover costs on future films that might fail. As a result, Paramount argued that Groom was not entitled to a share of the overall success of the movie.

Payback   The **payback** on a project is a measure of how quickly the cash flows generated by the project cover the initial investment. Consider a project that has the following cash flows:

Cash Flow			$300	$400	$500	$600
Investment	$1,000					

The payback on this project is between two and three years and can be approximated, based on the cash flows to be 2.6 years.[2]

Payback: The payback for a project is the length of time it will take for nominal cash flows from the project to cover the initial investment.

As with the other measures, the payback can be estimated either for all investors in the project or just for the equity investors. To estimate the payback for the entire firm, the free cash flows to the firm are cumulated until they cover the total initial investment. To estimate payback just for the equity investors, the free cash flows to equity are cumulated until they cover the initial equity investment in the project.

 IN PRACTICE   ESTIMATING PAYBACK FOR THE BOEING AND HOME DEPOT PROJECTS

The following example estimates the payback from the viewpoint of the firm, using the Boeing 777 example, and from the viewpoint of equity, using the Home Depot example. In the Boeing 777 analysis, as shown in Table 7.7, only the $4 billion investment that is still to be made is considered the initial investment. Based on the free cash flows to the firm estimated for each year: The initial investment of $4 billion is made back by the fourth year, leading to a payback of approximately four years.

---

[2] This assumes that cash flows occur uniformly over time.

Table 7.7   BOEING 777: FIRM CASH FLOWS

Year	FCFF	Cumulative CF	Year	FCFF	Cumulative CF
0	$(4,000)	$(4,000)	9	1,972	8,660
1	(711)	(4,711)	10	588	9,248
2	1,755	(2,956)	11	1,432	10,680
3	1,868	(1,088)	12	1,840	12,519
4	1,626	537	13	826	13,345
5	1,772	2,309	14	641	13,986
6	1,466	3,775	15	5,385	19,370
7	1,666	5,441			
8	1,247	6,688			

This analysis is repeated using cash flows to equity in the Home Depot example shown in Table 7.8.

Table 7.8   FREE CASH FLOWS TO EQUITY: THE HOME DEPOT—STORE ANALYSIS

Year	FCFE	Cumulative CF	Year	FCFE	Cumulative CF
0	$(7,500,000)	$(7,500,000)	6	$1,435,817	$(567,848)
1	1,125,000	(6,375,000)	7	1,507,608	939,760
2	1,181,250	(5,193,750)	8	1,582,988	2,522,747
3	1,240,313	(3,953,438)	9	1,662,137	4,184,885
4	1,302,328	(2,651,109)	10	4,122,787	8,307,672
5	647,445	(2,003,665)			

Based on the cumulative cash flows, the initial equity investment is recouped by year 7, leading to a payback to equity investors of between six and seven years.

Using payback in decision making   It is uncommon for firms to make investment decisions based solely on the payback, yet surveys reveal that some businesses do in fact use payback as their primary decision mechanism. In those situations where payback is used as the primary criterion for accepting or rejecting projects, a "maximum" acceptable payback period is typically set. Projects that pay back their initial investment sooner than this maximum are accepted, whereas projects that do not are rejected.

Firms are much more likely to employ payback as a secondary investment decision rule and use it either as a constraint in decision making (e.g., accept projects that earn a return on capital of at least 15%, as long as the payback is less than 10 years) or as a way to choose between projects that score equally well on the primary decision rule (e.g., when two mutually exclusive projects have similar returns on equity, choose the one with the lower payback).

Biases, limitations, and caveats   The payback rule is a simple and intuitively appealing decision rule, but it does not use a significant proportion of the information that is available on a project.

- By restricting itself to answering the question "When will this project make its initial investment?" It ignores what happens after the initial investment is recouped.

This is a significant shortcoming when deciding between mutually exclusive projects. To provide a sense of the absurdities this can lead to, assume that you are picking between two mutually exclusive projects with the cash flows shown in Figure 7.3. On the basis of the payback alone, project B is preferable to project A, since it has a shorter payback period. Most decision makers would pick project A as the better project, however, because of the high cash flows that result after the initial investment is paid back.

Concept Check   Payback is often used as a proxy for riskiness on a project. Why is payback a measure of risk? For what types of projects is it likely to be most useful?

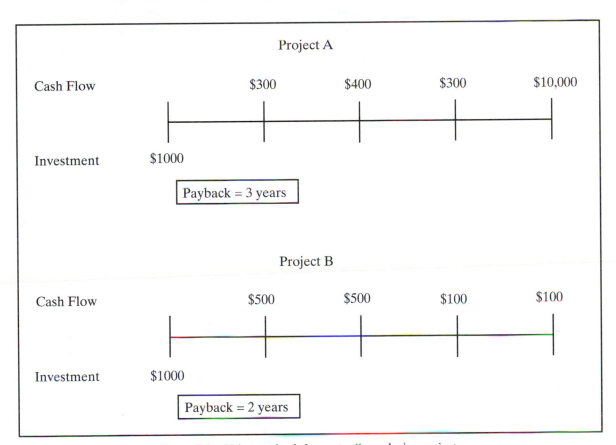

Figure 7.3   Using payback for mutually exclusive projects

- The payback rule is designed to cover the conventional project that involves a large up-front investment followed by positive operating cash flows. It breaks down, however, when the investment is spread over time or when there is no initial investment.
- The payback rule uses nominal cash flows and counts cash flows in the early years the same as cash flows in the later years. Since money has time value, however, recouping the nominal initial investment does not make the business whole again, since that amount could have been invested elsewhere and earned a significant return.

Discounted Cash-Flow Measures

As noted above, money has time value—cash flows that occur earlier in time are worth more than cash flows that occur later, differences that are accentuated as inflation and interest rates increase. Investment decision rules based on discounted cash flows not only replace accounting income with cash flows, but also explicitly factor in the time value of money. The first of these rules is *discounted payback,* which is an extension of nominal payback. The other two rules, which are more widely applied, are *net present value* and the *internal rate of return.*

Discounted payback   The **discounted payback** period for a project is the number of periods at the end of which the discounted cash flows cumulate to cover the initial investment. This approach, though a mild variant of the payback, attempts to examine when the initial investment is recouped with the opportunity costs. This concept can be illustrated easily by returning to the last example of Boeing and the Home Depot; the discounted payback for the Boeing 777 project is between five and six years. It is estimated by first discounting the cash flows, in each period, then cumulating these discounted cash flows, and finally calculating when these cumulated cash flows exceed the initial investment.

Discounted Payback: The discounted payback for a project measures the length of time needed for discounted cash flows on a project to cover the initial investment.

Net present value (NPV)   The net present value rule is an extension of the present value concepts developed in Chapter 3. The **net present value** of a project is the cumulation of the present values of each of the cash flows—positive as well as negative—that occur over the life of the project. The general formulation of the NPV rule is as follows:

$$\text{NPV of Project} = \sum_{t=1}^{t=N} \frac{CF_t}{(1 + r)^t} - \text{Initial Investment}$$

where

$$CF_t = \text{Cash flow in period } t$$
$$r = \text{Discount rate}$$
$$N = \text{Life of the project}$$

Net Present Value (NPV):   The net present value of a project is the sum of the present values of the expected cash flows on the project, net of the initial investment.

Thus, the net present value of a project with the cash flows depicted in Figure 7.4 and a discount rate of 12% can be written as shown in the figure.

The net present value of a project can be computed from one of two standpoints.

1.   It can be calculated from the perspective of all investors in the project, by discounting *free cash flows to the firm* at the *cost of capital,* and netting out the *total initial investment* in the project.

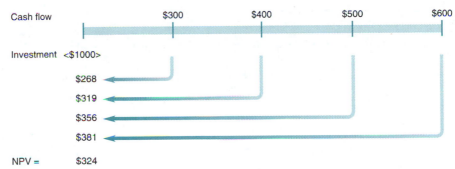

Figure 7.4   NPV of a project

2. It can be calculated from the perspective of equity investors in the project, by discounting *free cash flows to equity* at the *cost of equity,* and netting out the *initial equity investment* in the project. The cost of equity should reflect the riskiness of the project.

The key is to remain consistent in matching up discount rates and cash flows. Once the net present value is computed, the decision rule is extremely simple since the hurdle rate is already factored in the present value.

Note that a net present value that is greater than zero implies that the project makes a return greater than the hurdle rate.

Decision Rule for NPV for Independent Projects

If the NPV > 0 → Accept the project
If the NPV < 0 → Reject the project

 IN PRACTICE   NPV FROM THE FIRM STANDPOINT—BOEING

Table 7.9 calculates the present value of the cash flows to Boeing, as a firm, from the Boeing 777 project, using the cost of capital of 12% as the discount rate on the cash flows.

This project has a net present value of $5,220 million, suggesting that it is a project that should be accepted, based on the projected cash flows and the cost of capital of 12%.

 IN PRACTICE   NPV FROM THE EQUITY INVESTOR'S STANDPOINT—THE HOME DEPOT

The net present value is computed from the equity investors' standpoint in Table 7.10, using the projected cash flows for a prospective store opening for the Home Depot.

Based on the cost of equity of 15%, and the projected cash flows to equity investors from this store, the net present value is negative, suggesting that the store is not a good investment for the Home Depot.

Properties of the NPV rule   The net present value has several important properties that make it an attractive decision rule.

1. Net present values are additive. The net present values of individual projects can be aggregated to arrive at a cumulative net present value for a business or a division. No other investment decision rule has this property. The property itself has a number of implications.

Table 7.9   FCFF ON BOEING 777 INVESTMENT

Year	EBIT (1-t)	Capital Expenditures	Depreciation	Δ WC	FCFF	PV of FCFF
0		$4,000			$(4,000)	$(4,000)
1	$929		$82	$1,722	(711)	$(635)
2	1,666		72	(17)	1,755	1,399
3	1,458		67	(343)	1,868	1,330
4	1,615		62	51	1,626	1,033
5	1,620		61	(91)	1,772	1,005
6	1,507		61	102	1,466	742
7	1,647		61	42	1,666	754
8	1,922	$489	61	247	1,247	504
9	1,658		102	(212)	1,972	711
10	922		98	431	588	189
11	1,718		90	376	1,432	412
12	1,899		78	137	1,840	472
13	1,640	500	75	389	826	189
14	1,172		73	604	641	131
15	1,895		52	119	5,385	984
NPV						5,220

Table 7.10   FCFE ON THE HOME DEPOT STORE

Year	Net Income	Equity Investment	Depreciation	Δ WC	FCFE	PV of FCFE
0		$7,500,000			$(7,500,000)	$(7,500,000)
1	($250,000)		$1,500,000	$125,000	1,125,000	978,261
2	112,500		1,200,000	131,250	1,181,250	893,195
3	418,125		960,000	137,813	1,240,313	815,526
4	679,031		768,000	144,703	1,302,328	744,610
5	904,983	$720,000	614,400	151,938	647,445	321,894
6	1,103,832		491,520	159,535	1,435,817	620,743
7	1,281,904		393,216	167,512	1,507,608	566,766
8	1,444,303		314,573	175,888	1,582,988	517,482
9	1,595,161		251,658	184,682	1,662,137	472,483
10	1,737,834		201,327	193,916	4,122,787	1,019,090
					NPV =	($549,951)

Assets in Place: These are the assets already owned by a firm, or projects that it has already taken.

- The value of a firm can be written in terms of the net present values of the projects it has already taken on as well as the net present values of prospective future projects. The first term in this equation captures the value of **assets in place,** and the second term measures the value of *expected future growth*. Note that the present value of projects in place is based on anticipated future cash flows on these projects.

$$\text{Value of a Firm} = \sum \text{Present Value of Projects in Place} + \sum \text{NPV of expected future projects}$$

- When a firm terminates an existing project that has a negative present value based on anticipated future cash flows, the value of the firm will increase by that amount. Similarly, when a firm takes on a new project with a negative net present value, the value of the firm will decrease by that amount.

- When a firm divests itself of an existing asset, the price received for that asset will affect the value of the firm. If the price received exceeds the present value of the anticipated cash flows on that project to the firm, the value of the firm will increase with the divestiture; otherwise, it will decrease.

- When a firm takes on a new project with a positive net present value, the value of the firm will be affected, depending on whether the NPV meets expectations. For example, a firm like Microsoft is expected to take on high positive NPV projects, and this expectation is built into value. Even if the new projects taken on by Microsoft have positive NPV, there may be a drop in value if the NPV does not meet the high expectations of financial markets.

- When a firm makes an acquisition and pays a price that exceeds the present value of the expected cash flows from the firm being acquired, it is the equivalent of taking on a negative net present value project and will lead to a drop in value.

Concept Check

A firm that takes on a positive net present value project should see its value go up. Comment.

2. Intermediate cash flows are invested at the hurdle rate. Implicit in all present value calculations are assumptions about the rate at which intermediate cash flows get reinvested. The net present value rule assumes that intermediate cash flows on a projects—that is, cash flows that occur between the initiation and the end of the project—get reinvested at the **hurdle rate**, which is the cost of capital if the cash flows are to the firm and the cost of equity if the cash flows are to equity investors. Given that the cost of both equity and capital are based on the returns that can be made on alternative investments of equivalent risk, this assumption should be a reasonable one.

Hurdle Rate: This is the minimum acceptable rate of return that a firm will accept for taking a given project.

3. NPV calculations allow for expected term structure and interest rate shifts. In all the examples given in this chapter, we have assumed that the discount rate remains unchanged over time. This is not always the case, however; the net present value can be computed using time-varying discount rates. The general formulation for the NPV rule is as follows

$$\text{NPV of Project} = \sum_{t=1}^{t=N} \frac{CF_t}{\prod_{j=1}^{j=t}(1 + r_t)} - \text{Initial Investment}$$

where

$$CF_t = \text{Cash flow in period } t$$
$$r_t = \text{One-period Discount rate that applies to period } t$$
$$N = \text{Life of the project}$$

The discount rates may change for three reasons:

- The level of interest rates may change over time, and the term structure may provide some insight on expected rates in the future.
- The risk characteristics of the project may be expected to change in a predictable way over time, resulting in changes in the discount rate.
- The financing mix on the project may change over time, resulting in changes in both the cost of equity and the cost of capital.

To illustrate, assume that you are analyzing a four-year project, investing in computer software development. Furthermore, assume that the technological uncertainty associated with the software industry leads to higher discount rates in future years.

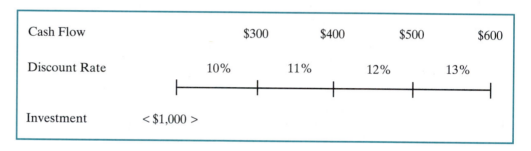

Cash Flow		$300	$400	$500	$600
Discount Rate		10%	11%	12%	13%
Investment	< $1,000 >				

The present value of each of the cash flows can be computed as follows:

PV of Cash Flow in year 1 = $300 / 1.10   = $272.72
PV of Cash Flow in year 2 = $400/ (1.10 * 1.11)   = $327.60
PV of Cash Flow in year 3 = $500/ (1.10 * 1.11 * 1.12)   = $365.63
PV of Cash Flow in year 4 = $600/ (1.10 * 1.11 * 1.12 * 1.13) = $388.27
            NPV of Project = $272.72+ $327.60+ $365.63+ $388.27 − $1000.00
                                                                = $354.23

☐ **Concept Check**

In the problem above, would using an average discount rate across the four years to calculate the net present value yield the same result? Why or why not?

Biases, limitations, and caveats   In spite of its advantages and its linkage to the objective of value maximization, the net present value rule continues to have its detractors, who point out some limitations. First, the net present value is stated in absolute rather than relative terms and does not, therefore, factor in the scale of the projects. Thus, project A may have a net present value of $200, while project B has a net present value of $100, but project A may require an initial investment that is 10 or 100 times larger than project B. Proponents of the NPV rule argue that it is surplus value, over and above the hurdle rate, no matter what the investment. Second, the net present value rule does not control for the life of the project. Consequently, when comparing mutually exclusive projects with different lifetimes, the NPV rule is biased toward accepting longer term projects.

Internal rate of return   The **internal rate of return** is also based on discounted cash flows. Unlike the net present value rule, however, it takes into account the project's scale. It is the discounted cash flow analog to the accounting rates of return. Again, in general terms, the internal rate of return is that discount rate that makes the net present value of a project equal to zero. To illustrate, consider again the project described at the beginning of the net present value discussion:

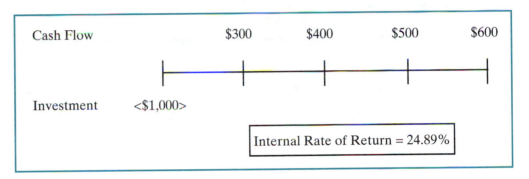

At the internal rate of return, the net present value of this project is zero. The linkage between the net present value and the internal rate of return is most visible when the net present value is graphed as a function of the discount rate in a *net present value profile*. A net present value profile for the project described is illustrated in Figure 7.5.

Internal rate of return (IRR):   The IRR of a project measures the rate of return earned by the project based upon cash flows, allowing for the time value of money.

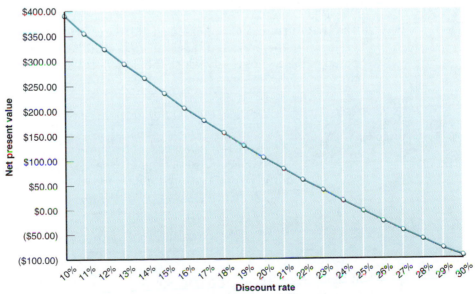

Figure 7.5   NPV profile

The net present value profile provides several insights on the project's viability. First, the internal rate of return is clear from the graph—it is the point at which the profile crosses the *x*-axis. Second, it provides a measure of how sensitive the NPV—and, by extension, the project decision—is to changes in the discount rate. The slope of the **NPV profile** is a measure of the discount rate sensitivity of the project. Third, when mutually exclusive projects are being analyzed, graphing both NPV profiles together provides a measure of the breakeven discount rate—the rate at which the decision maker will be indifferent between the two projects.

NPV Profile: This measures the sensitivity of the net present value to changes in the discount rate.

Concept Check

In the net present value profile above, higher discount rates lead to lower net present values. Is this always the case? If not, under what conditions will the net present value increase as discount rates are increased?

Using the internal rate of return   One reason often given for using the internal rate of return is that it can be used even in cases in which the discount rate is unknown. While this is true for the calculation of the IRR, it is *not true* when the decision maker has to use the IRR to decide whether or not to take a project. At that stage in the process, the internal rate of return has to be compared to the discount rate—if the IRR is greater than the discount rate, the project is a good one; alternatively, the project should be rejected.

Like the net present value, the internal rate of return can be computed in one of two ways:

- The IRR can be calculated based on the free cash flows to the firm and the total investment in the project. If so calculated, the IRR has to be compared to the cost of capital.

- The IRR can be calculated based on the free cash flows to equity and the equity investment in the project. If it is estimated with these cash flows, it has to be compared to the cost of equity, which should reflect the riskiness of the project.

Decision Rule for IRR for Independent Projects

A. IRR *is computed on cash flows to the firm*
If the IRR > Cost of Capital ⟶ Accept the project
If the IRR < Cost of Capital ⟶ Reject the project

B. IRR *is computed on cash flows to equity*
If the IRR > Cost of Equity ⟶ Accept the project
If the IRR < Cost of Equity ⟶ Reject the project

When choosing between projects of equivalent risk, the project with the higher IRR is viewed as the better project.

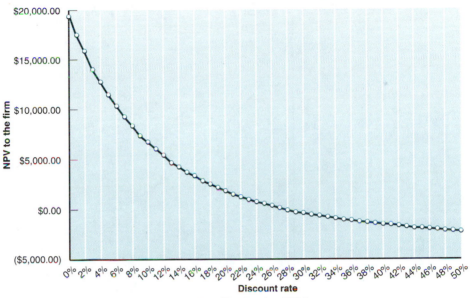

Figure 7.6   NPV profile: Boeing 777 investment

 IN PRACTICE   ESTIMATING THE IRR BASED ON FCFF—THE BOEING 777 INVESTMENT

The cash flows to the firm from the Boeing 777 investment, described earlier are used to arrive at a NPV profile for the project in Figure 7.6.

The internal rate of return on this project is 27.82%, which is significantly *higher* than the cost of capital, which is 12%. This confirms the conclusion, arrived at based on the NPV rule, that this is a worthwhile project.

 IN PRACTICE   ESTIMATING IRR BASED ON FCFE—THE HOME DEPOT

The net present value profile depicted in Figure 7.7 is based on the equity investment and the free cash flows to equity estimated for the Home Depot store analysis described earlier.

The internal rate of return on this project is 13.35%, which is *lower* than the cost of equity of 15%. Again, these results are consistent with the findings from the NPV rule, which also recommended rejection of this store.

Biases, limitations, and caveats   The internal rate of return is the most widely used discounted cash flow rule in investment analysis, but it does have some serious limitations.

- Since the IRR is a scaled measure, it tends to bias decision makers toward smaller projects, which are much more likely to yield high percentage returns, over larger ones.
- There are a number of scenarios whereby the internal rate of return cannot be computed or is not meaningful as a decision tool. The first occurs when there is no or only a very small initial investment and the investment is spread over time. In such cases, the IRR cannot be computed, or, if computed, it is likely to be meaningless. The second occurs when there is more than one internal rate of return for a project and it is not clear which one the decision maker should use.

To illustrate, consider a project to manufacture and sell a consumer product, with a hurdle rate of 12%, which has a four-year life and the following cash flows over those

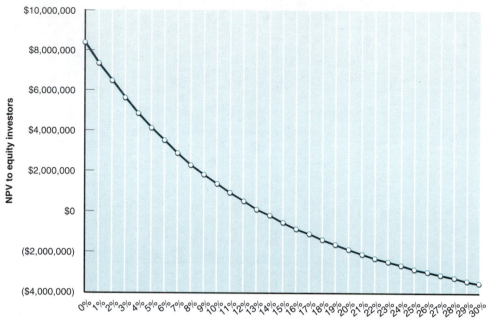

Figure 7.7   NPV profile for the Home Depot

four years. The project, which requires the licensing of a trademark, requires a large negative payment at the end of the fourth year:

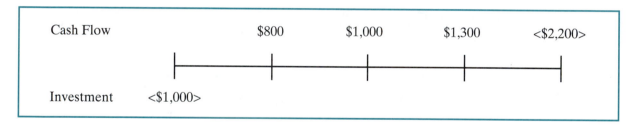

| Cash Flow | | | $800 | $1,000 | $1,300 | <$2,200> |

| Investment | <$1,000> |

The net present value profile for this project reflects the problems that arise with the IRR measure, as shown in Figure 7.8.

As you can see, this project has two internal rates of return —6.60% and 36.55%. Since the hurdle rate falls between these two IRRs, the decision on whether or not to take the project will change depending on which IRR is used. In order to make the right decision, the decision maker would have to look at the NPV profile. If, as in this case, the net present value is positive at the hurdle rate, the project should be accepted. If the net present value is negative at the hurdle rate, the project should be rejected.

Comparing NPV and IRR

The net present value and the internal rate of return, though viewed as competing investment decision rules, generally yield similar conclusions in most cases. The differences between the two rules are most visible when decision makers are choosing between mutually exclusive projects.

Differences in scale   The net present value of a project is stated in dollar terms and does not factor in the scale of the project. The internal rate of return, by contrast, is a percentage rate of return, which is standardized for the scale of the project. When

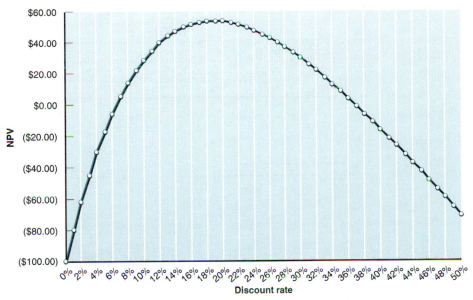

Figure 7.8 NPV profile for multiple IRR project

Multiple IRRs: Why They Exist and What to Do About Them

The internal rate of return can be viewed mathematically as a root to the present value equation for cash flows. The conventional project, in which there is an initial investment and positive cash flows thereafter, has only one sign change in the cash flows and one root—that is, there is a unique IRR. When there is more than one sign change in the cash flows, there will be more than one internal rate of return.[3] In Figure 7.8, for example, the cash flow changes sign from negative to positive in year 1 and from positive to negative in year 4, leading to two internal rates of return.

Lest this be viewed as some strange artifact that is unlikely to happen in the real world, note that many long-term projects require substantial reinvestment at intermediate points in the project and that these reinvestments may cause the cash flows in those years to become negative. When this happens, the IRR approach may run into trouble.

A number of solutions have been suggested to the multiple IRR problems. One is to use the hurdle rate to bring the negative cash flows from intermediate periods back to the present. Another is to construct an NPV profile. In either case, it is probably much simpler to estimate and use the net present value.

---

choosing between mutually exclusive projects with very different scales, this can lead to very different results.

Assume that you are a small bank, for example, and that you are comparing two mutually exclusive projects. The first project (Project A), which is to hire four extra tellers at the branches that you operate, requires an initial investment of $1 million and produces

---

[3]The number of internal rates of return will be equal to the number of sign changes, but some internal rates of return may be so far out of the realm of the ordinary (e.g., 10,000%) that they may not create the kinds of problems described here.

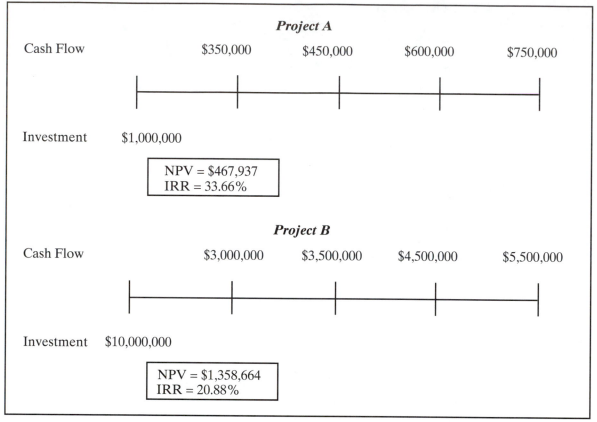

Figure 7.9   NPV and IRR-different scale projects

the cash-flow revenues shown in Figure 7.9. The second project (Project B) requires investment of $10 million in an automated teller machine and is likely to produce the much higher cash flows shown in Figure 7.9. The hurdle rate is 15% for both projects.

Another Approach to Scaling NPV: The Profitability Index

Another way of scaling the net present value is to divide it by the initial investment in the project. Doing so provides the **profitability index,** which is another measure of project return.

$$\text{Profitability Index} = \frac{\text{Net Present Value}}{\text{Initial Investment}}$$

In the bank example, for instance, the profitability index can be computed as follows for each project:

Profitability Index for Project A = $467,937/$1,000,000 = 46.79%
Profitability Index for Project B = $1,358,664/ $10,000,000 = 13.59%

Based on the profitability index, Project A is the better project, after scaling for size.

In most cases, the profitability index and the internal rate of return will yield similar results. The differences between these approaches can be traced to differences in reinvestment assumptions.

Profitability Index (PI): The profitability index is the net present value of a project divided by the initial investment in the project[3] it is a scaled version of NPV.

The two decision rules yield different results. The net present value rule suggests that Project B is the better project, while the internal rate of return rule leans toward Project A. This is not surprising, given the differences in scale.

Which rule yields the better decision? The answer depends on the **capital rationing** constraints faced by the business making the decision. When there are no capital rationing constraints (i.e., the firm has the capacity to raise as much capital as it needs to take prospective projects), the net present value rule provides the right answer—Project B should be picked over Project A. If there are capital rationing constraints, however, then taking Project B may lead to the rejection of good projects later on. In those cases, the internal rate of return rule may provide the better solution. The capital rationing question is dealt with in more detail in Chapter 9.

Capital Rationing: This refers to a scenario whereby a firm does not have sufficient funds—either on hand or in terms of access to markets—to take on all of the good projects it might have.

Differences in reinvestment rate assumption The differences between the NPV rule and the IRR rules due to scale are fairly obvious. However, there is a subtler, and much more significant, difference between the two rules, relating to the reinvestment of intermediate cash flows. As pointed out earlier, the net present value rule assumes that intermediate cash flows are reinvested at the discount rate, whereas the IRR rule assumes that intermediate cash flows are reinvested at the IRR. As a consequence, the two rules can yield different conclusions, even for projects with the same scale, as illustrated in Figure 7.10.

In this case, the net present value rule ranks Project B higher, whereas the IRR rule ranks Project A as the better project. The differences arise because the NPV rule assumes that intermediate cash flows get invested at the hurdle rate, which is 15%. The IRR rule assumes that intermediate cash flows get reinvested at the IRR of that project. Although both projects are impacted by this assumption, it has a much greater effect for Project A, which has higher cash flows earlier on. The reinvestment assumption is made clearer if the expected end balance is estimated under each rule:

End Balance for Project A with IRR of 21.41% $= \$10,000,000 * 1.2141^4 = \$21,729,904$
End Balance for Project B with IRR of 20.88% $= \$10,000,000 * 1.2088^4 = \$21,350,980$

To arrive at these end balances, however, the cash flows in years 1, 2, and 3 will have to be reinvested at the IRR. If they are reinvested at a lower rate, the end balance on these projects will be lower than the values stated above, and the actual return earned will be lower than the IRR, even though the cash flows on the project came in as anticipated.

The reinvestment rate assumption made by the IRR rule creates more serious consequences the longer the term of the project and the higher the IRR, because it implicitly assumes that the firm has and will continue to have, a fountain of projects yielding returns similar to that earned by the project under consideration.

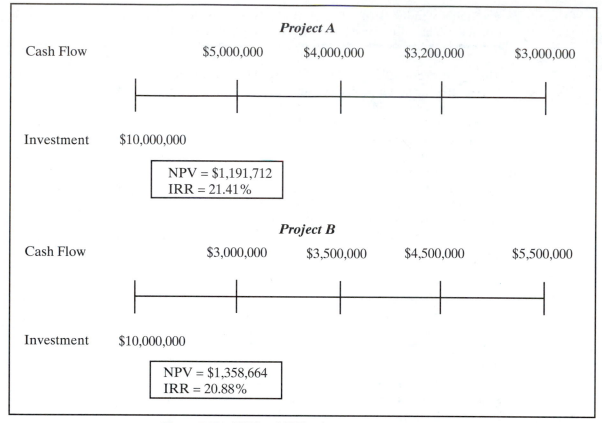

Figure 7.10   NPV and IRR-reinvestment assumption

■ **Modified Internal Rate of Return (MIRR):**   This is the internal rate of return, computed on the assumption that intermediate cash flows are reinvested at the hurdle rate.

A Solution to the Reinvestment Rate Problem: The Modified Internal Rate of Return

One solution that has been suggested for the reinvestment rate assumption is to assume that intermediate cash flows get reinvested at the hurdle rate—the cost of equity if the cash flows are to equity investors, and the cost of capital if they are to the firm—and to calculate the internal rate of return from the initial investment and the terminal value. This approach yields what is called the **modified internal rate of return (MIRR)**, as illustrated in Figure 7.11.

WHAT DO FIRMS USE IN INVESTMENT ANALYSIS?

A number of points must be made about investment analysis. First, firms generally use more than one technique in analyzing projects. Second, there are wide differences, even within firms, in usage.

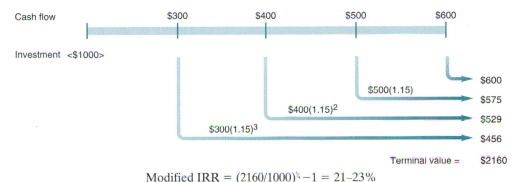

$$\text{Modified IRR} = (2160/1000)^{\frac{1}{4}} - 1 = 21\text{–}23\%$$

Figure 7.11   NPV and IRR-reinvestment assumption

Survey Results

Periodic surveys of financial managers have been conducted to find out which invest-ment techniques are being used. These surveys serve two useful purposes. First, they pro-vide a sense of what practitioners are using at any point in time. Second, comparisons of surveys across time provide a measure of changes in investment analysis. The survey re-ported in Table 7.11 was done in 1976 and focused on the financial managers of some of the largest companies in the United States.

Table 7.11   A SURVEY OF INVESTMENT DECISION TECHNIQUES IN 1976

| | Capital Budgeting Technique in Use | | | |
| | Primary | | Secondary | |
TECHNIQUE	Number	Percent	Number	Percent
Internal Rate of return	60	53.6	13	14.0
Accounting Rate of return	28	25.0	13	14.0
Net Present Value	11	9.8	24	25.8
Payback period	10	8.9	41	44.0
Profitability Ratio	3	2.7	2	2.2
Total Responses	112	100.0	93	100.0

This survey provided several interesting insights into the state of the art of in-vestment analysis in 1976. First, it provided evidence of the enduring popularity of accounting return measures, such as return on equity and assets, in spite of the em-phasis placed on cash flows over earnings in textbooks on investment analysis. Second, even when discounted cash-flow measures were used, the internal rate of re-turn was much more likely to be used as a primary decision technique than was net present value. Clearly, notwithstanding the problems with multiple internal rates of return and faulty reinvestment rate assumptions, decision makers preferred a scaled measure of investment performance to an unscaled one as a primary decision rule. Third, a surprisingly large number of respondents claimed that they used the pay-back period as the primary investment decision rule, despite all of its limitations and problems. Finally, most respondents used more than one investment analysis mea-sure in deciding on projects.

The survey was expanded and updated in 1986, and the results are summarized in Table 7.12.

Table 7.12 UPDATED SURVEY IN 1986

| | Capital Budgeting Technique in Use | | | |
| | Primary | | Secondary | |
TECHNIQUE	Number	Percent	Number	Percent
Internal Rate of return	288	49.0	70	15.0
Accounting Rate of return	47	8.0	89	19.0
Net Present Value	123	21.0	113	24.0
Payback period	112	19.0	164	35.0
Benefit/Cost Ratio	17	3.0	33	7.0
Total Responses	587	100.0	469	100.0

This survey shows that the net present value rule gained a significant proportion of adherents in the intervening decade, mostly at the expense of the accounting measures. This shift to discounted cash-flow models over time may be explained as a logical shift to more sophisticated investment analysis techniques and may be attributed to a recognition of the importance of value maximization. Yet, there is a puzzling anomaly that emerges from these findings in the doubling of those respondents using the payback period as their primary investment rule. This finding is confirmed by Ross (1986), who examined the capital budgeting practices of 12 large manufacturing firms and found that the payback method was widely used, especially among smaller firms. Some have suggested that this may have arisen because of the increased leverage taken on by some firms in the 1980s, which, in turn, increased the need for current or near term cash flows to meet debt obligations.

Discussion of Findings

None of the surveys mentioned above will ever end the debate on the right investment analysis technique, but, collectively, they provide some useful lessons. First, it is dangerous to insist dogmatically that one and only one technique is right and that all others are flawed. All investment analysis techniques have limitations, and no one technique works equally well for all organizations. Second, the reasons why decision makers choose the techniques they use for investment analysis may go beyond the mere theoretical pros and cons developed in this chapter and may depend on a number of real-world concerns, including the history of the business and the reward-punishment mechanism employed by the firm. Third, the use of multiple investment analysis techniques should not blind us to the fact that one technique still has to be the primary technique in making decisions.

CONCLUSION

Investment analysis is arguably the most important part of corporate financial analysis. In this chapter, we have defined the scope of investment analysis and examined a range of investment analysis techniques, ranging from accounting rate of return measures, such as return of equity and return on assets, to discounted cash-flow techniques, such as net present value and internal rate of return. In general, it can be argued that:

- Any decision that requires the use of resources is an investment decision; thus, investment decisions cover everything from broad strategic decisions, at one extreme, to decisions on how much inventory to carry, at the other.

- There are two basic approaches to investment analysis; in the equity approach, the returns to equity investors from a project are measured against the cost of equity to decide whether or not to take a project; in the firm approach, the returns to all investors in the firm are measured against the cost of capital to arrive at the same judgment.

- Accounting rate of return measures, such as return on equity or return on capital, generally work better for projects that have large initial investments, earnings that are roughly equal to the cash flows, and level earnings over time. For most projects, accounting returns will increase over time, as the book value of the assets is depreciated.

- Payback, which looks at how quickly a project returns its initial investment in nominal cash-flow terms, is a useful secondary measure of project performance or a measure of risk, but it is not a very effective primary technique because it does not consider cash flows after the initial investment is recouped.

- Discounted cash-flow methods provide the best measures of true returns on projects because they are based on cash flows and consider the time value of money.

- Among discounted cash-flow methods, net present value provides an unscaled measure, whereas internal rate of return provides a scaled measure of project performance. Both methods require the same information, and, for the most part, they arrive at the same conclusions when used to analyze independent projects. The internal rate of return does tend to overstate the return on good projects because it assumes that intermediate cash flows get reinvested at the internal rate of return. When analyzing mutually exclusive projects, the internal rate of return is biased toward smaller projects and may be the more appropriate decision rule for firms that have capital constraints.

- Firms seem much more inclined to use internal rate of return than net present value as an investment analysis tool; this can be attributed partly to the fact that IRR is a scaled measure of return, and partly to capital rationing constraints firms may face.

QUESTIONS AND PROBLEMS

1. A firm in Oklahoma is considering an investment project that needs an initial investment capital of $500,000. The project is to last 10 years with no salvage value. The EBIT is estimated to be $120,000 per year. What is the after-tax return on capital if the marginal tax rate is 34%?

2. A project calls for an initial investment of $1.2 million. This project will be completely depreciated over three years by the use of straight-line method, although its estimated market value at year 5 will be $400,000. It is estimated that the project will bring in $200,000 a year as EBIT for five years. The tax rate is 34%.

   a. Calculate after-tax ROC for each of the next five years.

   b. Find the geometric average return on capital.

   c. If the cost of capital is 25%, should the project be accepted?

3. Your company uses return on equity in the capital budgeting process. A project under evaluation needs an initial outlay of $1 million. Forty percent of the investment will be financed by bonds, with the balance of needed funding coming from equity. This project will generate an additional $50,000 in net income a year. What is the return on equity if the salvage value is 0 when the project is terminated five years later?

4. A company's acceptable minimum return on capital is 12%. If the debt/equity ratio is 100%, and the

after-tax interest rate is 5%. What is the corresponding acceptable minimum return on equity?

5. Stock analysts often treat the price/earnings ratio as a kind of payback period for investment in stocks. Under what assumptions concerning the earnings growth rate and dividend payout policy would you think it appropriate to call the P/E ratio as the payback period?

6. When a company uses the payback period as the decision rule in the capital budgeting process, it is necessary to compare the projected payback period of a particular project to a "maximum" acceptable payback period. What factors concerning financial markets, the company, and the project itself might affect this "maximum" acceptable payback period as the criterion in determining whether to accept or reject a project?

7. A company is considering building a hotel in Beijing, China. Because of the political risk involved, the company wants to have a small payback period. The cash flows are estimated to be as follows:

Year	Cash Flows
0	−3,000,000
1	250,000
2	500,000
3	750,000
4	750,000
5–20	750,000

a. Find the payback period for the project.

b. Find the discounted payback period if the discount rate is 10%.

8. Your company is considering a potential project that needs $1 million of initial investment. The initial outlay would be depreciated over the 10-year period by the straight-line method. The project is estimated to generate $300,000 of additional EBIT to the company per year. The marginal tax rate would be 34%. What is the payback period of this project? If the "maximum" acceptable payback period for this kind of projects is four years, would this project be accepted?

9. A project under evaluation is estimated to generate free cash flow to the firm as follows:

Year	FCFF
0	−2,000,000
1	100,000
2–10 per year	300,000

Calculate the net present value if (1) the cost of capital is 10%; or (2) the cost of capital is 15%. Should the firm accept the project?

10. Your company is considering a project that will bring in annual free cash flow to equity in the amount of $50,000 for 10 years. If the cost of equity is 14%, what would be the maximum initial investment on the project below which the project would be accepted based on the NPV rule?

11. Your company has decided to invest in a project with estimated NPV of $2 million. The financing of the project is a combination of retained earnings and bonds. If the company has 1 million shares outstanding and the financial market seems to accept the management's estimate on the NPV of this project, what would be the impact of this project on the company's stock price per share?

12. It is sometimes argued that net present value should be based on time-varying discount rates. As an example, consider a project with projected cash flows as follows:

Year	Cash Flows	Appropriate Discount Rate
0	−500,000	
1	300,000	10%
2	350,000	12%

What is the NPV of this project?

13. A project is estimated to have the cash flows to firm as follows:

Year	Cash Flow to Firm
0	−200,000
1–9 per year	25,000
10	75,000

a. What is the internal rate of return of this project?

b. Should the project be accepted if the cost of capital is 10%?

c. Is the NPV positive or negative?

14. There are two mutually exclusive projects with estimated cash flows to firm as follows:

Year	Project A	Project B
0	−500	−2,000
1–19	50	190
20	100	340

a. What is the IRR for Project A?

b. What is the IRR for Project B?

c. Which project should be accepted based on the IRR rule?

d. What are the NPVs of Project A and Project B if the cost of capital is 5%? Which project should be accepted based on the NPV rule?

e. What are the NPVs of Project A and Project B if the cost of capital is 7.5%. Which project should be accepted based on the NPV rule?

f. Do the IRR rule and NPV rule always reach the same conclusion with regard to the selection of two mutual exclusive projects? Which method is more consistent with the objective of corporate finance to maximize shareholders' wealth?

15. Can you name the term used in bond valuation equation which is also called IRR in capital budgeting? Can you use knowledge of bond valuation to better understand capital budgeting decision based on the IRR rule, and how?

CHAPTER 8

ESTIMATING CASH FLOWS

Both discounted cash-flow rules, such as net present value and internal rate of return, and nominal cash-flow rules, such as payback and cash-flow return on investment, are driven by estimates of cash flows. Thus, in order for these rules to accomplish their purpose, the cash flows have to be estimated correctly. This chapter looks at cash flow estimation in more detail. It examines several elements of cash-flow estimation and provides answers to the following questions:

- What are the effects of taxes on cash flows? In particular,

  How does a firm's tax status—that is, whether it is making or losing money—affect the cash flows on a project it is considering?

  What are non-cash charges, and how do they affect the cash flows on a project?

  What is the difference between tax deductible noncash charges such as depreciation and non-tax deductible noncash charges?

- What is an incremental cash flow, and why do only incremental cash flows matter? In particular,

  What are sunk costs, and how should they be considered in capital budgeting?

  What is the effect of working capital on cash flows?

  How do you price in project resources that may already be owned by a firm?

- How do you deal with inflation and leverage in estimating cash flows?

In reality, the bulk of the work in capital budgeting is in the estimation of cash flows, and a good investment analysis begins with a careful estimation of cash flows.

CASH-FLOW INGREDIENTS FOR A PROJECT

Let us start with a conventional project, where the outlay for the project occurs at the beginning, and cash flows are generated for the life of the project, at the end of which there is a liquidation of the remaining assets in the project. In this conventional project, cash flows can be classified into three categories:

1. The outlay in the project is called the **initial investment.** The word "initial" may be a misnomer because the outlay could either occur right now (in an instant) as is the case of the purchase of equipment, or take several periods, as is the case of building a new factory.

Initial Investment: This is the cash outlay needed to get a project operational. While it is often assumed to occur at the start of a project's life, it could occur at any time during its life.

2. The cash flows generated during the life of the project are called *operating cash flows.* Although they are generally positive for most conventional revenue-generating projects, there are some cost-minimization projects whereby all of these cash flows can be negative. This would be the case, for instance, for a firm considering whether to buy or lease a phone system for use in the business.

3. At the end of the project life, the remaining assets in the project, both fixed and current, are assumed to be liquidated; the cash flow generated by this liquidation is called the **salvage value.**

Salvage Value: This is the expected cash flow from liquidating the assets invested in a project, at the end of its life.

First Principles of Cash-Flow Estimation

The following three principles should be adhered to when cash flows are estimated for the purposes of analyzing a project.

1. *Cash flows should be after taxes.* All investment analysis should be done in after-tax terms. This implies that all items that affect taxes, even noncash items, such as depreciation, should be considered in the analysis.

2. *Cash flows should be incremental.* Only the **incremental cash flow** should be considered in project analysis. This implies that any cash inflow or outflow that can be directly or indirectly traced to a project has to be attributed to the project, for purposes of analysis. Less obviously, it also implies that any reduction in cash inflows and outflows that occurs as a consequence of a project should be considered in the course of the analysis.

3. *Cash flows and discount rates should be consistent.* As emphasized in the previous chapter, cash flows and discount rates must be matched up in terms of the investor group that is being analyzed—if the discount rate is a cost of equity, the cash flow has to be a cash flow to equity investors; if the discount rate is the cost of capital, the cash flow has to be a cash flow to the firm. Cash flows and discount rates should also be consistent in terms of how they deal with inflation—if cash flows are nominal, discount rates should be too.

Incremental Cash Flow: This refers to any cash flow, positive or negative, that arises as a consequence of taking a project.

Cash Flows Should Be After Taxes

When a project is expected to generate income, it can also be expected to create a tax liability. The questions of what tax rate to use in assessing this tax liability and how to deal with losses are central to assessing the impact of taxes.

Tax Rate

Let us begin by laying out the choices in terms of tax rates. The *average or effective tax rate,* often reported in financial statements, is the total tax paid as a proportion of the total income generated by a business. The **marginal tax rate** is the tax rate on the next dollar in income that will be generated by the business; it will generally be higher than the average tax rate because of the progressivity in tax schedules. The *statutory tax rate* is the rate specified in the tax rate schedules for a given level of income.

Marginal Tax Rate: The marginal tax rate is the tax rate that the firm will face on the next dollar of taxable income it generates.

In most cases, the income from a project is marginal; that is, it is additional to other income generated by the firm's existing assets and projects. The correct rate to use in estimating tax liability is therefore the marginal tax rate for the firm, which should include taxes at every level—federal, state, and local—on the marginal dollar of income generated.

IN PRACTICE ESTIMATING THE TAX LIABILITY ON PROJECT INCOME—THE BOEING CORPORATION

The Boeing Corporation performed an investment analysis on the Boeing 777 in 1990 and estimated the taxable income for the first 15 years of the project. Boeing reported an average tax rate of 29.6% in its annual report, but a marginal tax rate on income of 36%. Table 8.1 summarizes the tax liability (in millions) incurred by the project each year, as well as the present value of the tax liability at the cost of capital of 12%.

Table 8.1 **PRESENT VALUE OF TAX BENEFITS ON BOEING 777 PROJECT**

Year	Taxable Income	Taxes	PV of Taxes
1	$1,452	$(523)	$(467)
2	2,603	(937)	(747)
3	2,278	(820)	(584)
4	2,523	(908)	(577)
5	2,531	(911)	(517)
6	2,354	(847)	(429)
7	2,574	(927)	(419)
8	3,003	(1,081)	(437)
9	2,590	(932)	(336)
10	1,440	(518)	(167)
11	2,684	(966)	(278)
12	2,967	(1,068)	(274)
13	2,562	(922)	(211)
14	1,831	(659)	(135)
15	2,961	(1,066)	(195)
Sum		(13,087)	(5,773)

As you can see from this table, the project creates a substantial tax liability in both nominal terms ($13.09 billion) and present value terms ($5.77 billion).

How Do Businesses Deal with Different Tax Rates?

Some businesses operate in multiple locales, with different tax rates. For instance, multinational companies generate income in a number of countries, with very different marginal tax rates. Even when they can claim a tax credit in the United States for taxes paid in other countries, the different marginal tax rates raises a question: Which, if any, of the marginal tax rates should be used to compute the tax liability in each period? The answer is an *average* of the marginal tax rates of the different countries in which the project will generate profits, weighted by the profits in each country.

Dealing with Losses

Because both the firm and the project have the potential to generate losses, it is important that we look at all possible combinations and ways to deal with each. The following table summarizes the different scenarios.

Scenario	Project makes	Firm makes	Action
1	losses	losses	Defer tax saving until both profit
2	losses	profits	Take tax savings in year of loss
3	profits	losses	Defer taxes until firm profits
Stand alone	losses	—	Defer tax savings until project profits

The Effect of Noncash Charges

One consequence of dealing with cash flows after taxes is that **noncash charges** can have a significant impact on cash flows, if they affect the tax liability. Some noncash charges reduce the taxable income and the taxes paid by a business. The most important of such charges is depreciation, which, while reducing taxable and net income, does not cause a cash outflow. Consequently, depreciation is added back to net income to arrive at the cash flows on a project.

Noncash Charge: A noncash charge is an accounting expense that reduces income but does not create a cash outflow for the firm.

For projects that generate large depreciation charges, a significant portion of the net present value can be attributed to the tax benefits of depreciation, which can be written as follows:

$$\text{Tax Benefit of Depreciation} = \text{Depreciation*Marginal Tax Rate}$$

While depreciation is similar to other tax deductible expenses in terms of the tax benefit it generates, its impact is more positive because it does not generate a concurrent cash outflow.

Depreciation methods The many different depreciation methods used by firms can be classified broadly into two groups. The first is *straight-line depreciation*, whereby equal amounts of depreciation are claimed each period for the life of the asset. The second group includes *accelerated depreciation methods,* such as double-declining balance depreciation, which results in more depreciation early in the asset life and less in the later years. Because the nominal cumulative depreciation claimed under both methods is the same, the effect of switching from straight line to accelerated depreciation, or vice versa, is generally seen only when the present value of the tax savings is considered. Accelerated depreciation methods provide the tax benefits earlier than straight-line methods, and so the net present value will usually increase with the use of the former.

 IN PRACTICE DEPRECIATION, CASH FLOWS, AND NET PRESENT VALUE—BOEING

Assume that you are evaluating an investment proposal for the manufacture of an executive jet for Boeing Corporation, with the following details:

- The project will require an initial investment of $100 million in plant and equipment; this investment will be depreciated straight line down to a salvage value of $20 million at the end of 10 years.
- The project will generate revenues of $30 million and incur operating expenses (other than depreciation) of $10 million in the first year. These revenues and expenses are expected to grow 5% a year over the remaining nine years of the project.
- The marginal tax rate is 36%.
- The cost of capital is 12%.

The effects of depreciation on the tax liability can be highlighted by comparing the after-tax cash flow and tax liability, in year 1, with and without depreciation, as shown in Table 8.2.

Table 8.2   CASH FLOW WITH AND WITHOUT DEPRECIATION : YEAR 1

	Without Depreciation	**With Depreciation**	**Effect of Depreciation**
Revenues	$30,000,000	$30,000,000	-
−Operating Expenses	10,000,000	10,000,000	-
−Depreciation		8,000,000	8,000,000
=EBIT	20,000,000	12,000,000	(8,000,000)
−Taxes	7,200,000	4,320,000	(2,880,000)
=EBIT (1-t)	12,800,000	7,680,000	(5,120,000)
+Depreciation		8,000,000	8,000,000
=FCFF	12,800,000	15,680,000	2,880,000

The depreciation allowance of $8 million reduces taxes by $2.88 million and increases the after-tax cash flow by the same amount. Not coincidentally, the tax saving amounts to:

$$\text{Tax Savings from Depreciation} = \$8,000,000 * 0.36 = \$2,880,000$$

With the depreciation the same each year for the 10 years of the project, the present value of the depreciation tax benefits can be written as follows:

$$\begin{aligned}\text{Present Value of Tax Savings from Depreciation} &= \$2.88 \text{ million} \\ &\quad *PV(A,12\%,10 \text{ years}) \\ &= \$16.273 \text{ million}\end{aligned}$$

The overall NPV of the project can be estimated based on the initial investment, the annual after-tax cash flows, and the salvage value as in Table 8.3.

Initial Investment in the Project = $100 million

Table 8.3 ANNUAL AFTER-TAX CASH FLOWS ON PROJECT (IN '000s)									
	1	2	3	4	5	6	7	8	9	10
Revenues	$30,000	$31,500	$33,075	$34,729	$36,465	$38,288	$40,203	$42,213	$44,324	$46,540
−Operating Expenses	10,000	10,500	11,025	11,576	12,155	12,763	13,401	14,071	14,775	15,513
−Depreciation	8,000	8,000	8,000	8,000	8,000	8,000	8,000	8,000	8,000	8,000
=EBIT	12,000	13,000	14,050	15,153	16,310	17,526	18,802	20,142	21,549	23,027
−Taxes	4,320	4,680	5,058	5,455	5,872	6,309	6,769	7,251	7,758	8,290
=EBIT (1−t)	7,680	8,320	8,992	9,698	10,438	11,216	12,033	12,891	13,791	14,737
+Depreciation	8,000	8,000	8,000	8,000	8,000	8,000	8,000	8,000	8,000	8,000
=FCFF	15,680	16,320	16,992	17,698	18,438	19,216	20,033	20,891	21,791	22,737
PV of FCFF	14,000	13,010	12,095	11,247	10,462	9,736	9,062	8,437	7,858	7,321

PV of After-Tax Operating Cash Flows = $103.228 million
Salvage Value of Project = $20 million
PV of Salvage Value of Project = $20 mil/$1.12^{10}$ = $6.439 million
NPV of the Project = − 100 million + $103.228 million + $6.439 million
= $9.668 million

Without the depreciation tax benefits of $16.273 million, this project would have had a negative net present value.

 Concept Check

Since the tax benefits from depreciation increase with the tax rate, does it follow that the net present value of the project will increase with the tax rate as well?

 IN PRACTICE   SWITCHING DEPRECIATION METHODS—EFFECT ON NPV

Returning to the executive jet example described above, let us consider the consequences of switching from straight-line to double-declining balance depreciation for the net present value of the project. Double-declining balance depreciation can be estimated by doubling the straight-line rate and applying this rate to the remaining book value of the asset, as shown in Table 8.4. The user is usually given the option to switch to straight-line depreciation, if it provides more depreciation, during the asset life.

Table 8.4 BOOK VALUE AND DEPRECIATION ON ASSET			
Year	Starting Book Value	Depreciation	Ending Book Value
1	$100.00	$20.00	$80.00
2	80.00	16.00	64.00
3	64.00	12.80	51.20
4	51.20	10.24	40.96
5	40.96	8.19	32.77
6	32.77	6.55	26.21
7	26.21	5.24	20.97

(continues)

Table 8.4   (CONTINUED)

Year	Starting Book Value	Depreciation	Ending Book Value
8	20.97	0.97	20.00
9	20.00	-	20.00
10	20.00	-	20.00

Under this accelerated depreciation method, the total nominal depreciation is equal to the nominal depreciation under the straight-line approach, but the timing of the depreciation is different, with more depreciation earlier and less later on.

The present value of the depreciation under both the straight-line and the double-declining balance methods is calculated in Table 8.5.

Table 8.5   PRESENT VALUE OF DEPRECIATION TAX BENEFITS

Year	DDB Depreciation	Tax Savings	PV of DDB Depreciation	SL Depreciation	Tax Savings	PV of SL Depreciation
1	$20.00	$7.20	$6.43	$8.00	$2.88	$2.57
2	16.00	5.76	4.59	8.00	2.88	2.30
3	12.80	4.61	3.28	8.00	2.88	2.05
4	10.24	3.69	2.34	8.00	2.88	1.83
5	8.19	2.95	1.67	8.00	2.88	1.63
6	6.55	2.36	1.20	8.00	2.88	1.46
7	5.24	1.89	0.85	8.00	2.88	1.30
8	0.97	0.35	0.14	8.00	2.88	1.16
9	—	—	—	8.00	2.88	1.04
10	—	—	—	8.00	2.88	0.93
Sum	80.00	28.80	20.51	80.00	28.80	16.27

Although the nominal depreciation and tax savings are the same under both the straight-line and double-declining balance methods, the present value of the tax benefits is greater under the accelerated method:

Increase in PV of Tax Benefits = $20.51 million − $16.27 million = $4.24 million

The overall net present value of the project, which was $9.668 million, will increase by $4.24 million if the depreciation is changed from a straight-line to a double-declining balance.

Exceptions to the rule   There are two exceptions to the rule that switching from straight-line to accelerated depreciation methods results in an increase in the net present value of a project.

1. The first exception arises when the firm is losing money currently and cannot take advantage of the depreciation on the project anyway. If there is a danger that the firm might be unable to carry forward its losses, it might be advantageous to claim as little in depreciation in the early years as possible.

2. The second exception occurs when the marginal tax rate of the decision-making entity is expected to rise substantially in the future, either because the firm has moved

to a higher tax bracket or because tax rates have increased. Since the tax benefit from depreciation increases with the marginal tax rate, this may tilt the balance towards claiming less depreciation in the early years and more in the later periods.

The tradeoff between net income and cash flows   Switching to an accelerated depreciation method increases cash flows on a project at the expense of net income, which will decline in the earlier years as a consequence of the switch. For managers who are concerned about stockholders' reactions to the drop in earnings, this creates quite a conundrum. Many are able to eat their cake and have it too, however, by employing accelerated depreciation methods for tax purposes and straight-line depreciation methods for reporting net income to stockholders.

ACRS and MACRS systems   The 1986 Tax Reform Act essentially laid out specifics of depreciation systems that the Internal Revenue Service views as acceptable. The Modified Accelerated Cost Recovery System (MACRS) classifies assets into classes based on type and industry and specifies the depreciation that can be claimed in each year of an asset's life. Table 8.6 provides the categorization of assets, asset lives, and the methods used to estimate depreciation rates.

Table 8.6   **CLASSIFICATION OF ASSETS**

Type of Asset	Method	Lives (Class)
Property with ADR of 4 years or less, excluding automobiles and light trucks.	Double-declining balance	3-year
Property with ADR of more than 4 years and less than 10 years. Automobiles, light trucks, and R&D property are to be included.	Double-declining balance	5-year
Property with ADR of 10 years or more and less than 16 years, and property without and ADR that is not classified elsewhere are to be included.	Double-declining balance	7-year
Property with ADR of 16 years or more and less than 20 years.	Double-declining balance	10-year
Property with ADR of 20 years or more and less than 25 years.	150% declining balance	15-year
Property with ADR of 25 years or more, other than real property, such as buildings.	Straight-line	27.5-year
Real property (buildings) with ADR greater than 25 years.	Straight-line	31.5-year

The combination of depreciation methods and asset lives can be used to compute the depreciation percentages by year for different assets as shown in Table 8.7.

Table 8.7   **DEPRECIATION RATES FOR PROPERTY**[A]

Recovery Year	3-Year (200% DDB)	5-Year (200% DDB)	7-Year (200% DDB)	10-Year (200% DDB)	15-Year (150% DB)	20-Year (150% DB)
1	33.0%	20.0%	14.3%	10.0%	5.0%	3.8%
2	45.0	32.0	24.5	18.0	9.5	7.2
3	15.0	19.2	17.5	14.4	8.6	6.7
4	7.0	11.5[b]	12.5	11.5	7.7	6.2

(*continues*)

Recovery Year	3-Year (200% DDB)	5-Year (200% DDB)	7-Year (200% DDB)	10-Year (200% DDB)	15-Year (150% DB)	20-Year (150% DB)
				Table 8.7 (*Continued*)		
5		11.5	8.9[b]	9.2[b]	6.9	5.7
6		5.8	8.9	7.4	6.2	5.3
7			8.9	6.6[b]	5.9[b]	4.9
8			4.5	6.6	5.9	4.5[b]
9				6.5	5.9	4.5
10				6.5	5.9	4.5
11				3.3	5.9	4.5
12					5.9	4.5
13					5.9	4.5
14					5.9	4.5
15					5.9	4.5
16					3.0	4.5
17						4.5
18						4.5
19						4.5
20						4.5
21						1.7
Total	100.0	100.0	100.0	100.0	100.0	100.0

[a]Assumes half-year convention applies.
[b]Switch over to straight-line depreciation over remaining useful line.

Finally, the tax law specified limitations on the amount that can be claimed as depreciation in the year in which an asset was acquired or sold, by assuming that personal property, such as machinery, is placed in service at the midpoint of the taxable year in which it is acquired.

 IN PRACTICE   ESTIMATING MACRS DEPRECIATION AND TAX BENEFITS—BOEING

Returning to the executive jet example used in the previous two applications, we can estimate the depreciation using the ACRS tables as shown in Table 8.8.

Table 8.8   MACRS DEPRECIATION TAX BENEFITS FOR BOEING EXECUTIVE JET

Year	MACRS rate (%)	MACRS Depreciation	Tax Savings	PV of MACRS Depreciation	SL Depreciation	Tax Savings	PV of SL Depreciation
1	10.00%	$8.00	$2.88	$2.57	$8.00	$2.88	$2.57
2	18.00	14.40	5.18	4.13	8.00	2.88	2.30
3	14.40	11.52	4.15	2.95	8.00	2.88	2.05
4	11.50	9.20	3.31	2.10	8.00	2.88	1.83
5	9.20	7.36	2.65	1.50	8.00	2.88	1.63
6	7.40	5.92	2.13	1.08	8.00	2.88	1.46
7	6.60	5.28	1.90	0.86	8.00	2.88	1.30
8	6.60	5.28	1.90	0.77	8.00	2.88	1.16
9	6.50	5.20	1.87	0.68	8.00	2.88	1.04
10	6.50	5.20	1.87	0.60	8.00	2.88	0.93
11	3.30	2.64	0.95	0.27	—	—	—
Sum	100.00	80.00	28.80	17.52	80.00	28.80	16.27

Note that the half-year convention leads to an extra year of depreciation on the 10-year asset and that the nominal value of both the depreciation and the tax savings is the same as under straight-line depreciation. The higher depreciation in the earlier years leads to an increase in the present value of the tax savings from $16.27 million to $17.52 million.

Dealing with salvage value   The accounting convention maintains that equipment should be depreciated down to salvage value and that claiming too much depreciation will result in a tax liability when the asset is sold. Although a tax liability is indeed created if an asset is depreciated below salvage value, the present value of this tax liability will be lower than the tax benefits generated by claiming the excess depreciation. Thus, a project will generally gain in terms of net present value if the salvage value is ignored and the maximum depreciation is claimed on the asset. This gain will become even larger if the capital gains tax rate, which applies when the asset is sold, is lower than the marginal tax rate on ordinary income.

   IN PRACTICE   EFFECTS OF IGNORING SALVAGE VALUE ON NPV

In the executive jet example on page 198, the depreciation was stopped when the book value of the equipment reached the salvage value of $20 million. If the equipment had been depreciated down to zero, the project would have claimed more depreciation and higher tax benefits from depreciation as shown in Table 8.9.

Table 8.9   SALVAGE VALUE AND TAX EFFECTS

Year	DDB without Salvage	Tax Savings	PV of DDB without Salvage	DDB with Salvage	Tax Savings	PV with Salvage
1	$20.00	$7.20	$6.43	$20.00	$7.20	$6.43
2	16.00	5.76	4.59	16.00	5.76	4.59
3	12.80	4.61	3.28	12.80	4.61	3.28
4	10.24	3.69	2.34	10.24	3.69	2.34
5	8.19	2.95	1.67	8.19	2.95	1.67
6	6.55	2.36	1.20	6.55	2.36	1.20
7	6.55	2.36	1.07	5.24	1.89	0.85
8	6.55	2.36	0.95	0.97	0.35	0.14
9	6.55	2.36	0.85	—	—	—
10	6.55	2.36	0.76	—	—	—
Sum	100.00	36.00	23.14	80.00	28.80	20.51

Note the switch to straight-line depreciation in year 6, as it allows for a higher amount of depreciation in that year. The higher nominal depreciation ($100 million) leads to a higher tax saving ($36 million) and an increase in the present value of the tax savings from $20.51 million to $23.14 million.

The depreciation of the asset to a book value of zero does create a tax liability when it is salvaged. Even under the most extreme assumption, when the capital gains tax rate is also 36%, the present value effects will be smaller than the gain in depreciation tax benefits.

$$\text{Capital Gains Taxes on Sale of Asset} = (\text{Salvage Value} - \text{Book Value})* \text{Tax Rate}_{\text{cap gains}}$$
$$= (\$20 \text{ million} - \$0)*0.36 = \$7.2 \text{ million}$$
$$\text{Present Value of Capital Gains Taxes} = \$7.2 \text{ million}/1.12^{10}$$
$$= \$2.32 \text{ million}$$

$$\text{Present Value of Depreciation Tax Benefits}$$
$$= \$23.14 \text{ million} - \$20.51 \text{ million}$$
$$= \$2.63 \text{ million}$$
$$\text{Present Value Gain from switch} = \$2.63 \text{ million} - \$2.32 \text{ million}$$
$$= \$0.31 \text{ million}$$

Concept
Check

Estimate the gain from not having salvage if the firm faces a capital gains tax rate of 20% instead of 36%.

To expense or capitalize   In special cases firms have the option of either expensing an item or capitalizing it and depreciating it over time. Drawing on the discussion of accelerated and straight-line depreciation methods, it should be quite clear that the present value of the benefits that will accrue will be much larger from expensing an item rather than depreciating it, *as long as*

- The firm has enough taxable income to set off against the expenses.
- Marginal tax rates are not expected to rise over time.

Again, a distinction must be drawn between what firms do for tax purposes and what they do for reporting purposes. Many firms, wary of showing large drops in net income in those years in which they have these discretionary expenses, will choose to capitalize them for reporting purposes and expense them for tax purposes.

✈ **IN PRACTICE**   EXPENSING VERSUS CAPITALIZING—THE NPV EFFECT

Using the executive jet example once again, assume that Boeing was allowed, under a special provision in the tax code, to expense the entire investment of $100 million, when made. The tax savings from expensing the investment would have been:

Tax Savings from Expensing Investment = $100 million * 0.36 = $36 million

This is already in present value terms and can be compared to the present value of depreciating the $100 million over the 10-year period of $23.14 million. The firm can therefore gain $12.86 million by expensing the investment rather than capitalizing it. This is based, however, on the assumption that Boeing has at least $100 million in taxable income against which it can set off the expense to claim the tax credit.

Concept
Check

How would your answer change if Boeing had to wait until the end of the next taxable year to claim the tax deduction?

Nontax deductible noncash charges   There is a separate category of noncash charges that reduce net income but do not affect taxes. These charges do not create the tax benefits that the tax deductible charges do, but they do depress net income. Examples of these charges include the following.

- *Provisions for future losses:* Often, companies will set aside a portion of current profits to meet losses that are expected in future periods. This might be a prudent practice, but it does not provide a tax deduction for the users.

• *Amortization of goodwill:* When companies acquire other companies, in the context of a purchase of assets at or above their book value, they create an intangible asset called *goodwill,* which is amortized over long periods. While this amortization reduces reported net income, it is not tax deductible and therefore does not affect taxes.

These noncash charges should also be added back to net income to arrive at cash flow, but they provide no tax benefits to the firm using them.

CASH FLOWS SHOULD BE INCREMENTAL

One of the most important principles governing the estimation of cash flows is that only incremental cash flows belong in an investment analysis. An incremental cash flow includes any cash inflow or outflow that is a direct or indirect consequence of taking a project. Although a number of techniques can be used to assess whether an item of cash flow is incremental, one of the most effective ones is to ask the question: *What will happen to this item of cash flow if this project is not taken?* If the answer is that the cash flow will remain unaffected, it is not an incremental cash flow and does not belong in the investment analysis. If the answer is that it will change, the amount of the change should then become part of the analysis.

The incremental cash-flow principle is useful in dealing with a number of different factors that may arise in the context of capital budgeting, including sunk costs, working capital, opportunity costs, allocated costs, and product cannibalization.

Sunk Costs

Some expenses related to a project may be incurred before the project analysis is done. One example would be expenses associated with a test market done to assess the potential market for a product prior to conducting a full-blown investment analysis. Such expenses are called **sunk costs.** Since they will not be recovered if the project is rejected, sunk costs are not incremental and therefore should not be considered as part of the investment analysis. This contrasts with their treatment in accounting statements, which do not distinguish between expenses that have already been incurred and expenses that are still to be incurred.

Sunk Costs: Any expense that has been incurred already, and cannot be recovered if the project is not taken, is a sunk cost.

One category of expenses that consistently falls into the sunk cost column in project analysis is research and development, which occurs well before a product is even considered for introduction. Firms that spend large amounts on research and development, such as Merck and Intel, have struggled to come to terms with the fact that the analysis of these expenses generally occur after the fact, when little can be done about them.

❏ Concept Check

Would your analysis of test market expenses change if the research could be sold to a competitor for a reasonable price?

✈ **IN PRACTICE** SUNK COSTS IN A PROJECT—BOEING

When Boeing did the investment analysis on the Boeing 777 in 1990, it had already expended $2 billion in research and development expenses on the plane. It expected to incur an additional $4 billion in new investments before production could be started. Cumulatively, the total investment on the project was expected to amount to $6 billion.

From the viewpoint of an accounting analysis of this project, no distinction will be made between the $2 billion already expended and the $4 billion still to be expended. From an incremental cash-flow standpoint, however, the money spent on research and development prior to this analysis is a sunk cost and will not be recovered if the project is rejected. Thus, as long as the present value of the expected operating cash flows of the project exceeds the investment still to be made ($4 billion), the project should be accepted. For instance, if the present value of the operating cash flows over the project life amounts to $ 4.5 billion, this project has a positive net present value of $500 million. The fact that this net present value does not cover the sunk cost does not impact the investment decision on the project. In fact, if it had been factored in, and the project had been rejected, the firm would have actually turned away an opportunity to reduce its "losses" on the project from $2 billion to $1.5 billion.

Who Will Pay the Sunk Costs?

Although sunk costs should not be treated as part of investment analysis, a firm does need to cover its sunk costs over time or it will cease to exist. Consider, for example, a firm like McDonald's, which expends considerable resources in test marketing products before introducing them. Assume, on the ill-fated McLean Deluxe (the low-fat hamburger introduced in 1990), that the test market expenses amounted to $30 million and that the net present value of the project, analyzed after the test market, amounted to $20 million. On this basis, the project should be taken. If this pattern holds for every project McDonald's takes on, however, it will collapse under the weight of its test marketing expenses. To be successful, the *cumulated* net present value of its successful projects will have to exceed the *cumulated* test marketing expenses on both its successful and unsuccessful products.

Working Capital

Another item that affects cash flows but does not affect accounting income is working capital, or, more precisely, changes in working capital. According to the accounting definition, *working capital* is the difference between current assets and current liabilities. Current assets generally include inventory, accounts receivable, and cash, whereas current liabilities include accounts payable, taxes payable, and the current portion of long-term debt. From the viewpoint of project analysis, we can eliminate the current portion of long-term debt on two grounds. First, it will be considered as part of the overall financing for the project, and considering it as part of working capital will count it twice. Second, the objective in the analysis is to estimate future working capital needs, and the current portion of long-term debt is generally an unpredictable and highly variable component of working capital. Since we are attempting to estimate the effect of changes on cash flows, we can also eliminate cash from the definition,[1] reducing working capital to

---

[1]It would be difficult to argue that an increase in the cash balance is a cash outflow and that a decrease in the cash balance is a cash inflow. Furthermore, firms no longer need to keep large amounts of idle cash, and they can earn interest on their cash balances. It would therefore be inappropriate, in these cases, to consider changes in cash balances in calculating cash flows.

> Noncash Working Capital = (Inventory + Accounts Receivable) − (Accounts Payable + Taxes Payable)

Any investment in **noncash working capital** cannot be used elsewhere and is therefore similar to an investment in land or buildings or equipment. Thus, it has to be viewed as a cash outflow when it is made. Any increase in the noncash working capital will result in further cash outflow since more money is tied up in those assets, whereas a decrease in the noncash working capital can be viewed as a release of cash, or a cash inflow.

Noncash Working Capital: This is the difference between current assets, not including cash, and current liabilities (not including the current portion of long-term debt).

Cash Needed for Day-to-Day Operations

There is one exception to the rule that only noncash working capital needs should be considered in investment analysis. If a business needs a ready cash balance to run its day-to-day operations, this cash balance should be considered as part of working capital because

- It is a requirement for the operations of the business.
- It does not earn interest for the business.

Conversely, any cash that is not required for the day-to-day operations of the business or earns interest for the business should not be considered part of working capital for purposes of estimating cash flows.

Estimating net working capital needs for a project Because changes in working capital affect cash flows, it is important that the working capital requirements on every project be analyzed and factored into the cash flows. Generally speaking, the working capital requirements on a project will be a function of the expected growth in revenues and expenses on that project, although the exact linkage will vary from business to business. Some businesses, such as retailing, will require high working capital, whereas service businesses might be able to sustain themselves with very little. In addition, the following factors will determine working capital requirements:

- *Credit policy:* Businesses that offer more liberal credit tend to have larger working capital requirements than those that operate on cash.
- *Pricing policy:* Businesses that have low profit margins and high turnover typically have lower working capital requirements, relative to revenue, than businesses that operate with high profit margins and low turnover.
- *Product choice:* Businesses that offer a much wider array of products generally have to maintain much larger inventories, and thus have higher working capital requirements, than those that offer a limited array of products
- *Size and credit standing of the business:* Because working capital requirements are also affected by the capacity to finance current assets with accounts payable, those businesses that have the capacity to get generous credit terms from their suppliers,

either because of their size or their good credit history, typically have lower working capital requirements than firms that are in financial trouble.

It should be pointed out that different projects within the same business can have different working capital requirements and that the requirements themselves may be a function of how well working capital is managed. In Chapter 14, we will examine some of the ways in which the cash drain from working capital can be minimized over time.

Building working capital changes into cash flows   Some working capital investments may need to be made initially, before the project starts generating cash flows. For instance, a retail business has to invest in an inventory before it opens its doors for business. This is the *initial working capital investment,* and it creates a negative cash flow. This working capital requirement may change over time, for a number of reasons—the project may get larger over time, or the working capital needs may shift as the project matures. Any increases in working capital generate cash outflows, whereas decreases in working capital generate cash inflows. Finally, the entire working capital investment over the life of the project will have to be evaluated for potential salvage value at the end of the project's life, creating a positive cash flow. In estimating this salvage value, a contrast has to be drawn between working capital investments and investments in fixed assets. While the fixed assets investments are made during the early years of a project and depreciate in value over time as they age, working capital investments are renewed constantly. Thus, the working capital at the end of the project life, whether it takes the form of inventory or accounts receivable, is recent and should retain much more of its value than fixed assets. In many investment analyses, it is assumed that 100% of the working capital is salvaged at the end of the project life.

□ Concept
Check

> What will happen to the net present value of a project if working capital needs are factored into the cash flows but the salvage value of working capital is ignored?

 IN PRACTICE   ESTIMATING WORKING CAPITAL REQUIREMENTS FOR A PROJECT—THE HOME DEPOT

The Home Depot is considering a new store opening, with the following characteristics.

- The store will be approximately 85,000 square feet and will require an initial investment of $11 million. An additional investment of $1.5 million will be needed at the end of year 5. There is an estimated salvage value of $8.5 million at the end of the project life of 10 years.

- The store will be approximately 85,000 square feet and will generate $30 million in sales in the first year, and these sales are expected to grow 5% a year over the 10-year life of the project.

- The store is expected to generate the after-tax operating income and depreciation depicted in Table 8.10 for the 10-year life.

- The net working capital requirements, based on companywide figures in the latest fiscal year, are expected to be 8% of revenues and to be entirely salvageable at the end of the 10 years. The working capital investments are assumed to be made at the beginning of each year.

- The cost of capital is 12.5%.

We begin by estimating working capital requirements over the 10-year life of the project, based on 8% of the expected revenue change in each year (Table 8.11).

Table 8.10 OPERATING INCOME AND DEPRECIATION ON THE HOME DEPOT STORE

Year	EBIT (1 − t)	Depreciation
1	$212,500	$532,000
2	355,000	720,000
3	512,000	576,000
4	800,000	460,000
5	1,150,000	368,000
6	1,750,000	296,000
7	2,330,000	264,000
8	2,700,000	260,000
9	3,130,000	260,000
10	3,350,000	260,000

Table 8.11 WORKING CAPITAL REQUIREMENTS—THE HOME DEPOT STORE

Year	Revenues	Change in Revenues	Change in WC	Total WC
1	$30,000,000	$30,000,000	$2,400,000	$2,400,000
2	31,500,000	1,500,000	120,000	2,520,000
3	33,075,000	1,575,000	126,000	2,646,000
4	34,728,750	1,653,750	132,300	2,778,300
5	36,465,188	1,736,438	138,915	2,917,215
6	38,288,447	1,823,259	145,861	3,063,076
7	40,202,869	1,914,422	153,154	3,216,230
8	42,213,013	2,010,143	160,811	3,377,041
9	44,323,663	2,110,651	168,852	3,545,893
10	46,539,846	2,216,183	177,295	3,723,188

The changes in working capital occur at the beginning of each year. Therefore, the investment of $2.4 million for year 1 is assumed to be made at the beginning of the first year; the investment of $120,000 for year 2 is assumed to be made at the beginning of the second year, and so on.

Incorporating the investment needs, the operating income projections, and the working capital requirements, we can estimate the after-tax cash flow to the firm as follows:

After-tax Cash Flow to Firm = EBIT (1 - t) + Depreciation − Capital Expenditures − Change in Working Capital

The after-tax cash flow for the project for each year of the project is shown in Table 8.12.

Note that the cash flow in year 10 includes the salvage of the entire working capital [$3,723,188] and capital investments [$8,500,000].

The net present value of this project can be estimated by discounting the cash flows back at the cost of capital of 12.5% (Table 8.13).

Table 8.12 AFTER-TAX CASH FLOWS ON PROJECT—THE HOME DEPOT STORE

Year	Capital Investment	EBIT (1-t)	Depreciation	Change in WC	ATCF
0	$(11,000,000)	0	0	$(2,400,000)	$(13,400,000)
1		212,500	532,000	(120,000)	624,500
2		355,000	720,000	(126,000)	949,000
3		512,000	576,000	(132,300)	955,700
4		800,000	460,000	(138,915)	1,121,085
5	(1,500,000)	1,150,000	368,000	(145,861)	(127,861)
6		1,750,000	296,000	(153,154)	1,892,846
7		2,330,000	264,000	(160,811)	2,433,189
8		2,700,000	260,000	(168,852)	2,791,148
9		3,130,000	260,000	(177,295)	3,212,705
10	8,500,000	3,350,000	260,000	3,723,188	15,833,188

Table 8.13 PRESENT VALUE OF ATCF—THE HOME DEPOT STORE

Year	ATCF	PV of ATCF
0	$(13,400,000)	$(13,400,000)
1	624,500	555,111
2	949,000	749,827
3	955,700	671,219
4	1,121,085	699,888
5	(127,861)	(70,954)
6	1,892,846	933,685
7	2,433,189	1,066,862
8	2,791,148	1,087,834
9	3,212,705	1,113,008
10	15,833,188	4,875,769
	NPV =	$(1,717,752)

The net present value of this store is −$1.718 million. Based on the net present value, the store should not be opened.

The consequences of ignoring working capital needs Failing to consider working capital needs in investment analysis can have two serious consequences.

- Since working capital tends to increase during the initial years of growth on a project, and these increases cause cash outflows, not including working capital needs in an analysis will lead to an overestimation of the after-tax cash flows during these years.
- Even if working capital is salvaged fully at the end of the project lifetime, the present value of the cash flows created by working capital changes will be negative. Consequently, the net present value of a project will be overstated if working capital is not included in the analysis. Some projects that show positive net present values when working capital is ignored may become negative net present value projects when working capital needs are incorporated.

IN PRACTICE   EFFECTS OF IGNORING WORKING CAPITAL ON NPV

Consider again the Home Depot Store analysis above. Assume that working capital had been mistakenly ignored in the analysis. The after-tax cash flows would then have been calculated as shown in Table 8.14.

Table 8.14   ATCF ON PROJECT WITHOUT WORKING CAPITAL REQUIREMENTS

Year	Capital Investment	EBIT (1 -*t*)	Depreciation	ATCF	PV of ATCF
0	$(11,000,000)	0	0	$(11,000,000)	$(11,000,000)
1		$212,500	$532,000	$744,500	$661,778
2		355,000	720,000	1,075,000	849,383
3		512,000	576,000	1,088,000	764,137
4		800,000	460,000	1,260,000	786,612
5	(1,500,000)	1,150,000	368,000	18,000	9,989
6		1,750,000	296,000	2,046,000	1,009,231
7		2,330,000	264,000	2,594,000	1,137,371
8		2,700,000	260,000	2,960,000	1,153,643
9		3,130,000	260,000	3,390,000	1,174,430
10	8,500,000	3,350,000	260,000	12,110,000	3,729,228
				NPV =	$275,801

Note that the after-tax cash flows are higher in every year, other than year 10, as a consequence of ignoring working capital. The after-tax cash flow in year 10 is lower because it does not include the salvage value of working capital. The net present value of the project, which was negative with the working capital needs incorporated into cash flows, is now positive. The shift can be traced directly to the present value impact of the working capital changes, as shown in Table 8.15.

Table 8.15   PRESENT VALUE OF WORKING CAPITAL CHANGES ON PROJECT

Year	Change in WC	PV of WC Change
0	$(2,400,000.00)	$(2,400,000.00)
1	(120,000.00)	(106,666.67)
2	(126,000.00)	(99,555.56)
3	(132,300.00)	(92,918.52)
4	(138,915.00)	(86,723.95)
5	(145,860.75)	(80,942.35)
6	(153,153.79)	(75,546.20)
7	(160,811.48)	(70,509.78)
8	(168,852.05)	(65,809.13)
9	(177,294.65)	(61,421.86)
10	3,723,187.72	1,146,541.31
	PV of WC Changes =	(1,993,552.70)

Thus, the failure to consider working capital changes inflated the net present value by $1,993,553.

Opportunity Costs

In many of the project analyses that we have presented in this chapter, we have assumed that the resources needed for a project are newly acquired; this includes not only the building and the equipment, but also the personnel needed to get the project going. For most businesses considering new projects, this is an unrealistic assumption, for many of the resources used on these projects are already part of the business and will just be transferred to the new project. When a business uses such resources, there is the potential for an **opportunity cost**—the cost created for the rest of the business as a consequence of this project. This opportunity cost may be a significant portion of the total investment needed on a project.

Opportunity Cost: This is the cost assigned to a project resource that is already owned by the firm. It is based on the next best alternative use.

A general framework for analyzing opportunity costs   The general framework for analyzing opportunity costs begins by asking the question, "Is there any other use for this resource right now?" For many resources, there will be an alternative use if the project being analyzed is not taken.

- The resource might be rented out, in which case the rental revenue is the opportunity lost by taking this project. For example, if the project is considering the use of a vacant building owned by the business already, the potential revenue from renting out this building to an outsider will be the opportunity cost.
- The resource could be sold, in which case the sales price, net of any tax liability and lost depreciation tax benefits, would be the opportunity cost from taking this project.
- The resource might be used elsewhere in the firm, in which case the cost of replacing the resource is considered the opportunity cost. Thus, the transfer of experienced employees from established divisions to a new project creates a cost to these divisions, which has to be factored into the decision making.

Sometimes, decision makers have to decide whether the opportunity cost will be estimated based on the lost rental revenue, the foregone sales price, or the cost of replacing the resource. When such a choice has to be made, it is the highest of the costs—that is, the best alternative foregone—that should be considered as an opportunity cost.

 IN PRACTICE   ESTIMATING THE OPPORTUNITY COST FOR A RESOURCE WITH A CURRENT ALTERNATIVE

Working again with the Home Depot analysis, assume that the new store being considered will use the following resources already owned by the company:

- Two experienced managers, working at another established Home Depot store, will be transferred to this store. They will be replaced by their immediate subordinates at that store, but the shift is expected to incur an additional salary expenditure of $100,000 a year for the next three years as a consequence.
- Two trucks, currently owned but not used by another Home Depot store, will be moved to the new store. These trucks, which collectively have a book value of $25,000, are estimated to have a collective market value of $30,000. If the new store is not opened, the company plans to sell these trucks. (For purposes of simplicity, assume that these trucks are being depreciated straight line to a salvage value of zero and have a remaining depreciable life of five years. Also assume that the capital gains tax rate is 20%.)

The opportunity cost of transferring the two managers from another store to the new store lies in the additional salary expenditure that will be incurred as a consequence:

$$
\begin{aligned}
\text{Additional Salary Expenditure per year} &= \$100{,}000 \\
\text{After--tax Additional Salary Expenditure per year} &= \$100{,}000(1 - .36) \\
&= \$64{,}000 \\
\text{PV of After--tax Salary Expenditures for 3 years} &= \$64{,}000 \\
&\quad *PV\,(A, 12.5\%, 3 \text{ years}) \\
&= \$152{,}406
\end{aligned}
$$

With regard to the second resource—the company's trucks—if this project is taken, the opportunity to sell the trucks at the market value of $30,000 will clearly be lost. Such a sale will expose the firm to capital gains taxes, however, since the market value exceeds the book value:

$$
\begin{aligned}
\text{Capital Gains Taxes on Sale} &= (\text{Market Value} - \text{Book Value}) \\
* \text{Capital Gains Tax Rate} &= (\$30{,}000 - \$25{,}000) * 0.20 = \$1{,}000
\end{aligned}
$$

The sale will also lead to a loss of the tax benefits from depreciation that could have been claimed on the trucks. Since the depreciation method is straight line, and the remaining depreciable life is five years:

$$
\begin{aligned}
\text{Depreciation Allowance per year} &= \text{Book Value/Remaining Life} \\
&= \$25{,}000/5 = \$5{,}000 \\
\text{Tax Benefit per year} &= \text{Depreciation Allowance} * \text{Ordinary Tax Rate} \\
&= \$5{,}000 * 0.36 \\
&= \$1{,}800 \\
\text{PV of Tax Benefits over 5 years} &= \text{Tax Benefit} * PV\,(A, 12.5\%, 5 \text{ years}) \\
&= \$6{,}409
\end{aligned}
$$

Netting the capital gains tax and the lost tax benefits from the sale price provides an estimate of the net opportunity cost:

$$
\begin{aligned}
\text{Net Opportunity Cost of Trucks} &= \text{Sale Price} - \text{Capital Gains Tax} \\
&\quad - \text{PV of Depreciation tax} \\
\text{Benefits} &= \$30{,}000 - \$1{,}000 - \$6{,}409 = \$22{,}591
\end{aligned}
$$

The opportunity costs estimated for the two transferred managers ($152,406) and the trucks ($22,591) are in present value terms and can be added on to the initial investment in the store—$11 million for capital investments and $2.4 million for working capital investment—and the net present value from page 210 can be reestimated, as shown in Table 8.16.

Table 8.16   **NET PRESENT VALUE WITH OPPORTUNITY COSTS**

Year	ATCF	PV of ATCF
0	$(13,574,997)	$(13,574,997)
1	624,500	555,111
2	949,000	749,827
3	955,700	671,219
4	1,121,085	699,888
5	(127,861)	(70,954)
6	1,892,846	933,684
7	2,433,189	1,066,862
8	2,791,148	1,087,834
9	3,212,705	1,113,008
10	15,833,188	4,875,769
	NPV =	(1,892,749)

The net present value becomes more negative.

   The cash flows associated with the opportunity costs could alternatively have been reflected in the years in which they occurred. Thus, the $100,000 in additional salary expenses could have been added to the operating expenses of the store in each of the first three years and the depreciation on the truck added on to the store depreciation each year for the first five years. As Table 8.17 indicates, this approach would yield the same net present value and would have clearly been the appropriate approach if the internal rate of return were to be calculated.

Table 8.17   **NET PRESENT VALUE WITH OPPORTUNITY COSTS—ALTERNATE APPROACH**

Year	ATCF	PV of ATCF
0	($13,429,000)	($13,429,000)
1	562,300	499,822
2	886,800	700,681
3	893,500	627,534
4	1,122,885	701,012
5	($126,061)	($69,955)
6	1,892,846	933,684
7	2,433,189	1,066,862
8	2,791,148	1,087,834
9	3,212,705	1,113,008
10	15,833,188	4,875,769
	NPV =	($1,892,749)
	IRR =	10.28%

Note that this net present value and IRR both confirm our earlier finding—this store should not be opened.

Resources with no current alternative use   In some cases, a resource that is being considered for use in a project will have no current alternative use, but the business will have to forgo alternative uses in the future. One example would be **excess capacity** on a machine or a computer. Most firms do not have the capacity or the willingness to lease or sell excess capacity, but using it now for a new product may cause the businesses to run out of capacity much earlier than otherwise, leading to one of two costs:

Excess Capacity: This is the difference between the capacity available on a resource and the capacity in use.

- New capacity will have to be bought or built when capacity runs out, in which case the opportunity cost will be the higher cost in present value terms of doing this earlier rather than later.
- Production will have to be cut back on one of the product lines, leading to a loss in cash flows that would have been generated by the lost sales.

Again, this choice is not random, for the logical action to take is the one that leads to the lower cost, in present value terms, for the firm. Thus, if it is cheaper to lose sales rather than build new capacity, the opportunity cost for the project being considered should be based on the lost sales.

This approach to estimating opportunity cost for excess capacity has to be contrasted with the conventional accounting approach of allocating a portion of the book value of the capacity to the new project. Because this allocation has no relationship with the cash flows, it is meaningless as an opportunity cost.

Concept Check

Is the accounting approach to dealing with excess capacity a more conservative way of dealing with the issue—that is, will it always lead to a higher cost than using the cash-flow approach described in this section? Why or why not?

Framework for analyzing excess capacity   A general framework for pricing excess capacity for purposes of investment analysis asks three questions:

1.   If the new project is not taken, when will the firm run out of capacity on the equipment or space that is being evaluated?
2.   If the new project is taken, when will the firm run out of capacity on the equipment or space that is being evaluated? Presumably, with the new project using up some of the excess capacity, the firm will run out of capacity sooner than it would have otherwise.
3.   What will the firm do when it does run out of capacity? The firm has two choices:

- It can cut back on production of the less profitable product line and make less profits than it would have without a capacity constraint. In this case, the opportunity cost is the present value of the cash flows lost as a consequence.
- It can buy or build new capacity, in which case the opportunity cost is the difference in present value between investing earlier rather than later.

To illustrate, suppose that a food processing firm is considering using excess capacity in an existing cereal plant to manufacture a new brand of cereal called Cinnamon Bran. The current capacity of the plant is for 1 million boxes. In addition, you have the following information.

- The sales in units of the existing brand, Raisin Bran, is currently 500,000 units, and unit sales are expected to grow 5% a year. The current sales price per unit is $3, and the variable cost per unit is $2; both are expected to grow 3% a year.

- The sales in units of the new brand, Cinnamon Bran, is expected to be 300,000 units in year 1, and unit sales are expected to grow 10% a year. The expected sales price per unit is $3.25, and the variable cost per unit is $2.00; both are expected to grow 3% a year.

- The project analysis for Cinnamon Bran assumes a lifetime of 15 years for the brand.

- The tax rate is 40%.

- If the firm decides to build a new plant, the minimum economic size is 1 million units. The cost of building such a plant is $5 million currently, and these costs are expected to increase 3% a year. The plant will have a depreciable life of 25 years, and the depreciation method is straight line.

- The cost of capital is 11%.

Table 8.18 examines capacity usage with and without Cinnamon Bran.

Table 8.18   LOST SALES FROM CAPACITY CONSTRAINT

Year	Raisin Bran (in units)	Cinnamon Bran (in units)	Total Usage	Excess/ Shortfall Capacity	Lost Sales in Units	Lost AT Profit per Unit	Lost AT Profit in Dollars	Lost AT Profit in PV $
1	525,000	300,000	825,000	175,000				
2	551,250	330,000	881,250	118,750				
3	578,813	363,000	941,813	58,188				
4	607,753	399,300	1,007,053	−7,053	7,053	$0.68	$4,763,01	$3,137.54
5	638,141	439,230	1,077,371	−77,371	77,371	0.70	53,816.36	31,937.39
6	670,048	483,153	1,153,201	−153,201	153,201	0.72	109,757.87	58,681.04
7	703,550	531,468	1,235,019	−235,019	235,019	0.74	173,425.87	83,532.03
8	738,728	584,615	1,323,343	−323,343	323,343	0.76	245,760.63	106,642.05
9	775,664	643,077	1,418,741	−418,741	418,741	0.78	327,817.02	128,151.79
10	814,447	707,384	1,521,832	−521,832	521,832	0.81	420,778.84	148,191.78
11	855,170	778,123	1,633,292	−633,292	633,292	0.83	525,974.89	166,883.06
12	897,928	855,935	1,753,863	−753,863	753,863	0.86	644,897.18	184,337.94
13	942,825	941,529	1,884,353	−884,353	884,353	0.88	779,221.39	200,660.62
14	989,966	1,035,681	2,025,647	−1,025,647	1,025,647	0.91	930,830.02	215,947.75
15	1,039,464	1,139,250	2,178,714	−1,178,714	1,178,714	0.93	1,101,838.42	230,289.02
								1,558,392.01

The lost profit per unit is presented in after-tax terms. The analysis can be broken down as follows:

- Without the production of Cinnamon Bran, the firm will run out of capacity in year 15.
- If Cinnamon Bran is introduced, the firm will run out of capacity in year 4.
- When the firm runs out of capacity, it has two options. The first option is to cut back on production on the less profitable Raisin Bran from years 4 to 15, leading to a present value of lost after-tax cash flows of $1.558 million. The second option is to build new capacity in year 4 instead of in year 15.

Cost of Building Capacity in year 4 = $5 million * 1.03^4 = $5.63 million
Cost of Building Capacity in year 15 = $5 million * 1.03^{15} = $ 7.79 million

$$\text{Difference in PV} = \frac{\$5.63 \text{ mil}}{(1.11)^4} - \frac{\$7.79 \text{ mil}}{(1.11)^{15}} = \$2.09 \text{ million}$$

If the investment is made earlier, there will be additional depreciation amounting to $225,102 ($5.63 million/25 years) each year, leading to

$$\text{PV of Tax Benefits} = \frac{\$225,102*0.4*PV(A,11\%,11 \text{ years})}{(1.11)^4} = \$0.37 \text{ mil}$$

Net Cost of Building Early = $2.09 million − $0.37 million = $1.72 mil

- The cost that should be assigned to the excess capacity is therefore $ 1.558 million, the less expensive of the two options. This cost has to be compared to the benefits that will accrue from the production of Cinnamon Bran, leading to the after-tax cash flows and net present value presented in Table 8.19.

Table 8.19 **AFTER-TAX CASH FLOWS ON CINNAMON BRAN PROJECT**

Year	Initial Investment	Cinnamon Bran (in units)	Profit per Unit	BTCF	ATCF	PV of ATCF
0	$(1,558,392)					$(1,558,392)
1		300,000	$1.29	$386,250	$231,750	208,784
2		330,000	1.33	437,621	262,573	213,110
3		363,000	1.37	495,825	297,495	217,526
4		399,300	1.41	561,770	337,062	222,033
5		439,230	1.45	636,485	381,891	226,634
6		483,153	1.49	721,137	432,682	231,330
7		531,468	1.54	817,049	490,229	236,123
8		584,615	1.58	925,716	555,430	241,016
9		643,077	1.63	1,048,836	629,302	246,010
10		707,384	1.68	1,188,332	712,999	251,107
11		778,123	1.73	1,346,380	807,828	256,310
12		855,935	1.78	1,525,448	915,269	261,621
13		941,529	1.84	1,728,333	1,037,000	267,042
14		1,035,681	1.89	1,958,201	1,174,921	272,576
15		1,139,250	1.95	2,218,642	1,331,185	278,223
					NPV =	2,071,052

The net present value of introducing Cinnamon Bran is $2.071 million. Thus, in spite of the charge for excess capacity usage, the firm should introduce Cinnamon Bran as a new product.

 Concept Check

Of the two options—cutting back on sales versus building new capacity—which one will become more attractive if the project life for Cinnamon Bran were increased? Why?

Allocated Costs

Another accounting device created to ensure that every part of a business bears its fair share of costs is *allocation,* whereby costs that are not directly traceable to revenues generated by individual products or divisions are charged across these units, based on revenues, profits, or assets. Although the purposes of such allocations may be rational, their effect on investment analyses have to be viewed in terms of whether they create "incremental" cash flows. An **allocated cost** that will exist with or without the project being analyzed does not belong in the investment analysis.

Allocated Cost: This is a cost that cannot be directly traced to business units in a firm. Instead, it is charged to business units based on other observable measures.

Any increase in administrative or staff costs that can be traced to the project is an incremental cost and belongs in the analysis. One way to estimate the incremental component of these costs is to break them down on the basis of whether they are fixed or variable, and, if they are variable, what they are a function of. Thus, a portion of administrative costs may be related to revenue, and the revenue projections of a new project can be used to estimate the administrative costs to be assigned to it.

To illustrate, assume that you are analyzing a project for a retail firm with general and administrative (G&A) costs currently of $600,000 a year. The firm has five stores, and the new project will create a sixth store. The G&A costs are allocated evenly across the stores; with five stores, the allocation to each store will be $120,000. The firm is considering opening a new store; with six stores, the allocation of G&A expenses to each store will be $100,000. In this case, assigning a cost of $100,000 for general and administrative costs to the new store in the investment analysis would be a mistake, since it is not an incremental cost. The total G&A cost will be $600,000, whether or not the project is taken.

Now assume that all the facts remain unchanged except for one: the total general and administrative costs are expected to increase from $600,000 to $660,000 as a consequence of the new store. Each store is still allocated an equal amount; the new store will be allocated one-sixth of the total costs, or $110,000. In this case, the allocated cost of $110,000 should not be considered in the investment analysis for the new store. The *incremental* cost of $60,000 [$660,000−$600,000], however, should be considered as part of the analysis.

Who will pay for headquarters?   As in the case of sunk costs, the right thing to do in project analysis (i.e., considering only direct incremental costs) may not add up to create a firm that is financially healthy. Thus, if a retail chain like the Home Depot does not require any individual store that it analyzes to cover the allocated costs of general administrative expenses, it is difficult to see how these costs will be covered at the level of the firm. Assuming that these general administrative costs serve a purpose, which otherwise would have to be borne by each store, and that there is a positive relationship between the magnitude of these costs and the number of stores, it seems reasonable to argue that the firm should estimate a fixed charge for these costs that every new store has to cover, even though this cost may not occur immediately or as a direct consequence of the new store.

 IN PRACTICE ESTIMATING ALLOCATION CHARGE FOR A NEW PROJECT—THE HOME DEPOT

In 1993, the Home Depot had total general and administrative expenses of $185 million and 264 stores, resulting in expenses of $700,758 per store. The new store analyzed in the prior example was allocated this amount in general and administrative costs, for purposes of investment analysis.

- Assume that 30% of the general and administrative costs for the Home Depot are fixed, that 40% are a function of the number of stores open, and 30% are a function of total revenues.

- In 1993, the Home Depot had total revenues of $9,238 million.

Using this information, we can analyze the general and administrative costs that should be charged to the new store as follows:

Portion of G & A Costs	Allocation Method	Allocation to New Store
Fixed Costs	No allocation	$0.00
Function of Store Number	Number of Stores	$185 million * 0.40* (1/265) = $279,245
Function of Revenues	Proportion of Revenues	$185 million * 0.30 * (30/9238) = $180,234
Total Allocated Costs		= $279,245 + $180,234 = $459,479

Note that the new store has expected revenues of $30 million. The allocation of $459,479 is the amount that should be charged to the new store as part of the cash outflows. Similar analyses can be done on other costs that are not directly related to the new store, such as advertising costs.

 Concept Check

Under what conditions would you not allocate any G&A cost to this new store?

Product Cannibalization

Product cannibalization refers to the phenomenon whereby a new product introduced by a firm competes with and reduces sales of the firm's existing products. On one level, it can be argued that this is a negative incremental effect of the new product, and the lost cash flows or profits from the existing products should be treated as costs in analyzing whether or not to introduce the product. Doing so introduces the possibility that the new product will be rejected, however. If this happens, and a competitor now exploits the opening to introduce a product that fills the niche that the new product would have and consequently erodes the sales of the firm's existing products, the worst of all scenarios is created—the firm loses sales to a competitor rather than to itself.

Product Cannibalization: These are sales generated by one product, which come at the expense of other products manufactured by the same firm.

Thus, the decision whether or not to build in the lost sales created by product cannibalization will depend on the potential for a competitor to introduce a close substitute to the new product being considered. Two extreme possibilities exist: the first is that close substitutes will be offered almost instantaneously by competitors; the second is that substitutes cannot be offered.

- If the business in which the firm operates is extremely competitive and there are no barriers to entry, it can be assumed that the product cannibalization will occur anyway, and the costs associated with it have no place in an incremental cash-flow analysis. For example, in considering whether to introduce a new brand of cereal, a company like Kellogg's can reasonably ignore the expected product cannibalization that will occur because of the competitive nature of the cereal business and the ease with which Post or General Foods could introduce a close substitute. Similarly, it would not make sense for Compaq to consider the product cannibalization that would occur as a consequence of introducing a Pentium notebook PC. It can be reasonably assumed that a competitor, say IBM or Dell, would create the lost sales anyway with their versions of the same product if Compaq did not introduce the product.

- If a competitor cannot introduce a substitute, because of legal restrictions such as patents, for example, the cash flows lost as a consequence of product cannibalization belong in the investment analysis, at least for the period of the patent protection. For example, Glaxo, which owns the rights to Zantac, the top selling ulcer drug, should consider the potential lost sales from introducing a new and perhaps even better ulcer drug in deciding whether and when to introduce it to the market.

In most cases, there will be some barriers to entry, ensuring that a competitor will either introduce an imperfect substitute, leading to much smaller erosion in existing product sales, or that a competitor will not introduce a substitute for some period of time, leading to a much later erosion in existing product sales. In this case, an intermediate solution, whereby *some* of the product cannibalization costs are considered, may be appropriate. Note that brand-name loyalty is one potential barrier to entry. Firms with stronger brand-name loyalty should therefore factor into their investment analysis more of the cost of lost sales from existing products as a consequence of a new product introduction.

 IN PRACTICE ESTIMATING THE COSTS OF PRODUCT CANNIBALIZATION—THE HOME DEPOT

In the Home Depot store analysis, assume that 25% of the sales in the new store will be drawn from another Home Depot store 15 miles away and that the lost profits attributable to these sales have already been factored into the after-tax profits shown on page 209. Table 8.20 summarizes the after-tax operating income prior to the adjustment for lost sales, the adjustment made to that income to reflect the sales lost in the nearby store, and the adjusted after-tax operating income used in the investment analysis.

Table 8.20   **EBIT AND ADJUSTED EBIT FOR THE HOME DEPOT**

Year	EBIT$(1-t)$ Unadjusted	EBIT$(1-t)$ Lost Sales	EBIT$(1-t)$ Adjusted
0			$ -
1	$283,333	$70,833	$212,500
2	473,333	118,333	355,000
3	682,667	170,667	512,000
4	1,066,667	266,667	800,000
5	1,533,333	383,333	1,150,000
6	2,333,333	583,333	1,750,000
7	3,106,667	776,667	2,330,000
8	3,600,000	900,000	2,700,000
9	4,173,333	1,043,333	3,130,000
10	4,466,667	1,116,667	3,350,000

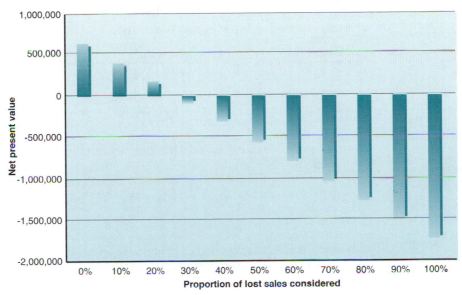

Figure 8.1   NPV and profits from lost sales

As you can see, the unadjusted estimate of $283,333 of after-tax operating income on the store was reduced by the lost after-tax operating profit from the lost sales at the existing store, leading to an estimate of $212,500 as the adjusted estimate for the year. The net present value of this project is estimated at −$1.718 million, using the adjusted operating income, with the entire lost sales factored in. Figure 8.1 graphs the net present value as a function of the proportion of the lost sales considered in the analysis.

At the other extreme, where all of the lost sales are ignored, the net present value of this project is $622,150. It can be reasonably argued that given the absence of barriers to entry in the home improvement material market and the ease with which new entrants can exploit openings, little of the lost sales should be considered in the analysis. The store should therefore be opened, notwithstanding the loss of sales at the existing store.

CASH FLOWS SHOULD BE ESTIMATED CONSISTENTLY

As we noted earlier in the chapter, the cash flows and the discount rates used on these cash flows have to be estimated consistently, in terms of both the investor group being analyzed and inflation.

Dealing with Leverage

As outlined in Chapter 7, two basic approaches can be used to deal with leverage. The first is to estimate the cash flows associated with debt financing—interest expenses and principal payments—and to calculate the residual cash flows left over for equity investors. This residual cash flow, which is the cash flow to equity, has to be discounted at a return that reflects the expectations of the equity investors (the cost of equity). The resulting present value is compared to the equity investment in the project, resulting in a net present value or internal rate of return. The second approach is to calculate the cumulated cash flows to both equity investors and lenders in the firm—that is, the cash flows prior to the cash flows associated with debt financing—and to discount these cash flows at the cost of capital, which is the weighted average of the return the equity investors demand and the after-tax cost of borrowing. The resulting present value is compared to the total investment required in the project to calculate net present value or internal rate of return.

Cash Flow	Discount Rate	Investment	Yields
Cash Flow to Equity	Cost of Equity	Equity Investment	NPV to Equity IRR to Equity
Cash Flow to Firm	Cost of Capital	Total Investment	NPV to Firm IRR to Firm

Chapter 7 provides an expanded definition of both the cash flows to equity and the cash flows to the firm.

IN PRACTICE   ESTIMATING THE CASH FLOWS FROM DEBT AND CASH FLOWS TO EQUITY

In the Home Depot Store analysis described on page 209, assume that $5 million out of the initial investment of $13.4 million will be borrowed at an interest rate of 8%. The following application estimates the cash flows on the debt and the effect on cash flows to equity under two scenarios—a 10-year balloon payment loan and a 10-year term loan.

In a **balloon payment loan,** only interest payments are made during the first nine years, and the entire principal is repaid with interest at the end of the year 10. The cash flows attributable to debt are shown in Table 8.21.

Table 8.21   **DEBT PAYMENTS ON BALLOON PAYMENT LOAN**

Year	Interest Expenses	Principal Payments
1	$400,000	
2	400,000	
3	400,000	
4	400,000	
5	400,000	
6	400,000	
7	400,000	
8	400,000	
9	400,000	
10	400,000	$5,000,000

The interest expenses are tax deductible, but the principal payments are not. Allowing for the $5 million inflow initially from the borrowing, and the interest and principal payments due, the cash flows to equity can be estimated as shown in Table 8.22.

The cash flows to equity have to be discounted at the cost of equity to arrive at a net present value on the project.

In a term loan, interest and principal are repaid in equal annual installments over the life of the loan. Table 8.23 shows estimates of the interest and principal payments on the loan.

The annual payment is $745,147 and is calculated as an annuity based on an 8% interest rate on a principal amount of $5 million. The cash flows to equity can then be estimated as indicated in Table 8.24.

Balloon Payment Loan: This is a loan whereby only interest is paid during the life of the loan, and the entire principal payment is made at the end of the loan's life.

Table 8.22 ATCF WITH BALLOON PAYMENT LOAN

Year	FCFF	Borrowing	Interest $(1-t)$	Principal Repaid	FCFE
0	$(13,400,000)	$5,000,000	$—		$(8,400,000)
1	624,500		256,000		368,500
2	949,000		256,000		693,000
3	955,700		256,000		699,700
4	1,121,085		256,000		865,085
5	(127,861)		256,000		(383,861)
6	1,892,846		256,000		1,636,846
7	2,433,189		256,000		2,177,189
8	2,791,148		256,000		2,535,148
9	3,212,705		256,000		2,956,705
10	15,833,188		256,000	$5,000,000	10,577,188

FCFE = FCFF + Borrowing − Interest Expense $(1-t)$ − Principal Repaid

Table 8.23 DEBT PAYMENTS ON TERM LOAN

Year	Interest Expenses	Principal Payments	Principal Remaining
1	$400,000	$345,147	$4,654,853
2	372,388	372,759	4,282,093
3	342,567	402,580	3,879,513
4	310,361	434,786	3,444,727
5	275,578	469,569	2,975,158
6	238,013	507,135	2,468,023
7	197,442	547,706	1,920,317
8	153,625	591,522	1,328,795
9	106,304	638,844	689,951
10	55,196	689,951	0

Table 8.24 CASH FLOWS TO EQUITY WITH DEBT PAYMENTS

Year	FCFF	Borrowing	Interest $(1-t)$	Principal Repaid	FCFE
0	$(13,400,000)	$5,000,000	$—		$(8,400,000)
1	624,500		256,000	345,147	23,353
2	949,000		238,328	372,759	337,912
3	955,700		219,243	402,580	333,877
4	1,121,085		198,361	434,786	487,668
5	(127,861)		176,370	469,569	(773,800)
6	1,892,846		152,328	507,135	1,233,383
7	2,433,189		126,363	547,706	1,759,121
8	2,791,148		98,320	591,522	2,101,306
9	3,212,705		68,034	638,844	2,505,827
10	15,833,188		35,326	689,951	15,107,911

The cash flows to equity, when discounted at the cost of equity, will yield the net present value for this project.

Which approach works better?   With consistent assumptions about growth, and debt that is correctly priced,[2] the net present value computed using the firm approach should be equal to the net present value computed using the equity approach. If the cash flows and the discount rates are mismatched, however, the net present value is meaningless. In particular, if cash flows to equity are discounted at the cost of capital, the net present value will be overstated, since the cost of capital is generally much lower than the cost of equity. If the cash flows to the firm are discounted at the cost of equity, the net present value will be understated, and a good project might end up being rejected.

To illustrate, assume that you have a project that requires a $100 million investment and produces after-tax cash flows to the firm of $20 million forever. Also, assume that you borrow $50 million, using perpetual bonds with an interest rate of 8%, and raise the rest from internal funds; the cost of equity is 15%. Finally, assume that the tax rate is 40%. The project can be evaluated in one of two ways.

In the equity approach, the cash flows to equity have to be estimated first. Because the bonds are perpetual, there is no principal repaid in any time period, leading to the following cash flow to equity each year:

$$\text{Cash flows to Equity} = \text{Cash flows to Firm} - \text{Interest} (1 - \text{tax rate})$$
$$- \text{Principal repaid}$$
$$= 20 \text{ million} - 4 \text{ million} (1 - 0.4) - 0 = 17.6 \text{ million}$$

The present value of the cash flows to equity are estimated using the cost of equity. Because the cash flow is a perpetuity, the present value is

$$\text{PV of Cash flows to Equity} = \text{Cash flows to Equity / Cost of Equity}$$
$$= 17.6/0.15 = 117.33$$

The net present value can be computed by factoring in the equity investment in the project, which is $50 million.

$$\text{NPV of Project} = \text{PV of Cash flows to Equity} - \text{Equity investment}$$
$$= 117.33 - 50 = 67.33$$

In the firm approach, the first step in computing the present value using the firm approach is to compute the cost of capital, based on the market values of debt and equity. The market value of debt is $50 million, and the market value of equity is assumed to be the present value of the cash flows to equity, which is $117.33 million.

---

[2]By "correctly priced," we mean that the market value of the debt is equal to the present value of the interest payments and the principal payments, discounted at the correct cost of debt.

Weighted Average cost of capital = (117.33/167.33) (15%)+(50/167.33) (8% (1 − 0.4))
= 0.1195

The cash flows to the firm from the project are $20 million each year, forever. The present value of this perpetuity is then

> PV of Cash flows to Firm = Cash flow to the Firm / Cost of Capital
> = 20 million / 0.1195 = 167.33

The net present value of this project can be computed by netting out the total investment in the project:

> NPV of Project = 167.33 − 100 = 67.33

The net present values are equivalent under both approaches. This equivalence becomes much more difficult to prove when projects have finite lives and cash flows grow over time, but it remains true, nevertheless.

Differences between NPV from the Equity Approach and NPV from the Firm Approach

It is difficult to ensure that the assumptions in both approaches are consistent since doing so requires that growth rates be estimated identically and that changes in leverage are reflected in the cost of capital over time. Even with consistent assumptions, however, there will be projects where the net present value computed using the firm approach will be different from the net present value computed using the equity approach. The difference can be viewed as a reflection of the market pricing of debt. If debt is underpriced, the net present value to equity can exceed the net present value to the firm.[3] If debt is overpriced, the net present value to equity will be lower than the net present value to the firm.

Real Cash Flows (Discount Rates): These are projected cash flows (discount rates) for future periods, without inflation expectations built into them.

Dealing with Inflation

In dealing with inflation, an analyst has two choices. The first is to incorporate expected inflation into the estimates of future cash flows, resulting in nominal cash flows for the project, and to discount these cash flows at a discount rate that also incorporates expected inflation (i.e., the nominal discount rate). The second is to estimate cash flows in real dollars, without building in inflationary effects, and to discount these **real cash flows** at a *real discount rate*. The relationship between nominal and real cash flows is determined entirely by the expected inflation rate:

---

[3] Another way of putting this is to specify that the interest rate on the debt is too low, given the default risk of the firm.

$$\text{Real Cash Flow}_t = \text{Nominal Cash Flow}_t / (1 + \text{Expected inflation Rate})^t$$

Similarly, the relationship between nominal and real rates is also determined by the expected inflation rate:

$$1 + \text{Nominal Discount Rate} = (1+\text{Real Discount Rate})$$
$$(1 + \text{Expected inflation Rate})$$

The consistency principle then suggests the following matchup of cash flows and discount rates.

Cash Flow	Discount Rate	Yields
Nominal Cash Flow	Nominal Rate	Present Value in nominal terms
Real Cash Flow	Real Rate	Present Value in real terms

The consequences of a mismatch can be dire. If nominal cash flows are discounted at the real rate, the resulting net present value will be overstated. If real cash flows are discounted at the nominal rate, the resulting net present value will be understated. Done consistently, however, the net present value will be identical under both approaches.

IN PRACTICE   NOMINAL AND REAL CASH FLOWS—EFFECTS ON NPV

Consider the Home Depot Store analysis once again. The cash flows given on page 210 were in nominal terms, building in an expected inflation rate of 3%. The cost of capital, which was 12.5%, is also stated in nominal terms. The entire analysis could have been done in real terms, in which case the cash flows would not have included the 3% inflation rate, and the discount rate would have been in real terms:

$$\text{Real Cost of Capital} = \frac{(1 + \text{Nominal Cost of Capital})}{(1 + \text{Real Cost of Capital})} - 1 = \frac{1.125}{1.03} - 1 = 9.22\%$$

In Table 8.25, the net present values are computed for the Home Depot Store, using both real and nominal cash flows:

Table 8.25   NOMINAL AND REAL ATCF ON THE HOME DEPOT STORE

Year	Nominal ATCF	PV of Nominal CF at Nominal Rate	Real ATCF	PV of Real CF at Real Rate
0	$(13,400,000)	$(13,400,000)	$(13,400,000)	$(13,400,000)
1	624,500	555,111	606,311	555,111
2	949,000	749,827	894,524	749,827
3	955,700	671,219	874,601	671,219
4	1,121,085	699,888	996,070	699,888
5	(127,861)	(70,954)	(110,294)	(70,954)
6	1,892,846	933,684	1,585,229	933,684
7	2,433,189	1,066,862	1,978,405	1,066,862

(*continues*)

Table 8.25 (*continued*) Year	Nominal ATCF	PV of Nominal CF at Nominal Rate	Real ATCF	PV of Real CF at Real Rate
8	2,791,148	1,087,834	2,203,358	1,087,834
9	3,212,705	1,113,008	2,462,271	1,113,008
10	15,833,188	4,875,769	11,781,379	4,875,769
NPV		(1,717,752)		(1,717,752)

As you can see, the net present value is the same, whether nominal cash flows are discounted at the nominal rate or real cash flows are discounted at the real rate.

Effects of inflation on net present value   Do increases in inflation increase, decrease or leave unchanged the net present value of a project? Many analysts believe that firms that can index their prices and costs to inflation are protected against changes in inflation. This is not a sufficient condition, however, for depreciation tax benefits might not be indexed to inflation. In particular, in low-inflation economies like the United States, depreciation is based on the original price paid on asset, and the tax benefits are therefore fixed and not a function of the inflation rate. As the inflation rate increases, the depreciation tax benefits become less valuable in present value terms, resulting in a loss of value on projects.

To evaluate the effects of inflation on the net present value of a project, assume that you first operate in an environment with no inflation. Consider an investment in equipment that requires an initial investment of $24 million and has pretax operating income, prior to depreciation, of $10 million a year over its four-year life, together with straight-line depreciation of $6 million a year. The cash flows, real as well as nominal, on the project can be estimated as shown in Table 8.26.

Table 8.26   ESTIMATED CASH FLOWS ON PROJECT—NO INFLATION ENVIRONMENT (MILLIONS)

Year	Investment	EBITDA	Depreciation	EBIT(1-t)	ATCF
0	−24				
1		10	6	2.4	8.4
2		10	6	2.4	8.4
3		10	6	2.4	8.4
4		10	6	2.4	8.4

Assuming that the discount rate is 5%, real as well as nominal, since the inflation rate is zero, we can estimate the net present value of this project as shown in Table 8.27.

Table 8.27   PRESENT VALUE OF CASH FLOWS— NO INFLATION ENVIRONMENT

Year	ATCF	PV of ATCF
0		$(24,000,000)
1	8,400,000	$8,000,000
2	8,400,000	$7,619,048
3	8,400,000	$7,256,236
4	8,400,000	$6,910,701
	NPV =	$5,785,984

Assume now that inflation increases to 5% a year and that the pretax operating income of the project keeps pace with inflation. According to Table 8.28, the nominal cash flows on the project can be estimated as follows:

Table 8.28 ESTIMATED ATCF WITH EXPECTED INFLATION RATE OF 5%

Year	Investment	EBITDA	Depreciation	EBIT(1 − t)	ATCF
0	−24,000,000				
1		$10,500,000	$6,000,000	$2,700,000	$8,700,000
2		11,025,000	6,000,000	3,015,000	9,015,000
3		11,576,250	6,000,000	3,345,750	9,345,750
4		12,155,063	6,000,000	3,693,038	9,693,038

The nominal discount rate for this project can be estimated from the real discount rate of 5% and the expected inflation rate of 5%:

$$\text{Nominal Discount Rate} = (1 + \text{Real Rate})(1 + \text{Expected Inflation}) - 1$$
$$= (1.05)(1.05) - 1 = .1025 \text{ or } 10.25\%$$

The net present value of this project can be estimated based on nominal cash flows and discount rates as follows (Table 8.29):

Table 8.29 PRESENT VALUE OF NOMINAL CASH FLOWS AT NOMINAL RATE

Year	ATCF	PV of ATCF
0		$(24,000,000)
1	$8,700,000	7,891,156
2	9,015,000	7,416,663
3	9,345,750	6,973,943
4	9,693,038	6,560,629
		4,842,391

The net present value of this project is $4,842,391. This entire analysis could have been done in terms of real cash flows, with the discounting at the real discount rate, as shown in Table 8.30.

Table 8.30 PRESENT VALUE OF REAL CASH FLOWS AT REAL DISCOUNT RATE

Year	Nominal ATCF	Real ATCF	PV of Real ATCF
0			$(24,000,000)
1	$8,700,000	$8,285,714	7,891,156
2	9,015,000	8,176,871	7,416,663
3	9,345,750	8,073,210	6,973,943
4	9,693,038	7,974,486	6,560,629
		NPV =	$4,842,391

Discounting the real cash flows at the real discount rate yields exactly the same net present value as the nominal approach. The interesting finding is that the net present value, with inflation of 5%, is lower than the net present value of the same project, without inflation, even though the operating income keeps pace with inflation. The loss can be traced to the present value of the tax benefits from depreciation, which is much lower after inflation (Table 8.31).

Table 8.31 **PRESENT VALUE OF DEPRECIATION TAX BENEFITS**

Year	Tax Benefit from Depreciation	PV at Discount Rate of 5%	PV of Discount Rate of 10.25%
1	$2,400,000	$2,285,714	$2,176,871
2	2,400,000	2,176,871	1,974,486
3	2,400,000	2,073,210	1,790,917
4	2,400,000	1,974,486	1,624,414
		8,510,281	7,566,688

The decline in the present value benefits from depreciation is equal to the drop in net present value for the project when the inflation rate increased from zero to 5%.

Inflation and Stock Prices

The negative effect of inflation on a project's net present values also casts some light on the empirical finding that stock prices are negatively affected by unexpected increases in inflation. A study by Fama and Schwert, for instance, noted that stock prices, on average, declined 4.25% for every 1% increase in the inflation rate. If this is partially due to the loss in value in tax benefits from depreciation and other tax shields, equity in manufacturing firms, which have large fixed asset bases, should be impacted much more negatively than equity in less capital-intensive firms. Feldstein reports evidence that is consistent with this hypothesis.

Dealing with Hyperinflation

Although the principles for dealing with inflation in investment analysis are straightforward, uncertainty about future inflation creates an additional risk factor in capital budgeting. The level of inflation and uncertainty about inflation are highly correlated, and as a result, investment analysis in high-inflation economies is generally much more difficult to do than investment analysis in economies with stable inflation. From a practical standpoint, these difficulties exist whether nominal cash flows are discounted at the nominal discount rate or real cash flows are discounted at the real rate. The expected inflation rate is incorporated in either analysis, and uncertainty about the rate will therefore affect both. An alternative is to estimate the cash flows for the project in a more stable currency and to calculate net present values based on these cash flows. If this is done, the consistency principle requires that the discount rates also be estimated in that currency. Thus, a Brazilian firm that does its investment analysis in U.S. dollars will also have to estimate its costs of equity and capital in dollar terms.

The additional uncertainty associated with high inflation can have real consequences. Projects that would have been accepted with low and stable inflation might be rejected in a high-inflation scenario. Because the uncertainty about inflation compounds over time, long-term projects will be penalized more than short-term projects, and firms will be much less willing to make commitments for extended periods of time.

Conclusion

This chapter examines the nuts and bolts of estimating cash flows, and emphasizes three principles:

1. *Cash flows should be estimated after taxes.* The effect of noncash charges, such as depreciation, which are tax deductible, can be calculated in terms of the tax benefits they create for the business.

2. *Cash flows should be incremental.* Using this principle, we find that

   • Sunk costs do not belong in capital budgeting.
   • Changes in working capital affect cash flows and net present value.
   • Using resources already owned by the firm can create opportunity costs.
   • Allocating existing costs to projects should not affect cash flows.
   • Sales lost on existing product lines as a consequence of introducing a new product may or may not be incremental, depending on the barriers to entry in the business.

3. *Cash flows and discount rates should be estimated consistently.* Cash flows to equity should be discounted at the cost of equity, and cash flows to the firm, at the cost of capital. Nominal cash flows should be discounted at a nominal discount rate, whereas real cash flows get discounted at a real rate.

Questions and Problems

1. You have acquired new equipment for a project costing $15 million. The equipment is expected to have a salvage value of $3 million and a depreciable life of 10 years. The cost of capital is 12%, and the firm faces a tax rate of 40%.

   a. Estimate the present value and the nominal value of the tax benefits from depreciation, assuming that you use straight-line depreciation.

   b. Estimate the present value and the nominal value of the tax benefits from depreciation, assuming that you use double-declining balance depreciation.

   c. Why does double-declining balance depreciation yield a higher present value?

2. You are analyzing the depreciation tax benefits from acquiring an asset that cost $2.5 million and has a salvage value of $0.5 million. The asset is classified as an asset with a five-year depreciable life in the ACRS system. Using the depreciation rates provided in Table 8.7:

   a. Estimate the depreciation tax benefits each year on this asset, assuming that the tax rate is 40%.

   b. Estimate the present value of these tax benefits, assuming a cost of capital of 10%.

   c. If you could expense this asset instead of using the ACRS rates, how much would you gain in present value terms from tax benefits?

3. In both examples above, there is an estimated salvage value. Assuming that you have to pay capital gains taxes at 20% on any excess of salvage value over book value, would you gain or lose by depreciating the assets down to zero and paying the capital gains taxes. Illustrate using straight-line depreciation in Problem 1 and ACRS depreciation in Problem 2.

4. You have just acquired equipment for $10 million, with a depreciable life of five years and no salvage value. You must decide whether you should be using the straight-line or double-declining balance method in estimating taxes and cash flows. Your tax rate is expected to increase over the five years:

Year	Tax Rate
1	20%
2	25%
3	30%
4	35%
5	40%

   a. Which depreciation method provides the larger nominal tax benefits?

   b. Which depreciation method provides the larger present value in tax benefits, assuming your cost of capital is 12%?

5. You are analyzing a project with a life of five years, which requires an initial investment in equipment

and machinery of $10 million. The equipment is expected to have a five-year lifetime and no salvage value and to be depreciated straight line. The project is expected to generate revenues of $5 million each year for the five years and have operating expenses (not including depreciation) amounting to 30% of revenues. The tax rate is 40%, and the cost of capital is 11%.

a. Estimate the after-tax operating cash flow each year on this project.

b. Estimate the net present value for this project.

c. How much of the net present value can be attributed to the tax benefits accruing from depreciation?

d. Assume that the firm that takes this project is losing money currently and expects to continue losing money for the first three years. Estimate the net present value of this project.

6. You are considering a capital budgeting proposal to make glow-in-the-dark pacifiers for anxious first-time parents. You estimate that the equipment to make the pacifiers would cost you $50,000 (which you can depreciate straight line over the lifetime of the project, which is 10 years) and that you can sell 15,000 units a year at $2 a unit. The cost of making each pacifier would be $0.80, and the tax rate you would face would be 40%. You also estimate that you will need to maintain an inventory at 25% of revenues for the period of the project and that you can salvage 80% of this working capital at the termination of the project. Finally, you will be setting up the equipment in your garage, which means you will have to pay $2,000 a year to have your car garaged at a nearby private facility. (Assume that you can deduct this cost for tax purposes.) To estimate the discount rate for this project, you find that comparable firms are being traded on the financial markets with the following betas:

Company	Debt-Equity ratio	Tax rate	Beta
Nuk-Nuk	0.50	0.40	1.3
Gerber	1.00	0.50	1.5

You expect to finance this project entirely with equity, and the current Treasury Bond rate is 11.5%.

a. What is the appropriate discount rate to use for this project?

b. What is the after-tax operating cash flow each year for the lifetime of the project?

c. What is the NPV of this project?

7. You are a financial analyst for a company that is considering a new project. If the project is accepted, it will use 40% of a storage facility that the company already owns but currently does not use fully. The project is expected to last 10 years, and the discount rate is 10%. You research the possibilities and find that the entire storage facility can be sold for $100,000 and a smaller facility can be acquired for $40,000. The book value of the existing facility is $60,000, and both the existing and the new facilities (if it is acquired) would be depreciated straight line over 10 years. The ordinary tax rate is 40%, and the capital gains rate is 25%. What is the opportunity cost, if any, of using the storage capacity?

8. You have been observing the progressive gentrification of your city with interest. You realize that the time is ripe for you to open and run an aerobic exercise center. You find an abandoned warehouse that will meet your needs and rents for $48,000 a year. You estimate that it will initially cost $50,000 to renovate the place and buy Nautilus equipment for the center. (There will be no salvage and the entire initial cost is depreciable.) Your market research indicates that you can expect to get 500 members, each paying $500 a year. You have also found five instructors you can hire for $24,000 a year each. Your tax rate, if you start making profits, will be 40%, and you choose to use straight-line depreciation on your initial investment. If your cost of capital is 15% and you expect to retire to the Bahamas in 10 years, answer the following questions:

a. Estimate the annual after-tax cash flows on this project.

b. Estimate the net present value and internal rate of return for this investment. Would you take it?

9. Brooks Brothers is thinking of investing in a new line of "punk rocker" clothes for the new executive. You have been hired to evaluate the project. You find that, if the project is accepted, you could use an abandoned warehouse already owned by Brooks Brothers, with a book value of $500,000. Your superior had been planning to rent this warehouse out to another firm for $100,000 a year. If your tax rate is 40%, your discount rate is 15%, your project lifetime is 10 years, and you use straight-line depreciation, what is the opportunity cost of using this warehouse?

10. You are graduating in June and would like to start your own business manufacturing wine coolers. You collect the following information on the initial costs:

Cost of Plant and Equipment = $500,000
Licensing and Legal Costs = $50,000

You can claim an investment tax credit of 10% on plant and equipment. You also have been left a tidy inheritance that will cover the initial cost, and your estimated opportunity cost is 10%.

You estimate that you can sell 1 million bottles a year at $1 a bottle. You estimate your costs as follows:

$$\text{Variable costs/bottle} = 50 \text{ cents}$$
$$\text{Fixed Costs/ year} = \$200,000$$

Adding up state, local, and federal taxes, you note that you will be in the 50% tax bracket. To be conservative, you assume that you will terminate the business in five years and that you will get nothing from the plant and equipment as salvage. (You also use straight-line depreciation.) As a final consideration, you note that starting this business will mean that you will not be able to take the investment banking job you have been offered (which offered $75,000 a year for the next five years). Should you take on the project?

11. You are an expert at working with PCs and are considering setting up a software development business. To set up the enterprise, you anticipate that you will need to acquire computer hardware costing $100,000. (The lifetime of this hardware is five years for depreciation purposes, and straight-line depreciation will be used.) In addition, you will have to rent an office for $50,000 a year. You estimate that you will need to hire five software specialists at $50,000 a year to work on the software and that your marketing and selling costs will be $100,000 a year. You expect to price the software you produce at $100 per unit and to sell 6,000 units in the first year. The actual cost of materials used to produce each unit is $20. The number of units sold is expected to increase 10% a year for the remaining four years, and the revenues and costs are expected to increase at 3% a year, reflecting inflation. The actual cost of materials used to produce each unit is $20, and you will need to maintain working capital at 10% of revenues. (Assume that the working capital investment is made at the beginning of each year.) Your tax rate will be 40%, and the cost of capital is 12%.

   a. Estimate the cash flows each year on this project.

   b. Should you accept the project?

12. You are an analyst for a sporting goods corporation that is considering a new project that will take advantage of excess capacity in an existing plant. The plant has a capacity to produce 50,000 tennis racquets, but only 25,000 are being produced currently, although sales of the rackets are increasing 10% a year. You want to use some of the remaining capacity to manufacture 20,000 squash rackets each year for the next 10 years (which will use up 40% of the total capacity), and this market is assumed to be stable (no growth). An average tennis racquet sells for $100 and costs $40 to make. The tax rate for the corporation is 40%, and the dis-

count rate is 10%. Is there an opportunity cost involved? If so, how much is it?

13. You are examining the viability of a capital investment in which your firm is interested. The project will require an initial investment of $500,000 and the projected revenues are $400,000 a year for five years. The projected cost-of-goods-sold is 40% of revenues, and the tax rate is 40%. The initial investment is primarily in plant and equipment and can be depreciated straight-line over five years. (The salvage value is zero.) The project makes use of other resources that your firm already owns:

- Two employees of the firm, each with a salary of $40,000 a year and who are currently employed by another division, will be transferred to this project. The other division has no alternative use for them, but they are covered by a union contract that will prevent them from being fired for three years (during which they would be paid their current salary).

- The project will use excess capacity in the current packaging plant. While this excess capacity has no alternative use now, it is estimated that the firm will have to invest $250,000 in a new packaging plant in year 4 as a consequence of this project using up excess capacity (instead of year 8 as originally planned).

- The project will use a van currently owned by the firm. Although the van is not currently being used, it can be rented out for $3,000 a year for five years. The book value of the van is $10,000, and it is being depreciated straight-line (with five years remaining for depreciation). The discount rate to be used for this project is 10%.

   a. What (if any) opportunity cost is associated with using the two employees from another division?

   b. What, if any, opportunity cost is associated with the use of excess capacity of the packaging plant?

   c. What, if any, opportunity cost is associated with the use of the van?

   d. What is the after-tax operating cash flow each year on this project?

   e. What is the net present value of this project?

14. You have been hired as a capital budgeting analyst by a sporting goods firm that manufactures athletic shoes and has captured 10% of the overall shoe market. (The total market is worth $100 million a year.) The fixed costs associated with manufacturing these shoes is $2 million a year, and variable costs are 40% of revenues. The company's tax rate is 40%.

Product line	Capacity Used Currently	Growth Rate/Year	Current Revenues	Fixed Cost/Year	Variable Cost/Year
Old product	50%	5%/year	100 mil	25 mil	50 mil/yr
New product	30%	10%/year	80 mil	20 mil	44 mil/yr

The firm believes that it can increase its market share to 20% by investing $10 million in a new distribution system (which can be depreciated over the system's life of 10 years to a salvage value of zero) and spending $1 million a year in additional advertising. The company proposes to continue to maintain working capital at 10% of annual revenues. The discount rate to be used for this project is 8%.

a. What is the initial investment for this project?

b. What is the annual operating cash flow from this project?

c. What is the NPV of this project?

15. Your company is considering producing a new product. You have a production facility that is currently used to only 50% of capacity, and you plan to use some of the excess capacity for the new product. The production facility cost $50 million five years ago when it was built and is being depreciated straight-line over 25 years (in real dollars, assume that this cost will stay constant over time).

The new product has a life of 10 years, the tax rate is 40%, and the appropriate discount rate (real) is 10%. (Use table at top of page.)

a. If you take on this project, when will you run out of capacity?

b. When you run out of capacity, what will you lose if you choose to cut back production (in present value after-tax dollars)? You have to decide on which product you are going to cut back production.

c. What opportunity cost would be assigned to this new product if you chose to build a new facility when you ran out of capacity instead of cutting back on production?

16. You run a mail-order firm, selling upscale clothing. You are considering replacing your manual ordering system with a computerized system to make your operations more efficient and to increase sales. (All the cash flows given below are in real terms.)

- The computerized system will cost $10 million to install and $500,000 to operate each year. It will replace a manual order system that costs $1.5 million to operate each year.

- The system is expected to last 10 years and to have no salvage value at the end of the period.

- The computerized system is expected to increase annual revenues from $5 million to $8 million for the next 10 years.

- The cost of goods sold is expected to remain at 50% of revenues.

- The tax rate is 40%.

- As a result of the computerized system, the firm will be able to cut its inventory from 50% of revenues to 25% of revenues *immediately*. No change is expected in the other working capital components.

The real discount rate is 8%.

a. What is your expected cash flow at time = 0?

b. What is the expected incremental annual cash flow from computerizing the system?

c. What is the net present value of this project?

17. A multinational firm is considering a project which will generate net cash flows in five different countries. The marginal tax rates are all different in these countries.

Country	Cash flow before taxes	Marginal tax rate
A	$20 m	60%
B	$15 m	50%
C	$10 m	40%
D	$5 m	40%
E	$3 m	35%

a. Find the net combined after-tax cash flow generated by this project.

b. Find the weighted marginal tax rate.

18. Your company is considering a project proposal. The following information is gathered for analysis:

Year	Cash flow before tax	Marginal tax rate
1	$10 m	25%
2	20 m	30%
3	50 m	30%
4	50 m	30%
5	100 m	40%

If the initial outlay is $120 m, and the cost of capital is 12%, should this project be accepted?

CHAPTER 9

ISSUES IN CAPITAL BUDGETING

In the last two chapters, we laid the groundwork for analyzing investment decisions by developing the basic decision rules and the process for estimating cash flows. In this chapter, we expand our discussion to cover a number of important issues in investment analysis. First, we look at the effects of having limited access to capital and funds on hand on project choice. Second, we examine the process by which firms pick between mutually exclusive projects, especially when the projects have unequal lives.

This chapter expands on the basics of capital budgeting developed in the previous two chapters by exploring the following questions:

- What is the source of capital rationing? Why do some firms face tighter capital rationing constraints than others? What modifications, if any, need to be made to capital budgeting techniques to deal with capital rationing?

- How do you choose between mutually exclusive projects? How do you choose between projects with different lives?

- How do you analyze replacement or expansion decisions?

- How do you consider interactions between projects and project synergies in investment analysis?

- Are there decision rules that can be used to determine the optimal timing of a project?

CAPITAL RATIONING

A firm faces *capital rationing* when it finds itself unable to take on projects that earn returns greater than the hurdle rates that would be justified based on their riskiness because it does not have the capital on hand *or the capacity to raise the capital needed to finance these projects*. In the context of net present value, this implies that the firm does not have—and cannot raise—the capital to take all the positive net present value projects that are available. Thus, the fact that a firm has many projects and limited resources on hand does not necessarily imply that it faces capital rationing, for it might still have the capacity to raise the resources from financial markets to finance all these projects.

There Is No Capital Rationing When . . .
In theory, there will be no capital rationing constraint as long as events take the following sequence:

1. The firm uncovers a lucrative investment opportunity.

2. The firm goes to financial markets with a description of the project.

234

3. Financial markets attach credibility to the firm's description of the project.

4. The firm issues securities—that is, stocks and bonds—to raise the capital needed to finance the project at "fair" market prices. Implicit here is the assumption that markets are efficient and that expectations of future earnings and growth are built into these prices.

5. The flotation cost associated with issuing these securities is minimal.

If this were the case for every firm, then every worthwhile project would be financed, and no good project would ever be rejected for lack of funds. In other words, there would be no capital rationing constraint.

There Is Capital Rationing When . . .
The reality is that the sequence described above is built on a series of assumptions, some of which are clearly unrealistic, at least for some firms. Let's consider each step even more closely.

1. Project Discovery: The implicit assumption that firms know when they have good projects on hand underestimates the uncertainty and the noise associated with project analysis. In very few cases can firms say with complete certainty that a prospective project will be a good one.

2 & 3. Firm Announcements and Credibility: Financial markets tend to be skeptical about announcements made by firms, especially when such announcements contain good news about future projects. It is easy for any firm to announce that its future projects are good, regardless of whether or not this is true. Therefore, financial markets often require more substantial proof of the viability of projects.

4. Market Efficiency: If a firm's securities are underpriced, there is a clear barrier to using external financing for a project, since the gains from taking on the project to existing stockholders may be overwhelmed by the loss from having to sell securities at or below their estimated true value. To illustrate, assume that a firm is considering a project that requires an initial investment of $100 million and has a net present value of $10 million. Also assume that the stock of this company, which management believes should be trading for $100 per share, based on the company's fundamentals, is actually trading at $80 per share. If the company issues $100 million of new stock to take on the new project, its existing stockholders will gain their share of the net present value of $10 million, but they will lose $20 million ($100 million - $80 million) to new investors in the company. One solution to this problem would be for the firm to make a rights issue to raise the stock, for this would ensure that existing stockholders would get first rights on the new issue. There is an interesting converse to this problem. When securities are overpriced, there may be a temptation to overinvest, inasmuch as existing stockholders gain from the very process of issuing equities to new investors.

5. Flotation Costs: The costs associated with raising funds in financial markets can be substantial. If these costs are larger than the net present value of the projects being considered, it would not make sense to raise these funds and finance the projects.

Flotation Cost: This is the cost associated with issuing new securities or raising external financing.

In summary, the contrast between the theoretical construct—where there is no capital rationing—and the real world—where there is—is illustrated in Table 9.1.

	In Theory	In Practice	Source of Rationing
Table 9.1 CAPITAL RATIONING: THEORY VS. PRACTICE			
1. *Project Discovery*	A business uncovers a good investment opportunity.	A business believes, given the underlying uncertainty, that it has a good project.	Uncertainty about true value of projects may cause capital rationing.
2. *Information Revelation*	The business conveys information about the project to financial markets.	The business attempts to convey information to financial markets.	Difficulty in conveying information to markets may cause rationing.
3. *Market Response*	Financial markets believe the firm; that is, the information is conveyed credibly.	Financial markets may not believe the announcement.	The greater the "credibility gap," the greater the rationing problem.
4. *Market Efficiency*	The securities issued by the business (stocks and bonds) are fairly priced.	The securities issued by the business may not be correctly priced.	With underpriced securities, firms will be unwilling to raise funds for projects.
5. *Flotation Costs*	There are no costs associated with raising funds for projects.	There are significant costs associated with raising funds for projects.	The greater the flotation costs, the larger the capital rationing problem.

Sources of Capital Rationing

The three primary sources of capital rationing constraints, therefore, are lack of credibility, underpricing of securities, and flotation costs.

Lack of credibility   The capacity of a firm to raise funds for good projects and avoid a capital rationing problem depends largely on the firm's credibility with financial markets. Obviously, a firm in good standing with financial markets is less likely to face capital rationing constraints than is a firm with credibility problems. A firm is able to build up credibility by delivering results over a long period of time that are consistent with its claims that it not only has good projects, but it also knows how to take on and manage these projects. We can therefore draw three implications:

1. Smaller firms with shorter histories should have much greater credibility problems and more capital rationing constraints than do larger firms with longer histories of project success.

2. Firms that have had recent problems in terms of project choice and financial results will have greater credibility problems and more capital rationing constraints than will firms that have had recent successes.

3. Firms that have to return repeatedly to financial markets to raise more funds should be more concerned about their credibility and, accordingly, should be less likely to lie to financial markets.

Underpricing of securities   Because firms with severely underpriced securities face more capital rationing constraints, the efficiency of markets will affect the prevalence of capital rationing. To the degree that market efficiency itself depends on the quality and quantity of information made available to financial markets, we would expect more significant errors in market pricing and more capital rationing for firms about which less or poorer quality information is available. For instance, using the number of analysts as a rough proxy for information availability, we would expect firms that are followed by relatively few analysts to be much more exposed to capital rationing constraints than firms that are heavily followed by analysts and institutional investors.

Flotation costs   The larger the cost of issuing external securities, the greater the chance that a firm will face capital rationing. The size of the flotation costs tends to vary inversely with the size of the issue; that is, larger issues tend to have much lower costs. This is true for both stocks and bonds, as is shown in Table 9.2.

Size of Issue	Cost of Issuing Securities (%)		
	Bonds (%)	Preferred Stock	Common Stock (%)
Under $1 mil	14.0	—	22.0
$1.0–1.9 mil	11.0	—	16.9
$2.0–4.9 mil	4.0	—	12.4
$5.0–9.9 mil	2.4	2.6	8.1
$10–19.9 mil	1.2	1.8	6.0
$20–49.9 mil	1.0	1.7	4.6
$50 mil and over	0.9	1.6	3.5

Table 9.2   FLOTATION COSTS FOR SECURITY ISSUES

Two findings emerge from this table. First, *smaller firms* are more likely to face capital rationing constraints than are larger firms because they have higher flotation costs. Second, firms that are primarily dependent on *equity financing* for projects are more likely to face capital rationing constraints than are firms that are dependent on debt financing because the issuance costs of raising equity are much higher than the costs of raising an equivalent amount of debt.

As you can see, different firms will face different degrees of capital rationing. A firm like AT&T would likely face few capital rationing constraints because of its large size, long history, greater dependence on debt, and repeated forays into financial markets. A smaller firm, like Adobe Systems, would face far more constraints because of its dependence on the equity markets for funds, its smaller size, and its shorter history.

Concept Check

Is it always true that small, high-growth firms face capital rationing constraints? If not, what are the exceptions?

Empirical Evidence on Capital Rationing Constraints

Attempts have been made to survey whether firms believe they face capital rationing constraints and, if so, to identify the sources of such constraints. One such survey was conducted by Scott and Martin and is summarized in Table 9.3.

This survey suggests that, although some firms face capital rationing constraints as a result of external factors largely beyond their control, such as frictions in financial markets and credibility problems, most firms face self-imposed constraints, such as restrictive policies to avoid overextending themselves by investing too much in any period.

Table 9.3 **THE CAUSES OF CAPITAL RATIONING**

Cause	Number	%
Debt limit imposed by outside agreement	10	10.7
Debt limit placed by management external to firm	3	3.2
Limit placed on borrowing by internal management	65	69.1
Restrictive policy imposed on retained earnings	2	2.1
Maintenance of target EPS or PE ratio	14	14.9

❏ Concept
Check

> Does it matter whether a capital rationing constraint is internally or externally imposed? Explain.

Dealing with Capital Rationing

Whatever the reason, many firms have capital rationing constraints, thereby limiting the funds available for investment. Consequently, the techniques developed in Chapter 7, such as net present value and internal rate of return, may prove inadequate since they are constructed on the premise that all good projects (i.e., projects with positive net present value and projects with an IRR greater than the hurdle rate) will be accepted. In this section, we examine some of the techniques that can be used to deal with the capital rationing constraint.

Profitability index   The first, and simplest, approach to dealing with capital rationing, especially for firms that have a constraint for the current period only, and relatively few projects, is the profitability index approach.

The profitability ratio, described in Chapter 7, is a scaled version of the net present value. It is computed by dividing the net present value of the project by the initial investment in the project.[1]

Profitability Index = Net Present Value / Initial Investment

In a very rough sense, the profitability index provides a measure of the net present value the firm gets for each dollar of investment. In the context of limited capital, where every positive net present value project cannot be accepted, this provides a way to get the highest cumulative net present value from the funds available for capital investment.

The steps involved in using the profitability index to choose projects are as follows:

1. The funds available for capital investment are clearly identified. This represents the capital budgeting constraint.

2. The net present values of all available projects are computed, and the initial investments required for each are estimated.

3. The profitability index is computed for all available projects.

---

[1]There is another version of the profitability index, whereby the present value of all cash inflows is divided by the present value of cash outflows. The resulting ranking will be the same as with the profitability index, as defined in this chapter.

4. The projects are ranked in the order of the profitability index.

5. Projects are chosen, starting with the highest profitability index and moving down, while tracking the cumulated initial investment and comparing it to the funds available for investment.

6. When the cumulated initial investment in the project reaches the capital funding constraint, investments are stopped and no further projects are taken.

Limitations of the approach   Although this approach to choosing among investments is intuitive, it has several limitations. First, it assumes that the capital rationing constraint applies the current period only and does not factor in investment requirements in future periods. Thus, a firm may choose projects with a cumulated initial investment that is less than the current period's capital constraint, but it may expose itself to capital rationing problems in future periods if these projects have outlays in those periods. A related problem with this approach is its classification of cash flows into an initial investment that occurs now and positive operating cash flows that occur in future periods. To the extent that projects have investments spread over multiple periods and operating cash flows that are negative, this may be unrealistic. Finally, this approach does not guarantee that the cumulated investment will add up to the capital rationing constraint; if it does not, the user of the approach will have to consider other combinations of projects, which may yield a higher net present value. This may be feasible for firms with relatively few projects, but it becomes increasingly unwieldy when the number of projects increases.

☐ Concept
Check

The internal rate of return is also a scaled measure of project quality. Will the projects picked using the profitability index be the same as the projects that would have been picked based on an IRR ranking? Why or why not?

Using the profitability index to pick projects   Consider a growing computer software firm with a capital budget of $100 million available for projects in the current period. The projects available to the firm are listed in Table 9.4.

Table 9.4   **AVAILABLE PROJECTS**
(MILLION DOLLARS)

Project	Initial Investment	NPV
A	$25	$10
B	60	30
C	5	5
D	100	25
E	50	15
F	70	20
G	35	20

Note that all the projects have positive net present values and that a firm would have accepted them without a capital rationing constraint.

In order to choose among these projects, the profitability index of each project is computed in Table 9.5.

Table 9.5   **PROFITABILITY INDEX FOR PROJECTS**

Project	Initial Investment	NPV	Profitability Index	Ranking
A	$25	$10	0.40	4
B	60	30	0.50	3
C	5	5	1.00	1
D	100	25	0.25	7
E	50	15	0.30	5
F	70	20	0.29	6
G	35	20	0.57	2

The profitability index of 0.40 for Project A implies that the project earns a net present value of 40 cents for every dollar of initial investment. Based on the profitability index, Projects B, C, and G should be accepted; this would exhaust the capital budget of $100 million while maximizing the net present value of the projects accepted.

This analysis is based on the assumption that the capital constraint is for the current period only and that the initial investments on all these projects will occur in the current period. It also highlights the cost of the capital rationing constraint for this firm; the net present value of the projects rejected as a consequence of the constraint is $70 million.

☐ Concept Check

> Assume that the initial investment required for Project B was $40 million (the NPV stays at $30). How would that change your analysis?

Using a higher hurdle rate   Some firms choose what seems to be a more convenient way of dealing with the capital rationing constraint—they raise the hurdle rate to reflect the severity of the constraint. If the definition of capital rationing is that a firm cannot take all the positive net present value projects that it faces, raising the hurdle rate sufficiently will ensure that the problem disappears or at least is hidden. For instance, assume that a firm has a true cost of capital of 12%, a capital rationing constraint of $100 million, and positive net present value projects requiring an initial investment of $250 million.[2] At a higher cost of capital, fewer projects will have positive net present values; at some cost of capital, say 18%, the positive net present value projects remaining will require an initial investment of $100 million or less.

The dangers of building in the capital rationing constraint into the cost of capital are threefold. First, once the adjustment is made, the firm may fail to correct it for shifts in the severity of the constraint. Thus, a small firm may adjust its cost of capital from 12% to 18% to reflect a severe capital rationing constraint. As the firm gets larger, the constraint will generally become less severe, but the firm, operating on auto-pilot, may not adjust its cost of capital accordingly. Second, increasing the discount rate to reflect the capital rationing constraint will yield net present values that do not convey the same information as those computed using the correct discount rates (i.e., the adjusted net present value cannot be viewed as an increase in firm value). Finally, adjusting the discount rate penalizes all projects equally, whether or not they are capital intensive.

---

[2]By "true cost of capital," we mean a cost of capital that reflects the riskiness of the firm and its financing mix.

> How would you go about adjusting the hurdle rate to reflect your capital rationing constraint?

Building capital rationing constraints into analysis   In closing, it is a good idea for firms to keep the capital rationing constraint separate from traditional investment analysis so that they can get an idea about how much these constraints are costing them. In the simplest terms, the cost of a capital rationing constraint is the cumulated net present value of the good projects that could not be taken for lack of funds. There are two reasons why this is useful. First, if the firm is faced with the opportunity to relax these constraints, knowing how much these constraints are costing the firm may be useful. For instance, the firm may be able to enter into a strategic partnership with a larger firm with excess funds, use the cash to take the good projects that would otherwise have been rejected, and share the net present value of these projects. Second, if the capital rationing is self-imposed, the decision makers are forced to confront the cost of the constraint. In some cases, the sheer magnitude of this cost may be sufficient for them to drop or relax the constraint.

MUTUALLY EXCLUSIVE PROJECTS

A set of projects is said to be *mutually exclusive* when a firm can accept only one of the set. Projects may be mutually exclusive for different reasons. They may each provide a way of getting a needed service, but any one of them is sufficient for the service. An example would be choosing among a number of different air-conditioning or heating systems for a building. Or, they may provide alternative approaches to the future of a firm; a firm that has to choose between a "high-margin, low-volume" strategy and a "low-margin, high-volume" strategy for a product can choose only one of the two.

In choosing among mutually exclusive projects, many of the principles that concern independent projects continue to apply. The business should choose the project that adds the most to its value. This concept, though relatively straightforward when the projects have the same lives, can become more complicated when the projects have different lives.

Projects with Equal Lives

When comparing projects with the same lives, a business can make its decision in one of two ways. It can compute the net present value of each project and choose the one with the highest positive net present value (if the projects are revenue generating) or the one with the lowest negative net present value (if the projects are cost minimizing), or it can compute the differential cash flow between two projects and base its decision on the net present value or the internal rate of return of the differential cash flow.

Comparing net present values   The simplest way of choosing among mutually exclusive projects with equal lives is to compute the net present values of the projects and choose the one with the highest net present value. This decision rule is consistent with firm value maximization. If the firm faces a capital rationing constraint, however, the profitability index or the internal rate of return of each of the projects can be computed instead.

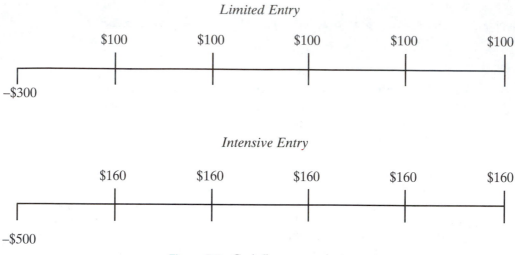

Limited Entry

$100 $100 $100 $100 $100

−$300

Intensive Entry

$160 $160 $160 $160 $160

−$500

Figure 9.1   Cash flows on projects

To illustrate, suppose a consumer products firm is considering two alternative strategies for a new product it is planning to introduce, as shown in Figure 9.1. Under the first plan (limited entry), the firm will invest $300 million in advertising and promotion and it expects to make $100 million a year for the next five years. Under the second plan (intensive entry), the firm will spend more on advertising and promotion ($500 million), and it expects to make $160 million a year for the next five years. The firm has a discount rate of 12%.

The net present values of these projects can be estimated as follows:

Net Present Value of Limited Entry = - $300 + $100 [PV(A,12%,5 years)] = $60.48 million

Net Present Value of Intensive Entry = - $500 + $160 [PV(A,12%,5 years)] = $76.76 million

Based on the net present value, the intensive entry option (with the higher advertising and promotion expenses) is the better project and should be picked over the limited entry option because it will provide $16.28 million more in value to the firm.

Now consider a small business that is choosing between alternative vendors who are offering phone systems. Both systems have five-year lives, and the appropriate cost of capital is 10% for both projects, as shown in Figure 9.2.

The more expensive system is also more efficient, resulting in lower annual costs. The net present values of these two systems can be estimated as follows:

Net Present Value of Less Expensive System = - $20,000 - $8,000 [PV(A,10%,5 years)]
= - $50,326

Net Present Value of More Expensive System = - $30,000 - $3,000 [PV(A,10%,5 years)]
= - $41,372

The net present value of all costs is much lower with the second system, making it the better choice.

Differential cash flows   An alternative approach to picking between mutually exclusive projects is to compute the difference in cash flows each period between the two investments being compared. Thus, if A and B are mutually exclusive projects with estimated cash flows over *n* years, the **differential cash flows** can be computed as shown in Figure 9.3.

Vendor 1: Less Expensive System

−$8000   −$8000   −$8000   −$8000   −$8000

−$20,000

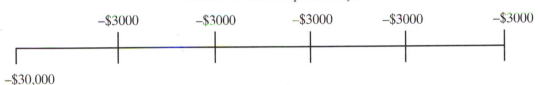

Vendor 2: More Expensive System

−$3000   −$3000   −$3000   −$3000   −$3000

−$30,000

Figure 9.2   Cash flows on phone systems

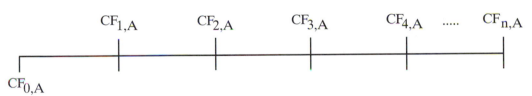

Project A

$CF_{1,A}$ $CF_{2,A}$ $CF_{3,A}$ $CF_{4,A}$ ..... $CF_{n,A}$

$CF_{0,A}$

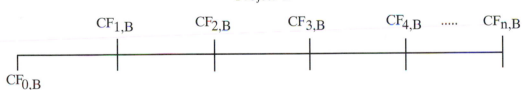

Project B

$CF_{1,B}$ $CF_{2,B}$ $CF_{3,B}$ $CF_{4,B}$ ..... $CF_{n,B}$

$CF_{0,B}$

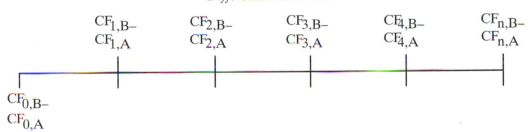

Differential Cash Flow

$CF_{1,B-}$ $CF_{1,A}$ $CF_{2,B-}$ $CF_{2,A}$ $CF_{3,B-}$ $CF_{3,A}$ $CF_{4,B-}$ $CF_{4,A}$ $CF_{n,B-}$ $CF_{n,A}$

$CF_{0,B-}$ $CF_{0,A}$

Figure 9.3   Differential cash flows

Differential Cash Flows: These are the differences between cash flows, in each period, on two mutually exclusive projects.

In computing the differential cash flows, the project with the larger initial investment becomes the index project against which the comparison is made. In practical terms, this means that the Cash Flow$_{B-A}$ is computed if B has a higher initial investment than A, and the Cash Flow$_{A-B}$ is computed if A has a higher initial investment than B. If more than two projects are being compared, comparisons are still made between projects, two at a time, and the less attractive project is dropped at each stage.

The differential cash flows can be used to compute the net present value, and the decision rule can be summarized as follows:

If $NPV_{B-A} > 0$:   Project B is better than Project A

                    $NPV_{B-A} < 0$:   Project A is better than Project B

Two points need to be made about this differential net present value. The first is that it provides the same result as would have been obtained if the business had computed net present values of the individual projects and then taken the difference between them.

$$NPV_{B-A} = NPV_B - NPV_A$$

The second is that this approach works only when the two projects being compared have the same risk level and discount rates, since only one discount rate can be used on the differential cash flows. By contrast, computing project-specific net present values allows for the use of different discount rates on each project.

The differential cash flows can also be employed to compute an internal rate of return, which can be used to select the better project.

If $IRR_{B-A} > $ Discount Rate   :   Project B is better than Project A

        $IRR_{B-A} < $ Discount Rate   :   Project A is better than Project B

Again, this approach works only if the projects are of equivalent risk.

☐ Concept
Check

If differential cash flows are computed across two projects with different risk levels and discount rates, can the average of the two discount rates be used to calculate the net present value. Why or why not? Can the internal rate of return be computed and used in such a case?

Consider again the small business choosing between two phone systems. The differential cash flows can be estimated as shown in Figure 9.4.

The more expensive system costs $10,000 more to install but saves the firm $5,000 a year. Using the 10% discount rate, the net present value of the differential cash flows can be estimated as follows:

Net Present Value of Differential Cash Flows =- $10,000 + $5,000 [PV(A,10%,5 years)]
= + $8,954

This net present value is equal to the difference between the net present values of the individual projects and indicates that the system that costs more up front is also the better system from the viewpoint of net present value. The internal rate of return of the differential cash flows is 41.04%, which is higher than the discount rate of 10%. This once again suggests that the more expensive system is the better one, from a financial standpoint.

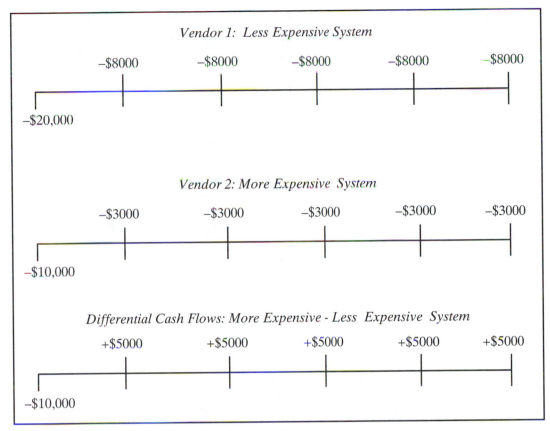

Figure 9.4   Cash flows on phone systems

Assume now that the differential cash flows had been computed using the less expensive system as the index project. What would the net present value have been? What about the internal rate of return?

Projects with Different Lives

In many cases, firms have to choose among projects with different lives. In doing so, the firms cannot rely solely on just the net present value, since it is a dollar figure and is likely to be higher for longer term projects. For instance, assume that you are choosing between a 5-year and a 10-year project, with the cash flows shown in Figure 9.5 and that a discount rate of 12% applies for each.

The net present value of the first project is $442, whereas the net present value of the second project is $478. On the basis of net present value alone, the second project is better, but this analysis fails to factor in the additional net present value that the firm could make from years 6 to 10 in the project with a five-year life.

In comparing a project with a shorter life to one with a longer life, the firm must consider the fact that it will get a chance to invest again sooner with the shorter term project. Two conventional approaches—project replication and equivalent annuities—assume that when the current project ends, the firm will be able to invest in the same project or a very similar one. We will also consider an alternate approach that allows for changes in project characteristics over time.

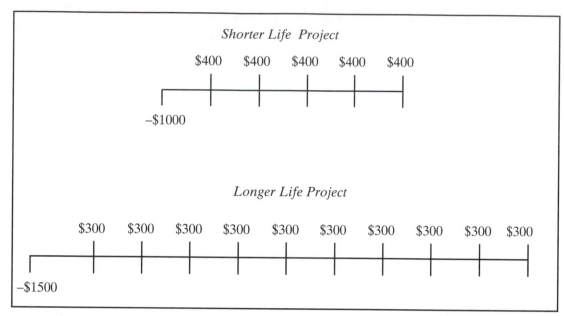

Figure 9.5 Cash flows on projects with unequal lives

Project replication   One way of getting around the problem of different lives is to assume that projects can be replicated until they have the same lives. Thus, instead of comparing a 5-year to a 10-year project, an estimate of net present value can be obtained from doing the 5-year project twice and compared to the net present value of the 10-year project.

   This approach has met with criticism, however. On a practical level, it can become tedious to use when the number of projects increases and the lives do not fit neatly into multiples of each other. For example, an analyst using this approach to compare a 7-year, a 9-year, and a 13-year project would have to replicate these projects 819 years to arrive at an equivalent life on all three projects. Theoretically, it is also difficult to argue that a firm's project choice will essentially remain unchanged over time, especially if the projects being compared are very attractive in terms of net present value.

❏ Concept
Check

> Project replication is obviously done in real dollars; if it were done in nominal dollars, and there was inflation in the economy, how would the analysis differ?

Project replication to compare projects with different lives: an illustration   Suppose you are trying to choose between buying a used car, which costs less but does not give very good mileage, and a new car, which is more expensive but is more economical in its mileage. The two options are listed in Table 9.6.

Table 9.6   EXPECTED CASH FLOWS ON NEW VERSUS USED CAR

	Used Car	New Car
Initial cost	$3,000	$8,000
Maintenance costs/year	$1,500	$1,000
Fuel costs/mile	$ 0.20/ mile	$ 0.05/mile
Lifetime	4 years	5 years

Ignoring taxes, which car would you buy if you drove 5,000 miles a year and had an opportunity cost of 15%?

Step 1   Replicate the projects until they have the same lifetime; in this case, that would mean buying used cars five consecutive times and new cars four consecutive times.

A.   Buy a used car every four years for 20 years.

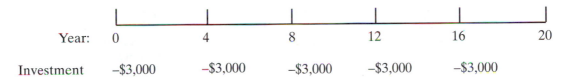

Year:	0	4	8	12	16	20
Investment	−$3,000	−$3,000	−$3,000	−$3,000	−$3,000	

Maintenance costs: $1,500 every year for 20 years
Fuel costs: $1,000 every year for 20 years (5,000 miles at 20 cents a mile)

B.   Buy a new car every five years for 20 years

Year:	0	5	10	15	20
Investment:	−$8,000	−$8,000	−$8,000	−$8,000	

Maintenance costs: $1,000 every year for 20 years
Fuel costs: $250 every year for 20 years (5,000 miles at 5 cents a mile)

Step 2   Compute the NPV of each stream.

NPV of replicating used cars for 20 years = -22225.61
NPV of replicating new cars for 20 years = -22762.21

The net present value of the costs incurred by buying a used car every four years is less negative than the net present value of the costs incurred by buying a new car every five years, given that the cars will be driven 5,000 miles every year. As the mileage driven increases, however, the relative benefits of owning and driving the more efficient new car will also increase.

Equivalent Annuity: This is an annuity that if paid or received over each year of a specified project would yield the same net present value as the project.

Equivalent annuities   The net present values of projects with different lives can be made comparable in another way. They can be converted into an **equivalent annuity,** which can be considered the annualized net present value; because the NPV is annualized, it can be compared legitimately across projects with different lives. The net present value of any project can be converted into an annuity using the following calculation.

Equivalent Annuity = Net Present Value * [A(PV , *r, n*)]

where

$$r = \text{Project discount rate}$$
$$n = \text{Project lifetime}$$
$$A(PV, \text{r}, \text{n}) = \text{annuity factor}$$

Note that the net present value of each project is converted into an annuity using that project's life and discount rate. Thus, this approach is flexible enough to deal with projects with different discount rates and lifetimes.

This approach does not *explicitly* make the assumption of project replication; rather it does so implicitly. Consequently, it will always lead to the same decision rules as the replication approach. The advantage is that the equivalent annuity approach is less tedious and will continue to work even in the presence of projects with infinite lives.

Consider again the choice between a new car and a used car described earlier. The equivalent annuities can be estimated for the two options as follows:

Step 1 Compute the net present value of each project individually (without replication).

Net present value of buying a used car = - $3,000 - $2,500 * PV(A,15%,4 years)
= - $10,137
Net present value of buying a new car = - $8,000 - $1,250 * PV(A,15%,5 years)
= - $12,190

Step 2 Convert the net present values into equivalent annuities.

Equivalent annuity of buying a used car = -$10,137 * (A(PV,15%, 4 years))
= -$3,551
Equivalent annuity of buying a new car = -12,190 * (A(PV,15%, 5 years))
= -$3,637

Based on the equivalent annuities of the two options, buying a used car is more economical than buying a new car.

IN PRACTICE USING EQUIVALENT ANNUITIES AS A GENERAL APPROACH FOR MULTIPLE PROJECTS

The equivalent annuity approach can be used to compare multiple projects with different lifetimes. For instance, assume that the Home Depot is considering three storage options:

Option	Initial Investment	Annual Cost	Project Life
Build own storage system	$10 million	$0.5 million	Infinite
Rent storage system	$2 million	$1.5 million	12 years
Use third-party storage	—	$2.0 million	1 year

These options have different lives; thus, the equivalent annual costs have to be computed for the comparison. If the cost of capital is 12.5%, the equivalent annual costs can be computed as follows.

Option	Net Present Value	Equivalent Annual Cost
Build own storage system	$14.00 million	$1.75 million
Rent storage system	$11.08 million	$1.83 million
Use third-party storage	$2 million	$2.00 million

Based on the equivalent annual costs, the Home Depot should build its own storage system, even though the initial costs are highest for this option.

Calculating Breakeven

When an option that costs more up front but is more efficient and economical on an annual basis is compared with a less expensive and less efficient option, the choice will depend on usage. For instance, in the analysis above, the less expensive used car is the more economical option if the mileage driven stays at 5,000 miles. The used car will become even more economical if the number of miles driven decreases, but the more efficient new car will become the better option if the car is driven more. The *breakeven* point is the number of miles at which the two options provide the same equivalent annual cost, as illustrated in Figure 9.6.

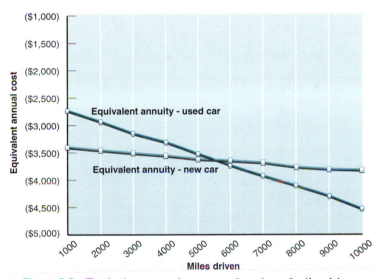

Figure 9.6   Equivalent annual costs as a function of miles driven

The breakeven occurs at roughly 5500 miles; if there is a reasonable chance that the mileage driven will exceed this break-even, the new car becomes the better option.

Concept Check

Assume that the cost of the third-party storage option will increase 3% a year forever. Compute the equivalent annual cost of that option.

A general framework   In a general framework for dealing with projects with different lives, a user can make specific assumptions about the types of projects that will be available when the shorter term projects end. To illustrate, an assumption that the firm will have no positive net present value projects when its current projects end will lead to a decision rule whereby the net present values of projects can be compared, even if they have different lives. Alternatively, specific assumptions can be made about the availability and the attractiveness of projects in the future, leading to cash-flow estimates and present value computations. Returning to the 5-year and 10-year projects described earlier in this chapter, assume that future projects will not be as attractive as current projects. More specifically, assume that the annual cash flows on the second 5-year

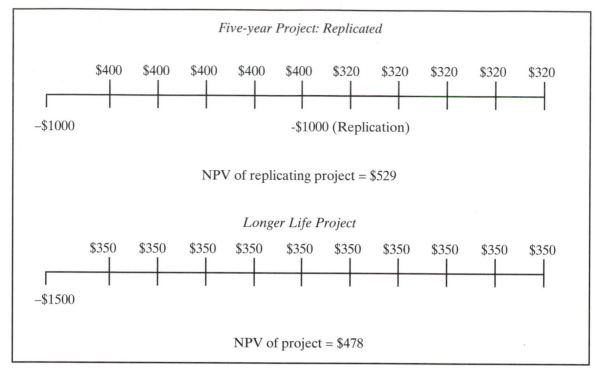

Figure 9.7   Cash flows on projects with unequal lives: replicated with poorer project

project that will be taken when the first 5-year project ends will be $320 instead of $400. The net present values of these two investment streams can be computed as shown in Figure 9.7. The firm will still pick the shorter-life project, although the margin in terms of net present value has shrunk.

This problem is not avoided by using internal rates of return. When the internal rate of return of a short-term project is compared to the internal rate of return of a long-term project, there is an implicit assumption that future projects will continue to have similar internal rates of return.

OTHER INVESTMENT DECISIONS

In this section, we explore a number of other investment decisions that do not fit neatly into any of the discussions we have had so far. In particular, we explore the dynamics of

- The *replacement decision,* whereby an existing machine, building, or equipment is replaced with a new one.
- The *expansion decision,* whereby an existing facility is expanded to meet increased demand.
- The *timing decision,* whereby the decision maker might have to decide when to take or terminate a project.

Replacement Decision

A **replacement decision,** involves replacing an existing investment with a new one, generally because the existing investment has aged and become less efficient. In a typical replacement decision

Replacement Decision: This is the decision whether to replace an existing asset with a newer one that performs the same functions.

- The replacement of old equipment with new equipment will involve a cash outflow, because the money spent on the new equipment will exceed any proceeds obtained from the sale of the old equipment.
- There will be cash inflows during the life of the new machine as a consequence of either the lower costs of operation arising from the newer equipment or the higher revenues flowing from the decision. These cash inflows will be augmented by the tax benefits accruing from the additional depreciation that will arise from the new investment.
- The salvage value at the end of the life of the new equipment will be the differential salvage value—that is, the excess of the salvage value on the new equipment over the salvage value that would have been obtained if the old equipment had been kept for the entire period and not replaced at the beginning.

This approach has to be modified if the old equipment has a remaining life that is much shorter than the life of the new equipment replacing it.

To illustrate, suppose a mail-order company is considering replacing an antiquated packaging system with a new one. The old system has a book value of $50,000 and a remaining life of 10 years and could be sold for $15,000, net of capital gains taxes, right now. It would be replaced with a new machine that costs $150,000 and has a depreciable life of 10 years and annual operating costs $40,000 lower than with the new machine. Assuming straight-line depreciation for both the old and the new system, a 40% tax rate, and no salvage value on either machine in 10 years, the replacement decision cash flows can be estimated as follows:

$$\text{Net Initial Investment in New Machine} = -\$150,000 + \$15,000 = \$135,000$$
$$\text{Depreciation on the old system} = \$5,000$$
$$\text{Depreciation on the new system} = \$15,000$$
$$\text{Annual Tax Savings from Additional Depreciation on New Machine}$$
$$= (\$15,000 - \$5,000)*0.4 = \$4000$$
$$\text{Annual After-tax Savings in Operating Costs} = \$40,000 (1-0.4) = \$24,000$$

The cost of capital for the company is 12%, resulting in a net present value from the replacement decision of:

$$\text{Net Present Value of Replacement Decision} = -\$135,000 + \$28,000 *$$
$$\text{PV(A,12\%,10 years)} = \$23,206$$

This suggests that replacing the old packaging machine with a new one will have a net present value of $23,206 and would be a wise move to make.

 Concept Check

Assume that you are unsure about how much operating expenses will drop as a consequence of the replacement decision. How much would they need to drop, at the minimum, for you to break even on this decision?

Expansion Decision

An **expansion decision** involves considering an additional investment in order to expand an existing facility, generally because it is at or near capacity. The cash flows in such a decision can be categorized as follows:

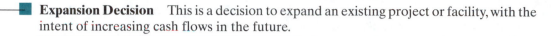

Expansion Decision   This is a decision to expand an existing project or facility, with the intent of increasing cash flows in the future.

- The expansion itself will create a cash outflow as the facility is expanded and new equipment is acquired to facilitate the expansion.
- As a result of the expansion, additional revenue will be generated in periods whereby the new capacity enables the firm to meet demand it could not have met with the existing facility. These revenues will provide cash inflows in future periods and will be augmented by the tax benefits from the incremental depreciation.
- At the end of the project life, the incremental salvage value from the expansion will have to be considered as a cash inflow.

IN PRACTICE   ANALYZING AN EXPANSION DECISION—THE HOME DEPOT

Assume that the Home Depot is considering an expansion of an existing store from 60,000 square feet to 100,000 square feet. The expansion is expected to cost $5 million, which will be depreciated straight-line over 10 years to a salvage value of zero. The expansion will increase revenues next year at the store from $15 million to $25 million, and the pretax operating margin is 20%. This is expected to grow 7% a year for the next 10 years. The tax rate is 36%, and the cost of capital is 12.5%.

$$\text{Initial investment associated with expansion} = -\$5 \text{ million}$$

The operating cash flows from the expansion can be computed as shown in Table 9.7.

Table 9.7   **AFTER-TAX CASH FLOWS FROM EXPANSION DECISION: THE HOME DEPOT**

Year	Incremental Pretax OI	Incremental After-tax OI	Depreciation Tax Benefit	ATCF	PV of ATCF
1	$2,000,000	$1,280,000	$180,000	$1,460,000	$1,297,778
2	2,140,000	1,369,600	180,000	1,549,600	1,224,375
3	2,289,800	1,465,472	180,000	1,645,472	1,155,668
4	2,450,086	1,568,055	180,000	1,748,055	1,091,302
5	2,621,592	1,677,819	180,000	1,857,819	1,030,958
6	2,805,103	1,795,266	180,000	1,975,266	974,340
7	3,001,461	1,920,935	180,000	2,100,935	921,181
8	3,211,563	2,055,400	180,000	2,235,400	871,235
9	3,436,372	2,199,278	180,000	2,379,278	824,276
10	3,676,918	2,353,228	180,000	2,533,228	780,098
					$10,171,209

Net Present Value of Expansion Decision = - $5,000,000 + $10,171,209
= $5,171,209

Expanding the store will result in a positive net present value and should be done.

Timing Decisions

A **timing decision** allows the decision maker to decide when to take an action. For instance, the owner of a lumber tract may have to decide when to harvest the trees for lumber. Similarly, the owner of a product patent may have to decide when to introduce the product. In decisions of this type, there is generally both a cost and a benefit to waiting. By waiting, the firm may be able to get better information on the market or get a higher price for its product, or it may have time to improve the product itself. These advantages have to be weighed against the time value of waiting an extra period as well as the risk of a competitor entering the market first. In addition, the costs may increase over time. If the benefits of waiting exceed the costs, it pays to wait.

Timing Decision: This is the decision of when to act on or take a project.

Another way of thinking about the timing decision is in terms of net present value. If the net present value is a function of when an action is taken, the optimal time to take the action is the one that maximizes the net present value.

To illustrate, assume that you own an area of land on which you have the rights to cut the trees for lumber. It will cost you $1 million to clear the land, and the lumber harvested right now will yield $1.1 million. These costs are expected to grow 3% a year over time. Your cost of capital is 10%. Furthermore, assume that the trees will become more valuable over time and that the growth rates in value will be as shown in Table 9.8.

Table 9.8 **PRESENT VALUE OF LUMBER AT DIFFERENT HARVESTING PERIODS**

Year	Growth Rate (%)	Value of Lumber	Cost of Harvesting	NPV
0		$1,100,000	$1,000,000	$100,000
1	10	1,210,000	1,030,000	163,636
2	9	1,318,900	1,060,900	213,223
3	8	1,424,412	1,092,727	249,200
4	7	1,524,121	1,125,509	272,257
5	6	1,615,568	1,159,274	283,323
6	5	1,696,346	1,194,052	283,532
7	4	1,764,200	1,229,874	274,194
8	3	1,817,126	1,266,770	256,745
9	2	1,853,469	1,304,773	232,701
10	1	1,872,004	1,343,916	203,600
11	1	1,890,724	1,384,234	177,522
12	1	1,909,631	1,425,761	154,176

To understand how the net present value is computed, assume that you delay harvesting the lumber until the end of the first year. The value of the lumber will increase to $1.21 million, while the cost of harvesting will increase to $1.03 million, resulting in a net gain of $180,000. Discounted back one year at 10% yields a net present value of $163,236. Based on similar computations for the other periods, the net present value is maximized if the lumber is harvested in the sixth year.

DEALING WITH PROJECT INTERACTIONS

In many cases, projects that are considered by a firm are intertwined with the revenues and cash flows of other projects being considered contemporaneously and with exisiting projects. Sometimes the effects are positive, with one project gaining from another project under consideration; other times the effects are negative, with one project draining cash flows from another project that has already been taken or is under consideration. From the viewpoint of incremental cash flows to the firm, these intraproject effects must be considered.

Project Synergies

When a project under consideration creates positive benefits (in the form of cash flows) for other projects that a firm may have, there are **project synergies.** For instance, assume that you are a clothing retailer considering whether to open an upscale clothing store for children in the same shopping center where you already own a store that caters to an adult audience. In addition to generating revenues and cash flows on its own, the children's store might increase the traffic into the adult store and increase profits at that store. That additional profit, and its ensuing cash flow, have to be factored into the analysis of the new store.

Project Synergy: These are the increases in cash flows that accrue to other projects, as a consequence of the project under consideration.

Sometimes the project synergies are not with existing projects but with other projects that are being considered contemporaneously. In such cases, the best way to analyze the projects is jointly, since examining each separately will lead to a much lower net present value. Thus, a proposal to open a children's clothing store and an adult clothing store in the same shopping center will have to be treated as a joint investment analysis, and the net present value will have to be calculated for both stores together. A positive net present value would suggest opening both stores, whereas a negative net present value would indicate that neither should be opened.

 IN PRACTICE   CASH-FLOW SYNERGIES WITH EXISTING PROJECTS—THE HOME DEPOT

Assume that the Home Depot is considering adding a restaurant to one of its stores to take advantage of the substantial traffic through the store. The restaurant will cost $300,000 to build and is expected to generate sales of $60,000 in the first year. The following additional information is available on the store:

- The revenue is expected to increase 7% a year.
- The cost of running the restaurant, including the cost of the food, will be 60% of the revenue.
- The store life is assumed to be 10 years, at the end of which there will be no salvage from the investment in the restaurant (there is no depreciation).
- The cost of capital is 12.5%, and the tax rate is 36%.

Based on this information, the estimated cash flows on the restaurant are shown in Table 9.9.

The present value of the cash inflows is less than the initial investment of $300,000, suggesting that this is not a good investment, based on the cash flows it would generate. Assume, however, that the restaurant will attract some customers into the store who otherwise would not have shopped there. These customers are expected to generate about $300,000 in additional

Table 9.9   ESTIMATED CASH FLOWS ON THE HOME DEPOT RESTAURANT

Year	Revenues	Operating Costs	BTCF	ATCF	PV of ATCF
1	$60,000	$36,000	$24,000	$15,360	$13,653
2	64,200	38,520	25,680	16,435	12,986
3	68,694	41,216	27,478	17,586	12,351
4	73,503	44,102	29,401	18,817	11,747
5	78,648	47,189	31,459	20,134	11,173
6	84,153	50,492	33,661	21,543	10,627
7	90,044	54,026	36,018	23,051	10,107
8	96,347	57,808	38,539	24,665	9,613
9	103,091	61,855	41,236	26,391	9,143
10	110,308	66,185	44,123	28,239	8,696
					$110,096

sales in the first year, and this amount is expected to grow 7% a year. The pretax operating margin for the store is 20%. The incremental cash flows from the "synergy" are shown in Table 9.10.

Table 9.10:   INCREMENTAL CASH FLOWS FROM SYNERGY

Year	Incremental Revenue	Incremental After-tax OI	PV of Incremental OI
1	$300,000	$36,000	$32,000
2	321,000	38,520	30,436
3	343,470	41,216	28,948
4	367,513	44,102	27,532
5	393,239	47,189	26,186
6	420,766	50,492	24,906
7	450,219	54,026	23,688
8	481,734	57,808	22,530
9	515,456	61,855	21,429
10	551,538	66,185	20,381
			258,036

The present value of the incremental cash flows generated for the store as a consequence of the restaurant is $258,036. Incorporating this into the present value analysis yields the following:

Net Present Value of Restaurant = - $300,000 + $110,096 + $258,036 = $68,132

Incorporating the cash flows from the synergy into the analysis, the restaurant is a good investment for the Home Depot.

Project Costs

A new project may sometimes generate costs for other ventures the business has. Chapter 8 provided an analysis of two fairly common components of these costs—opportunity costs and lost sales from product cannibalization. In general, however, intraproject costs can be estimated as follows:

Step 1   Estimate any incremental costs that will be incurred by other projects at the firm as a consequence of taking the new project.

Step 2 Either incorporate these costs into the operating cash flows of the project or estimate the present value of the after-tax incremental costs.

Step 3 Estimate the net present value of the new project, incorporating the incremental costs into the cash flows or adding them to the initial investment. If the new project still has a positive net present value, accept the project.

As an example, assume that the restaurant described in the previous example also created a parking constraint, that is, there are not enough parking spots for the customers in the store and the restaurant. This constraint may result in the store losing some sales; the present value of the after-tax cash flows from these lost sales will have to be subtracted from the present value of the project in order to decide whether it should be taken. In this case, if the present value of the cash flows from the lost sales is greater than $68,132, the Home Depot should not open the restaurant.

CONCLUSION

This chapter builds on the concepts of capital budgeting introduced in the last two chapters and develops the following concepts:

- Firms face capital rationing constraints for a number of reasons, some internal and some external. Generally, firms that are smaller and use equity rather than debt will face tighter capital rationing constraints than will larger firms with greater access to the debt markets. In the presence of capital rationing, the net present value of projects has to be scaled to account for size; those projects that yield the highest net present value given the limited investment funds should be chosen.

- When choosing among projects, the net present values can be compared only if the projects have the same lives. When comparing projects with different lives, the net present value has to be converted into an annuity, or the projects have to be replicated until they have equivalent lives.

- Replacement and expansion decisions can be made by looking at the incremental cash flows from these decisions to the business.

- Projects that create benefits or costs for other parts of the business have to be considered on an after-tax basis, when these projects are evaluated.

QUESTIONS AND PROBLEMS

1. A small manufacturing firm that has limited access to capital has a capital rationing constraint of $150 million and is faced with the following investment projects:

Project	Initial Investment	NPV
A	$25	$10
B	$30	$25
C	$40	$20
D	$10	$10
E	$15	$10
F	$60	$20
G	$20	$10

Project	Initial Investment	NPV
H	$25	$20
I	$35	$10
J	$15	$5

a. Which of these projects would you accept? Why?

b. What is the cost of the capital rationing constraint?

2. A closely held, publicly traded firm faces self-imposed capital rationing constraints of $100 million in this period and $75 million in the next period. It has to choose among the following projects:

Investment Outlay

Project	Current Period	Next Period	NPV
A	$20	$10	$20
B	$25	$15	$20
C	$30	$30	$15
D	$15	$15	$20
E	$40	$25	$30
F	$10	$10	$10
G	$20	$15	$20
H	$30	$25	$35
I	$35	$25	$25
J	$25	$15	$10

Set up the capital rationing problem, assuming that fractions and multiples of projects cannot be taken.

3. You own a rental building in the city and are interested in replacing the heating system. You are faced with the following alternatives:

  a. A solar heating system, which will cost $12,000 to install and $500 a year to run and will last forever (assume that your building will too).

  b. A gas-heating system, which will cost $5,000 to install and $1,000 a year to run and will last 20 years.

  c. An oil-heating system, which will cost $3,500 to install and $1,200 a year to run and will last 15 years.

If your opportunity cost is 10%, which of these three options is best for you?

4. You are trying to choose a new siding for your house. A salesman offers you two choices:

  a. Wooden siding, which will last 10 years and cost $5,000 to install and $1,000/year to maintain.

  b. Aluminium siding, which will last forever, cost $15,000 to install, and will have a lower maintentance cost per year.

If your discount rate is 10%, how much would your maintenance costs have to be for you to choose the aluminium siding?

5. You have just been approached by a magazine with an offer for to renew your subscription. You can renew for one year at $20, two years at $36, or three years at $45. Assuming that you have an opportunity cost of 20% and the cost of a subscription will not change over time, which of these three options should you choose?

6. You have been hired as a capital budgeting analyst by a sporting goods firm that manufactures athletic shoes and has captured 10% of the overall shoe market. (The total market is worth $100 million a year.) The fixed costs associated with manufacturing these shoes is $2 million a year, and variable costs are 40% of revenues. The company's tax rate is 40%. The firm believes that it can increase its market share to 20% by investing $10 million in a new distribution system (which can be depreciated over the system's life of 10 years to a salvage value of zero) and spending $1 million a year in additional advertising. The company proposes to continue to maintain working capital at 10% of annual revenues. The discount rate to be used for this project is 8%.

  a. What is the initial investment for this project?

  b. What is the annual operating cash flow from this project?

  c. What is the NPV of this project?

  d. How much would the firm's market share have to increase for you to be indifferent to taking or rejecting this project?

7. You are considering the possibility of replacing an existing machine that has a book value of $500,000, a remaining depreciable life of five years, with a new machine that will cost $2 million and have a 10-year life. The existing machine can be sold for $300,000 now, and the discount rate is 10%. Assuming that you use straight-line depreciation and that neither machine will have any salvage value at the end of the next 10 years, how much would you need to save each year to make the change (the tax rate is 40%)?

8. You are helping a bookstore decide whether it should open a coffee shop on the premises. The details of the investment are as follows:

  • The coffee shop will cost $ 50,000 to open; it will have a five-year life and be depreciated straight-line over the period to a salvage value of $10,000.

  • The sales at the shop are expected to be $15,000 in the first year and to grow 5% a year for the following five years.

  • The operating expenses will be 50% of revenues.

  • The tax rate is 40%.

  • The coffee shop is expected to generate additional sales of $20,000 next year for the book shop, and the pretax operating margin is 40%. These sales will grow 10% a year for the following four years.

  • The discount rate is 12%.

  a. Estimate the net present value of the coffee shop without the additional book sales.

  b. Estimate the present value of the cash flows accruing from the additional book sales.

  c. Would you open the coffee shop?

9. The lining of a plating tank must be replaced every three years at the cost of approximately $2,000. A new lining material has been developed that is more resistant to the corrosive effects of the plating liquid and will cost approximately $4,000. If the required rate of return is 20% and annual property taxes and insurance amount to about 4% of the initial investment, how long must the new lining last to be more economical than the present one?

10. You are a small-business owner and are considering two alternatives for your phone system.

	Plan A	Plan B
Initial cost	$50,000	$120,000
Annual maintenance cost	$9,000	$6,000
Salvage value	$10,000	$20,000
Life	20 years	40 years

The discount rate is 8%. Which alternatve would you pick?

11. You have been asked to compare three alternative investments and make a recommendation.

- Project A has an initial investment of $5 million and after-tax cash flows of $2.5 million a year for the next 5 years.

- Project B has no initial investment, after-tax cash flows of $1 million a year for the next 10 years, and a salvage value of $2 million (from working capital).

- Project C has an initial investment of $10 million, another investment of $5 million in 10 years, and after-tax cash flows of $2.5 million a year forever.

The discount rate is 10% for all three projects. Which of the three projects would you pick? Why?

12. You are the manager of a pharmaceutical company and are considering what type of laptops to buy for your sales representatives to take with them on their calls.

- You can buy fairly inexpensive (and less powerful) older machines for about $2,000 each. These machines will be obsolete in three years and are expected to have an annual maintentance cost of $150.

- You can buy newer and more powerful laptops for about $4,000 each. These machines will last five years and are expected to have an annual maintenance cost of $50.

If your cost of capital is 12%, which option would you pick and why?

13. You are the supervisor of a town in which the roads are in need of repair. You have a limited budget and are considering two options:

- In the first option, you will patch up the roads for $100,000, but you will then have to repeat this ex-penditure every year to keep the roads in reasonable shape.

- Alternatively, you can spend $400,000 to repave and repair the roads, in which case, the annual expenditures on maintenance will drop.

If your discount rate is 10%, how much would the annual expenditures have to drop in the second option for you to consider it?

14. You are the manager of a specialty retailing firm that is considering two strategies for getting into the Malaysian retail market. Under the first strategy, the firm will make a small initial investment of $10 million and can expect to capture about 5% of the overall market share. Under the second strategy, the firm will make a much larger commitment of $40 million for advertising and promotion and can expect to capture about 10% of the market share. If the overall size of the market is $200 million, the firm's cost of capital is 12%, the tax rate is 40%, and the typical life of a project in the firm is 15 years, what would the operating margin have to be for the firm to consider the second strategy? (You can assume that the firm leases its stores and has no depreciation or capital expenditures.)

15. You work for a firm that has limited access to capital markets. As a consequence, it has only $20 million available for new investments this year. The firm does have a ready supply of good projects, and you have listed out all of the projects.

Project	Initial Investment	NPV	IRR
I	$10 million	$3 million	21%
II	$5 million	$2.5 million	28%
III	$15 million	$4 million	19%
IV	$10 million	$4 million	24%
V	$5 million	$2 million	20%

a. Based on the profitability index, which of these projects would you take?

b. Based on the IRR, which of these projects would you take?

c. Why might the two approaches give you different answers?

16. You are the owner of a small hardware store, and you are considering opening a gardening shop in a vacant area in the back of the store. You estimate that it will cost you $50,000 to set up the store and that you will generate $10,000 in after-tax cash flows for the life of the store (which is expected to be 10 years). The one concern you have is that you have limited parking; by opening the gardening shop you run the risk of not having enough parking for customers who shop at your hardware store. You estimate that the lost sales would amount to $3,000 a

year and that your after-tax operating margin on sales at the hardware store is 40%. If your discount rate is 14%, would you open the gardening shop?

17. You are the manager of a grocery store and you are considering offering baby-sitting services to your customers. You estimate that the licensing and set-up costs will amount to $150,000 initially and that you will be spending about $60,000 annually to provide the service. As a result of the service, you expect sales at the store, which are $5 million currently, to increase by 20%; your after-tax operating margin is 10%. If your cost of capital is 12%, and you expect the store to remain open for 10 years, would you offer the service?

18. You run a financial service firm and you replace your employees' computers every three years. You have 5000 employees, and each computer costs $2,500 currently; the old computers can be sold for $500 each. The new computers are generally depreciated straight-line over their three-year lives to a salvage value of $500. A computer service firm offers to lease you the computers and replace them for you at no cost if you will pay a leasing fee of $5 million a year (which is tax deductible). If your tax rate is 40% and your discount rate is 12%, would you accept the offer?

CHAPTER 10

UNCERTAINTY AND RISK IN CAPITAL BUDGETING: PART I

Decisions on projects almost always involve uncertainty. This chapter describes the probabilistic approaches to dealing with uncertainty, which examine the effect of changing assumptions on investment decisions. In the process, it attempts to answer the following questions:

- In doing investment analysis, how sensitive are the conclusions to changes in the key assumptions underlying the analysis?

- How can investment analysis be done under different scenarios for the future?

- How is breakeven analysis done from the viewpoint of present value analysis different from traditional breakeven analysis, which looks at net income?

- Under what conditions can simulations be done to analyze projects, and how can the results from these simulations be used in decision making?

- What types of risk does a typical project carry? What portion of this risk is relevant when analyzing the project?

- How can this risk be factored into discount rates and expected cash flows?

- What are some of the most common errors made by firms when analyzing the riskiness of projects?

BASIC APPROACHES TO DEALING WITH UNCERTAINTY

There are two basic approaches to dealing with uncertainty. In the first approach, the robustness of the analysis tested by changing the assumptions and examining the effects of these changes on the conclusions. This information is then used to make a final decision on a project. Typical examples of this approach include sensitivity analysis, scenario analysis, breakeven analysis, simulation analysis, and decision trees. In all these approaches, the analysis adds information to that provided by the **base case analysis**. But it is still up to the decision maker to weigh this information intelligently and make the final decision. The subjective judgments of analysts and their tolerance for uncertainty will therefore affect their decisions. The same sensitivity analysis, for example, might result in one analyst rejecting a project and another analyst accepting the same project.

The second approach to dealing with risk adjusts for it either in the discount rate used in the base case analysis or in the expected cash flows used to measure the project's viability. The advantage of this approach is that it yields one measure (i.e., a base case net present value or internal rate of return) that already reflects the riskiness of the project. For the most part, it takes out the subjective element from the risk analysis. At the same time, this approach puts a larger onus on the analyst to estimate and adjust for risk correctly. This approach is examined in the next chapter.

Base Case Analysis: This is the project analysis done with the most likely values used for the inputs.

PROBABILISTIC APPROACHES TO DEALING WITH RISK

In the traditional investment analysis, described in the last few chapters of this book, the investment decision has been based on a single NPV or IRR, which, in turn, is based on a set of assumptions made about the future prospects of the project. Each of these assumptions by itself may be reasonable and justifiable, but each also represents a single estimate, often drawn from a range of possible outcomes. In the approaches described here, risk is assessed by estimating the net present value or the internal rate of return for a *range of outcomes* for the underlying variables.

SENSITIVITY ANALYSIS

Most investment analyses are based on expectations about future cash flows and earnings, which, in turn, provide the forecasts for the "base case" analysis. Uncertainty is associated with most of these forecasts, and the conclusions may be affected by changes in one or more of the assumptions underlying the base case analysis. In **sensitivity analysis,** the effect of changes in one or more of the assumptions on net present value, internal rate of return, or return on investment are considered in deciding whether or not to take the project.

Sensitivity Analysis: This is an analysis that examines the sensitivity of the decision rule (NPV, IRR, etc.) to changes in the assumptions underlying a project.

Sensitivity analysis is conducted as follows:

Step 1   Based on expectations for the future, the earnings and cash flows are estimated for a base case analysis.

Step 2   The key assumptions made in the base case analysis are identified. In general, these assumptions can be:

- *Firm specific*—related to revenue levels, operating margins, project life, and working capital needs, among others.
- *Macroeconomic*—related to variables such as tax rates and overall economic growth, which, though not under the control of the firm, may still have a major impact on the cash flows and conclusions of the analysis.

Step 3   Each assumption in the analysis is changed, while keeping all other assumptions unchanged, and the net present value, IRR, or return on capital is estimated after the change. To illustrate, in a project involving product sales, the number of units sold will vary while the price, costs, and discount rate will remain fixed.

Step 4   The findings are presented in the form of either graphs or tables, summarizing the effect on NPV or IRR of changes in each variable.

Step 5 This information is used in conjunction with the base case analysis to decide whether or not to take the project. This process can either be subjective and left to the discretion of the decision maker, or it can be based on specific quantitative criteria.

 IN PRACTICE THE HOME DEPOT: A SENSITIVITY ANALYSIS

The following is an analysis of a new store being considered by the Home Depot, with the following assumptions governing the base case:

- Initial Investment in the Store (100,000 square feet) = $12.5 million
- Expected Life of the Store = 10 years
- Salvage Value of the Store Premises at the end of 10 years = $5.5 million
- Expected Revenues/Square Foot in first year = $300 / square foot; Growth rate = 5%;
- Pretax Operating Margin (EBIT/Sales) = 10.00%
- Working Capital as a percentage of Revenues = 10.00%; investment is at beginning of each year and is completely salvageable at the end of the project life.
- The depreciation each year is computed using MACRS depreciation rates.
- The corporate tax rate is 36.00%; The cost of capital is 12.5%

With these assumptions, the expected cash flows can be computed for the project life, as shown in Table 10.1.

TABLE 10.1 FCFF ON THE HOME DEPOT STORE

Year	Investment	Revenues	EBIT (1-t)	Depreciation	Change in WC	FCFF
0	$(12,500,000)				$(3,000,000)	$(15,500,000)
1		$30,000,000	$1,920,000	$540,000	(150,000)	2,310,000
2		31,500,000	2,016,000	432,000	(157,500)	2,290,500
3		33,075,000	2,116,800	345,600	(165,375)	2,297,025
4		34,728,750	2,222,640	276,480	(173,644)	2,325,476
5		36,465,188	2,333,772	221,184	(182,326)	2,372,630
6		38,288,447	2,450,461	176,947	(191,442)	2,435,966
7		40,202,869	2,572,984	141,558	(201,014)	2,513,527
8		42,213,013	2,701,633	113,246	(211,065)	2,603,814
9		44,323,663	2,836,714	90,597	(221,618)	2,705,693
10	$5,500,000	$46,539,846	$2,978,550	$72,478	$4,653,985	$13,205,012

FCFF = EBIT (1-t) + Depreciation + Change in Working Capital - Capital expenditure

These estimated cash flows to the firm are discounted back at the cost of capital of 12.5%, to arrive at a net present value of $1,067,099, which would suggest accepting the project. The internal rate of return, based on the cash flows, is 13.83%, which would confirm this conclusion.

Because these conclusions are affected by the assumptions made in the base case, we examine the sensitivity of the conclusions to changes in the assumptions. We focus on four assumptions: (1) the level of revenues, (2) the expected growth rate in revenues, (3) the operating margin, and (4) the working capital as a percentage of revenues. With each assumption, we estimate the net present value and the IRR as the assumption changes, keeping other assumptions unchanged.

Choice of Variables

Although it is always tempting to change each and every assumption underlying an analysis, it makes sense to focus on two sets of assumptions in particular:

1. Those that matter the most, in terms of affecting cash flows and, thus, net present value and internal rate of return (e.g., the level of revenues, revenue growth, and operating margin); and

2. Those with the most uncertainty (e.g., it does not make sense to vary depreciation if the depreciation rates are governed by the ACRS schedule and are thus fixed).

In addition, some assumptions are subject to management control, where the sensitivity analysis might help the management increase the project's value. In the above Home Depot example, the working capital as a percentage of revenues would qualify under this criterion because the Home Depot may be able to reduce this working capital investment, either by maintaining lower inventory or by using more short-term financing and accounts payable.

In addition, a range of values has to be specified for the chosen variables. This range is a function of past experience (e.g., revenues/square foot at existing stores may range anywhere from $200 per square foot at the poorer performing stores to $400 per square foot at the very best stores) and is constrained by reasonable values. Thus, when estimating working capital as a percentage of revenues, the minimum would be set at zero percent, rather than allowing working capital to become negative.[1]

Level of revenues   The base case analysis assumes that the revenues at the store will be $30 million, or $300 per square foot, in the first year. In Figure 10.1, the net present

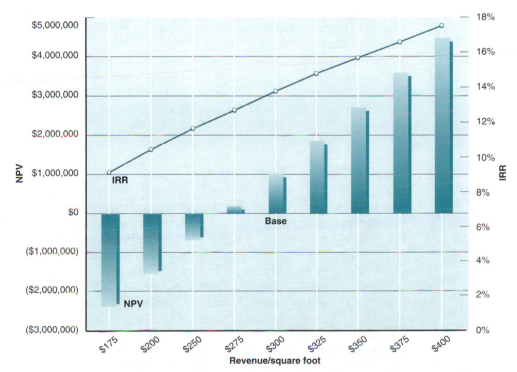

Figure 10.1   The Home Depot: NPV and IRR as a function of revenues/square foot

---

[1]It could be argued that even zero percent is unreasonable, since the company has to maintain *some* working capital for its stores to succeed.

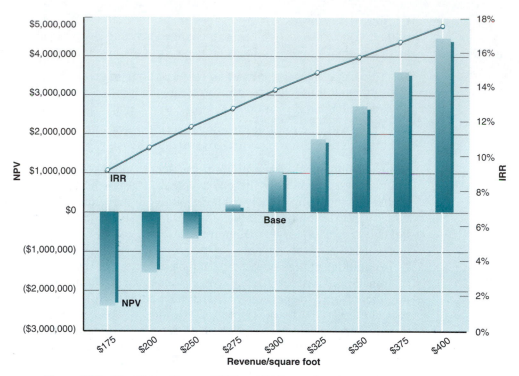

Figure 10.2   The Home Depot: NPV and IRR as a function of expected growth rate

value for the Home Depot store is computed as the revenues per square foot and increased from $200 to $400, while the expected growth rates and the operating margin remain at the base case levels.

The net present value of the store remains positive if the revenue per square foot drops from $300 to $275, but it becomes negative at levels below that, with a net present value below minus $2 million at $200 per square foot. Conversely, the net present value increases fairly dramatically if the revenues per square foot are increased above $300 per square foot. Similar conclusions emerge from the analysis of the IRR as a function of revenue growth.

Expected revenues growth rate   In the base case analysis, we assumed that revenues would grow 5% a year for the 10-year life of the project. In Figure 10.2, we examine the effects on the net present value and the internal rate of return of changing this growth rate while keeping other assumptions at base case levels. (Revenues revert to $300 per square foot, and operating margins are assumed to remain at 10%.)

Not surprisingly, the net present value decreases as the growth rate drops below 5%, but not by as much as it did when the level of revenues was changed. In fact, at growth rates of 2% or greater, the net present value remains positive. The IRR does not change as much either and is approximately 12%, even at a growth rate of zero.

Operating margins   The base case analysis is based on the assumption that the pretax operating margin will be 10% of revenues. In Figure 10.3, the net present value and the IRR are computed as a function of the pretax operating margin.

The effects on net present value and the IRR are dramatic, as the net present value drops to about minus $10 million at a pretax operating margin of 2% and the IRR drops to close to zero.

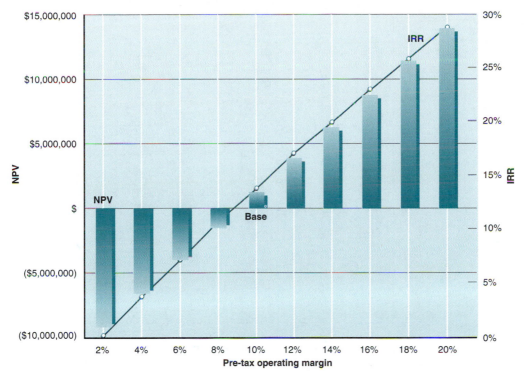

Figure 10.3   The Home Depot: NPV and IRR as a function of operating margin

Working capital as a percentage of revenues   In the base case analysis, working capital was assumed to be 10% of revenues, and the investments were made at the beginning of each year. Consequently the new store requires an initial investment of $3 million in working capital and makes additional investments totaling $1.65 million over the next 10 years; the entire amount—$4.65 million—is salvaged at the end of the tenth year. As a result of the difference in timing, however, the net present value decreases. Figure 10.4 computes the net present value as a function of the working capital investment. As you can see, the net present value increases (decreases) by approximately $625,000 for every 2.5% drop (rise) in the working capital as a percentage of revenues.

Making a Final Decision
The final decision on whether or not to take the project will be based on both the base case analysis and the additional information generated by the sensitivity analysis. It is entirely feasible that a decision maker, when faced with the results from the sensitivity analysis, might decide to override the base case and reject the project. As a rationale, he or she might point out that small drops in the operating margin make the project unacceptable and that there is substantial variability in operating margins across time.

Project Life and NPV: Another Assumption?
The life of a project, which is often taken as given, is usually an assumption just like the other assumptions listed above. In fact, the life of a project can sometimes have a much larger effect on the decision to take or reject the project than more conventional assumptions. The project life is based on a mixture of factors, including:

Concept
Check

Given the sensitivity of net present value to each of these assumptions, would your decision on this project change from the base case? Why or why not?

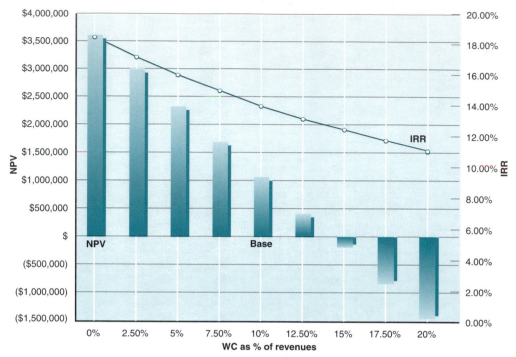

Figure 10.4   The Home Depot: Working capital as percent of revenues

- The company's past experience with projects and how long these projects have survived and produced cash flows.
- The intensity of the competition; the more intense the competition, the shorter the project life should be in order to reflect the fact that excess returns (which create positive net present value) are unlikely to persist over long periods.
- The uncertainty associated with cash-flow estimates; it is much more difficult to estimate cash flows well into the future, and many companies cut their analysis off at some point in time (such as 10 years) to prevent getting bogged down in this uncertainty.
- The length of leases or rentals that might govern the project; for instance, a retail store may set its project life to the life of its typical lease (10 or 12 years).

No matter what the rationale, some uncertainty is associated with the estimate of project life. Consequently, it makes sense to calculate the performance measures (such as NPV or IRR) as a function of the project life.

When the project life is extended, the analyst is burdened with the responsibility of estimating cash flows even further into the future. This estimation process can be simplified in one of two ways:

1. By assuming that cash flows will continue to grow at a specific rate beyond the final year of the initial analysis, or
2. By assuming that the cash flows will be fixed at the level they reached in the final year of the initial analysis.

In either case, the salvage value of plant and working capital cannot be shown as a positive cash flow in the final year of the original analysis, for a project cannot be salvaged and still continue to earn cash flows. If the project is expected to continue for a fixed period, the salvage must be shown at the end of the project life. If the project is expected to last forever (i.e., be a perpetuity), the salvage value will be ignored and replaced with a terminal value that captures the present value of all future cash flows.

 Concept Check

> It is often argued that forcing a fixed life for all projects under consideration affects all the projects equally and thus should not matter if they are being compared for investment purposes. Do you agree with this statement? Why or why not?

IN PRACTICE   EFFECT OF CHANGING PROJECT LIFE: THE HOME DEPOT STORE

The project lifetime assumed for the store in the previous example was 10 years. In general, the net present value will increase if the project life is increased and will decrease if the project life is reduced. In this case, assume the following:

- Revenue will continue to grow 5% a year, for each additional year of the project, until 15 years. After that, if the project continues, the cash flows will remain constant.
- The pretax operating margin and the working capital as a percentage of revenues will both continue to be 10%.
- The working capital will be salvaged at the end of the project life.
- The salvage value of the store is assumed to remain at $5.5 million, but it too will be collected at the end of the project life.

Using these assumptions, we can compute the net present value for project lives ranging from 5 to 15 years, as shown in Figure 10.5.

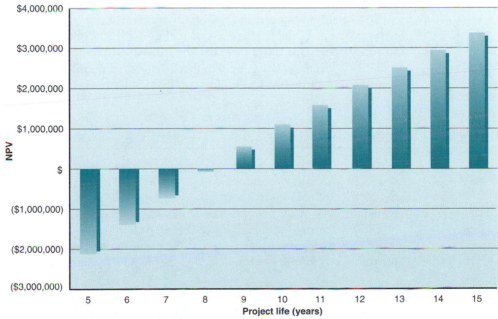

Figure 10.5   The Home Depot: Project life vs. NPV

Note that the net present value of the store increases at a decreasing rate as the project life is extended, largely because of the present value effects.

In the above example, if the store is assumed to last forever, the analysis can be extended fairly simply by replacing the salvage value (of working capital and the store) with a terminal value, which captures the present value of cash flows forever after the last year. In this case, for instance, if we assume that the cash flows after year 15 will remain constant forever, the terminal value can be computed as follows:

$$\text{Terminal Value of the Store} = \text{Cash Flow to Firm in Year 15/Cost of Capital}$$
$$= \$3,801,469/.125 = \$30,411,749$$

The net present value of the store can then be calculated, based on receiving this terminal value in year 15, as $6,015,193.

Limitations (and Possible Fixes) for Sensitivity Analysis

Several limitations are associated with traditional sensitivity analysis. The first is that the analysis presents results for a range of values, without providing any sense of the likelihood of these values occurring. Thus, the net present value of the Home Depot store in the previous example is $2.5 million when working capital is 2.5% of revenues, but this may actually be a very unlikely scenario. Similar arguments could be made about the extremes for the values in each of the preceding figures.

The second limitation is based on the requirement that only one assumption be changed at a time, keeping all other assumptions unchanged. In the real world, variables often move together. Revenues may be lower in precisely the same cases that growth rates are low, for example. This can be dealt with in one of two ways. First, the net present value can be computed as a function of two variables and presented on a three-dimensional graph rather than the two-dimensional graph used above. Second, the correlated variables can be combined to create a single variable, which can then be manipulated. For instance, the entire revenue stream, which incorporates both the level and growth in revenues, can be changed and the net present value computed.

The final limitation is the essentially subjective use of the analysis. The same sensitivity analysis that leads one decision maker to reject a project might be used by another to accept it, and the differences may be traceable to the risk preferences of the decision makers. It can also be argued that the risk is being double counted, if the discount rate is also risk-adjusted. We will return to this point later in this chapter.

BREAKEVEN ANALYSIS

Traditional breakeven analysis attempts to estimate the revenues that will be needed in order for a project or a company to break even in accounting terms—that is, to make a net income of zero. In this section, we examine an alternative to accounting breakeven by asking how much revenue will be needed for a project or a company to break even in *financial* terms—that is, to make the *net present value* zero. We would argue that this is not only a higher hurdle, but it is also a more *realistic* hurdle since it factors in the opportunity cost of the funds invested in the project.

Accounting Breakeven: This is the number of units a firm has to sell to ensure that it does not have an accounting loss (or make accounting profit zero).

Accounting versus Financial Breakeven

We begin by defining an **accounting breakeven** as the number of units (or dollar revenue, if the units are not standard) that will have to be sold in order to make the net income of a project zero. If the costs on the project can be broken up into fixed and variable costs, and the contribution margin per unit is the difference between the sales price per unit and the variable cost per unit, then the accounting breakeven can be calculated as follows:

> Breakeven Units (Accounting) = Fixed Costs /
> (Sales Price/Unit - Variable Cost/Unit)

This number will change from year to year as the fixed costs and the contribution margin per unit change (see Figure 10.6).

The **financial breakeven** is computed by first estimating the annual cash flow needed to make the net present value zero, then backing out the revenues needed to generate this annual cash flow, and finally estimating the number of units that have to be sold to create this revenue. Figure 10.7 illustrates this computation graphically.

Financial Breakeven: This is the number of units a firm has to sell to arrive at a NPV of zero.

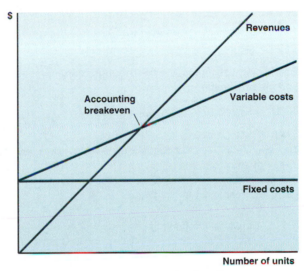

Figure 10.6   Accounting breakeven

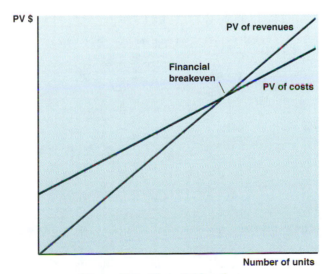

Figure 10.7   Financial breakeven

As a general rule of thumb, the financial breakeven is a higher hurdle because it requires the firm to make sufficient returns to cover the hurdle rate on the funds invested in the project. Consequently, the financial breakeven will be higher (in units and dollars) than the accounting breakeven.

 Concept Check

> Can you think of a scenario under which the financial breakeven may be lower than the accounting breakeven?

✈ IN PRACTICE THE BOEING 777 EXAMPLE: ACCOUNTING VERSUS FINANCIAL BREAKEVEN

The accounting and financial breakeven can be estimated approximately for the Boeing 777 project, using the following information:

$$\text{Sales Price per plane} = \$130 \text{ million}$$
$$\text{Variable Cost per plane} = \$97.50 \text{ million}$$
$$\text{Total Fixed Costs} = \$2.35 \text{ billion}$$

Based on these inputs, the **contribution margin** per plane can be estimated to be $32.50 million and the breakeven is:

$$\text{Breakeven (accounting)} = \text{Fixed Costs} / (\text{Sales Price/Unit} - \text{Variable Costs/Unit})$$
$$= \$2,350 / (\$130 - \$97.5) = 72.31 \text{ planes a year}$$

This calculation would suggest that Boeing has to sell at least 73 planes a year to ensure that it does not show an accounting loss. It is important to note that the revenue and cost estimates in this calculation were based on 1990 numbers, and the breakeven might be different for future years as these estimates change.

Similarly, the financial breakeven can be estimated using the cash flows estimated for the project. Drawing on the analysis done in Chapter 7, the cash flows and the net present value of the project, based on Boeing's estimates for the Boeing 777 and a cost of capital of 12%, are shown in Table 10.2.

Table 10.2		FREE CASH FLOWS TO FIRM ON BOEING 777 PROJECT				
Year	EBIT (1 - t)	Capital Expend.	Depreciation	Δ WC	FCFF	PV of FCFF
0		$4,000			$(4,000)	$(4,000)
1	$929		$82	$1,722	(711)	(635)
2	1,666		72	(17)	1,755	1,399
3	1,458		67	(343)	1,868	1,330
4	1,615		62	51	1,626	1,033
5	1,620		61	(91)	1,772	1,005
6	1,507		61	102	1,466	742
7	1,647		61	42	1,666	754
8	1,922	489	61	247	1,247	504
9	1,658		102	(212)	1,972	711
10	922		98	431	588	189
11	1,718		90	376	1,432	412
12	1,899		78	137	1,840	472

(continues)

(Table 10.2 *continued*)

Year	EBIT (1 - *t*)	Capital Expend.	Depreciation	Δ WC	FCFF	PV of FCFF
13	1,640	500	75	389	826	189
14	1,172		73	604	641	131
15	1,895		52	3,438	5,385	984
NPV						5,220

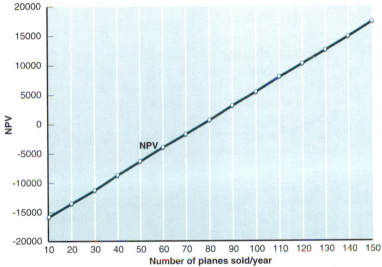

Figure 10.8   Financial breakeven: NPV as a function of number of planes sold

While the net present value is positive, it is based on Boeing's ability to sell 100 planes a year, on average. As shown in Figure 10.8, the net present value is computed as a function of the number of planes sold each year. The financial breakeven is approximately 78 planes a year, at which point the net present value is zero.

Contribution Margin: This is the difference between the sales price and variable cost per unit.

Extending and Using the Breakeven Concept

The breakeven analysis is generally calculated in terms of units sold and revenues; it can also be done using any assumption in the analysis. Thus, in the Home Depot example, the breakeven could have been computed for any of the assumptions used in the sensitivity analysis—the level of revenues, the expected growth rate, the operating margin, the working capital as a percentage of revenues, and the project life. In fact, using the figures from the sensitivity analysis, we can arrive at a breakeven table for the variables analyzed as shown in Table 10.3. The margin for error is the difference between the base case assumption and the breakeven point.

Again, by itself a breakeven analysis does not answer the question of whether a project should be accepted or rejected, but it does provide additional information to use in making that decision. In both the Boeing and Home Depot examples, knowing the breakeven will help at two levels. At the decision level, it can provide a measure of the

272   PART TWO   INVESTMENT ANALYSIS

Table 10.3   **Breakeven Points on Assumptions for the Home Depot Store**

Variable	Breakeven Point	Margin of Error
1. Revenues/Square Foot	Approximately $270	Approximately $30
2. Expected Growth Rate	2%	3%
3. Operating Margin	Approximately 9%	Approximately 1%
4. Working Capital as % of Revenue	Approximately 14%	Approximately 4%
5. Project Life	Approximately 8 years	Approximately 2 years

margin of safety the decision maker has if the project is accepted, and it can help make the final judgment. Once the project is accepted, it provides a useful benchmark against which actual performance can be compared, to measure whether the project is indeed adding value to the firm. Thus, if Home Depot opens the new store, and operating margins are only 7% after the first year, it would be a warning sign that the store is not measuring up to expectations and delivering value.

 Concept Check

Assume that you have done a breakeven analysis on each of the variables driving the project. Assume also that you now intend to collect more information on the project, either through direct research or market testing. How would the results of the breakeven analysis help in planning the information collection?

SCENARIO ANALYSIS

Scenario analysis is a version of sensitivity analysis, whereby specific scenarios are developed for the future, and the viability of the investment is considered under each scenario. These scenarios can be based on macroeconomic factors, relating to overall economic growth, interest rates, or inflation; industry-specific factors, relating to competitive dynamics; or firm-specific factors, such as working capital policies or operating margins.

 Scenario Analysis: This is an analysis of the NPV or IRR of a project under a series of specified scenarios, based on macroeconomic, industry, and firm-specific factors.

The steps involved in a scenario analysis are as follows:

Step 1   The factor around which scenarios will be built is selected, generally based on the type of business the firm is in and the biggest source of uncertainty for the future success of the project. Thus, a cyclical firm may choose to construct scenarios around the state of the economy, a financial service firm may consider different interest rate scenarios, and a computer manufacturing firm may build scenarios around different technological developments.

Step 2   The values each of the variables in the investment analysis (revenues, growth, operating margin, etc.) will take on under each scenario are estimated.

Step 3   The net present value and internal rate of return under each scenario are estimated.

Step 4   A decision is made on the project, based on the net present values under all the scenarios, rather than just the base case.

IN PRACTICE   SCENARIO ANALYSIS FOR THE BOEING 777 AIRPLANE

The health of the airline industry can be used to evaluate the future success of the Boeing 777. If airline companies are in financial trouble, they are unlikely to buy as many new planes as they would have otherwise, or they might require better financial terms to buy the same number of planes. Although the health of the overall industry is a continuous variable, we consider three discrete scenarios, defined as follows. *If the aggregate profitability of all airlines exceeds $5 billion,* the financial health of airlines has improved. We can then assume that the number of planes sold will increase from the base case to 120 planes a year and that the price per plane will also increase marginally to $135 million. *If the aggregate profitability of all airlines is between $0.5 billion and $5 billlion,* the financial health of airlines has not changed, and the base case assumptions will apply (100 planes a year; $130 million a plane). *If the aggregate profitability drops below $0.5 billion,* the financial health of airlines has worsened, and the number of planes sold will drop to 80 a year, and the price per plane to $125 million:

Scenario	Planes sold/year	Sales Price/Plane
Airline firms' financial health improves	120	$135 million
Airline firms' financial health remains unchanged	100	$130 million
Airline firms' financial health worsens	80	$125 million

Under these scenarios, the net present value for the Boeing 777 can be computed as follows:

Scenario	NPV	IRR
Airline firms' financial health improves	$10,971 million	43.42%
Airline firms' financial health remains unchanged	$5,220 million	27.82%
Airline firms' financial health worsens	- $171 million	11.42%

Clearly, the Boeing 777, which is a worthwhile project under the base case assumptions, is not an attractive project if the airline business worsens significantly. This will have to be weighed into the final decision on whether to take the project.

 Concept
Check

Since this project becomes unattractive if the airline business worsens, is it possible to protect against that eventuality? If so, how would you do it?

Limitations of Scenario Analysis

Much of scenario analysis is predicated on the assumption that there are clearly delineated scenarios, under which outcomes will differ. In many cases, however, this is not true. For instance, the economy does not take one of three discrete states—boom, recession, or stability—but can lie anywhere on a continuum between the extremes. By converting this continuum into discrete levels, some information is lost. Consequently, scenario analysis is more likely to work in cases with discrete outcomes. For instance, a pharmaceutical company may analyze a new product under two scenarios—either the competitors will come up with a substitute or they will not.

Another limitation of scenario analysis is the fact that it expands the notion of estimating expected values for the variables in the investment analysis beyond just the base case. Thus, in a case where there are three scenarios, and the investment analysis requires inputs for 15 variables, the analyst will have to estimate 45 expected values (3 × 15) to conduct the scenario analysis.

Finally, there is no clear roadmap to indicate how the decision maker will use results of the investment analysis. The fact that the net present value of a project is much lower—even negative—under the economic recession scenario should come as no surprise to a cyclical firm and should not be an automatic basis for rejecting a project.

Best Case and Worst Case Analysis: A Discourse

One popular variant of scenario analysis is **best case and worst case analysis.** Among the several forms it may take, one of the most common involves setting all the assumptions at the *optimistic* end of the spectrum and calculating the net present value and the internal rate of return in order to compute a best-case return on the project. The analysis is then repeated, setting the assumptions at the *pessimistic* end of the spectrum in order to compute the worst-case return. Not surprisingly, the best-case return is extremely high for most projects, and the worst-case return is abysmal.

Best (Worst) Case Analysis: This is an analysis where by all the inputs are set at their most optimistic (pessimistic) levels, and the NPV and IRR are computed.

The rationale for conducting such an analysis includes the following. By doing a worst-case analysis, it is argued, firms can be made aware of the potential downside on a project in terms of cash flows and net present value; this information can be factored into the decision making. It is also argued that a worst-case analysis may enable firms to buy some protection against the worst-case scenario. If Boeing analyzes a new plane for production and finds the potential downside to be too large, for example, it may choose to share the risk with another company rather than go it alone.

SIMULATIONS

In traditional investment analysis, we make point estimates for each of the variables. For instance, in the Home Depot illustration, we assumed that the revenues would be $30 million and that the operating margin would be 10%. In reality, each of these variables has a distribution of values, which we condense into an expected value. **Simulations** attempt to utilize the information in the entire distribution, rather than just the expected value, to arrive at a decision to accept or reject the project.

Simulations: In a simulation, the outcomes for the variables are drawn from prespecified distributions for these variables, and the NPV or IRR are computed based on these outcomes.

The steps involved in a simulation are the following:

Step 1 The first step in a simulation involves choosing those variables whose expected values will be replaced by distributions. While uncertainty may be associated with every variable in an investment analysis, only the most critical variables might be chosen at this stage.

Step 2 The correct distribution is chosen for each of the variables. A number of choices are available here are, ranging from discrete probability distributions (probabilities are assigned to specific outcomes) to continuous distributions (the normal or exponential distribution). In making this choice, the following factors should be considered:

- The range of feasible outcomes for the variable (e.g., the revenues cannot be less than zero, ruling out any distribution that allows the variable to take on large negative values, such as the normal distribution)

- The experience of the company on this variable, with similar projects in the past; data on a variable, such as operating margins on past projects, may be plotted to see what distribution best fits the data—statistical techniques exist that check for this fit

No distribution will provide a perfect fit, so the distribution that *best* fits the data should be used.

Step 3   Next, the parameters of the distribution chosen for each variable are estimated. The number of parameters will vary from distribution to distribution; for instance, the mean and the variance have to be estimated for the normal distribution, whereas the uniform distribution requires estimates of the minimum and maximum values for the variable.

Step 4   One outcome is drawn from each distribution; the variable is assumed to take on that value for that particular simulation.

Step 5   The investment statistics (NPV, IRR, ROI) are computed for the set of outcomes drawn in step 4.

Step 6   Steps 4 and 5 are repeated until a sufficient number of simulations have been conducted. In general, the more complex the distribution (in terms of the number of values the variable can take on and the number of parameters needed to define the distribution) and the greater the number of variables that have to be varied, the larger this number will be.

Step 7   The summary statistics for the investment statistics across all the simulations run are reported and used by decision makers in investment analysis. A number of statistics might be used, including:

- *Variance (or standard deviation) in the net present value or the internal rate of return:* This is a measure of the uncertainty associated with the project and can be used to choose between mutually exclusive projects. A scaled version of this statistic is the **coefficient of variation,** whereby the standard deviation is divided by the average net present value.

- *Percentage of outcomes that are unacceptable:* This is a measure of the likelihood that the project will be unacceptable. Its definition depends on the investment measure used—for the NPV, it is the percentage of net present values, from the simulations, that are below zero; for the IRR, it is the percentage of internal rates of return that are below the discount rate.

Coefficient of Variation: This is the standard deviation of a data series, divided by its average.

IN PRACTICE   SIMULATION ANALYSIS FOR THE HOME DEPOT

Steps 1-3   In the Home Depot example, assume the distributions for each of the key variables as shown in Table 10.4.

Table 10.4 **PROBABILITY DISTRIBUTIONS FOR KEY VARIABLES: THE HOME DEPOT STORE**

Variable	Distribution	Expected Value	Characteristics of the Distribution	
1. Revenues	General	$30 million	*Value*	*Probability*
			$20 million	0.125
			$25 million	0.1875
			$30 million	0.375
			$35 million	0.1875
			$40 million	0.125
2. Growth Rate	Normal	5.00%	Standard Deviation = 2.00%	
3. Operating Margin	Uniform	10.00%	Minimum of 0%	
			Maximum of 20.00%	
4. WC as % of Rev.	Normal	10.00%	Standard Deviation = 2.50%	

The Home Depot has opened hundreds of stores and can use the values for the variables from these stores to develop distributions. Thus, the operating margins of the stores can be plotted on a distribution, and a standard distribution can be matched up to it.

Step 4 Draw one outcome from each distribution. In the Home Depot example, assume the following outcomes on the first simulation:

Variable	Drawn Outcome
1. Revenues	$25 million
2. Growth Rate	6.35%
3. Operating Margin	10.00%
4. WC as % of Rev.	9.16%

Step 5 Estimate a net present value, based on the outcomes drawn. In the Home Depot example, calculate the net present value based on the outcomes drawn in step 3:

Net Present Value from simulated outcomes = - $13,423
Internal Rate of Return for simulated outcomes = 12.48%

Step 6 Repeat steps 4 and 5 a sufficient number of times. In the Home Depot example, the simulations were repeated 5,000 times. A fairly large number was chosen for two reasons: the distributions were complex, and four variables were changing in the project.

Compute the summary statistics for the net present values across all the simulations (expected value, standard deviation, minimum, maximum, percentage of time under zero) and plot the net present values on a graph.

Example: In the Home Depot example, calculate the summary statistics for net present value based upon the simulations as shown in Figure 10.9.

Net Present Value	**Internal Rate of Return**
Expected Value = $1,067,150	Expected Value = 13.84%
Standard Deviation = $451,335	Standard Deviation = 0.55%
CV of NPV = $451,335/1,067,150	CV of IRR = 0.55%/13.84%
Minimum = -$9,504,201	Minimum = -1.21%
Maximum = $31,013,450	Maximum = 47.95%
% of time below zero = 20.16%	% of time below Discount rate = 20.16%

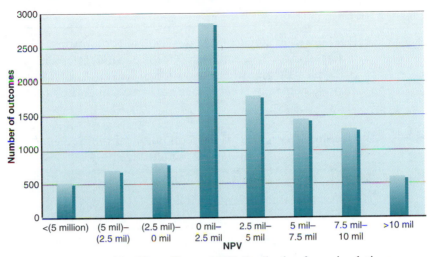

Figure 10.9   The Home Depot: NPV distribution from simulations

Step 7   Use the distribution of net present values, rather than just the base case net present value, to make your decision. In the Home Depot example, a number of questions can be answered with this simulation:

- What is the likelihood that this will be a bad project? (The net present value is less than zero in 20.16% of the simulations.)

- What are the worst-case and best-case scenarios? (The lowest net present value computed is -$9.5 million, which is the worst-case scenario; the highest net present value computed is $31.01 million, which is the best-case scenario.)

- What is the riskiness of this project relative to other projects? (The standard deviation in the net present values is $451,335; when standardized by dividing by the net present value, it is 0.4226. Although these statistics, by themselves, are difficult to use, they could be computed for other stores that the Home Depot is considering opening or has opened already and compared across these investment alternatives as a measure of risk.)

Limitations of Simulation Analysis

The primary limitation of simulation analysis is the information that is required for it to work. In particular, it is difficult to choose both the right distribution to describe a variable and the parameters of that distribution. When these choices are made carelessly or randomly, the output from the simulation may look impressive but actually convey no valuable information.

Traditional simulation analysis also does not permit interaction between variables (e.g., such as revenues and growth rates, in the Home Depot example). This limitation can be overcome by building in linkages into the simulation that take these interactions into account.

Finally, like the other approaches described earlier in this chapter, no clear decision rule emerges from the simulation analysis. Instead, the subjective judgments and risk preferences of the person using the simulation will determine whether the project will end up being accepted or rejected.

DECISION TREES

Decision trees allow firms to deal with uncertainty in projects. The project is considered in stages; the decision at each stage is dependent on the outcome from the prior stage. In a typical decision tree, the project is broken down into clearly defined stages, and the possible outcomes at each stage are listed along with probabilities and cash-flow effects of each outcome.

Decision Tree: This is a presentation of the decisions and possible outcomes, with probabilities, at each stage of a multistage project.

Decision trees operate as follows:

Step 1   Break the project into clearly defined stages. In some cases, this is fairly easy to do. For instance, a computer software company may look at four stages in the introduction of a new software package: research and development, market testing, limited production, and full production. At each stage, the decision whether or not to go on to the next stage will be based on the outcome at the prior stage.

Step 2   List all possible outcomes at each stage. This is done much more easily if the outcomes are discrete. For instance, a pharmaceutical company considering a new drug can put the product into production only if the FDA approves it. Thus, at the stage of FDA approval, only two outcomes are possible—either the FDA will approve, or it will not. In many cases, however, the outcomes are continuous, as is the case with a market test, where the results can range anywhere from an extraordinary success to a total failure. In such a case, the set of outcomes (which may be very large) has to be condensed to a few discrete outcomes. Thus, the firm might classify a "great" success as one in which the revenues exceed a certain amount; a "moderate success" as one in which revenues fall within a lesser range; and a "failure" as one in which revenues fall below a defined floor.

Step 3   Specify the probabilities of each outcome at each stage, based on information available now. This task will become progressively more difficult the further down the decision tree (and in later stages) in the process, because the firm may have limited information at the start of the process.

Step 4   Specify the effect of each outcome on expected project cash flows. In market testing, for instance, a "great" success should generally imply higher expected cash flows in the future. To use decision trees well, these cash flows must be specified. In addition, the discount rate may vary, depending on the outcome, and thus influence the decision.

Step 5   Evaluate the optimal action to take at each stage in the decision tree, based on the outcome at the previous stage and its effect on cash flows and discount rate, beginning with the final stage and working backward.

Step 6   Estimate the optimal action to take at the very first stage, based on the expected cash flows over the entire project, and all of the likely outcomes, weighted by their relative probabilities.

IN PRACTICE   USING DECISION TREES TO ANALYZE A PROPOSED SERVICE

Assume that the Home Depot is considering introducing a new in-home computer shopping service. Knowing little about the business, the company is proposing making the investment in three stages: a market test, a partial introduction, and, ultimately, full introduction.

In the first stage, the Home Depot considers market testing the service on a fairly small number of consumers. The development and the market test are expected to cost $1 million (to be spent right away), and the likelihood of success is believed to be high (about 75%).

If the market test (which is expected to last a year) succeeds, the Home Depot plans to put a few of its most widely ordered items on line on the shopping service and market it to a much wider audience—all consumers who have spent more than $1,000 at the Home Depot over the prior year, for example. This is expected to cost $2.5 million and be a much tougher test of the viability of the service. (The chances of success and failure are expected to be even.)

If the partial introduction is a success, the Home Depot plans to spend $15 million to provide its on-line shopping service for a full range of products to all consumers. This is not expected to happen until the end of the second year, and the service itself will not start generating revenues until the following year. There are three possible outcomes of the full introduction (see Figure 10.10):

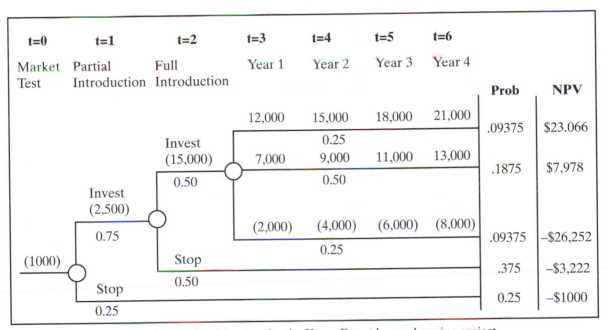

Figure 10.10   Decision tree for the Home Depot home shopping project

1. *Huge success:* Under this scenario, the Home Depot expects an after-tax operating income of $12 million in the first year of full introduction (three years from now) and for this operating income to grow $3 million a year each year for the following three years. The odds of this happening, given full introduction, are one in four.

2. *Moderate success:* Under this scenario, the Home Depot expects an after-tax operating income of $7 million in the first year of full introduction and for this operating income to grow $2 million a year each year for the following three years. The odds of this happening, given full introduction, are one in two.

3. *Disaster:* Under this scenario, the Home Depot expects an after-tax loss of $2 million in the first year and for this loss to increase by $2 million each year for the following three years.

The probability of each of the branches in Figure 10.9 is estimated by taking the cumulative probabilities. To illustrate, the probability of a "huge success" after full introduction can be estimated as follows:

Probability of huge success = Probability of success on market test
* Probability of success on partial introduction
* Probability of huge success on full introduction
= 0.75 * 0.5 * 0.25 = 0.09375

The net present value of the cash flows for each of the branches is estimated using the cost of capital of the Home Depot (12.5%) and factoring in when the cash flows occur. Again, using the "huge success" branch of the tree:

$$\text{NPV of huge success} = -\$1{,}000 - \$2{,}500/1.125^1 - \$15{,}000/1.125^2 + \$12{,}000/1.125^3$$
$$+ \$15{,}000/1.125^4 + \$18{,}000/1.125^5 + \$21{,}000/1.125^6 = \$23{,}066$$

The expected net present value for all of the possible outcomes can then be estimated using the following probabilities and net present values:

Outcome	Probability	NPV
Full Investment: Huge Success	0.09375	$23,066
Full Investment: Moderate Success	0.18750	$7,978
Full Investment: Disaster	0.09375	-$26,252
Partial Investment and then stop	0.37500	-$3,222
Stop after market test	0.25000	-$1,000

> Expected NPV across all outcomes = 0.09375 ($23,066) + 0.1875 ($7978)
> + 0.09375 (-$26,252) + 0.375 (-$3,222) + 0.25 (-$1,000) = - $261

This would imply that the Home Depot should not embark on this process because the expected net present value is negative.

The Option to Abandon a Project

In some cases, firms have the option to abandon a project sometime during the life of the project, if the cash flows do not measure up to expectations. By providing the firm with a chance to cut its losses, this option has value. In Chapter 28, we will examine the value of this option using option pricing models. Decision trees, however, offer another way of examining the value of this option.

The first step in using decision trees to analyze the value of the option to abandon is to specify both the stage(s) at which the project can be abandoned and the cost of abandonment. The next step is to calculate the expected value of the project over its entire life, assuming no abandonment. The third step is to calculate the expected value of the project, allowing the option to abandon. The value of the option to abandon is the difference in the expected values obtained in steps 2 and 3.

IN PRACTICE   USING DECISION TREES TO ANALYZE THE OPTION TO ABANDON

In the computer shopping service example we have described, the disaster scenario weighs heavily on the final outcome, because of the very negative cash flows that occur in this scenario. Assume that the Home Depot could abandon the project at the end of the third year (the first year of the full introduction) after having observed the negative cash flows in that year. The decision tree and net present values can be reestimated, as shown in Figure 10.11. The expected net present value can then be estimated as follows:

Outcome	Probability	NPV
Full Investment: Huge Success	0.09375	$23,066
Full Investment: Moderate Success	0.18750	$7,978
Full Investment: Disaster	0.09375	-$16,479
Partial Investment and then stop	0.37500	-$3,222
Stop after market test	0.25000	-$1,000

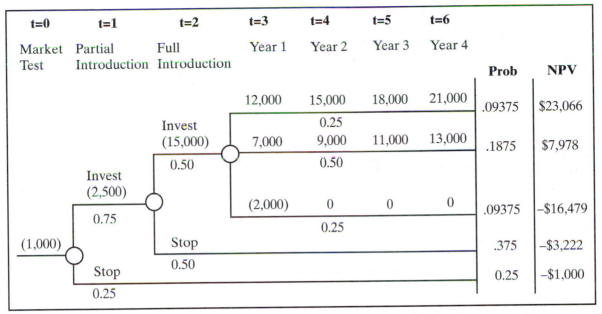

Figure 10.11   Decision tree for the Home Depot home shopping with abandonment option

Expected NPV across all outcomes = 0.09375 ($23,066) + 0.1875 ($7978)
+ 0.09375 (-$16,479) + 0.375 (-$3,222) + 0.25 (-$1,000) = + $655

The value of the abandonment option can then be estimated by taking the difference in net present values between the two cases (with and without the abandonment option):

Value of abandonment option = NPV of Decision with abandonment
- NPV of Decision without abandonment
= $655 −(−261) = $916

The value of the abandonment option is $916,000. In this case, having the option makes this a viable project.

Limitations of Decision Trees
Decision trees provide a wealth of information to a decision maker considering a new project or product, but they also *require* a wealth of information. In particular, the requirement that the project be analyzed in stages, and that the outcome be discrete at each stage, reduces the number of projects for which it is feasible to use this approach. In particular, decision trees are most likely to work when:

- The firm considering the project will be making decisions on continuing the project in clear stages.
- The outcomes at each stage can at least be classified into broader classes.
- The probabilities of the outcomes and the effect on cash flows is known at the start; this usually implies that the firm has done similar projects in the past.

One case in which decision trees could be used arises when oil companies evaluate an opportunity to drill for oil. The drilling is usually done in stages, with exploration followed by a small rig and ending with the final investment in a production rig. The company (or other oil companies) has generally drilled for oil in the vicinity (say, the Gulf of Mexico) in the recent past, and thus has a sense of the probability of finding oil, as well as what comprises a "great" well, an "average" well, and a "poor" well.

In contrast, decision trees are much more difficult to apply in cases where the product or service is new or unique and the firm has very little information on whether consumers will like it or how much they are willing to pay for it, at least until the market test is done. Decision trees are also difficult to apply when investments occur initially or gradually over time, rather than in clear stages.

❏ Concept Check

Assume that you have done similar projects before. How would you use the information from your experience with these projects to draw a decision tree?

CONCLUSION

This chapter provides an overview of the probabilistic approaches that can be used to evaluate risk in projects. It provides an introduction to five basic approaches—sensitivity analyses, breakeven analyses, scenario analyses, simulations, and decision trees—and summarizes the advantages and limitations of each approach. The following general propositions can be drawn about all these approaches:

- All these approaches are designed to provide a decision maker with additional information to make better decisions.
- Sensitivity analysis and breakeven analysis attempt to vary one variable at a time, keeping all other variables fixed, which is an unrealistic assumption.
- Simulations and decision trees provide valuable output about the uncertainty in the project, but they both require substantial new information that may not always be readily available.

All the approaches described in this chapter share some advantages and disadvantages. Their strength lies in their intuitive appeal; all decision makers like answers to "what-if" questions about assumptions and can use information relating to best-case and worst-case outcomes. They also allow decision makers to exercise subjective judgments about accepting or rejecting projects, enabling them to use the knowledge they might have accumulated from past experience in making similar decisions, rather than trusting a mechanical rule.

It is the subjective use of these approaches that also exposes them to the most criticism, however. The fact that none of the rules provides a clean-cut decision rule means that base case analysis can be overridden on the whim (or bias) of the person doing the investment analysis. In addition, the decision rules that yield the most information, such as simulation and decision trees, are also those that require the most information. To the extent that this information is difficult to obtain, these approaches will not provide much additional information.

QUESTIONS AND PROBLEMS

1. Suppose you are analyzing a new store for the Limited, a leading clothing retailer, and the store is expected to have the following characteristics:

    Size of the store = 10,000 square feet
    Sales/square foot = $500/square foot

    Cost of setting up store = $2.5 million (depreciated straight line over 10 years to $500,000)

    Variable Costs = 40% of revenues

    Fixed Costs = $1 million/ year

The store is expected to have a life of 10 years, and the firm is expected to pay 40% of its income as taxes and has a cost of capital of 14%.

a. Estimate the base case net present value and IRR.

b. Estimate the sensitivity of both measures to sales/square foot and the variable costs as a percentage of revenues.

c. Estimate the breakeven in financial and accounting terms, in terms of sales per square foot.

2. Suppose you are analyzing the cash flows on a manufacturing plant to produce a new type of computer disk drive. The plant will cost $10 million to build and will have the capacity to sell 20,000 drives a year. Each drive is expected to retail for $250, and the cost of making each drive is expected to be $100. The fixed costs amount to $500,000 a year, not including depreciation, which is assumed to be straight-line over five years on the initial investment of $10 million, with no salvage value. The inflation rate in both revenues and costs is expected to be 5%, and the cost of capital is 15%. (Tax rate = 40%)

a. Estimate the NPV and IRR for the base case analysis.

b. Estimate the sensitivity of these measures to changes in assumptions on the number of units sold and the sales price per unit.

c. Estimate the accounting and financial breakeven on this project.

3. Consider again the example described above. Instead of providing base case estimates, assume that you are given the following probability distributions for each of the following variables:

Number of Units Sold		Sales Price/Unit	
# Units Sold	Probability	Sales Price	Probability
15,000	0.25	$200	0.20
20,000	0.50	$225	0.20
25,000	0.25	$250	0.20
		$275	0.20
		$300	0.20

Assume that all of the other base case assumptions hold.

a. How would you go about structuring the simulation for this problem?

b. If you repeated this simulation for a large number of times and calculated the expected net present value and IRR across these simulations, what would you expect to find (relative to the base case)?

c. What other information from the simulation would you use in your decision making?

4. You have just analyzed a project requiring an initial investment in plant and equipment and with a 10-year life and estimated the cash flows over the 10 years:

Year	Initial Investment	AT Operating CF	Salvage Value
0	$(10,000,000.00)		
1		$1,500,000	
2		1,575,000	
3		1,653,750	
4		1,736,438	
5		1,823,259	
6		1,914,422	
7		2,010,143	
8		2,110,651	
9		2,216,183	
10		2,326,992	$1,000,000.00

a. Estimate the net present value, assuming a cost of capital of 12%.

b. Since the life of the project is arbitrarily set at 10 years, recalculate the net present value, assuming that

(1) The project continues for five more years and that cash flows continue to grow 5% a year during this period. (The salvage value remains unchanged.)

(2) The project continues for 10 more years and cash flows are frozen at year 10 levels. (The salvage value remains unchanged.)

(3) The project continues forever and cash flows are frozen at year 10 levels.

5. Assume that you are analyzing a new menu entry for a fast-food chain, which has three stages:

Stage 1 The project requires a test-marketing expense of $5 million. This test market is expected to last a year, and there is a 60% chance of success.

Stage 2 If the test market is a success, the firm plans an introduction into one region of the country at a cost of $20 million (at the start of the second year), and there is a 75% chance of success.

Stage 3 If the regional introduction succeeds, the firm plans to introduce the product countrywide at a cost of $50 million (at the start of the third year). If it does so, there are three possibilities:

a. The product sells much better than expected and generates $40 million in after-cash flows for the next five years.

b. The product sells as well as expected and generates $20 million in after-tax cash flows for the next five years.

c. The product sells less well than expected and generates $5 million in after-tax cash flows for the next five years.

Each has an equal probability of occurring. The cost of capital is 10%.

a. Draw the decision tree for this project.

b. Estimate the expected net present value of this decision.

c. If you were given the right to abandon the project one year into the full introduction, estimate the value of the option to abandon.

6. You are helping Hershey's, the chocolate manufacturer, decide whether it should introduce a new low-fat candy. To help the company make this decision, you have done simulations of the cash flows from introducing the new product and arrived at the following distribution of net present values:

NPV	Number of Simulations
< -10 million	150
-10 million to 0	350
0 to + 10 million	500
10 to 20 million	1000
20 to 30 million	1000
30 to 40 million	500
40 to 50 million	300
> 50 million	200

a. Estimate the expected net present value of this project.

b. What is the likelihood that this project is a bad one?

c. How would you use the output from these simulations in your decision making?

7. You work for a newspaper and magazine publisher who has asked you to look into the feasibility of introducing a weekly magazine directed to reporting financing news from overseas for U.S. investors. After your research, you conclude the following:

- Depreciation is straight line to salvage value of zero.

- It will cost you approximately $20 million to start the newspaper. (Depreciation is straight line; no salvage)

- The annual fixed cost of preparing the magazine will be approximately $10 million; there will be a production cost of a $1 for every issue sold.

- Based on the overall market size, you expect to sell about 100,000 copies of your magazine each week and receive about $2.50 per issue sold. You also expect advertising revenues to be about $15 million a year.

- You have estimated a life of five years for the magazine.

- You have estimated a tax rate of 40% for the firm, and your cost of capital is 12%.

a. Estimate the base case NPV and IRR for this project.

b. How sensitive is your conclusion to the number of magazines you sell a week?

c. How many magazines would you have to sell to break even on an accounting basis? on a financial basis?

8. You have the opportunity to invest in a real estate project with significant risks associated with it. The investment is only marginally acceptable, and you are considering rejecting it. The promoter of the project offers you the option to sell back your share of the project at 75% of your investment anytime in the first five years of the project. Would it make a difference to your decision? Why or why not?

9. You are considering test marketing a new breakfast bar that you have just developed. It is estimated that the test marketing will cost approximately $10 million. Based on your prior experiences with similar products, there is a 60% chance that the test market will be successful; if it is, a plant will be built at a cost of $50 million and the product can expect to generate after-tax cash flows of $10 million a year for 10 years; if it is not, the product will be abandoned. The cost of capital is 10%.

a. Draw the decision tree for this project.

b. Would you do the test market for the project? Why?

10. Coca-Cola Corporation is considering the introduction of a grape-flavored cola and has asked you to do the analysis of the feasibility of the project. The initial cost of promotion and advertising is expected to be $100 million; the advertising cost per year after that is expected to be $10 million. All advertising costs are tax deductible in the year in which they are made. The cost per can sold is $0.20, and the expected revenue per can to the company is $0.50. The product is expected to have a 20-year life, and the cost of capital for Coca-Cola is 11%. The corporate tax rate is 40%.

a. Estimate how many cans of the new soda Coca-Cola will have to sell to reach an accounting breakeven.

b. Estimate how many cans of the new soda Coca-Cola will have to sell to reach a financial break-even.

11. You are the owner of a small appliance store and are thinking of ways to increase your sales. One option that you are considering is to start offering credit to your customers. By doing so, you expect to increase your sales from $4 million a year to $6 million and for your after-tax operating margins to remain un-changed at 10%. The credit, however, will increase your working capital needs from 10% of revenues to 20% of revenues. Your cost of capital is 14%.

a. Assuming that you plan to stay in business for 10 years, should you offer credit?

b. How much would your sales have to increase for you to reach breakeven (from a financial standpoint)?

c. How many years would you have to stay in business to recoup your investment in working capital?

12. You are looking at the results of a sensitivity and breakeven analysis done on the new chemical plant your firm is considering:

Variable	Base Case Assumption	Breakeven for NPV=0
Volume Sold	100,000 tons	92,000 tons
Price/unit	$1000/ton	$875/ton
Operating Margin	15%	14.1%
Discount Rate	12.5%	14.0%
Life of Project	15 years	12.7 years

a. Estimate the margin for error you have on each of these assumptions.

b. How would you use this information in your decision making?

c. If you were concerned about the small margin for error on operating margin, how would you go about reducing your discomfort with that assumption?

13. GellComm Corporation is a new Internet service company that is planning to offer subscribers unlimited access to the Internet for $15 a month. It will cost the company $10 million initially to set up the service and $5 a month to provide the service to each subscriber. GellComm is not sure how long it will be able to stay in business before it is overwhelmed by the competition from phone companies. It has a cost of capital of 14% and a tax rate of 40%.

a. Assuming that it stays in business for two years, how many subscribers will it need to break even on a NPV basis?

b. Assuming that it signs up 500,000 subscribers, how long will it need to stay in business to break even on a NPV basis?

14. Doing sensitivity analysis on a project can lead to the double counting of risk, for the discount rates used already reflect the project risk. Comment.

15. You run a software firm and are considering a major upgrade of your product. The upgrade will cost $15 million, but it will increase the sales significantly. You will keep the price per unit at $200, and your after-tax operating margin is expected to remain at 40%. Your cost of capital is 15%.

a. If your product has an expected life of three years (before becoming obsolete), how many additional units would you have to sell to break even?

b. How would your answer to (a) change if you are extremely uncertain about the remaining life of your product?

16. An oil company is considering whether it should drill for oil in the Gulf of Mexico. Based on prior experience, it has estimated the following:

- The initial cost of the exploratory rig is $10 million; the probability of finding sufficient oil with the exploratory rig is 60%.

- The cost of the full rig is $50 million; if this investment is made, there are three equally possible scenarios:

- Mega Well: The well will yield 500,000 barrels of oil a year for 20 years.

- Typical Well: The well will yield 250,000 barrels of oil a year for 20 years.

- Bust Well: The well will yield only 50,000 barrels of oil a year for 20 years.

The company has a pretax operating profit of $12 per barrel currently, and this is expected to grow 3% a year over the next 20 years. The annual fixed cost of operating the rig is $1 million, and the rig will be depreciated straight-line over 20 years. The cost of capital is 10%, and the corporate tax rate is 40%.

a. Show the decision tree for this investment.

b. Should the oil company invest in the exploratory rights?

c. How much is the value of the option to abandon the well? (Assume that there is no salvage.)

CHAPTER 11

UNCERTAINTY AND RISK IN CAPITAL BUDGETING: PART II

This chapter explores the second approach to dealing with uncertainty, which is to factor the risk into either the discount rate or the expected cash flows and calculate performance measures, such as net present value and internal rate of return, with these risk-adjusted measures. In the process of making these risk adjustments, we attempt to answer the following questions:

- What types of risk does a typical project carry? What portion of this risk is relevant when analyzing the project?
- How can this risk be factored into discount rates and expected cash flows?
- What are some of the most common errors made by firms when analyzing the riskiness of projects?

ANALYZING PROJECT RISK

One approach to dealing with risk involves adjusting discount rates and cash flows for the risk. In doing so we have to:

- Examine the sources of risk in a project and differentiate between risk that matters and risk that does not.
- Measure the risk that matters and estimate the effect on discount rates or cash flows.

The risk in a project comes from a number of sources, including the project itself, competition, shifts in the industry, international considerations, and macroeconomic factors.

Project Specific Risk

The first source of risk is *project-specific*; an individual project may have higher or lower cash flows than expected, either because the analyst misestimated the cash flows for that project or because of factors specific to that project. When firms take a large number of similar projects, it can be argued that much of this **project risk** should be diversified away in the normal course of business. For instance, some of the project risk in a Home Depot store analysis comes from the estimation error embedded in the projections of revenue, operating margins, and working capital. Other risk comes from factors specific to that store, such as its location and the quality of its personnel. Because the Home Depot opens several new stores every year across the country, it can be argued that this risk should be less important looking at all the stores together—for every store where the location turns out to be less attractive than expected, there should be some other store where the opposite is true. In contrast, firms that take on relatively few projects will be unable to diversify across projects. For example, Boeing faces project risk on its Boeing 777 project, but it cannot diversify this risk away because it takes on relatively few projects every year.

Project Risk: This is risk that affects only the project under consideration and may arise from factors specific to the project or estimation error.

Competitive Risk

The second source of risk is **competitive risk,** whereby the earnings and cash flows on a project are affected (positively or negatively) by the actions of competitors. Although a good project analysis might factor in the expected reactions of competitors into estimates of profit margins and growth, the actual actions taken by competitors may differ from these expectations. In most cases, this component of risk will affect more than one project and is therefore more difficult to diversify away in the normal course of business by the firm. The Home Depot, for instance, may face much more aggressive competition from existing competitors in the home improvement retail market or from new competitors (Wal-Mart might decide to offer expanded home improvement sections in its existing stores), resulting in lower earnings and cash flows than expected on many of its stores. Firms cannot diversify away much of their competitive risk, but their stockholders can, if they have the capacity and willingness to hold stock in their competitors.[1]

Competitive Risk: This is the unanticipated effect (positive or negative) on the cash flows in a project of competitor actions.

Industry-specific Risk

The third source of risk is **industry-specific risk**—those factors that primarily impact the earnings and cash flows of a specific industry. There are three sources within this category. The first is *technology risk,* which reflects the effects of technologies that change or evolve in ways different from those expected when the project was originally analyzed. In estimating earnings and cash flows for new stores, for instance, the Home Depot might operate under the assumption that people will continue to shop for home improvement products at traditional stores. If enough consumers turn to computer online shopping services for the same products, however, the actual sales and earnings at the Home Depot's stores may not measure up to expectations.

The second source is *legal risk,* which reflects the effect of changing laws and regulations. For instance, on the one hand, automobile firms reaped a windfall in the 1980s as a consequence of the trade quotas imposed on Japanese cars. Boeing, on the other hand, may be adversely impacted by laws passed by European countries, requiring their local airlines to buy only from Airbus.

Industry-Specific Risk: These are unanticipated effects on project cash flows of industrywide shifts in technology or changes in laws or in the price of a commodity.

---

[1]Firms could conceivably diversify away competetive risk by acquiring their existing competitors. Doing so would expose them to attacks under the antitrust law, however, and would not eliminate the risk from as yet unannounced competitors.

The third source is *commodity risk,* which reflects the effects of price changes in commodities and services that are used or produced disproportionately by a specific industry. Diamond mining companies, for example, will be particularly sensitive to developments in South Africa and the resulting impact on the price of diamonds. A firm cannot diversify away its industry-specific risk without diversifying across industries, either with new projects or through acquisitions. Stockholders in the firm should be able to diversify away industry-specific risk by holding portfolios of stocks from different industries.

International Risk

The fourth source of risk is **international risk.** A firm faces this type of risk when it takes on projects outside its domestic market. In such cases, the earnings and cash flows might be different than expected owing to exchange rate movements or political risk. Some of this risk may be diversified away by the firm in the normal course of business by taking on projects in different countries whose currencies may not all move in the same direction. Citibank and McDonald's, for instance, operate in many different countries and are much less exposed to this type of risk than was Wal-Mart in 1994, when its foreign operations were restricted primarily to Mexico. Companies can also reduce their exposure to the exchange rate component of this risk by choosing a financing mix for projects which matches the cash flows on these projects—for instance, by borrowing money in deutsche marks to take projects in Germany. Investors who are restricted to domestic investments because of transactions costs or other constraints will also be exposed to currency and political risk if they hold stock in the company. An international investor who holds investments in multiple countries and currencies may be able to diversify away the international risk.

International Risk: This is the additional uncertainty created in cash flows of projects by unanticipated changes in exchange rates and by political risk in foreign markets.

Market Risk

The final source of risk is **market risk**—macroeconomic factors that affect essentially all companies and all projects, to varying degrees. For example, changes in interest rates will affect the value of projects already taken and those yet to be taken both directly, through the discount rates, and indirectly, through the cash flows. Other factors that affect all investments include the term structure (the difference between short- and long-term rates), the risk preferences of investors (as investors become more risk averse, more risky investments will lose value), inflation, and economic growth. Although the expected values of all these variables enter into project analysis, changes in these variables will affect the values of these investments. Firms cannot diversify away this risk in the normal course of business, although they could conceivably do so by using interest rate or market derivatives. Investors also cannot diversify away this risk by creating portfolios of risky investments (such as stocks), for all risky investments bear some exposure to this risk.

Market Risk: Market risk refers to the unanticipated changes in project cash flows created by changes in interest rates, inflation rates, and the economy.

Table 11.1 summarizes the different components of risk and the actions that the firm and its investors can take to reduce or eliminate this risk. The basic rule for risk bearing is that the firm should take actions to eliminate this risk, *if and only if it can do so more economically than investors can.* It can be argued that investors can deal with competitive and technology risk more cheaply than can the firm, because portfolio diversification is cheaper than acquisitions. At the same time, the firm could argue that any risk that it can eliminate in the normal course of business is essentially costless.

This differentiation is critical because the expected return on a project should reflect only that risk which investors in the company (which is considering the project) cannot diversify away in the course of building a diversified portfolio of risky investments. If the investors in the company are primarily international investors, for example, the only risk that should affect the expected return is the macroeconomic risk or market risk.[2] If the investors are primarily domestic investors, there may be an additional premium for international risk (i.e., exchange rate and political risk). If the company is private or closely held, and the investors in the company do not have the capacity to diversify, there may be a further premium for industry and competitive risk.

⬚ Concept
Check

> Consider the acquisition of a small private firm in a high-growth and high-return industry by a large, publicly traded company. Given the discussion above, how would you factor in the benefits that accrue from this acquisition?

MEASURING PROJECT RISK

Estimating the expected return on a project begins by indentifying the investor base in the company, followed by the risk factors that matter and measures of these risk factors.

Measuring Market Risk

The risk measure that matters for all companies is the *market risk measure.* The risk and return models developed and discussed in Chapters 5 and 6 attempt to identify and measure this market risk; the CAPM estimates a beta relative to a market portfolio, which is assumed to capture all market risk, whereas, the APM estimates betas relative to each of the macroeconomic factors. Both models do so at the level of the firm, however. In estimating *project* risk, one of two approaches can be used: the firm's risk measures can be applied to the project, or the project's own risk characteristics can be estimated.

If project risk is constant across the firm   One way of estimating market risk parameters for a specific project is to assume that its exposure to market risk is similar to the firm's overall exposure to the same risk. In practical terms, the firm would use its overall cost of equity (estimated using the market beta in the CAPM and the factor betas in the APM) as the cost of equity for the project. The advantage of this approach is that it does not require risk estimation prior to every project, providing managers with a fixed benchmark for their project investments. This advantage is acquired at a high cost, however, for the assumption that the project has a risk profile similar to that of the company as a whole may not apply to companies in multiple lines of business. This approach is

---

[2]The macroeconomic factors that drive market risk are identified using past data on stock returns. Recent studies on past returns identify the level of rates, the term structure, the default spread, the inflation rate, and economic growth as the five factors that drive stock returns.

Table 11.1   AN ANALYSIS OF RISK

Type of Risk	Examples	Firm Can Mitigate by	Investor Can Mitigate by	Effects on Analysis		
				Private Firm	Public Firm with Domestic Investors	Public Firm with International Investors
Project-specific	Estimation mistakes Errors specific to product or location	Taking a large number of projects	Holding a diversified portfolio.	Should not matter if firm takes many projects May matter if firm takes few projects	Should not matter	Should not matter
Competitive	Unexpected response or new product/service from competitor	Acquiring competitors	Investing in the equity of competitors	Will matter since owner is generally not well diversified	Should not matter	Should not matter
Industry	Changes that affect all companies in a industry	Diversifying into other businesses, through acquisitions/investments	Holding a portfolio diversified across industries	Will matter since owner is generally not well diversified	Should not matter	Should not matter
International	Currency changes Political changes	Investing in multiple countries/currencies	Holding a portfolio diversified across countries	Will matter since owner is generally not well diversified	Will matter since investors are not internationally diversified.	Should not matter
Market/Macro	Interest rate changes Inflation changes Economy			Should matter	Should matter	Should matter

useful to companies that are in one line of business and take on homogeneous projects, however. The Home Depot, for instance, has made nearly all of its investments in one kind of project: opening new retail stores to sell home improvement products. Consequently, it can be argued that it is entirely appropriate for the Home Depot to use its beta (or betas, in the APM) as a firm for each and every one of these projects, at least as its measure of market risk.

IN PRACTICE   USING A COMPANY'S RISK PROFILE FOR THE PROJECT—THE HOME DEPOT AND BOEING

In the Home Depot example, we would argue that it is entirely appropriate to use the company's beta and cost of equity for the store analysis as well:

$$\text{Beta for the Home Depot} = \text{Beta for the Store} = 1.60$$
$$\text{Cost of Equity for the Home Depot} = \text{Cost of Equity for the Store}$$
$$= 7\% + 1.60\,(5.5\%) = 15.80\%$$
$$[\text{Based on a Treasury bond rate of } 7\% \text{ and a risk premium of } 5.5\%]$$

We would argue that Boeing, too, in the light of the preponderance of its investments in the aerospace industry, can also use its beta and cost of equity for analyzing the Boeing 777 project.[3]

$$\text{Beta for Boeing} = \text{Beta for Boeing 777 project} = 1.00$$
$$\text{Cost of Equity for Boeing} = \text{Cost of Equity for Boeing 777 project}$$
$$= 7\% + 1\,(5.5\%) = 12.50\%$$

If project risk varies across the firm   When firms operate in more than one line of business or take on projects that are different in their risk characteristics, they should estimate market risk parameters, if not for each individual project, at least for divisions or classes of projects. These market risk parameters will be higher than those of the firm (leading to a higher cost of equity) for riskier divisions and projects, and lower than those of the firm for safer divisions and projects. Imposing the same market risk parameters across projects with different risk characteristics will lead to overinvesting in the riskiest projects (since the cost of equity will be artificially low) and underinvesting in the safest projects (since the cost of equity will be too high, relative to the risk in these projects).

The realization that different divisions and projects have different market risk characteristics raises a question: How do you estimate the market risk parameters for different divisions and projects, when most risk estimation techniques require assets that are traded and past prices? Unlike companies that are publicly traded, divisions and projects are seldom traded. In Chapter 6, we discussed some approaches to estimating market risk parameters for assets that are not traded: the comparable firm approach, accounting betas, and cross-sectional regression. We will revisit them here and focus exclusively on the issue of estimation of risk for individual projects.

Using comparable firms   The most widely used approach, often called the **pure play approach,** to estimating market risk parameters for projects or divisions is the "comparable firm" approach, whereby the market risk parameters are estimated as follows:

Step 1:   The business in which the division or project operates is identified.
Step 2:   Companies that are involved primarily in this business and are publicly traded are identified.

---

[3]In 1994, Boeing received 92% of its revenues from aerospace and only 8% from defense.

Step 3: The market risk parameters are estimated or gathered for these companies. If the CAPM is used, the market betas for each of these companies is collected.

Step 4: The market risk parameters are corrected for systematic differences in financial leverage between the comparable firms and the division or project in question. If the division does not carry debt, the financial leverage of the firm considering it is used.

Step 5: The corrected market risk parameters, estimated using comparable firms, is used to estimate a cost of equity for the division or project.

Pure Play Approach: In the pure play approach, the beta for a firm or division is estimated by looking at publicly traded firms operating in the same line of business.

The key step in this process is undoubtedly the second step, whereby comparable firms are identified. In cases where there are directly comparable firms, this is a fairly simple approach to use. In cases where there are no directly comparable firms, however, it is much more difficult to apply and justify.

☐ Concept
   Check

> Once you have put together a list of "comparable firms," how would you check to see if they are in fact comparable to the project or division that you are analyzing?

IN PRACTICE   THE PURE PLAY APPROACH TO ESTIMATING PROJECT BETAS—THE HOME DEPOT

In 1995, the Home Depot announced its intention to open a new line of stores, called Home Depot Expo, carrying upscale home furnishings to appeal to a different market than that attracted by the traditional Home Depot stores. The Expo stores might have a different risk profile from the traditional stores because

- Their prices and profit margins are likely to be larger than the profit margins at the traditional Home Depot stores.

- Their customers are likely to be more affluent.

- They are more likely to be clustered in urban and suburban markets, where the demand for their products is likely to be higher.

The following is a list of publicly traded companies that draw the preponderance of their revenues from home furnishings and that serve the same (or a similar) customer base as the proposed Expo stores (with betas and debt/equity ratios estimated for each):

Comparable Firm	Beta	Debt/Equity Ratio
Bed, Bath and Beyond	1.90	2.00%
Bombay Company	1.55	0.00%
Michaels Stores	1.65	15.00%
Pier 1 Imports	1.60	10.00%
Average	1.675	6.75%

Unlevered Beta for Home Furnishings = 1.675/[1+0.64 (.0675)] = 1.606

The average beta across these companies, in conjunction with the average debt/equity ratio, can be used to estimate an unlevered beta.

This beta can be re-levered back up using the Home Depot's proposed debt/equity ratio (25%) to arrive at a beta for the Expo stores:

$$\text{Beta for Expo stores} = \text{Unlevered Beta} \left[1 + (1 - \text{tax rate})(D/E) \right]$$
$$= 1.606 \left(1 + 0.36 \left(0.25 \right) \right) = 1.86$$
$$\text{Cost of Equity for Expo stores} = 7\% + 1.86 \left(5.5\% \right) = 17.24\%$$
[The Treasury bond rate is assumed to be 7%, and
the risk premium is assumed to be 5.5%.]

The Home Depot, in evaluating whether to take the Expo stores, should ensure that the returns it earns for equity investors on these stores is at least 17.24%.

☐ Concept
Check

> Can you think of an exception to the rule that the firm's debt/equity ratio should be used to calculate the beta for a division?

Accounting betas   A second approach is to estimate the market risk parameters for divisions or projects from accounting earnings rather than from traded prices. Thus, changes in earnings at a division, on a quarterly or annual basis, can be regressed against changes in earnings for the market, in the same periods, to arrive at an estimate of an **accounting beta** to use in CAPM. Although the approach has some intuitive appeal, it suffers from three potential pitfalls. First, accounting earnings tend to be smoothed out relative to the underlying value of the company, resulting in betas that are "biased down," especially for risky firms, or "biased up," for safer firms. In other words, betas are likely to be closer to one using accounting data. Second, accounting earnings can be influenced by nonoperating factors, such as changes in depreciation or inventory methods, which can affect the earnings, and by allocations of corporate expenses at the divisional level. Finally, accounting earnings are measured, at most, once every quarter, and often only once every year, resulting in regressions with few observations and not much power.

Accounting Beta: This is a beta estimated by regressing the accounting earnings of an asset against the accounting earnings of the market.

 IN PRACTICE   ESTIMATING ACCOUNTING BETAS—BOEING

Assume that Boeing is considering bidding on a defense project and needs an estimate of beta and cost of equity for the project. Having operated in the defense business for decades, Boeing

Table 11.2 **EARNINGS ON DEFENSE BUSINESS—BOEING (PERCENTAGE DISTRIBUTION)**		
Year	**S&P 500 (%)**	**Defense Business (%)**
1980	−2.10 (%)	−12.70 (%)
1981	−6.70	−35.56
1982	−45.50	27.59
1983	37.00	159.36
1984	41.80	13.11

(continues)

(Table 11–2 *continued*)	Year	S&P 500	Defense Business
	1985	−11.80	−26.81
	1986	7.00	−16.83
	1987	41.50	20.24
	1988	41.80	18.81
	1989	2.60	−29.70
	1990	−18.00	−40.00
	1991	−47.40	−35.00
	1992	64.50	10.00
	1993	20.00	−7.00
	1994	25.30	11.00

has a historical record of its profitability. These profits are reported in Table 11.2, together with earnings changes for the S&P 500 going back to 1980.

Regressing the changes in profits in the defense division against changes in profits for the S&P 500 yields the following:

Defense Business Earnings Change $= -0.03 + 0.65$ (S&P 500 Earnings Change)

Based on this regression, the beta for the defense division is 0.65. We can now estimate the cost of equity for the defense project as follows:

Cost of Equity for the Defense project $= 7\% + 0.65 \ (5.5\%) = 10.58\%$
[The Treasury bond rate is assumed to be 7%, and the risk premium is 5.5%.]

Thus, in bidding for this project, Boeing has to ensure that the returns to equity investors exceeds 10.58%.

☐ Concept Check

In calculating betas, we used net income rather than operating income. Why is that the right choice? Explain.

Betas from cross-sectional regressions The final way of estimating risk parameters is to use a cross-sectional regression, whereby the betas of publicly traded firms are regressed against firm characteristics that have been shown to affect betas, such as dividend payout, earnings variability, and cash flow-generating capacity. Once the cross-sectional regression has been estimated, the specific characteristics of the division or project can be plugged into the regression to arrive at an estimate of a beta.

A number of researchers have examined the relationship between betas and fundamental variables.[4] The following is an updated regression relating the betas of NYSE and AMEX stocks in 1994 to four variables: coefficient of variation in operating income, size, debt/equity, and growth in earnings.

Beta $= 0.6507 + 0.25$ (CV in Operating Income) $+ 0.09$ (Debt/Equity Ratio) $+ 0.54$ (Earning Growth) $- 0.000009$ [Total Assets (millions)]

[4]Beaver, Kettler, and Scholes (1970) examined the relationship between betas and seven variables: dividend payout, asset growth, leverage, liquidity, asset size, earnings variability, and the accounting beta. Rosenberg and Guy conducted a similar analysis of the relationship between betas and financial fundamentals.

where

$$\text{CV in Operating Income} = \text{Coefficient of Variation in Operating Income}$$
$$= \text{Standard Deviation in Operating Income/ Average Operating Income}$$

In more general terms, Rosenberg and Marathe suggest that fundamental information about a firm can be used in conjunction with historical beta estimates to provide superior predictors of future betas.

Concept Check

Assume that you regress betas against the fundamental characterstics of the firm and that you get a regression with low explanatory power (R-squared is low). How would that affect your use of the regression?

IN PRACTICE   USING FUNDAMENTAL INFORMATION TO PREDICT BETAS FOR PROJECTS—THE HOME DEPOT

To apply this approach to estimating betas and costs of equity, consider the Home Depot's planned foray into computerized home shopping. Assume that the home shopping business has the following characteristics:

CV of Operating Income = 1.74 (based on other home shopping firms income)
Debt/Equity Ratio = 25.00% (Home Depot's planned debt/equity ratio)
Earnings Growth Rate = 45% (Growth in earnings for home shopping business)
Total Assets = $500 million (Expected size of Home Depot's ultimate investment)

How does one know the characteristics of a business before entering into it? In this case, the information can come from looking at the characteristics of private or public companies that have operated in this business. Plugging in these values into the regression yields the following beta:

$$\text{Beta} = 0.6507 + 0.25\,(1.74) + 0.09\,(25\%) + 0.5406\,(.45) - 0.000009\,(500)$$
$$= 1.35$$

Note that the beta for this project could have been estimated more directly by looking at the betas of comparable firms and adjusting for differences in leverage. If that approach had been used, the beta would have been computed as follows:

Average Beta of comparable firms = 1.40
Average D/E Ratio of comparable firms = 10%
Unlevered Beta for comparable firms = 1.32
Beta for Home Shopping business = 1.32 (1 + 0.64 (0.25)) = 1.53
[This is estimated using Home Depot's target debt/equity ratio of 25% and a tax rate of 36%.]

This beta can be used to estimate a cost of equity for this project; the returns to equity investors on the home shopping project must be greater than the cost of equity.

RISK-ADJUSTED INVESTMENT ANALYSES

Once the relevant risk has been identified and measured at the project level, it can be factored into the analysis in one of two ways. The first, and more conventional approach is to *adjust the discount rates to reflect the risk*; the cost of equity will be adjusted to reflect risk if the cash flows being discounted are cash flows to equity, and the cost of capital will be changed to reflect risk if the cash flows are those to the firm. The other approach is to *adjust the cash flows to reflect the risk* and to use a riskless rate as the discount rate.

Adjusting Discount Rates

Once the risk parameters have been estimated for a project, the discount rate can be adjusted to reflect its riskiness. The adjustment will also vary depending on whether the discount rate is the cost of equity or the cost of capital; this will be determined depending on whether the cash flows being discounted are cash flows to equity or cash flows to the firm.

Adjusting the cost of equity   The adjustment to the cost of equity will depend on both the risk/return model being used and the preceding analysis of which types of risk matter and which do not. If the only risk that matters is market risk, and the capital asset pricing model is used, the cost of equity for the project will be:

Project Cost of Equity = Risk-free Rate + Project Beta (Market Risk Premium)

where the project beta is estimated using one of the three approaches described in the previous section—the pure play approach, the accounting approach, or the cross-sectional regression.

   This cost of equity will be understated, however, if other sources of risk that investors in the company care about are not reflected in the beta. For instance, if the investors in the company are primarily domestic investors who consider currency risk to be a priced risk (rather than a diversifiable risk), an additional premium will have to be added on for projects taken on in currencies other than the company's domestic currency. The magnitude of this premium will be an increasing function of the volatility of the currency. Although there are no widely accepted models for estimating this premium, some practical approaches can be used. One is to look at the historical premiums earned by equity investors in financial investments (stocks and bonds) in the desired currency over and above equivalent domestic investments. Based on this approach, it can be argued that a company planning to make real investments in Brazil should demand a 4% **currency risk premium** because that is the premium that U.S. investors have made on Brazilian stocks, relative to U.S. stocks over the last 10 years. The limitation of this approach, when historical data are limited and volatile, is that it can yield unsustainable and unrealistic premiums. The second practical approach to estimating this premium is to look at expected returns on investments in that country. **Brady bonds,** for example, are dollar-denominated bonds issued by many emerging economies, and they generally carry yields much higher than the Treasury yields. This yield differential can be viewed as a risk premium reflecting both currency and political risk.

Currency Risk Premium: This is a premium added on to discount rates to reflect the additional risk created by exchange rate movements and political risk.

Brady Bonds: These are dollar-denominated bonds trading in many emerging economies; they are partially backed by the U.S. government.

Let us take this one step further: a private company may add an extra premium to reflect other risk (that normally would be classified as diversifiable) to arrive at a cost of equity that is significantly higher, reflecting the risk concerns of the owners of the company, who do not have the capacity to diversify. Because this will be a subjective estimate, it will be determined by the risk aversion of the owner; the more risk averse he or she is, the greater will be the additional premium.

Concept Check

If you were analyzing a private company for sale to a publicly traded firm, which of the above estimates would you end up using in your valuation?

IN PRACTICE   ESTIMATING COST OF EQUITY FOR A PROJECT—THE HOME DEPOT

In this application, we estimate the cost of equity for the same project from three perspectives—that of a large publicly traded firm with an international investor base; that of a publicly traded firm with a domestic investor base and that of a private or closely held firm.

Assume that the project is a proposed store to sell upscale home furnishings in Mexico and that the firm is a U.S.-based firm, like the Home Depot. In addition, assume that the analysis is being done in dollars and that the appropriate beta is 1.84. Given a risk-free rate of 7% and a risk premium of 7.5% (reflecting the higher political and economic risk of investing in Mexico), the base cost of equity for this project, based on the beta alone, is

$$\text{Base Cost of Equity} = 7\% + 1.84\,(7.50\%) = 20.80\%$$

This would be the cost of equity that would be used by the large publicly traded firm with an international investor base.

A publicly traded firm with a predominantly domestic investor base might demand a premium for currency risk, over and above the base cost of equity, leading to a higher cost of equity:

$$\text{Cost of Equity with Currency Risk Premium} = 20.80\% + 3.00\% = 23.80\%$$

The currency risk premium used reflects the volatility of the Mexican peso. Although the premium can be estimated in a number of ways, we use the premium on dollar-denominated Mexican Brady bonds, relative to U.S. Treasury bonds.

A private firm with relatively few nondiversified investors might demand a further premium to cover another potentially diversifiable risk, such as competitive or industrywide risk:

$$\text{Cost of Equity with Currency Risk and Other Risk Premium}$$
$$= 20.80\% + 3.00\% + 3.50\% = 27.30\%$$

The additional premium is based on subjective factors. These differences in costs of equity will therefore provide the company with the international investor base, a decided advantage when it comes to analyzing this project.

Concept Check

If you were advising the owner of a private firm on how to overcome the disadvantage of having a higher discount rate, outlined above, how would you suggest he or she eliminate or at least mitigate this disadvantage?

Estimating cost of capital   Getting from cost of equity to cost of capital requires two additional inputs—an after-tax cost of debt, and the relative weights of debt and equity in the financing mix:

Project Cost of Capital = Project Cost of [Equity/(Debt + Equity)]
+ After-tax Cost of Debt [Debt/(Debt + Equity]

Two estimation issues arise in the context of estimating project cost of capital. The first relates to the estimation of the *after-tax cost of debt*. In most cases, it is reasonable to assume that all projects taken on by a firm carry the same after-tax cost of debt and that it is the firm's after-tax cost of debt. The exception to this rule is a division of a firm, which may carry its own debt and have its own rating, enabling it to have a cost of debt different from the firm's. The most common examples are the finance arms of major manufacturing companies, such as GE Capital and GMAC, which issue commercial paper and long-term debt and are rated separately from their parent companies. The second estimation issue concerns the *debt ratio* to use for a project. There are potentially three choices: (1) the specific mix of debt and equity used for the project. (2) the financing mix used by the division taking the project; or (3) the debt and equity proportions for the overall firm. The project's financing mix should be used if, and only if, the project is a standalone venture with independent financing, which is generally the case only for very large and long-term projects. The division's mix of debt and equity can be used if the division has a target debt ratio and carries its own debt. In all other cases, it is reasonable to use the company's financing mix to come up with the weights to use in arriving at the cost of capital.

Even if all projects taken by a firm share the same after-tax cost of debt and financing mix, they can still have different costs of capital, as a result of their different risk characteristics and costs of equity.

To illustrate, we consider three distinct cases, reflecting the use of project-specific, division-specific, and firm-wide costs and weights for debt. In the first case, assume that you are analyzing a project for a phone company considering investing in developing infrastructure for telecommunication in China. The project is expected to last decades and to cost billions, and will be financed independently using 75% debt (at an after-tax rate of 4.5%) and 25% equity. Assuming a 12% cost of equity, the cost of capital for this project can be written as

Cost of Capital for project = 12% (0.25) + 4.5% (0.75) = 6.375%

In the second case, assume that you are analyzing a project for GE Capital, which carries its own debt (at an after-tax rate of 4.25%) and has a debt ratio of 80%. Furthermore, assume that the cost of equity for GE Capital is based on a beta of 0.75, which, in turn, is estimated by looking at other financial service firms. The cost of capital on this project can be estimated as follows

Cost of Equity for the project = 7% + 0.75 (5.5%) = 11.125%
Cost of Capital for the project = 11.125% (0.2) + 4.25% (0.8) = 5.625%

In the final example, consider the Home Depot Expo stores the Home Depot is considering. These stores will operate under the auspices of the overall company rather than under a separate division. The after-tax cost of debt for the Home Depot is 5%, and the debt ratio for the firm is expected to be 20%, looking forward. The cost of equity for the

Home Depot Expo stores, based on the analysis in the previous section, is expected to be 17.24%. This results in a cost of capital for the Home Depot Expo stores of

$$\text{Cost of Capital} = 17.24\% \ (0.80) + 5.00\% \ (0.20) = 14.792\%$$

Adjusting Expected Cash Flows

An alternative approach to adjusting for risk is to adjust the expected cash flows to reflect their riskiness. Intuitively, more risky cash flows will be adjusted down than will less risky cash flows. The extent of the adjustment will vary depending on the approach used, and the adjustments can either be subjective or based on a risk/return model.

Subjective estimates   A project analyst will sometimes build in risk into cash-flow estimates by lowering expected cash flows if they are riskier. Although this approach has the advantage of flexibility, it gives rise to several problems:

- The adjustment is essentially subjective and will vary from analyst to analyst, depending on his or her risk aversion. Thus, there will be little uniformity in the way decision makers deal with risk within the same organization.
- There is always the danger that the analyst may adjust for risk, which may be diversifiable, either at the firm level or at the level of the investor in the firm. For instance, an analyst at the Home Depot may adjust the expected cash flow estimates of a store because it is in a risky location. This risk can, be diversified away by the Home Depot, however, because of the number of stores it opens in a year.
- Because the adjustment is often hidden in the estimates, there is the chance that the same risk may be factored in several times. To illustrate, the project analyst may lower the cash flows to reflect perceived risk. When the cash flows get to a decision maker, he or she may lower them further to adjust for the same risk, unaware that the adjustment has already been made.
- It undercuts the notion of a base case analysis, for the project diagnostics will also be affected adversely by the risk adjustment.
- In many cases, firms also adjust the discount rates to reflect the risk. It can be argued that this will result in a double counting of the same risk.

Certainty equivalent approaches   An alternative to the subjective adjustment is the **certainty equivalent** approach, whereby risky cash flows are stated in terms of the riskless cash flows to which they would be equivalent. For instance, a risky cash flow of $120 may be equivalent to a riskless cash flow of $100. While the riskless cash flow will always be smaller than the risky cash flow, the difference is a function of the riskiness of the cash flows.

Certainty Equivalent: This is the riskless cash flow that is the equivalent, in value to the receiver, of a larger risky cash flow.

The models for risk and return, though traditionally used to estimate discount rates, can also be used to estimate certainty equivalent cash flows on projects. If the risk-adjusted discount rate and the risk-free rate are known, for instance, the certainty equivalent cash flow for a risky cash flow can be written as

$$CF \ (\text{Certainty Equivalent})_t = \text{Expected Cash flow}_t \ (\lambda)^t$$

where

$$\lambda = (1+R_f) / (1+ \text{Risk-adjusted Rate})$$

Note that the certainty equivalent is determined by the following variables:

- *Risk measure*: The higher the riskiness of the cash flow, the lower the certainty equivalent.
- *Risk premium*: As the risk premium rises, the certainty equivalent cash flow decreases.

Once all the cash flows are reduced to their certainty equivalents, they can be discounted back at the *riskless rate* to arrive at a net present value. Done right, it should always be equal to the net present value computed using expected cash flows and a risk-adjusted discount rate.

 Concept Check

> What would be the end result of an analysis whereby certainty equivalent cash flows are discounted at a risk-adjusted discount rate? Is there a cost to being too conservative in investment analysis?

 IN PRACTICE   USING CERTAINTY EQUIVALENT CASH FLOWS—BOEING

The Boeing 777 project is analyzed using both risk-adjusted discount rates and certainty equivalent cash flows in Table 11.3.

Table 11.3   **CERTAINTY EQUIVALENT CASH FLOWS AND PRESENT VALUES**

Year	FCFF	PV at Risk-Adjusted Rate	Certainty Equivalent Cash Flow	PV at Risk-free Rate
0	$(4,000)	$(4,000)	$(4,000)	$(4,000)
1	(711)	(635)	(679)	(635)
2	1,755	1,399	1,602	1,399
3	1,868	1,330	1,629	1,330
4	1,626	1,033	1,354	1,033
5	1,772	1,005	1,410	1,005
6	1,466	742	1,114	742
7	1,666	754	1,210	754
8	1,247	504	865	504
9	1,972	711	1,307	711
10	588	189	372	189
11	1,432	412	866	412
12	1,840	472	1,064	472
13	826	189	456	189
14	641	131	338	131
15	5,385	984	2,714	984
	NPV	5,220	NPV =	5,220

The adjustment factor for estimating certainty equivalent cash flows is estimated from Boeing's risk-adjusted cost of capital (12%) and the risk-free rate (7%).

Adjustment Factor for year 1 = (1 + Risk-free Rate) / (1 + Risk-adjusted Rate)

$$= 1.07/1.12 = 0.9554$$

Adjustment Factor for year 2 = 0.95542^2

Note that the net present value is the same under both approaches.

RISK ADJUSTMENT PRACTICES

Most firms consider risk in the process of investment analyses, but the techniques used vary widely. A survey by Kim, Crick, and Kim (1986) questioned 320 firms about how they adjusted for risk in investment analysis. The results are shown in Table 11.4.

Table 11.4   RISK-ADJUSTMENT TECHNIQUES USED BY RESPONDENTS

Technique	Percentage
No adjustment is made	14%
Adjustment is made subjectively	48%
Certainty-equivalent method	7%
Risk-adjusted Discount Rate	29%
Shortening Payback Period	7%
Others	5%

The majority of the firms adjusted for risk "subjectively," and a significant number used risk-adjusted discount rates. A surprisingly large number did not adjust for risk at all in investment analysis.

Examining both formal and informal surveys of risk-adjustment techniques over time, the following conclusions emerge:

- Firms are much more likely to adjust discount rates to reflect risk today than they were 10 or 20 years ago; often, the adjustment is made using a risk/return model like the capital asset pricing model.

- As firms enter diverse businesses, they are at least recognizing the need for different risk adjustments in different business lines.

- Many firms also continue to use the probabilistic techniques, such as breakeven and sensitivity analyses, to provide decision makers with more information on which to base their decisions.

COMMON ERRORS IN PROJECT RISK ASSESSMENT

A number of common errors are made in project risk assessment:

1. *Failure to consider risk entirely*: Any firm that completely ignores risk in its decision making is asking for trouble. Decision makers, if they are not penalized for the riskiness of the projects they take on, will consider and take on riskier and riskier projects, betting on the higher returns.

2. *Counting the same risk more than once*: When firms use more than one risk-adjustment technique, they might end up counting the same risk more than once. Consequently, they will end up rejecting some good risky projects.

3. *Applying the firm's risk profile to a project with different risk characteristics*: Many firms continue to use one risk premium (and one cost of equity) across projects. Doing so will clearly tilt the scale toward the riskier projects, resulting in overinvestment in these projects. Conversely, it will be unfair to safer projects (and divisions), leading to underinvestment in these projects.

4. *Considering "diversifiable" risk in project analysis*: When a decision maker at a large publicly traded firm considers diversifiable risk in project analysis, he or she increases the likelihood that the project will be rejected for the wrong reasons.

CONCLUSION

The discount rates or expected cash flows on a project can be adjusted to reflect the riskiness of the project. In the process of doing so, however, firms must analyze or address the following issues:

- The different sources of risk in investments must be examined, ranging from risk that is specific to a project (which can be effectively eliminated if the firm considers a large number of similar projects every year) to competitive and industry factors (which investors in the firm should be able to diversify away) to market factors (which affects all firms, albeit to varying degrees).

- Among the different sources of risk, only that risk which the investors cannot diversify away or eliminate more economically than the firm can should be considered in investment analysis. What portion of the risk meets this condition will vary across firms, depending on whether they are publicly traded or private firms and, even among publicly traded firms, on the type of investors.

- Once the relevant risk is identified, it has to be measured using a specified risk and return model and then built into either the cash flows or discount rates in the analysis. In the process, the risk of a project that has a very different risk profile than the firm that takes it might have to be assessed separately, based on either comparable firms, accounting data, or cross-sectional regressions.

QUESTIONS AND PROBLEMS

1. Examine the following sources of risk and list whether you would consider them as part of an investment analysis if you were a large publicly traded clothing retail firm:

   a. The project analyst might have overestimated the revenues on the store.

   b. There might be a natural disaster (hurricane or flood) in the area in which the project is located, resulting in major losses.

   c. A competitor might open a store close by and drive down margins and sales.

   d. A manufacturing plant that employs most of the people who live in the area around the store might close down.

   e. An economic recession leads to layoffs at the plant, resulting in lower sales and profits at the store.

   f. A national sales tax might be passed, decreasing sales.

   g. Inflation increases, increasing interest rates.

2. Would any of your answers be different if you were a small private company considering a similar store opening?

3. The Limited is considering expanding into South America. In making its project analyses, the following information is available:

   - The beta for the Limited is 1.40.
   - The Treasury bond rate is 7%, and the project analyses will be done in dollars.
   - The risk premium for South American countries is expected to be 7.5%.
   - Brady bonds issued by South American countries trade at a premium of 2% over the Treasury bond rate.

a. Estimate the cost of equity to use in evaluating the new South American stores.

b. Explain your reasoning and the conditions under which you might have decided differently.

4. You have been asked to estimate the cost of capital for a power plant being considered in Thailand by a U.S.-based utility. The plant will require an initial investment of $1 billion and will be independently financed using 60% debt (carrying an after-tax rate of 4.5%) and 40% equity. The beta for power plants is 0.8, and the Treasury bond rate is 7%.

a. Estimate the cost of equity for this power plant, in U.S. dollars.

b. Estimate the cost of capital for this power plant, in U.S. dollars.

c. How would your analysis differ, if it were done in the local currency?

5. You are advising a phone company that is planning to invest in multimedia projects. The beta for the telephone company is 0.75 and it has a debt/equity ratio of 1.00; the after-tax cost of borrowing is 4.25%. The multimedia business is considered much riskier than the phone business; the average beta for comparable firms is 1.30, and the average debt/equity ratio is 50%. Assuming that the tax rate is 40%, and the Treasury bond rate is 7%,

a. Estimate the unlevered beta of being in the multimedia business.

b. Estimate the beta and cost of capital if the phone company finances its multimedia projects with the same debt/equity ratio as the rest of its business.

c. Assume that a multimedia division is created to take these projects, with a debt/equity ratio of 40%. Estimate the beta and cost of capital for the projects with this arrangement.

6. Intel is exploring a joint venture with Ford to develop computer chips to use in automobiles. Although Intel had traditionally used a cost of equity based on its beta of 1.50, and a cost of capital based on its debt ratio of 5%, it is examining whether it should use a different approach for this project. It has collected the following information:

- The average beta for automobile component firms is 0.90, and the average debt/equity ratio across these firms is 40%. (Tax Rate = 36%).

- The joint venture will be financed 70% with equity from Ford and Intel, and 30% with new debt raised at a market interest rate of 7.5%.

- The T-Bond rate is 7%.

a. Estimate the beta that Intel should use for this project.

b. Estimate the cost of capital that Intel should use for this project.

c. What would the consequences be of Intel using its current cost of equity and capital on this project?

7. Hershey's is considering expanding its operations into Malaysia. It is trying to estimate the appropriate cost of capital to use in evaluating this expansion option and has collected the following information:

- The beta for Hershey stock is 0.95.
- Hershey has traditionally used only a small amount of debt; its current debt ratio is 12%. It is planning to raise this debt ratio to 20%.
- The cost of debt for Hershey's is 8%. (Tax Rate = 36%)
- Institutional investors hold 65% of the outstanding stock at Hershey's.

a. Estimate the cost of capital, in U.S. dollars, for this project, if the Treasury bond rate is 7.5%.

b. Did you charge a premium for currency risk? Why or why not?

c. Did you charge a premium for political risk? Why or why not?

d. Would your analysis have been any different if Hershey was privately held?

8. You are analyzing a line of cosmetics that the Gap is proposing to introduce and are trying to arrive at a reasonable estimate for the cost of equity for this project. The Gap has no debt and a beta of 1.45. In contrast, cosmetics firms have an average beta of 1.75 and an average debt/equity ratio of 10%. The Treasury bond rate is 7%, and the corporate tax rate is 40%. What would your estimate of cost of equity be for this project and why?

9. Returning to the cosmetics project for the Gap, assume that you have the following estimates of the cash flows on the project:

Year	After-tax Cash Flows (to Equity)
0	−$10,000,000
1	3,500,000
2	4,000,000
3	4,500,000
4	5,000,000
5	5,000,000

The project ends after five years, and there is no salvage value.

a. Estimate the net present value of the project, using the cost of equity estimated in the previous problem.

b. Estimate the certainty equivalent cash flows in each year, and the net present value based on these certainty equivalents.

10. The New York Yankees baseball franchise is considering introducing a new line of clothes carrying the Yankee logo. The Yankees are a privately owned firm and therefore have no risk parameters estimated for them. Publicly traded firms involved in the apparel business have an average beta of 1.15 and an average debt/equity ratio of 20%. The Treasury bond rate is 7%, and the corporate tax rate is 40%.

a. Estimate the beta and cost of equity for this project.

b. Should there be a premium for the fact that Yankees are a privately owned business? Why or why not?

11. You are helping the financial managers of a grocery store estimate a cost of capital to use in assessing new stores. The grocery store, which is publicly traded, has a beta of 1.40 and a debt/equity ratio of 70%; the after-tax cost of debt is 5.5%. The managers are trying to estimate costs of capital at two different stores. One is a suburban store, with little competition, whose cash flows can be estimated fairly accurately. The other is a store in New York City, where the estimates have much more potential for error. (T. Bond rate = 7%)

a. What cost of capital would you charge for these two stores?

b. Would you charge a higher cost of capital for the New York City store? Why or why not?

12. Compaq is trying to estimate a cost of capital to use in assessing its entry into the high-end workstation market. The publicly traded firms in this market have an average beta of 1.20 and an average debt/equity ratio of 20%. There is intense competition within the industry for business. Compaq itself has a beta of 1.45 and has a debt ratio of only 10%. It plans to maintain this debt ratio on its new venture. The T-Bond rate is 7%, and Company's cost of debt is 7.5%. (Tax Rate = 36%)

a. Estimate the cost of capital for this new venture.

b. Would you charge a premium for the fact that this is an intensively competitive industry? Why or why not?

13. Philip Morris is reexamining the costs of equity and capital it uses to decide on investments in its two primary businesses—food and tobacco. It has collected the following information on each business:

- The average beta of publicly traded firms in the tobacco business is 1.10, and the average debt/equity ratio of such firms is 20%.

- The average beta of publicly traded firms in the food business is 0.80, and the average debt/equity ratio of such firms is 40%.

Philip Morris has a beta of 0.95 and a debt ratio of 25%; the pretax cost of debt is 8%. The Treasury bond rate is 7%, and the corporate tax rate is 40%. Assume the two divisions are of equal market value.

a. Estimate the cost of capital for the tobacco business.

b. Estimate the cost of capital for the food business.

c. Estimate the cost of capital for Philip Morris, as a firm.

14. Having looked at your estimates of cost of capital for the tobacco and food divisions at Philip Morris, the financial managers at Philip Morris have come back with a question: Where is the substantial risk posed by tobacco lawsuits showing up in the costs of capital that you have estimated? How would you respond?

15. Now assume that Philip Morris is considering separating into two companies—one holding the tobacco business and one the food business.

a. Assuming that the debt is allocated to both companies in proportion to the market values of the divisions, estimate the cost of capital for each of the companies. Will it be the same as the costs of capital calculated for the divisions? Why or why not?

b. Assuming that the tobacco firm is assigned all of the debt and that both firms are of equal market value, estimate the cost of capital for each company. (Assume that the pretax cost of debt will increase to 10% if this allocation is made.)

16. You are assisting First Global, an international bank, in deciding on the costs of equity it should be using to evaluate its various divisions. It has three divisions currently—commercial banking, real estate, and investment banking. The betas of comparable firms in each division are provided below:

Division	Comparable Firms' Beta
Commercial Banking	1.05
Real Estate	0.70
Investment Banking	1.40

The T-Bond rate is 7%.

a. Estimate the costs of equity for each division.

b. What would happen if you used First Global's beta of 0.95 to estimate the cost of equity for all three divisions?

CHAPTER 12

ORGANIZING AND FOLLOWING UP ON INVESTMENT ANALYSIS

In the last five chapters, we examined and developed the techniques that can be used for analyzing investment opportunities. Although the decision rules provided in those chapters are indeed valuable, this chapter provides added insight into both the sources of good projects and the process by which projects are analyzed. It also examines how project choice can be followed up and monitored. In particular, the following questions are analyzed:

- What are the determinants of project success? Why do some firms have more good projects than others? How can a business increase its likelihood of finding and exploiting good projects?
- What are some of the more common errors made in investment analysis, and how can firms organize to prevent or at least minimize these errors?
- How do you follow up on investment analysis? When should a project be terminated or divested?
- How do you analyze a firm's overall success at investment analysis?

WHERE DO GOOD PROJECTS COME FROM?

In the process of analyzing new investments in the preceding chapters, we have examined some of the characteristics of good projects. Depending on the investment criteria used, good projects will

- have a positive net present value
- earn an internal rate of return greater than the hurdle rate
- have an accounting rate of return greater than the hurdle rate

Although these criteria are certainly valid from a measurement standpoint, they do not address the deeper questions about good projects, including:

- What is it that makes a project good? Is it purely a function of serendipity, or is it the result of careful planning by management?
- Why do some businesses have more good projects available to them than others?
- How can businesses that do not have a ready supply of good projects increase their access to them? How can businesses with more than enough good projects maintain their status?

Competitive Product Markets and Project Quality

Implicit in the definition of a good project—one that earns a return that is greater than that earned on investments of equivalent risk—is the existence of super-normal returns to the business considering the project. In a competitive market for real investments, the existence of these excess returns should act as a magnet, attracting competitors to take on similar investments. In the process, the excess returns should dissipate over time; just how quickly they dissipate will depend on the ease with which competition can enter the market and provide close substitutes and on the magnitude of any differential advantages that the business with the good projects might possess. Take an extreme scenario, whereby the business with the good projects has no differential advantage in cost or product quality over its competitors, and new competitors can enter the market easily and at low cost to provide substitutes. In this case, the super-normal returns on these projects should disappear very quickly.

❑ Concept
Check

In a perfectly competitive product market, what type of projects should firms expect to have? What type of returns should they expect to make?

Barriers to Entry and Project Quality

As noted above, an integral basis for the existence of a "good" project is the creation and maintenance of barriers to new or existing competitors taking on equivalent or similar projects. These barriers can take different forms, including economies of scale, cost advantages, capital requirements, product differentiation, access to distribution channels, and legal and government barriers.

Economies of scale   Some projects might earn high returns only if they are done on a "large" scale, thus restricting competition from smaller companies. In such cases, large companies in this line of business may be able to continue to earn super-normal returns on their projects because smaller competitors will not be able to replicate them. Consider the example of a company like Wal-Mart, whose success at discount retailing has been well documented. Although Wal-Mart made extraordinary returns on its strategy of opening huge retail stores that offer a wide range of products at the lowest prices, it has been able to preserve these returns over an extended period, because competitors with smaller stores are unable to match Wal-Mart's prices and make equivalent returns.

Size alone does not guarantee that any company will continue to earn excess returns on projects, however, for large firms may compete with one another for available projects and, consequently, drive down the returns on these projects. A good example is the automotive sector, where clearly **economies of scale** are associated with producing cars. The strong competition among both domestic and foreign manufacturers for the automobile market has driven down the returns earned by these manufacturers on their projects.

Economies of Scale: Economies of scale refer to savings in costs that arise as an entity gets larger.

Cost advantages   A business might work at establishing a cost advantage over its competitors, either by being more efficient or by taking advantage of arrangements that its competitors cannot use. For example, in the late 1980s, Southwest Airlines was

> **Proposition 1:**   The greater the economies of scale associated with a type of investment, the greater the likelihood that larger businesses taking on this type of investment will continue to earn super-normal returns, relative to smaller businesses. In other words, larger firms are much more likely to find positive net present value projects in those areas where their size works to their advantage—that is, in areas where there are economies of scale.

able to establish a cost advantage over its larger competitors, such as American and United Airlines, by using nonunion employees; the company exploited this cost advantage to earn much higher returns.

> **Proposition 2:**   Firms that have established a cost advantage over their competitors in a particular line of business are much more likely to find good projects. As their cost advantage deteriorates, the number of "good" projects will also decline.

Capital requirements   Entry into some businesses might require such large investments that it discourages competitors from entering, even though projects in those businesses may earn above-market returns. Assume that Boeing is faced with a large number of high-return projects in the aerospace business, for example. This scenario would normally attract competitors, but the huge initial investment needed to enter this business would enable Boeing to continue to earn these high returns. The immunity from competition is not permanent, however. Airbus Industries, formed and financed by the European countries in response to Boeing's dominance of the sector prior to 1980, eventually was able to compete with Boeing and drive down the excess returns.

When there are relatively few firms competing in a business, and the capital requirements for new entrants are prohibitive, the chances of collusion among these firms to keep their returns high will increase, because they do not have to fear the threat of new competitors. It can be argued that the super-normal profits earned by the U.S. automobile firms until the Japanese incursion in the early 1970s can be attributed to this factor. By contrast, the chances of colluding successfully will decrease when new firms can enter a business easily.

> **Proposition 3:**   Firms involved in businesses that require a substantial initial investment for competitors to enter are much more likely to earn excess returns on their projects, relative to businesses where new firms can enter at low cost.

Product differentiation   Some businesses continue to earn excess returns by differentiating their products from those of their competitors, leading to either higher profit margins or higher sales. This differentiation can be created in a number of ways.

- *Extensive advertising and promotion:* The objective of advertising and promotion is to endow the product with special features that the competitors' products do not possess. Thus, Kellogg and General Foods continue to earn excess returns on their projects in the cereal business by advertising heavily and charging much higher prices for their brand names than do generic competitors. Spending more on advertising and promotion may be an integral part of creating a valuable brand name, but it is by no means a sufficient condition. For a brand name to acquire value, there has to be some consistency in product delivery and a genuine concern for customer needs.

> **Proposition 4:** Companies that have recognized and valuable brand names are much more likely to earn excess returns on their projects than are companies that

- *Technical expertise:* Large research and development expenditures, better trained personnel, or superior production facilities are all sources of technical expertise. In this case, the products sold by the company will be of better quality or will use more advanced technology than those of its competitors, enabling the firm to capture more of the market or to charge higher prices and earn higher returns. Sony, for instance, has developed a reputation for making superior consumer electronic goods, allowing the company to charge higher prices.

> **Proposition 5:** The likelihood of earning excess returns on a project will increase if the company considering the project has the technical expertise and the production facilities to create a product that is qualitatively better than those produced by its competitors.

- *Better service:* Some firms earn excess returns on their projects because their reputation for good service enables them to sell more of their products than their competitors. The Home Depot, for instance, registered impressive growth in the home-improvement retail market not only by offering products at competitive prices, but also by providing better customer service than its competitors.
- *Responsiveness to customer needs:* Companies that focus on the customer are arguably more likely to offer products that sell better and make higher returns, because they supply products that more closely meet their customers' needs.

> **Proposition 6:** Firms with a reputation for good customer relations are much more likely to earn excess returns on projects than their competitors.

Access to distribution channels   Those firms that have much better access to the distribution channels for their products than their competitors are better able to earn excess returns. In some cases, the restricted access to outsiders is due to tradition or loyalty to existing competitors. For instance, in Japan, the inability of foreign automobile manufacturers to get Japanese dealers to carry their cars in showrooms has enabled Japanese car manufacturers to charge higher prices in that country and presumably earn higher returns than they would have otherwise. In other cases, the firm may actually own the distribution channel, and competitors may not be able to develop their own distribution channels because the costs are prohibitive. For example, telephone companies that own the phone lines might have a decided advantage in providing online services than their competitors.

> **Proposition 7:** Firms that have preferential access to distribution channels have a much greater chance of making excess returns on projects that utilize these chan-

Concept Check

New avenues are opening up for consumer shopping every day; in particular, shopping on line (from personal computers) has become increasingly popular. What implications does this technology have for returns in retailing? What do you think will characterize successful retailing firms in the future, assuming that this trend continues?

Legal and government barriers In some cases, a firm may be able to exploit investment opportunities without worrying about competition because of restrictions on competitors, from product patents the firm may own or from government restrictions.

- *Product patents:* A product patent gives a firm more power over the pricing of its product as well as the returns it will earn on related projects because it protects it against competitors. For example, Glaxo has been able to earn extraordinary returns on its ulcer drug, Zantac, because it owns the patent rights to the drug. Note that having the product patent does not ensure project success, inasmuch as other companies may come up with their own products that are close substitutes, thereby eliminating the excess returns.

> **Proposition 8:** A firm that possesses a patent on a product increases its likelihood of earning excess returns on related projects, at least for the life of the patent. The excess returns are likely to increase if the capacity of competitors to produce close substitutes decreases.

- *Government restrictions on entry:* In some cases, government restrictions on entry into a business may help existing firms earn excess returns. For instance, many countries restrict ownership of their media companies to domestic citizens. Although one may debate the social implications and rationale for such a policy, it does serve the interests of existing firms by restricting competition from outside. Similarly, government tariffs or quota restrictions on foreign goods allow domestic producers of these goods to charge higher prices and earn higher returns.

> **Proposition 9:** Firms operating in businesses where entry is restricted by the government are much more likely to earn excess returns than are firms operating in businesses where there are no such restrictions.

Concept Check

You are analyzing a firm that has made extraordinary returns on its projects over the last 10 years, largely as a consequence of a few products that are patent protected. You know that the patent protection will end in two years. How will that affect future returns for the firm?

Quality of Management and Project Quality

In the preceding section, we examined some of the factors that determine the attractiveness of the projects a firm will face. Some factors, such as government restrictions on entry, may largely be out of the control of incumbent management. There are other factors, however, that can clearly be influenced by management.[1] Considering each of the factors discussed above, for instance, we would argue that a good management team can increase both the number of and the returns on available projects by

- *Taking projects that exploit any economies of scale that the firm may possess:* In addition, management can look for ways it can create economies of scale in the firm's existing operations.

- *Establishing and nurturing cost advantages over its competitors:* Some cost advantages may arise from labor negotiations, whereas others may result from long-term strategic decisions made by the firm. For instance, by owning and developing SABRE, the airline reservation system, American Airlines has been able to gain a cost advantage over its competitors.

- *Taking actions that increase the initial cost for new entrants into the business:* One of the primary reasons Microsoft was able to dominate the computer software market in the early 1990s was its ability to increase the investment needed to develop and market software programs.

- *Increasing brand-name recognition and value through advertising and by delivering superior products to customers:* A good example is the success that Snapple experienced in the early 1990s in promoting and selling its iced tea beverages.

- *Nurturing markets in which the company's differential advantage is greatest, in terms of either cost of delivery or brand-name value:* In some cases, this will involve expanding into foreign markets, as both Levi Strauss and McDonald's did in the 1980s in order to exploit their higher brand-name value in those markets. In other cases, this may require concentrating on segments of an existing market, as the Gap did when it opened its Banana Republic division.

- *Improving the firm's reputation for customer service and product delivery:* This will enable the firm to increase both profits and returns. One of the primary factors behind Chrysler's financial recovery in the 1980s was the company's ability to establish a reputation for producing quality cars and minivans.

- *Developing distribution channels that are unique and cannot be easily accessed by competitors:* Avon, for instance, employed a large sales force to go door-to-door to reach consumers who could not be reached by other distribution channels.

- *Getting patents on products or technologies that keep out the competition and earn high returns:* Doing so may require large investments in research and development over time. It can be argued that Intel's success in the market for semiconductors can be traced to the strength of its research and development efforts and the patents it consequently obtained on advanced chips, such as the Pentium.[2]

The quality of management is typically related to the quality of projects a firm possesses, and yet a good management team does not guarantee the existence of good projects. In fact, a rather large element of chance is involved in the process; even the best

---

[1]When government policy is influenced by lobbying by firms, it can be argued that even these factors may be affected by the management of a firm.

[2]It is estimated that Intel spent between $3 billion and $5 billion developing the Pentium chip.

laid plans of the management team to create project opportunities may come to naught if circumstances conspire against them—a recession may upend a retailer, or an oil-price shock may cause an airline to lose money.

Concept Check

In the late 1980s, commercial banks in the United States increasingly turned to securities trading as a way of increasing their returns. What are the potential sources of excess returns from trading? What implications would you draw for commercial banks from this analysis?

The Role of Acquisitions

As firms mature and increase in size, they are often confronted with a quandary. Instead of being cash poor and project rich, they find that their existing projects generate far more in cash than they have available projects in which to invest. This can be attributed partly to size and partly to competition. As they face up to their new status as cash-rich companies, with limited investment opportunities, acquiring other firms with a ready supply of high-return projects looks like an attractive option, but there is a catch. If these firms are publicly traded, the market price already reflects the expected higher returns not only on existing projects but also on expected future projects. In terms of present value, the value of a firm can be written as

Value of Firm = Present Value of Cash Flows from Existing Projects
+ Net Present Value of Cash Flows from Expected
Future Projects

Super-Normal Returns: These are returns that are greater than the returns that would normally be earned for an investment of equivalent risk.

Thus, firms that are earning super-normal returns on their existing projects and are expected to maintain this status in the future will sell at prices that reflect these expectations. Accordingly, even if the cash-rich firm pays a "fair" price to acquire one of these firms, it has to earn more than the expected **super-normal returns** to be able to claim any premium from the acquisition. To put all this in perspective, assume that you are considering the acquisition of a firm that is earning 25% on its projects, when the hurdle rate on these projects is 12%, and that it is expected to maintain these high returns for the foreseeable future. A fair price attached to this acquisition will reflect this expectation. All this implies that an acquisition will earn super-normal returns for the acquirer if, and only if, one of the following conditions holds:

- The acquisition is done at a price below the fair price (i.e., the company is significantly undervalued).
- The acquisition is done at a price that reflects the expectation that the firm will earn 25%, but the acquirer manages to earn an even higher return, say 30%, on future projects.
- The acquisition enables the firm to take on projects that it would not have taken on as an independent firm; the net present value of these additional projects will then be a bonus that is earned by the acquiring firm. This is the essence of **synergy.**

- The acquisition lowers the discount rate on projects, leading to an increase in net present value, even though the returns may be unchanged.

Overall, it is clear that internally generated projects have better odds of success than do acquisitions since no premium is paid for market expectations up front.

Synergy: This is the increase in the value that results from combining two firms.

❑ Concept
  Check

> Given a choice between acquiring a publicly traded or a private firm, where would you suppose the odds of success (in terms of eventual returns to the acquiring company) would be greater? Why? If you were mapping out an acquisition strategy designed to increase your access to good projects, how would you go about maximizing your odds for success?

COMMON ERRORS IN INVESTMENT ANALYSIS

There is always the possibility of errors in investment analysis. Some are conceptual; others are more quantitative, involving measurement and estimation. There is also the very real likelihood that the analysis reflects the biases of the analysts and decision makers using it, leading to skewed results.

Conceptual Errors

The fundamentals of investment analysis are simple: The *cash flows* from making an investment should always be *incremental* and *after taxes*, whereas the *hurdle rate* used for the project should be defined *consistently* with the cash flows and reflect the *riskiness* of the project being analyzed. The most common conceptual errors in investment analysis violate one or another of these basic principles.

Violation of the cash-flow principle   Cash flows may be estimated incorrectly in a number of ways:

- Noncash charges that have to be added back to earnings to arrive at cash flows may be overlooked.
- Changes in working capital that do not affect earnings but affect cash flows may be ignored.
- Additional capital investments that have to be made to keep the project going may not be adequately considered.

Although the net income on a project is generally lower than its cash flows, largely because of depreciation and amortization, there are exceptions to this rule, especially when it comes to long-term projects that require large working capital investment. Thus, a specialty retail firm that is considering a long-term project might find its cash flows lower than its net income, after factoring in increases in working capital on the project.

Violations of the incremental cash-flow principle   The cash flows used to analyze a project should be incremental; that is, they should result from the project. This principle can be violated in several ways, however.

Considering sunk costs as cash outflows   In Chapter 8, we defined a sunk cost as an expense that has already been incurred prior to the investment analysis and, consequently, cannot be reversed by not taking the project. Because these costs are unaffected by whether or not the project is taken, they should not be considered in the course of an investment analysis. Some investment analyses consider sunk costs, however, either because they are based on accounting statements (which do not distinguish between sunk costs and costs yet to be incurred) or because of a misplaced sense of fairness that every project should to be forced to carry its own weight. This behavior increases the likelihood that the project will be rejected, even though such a rejection might be to the detriment of the firm.

Considering allocated costs as cash outflows   Another consequence of using accounting statements as the basis for investment analysis is the consideration of allocated expenses as cash outflows. Again drawing on the discussion in Chapter 8, any increase in allocated expenses should be considered in investment analysis, whereas a reallocation of an existing expense to a project is *not* considered a cash outflow. Those investment analyses that build in allocated expenses that do not pass the incremental test are likely to result in more projects being rejected, which may be a mistake.

Not considering the opportunity costs of resources used in the project   A new project often utilizes resources that are already owned by the firm. These resources may not need to be acquired anew, but they might have opportunity costs; that is, by taking this project, an opportunity to use the resources elsewhere may be lost, resulting in lost profits or cash flows. As we noted in Chapter 8, these costs can be estimated based on cash flows for a wide range of resources, ranging from equipment to individuals to excess capacity. In some investment analyses, these resources are viewed as free because they are already owned by the firm. Doing so underestimates the costs of the project, however; as a result, some bad projects may be accepted. In other investment analyses, the book value of assets used by the project are considered a measure of their cost. Because book value and cash flows are often unrelated, however, cash flows on the project may be either under- or overestimated.

Not considering the benefits that accrue to other projects   In some cases, a project may create benefits for other projects. These synergies, which should be considered part of the project cash flows, are often ignored because they do not fit neatly into the items that make up a typical investment analysis. Consequently, some projects that should be accepted may wind up rejected.

Violation of the after-tax principle   The cash flows used in investment analysis should be considered after taxes. This may seem straightforward, but there are a number of details which, if ignored, can result in erroneous investment decisions.

Not using the marginal tax rate   When firms consider new projects, they have to consider all income and expenses arising from the project *at the margin*; that is, they add on to the cumulated income and expenses the firm has from its existing projects. Consequently, it is the *marginal tax rate* that should be used in estimating cash flows, not the average tax rate, which some analysts use.

By the same principle, any losses incurred by a project should be construed as creating a tax benefit in that year for a firm that makes enough income on its other projects to claim that loss as a deduction. A common error in investment analysis involves carrying losses on projects forward to set off against forecasted project income in future years when, in fact, the benefit is received right away. Thus, a project that creates a tax loss of $10 million in the first year for a profit-making firm with a marginal tax rate of 40% will create a tax savings of $4 million in that year. Delaying this tax benefit until future years will reduce the net present value of the project.

Failure to consider tax factors   Because all cash flows used should be after taxes, any items that may affect the taxes should be built into the investment analyses. For instance, when equipment is salvaged, capital gains taxes may be due that are based on the difference between the salvage value and the book value at the time of the sale. Similarly, the choice of depreciation method has significant implications for both the timing and the present value of the cash flows. Any investment analysis that ignores the nuances of these tax choices will misestimate the cash flows and may result in erroneous investment decisions.

Violations of the consistent discount rate principle   Once cash flows have been estimated on an incremental, after-tax basis, they must be matched up with discount rates that are defined consistently. Failure to do so will result in significant errors, as discussed in Chapters 7 and 8. The two most common mismatches are highlighted in this section.

Mismatching equity and firm cash flows and discount rates   As noted in the previous chapter, the two approaches to investment analysis are the *equity approach,* whereby returns to equity investors are compared to the cost of equity, and the *firm approach,* whereby returns to all investors in the firm are compared to the cost of capital. Any analysis that mixes and matches returns to one group with the costs of the other is fundamentally flawed and cannot be depended on to yield the right decision. Thus, discounting cash flows to equity at the cost of capital will significantly overestimate the net present value; and discounting cash flows to the firm at the cost of equity will significantly underestimate the net present value.

Mismatching nominal and real cash flows and discount rates   Both the cash flows and the discount rates must be stated either in nominal terms (incorporating expected inflation) or real terms for the analysis to have any meaning. Analysts who use nominal discount rates with cash flows that do not build in expected inflation will underestimate the project's net present value, whereas those who use real discount rates with nominal cash flows will overestimate the project's net present value.

Failure to consider project risk correctly   The discount rate for a project should reflect its risk—higher risk projects should have higher discount rates. This principle may be violated in a number of ways, however. First, some firms use the same discount rate on all their projects, even though the projects may have very different risk characteristics. As a result, cash flows on some projects may be discounted at rates much too high given their risk levels, whereas cash flows from other projects may be discounted at rates much too low. Second, most models of risk and return suggest that only the market risk component should be considered for setting the discount rate. Considering any firm-specific risk that should not be rewarded, such as project or industry risk, while setting the discount or hurdle rate, leads to incorrect decisions.

Estimation Errors

The potential for estimation errors within the confines of an investment analysis is great. Certain assumptions need to be made about almost every item in a capital budgeting analysis—the project life, revenues, expenses, working capital needs, and taxes. These assumptions may reflect the best information available to the analyst, but they are also likely to contain significant estimation errors. These errors are likely to increase with

- The riskiness of the project,
- The project life: longer-term projects require more assumptions than shorter-term projects.

In many ways, **estimation errors** reflect the uncertainty of dealing with the future, which is an integral part of running a business. We would argue that estimation errors, though creating discomfort for the analyst and the decision maker, are much less of a problem than the conceptual errors listed above or the bias errors listed below because they tend to average out, especially for firms with large numbers of projects. Thus, the Home Depot might overestimate the cash flows on one of its home improvement stores, but it will probably underestimate the cash flows on another. Given that the Home Depot opens several new stores each year, the estimation errors across these stores are expected to average out. However, it is still entirely possible for a business to do everything right conceptually from an investment standpoint and still end up losing because of an input that was erroneously estimated. Thus, the Home Depot may build a store on a highway on the basis of expected traffic and may find itself with an empty store if the highway is diverted.

Estimation Errors: These are mistakes made in the forecasts of cash flows on a project.

□ Concept Check

> You are comparing two companies. The first is a manufacturing company that makes only two or three large investments each year. The second is a service company that makes dozens of smaller investments each year. Which of these two companies should worry more about estimation error and why?

Bias in Investment Analysis

Visualizing investment analysis as the objective search for the truth about projects may make it seem more appealing. Clearly, however, biases, positive as well as negative, enter into every analysis. **Estimation bias** arises from decision makers' and analysts' preconceptions about projects and investment choices, which percolate through the assumptions into the forecasts and, ultimately, into the decisions. It is not surprising, therefore, that a decision maker or analyst who starts off with a presumption that a project is good will generally find that the analysis backs up his or her prior opinion.

Estimation Bias: Estimation bias occurs when the estimated cash flows on a project are systematically different (higher or lower) than expected values.

Empirical evidence on bias   There is substantial evidence of a positive forecasting bias in investment analysis. This suggests that some projects that should not be accepted will be taken because of optimistic estimates of cash flows. Mansfield, Rapoport, Schnee, Wagner, and Hamburger examined the accuracy of development cost forecasts in two drug firms and found that the average ratio of actual to forecasted costs was 2.25 for the development of new chemical products, 1.70 for compounded products, and 1.51 for alternative dosage forms. In other words, the actual costs in all three cases were significantly higher than those estimated at the time of the initial analysis, by margins ranging from 51% for dosage forms to 125% for new products. Similar results are reported by Meadows and Allen and Norris. Tull reports on the actual sales of new products introduced by 24 companies and found that actual sales fell below forecasts in 66% of the cases.

The source of this bias often lies in the ways in which investment analysis is done in firms. A project advocate is often responsible for preparing the cash flows on the project, and there typically is no counteravailing force—a devil's advocate—pointing out the inconsistencies in the assumptions and the analysis.

Dealing with bias This optimistic bias seems to be most pronounced when the same person preparing the forecast is responsible for evaluating the forecast and making the investment decision. Statman and Tyebjee report that separating the forecasting from the evaluation decisions reduces bias considerably; the evaluators simply assume that the forecasts are biased and adjust them accordingly. The researchers reported the following conclusions to an experiment they conducted:

- Individuals with extensive work experience seem to allow for a much larger bias in forecasts than do those with less experience and adjust the cash flows accordingly, increasing cost forecasts and reducing revenue forecasts.
- The adjustments made for bias seem to be insufficient because the forecasts continue to be optimistic even after adjustments are made.

Concept Check

An optimistic bias is dangerous because it encourages firms to take bad projects. By contrast, a pessimistic bias, whereby cash flows are underestimated, is beneficial because it provides a way to be more conservative in investment analyses. Do you agree or disagree with this statement? Why?

ORGANIZING FOR INVESTMENT ANALYSIS

Investment analysis is a critical part of managing any business. Firms often create formal processes for analyzing projects and deciding whether they should be accepted or rejected. Large firms generally have more formal capital budgeting processes than do smaller firms, for three reasons: (1) They have more projects to analyze; (2) to ensure uniformity in how projects are analyzed; and (3) to maintain control. Although it is difficult to generalize these processes, most firms use a combination of top-down and bottom-up analysis to pick projects. In **top-down budgeting,** the firm decides on its capital budget, which is the amount that will be available for capital investments during the period. This allocation is determined by several factors. First, it is a function of the cash flows generated from operations by the firm, net of any dividends and financing costs the firm plans to incur. Second, it is likely to be affected by capital budgeting allocations in prior years; for instance, a firm that allocated $200 million to projects last year is unlikely to increase its capital budget to $600 million this year. Third, it is influenced by managers' perceptions not only of the economy but also of the availability of good projects. Finally, it will reflect the firm's capacity to raise external financing at a reasonable cost.

Top-down Budgeting: In top-down budgeting, capital allocations are made by a central entity at the firm level for divisions of the firm.

In **bottom-up budgeting,** individuals and divisions within a firm make requests for *capital authorizations* for projects, and back up their requests with financial analyses showing the viability of these projects. In some firms, the decision to accept or reject these projects is made at the divisional level by local managers, subject to the overall budget constraints set at the corporate level. In other firms, decisions concerning at least the large projects are made at the corporate level, in order to keep control over the investment process.

> **Bottom-up Budgeting:**   In bottom-up budgeting, capital allocations are based on requests that flow from individuals or divisions to the firm.

If the authorizations exceed the budget, one possible solution is to increase the capital budget to allow more projects to be taken. The second solution is to select a subset of the projects, using the capital rationing criteria developed in the earlier chapters.

Smaller firms tend to get away with less formal processes by centralizing investment decisions with one or a few individuals because they have far fewer projects to analyze. As they grow, however, the stress on this centralized decision process tends to increase. In fact, the failure of many small firms on a growth path can be attributed to the inability of owner-managers to delegate this authority.

☐ Concept
Check

> Think of some of the constraints corporate headquarters add to investment analysis. What is the rationale for these constraints? What are some of the negative consequences?

Organizing for Best Effect in Investment Analysis

In theory, investment analysis should begin with an overview of the available projects, proceed with unbiased and thorough analysis of the viability of these projects, and end with an assessment of the financing options available for these projects. In practice, however, the competition among divisional managers for limited resources often results in biased project analysis. Corporate headquarters typically react by constraining resource allocations, even though they risk rejecting good projects.

Firms attempt to exercise control over the investment process by adding more constraints on project decisions, including size constraints (e.g., projects costing more than a certain amount will have to be run past corporate headquarters) and payback requirements (e.g., only projects that pay off within 10 years can be accepted). These constraints may protect the firm against decision makers at lower levels committing the firm's funds to projects that are long term, risky, and often poor investments, but they also create several costs:

- Good projects may be rejected because they do not meet one or more of the arbitrary constraints created to control the process.
- Decision makers may spend considerable time and resources figuring out ways to get around the constraints and end up accentuating the problems. For instance, investment requests in firms with size constraints are often broken up into smaller components to enable divisions to preserve their decision-making authority on these projects.
- The process may be delayed, allowing competitors to preempt the firm and introduce similar products.

Thus, investment analysis must be organized in such a way that it not only minimizes the bias inherent in investment analysis but also holds decision makers responsible for the forecasts they use to justify their decisions. Although the first objective can be accomplished by separating the forecasting from the evaluation decisions, the second can be accomplished only if the firm follows up project decisions with *postaudits* whereby the actual numbers on projects are measured up against their forecasts and the forecasters are held responsible for deviations.

FOLLOWING UP ON INVESTMENT ANALYSIS

The investment analysis is the start of the investment process. Many firms follow up project acceptance with **postaudits,** which allow them to keep tabs on the actual cash flows of projects, for two reasons. First, postaudits enable the firm to evaluate the investment process and hold forecasters responsible when the actuals deviate from the forecasts. Second, postaudits help the firm decide whether projects in place should be continued, divested, or terminated.

Postaudit: A postaudit is an analysis of how a project taken in the past has performed relative to expectations.

Measuring Up Actuals

All investment analyses are based on forecasts of revenues and expenses. In the prior section, we pointed out the prevalence of estimation errors and bias in these forecasts. Once a project has been accepted and implemented, the firm can and should compare the actual revenues and expenses to the forecasted revenues and expenses. The two will almost never be equal, but the differences may provide some insight into a number of critical issues.

Measuring error and bias in forecasts The actual cash flows and earnings may be above or below the forecasts on a project for a number of reasons. First, the economy might have taken a turn for the worse or the better after the project was accepted, affecting earnings and cash flows. Second, the forecaster might have erred in his or her forecasts on the basis of one or more incorrect assumptions. If this is the case, the errors should average out across projects—some projects will have actual earnings that exceed forecasts, whereas others will underperform expectations. Third, the forecaster might have been overly optimistic in his or her forecasts. In this case, the errors will not average out, and the actual earnings will, on average, be less than forecast across projects.

Holding forecasters responsible The postaudit introduces some responsibility into the forecasting process by ensuring that the forecasts are measured up against actuals. That said, we would hasten to add that the failure of actual earnings to measure up to forecasts *on any one project* should not be used as a measure of the bias or the skills of a forecaster. *Consistent* failures, however, would reflect unfavorably on the analyst making these forecasts.

Project followup Measuring the actual earnings against forecasts enables managers to take corrective action to rescue projects that might be in trouble and to provide additional resources for projects that might be doing better than expected. For instance, if the actual revenues on a project are coming in 20% below expectations, the firm may shift its marketing strategy or its target market to increase revenues. Similarly, if actual revenues are coming in 50% above expectations, the firm may have to make arrangements to increase its production capacity and its working capital investment to accommodate the higher growth.

Measuring up forecasts against actuals is only one part of the evaluation. The actual return on a project must be measured against the required return in order to evaluate whether or not the project added value to the firm during the period of the evaluation.

Analyzing Existing Projects

Many of the same techniques used for analyzing new projects can be used to analyze existing projects to decide whether they should be continued or terminated. There are some differences between the analysis of an existing project and that of a new project, however:

- Most of the investment cost for a new project is still to be made and, hence, has to be factored into the analysis as a cash outflow. By contrast, much of the investment for an existing project has already been made and is a sunk cost and should not be considered in the project analysis. Similarly, any other operating cash flows that might have already been incurred for an existing project will have to be ignored.

- The estimates of revenues and cash flows for a new project are based entirely on projections. If the project involves a new product in a new market, considerable uncertainty characterizes the estimates. By contrast, the firm has much more information on both the product and the market for an existing project, allowing more precise estimates of future earnings and cash flows.

- The discount rate used on an existing project may be different from that used to analyze the same project at initiation and will reflect the new information the firm has collected on the project.

- The cash flows on an existing project have to be evaluated entirely on an incremental basis. Thus, if there is an option to terminate the project, the incremental cash flow is the difference between the cash flow the firm can expect from continuing the project and the cash flow it could lose if the project is terminated. If the firm is pre-committed to the expenses on the project, for contractual or legal reasons, it may not save much by terminating the project. In contrast, firms have far fewer commitments on new projects, and most cash flows are therefore incremental.

If the incremental cash flows on the existing project are estimated and discounted at an appropriate rate, the firm is in a position to decide whether the project should be continued, terminated, or divested. For example, assume that you are analyzing a 10-year project two years into its life and that the cash flows are as shown in Figure 12.1.

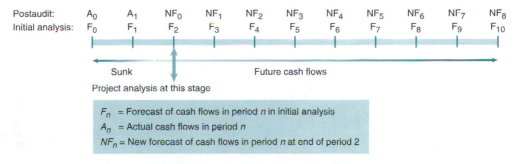

Figure 12.1   Analysis of existing project

In particular, the following general decision rules should apply:

- If the present value of the expected future cash flows is negative, and there are no offers from third parties to acquire the project, the project should be terminated:

$$\sum_{t=0}^{t=n} \frac{NF_n}{(1 + r)^n} < 0 \qquad \ldots\ldots\text{Terminate the project}$$

where r is the discount rate that applies to the cash flows, based on perceived risk at the time of the analysis.

- If the present value of the expected future cash flows is positive but it is less than the salvage value (SLVG) that can be obtained by terminating the project today, the project should be terminated:

$$\sum_{t=0}^{t=n} \frac{NF_n}{(1 + r)^n} < \text{SLVG} \qquad \ldots\ldots\text{Terminate the project}$$

where r is the discount rate that applies to the cash flows, based on perceived risk at the time of the analysis.

- If the present value of the expected future cash flows is positive but there is an offer from a third party to buy the project for a higher price, the project should be divested (DIV):

$$\sum_{t=0}^{t=n} \frac{NF_n}{(1 + r)^n} < \text{DIV} \qquad \ldots\ldots\text{Divest the project}$$

- If the present value of the expected future cash flows is positive (even though it may be well below expectations and below the initial investment) and there are no better offers from third parties, the project should be continued:

$$\sum_{t=0}^{t=n} \frac{NF_n}{(1 + r)^n} > 0 > \text{DIV} \qquad \ldots\ldots\text{Continue the project}$$

Existing projects should not be terminated simply because the actual returns do not measure up to either the forecasts or the original investment. They should be terminated if, and only if, the forecasted incremental cash flows on the project have a negative present value.

❏ Concept
Check

A restructuring specialist argues that firms should always divest or terminate underperforming divisions (i.e., divisions that earn less than the cost of capital). Do you agree? Why or why not?

A postmortem analysis on a completed project   Assume that you are analyzing a just-completed 10-year project involving the introduction of a new breakfast cereal mix for a food products company. The original forecasts of the cash flows as well as the actual cash flows over each of the 10 years are reported in the Table 12.1.

Table 12.1 **PROJECTED AND ACTUAL CASH FLOWS ON CEREAL PROJECT**

	Initial Analysis				Actual Cash Flows			
Year	Investment	Operating CF	Salvage	Total	Investment	Operating CF	Salvage	Total
0	$(10,000,000)			$(10,000,000)	$(10,500,000)			$(10,500,000)
1		$2,000,000		2,000,000		$1,800,000		1,800,000
2		2,100,000		2,100,000		1,872,000		1,872,000
3		2,205,000		2,205,000		1,946,880		1,946,880
4		2,315,250		2,315,250		2,024,755		2,024,755
5		2,431,013		2,431,013		2,105,745		2,105,745
6		2,552,563		2,552,563		2,189,975		2,189,975
7		2,680,191		2,680,191		2,277,574		2,277,574
8		2,814,201		2,814,201		2,368,677		2,368,677
9		2,954,911		2,954,911		2,463,424		2,463,424
10		3,102,656	$2,000,000	5,102,656		2,561,961	$1,800,000	4,361,961
	Internal Rate of Return (Initial) =			20.39%	Actual Rate of Return on Project =			15.71%

Initally, the project was expected to earn an internal rate of return of 20.39%. In the ex-post analysis, however, it actually earned only 15.71%.

   Taking this analysis one step further, assume that the cost of capital at the time of the initial analysis was 13%. This project would have been viewed as a good one, inasmuch as it was expected to earn a return (20.39%) much greater than this hurdle rate. In hind-sight, the project did not do as well as expected, but it still earned a return (15.71%) greater than the hurdle rate, suggesting that it added value to the company.

 IN PRACTICE   ANALYZING AN EXISTING PROJECT: THE HOME DEPOT

Assume that you are analyzing a store opened by the Home Depot five years ago, which has a remaining life of five years. Table 12.2 summarizes the original forecasts of cash flows used when the store was opened to justify the project, as well as the actual cash flows generated by the store over the first five years of its existence.

Table 12.2   **ANALYZING AN EXISTING PROJECT: THE HOME DEPOT**

	Initial Analysis			Analysis in Year 5		
Year	Initial Forecast of CF	PV of CF	Year	Actual Cash Flow	Forecast in year 5	PV of CF
0	$(13,574,997)	$(13,574,997)		$(14,100,000)		
1	1,050,000	937,500		900,000		
2	1,175,000	936,703		920,000		
3	1,355,000	964,462		1,050,000		
4	1,521,000	966,623		1,125,000		
5	1,727,000	979,946		1,220,000		
6	1,892,846	958,975	1		$1,350,000	$1,200,000
7	2,433,189	1,100,651	2		1,500,000	1,185,185

(continues)

Table 12.2   (*CONTINUED*)

	Initial Analysis			Analysis in Year 5		
Year	Initial Forecast of CF	PV of CF	Year	Actual Cash Flow	Forecast in year 5	PV of CF
8	2,791,148	1,127,298	3		1,750,000	1,229,081
9	3,212,705	1,158,534	4		1,900,000	1,186,161
10	15,833,188	5,097,863	5		12,000,000	6,659,147
	Initial NPV =	$653,557		NPV for analysis at end of Year 5 =	$11,459,574	
	Initial IRR	12.77%				

Based on the initial analysis, with a cost of capital of 12%, the store clearly seemed to be a good investment, with a net present value of $653,557 and an internal rate of return of 12.77%.

In the second analysis, done five years later, the data indicate that the actual cash flows for the first five years had come in well below expectations and the forecasted cash flows for the remaining five years had been scaled down accordingly from the initial estimates. Assume also that interest rates have gone up since the initial analysis and that the new cost of capital is 12.5%. This postaudit can answer several questions:

- *In hindsight, how did the actual cash flows compare to the forecasts?*

The actual cash flows on this store deviated significantly from the forecasts in each of the five years the store had been in existence. Even more troubling is the fact that the forecasts were below expectations in each of the five years, as shown in Table 12.3.

Table 12.3   **ACTUAL VERSUS FORECASTED CASH FLOWS**

Year	Forecast	Actual	Actual Relative to Forecast	% Forecast Error
0	$(13,574,997)	$(14,100,000)	$(525,003)	3.87
1	1,050,000	900,000	(150,000)	−14.29
2	1,175,000	920,000	(255,000)	−21.70
3	1,355,000	1,050,000	(305,000)	−22.51
4	1,521,000	1,125,000	(396,000)	−26.04
5	1,727,000	1,220,000	(507,000)	−29.36

The initial investment exceeded the forecast by 3.87%, and the first year's after-tax cash flow fell below expectations by 14.29%. The discrepancy increased over time.

- *Why did the actual cash flows fall below expectations?*

There are a number of reasons why forecasts and actuals may deviate from each other.

1. *Economy-wide factors:* The economy might have underperformed expectations. Although this may explain shortfalls in one or two periods, it is unlikely that it can be used to justify a large and increasing shortfalls over a five-year period.

2. *Project-specific factors:* This particular store might have been affected by locational factors (such as traffic on the highway running past the store), or the analyst making projections for this store might have made incorrect assumptions. If this is the case, the shortfall of actuals relative to forecasts should not be repeated across project analyses. In fact, the actuals will likely have *exceeded* forecasts in other stores.

3. *Analyst-specific factors:* The analyst who made the projections for this store may have had a systematic bias toward optimistic projections. If so, most of the stores on which he or she made projections should exhibit this pattern of actuals lagging forecasts.

4. *Company-wide factors:* The company itself may have come under increasing competition, which has driven down sales and returns on all its stores. If this is the case, there should be a companywide pattern of declining earnings and cash flows.

• *What corrective action can the Home Depot take, given the postaudit?*

The corrective action Home Depot can take will depend on the cause of the shortfall. If the shortfall is attributed to the economy, the company clearly cannot do much beyond hope for an economic revival and attempt to be more realistic in assessing economic prospects on future analyses. If localized factors caused the shortfall, the company should chalk this up to the price of being in business and attempt to mitigate some of the risk by spreading its store openings over more diverse areas. If analyst bias created the shortfall, the company should hold the analyst responsible for the shortfall and improve its capital budgeting process. Finally, if the shortfall can be attributed to increasing competition, the company must be more cautious about future expansion and come up with new ways of differentiating itself from its competition.

• *Did the project add value to the firm during the period of its existence?*

It is possible for a project to deliver forecasted cash flows that are well below expectations and still add value to the firm. The distinction is made by delineating the three rates of return that come into play in a postaudit—the internal rate of return on the project from the initial analysis, the actual rate of return earned by the project during its existence, and the required rate of return (the hurdle rate) during that period. A project may earn an actual rate of return that is below the initially estimated internal rate of return, for example, but still exceed the hurdle rate.

In the case of the Home Depot store, the actual returns made by the store during the five years of its existence can be computed from either an accounting standpoint (using average return on capital) or a cash-flow standpoint (using average cash-flow return on capital) and compared to the cost of capital during the five-year period:

$$\text{Accounting Return on Capital} = \text{EBIT } (1 - t)/$$
$$\text{Average Book Value of Capital Invested}$$
$$\text{Cash Flow Return on Capital} = \text{FCFF}/\text{Cash Flow Investment in Project}$$

Estimates for the Home Depot Store are summarized in Table 12.4.

Table 12.4   RETURN ON CAPITAL AT THE HOME DEPOT STORE

Year	Actual Cash Flow	CF Return on Capital (%)	BV of Investment	EBIT(1 − t)	Return on Capital (%)
0	$(14,100,000)		$11,000,000		
1	900,000	6.38	10,300,000	$200000	1.82
2	920,000	6.52	9,700,000	320000	3.11
3	1,050,000	7.45	9,200,000	550000	5.67
4	1,125,000	7.98	8,800,000	725000	7.88
5	1,220,000	8.65	8,500,000	920000	10.45

Return on Capital = EBIT $(1 - t)$/BV of Investment from previous year

The average accounting return on capital on this store during the five years of its operation was 5.79%, and the average cash-flow return on capital was 7.40%. Neither rate measures up to the cost of capital of 12%, suggesting that the project did not add value to the firm.

Again, it is important to note that this is an ex-post analysis (i.e., it is done after the project is taken), and although it indicates that the store did not add value to the company, it does not imply that the store should be closed.

• *Should the store be closed or should it continue to exist?*

The decision of whether or not the store should continue to remain open should be based on expected future cash flows. The present value of the cash flows from continuing operations can be estimated by discounting expected future cash flows at the current cost of capital of 12.5%, as shown in Table 12.5.

Table 12.5   **PRESENT VALUE OF CONTINUING OPERATIONS**

Year	New Forecast	PV of CF
1	$1,350,000	$1,200,000
2	1,500,000	1,185,185
3	1,750,000	1,229,081
4	1,900,000	1,186,161
5	12,000,000	6,659,147
	NPV of expected future cash flows =	$11,459,574

This present value should be compared to the cash flow that would be received by the firm if it closed the store and sold the facilities (land, building, and equipment). If the firm can receive more that $11.46 million for these facilities, it should close the store. If not, it makes sense to keep the store open, even though the returns do not match up to expectations.

Deciding on a divestiture: an illustration   Assume that you are analyzing the food division of a tobacco firm. The food division has earned a return on capital of only 7.5% over the last five years, well below the cost of capital of 12.5%. Table 12.6 shows the projected free cash flows to the firm from keeping the food division.

Table 12.6   **CASH FLOWS ON DIVISION**

Year	EBIT $(1 - t)$	Terminal Value	Present Value
1	$2,500,000		$2,222,222
2	2,750,000		2,172,840
3	3,025,000		2,124,554
4	3,327,500		2,077,342
5	3,660,250	$51,243,500	30,467,681
	Value of CF from Division =		39,064,639

As long as there is no offer from a third party to buy the division for more than $39.06 million, it pays for the firm to keep the division, even though it earns a substandard return on capital.

Investment Analysis at the Firm Level

An ex-post analysis can be done not only on individual projects but on aggregates of projects as well. The collective cash flow on all the projects a firm has taken can be evaluated against both forecasts (to evaluate whether the firm did as well as expected) and required returns (to examine whether the firm succeeded in aggregate in picking good projects). In many cases lacking project-specific information, analysts adopt shortcuts based on companywide accounting earnings to measure a firm's success at investment analysis.

In one comparison, the return on equity earned on existing projects is compared to the cost of equity; if the return on equity exceeds the cost of equity, it can be argued that, at least in the aggregate, the firm picked good projects and delivered on them. Alternatively, the actual return on equity can be compared to the forecasted return on equity to determine whether the firm did as well as expected. A firm may pass the first test but fail the second. To illustrate, assume that the Gap made a return on equity of 25% in 1995 and that the firm had a cost of equity of 16%. It can be argued that, on average, the firm's projects earned more than the hurdle rate and thus added value to the firm. However, if the forecasted return on equity for 1995 was 28%, it can also be argued that the firm underperformed relative to expectations, which would then decrease the stock price. In the final comparison, the firm's return on equity is compared to the average return on equity earned by its peer group in order to separate those effects that are specific to the firm from those that are industrywide.

The same analysis can be repeated at the level of the firm using the return on capital and the cost of capital, comparing

- *The actual return on capital to the cost of capital* to determine whether the projects overall beat the hurdle rate.
- *The actual return on capital to the forecasted return on capital* to determine whether the firm's choice of projects is improving or worsening.
- *The actual return on capital earned by the firm to the average return on capital earned by its peer group,* to determine whether the firm did better or worse than its competitors.

 IN PRACTICE EVALUATING PROJECT CHOICE AT BOEING AND THE HOME DEPOT

Table 12.7 analyzes project choice at Boeing and the Home Depot, for 1994, using all three approaches.

Table 12.7 **ANALYZING PROJECT CHOICE AT BOEING AND THE HOME DEPOT**

Company	Return on Capital			
	Actual for Firm	Actual for Industry	Cost of Capital	Forecasted for Firm
Boeing	6.03%	10.12%	9.65%	10.65%
The Home Depot	15.11%	10.62%	14.37%	15.00%

Company	Return on Equity			
	Actual for Firm	Actual for Industry	Cost of Equity	Forecasted for Firm
Boeing	8.80%	13.00%	12.50%	13.60%
The Home Depot	17.50%	12.00%	14.65%	16.30%

The three comparisons yield the following results:

1. *Actual returns versus forecasts:* Using both the equity and the firm measures, Boeing did worse than expected in 1994, whereas the Home Depot did slightly better than expected. Not surprisingly, an investment in Boeing stock during 1994 would have underperformed the market, but an investment in Home Depot stock would have outperformed the index.

2. *Actual returns versus hurdle rates:* Using both the equity and firm approaches, Boeing earned a return lower than the hurdle rate in 1994. The Home Depot, by contrast, earned a return higher than the hurdle rate on its projects in 1994.

3. *Actual returns versus industry averages:* Using both the equity and firm approaches, the Home Depot did much better than its peer group in 1994, whereas Boeing did much worse than its peer group in the same year.

The results must be considered with some caution, however, since they are based on one year of performance. If the results persist over several years, stronger conclusions can be drawn about the investment choices of both these firms.

 Concept Check

In this analysis, we have used actual returns on equity and capital to judge a firm's performance at picking projects. What are some of the limitations of this approach? How would you modify the approach to make it more robust?

Conclusion

In this chapter, we have moved beyond the mechanics of investment analysis to investigate several issues:

- The capacity to generate good projects (i.e., projects that earn super-normal returns), stems from a firm's ability to differentiate itself from its competition, either by creating a cost advantage or a better product or both, and from barriers to entry that it creates to keep existing competitors and new entrants from imitating it and driving down these high returns.

- Investment analysis, by its very nature, is fraught with uncertainty and estimation error.

- There is evidence that investment analysis reflects an optimistic bias that can be countered by holding investment analysts responsible for their forecasts and by separating the forecasting from the decision making.

- Once a project has been accepted, it has to be followed up to (1) evaluate the quality of and bias (if any) in the forecasts used in the initial analysis; (2) examine whether the project should be continued, divested, or terminated; and (3) estimate whether the project has added value to the firm during its existence.

- At the level of the firm, the quality of investment analysis can be judged by comparing the firm's actual returns to forecasted returns, required returns, and peer-group returns, either on an equity or a firm basis.

Questions and Problems

1. Most utilities in the United States are regulated monopolies. Why are they regulated? What are the implications of removing the regulations for excess returns at these firms?

2. Assume that you are the leading manufacturer of industrial chemicals and that there is a long lead time for a new entrant to become an established competitor. You have a decided advantage over your existing competitors in terms of access to funds. What is your differential advantage and how will it manifest itself in project analysis? What are some of the ways in which you might lose this differential advantage?

3. You are a private firm in the environmental waste disposal industry in which the rest of your competitors are publicly traded. What, if any, differential advantages would you have over your competitors? What, if any, are the differential advantages your competitors would have over you?

4. In the early 1980s, Lotus Corporation introduced Lotus 1-2-3 and dominated the spreadsheet market. In the late 1980s, as Lotus failed to introduce newer versions of its program, Microsoft stepped in and offered its version, Excel, and took away a significant portion of Lotus's market share.

   a. What was the differential advantage that Lotus offered in the early 1980s that allowed it to dominate and profit from this market?

   b. What was the differential advantage that Microsoft offered that allowed it to overtake Lotus?

   c. Assume that you are advising a small software firm that plans to offer its own spreadsheet program. What differential advantages can a product from such a firm offer?

5. The pharmaceutical firms in the United States have historically been able to maintain high returns on equity and earn surplus returns. It has been argued by many that this is due to the protection that the patent system offers them against competition.

   a. Why would patents lead to higher returns on equity and capital?

   b. Assume that a law is passed weakening patent protection against competition. What implications would this law have for the profitabity of pharmaceutical firms?

   c. In the absence of patent protection, what differential advantages would a pharmaceutical firm have over its competitors? What types of firms are likely to succeed under this scenario?

6. In the consumer product sector, brand names have traditionally allowed a firm to charge higher prices and have much larger profit margins.

   a. In a project analysis, how does the effect of a brand name show up in the estimates?

   b. What are the implications of declining brand-name loyalty for the capacity of a consumer product firm, like Procter and Gamble or Unilever, to maintain high returns on its projects?

7. Assume that a friend of yours, who has substantial technical experience in computers, is considering starting a firm to manufacture personal computers and has lined up investors who are willing to back her up. She has come to you for advice on how to make this venture succeed.

   a. Outline the potential differential advantages in the personal computer market.

   b. Specify what your friend would need to do to achieve these differential advantages.

   c. What path would you suggest offers the greatest chance for success for a small firm with significant technical expertise?

8. In 1995, Iomega, a small firm manufacturing disk storage systems for personal computers, introduced a new product called the Zip Drive. Priced at around $200, the Zip Drive allows computer users to store up to 100 MB of data on small disks and access the data easily. The demand for the Zip drive surged ahead of the supply, and the company reported a surge in profits and an increase in the stock price.

   a. If the Zip drive had no patent protection, what would you expect to happen in the market over the months following its introduction?

   b. If you were an analyst looking at Iomega as a firm, would you expect the surge in profitability to continue into the future? Why or why not?

9. In one of the greatest business success stories of the twentieth century, Ray Kroc bought the rights to a hamburger chain in the late 1950s and converted it into a chain of hundreds of franchises around the world. As one of the first fast-food chains with standardized menus and food, McDonald's clearly succeeded in meeting a need and profiting from it.

   a. To what factors would you attribute the early success of McDonald's? What differential advantage did it offer that allowed it to be profitable?

   b. Given that there is far more competition from other fast-food chains now, what differential advantages does McDonald's have looking forward? How can it exploit these advantages?

10. Firms spend large amounts of money on advertising to increase brand-name awareness and value. How would you measure the payoff to advertising in terms of project characteristics?

11. Assume that you are analyzing a five-year project for a manfacturing firm after its completion. The following table summarizes the original forecasts and the actual cash flows over each of the five years:

Year	Forecasted CF	Actual CF
0	−$100,000	−$105,000
1	20,000	15,000
2	25,000	20,000
3	30,000	25,000
4	35,000	30,000
5	40,000	35,000

   a. Estimate the internal rate of return on the project, based on the initial forecasts of cash flows.

   b. Estimate the actual rate of return on the project.

   c. Assuming that the cost of capital is 12%, did the project add value to the firm during the period of the analysis?

12. Assume that you are analyzing a 10-year project for a consumer product company, five years into the project and that you have the following information on the project: (Table 12.8, p. 328)

   a. Assuming that the cost of capital was 11% at the time of the initial analysis, would you have taken this project?

   b. Estimate the forecast error, by year, for the five years the project has been in existence.

   c. Estimate the cash-flow return earned by this project during the five years of its existence.

   d. Based on these forecast errors, reestimate the cash flows you will have on the remaining five years of the project.

   e. Estimate the net present value of continuing this project, assuming that the cost of capital is now 12%.

13. Assume that you are analyzing the performance of two companies, one a computer software firm and the other an automobile manufacturer, in picking projects. You have collected the following information on the two companies: (Table 12.9, p. 328)

TABLE 12.8

Year	Forecasts Investment	EBIT (1 − t)	Cash Flow	Actuals Investment	EBIT (1 − t)	Cash Flow
0	$(10.50)			$(10.00)		
1		$1.50	$3.00		$1.60	$3.10
2		1.60	2.80		1.65	2.85
3		1.70	2.60		1.75	2.65
4		1.80	2.40		1.85	2.45
5		1.90	2.40		2.00	2.50
6		2.00	2.40			
7		2.10	2.40			
8		2.20	2.40			
9		2.30	2.40			
10		2.40	2.40			

TABLE 12.9

Company	Actual ROE	Beta	ROE of Peer Group	Forecasted ROE
Software firm	20.5%	1.2	16%	22.0%
Auto firm	12.5%	1.4	10%	10.5%

The Treasury bond rate is 7%. Evaluate the performance of each of these companies relative to

a. The required rate of return

b. The return on equity of the peer group

c. The forecasted return on equity

What conclusions would you draw about the investment choices made by these firms?

14. The following table summarizes net income and average book value of equity each year for the Gap between 1991 and 1995:

Year	Net Income	Average BV of Equity
1991	$230 million	$576 million
1992	$211 million	$773 million
1993	$258 million	$1,001 million
1994	$320 million	$1,260 million
1995	$343 million	$1,480 million

(T Bond rate = 7%)

a. If the firm had a beta of 1.45 during the period, how would you evaluate the quality of the Gap's investments during the period?

b. Is the trend in return on equity a relevant factor to consider in the analysis?

c. If the market had been anticipating that the Gap would earn a return on equity of 28%, would your conclusions change?

d. Would your conclusions be affected by the fact that all specialty retailers reported declines of 5% or greater in return on equity during the period?

15. The following table summarizes returns on equity and betas at major automobile firms in 1995: (T. Bond rate = 8%)

Firm	Return on Equity	Beta
Chrsyler	14.0%	1.20
Ford Motor	16.0%	1.10
General Motors	11.5%	1.15

(The T Bond rate is 8%)

a. Estimate the differential between return on equity and cost of equity in 1995.

b. What conclusions would you draw about project choice at these companies in 1995?

c. What concerns would you have about using this approach to measure project quality?

16. Cooper Tire, the ninth largest tire manufacturer in the world in 1995, reported earnings before interest and taxes of $175 million. It had a book value of equity of $750 million (market value of equity was $2.4 billion) and debt outstanding of $38 million in 1995. The beta for the stock was 1.25, while the pre-tax cost of debt was 8%. The T bond rate is 7%. Evaluate whether Cooper made surplus returns during 1995. (Corporate tax rate = 36%).

17. Kollmorgen Corporation, a diversified technology company in motion technologies and electro-optical instruments, is evaluating what might have gone wrong in an investment that it made 10 years ago in photo research. The original forecasts of cash flows, made when the project was taken, and the actual cash flows on the project are summarized below:

Year	Forecasted CF	Actual CF
1986	−1,500	−2,200
1987	+100	−150
1988	+150	+50
1989	+200	+100
1990	+250	+150
1991	+275	+100
1992	+300	+175
1993	+325	+200
1994	+350	+200
1995	+350	+175

a. Estimate the net present value of the project, using the original forecasted cash flows and a discount rate of 12%.

b. Estimate the net present value of the project, using the actual cash flows and a discount rate of 11.5%.

c. You have a choice of continuing the project now or abandoning it. If cash flows are expected to remain at 1995 levels in perpetuity and the assets invested in the project have a salvage value of $1,000, would you continue the project? Why or why not?

18. Folly Industries, a consumer product firm in cosmetics and appliances, is in serious fiscal trouble and is unable to meet its debt obligations. It is considering whether to divest itself of its cosmetic division, and the division is projected to have the following expected cash flows for the next five years:

Year	Expected Cash Flow
1	$10 million
2	$12.5 million
3	$15 million
4	$17.5 million
5	$120 million

The cost of capital for the division is 12.5%.

a. How much is the division worth to Folly Industries?

b. If there is an offer of $150 million for this division, should Folly accept it?

19. Economies of scale restrict competition from smaller firms. Does economy of scale have any limit on its effect? In the other word, does it mean that the bigger is better in producing above-normal returns?

20. Critics of capitalist economies often argue that economy of scale leads to monopoly. This argument implies that without government regulation most industries will be controlled by monopolists which can earn extremely high returns on their projects. What are the flows of this logic? (Pay attention to the role of technological changes)

21. The same project may be a "good" project to one firm and at the same time be a "bad" project to another. In the 1970's, Japanese firms took on many projects which were abandoned by American firms. Explain why both the American firms and Japanse firms made the right decisions based on the observation that both the labor costs and capital costs were much lower in Japan than in the U.S.A. in the 1970's.

22. List explicit or implicit barriers a country may impose on foreign competitors to protect their domestic industries.

CHAPTER 13

THE LEASING DECISION

One of the most common capital budgeting choices that many firms face in the course of business is whether to buy or lease an asset. In making this decision, firms have to weigh many factors, including the size of the lease payments, any flexibility that may come with a leasing arrangement, and the availability of funds to buy the asset. In addition, firms have to consider the tax implications of leasing and the effects of leasing on the balance sheet. This chapter examines this choice and attempts to answer the following questions:

- What are the different types of lease arrangements that can be made, and what are the financial implications of each arrangement?

- How are leases treated in financial statements, and how do they affect financial ratios?

- What are the nonfinancial advantages of leasing?

- How should a firm financially analyze the lease versus buy decision? In particular,

  What are the cash flows associated with the lease decision?

  What are the cash flows associated with a comparable buy decision?

  What are the appropriate discount rates to use with each decision and why?

- How does this analysis differ when done from the viewpoint of the investor who owns the asset (i.e., the lessor)?

TYPES OF LEASES

A lease involves two parties—the owner of the asset, who buys it and leases it out—and the user of the asset, who uses the asset during the life of the lease. The first party, the **lessor,** charges the second party, the **lessee,** an agreed upon charge—a *lease payment*—in every period (usually monthly or semiannually). Although this is the typical structure, leases take a number of different forms, with different implications for ownership and tax benefits to both parties.

Lessor: The lessor is the owner of the leased asset; in return, he or she receives an agreed upon payment from the entity leasing the asset.

Lessee: The lessee is the entity that uses the leased asset and makes agreed upon payments to the owner of the asset (lessor).

330

Operating versus Financial Leases

An **operating** or **service lease** is usually signed for a period much shorter than the actual life of the asset, and the present value of lease payments is generally much lower than the actual price of the asset. At the end of the life of the lease, the equipment reverts back to the lessor, who will either offer to sell it to the lessee or lease it to somebody else. The lessee usually has the option to cancel the lease and return the asset to the lessor. Thus, the ownership of the asset in an operating lease clearly resides with the lessor, with the lessee bearing little or no risk if the asset becomes obsolete. Examples of operating leases are the store spaces that are leased out by specialty retailing firms like the Gap.

Operating Lease: In an operating lease, the ownership of the asset remains with the owner of the asset. The lessee makes a lease payment that is tax deductible but does not show the asset on its balance sheet.

A **financial** or **capital lease** generally lasts for the life of the asset, with the present value of lease payments covering the price of the asset. A financial lease generally cannot be canceled, and the lease can be renewed at the end of its life at a reduced rate or the asset can be acquired at a favorable price. In many cases, the lessor is not obligated to pay insurance and taxes on the asset, leaving these obligations up to the lessee. Consequently, the lessee reduces the lease payments, leading to what are called *net leases*. In summary, a financial lease imposes substantial risk on the lessee.

Capital Lease: In a capital lease, the lessee is viewed as the owner of the asset and has to show the asset on its balance sheet.

Although the differences between operating and financial leases are obvious, some lease arrangements do not fit neatly into one or another of these extremes. Rather, they share some features of both types of leases. These leases are called *combination leases*.

Direct versus Sale and Leaseback Leases

When a new asset is leased, the subsequent lease is described as a *direct lease*. In some cases, however, a firm that owns an asset will sell it to another entity and then lease it back; this is known as a **sale and leaseback lease.** In return for receiving the purchase price of the asset, the leasing firm agrees to make lease payments for the period of the lease. This arrangement provides cash-flow effects similar to those that would have been created if the firm had borrowed and bought the asset: the borrowing would have created a cash inflow immediately, but the firm would have been obligated to make interest and principal payments for the life of the loan. For example, an airline in urgent need of cash may sell planes to another firm, say GE Capital, and then lease them back. By doing so, the airline gets a large cash inflow now in return for obligated payments to GE Capital in the future.

Sale and Leaseback Lease: This is a lease where an entity sells an asset to another and then leases it back.

ACCOUNTING FOR LEASES

The effects of leasing an asset on accounting statements will depend on how the lease is categorized by the Internal Revenue Service (for tax purposes) and by generally accepted accounting standards (for measurement purposes). Leasing an asset rather than buying it substitutes lease payments as a tax deduction for the payments that the firm would have claimed as tax deductions if had owned the asset (depreciation and interest expenses on debt). The IRS is therefore wary of lease arrangements that are designed purely to speed up tax deductions. Some of the issues the IRS considers in deciding whether lease payments are tax deductible include the following.

- Are the lease payments on the asset spread out over the life of the asset, or are they accelerated over a much shorter period?
- Can the lessee continue to use the asset after the life of the lease at preferential rates or nominal amounts?
- Can the lessee buy the asset at the end of the life of the lease at a price well below market?

If lease payments are made over a period much shorter than the asset's life and the lessee is allowed either to continue leasing the asset at a nominal amount or to buy the asset at a price below market, the IRS may view the lease as a loan and prohibit the lessee from deducting the lease payments in the year(s) in which they are made.

Lease arrangements also allow firms to take assets off the balance sheet and reduce their leverage, at least in cosmetic terms. In other words, leases are sometimes a source of **off-balance sheet financing.** Consequently, the Financial Accounting Standards Board (FASB) has specified that firms must treat leases as capital leases if any one of the following four conditions holds.

1. The life of the lease is at least 75% of the asset's life.

2. The ownership of the asset is transferred to the lessee at the end of the life of the lease.

3. There is a "bargain purchase" option, whereby the purchase price is below expected market value, increasing the likelihood that ownership in the asset will be transferred to the lessee at the end of the lease.

4. The present value of the lease payments exceeds 90% of the initial value of the asset.

All other leases are treated as operating leases.

Off-Balance Sheet Financing: This is financing used by a firm which does not show up as a liability on the balance sheet of that firm.

 Concept Check

The IRS and FASB have different definitions of what constitutes an operating lease. What are the objectives of each of these entities, and how would they help explain the differences in the definitions?

Effect on Expenses, Income, and Taxes

Effect of operating leases   If, under the above criteria, a lease qualifies as an operating lease, the lease payments are operating expenses, which are tax deductible. Thus, although lease payments reduce income, they also provide a tax benefit. The after-tax impact of the lease payment on income can be written as

$$\boxed{\text{After-tax Effect of Lease on Net Income} = \text{Lease Payment} (1 - t)}$$

where t is the marginal tax rate on income.

Note the similar impact, on after-tax income, of lease payments and interest payments. Both create a cash outflow while creating a concurrent tax benefit, which is proportional to the marginal tax rate.

On the other side of the transaction, the lessor counts the lease payment as revenue, which is taxable. In addition, the lessor can generally claim depreciation, interest, and other deductions associated with the lease as expenses. To do so, however, the lease has to fulfill five criteria:

1. The asset can still be used by someone other than the lessee at the end of the life of the lease.
2. The lessee cannot buy the asset at below-market value at the end of the life of the lease.
3. The lessor has at least 20% of the asset at risk; in other words, the present value of the lease payments is less than 80% of the asset's value.
4. The lessor has a positive cash flow from the lease, not counting the tax benefits.
5. The lessee has not lent any money to the lessor to buy the asset.

The after-tax income generated by the lease can then be written as a function of the lessor's tax rate, which may be different from the lessee's tax rate.

Effect of capital leases   A capital lease on operating and net income has a different effect from that of an operating lease because capital leases are treated similarly to assets that are bought by the firm. That is, the firm is allowed to claim depreciation on the asset and an **imputed interest payment** on the lease as tax deductions rather than the lease payment itself. The imputed interest payment is computed by assuming that the lease payment is a debt payment and by apportioning it between interest and principal repaid. Thus, a five-year capital lease with lease payments of $1 million a year for a firm with a 10% cost of debt will have the interest payments and depreciation imputed to it shown in Table 13.1.

Imputed Interest Payment: This is the interest payment that would provide the equivalent of the lease payment on an asset; it is calculated by apportioning the lease payment between interest and principal payments.

Table 13.1   LEASE PAYMENTS, IMPUTED INTEREST, AND DEPRECIATION

Year	Lease Payment	Interest Expense	Reduction in Liability	Imputed Lease Liability	Depreciation	Total Tax Deduction
1	$1,000,000	$379,079	$620,921	$3,169,865	$758,157	$1,137,236
2	1,000,000	316,987	683,013	2,486,852	758,157	1,075,144
3	1,000,000	248,685	751,315	1,735,537	758,157	1,006,843
4	1,000,000	173,554	826,446	909,091	758,157	931,711
5	1,000,000	90,909	909,091	(0)	758,157	849,066

The lease liability is estimated by taking the present value of $1 million a year for five years at a discount rate of 10% (the pretax cost of debt), assuming that the payments are made at the end of each year.

> Present Value of Lease Liabilities = $1 million (PV of Annuity, 10%, 5 years)
> = $3,790,787

The imputed interest expense each year is computed by calculating the interest on the remaining lease liability:

> In year 1, the imputed interest expense = $3,790,787 * .10 = $379,079

The balance of the lease payment in that year is considered a reduction in the lease liability:

> In year 1, reduction in lease liability = $1,000,000 − $379,079 = $620,921

The lease liability is also depreciated over the life of the asset, using straight-line depreciation in this example.

If the imputed interest expenses and depreciation, which comprise the tax deductible flows arising from the lease, are aggregated over the five years, the total tax deductions amount to $5 million, which is also the sum of the lease payments. The only difference is in timing—the capital lease leads to more deductions earlier and fewer deductions later on.

 Concept
Check

Given that the differences between capital lease deductions and operating lease deductions are in the timing rather than the amount, which approach will yield

- Higher net income in the earlier years?
- Higher cash flows in the earlier years?

 IN PRACTICE   EFFECT OF LEASING ON INCOME—THE HOME DEPOT

The Home Depot is considering leasing a distribution system to service its stores on the east coast. The lease expenses are expected to be $5.5 million a year for the next 15 years, and the corporate tax rate is 36%.

If treated as an operating lease . . .

Table 13.2 shows the effect of lease expenses on pretax income and taxes for 1995 (in millions).

Table 13.2 EFFECT OF LEASE PAYMENTS ON PRETAX INCOME AND TAXES (IN 000s)

	Without Lease	With Lease	Effect of Lease
Revenues	$15,000.00	$15,000.00	$—
− Expenses	13,749.06	13,749.06	—
− Lease Payments	—	5.50	5.50
= EBIT	1,250.94	1,245.44	(5.50)
− Interest Expenses	40.00	40.00	—
= Taxable Income	1,210.94	1,205.44	(5.50)
− Taxes	435.94	433.96	(1.98)
= Net Income	775.00	771.48	(3.52)

The lease payment reduces the taxable income by $5.5 million, the taxes due by $1.98 million, and the net income by $3.52 million.

If treated as a capital lease . . .

If the lease is treated as a capital lease, and the pretax cost of debt for the Home Depot is 8.5%, the present value of the lease payments of $5.5 million a year for 15 years can be estimated as follows (assuming the payments are at the end of each year):

$$\text{Present Value of Lease Payments} = \$5.5 \text{ million (PV of Annuity, 8.5\%, 15 years)}$$
$$= \$45.67 \text{ million}$$

The imputed interest expense for 1995 (which is assumed to be the first year) can be calculated as follows:

$$\text{Imputed Interest Expense} = \$45.67 \text{ million} * .085 = \$3.88 \text{ million}$$

The imputed depreciation can be computed as follows, assuming that the depreciation is straight-line over 15 years:

$$\text{Imputed Depreciation} = \$45.67 \text{ million} / 15 = \$3.04 \text{ million}$$

The effect on operating and net income can then be computed as shown in Table 13.3.

Table 13.3 EFFECT OF IMPUTED DEPRECIATION AND INTEREST ON INCOME (IN 000s)

	Without Lease	With Lease	Effect of Lease
Revenues	$15,000.00	$15,000.00	$—
− Expenses	13,749.06	13,749.06	—
− Imputed Depreciation	—	3.04	3.04
= EBIT	1,250.94	1,247.89	(3.04)
− Interest Expenses	40.00	40.00	—
− Imputed Interest		3.88	3.88
= Taxable Income	1,210.94	1,204.01	(6.93)
− Taxes	435.94	433.44	(2.49)
= Net Income	775.00	770.57	(4.43)

Note that the net income is lower because the cumulative tax deduction from depreciation and interest expenses ($6.93 million) is greater than the tax deduction from the lease payment ($5.5 million). This will be reversed later in the life of the lease.

☐ Concept
Check

> In this example, we assumed straight-line depreciation. How would the results have changed (in terms of effects on net income, taxes, and cash flows) if the firm had used an accelerated depreciation method?

Effect on Balance Sheet

The effect of leased assets on the balance sheet will depend on whether the lease is classified as an operating lease or a capital lease. In an operating lease, the leased asset is not shown on the balance sheet; in such cases, leases are a source of off-balance sheet financing. In a capital lease, the leased asset *is* shown as an asset on the balance sheet, with a corresponding liability capturing the present value of the expected lease payments. Given the discretion, many firms prefer the first approach, because it hides the potential liability to the firm and understates its effective financial leverage.

What prevents firms from constructing lease arrangements to evade these requirements? The lessor and the lessee have very different incentives, for the arrangements that would provide the favorable "operating lease" definition to the lessee are the same ones under which the lessor cannot claim depreciation, interest, or other tax benefits on the lease. In spite of this conflict of interest, the line between operating and capital leases remains a thin one, and firms constantly figure out ways to cross the line.

These conditions for classifying operating and capital leases apply in most countries; France and Japan are major exceptions—in these countries, all leases are treated as operating leases.

 IN PRACTICE EFFECT OF LEASING ON THE BALANCE SHEET: OPERATING VERSUS CAPITAL LEASES

The effects of leasing on the balance sheet can be illustrated using the lease from the previous Home Depot application. The balance sheet for the Home Depot is reproduced in Table 13.4 for 1995; the effects of the lease are treated first as an operating lease and then as a capital lease.

Table 13.4 **BALANCE SHEET FOR THE HOME DEPOT WITH AND WITHOUT OPERATING LEASE**

Assets	Without Lease	With Operating Lease	With Capital Lease
Current Assets	$2,379.00	$2,379.00	$2,379.00
Fixed Assets	4,287.00	4,287.00	4,287.00
Capitalized Asset (from Lease)	—	—	45.67
Total Assets	6,666.00	6,666.00	6,711.67
Liabilities			
Current Liabilities	1,512.00	1,512.00	1,512.00
Debt	899.00	899.00	899.00
Lease Liability	—	—	45.67
Equity	4,255.00	4,255.00	4,255.00
Total Liabilities	6,666.00	6,666.00	6,711.67

The operating lease does not affect any of the items on the balance sheet; this is why it is termed off-balance sheet financing. By contrast, the capital lease creates both an asset and a liability equal to the present value of the lease payments. The lease liability is treated as debt.

This example also illustrates the fine line that separates operating leases from capital leases. A firm that uses operating leases may not show the liability on the balance sheet, but it has in fact created one by obligating itself to make lease payments.

☐ Concept Check

> As an analyst, would you distinguish between debt created by borrowing and the liability created by operating lease payments, when measuring a firm's effective leverage? Why or why not?

Effect on Financial Ratios

The effect of leases on the firm's financial ratios depends on whether the lease is classified as an operating or a capital lease. Table 13.5 summarizes types of profitability, solvency, and leverage ratios and the effects of operating and capital leases on each. (The effects are misleading, in a way, because they do not consider what would have happened if the firm had bought the asset rather than leased it.)

Table 13.5   EFFECTS OF OPERATING AND CAPITALIZED LEASES

Ratio	Effect of Operating Lease	Effect of Capitalized Lease
Return on Capital	• Decreases EBIT • Assets unaffected • ROA decreases	• Decreases EBIT • Increases Assets • ROA decreases more
Return on Equity (ROE)	• Decreases Net Income • BV of Equity Unaffected • ROE decreases	• Decreases Net Income • BV of Equity Unaffected • ROE decreases
Interest Coverage Ratio	• EBIT decreases • Interest Exp. unaffected • Coverage Ratio drops	• EBIT decreases • Interest Exp. increases • Coverage Ratio drops more
Debt Ratio	• Debt is unaffected • Debt Ratio is unchanged	• Debt increases (to account for capitalized leases) • Debt Ratio increases

The level of financial ratios, and subsequent predictions, can vary depending on whether leases are treated as operating or capital leases. Accordingly, it may make sense to convert operating leases into capitalized leases when comparing these ratios across firms.

☐ Concept Check

> In the earlier section, we mentioned that all leases are treated as operating leases in France and Japan. Assume that you are comparing the financial ratios of a U.S. company, which capitalizes leases, to a Japanese company, which does not. What biases would you expect to observe in the profitability and leverage ratios as a consequence, and how would you correct for these biases?

 IN PRACTICE   EFFECT OF LEASING ON FINANCIAL RATIOS—THE HOME DEPOT

The Home Depot lease example can be extended to examine the effect on profitability and leverage ratios of operating and capital leases, as shown in Table 13.6.

Table 13.6   **EFFECTS OF OPERATING AND CAPITAL LEASES ON FINANCIAL RATIOS**

	Operating Lease	Capital Lease
Return on Capital	15.47%	15.36%
Return on Equity	18.13%	18.11%
Interest Coverage Ratio	31.14	28.44
Debt Ratio	17.44%	18.17%

$$\text{Return on Capital} = \text{EBIT} (1 - \text{tax rate}) / (\text{BV of Debt} + \text{BV of Equity})$$
$$\text{Return on Equity} = \text{Net Income} / \text{BV of Equity}$$
$$\text{Interest Coverage Ratio} = \text{EBIT} / \text{Interest Expenses}$$
$$\text{Debt Ratio} = (\text{Debt} + \text{Capital Lease})/(\text{BV of Debt} + \text{Capital Lease} + \text{BV of Equity})$$

Note that, if the lease is treated as an operating lease, the profitability ratios are higher, and the leverage ratios decline, at least in the early years of the lease.

Again, since the difference lies more in the accounting treatment than in the cash-flow consequences to the firm, it can be argued that analysts should convert all operating leases into capital leases before computing these ratios, especially if they are being compared across firms.

RATIONALE FOR LEASING

Firms lease assets—rather than buy them—for a number of reasons. Some of these reasons make sense from a financial standpoint, and some do not.

Cash Flow and Financing Reasons

It has been argued that firms that do not have the capacity to borrow enough to purchase an asset may be able to lease it instead. This is based on the fairly shaky presumption that the same conditions that prevented the firm from borrowing in the first place will not act as an impediment when it attempts to lease; the lessor, after all, is just as interested in the creditworthiness of the firm as a lessee as the lender is in the firm as a borrower.

This argument is an extension of another one, which states that leases provide a source of off-balance sheet financing for heavily levered firms that may have used up their borrowing capacity or whose analysts are concerned about their level of leverage. In either case, the fact that some leases are off-balance sheet does not reduce the financial risk faced by the firm. If analysts and lenders are careful about considering the cash-flow effects of these leases, leasing an asset should not provide any benefits to firms from a leverage standpoint. If they are not careful, however, leasing may provide a way for a firm to hide its financial weakness *in the short term,* but the long-term exposure to risk remains.

In a third version of this argument, it is noted that bond covenants that restrict firms from further borrowing may not cover leases in some instances. In such cases, it is argued, leasing may be a way for a firm to wiggle its way out of an otherwise binding constraint.

All these arguments are based on the assumption that financial markets, analysts, and lenders are either incapable of or unwilling to consider the effects of operating leases on borrowing capacity and financial leverage. In the Home Depot example presented earlier, the lease creates an obligation to pay $5.5 million a year for the next 15 years. In present value terms, this works out to $45.67 million. Even if the lease is treated as an operating lease and this obligation is not shown on the balance sheet, it is the equivalent of borrowing $45.67 million.

Profitability Reasons

The perception gap between a firm's true performance and the views of analysts and other outsiders of its performance provides a second rationale for leasing. Because lease payments are generally lower than the expenses that would have been incurred by buying the asset—at least in the first few years of the asset's life—the reported net income for a firm may be higher if assets are leased instead of bought. This effect can be accentuated if profitability ratios such as return on assets are used to evaluate firm performance, since the leased assets will not be shown as part of the total assets of the firm (which is the denominator in this ratio).

Again, it can be argued that these effects are likely to be illusory and short-lived, for the value of the company should ultimately be determined by the cash flows generated by its assets and not by whether they are leased or bought. More generally, firms such as the Gap and the Limited, with substantial leased assets, will report high returns on assets, because their leases are primarily operating leases and do not show up in the asset base.

Service Reasons

In some cases, the lessor of an asset will bundle service agreements with the lease agreements and offer to provide the lessee with service support during the life of the lease. If this service is unique, either because of the lessor's reputation or because the lessor is also the manufacturer of the asset, and the cost of obtaining this service separately is high, the firm may choose to lease rather than buy the asset. IBM, for instance, has traditionally leased computers to users, with an offer to service them when needed.

Flexibility Reasons

Some lease agreements provide the lessee with the option to exchange the asset for a different or an upgraded version during the life of the lease. This flexibility is particularly valuable when the firm is unsure of its needs and the technology is evolving rapidly. Computers are a good example of the value of this flexibility, for upgraded models are introduced rapidly.

Flexibility is also useful when the asset is required for a period much shorter than the life of the asset; buying the asset and selling it again is costly in terms of transactions time and cost. Thus, a firm that needs the use of a car for six months might be better off leasing the car for that period. In a similar vein, the cancellation option that is embedded in some leases makes them valuable to firms that are uncertain about the extent of and length of their need for the asset.

Tax Reasons

The classic rationale provided for leasing is grounded in differences in tax rates—an entity with a high tax rate buys an asset and leases it to an entity with no or a low tax rate. By doing so, the lessor obtains the tax benefits, which are greater because of its higher tax rate. The lessee, in turn, gets the use of the asset and also gains by sharing in some of the tax benefits. The following conclusions, which are supported by empirical data, can then be drawn:

- Firms that are losing money, and hence do not have the capacity to use the tax benefits that accrue from buying, are more likely to lease their assets than buy them.
- Leasing for tax purposes will be much greater when there are large differences in tax rates across different taxpaying entities. Thus, the practice of leasing boomed in the 1960s and 1970s in the United States, when the highest marginal tax rate for individuals was in excess of 70% and the highest marginal tax rate for corporations was 38%. The narrowing of this differential in the 1980s caused a dropoff in leasing activity.

LEASING VERSUS BUYING—THE LESSEE'S POINT OF VIEW

In comparing investment alternatives, differences in risk and investment life must be considered. That is, in deciding whether to lease or buy, firms have to control for the differences in risk flowing from each decision. Firms also have to factor in the differences in the period for which they will get to use the asset under the buy and lease options. In this section, we begin with the assumption that the firm has decided it needs an asset based on a conventional capital budgeting analysis of a project. We then consider whether to buy or lease the asset.

Cash Flows

The cash flows on an operating lease to the lessee include only the lease payments. As specified earlier in the chapter and shown in Figure 13.1, these cash flows can be written in after-tax terms for a four-year lease, with the lease payments being made at the beginning of each period.

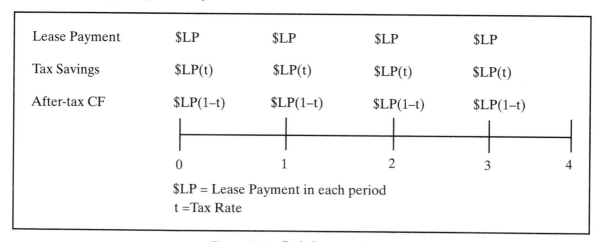

Figure 13.1   Cash flows on a lease

The alternative to leasing the asset is buying it. However, buying the asset entirely, even substantially, with equity would expose the firm to far less risk than leasing the asset, inasmuch as lease payments represent a contractual commitment, whereas cash flows on equity do not. In general, therefore, leasing should be compared to borrowing all of the value of the asset and buying it. Doing so generates the following cash flows during the asset's life to the firm:

- Interest expenses on the debt, which are tax deductible.
- Principal payments on the debt, which are not tax deductible.

- Tax savings accruing from the depreciation on the asset.
- Any other operating expenses, such as service and maintenance, arising as a consequence of buying the asset.
- Any salvage value that may be incurred from selling the asset at the end of its life.

The net cash flow each year from borrowing the money and buying the asset can then be written as shown in Figure 13.2.

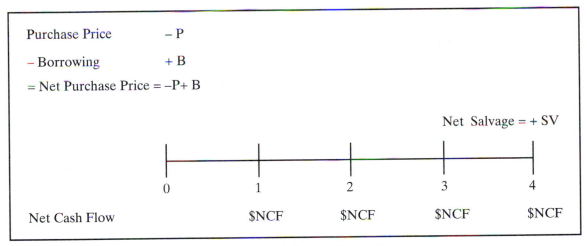

Figure 13.2   Cash flows on borrow/buy

Note that when the entire price of the asset is borrowed, the **net purchase price** is zero. The differential cash flow can then be computed, assuming that the life of the lease and the life of the asset are the same, as shown in Figure 13.3.

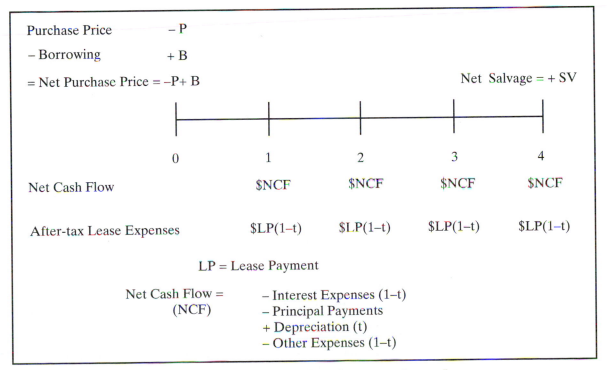

Figure 13.3   Differential cash flows: lease versus borrow/buy

The differential cash flows can be computed from the lease and the buy decisions.

■ **Net Purchase Price:**   This is the difference between the purchase price and the debt taken on to finance the purchase.

 IN PRACTICE   CASH FLOWS ON A LEASE VERSUS BUY DECISION

With regard to the Home Depot example again, the payments on the lease the firm is considering are expected to be $5.5 million a year for 15 years, and payments are due at the end of each year. The company is assumed to have a tax rate of 36%.

As an alternative, the Home Depot can buy the distribution system for $50 million, with a pretax cost of debt of 8.5%. At the end of 15 years, the system can be salvaged for $15 million. In addition, assume that the system will be depreciated using straight-line depreciation over 15 years. Finally, the Home Depot will have to incur $500,000 in annual maintenance costs if it buys the system—an expense it would not have to incur if the system were leased. The cash flows on the two alternatives are shown in Table 13.7.

Table 13.7   CASH FLOWS ON LEASE AND BUY OPTIONS—THE HOME DEPOT DISTRIBUTION SYSTEM

Year	Lease Option		Borrow and Buy Option				
	Lease Payment	Lease Payment $(1 - t)$	Interest $(1 - t)$	Depreciation (t)	Principal Payment	Maintenance Expenses $(1 - t)$	ATCF
1	$(5,500,000)	$(3,520,000)	$2,720,000	$840,000	$1,771,023	$320,000	$(3,971,023)
2	(5,500,000)	(3,520,000)	2,623,656	840,000	1,921,560	320,000	(4,025,216)
3	(5,500,000)	(3,520,000)	2,519,123	840,000	2,084,893	320,000	(4,084,016)
4	(5,500,000)	(3,520,000)	2,405,705	840,000	2,262,109	320,000	(4,147,814)
5	(5,500,000)	(3,520,000)	2,282,647	840,000	2,454,388	320,000	(4,217,034)
6	(5,500,000)	(3,520,000)	2,149,128	840,000	2,663,011	320,000	(4,292,139)
7	(5,500,000)	(3,520,000)	2,004.260	840,000	2,889,367	320,000	(4,373,627)
8	(5,500,000)	(3,520,000)	1,847,079	840,000	3,134,963	320,000	(4,462,041)
9	(5,500,000)	(3,520,000)	1,676,537	840,000	3,401,435	320,000	(4,557,971)
10	(5,500,000)	(3,520,000)	1,491,499	840,000	3,690,557	320,000	(4,662,055)
11	(5,500,000)	(3,520,000)	1,290,732	840,000	4,004,254	320,000	(4,774,986)
12	(5,500,000)	(3,520,000)	1,072,901	840,000	4,344,615	320,000	(4,897,516)
13	(5,500,000)	(3,520,000)	836,554	840,000	4,713,908	320,000	(5,030,462)
14	(5,500,000)	(3,520,000)	580,117	840,000	5,114,590	320,000	(5,174,707)
15	(5,500,000)	(3,520,000)	301,884	840,000	5,549,330	320,000	9,668,786
	NPV =	($35,473,595)					($37,983,007)

The after-tax cash flows in year 15 include the salvage value of $15 million from selling the distribution center.

ATCF from Buy Decision = −Interest Expenses $(1 - t)$ + Depreciation (t) − Principal Payments − Maintenance Expenses $(1 - t)$

The buy option has more negative cash flows each year throughout the entire period, but it has a positive cash flow in the last year, as a consequence of the salvage value.

Concept Check

How would your cash flows have changed if the value of the asset had been depreciated to zero instead of the salvage value? (Assume that your capital gains tax rate is 20%.)

Risk and Discount Rates

Lease payments and interest payments create similar commitments for the firm. Consequently, it can be argued, they should be treated similarly, in terms of risk, for purposes of estimating discount rates. Because the discount rate for debt is the after-tax cost of borrowing for the firm, the discount rate for the lease payments should also be the after-tax cost. The discount rate can then be used in two ways:

1. The *net present value* of the lease option and the borrow-and-buy option cash flows can be calculated at the after-tax cost of debt. The option with the lower present value of costs can be considered the less expensive option.

2. The *internal rate of return* of the differential cash flows (between leasing and borrowing and buying) can be calculated and compared to the after-tax cost of debt. In doing so, the borrowing and the cash flows associated with it can be ignored, because the present value of the debt payments at the cost of debt will be equal to the initial borrowing.

If $IRR_{Borrow - Lease}$ > After-tax Cost of Debt   Borrow and Buy the asset
If $IRR_{Borrow - Lease}$ < After-tax Cost of Debt   Lease the asset

Either approach should provide the same answer.

IN PRACTICE   ANALYZING A LEASE DECISION—THE HOME DEPOT

The cash flows that the Home Depot can expect from leasing the distribution system versus buying it were estimated in the previous application. These cash flows are discounted at the after-tax cost of debt as follows:

Net Advantage to Leasing = NPV of Lease Option − NPV of Buy Option
= (35,473,595) - (37,983,007) = $2,509,412

The present value of the cash flows is computed in Table 13.8. The cash flows in year 15 include a salvage value of $15 million. In present value terms, the lease option is the less expensive option, costing $2,509,412 less than the buy option. This is often termed the **net advantage to leasing.** In this case:

Net Advantage to Leasing: This is the difference between the net present value of lease payments and the net present value of the payments associated with borrowing and buying the same asset.

Table 13.8   **DIFFERENTIAL CASH FLOWS BETWEEN LEASING AND BUYING**

Year	Lease Payment $(1 - t)$	ATCF	Differential CF
1	$(3,520,000)	$(3,971,023)	$(451,023)
2	(3,520,000)	(4,025,216)	(505,216)
3	(3,520,000)	(4,084,016)	(564,016)
4	(3,520,000)	(4,147,814)	(627,814)
5	(3,520,000)	(4,217,034)	(697,034)
6	(3,520,000)	(4,292,139)	(772,139)
7	(3,520,000)	(4,373,627)	(853,627)
8	(3,520,000)	(4,462,041)	(942,041)
9	(3,520,000)	(4,557,971)	(1,037,971)
10	(3,520,000)	(4,662,055)	(1,142,055)
11	(3,520,000)	(4,774,986)	(1,254,986)
12	(3,520,000)	(4,897,516)	(1,377,516)
13	(3,520,000)	(5,030,462)	(1,510,462)
14	(3,520,000)	(5,174,707)	(1,654,707)
15	(3,520,000)	9,668,786	13,188,786
NPV	($35,473,595)	($37,983,007)	($2,509,412)

> After-tax Cost of Debt = Pretax Cost of Debt $(1 - \text{tax rate})$
> $= 8.5\% \ (1 - 0.36) = 5.44\%$

The two options can also be evaluated by calculating the IRR of the differential cash flows, ignoring interest and principal payments, and allowing for an initial investment of $50 million, which amounts to 4.12% in this case. This scenario confirms that the buy option is not as economical as the lease option, because the internal rate of return is lower than the after-tax cost of debt, which is 5.44%.

Concept Check

Assume that you will receive a discount on the purchase price of an asset, if you buy it instead of leasing it. What would the discount have to be for you to be indifferent between buying and leasing the distribution system?

Capital Budgeting Analysis and the Lease Option

In the above analysis, we began with the assumption that the firm had decided that it needed the asset, based on a project analysis. In some cases, the option to lease an asset may change a project from "unacceptable" to "acceptable." For this to happen, the following sequence of events has to unfold. First, the project analysis, done on the assumption that the asset would be bought, should have yielded a negative net present value. Second, the lease option should be specific to this project and should not reflect a companywide advantage to leasing versus buying. Finally, the lease decision should yield savings in present value relative to the buy decision, which exceed the negative net present value from the first step.

To illustrate, assume that the net present value to the Home Depot of the distribution system, based on the purchase of the land and buildings described earlier, is −$2 million and that the lease option is available only on this project. The net advantage to leasing is $2.509 million, which is greater than the negative net present value of the project based on buying the asset. Assuming the asset is leased, we can then compute the modified net present value of the project, assuming the asset is leased:

$$
\begin{aligned}
\text{Modified NPV of Project} &= \text{NPV of Project with the buy decision} \\
&\quad + \text{Net Advantage to Leasing} \\
&= -\$2 \text{ million} + \$2.509 \text{ million} = \$0.509 \text{ million}
\end{aligned}
$$

Thus, it is possible that the opportunity to lease project-specific assets at attractive rates may turn some bad projects into good ones. It would be dangerous, however, for a firm to use leasing opportunities that are not project specific to justify taking negative net present value projects; the firm would gain even more by using the opportunities to take projects with positive net present value.

Differences in Risk: Buying versus Leasing

Our analysis is based on the assumption that the two approaches are equivalent in terms of generating a risk exposure to the firm. In some cases, however, there may be differences between the two options.

- There are differences in terms of **priority in claims** to cash flows between lenders and lessors. Usually, lenders get a prior claim to the cash flows due to them (interest and principal payments) than do lessors. Consequently, it can be argued that lease payments should be treated as riskier than cash flows associated with debt, and thus should be charged a rate higher than the after-tax cost of debt. (Note that subordinated debt issued by companies carries a higher interest rate than senior debt, because of its lower priority in claims.)

Priority in Claims: The priority in claims refers to the sequence in which different claimholders in the firm will get paid out of cash flows or in the event of bankruptcy.

- The buy option exposes the firm to **ownership risk,** represented in the salvage value at the end of the analysis period. For depreciable assets such as equipment (airplanes, cars, machinery), this salvage value may be small and would not expose the firm to much risk. For nondepreciable or long-lived assets, such as real estate and buildings, the salvage value may be a significant source of uncertainty. The best way to deal with this risk is to use a different and higher discount rate, reflecting the uncertainty in the specific asset's value, for the salvage value.

Ownership Risk: Ownership risk refers to the uncertainty about the value of an asset at the end of the period of analysis.

- When the project is expected to continue beyond the period of the analysis and the lease has to be renewed, the lease may actually expose the firm to more risk than the buy decision, inasmuch as the renewal may be at less favorable terms. Some analysts argue that such **renewal risk** offsets the "salvage value" risk specified above and that the analysis therefore reverts back to that described earlier.

Renewal Risk: The renewal risk refers to the uncertainty associated with the specific terms at which a lease can be renewed.

- The option to *renew or cancel a lease* can add value as a result of flexibility, which is not captured in the conventional present value. These options can be brought into the analysis by valuing them using option pricing models and considering them explicitly. Another, more common, approach is to use these options to tilt the balance toward leasing if the net present values from leasing and buying are similar.

IN PRACTICE   DIFFERENT RISK LEVELS IN LEASES—THE HOME DEPOT

Consider once again the financial analysis of the system lease being considered by the Home Depot. Initially, the after-tax cost of debt of 5.44% was used to discount both the lease and the borrow-and-buy cash flows. Assume that there are differences in risk and that these differences lead to the following adjustments in the discount rates:

- The lease payments are slightly more risky than the debt payments, because of the difference in priority in claims. Assume that this difference will lead to a slightly higher pretax discount rate of 9% (instead of the cost of debt of 8.5%) for the leasing cash flows.

- The salvage value of $15 million in year 15 is assumed to have more uncertainty associated with it than the other cash flows from the buy decision; an after-tax discount rate of 8% is used for this cash flow alone.

With these adjustments to the discount rate, the net present values of the two options are recalculated as follows.

$$\text{After-tax Discount Rate for Lease Option} = 9\% \ (1-.36) = 5.76\%$$
$$\text{NPV of the Lease Option} = \$5.5 \text{ million} \ (1 - 0.36) \ (\text{PV of Annuity, 5.76\%, 15 years})$$
$$= (\$34,729,668)$$
$$\text{NPV of Buy Option} = \text{Present Value of Operating Cash Flows @ discount rate}$$
$$\text{of 5.44\% + Present Value of Salvage Value @ discount rate of 8\%} = (\$40,030,957)$$
$$\text{Net Advantage to Leasing} = \text{NPV of Leasing} - \text{NPV of Buy Decision}$$
$$= (\$34,729,668) - (\$40,030,957) = \$5,301,289$$

With the adjustments to the discount rate, the advantage to leasing increases.

Concept Check

How would you estimate these risk-adjusted discount rates for the "riskier" lease payments and the salvage value?

Differences in Lives: Buying versus Leasing

In analyzing the lease versus buy decision, we have implicitly assumed a lease that lasts the length of the life of the asset. If the life of the lease is different from the life of the asset, however, the analysis changes. Analysts often skirt the issue by assuming that the lessee will buy the asset at the end of the lease life or that the asset will be sold at the end of the lease life, under the buy option. An alternative is to use the approaches described in Chapter 9 for choosing between projects with different lives. In particular, the analyst can do one of the following:

- Assume that the lease will be renewed to cover the life of the asset. For an asset with a 15-year life, where the lease life is five years, this will require renewing the lease twice. Once this assumption is made, the net present values of the lease (thrice) option and the buy option can be compared.

- Estimate the equivalent annual costs of leasing and buying using the appropriate discount rate for each. These annuities can then be compared to determine the cheaper option.

 IN PRACTICE   ESTIMATING EQUIVALENT ANNUAL COSTS—THE HOME DEPOT

Completing the analysis of the Home Depot's proposed lease of a distribution system, consider once again the net present values of each option computed on page 342.

$$\text{NPV of the Lease Option} = (\$35,473,595)$$
$$\text{NPV of Buy Option} = (\$37,983,007)$$

These net present values can be compared because both the lease and the buy option have 15-year lives. The equivalent annual costs could have been computed from these net present values using the after-tax discount rate of 5.44%:

$$\text{Equivalent Annual Cost of Lease Option} = (\$3,520,000)$$
$$\text{Equivalent Annual Cost of Buy Option} = (\$3,769,006)$$

On an equivalent annual cost basis, the decision to lease is still the better one, at least in terms of the cash-flow implications for the firm.

❏ Concept
Check

> Under what conditions would you override this analysis and choose to buy rather than lease? Conversely, if the buy decision looks better than the lease decision, based on the present value of the cash flows, what might lead you to override the analysis and lease the asset anyway?

LEASING VERSUS BUYING—THE LESSOR'S POINT OF VIEW

An analysis of leasing versus buying from the lessor's standpoint must consider the lease payment as revenue as well as any factors in the tax benefits associated with ownership, such as depreciation. In addition, if the lessor borrows the funds to acquire the asset (creating a leveraged lease), the interest expenses and principal payments associated with the borrowing should also be considered.

In general, cash flows to the lessor include the following components (see Figure 13.4). There may be an *initial cash outflow* associated with buying the asset, which is the purchase price of the asset net of any borrowing used to finance the acquisition. During the life of the lease, the lease payments become the *operating revenues,* and *interest expenses* and any costs associated with *maintenance and service* that are offered as part of the lease deal are tax deductible expenses. In addition, the lessor receives the

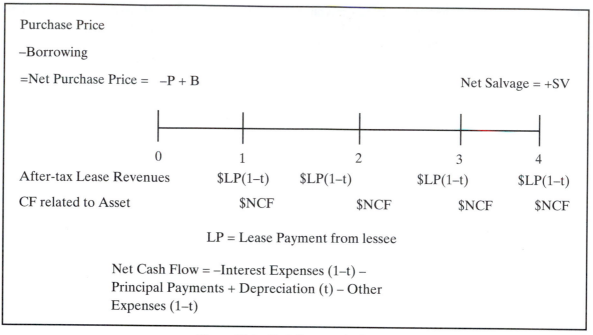

Figure 13.4   Cash flows to the lessor

tax benefits associated with depreciation in each period and has to repay the principal on the loan. At the end of the lease life, the lessor receives the *salvage value* on the leased asset.

These cash flows must be discounted back at a rate that reflects their riskiness. The lease payments (which are the operating revenues) should be discounted back at the after-tax cost of debt of the lessee, whose default risk determines whether the lease payments will be made in the first place. All other cash flows should be discounted back at the cost of capital of the lessor; if the lessor borrows the entire purchase price, the appropriate discount rate is the lessor's after-tax cost of debt. In many cases, firms use the same discount rate for both the lessor and lessee. This may not create much of a problem if the two firms have similar default risk, but will provide an erroneous estimate of value if the two firms have different default risk characteristics. To illustrate, if GE Capital leases equipment to a small, risky firm with high default risk, it would make sense to consider the cash flows separately, for discounting purposes.

 IN PRACTICE   THE LESSOR'S VIEW OF A LEASE—THE HOME DEPOT

Suppose that the distribution system that the Home Depot is considering leasing will be acquired by LF Capital. The lease has the following characteristics:

- The distribution system will be acquired for $50 million. The entire purchase price will be borrowed at a pretax cost of debt of 7.5% and repaid over the life of the system (15 years). At the end of the period, the system can be salvaged for $15 million.

- LF Capital will have maintenance expenses of $500,000 a year for the leased distribution system; it will bear the entire cost.

- LF Capital will receive the lease payment of $5.5 million a year from the Home Depot.

- LF Capital faces a tax rate of 48% on its operating income.

The cash flows to LF Capital from buying the system and leasing it out to the Home Depot can be estimated as shown in Table 13.9.

	Lease Revenue	Lease Revenue $(1-t)$	Interest $(1-t)$	Depreciation (t)	Principal Payment	Maint. Expenses $(1-t)$	ATCF
	Table 13.9 CASH FLOWS TO LF CAPITAL FROM LEASING THE ASSET						
1	$5,500,000	$2,860,000	$1,950,000	$1,120,000	$1,914,362	$260,000	$(144,362)
2	5,500,000	2,860,000	1,875,340	1,120,000	2,057,939	260,000	(213,279)
3	5,500,000	2,860,000	1,795,080	1,120,000	2,212,284	260,000	(287,365)
4	5,500,000	2,860,000	1,708,801	1,120,000	2,378,206	260,000	(367,007)
5	5,500,000	2,860,000	1,616,051	1,120,000	2,556,571	260,000	(452,622)
6	5,500,000	2,860,000	1,516,345	1,120,000	2,748,314	260,000	(544,659)
7	5,500,000	2,860,000	1,409,161	1,120,000	2,954,438	260,000	(643,598)
8	5,500,000	2,860,000	1,293,938	1,120,000	3,176,020	260,000	(749,958)
9	5,500,000	2,860,000	1,170,073	1,120,000	3,414,222	260,000	(864,295)
10	5,500,000	2,860,000	1,036,918	1,120,000	3,670,288	260,000	(987,207)
11	5,500,000	2,860,000	893,777	1,120,000	3,945,560	260,000	(1,119,337)
12	5,500,000	2,860,000	739,900	1,120,000	4,241,477	260,000	(1,261,377)
13	5,500,000	2,860,000	574,482	1,120,000	4,559,588	260,000	(1,414,070)
14	5,500,000	2,860,000	396,659	1,120,000	4,901,557	260,000	(1,578,216)
15	5,500,000	2,860,000	205,498	1,120,000	5,269,174	260,000	13,245,328
						NPV =	$101,143

In this case, the lease provides a positive net present value to the lessor. Note that the purchase price, nominal depreciation, and maintenance costs are the same for the lessor as they would have been for the Home Depot if it had bought the system itself. Where does the additional value come from? In this case, it is comes from two sources:

1. LF Capital has a much lower pretax cost of debt than the Home Depot, being able to borrow at 7.5% instead of 8.5%. This enables LF Capital to pay markedly lower interest expenses on the same borrowing ($50 million).

2. LF Capital has a much higher tax rate, enabling it to gain a bigger tax benefit from the same depreciation and interest expenses. This benefit will increase if an accelerated depreciation method is used. It also lowers the after-tax cost of debt:

$$\text{After-tax Cost of Debt} = 7.5\% \ (1-0.48) = 3.9\%$$

These advantages enable LF Capital to create additional value of $2.61 million from the buy option, relative to the Home Depot. This analysis can be used to develop two propositions:

> **Proposition 1:**   There will be a benefit to leasing if the lessor has *lower default risk* than the lessee. This benefit increases as the difference in default risks increases.
>
> **Proposition 2:**   There will be a benefit to leasing if the lessor has a *higher tax rate* than the lessee. This benefit increases as the difference in tax rates increases.

❑ Concept
   Check

> Assuming that LF Capital is willing to lower the lease payments on this asset, what is the breakeven lease payment (the lease payment at which LF Capital makes sufficient but no excess returns)?

CONCLUSION

This chapter examines the decision of whether to lease an asset or to buy it. In summary, it makes the following points.

- There are many different types of leases, with different implications for net income, cash flows, and financial leverage (as revealed on a balance sheet). Operating leases, which create off-balance sheet financing, reduce net income less than do capital leases, at least in the initial years of the lease. Capital leases create effects very similar to those that would have been created if the firm had borrowed money and bought the asset.

- In real terms, both operating and capital leases create cash-flow obligations for the firm and therefore affect its financial leverage. To be safe, therefore, even operating leases should be capitalized for purposes of comparing leverage and income across firms.

- Firms choose to lease assets for a number of reasons, some of which are based on the real advantages that leasing bestows on the firm, including greater flexibility, tax savings, and lower maintenance costs, and others of which are based on purely cosmetic factors, such as the ability of the firm to not reveal as much in liabilities on the balance sheet or to improve reported net income.

- In analyzing a lease versus buy decision, firms should compare leasing to borrowing the purchase price and buying the asset (rather than using equity to buy the asset). This is because leasing creates obligations for the firm which are very similar to those created by borrowing.

- The cash flows associated with leasing and borrowing-and-buying are discounted at the after-tax cost of debt to yield net present values to each option. The difference is referred to as the *net advantage to leasing.* In some cases, projects that do not pass muster when the assets are bought may become acceptable when the same assets are leased.

- There may be differences in risk associated with leasing as opposed to buying. If so, these differences should be reflected in the discount rate.

- Leasing may provide benefits to both the lessor and the lessee because of differences in tax rates and default rates between the two parties.

QUESTIONS AND PROBLEMS

1. LMN Corporation is considering leasing copier machines at a cost of $500,000 a year for the next five years. (Tax rate = 40%) Its income statement and balance sheet prior to the lease are shown on pg. 351:

   a. Assuming that LMN Corporation has a pretax cost of borrowing of 10%, estimate the effect this lease will have on the net income and balance sheet if it is treated as an operating lease.

   b. Estimate the effect if the lease is treated as a capital lease, assuming that straight-line depreciation will be used.

2. Using the numbers in the example above, calculate the following ratios under both the operating and capital lease assumptions:

   a. Return on Capital

   b. Return on Equity

INCOME STATEMENT		BALANCE SHEET	
Revenues	$10,000,000	Current Assets	$3,000,000
− Operating Expenses	6,000,000	Fixed Assets	7,000,000
= EBIT	4,000,000	Total Assets	10,000,000
− Interest Expenses	1,000,000	Current Liabilities	2,000,000
= Taxable Income	3,000,000	Debt	2,000,000
− Taxes	1,200,000	Equity	6,000,000
= Net Income	1,800,000	Total Liabilities	$10,000,000

   c. Interest Coverage Ratio

   d. Debt Ratio

3. You are comparing two retail firms, QuickShop Corporation and LoMart Corporation, which follow very different policies on leasing versus buying their retail sites. Quickshop Corporation uses operating leases to acquire retail sites and has expected lease payments of $10 million for the next 10 years on its existing sites and no debt outstanding. LoMart Corporation has borrowed money to buy retail sites and has outstanding debt of $50 million and a pre-tax cost of debt of 9%. (The two firms face similar default risk and tax rates.) Assuming that the two firms have $100 million in equity each, estimate

   a. The debt ratio for each firm, using conventional measures of debt and equity.

   b. A corrected debt ratio, which takes into account the operating leases. Which firm is more highly levered using this measure?

4. You are considering a five-year lease of storage space, and your payments each year would amount to $1 million, with the payments made at the end of each year. Assuming that you have a pretax cost of debt of 9% and a tax rate of 40% and that you use straight-line depreciation, estimate

   a. The tax deductions you would have, assuming that the lease is treated as an operating lease.

   b. The tax deductions you would have, assuming that the lease is treated as a capital lease.

   c. The difference in nominal and present value dollars in the tax deductions.

5. Compare the following alternatives that GMIC Inc. faces in acquiring equipment for its factories.

Alternative 1: It can buy the equipment for $10 million, using a 10-year term loan at an interest rate of 10%. The equipment will be depreciated straight-line over its 10-year life to a salvage value of $2 million. Maintenance expenses will be $100,000 a year.

Alternative 2: It can lease the asset for $1.5 million a year; the lessor will cover all maintenance expenses.

GMIC has a tax rate of 30% on its income.

   a. Estimate the after-tax cash flows from leasing for the next 10 years.

   b. Estimate the after-tax cash flows from buying for the next 10 years.

   c. Estimate the net present values of the two options.

   d. Estimate the net advantage to leasing this asset.

6. If GMIC leases the asset described above, MC Capital will be the lessor. Although the purchase price, salvage value, and depreciation method are the same for both firms, MC Capital can borrow at 8% (pretax) and has a tax rate of 50%.

   a. Estimate whether the lease makes sense from the viewpoint of MC Capital.

   b. How would you explain the differences between the present value of buying the asset to GMIC and MC Capital?

7. CEF Inc. is a company that has large accumulated losses and does not expect to pay taxes for the next five years. It is debating whether to acquire equipment costing $5 million, with a five-year life and no salvage value. If it does so, it will borrow the purchase price at 12% and depreciate the equipment straight-line over the five-year period. DP Capital, a financing and leasing firm that can borrow at 8% and faces a 40% tax rate, is willing to lease the equipment to CEF.

   a. Estimate the minimum lease payment DP Capital will have to charge for this to be a viable lease.

   b. Estimate the maximum lease payment CEF will be willing to pay, given its buy alternative.

8. Based on the principles of leasing developed in this chapter, explain the following phenomena:

   a. Car rental companies generally lease their cars from the automobile manufacturers, rather than buy them.

   b. Highly levered firms are more likely to lease assets than are firms with low leverage.

c. Large companies often lease computers rather than buy them.

d. Finance companies that often operate as lessors have high bond ratings.

9. You are looking at the financial statements of Jan Taylor Corporation, a specialty retailer of apparel. The firm leases store space and had operating lease expenses of $120 million last year. These lease expenses are expected to increase 3% a year for the next five years and then stabilize at that level in the long term. The firm has no debt, but it could borrow long term at 8%; it has 100 million shares outstanding, trading at $25 per share. The corporate tax rate is 40%.

a. Estimate the capitalized value of the operating lease payments.

b. Calculate the debt ratios with and without the capitalized lease payments.

10. Service International, a firm that provides data processing support to other firms, is debating whether it should buy or lease computers for its office staff. It requires 1,000 computers, and the details of the two options are as follows:

• The cost per computer is $2,000, and the average life of the computers is three years. At the end of the period, the salvage value is expected to be $500 for each computer. The maintenance cost is $200 each year. The computers will be depreciated straight-line over the three-year life down to the salvage value.

• The firm can lease the computers at a cost of $800 a year. The lessor will maintain the computers at no cost.

• The firm can borrow money at 8% a year; its tax rate is 40%.

a. Would you buy or lease the computers?

b. What would the lease payments have to be to make leasing the better option?

11. You are debating whether to buy or lease office space for a new consulting business you plan to operate. The cost of buying the office space is $200,000, and you could borrow money at 8.5%. You expect real estate to appreciate 3% a year. You could lease similar office space for $2,000 a month. You will have to pay $500 in maintenance costs in either scenario. (Tax rate = 40%)

a. If you were planning to stay in business for 10 years, would you lease or buy the office space?

b. If you were uncertain about how long you would be in business, would you lease or buy the office space?

12. How would your answer to the previous problem change, if you were given the following additional information?

a. The lease agreement runs for three years. At the end of each three-year period, the lease is expected to be renewed, with a 7% appreciation in annual lease payments.

b. The expected appreciation in real estate prices is 3%, but there is uncertainty about this estimate resulting in an increase in the pretax discount rate of 2%.

13. A grocery firm, which is losing money and is in urgent need of cash, is considering selling its entire fleet of trucks and leasing them back. GE Capital has offered to buy the trucks for $50 million (which is their estimated market value) and lease them back to the firm for an annual cost of $4 million. The book value of the trucks is also $50 million, and they can be depreciated straight-line over the next 10 years to a salvage value of $10 million. The grocery firm has a pretax cost of debt of 10% and does not expect to have taxable income in the foreseeable future. Should the grocery firm do the sale and leaseback?

14. Now consider the lease from the viewpoint of GE Capital, which has a pretax cost of debt of 7% and faces a corporate tax rate of 40%.

a. Should it agree to buy the trucks and lease them back?

b. How is it possible for both GE Capital and the grocery store to gain from the lease?

15. You are negotiating terms with the automobile dealer in your town to buy a Ford Explorer. The vehicle costs $30,000 and you can get a five-year term loan, with annual payments, at 8%; at the end of five years the van is expected to have a value of $10,000. The dealer is willing to lease you the van for $5,000 a year.

a. Assuming that the van is for personal use and that none of these payments are tax deductible, would you lease the van?

b. Would it make any difference if you were a business and had a tax rate of 35%? (Assume that the van will be depreciated straight-line over the five-year period down to a salvage value of $10,000.)

16. You are the owner of the Spokane Skins, a semiprofessional football team, and you have convinced the city to grant you a 25-year lease for land to build a football stadium on, for $1 million a year; you also have the option to buy the land at a bargain price at the end of the twenty-fifth year. The lease will be treated as a capital lease, because of the terms involved.

a. Estimate the value of the capital lease.

b. Estimate the imputed interest payments and depreciation.

CHAPTER 14

WORKING CAPITAL: INVESTMENT DECISIONS AND FINANCING

The importance of working capital has been noted in passing in the previous chapters on capital budgeting in the context of its effect on cash flows and, consequently, on net present value. In most of our analyses so far, we have assumed either a given dollar amount or a specific percentage of revenues for working capital. This chapter goes beyond these numbers and tries to answer the following questions:

- What is working capital and how is it measured?
- What are the basic tradeoffs on working capital? Is there an optimal amount of working capital that a firm should maintain?
- What are the benefits and the costs of holding cash? What is the optimal cash balance for a firm?
- What are the benefits and costs of holding inventory? What are the determinants of an optimal inventory balance?
- What are the determinants of a firm's credit policy?

THE BASICS OF WORKING CAPITAL

We begin our discussion with an introduction to the basics of working capital, starting with a definition of working capital, continuing with a look at some common measures of the magnitude of working capital investment, and concluding with an analysis of the tradeoffs that determine the optimal amount to be invested in working capital.

Defining Working Capital

The net working capital, often referred to simply as working capital, is the difference between a firm's current assets and current liabilities. The *current assets* of a firm are those that either are in the form of cash or are expected to be converted into cash in the short term (usually defined to be less than one year). They generally include the following.

- *Cash and marketable securities:* These are the most liquid assets a firm possesses; marketable securities, such as government bonds, can generally be converted into cash quickly, at low cost, and with little or no loss of value.
- *Inventory:* The inventory of a firm usually turns over at frequent intervals and, thus, can be expected to be converted into cash rather quickly. The speed with which inventory is turned into cash depends on the business in which the firm operates; a

firm in the grocery business is likely to turn over inventory much more quickly than is an appliance retailer, for example.

- *Accounts receivable:* When a firm sells goods on credit, it creates accounts receivable; as it receives payment on these credit sales, accounts receivable are converted into cash.

The *current liabilities* of a firm include those that are expected to come due within the year; they generally include the following:

- *Accounts payable:* When a firm buys goods or services on credit, it creates accounts payable, which come due in the short term.
- *Accrued wages, salaries, and taxes:* In the normal course of doing business, firms accrue wages and salaries to their employees and taxes to the government.
- *Current portion of long-term debt:* Any long-term debt (bonds, bank debt) that is expected to come due within the year is classified as a current liability; it differs qualitatively from accounts payable because it is usually refinanced with new long-term debt.

The Tradeoff on Working Capital

Like most corporate finance decisions, the decision on how much working capital to hold involves a tradeoff—having a large net working capital (i.e., current assets that significantly exceed current liabilities) may reduce the liquidity risk faced by the firm, but it can have a negative effect on cash flows. Therefore, the *net effect on value* should be used to determine the optimal amount to be held in working capital.

The cash-flow effect   As discussed in Chapter 8, changes in working capital affect cash flows: an increase in working capital reduces cash flows, for cash invested in working capital cannot be used elsewhere, whereas a decrease in working capital increases cash flows. The effect of working capital changes on cash flows will depend on a number of factors, including the following.

- *Magnitude of working capital investment needed for operations:* The effects of working capital changes on cash flows are likely to be larger, at least relative to overall cash flows and value, for firms that have to maintain large investments in working capital relative to operating cash flows and sales. For instance, a car dealer is likely to experience much larger changes in cash flows as a consequence of increases or decreases in his or her inventory than will a service business, such as a temp agency, which has lower working capital requirements.
- *Makeup of working capital:* Not all working capital items are created equal in terms of their effects on cash flows. Increases in marketable securities, for instance, have a less negative impact on cash flows because they earn a positive return (interest or dividends on these securities) while they are held. Increases in inventory, on the other hand, have a more negative impact on cash flows because they do not earn any positive returns while held and might create additional storage and administrative costs.

The liquidity effect and operating effect   The traditional view of working capital as a measure of liquidity risk suggests that increasing working capital will generally reduce the liquidity risk faced by the firm, whereas decreasing working capital will generally increase the liquidity risk. The effects of working capital changes on liquidity risk depend on a number of factors, including the following.

- *Access to financing:* A firm with ready access to external financing is much less exposed to liquidity risk than a firm that does not have access, because it can tap these external sources if it needs to cover liabilities coming due. Accordingly, small private firms tend to have much greater increases in liquidity risk from decreases in net working capital than do large, publicly traded firms that have lines of credit available or access to commercial paper (short-term borrowing from financial markets).

- *State of the economy:* Holding other factors constant, firms typically experience much larger changes in liquidity risk as a consequence of working capital changes when the economy is in recession than when it is doing well.

- *Uncertainty about future cash flows:* Firms often plan on using cash flows from operations to meet current liabilities that come due. To the degree that these cash flows are predictable and stable, the firm can survive with lower investments in working capital than could otherwise similar firms that experience more uncertainty about future cash flows.

A second benefit of maintaining high working capital is its potential effect on revenues and future growth. That is, although increasing inventory will tie up more cash, it might also enable the firm to increase sales or at least avoid lost sales as a consequence of not having the desired item in stock when a customer wants it. A similar argument can be made about accounts receivable: though offering more generous credit increases investment in accounts receivable, which impacts cash flow negatively, it might also increase sales and operating profits.

An optimal level of working capital?   Given the tradeoff between the negative effects on cash flows of increasing working capital and the positive effects of reducing liquidity risk and potentially increasing revenues and operating cash flows, it can be argued that working capital should be increased *if, and only if, the benefits exceed the costs.* To put this in perspective, there is a correlation between firm value and the level of working capital investment. At least initially, increases in working capital typically lead to increases in firm value, because the marginal benefits are likely to exceed the costs. At some level of working capital investment, holding all other factors constant, the firm value should be maximized. This is the optimal level for working capital investment.

To illustrate, assume that you are analyzing the working capital investment for a mail-order retail firm with current revenues of $1 billion and operating profits after taxes of $100 million. If the firm maintains no working capital, its operating profits after taxes are expected to grow 3% a year forever and it will have a cost of capital of 12.50%. As the working capital is increased as a percentage of revenues, the expected growth in operating profits will increase (at a decreasing rate) and the cost of capital will decrease (by 0.05% for every 10% increase in working capital as a percentage of revenues). Table 14.1 summarizes the expected effects of maintaining different levels of working capital on revenue growth, risk, and value.

To illustrate the effect of changing working capital as a percentage of revenues, let us first value the firm with no working capital investment:

Expected cash flow to firm next year = Expected operating income next year −
Expected increase in working capital next year = $100 (1.03) − $0 = $103
Value of the firm with no working capital investment =
$103/(.125−.03) = $1,084.21

Table 14.1 VALUE OF FIRM AS FUNCTION OF WORKING CAPITAL INVESTMENT (IN '000s)

Working Capital as a pct. of Revenues (%)	Expected Growth in Operating Income (%)	Cost of Capital (%)	Value of Firm
0	3.00	12.50	$1,084.21
10	4.00	12.45	$1,183.43
20	4.50	12.40	$1,208.86
30	4.83	12.35	$1,201.77
40	5.08	12.30	$1,174.36
50	5.28	12.25	$1,132.06
60	5.45	12.20	$1,077.78
70	5.59	12.15	$1,013.29
80	5.72	12.10	$939.73
90	5.83	12.05	$857.87
100	5.93	12.00	$768.23

If working capital increases to 10% of revenues, the growth rate is expected to increase from 3% to 4%, whereas the cost of capital is expected to drop from 12.5% to 12.4%. But the expected cash flow to the firm next year will be reduced by the expected increase in working capital investment:

Expected cash flow to firm next year = Expected operating income next year − Expected increase in working capital next year = $100 (1.04) − $1,000 (0.04) (0.10) = $100

[Note that Increase in working capital = Increase in revenues * Working capital as a percent of revenues.]

Value of the firm with working capital as 10% of revenues = $100/(.1245−.04) = $1,183.43

The firm value increases as a consequence of the working capital increase. In Figure 14.1, the firm value is computed as a function of working capital for a range of working capital ratios.

As you can see, the firm value is maximized when working capital is 20% of revenues. This example assumes that the effects of working capital changes on risk and growth are known, but it might be difficult to put this into practice if they cannot be estimated.

Concept Check

From a practical standpoint, how would you go about estimating the effect of changing working capital investment on growth rates and discount rates? In the above example, how would your answer change if changing working capital *did not* affect discount rates?

Industry differences on working capital management   As a result of the difficulty in coming up with the inputs needed to estimate optimal working capital, companies often adopt much more simplistic approaches to working capital management. One approach is to pattern working capital ratios on comparable firms operating in the same line of business. This approach can be justified on the following bases.

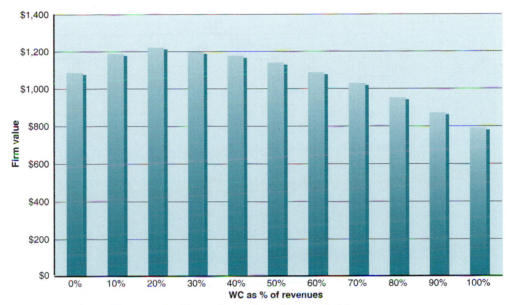

Figure 14.1   Firm value and working capital investment

1. Although individual companies might make errors by under- or overinvesting in working capital, these errors should average out across firms and the average should provide a better estimate of the optimal working capital ratio. This is only true, however, if firms are attempting to manage their working capital investments optimally and if the errors are not correlated across firms, both of which are daunting assumptions.

2. Analysts following the company will measure it against these comparable companies. Thus, the company will be penalized for having a working capital investment that is out of line—either too high or too low—with these comparable firms.

Table 14.2 summarizes working capital ratios as a proportion of revenues in different industries.

Table 14.2   **WORKING CAPITAL (IN $) AND AS PERCENTAGE OF REVENUES—BY INDUSTRY**

Industry	Working Capital	Working Capital as % of Revenues
Agricultural Products	$204.83	31.30
Mining	102.66	39.48
Petroleum Production and Refining	209.59	15.95
Building Contractors and Related Areas	146.87	17.67
Food Production	175.62	8.53
Beverages	103.93	7.26
Tobacco	112.91	3.36
Textile and Clothing Manufacturers	165.97	27.57
Furniture	209.60	23.68
Paper and Plastic Production	114.73	8.77
Publishing	100.53	18.25
Chemicals	410.32	18.42
Pharmaceuticals	383.78	43.15

(continues)

Table 14.2   (*Continued*)

Industry	Working Capital	Working Capital as % of Revenues
Consumer Products	134.93	13.72
Autos and Related	458.53	18.92
Miscellaneous Manufacturing	112.38	15.92
Equipment Manufacturing	231.39	25.11
Computers and Office Equipment	443.04	34.22
Consumer Electronics	905.78	12.28
Other Consumer Durables	114.82	30.22
Transportation	(80.93)	3.62
Telephone Utilities	(368.70)	−1.72
Entertainment (TV and Movies)	170.57	22.75
Electric and Gas Utilities	(64.81)	−0.13
Wholesalers	121.05	17.36
Retailers	330.54	13.95
Restaurants and Eating Places	(53.74)	−6.04
Banks and Financial Service	21.76	9.84
Insurance	91.74	17.44
Real Estate	24.95	46.03
Other Services	35.40	12.80
Computer Software and Services	167.94	28.56
Health Services	48.95	20.66
AVERAGE	**179.60**	**18.81**

It is not unusual for firms to follow their peer group in setting working capital policy. Yet there is the possibility of "herd behavior" arising as a consequence, with all firms within a group over- or underinvesting in working capital. Thus, it might pay to try to collect the information needed to determine the optimum working capital for a firm first and then consider the working capital policies of the peer group.

Despite the attempts by firms to pattern their working capital management after other firms in the industry, significant differences in working capital ratios remain, even within the same industry groups. Referring back to the discussion of the determinants of net working capital investment, we would argue that working capital should be larger for firms that

- Have more volatile revenues and cash flows.
- Experience higher risk from other sources, business or financial, and hence want to restrict any incremental risk from working capital.
- Are smaller and have less access to external financing.

Although this list is by no means comprehensive, the working capital ratios within an industry can be estimated as a function of these and other characteristics, and this relationship can be used both to examine outliers within the group and to estimate optimal working capital for an individual firm.

 Concept
Check

Examine Table 14.2 and try to explain why the industries with the highest and lowest working capital ratios exhibit these behaviors.

IN PRACTICE   COMPARING WORKING CAPITAL RATIOS ACROSS FIRMS—BOEING AND THE AEROSPACE/DEFENSE INDUSTRY

Table 14.3 reports working capital as a percentage of revenues in the aerospace/defense sector, together with information on the expected growth rates, betas, and revenues of these firms.

Table 14.3   WORKING CAPITAL RATIOS ACROSS AEROSPACE FIRMS

Firm	Net Working Capital	Revenues	Beta	Expected Growth (%)	Working Capital as % of Revenues
AAR Corporation	$240	$408	1.35	12.50	58.82
Boeing Corporation	3,587	21,924	1.00	9.00	16.36
Bombardier	1,771	4,672	1.00	21.50	37.91
CAE Inc.	(25)	1,027	0.55	−8.00	−2.43
E-Systems	584	2,028	0.60	7.00	28.80
EDO Corp	41	105	0.85	6.00	39.05
GRC International	25	130	1.20	18.00	19.23
General Dynamics	1,171	3,058	1.10	9.00	38.29
Hexcel Corporation	55	339	0.65	−8.00	16.11
Hughes Electronics	2,696	14,062	0.95	9.00	19.17
Litton Industries	37	3,446	0.90	−2.00	1.07
Loral Corporation	555	4,009	0.85	13.00	13.84
McDonnell Douglas	2,239	13,176	1.25	24.00	16.99
Average					23.33%
Standard Deviation					16.82%

The fact that a firm has a working capital ratio that is higher or lower than the average, which is 23.33%, should not be taken as an indication that the firm has over or underinvested in working capital since the ratio is affected by differences in firm characteristics. A regression of the working capital ratio against three independent variables—revenues, risk, and expected growth— yields the following equation:

Working Capital as % of Revenues = −0.01 − .00001
Revenues + 0.27 Beta + 0.44 Growth Rate
[R-squared = 39.55%]

For instance, based on this regression, the predicted working capital ratio for Boeing would be

Working Capital as % of Revenues = − .01 − .00001(21,924) + 0.27(1.00)
+ 0.44(.09) = .0804 or 8.04%

Thus, given Boeing's revenues, risk characteristics, and growth profile, its working capital investment of 16.36% would be considered too high. This recommendation should be taken with a grain of salt, however, given the low R-squared on the regression. It might be improved by looking at working capital investment over time, rather than for just one year, and by expanding the sample to include more firms.

Financing Current Assets

An investment in current assets creates a need for financing, first from current liabilities and then from either long- or short-term financing sources for the balance. In this section, we examine the question of how much to take on in the form of current liabilities and whether to use short-term or long-term financing to cover net working capital investments.

Permanent versus transitory components   The need for current assets tends to shift over time. Some of these changes reflect permanent changes in the underlying firm, as is the case when inventory and accounts receivable increase as revenues grow and the firm becomes larger. Other changes are seasonal, as is the case with increased inventory around the Christmas holiday season for retail firms. Still others are random, reflecting the uncertainty associated with revenue growth owing to firm-specific or economywide factors. A small mail-order firm, for example, may find that its working capital increases dramatically if its sales surge above expectations, putting pressure on it to increase both inventory and credit sales. The investment in current assets is traced over time and broken down into these three components for a firm in Figure 14.2.

In Figure 14.2, the permanent component of current assets increases over time as the firm becomes larger. The seasonal component changes over the course of the year but in a predictable way. The sum of the permanent and the seasonal component is different from the total current assets as a result of the random component that also changes over the course of time but does not follow a predictable pattern.

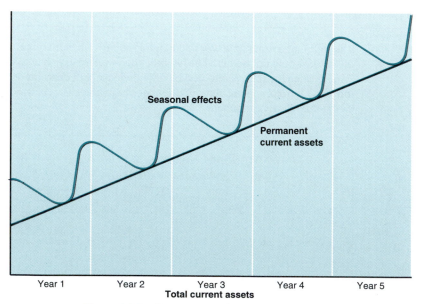

Figure 14.2   Current asset investment over time

🔲 Concept Check

What are some of the factors that might cause random changes in current assets over time?

Short-term versus long-term financing Breaking down working capital needs into permanent, seasonal, and random components over time provides a useful byproduct in terms of financing choice. The permanent component is predictable insofar as it is linked up to expected changes in revenues or cost of goods sold over time. The seasonal component is also predictable because it follows the same pattern every year. The random component, by definition, is unpredictable.

The permanent and seasonal components are both predictable, yet they differ on at least one dimension: the permanent component of working capital is similar to an investment in fixed assets because it has to be replenished over time and thus requires financing for the long term. Consequently, it can be argued that this component should be financed with a *combination of current liabilities and long-term financing*—either debt or equity, or more likely, a combination of the two, depending on the financing mix the firm chooses to use for financing long-term assets. The exact breakdown of current liabilities and long-term financing will depend on the tradeoff between the perceived liquidity risk of having too much in current liabilities and the costs associated with using long-term financing. The seasonal component should be financed with *prearranged lines of short-term credit* and with accounts payable. The random component has to be financed with either *spontaneous credit*—trade credit arising from day-to-day operations of the firm—or from short-term liabilities.

Figure 14.3 analyzes the financing of current assets using the framework suggested above. This strategy will require the firm to borrow short term to cover its temporary working capital needs. For firms that have a deep aversion to short-term financing, an alternative strategy is to raise sufficient long-term financing to cover the temporary needs as well. This strategy will result in excess cash in periods in which the temporary needs subside, as shown in Figure 14.4.

An intermediate strategy would involve financing a portion of the temporary working capital needs with long-term financing and the balance with short-term financing. This strategy would still create excess cash in some periods, though not of the same magnitude.

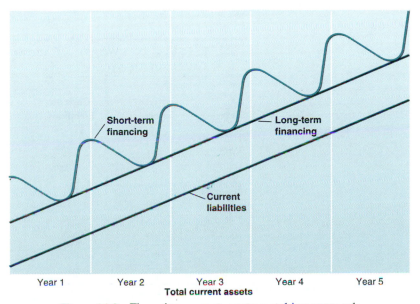

Figure 14.3 Financing current assets: matching approach

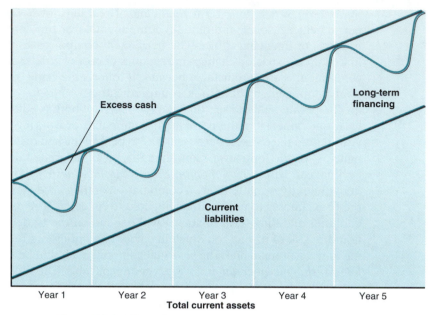

Figure 14.4 Financing current assets: a conservative strategy

 Concept Check

Of the strategies described above for financing current assets, which one would minimize the interest costs paid? Which would minimize risk?

IN PRACTICE NET WORKING CAPITAL CHANGES OVER TIME—THE HOME DEPOT

Table 14.4 summarizes total current assets and total current liabilities at the Home Depot from 1987 to 1995.

Table 14.4 NET WORKING CAPITAL—THE HOME DEPOT

Year	Current Assets	Current Liabilities	Net Working Capital
1987	$198	$107	$91
1988	257	147	111
1989	337	194	143
1990	566	292	274
1991	714	413	301
1992	1,158	534	624
1993	1,562	755	807
1994	1,967	973	994
1995	2,133	1,214	919

The current assets and current liabilities have grown over time as the firm's revenues have grown, as shown in Figure 14.5.

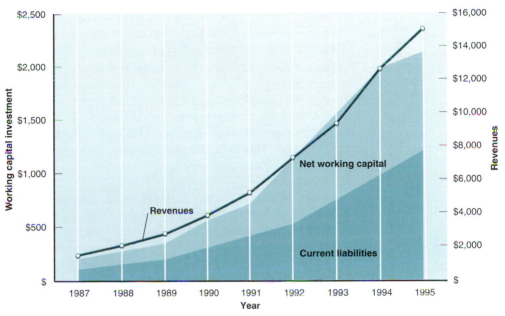

Figure 14.5 The Home Depot: working capital from 1987 to 1995

MANAGING CURRENT ASSETS

Significant differences and similarities exist in the way current assets are managed. In this section, we examine management considerations on three of the most important items: cash and marketable securities, inventory, and accounts receivable.

Managing Cash and Cash Equivalents

Every business has to maintain a cash balance to meet needs that can be managed only with cash. The convenience and liquidity associated with keeping cash also carries a clear cost, however, for cash does not earn a return for the business. Some businesses hold cash equivalents, such as Treasury bills, which provide almost all of the convenience of cash but also earn a return for the holder, albeit one lower than that earned by the business on real projects.[1]

Motivations for holding cash Keynes suggested three motives for holding cash (and cash equivalents): (1) a *transactions motive*, to meet the needs that arise in the course of doing business; (2) a *precautionary motive*, to meet unspecified and unexpected contingencies that may arise; and (3) *a speculative motive*, to take advantage of profit-making opportunities that may develop. On each of these motives, firms differ significantly in terms of their needs:

- The greater the uncertainty about operating cash-flow needs, the greater should be the cash requirements for transactions and precautionary motives.
- The transactions demand for cash is affected by any seasonal factors that may affect demand. For instance, retail firms are likely to maintain higher cash balances in the last couple of months of each year, reflecting the higher sales they anticipate around the Christmas season.

---

[1]A money market account, which allows checks to be written against the balance, is an intermediate solution available to smaller businesses that might not want to hold Treasury bills.

- The demand for cash to cover unanticipated contingencies is affected by the firm's access to external financing; firms that can borrow easily and at low cost are much less likely to keep large cash balances to cover unexpected events.

- The speculative motive for cash typically is not a large factor for firms with long-term projects, but it may be a factor for firms that are faced with the possibility of short-term profit-making opportunities that have to be taken advantage of quickly or will be lost to the competition. A good example is a small financial service firm that makes its profits from short-term trading opportunities that may arise in financial markets. This firm will need to have cash on hand to take advantage of these opportunities as they arise.

Managing float   When businesses make or receive payments in the form of checks, there is usually a time lapse between the time the check is written and when it is cleared. This is referred to as the **float**, and it can have either a positive or a negative impact on the firm, depending on whether the firm receives or provides the benefit of the float. When the firm makes the payment, it receives the benefit of the *payment* or *disbursement float;* that it, it gets to use the money for the period between when the check is written and when it clears. When the firm receives a check as payment for goods or services rendered, it is at the receiving end of the *processing* or *availability float* and cannot use the funds until the check clears. The difference between the two is the net float—the net benefit or cost to the firm as a result of float.

Float: This is the time that lapses between when a check is written and when is cleared. If the firm makes the payment, it is called *payment float.* If it receives the payment, it is a *processing float.* The *net float* is the difference between the two.

A firm with a positive net float can use it to advantage and maintain a smaller cash balance than it would have in the absence of the float. To illustrate, assume that a firm makes payments of $1 million a day, and it takes five days for the checks to clear; and the firm receives $800,000 a day in checks, and it takes four days for these checks to clear. This firm has a positive net float, which can be computed as follows.

$$\text{Net Float} = \text{Payment Float} - \text{Processing Float} = \$1 \text{ mil } (5) - \$800,000 (4)$$
$$= \$1.8 \text{ million}$$

Conceivably, the firm could hold $1.8 million less as a cash balance and save in opportunity costs as a consequence. The effects of speeding up collections can be illustrated fairly easily within this context. If the firm can reduce the number of days its takes to collect on checks received from four to three, the net float will increase by $800,000, as will the value of the firm.

In recent years, firms have focused on ways to increase their net float. Some have worked on speeding up collections

- By encouraging customers to use *debit cards, preauthorized checks, and wire transfers* to speed the receipt of cash.

- By switching to **lock-box arrangements**, whereby checks written by customers are processed by a local bank rather than being sent to headquarters before the processing, saving on the processing time.

Others have concentrated on controlling and slowing disbursements. In either case, they are *playing the float*, hoping to maintain lower cash balances.

Lock-box Arrangement: This is an arrangement with a bank, whereby checks received by a firm are processed at a local bank, saving time.

* By using *concentration banking*, whereby payments are made to regional collection centers for funds.

☐ Concept
   Check

> Do you think technological advances will increase or decrease net float for firms? Are some firms more likely to benefit than others? Explain.

Tradeoffs on holding cash and marketable securities Traditional models of cash balances focus on the cost of holding cash relative to holding interest-bearing securities. In these models, the cost of holding cash is the interest foregone, and liquidity needs exist that can be met only with available cash. Consequently, a firm faced with these needs must either have the cash on hand or sell securities, which is assumed to create a fixed cost. Thus, a firm that does not have enough cash will have to sell its securities more frequently, resulting in transactions costs that exceed any interest earned by virtue of maintaining a low cash balance.

A more expansive analysis would consider the costs of holding cash-equivalent securities relative to making real investments in plant, equipment, and inventory. In this case, the firm earns a return on the securities, but the return is lower than that it would have made on these alternative investments; this is the cost of holding too much in cash equivalent securities. This cost has to be weighed against the substantial costs associated with having insufficient cash and equivalent securities to meet liabilities coming due, for plant, equipment, and inventory cannot be converted into cash at short notice without paying a substantial price.

The two tradeoffs are illustrated in Figure 14.6. The first tradeoff is between investing in real assets and cash or cash equivalents; the second is the more traditional trade-off between cash and marketable securities.

At the end of this process, the firm should have a sense not only of what the optimal balance for cash and cash equivalents should be, but also of the breakdown of this balance into cash and marketable securities. The final step is the composition of the marketable securities component. Firms have several choices when it comes to marketable securities:

* *Treasury bills*, which are short-term obligations of the U.S. government and, hence, not only carry the least risk (default and interest rate risk) but also provide the most liquidity.
* *Federal agency securities*, which have slightly more default risk and may be slightly less liquid than Treasury bills.
* *Commercial paper*, which are short-term obligations of other firms, generally large and safe, but which still have some default risk.
* *Repurchase agreements*, whereby U.S. government securities are purchased by the firm from commercial banks or other financial institutions, with the agreement that these securities will be sold back at the contract price plus accrued interest.

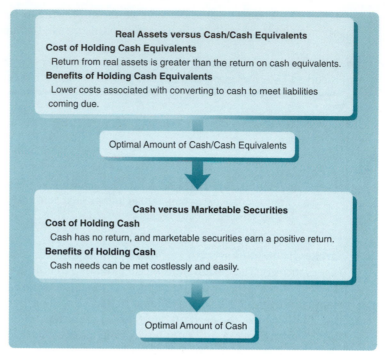

Figure 14.6   Determining optimal cash policy

In choosing among these alternatives, firms have to trade off the higher returns they are likely to make on commercial paper against the higher default and liquidity risk to which these securities expose them. Some firms take on even larger amounts of risk, both default and interest rate, by investing in long-term Treasury bonds and corporate bonds, because they feel that the higher returns justify doing so.[2] Given that one motive for holding marketable securities is to have liquid assets, in case the need arises, that seems like a rather risky strategy.

Determining an optimal cash balance   The traditional tradeoff between the costs and benefits of holding cash is considered in the Baumol model. This model trades off the interest foregone by holding cash instead of marketable securities against the cost associated with selling marketable securities, and it estimates an optimal cash balance based on the firm's cash usage rate. In this model, developed by William Baumol, the optimal cash balance can be written as follows.

$$\text{Optimal Cash Balance} = \sqrt{\frac{2 * \text{Annual Cash Usage Rate} * \text{Cost per Sale of Securities}}{\text{Annual Interest Rate}}}$$

The optimal cash balance is an increasing function of the annual cash usage and the cost per sale of security and a decreasing function of the annualized interest rate. Note, however, that this model assumes that the firm uses up cash: in reality, most firms have both cash inflows and outflows.

---

[2]Some firms have even invested in the stock of other companies; one example is Seagram's investment in Du Pont in the 1980s.

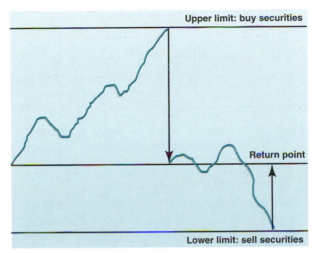

Figure 14.7   Upper and lower limits: the Miller–Orr model

An alternative model is provided by Miller and Orr for firms with uncertain cash inflows and cash outflows to develop lower and upper limits for cash balances. This model is shown in Figure 14.7.

The spread between the lower and the upper limit computed by the model is that which minimizes the sum of transactions costs and interest costs. The firm buys securities when it gets to the upper limit and reduces its cash balance to the return point and sells securities when it gets to the lower limit and raises its balance to the same point. This spread is an increasing function of the variability in cash flows and can be written as follows.

$$\text{Spread between upper and lower cash balance limits} =$$
$$3\left(\frac{3}{4} * \frac{\text{Transactions Cost} * \text{Variance of Cash Flows}}{\text{Interest Rate}}\right)^{1/3}$$

Putting the Miller–Orr approach to use requires three steps. The first step involves specifying a minimum cash balance, which comprises the lower limit for the cash flows; this could be zero. The second step involves estimating the variability in future cash flows, by looking at either historical data on cash flows or comparable firms. The final step involves computing the spread as a function of the variability, the transactions cost, and the market interest rate. Adding this spread to the lower limit yields the upper limit for the cash flows.

☐ Concept
Check

As it becomes easier for firms to preserve liquidity and still earn interest (as in the case of money market accounts), will optimal cash balances increase, decrease, or remain unchanged? Explain.

Optimal cash balance for a firm with a steady cash usage rate   Assume that you want to estimate the optimal cash balance for an automobile supplies firm that has the following characteristics:

- The annual cash usage rate for the firm is $10 million.
- The cost per sale of securities is $50.
- The annual interest rate is 10%.

The optimal cash balance can be computed from the Baumol model:

$$\text{Optimal Cash Balance} = \sqrt{\frac{2 * \$10{,}000{,}000 * \$50}{.10}} = \$100{,}000$$

Optimal cash balance for a firm with uncertain cash flows   Now assume that you are estimating the optimal cash balance for a computer software firm with uncertain future cash flows. The firm has the following characteristics:

- The standard deviation in daily cash balances is $10,000; the variance is $100 million.
- The minimum cash balance this firm has to maintain is $100,000.
- The interest rate, on a daily basis, is .01%.
- The transactions costs for each sale or purchase of securities is $50.

The spread between the lower and the upper limit can be computed using the Miller–Orr model:

$$\text{Spread between upper and lower cash balance limits} =$$
$$3\left(\frac{3}{4} * \frac{\$50 * \$100{,}000{,}000}{.0001}\right)^{1/3} = \$100{,}415$$

The upper limit for cash balances is $200,415 [$100,000 + $100,415]; the return point after the firm reaches the limits is $133,472 [$100,000 + $100,415/3].

☐ Concept
Check

> **Estimate the spread between the lower and upper limits as a function of the variance in operating cash flows. Discuss the relationship.**

Cash management practices   A handful of studies have examined the actual cash management practices used by firms in the United States. Gitman, Moses and White surveyed 300 large U.S. companies in 1975 and found that 80% of the respondents used lock-box systems to increase their net float. The most favored marketable security for firms was commercial paper, followed by repurchase agreements and Treasury bills; most firms invested in several types of marketable securities. Similar results were reported by Mathur and Loy in a study of 200 large U.S. companies in 1979.

Table 14.5 summarizes cash balances as a percentage of total assets in different industries in the United States in 1994. As the table indicates, clear differences exist between industries; it would be a mistake, however, to attribute these differences entirely to the cost/benefit tradeoff, for a number of other factors may affect cash balances. For instance, the cash balances of cyclical firms are much more likely to decrease during re-

Table 14.5   CASH AND SHORT-TERM INVESTMENTS AS A PERCENTAGE OF TOTAL ASSETS—BY INDUSTRY

Industry	Cash as % of Total Assets
Agricultural Products	9.18
Mining	18.12
Petroleum Production and Refining	8.48
Building Contractors and Related	9.20
Food Production	5.83
Beverages	5.17
Tobacco	3.35
Textile and Clothing Manufacturers	8.35
Furniture	6.50
Paper and Plastic Production	3.72
Publishing	9.35
Chemicals	7.02
Pharmaceuticals	26.73
Consumer Products	9.40
Autos and Related	7.99
Miscellaneous Manufacturing	6.78
Equipment Manufacturing	8.89
Computers and Office Equipment	15.47
Consumer Electronics	8.25
Other Consumer Durables	14.91
Transportation	7.55
Telephone Utilities	4.80
Entertainment (TV and Movies)	13.83
Electric and Gas Utilities	2.73
Wholesalers	7.63
Retailers	7.30
Restaurants and Eating Places	7.52
Banks and Financial Service	8.05
Insurance	9.02
Real Estate	10.32
Other Services	13.21
Computer Software and Services	21.03
Health Services	12.64
Average	**9.31**

cessions, as earnings dip. Furthermore, closely held firms may keep much larger cash balances than needed to provide more power to incumbent managers and to protect insiders from significant tax liabilities.

 Concept Check

Assume that you want to isolate those firms that have unusually high cash balances. How would you control for differences across industries in cash balances?

Managing Inventory

Most firms build up and maintain inventories in the course of doing business. For manufacturing firms, the inventories may be of raw materials, intermediate goods, and finished products. For financial service firms, the inventory tends to be of marketable securities. We now turn to a discussion of how much a firm should hold in inventory and the costs and benefits of holding inventory.

Motivation for holding inventory   The motivation for holding inventory varies, depending on the type of inventory. As noted earlier, a manufacturing firm may have inventories at different stages in the production process:

1. *Inventories of raw materials are held to ensure that the production process is not stymied by a shortage of these materials.* The amount of this inventory will depend on a number of factors, including the speed with which raw materials can be ordered and delivered (the greater the speed, the lower the required inventory for raw materials) and the uncertainty in the supply of these raw materials (the larger the uncertainty, the greater the need for inventories of these materials). For instance, in the aftermath of the OPEC oil embargo, airlines that used substantial amounts of oil increased their inventories of oil.

2. *Inventories of intermediate goods arise in the process of production.* As the production process becomes more complicated and lengthy, the intermediate goods inventory will also increase.

3. *Inventories of finished goods arise because of the time involved in the production process and the need to meet customer demand promptly.* If firms do not maintain a sufficient finished good inventory, they run the risk of losing sales, as customers who are unwilling to wait turn to competitors. Alternatively, firms have to replenish their inventory, leading to ordering and administrative costs, which may be large. The magnitude of the finished good inventory will depend on

   - *The time it takes to fill an order from a customer.* If orders cannot be filled quickly and at low cost, the firm will need to maintain a higher finished goods inventory. A clothing manufacturer can maintain a lower inventory than an automobile manufacturer, for instance, because it can meet sudden demand much more promptly.

   - *The diversity of the product line.* Firms that sell a wide variety of goods generally need to invest more in finished goods inventory than do firms that have a single or only a few lines of goods. For example, a retail store that sells a wide range of goods and multiple brands invests more in inventory than one that specializes in a few items and only one or two brand names.

   - *The strength of the competition.* When competitors offer close or perfect substitutes at similar prices, the firm is much more likely to suffer from lost sales if it does not have sufficient inventory. A new car dealer that does not have a sufficient inventory of cars, for instance, will lose sales to competitors. On the other hand, if there are no close substitutes, the firm can afford to keep a lower inventory because it does not have to worry about losing sales to competitors.

❑ Concept
Check

A retail firm decides to reduce the number of brand names it carries in its stores from seven to three. What implications does this action have for inventory at this firm and why?

Cost of holding inventory   Two costs are associated with holding inventory. The first is the cost of the interest foregone on the cash invested in inventory, because it does not earn a return. This cost will increase with

- *The value of the inventory*, relative to sales. The greater the value, the greater is the cost associated with holding that inventory.
- *The level of interest rates*. As interest rates increase, the cost of holding inventory increases.

The second cost is the storage and tracking cost associated with maintaining the inventory. The sum of the storage cost and the cost of interest foregone is called the **carrying cost.**

Carrying Cost: This is the cost associated with holding inventory; it includes the storage cost and the cost of interest foregone.

Determining an optimal inventory   The tradeoff on inventory is fairly clear. On the one hand, having too high an investment in inventory results in large carrying costs, which will drag down the value of the firm. On the other hand, having too small an inventory results in either lost sales or higher ordering costs, for the firm has to replenish its inventory on a more frequent basis. One model used to estimate economic order quantities, and consequently inventory levels, minimizes the sum of the carrying and the ordering costs. This model yields an estimate similar to the Baumol model:

$$\text{Optimal Order Quantity} = \sqrt{\frac{2 * \text{Annual Demand in Units} * \text{Ordering Cost per Order}}{\text{Carrying Cost per Unit}}}$$

where the carrying cost per unit includes both the interest foregone and the storage and administrative costs per unit stored, and the ordering cost is the cost associated with filling an order on short notice. The inventory and replenishment policy that follows from this model is depicted in Figure 14.8.

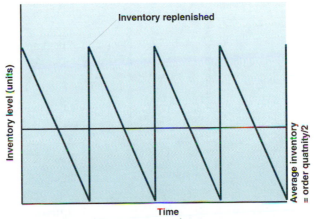

Figure 14.8   Economic order quantity and inventory replenishment

This model, though simple, suffers from several shortcomings, largely as a consequence of its restrictive assumptions:

1. *It assumes that the demand is constant over time.* If some uncertainty is associated with the demand, the model will not work.

2. *It assumes that inventory can be replenished instantaneously.* This is an unrealistic assumption for both manufacturing firms (where production can take time) and retail firms (where delivery can take time). Consequently, inventory in this model can drop to zero before a new order is made.

3. *It assumes that the ordering costs are fixed and not a function of the size of the order.* This is unlikely to be true when there are economies of scale or volume discounts associated with larger orders.

Some of these assumptions can be modified within the context of the economic order model. The assumptions of instantaneous replenishment and predictable demand can be eliminated by allowing firms to maintain a **safety inventory,** which would cover the demand while the order is being replenished. The size of this safety inventory is an increasing function of the time it takes to replenish inventory and of the uncertainty associated with demand. The presence of a safety stock is illustrated in Figure 14.9.

Safety Inventory: This is the level below which the firm does not want its inventory to fall, and is set to cover demand while the order is filled.

Optimal inventory estimation—an illustration   Suppose you are estimating the optimal order quantity for a new car dealer with the following characteristics:

- The annual expected sales, in units, is 1,200 cars; some uncertainty is associated with this forecast, and monthly sales are normally distributed with a mean of 100 cars and a standard deviation of 15 cars.

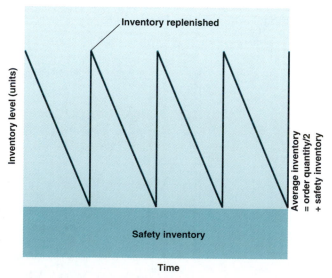

Figure 14.9   Economic order quantity and inventory replenishment

- The cost per order is $10,000, and it takes 15 days for new cars to be delivered by the manufacturer.
- The carrying cost per car, on an annualized basis, is $1,000.

Step 1: Estimate the Safety Inventory The safety inventory has two components. The first is the delivery lag; a 15-day lag in conjunction with the monthly expected sales of 100 cars yields a safety inventory of 50 cars [100/2]. The second reflects the uncertainty associated with the demand. Assuming that the firm wants to ensure, with 99% probability, that it does not run out of inventory, the safety inventory would have to be increased by 30 cars (which is twice the standard deviation).

$$\text{Safety Inventory} = \text{Delivery Lag Effect} + \text{Uncertainty Effect} = 50 + 30 = 80 \text{ cars}$$

The safety inventory would be lower if the firm were willing to accept a greater chance of running out of inventory.

Step 2: Estimate the Economic Order Quantity The economic order quantity can be estimated using the Economic Order Quantity (EOQ) model described above:

$$\text{Optimal Order Quantity} = \sqrt{\frac{2 * 1200 * 10{,}000}{1000}} = 155 \text{ cars}$$

Incorporating the safety inventory of 80 cars, we can estimate the following statistics for the dealership's inventory policy:

$$\text{Minimum Balance (Ordering Point)} = 80 \text{ cars}$$
$$\text{Average Inventory} = 155/2 + 80 = 157.5 \text{ cars}$$

Concept Check Estimate the average inventory as a function of the carrying cost and the ordering cost. As interest rates increase, what will be the effect be on optimal average inventory?

Inventory management practices Wide variations exist in both the investment in inventory and inventory management practices across industries. Table 14.6 summarizes the average investment made in inventory by firms and inventory turnover ratios in different industries.

As the costs of maintaining inventory have increased, and the costs of creating and maintaining computerized information systems have decreased, firms have begun using more sophisticated technology to manage inventory more efficiently. A number of inventory management techniques have been developed in recent years to take advantage of both trends:

1. The *just-in-time inventory system* focuses on keeping the minimum level of inventory and relying on suppliers who can supply goods on short notice.

Table 14.6   INVENTORY RATIOS—BY INDUSTRY

Industry	Inventory Turnover Ratio	Days of Inventory
Agricultural Products	44.74	8.16
Mining	9.64	37.86
Petroleum Production and Refining	26.08	14.00
Building Contractors and Related	16.62	21.96
Food Production	13.87	26.32
Beverages	17.19	21.23
Tobacco	7.48	48.80
Textile and Clothing Manufacturers	5.82	62.71
Furniture	9.21	39.63
Paper and Plastic Production	9.14	39.93
Publishing	37.10	9.84
Chemicals	18.63	19.59
Pharmaceuticals	6.80	53.68
Consumer Products	9.82	37.17
Autos and Related	9.17	39.80
Miscellaneous Manufacturing	9.20	39.67
Equipment Manufacturing	6.42	56.85
Computers and Office Equipment	6.66	54.80
Consumer Electronics	11.71	31.17
Other Consumer Durables	9.46	38.58
Transportation	56.98	6.41
Telephone Utilities	47.11	7.75
Entertainment (TV and Movies)	69.36	5.26
Electric and Gas Utilities	23.86	15.30
Wholesalers	49.66	7.35
Retailers	8.29	44.03
Restaurants and Eating Places	69.72	5.24
Banks and Financial Service	32.63	11.19
Insurance	2.14	170.56
Real Estate	1.15	317.39
Other Services	29.88	12.22
Computer Software and Services	21.44	17.02
Health Services	31.34	11.65
Average	**18.36**	**19.88**

2. Computers have been used to schedule delivery of raw materials closer to actual production in systems that are referred to as *material requirements planning,* or *MRP.*

3. Many firms have turned to *reengineering* their production processes to speed up production and reduce the inventory of work in progress they maintain.

4. Some firms, particularly retailing firms, have focused on *reducing the number* of items and brand names they carry, in order to maintain control of inventory.

Managing Accounts Receivable

Many firms offer credit to their customers to increase sales and, hopefully, profits. There is a cost to offering credit, however; the firm may report the credit sales when they occur, but it does not receive the cash until the customer pays. Consequently, credit sales and the accounts receivable that arise from them tie up cash, just as inventory does. We now turn to a discussion of the motivations for offering credit, the cost of offering credit, and the credit decision itself.

Tradeoff on offering credit Firms offer credit to customers for a number of reasons, but the ultimate objective is to generate sales that would not have occurred otherwise— either because customers do not have the cash to pay for the product or because credit increases the likelihood of selling the product. The payoff to offering credit varies across businesses; it is likely to be large for high-priced items, like cars, and smaller for less expensive items, like clothing.

The costs associated with offering credit are twofold. First, granting credit exposes the firm to the possibility that the customer will *default* on the payment, resulting in losses (from bad debts and collection costs) for the firm, even if it is able to reclaim the item that was sold. The second cost is the *interest foregone* between the time of the sale and the time of payment by the customer. This cost can be partially or fully offset by charging customers interest costs for buying items on credit. In fact, in cases where the firm can charge high interest rates on customer borrowings, the interest income becomes a revenue generator rather than a cost creator for the firm.

This tradeoff can be applied to the decision of whether or not to liberalize credit terms. More liberal credit terms (including lower interest rates and longer payment periods) may be expected to generate higher revenues, but they increase the potential costs as well. If the net benefit is positive, the firm should offer more liberal credit; if it is negative, it should not.

Decision to offer credit—an illustration Uncle Tech is a retailer of stereo and video products which traditionally has not allowed its customers to use credit and accepted only cash payment. In the current year, it had revenues of $10 million and pretax operating income of $2 million. Assume that Uncle Tech is now considering offering 30-day credit to its customers. Consequently:

- sales are expected to increase by $1 million each year, with the pretax operating margin remaining at 20% on these incremental sales.
- the store expects to charge an annualized interest rate of 12% on these credit sales.
- the bad debts (including the collection costs and net of any repossessions) is expected to be 5% of the credit sales.
- the cost of administration associated with credit sales is expected to be $25,000 a year, along with an initial investment in a computerized credit-tracking system of $100,000. The computerized system will be depreciated straight-line over 10 years.
- the tax rate is 40%.
- the store is expected to be in business in 10 years; at the end of that period, it is expected that 95% of the accounts receivable will be collected (and salvaged).
- the store is expected to face a cost of capital of 10%.

Initial investment The initial investment needed to generate the credit has two components: the cost of the computerized system needed for the credit sales, which is $100,000; and the investment in accounts receivable created as a consequence of the credit sales, which is $1 million. Because no growth in sales is expected, no more investment will be needed over time.

Operating cash flows   During the 10-year life of the store, it is expected to generate additional operating income as a result of the credit sales, but it is also expected to generate additional costs in terms of administration and bad debts. The firm can also expect to receive interest income from the credit sales, net of bad debts:

Incremental Revenues	$1,000,000	
Incremental Pretax Margin (20%)	200,000	
+ Interest Income from Credit	114,000	[12% of $950,000]
− Bad Debts	50,000	
− Annual Administrative Costs	25,000	
Incremental Pretax Operating Profit	239,000	
− Taxes (at 40%)	95,600	
Incremental After-tax Operating Profit	143,400	
+ Tax Benefit from Depreciation	4,000	[$10,000 * 0.4]
Incremental After-tax Cash Flow	147,400	

Salvage value   The salvage value comes from the collection of outstanding accounts receivable at the end of the store's life, which amounts to 95% of $1 million.

Present value of credit decision   The present value of the credit decision can be computed using the cost of capital of 10%:

NPV of Credit Decision = −1,100,000 + $147,400 (PV of Annuity, 10 years, 10%) + $950,000/1.10^{10} = $171,975

Based on the net present value, it makes sense for the firm to start offering credit.

Concept Check

As long as the firm charges a higher interest rate on credit sales than its cost of capital, the firm value will increase with credit sales. Do you agree? Why or why not?

Credit analysis and the credit decision   Although the decisions of whether or not to offer credit and how much to liberalize credit can be evaluated by looking at the overall costs and benefits to the firm, the decision to offer credit will generally have to be followed by additional decisions regarding which customers will be offered credit and on what terms. In making these decisions, firms generally rely on **credit analysis**, which is intended to evaluate the creditworthiness of individual customers. The question of whether or not to do a credit analysis will depend on the size of the credit. Because an administrative cost is associated with it, it might not pay to do a credit analysis if the credit being offered is small or if the risk of default is very low.

Credit Analysis: This is an analysis designed to evaluate the creditworthiness of a customer.

In a typical credit analysis, customers are asked to provide information concerning the five C's of credit: the customer's *c*haracter, *c*apacity to pay, and *c*apital; the collateral offered for the credit; and the *c*ondition of the customer's employment. These characteristics have been shown to correlate with creditworthiness (or, alternatively, default rates) in the past.

Terms of sale and credit The terms of sale specify how the credit will be offered, including the length of the period for which the credit will be offered, the interest rate on the credit, and the cost of default. In some cases, the discount that will be provided if the customer pays cash instead of using credit is also specified. For instance, if the terms of sale are 4/15 net 60:

4	/	15	net 60
Percent discount for early payment		Number of days that discount is available	Number of days before payment is due

Thus, a customer who makes payment within 15 days of the sale will receive a 4% discount; if the customer chooses not to take advantage of this discount, he or she has an extra 45 days to make the payment. Although no interest rate on the credit is specified as part of the agreement, the cash discount can be translated into an effective interest rate. Consider the case described above: For an item costing $1,000, the customer pays only $960 if the payment is made within 15 days; if the customer waits, he or she gets an extra 45 days but has to pay $40 more. This yields an effective annualized interest rate:

$$\text{Effective interest rate} = \left(1 + \frac{\text{Cash Discount}}{\text{Price} - \text{Cash Discount})}\right)^{365/number \text{ of extra days to make payment}} - 1$$

$$= \left(1 + \frac{40}{(1000 - 40)}\right)^{365/45} - 1 = 39.25\%$$

Thus, a policy of providing a cash discount of 4% and allowing an extra 45 days for payment is the equivalent of offering credit at an annualized interest rate of 39.25%.

To illustrate, suppose you run a plumbing service and you are considering offering 30-day credit to your customers and would like to charge them an annualized rate of 24%. If you want to structure the credit in terms of a cash discount for immediate payment, how much would the discount have to be?

To solve for the cash discount rate, note the following:

$$\left(1 + \frac{\text{Cash Discount}}{(1 - \text{Cash Discount})}\right)^{365/30} = 1.24$$

Solving for the cash discount rate,

$$\left(\frac{\text{Cash Discount}}{1 - \text{Cash Discount})}\right) = 1.24^{(30/365)} - 1 = .01784$$

This results in a cash discount rate of 1.753%. In other words, offering customers who pay cash a 1.75% discount is the equivalent of charging customers who use credit 24% as an interest rate.

Collection policy Once a firm decides to offer credit and defines the terms of credit sales, it must develop a policy for dealing with delinquent or slow-paying customers. There is a cost to both: delinquent customers create bad debts and other costs associated with repossession, whereas slow-paying customers cause more cash to be tied up in accounts receivable and in increased interest costs. For instance, if the customer in the above example takes an extra 75 days to pay instead of the agreed-upon 45 days, the implicit interest earned on credit will drop:

$$\text{Effective interest rate} = \left(1 + \frac{\text{Cash Discount}}{\text{Price} - \text{Cash Discount}}\right)^{365/\text{number of extra days to make payment}} - 1$$

$$= \left(1 + \frac{40}{1000 - 40}\right)^{365/75} - 1 = 21.98\%$$

The decision of whether to give the customer extra time to pay—which costs the firm in terms of interest foregone—or to force repossession or bankruptcy—which costs the firm in terms of bad debt and administrative costs as well as any potential repeat sales from that customer—will create friction between the collection department and the sales department. It can be resolved, however, in purely economic terms. The quality of a firm's accounts receivable can be measured by looking at the age of accounts receivable—the older the accounts receivable, the lower the quality, and the greater the likelihood of default. An **aging analysis,** an example of which is shown in Table 14.7, provides this breakdown.

Table 14.7 **AGING ANALYSIS OF ACCOUNTS RECEIVABLE**

Age of Account	$ Value	% of Outstanding Receivables
0–15 days	10.50	35.59
15–30 days	7.00	23.73
30–60 days	5.00	16.95
60–90 days	3.00	10.17
> 90 days	4.00	13.56
Total	29.50	100.00

In this aging analysis, for instance, more than 25% of the customers have owed the firm for more than three months. When compared with past aging analyses done by the firm and the aging analysis done by comparable firms right now, this may provide an indication of whether the firm should start worrying about its collections.

Aging Analysis: This is a breakdown of a firm's accounts receivable by age—length of time the amount has been owed to the firm.

Credit practices of firms Firms vary widely on credit practices, reflecting differences in the businesses in which they operate and the customers they serve. Table 14.8 summarizes average accounts receivable turnover and collection periods in a number of industries in the United States, based on 1994 data.

Table 14.8 ACCOUNTS RECEIVABLE RATIOS: BY INDUSTRY		
Industry	**Receivable Turnover**	**Days Receivables**
Agricultural Products	4.91	74.34
Mining	22.68	16.09
Petroleum Production and Refining	7.20	50.69
Building Contractors and Related	19.65	18.58
Food Production	11.99	30.44
Beverages	11.49	31.77
Tobacco	13.47	27.10
Textile and Clothing Manufacturers	8.00	45.63
Furniture	6.09	59.93
Paper and Plastic Production	9.20	39.67
Publishing	8.41	43.40
Chemicals	6.48	56.33
Pharmaceuticals	7.33	49.80
Consumer Products	9.00	40.56
Autos and Related	8.05	45.34
Miscellaneous Manufacturing	7.40	49.32
Equipment Manufacturing	6.60	55.30
Computers and Office Equipment	5.38	67.84
Consumer Electronics	8.01	45.57
Other Consumer Durables	6.99	52.22
Transportation	13.36	27.32
Telephone Utilities	5.95	61.34
Entertainment (TV and Movies)	28.43	12.84
Electric and Gas Utilities	12.18	29.97
Wholesalers	9.94	36.72
Retailers	76.82	4.75
Restaurants and Eating Places	157.97	2.31
Banks and Financial Service	1.11	328.83
Insurance	4.52	80.75
Real Estate	8.13	44.90
Other Services	10.17	35.89
Computer Software and Services	4.98	73.29
Health Services	5.48	66.61
Average	**10.79**	**33.83**

MANAGING ACCOUNTS PAYABLE AND SHORT-TERM FINANCING

The current asset needs of a firm are financed partially using current liabilities and short-term financing sources. In this section, we examine some of the choices available in terms of short-term financing and the considerations involved in choosing among them.

Trade Credit

Trade credit arises as a result of the firm's purchase of goods and services. Thus, the purchase of computer chips on credit by Compaq from Intel would create trade credit for

Compaq. Because these goods and services then go on to produce revenues for the firm, trade credit tends to move with both revenues and current asset items, such as inventory and accounts receivable, that are linked up to revenues. By using trade credit judiciously, a firm can reduce the effect of growth on working capital needs. To illustrate, assume that a firm has revenues of $20 million and inventory of $5 million and it uses no trade credit. If this firm doubles its sales, and its inventory as a percentage of sales remains unchanged, the firm will have to invest $5 million more in inventory. If this firm had used trade credit amounting to 50% of inventory, its working capital investment would have increased from $2.5 million to $5 million, resulting in an incremental investment of only $2.5 million.

The tradeoff on trade credit   As illustrated above, trade credit reduces working capital investment and provides a buffer against growth. Consequently, it saves the firm's resources and reduces the interest foregone in working capital investments. There may be a cost, however: there is often a discount on the price the firm foregoes when it uses trade credit. This discount can translate into a high implicit interest cost, as evidenced by the discussion of customer credit in the previous section. Table 14.9 summarizes the implicit interest rate in various trade credit arrangements for a firm with a 40% tax rate.

Table 14.9   IMPLIED INTEREST RATES IN CREDIT ARRANGEMENTS

Credit Arrangement	Implicit Interest Rate (%)	After-tax Rate (%)
1/10 net 30	20.13	12.08
2/10 net 30	44.59	26.75
1/10 net 60	7.61	4.57
2/10 net 60	15.89	9.53
1/10 net 90	4.69	2.82
2/10 net 90	9.66	5.79

The implicit interest rate is adjusted for the tax deduction the firm obtains when it purchases goods and services.

Thus, a firm that chooses to take advantage of trade credit (where the terms are 1/10 net 30) will reduce its working capital requirements, but at an implicit annualized interest rate of 12.08%. If its cost of capital is only 11%, this will clearly work to its detriment. However, if it is able to negotiate better terms (say, 2/10 net 90), the value of the firm will increase if it uses trade credit. Alternatively, some firms attempt to stretch out payments beyond the agreed-upon payment date, but this might result in the loss of credit.

Lines of Credit

A second source of short-term financing available to firms is a *line of credit*, on which the firm can draw if it needs financing to meet unanticipated or seasonal working capital needs. In most cases, a line of credit specifies an amount the firm can borrow and links the interest rate on the borrowing to a market rate, such as the prime rate or Treasury rates.

The advantage of a line of credit is that it provides the firm with access to the funds without having to pay interest costs if the funds remain unused. Thus, it is a useful type of financing for firms with volatile working capital needs. In many cases, however, the firm is required to maintain a compensating balance on which it earns either no interest or below-market rates. The opportunity cost of having this compensating balance must be weighed against the higher interest costs that will be incurred by taking on a more conventional loan to cover working capital needs.

To illustrate, assume that a restaurant has net working capital need that averages $300,000 a month but could increase in some months to $500,000. Assume, furthermore, that this firm has two choices:

1. It can borrow $500,000, using a short-term loan, for the entire year, and pay 10% on the loan.

2. It can borrow $300,000, using a short-term loan, for the entire year, and pay an annual rate of 10% on this loan. In addition, it can arrange a line of credit, with a rate that is expected to be 2% higher than the prevailing prime rate (currently at 8%). The firm will be required to maintain a compensating balance amounting to 20% of the loan. Based on past history, the firm expects to raise $200,000 in funds from the line of credit in 6 out of the 12 months of the year.

The expected interest cost on the two options can be estimated as follows:

$$\text{Expected Interest Cost from Option 1} = \$500,000 * .10 = \$50,000$$
$$\text{Expected Interest Cost from Option 2} = \$300,000 * .10 + \$250,000 * (6/12) * .10$$
$$= \$30,000 + \$12,500 = \$42,500$$

Note that the firm has to borrow $250,000 in order to have access to $200,000 because of the need to maintain a compensating balance (20% of $250,000).

Commercial Paper

Some large companies with excellent credit records can raise short-term financing using *commercial paper*. Commercial paper generally has a maturity of less than six months and is sold on a discounted basis (like Treasury bills). Thus, an issue of six-month commercial paper sold at a discount of 3% at issue has a yield of

$$\text{Annualized Rate on Commercial Paper} = \left(\frac{1}{(1 - \text{Discount})}\right)^{1/n} = (1/.97)^2 = 6.28\%$$

where n is the maturity of the commercial paper stated as a fraction of a year.

Commercial paper carries rates that are generally lower than comparable bank loans, but its use is restricted to only a few firms, and it carries a large fixed cost in terms of issue, which makes it economical only if the firm raises large amounts in short-term financing. For instance, the financing arms of automobile (Ford, GMAC) and appliance companies (GE Capital), which have the advantages of high credit ratings and substantial financing needs, are heavy users of commercial paper. The buyers of commercial paper tend to be other companies with substantial excess cash, and portfolio managers who want to invest short term and at low risk.

Asset-Backed Borrowing and Securities

A firm with substantial accounts receivable can borrow on its basis from a bank. Alternatively, it can sell the accounts receivable at a discount to another entity, usually a bank, which then takes on the task of collecting the accounts receivable and bearing the risk of bad debt. This is called *factoring*. The size of the discount will increase with the perceived default risk in the accounts receivable and the administrative costs associated with the collection. Similarly, firms with high inventory can borrow on its basis and use the funds to meet immediate needs.

In recent years, asset-backed securities have made it easier for firms with substantial current assets to raise funds, using these assets as backing. Thus, a financial service firm with substantial credit card dues might reduce its working capital exposure by issuing bonds backed by credit cards.

CONCLUSION

This chapter covers an important aspect of financial management—the management and financing of working capital needs. In the process, we have developed the following points:

- The net working capital of a firm—the difference between current assets and current liabilities—represents an investment for the firm. An increase in working capital will reduce the firm's cash flows, and a decrease will increase cash flows.

- The tradeoff on working capital is straightforward: increasing working capital reduces liquidity risk and can also increase growth (through looser credit and higher inventory), but it creates a cash outflow; the net effect can be either positive or negative. The optimum working capital investment is the one that maximizes firm value.

- The amount a firm should hold in cash or cash equivalents is determined by the tradeoff between having the additional liquidity to meet transactions, speculative or precautionary motives, and the interest foregone by holding cash.

- Similarly, firms have to decide on inventory policy by trading off the higher sales and lower ordering costs that arise from having a larger inventory against the higher carrying costs that follow. The optimal inventory policy for the firm can be determined if the information on ordering and carrying cost is available.

- In offering credit, firms have to trade off the higher sales and interest income that may accrue from loosening credit against the possibility of default.

- On the other side of the equation, firms should try to use trade credit to finance some of their current asset needs, but only if the cost of using trade credit is lower than the cost of capital.

QUESTIONS AND PROBLEMS

1. The balance sheet for Ford Motor Company as of December 31, 1994 (in millions) is shown on pg. 383:

The firm had revenues of $154,951 million in 1994 and cost of goods sold of $103,817 million.

   a. Estimate the current ratio.
   b. Estimate the quick ratio.
   c. Estimate the accounts receivable and inventory turnover ratios.
   d. Estimate the required financing period.

2. You are analyzing the balance sheet on pg. 383 for Bed, Bath and Beyond, a retail firm that sells home furnishings, from February 26, 1995 (in millions):

The firm had revenues of $440.3 million in 1994 and cost of goods sold of $249.2 million.

   a. Estimate the current ratio.
   b. Estimate the quick ratio.
   c. Estimate the accounts receivable and inventory turnover ratios.
   d. Estimate the required financing period.

3. Assume, in the previous problem, that Bed, Bath and Beyond was able to halve its inventory requirement by adopting better inventory policies. Estimate the following:

   a. The investment in working capital, after the change.

Ford

Assets		Liabilities	
Cash	$19,927	Accounts Payable	$11,635
Receivables	61,469	Debt due within one year	36,240
Inventory	10,128	Other Current Liabilities	2,721
Current Assets	*91,524*	*Current Liabilities*	*50,596*
Fixed Assets	45,586	Short-Term Debt	36,200
		Long-Term Debt	37,490
		Equity	12,824
Total Assets	137,110	Total Liabilities	137,110

Bed, Bath & Beyond

Assets		Liabilities	
Cash	$6.5	Accounts Payable	27.5
Receivables	3.1	Other Current Liabilities	18.6
Inventory	108.4		
Current Assets	*118.0*	*Current Liabilities*	*46.1*
Fixed Assets	53.8	Long-Term Debt	16.8
		Equity	108.9
Total Assets	171.8	Total Liabilities	171.8

b. The savings in cash flow that would accrue from this change.

How would you estimate the increase in firm value that would arise from the better inventory policy, if revenues at the firm were expected to grow 6% a year forever, and the firm had a cost of capital of 11%?

4. You have been asked to estimate the optimal working capital, as a percentage of revenues, for an auto-parts manufacturing firm that currently maintains a net working capital of 10% of revenues. The firm currently has revenues of $100 million and after-tax operating income of $10 million, and it expects the latter to grow 5% a year in perpetuity. The current cost of capital is 11%. The following table provides estimates of growth and costs of capital at different levels of working capital, ranging from 0% to 100%

a. Estimate the value of the firm at the current working capital ratio.

b. Estimate the optimal working capital policy for this firm.

Working Capital as % of Revenue	Expected Growth (%)	Cost of Capital (%)
0	4.50	10.90
10	5.00	11.00
20	5.20	11.11
30	5.35	11.23
40	5.45	11.36
50	5.50	11.50
60	5.54	11.65
70	5.55	11.80

Working Capital as % of Revenue	Expected Growth (%)	Cost of Capital (%)
80	5.55	11.95
90	5.55	12.10
100	5.55	12.35

c. What would the optimal working capital proportion for this firm be if the cost of capital were unaffected by the changes in working capital?

5. You are advising a small retailing firm that is considering a significant change in inventory policy. The firm currently has inventory of $20 million on revenues of $100 million; it had net after-tax operating income of $5 million. The firm is considering reducing its inventory by 40%, but revenues might be affected adversely by the change. If the expected growth rate in the firm's revenues and operating income is 5%, and the cost of capital is 12%, how much would the revenues have to drop for this change in inventory to negatively affect value? Assume the working capital is entirely inventory.

6. The following table summarizes working capital and revenue for the following firms in the chemical industry, as well as information on betas, expected growth, and size.

a. Estimate the average and standard deviation in working capital ratios across these firms.

b. What proportion of the differences in net working capital investments across firms can you explain using the information you have been provided in the table?

Firm	Net Working Capital	Revenues	Expected Beta	Expected Growth (%)	Market Value
Arco Chemical	$579	$3,423	0.80	13.00	$4,517
Dow Chemical	2,075	20,015	1.25	16.00	19,398
Du Pont	3,543	39,333	1.00	17.50	44,946
Georgia Gulf	127	955	1.70	26.50	1,386
Lyondell Petro	264	3,857	1.10	23.50	2,080
Monsanto	2,948	8,272	1.10	11.50	9,296
Olin Corp.	749	2,658	1.00	22.00	1,205
Sterling Chemical	21	701	0.95	43.00	724
Union Carbide	329	4,865	1.30	16.00	4,653

c. How would you use this information to estimate the optimal working capital as a percentage of revenues for an Monsanto?

7. You have been provided with the current assets and current liabilities of a retailing firm each quarter for the last five years, together with the revenues in each quarter:

    a. Based on this information, estimate the permanent, seasonal, and transitory components of current assets.

    b. How would you propose financing these current assets? Why?

Period	Current Assets	Current Liabilities	Revenues
1990–1	$300	$150	$3,000
1990–2	325	160	3,220
1990–3	350	180	3,450
1990–4	650	300	6,300
1991–1	370	170	3,550
1991–2	400	200	4,100
1991–3	420	220	4,350
1991–4	755	380	7,750
1992–1	450	220	4,500
1992–2	480	240	4,750
1992–3	515	265	5,200
1992–4	880	460	9,000
1993–1	550	260	5,400
1993–2	565	285	5,600
1993–3	585	300	5,900
1993–4	1,010	500	10,000
1994–1	635	330	6,500
1994–2	660	340	6,750
1994–3	665	340	6,900

8. You have been asked to estimate the effect of float on a small manufacturing company. Each day the company receives about $5 million in checks from customers and takes four days to clear these checks. It pays out $4 million in checks, and the recipients generally take five days to clear these checks. If the firm faces an interest rate of 10%,

    a. Estimate the processing float for the company.

    b. Estimate the disbursement float for the company.

    c. Estimate the net float for the firm.

    d. How much would the net float change if the firm can reduce the number of days it takes to clear checks to three days?

9. You have been asked to estimate the optimal cash balance for a firm that

- Uses up $25 million in cash, at a steady rate, on an annual basis.
- Could earn interest at an annualized rate of 12%, if its funds were not tied up in a cash balance
- Spends $100 every time it has to convert interest-bearing securities into cash.

    a. Estimate the optimal using the Baumol Model.

    b. How would your answer change if the firm were able to earn 3% on cash (i.e., it uses an interest-bearing checking account)?

10. Assume that interest rates increase significantly from current levels. What effect would you expect this change to have on optimal cash balances? Why?

11. Miller Electronics has used the Baumol Model to estimate its optimal cash balance to be $1 million. Its opportunity cost is 10%, and there is a cost of $125 every time marketable securities have to be converted into cash. Estimate the weekly cash usage rate.

12. A firm that has a standard deviation in daily cash flows of $12,000, pays $75 every time it buys or sells securities, and faces a daily interest rate of .0125%

is trying to estimate the upper and lower limits for its cash balance.

a.   Estimate the spread using the Miller–Orr Model.

b.   What will be the average cash balance?

c.   How would your answers change if there were a minimum cash balance of $50,000?

13.   How would the spread and average cash balance you computed in the previous problem change if the standard deviation doubled? Provide an intuitive rationale for your findings.

14.   You are analyzing the inventory policy of HighTech Retail, a retailer of stereo systems. You collect the following information:

- The annual expected sales, in units, is 18,000 units.
- The cost of placing a new order is $1,000, and it takes a month to receive delivery.
- The interest rate (foregone on inventory) is 10%, and each stereo costs about $1,000. Other storage and administrative costs, on an annualized basis, will amount to $100 per unit.

a.   Estimate the optimal order quantity for this firm.

b.   When would you reorder units for this firm? What is your safety inventory?

c.   Estimate the average inventory the firm will maintain.

15.   An electronics retail firm that has traditionally required customers to pay cash for items is considering introducing credit sales. The firm currently has revenues of $30 million and operating income of $15 million. Without the credit sales, the growth in earnings and cash flows is expected to be 5%, whereas the cost of capital is 12%. With the introduction of credit sales, there is expected to be an increase in revenues of $5 million, from $30 million to $35 million. The cost of goods sold will remain at 50% of revenues, and the firm faces a tax rate of 40%. The accounts receivable will be 10% of total sales. The cost of capital will remain unchanged.

a.   Estimate the cash flows associated with introduction of credit sales.

b.   Estimate the net present value of the credit sales decision.

16.   You are considering offering your customers a 2% discount if they pay cash on their purchases within 10 days; if they do not pay cash, the balance will be due within 50 days. The trade credit deal is 2/10 net 50.

a.   Estimate the implied interest rate (annualized) being charged credit customers.

b.   Estimate the actual interest rate earned if customers take 100 days to make payment instead of 50 days.

17.   A firm that has an average monthly working capital requirement of $10 million is evaluating two options for financing this requirement:

- It can borrow $12 million long term to cover not only the average requirement but also any seasonal and random requirements that may arise. The interest rate on the borrowing is 9%.
- It can borrow $8 million long term to cover the permanent component of working capital and use a $4 million line of credit to cover any seasonal or random changes, which are expected (based on past history) to occur in 4 out of the 12 months of the year. The line of credit will be at 1.5% above the prime rate (which is currently 6.5%), but it requires that the firm maintain a compensating balance of 20%.

a.   Estimate the interest cost associated with the first option.

b.   Estimate the interest cost associated with the second option.

18.   Calculate the amount in average accounts payable if you are given the following information:

$$\text{required financing period} = 40 \text{ days}$$
$$\text{sales} = \$150,000$$
$$\text{average accounts receivable} = \$20,548$$
$$\text{cost of goods sold} = 50\% \text{ of sales}$$
$$\text{average inventory} = \$4,110$$
$$\text{purchases} = 60\% \text{ of sales}$$

19.   Your company has annual sales of $100 million. Almost all of them are credit sales. The current credit policy allows customers to mail their checks 30 days after sales are made. It is found that on average customers mail their checks 36 days after the sales and it takes another 7 days before the checks are processed, deposited and collected. The company is considering the use of a new collection system which will cost the company $65,753 a year to operate. How many days of float should the new collection system be able to reduce in order to make it cost effective. Assume that the cost of capital is 12%.

20.   ATM machines are widely used in U.S.A. for the convenience of use. Baumol model can be used to determine the optimal cash balance a person should hold. Suppose that the annual cash usage rate is $1,200, annual interest rate is 3% and it costs

$1.00 for using ATM machine to get cash each time. Calculate the optimal cash level.

21. A company is considering whether to take a price discount of 1% in purchase of raw materials. The discount would be given if each order is 2,000 units or larger. Its annual demand in units is 16,000, ordering cost per order is $100 and carrying cost per unit is $12.8. The original price per unit before discount is $100. Should the company take the discount?

22. A well known company always pays on day 35 even though its supplier has a credit policy of 2/10, net 30. If the average accounts payable balance is $10

m and its cost of short-term borrowing is 10% per year, how much can the company save a year if it pays on day 10 and takes the discount?

23. Your company is negotiating with Citizens Bank to get a one-year loan. The bank offers two options. One loan has interest rate 10% with quarterly payment of interests and repayment of principal at maturity. The other loan has 9% interest rate but all the interests have to be paid when the loan is taken out.

a. What are the effective interest rates for both types of loans?

b. Which loan is less expensive?

PART THREE

THE FINANCING DECISION

Of the three decisions covered in corporate finance, the investment decision is arguably the most critical, especially in the growth stage of a firm's life cycle. As firms mature and growth opportunities become less abundant, the question of how projects should be financed becomes more critical. In this section, we look at financing options and the financing decision in more detail. In Chapter 15, we consider the financing choices firms have to make in raising funds in both private and public markets. We also examine historical patterns in financing. In Chapter 16, we evaluate some lessons that can be learned from studies of market efficiency by firms considering what types of financing to use and when to use them. In Chapter 17, we establish the basic tradeoff on the use of debt—the tax benefits and discipline that debt creates against the bankruptcy risk and loss of flexibility that may flow from using too much debt. We also examine the specific conditions under which debt is irrelevant. In Chapter 18, we introduce several practical approaches that can be used to determine the optimal debt ratio for a firm, and consider their limitations. In Chapter 19, we provide a framework for determining the right kind of financing for a firm—short term or long term, fixed rate or floating rate—based on its asset mix.

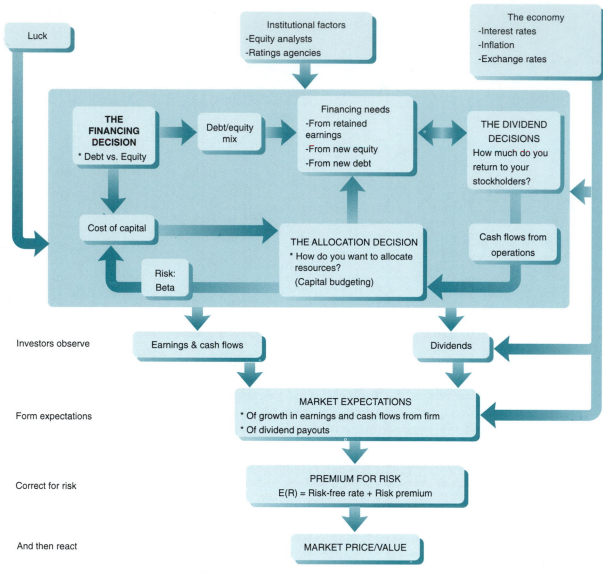

The financing decision in the big picture

CHAPTER 15

CAPITAL STRUCTURE: AN OVERVIEW OF FINANCING CHOICES

Every business needs financing to keep existing projects going and to take on new projects. This chapter explores the financing choices that firms have, both in terms of the types of securities that they can use to raise the funds and in terms of the process by which they can issue these securities. In the process, we examine the following questions:

- What are the fundamental characteristics of debt and equity, and what are the different types of debt and equity securities? What are hybrid securities, and why do firms issue them?

- How do private and public firms differ in terms of their access to new financing? How and why would a private firm become a publicly traded firm?

- What is the difference between internal and external equity financing?

- How have firms used different types of financing over time?

- What are the ways in which securities can be issued? Why do some firms use private placements or rights issues?

THE CHOICES: TYPES OF FINANCING

In this section, we will explore the types of financing that are available to both privately owned businesses and publicly traded firms. We will begin with a discussion of a broad distinction between debt and equity, and then look at a range of financing vehicles available within each of these categories. We then examine a range of securities that share some characteristics with debt and some with equity, and are therefore called **hybrid securities.**

Hybrid Security: This refers to any security that shares some characteristics of debt and some characteristics of equity.

The Continuum Between Debt and Equity

Although the distinction between debt and equity is often made in terms of bonds and stocks, its roots lie in the nature of the cash-flow claims of each type of financing. The first distinction is that a *debt claim* entitles the holder to a contracted set of cash flows (usually interest and principal payments), whereas an *equity claim* entitles the holder to any residual cash flows left over after meeting all other promised claims. While this remains the fundamental difference, other distinctions have arisen, partly as a result of the tax code and partly as a consequence of legal developments.

The second distinction, which is a logical outgrowth of the nature of the cash-flow claims (contractual versus residual), is that debt has a prior claim both on both cash flows on a period-to-period basis, (for interest and principal payments), and on the assets of the firm, (in the case of liquidation). Third, the tax laws have generally treated interest expenses, which accrue to debtholders, very differently and often much more advantageously than dividends or other cash flows that accrue to equity. In the United States, for instance, interest expenses have been tax deductible and thus create tax savings, whereas dividend payments have to be made out of after-tax cash flows. Fourth, debt has a fixed maturity date, at which point the principal is due, whereas equity generally has an infinite life.

A Financing Checklist Some new securities, at first sight, are difficult to categorize as either debt or equity. To check where on the spectrum between straight debt and straight equity, these securities fall, answer the following questions:

1. *Are the payments on the securities contractual or residual?*
   - If contractual, it is closer to debt.
   - If residual, it is closer to equity.
2. *Are the payments tax deductible?*
   - If yes, it is closer to debt.
   - If no, it is closer to equity.
3. *Do the cash flows on these security have a high priority or a low priority if the firm is in financial trouble?*
   - If it has high priority, it is closer to debt.
   - If it has low priority, it is closer to equity.
4. *Does the security have a fixed life?*
   - If yes, it is closer to debt.
   - If no, it is closer to equity.
5. *Does the owner of the security get a share of the control of management of the firm?*
   - If no, it is closer to debt.
   - If yes, it is closer to equity.

Finally, equity investors, by virtue of their claim on the residual cash flows of the firm, are generally given the bulk of or all of the control of the management of the firm. Debt investors, on the other hand, play a much more passive role in management, exercising, at most, veto power over significant financial decisions.[1] These differences are summarized in Figure 15.1.

To summarize, debt is defined as any financing vehicle that is a contractual claim on the cash flows of the firm (and not a function of its operating performance), creates tax deductible payments, has a fixed life, and has priority in both operating periods and in

---

[1]The veto power is usually exercised through covenants in bond agreements.

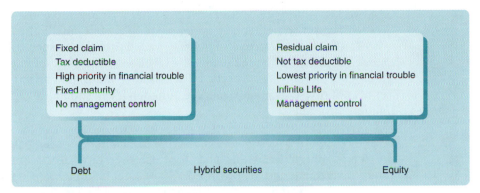

Figure 15.1   Debt versus equity

bankruptcy. Conversely, equity is defined as any financing vehicle that is a residual claim on the cash flows of the firm, does not create a tax advantage from its payments, has an infinite life, does not have priority in bankruptcy, and provides management control to the owner. Any security that shares characteristics with both is a hybrid security.

EQUITY

Although most people think of equity in terms of common stock, the equity claim can take a variety of forms, depending partly on whether the firm is a privately owned firm or a publicly traded firm, and partly on the firm's growth and risk characteristics.

Equity Choices for Private Firms

Private firms have fewer choices available than do publicly traded firms, since they cannot issue securities to raise equity. Consequently, they have to depend either on the owner or a private entity, usually a venture capitalist, to bring in the equity needed to keep the business operating and expanding.

Owner's equity   Most businesses, including the most successful companies of our time, such as Microsoft and Wal-Mart, started off as small businesses with one or a few individuals providing the seed money and plowing back the earnings of the firm into the businesses. These funds, brought in by the owners of the company, are referred to as the *owner's equity* and provide the basis for the growth and eventual success of the businesses. Although owner's equity may not be **securitized** like common stock, its counterpart in publicly traded firms, the two sources share several characteristics. First, both entitle the holder to the residual cash flows of the business. The difference is that this cash flow is often funneled through a manager as dividends in publicly traded firms, whereas the claim is much more direct for privately owned firms. Second, the cash flows to equity are not tax deductible for both private and publicly traded firms. Third, lenders to the firm have prior claims on the operating cash flows and the assets of the firm in both cases. Finally, in both cases, the holders of the equity maintain management control of the firm, although the control may be more indirect for publicly traded firms.

Securitized: This refers to the conversion of an asset into a security or securities that can be traded on a financial market.

Two key differences exist between owner's equity and common stock in a publicly traded firms. The first is that owner's equity is generally limited to the wealth of the owner; the common stock in a publicly traded firm has no such constraint, because new stock can always be issued to investors. The second is that common stock is traded and thus has a market value attached to it, based on the traded price. Owner's equity is generally not priced in a public market, although it can still be valued using traditional valuation techniques.

Venture capital As small businesses succeed and grow they typically run into a funding constraint whereby the funds to which they have access are insufficient to cover their investment and growth needs. Some may be able to go public at this stage and relieve this constraint by issuing common stock in financial markets. To do so, however, the business has to be large enough and have sufficient appeal to investors to be offered to the public. For example, Netscape Communications, a relatively small company providing access to the Internet, with revenues of $16.6 million, was able to go public in 1995 because of the perception that it was poised for very high growth. Many private businesses find themselves unable to take advantage of this option to raise equity, however. For these businesses, an alternative is to raise equity financing from private investors or funds in the form of **venture capital.**

Venture Capital: This is usually equity capital provided to a private firm by an investor or investors, in exchange for a share of the ownership of the firm.

A *venture capitalist* provides equity financing to small and often risky businesses in return for a share of the ownership of the firm. The proportion of the firm that ends up with the venture capitalist will depend on a number of factors:

1. *Amount of venture capital financing:* At the minimum, the venture capitalist will demand the venture capital contribution as a proportion of the firm value. If the venture capital provided is $2 million, for instance, and the estimated value of the firm is $10 million, the proportion of ownership that will be demanded as an absolute minimum is 20%.

2. *Alternative sources of funding:* To the extent that the business can raise the funds from other sources, its bargaining position with the venture capitalist will be stronger, and it may be able to keep the venture capitalist's share down to a small premium over the minimum specified above. If a business has no other options available to raise the equity financing, however, its bargaining position is considerably weaker, and the only competition it can hope for is between venture capitalists. In such cases, the owner of the business will have to give up a disproportionate share of the ownership to get the required funding.

Generally speaking, the capacity to raise funds from alternative sources or to go public will increase with the size of the firm and decrease with the uncertainty about its future prospects. Thus, smaller and riskier businesses are more likely to seek venture capital and are also more likely to be asked to give up a greater share of the value of the firm when receiving the venture capital.

Note that the act of seeking and receiving venture capital is voluntary, and both sides enter into the relationship with the hope of gaining. The business gains access to funds that would not have been available to it otherwise; these funds, in turn, might enable the firm to bridge the gap until it can go public. The venture capitalist might also contribute management and organizational skills to the venture and provide the credibility needed for the business to go out and raise more financing. Finally, the venture capitalist might provide the know-how ultimately needed to go public.

The venture capitalist gains as well. If the venture capitalist picks the right businesses to fund and provides good management skills and advice in the aftermath, there can be large returns on the initial investment. Although the venture capitalist may reap returns from the private business itself, the largest payoff occurs if and when the business goes public and the venture capitalist is able to convert his or her stake into cash at the market price. Barry, Muscarella, Peavey, and Vetsuypens (1990) note, however, that venture capitalists do not usually sell shares at the initial public offering, choosing instead to play a more active role in management.

It is also interesting to note the change in composition of the typical venture capitalist, at least in the United States. Venture capital was initially provided by wealthy individuals and small venture capital firms. Recently, however, pension funds and institutional investors have become more important players, setting aside a small portion of their vast resources explicitly for venture capital investing. For instance, both Citicorp and Chemical Bank have venture capital arms that fund start-up and growth companies.

☐ Concept
  Check

> Venture capitalists often make investments in a large number of private companies in a variety of businesses. How would this affect the way in which venture capitalists evaluate their investments?

Equity Choices for Publicly Traded Firms

Once a firm decides to go public, and issue securities in financial markets, it has a number of options for raising equity, including common stock, warrants, contingent value rights, and other equity innovations.

Common stock   The conventional way for a publicly traded firm to raise equity is to issue common stock at a price that the market is willing to pay for it. For a newly listed company, this price is estimated by the issuing entity (such as an investment banker); for an existing company, it is based on the current market price. In some cases, the common stock issued by a company is uniform; that is, each share receives a proportional share of both the cash flows (such as dividends) and the voting rights. In other cases, different classes of common stock will provide different cash flows and voting rights.

Warrants   In recent years, firms have started looking at equity alternatives to common stock. One alternative used successfully by the Japanese companies in the late 1980s involved **warrants**—the holders received the right to buy shares in the company at a fixed price in return for paying for the warrants up front. Because their value is derived from the price of the underlying common stock, warrants have to be treated as another form of equity. We will return to the issue of how best to price a warrant later in this book.

Warrants: A warrant is a security issued by a company which provides the holder with the right to buy a share of stock in the company at a fixed price during the life of the warrant.

Why might a firm use warrants rather than common stock to raise equity? We can think of several reasons. Warrants are priced based on the implied volatility assigned to the underlying stock; the greater the volatility, the greater the value. To the degree that the market overestimates the firm's volatility, the firm may gain by using warrants and option-like securities. Moreover, warrants, by themselves, create no financial obligations at the time of the issue. Consequently, issuing warrants is a good way for a high-growth firm to raise funds, especially when current cash flows are low or non-existent. Finally, for financial officers who are sensitive to the dilution created by issuing common stock, warrants seem to provide the best of both worlds—they do not create any new additional shares currently, while they raise equity investment funds for current use.

Contingent value rights Contingent value rights provide investors with the right to sell stocks for a fixed price, and thus derive their value from the volatility of the stock and the desire on the part of investors to protect themselves against losses. *Put options,* which are traded on the option exchanges, give their holders a similar right to sell the underlying stock at a fixed price. There are two primary differences between contingent value rights and puts. First, the proceeds from the contingent value rights sales go to the firm, whereas those from the sale of listed puts go to private parties. Second, **contingent value rights** tend to be much more long term than typical listed puts.

Contingent Value Rights: A contingent value right (CVR) provides the holder with the right to sell a share of stock in the underlying company at a fixed price during the life of the right.

A firm may choose to issue contingent value rights primarily because it believes it is significantly undervalued by the market. In such a scenario, the firm may offer contingent value rights to take advantage of its belief and to provide a signal to the market of the undervaluation. Contingent value rights are also useful if the market is overestimating volatility, and the put price reflects this misestimated volatility. Finally, the presence of contingent value rights as insurance may attract new investors to the market for the common stock.

Concept Check Both warrants and contingent value rights are equity options. Why might some firms use warrants and others contingent value rights?

DEBT

The clear alternative to using equity, which is a residual claim, is to borrow money. This option both creates a fixed obligation to make cash-flow payments and provides the lender with prior claims if the firm is in financial trouble.

Bank Debt

Historically, the primary source of borrowed money for all private firms and many publicly traded firms have been banks, with the interest rates on the debt based on the perceived risk of the borrower. Bank debt provides the borrower with several advantages. It can be used for borrowing relatively small amounts of money; in contrast, bond issues thrive on economies of scale, with larger issues having lower costs. Moreover, if the company is neither well known nor widely followed, bank debt provides a convenient framework to convey information to the lender which will help in both pricing and evaluating the loan. The presence of hundreds of investors in bond issues makes this both costly and infeasible if bonds are issued as the primary vehicle for debt. Finally, in order to issue bonds, firms have to submit to being rated. The added dynamic of ratings agencies' screening decisions, in addition to the equity investors, may create conflicts between the two, which the manager then has to resolve. In contrast, firms have to deal only with the lending bank when they take on bank debt, which may be simpler to do in some cases and minimizes the amount of information they have to make public.[2]

Concept Check

> A firm has a choice of taking on bank debt or issuing bonds. Under what conditions will it take on bank debt?

Bonds

For larger publicly traded firms, an alternative to bank debt is to issue bonds. Generally speaking, bond issues have several advantages. Bonds usually carry more favorable financing terms than equivalent bank debt, largely because risk is shared by a larger number of financial market investors. Bond issues also might provide a chance for the issuer to add on special features that could not be added on to bank debt. For instance, bonds can be convertible into common stock or have commodity options attached to them. In this section, we examine a variety of choices the firm has to make when anticipating borrowing money.

Choices on maturity   Corporate borrowing in financial markets can be either short or long term. Corporate borrowing in financial markets with a maturity less than one year is classified as commercial paper and is generally sold at a discount on face value, like Treasury bills. Only the largest and safest companies have the capacity to issue commercial paper. Most corporate bonds are issued with maturities ranging from the medium to the long term. Although the conventional wisdom holds that financial markets are not receptive to corporate bonds with maturities greater than 15 or 20 years, companies like Disney and Boeing have issued bonds with maturities of 50 to 100 years in recent years.

The question of what maturity the bonds that a company is planning to issue should have cannot be answered without looking at the kinds of assets and projects that are being financed with the borrowing. In general, projects and assets with long lives should be financed with long maturity debt. This issue will be examined in more depth in Chapter 19.

Fixed versus floating rate debt   Another decision the firm issuing the bonds has to make concerns the interest paid on the debt. The conventional straight bond, which was the primary vehicle for long-term borrowing by companies until the 1970s, had a fixed coupon rate that did not change during the life of the bond. In the aftermath of the higher inflation and greater interest rate volatility of the last two decades, however, more firms have started issuing bonds or borrowing from banks, with floating interest rates, whereby the interest paid may vary from period to period, depending on the market rate at which it is indexed, such as the **LIBOR** rate or the Treasury bill rate.

LIBOR (London Interbank Borrowing Rate):   This is a short-term rate at which banks can lend to and borrow from each other on an overnight basis. It is used as the index for many floating rate instruments.

---

[2]This is especially true if the bank is a local bank and knows the firm well. This knowledge may allow the bank to grant more freedom to the borrowing firm.

Floating rate bonds insulate bond values from changing interest rates while linking up the firm's interest payments to the level of market interest rates. This clearly is an advantage when the operating cash flows of the firm increase and decrease with interest rates; this is more likely to happen when changes in inflation are driving the changes in interest rates, and the firm's own cash flows are positively related to inflation. The other advantage of issuing floating rate bonds is that they provide a firm that is unsure about the life of its projects or about its future investment prospects with a way to buy time. The firm can issue floating rate bonds until it has a clearer idea of its investment options and then switch to fixed rate bonds with maturities that match up to the project life.

Choices on security   Lenders have a prior claim over equity investors on the assets of the firm, but in the event of bankruptcy or liquidation, not all lenders have equal claims. In many firms, the bonds with the lowest claim on the assets are *unsecured bonds,* which are backed up not by specific assets of the firm, but by its general credit. These unsecured bonds are called **debentures**, if they have a maturity greater than 15 years, or *notes,* if they have a maturity less than 15 years. Although these bonds are backed up only by the earning power of the firm, they usually have a *negative pledge clause,* which prevents their claim on the assets from being superseded by future debt that might be taken on by the firm. Unsecured debt yields the borrower the greatest flexibility in terms of using its debt capacity, but it is also viewed as riskier by lenders, leading to higher interest rates.

Debentures: These are bonds, secured by the general credit of a firm, with a maturity greater than 15 years.

The next set of securities are unsecured securities with claims on assets that are subordinated to the claims of specified senior debt on the same assets. These unsecured bonds are called *subordinated debentures;* they are viewed favorably by firms, for they provide the opportunity to issue debt without affecting the firm's senior claimholders. The buyers of the subordinated debentures recognize that their cash flows can be claimed by senior debtholders in the case of default; accordingly, they demand a higher interest rate on them. Another category of unsecured bonds, wherein the interest payments on the bond are due only to the extent that the firm makes income are called **income bonds.** Income bonds typically have a cumulative feature—interest is cumulated and paid when earnings are realized in the future. These bonds are also riskier and should carry a higher interest rate.

Income Bonds: These are bonds on which interest is paid only when the firm makes income.

Secured debt occupies the top rung in terms of priority, in case of default, because specific assets are pledged as security on the debt. In the event of default, these assets provide the basis for claims made by these debtholders. Furthermore, the firm cannot replace or sell these assets without the agreement of the secured bondholders, thereby reducing the firm's flexibility to make investment or divestiture decisions. In return, however, the firm is able to reduce the interest it pays on its debt, because the security is perceived to be less risky. One special case of secured debt is a *mortgage bond,* which is secured with real property, such as land or buildings. Another case is a *collateral bond,* which is secured in the form of marketable securities. A company that has accumulated

$100 million in government bonds, for example, may use this portfolio as the basis for a collateral bond, secured by the bonds.

Choices on currencies   Until recently, firms issued debt in their domestic currency and often only to domestic investors, for two reasons: (1) foreign operations accounted for a relatively small proportion of overall revenues; and (2) only domestic investors had the information necessary to assess the default risk of firms. In the last two decades, however, three trends have stimulated a move away from these restrictions. First, foreign operations account for a much larger proportion of the business mix for most firms; as a result, both revenues and earnings are influenced by currency rate movements. Second, the dissemination of information on both the health and the financial standing of firms internationally has enabled firms to cross borders and issue securities in other markets. In addition, ratings agencies have also expanded their reach beyond the U.S. market and started assigning bond ratings for companies in other countries. Third, firms have become more sophisticated in their consideration and management of exchange rate risk and tax liabilities through the structuring of their liabilities.

Choices on repayment   Bonds have fixed maturities, at the end of which they have to be repaid. Firms set up a variety of arrangements to facilitate repayment. Some firms set up *sinking funds,* whereby a set amount is set aside each year to allow for the repayment of bonds; the bonds that are retired are usually picked at random among the outstanding bonds. Although this creates an obligation for the firm, its advantages include lower perceived risk and lower interest rates on the bonds. Some firms have *serial bonds,* whereby a percentage of the outstanding bonds mature each year, and the maturity is specified on the serial bond. This allows investors to choose the bond maturity that best fits their needs. Finally, some firms have *balloon payment debt,* whereby no repayment is made during the life of the bond.

Choices on special features   When issuing bonds, companies can add on special features designed to make them less risky to the issuers or more attractive to the buyers. One of the more common features is *callability,* whereby the issuer can call back the bonds at any time before maturity, if a premium over the face value is paid. By making bonds callable, the issuer is no longer locked into making high interest payments if interest rates decline; instead, the high-rate bonds can be called back, and lower rate bonds can be issued in their place. Understandably, these bonds are not as attractive as noncallable bonds to buyers, who pay a lower price (and charge a higher rate).

In the case of floating rate bonds, companies often add *caps* and *floors,* with caps preventing interest rates from moving above specified maximum rates, and floors preventing them from falling below minimum rates, to ensure that both the company and the buyers of the bonds have some protection if the rates move outside these limits.

Debt Innovations

The past two decades have seen an explosion in new features added on to bonds. Some, such as floating rates and caps and floors, arose as a consequence of the high inflation and interest rate volatility that characterized the late 1970s. Some of these features take advantage of the better understanding that issuers (or their agents) have of how to price options. Table 15.1 summarizes some of the most important innovations, as well as the rationale for their introduction.

These innovations provide both companies and buyers with more options and the capacity to tailor bonds to their specific needs. They also carry a downside, however. The

Table 15.1 INNOVATIONS IN BOND MARKET		
Innovation	**Description/Year Introduced**	**Rationale for Innovation**
Floating rate loans	Interest rate varies with index. [introduced in 1973–74]	To avoid volatility in inflation and interest rates
Puttable bonds	Bondholders can put bond back to firm, and get face value, under specified events. [introduced in 1976]	To protect bondholder interests
Convertible/exchangeable floating rate notes	Floating rate note can be converted into equity. [introduced in 1978]	To provide flexibility to buyer of bond
Extendable bonds	Life of the bond can be extended at the option of the issuer. [introduced in 1980]	To provide more flexibility to the issuer
Caps and floors	They limit interest rate movements on a floating rate loan. [introduced in 1983]	To limit risk to issuer and buyer
Swaps	Bonds can be exchanged for bonds with different characteristics (fixed to floating, different currency). [introduced in 1983]	To allow firms to alter their financing mix
Reverse floating rate notes	Interest rate varies inversely with an index; as index rate goes up, rate on bond goes down. [introduced in 1985]	To increase duration and price sensitivity of bond
Swaptions	Option on a swap [introduced in 1989–90]	To allow firms to buy options to do swaps

special features, especially when combined, become more and more difficult to value and keep track of over time.

HYBRID SECURITIES

In summary, equity represents a residual claim on the cash flows and assets of the firm and is generally associated with management control. Debt, on the other hand, represents a fixed claim on the cash flows and assets of the firm, and is usually not associated with management control. A number of securities do not fall neatly into either of these two categories; rather, they share some characteristics with equity and some with debt. These securities are called *hybrid securities*.

Convertible Debt

A **convertible bond** is a bond that can be converted into a predetermined number of shares, at the discretion of the bondholder. Although it generally does not pay to convert at the time of the bond issue, conversion becomes a more attractive option as stock prices increase. Firms generally add conversions options to bonds to lower the interest rate paid on the bonds.

Convertible Bond: This is a bond that can be converted into equity at a rate that is specified as part of the debt agreement (conversion rate).

The conversion option In a typical convertible bond, the bondholder is given the option to convert the bond into a specified number of shares of stock. The *conversion ratio* measures the number of shares of stock for which each bond may be exchanged. Stated differently, the *market conversion value* is the current value of the shares for which the bonds can be exchanged. The *conversion premium* is the excess of the bond value over the conversion value of the bond.

Thus, a convertible bond with a par value of $1,000, which is convertible into 50 shares of stock, has a conversion ratio of 50. The conversion ratio can also be used to compute a conversion price—the par value divided by the conversion ratio—yielding a conversion price of $20. If the current stock price is $25, the market conversion value is $1,250 (50 * $25). If the convertible bond is trading at $1,300, the conversion premium is $50. The effect of including a conversion option in a bond is illustrated in Figure 15.2.

Determinants of value The conversion option is a call option on the underlying stock; its value is therefore determined by the variables that affect call option values: the underlying stock price, the conversion ratio (which determines the strike price), the life of the convertible bond, the variance in the stock price, and the level of interest rates. We will explore the use of option pricing models to value the conversion option in Chapter 28. Like a call option, the value of the conversion option will increase with the price of the underlying stock, the variance of the stock, and the life of the conversion option; it will decrease with the exercise price (determined by the conversion option).

The effects of increased risk in the firm can cut both ways in a convertible bond: it will decrease the value of the straight bond portion, while increasing the value of the conversion option. These offsetting effects mean that convertible bonds will be less exposed to changes in the firm's risk than are other types of securities.

The value of a convertible bond is also affected by a feature shared by most convertible bonds, which allows for the adjustment of the conversion ratio (and price) if the firm issues new stock below the conversion price or has a stock split or dividend. In some cases, the conversion price has to be lowered to the price at which new stock

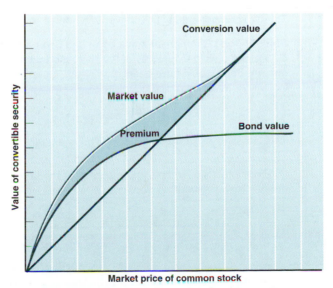

Figure 15.2 Bond value and conversion option

is issued. This is designed to protect the convertible bondholder from misappropriation by the firm.

A simple approach to decomposing debt and equity   The value of a connectible debt can be decomposed into straight debt and equity components using a simple approach. Because the price of a convertible bond is the sum of the straight debt and the call option components, the value of the straight bond component in conjunction with the market price should be sufficient to estimate the call option component, which is also the equity component:

Value of Equity Component = Price of Convertible Bond − Value of Straight Bond Component

The value of the straight bond component can be estimated using the coupon payments on the convertible bond, the maturity of the bond, and the market interest rate the company would have to pay on a straight debt issue. This last input can be estimated directly if the company also trades straight bonds in the marketplace, or it can be based on the bond rating, if any, assigned to the company.

 IN PRACTICE   DECOMPOSING A CONVERTIBLE BOND—DEBT AND EQUITY COMPONENTS

General Signal is a leading maker of equipment and systems for industrial process and electrical control and for the telecommunication industry. In December 1994, General Signal had convertible bonds outstanding with the following features:

- The bonds are to mature in June 2002. There were 100,000 bonds outstanding.
- They had a face value of $1,000 and were convertible into 25.32 shares per bond until June 2002.
- The coupon rate on the bond was set at 5.75%.
- The company was rated A−. Straight bonds of similar rating and similar maturity were yielding 9.00%.
- The convertible bonds were trading at $1,135 per bond in December 1994.

The two components of the convertible bond can be valued as follows.

1. *Straight Bond Component* If this bond had been a straight bond, with a coupon rate of 5.75% and a yield to maturity of 9.00% (based on the bond rating), the value of this straight bond would have been:

$$\text{PV of Bond} = \sum_{t=1}^{t=15} \frac{28.75}{(1.045)^t} + \frac{1,000}{(1.045)^{15}} = \$825.48$$

This is based on semiannual coupon payments (of $28.75 for semiannual periods).

2. *Conversion Option* Because the convertible bond is a combination of the straight bond and the conversion option, and the price of the convertible bond is known, the conversion option can be valued:

Conversion Option = Price of Convertible Bond − Value of Straight Bond
= $1135 − $825.48 = $309.52

The conversion option is valued at $309.52

3. *Decomposition into Debt and Equity* Once the convertible bond has been broken up into straight bond and conversion option components, their values can be used to calculate the debt and equity components of the convertible bonds outstanding. In the case of General Signal, the debt component is the value of the straight bond component:

$$\text{Debt Component of Convertible Bonds} = 100,000 * \$825.48 = \$82.548 \text{ million}$$

This can be added on to the remaining debt of the firm to compute the debt ratio.

The equity component is the value of the conversion option embedded in the convertible bond:

$$\text{Equity Component of Convertible Bonds} = 100,000 * \$309.52 = \$30.952 \text{ million}$$

This can be added on to the market value of the outstanding common stock to compute the total market value of equity.

Why do companies issue convertible debt?   There are a number of reasons why companies might issue convertible debt, but there is one reason often given that does not make much sense—that is, that it is cheaper for a firm to borrow using convertible debt than it is for it to issue straight debt. If, by "cheaper," the implication is that the interest rate on the convertible debt will be lower than the interest rate on straight debt, this is true;, but there is a good reason why the convertible debt is "cheaper": the firm is packaging a valuable call option on the equity with the straight debt to create the convertible debt, and it is the value of the option that is pushing down the stated interest rate on the debt.

Having dispensed with the one reason that does not make sense, let us consider some that do. First, convertible debt provides an attractive alternative to straight debt for high-growth companies that do not currently have high operating cash flows. The high growth and risk combine to increase the value of the conversion option, which, in turn, pushes down the interest rate and relieves the cash-flow pressures on the firm. This is confirmed by studies; one study by Wayne Mikkelson found that highly levered and high-growth firms are more likely to issue convertibles. Second, convertible debt is one way of reducing the conflict between equity- and debtholders in a firm. Equity investors have an incentive to expropriate wealth from bondholders by taking on riskier projects and new financing. If they do so with convertible debt, debtholders can always exercise their conversion options and become equity investors, thus removing themselves as a target for expropriation.

Concept Check

Assume that a company issues convertible debt and that the stock price increases over the following years. Assume, further, that the convertible debt is not converted. What will happen to the debt ratio over time, and why?

Preferred Stock

Preferred stock is another security that shares some characteristics with debt and some with equity. Like debt, preferred stock has a fixed dollar dividend; if the firm does not have the cash to pay the dividend, it is cumulated and paid in a period when there are sufficient earnings. Like debt, preferred stockholders do not have a share of control in the firm, and their voting privileges are strictly limited to issues that might affect their claims on the firm's cash flows or assets. Like equity, payments to preferred stockholders are not tax deductible and have to come out of after-tax cash flows. Also like equity, preferred stock does not have a maturity date at which time the face value is due. In terms of priority, in the case of bankruptcy, preferred stockholders have to wait until the debtholders' claims have been met before receiving any portion of the assets of the firm.

Preferred Stock: This is a hybrid security. Like debt, it has a promised payment (the preferred dividend) in each period. Like equity, its cash flows are not tax deductible, and it has an infinite life.

Preferred stock: equity or debt?   Accountants and ratings agencies continue to treat preferred stock as equity. It can be argued, however, that the fixed commitments that preferred stock create are like debt obligations and have to be dealt with likewise. The obligations created by preferred stock are generally less onerous than those created by debt; however, they are generally cumulated, cannot cause default, and do not have priority over debt claims in the case of bankruptcy.

Unlike convertible debt, which can be decomposed into equity and debt components, preferred stock cannot be treated as debt, because preferred dividends are not tax deductible and certainly cannot be viewed as the equivalent of equity, because of the differences in cash-flow claims and control. Consequently, preferred stock is treated as a third component of capital, in addition to debt and equity, for purposes of performing capital structure analysis and estimating the cost of capital.

Why do companies issue preferred stock?   In many ways, it is difficult to understand the rationale for issuing preferred stock, if the firm also has the option to issue straight debt, inasmuch as preferred stock generally costs more (since it is riskier) and provides no tax benefits. It makes much more sense, however, if we consider a couple of additional factors in its favor. First, preferred stock is treated as equity by many analysts and ratings agencies for the purposes of calculating leverage. For firms that are concerned about being viewed as overlevered, it offers a way of raising money without giving up control (as would have been the case if they had issued equity) and without increasing their debt ratios. Second, companies do not have to pay taxes on 70% of the preferred dividends that they receive on preferred stock investments they might have made in other firms. In contrast, if they lend the money out, they would have had to pay taxes on the entire interest received. This tax saving might be shared with the issuing company, enabling them to bring the preferred dividend rate down. The same argument can also be made about common stock, however, since common stock dividends are also covered by the same exemption. Finally, preferred stock may offer a way of raising money for companies that have no other options—debt or equity—available to them.

❏ Concept
Check

Can preferred stock ever have a lower cost than straight debt to a company? Explain your answer.

Special features of preferred stock   In recent years, special features have often been added on to preferred stock to make it more attractive to buyers or less risky to issuers. One variant is *convertible preferred stock,* whereby the preferred shares can be converted into common stock at a fixed price. This is analogous to the convertible debt discussed earlier, and convertible preferred stock should sell for a higher price than otherwise similar straight preferred stock. Another variant is *adjustable rate preferred stock,* whereby the dividend rate on the preferred stock is pegged to an index rate, such as the Treasury bill or Treasury bond rate, instead of being a fixed rate. This, again, is comparable to floating rate debt, and has the same advantages and disadvantages.

Option-linked Bonds

In recent years, firms have recognized the value of combining options with straight bonds to create bonds that more closely match the firm's specific needs. Consider two examples. In the first, commodity companies issued bonds linking the principal and even interest payments to the price of the commodity. Thus, interest payments would rise if the price of the commodity increased, and fall if the price fell. The benefit for the company was that it tailored the cash flows on the bond to the cash flows of the firm, and reduced the likelihood of default. These **commodity-linked bonds** can be viewed as a combination of a straight security, and a call option on the underlying commodity. In the second example, consider insurance companies that have recently issued bonds whereby the principal on the bond is reduced in the case of a specified catastrophe and remains unaffected in its absence. For instance, an insurance firm for whom the bulk of its revenues come from homeowners' insurance in California might attach a provision that reduces principal or interest in the case of a major earthquake. Again, the rationale is to provide the firm with some breathing room, when it needs it the most—when a catastrophe creates huge cash outflows for the firm.

Commodity-linked Bonds: Commodity bonds are bonds in which the interest or the principal payments are linked to the price of the commodity. In most cases, the payments will increase with the price of the commodity and decrease if it drops.

THE HISTORICAL EXPERIENCE: HOW FIRMS HAVE ACTUALLY RAISED FUNDS

Firms have historically raised funds from a variety of sources—debt, equity, and hybrid securities—but their dependence on these sources varies both across time and countries. In the United States, for instance, firms have generally raised external financing through debt issues rather than equity issues and have primarily raised equity funds internally from operations. Figure 15.3 illustrates the proportion of funds from new debt and equity issues, as well as from internal funds for U.S. corporations between 1975 and 1990.

In every year, the dependence on internal financing to meet funding needs is clear. Furthermore, when external financing is used, it is more likely to be new debt rather than new equity or preferred stock. In fact, some note that the equity issues reported in this figure have to be netted out against equity repurchases in each year. This is illustrated in Figure 15.4, which reports net equity issues by U.S. companies from 1981 to 1990; between 1984 and 1990, the net equity issues were negative in every year, indicating that equity repurchases exceeded new equity issues in each of those years.

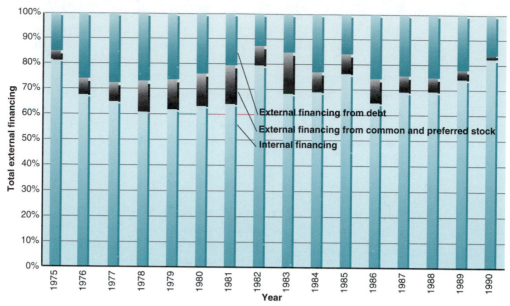

Figure 15.3   Breakdown of financing for U.S. firms: 1975–1990

A Cross-Cultural Comparison of Financing Ratios

In comparing the financing patterns of U.S. companies to companies in other countries, there is some evidence that U.S. companies are much more heavily dependent on debt than equity for external financing than their counterparts in other countries. Figure 15.5 summarizes new security issues in each of the G-7 countires between 1984 to 1991.[3]

There is also some evidence that firms in Indonesia, India, Malaysia, and other emerging markets use equity (internal and equity) much more than debt to finance their operations. Some of this dependence can be attributed to government regulation that discourages the use of debt, either directly, by constraining the debt ratios of firms to be below specified limits, or indirectly, by limiting the deductibility of interest. Some of it is due to the absence of corporate bond markets in many of these countries, which leads to an almost complete dependence on bank debt.

There are several possible explanations for the greater dependence of U.S. corporations on debt issues for raising external financing.

1.   Cost of Issue:

The first explanation concerns the differential cost between issuing new stock and debt; stock issues have flotation costs that are significantly higher than debt issues. Figure 15.7 summarizes the average flotation cost (issuance as well as underwriting spread) for stock and bond issues, by size of the issue.

2.   Dependence on Common Stock:

In our discussion of ways of raising equity, we noted several options, ranging from common stock to warrants. Companies in the United States have generally been reluctant to

---

[3]This is based on OECD data, summarized in the OECD publication "Financial Statements of Non-Financial Enterprises." These data are excerpted from Rajan and Ziingales (1995).

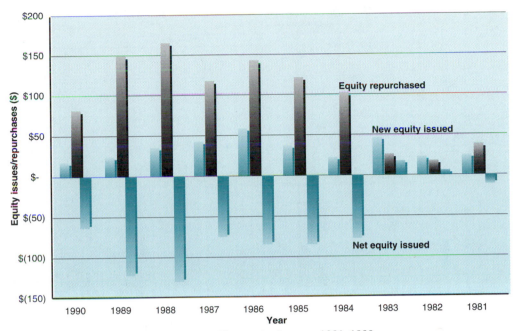

Figure 15.4   Net equity issues—1981–1990

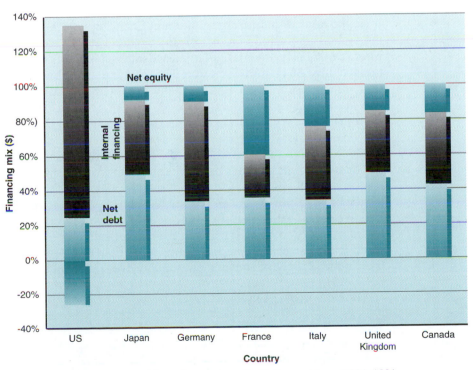

Figure 15.5   Financing patterns in G-7 countries—1984–1991

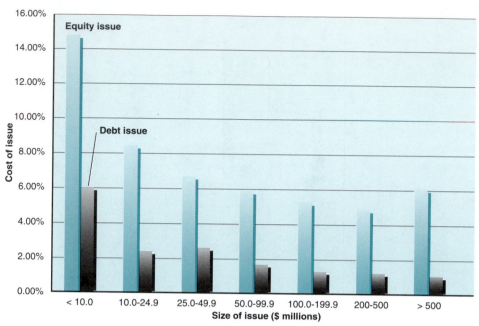

Figure 15.6   Cost of debt and equity issues

use equity instruments other than common stock, and have also shown an aversion to issuance procedures, such as rights issues, that may lower the flotation costs. This tendency, in conjunction with the fear of dilution, has kept issues of common stock to a minimum.

3.   Stage in Life Cycle:

It can be argued that firms use different financing vehicles at different stages in their life cycle, as shown in Figure 15.7. In the initial stages of high growth and high risk, where capital investments tend to exceed internal funds, firms are most likely to use external equity. As their projects start paying off and cash flows from operations increase, they shift to use internal equity. Finally, as they mature, and growth and risk decline, they start using external debt.

In this framework, firms in large and stable economies, like the United States, should depend much more on external debt and internal funds than should firms in smaller, higher growth economies, such as Indonesia and India, where external equity would be the choice.

The other trend that has been especially noted in the press has been the increasing leverage at U.S. companies, at least during the 1980s. The leverage, when measured using the book values of debt and equity, has increased over time, as is evidenced in Figure 15.6. We would argue that the book value leverage is a poor measure of the financial leverage at U.S. companies and that the market value leverage is a more relevant measure. Figure 15.8 also graphs the market value debt ratios for firms in the United States; these debt ratios have shown more stability over time. Thus, the increase in the market value of equity which many firms enjoyed in the 1980s might have been the trigger for additional borrowing in that decade.

❑ Concept
Check

Assume that you are comparing the financing mix used by firms in the United States and Japan. What are some of the factors that might cause differences between the countries?

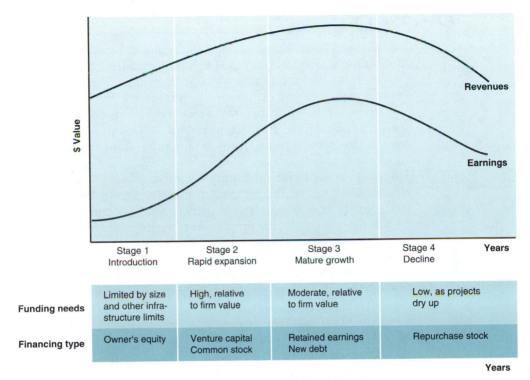

Figure 15.7   Life cycle analysis of financing

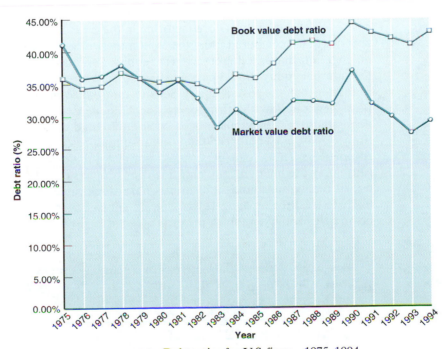

Figure 15.8   Debt ratios for U.S. firms—1975–1994

WAYS OF RAISING FINANCING

Not only can firms choose among debt, equity, or some hybrid of the two, but they can also choose how to raise the funds. Private companies generally have fewer choices than public firms—they can raise funds either internally, from operations, or externally, from venture capitalists and the owner's own resources. In this section, we will examine the options available to private firms to raise funds, the process by which private firms make their first public issue and become publicly traded firms, and the range of choices that open up for publicly traded firms to raise funds from debt and equity.

Internal versus External Equity Financing

Studies that examine the patterns of financing among firms in the United States point to their dependence on internal equity to finance operations. This is evident in Figure 15.4, which shows that the proportion of funds raised from internal equity was consistently greater than that from external financing. *Internal equity* refers to the earnings (and cash flows) of a firm that are plowed back into the firm instead of being paid out as dividends. Using the reasonable presumption that the earnings of a firm belong to its stockholders, it can be argued that any portion of these earnings that is not paid out as dividends is still equity being reinvested back in the firm. *External equity,* on the other hand, refers to funds raised by issuing common stock, warrants, contingent value rights, or other equity instruments in financial markets.

A firm may prefer internal to external financing for a number of reasons. For private firms, external equity is typically difficult to access, and even when it is available (through a venture capitalist, for instance) the trade off is a loss of control and flexibility. For publicly traded firms, external equity may be easier to tap into, but it is still costly in terms of transactions costs and potential price impact. Internal equity, on the other hand, can be used to finance operations without incurring large transactions costs and loss of flexibility.

These advantages notwithstanding, there are caveats to the use of internal equity for funding projects. First, firms have to recognize that internal equity has the same cost as external equity, before factoring in the transactions cost differences. Thus, the cost of equity, computed using the capital asset or arbitrage pricing model, applies as much to internal as it does to external equity. This implies that the projects taken with the internal equity should pass muster and earn a return for equity for investors that is greater than the cost of equity. Second, internal equity is clearly limited to the cash flows generated by the firm for its stockholders. Even if the firm does not pay dividends, these cash flows may not be sufficient to fund the firm's projects. Depending entirely on internal equity can therefore result in project delays or their possible loss to competitors. Third, managers should not make the mistake of thinking that just because they use internal equity for financing projects that the stock price does not matter. In reality, stockholders in firms whose stock prices have dropped are much less likely to trust their managers to reinvest their cash flows for them than are stockholders in firms with rising stock prices.

❏ Concept
Check

Some argue that internal equity financing is cheaper than external equity financing, because of the flotation costs. How would you quantify the difference?

From Private to Publicly Traded Firm: The Initial Public Offering

A private firms is clearly restricted in its access to external financing, both for debt and for equity. In our earlier discussion of equity choices, we pointed out the hard bargain venture capitalists extract for investing equity in a private business. Some private firms have the choice of going public and take advantage of this option.

The tradeoff: staying private versus going public   When a private firm goes public, the primary benefit is an increased access to financial markets and funds for projects. This is a significant gain for high-growth businesses with large and lucrative investment opportunities. A secondary benefit is that the owners of the private firm are able to cash in on their success by attaching a market value to their holdings. Owners can become very wealthy individuals overnight. To illustrate, in a recent and well-publicized public offering, Netscape, a company servicing the Internet, was valued at $2.1 billion on the day that it went public. Jim Clark, the CEO and co-founder of the firm, who owned about 25% of the outstanding shares in the firm, found his stake valued at $565 million, while Marc Andreesen, the 24-year-old programmer, found his million shares to be worth $58.25 million.

These benefits have to be weighed against the potential costs, however, the most significant of which is the loss of control that may ensue from being a publicly traded firm. As firms get larger, and the owners are tempted to cash in their holdings over time, the owner's share of the outstanding shares will generally decline. If the stockholders in the firm come to believe over time that the owner's association with the firm is hurting rather than helping it, they may decide to push for the owner's removal. In the case of Apple Computers, for instance, the two founders, Steve Jobs and Steve Wozniak, were eventually removed from management positions, largely as a consequence of stockholder disapproval of their actions.

Other costs associated with a publicly traded firm are exposure to information and legal requirements associated with being publicly traded. A private firm going through a bad patch may be able to protect itself from exposure, whereas a publicly traded firm may have no choice but to reveal the information. Yet another cost is the increase in the different and often competing interests that have to be kept abreast of decisions made at the firm; the two most powerful are equity research analysts and bond rating agencies.

Finally, firms may not be able to go public if they do not meet the minimum listing requirements for the exchange on which they want to be traded. The listing requirements vary across exchanges, with the New York Stock Exchange imposing the strictest requirements (pretax income of at least $2.5 million, tangible assets of at least $18 million, and 2,000 or more stockholders). Most small firms, therefore, choose to get listed on the NASDAQ, which has far fewer restrictions on listing, and move to the NYSE later in the process.

Overall, the net trade off of going public will generally be positive for firms with large growth opportunities and funding needs, because a failure to go public will result in capital rationing constraints that end up costing a great deal in terms of foregone value.

Choosing an investment banker   Once the decision to go public has been made, the firm has to pick an intermediary to facilitate the transaction. These intermediaries are usually investment bankers, who provide several services. First, they help the firm meet the requirements of the Securities and Exchange Commission (SEC) in preparing and filing the necessary registration statements. Second, they provide the credibility that a small and unknown private firm may need to induce investors to buy their stocks. Third, they provide their "expert" advice on the valuation of the company and the pricing of the new issue. Fourth, they absorb some of the risk in the issue by "underwriting" the issue and guaranteeing the proceeds on the issue. Finally, they help sell the issue by assembling a syndicate of underwriters who try to place the issue with their clients.

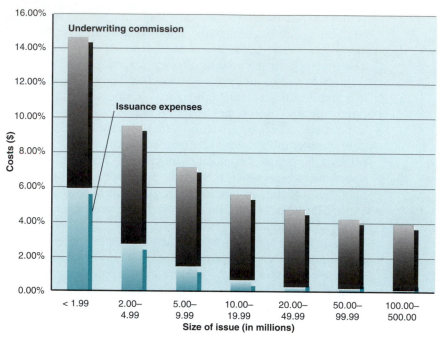

Figure 15.9   Issuance costs by size of issue

In deciding to go public, the firm has to consider is the cost of making the issue. The firm must consider the legal and administrative cost of making a new issue, including the cost of preparing registration statements and filing fees. The firm should also examine **underwriting commission**—the gross spread between the offering price and what the firm receives per share, which goes to cover the underwriting, management, and selling fees on the issue. This commission can be substantial, and is a decreasing function of the size of the issue. Yet another cost to consider is any *underpricing on the issue,* which provides a windfall to the investors who get the stock at the offering price and can then turn around and sell it at the much higher market price. Thus, for Netscape, whose offering price was $29 and the stock opened at $50, it can be argued that the difference of $21 per share is an implicit cost. Figure 15.9 summarizes the average issuance and underwriting costs for issues of different sizes.

Underwriting Commission: This is the difference between the offering price on a stock issue and the proceeds the firm receives on the issue.

The underpricing cost varies as well, and although precise estimates for seasoned issues are difficult to come by, the average initial public offering seems to be underpriced by 10% to 15%. Ibbotson, Sindelar, and Ritter (1993), in a study of the determinants of the magnitude of the underpricing, estimate the extent of the underpricing as a function of the size of the issue. Figure 15.10 summarizes the underpricing as a percentage of the price by size of issue.

If the only task for the issuing company were to find the investment banker who could deliver the lowest combined cost, the whole process could be opened up to auction and the investment banker that promised to deliver the highest net proceeds to the firm would be chosen. There are several problems, with this idealized scenario, however. First, the promised proceeds may not be delivered, and the investment

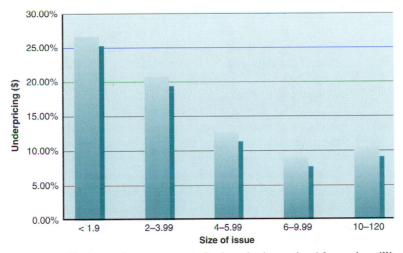

Figure 15.10   Underpricing as percent of price—by issue size (shown in millions)

bank may not have the capital to back up its guarantee. Second, we would argue that a bungled initial public offering—for example, the offering price is set too high—can create lasting damage to the firm's reputation and affect its ability to make future issues. Third, the investment banker of choice may not have the specialized expertise, say in biotechnology or software development, to provide the advice needed to help the issuing company decide on the particulars of the issue. Fourth, given that this is a private firm, no investment banker may be willing to estimate an offering price without receiving more information and valuing the firm. Finally, the presumption that there will be a large number of investment bankers contending for the issue may not hold true. A number of private firms have to seek out and convince an investment banker to take them public and do not have the luxury of choosing between multiple bidders.

Given these problems, private firms tend to pick investment bankers based on reputation and expertise rather than price. A good reputation provides the credibility and the comfort level needed for investors to buy the stock of the firm; expertise applies not only to the pricing of the issue and the process of going public, but also to other financing decisions that might be made in the aftermath of a public issue. The investment banking agreement is then negotiated, rather than opened up for competition.

Valuing the company and setting issue details   Once the firm chooses an investment banker to take it public, the next step is to estimate a value for the firm. The value is sometimes estimated using discounted cash-flow models. More often, however, the value is estimated using a multiple, like price earnings ratios, and by looking at the pricing (on the basis of these multiples) of comparable firms that are already publicly traded. Whichever approach is used, the absence of substantial historical information, in conjunction with the fact that these are small companies with high-growth prospects, makes the estimation of value a noisy one at best.

The other decision the firm has to make relates to the size of the initial issue and the use of the proceeds. In most cases, only a portion of the firm's stock is offered at the initial public offering; this reduces the risk on the underpricing front and enables the owners to test out the waters before they try to sell more stock. In most cases, the proceeds from the initial issue are invested back into the firm.

The next step in this process is to set the value per share for the issuer. To do so, the equity in the firm is divided by the number of shares, which is in many ways an arbitrary number that is determined by the price range that the issuer would like to have on the issue. If the equity in the firm is valued at $50 million, for example, the number of shares would be set at 5 million to get a target price range of $10, or at 1 million shares to get a target price range of $50 per share.

The final step in this process is to set the offering price per share. Most investment banks set the offering price below the estimated value per share for two reasons. First, it reduces the bank's risk exposure, since it guarantees that the shares will be acquired at the offering price. Second, it is a good sign if the stock increases in price in the immediate aftermath of the issue. For the clients of the investment banker, who get the shares at the offering price, there is an immediate payoff; for the issuing company, the ground has been prepared for future issues. In setting the offering price, investment bankers have the advantage of first testing the waters. They can gauge demand from individual and institutional buyers at different prices, before setting the offering price.

SEC requirements   In order to make a public offering in the United States, firms have to meet several requirements. First, they have to file a registration statement and **investment prospectus** with the SEC, providing information on the firm's financial history, its forecasts for the future, and its plans for the funds it raises from the initial public offering. The prospectus provides information on the riskiness and prospects of the firm for prospective investors in its stock. The SEC reviews this information, and either approves the registration or sends out a deficiency memorandum asking for more information. While the registration is being reviewed, the firm may not sell any securities, although it can issue a preliminary prospectus, titled a *red herring,* for informational purposes only.

Investment Prospectus: This is a document that lays out the information on the riskiness and prospects of a firm for prospective investors in its stock.

Once the registration has been approved by the SEC, the firm can take out a *tombstone advertisement,* which lists the details of the issue, the lead investment banker, and the names of other investment bankers involved in the issue. The order in which the investment bankers are listed is significant. At the top are the lead investment banker and the co-managers of the issue, followed by the *major bracket investment bankers.*[4] Then comes the *mezzanine bracket,* and at the bottom are the regional investment bankers involved with the issue.[5]

The investment banker and the issuer also mount a marketing blitz at this point, whereby they present their company to investors at road shows. The investment syndicate simultaneously starts the distribution phase by lining up interested investors.

The issue   Once the offering price has been set, and the tombstone advertisement has been taken, the die has been cast. If the offering price has indeed been set below the true value, the subscriptions will exceed the offering, and the investment banker will have to choose a rationing mechanism to allocate the shares. On the offering date—the

---

[4]The investment bankers are categorized into major investment bankers, based both on reputation and national focus. Generally speaking, investment banks that serve localized markets or sectors are not classified as "major."

[5]The mezzanine bracket generally includes smaller investment banks that operate nationally.

first date that the shares can be traded—there will generally be a spurt in the market price. If the offering price has been set too high, as is sometimes the case, the investment bankers will have to discount the offering to sell it and make up the difference to the issuer, because of the underwriting agreement.

The Choices for a Seasoned Firm

A publicly traded firm has a number of choices when it comes to issuing securities to financial markets, ranging from underwritten general subscriptions, which are very similar to the initial public offering described earlier, to private placements to rights offerings, to the recent phenomenon of shelf registrations, especially for bonds.

General subscriptions   In a general subscription, the issue is open to any member of the general public to subscribe. In that sense, it is very similar to an initial public offering, though there are some basic differences:

- *Underwriting Agreement:* The underwriting agreement of an initial public offering almost always involves a firm guarantee and is generally negotiated with the investment banker, whereas the underwriting agreements for seasoned issues take on a wider variety of forms. Competitive bids can be made on seasoned issues, because investment bankers do not have to estimate an offering price. There is evidence that competitive bids reduce the spread, though even seasoned firms continue to prefer negotiated offerings. Seasoned issues also offer a wider range of underwriting guarantees; some issues are backed up by a *best efforts guarantee,* which does not guarantee a fixed price; other issues come with *standby guarantees,* whereby the investment banker provides backup support, in case the actual price falls below the offering price. The payoff from relaxing the guarantee is in lower underwriting commissions.
- *Pricing of Issue:* The issuer of an initial public offering has to estimate the value of the firm and then the per-share value before pricing the issue, while the pricing of a seasoned issue starts with the current market price, simplifying the process.

The overall evidence on the cost of public offerings indicates that it is still clearly much more expensive to issue stock rather than bonds and the cost of the issue is a decreasing function of the size of the issue.

Private placements   An alternative to a general subscription is a **private placement**, whereby securities are sold directly to one or a few investors interested in holding these securities as investments. The terms for the securities are negotiated between the two parties. The primary advantage of private placements is the lower cost, inasmuch as there are fewer intermediaries and no need for underwriting guarantees or marketing. There are also a substantial savings in time and administrative costs because the SEC registration requirements are bypassed. The secondary advantages are that the terms of the bond can be tailored to meet the specific needs of the buyer, and that the firm can also convey proprietary information to the potential investors.

Private Placement: This is a security issue whereby securities are sold directly to private investors at a price negotiated with these investors.

The primary disadvantage of private placements is that there are relatively few potential investors since large private placements may expose the investor to firm-specific risks. Until the mid-1960s, private placements were very common, especially for corporate bonds, but higher interest rate volatility and shifts in default risk, even among the largest corporations, have made private placements less attractive to investors. The investors with whom private placements are made also impose more onerous constraints on the firms, partly because they need to protect their unique exposure to firm-specific risk, and partly because firms that make private placements tend to be riskier firms.

Rights offerings The third option available to seasoned issuers is to make a **rights offering,** whereby instead of trying to sell new stock at the current market price to all investors, the existing investors in the firm are given the right to buy additional shares, in proportion to their current holdings, at a price much lower than the current market price.

Rights Offering: A rights offering allows existing stockholders in the firm to buy additional stock in the firm, at a price that is usually lower than the current market price.

A company that uses a rights offering generally issues one right for each outstanding common share, allowing each stockholder to use his or her rights to buy additional shares in the company at a subscription price that is generally much lower than the market price. Rational stockholders will either exercise the right or sell it. Those investors who let it expire without doing either will find that the market value of their remaining holding shrinks—the market price will almost certainly drop when the rights are exercised for the subscription price is set much lower than the market price. In some cases, firms will get a standby agreement from an underwriting syndicate, allowing the underwriters to buy the shares that remain unsold at the end of the rights offering.

Value of a right Since rights are freely bought and sold by investors in the stock, the value of a right has to be estimated. In general, the value of a right should be equal to the difference between the stock price with the rights attached—or the rights-on price—and the stock price without the rights attached—the ex-rights price. The rationale is simple: if this were not true, there would be opportunities for easy profits on the part of investors, and the resulting price would not be stable. To illustrate, if the price of the right were greater than the difference between the rights-on price and the ex-rights price, every stockholder would be better off selling his or her right rather than exercising it. This, in turn, would push the price down toward the equilibrium price. If the price of the right were lower than the difference between the rights-on and the ex-right price, there would be an equally frenzied rush to buy the right and exercise it, which, in turn, would push the price up toward the equilibrium price. The value of a right can be estimated using the following formula:

$$\text{Rights Price} = (\text{Rights-on Price} - \text{Subscription Price})/(n + 1)$$

where n is the number of rights required for each new share.

 IN PRACTICE VALUING A RIGHTS OFFERING—TECH TEMP, INC.

Tech Temp, Inc. has 10 million shares outstanding, trading at $25 per share. It needs to raise $25 million in new equity, and decides to make a rights offering. Each stockholder is provided with one right for every share he or she owns, and five rights can be used to buy an additional share in the company at $12.50 per share. The value of a right can be calculated as follows:

	Before Rights Exercised	After Rights Exercised
Number of shares	10 million	12 million
Value of equity	$250 million	$275 million
Price per share	$25.00	$22.92

The rights-on price is $ 25.00 per share, and the ex-rights price is $22.92, leading to a per right value of $2.08. This can be confirmed by using the alternate formula:

$$\text{Value per Right} = (\text{Rights-on Price} - \text{Subscription Price})/(n + 1)$$
$$= (\$25 - \$12.50)/ (5 + 1)$$
$$= \$12.50 /6 = \$2.08$$

If the rights price were greater than this value, there would be a rush to sell the rights, pushing the price down. Alternatively, if the rights could be acquired for less than $2.08, there would be an opportunity to gain by acquiring the rights at the lower price and exercising them.

Concept Check

Assume that the rights are trading at $1.80 per right, in the above example. Trace the actions you would have to take in order to take advantage of this mispricing.

Rights offerings versus public issues Rights offerings are much less expensive than public issues, for two reasons. First, the underwriting commissions are much lower, for a rights offering has little risk of not receiving subscriptions if the subscription price is set well below the market price. Second, the other transactions and administrative costs should also be lower because the marketing and distribution are much less involved. Figure 15.11 illustrates the differences in issuance cost, classified by issue size, for rights and public issues.

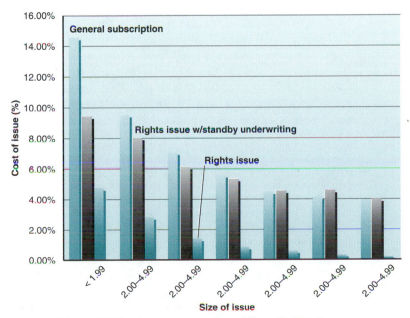

Figure 15.11 Issuance costs for public and rights issues

It can be argued that a rights offering preserves the control position of existing stockholders. There is an additional advantage. Even though the price in a rights offering is set below the current market price, there should be no transfer of wealth from existing stockholders since only they receive the rights. In contrast, in a public offering, existing stockholders can lose if the securities are underpriced since the benefit of the underpricing accrues to the new stockholders.

What is the downside of making a rights issue? The primary reservation seems to be that it dilutes the share holding and lowers the market price. Although this is true in a technical sense, the existing stockholders should not object since they are the only ones who receive the rights. In fact, it can be argued that a rights offering is very much like a stock split, insofar as a split also leads a drop in the market price.

In general, firms in the United States have been much more reluctant to use rights issues than European firms, in spite of the significant cost savings that could accrue from them. Part of this reluctance can be attributed to the fear of dilution in earnings that arise as a consequence of the rights issues. Some companies also argue that transactions costs are associated with having to contact stockholders on a rights offering and to administer the offering, although it does not seem likely that these costs would be greater than the marketing and distribution costs in a public offering. Other companies argue that a rights offering does not expand the investor base of the company; by expanding the base, it is argued, that the firm reduces its cost of capital. Finally, the very fact that a firm uses a rights offering rather than making a public issue may be viewed by the market as a signal that the firm does not want to open itself up to the scrutiny of financial markets that will ensue if it makes a public offering.

☐ Concept
Check

> Some financial managers argue that rights offerings dilute stockholders' holdings. Illustrate how an existing stockholder is unaffected by the price decrease wrought by a rights offering.

Shelf registrations   Firms that want to raise external financing have to go through the process of collecting the information required by the SEC and filing for approval. This process is costly and time consuming, and is one of the reasons why firms rely on internal financing. In response to this criticism, the SEC simplified its rules and allowed firms more flexibility in external financing. Rule 415, which was issued in 1982, allows firms to make a **shelf registration,** whereby a single prospectus can be filed for a series of issues that the firm expects to issue over the following two years.

Shelf Registration: This is a registration with the SEC, allowing a firm to make multiple security issues—usually debt—over a specified period of time.

Besides making the process less cumbersome, shelf registration also gives firms more flexibility in terms of timing, because issues can be made when windows of opportunity open up. Thus, a firm might make a shelf registration for $200 million in bonds and make the issue when interest rates are at a low point. This flexibility in timing also allows firms to open up the process to aggressive bidding from investment banks, reducing their transactions costs substantially. Some firms chose to make the issues themselves rather than use the investment bankers, since the process is simpler and faster.

Overall, the spreads on new issues, especially for bonds, have been under pressure since the passage of shelf registration, although the empirical evidence is mixed. In spite of its benefits, shelf registration is more likely to be used by large firms making bond issues and less by small firms making equity issues.

CONCLUSION

Firms have a number of options when it comes to financing, both in terms of the type of financing that they use and the way in which they raise the financing. In this chapter, we developed and discussed the following issues:

- We differentiated between debt and equity, at a generic level, by pointing out that any financing approach that results in fixed cash flows and has prior claims in the case of default, fixed maturity, and no voting rights is debt, whereas a financing approach that provides for residual cash flows and has low or no priority in claims in the case of default, infinite life, and a lion's share of the control is equity.

- Within the broad category of equity, there a number of choices that a firm can make besides the traditional mechanism of common stock for publicly traded firms and owners' equity for private firms. Private firms can access and use venture capital, whereas publicly traded firms can issue warrants and contingent value rights to raise equity.

- Within the broad category of debt, firms have to make a number of choices ranging from the maturity of the debt (long versus short term) to the interest rate (fixed versus floating) to the type of currency (domestic versus foreign) in which the debt is issued. They must also choose the special features to add on to the debt.

- Private firms generally have fewer choices for financing than do publicly traded firms; one of the main reasons for going public is to gain access to these additional funding sources.

- When it comes to making new security issues, firms in the United States are much more likely to make debt than equity issues and to use internal financing than external financing.

- Even though the costs of making a public issue are generally much higher than making a rights issue, many U.S. firms are still reluctant to make rights issues.

- Overall, the financing choices for firms are expanding, both in terms of the vehicles available for financing and the markets that can be tapped for this financing.

QUESTIONS AND PROBLEMS

1. An income bondholder receives interest payments only if the firm makes income. If the firm does not make interest payments in a year, the interest is cumulated and paid in the first year that the firm makes income. A preferred stockholder receives preferred dividends only if the firm makes income. If a firm does not make preferred dividend payments in a year, the dividend is cumulated and paid in the first year that the firm makes income. Are income bonds really preferred stock? What are the differences? For purposes of analyzing debt, how would you differentiate between income bonds and regular bonds?

2. A commodity bond links interest and principal payments to the price of a commodity. Differentiate a commodity bond from a straight bond, and then from equity. How would you factor these differences into your analysis of the debt ratio of a company that has issued exclusively commodity bonds?

3. You are analyzing a new security that has been promoted as equity, with the following features:

- The dividend on the security is fixed in dollar terms for the life of the security, which is 20 years.
- The dividend is not tax deductible.
- In the case of default, the holders of this security will receive cash only after all debtholders, secured as well as unsecured, are paid.
- The holders of this security will have no voting rights.

Based on the description of debt and equity in the chapter, how would you classify this security? If you were asked to calculate the debt ratio for this firm, how would you categorize this security?

4. You are analyzing a convertible preferred stock, with the following characteristics for the security:

- There are 50,000 preferred shares outstanding, with a face value of $100 and a 6% preferred dividend rate.
- The firm has straight preferred stock outstanding, with a preferred dividend rate of 9%.
- The preferred stock is trading at $105.

Estimate the preferred stock and equity components of this preferred stock.

5. You have been asked to calculate the debt ratio for a firm that which has the following components to its financing mix:

- The firm has 1 million shares outstanding, trading at $50 per share.
- The firm has $25 million in straight debt, carrying a market interest rate of 8%.
- The firm has 20,000 10-year convertible bonds outstanding, with a face value of $1,000, a market value of $1,100, and a coupon rate of 5%.

Estimate the debt ratio for this firm.

6. You have been asked to estimate the debt ratio for a firm, with the following financing details:

- The firm has two classes of shares outstanding; 50,000 shares of class A stock, with 2 voting rights per share, trading at $100 per share and 100,000 shares of class B stock, with 1/2 voting right per share, trading at $90 per share.
- The firm has $5 million in bank debt, and the debt was taken on recently.

Estimate the debt ratio. Why does it matter when the bank debt was taken on?

7. You are the owner of a small and successful firm with an estimated market value of $50 million. You are considering going public.

a. What are the considerations you would have in choosing an investment banker?

b. You want to raise $20 million in new financing, which you plan to reinvest back in the firm. (The estimated market value of $50 million is based on the assumption that this $20 million is reinvested.) What proportion of the firm would you have to sell in the initial public offering to raise $20 million?

c. How would your answer to (b) change if the investment banker plans to underprice your offering by 10%?

d. If you wanted your stock to trade in the $20 to $25 range, how many shares would you have to create? How many shares would you have to issue?

8. You have been asked for advice on a rights offering by a firm with 10 million shares outstanding, trading at $50 per share. The firm needs to raise $100 million in new equity. Assuming that the rights subscription price is $25, answer the following questions:

a. How many rights would be needed to buy one share at the subscription price?

b. Assuming that all rights are subscribed to, what will the ex-rights price be?

c. Estimate the value per right.

d. If the price of a right were different (higher or lower) than the value estimated in (c), how would you exploit the difference?

9. U.S. firms are heavily dependent on debt for external financing, and they are overleveraged. Comment.

10. You are a stockholder in SmallTech Inc., a company that is planning to raise new equity. The stock is trading at $15 per share, and there are 1 million shares outstanding. The firm issues rights to buy additional shares at $10 per share to its existing stockholders. (Two rights are needed to buy 1 share.)

a. What is the expected stock price after the rights are exercised?

b. If the rights are traded, what is the price per right?

c. As a stockholder, would you be concerned about the dilution effect lowering your stock price? Why or why not?

11. There is evidence that initial public offerings are underpriced. Which of the following statements would you agree with?

a. This indicates that investment bankers are making excess returns on initial public offerings.

b. Investors who subscribe to initial public offerings should make excess returns.

c. The companies issuing the stock in the initial public offering should try to find investment bankers who will overprice their issues.

d. The underpricing is compensation for the risk that investment bankers take.

e. The underpricing operates as a promotion, encouraging investors to buy more stock in this company.

f. None of the above.

g. All of the above.

12. Convertible bonds are often issued by small, high-growth companies to raise debt. Why?

13. A manager of NoZone Inc., a company in urgent need of financing, is debating whether to issue straight debt at 11% or convertible debt at 7%. He is leaning toward the convertible debt because it is cheaper. Is it? How would you check this proposition?

14. A company is trying to estimate its debt ratio. It has 1 million shares outstanding, trading at $50 per share, and had $250 million in straight debt outstanding (with a market interest rate of 9%). It also

has two other securities outstanding:

a. It has 200,000 warrants outstanding, conferring on its holders the right to buy stock in the Complex Inc., at $65 per share. These warrants are trading at $12 each.

b. It also has 10,000 20-year convertible bonds outstanding, with a coupon rate of 6% and 10 years to maturity.

Estimate the debt ratio in market value terms.

15. Venture capitalists take advantage of small businesses by demanding a disproportionate share of the ownership of the company for their investment. Comment.

16. Firms generally can borrow money by using bank debt or by issuing bonds. Why might a firm choose one method over the other?

17. Preferred stock is often considered as equity, when analysts calculate debt ratios. Is this appropriate? Under what conditions would you consider it to be more like debt?

18. Debt will always be cheaper than preferred stock, because of the tax advantage that it confers on the firm. What is the source of the tax advantage? Is this statement true?

CHAPTER 16

MARKET EFFICIENCY LESSONS FOR CORPORATE FINANCE

There is a substantial body of literature examining the efficiency of markets and the implications for portfolio management. Some of the evidence also concerns a firm's decision on whether to go public, when to go public, and, once publicly traded, what securities to issue and when. In particular, this chapter addresses the following questions:

- Are market prices based on earnings or cash flows? Do market prices reflect new information well and promptly?

- Should firms try to time their security issues (stock as well as bond issues), or is market timing a hopeless venture?

- How do markets react to different security issues? How can firms use this information to decide which securities they should use to raise funds?

- What happens if markets are inefficient? Can firms exploit these inefficiencies in their financing decisions?

- How much influence do equity research analysts and ratings agencies have on securities prices?

WHAT IS AN EFFICIENT MARKET?

Efficient Market: An **efficient market** is one in which the market price is an unbiased estimate of the true value of the investment.

Implicit in this characterization are several key concepts:

1. Contrary to popular view, market efficiency does not require that the market price be equal to true value *at every point in time.* All it requires is that errors in the market price be *unbiased;* that is, prices can be greater than or less than true value, as long as these deviations are random.[1]

2. The fact that the deviations from true value are random implies that there is *an equal chance* that stocks will be under- or overvalued at any point in time and that

---

[1]Randomness implies that there is an equal chance that stocks are under- or overvalued at any point in time.

these deviations are uncorrelated with any observable variable. For instance, in an efficient market, stocks with lower price/earnings (PE) ratios should be no more or less likely to be undervalued than stocks with high PE ratios.

3. If the deviations of market price from true value are random, it follows that no group of investors should be able *to consistently find under- or overvalued stocks* using any investment strategy.

Definitions of market efficiency have to be specific about both the market being considered and the investor group that is covered. It is extremely unlikely that *all* markets are efficient to *all* investors, but it is entirely possible that a particular market (for instance, the New York Stock Exchange) is efficient with respect to the average investor. It is also possible that some markets are efficient while others are not, and that a market is efficient with respect to some investors and not others. This is a direct consequence of differential tax rates and **transactions costs,** which confer advantages on some investors relative to others.

Transactions Cost: The cost of transacting includes broker commissions, the bid-ask spread, and any price impact from trading.

Definitions of market efficiency are also linked up with the information that is available to investors and reflected in the price. For instance, a strict definition of market efficiency that assumes that all information, public as well as private, is reflected in market prices would imply that even investors with precise inside information will be unable to beat the market. One of the earliest classifications of levels of market efficiency was provided by Fama (1971), who argued that markets could be efficient at three levels, depending on what information was reflected in prices. Under *weak-form efficiency,* the current price reflects the information contained in all past prices, suggesting that charts and technical analyses that use past prices alone would not be useful in finding undervalued stocks. Under *semistrong-form efficiency,* the current price reflects the information contained not only in past prices but also in all public disclosures (including financial statements and news reports), and no approach predicated on this information would be useful in finding undervalued stocks. Under *strong-form efficiency,* the current price reflects all information, public as well as private, and no investor will be able consistently to find undervalued stocks.

❑ Concept
Check

You are comparing two markets, one with low transactions costs and one with high transactions costs. Which of these two markets is likely to be more efficient and why?

EFFICIENCY IN RELATION TO PAST PRICES

A great deal of research has been conducted to explore whether there are patterns in prices and whether investors can time stock and bond markets. Much of this literature has relevance for corporate financial managers, who often have to make decisions on the timing of stock and bond issues for their firms.

The Empirical Evidence
Market timing has always been the holy grail of investing, since a successful market timer would undoubtedly beat the market and earn substantial excess returns. A financial

manager who can time either the stock or the bond market and make his or her stock issues when stock prices are at their peak, or bond issues when interest rates are at their lows, would undoubtedly save his or her firm substantial amounts of money in the long term. This potential payoff to successful market timing has to be weighed against the odds of success, however. In the words of Fisher Black, market timing may well be the impossible dream—attractive in the abstract but impossible to achieve.

Market Timing: Market timing refers to the forecasting of the direction of financial markets, usually in the short term.

Aggregate Market Timing

In the aggregate, can we make predictions about the future movements of equity and bond markets based on past prices or other macroeconomic information? Studies of aggregate market timing have looked at a variety of schemes ranging from simple schemes based on past prices to more elaborate ones involving macroeconomic information.

Price-based schemes
Investment strategies based on charts or technical analysis are generally founded on one of two diametrically opposed beliefs. The first is that prices have **momentum**; that is, markets that have gone up are more likely to keep going up, and markets that have gone down are more likely to keep going down. The second is that prices tend to *reverse* themselves, that is, periods of price increases are more likely to be followed by a price decrease, and vice versa.

Momentum: Momentum refers to the tendency of assets that have gone up (down) to keep going up (down).

These strategies can be tested in a number of ways. One is to look at the correlation in market price changes over time. In a momentum market, the price changes should be positively correlated, whereas in a reversal market, the price changes should be negatively correlated. At the aggregate market level, there is little evidence that either strategy works in the short-term, in terms of delivering excess returns. However, some interesting anomalies and patterns emerge that might still be useful for managers making financing decisions.

Calendar anomalies   There are systematic return patterns in the equity markets that are related to the calendar. For instance, there is clear evidence that stock prices go up more in January than in any other month of the year. Figure 16.1 reports average returns for U.S. stocks by month of the year, from 1926 to 1983. As you can see, returns in January are significantly higher than returns in any other month of the year. This phenomenon is called the *year-end* or *January effect,* and it can be traced to the first two weeks in January. The January effect is much more accentuated for small firms than for larger firms, and roughly half of the excess returns that small firms make over larger firms is earned in the first two weeks of January. Figure 16.2 graphs returns in January by size and risk class for data from 1935 to 1986.

A number of explanations have been advanced for the January effect, but few hold up to serious scrutiny. One is that investors engage in tax loss selling at the end of the year on stocks that have "lost money" in order to capture the capital gain, driving prices down, presumably below true value, in December, and then buying back the same stocks in January,

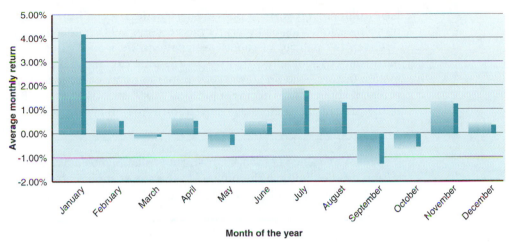

Figure 16.1   Average return by month of the year

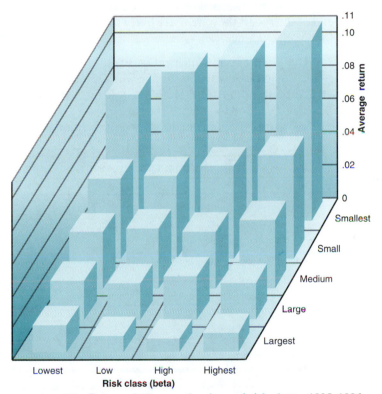

Figure 16.2   Returns in January by size and risk class—1935–1986

resulting in the high returns.[2] As proof of this explanation, some point to the fact that the January effect is accentuated for stocks that have done worse over the prior year. Several pieces of evidence contradict this theory, however. First, countries, such as Australia that

_____
[2]Since wash sales rules would prevent an investor from selling and buying back the same stock within 45 days, there has to be some substitution among the stocks. Thus, investor 1 sells stock A and investor 2 sells stock B, but when it comes time to buy back the stock, investor 1 buys stock B and investor 2 buys stock A.

have a different tax year also show a January effect. Second, the January effect is no greater, on average, following bad years for the stock market than following good years.

Given the paucity of robust explanations, we would categorize the January effect partly under "anomalies" that we cannot quite explain, and partly attribute it to information factors—the first few weeks of the year may be when substantial information is revealed about firms. This, in conjunction with cash inflows to portfolios around the turn of the year, may explain the positive returns in January.

> **Market Efficiency Lesson 1:** If a firm is planning to make a stock or bond issue and has flexibility in the timing of the issue, it should attempt to make the issue around the turn of the year to take advantage of the January effect.

Normal range of interest rates Some analysts hypothesize that market interest rates move within a normal range. Under this hypothesis, when interest rates approach the high end of the range, they are more likely to decrease, and when they approach the low end of the range, they are more likely to increase. This hypothesis is corroborated by the following evidence:

1. The **yield curve,** which reflects future expectations about interest rates, is more likely to be downward sloping when interest rates are high than when they are low. Thus, investors are more likely to expect interest rates to come down, if they are high now, and to go up, if they are low now. Table 16.1 summarizes the frequency of downward-sloping yield curves as a function of the level of interest rates.[3]

Table 16.1 YIELD CURVES AND THE LEVEL OF INTEREST RATES

One-year Corporate Bond Rate	Slope of Yield Curve		
	Positive	Flat	Negative
Above 4.40%	0	0	20
1900–1970 3.25%–4.40%	10	10	5
Below 3.25%	26	0	0
1971–1992 Above 8.00%	4	1	3
Below 8.00%	10	4	0

Yield Curve: This is a plot of spot interest rates against different maturities, ranging from short term to long term.

This evidence is consistent with the hypothesis that maintains interest rates move within a normal range. When they approach the upper end (lower end) of the normal range, the yield curve is more likely to be downward sloping (upward sloping).

2. More significantly, investors' expectations about future interest rate movements seem to be borne out by actual changes in interest rates. When changes in interest rates are regressed against the current level of interest rates, there is a negative and significant relationship between the level of the rates and the change in rates in sub-

[3]Some of this table is extracted from Wood (1984).

sequent periods. That is, there is a much greater likelihood of a drop in interest rates next period if interest rates are high in this one, and a much greater chance of rates increasing in future periods if interest rates are low in this one. For instance, using Treasury bond rates from 1970 to 1995 and regressing the change in interest rates (Δ Interest Rate$_t$) in each year against the level of rates at the end of the prior year (Interest Rate$_{t-1}$), we arrive at the following results:

$$\Delta\text{Interest Rate}_t = 0.0139 - 0.1456\ \text{Interest Rate}_{t-1} \quad R^2 = .0728$$
$$(1.29) \quad (1.81)$$

This regression suggests that the change in interest rates in this period is negatively correlated with the level of rates at the end of the prior year; if rates were high (low), they were more likely to decrease (increase). In addition, for every 1% increase in the level of current rates, the expected drop in interest rates in the next period increases by 0.1456%.

This evidence has to be considered with some caveats. The first is that the proportion of interest rate changes in future periods explained by the current level of rates is relatively small (about 7.28%). There are clearly a large number of other factors, most of which are unpredictable, that affect interest rate changes. The second is that the normal range of interest rates, which is based on past experience, might shift if the underlying inflation rate changes dramatically as it did in the 1970s in the United States. Consequently, many firms that delayed borrowing in the early part of that decade, because they thought that interest rates were at the high end of the range, found themselves facing higher and higher rates in the following years.

Market Efficiency Lesson 2:   Firms that have the capacity to delay bond issues should do so if interest rates are at historical highs. Firms that might need debt financing in the near future should consider issuing debt early if interest rates are at historical lows.

Market timing with macroeconomic and other information   Many investors would argue that, while market timing using past prices alone may not be feasible, future market movements in either the stock or the bond market can be forecast using a broader information set. For instance, some technical analysts and chartists maintain that future stock and bond price movements can be forecast using volume indicators and other market-based measures. The empirical evidence to back up such claims is scanty, however, and is presented selectively by its proponents.

A more reasoned argument comes from empiricists, who claim to have found patterns in both stock and bond market data that are related to broader macroeconomic factors. For instance, historical data seem to indicate that the more upward sloping the term structure, the greater the likelihood of stock price declines in future periods. Without examining every one of these claims in detail, we note the following concerns regarding these claims.

1.   As the data available expand, and more and more powerful computers are put to use to find patterns in the data, some variables will inevitably explain past stock price movements *based solely on chance*—hence, the oft-quoted and spurious correlation between such measures as hemlines and stock prices, and between Super Bowl winners and market performance.

2. There might be a statistically significant relationship between the variables and future market movements, but the proportion of the movement that is explained is usually *fairly small.*

3. Even when a study is done carefully to avoid **data mining,** and a strong relationship is established between the variable and market movements, the relationship tends to be unstable over time, and thus is not particularly useful as a predictive tool.

Data Mining: Data mining is the process of looking through a very large data set, without a clear theory or hypothesis, with the intent of finding patterns in the data.

> **Market Efficiency Lesson 3:** Even the best stock price and bond price forecasting models, while passing the statistical significance test, provide very noisy forecasts and do not provide a reliable basis for making corporate financial decisions. In most cases, firms will be better off making stock and debt issues based on their needs and financial characteristics and ignoring the model forecasts.

Individual Stocks

Many of the earlier studies that looked at price patterns examined short time intervals and concluded that past prices could not be used to predict future prices, at least not often enough for investors to make excess returns. In recent years, however, fairly decisive evidence has pointed to the existence of strong and systematic long-term patterns in price movements.

Short-term price movements: serial correlations The **serial correlation** measures the correlation between price changes in consecutive time periods—hourly, daily, or weekly—and is a measure of how much the price change in any period depends on the price change over the previous time period. A serial correlation of zero would therefore imply that price changes in consecutive time periods are uncorrelated with one another and can thus be viewed as a rejection of the hypothesis that investors can learn about future price changes from past ones. A serial correlation that is positive and statistically significant could be viewed as evidence of price momentum and would suggest that returns in a period are more likely to be positive (negative) if the prior period's returns were positive (negative). A serial correlation that is negative and statistically significant could be evidence of price reversals and would indicate a market in which positive returns are more likely to follow negative returns, and vice versa.

Serial Correlation: This is the correlation between a data time series and the same series lagged by one or more periods.

From the viewpoint of investment strategy, serial correlations can be exploited to earn excess returns. A positive serial correlation would be exploited by a strategy of buying after periods with positive returns and selling after periods with negative returns. A negative serial correlation would suggest a strategy of buying after periods with negative returns and selling after periods with positive returns. Because these strategies generate transactions costs, the correlations have to be large enough to allow investors to generate profits to cover these costs. It is therefore entirely possible for there to be serial correlation in returns, without any opportunity to earn excess returns for most investors.

Table 16.2 summarizes the evidence from a number of studies that have examined the serial correlation of returns in short periods in financial markets.

Table 16.2 SERIAL CORRELATION IN SHORT-PERIOD RETURNS

Author	Data	Variables	Time Interval	Correlation
Kendall & Alexander (28)	19 indices—U.K.	price	1 week	0.131
			2 weeks	0.134
			4 weeks	0.006
Moore (28)	30 companies—U.S.	log prices	1 week	−0.056
Cootner (28)	45 companies—U.S.	log prices	1 week	−0.047
Fama (46)	30 companies—U.S.	log prices	1 day	0.026
			4 days	−0.039
			9 days	−0.053
King (28)	63 companies—U.S.	log prices	1 month	0.018
Niarchos (119)	15 companies—Greece	log prices	1 month	0.036
Praetz (128)	16 indices	log prices	1 week	0.000
	20 companies		1 week	−0.118
Griffiths (73)	5 companies—U.K.	prices	9 days	−0.026
			1 month	0.011
Jennergren (90)	15 companies—U.K.	log prices	1 day	0.068
			2 days	−0.070
			5 days	−0.004
Jennergren & Kosvold (91)	30 companies—Sweden	log prices	1 day	0.102
			3 days	−0.021
			5 days	−0.016

As the evidence indicates, the serial correlation in most markets is small. Although statistical significance may be associated with some of these correlations, it is unlikely that there is enough correlation to generate excess returns.

> **Market Efficiency Lesson 4:** Firms are better off not trying to make and take advantage of short-term forecasts of their stock prices based purely on past price movements.

Long-term price movements Most of the earlier studies of price behavior focused on shorter return intervals, but in recent years attention has been paid to price movements over longer periods (one to five years). Part of this attention can be attributed to the fact that there is substantial negative correlation in longer term return intervals, suggesting that prices reverse themselves over very long periods. Because such behavior would be a serious challenge to market efficiency, the phenomenon has been examined in extensive detail. Studies that break down stocks on the basis of market value have found that the serial correlation is more negative in five-year returns than in one-year returns and is much more negative for smaller stocks than for larger stocks. Figure 16.3 summarizes one-year and five-year serial correlations by size class for stocks on the New York Stock Exchange.

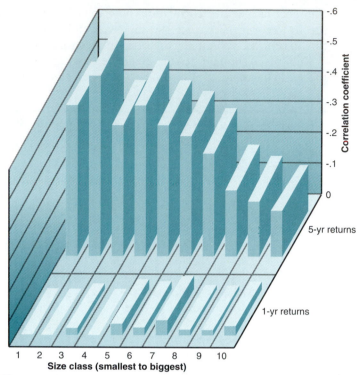

Figure 16.3 One-year and five-year serial correlations—by size class

This phenomenon has been examined in other markets as well, and the findings are similar—returns reverse themselves over long time periods.

Winner and loser portfolios Given the evidence that prices reverse themselves in the long term for entire markets, it might be worth examining whether such price reversals occur on certain classes of stock within a market. For instance, are stocks that have gone up the most over the last period more likely to go down over the next period, and vice versa? To isolate the effect of such price reversals on the extreme portfolios, DeBondt and Thaler constructed a winner portfolio of 35 stocks that had gone up the most over the prior year and a loser portfolio of 35 stocks that had gone down the most over the prior year, each year from 1933 to 1978. They then examined returns on these portfolios for the 60 months following the creation of the portfolio. Figure 16.4 summarizes the excess returns for winner and loser portfolios.

This analysis suggests that loser portfolios clearly outperform winner portfolios in the 60 months following creation. This evidence is consistent with market overreaction and correction in long return intervals.

Many academics and practitioners suggest that, although these findings may be interesting, they overstate potential returns on "loser" portfolios. For instance, there is evidence that loser portfolios are more likely to contain low-priced stocks (selling for less than $5), which inherently generate higher transactions costs and are more likely to offer heavily skewed returns (i.e., the excess returns come from a few stocks making phenomenal returns rather than from consistent performance). One study attributes the bulk of the excess returns of loser portfolios to low-priced stocks and finds that the results are sensitive to the time at which the portfolios are created. Loser portfolios created every December earn significantly higher returns than do portfolios cre-

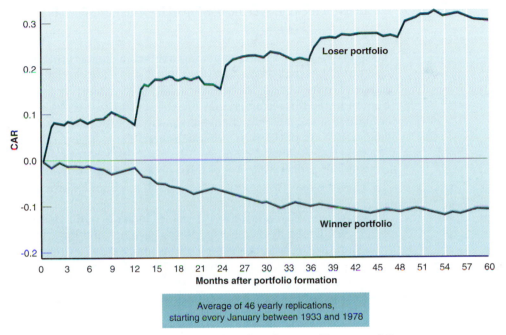

Figure 16.4 Excess returns for winner and loser portfolios

ated every June; this may be due to the January effect and its link to tax effects, which we mentioned earlier in this chapter.

Market Efficiency Lesson 5:   A firm whose stock price has gone down much more than the market in recent periods, while the fundamentals are still perceived to be sound, will generally gain by waiting to make equity issues, assuming such a delay is feasible.

Market Efficiency Lesson 6:   All of the lessons noted above should be at the margin; no firm should override the more important considerations of funding projects as needed and matching up assets to liabilities in order to exploit a market timing possibility. The gains are too low and the noise is too high to justify such

---

INFORMATION EFFICIENCY

Information efficiency examines three questions: (1) What information affects prices? (2) How quickly do prices react to this information? (3) How appropriate is the price adjustment to the information?

What Information Affects Prices?

The question of what information affects prices is a broad one, for any information that affects any aspect of value should also affect prices. This includes firm-specific information on future earnings, cash flows, and growth prospects; macro-economic information on inflation, interest rates, and the economy; and industry-specific information. We will focus on the firm specific portion of information, since managers do not have much control over the other two.

Cosmetic changes   Firms sometimes announce changes that are purely cosmetic and have no real impact on cash flows or value, and they expect markets to react to these changes. For instance, a change in accounting for inventory in the reporting statements (but not in the tax accounts) may increase earnings but not affect cash flows or value. Similarly, a stock split may change the number of shares outstanding but not the underlying cash flows of the firm. Although these changes generally do not impact current earnings or cash flows, they might affect market perceptions of future cash flows and, consequently, value. We consider three of these changes in the following section, two of which seem to have a negative effect on value, while the other has a positive effect.

Change in depreciation method   A change in depreciation method from accelerated to straight line generally increases reported earnings and lowers cash flows if the change is made in the tax accounts as well. Firms making this switch often do so only for purposes of reporting earnings to stockholders and continue to use **accelerated depreciation** methods for tax purposes. Thus, the switch has the purely cosmetic effect of inflating earnings without affecting cash flows, with the hope that stockholders will react positively to the increase in earnings.

Accelerated Depreciation: Any depreciation method that results in higher depreciation in the earlier years and less later on.

The evidence suggests the contrary, however. Kaplan and Roll (1972) examined the stock price reaction in the 60 weeks surrounding earnings announcements by firms that switched from the accelerated to the straight-line method for reporting purposes alone. They found that, although the prices increased temporarily in the aftermath of the earnings reports, they ended up significantly lower at the end of the analysis period, as shown in Figure 16.5.

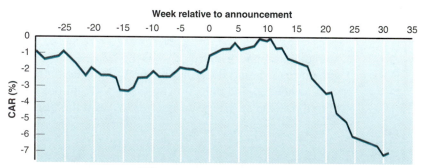

Figure 16.5   Effects of switch in depreciation methods

The negative market reaction can be explained partly by market disappointment at being fooled and partly by the realization that a firm that has to resort to such techniques to inflate earnings must not have very good projects or prospects, which translates into lower expected future cash flows and value.

Pooling versus purchase   Firms that make acquisitions often attempt to use the pooling approach, because the income statements and the balance sheets of the two companies are merged and any premium paid above book value for the acquired company is not reflected in the statements. In contrast, in the purchase approach, the excess of market over book value has to be shown on the acquiring company's balance sheet as **goodwill** and amortized over an extended period (not to exceed 40 years.) Because the amortization is after taxes (i.e., it does not create a tax deduction or affect the cash flows), it does lower reported earnings.

Goodwill: This is an accounting entry on a balance sheet, designed to capture the difference between the market value of an acquisition and its book value.

Hong, Kaplan, and Mandelkar (1978) examined the monthly excess returns of 122 firms that acquired other firms between 1954 and 1964 using the pooling technique. They compared these findings to 37 acquisitions that used the purchase approach to determine whether markets were misled by the "pooling" technique. They found no evidence that the pooling technique raised stock prices or that the purchase technique lowered prices. The results are summarized in Figure 16.6.

Panel A: Excess returns for 122 firms that used pooling

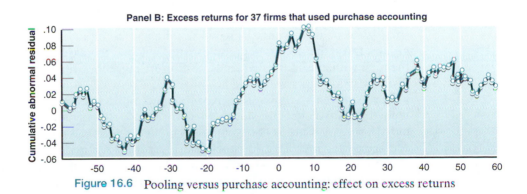

Panel B: Excess returns for 37 firms that used purchase accounting

Figure 16.6 Pooling versus purchase accounting: effect on excess returns

Note that no positive excess returns are associated with pooling in the 60 months following the merger, nor are negative excess returns associated with purchase in the same time period. Thus, markets seem to discount the negative earnings effect of amortizing goodwill.

> **Market Efficiency Lesson 7:** Firms that attempt to fool markets using accounting gimmicks generally find that these attempts backfire. (You can fool some investors all the time, all investors some of the time, but not all investors all the time.)

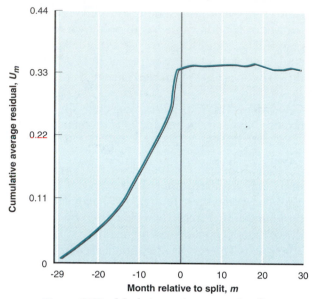

Figure 16.7   Market reaction to stock splits

Stock splits   A stock split increases the number of shares outstanding, without changing the current earnings or cash flows of the firm. As a purely cosmetic event, a stock split should not affect the value of the firm or of outstanding equity. Rather, the price per share will go down to reflect the stock split, because there are more shares outstanding. An early and oft-cited study by Fama, Fisher, Jensen, and Roll examined the stock price reaction to 940 stock splits between 1927 and 1959 by cumulating excess returns in the 60 months around the actual split date. The results are shown in Figure 16.7.
On average, their study found that stock splits tended to follow periods of excess returns; this is not surprising, inasmuch as splits typically follow price runups. They also found no evidence of excess returns around the splits themselves, suggesting that the splits were neutral events. Fama et al. followed up and classified the firms into two groups: those that followed the splits with dividend increases, and those that followed them up with cuts in the dividends. Not surprisingly, they found that the firms that cut dividends after stock splits had negative excess returns, as shown in Figure 16.8.

In recent years, a few studies have pointed out that stock splits may have an unintended negative effect on stockholders by raising transactions costs. For instance, the bid-ask spread, which is one component of the transactions costs, is a much larger percentage of the price for a $20 stock than it is for a $40 stock.[4] Copeland (1979) chronicles the increase in transactions costs and the decline in trading volume following splits. This additional cost has to be weighed against the potential signaling implications of a stock split; investors may view a stock split as a positive signal about future prospects. This may explain the small positive returns some researchers have found around stock split announcement dates.[5]

Earnings announcements   Earnings announcements are made by publicly traded firms in the United States every quarter, making them the most common vehicles for convey-

---

[4]The *bid-ask spread* refers to the difference between the price at which a security can be bought (the ask price) or the sold (the bid price) at any point in time.

[5]See Charest (1978) and Grinblatt, Masulis, and Titman (1984).

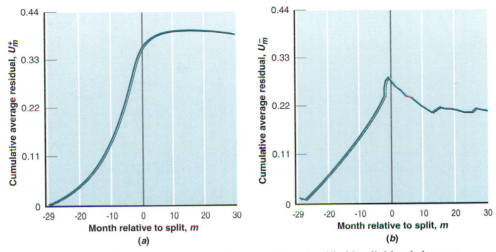

Figure 16.8 Excess returns around stock splits—classified by dividend changes

ing information about current operations. Earnings reports, which summarize the firm's performance over the prior quarter in an accounting statement, are significant because (1) they provide information on the current financial health of the firm, and (2) they contain information about future prospects. The magnitude of the information and the size of the market reaction depend on how much the earnings report exceeds or falls short of investor expectations. In an efficient market, we would predict an instantaneous reaction to the earnings report if it contained surprising information: an increase in prices following positive surprises, and a decrease in prices following negative surprises.

Because actual earnings are compared to investor expectations, a key part of an earnings event study is the measurement of these expectations. Some of the earlier studies used earnings from the same quarter in the prior year as a measure of expected earnings (i.e., firms that report increases in quarter-to-quarter earnings provide positive surprises, and those that report decreases in quarter-to-quarter earnings provide negative surprises). In more recent studies, analyst estimates of earnings have been used as a proxy for expected earnings and compared to the actual earnings.

Figure 16.9 provides a graph of price reactions to earnings surprises from "most negative" earnings reports (Group 1) to "most positive" earnings reports (Group 10). The evidence contained in this graph is consistent with the evidence in most earnings announcement studies:

1. The earnings announcement clearly conveys valuable information to financial markets: positive excess returns (cumulative abnormal returns) follow positive announcements, and negative excess returns follow negative announcements.

2. There is some evidence of a market reaction the day immediately prior to the earnings announcement, which is consistent with the nature of the announcement: prices tend to increase the day before positive announcements and to decrease the day before negative announcements. This can be viewed either as evidence of insider trading or as a consequence of using the wrong announcement date in the study.[6]

---

[6]The *Wall Street Journal* and COMPUSTAT are often sources of announcement dates for earnings. For some firms, news of the announcement may actually cross the news wire the day before the *Wall Street Journal* announcement, resulting in a misidentification of the report date and the drift in returns the day before the announcement.

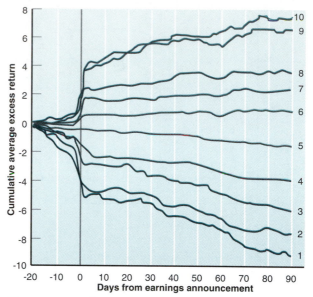

Figure 16.9   Price reactions to quarterly earnings report

3.   There is some evidence, albeit weak, of a **price drift** in the days following an earnings announcement. Thus, a positive report evokes a positive market reaction on the announcement date, and there are mildly positive excess returns in the days following the earnings announcement. Similar conclusions emerge for negative earnings reports.

Price Drift: This refers to the tendency of prices to keep increasing (decreasing) in the periods after a positive (negative) announcement.

The management of a firm has some discretion on the timing of earnings reports, and there is evidence that the timing affects expected returns. A study of earnings reports, classified by the day of the week the earnings are reported, reveals that earnings and dividend reports on Fridays are much more likely to contain negative information than are announcements on any other day of the week, as shown in Figure 16.10.

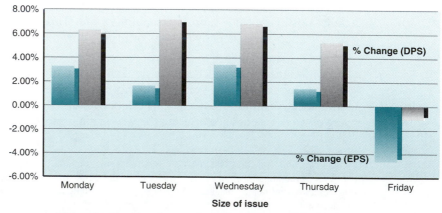

Figure 16.10   Earnings and dividend reports by day of the week

One explanation that has been advanced for this phenomenon is that managers do not like revealing bad news when markets are open and choose to reveal this news after markets are closed on Friday.

There is also some evidence that earnings announcements that are delayed, relative to the expected announcement date, are much more likely to contain bad news than those that are early or on time, as shown in Figure 16.11.

Figure 16.11   Cumulated abnormal returns and earnings delay

Furthermore, earnings announcements that are more than six days late, relative to the expected announcement date, are much more likely to contain bad news and to evoke negative market reactions than are earnings announcements that are on time or early. Here, again, the evidence suggests that managers try to delay bad news as long as possible, hoping either that they will be able to package it with some good news, or that they will find a better time to reveal the bad news.

> **Market Efficiency Lesson 8:**   Markets expect the worst, and no news is often viewed as bad news. Firms are generally better off revealing bad news immediately rather than delaying or suppressing it.

Earnings versus cash flows   As the evidence thus far indicates, financial markets tend to greet unexpected increases in earnings positively and unexpected decreases negatively. For the most part, earnings and cash flows move in the same direction; when earnings increase (decrease), cash flows do too. However, firms can take certain actions to increase earnings while reducing cash flows, and other actions to decrease earnings while increasing cash flows. For instance, a firm that switches its inventory method from **FIFO** to **LIFO** may decrease earnings but will increase cash flows. Similarly, a firm that chooses to capitalize an item and depreciate it, rather than expensing it, increases earnings at the expense of cash flows. The interesting question in these cases is whether the market reacts to the earnings effect or the cash-flow effect.

FIFO and LIFO: These are both methods used to value inventory. With First-in First-out (FIFO), inventory is valued at the end of each period on the basis of the cost of the most recently added items. With Last-in First-out (LIFO), it is valued based on the earliest items bought.

Sunder (1975) examined the market reaction to changes in inventory methods by 110 firms that switched from FIFO to LIFO, thereby increasing their cash flows, and by 22 firms that switched from LIFO to FIFO, thus increasing earnings, between 1946 and 1966. He found that the firms switching to LIFO posted a positive excess return of 5.3% in the year following the switch, whereas the firms switching to FIFO experienced negative returns, as shown in Figure 16.12.

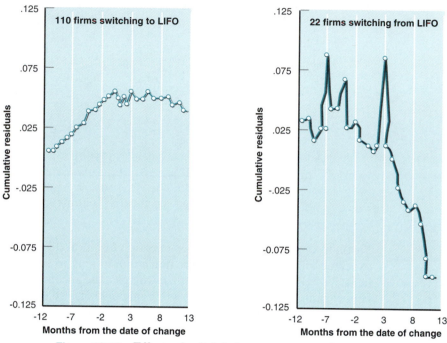

Figure 16.12 Effects of switch in inventory accounting methods

Note that, while the *initial* reaction to the earnings increase reported by firms switching to FIFO is positive, the reaction is reversed as investors learn more about the reason for the increase.

Market Efficiency Lesson 9: Given a choice between increasing earnings and increasing cash flows, firms that want to maximize value will be better off focusing on cash flows.

Other information Earnings and dividends announcements are not the only announcements made by firms to financial markets. Firms announce projects, acquisitions, joint ventures, and management changes to financial markets, and the market reaction to each of these announcements has been chronicled. Without going into the details on each study, the evidence can be summarized as follows:

- Financial markets seem to weigh the *long-term effects* of decisions in their reactions to them. Thus, on average, investments, R & D, and joint venture announcements tend to evoke positive reactions, even though these actions may reduce the current earnings of the company.

- Financial markets do not seem to buy in as easily into the management hype surrounding announcements of *acquisitions.* In a significant proportion of the cases (about 50%), the stock price of the acquiring company declines following the announcement of the acquisition.

- Financial markets seem to like *change,* especially in underperforming firms. Management changes at firms that have underperformed the market and their peer group are generally accompanied by stock price increases.

- Financial markets deal with *complex information* surprisingly well. For instance, when firms announce restructuring packages that involve changes in every aspect of the firm, from its asset base to its capital structure, markets respond instantaneously by adjusting the price to reflect the changes.

> **Market Efficiency Lesson 10:** Firms often underestimate the capacity of financial markets to assimilate, deal with, and react to complex information.

The Speed and Appropriateness of the Price Adjustment

The other questions relating to information efficiency concern how quickly the price adjustment is made and whether it appropriately reflects the information. This point is illustrated in Figure 16.13 by contrasting three different market reactions to information announcements.

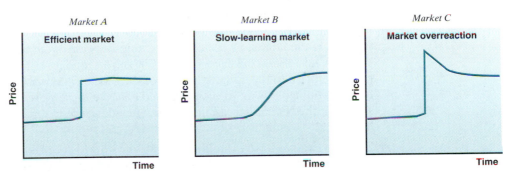

Figure 16.13   Contrasting market reactions to information announcements

Of the three market reactions pictured here, only market A is consistent with an efficient market. In market B, the information announcement is followed by a gradual increase in prices, allowing investors to make excess returns after the announcement. This is a slow-learning market in which some investors will make excess returns on the price drift. In market C, the price reacts instantaneously to the announcement but corrects itself in the days that follow, suggesting that the initial price change was an overreaction to the information. Here, again, an enterprising investor could have sold short after the announcement and have expected to make excess returns as a consequence of the price correction.

In general, studies that look at the market reaction to information announcements conclude that prices adjust quickly even to complex information.

- Studies of the price reaction to large block trades on the floor of the exchange conclude that prices adjust within a few minutes to such trades. Dann, Mayers, and Rabb examined the speed of the price reaction by looking at the returns an investor could

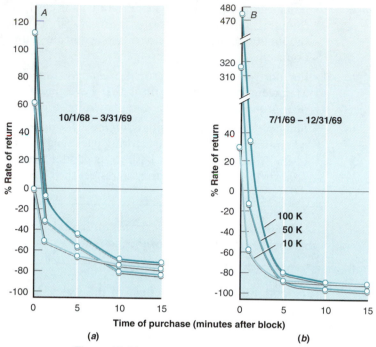

Figure 16.14   Returns around block trades

make by buying stock right around the block trade and selling later. They estimated the returns as a function of how many minutes the trade took place after the block trade and found that only trades made within a couple of minutes of the block trade had a chance of making excess returns, as shown in Figure 16.14. Put another way, prices adjusted to the liquidity effects of the block trade within five minutes of the block. Although this may be understated because these were block trades on large stocks on the NYSE, it is still fairly strong evidence of the market's capacity to adjust quickly to imbalances between demand and supply.

- Similarly, studies have examined the speed with which prices react to earnings announcements in the same day. There, the evidence is mixed. Woodruff and Senchack examined price adjustment by transaction after favorable (surprise > 20%) and unfavorable (surprise < −20%) earnings reports and reported the proportion of the eventual adjustment that has occurred by the hour after the earnings report for each category. As Figure 16.15 illustrates, approximately 91% of the eventual adjustment occurs within three hours of the report for the most positive earnings surprises, whereas only 76% of the eventual adjustment occurs during the same period for the most negative earnings announcements.

- Markets overreact to new information. This thesis is supported indirectly by the studies cited earlier, which note the excess returns made by stocks that have done badly in the past. It is also supported more directly by studies that look at the stock price performance for companies that report exceptionally good or bad news in the months following the announcements.

MARKET REACTION TO SECURITY ISSUES

As we discussed in detail in the previous chapter, firms can choose to issue one of a variety of securities—equity, debt, or hybrid securities—and they can choose from a vari-

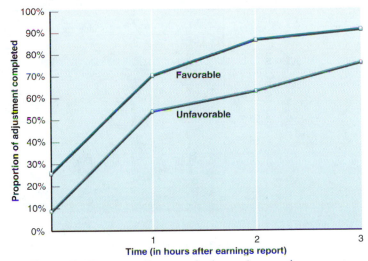

Figure 16.15   Price adjustment by hour after earnings report

ety of paths—from rights issues to general subscriptions. They typically have very good reasons for these choices, which they might convey to financial markets. However, financial markets react to these decisions based on not only the firm's reasoning, but also on their perception of the real reasons for the issues and the signals the firm's choices convey about future prospects. Thus, a firm may make an equity issue and justify its actions by pointing out that it is overlevered relative to its peer group. Markets, on the other hand, may respond negatively, seeing the equity issue as a signal that the managers of the firm do not believe that their future cash flows will be sufficient to make interest payments on debt.

Initial Public Offerings

In Chapter 15, we also described the process by which private firms go public and noted that investment banks often underprice new issues to reduce their risk and increase the appeal of the company for future issues. Not surprisingly, studies of the market response to initial public offerings report that there are excess returns to be made in the immediate aftermath of an issue. In a study of all initial public offerings made between 1960 and 1987, Ibbotson, Sindelar, and Ritter report an average initial return of 16.37% in the month following the initial offering. They also find that the initial return is larger for smaller and more speculative issues, as shown in Figure 16.16. This evidence suggests that at least a portion of the underpricing can be attributed to the riskiness associated with the issue.

In recent years, much more has been learned about the price behavior of initial public offerings, largely as a consequence of a series of empirical studies on the issue. Summarizing the evidence from these studies, we note the following:

- Much of the excess return made by initial public offerings occurs on the opening day of trading and thus reflects the deliberate underpricing of these issues.
- The risk adjustment made to calculate these excess returns may understate the riskiness of these offerings, and the higher transactions costs may overwhelm the excess returns, for average investors.
- Hot and cold performance in new issue markets seems to occur in waves, and there are fewer issues and lower returns in cold markets.

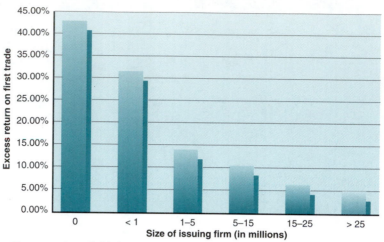

Figure 16.16   Initial returns in month following initial public offering

• The underpricing does not seem to represent surplus or unfair returns for investment bankers, who underwrite the issue. Muscarella and Vetsuypens (1988) report underpricing of roughly 7.1% for 38 investment banks that went public between 1970 and 1987.

> **Market Efficiency Lesson 11:**   Firms that make initial public offerings face a cost, on average, from having their issues underpriced; this cost is an increasing function of the riskiness and a decreasing function of the size of the issue. Firms can reduce their exposure to the underpricing cost by limiting the size, relative to firm value, of the initial issue.

Seasoned Security Issues

A number of studies have looked at the impact of changes in capital structure, either through the issue of new securities or through exchange offers, such as stock repurchases or debt for equity swaps. In a review article, Smith (1993) summarizes the results from the numerous studies looking at the valuation effects of these changes.

Type of security issued   Table 16.3, reproduced from Smith's paper, reports the two-day abnormal returns on common stock around various types of security offerings.

Table 16.3 ABNORMAL RETURNS AROUND SECURITY ISSUES		
	Type of Issuer	
Type of Security Offering	**Industrial**	**Utility**
Common stock	−3.14%	−0.75%
Preferred stock	−0.19%	+0.08%
Convertible preferred stock	−1.44%	−1.38%
Straight bonds	−0.26%	−0.13%
Convertible bonds	−2.07%	n.a.

Although none of the security issues elicits a positive stock price response, the market's response to common stock issues is much more negative than is its response to preferred or bond offerings. The surprising finding that all security issues elicit negative market responses does not bode well for a theory of optimal capital structure, for it implies that all such issues move firms away from their optimal.

Effect of offering on leverage   Smith also summarizes the results of numerous studies that look at exchange offers and other transactions that affect leverage. He concludes that transactions that increase leverage generally elicit positive abnormal returns for equity investors, whereas transactions that reduce leverage usually cause negative abnormal returns. For instance, issuing debt to repurchase equity creates a two-day return, on average, of 21.9%, whereas issuing equity to retire debt results in a two-day abnormal return of −9.9%. Table 16.4 provides a summary of academic findings on leverage-changing transactions.

Table 16.4   EFFECT OF LEVERAGE-INCREASING AND DECREASING TRANSACTIONS

Type of Transaction	Security Issued	Security Retired	Sample Size	Two-day Abnormal Return (%)
Leverage-Increasing Transactions				
Stock repurchase	Debt	Common	45	21.9%
Exchange offer	Debt	Common	52	14.0
Exchange offer	Preferred	Common	9	8.3
Exchange offer	Debt	Preferred	24	2.2
Exchange offer	Bonds	Preferred	24	2.2
Transactions with no Change in Leverage				
Exchange offer	Debt	Debt	36	0.6
Security sale	Debt	Debt	83	0.2
Leverage-Reducing Transactions				
Conversion-forcing call	Common	Convertible	57	−0.4
Conversion-forcing call	Common	Preferred	113	−2.1
Security sale	Convertible debt	Convertible debt	15	−2.4
Exchange offer	Common	Debt	30	−2.6
Exchange offer	Preferred	Preferred	9	−7.7
Security sale	Common	Debt	12	−4.2
Exchange offer	Common	Debt	20	−9.9

Again, this evidence is difficult to reconcile with a theory of optimal capital structure, unless we assume that firms are generally underleveraged and that increases in leverage are therefore more likely to push a firm toward its optimal.

> **Market Efficiency Lesson 12:**   Every financing choice made by a firm conveys information to financial markets and, consequently, affects prices.

THE INFLUENCE OF EQUITY RESEARCH ANALYSTS AND BOND RATINGS AGENCIES

Firms typically view equity research analysts and bond rating agencies as key players because of their capacity to influence market opinion and prices. Consequently, firms spend a great deal of time catering to the needs of these parties and worrying about their response to investment, financing, and payout decisions.

Analyst Recommendations

Analysts clearly hold a privileged position in the market for information, operating at the nexus of private and public information. Using both types of information, analysts issue buy and sell recommendations to their clients, who trade on its basis. Figure 16.17 reveals the price impact that analysts' recommendations have on stock prices in the United States and Britain.

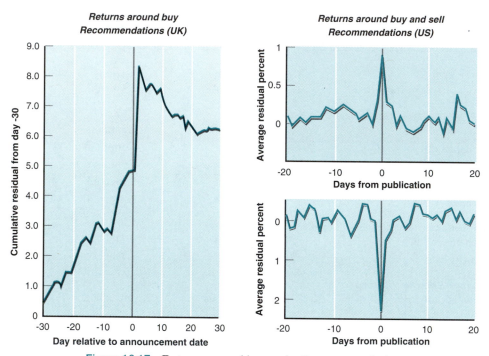

Figure 16.17   Returns around buy and sell recommendations

Although both recommendations affect stock prices, sell recommendations affect prices much more adversely than buy recommendations affect them positively. Furthermore, the price effect is restricted to the day of the recommendation, and there is no evidence in the prices of *front running* (whereby analysts buy or sell stocks on their own account before issuing recommendations) or *drifts* (whereby buy and sell recommendations affect prices in the days after they are issued).

The fact that analyst recommendations affect prices should not come as a surprise to financial managers. The more important question is whether these price effects are permanent or temporary. There is contradictory evidence on this point, and yet a recent working paper by Womack (1995) suggests that the price effects can be lasting, with negative recommendations causing a price drop, on average, of 13.8% in the six months following, and positive recommendations resulting in a price increase of 2.4% in the same time span. This finding has to be tempered by others that show that the price impact is permanent only if the analyst report is based on substance. In other words, analyst reports based on bad information or faulty analysis do not seem to have any lasting impact on prices.

> **Market Efficiency Lesson 13:** Because analyst recommendations create permanent price changes, *only if based on substance,* firms may find their time better spent focusing on improving their cash flows and earnings than on keeping analysts happy.

Bond Rating Agencies

Bond rating agencies determine ratings, and ratings determine interest rates. Accordingly, bond ratings agencies hold the key to lower interest rates, and decisions have to be made with an eye to meeting their specific criteria and needs. But is this premise correct? Bond ratings agencies do determine ratings, but do ratings determine interest rates? This may sound like an absurd question, especially given the empirical fact that a very high correlation exists between ratings and interest rates. But there is evidence that the ratings do not determine interest rates, but that interest rates determine ratings.

A series of studies on bond price changes in response to ratings changes concluded that bond prices are unaffected by ratings changes; rather, the price changes occur well in advance of the ratings change. This premise was also tested by Hand, Holthausen, and Leftwich (1992), who examined bond and stock price changes around ratings changes. They report that downgrades by ratings agencies have a negative effect on stock prices but not on bond prices, and that upgrades have no effect on stock prices while benefiting bond prices. Their findings suggest that the effect is small, however, and that the ratings change might occur after the market has already priced in the bulk of the change into security prices.

This evidence seems to indicate that ratings agencies follow the market rather than lead it, at least on average. In addition, firms that tailor their financing needs to meet ratings agency concerns and measurement quirks may not receive the payoff they expect because financial markets are not only much smarter, but are also much quicker in responding to underlying changes in the firm.

> **Market Efficiency Lesson 14:** A firm might fool the ratings agency all the time, but it will not fool markets much of the time.

CONCLUSION

In this chapter, we have examined studies of market efficiency from the perspective of corporate finance. We began with a generic definition of market efficiency and then proceeded to examine four broad areas of empirical research:

1. On the issue of *market timing,* at either the aggregate market level or the level of the firm, we concluded that there are some disquieting patterns in stock prices. In particular, we noted the positive returns in January for small stocks, the tendency of

interest rates to move in a normal range, and the long-term reversals in stock prices. Although managers may take advantage of some of these patterns in financing, we also noted that there is a great deal of noise in both stock and bond prices, and that these effects should be considered marginal and not override more important fundamental considerations.

2. On the issue of *information efficiency,* we examined three questions. The first related to the types of information that move markets. We noted that cosmetic changes have little effect on prices, that they do not fool markets for extended periods, and that markets seem to value cash flows more than earnings. The second question considered the speed of the price adjustment in response to new information. There seems to be sufficient evidence that markets respond quickly to new information and that they seem to do a reasonably good job in evaluating and pricing complex information. The third related to the prevalence of price drifts and market overreaction; there seems to be some evidence of both phenomena in financial markets. Overall, we concluded that managers should trust financial markets with information, good as well as bad, and that markets are fair for the most part in assessing the effects of the information.

3. On the issue of *market reactions* to security issues, we noted two findings. First, initial public offerings are, on average, underpriced, but the underpricing does not seem to be as much an inefficiency as a price paid for the uncertainty associated with the issue. Second, security issues made by firms are perused by markets for signals about future earnings and cash flows and can thus affect prices. Overall, leverage-increasing transactions evoke more positive market reactions than do leverage-decreasing transactions.

4. Finally, we examined the *influence of equity research analysts and bond ratings agencies* on security prices and concluded that, although they do affect prices with their recommendations and actions, the price effect is small and unlikely to persist unless it is based on substance. Moreover, market prices seem to influence analysts and ratings agencies at least as much as, if not more than, they influence markets. This suggests that firms will get a much larger payoff by focusing on improving their underlying prospects and increasing value than by expending the same effort to keep analysts and ratings agencies happy.

QUESTIONS AND PROBLEMS

1. You have been asked for your advice by XYTEL Inc., a small software firm that is planning to make an equity issue in November, as to whether it should wait until January to make the issue. What would you advise? Would your advice be any different if the firm were planning to make the issue in June? Why or why not?

2. Interest rates are rising because of a surge in inflation. FinBank, a large financial service firm that had been planning to make a bond issue, asks you whether the bond issue should be delayed until rates come down. Assuming that the delay will cost the firm in terms of lost projects, what would you advise?

3. You have been approached by FutureFin, an investment bank that claims to have a model that predicts stock and bond market movements. The bank offers its services to help in timing your security issues. Would you accept the offer? Why or why not?

4. DownSize Inc, a large auto parts manufacturing firm, announces that it will be closing an unprofitable plant and taking a charge against earnings, causing a big drop in earnings per share. Based on the empirical evidence surveyed in this chapter, what would you expect the stock price response to be?

5. Mintel, a firm that manufactures semiconductor chips for computers, has just uncovered a flaw in one of its most widely used products. You have been asked to advise the firm on whether it should announce this bad news to financial markets or suppress it for as long as it can. What would you advise? Why?

6. A firm makes a very negative earnings announcement, and, as a result, stock prices plummet. The managers of the firm feel that the market response is much too negative, given the report. Given the historical evidence, are they likely to be right?

7. NeedCap, a small, fast-growing firm decides to raise new equity by making a rights offering and is surprised to see its stock price go down upon the announcement. How would you explain the market reaction? Can you counter the reaction?

8. A well-known equity research analyst has issued a sell recommendation on your company but has based it on faulty data. What would you expect to happen to your stock price when the sell recommendation comes out? What would you expect the price to be six months later?

9. A firm comes up with a security, with fixed life, fixed dollar dividend payments that are tax deductible and no voting rights (and therefore has all of the characteristics of debt), but it is classified as equity by ratings agencies in calculating leverage. The firm believes it is pulling off a coup because it is getting all the benefits of leverage without increasing its leverage. Is it right? Why or why not?

10. Daimler Benz reported a loss of $4.2 billion in January 1996 for the 1995 fiscal year. Much of the loss was attributed to the writeoff of the Fokker Aircraft division it owned. The stock price increased by 1.25 DM on the report. How would you explain the reaction? Under what conditions would you expect the stock price to react negatively?

11. The Gap, a specialty retailing firm, announces that it will be splitting its stock two-for-one, while increasing its cash dividend by 25%. How would you expect the stock price to react? Why?

12. You own a small software company that is planning to make an initial public offering. The value of the company is estimated to be $25 million, and there will be 2.5 million shares outstanding. The investment banker proposes to price the issue at $9.00 per share. How would you react to the pricing? Would your response be any different if you planned to offer only 10% of the stock on the initial offering date, and the remaining stock six months later?

13. You are the manager of Telefax Inc, a company that manufactures fax modems for computers. You need to raise fresh equity for your firm, which is publicly traded. Your investment banker argues against doing so now, suggesting that your stock, which has gone up 75% in the last six months, is likely to keep going up because of price momentum. Would you follow her advice? Why or why not?

14. You are a manager at a large manufacturing company, and you have information that your next earnings report is going to come in well below analyst expectations. Should you try to reveal the information to financial markets? Why or why not?

15. Swimmees Inc., a company that manufacturers swimming wear, makes almost 65% of its operating income in the summer months. It needs to raise fresh equity to finance its projects and is considering delaying the issue until the summer when its sales will be greatest, because it assumes that its stock price will also be highest in those months. What would your advice be? Under what conditions will the stock price increase during the summer months?

CHAPTER 17

CAPITAL STRUCTURE: TRADEOFFS AND THEORY

In the last two chapters, we examined many of the financing choices available to businesses and the lessons that can be learned from studies of market efficiency in making these choices. In this chapter, we introduce the basic tradeoff between using debt and equity in financing a firm's needs, as well as the underlying theory and hypotheses relating to the "right mix" of debt and equity. In the process, we attempt to answer the following questions:

- What are the primary benefits and costs of using debt financing rather than equity financing?

- What types of firms are most likely to benefit from debt financing?

- When is there no optimal mix of debt and equity? (In other words, when is the capital structure decision irrelevant?)

- How do firms make capital structure decisions?

THE BENEFITS OF DEBT

When firms choose between borrowing money or using equity to finance their projects, they are making a tradeoff between the benefits of using debt, relative to using equity, against the costs borrowing poses for them. In the broadest terms, debt provides two differential benefits over equity. The first is the *tax benefit*: interest payments on debt are tax deductible, whereas cash flows on equity are not. The second is the *added discipline imposed on management* by having to make payments on debt. Both benefits can and should be quantified if firms want to make reasonable judgments on debt capacity.

The Tax Advantage of Debt

The primary benefit of debt is the tax advantage it confers on the borrower. In the United States, interest paid on debt incurred by businesses is tax deductible, whereas cash flows on equity (such as dividends) have to be paid out of after-tax cash flows. For the most part, this is true in other countries as well, although some countries try to provide partial protection against the **double taxation** of dividends by providing a tax credit to investors who receive the dividends for the corporate taxes paid (Britain) or by taxing retained earnings at a rate higher than dividends (Germany).

Double Taxation: Double taxation exists when the same income is taxed twice—once at the entity level and once at the individual level. Thus, dividends, which are paid out of after-tax corporate profits, are double taxed when individuals have to pay taxes on them as well.

The tax benefits from debt can be presented in two ways. In the first approach, the present value of tax savings arising from interest payments is computed and added on to firm value. In the second approach, the savings from the tax deduction are shown as the difference between the pretax rate of borrowing and the after-tax rate.

The dollar tax savings Consider a firm that borrows $B to finance its operations, on which it faces an interest rate of $r\%$, and assume that it faces a **marginal tax rate** of t on income. The annual tax savings from the interest tax deduction can be calculated as follows:

$$\text{Annual Interest Expense arising from the Debt} = r\,B$$
$$\text{Annual Tax Savings arising from the Interest Payment} = t\,r\,B$$

Marginal Tax Rate: This is the tax rate that applies on the marginal dollar of income at a firm. In general, it will be higher than the average tax rate.

The present value of the annual tax savings can be computed by making three other assumptions. (1) The debt is perpetual, which also means that the dollar savings are a perpetuity. (2) The appropriate discount rate for this cash flow is the interest rate on the debt because it reflects the riskiness of the debt. (3) The expected tax rate for the firm will remain unchanged over time, and the firm is in a taxpaying position. With these three assumptions, the present value of the savings can be computed as follows:

$$\text{Present Value of Tax Savings from Debt} = t\,r\,B\,/\,r = t\,B$$
$$= \text{Marginal tax rate} * \text{Debt}$$

Although the conventional view is to look at the tax savings as a perpetuity, the approach is general enough to be used to compute the tax savings over a shorter period (say, 10 years.) Thus, a firm that borrows $100 million at 8% for 10 years and has a tax rate of 40% can compute the present value of its tax savings as follows:

$$\text{Present Value of Interest Tax Savings} = \text{Annual Tax Savings (PV of Annuity)}$$
$$= (.08 * 0.4 * \$100 \text{ million}) \text{ (PV of Annuity, 8\%,10 years)} = \$21.47 \text{ million}$$

In addition, the net tax benefit can be computed if dividends also provide a tax benefit, albeit one that is smaller than that conferred by debt. In such a case, the present value of the net tax savings from debt can be written as:

$$\text{Present Value of Net Tax Savings from Debt}$$
$$= \text{PV of Tax Savings from Debt} - \text{PV of Tax Savings from Dividend Payments}$$

To illustrate, consider the example of a country whose tax rate on cash paid out as dividends (t_{div}) is less than the tax rate on retained earnings (t_{re}). The present value of the tax savings arising from dividends can be written as follows, assuming a growth rate of g in dividends and a cost of equity of k_e:

Present Value of Tax Savings from Dividends $= (t_{\text{re}} - t_{\text{div}})$ Dividend $(1 + g) / (k_e - g)$

Note that this is the present value of a growing perpetuity.

When asked to analyze the effect of adding debt on value, some analysts use a shortcut and simply add the tax benefit from debt to the value of the firm with no debt:

Value of Levered Firm with debt B $=$ Value of Unlevered Firm $+ t\,B$

The limitation of this approach is that it considers only the tax benefit from borrowing and none of the additional costs. It also yields the unrealistic conclusion that firm value increases monotonically with more debt.

Pretax and after-tax costs   The tax benefit from debt can also be expressed in terms of the difference between the pretax and after-tax cost of debt. To illustrate, if r is the interest rate on debt and t is the marginal tax rate, the after-tax cost of borrowing (k_d) can be written as follows:

After-tax Cost of Debt (k_d) $= r\,(1 - t)$

This is the familiar formula used for calculating the cost of debt in the cost of capital calculation. In this formula, the after-tax cost of debt is a decreasing function of the tax rate. A firm with a tax rate of 40%, which borrows at 8%, has an after-tax cost of debt of 4.8%. Another firm with a tax rate of 70%, which borrows at 8%, has an after-tax cost of debt of 2.4%. There are two points to be emphasized in this calculation. First, the tax rate to be used is the *marginal rate* and not the average rate, since interest tax deductions are set off against the marginal dollar of income. Second, this calculation makes sense only if the firm is making money and paying taxes; a firm that has large accumulated losses and no taxable income may not get a tax benefit from debt.

❏ Concept
Check

Assume that you are examining the debt capacity of a firm that has large accumulated net losses. How would you calculate the after-tax cost of debt for such a firm? Would this calculation change over time?

Implications for optimal capital structure   Other things remaining equal, the benefits of debt are much greater when tax rates are higher. Consequently, four predictions can be made about debt ratios across companies and across time.

1.   The debt ratios of entities facing higher tax rates should be higher than the debt ratios of comparable entities facing lower tax rates.

2.   Firms that have substantial nondebt tax shields, such as depreciation, should be less likely to use debt than firms that do not have these tax shields.

3.   If tax rates increase over time, we would expect debt ratios to go up over time as well, reflecting the higher tax benefits of debt.

4.   Although it is always difficult to compare debt ratios across countries, we would expect countries whose debt has a much larger tax benefit or whose tax rates are higher to have higher debt ratios than countries whose debt has a lower tax benefit.

☐ Concept
Check

> What type of debt policy would you advise a nonprofit organization to follow? Why?

The Discipline of Debt

In the 1980s, in the midst of the leveraged buyout boom, a group of practitioners and academics, led by Michael Jensen at Harvard, developed and expounded a new rationale for borrowing, based on improving the firm's efficiency in utilizing its free cash flows. **Free cash flows** represent cash flows made on operations over which managers have discretionary spending power; they may use them to take projects, pay them out to stockholders, or hold them as idle cash balances. The group argued that managers in firms that have substantial free cash flows and no or low debt have such a large cash cushion against mistakes that they have no incentive to be efficient in either project choice or project management. One way to introduce discipline into the process is to force these firms to borrow money; borrowing creates the commitment to make interest and principal payments, increasing the risk of default on projects with substandard returns. This difference between the forgiving nature of the equity commitment and the inflexibility of the debt commitment has led some to call equity a *cushion* and debt a *sword.*

Free Cash Flows (Jensen's):   These cash flows are the operating cash flows after taxes but before discretionary capital expenditures.

The underlying assumptions in this argument are that there is a separation of ownership and management and that managers will not maximize shareholder wealth without some prodding (debt). From our discussion in Chapter 2, it is clear that both assumptions are grounded in fact. Most large U.S. corporations employ managers who own only a very small portion of the outstanding stock in the firm; they receive most of their income as managers rather than stockholders. Furthermore, evidence indicates that managers, at least sometimes, put their interests ahead of those of stockholders.

While conceding the need for discipline, we would also add that debt may have a beneficial effect *only up to a certain point.* At some point, the risk added by the leverage may be so great that managers become reluctant to take even the slightest risks, for fear of bankruptcy, and turn down even good projects.

☐ Concept
Check

> You are examining two firms, one in a sector with high returns and one in a sector with low returns. Which one would you expect to benefit more from the discipline of debt and why?

Management perspectives on using debt   The argument that debt adds discipline to the process also provides an interesting insight into management perspectives on debt. Based purely on managerial incentives, the optimal level of debt may be much lower than that estimated based on shareholder wealth maximization. Left to themselves, why would managers want to burden themselves with debt, knowing full well that they will have to become more efficient and pay a larger price for their mistakes?

The corollary to this argument is that the debt ratios of firms in countries in which stockholder power to influence or remove managers is minimal will be much lower than optimal because managers enjoy a more comfortable existence by carrying less debt than they can afford. Conversely, as stockholders acquire power, they will push these firms to borrow more money and, in the process, increase their stock prices.

❑ Concept
Check

> In many hostile acquisitions, the debt ratios of the acquired firms are increased substantially after the acquisition. How would you explain this phenomenon?

The empirical evidence   Do increases in leverage lead to improved efficiency? The answer to this question should provide some insight into whether the argument for added discipline has some basis. A number of studies have attempted to answer this question, though most have done so indirectly:

- Firms that are taken over in hostile takeovers are generally characterized by poor performance in both accounting profitability and stock returns. Bhide (1993), for instance, notes that the return on equity of these firms is 2.2% below that of their peer group, while the stock returns are 4% below the peer group's returns.

- Whereas the poor performance, does not itself constitute support for the free cash-flow hypothesis, Palepu (1986) presents evidence that target firms in acquisitions are underleveraged relative to similar firms that are not taken over.

- Increases in leverage are followed by improvements in operating efficiency. Palepu (1990) presents evidence of modest improvements in operating efficiency at firms involved in leveraged buyouts. Kaplan (1989) and Smith (1990) also report improvements in operating efficiency at firms following leveraged buyouts. Denis and Denis (1993) present more direct evidence of improvements in operating efficiency after **leveraged recapitalizations.** In their study of 29 firms that increased debt substantially, they report a median increase in the return on assets of 21.5%. Much of this gain seems to arise out of cutbacks in unproductive capital investments, since the median reduction in capital expenditures of these firms is 35.5%.

Leveraged Recapitalization: In a leveraged recapitalization, a firm borrows money and either buys back stock or pays a dividend, thus increasing its debt ratio substantially.

Of course, we must consider that this evidence to be consistent with a number of different hypotheses, among them the free cash-flow hypothesis. Moreover, acquisitions, which often comprise the samples in most of these studies, are accompanied by a number of changes, including leverage shifts, making it difficult to isolate the impact of leverage on firm performance.

THE COSTS OF DEBT

As any borrower will attest, debt certainly has disadvantages. In particular, borrowing money can expose the firm to default and eventual liquidation, increase the agency problems arising from the conflict between the interests of equity investors and lenders, and reduce the firm's flexibility to take actions now or in the future.

Bankruptcy Costs

The primary concern when borrowing money is the increase in expected bankruptcy costs that typically follows. The expected bankruptcy cost can be written as a product of the probability of bankruptcy and the direct and indirect costs of bankruptcy.

The probability of bankruptcy   The probability of bankruptcy is the likelihood that a firm's cash flows will be insufficient to meet its promised debt obligations (interest or principal). Although such a failure does not automatically imply bankruptcy, it does trigger default, with all its negative consequences. Based on this definition, the probability of bankruptcy is a function of the following:

1. *Size of operating cash flows relative to size of cash flows on debt obligations:*   Other things remaining equal, the larger the operating cash flows relative to the cash flows on debt obligations, the smaller the likelihood of bankruptcy. Accordingly, the probability of bankruptcy increases marginally for all firms as they borrow more money, regardless of how large and stable their cash flows might be.

2. *Variance in operating cash flows:*   Given the same cash flows on debt, a firm with more stable and predictable cash flows has a lower probability of bankruptcy than does another firm with a similar level of operating cash flows, but with far greater variability in these cash flows.

□ Concept Check

> A firm that has traditionally operated in a regulated environment (say, phone service) decides to enter a higher-return but unregulated business. What are the consequences for its leverage?

The cost of bankruptcy   The cost of going bankrupt is neither obvious nor easily quantified. It is true that bankruptcy is a disaster for all involved in the firm—lenders often get only a fraction of what they are owed, and equity investors get nothing—but the overall cost of bankruptcy also includes the *indirect* costs on operations of being perceived as having high default risk.

Direct costs   The direct, or deadweight, costs of bankruptcy are those which are incurred in terms of cash outflows at the time of bankruptcy. These costs include the legal and administrative costs of a bankruptcy, as well as the present value effects of delays in paying out the cash flows. Warner (1977) estimated the legal and administrative costs of 11 railroads to be, on average, 5.3% of the value of the assets at the time of the bankruptcy. He also estimated that it took, on average, 13 years before the railroads were reorganized and released from the bankruptcy costs. These costs, though not negligible, are not overwhelming, especially in light of two additional factors. First, the direct cost as a percentage of the value of the assets decreases to 1.4% if the asset value is computed five years before the bankruptcy. Second, railroads, in general, are likely to have higher bankruptcy costs than other companies because of the nature of their assets (real estate and fixed equipment).

□ Concept Check

> Some argue that bankruptcy costs are huge, especially when one considers the loss in the value of the securities of firms that go bankrupt. Do you agree? Why or why not?

Indirect costs If the only costs of bankruptcy were the direct costs, the low leverage maintained by many firms would be puzzling. However, much larger costs are associated with taking on debt and increasing default risk, which arise prior to the bankruptcy, largely as a consequence of the perception that a firm is in financial trouble. The first is the perception on the part of the *customers of the firm* that the firm is in trouble. When this happens, customers may *stop buying the product or service,* for fear that the company will go out of business. In 1980, for example, when car buyers believed that Chrysler was on the verge of bankruptcy, they chose to buy from Ford, GM, and other car manufacturers, largely because they were concerned about receiving service and parts for their cars after their purchases. Similarly, in the late 1980s, when Continental Airlines found itself in financial trouble, business travelers switched to other airlines because they were unsure about whether they would be able to accumulate and use their frequent flier miles on the airline. The second indirect cost is the stricter terms that *suppliers start demanding* to protect themselves against the possibility of default, leading to an increase in working capital and a decrease in cash flows. The third cost is the difficulty the firm may experience trying to *raise fresh capital* for its projects; both debt and equity investors are reluctant to take the risk, leading to capital rationing constraints and the rejection of good projects.

Shapiro and Titman point out that the indirect costs of bankruptcy are likely to be higher for the following types of firms:

- *Firms that sell durable products with long lives that require replacement parts and service*: Thus, a personal computer manufacturer would have higher indirect costs associated with bankruptcy than would a grocery store.

- *Firms that provide goods or services for which quality is an important attribute but is difficult to determine in advance*: Because the quality cannot be determined easily in advance, the reputation of the firm plays a significant role in whether the customer will buy the product in the first place. For instance, the perception that an airline is in financial trouble may scare away customers who worry that the planes belonging to the airline will not be maintained in good condition.

- *Firms that produce products whose value to customers depends on the services and complementary products supplied by independent companies*: With regard to the example of personal computers, a computer system is valuable only insofar as software is available to run it. If the firm manufacturing the computers is perceived to be in trouble, it is entirely possible that the independent suppliers that produce the software might stop providing it. Thus, if Apple Computers gets into financial trouble, many software manufacturers might stop producing software for its computers, leading to an erosion in its potential market.

- *Firms that sell products that require continuous service and support from the manufacturer*: A manufacturer of copying machines, for which constant service seems to be a necessary operating characteristic, would be affected more adversely by the perception of default risk than would a furniture manufacturer, for example.

Implications for optimal capital structure If the expected bankruptcy cost is indeed the product of the probability of bankruptcy and the direct and indirect bankruptcy cost, interesting and testable implications emerge for capital structure decisions:

1. Firms operating in businesses with volatile earnings and cash flows should use debt less than should otherwise similar firms with stable cash flows. For instance, regulated utilities in the United States have high leverage because the regulation and the monopolistic nature of their businesses result in stable earnings and cash flows. At the other extreme, toy manufacturing firms, such as Mattel, can have large shifts in income from one year to another, based on the commercial success or failure of a single toy;[1] these firms should make far less use of leverage in meeting their funding needs.

2. If firms can structure their debt in such a way that the cash flows on the debt increase and decrease with their operating cash flows, they can afford to borrow more. This is because the probability of default is greatest when operating cash flows decrease, and the concurrent reduction in debt cash flows makes the default risk lower. In Chapter 15, we examined several features that can be added to debt to create this feature. Commodity companies, whose operating cash flows increase and decrease with commodity prices, may be able to use more debt if the debt payments are linked to commodity prices. Similarly, a company whose operating cash flows increase as interest rates (and inflation) go up and decrease when interest rates go down may be able to use more debt if the debt has a floating rate feature.

3. If an external entity provides protection against bankruptcy, by providing either insurance or bailouts, firms will tend to borrow more. To illustrate, the deposit insurance offered by the FSLIC and the FDIC enables savings & loans and banks to maintain higher leverage than they otherwise could. Although one can argue for this insurance on the grounds of preserving the integrity of the financial system, undercharging for the insurance will accentuate this tendency and induce high-risk firms to take on too much debt, letting taxpayers bear the cost. Similarly, governments that step in and regularly bail out firms on social grounds (e.g., to save jobs) will encourage all firms to overuse debt.

4. The direct bankruptcy costs are higher when the firm's assets are not easily divisible and marketable. Firms with assets that can be easily divided and sold should therefore be able to borrow more than firms with assets that do not share these features. Thus, a firm, such as Weyerhauser, whose value comes from its real estate holdings, should be able to borrow more money than a firm such as Coca-Cola, which derives a great deal of its value from its brand name.

5. Firms that produce products that require long-term servicing and support generally have lower leverage than do firms whose products do not share this feature, as we discussed earlier.

> ❑ Concept
> Check
>
> In the German and Japanese systems of corporate governance, loosely organized firms invest in one another, creating complex cross-holdings. If any of the companies in the group get into trouble, the stronger companies will step in and provide support and, if necessary, help extract the company from its financial predicament. What are the implications of this arrangement for capital structure?

Agency Costs

Equity investors and lenders do not always agree on the best course of action for a firm, largely because they have very different cash-flow claims to the firm. Equity investors, who receive a residual claim on the cash flows, tend to favor actions that increase the value of their holdings, even if that means increasing the risk that the bondholders (who have a fixed claim on the cash flows) will not receive their promised payments. Bondholders, on the other hand, want to preserve and increase the security of their

---

[1] In years past, a single group of toys, such as the Teenage Mutant Ninja turtles or the Power Rangers, could account for a substantial proportion of a major toy manufacturer's profits.

claims. Because the equity investors generally control the firm's management and decision making, their interests will dominate bondholder interests, unless bondholders take some protective action. By borrowing money, a firm exposes itself to this conflict and its negative consequences and pays the price in terms of both real costs and a loss of freedom in decision making.

The conflict between stockholders and bondholders   The conflict between bondholder and stockholder interests manifests itself in all three aspects of corporate finance: (1) choosing which projects to take (investment decisions), (2) determining how to finance these projects, and (3) deciding how much to pay out as dividends.

Investment decisions   Earlier in this book, we emphasized that any project that earns a return that exceeds the hurdle rate, adjusted to reflect the riskiness of the project, is a good project that should increase the firm's value. It would seem logical that both stockholders and bondholders would favor taking all such projects, but this is not always so. Although stockholders may enthusiastically support this proposition, bondholders may find themselves worse off after some of these projects are taken. This is because bondholders lend money to the firm with the expectation that the projects taken will have a certain risk level and set the interest rate on the bonds accordingly. If the firm takes projects that are riskier than expected, however, the bondholder will lose on his or her existing holdings because the price of the holdings will decrease (and the interest rate will increase) to reflect the higher risk. The bondholder's loss is the stockholder's gain. Although the project may have a positive net present value, the stockholders not only gain the entire present value, but they expropriate wealth from the bondholders as well. This wealth expropriation can sometimes lead to perverse decision making, whereby stockholders take projects that do not earn the hurdle rate (i.e., have negative net present value), but the value of equity actually increases because the wealth transferred from bondholders exceeds the negative net present value.

Bondholders and lenders often attempt to protect themselves against the **risk shifting** that occurs with investment decisions by constraining the firm from increasing the riskiness of its investments. These constraints which take the form of covenants may range from mild limits on investments in new businesses to tighter limits giving bondholders veto power over investment decisions.

Risk Shifting: Risk shifting refers to the tendency of stockholders in firms and their agents (managers) to take on much riskier projects than bondholders expect them to.

Concept Check   The loss in market value of bonds which arises when firms increase their risk is not a real loss if lenders are willing to hold on until maturity and collect their cash flows. Do you agree with this argument? Explain.

Financing decisions   The conflict between stockholder and bondholder interests also comes to the fore when new projects have to be financed. Left to their own devices, the equity investors in a firm would like to take on new debt, using the assets of the firm as security and providing the new lenders with prior claims over existing lenders, because doing so reduces the interest rate on the new debt. Obviously, the existing lenders in a firm do not want to provide new lenders with priority over their claims because it makes their debt riskier.

Similarly, a firm may adopt a conservative financial policy and borrow money at low rates, with the implicit expectation of keeping its default risk low. Once it has borrowed the money, however, the firm might choose to shift to a strategy of higher leverage and default risk, leaving the original lenders worse off. In 1988, for example, RJR Nabisco rocked the corporate bond markets by announcing its intention to do a leveraged buy-out. The company's existing debt, which had enjoyed a high rating, dropped dramatically in price upon the announcement, as shown in Figure 17.1.

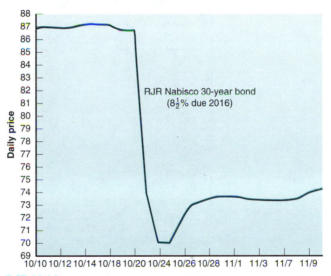

Figure 17.1   RJR Nabisco: Bond prices around LBO announcement (October 20, 1988)

The decline in the market value of the bonds can be seen as a transfer of wealth from existing bondholders to stockholders.

Bondholders cannot protect themselves against all such eventualities, but they can at least protect themselves against a specified set of actions that stockholders might take by inserting a **"protective put"** clause in the bonds, allowing them to sell the bonds back to the firm at face value, if these actions are taken.

Protective Puts (*in bonds*):   A protective put in a bond allows a bondholder to return the bonds to the issuer before maturity and receive the face value, under a series of conditions that are enumerated in the bond covenants. For instance, the put may be triggered by an increase in the leverage.

Dividend decisions   Dividend payments and equity repurchases also divide stockholders and bondholders. Consider a firm that has built up a large cash reserve but has very few good projects available. The stockholders in this firm may benefit if the cash is paid out as a dividend or used to repurchase stock. The bondholders, on the other hand, will prefer that the firm retain the cash because it can be used to make payments on the debt, reducing default risk.

Not surprisingly, stockholders, if not constrained, will go ahead and pay the dividends or buy back stock, overriding bondholder concerns. In some cases, the payments are large and can increase the firm's default risk dramatically. In 1989, for example, Colt Industries sold its most liquid assets and used the cash to pay a dividend that was 50% of the stock price. As a result, its bond rating dropped from investment grade to junk bond status.

If increases in dividends are indeed bad news for bondholders, bond prices should react negatively to the announcement of such increases. The empirical evidence supports this hypothesis. As illustrated in Figure 17.2, bond prices decrease following the announcement of dividend increases, whereas they are relatively unaffected by dividend decreases. At the same time, empirical evidence indicates that stock prices increase following the announcement of dividend increases.

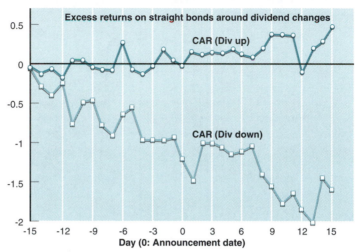

Figure 17.2 Effects of dividend changes on bond prices

Bondholders can protect themselves against such loss by restricting dividends in the bond covenants to a certain percentage of earnings or by limiting dividend increases to a specified amount. Hybrid securities also provide an appealing way of dealing with agency costs. Convertible bonds give bondholders some protection against expropriation by stockholders, for instance, because they can convert their holdings into equity.

☐ Concept
Check

> Some firms increase dividends because of improvements in earning power, and other firms increase dividends because they have large cash balances. As a bondholder in a firm, would you differentiate the two in terms of the impact on your holdings?

Where does the agency cost show up? The agency cost of this disagreement can show up in two ways as real costs:

1. If bondholders believe there is a significant chance that stockholder actions might make them worse off, they can build this expectation into bond prices by demanding much higher rates on debt.

2. If bondholders can protect themselves against such actions by writing in restrictive covenants, two costs follow:

- The *direct cost* of monitoring the covenants, which increases as the covenants become more detailed and restrictive.
- The *indirect cost* of lost flexibility, because the firm is not able to take certain projects, use certain types of financing, or change its payout; this cost will also increase as the covenants become more restrictive.

As firms borrow more and more and expose themselves to greater agency costs, these costs will also increase.

Because agency costs can be substantial, several implications relating to optimal capital structure follow:

1. The agency cost arising from risk shifting is likely to be greatest in firms whose investments cannot be easily observed and monitored. For example, a lender to a firm that invests in real estate is less exposed to agency cost than is a lender to a firm that invests in people or intangible assets. Consequently, it is not surprising that manufacturing companies and railroads, which invest in substantial real assets, have much higher debt ratios than do service companies.

2. The agency cost associated with monitoring actions and second-guessing investment decisions is likely to be largest for firms whose projects are long term, follow unpredictable paths, and may take years to come to fruition. Pharmaceutical companies in the United States, for example, which often take on research projects that may take years to yield commercial products, have historically maintained low debt ratios, even though their cash flows would support more debt.

Loss of Flexibility

As noted earlier, one of the byproducts of the conflict between stockholders and bondholders is the introduction of strict bond covenants that reduce the flexibility of firms to make investment, financing, or dividend decisions. It can be argued that this is part of a much greater loss of **financial flexibility** arising from taking on debt. One of the reasons firms do not use their debt capacity is that they like to preserve it for a rainy day, when they might need the debt to meet funding needs or specific contingencies. Firms that borrow to capacity lose this flexibility and have no fallback funding if they do get into trouble.

Financial Flexibility: Financial flexibility refers to the capacity of firms to meet any unforeseen contingencies that may arise (such as recessions and sales downturns) and take advantage of unanticipated opportunities (such as great projects), using the funds they have on hand and any excess debt capacity that they might have nurtured.

Firms value flexibility for two reasons. First, the value of the firm may be maximized by preserving some flexibility to take on future projects as they arise. Second, flexibility provides managers with more breathing room and more power, and it protects them from the monitoring that comes with debt. Thus, although the argument for maintaining flexibility in the interests of the firm is based on sound principles, managers pursuing their own interests sometimes use it as camouflage. There is also a tradeoff between not maintaining enough flexibility (because a firm has too much debt) and having too much flexibility (by not borrowing enough).

Concept Check

The argument for preserving flexibility is in many ways the polar opposite of the free cash-flow argument for increasing debt. Which of the two views do you buy into? Why?

Valuing flexibility   Although firms clearly value flexibility, it is difficult to attach a precise dollar value to it. We will attempt to do so more fully in Chapter 28 which discusses option pricing applications. Here we argue that, other things remaining equal, the value of flexibility should be a function of the following variables:

- *Availability of projects*: Firms with substantial investment opportunities value flexibility more than do stable firms without these same opportunities.
- *Excess returns on projects*: The more lucrative the projects that would be turned away in the absence of the funding, the greater the value of preserving the flexibility.
- *Uncertainty about project needs and cash flows*: The greater the uncertainty about future project needs, the greater the value of preserving flexibility.

These variables have the following implications for optimal capital structure:

- Firms that have large and unpredictable demands on their cash flows to take on projects with high excess returns will value flexibility more and borrow less than firms with stable investment requirements and low-return projects. Thus, even the most successful firms in the high-technology arena (which is characterized by high returns and uncertainty about investment requirements), such as Intel and Microsoft, use very little debt in their capital structure.
- As firms and industries mature, the returns on projects drop off and project requirements become more stable. These changes increase the capacity of firms to borrow money. Intel and Microsoft, by this reasoning, will find the value of flexibility decrease over time, increasing their debt capacities. This provides an explanation for the financing life cycle, introduced in Chapter 16.

THE TRADEOFF IN A BALANCE SHEET FORMAT

Bringing together the benefits and the costs of debt, we can present the tradeoff in a balance sheet format:

Advantages of Borrowing	Disadvantages of Borrowing
1. Tax Benefit: Higher tax rates → Higher tax benefit *2. Added Discipline:* Greater the separation between managers and stockholders → Greater the benefit	*1. Bankruptcy Cost:* Higher business risk → Higher cost *2. Agency Cost:* Greater the separation between stockholders and lenders → Higher cost *3. Loss of Future Financing Flexibility:* Greater the uncertainty about future financing needs → Higher cost

Overall, if the marginal benefits of borrowing exceed the marginal costs, the firm should borrow money. Otherwise, it should use equity.

Survey Results
What do firms consider when they make capital structure decisions? To answer this question, Pinegar and Wilbricht surveyed financial managers at 176 firms in the United States. They concluded that the financial principles listed in Table 17.1 determine capital structure decisions, in the order of importance in which they were given.

The foremost principles the survey participants identified were maintaining financial flexibility and ensuring long-term survivability (which can be construed as avoiding bankruptcy). Surprisingly few managers attached much importance to maintaining comparability with other firms in their industries or maintaining a high debt rating.

Table 17.1   **FINANCIAL PRINCIPLES DETERMINING CAPITAL STRUCTURE DECISIONS**

Planning Principle by Order of Importance	Percentage of Responses Within Each Rank						
	Unimportant	2	3	4	Important	Not Ranked	Mean
1. Maintaining financial flexibility	0.6	0.0	4.5	33.0	61.4	0.6	4.55
2. Ensuring long-term survivability	4.0	1.7	6.8	10.8	76.7	0.0	4.55
3. Maintaining a predictable source of funds	1.7	2.8	20.5	39.2	35.8	0.0	4.05
4. Maximizing security prices	3.4	4.5	19.3	33.5	37.5	1.7	3.99
5. Maintaining financial independence	3.4	4.5	22.2	27.3	40.9	1.7	3.99
6. Maintaining a high debt rating	2.3	9.1	32.4	43.2	13.1	0.0	3.56
7. Maintaining comparability with other firms in the industry	15.9	36.9	33.0	10.8	2.8	0.6	2.47

THERE IS NO OPTIMAL CAPITAL STRUCTURE—THE MILLER-MODIGLIANI THEOREM

In spite of the arguments presented above, there is a large and fairly influential school of thought that argues that capital structure decisions do not really affect the value of the firm. The seeds of this argument were sown in one of the most influential papers ever written in corporate finance, containing one of corporate finance's best-known theorems, the *Miller–Modigliani Theorem*.

In their initial work, Miller and Modigliani operated in an environment void of taxes, transactions costs, and the possibility of default. In that environment, they concluded that the value of a firm was unaffected by its leverage and that investment and financing decisions could be separated. Their conclusion can be confirmed in several ways; we present two below.

The Irrelevance of Capital Structure: Balance Sheet Proof

Miller and Modigliani made the following assumptions about the markets in which they were working:

1. There are no taxes.
2. Markets are frictionless and there are no transactions costs.
3. There are no direct or indirect bankruptcy costs. (The expected bankruptcy costs are zero.)

In such an environment, reverting back to the balance sheet format on page 458, it is quite clear that all of the advantages and disadvantages disappear, leaving debt with no marginal benefits and costs. Accordingly, we can conclude that debt does not affect value.

In a later paper, Miller and Modigliani preserved the environment they introduced above but made one change, allowing for a tax benefit for debt. In this scenario, where debt continues to have no costs, the optimal debt ratio for a firm is 100% debt. In fact, in such an environment, the value of the firm increases by the present value of the tax savings for interest payments (see Figure 17.3):

$$\text{Value of Levered Firm} = \text{Value of Unlevered Firm} + t_c B$$

where t_c is the corporate tax rate and B is the dollar borrowing.

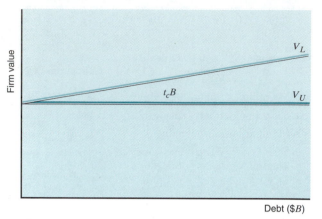

Figure 17.3 Value of levered firm: MM with taxes

An Alternate Proof

Miller and Modigliani presented an alternative proof of the irrelevance of leverage, grounded in the notion that debt does not affect the underlying operating cash flows of the firm, in the absence of taxes. Consider two firms that have the same cash flow (X) from operations. The first firm is an all-equity firm, whereas the second firm has both equity and debt. The interest rate on debt is r.

	Firm A	Firm B
Type of firm	All equity firm ($V_u = E$)	Has some equity and debt
Actions now	Investor buys a fraction α of the firm (αV_u)	Investor buys a fraction α of both equity and debt of the firm $\alpha E_L + \alpha D_L$
Next period	Investor receives a fraction of the cash flow (αX)	Investor receives the following: $\alpha(X - rD_L) + \alpha rD_L = \alpha X$

Because the investor receives the same cash flows in both firms, the price he or she will pay for either firm has to be the same. This implies that leverage is irrelevant.

Note that this proof works only if the firm does not receive a tax benefit from debt; a tax benefit would give Firm B a higher cash flow than Firm A.

The Effect of Taxes: The Miller Proof of Irrelevance

The Miller–Modigliani model shows that introducing the tax benefit of debt into the mix undercuts the conclusion that debt is irrelevant. In an address in 1979, however, Merton Miller argued that the debt irrelevance theorem could be resuscitated even in the presence of corporate taxes if taxes on the dividend and interest income that individuals receive from firms were factored into the analysis.

To see the Miller proof of irrelevance, assume that investors face a tax rate of t_d on interest income and a tax rate of t_e on equity income. Assume also that the firm pays an interest rate of r on debt and faces a corporate tax rate of t_c. The after-tax return to the investor from owning debt can then be written as follows:

$$\text{After-tax Return from owning Debt} = r(1 - t_d)$$

The after-tax return to the investor from owning equity (where r_e is the pre-corporate tax return to equity inventory's) can be written after the double taxation—once at the corporate level and once at the equity level:

$$\text{After-tax Return from owning Equity} = r_e\,(1 - t_c)\,(1 - t_e)$$

The returns to equity can take two forms—dividends or capital gains; the equity tax rate is a blend of the tax rates on both. In such a scenario, Miller noted that the value of the firm, with leverage, could be written as

$$V_L = V_u + [(1 - t_c)\,(1 - t_e))/(1 - t_d)]\,B$$

where V_L is the value of the firm with leverage, V_U is the value of the firm without leverage, and B is the dollar debt.

As Miller noted, several possible scenarios can be considered here:

1. The tax rate on equity income is the same as the tax rate on debt income: If this were the case, the result reverts back to the original one—the value of the firm increases monotonically with the debt.

2. The tax rate on debt income is higher than the tax rate on equity income: In such a case, the differences in the tax rates may more than compensate for the double taxation of equity cash flows. To illustrate, assume that the tax rate on ordinary income is 70%, the tax rate on capital gains on stock is 28%, and the tax rate on corporations is 35%. In such a case, the tax liabilities for debt and equity can be calculated for a firm that pays no dividend as follows:

$$\text{Tax Rate on Debt Income} = 70\%$$
$$\text{Tax Rate on Equity Income} = 1 - (1 - 0.35)\,(1 - .28) = 0.532 \text{ or } 53.2\%$$

This is not an implausible scenario, especially considering tax law in the United States until the mid-1980s.

3. The tax rate on equity income is just low enough to compensate for the double taxation: in this case, we are back to the original debt irrelevance theorem.

$$(1 - t_d) = (1 - t_c)\,(1 - t_e) \text{ .... Debt is irrelevant.}$$

Miller's analysis brought investor tax rates into the analysis for the first time and provided some insight into the effect of investor tax preferences on a firm's capital structure. As Miller himself notes, however, this analysis does not reestablish the irrelevance of debt under all circumstances. Rather, it opens up the possibility that debt could still be irrelevant, despite its tax advantages.

☐ Concept
   Check

> The 1986 tax act eliminated the capital gains tax rate and made the tax rate on all income 28%, at the margin. What were the implications of this law for the Miller thesis?

The Consequences of Debt Irrelevance

If the financing decision is irrelevant, as posited by Miller and Modigliani, corporate financial analysis is simplified in a number of ways:

- *The cost of capital, which is the weighted average of the cost of debt and the cost of equity, is unaffected by changes in the proportions of debt and equity.* This might seem unreasonable, especially since the cost of debt is much lower than the cost of equity. In the Miller–Modigliani world, however, any benefits incurred by substituting cheaper debt for more expensive equity are offset by increases in both their costs, as shown in Figure 17.4.

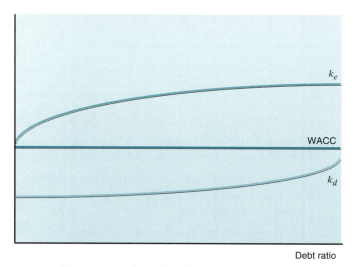

Figure 17.4   Cost of capital in the MM world

- *The value of the firm is unaffected by the amount of leverage it has.* Thus, if the firm is valued as an all-equity entity, its value will remain unchanged if it is valued with any other debt ratio. (This actually follows from the implication that the cost of capital is unaffected by changes in leverage and from the assumption that the operating cash flows are determined by investment decisions rather than financing decisions.)
- *The investment decision can be made independently of the financing decision.* In other words, if a project is a bad project when evaluated as an all-equity project, it will remain so using any other financing mix.

Some Closing Thoughts

It is unlikely that capital structure is irrelevant in the real world, given tax preferences for debt and default risk. Nonetheless, Miller and Modigliani were pioneers in moving capital structure analysis from an environment in which firms picked their debt ratios based on their peer groups and management preferences to one that recognized the tradeoffs on debt. They also emphasized that good investment decisions comprise the core of value creation for firms. To be more precise, a firm that takes bad projects cannot hope to recoup the lost value by making better financing decisions; a firm that takes good projects will succeed in creating value, even if its capital structure choices are suboptimal. Finally, although the concept of a world with no taxes, default risk, or agency problems may seem a little far-fetched, in some environments the description might hold. Assume, for instance, that the U.S. government decides to encourage small businesses to invest in urban areas by relieving them of their tax burden and providing a backup guarantee on loans (default protection). Firms that respond to these initiatives might find that their capital structure decisions do not affect their value.

Finally, surveys of financial managers indicate that, in practice, they do not attach as much weight to the tradeoff mentioned above as we do in theory. In a survey by Pinegar and Wilbricht, managers were asked to cite the most important inputs governing their financial decisions. Their responses are ranked in the order of the importance managers attached to them in Table 17.2.

Inputs/Assumptions by Order of Importance	1	2	3	4	5	Not Ranked	Mean
1. Projected cash flow from asset to be financed	1.7%	1.1%	9.7%	29.5%	58.0%	0.0%	4.41
2. Avoiding dilution of common equity's claims	2.8%	6.3%	18.2%	39.8%	33.0%	0.0%	3.94
3. Risk of asset to be financed	2.8%	6.3%	20.5%	36.9%	33.0%	0.6%	3.91
4. Restrictive convenants on senior securities	9.1%	9.7%	18.7%	35.2%	27.3%	0.0%	3.62
5. Avoiding mispricing of securities to be issued	3.4%	10.8%	27.3%	39.8%	18.7%	0.0%	3.60
6. Corporate tax rate	4.0%	9.7%	29.5%	42.6%	13.1%	1.1%	3.52
7. Voting control	17.6%	10.8%	21.0%	31.2%	19.3%	0.0%	3.24
8. Depreciation and other tax shields	8.5%	17.6%	40.9%	24.4%	7.4%	1.1%	3.05
9. Correcting mispricing of securities	14.8%	27.8%	36.4%	14.2%	5.1%	1.7%	2.66
10. Personal tax rates of debt and equityholders	31.2%	34.1%	25.6%	8.0%	1.1%	0.0%	2.14
11. Bankruptcy costs	69.3%	13.1%	6.8%	4.0%	4.5%	2.3%	1.58

Table 17.2   INPUTS INTO CAPITAL STRUCTURE DECISIONS. Percentage of Responses Within Each Rank, Least Important...Most Important.

Notice that, while the capital structure tradeoff theory would predict that bankruptcy cost and tax-related variables would be the most important variables, this survey suggests that they are not actually given as much weight by financial managers making capital structure decisions as the theory suggests. Instead, financial managers seem to weigh financial flexibility and potential dilution much more heavily in their capital structure decisions.

THERE IS AN OPTIMAL CAPITAL STRUCTURE

The counter to the Miller–Modigliani proposition is that the tradeoffs on debt may work in favor of the firm, at least initially, and that borrowing money may lower the cost of capital and increase firm value. We will examine the mechanics of putting this argument into practice in the next chapter. Here, we make a case for the existence of an optimal capital structure and look at some of the empirical evidence for and against it.

The Case for an Optimal Capital Structure
If the debt decision involves a tradeoff between the benefits of debt (tax benefits and added discipline) and the costs of debt (bankruptcy costs, agency costs, and lost flexibility), it can be argued that the marginal benefits will be offset by the marginal costs *only in exceptional cases,* and not always (as argued by Miller and Modigliani). In fact, under most circumstances, the marginal benefits will either exceed the marginal costs (in which case, debt is good and will increase firm value) or fall short of marginal costs

(in which case, equity is better). Accordingly, there is an optimal capital structure for most firms at which firm value is maximized.

Of course, it is always possible that managers may be operating under an *illusion* that capital structure decisions matter, when the reality might be otherwise. Consequently, we examine some of the empirical evidence to see if it is consistent with the theory of an optimal mix of debt and equity.

Empirical Evidence

The question of whether there is an optimal capital structure can be answered in a number of ways. The first is to see if differences in capital structure across firms can be explained systematically by differences in the variables driving the tradeoffs. Other things remaining equal, we would expect to see the relationships listed in Table 17.3.

Table 17.3   **DEBT RATIOS AND FUNDAMENTALS**

Variable	Effect on Debt Ratios
Marginal tax rate	As marginal tax rates increase, debt ratios increase.
Separation of ownership and management	The greater the separation of ownership and management, the higher the debt ratio.
Variability in operating cash flows	As operating cash flows become more variable, bankruptcy risk increases, resulting in lower debt ratios.
Debtholders' difficulty in monitoring firm actions, investments, and performance	The more difficult it is to monitor the actions taken by a firm, the lower the optimal debt ratio.
Need for flexibility	The greater the need for decision-making flexibility in future periods, the lower the optimal debt ratio.

Although this may seem to be a relatively simple test to run, keeping all other things equal in the real world is often close to impossible. In spite of this limitation, attempts to determine whether the direction of the relationship is consistent with the theory have produced mixed results.

Bradley, Jarrell, and Kim (1984) analyzed whether differences in debt ratios can be explained by proxies for the variables involved in the capital structure tradeoff. They noted that the debt ratio is

- *Negatively correlated with the volatility in annual operating earnings,* as predicted by the bankruptcy cost component of the optimal capital structure tradeoff.

- *Positively related to the level of nondebt tax shields,* which is counter to the tax hypothesis, which argues that firms with large nondebt tax shields should be less inclined to use debt.

- *Negatively related to advertising and R&D expenses used as a proxy for agency costs*, which is consistent with optimal capital structure theory.

Others who have attempted to examine whether cross-sectional differences in capital structure are consistent with the theory have come to contradictory conclusions.

A second test of whether differences in capital structure can be explained by differences in firm characteristics involves examining differences in debt ratios across industries. Table 17.4 summarizes debt ratios, by industry, in both book value and market value terms at the end of 1994. The table provides relevant information on average tax rates, variability in operating income, and investment needs for each industry.

Table 17.4 DEBT RATIOS BY INDUSTRY, 1995 (PERCENTAGE)

Industry	Debt Ratio: MV	Debt Ratio: BV	Op. Income Variance	Insider Holdings(%)	Cap Ex/ MV(%)	ROE(%)	FCF/ Price(%)
Agricultural products	35.05	47.05	30.86	30.16	7.18	24.35	11.72
Mining	26.33	36.64	34.50	14.28	6.55	13.86	6.70
Petroleum production and refining	27.08	39.88	28.91	26.00	13.05	16.11	7.45
Building contractors and related area:	28.21	36.16	42.19	33.34	6.51	15.16	7.72
Food production	22.90	39.89	39.27	28.38	7.77	24.12	5.06
Beverages	25.07	40.19	38.07	33.20	7.13	17.52	5.36
Tobacco	31.42	49.82	37.59	4.28	3.48	33.16	6.98
Textile and clothing manufacturers	21.89	27.23	46.01	33.97	5.98	14.84	7.12
Furniture	16.66	22.83	47.80	42.89	7.59	19.69	7.85
Paper & plastic production	30.41	46.81	42.48	20.64	8.74	20.96	5.96
Publishing	16.29	32.38	42.39	30.75	6.92	26.82	6.28
Chemicals	17.30	31.57	42.88	21.66	7.17	37.80	6.19
Pharmaceuticals	8.52	24.63	39.12	27.62	10.35	26.25	2.76
Consumer products	18.62	39.23	44.38	29.05	6.94	26.45	4.36
Autos and related	26.91	38.00	47.17	28.23	6.67	21.66	7.71
Miscellaneous manufacturing	24.00	37.75	47.91	26.05	8.71	21.10	8.45
Equipment manufacturing	19.06	29.57	49.32	25.60	6.52	18.45	6.83
Computers and office equipment	8.44	17.29	51.26	25.84	7.34	18.89	5.50
Consumer electronics	9.48	15.79	59.81	23.96	7.30	14.22	4.82
Other consumer durables	15.89	25.18	41.72	39.32	6.71	18.71	5.02
Transportation	33.57	44.97	41.62	29.22	8.64	18.09	7.26
Telephone utilities	19.83	38.54	25.24	19.34	12.28	16.21	3.37
Entertainment (TV & Movies)	19.60	39.83	38.78	41.59	7.24	26.68	10.80
Electric and gas utilities	43.22	52.90	32.25	19.49	6.51	12.31	5.29
Wholesalers	19.16	28.18	46.94	33.12	4.79	15.22	6.95
Retailers	21.65	30.01	45.21	35.39	9.24	20.42	5.49
Restaurants and eating places	20.21	32.28	42.94	29.45	16.12	18.19	7.45
Banks and financial service	17.23	28.40	67.01	30.13	2.07	18.99	11.39
Insurance	14.35	31.71	39.84	34.15	5.15	19.11	5.51
Real Estate	30.85	40.97	39.49	29.15	3.08	19.15	7.75
Other Services	20.17	34.86	39.92	36.07	7.18	24.67	6.99
Computer software and services	3.48	10.10	43.58	34.16	9.28	19.07	3.80
Health services	17.30	27.97	44.72	30.13	5.83	12.30	6.12
Average	**21.52**	**33.90**	**42.46**	**28.69**	**7.46**	**20.32**	**6.61**

An alternative test of the optimal capital structure hypothesis is to examine the stock price reaction to actions taken by firms either to increase or decrease leverage. In evaluating the price response, we have to make some assumptions about the motivation of the firms making these changes. If we assume that firms are rational and that they make these changes to get closer to their optimal, both leverage-increasing and-decreasing actions should be accompanied by positive excess returns, at least on average. In a study cited in the previous chapter, Smith (1988) notes that the evidence is *not* consistent with an optimal capital structure hypothesis, however: leverage-increasing actions seem to be accompanied by positive excess returns, and leverage-reducing actions seem to be followed by negative returns. The only way to reconcile this tendency with an optimal capital structure argument is to assume that managerial incentives (desire for stability and flexibility) keep leverage below the optimal for most firms and that actions by firms to reduce leverage are seen as serving managerial interests rather than stockholder interests.

HOW FIRMS CHOOSE THEIR CAPITAL STRUCTURES

Although the theory suggests that firms should pick the mix of debt and equity that maximizes firm value, the most common approach is to set leverage close to that of the peer group to which the firm belongs. If firms in the peer group are similar on the fundamental characteristics (tax rates and cash-flow variability) and tend to be right, at least on average, it can be argued that this approach provides a shortcut to arriving at the optimal. It is likely to fail, however, when firms differ on these characteristics.

A Financing Hierarchy

It can be argued that firms follow a financing hierarchy: retained earnings are the most preferred choice for financing, followed by debt, new equity and common; preferred stock is the least preferred choice. The argument is supported as follows. First, managers value *flexibility and control.* To the extent that external financing reduces flexibility for future financing (especially if it is debt) and control (bonds have covenants; new equity attracts new stockholders into the company and may reduce insider holdings as a percentage of total holdings), managers prefer retained earnings as a source of capital. Second, although it costs nothing in terms of flotation costs to use retained earnings, *it costs more* to use external debt, and even more to use external equity.

Survey results   There is some evidence to support a financing hierarchy. For instance, in the survey by Pinegar and Wilbricht (Table 17.5), managers were asked to rank six different sources of financing from most preferred to least preferred: internal equity, external equity, external debt, preferred stock, and hybrids (convertible debt and preferred stock).

Table 17.5   SURVEY RESULTS ON PLANNING PRINCIPLES

Ranking	Souce	Planning Principle cited	Score
1	Retained Earnings	None	5.61
2	Straight Debt	Maximize security prices	4.88
3	Convertible Debt	Cash flow & survivability	3.02
4	External Common Equity	Avoiding dilution	2.42
5	Straight Preferred Stock	Comparability	2.22
6	Convertible Preferred	None	1.72

Retained earnings (internal equity) emerged as the clear first choice for financing projects. The survey yielded some other interesting conclusions as well:

- External debt is strongly preferred over external equity as a way of raising funds. The values of external debt and external equity issued between 1975 and 1990 by U.S. corporations are shown in Figure 17.5.

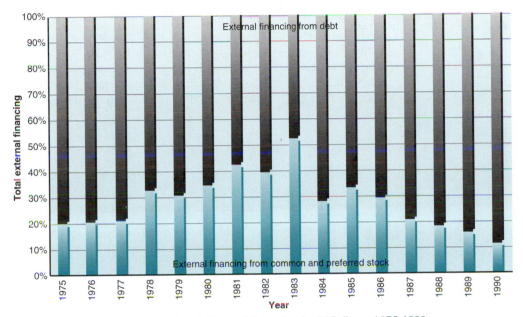

Figure 17.5   Breakdown of financing for U.S. firms: 1975-1990

- Given a choice, firms would much rather use straight debt than convertible debt, in spite of the lower interest cost on convertible debt. Managers perhaps have a much better sense of the value of the conversion option than is recognized, since the conventional wisdom holds that the lure of lower rates will result in more convertibles being issued than are justified by theory.

- The primary reason for *not* issuing external equity seems to be the avoidance of dilution, and the main reason *for using* debt is the maximization of stock prices.

- A firm's choices may say a great deal about its financial strength. Thus, the decisions by RJR Nabisco and GM, in 1993, to raise new funds through convertible preferred stock were seen by markets as an admission by these firms of their financial weakness. Not surprisingly, the financial market response to the issue of the securities listed above mirrors the preferences: the most negative responses are reserved for securities near the bottom of the list, and the most positive (or at least the least negative) for those at the top of the list.

Information asymmetry and financing hierarchy   In the discussion of financing choices so far, we have steered away from questions about how firms convey information to financial markets about their future choices and how well the securities the firms issue are priced. Firms know more about their future prospects than do the financial markets with which they deal; markets may under- or overprice securities issued by firms. Myers and Majluf (1984) note that, in the presence of this asymmetric information, firms that believe their securities are underpriced, given their future prospects, may be inclined to reject good projects rather than raise external financing. Alternatively, firms that believe their securities are overpriced are more likely to issue these securities, even if they have no projects available. In this environment, the following implications emerge:

- Managers prefer retained earnings to external financing, because it allows them to consider projects on their merits, rather than depending on whether markets are pricing their securities correctly. It follows that firms will be more inclined to retain earnings over and above their current investment requirements to finance future projects.
- When firms issue securities, markets will consider the issue a signal that these securities are overvalued. This signal is likely to be more negative for securities, such as stocks, in which the asymmetry of information is greater, and smaller for securities, such as straight bonds, in which the asymmetry is smaller. This would explain both the rankings in the financial heirarchy and the market reaction to these security issues.

CONCLUSION

This chapter lays the groundwork for analyzing a firm's optimal mix of debt and equity by presenting the benefits and costs of borrowing money.

- The primary benefit of debt is a tax benefit: interest expenses are tax deductible, whereas cash flows to equity (dividends) are not. This benefit increases with the tax rate of the entity taking on the debt.
- A secondary benefit of debt is that it forces managers to be more disciplined in their choice of projects by increasing the costs of failure; a series of bad projects may create the possibility of defaulting on interest and principal payments.
- The primary cost of borrowing is an increase in the expected bankruptcy cost—the product of the probability of default and the cost of bankruptcy. The probability of default is greater for firms that have volatile cash flows. The cost of bankruptcy includes both direct costs (legal and time value) and indirect costs (lost sales, tighter credit, and less access to capital).
- Borrowing money exposes the firm to the possibility of conflicts between stock- and bondholders over investment, financing, and dividend decisions. The covenants that bondholders write into bond agreements to protect themselves against expropriation cost the firm in both monitoring costs and lost flexibility.
- The loss of flexibility that arises from borrowing money is more likely to be a problem for firms with substantial and unpredictable investment opportunities.
- In the special case where there are no tax benefits, default risk, or agency problems, the financing decision is irrelevant. This is known as the Miller–Modigliani theorem.
- In most cases, however, the tradeoff between the benefits and costs of debt will result in an optimal capital structure whereby the value of the firm is maximized.

QUESTIONS AND PROBLEMS

1. MVP Inc., a manufacturing firm with no debt outstanding and a market value of $100 million is considering borrowing $40 million and buying back stock. Assuming that the interest rate on the debt is 9% and that the firm faces a tax rate of 35%, answer the following questions:

   a. Estimate the annual interest tax savings each year from the debt.

b. Estimate the present value of interest tax savings, assuming that the debt change is permanent.

c. Estimate the present value of interest tax savings, assuming that the debt will be taken on for 10 years only.

d. What will happen to the present value of interest tax savings if interest rates drop tomorrow to 7% but the debt itself is a fixed rate debt?

2. A business in the 45% tax bracket is considering borrowing money at 10%.

a. What is the after-tax interest rate on the debt?

b. What is the after-tax interest rate if only half of the interest expense is allowed as a tax deduction?

c. Will your answer change if the firm is losing money now and does not expect to have taxable income for three years?

3. WestingHome Inc. is a manufacturing company that has accumulated a net operating loss of $2 billion over time. It is considering borrowing $5 billion to acquire another company.

a. Based on the corporate tax rate of 36%, estimate the present value of the tax savings that could accrue to the company.

b. Does the existence of a net operating loss carry-forward affect your analysis? (Will the tax benefits be diminished as a consequence?)

4. Answer true or false to the following questions relating to the free cash-flow hypothesis.

a. Companies with high operating earnings have high free cash flows.

b. Companies with large capital expenditures, relative to earnings, have low free cash flows.

c. Companies that are committed to paying a large portion of their free cash flow as dividends do not need debt to add discipline.

d. The free cash-flow hypothesis for borrowing money makes more sense for firms in which there is a separation of ownership and management.

e. Firms with high free cash flows are run inefficiently.

5. Assess the likelihood that the following firms will be taken over, based on your understanding of the free cash-flow hypothesis.

a. A firm with high-growth prospects, good projects, low leverage, and high earnings.

b. A firm with low-growth prospects, poor projects, low leverage, and poor earnings.

c. A firm with high-growth prospects, good projects, high leverage, and low earnings.

d. A firm with low-growth prospects, poor projects, high leverage, and good earnings.

e. A firm with low-growth prospects, poor projects, low leverage, and good earnings.

You can assume that earnings and free cash flows are highly correlated.

6. Nadir, Inc., an unlevered firm, has expected earnings before interest and taxes of $2 million per year. Nadir's tax rate is 40%, and the market value is $V = E = \$12$ million. The stock has a beta of 1, and the risk-free rate is 9%. (Assume that $E(R_m) - R_f = 6\%$.) Management is considering the use of debt; debt would be issued and used to buy back stock, and the size of the firm would remain constant. The default-free interest rate on debt is 12%. Because interest expense is tax deductible, the value of the firm would tend to increase as debt is added to the capital structure, but there would be an offset in the form of the rising cost of bankruptcy. The firm's analysts have estimated that the present value of any bankruptcy cost is $8 million and that the probability of bankruptcy will increase with leverage according to the following schedule:

Value of Debt	Probability of Failure (%)
$2,500,000	0.0
5,000,000	8.0
7,500,000	20.5
8,000,000	30.0
9,000,000	45.0
10,000,000	52.5
12,500,000	70.0

a. What is the cost of equity and cost of capital at this time?

b. What is the optimal capital structure when bankruptcy costs are considered?

c. What will the value of the firm be at this optimal capital structure?

7. Agency costs arise from the conflict between stockholders and bondholders, but they do not impose any real costs on firms. Comment.

8. Two firms are considering borrowing. One firm has excellent prospects in terms of future projects and is in an area in which cash flows are volatile and future needs are difficult to assess. The other firm has more stable cash flows and fewer project opportunities and predicts its future needs with more precision. Other things remaining equal, which of these two firms should borrow more?

9. How would you respond to a claim by a firm that maintaining flexibility is always good for stockholders, although they might not recognize it in the short term?

10. A firm that has no debt has a market value of $100 million and a cost of equity of 11%. In the Miller–Modigliani world:

   a. What happens to the value of the firm as the leverage is changed (assume no taxes)?

   b. What happens to the cost of capital as the leverage is changed (assume no taxes)?

   c. How would your answers to (a) and (b) change if there were taxes?

11. XYZ Pharma Inc. is a pharmaceutical company that traditionally has not used debt to finance its projects. Over the last 10 years, it has also reported high returns on its projects and growth rates, and has incurred substantial research and development expenses over the time period. The health-care business overall is growing much slower now, and the projects the firm is considering have lower expected returns.

   a. How would you justify the firm's past policy of not using debt?

   b. Do you think the policy should be changed now? Why or why not?

12. Stockholders can expropriate wealth from bondholders through their investment, financing, and dividend decisions. Explain.

13. Bondholders can always protect themselves against stockholder expropriation by writing bond covenants. Therefore, no agency cost is associated with the conflict between stockholders and bondholders. Do you agree?

14. Unitrode Inc., which makes analog/linear integrated circuits for power management, has not used debt in the financing of its projects. The managers of the firm contend that they do not borrow money because they want to maintain financial flexibility.

   a. How does not borrowing money increase financial flexibility?

   b. What is the tradeoff you will be making if you have excess debt capacity and you choose not to use it because you want financial flexibility?

15. Consolidated Power is a regulated electric utility that has equity with a market value of $1.5 billion and debt outstanding of $3 billion. A consultant notes that this is a high debt ratio relative to the average across all firms, which is 27%, and suggests that the firm is overlevered.

   a. Why would you expect an electric utility to be able to maintain a higher debt ratio than the average company?

   b. Does the fact that the company is a regulated monopoly affect its capacity to carry debt?

16. Assume that legislators are considering a tax reform plan that will lower the corporate tax rate from 36% to 17%, while preserving the tax deductibility of interest expenses. What effect would this tax reform plan have on the optimal debt ratios of companies? Why? What if the tax deductibility of debt were removed?

17. Governments often step in to protect large companies that get into finanical trouble and bail them out. If this is an accepted practice, what effect would you expect it to have on the debt ratios of firms? Why?

18. The Miller–Modigliani theorem proposes that debt is irrelevant. Under what conditions is this true? If debt is irrelevant, what is the effect of changing the debt ratio on the cost of capital?

19. Based on the financing hierarchy described in this chapter, what types of securities would you expect financially strong firms to issue? What about financially weak firms? Why?

20. In general, private firms tend to take on much less debt than publicly traded firms. Based on the discussion in this chapter, how would you explain this phenomenon?

21. There is a significant cost to bankruptcy because the stock price essentially goes to zero. Comment.

22. Studies indicate that the direct cost of bankruptcy is small. What are the direct costs? What are the indirect costs of bankruptcy? What types of firms are most exposed to these indirect costs?

23. When stockholders have little power over incumbent managers, firms are likely to be underlevered. Comment.

24. Debt is always cheaper than equity. Therefore, the optimal debt ratio is all debt. How would you respond to this statement?

CHAPTER 18

CAPITAL STRUCTURE: MODELS AND APPLICATIONS

In the previous chapter, we examined the costs and benefits of borrowing and noted that the tradeoff will favor debt for some firms and equity for others. In this chapter, we move beyond generalities to practical tools for analyzing the capital structure and choosing an optimal debt level for a firm. We explore five ways of doing so. The first approach begins with a distribution of future operating income; we can then decide how much debt to carry by defining the maximum possibility of default we are willing to countenance. The second approach is to choose the debt ratio that minimizes the cost of capital. Here, we define the cost of capital, explain its role in analysis and valuation, and discuss its relationship to the optimal debt ratio. The third approach is to view leverage as a way of maximizing the return differential between the returns made by equity investors on the projects taken by the firm and the cost of equity. The fourth approach, like the second, attempts to maximize firm value, but does so by adding the value of the unlevered firm to the present value of tax benefits and then netting out the expected bankruptcy costs. The final approach is to look at the way comparable firms finance their operations.

OPERATING INCOME APPROACH

The *operating income approach* to setting debt capacity is the simplest and one of the most intuitive ways of setting debt policy. The firm begins with an analysis of its operating income and considers how much debt it can afford to carry based on its cash flows. The steps involved in the operating income approach are as follows:

1. The firm's capacity to generate operating income is assessed based on both current conditions and past history. The result is a distribution for expected operating income, with probabilities attached to different levels of income.

2. For any given level of debt, the interest and principal payments that have to be made on the debt are estimated over time.

3. Given the probability distribution of operating cash flows and the debt payments that have to be made, the firm can estimate the probability that it will be unable to make those payments.

4. The management of the firm specifies a limit on the probability of being unable to meet debt payments as a constraint. Clearly, the more conservative the management, the lower this probability will be.

5.   The estimated probability of default at a given level of debt is compared to the probability constraint. If the probability of default is higher than the constraint, the firm considers a lower level of debt; if it is lower than the constraint, the firm considers a higher level of debt.

Limitations of the Operating Income Approach

Although this approach may be intuitive and simple, it has some severe limitations. First, estimating a distribution for operating income is not as easy as it sounds, especially for firms in businesses that are changing and volatile. For instance, the operating income of toy manufacturers, such as Mattel and Hasbro, tends to swing wildly from year to year, depending on the success or failure of their newest products. Second, this is an extremely conservative approach to setting debt policy, since it assumes that debt payments have to be made out of a firm's cash balances and operating income and that the firm has no access to financial markets. Third, the probability constraint set by management is essentially a subjective one and may reflect management concerns more than stockholder interests. For instance, management may decide that it wants *no* chance of default and may refuse to borrow money as a consequence.

 **IN PRACTICE**   ESTIMATING DEBT CAPACITY BASED ON OPERATING INCOME DISTRIBUTION

In the following analysis, we apply this approach to setting debt capacity to Boeing in 1990.

Step 1:   We derive a probability distribution for expected operating income by drawing on Boeing's history and estimating operating income changes from 1976 to 1990 (Figure 18.1).

We then calculate the mean and standard deviation in these changes:

Mean Change in Operating Income = 10.89%   Standard Deviation = 30.49%

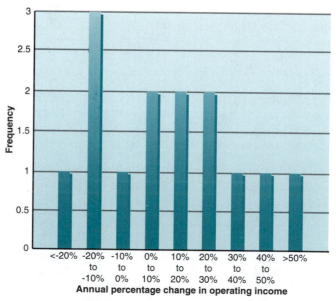

Figure 18.1   Boeing's operating income: Annual percentage changes, 1976-1990

If we assume that these changes are distributed normally, which is a strong assumption, these statistics are sufficient for us to compute the approximate probabilities of being unable to meet the specified debt payments.

Step 2: We estimate the interest and principal payment on a proposed bond issue of $2 billion by assuming that the interest rate on the debt is based on Boeing's current rating of AA, resulting in a rate of 10%. In addition, we assume that the sinking fund payment set aside to repay the bonds is 5% of the bond issue. This results in an annual debt payment of $300 million:

$$\text{Additional Debt Payment} = \text{Interest Expense} + \text{Sinking Fund Payment}$$
$$= 0.10 * 2,000 + .05 * 2,000 = \$300 \text{ million}$$

The total debt payment can then be computed by adding the interest payment on existing debt in 1990—$23 million—to the new debt payment that will be created by taking on $2 billion in additional debt.

$$\text{Total Debt Payment} = \text{Interest on Existing Debt} + \text{Additional Debt Payment}$$
$$= \$23 \text{ million} + \$300 \text{ million} = \$323 \text{ million}$$

T statistic: A *t* statistic measures the statistical significance of an estimate. If one assumes that the estimate is drawn from a normal distribution, the *t* statistic can be compared to specific values to measure significance.

Step 3: We can then estimate the probability of default[1] from the distribution of operating income by assuming that the percentage changes in operating income are distributed normally and considering the operating income of $2,063 million that Boeing earned in 1990 as the base year:

$$T \text{ statistic} = (\text{Current Operating Income} - \text{Debt Payment}) / \sigma_{OI} (\text{Current Operating Income})$$
$$= (\$2,063 - \$323 \text{ million}) / (.3049 * \$2,063) = 2.77$$

Based on the *t statistic,* the probability that Boeing will be unable to meet its debt payments is less than 1%.

Step 4: Assume that the management at Boeing sets a constraint that the probability of default be no greater than 5%.

Step 5: Since the estimated probability of default is indeed less than 5%, Boeing can afford to borrow more than $2 billion. Incidentally, if the distribution of operating income changes is assumed to be normal, we can estimate the level of debt payments Boeing can afford to make for a probability of default of 5%.

$$T \text{ statistic for 5\% probability level} = 1.645$$

Consequently, the breakeven debt payment can be estimated as follows:

$$(\$2,063 - X)/ (.3049 * \$2,063) = 1.645$$

This yields a breakeven debt payment of

$$\text{Breakeven Debt Payment} = \$1.028 \text{ billion}$$

If we assume that the interest rate remains unchanged at 10% and the sinking fund will remain at 5% of the outstanding debt, this yields an optimal debt level of $6,855 million:

[1]This is the probability of defaulting on interest payments on one period. The cumulative probability of default over time will be much higher.

> Optimal Debt Level = Breakeven Debt Payment / (Interest Rate + Sinking Fund Rate)
> = $1,028 / (.10 + .05) = $6,855 million

The optimal debt level will be lower if the interest rate increases as Boeing borrows more money.
Another limitation of the operating income approach is that the distribution does not really fit the parameters of a normal distribution, and the annual changes in operating income may not reflect the risk of consecutive bad years. This can be remedied by calculating the distributional statistics based on multiple years of data. For Boeing, if operating income is computed over rolling two-year periods,[2] the standard deviation jumps to 52.64%. This, in turn, will reduce the optimal debt level to $1,844 million.

Concept Check

What are some of the factors that would determine the maximum acceptable probability of default for the management of a firm? Would you expect closely held companies, in which managers hold a large percentage of the outstanding stock, to behave differently from widely held companies?

COST OF CAPITAL APPROACH

Intuitively, the *cost of capital* is the weighted average of the costs of the different components of financing—including debt, equity, and hybrid securities—used by a firm to fund its financial requirements. By altering the weights of the different components, firms might be able to change their cost of capital.[3]

Definition of the Weighted Average Cost of Capital (WACC)

The *weighted average cost of capital* is defined as the weighted average of the costs of the different components of financing used by a firm.

$$\text{WACC} = k_e\,[\,E/\,(D + E + PS)] + k_d\,[\,D/\,(D + E + PS)] + k_{ps}\,[\,PS/\,(D + E + PS)]$$

where WACC is the weighted average cost of capital; k_e, k_d, and k_{ps} are the costs of equity, debt, and preferred stock, respectively, and E, D, and PS are their respective market values.

Estimation of the costs of the individual components—equity, debt, and preferred stock—and of the weights in the cost of capital formulation is explored in detail in Chapter 6. To summarize:

- The cost of equity should reflect the riskiness of an equity investment in the company. The standard models for risk and return—the capital asset pricing model

[2]By rolling two-year periods, we mean 1980 and 1981, 1981 and 1982, 1982 and 1983, and so on. The resulting standard deviation is corrected for the multiple counting of the same observations.

[3]If capital structure is irrelevant, the cost of capital will be unchanged as the capital structure is altered.

(CAPM) and the arbitrage pricing model—measure risk in terms of market risk and convert the risk measure into an expected return.

- The cost of debt should reflect the default risk of the firm—the higher the default risk, the greater the cost of debt—and the tax advantage associated with debt— interest is tax deductible.

> Cost of Debt = Pretax Interest Rate on Borrowing (1 - tax rate)

- The cost of preferred stock should reflect the preferred dividend and the absence of tax deductibility.

> Cost of Preferred Stock = Preferred Dividend / Preferred Stock Price

- The weights used for the individual components should be market value weights rather than book value weights.

The Role of Cost of Capital in Investment Analysis and Valuation

In order to understand the relationship between the cost of capital and optimal capital structure, we first have to establish the relationship between firm value and the cost of capital. In Chapter 7, we noted that the value of a project to a firm could be computed by discounting the expected cash flows on it at a rate that reflected the riskiness of the cash flows, and that the analysis could be done either from the viewpoint of equity investors alone, by discounting cash flows to equity at the cost of equity, or from the viewpoint of the entire firm. In the latter approach, we discounted the **cash flows to the firm** on the project—that is, the project cash flows prior to debt payments but after taxes— at the project's cost of capital. Extending this principle, we can estimate the value of the entire firm by discounting the aggregate expected cash flows over time at the firm's cost of capital. The firm's aggregate cash flows can be estimated as cash flows left over after operating expenses, taxes, and any capital investments needed to create future growth in both fixed assets and working capital.

Cash Flows to Equity: The cash flow to equity investors is the cash flow left over after taxes, preferred dividends, cash flows to debtholders (interest payments, principal payments and new debt), net capital expenditures, and working capital needs.

Cash Flows to Firm: The cash flow to the firm is the cash flow left over after taxes, net capital expenditures, and working capital needs, but before debt payments or preferred dividends.

> Cash Flow to Firm = EBIT $(1 - t)$ - (Capital Expenditures - Depreciation) - Change in Working Capital

The value of the firm can then be written as

$$\text{Value of Firm} = \sum_{t=1}^{t=\infty} \frac{CF\ to\ Firm_t}{(1 + WACC)^t}$$

The value of a firm is therefore a function of its cash flows and its cost of capital. In the specific case where the cash flows to the firm are unaffected by the debt equity mix, and the cost of capital is reduced, the value of the firm will increase. If the objective in choosing the financing mix for the firm is the maximization of firm value, this can be accomplished, in this case, *by minimizing the cost of capital.* In the more general case where the cash flows to the firm are a function of the debt equity mix, the optimal financing mix is the one that *maximizes firm value.*[4]

The optimal financing mix for a firm is simple to compute if one is provided with a schedule that relates the costs of equity and debt to the leverage of the firm.

A PRACTICAL FRAMEWORK FOR ANALYZING CAPITAL STRUCTURE

As noted above, some compromises have to be made in order to apply the cost of capital approach to real-world problems. This section provides a general framework for analyzing these problems.

Cost of Equity
The primary task here is to estimate the cost of equity at different levels of debt. The approach described here applies if the CAPM is used to estimate cost of equity; the approach can be modified if the APM is used to estimate the cost of equity instead.

Step 1:   Obtain a current estimate of the equity beta and the debt equity ratio.

Step 2:   Estimate the **unlevered beta** (i.e., the beta that the firm would have had if it had no debt at all). If one uses the relationship between beta and leverage developed in Chapter 6, the unlevered beta can be written as

Unlevered Beta: The unlevered beta of an investment is a measure of only the business risk in that investment.

$$\beta_u = \beta_{\text{current}}/[1 + (1 - t)\ D/E]$$

where β_u is the unlevered beta of the firm, β_{current} is the current equity beta of the firm, t is the tax rate for the firm, and D/E is the current debt/equity ratio.

Step 3:   Reestimate the levered betas for different levels of debt.
$$\beta_{\text{levered}} = \beta_u\ [1 + (1 - t)\ D/E]$$

---

[4]In other words, the value of the firm might not be maximized at the point at which the cost of capital is minimized, if firm cash flows are much lower at that level.

where β_{levered} is the equity beta given new leverage and D/E is the debt/equity ratio. At each level of leverage, measured using the debt/equity ratio, the equity beta is reestimated.

Step 4: Estimate the costs of equity using this levered beta.

$$k_e = R_f + \beta_{\text{levered}} [E(R_m) - R_f]$$

where k_e is the cost of equity, $E(R_m)$ is the expected return on the market index, and R_f is the current risk-free rate.

The definition of levered beta is based on the assumption that all market risk is borne by the equity investors; this is unrealistic, however, especially at higher levels of debt. An alternative estimate of levered betas apportions some of the market risk to the debt:

$$\beta_{\text{levered}} = \beta_u [1 + (1-t)D/E] - \beta_{\text{debt}} (1-t) D/E$$

The beta of debt is based on the rating of the bond and is estimated by regressing past returns on each rating class against returns on a market index. The levered betas estimated using this approach will generally be lower than those estimated with the conventional model.

Costs of Debt

Once again, the task here is to estimate the firm's cost of debt at different levels of debt. As background to estimating the cost of debt, two schedules have to be developed. The first lays out the relationship between default risk and a firm's underlying characteristics. For instance, if bond ratings are used to measure default risk, this schedule will describe the relationship between ratings and financial ratios, using either general information or information pertaining to a particular industry. The other schedule includes current market interest rates on corporate bonds in each ratings class. These default premia will change over time and will have to be updated on a regular basis.

Given this background, the cost of debt for a firm can be estimated at different levels of debt by first estimating the bond rating for the firm at each debt level and then using the interest rate that corresponds to that rating.

Step 1: Prepare the latest income statement showing the current operating income and relevant financial ratios.

Step 2: Compute the current market value of the firm:

Market Value of Firm = Market Value of Equity + Market Value of Debt

Step 3: As the debt ratio is changed, compute the dollar value of debt:

Dollar Value of Debt = Debt/(Debt + Equity) * Current Market Value of Firm

Step 4: Compute the amount that will be paid as interest (Interest Rate*Dollar Value of Debt) and the financial ratios at each new debt ratio.

Step 5: Using the schedule that relates bond ratings to financial ratios, estimate what the firm's rating will be at each new debt ratio and the market interest rate that would correspond to that rating; this is the before-tax cost of debt.

Step 6: The after-tax cost of debt can then be computed using the firm's tax rate:

$$k_d = \text{After-Tax Cost of Debt} = \text{Before-Tax Cost of Debt} *(1 - \text{Tax Rate})$$

Cost of Capital

The costs of capital for different levels of debt can be estimated using the costs of equity and debt at each level. The debt ratio at which the cost of capital is minimized is the optimal debt ratio.

General Assumptions

The approach described earlier for estimating the cost of capital at different levels of debt rests on several assumptions. First, the effect of changing the capital structure on the firm's value is isolated by keeping the asset side fixed and changing the liability side. In practical terms, this implies that the debt ratio is increased (decreased) by issuing debt (equity) and repurchasing equity (debt). You may wonder whether the optimal debt ratio obtained by doing this can be generalized to cases in which the firm plans to invest the new funds in projects rather than in buying back securities. The answer is yes, on one condition: as long as the firm continues to make investments in the same line of business (or risk class) in which it has operated in the past, the optimal debt ratio obtained from this analysis can continue to be used. If the firm is planning to invest in new areas, with different risk profiles, however, the optimal debt ratio calculated, keeping the asset side fixed, may no longer be appropriate.

Second, the pretax operating income is assumed to be unaffected by the firm's financing mix and, by extension, its bond rating. If the operating income is a function of the firm's default risk, the basic framework will not change. Minimizing the cost of capital may not be the optimal course of action, however, since the value of the firm is determined by both the cash flows and the cost of capital. The value of the firm will have to be computed at each debt level, and the optimal debt ratio will be that which maximizes firm value.

 IN PRACTICE   ANALYZING THE CAPITAL STRUCTURE FOR BOEING—MARCH 1990

The general framework can be used to find the optimal capital structure for a firm, as we have for Boeing in March 1990. Boeing had only $277 million of debt on its books at that time,[5] whereas the market value of equity at the same point in time was $16.182 billion. The market price per share was $69.75, and there were 232 million shares outstanding. Proportionately, 1.68% of the overall financing mix was debt, and the remaining 98.32% was equity.

The beta for Boeing's stock in March 1990 was 0.95.[6] The Treasury bond rate at that time was 9.00%, and Boeing's senior debt was rated AA. While Boeing had no bonds outstanding, other long-term bonds with an AA rating were yielding 9.7%. The tax rate used for the analysis is 34%. The market premium used is 5.5%.

$$\text{Value of Firm} = 16{,}182 + 277 = \$16{,}459 \text{ million}$$
$$\text{Cost of Equity} = \text{Risk-free rate} + \text{Beta} * (\text{Market Premium})$$
$$= 9.00\% + 0.95 (5.5\%) = 14.23\%$$
$$\text{Cost of Debt} = \text{Pretax interest rate } (1\text{- tax rate})$$
$$= 9.70\% (1\text{- } 0.34) = 6.40\%$$
$$\text{WACC} = 14.23\% [16{,}182/(16{,}182+277)] + 6.40\% *[277/(16{,}182+277)] = 14.09\%$$

Boeing's cost of equity and leverage   Using the framework developed in the prior section, we can compute the unlevered beta and then recompute levered betas at each level of debt. These betas are used to estimate the cost of equity. The six-month Treasury

---

[5]This is the book value of the outstanding debt. Since the debt was recent and small relative to the equity, we assume that the book value was close to the market value.

[6]This was the beta reported in Value Line for Boeing in March 1990. It is based on a regression of five years of weekly returns for Boeing against the New York Stock Exchange Composite.

bond rate was 9.00% in March 1990, and the historical market premium of 5.5% was used to compute the cost of equity.

$$
\begin{aligned}
\text{Unlevered Beta} &= \text{Current Beta} / (1 + (1\text{-}t)\,\text{Debt/Equity}) \\
&= 0.95 / (1 + (1 - 0.34)\,(.0171)) \\
&= 0.94
\end{aligned}
$$

The recomputed betas are reported in Table 18.1.

Table 18.1   LEVERAGE, BETAS, AND THE COST OF EQUITY

Debt/ (Debt + Equity) (%)	$ Debt[a]	Levered Beta	Cost of Equity (%)
0	$0	0.94	14.17
10	1,646	1.01	14.55
20	3,292	1.09	15.02
30	4,938	1.21	15.63
40	6,584	1.35	16.44
50	8,230	1.56	17.58
60	9,876	1.94	19.67
70	11,522	2.59	23.23
80	13,168	3.95	30.72
90	14,814	7.90	52.44

[a]Dollar Value of Debt   = Debt/(Debt + Equity) * (Market Value of Equity + Market Value of Debt)
= Debt/(Debt + Equity) * (16,182 + 277)

Boeing's cost of debt and leverage   A number of financial ratios are correlated with bond ratings, and, ideally, we could build a sophisticated model to predict ratings. For purposes of this illustration, however, we use a much simpler version: We assume that bond ratings are determined solely by the **interest coverage ratio,** which is defined as follows:

Interest Coverage Ratio: The interest coverage ratio is the earnings before interest and taxes divided by the interest expense. It is a measure of the firm's capacity to service its interest payments, with higher coverage ratios representing more safety.

> Interest Coverage Ratio = Earnings before interest and taxes / Interest Expense

We chose the interest coverage ratio because it is an important ratio that both Standard and Poor's and Moody's use to determine ratings. In addition, there is significant correlation not only between the interest coverage ratio and bond ratings, but also between the interest coverage ratio and other ratios used in analysis, such as the debt coverage ratio and the funds flow ratios. Moreover, the interest coverage ratio changes as a firm changes its financing mix and decreases as the debt ratio increases.

The data in Table 18.2 were obtained based on an analysis of the financial ratios of manufacturing firms in different ratings classes (extrapolating for those ratings where no firms were listed).

Table 18.2 **BOND RATINGS AND INTEREST COVERAGE RATIOS**

Bond Rating	Interest Coverage Ratio	
	Low	High
AAA	9.65	∞
AA	6.85	9.649
A+	5.65	6.849
A	4.49	5.649
A-	3.29	4.489
BBB	2.76	3.289
BB	2.17	2.759
B+	1.87	2.169
B	1.57	1.869
B-	1.27	1.569
CCC	0.87	1.269
CC	0.67	0.869
C	0.25	0.669
D	-∞	0.249

Using this table as a guideline then, we see that a firm with an interest coverage ratio of 1.75 should have a rating of B for its bonds.

The relationship between bond ratings and interest rates in March 1990 was obtained by looking at yields of long-term bonds in each ratings class and averaging these yields. Table 18.3 summarizes the interest rates/rating relationship and reports the *default spread* for these bonds over Treasury bonds. (The Treasury bond rate in March 1990 was 9%.)

Table 18.3 **BOND RATINGS AND MARKET INTEREST RATES**

Bond Rating	Interest Rate on Debt (%)	Spread over Treasuries (%)
AAA	9.30	0.30
AA	9.70	0.70
A+	10.00	1.00
A	10.25	1.25
A-	10.50	1.50
BBB	11.00	2.00
BB	11.50	2.50
B+	12.00	3.00
B	13.00	4.00
B-	14.00	5.00
CCC	15.00	6.00
CC	16.50	7.50
C	18.00	9.00
D	21.00	12.00

Table 18.4 summarizes Boeing's operating income statement for the financial year 1989–1990. It shows that Boeing had earnings before interest, taxes, and depreciation of $2.063 billion and paid out interest of only $23 million. The financial ratios provide evidence of Boeing's capacity to meet its debt obligation.

Default Spread: This is the difference between the rate at which a firm with a specified default risk can borrow and the government bond rate on a bond of equivalent maturity.

Table 18.4 BOEING'S INCOME STATEMENT IN 1990		
Revenues	27,500	
- Operating expenses	25,437	
EBITDA	2,063	
- Depreciation	675	
- Interest expense	23	
Income before taxes	1,365	Interest coverage ratio = (1365+23)/23 = 60
- Taxes	396	Fund flow interest coverage = 1644/23 = 71
Income after taxes	969	Fund flow % of total debt = 1644 / 277 = 5
+ Depreciation	675	[The effective tax rate in 1989-90 was lower than 34%]
Funds from operations	1,644	

Note that the interest coverage ratio is 60, but Boeing's current rating is AA. Referring to Table 18.2, based on the coverage ratio alone, we see that Boeing should command a AAA rating. This does not take into account the fact that Boeing has almost no debt, however, and that even small increases in dollar debt will decrease the coverage ratio dramatically.

Finally, to compute Boeing's ratings at different debt levels, we redo the operating income statement at each level of debt, compute the interest coverage ratio at that level of debt, and find the rating that corresponds to that level of debt. For example, Table 18.5 provides operating income statements showing the debt ratio increased to 10% and 20% of the overall value of the firm.

Table 18.5 EFFECT OF MOVING TO HIGHER DEBT RATIOS		
	10% D/(D+E)	20% D/(D+E)
Debt	$1,646[a]	$3,292
EBITDA	2,063	2,063
- Depreciation	675	675
EBIT	1,388	1,388
- Interest expense	160	346
Taxable income	1,228	1,042
- Tax	418	354
Net income	810	688
Interest coverage ratio	8.69	4.02
Likely rating	AA	A-
Interest rate	9.70%	10.50%
After-tax cost of debt	6.40%	6.93%

[a]The value of the firm is $16,459 million. This is 10% of the value.

Note that an element of circular reasoning is involved here. The interest rate is needed to calculate the interest coverage ratio, and the coverage ratio is necessary to compute the interest rate. To get around the problem, we do a series of iterations until consistency is attained between the rate used to calculate the interest expense and the rate

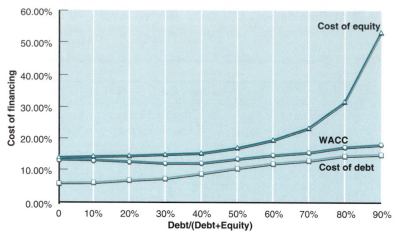

Figure 18.2   Boeing—Costs of financing as a function of leverage

that is obtained from the coverage ratio. If the interest expense exceeds the earnings before interest and taxes, the tax rate used to calculate the after-tax cost of debt is reestimated as follows:

$$\text{Effective Tax rate} = \text{Stated Tax Rate} \left(\frac{\text{EBIT}}{\text{Interest Expense}} \right)$$

This process is repeated for each level of debt from 10% to 90%, and the after-tax costs of debt are obtained at each level of debt.

Effects of leverage on Boeing's cost of capital   Now that we have estimated the cost of equity and the cost of debt at each debt level, we are in a position to compute Boeing's cost of capital. This is done for each debt level in Exhibit 18.1. The cost of capital, which is 14.17% when the firm is unlevered, decreases as the firm initially adds debt, reaches a minimum of 13.22% at 30% debt, and then starts to increase again. This is illustrated graphically in Figure 18.2.

To illustrate the robustness of this solution to alternative measures of levered betas, the costs of debt, equity, and capital were reestimated under the assumption that debt bears some market risk; the results are summarized in Table 18.6.

Table 18.6:   COSTS OF EQUITY, DEBT, AND CAPITAL WITH DEBT CARRYING MARKET RISK

Debt Ratio (%)	Bond Rating	Cost of Debt (%)	Beta of Debt	Beta of Equity	Cost of Equity (%)	Cost of Capital (%)
0	AA	6.40	0.00	0.94	14.17%	14.17%
10	AA	6.40	0.05	1.00	14.55%	13.71%
20	A-	6.93	0.10	1.08	14.93%	13.33%
30	BB	7.59	0.20	1.15	15.32%	13.00%
40	B-	9.24	0.30	1.22	15.71%	13.12%
50	CCC	9.90	0.40	1.30	16.12%	13.13%
60	CC	11.72	0.50	1.37	16.56%	13.66%
70	C	13.90	0.50	1.62	17.89%	15.10%
80	C	14.42	0.50	2.10	20.55%	15.64%
90	C	14.81	0.55	3.25	26.89%	16.02%

CAPITAL STRUCTURE

Current beta =	0.95		Current Equity =	$16,182		Current Depreciation =	$675
Current Debt =	$277		Current EBITDA =	$2,063		Current Interest rate (Company) =	10.00%
Tax Rate =	34.00%		Current Rating =	AA		Current T. Bond rate =	9.00%
						Six-month T. Bill rate =	8.33%

WORKSHEET FOR ESTIMATING RATINGS/INTEREST RATES

D/(D+E)	0.00%	10.00%	20.00%	30.00%	40.00%	50.00%	60.00%	70.00%	80.00%	90.00%
D/E	0.00%	11.11%	25.00%	42.86%	66.67%	100.00%	150.00%	233.33%	400.00%	900.00%
$ Debt	$0	$1,646	$3,292	$4,938	$6,584	$8,230	$9,875	$11,521	$13,167	$14,813
Beta	0.94	1.01	1.09	1.21	1.35	1.56	1.94	2.59	3.95	7.90
Cost of Equity	14.17%	14.55%	15.02%	15.63%	16.44%	17.58%	19.67%	23.23%	30.72%	52.44%
Operating Inc.	$2,063	$2,063	$2,063	$2,063	$2,063	$2,063	$2,063	$2,063	$2,063	$2,063
Depreciation	$675	$675	$675	$675	$675	$675	$675	$675	$675	$675
Interest	$0	$160	$346	$568	$922	$1,234	$1,629	$1,901	$2,370	$2,666
Taxable Income	$1,388	$1,228	$1,042	$820	$466	$154	($241)	($513)	($982)	($1,278)
Tax	$472	$418	$354	$279	$159	$52	($82)	($174)	($334)	($435)
Net Income	$916	$811	$688	$541	$308	$101	($159)	($339)	($648)	($844)
(+)Deprec'n	$675	$675	$675	$675	$675	$675	$675	$675	$675	$675
Funds from Op.	$1,591	$1,486	$1,363	$1,216	$983	$776	$516	$336	$27	($169)
Pretax Int. cov	∞	8.69	4.02	2.44	1.51	1.12	0.85	0.73	0.59	0.52
Funds Int. Cov	∞	9.31	3.94	2.14	1.07	0.63	0.32	0.18	0.01	-0.06
Funds/Debt	∞	0.90	0.41	0.25	0.15	0.09	0.05	0.03	0.00	-0.01
Likely Rating	AA	AA	A-	BB	B-	CCC	CC	CC	C	C
Interest Rate	9.70%	9.70%	10.50%	11.50%	14.00%	15.00%	16.50%	16.50%	18.00%	18.00%
Eff Tax Rate	34.00%	34.00%	34.00%	34.00%	34.00%	34.00%	28.96%	24.82%	19.91%	17.70%

WORKSHEET FOR CALCULATING WEIGHTED AVERAGE COST OF CAPITAL

D/(D+E)	0.00%	10.00%	20.00%	30.00%	40.00%	50.00%	60.00%	70.00%	80.00%	90.00%
D/E	0.00%	11.11%	25.00%	42.86%	66.67%	100.00%	150.00%	233.33%	400.00%	900.00%
$ Debt	$0	$1,646	$3,292	$4,938	$6,584	$8,230	$9,875	$11,521	$13,167	$14,813
Cost of Equity	14.17%	14.55%	15.02%	15.63%	16.44%	17.58%	19.67%	23.23%	30.72%	52.44%
Cost of Debt	6.40%	6.40%	6.93%	7.59%	9.24%	9.90%	11.72%	12.40%	14.42%	14.81%
WACC	14.17%	13.73%	13.40%	13.22%	13.56%	13.74%	14.90%	15.65%	17.68%	18.58%
Firm Value (C)	$16,378	$16,897	$17,313	$17,555	$17,110	$16,888	$15,570	$14,824	$13,126	$12,490
Firm Value (G)	$16,223	$17,805	$19,205	$20,082	$18,507	$17,776	$14,070	$12,354	$9,180	$8,194

If the debtholders bear some market risk, the cost of equity is lower at each level of debt, but Boeing's optimal debt ratio is still 30%, which is the same as the optimal calculated under the conventional calculation of the levered beta.

Firm Value and Cost of Capital The rationale for minimizing the cost of capital is that it maximizes the value of the firm. To illustrate the effects of moving to the optimal on Boeing's firm value, we start off with a simple valuation formula:

$$\text{Firm Value} = \text{CF to Firm } (1 + g) / (\text{WACC} - g)$$

where

g = Growth rate in the cash flow to the firm (steady state)

The current value of the firm is $16,459 million, and the weighted average cost of capital is 14.09%. The current cash flow to the firm is

$$
\begin{aligned}
\text{Cash Flow to Firm} &= \text{EBIT } (1 - \text{tax rate}) + \text{Depreciation} - \text{Capital Spending} \\
&= 1388 (1 - 0.34) + 675 - 800 = \$791 \text{ million}
\end{aligned}
$$

Solving for the implied growth rate:

$$
\begin{aligned}
\text{Growth Rate} &= (\text{Firm Value} * \text{WACC} - \text{CF to Firm})/(\text{Firm Value} + \text{CF to Firm}) \\
&= (16,459*.1409 - 791)/(16,459 + 791) = .0886 \text{ or } 8.86\%
\end{aligned}
$$

Now assume that Boeing moves to 30% debt and a WACC of 13.22%. The firm can now be valued using the following parameters:

$$
\begin{aligned}
\text{Savings in Cost from moving to optimal} \\
&= (\text{WACC}_{old} - \text{WACC}_{optimal})\text{Firm Value} \\
&= (.1409 - .1322)(16,459) \\
&= \$145
\end{aligned}
$$

$$
\begin{aligned}
&\text{Present Value of Savings in Perpetuity} \\
&= \frac{\text{Annual Savings } (1 + g)}{WACC_{optimal} - g} \\
&= \frac{145 (1.0886)}{.1322 - .0886} = \$3,623
\end{aligned}
$$

The value of the firm will increase from $16,459 million to $20,082 million if the firm moves to the optimal debt ratio:

$$\text{Increase in Firm Value} = \$20,082 - \$16,459 = \$3,623 \text{ million}$$

With 232 million shares outstanding, assuming that stockholders can rationally evaluate the effect of this refinancing, the increase in the stock price can be calculated:

$$
\begin{aligned}
\text{Increase in Stock Price} &= \text{Increase in Firm Value} / \text{Number of Shares Outstanding} \\
&= 3,623/232 = \$15.61
\end{aligned}
$$

Since the current stock price is $69.75, the stock price can be expected to increase to $85.36, which translates into a 22.39% increase in the price. Since the asset side of the balance sheet is kept fixed, and changes in capital structure are made by borrowing funds and repurchasing stock, this implies that the stock price would increase to $85.36

on the announcement of the repurchase. Note that all stockholders, including those who sell back shares, are assumed to share in the spoils.

Caveat Emptor—Some Considerations in Using the Model

Several considerations need to be taken into account when we use this approach to come up with an optimal debt ratio. First, the bond rating is assumed to be predictable, based on financial observables. The ratings agencies would argue, however, that certain subjective factors, such as the perceived quality of management, are part of the ratings process. One way to build these factors into the analysis would be to modify the ratings obtained from the financial ratio analysis across the board to reflect the ratings agencies' subjective concerns.[7]

Second, it is assumed that, at every debt level, all existing debt will be refinanced at the "new" interest rate that will prevail after the capital structure change. For instance, Boeing's existing debt of $277 million, which has a AA rating, is assumed to be refinanced at the interest rate corresponding to a BB rating, which is our estimate of Boeing's rating at the optimal debt level of 30%. This is done because existing debtholders might have protective puts that enable them to put their bonds back to the firm and receive face value.[8] Another reason is that it eliminates "wealth expropriation" effects—the effects of stockholders expropriating wealth from bondholders, when debt is increased, and vice versa, when debt is reduced—from the value calculations. These wealth transfer effects can be built in by locking in current rates on existing bonds and recalculating the optimal debt ratio.[9]

Third, the assumption that the operating income is unaffected by the bond rating is a key one. If the operating income is adversely affected by the drop in the bond rating, the value of the firm may not be maximized where the weighted average cost of capital is minimized. Again, the analysis can be modified so that the operating income is a function of the bond rating and estimating the value of the firm at each debt level.[10]

Finally, the unconstrained analysis leaves us with the uncomfortable finding that at its optimal debt ratio, Boeing has a bond rating below **investment grade**. Since most financial managers would be troubled by this sudden increase in default risk and its implications for the long-term survival of the firm, we introduce constraints into the analysis.

Investment Grade Bonds: An investment grade bond is one with a rating greater than or equal to BBB. Some institutional investors, such as pension funds, are constrained from holding bonds with lower ratings.

Building Constraints into the Analysis

The simplest solution to the ratings problem is a "bond rating constraint," whereby the debt level chosen is the one that has the lowest cost of capital, subject to the constraint

---

[7]For instance, assume that a firm's current rating is AA but that its financial ratios would result in an A rating. It can then be argued that the ratings agencies are, for subjective reasons, rating the company one notch higher than the rating obtained from a purely financial analysis. The ratings obtained for each debt level can then be increased by one notch across the board to reflect these subjective consideratons.

[8]If they do not have protective puts, it is in the stockholder's best interests not to refinance the debt (as in the leveraged buyout of RJR Nabisco) if debt ratios are increased.

[9]This will have the effect of reducing total interest cost, when debt is increased, and, thus, interest coverage ratios. This will lead to higher ratings, at least in the short term.

[10]For example, we assumed that Boeing's operating income would drop 10% if its rating dropped below A- and another 10% if it dropped below BBB. Consequently, the optimal debt ratio is reduced to 20%.

that the bond rating meets or exceeds a certain level. For example, in the previous illustration, if Boeing insisted on preserving a bond rating of A- or above, the optimal
debt ratio would be 20%.

Although this approach is simple, it is essentially subjective and is therefore subject
to manipulation. For instance, Boeing's management could insist that it wants to preserve a AA rating and, hence, justify the existing debt policy. One way to make managers more accountable in this regard is to measure the cost of a rating constraint.

$$\text{Cost of Rating Constraint} = \begin{array}{c} \text{Maximum Firm Value} \\ \text{without constraints} \end{array} - \begin{array}{c} \text{Maximum Firm Value} \\ \text{with constraints} \end{array}$$

If Boeing insisted on maintaining an A- rating, its constrained optimal debt ratio would
be 20%. The cost of preserving the constraint can then be measured as the difference in
firm value at 30% and at 20%.

$$\text{Cost of 20\% Rating Constraint} = \underset{\$20,082}{\text{Value at 30\% Debt}} - \underset{-\$19,205}{\text{Value at 20\% Debt (Boeing)}}$$
$$= \$877 \text{ million}$$

Managers could probably justify a loss in potential value of $877 million to stock-
holders, but it would be increasingly difficult to justify the larger losses that would accrue if the firm tightened its rating constraints any further.

Another approach to building in constraints is to analyze the effects of changes in
operating income on the optimal debt ratio. In the case described here, we used
Boeing's operating income in 1990 to find the optimal leverage. One could argue that
Boeing's operating income is subject to large swings, however, depending on the va-
garies of the economy and the fortunes of the airlines that order commercial aircraft
from the company, as shown in Table 18.7.

Table 18.7 BOEING'S OPERATING INCOME HISTORY, 1980–1990

Year	Sales	EBITDA	Change %
1980	9426	877	
1981	9788	715	-18.49
1982	9035	578	-19.07
1983	11129	701	21.25
1984	10354	725	3.37
1985	13636	968	33.58
1986	16341	1,095	13.09
1987	15355	706	-35.49
1988	16962	1,018	44.09
1989	21000	1,155	13.49
1990	27500	2,063	78.57

There are several ways of using such historical data to modify the analysis. One way is
to look at the firm's performance during previous "downturns." In Boeing's case, the re-

cession in 1980–1982 resulted in a drop in operating income of about 34% from $877 million to $578 million. Another way is to obtain a statistical measure of the volatility in operating income, so that we can be more conservative in choosing debt levels for firms with more volatile earnings. In Boeing's case, the standard deviation in percentage changes in operating income is 33.70%. Finally, it is a source of some concern that the EBITDA for Boeing registered a dramatic jump from $1,155 million in 1989 to $2,063 million in 1990. Table 18.8 illustrates the impact of lowering EBITDA from current levels on the optimal debt level.

Table 18.8 EFFECTS OF OPERATING INCOME ON OPTIMAL DEBT RATIO

% Lower	EBITDA	Optimal D/(D+E) (%)
-5	$1,960	30.00
-10	1,857	20.00
-15	1,754	20.00
-20	1,650	20.00
-25	1,547	20.00
-30	1,444	20.00
-40	1,238	10.00
-50	1,032	10.00

As you can see, the optimal debt ratio declines as the EBITDA decreases. It is striking to note, however, that Boeing can afford to carry a significantly higher amount of debt even with dramatically lower operating income. This suggests that even if its managers are conservative and want to avoid putting their firm at risk of default, they can increase debt and add value to both the firm and its stockholders.

Concept Check

How would one consider the implications of the higher agency costs and lost flexibility as a result of the higher leverage in the analysis described above?

Determinants of Optimal Debt Ratio

The preceding analysis highlights some of the determinants of the optimal debt ratio. We can divide these determinants into firm-specific and macroeconomic factors.

Firm-specific factors   Determinants specific to the firm include the firm's tax rate, pretax returns, and variance in operating income.

The firm's tax rate   In general, the tax benefits from debt increase as the tax rate goes up. In relative terms, firms with higher tax rates should have higher optimal debt ratios than do firms with lower tax rates, other things being equal. It also follows that a firm's optimal debt ratio will increase as its tax rate increases. In the preceding example, Boeing has an optimal debt ratio of 30% with a tax rate of 34%. Figure 18.3 illustrates the relationship between tax rates and optimal debt ratios for Boeing.

Pretax returns on the firm (in cash-flow terms)   This is defined as the EBITDA, as a percentage of the market value of the firm. It follows that a firm with higher pretax returns can sustain much more debt as a proportion of the market value of the firm, because debt payments can be met much more easily from prevailing cash flows.

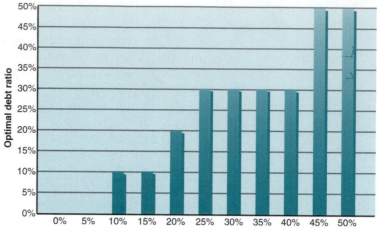

Figure 18.3   Optimal debt ratio for Boeing and tax rates

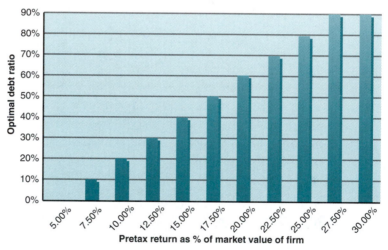

Figure 18.4   Optimal debt ratio as a function of pretax return (%)

Boeing, for example, has pretax cash flow returns of 12.53% in the base case and an optimal debt ratio of 30%. Figure 18.4 examines the relationship between pretax returns and optimal debt ratios for Boeing.

Variance in operating income   The variance in operating income enters the analysis in two ways. First, it plays a role in determining the current beta: firms with high (low) variance in operating income have high (low) betas. Second, the volatility in operating income can be one of the factors determining bond ratings at different levels of debt: ratings drop off much more dramatically for higher variance firms as debt levels are increased. It follows that firms with higher (lower) variance in operating income will have lower (higher) optimal debt ratios. The variance in operating income also plays a role in the constrained analysis, for higher variance firms are much more likely to register significant drops in operating income. Consequently, the decision to increase debt should be made much more cautiously for these firms.

☐ Concept Check	Considering the determinants of optimal debt ratios listed above, what kind of optimal capital structure would you expect a high-growth, high-technology firm to have?

Macroeconomic Factors   Macroeconomic determinants include the term structure of interest rates and default spreads.

Term structure of interest rates   The **term structure premium** in interest rates can be defined as the difference between long-term and short-term rates. We find that the optimal debt ratios of all firms increase as the premium decreases (or turns negative; i.e., an inverted term structure) and decrease as the premium increases. As the term structure becomes more upward sloping, long-term bonds become a less attractive way of raising funds to finance projects, whereas equity becomes more attractive.

Term Structure Premium: This is the difference between the long-term and short-term default-free rates at any point in time.

Default spreads   The default spreads commanded by different ratings classes tend to increase during recessions and decrease during recoveries. Keeping other things constant, as the spreads increase (decrease), optimal debt ratios decrease (increase), for the simple reason that higher spreads penalize firms that borrow more money and have lower ratings.

Extending the Cost of Capital Approach
The cost of capital approach, which works so well for manufacturing firms that are publicly traded and rated and stay financially healthy, may have to be adapted in other cases, such as for private firms that might not be rated; for financial service firms, such as banks, and insurance companies, and for firms in financial trouble.

Private firms that are not rated   Working with a publicly rated company like Boeing has some advantages. The current rating for the company provides information that can be used to assess its current default risk and how it might change as the debt ratio changes. It also provides a rationale for the process of estimating ratings and then using the ratings to estimate the interest rate on the debt. This does not imply that the approach cannot be used for unrated firms, however. We can deal with this deficit by estimating a bond rating for the firm, based on interest coverage or other financial ratios, and then use this rating to estimate an interest rate on debt. For private firms in the United States, this may provide a useful approximation of default risk. Another way to deal with the deficit is to develop an alternative measure of default risk, which can then be used to estimate an interest rate on the debt. This measure can be based on credit scoring approaches used by banks to determine default risk and interest rates; it can be as simple as classifying firms on a continuum from "very safe" to "very risky." This approach may provide better estimates of interest rates for firms in economies where ratings are not widely used, such as Germany.

Banks and insurance companies   Applying the cost of capital approach to financial service firms, such as banks and insurance companies presents several problems. The first is that the interest coverage ratio spreads, which are critical in determining the bond ratings, have to be estimated separately for financial service firms; applying manufacturing company spreads will result in absurdly low ratings for even the safest banks and very low optimal debt ratios. The second is a measurement problem that arises partly from the difficulty in estimating the debt on a financial service company's balance sheet. Given the mix of deposits, repurchase agreements, short-term financing, and other liabilities that may show up on the balance sheet, one solution may be to focus only on long-term debt, defined tightly, and to use interest coverage ratios defined consistently. The third problem is that financial service firms may find their operating income affected by their bond rating; as the rating drops, the operating income might drop too.

IN PRACTICE   APPLYING THE COST OF CAPITAL APPROACH TO J.P. MORGAN

Here, we analyze the optimal capital structure for J.P. Morgan, using data from 1994. To begin, we make the following assumptions:

- The earnings before long-term interest expenses and taxes amounted to $2,448 million.
- J. P. Morgan was ranked AA+ and paid 8.20% on its long-term debt in 1994. It had $9 billion in long-term debt outstanding at the end of the year.
- J.P. Morgan had 187.10 million shares outstanding, trading at $70 per share, and had a beta of 1.15. (The Treasury bond rate at that time was 8.00%.)
- The interest coverage ratios used to estimate the bond ratings were adjusted downward, based on the ratings of financial service firms.
- The operating income for J.P. Morgan is assumed to drop if its rating drops. Table 18.9 summarizes the interest coverage ratios and estimated operating income drops for different ratings classes.

Table 18.9   **INTEREST COVERAGE RATIOS, RATINGS, AND OPERATING INCOME DECLINES**

Long-Term Interest Coverage Ratio	Rating is	Spread is (%)	Operating Income Decline (%)
< 0.25	D	12.00	-50
0.25–0.50	C	9.00	-40
0.50–0.75	CC	7.50	-40
0.75–0.90	CCC	6.00	-40
0.90–1.00	B-	5.00	-25
1.00–1.25	B	4.00	-20
1.25–1.50	B+	3.00	-20
1.50–2.00	BB	2.50	-20
2.00–2.25	BBB	2.00	-10
2.25–3.00	A-	1.50	-5
3.00–3.90	A	1.25	-5
3.90–4.85	A+	1.00	-5
4.85–6.65	AA	0.70	-5
> 6.65	AAA	0.30	0

Thus, we assume that the operating income will drop 5% if J.P. Morgan's rating drops to AA, and 20% if it drops to BB.

Based on these assumptions, the optimal debt ratio for J.P. Morgan is estimated to be 30%, lower than the current debt ratio of 40%. Table 18.10 below summarizes the cost of capital and firm values at different debt ratios for the firm.

Table 18.10   DEBT RATIOS, WACC, AND FIRM VALUE: J.P. MORGAN

Debt Ratio (%)	Cost of Equity (%)	Cost of Debt (%)	WACC (%)	Firm Value
0	12.40	5.31	12.40	$17,944
10	12.71	5.31	11.97	$17,894
20	13.10	5.57	11.59	$18,712
30	13.60	5.92	11.30	$19,410
40	14.27	6.08	11.00	$16,993
50	15.21	7.68	11.45	$12,035
60	17.12	10.02	12.86	$10,244
70	20.40	12.09	14.58	$8,670
80	26.60	12.51	15.33	$8,126
90	46.82	14.79	17.99	$5,539

Concept Check

> Can you think of other industries in which the operating income is sensitive to the bond rating? What are the implications for optimal capital structure analysis for firms in these industries?

Firms in trouble   As we discussed earlier, a key input that drives the optimal capital structure is the current operating income. If this income is depressed, either because the firm is a cyclical firm or because of firm-specific factors that are expected to be temporary, the optimal debt ratio that will emerge from the analysis will be much lower than the firm's true optimal. For example, automobile manufacturing firms would have had very low optimal debt ratios if the debt ratios had been computed based on the operating income in 1991 and 1992, which were recession years. If the drop in operating income is permanent, however, this lower optimal debt ratio is, in fact, the correct estimate.

Normalized Operating Income   This is a measure of the income that a firm can make in a normal year, in which there are no extraordinary gains or losses either from firm-specific factors (such as write-offs and one-time sales) or macroeconomic factors (such as recessions and economic booms).

When faced with a firm with depressed current operating income, the first issue to address is whether the drop in income is temporary or permanent. If the drop is temporary, we must determine the normalized operating income for the firm. The **normalized operating income** is an estimate of how much the firm can be expected to earn in a normal year—that is, a year without the specific characteristics that depressed earnings this year. For a cyclical firm, this may require going back to a year in which the economy was healthy and either estimating the operating income in that year or using the return on capital from that year to arrive at an operating income in the current year. The latter approach will work better when the firm's size has changed. In other cases, profitability measures from comparable firms may be used to arrive at a normalized operating income. In either case, however, the optimal debt ratio arrived at using the normalized operating income has to be used cautiously, since the analysis is based on the assumption that earnings will recover to normalized levels.

IN PRACTICE ESTIMATING THE OPTIMAL DEBT RATIO FOR A FIRM IN FINANCIAL TROUBLE: BEN AND JERRY'S

In 1994, Ben & Jerry's reported earnings, before interest, taxes, and depreciation (EBITDA), of $7.44 million and a net loss of $1.90 million. Based on this operating income, the optimal debt ratio for the firm is 10%. This operating income was depressed, however, because of operating and management problems at Ben & Jerry's during the year. With a management change, it can be argued that the normalized operating income for Ben & Jerry's will be higher; we can estimate it by assuming that the pretax operating (EBITDA) margin will return to pre-1994 levels of 11%. Based on the revenues of $148.8 million in 1994, the normalized operating income is

Normalized EBITDA = 11% of $148.8 million = $16.37 million

Ben &and Jerry's was not rated in 1994; rather, we estimated the rating based on the interest coverage ratio derived from the normalized operating income: (Depreciation was $5 million.)

Estimated Interest Coverage Ratio for Ben and Jerry's = EBIT / Interest Expense
= ($16.37 million - $5 million) / $1.30 million = 8.74
Estimated Bond Rating, given interest coverage ratio = AA

In Table 18.11, the cost of capital and the firm value are estimated under both the current and the normalized operating income for different debt ratios.

Table 18.11   BEN & JERRY'S: COST OF CAPITAL, FIRM VALUE, AND DEBT RATIOS

Debt Ratio (%)	With Current Operating Income		With Normalized Operating Income	
	WACC (%)	Firm Value	WACC (%)	Firm Value
0	13.00	$152	13.00	$152
10	12.92	$154	12.58	$162
20	14.13	$129	12.26	$171
30	15.95	$104	12.18	$173
40	17.15	$92	12.67	$160
50	18.35	$82	12.71	$159
60	19.55	$74	15.26	$112
70	20.75	$67	16.16	$101
80	21.95	$61	17.06	$92
90	23.15	$56	17.96	$85

Using the normalized operating income, we find that the optimal debt ratio is 30%, which may be more representative of Ben & Jerry's true debt capacity in the long term.

THE RETURN DIFFERENTIAL APPROACH

Returning to our original discussion of ways of choosing an optimal debt level for a firm, we can present the trade-off between debt and equity in terms of returns on and the cost of equity. As illustrated in Chapter 4, the return on equity for a firm can be written in terms of its return on capital and its after-tax cost of borrowing:

$$ROE = ROA + D/E \, [(ROA - i \, (1 - t)]$$

where ROE is the return on equity, ROA is the return on assets (capital), D/E is the debt equity ratio, i is the interest rate on debt, and t is the tax rate. The return on assets (capital) is defined as the after-tax earnings before interest and taxes, divided by the book value of capital invested in the firm:

$$ROA = EBIT\ (1 - t)\ /\ (Debt + Equity)$$

If the return on assets (capital) is greater than the after-tax cost of borrowing, the return on equity will increase as the leverage increases. This is the benefit of borrowing, as illustrated in Figure 18.5.

Of course, this benefit has to be weighed against the additional risk equity investors face as a consequence of the borrowing. In the capital asset pricing model, this additional risk can be measured by reestimating the beta with the higher leverage, as shown in Figure 18.6.

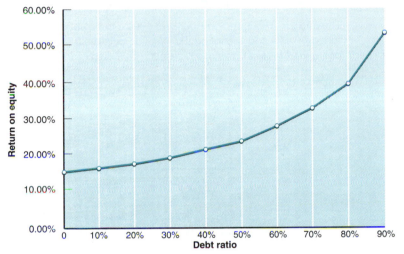

Figure 18.5   Leverage and return on equity

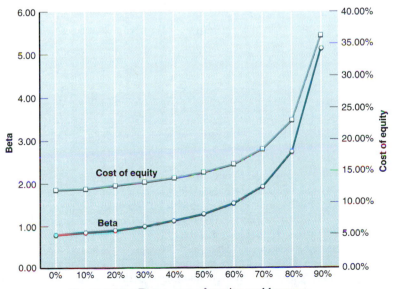

Figure 18.6   Betas, cost of equity, and leverage

As the firm borrows more money, the beta will increase, as will the cost of equity.

It makes sense to present the differential between the return and the cost of equity as a function of the leverage. At the risk of oversimplifying the capital structure decision, it can be argued that if the increase in leverage increases the differential between return on equity and cost of equity, the firm is better off taking on the debt.

There are some limitations to this approach, however. By measuring the return differential in percentage terms between return on equity and the cost of equity, the firm might underinvest. Moreover, simply maximizing the return differential might not maximize the stock price or firm value, unless other assumptions are made about the sustainability of growth and earnings.

 IN PRACTICE   EFFECTS OF LEVERAGE, ROE, AND COST OF EQUITY ON BOEING

The effects of leverage on Boeing in 1990 can be captured by estimating the effects on both return on equity and cost of equity. We first estimate the return on equity at different levels of debt, based on the return on assets earned by Boeing in 1990:

$$\text{Return on Assets at Boeing (1990)} = \text{EBIT}\,(1 - t)/\,(\text{Debt} + \text{Equity})_{\text{Book Value}}$$
$$= 1388\,(1 - 0.34)/(277 + \$6{,}835) = 12.88\%$$

Table 18.12 tracks the interest rates estimated at different levels of debt, from the capital structure analysis.

Table 18.12   INTEREST RATES, ROE AND DEBT RATIOS

Debt Ratio (%)	Interest Rate on Debt (%)	ROE (%)
0	9.70	12.88
10	9.70	13.60
20	10.50	14.37
30	11.50	15.15
40	14.00	15.31
50	15.00	15.86
60	16.50	15.87
70	17.25	16.37
80	18.00	16.88
90	18.00	21.89

The tax rate used to estimate the cost of equity is 34%. In addition, the betas and costs of equity can be estimated at different levels of debt for Boeing, by using the unlevered beta of 0.94, estimated earlier in this chapter (see Table 18.13).

The treasury bond rate used was 9%, and the risk premium was 5.5%.

The differential between the return on equity and the cost of equity at different debt levels can be computed as shown in Table 18.14.

The differential is always negative but is least negative at a 30% debt ratio, which is the optimal. Note that, although the optimal debt ratios under the cost of capital approach and this approach are the same for Boeing, this will not always be true.

Table 18.13   BETAS, COSTS OF EQUITY, AND DEBT RATIOS

Debt Ratio (%)	Beta	Cost of Equity (%)
0	0.94	14.17
10	1.01	14.55
20	1.10	15.02
30	1.21	15.63
40	1.35	16.44
50	1.56	17.58
60	1.87	19.29
70	2.39	22.13
80	3.40	27.82
90	6.52	44.86

Table 18.14   RETURN DIFFERENTIAL AND DEBT RATIOS

Debt Ratio (%)	ROE (%)	Cost of Equity (%)	ROE—Cost of Equity (%)
0	12.88	14.17	-1.29
10	13.60	14.55	-0.94
20	14.37	15.02	-0.65
30	15.15	15.63	-0.48
40	15.31	16.44	-1.13
50	15.86	17.58	-1.72
60	15.87	19.29	-3.41
70	16.37	22.13	-5.75
80	16.88	27.82	-10.93
90	21.89	44.86	-22.97

THE ADJUSTED PRESENT VALUE APPROACH

In the adjusted present value approach, the firm value and leverage are connected using the value of the firm without debt as the starting point and adding the positive and negative value effects of leverage. In particular, when the primary benefit of borrowing is a tax benefit and the most significant cost of borrowing is the risk of bankruptcy, the value of a levered firm can be written as the sum of the following:

> Value of Levered Firm = Value of Unlevered Firm + Present Value of Tax Benefits of Debt − Present Value of Expected Bankruptcy Costs

The value of the levered firm can then be estimated at different levels of the debt; the debt level that maximizes firm value is the optimal debt ratio.

Value of Unlevered Firm

The first step in this approach is to estimate the value of the unlevered firm. This can be accomplished by valuing the firm as if it had no debt—that is, by discounting the expected after-tax operating cash flows at the unlevered cost of equity. In the special case whereby cash flows grow at a constant rate in perpetuity

$$\text{Value of Unlevered Firm} = \text{FCFF}_0\,(1+g)/(\rho_u - g)$$

where FCFF_0 is the current after-tax operating cash flow to the firm, ρ_u is the unlevered cost of equity, and g is the expected growth rate.

The inputs needed for this valuation are the expected cash flows, growth rates, and the unlevered cost of equity. To estimate the unlevered cost of equity, we can draw on our earlier analysis and compute the unlevered beta of the firm:

$$\beta_{\text{unlevered}} = \beta_{\text{current}}/[1 + (1 - t)D/E]$$

where $\beta_{\text{unlevered}}$ is the unlevered beta of the firm, β_{current} is the current equity beta of the firm, t is the tax rate for the firm, and D/E is the current debt/equity ratio. This unlevered beta can then be used to arrive at the unlevered cost of equity.

Expected Tax Benefit from Borrowing

The second step in this approach is to calculate the expected tax benefit from taking on a given level of debt. This tax benefit is a function of the tax rate of the firm and is discounted back at the cost of debt to reflect the riskiness of this cash flow. If the tax savings are viewed as a perpetuity

$$\begin{aligned}
\text{Value of Tax Benefits} &= [\text{Tax Rate} * \text{Cost of Debt} * \text{Debt}] / \text{Cost of Debt} \\
&= \text{Tax Rate} * \text{Debt} \\
&= t_c\,D
\end{aligned}$$

The tax rate referred to here is the firm's marginal tax rate, and the approach is general enough to allow it to change over time.

Estimating Expected Bankruptcy Costs

The third step is to evaluate the effect of the given level of debt on both the default risk of the firm and expected **bankruptcy costs**. In theory, at least, this requires estimating the probability of default with the additional debt and the direct and indirect cost of bankruptcy. If π_a is the probability of default after the additional debt, and BC is the present value of the bankruptcy cost, the present value of expected bankruptcy cost can be estimated as follows:

PV of Expected Bankruptcy cost = Probability of Bankruptcy * PV of
Bankruptcy Cost = π_a BC

This component of the adjusted present value approach poses the most significant estimation problem, since neither the probability of bankruptcy nor the bankruptcy cost
can be estimated directly.

Bankruptcy Cost   This is the cost associated with going bankrupt. It includes both
direct costs (from going bankrupt) and indirect costs (arising from the *perception* that
a firm may go bankrupt).

There are two basic ways in which the probability of bankruptcy can be estimated indirectly. The first is to estimate a bond rating, as we did in the cost of capital approach,
at each level of debt and to use the empirical estimates of default probabilities for each
rating. For instance, Table 18.15, extracted from a study by Altman and Kishore, summarizes the probability of default over 10 years by bond rating class in 1995.[11]

Table 18.15   **DEFAULT RATES BY BOND RATING CLASSES**

Bond Rating	Default Rate (%)
D	100.00
C	80.00
CC	65.00
CCC	46.61
B-	32.50
B	26.36
B+	19.28
BB	12.20
BBB	2.30
A-	1.41
A	0.53
A+	0.40
AA	0.28
AAA	0.01

The second approach is to use a statistical approach, such as a **probit** model, to estimate the probability of default, based on the firm's observable characteristics, at each
level of debt.

The bankruptcy cost can be estimated, albeit with considerable noise in the estimate,
from studies that have looked at the magnitude of this cost in actual bankruptcies. In

[11]This study estimated default rates over 10 years for only some of the ratings classes. We extrapolated the
rest of the ratings.

chapter 17 we discussed two studies – one by Warner on direct bankruptcy costs at railroads and the other by Shapiro on indirect bankruptcy costs. Combining Warner's results on direct bankruptcy cost and Shapiro's results on indirect bankruptcy cost may provide a measure of the total bankruptcy costs faced by firms.

Probit Model: This is a statistical technique that allows the probability of an event to be estimated as a function of the observable characteristics.

The Net Effect

The net effect of adding debt can be calculated by aggregating the costs and the benefits at each level of debt.

$$\text{Value of Levered Firm} = \text{FCFF}_0\,(1+g)/(\rho_u - g) + t_c\,D - \pi_a\,\text{BC}$$

The debt level that maximizes firm value is the optimal debt ratio.

Benefits and Limitations of This Approach

This approach separates out the effects of debt into different components and allows the analyst to use different discount rates for each component. It does not make the assumption that the debt ratio stays unchanged forever, which is an implicit assumption in the cost of capital approach. Instead, it allows the analyst the flexibility to keep the dollar value of debt fixed and to calculate the benefits and costs of the fixed dollar debt.

These advantages have to be weighed against the difficulty of estimating probabilities of default and the cost of bankruptcy. In fact, many analyses that use the adjusted present value approach ignore the expected bankruptcy costs, leading them to the conclusion that firm value increases monotonically with leverage.

  IN PRACTICE   USING THE ADJUSTED PRESENT VALUE APPROACH TO CALCULATE OPTIMAL DEBT RATIO FOR BOEING IN 1990

This approach can be applied to estimate the optimal capital structure for Boeing. The first step is to estimate the value of the unlevered firm. We start with the value of Boeing as a firm in 1990 and net the effect of the tax savings and bankruptcy costs arising from the existing debt:

Value of Boeing in 1990 = Value of Equity + Value of Debt = 16182 + 277 = \$16,459
- PV of Tax Savings from Existing Debt = \$277 * 0.34 = \$94
        + PV of Expected Bankruptcy Cost = 0.28% * (0.35 * (16,459-94)) = \$16
                = Value of Boeing as an Unlevered Firm = \$16,381

The probability of bankruptcy is estimated using the bond rating for Boeing in 1990 (AA), and the default probabilities listed in Table 18.15. The bankruptcy cost is assumed to be 35% of the firm value, prior to the tax savings.[12] The cost is high because the perception of default risk is likely

---

[12]This estimate is based on the Warner study, which estimates bankruptcy costs for large companies to be 10% of the value, and on the qualitative analysis of indirect bankruptcy costs in Shapiro and Cornell.

to be very damaging for a firm like Boeing, whose customers depend on it for long-term service and support, and whose sales contracts are often spread out over a decade or more.

The next step in the process is to estimate the tax savings at different levels of debt (Table 18.16). Although we use the standard approach of assuming that the present value is calculated over a perpetuity, we reduce the tax rate used in the calculation if interest expenses exceed the earnings before interest and taxes. The adjustment to the tax rate is described more fully in the preceding section on the cost of capital.

Table 18.16   TAX SAVINGS FROM DEBT (T_cD)

Debt Ratio (%)	$ Debt	Tax Rate (%)	Tax Benefits (%)
0	$0	34.00	$0
10	1,646	34.00	560
20	3,292	34.00	1,119
30	4,938	34.00	1,679
40	6,584	34.00	2,238
50	8,230	34.00	2,798
60	9,875	28.96	2,860
70	11,521	24.82	2,860
80	13,167	19.91	2,622
90	14,813	17.70	2,622

The final step in the process is to estimate the expected bankruptcy cost, based on the bond ratings, probabilities of default, and the assumption that the bankruptcy cost is 35% of firm value. Table 18.17 summarizes these probabilities.

Table 18.17   EXPECTED BANKRUPTCY COST

Debt Ratio (%)	Bond Rating	Probability of Default (%)	Expected Bankruptcy Cost
0	AA	0.28	$16
10	AA	0.28	16
20	A-	1.41	81
30	BB	12.20	699
40	B-	32.50	1,863
50	CCC	46.61	2,672
60	CC	65.00	3,727
70	CC	65.00	3,727
80	C	80.00	4,587
90	C	80.00	4,587

The value of the levered firm is estimated in Table 18.18 by aggregating the effects of the tax savings and the expected bankruptcy costs.

The firm value is optimized at between 20% and 30% debt, which is consistent with the findings from the other approaches. These findings are very sensitive, however, to both the estimate of bankruptcy cost, as a percentage of firm value, and the probabilities of default.

Table 18.18 VALUE OF BOEING WITH LEVERAGE				
Debt Ratio (%)	Unlevered Firm Value	Tax Benefits	Expected Bankruptcy Cost	Value of Levered Firm
0	$16,411	$0	$16	$16,365
10	16,411	560	16	16,924
20	16,411	1,119	81	17,419
30	16,411	1,679	699	17,360
40	16,411	2,238	1,863	16,756
50	16,411	2,798	2,672	16,507
60	16,411	2,860	3,727	15,514
70	16,411	2,860	3,727	15,514
80	16,411	2,622	4,587	14,416
90	16,411	2,622	4,587	14,416

THE COMPARATIVE ANALYSIS APPROACH

The most common approach to analyzing the debt ratio of a firm is to compare its leverage to that of "similar" firms. A simple way of doing this is to compare a firm's debt ratio to the average debt ratio for the industry in which the firm operates. The underlying assumptions here are that firms within the same industry are comparable firms and that, on average, these firms are operating at or close to their optimal. Both assumptions can be contested, however. Firms within the same industry can have different product mixes, different amounts of operating risk, different tax rates, and different project returns; in fact, most do. For instance, Boeing is considered part of the aerospace/defense industry, but its mix of defense and commercial business is very different from that of McDonnell Douglas, Grumman Corporation, or Lockheed Corporation. Furthermore, Boeing's size and risk characteristics are very different from those of Lear Siegler, which is also considered part of the same industry group. There is also anecdotal evidence that since firms try to mimic the industry average, the average debt ratio across an industry might not be at or even close to its optimal. Thus the fact that the median debt ratio in the aerospace industry is 15% while Boeing's debt ratio is 1.68% is interesting, but it does not provide much information beyond that. One can always ascribe this divergence to fundamental differences between Boeing and the rest of the companies in the industry.

Comparable Firm: This is a firm that is similar to that which is being analyzed in terms of underlying characteristics—risk, growth, and cash-flow patterns. The conventional definition of a comparable firm is one that is the same business as the one being analyzed and is of similar size.

Controlling for Differences Between Firms

To ensure comparability on debt ratios, a firm with similar tax rates, pretax returns as a fraction of the market value of the firm, and variance in operating income has to be identified. Note, however, that the firm need not be in the same industry or produce the same product. The difficulty of finding such a firm gives rise to a second approach, whereby differences on these variables are controlled for when debt ratios are compared across firms. The simplest way to control for these differences, while using the maximum information available in the cross-section of firms, is to run a cross-sectional regression, regressing debt ratios against these variables:

$$\text{Debt Ratio} = \alpha_0 + \alpha_1 \text{ Tax Rate} + \alpha_2 \text{ Pretax Returns} + \alpha_3 \text{ Variance in Operating Income}$$

Once the regression has been run and the basic relationship established (i.e., the intercept and coefficients have been estimated), the predicted debt ratio for any firm can be computed quickly using the measures of the independent variables for this firm. If a task involves calculating the optimal debt ratio for a large number of firms in a short time period, this may be the only practical way of approaching the problem, since using the cost of capital approach is time intensive.[13]

This approach has severe limitations. The coefficients tend to be unstable and shift over time. Besides some standard statistical problems and errors in measuring the variables, these regressions also tend to explain only a portion of the differences in debt ratios between firms.[14] However, they do provide significantly more information than does a naive comparison of a firm's debt ratio to the industry average.

 IN PRACTICE AN ILLUSTRATION OF THE CROSS-SECTIONAL APPROACH

A cross-sectional regression of debt ratios against tax rates, pretax returns, and variance in operating income was run for nonfinancial-service firms, using the following measures:

Debt Ratio: Book Value of Debt / (Market Value of Equity + Book Value of Debt)
Tax Rate: Average tax rate reported on Compustat for 1989
Pretax Returns: EBITDA in 1989/ (Market Value of Equity at the end of 1989 + Book Value of Debt at the end of 1989)[15]
CV in Operating Income (CVOI): Standard Deviation in Operating income : 1985 to 1989 / Average Operating Income from 1985 to 1989

The output from the regression from 1989 is provided here, with t statistics in parentheses below the coefficients:

$$\text{Debt Ratio} = 0.2516 + 0.0178 \text{ Tax Rate} - 0.0810 \text{ CVOI} + 0.2538 \text{ Pretax Returns}$$
$$(12.50) \quad (1.96) \qquad\qquad (2.60) \qquad\qquad (3.57)$$

The R-Squared for this regression is 42%.
    The values for the independent variables were then obtained for Boeing at the end of 1989:

---

[13]Some analysts have hypothesized that underleveraged firms are much more likely to be taken over than firms that are overleveraged or correctly leveraged. If an analyst wants to find the 100 firms on the New York Stock Exchange that are most underleveraged, the cross-sectional regression and the predicted debt ratios that come out of this regression can be used to find this group.

[14]The independent variables are correlated with one another. This multicollinearity makes the coefficients unreliable, and they often have signs that run counter to intuition.

[15]If market values for debt had been available on the database, these would have been used.

Tax Rate = 0.2679   CVOI = 1.014   Pretax Returns = 0.0865

Using these values to obtain the predicted debt ratio:,

> Predicted Debt Ratio: Boeing = 0.2516 + 0.0178 * 0.2679 - 0.0810 * 1.014 + 0.2538 * 0.0865 = 0.1962 or 19.62%

Based on this analysis, Boeing is underleveraged in March 1990, with an actual debt ratio of 1.68% and a predicted debt ratio of 19.62%.

Improving the Cross- Sectional Regression

The cross-sectional regression reported earlier often yields noisy predictions. Although some of this noise is an unavoidable byproduct of the differences in how firms make their capital structure decisions, some of it can be eliminated through the judicious use of data aggregation and variable manipulation. To illustrate, consider a regression of debt ratios against a number of relevant variables, using 1994 data for 2,284 firms listed on the NYSE, AMEX, and NASDAQ databases. The regression provides the following results:

$$DFR = 0.2927 - 0.1832\ PRVAR - .0011\ CLSH + 0.3283\ CPXFR + .0058\ FCP$$
$$(26.41^a)\ (11.35)\qquad (7.45^a)\qquad (5.69^a)\qquad (14.76^a)$$

where

DFR	= Debt / (Debt + Market Value of Equity)
PRVAR	= Variance in Firm Value
CLSH	= Closely held shares as a percentage of outstanding shares
CPXFR	= Capital Expenditures / (Book Value of Debt + Book Value of Equity)
FCP	= Free Cash Flow to Firm / Market Value of Equity

While all the coefficients have the right sign and are statistically significant, the regression itself has an R-squared of only 13.57%.

SIC CODE: This is a four-digit industry code used by most services in the United States to classify firms. For a broader aggregation, the classification is often done using the first two digits of the code.

One way to improve the predictive power of the regression is to aggregate the data first and then do the regression. To illustrate using 1994 data, the firms are aggregated into two-digit **SIC** codes, and the same regression is rerun:

$$DFR = 0.4515 - 0.5505\ PRVAR - .0034\ CLSH + 0.3283\ CPXFR + .0058\ FCP$$
$$(5.26^a)\ (3.92)\qquad (2.41^a)\qquad (2.17^a)\qquad (3.70^a)$$

Note that while all the regression coefficients preserve their signs, the size of the coefficients has changed and the R-squared of the regression has increased to 55.64%.

The other way to improve the regression is to transform the variables to conform more closely to the regression ideal, which is that the variables should be normally distributed. That will require applying the log transformation to the debt ratio, since it cannot be lower than zero, and estimating the regression coefficients again.

CONCLUSION

This chapter has provided background on five tools that can be used to analyze capital structure.

- The first approach is the operating income approach, whereby a maximum acceptable probability of default is defined in conjunction with a distribution for operating income to arrive at an optimal debt ratio.

- The second approach is the cost of capital—the weighted average of the costs of equity, debt, and preferred stock—whereby the weights are market value weights and the costs of financing are current costs. The objective is to minimize the cost of capital, which also maximizes the value of the firm. A general framework is developed to use this model and applied to find the optimal financing mix for Boeing. We find that Boeing, which had almost no debt in 1990, would minimize its cost of capital at a debt level of 30%, leading to an increase in market value of the firm of about $3.6 billion. Even allowing for a much diminished operating income, we find that Boeing could have afforded to increase its debt ratio.

- The third approach focuses on finding the debt ratio that maximizes the spread between the return on equity and the cost of equity. By increasing the spread, we will generally increase the value per share.

- The fourth approach estimates the value of the firm at different levels of debt by adding the present value of the tax benefits from debt to the unlevered firm's value and then subtracting out the present value of expected bankruptcy costs. The optimal debt ratio is the one that maximizes firm value.

- The final approach is to compare a firm's debt ratio to "similar" firms. While comparisons of firm debt ratios to an industry average are commonly made, they are generally not very useful in the presence of large differences across firms within the same industry. A cross-sectional regression of debt ratios against underlying financial variables brings in more information from the general population of firms and can be used to predict debt ratios for a large number of firms.

QUESTIONS AND PROBLEMS

1. Rubbermaid Corporation, a manufacturer of consumer plastic products, is evaluating its capital structure. The balance sheet of the company is as follows (in millions):

Assets		Liabilities	
Fixed assets	4000	Debt	2500
Current assets	1000	Equity	2500

In addition, you are provided with the following information:

a. The debt is in the form of long-term bonds, with a coupon rate of 10%. The bonds are currently rated AA and are selling at a yield of 12%. (The market value of the bonds is **80%** of the face value.)

b. The firm currently has 50 million shares outstanding, and the current market price is $80

per share. The firm pays a dividend of $4 per share and has a price/earnings ratio of 10.

c. The stock currently has a beta of 1.2. The six-month Treasury bill rate is 8%.

d. The tax rate for this firm is 40%.

(1) What is the debt/equity ratio for this firm in book value terms? in market value terms?

(2) What is the debt/(debt+equity) ratio for this firm in book value terms? in market value terms?

(3) What is the firm's after-tax cost of debt?

(4) What is the firm's cost of equity?

(5) What is the firm's current cost of capital?

2. Now assume that Rubbermaid Corporation has a project that requires an initial investment of $100

million and has the following projected income statement:

EBIT	$20 million
- Interest	$4 million
EBT	$16 million
Taxes	$6.40 million
Net income	$9.60 million

(Depreciation for the project is expected to be $5 million a year forever.)

This project is going to be financed at the same debt/equity ratio as the overall firm and is expected to last forever. Assume that there are no principal repayments on the debt (it too is perpetual).

(1) Evaluate this project from the equity investors' standpoint. Does it make sense?

(2) Evaluate this project from the firm's standpoint. Does it make sense?

(3) In general, when would you use the cost of equity as your discount rate/benchmark?

(4) In general, when would you use the cost of capital as your benchmark?

(5) Assume, for economies of scale, that this project is going to be financed entirely with debt. What would you use as your cost of capital for evaluating this project?

3. Rubbermaid is considering a major change in its capital structure. It has three options:

Option 1: Issue $1 billion in new stock and repurchase half of its outstanding debt. This will make it a AAA rated firm. (AAA rated debt is yielding 11% in the marketplace.)

Option 2: Issue $1 billion in new debt and buy back stock. This will drop its rating to A-. (A- rated debt is yielding 13% in the marketplace.)

Option 3: Issue $3 billion in new debt and buy back stock. This will drop its rating to CCC. (CCC rated debt is yielding 18% in the marketplace.)

(1) What is the cost of equity under each option?

(2) What is the after-tax cost of debt under each option?

(3) What is the cost of capital under each option?

(4) What would happen to (a) the value of the firm; (b) the value of debt and equity; and (c) the stock price under each option, if you assume rational stockholders?

(5) From a cost of capital standpoint, which of the three options would you pick, or would you stay at your current capital structure?

(6) What role (if any) would the variability in Rubbermaid's income play in your decision?

(7) How would your analysis change (if at all) if the money under the three options listed above were used to make new investments (instead of repurchasing debt or equity)?

(8) What other considerations (besides minimizing the cost of capital) would you bring to bear on your decision?

(9) Intuitively, why doesn't the higher rating in option 1 translate into a lower cost of capital?

4. Rubbermaid Corporation is interested in how it compares with its competitors in the same industry.

	Rubbermaid Corporation	Other Competitors
Debt/Equity Ratio	50%	25%
Variance in EBITDA	20%	40%
EBITDA/MV of firm	25%	15%
Tax rate	40%	30%
R&D/sales	2%	5%

a. Considering each of these variables, explain at an intuitive level whether you would expect Rubbermaid to have more more or less debt than its competitors and why.

b. You have also run a regression of debt/equity ratios against these variables for all the firms on the New York Stock Exchange and have come up with the following regression equation:

$$D/E = .10 - .5 \text{ (Variance in EBITDA)} + 2.0 \text{ (EBITDA/MV)} + .4 \text{ (Tax rate)} + 2.5 \text{ (R\&D/sales)}$$

(All inputs to the regression were in decimals; that is, 20% was inputted as .20 ....)

Given this cross-sectional relationship, what would you expect Rubbermaid's debt/equity ratio to be?

5. As CEO of a major corporation, you have to make a decision on how much you can afford to borrow. You currently have 10 million shares outstanding, and the market price per share is $50. You also currently have about $200 million in debt outstanding (market value). You are rated as a BBB corporation now.

a. Your stock has a beta of 1.5 and the Treasury bond rate is 8%.

b. Your marginal tax rate is 46%.

c. You estimate that your rating will change to a B if you borrow $100 million. The BBB rate now is 11%. The B rate is 12.5%.

(1) Given the marginal costs and benefits of borrowing the $100 million, should you go ahead with it?

(2) What is your best estimate of the weighted average cost of capital with and without the $100 million in borrowing?

(3) If you do borrow the $100 million, what will the price per share be after the borrowing?

(4) Assume that you have a project that requires an investment of $100 million. It has expected before-tax revenues of $50 million and costs of $30 million a year in perpetuity. Is this a desirable project by your criteria? Why or why not?

(5) Does it make a difference in your decision if you are told that the cash flows from the project in (4) are certain?

6. You have been hired as a management consultant by AD Corporation to evaluate whether it has an appropriate amount of debt. (The company is worried about a leveraged buyout.) You have collected the following information on AD's current position:

 a. There are 100,000 shares outstanding, at $20 a share. The stock has a beta of 1.15.

 b. The company has $500,000 in long-term debt outstanding and is currently rated as a "BBB." The current market interest rate is 10% on BBB bonds and 6% on Treasury bills.

 c. The company's marginal tax rate is 40%.

You proceed to collect the data on what increasing debt will do to the company's ratings:

Additional Debt*	New Rating	Interest Rate
$500,000	BB	10.5
$1,000,000	B	11.5
$1,500,000	B-	13.5
$2,000,000	C	15

* In addition to the existing debt of $500,000:

 (1) How much additional debt should the company take on?

 (2) What will the price per share be after the company takes on new debt?

 (3) What is the weighted average cost of capital before and after the additional debt?

 (4) Assume that you are considering a project that has the following earnings in perpetuity, and is of comparable risk to existing projects.

Revenues/year	$1,000,000
Cost of goods sold	$400,000 (includes depreciation of $100,000)
EBIT	$600,000
Debt payments	$100,000 (all interest payments)
Taxable income	$500,000
Tax	$200,000
After-tax profit	$300,000

If this project requires an investment of $3 million, what is its NPV?

7. UB Inc. is examining its capital structure with the intent of arriving at an optimal debt ratio. It currently has no debt and has a beta of 1.5. The riskless interest rate is 9%. Your research indicates that the debt rating will be as follows at different debt levels.

D/(D+E)	Rating	Interest Rate
0%	AAA	10%
10%	AA	10.5%
20%	A	11%
30%	BBB	12%
40%	BB	13%
50%	B	14%
60%	CCC	16%
70%	CC	18%
80%	C	20%
90%	D	25%

The firm currently has 1 million shares outstanding at $20 per share (tax rate = 40%).

 a. What is the firm's optimal debt ratio?

 b. Assuming that the firm restructures by repurchasing stock with debt, what will the value of the stock be after the restructuring?

8. GenCorp, an automotive parts manufacturer, currently has $25 million in outstanding debt and has 10 million shares outstanding. The book value per share is $10, while the market value is $25. The company is currently rated A, and its bonds have a yield to maturity of 10%, and the current beta of the stock is 1.06. The six-month Treasury bond rate is 8% now, and the company's tax is 40%.

 a. What is the company's current weighted average cost of capital?

 b. The company is considering a repurchase of 4 million shares at $25 per share with new debt. It is estimated that this will push the company's rating down to a B (with a yield to maturity of 13%). What will the company's weighted average cost of capital be after the stock repurchase?

9. You have been called in as a consultant for Herbert's Inc., a sporting goods retail firm, which is examining its debt policy. The firm currently has a balance sheet that looks as follows:

Liability		Assets	
LT bonds	$100	Fixed assets	300
Equity	$300	Current assets	100
Total	$400	Total	400

The firm's income statement is as follows:

Revenues	250
COGS	175
Depreciation	25
EBIT	50
LT interest	10
EBT	40
Taxes	16
Net income	24

The firm currently has 100 shares outstanding, selling at a market price of $5 per share, and the bonds are selling at par. The firm's current beta is 1.12, and the six-month Treasury bond rate is 7%.

   a. What is the firm's current cost of equity?
   b. What is the firm's current cost of debt?
   c. What is the firm's current weighted average cost of capital?

Assume that management of Herbert's Inc. is considering doing a debt equity swap (i.e., borrowing enough money to buy back 70 shares of stock at $5 per share). It is believed that this swap will lower the firm's rating to C and raise the interest rate on the company's debt to 15%.

   d. What is the firm's new cost of equity?
   e. What is the effective tax rate (for calculating the after-tax cost of debt) after the swap?
   f. What is the firm's new cost of capital?

10. Terck Inc., a leading pharmaceutical company, currently has a balance sheet as follows:

Liability		Assets	
LT bonds	$1000	Fixed assets	1700
Equity	$1000	Current assets	300
Total	$1000	Total	1000

The firm's income statement looks as follows:

Revenues	1000
COGS	400
Depreciation	100
EBIT	500
LT interest	100
EBT	400
Taxes	200
Net income	200

The firm's bonds are all 20-year bonds with a coupon rate of 10% and are selling at 90% of face value. (The yield to maturity on these bonds is 11%.) The stocks are selling at a PE ratio of 9 and have a beta of 1.25. The six-month Treasury bond rate is 6%. Cost of debts 10%, tax rate = 40%

   a. What is the firm's current cost of equity?
   b. What is the firm's current after-tax cost of debt?
   c. What is the firm's current weighted average cost of capital?

Assume that management of Terck Inc., which is very conservative, is considering doing an equity-for-debt swap (i.e., issuing $200 more of equity to retire $200 of debt). This action is expected to lower the firm's interest rate by 1%.

   d. What is the firm's new cost of equity?
   e. What is the new WACC?
   f. What will the value of the firm be after the swap?

11. You have been asked to analyze the capital structure of DASA Inc., an environmental waste disposal firm, and to make recommendations on a future course of action. DASA Inc. has 40 million shares outstanding, selling at $20 per share, and a debt equity ratio (in market value terms) of 0.25. The beta of the stock is 1.15 and the firm currently has a AA rating, with a corresponding market interest rate of 10%. The firm's income statement is as follows:

EBIT	$150 million
Interest exp.	$20 million
Taxable income	$130 million
Taxes	$52 million
Net income	$78 million

The current Treasury bond rate is 8%. Tax rate = 40%.

   a. What is the firm's current weighted average cost of capital?
   b. The firm is proposing borrowing an additional $200 million in debt and repurchasing stock. If it does so, its rating will decline to A, with a market interest rate of 11%. What will the weighted average cost of capital be if the firm makes this move?
   c. What will the new stock price be if the firm borrows $200 million and repurchases stock (assuming rational investors)?
   d. Now assume that the firm has another option to raise its debt/equity ratio (instead of borrowing money and repurchasing stock). It has considerable capital expenditures planned for the next year ($150 million). The company also currently pays $1 in dividends per share. If the company finances all its capital expenditures

with debt and doubles its *dividend yield* from the current level for the next year, what would you expect the debt/equity ratio to be at the end of the next year?

12. You have been asked by JJ Corporation, a California-based firm that manufacturers and services digital satellite television systems, to evaluate its capital structure. They currently have 70 million shares outstanding trading at $10 per share. In addition, it has 500,000 ten-year convertible bonds, with a coupon rate of 8%, trading at $1000 per bond. JJ Corporation is rated BBB, and the interest rate on BBB straight bonds is currently 10%. The beta for the company is 1.2, and the current risk-free rate is 6%. The tax rate is 40%.

   a. What is the firm's current debt/equity ratio?

   b. What is the firm's current weighted average cost of capital?

JJ Corporation is proposing to borrow $250 million to use for the following purposes:

   Buy back $100 million worth of stock.

   Pay $100 million in dividends.

   Invest $50 million in a project with a NPV of $25 million.

The effect of this additional borrowing will be a drop in the bond rating to B, which currently carries an interest rate of 11%.

   c. What will the firm's cost of equity be after this additional borrowing?

   d. What will the firm's weighted average cost of capital be after this additional borrowing?

   e. What will the value of the firm be after this additional borrowing?

13. Baldor Electric, a company that gets 85% of its revenues from industrial electric motors, had 27.5 million shares at $25 per share and $25 million in debt outstanding at the end of 1995. The firm has a beta of 0.70, and it had earnings before interest and taxes of $63.3 million as well as a book value of equity of $200 million. The following table summarizes the ratings and interest rates for Baldor Electric at different levels of debt.

Debt Ratio (%)	Bond Rating	Interest Rate on Debt (%)
0	AA	6.70
10	A+	7.00
20	A-	7.50
30	BBB	8.00
40	BB	8.50
50	B+	9.00

Debt Ratio (%)	Bond Rating	Interest Rate on Debt (%)
60	B	10.00
70	B-	11.00
80	CCC	12.00
90	C	15.00

The tax rate is 35%. The T. Bond rate is 7%.

   a. Estimate the cost of equity at each level of debt.

   b. Estimate the return on equity at each level of debt.

   c. Estimate the optimal debt ratio based on the differential return.

   d. Will the value of the firm be maximized at this level of debt. Why or why not?

14. Pfizer, one of the largest pharmaceutical companies in the United States, is considering its debt capacity. In March 1995, Pfizer had an outstanding market value of equity of $24.27 billion, debt of $2.8 billion, and a AAA rating. Its beta was 1.47, and it faced a marginal corporate tax rate of 40%. The Treasury bond rate at the time of the analysis was 6.50%, and AAA bonds trade at a spread of 0.30% over the Treasury rate.

   a. Estimate the current cost of capital for Pfizer.

   b. It is estimated that Pfizer will have a BBB rating if it moves to a 30% debt ratio and that BBB bonds have a spread of 2% over the Treasury rate. Estimate the cost of capital if Pfizer moves to its optimal.

   c. Assuming a constant growth rate of 6% in the firm value, how much will firm value change if Pfizer moves its optimal? What will the effect be on the stock price?

   d. Pfizer has considerable research and development expenses. Will this fact affect whether Pfizer takes on the additional debt?

15. Upjohn, another major pharmaceutical company, is also considering whether it should borrow more. It has $664 million in book value of debt outstanding and 173 million shares outstanding at $30.75 per share. The company has a beta of 1.17 and faces a tax rate of 36%. The Treasury bond rate is 6.50%.

   a. If the interest expense on the debt is $55 million, the debt has an average maturity of 10 years, and the company is currently rated AA- (with a market interest rate of 7.50%), estimate the market value of the debt.

   b. Estimate the current cost of capital.

   c. It is estimated that if Upjohn moves to its optimal debt ratio, and no growth in firm value is assumed, the value per share will increase by $1.25. Estimate the cost of capital at the optimal debt ratio.

16. Nucor, an innovative steel company, has had a history of technical innovation and financial conservatism. In 1995, Nucor had only $210 million in debt outstanding (book as well as market value) and $4.2 billion in market value of equity (with a book value of $1.25 billion). In the same year, Nucor had earnings before interest and taxes of $372 million, and faced a corporate tax rate of 36%. The beta of the stock is 0.75, and the company is AAA rated (with a market interest rate of 6.80%). The T. Bond rate is 6.5%.

   a. Estimate the return differential between return on equity and cost of equity at the current level of debt.

   b. Estimate the return differential at a debt ratio of 30%, assuming that the bond rating will drop to A-, leading to market interest rate of 8.00%.

17. Bethlehem Steel, one of the oldest and largest steel companies in the United States, is considering the question of whether it has any excess debt capacity. The firm has $527 million in market value of debt outstanding and $1.76 billion in market value of equity. The firm has earnings before interest and taxes of $131 million, and faces a corporate tax rate of 36%. The company's bonds are rated BBB, and the cost of debt is 8%. At this rating, the firm has a probability of default of 2.30%, and the cost of bankruptcy is expected to be 30% of firm value. The T. Bond rate is 6.5%.

   a. Estimate the unlevered value of the firm.

   b. Estimate the levered value of the firm, using the adjusted present value approach, at a debt ratio of 50%. At that debt ratio, the firm's bond rating will be CCC, and the probability of default will increase to 46.61%.

18. Kansas City Southern, a railroad company, had debt outstanding of $985 million and 40 million shares trading at $46.25 per share in March 1995. It earned $203 million in earnings before interest and taxes and faced a marginal tax rate of 36.56%. The firm was interested in estimating its optimal leverage using the adjusted present value approach. The following table summarizes the estimated bond ratings and probabilities of default at each level of debt from 0% to 90%.

Debt Ratio (%)	Bond Rating	Probability of Default (%)
0	AAA	0.28
10	AAA	0.28
20	A-	1.41
30	BB	12.20

Debt Ratio (%)	Bond Rating	Probability of Default (%)
40	B-	32.50
50	CCC	46.61
60	CC	65.00
70	C	80.00
80	C	80.00
90	D	100.00

The direct and indirect bankruptcy cost is estimated to be 25% of the firm value. Estimate the optimal debt ratio of the firm, based on levered firm value. The T. Bond rate is 7%.

19. In 1995, an analysis of the capital structure of Reebok provided the following results on the weighted average cost of capital and firm value.

	Actual	Optimal	Change
Debt ratio	4.42%	60.00%	55.58%
Beta for the stock	1.95	3.69	1.74
Cost of equity	18.61%	28.16%	9.56%
Bond rating	A-	B+	
After-tax cost of debt	5.92%	6.87%	0.95%
WACC	18.04%	15.38%	-2.66%
Firm value (with no growth)	$3,343 mil	$3,921 mil	$578 mil
Stock price	$39.50	$46.64	$7.14

This analysis was based on the 1995 earnings before interest and taxes of $420 million and a tax rate of 36.90%.

   a. Why is the optimal debt ratio for Reebok so high?

   b. What might be some of your concerns in moving to this optimal?

20. Timberland Inc., a manufacturer and retailer of footwear and sportswear, is considering its highly levered status. In 1995, the firm had $237 million in market value of debt outstanding and 11 million shares outstanding at $19.88 per share. The firm had earnings before interest and taxes of $44 million, a book value of capital of $250 million, and a tax rate of 37%. The Treasury bond rate is 7.88%, and the stock has a beta of 1.26. The following table summarizes the estimated bond ratings and interest rates at different levels of debt for Timberland:

Debt Ratio (%)	Bond Rating	Interest Rate on Debt (%)
0	AAA	8.18
10	AAA	8.18
20	A+	8.88
30	A	9.13
40	A-	9.38
50	BB	10.38
60	BB	10.38

Debt Ratio (%)	Bond Rating	Interest Rate on Debt (%)
70	B	11.88
80	B-	12.88
90	CCC	13.88

a. Estimate the optimal debt ratio, using the cost of capital approach.

b. Estimate the optimal debt ratio, using the return differential approach.

c. Will the two approaches always give you identical results? Why or why not?

21. You are trying to evaluate whether United Airlines has any excess debt capacity. In 1995, UAL had 12.2 million shares outstanding at $210 per share and debt outstanding of approximately $3 billion (book as well as market value). The debt had a rating of B and carried a market interest rate of 10.12%. In addition, the firm had leases outstanding, with annual lease payments anticipated to be $150 million. The beta of the stock is 1.26, and the firm faces a tax rate of 35%. The Treasury bond rate is 6.12%.

a. Estimate the current debt ratio for UAL.

b. Estimate the current cost of capital.

c. Based on 1995 operating income, the optimal debt ratio is computed to be 30%, at which point the rating will be BBB, and the market interest rate is 8.12%. Estimate the cost of capital and firm value at the optimal.

d. Would the fact that 1995 operating income for airlines was depressed alter your analysis in any way? Explain why.

22. Intel has earnings before interest and taxes of $3.4 billion and faces a marginal tax rate of 36.50%. It currently has $1.5 billion in debt outstanding and a market value of equity of $51 billion. The beta for the stock is 1.35, and the pretax cost of debt is 6.80%. The Treasury bond rate is 6%. Assume that the firm is considering a massive increase in leverage to a 70% debt ratio, at which level the bond rating will be C (with a pretax interest rate of 16%).

a. Estimate the current cost of capital.

b. Assuming that all debt is refinanced at the new market interest rate, what would your interest expenses be at 70% debt? Would you be able to get the entire tax benefit? Why or why not?

c. Estimate the beta of the stock at 70% debt, using the conventional levered beta calculation. Reestimate the beta, on the assumption that C rated debt has a beta of 0.60. Which one would you use in your cost of capital calculation?

d. Estimate the cost of capital at 70% debt.

e. What will happen to firm value if Intel moves to a 70% debt ratio?

f. What general lessons on capital structure would you draw for other growth firms?

23. NYNEX, the phone utility for the New York Area, has approached you for advice on its capital structure. In 1995, NYNEX had debt outstanding of $12.14 billion and equity outstanding of $20.55 billion. The firm had earnings before interest and taxes of $1.7 billion, and faced a corporate tax rate of 36%. The beta for the stock is 0.84, and the bonds are rated A- (with a market interest rate of 7.5%). The probability of default for A-rated bonds is 1.41%, and the bankruptcy cost is estimated to be 30% of firm value. The T. Bond rate is 6.5%.

a. Estimate the unlevered value of the firm.

b. Value the firm if it increases its leverage to 50%. At that debt ratio, its bond rating would be BBB, and the probability of default would be 2.30%.

c. Assume now that NYNEX is considering a move into entertainment, which is likely to be both more profitable and riskier than the phone business. What changes would you expect in the optimal leverage?

24. A small, private firm has approached you for advice on its capital structure decision. It is in the specialty retailing business, and it had earnings before interest and taxes last year of $500,000.

- The book value of equity is $1.5 million, but the estimated market value is $6 million.
- The firm has $1 million in 5-year debt outstanding and paid an interest expense of $80,000 on the debt last year. (Based on the interest coverage ratio, the firm would be rated AA and would be facing an interest rate of 8.25%.)
- The equity is not traded, but the average beta for comparable traded firms is 1.05, and their average debt/equity ratio is 25%. The T. Bond rate is 7%.

a. Estimate the current cost of capital for this firm.

b. Assume now that this firm doubles it debt from $1 million to $2 million, and that the interest rate at which it can borrow increases to 9%. Estimate the new cost of capital, and the effect on firm value.

c. You also have a regression that you have run of debt ratios of publicly traded firms against firm characteristics:

DBTFR = 0.15 + 1.05 (EBIT/FIRM VALUE) - 0.10 (BETA)

Estimate the debt ratio for the private firm, based on this regression.

d. What are some of the concerns you might have in extending the approaches used by large publicly traded firms to estimate optimal leverage to smaller firms?

25. XCV Inc., which manufactures automobile parts for assembly, is considering the costs and the benefits of leverage. The CFO notes that the return on equity of the firm, which is only 12.75% now, based on the current policy of no leverage, could be increased substantially by borrowing money. Is this true? Does it follow that the value of the firm will increase with leverage? Why or why not?

CHAPTER 19

CAPITAL STRUCTURE— THE FINANCING DETAILS

In this chapter, we complete our analysis of the financing decision by building on the discussion of optimal capital structure initiated in the previous chapter. In particular, we examine the following questions:

- When the actual and optimal debt ratios differ, what is the best path for moving from the actual to the optimal?
- When and how should firms increase or decrease leverage *quickly*?
- When and how should firms increase or decrease leverage *gradually*?
- What is the appropriate financing mix for a firm? In particular, how should firms decide on the maturity, currency mix, and special features for their debt issues?
- How do tax, agency cost, and information asymmetry affect the financing mix?

A FRAMEWORK FOR CAPITAL STRUCTURE CHANGES

A firm whose actual debt ratio is very different from its optimal has several choices to make. It has to decide *whether to move toward the optimal or preserve the status quo*. Once it decides to move toward the optimal, the firm has to choose *between changing its leverage quickly or moving more deliberately*. This decision may also be governed by pressure from external sources, such as impatient stockholders or bond ratings agency concerns. Finally, if the firm decides to move gradually to the optimal, it has to decide whether to use new financing *to take new projects* or to shift its *financing mix on existing projects*.

In the last chapter, we presented the rationale for moving toward the optimal in terms of the value that could be gained for stockholders by doing so. Conversely, the cost of preserving the status quo is this potential value increment. Although managers nominally make this decision, they will often find themselves under some pressure from stockholders, if they are underlevered, or under threat of bankruptcy, if they are overlevered, to move toward their optimal debt ratios.

IMMEDIATE OR GRADUAL CHANGE

When firms are significantly underlevered or overlevered, they have to decide whether to adjust their leverage quickly or gradually over time. The advantage of a prompt movement to the optimal is that the firm immediately receives the benefits of the optimal leverage, which include a lower cost of capital and a higher value. The disadvantage

511

of a sudden change in leverage is that it changes both the way and the environment in which managers make decisions within the firm. If the optimal debt ratio has been mis-estimated, a sudden change may also increase the risk that the firm may have to back-track and reverse its financing decisions. To illustrate, assume that a firm's optimal debt ratio has been calculated to be 40% and that the firm moves to this optimal from its current debt ratio of 10%. A few months later, the firm discovers that its optimal debt ratio is really 30%. It will then have to repay some of the debt that it has taken on to get back to the optimal leverage.

☐ Concept Check

> Given the analysis of the optimal capital structure in the previous chapter, what are some of the variables that determine the degree of uncertainty about the optimal capital structure?

Underlevered Firms

For underlevered firms, the decision to increase the debt ratio to the optimal quickly or gradually is determined by a number of factors:

1. *Degree of Confidence in the Optimal Leverage Estimate:*   The greater the noise in the estimate of optimal leverage, the more likely it is that the firm will move gradually to the optimal.

2. *Comparability to Peer Group:*   When the optimal debt ratio for a firm is very different from that of its peer group, the firm is much less likely to move to the optimal quickly because analysts and ratings agencies might not look favorably on the change.

3. *Likelihood of a Takeover:*   Empirical studies of the characteristics of target firms in acquisitions have noted that underleveraged firms are much more likely to be acquired than are overleveraged firms.[1] Often, the acquisition is financed at least partially by the target firm's unused debt capacity. Consequently, firms with excess debt capacity which delay increasing debt run the risk of being taken over; the greater this risk, the more likely the firm will choose to take on additional debt quickly.

    A number of factors may determine the likelihood of a takeover. One is the prevalence of anti-takeover laws (at the state level) and amendments (at the firm level) designed specifically to prevent hostile acquisitions. Another is the size of the firm; the larger the firm, the more protected it may feel from hostile takeovers. Yet another is the extent of holdings by insiders and managers in the company; insiders and managers with substantial stakes may be able to preempt hostile acquisitions.

4. *Need for Financing Slack:*   On occasion, firms may require **financial slack** to meet unanticipated needs for funds, either to keep existing projects going or to take on new ones. Firms that need and value financial slack will be less likely to move quickly to their optimal debt ratios and use up their excess debt capacity.

Financing Slack: The financing slack is the difference between the debt a firm chooses to carry and the optimal debt it *could* carry, when the former is less than the latter.

---

[1]Palepu (1986) notes that one of the variables that seems to predict a takeover is a low debt ratio, in conjunction with poor operating performance.

Overlevered Firms

Similar considerations apply to overlevered firms that are considering how quickly they should lower their debt ratio. As in the case of underlevered firms, the precision of the optimal leverage estimate will play a role, with more precise estimates leading to quicker adjustments. The other factor in the case of overlevered firms is *the possibility of default*—the primary risk of having too much debt. Too much debt results in higher interest rates and lower ratings on the debt. Thus the greater the chance of bankruptcy, the more likely the firm is to move quickly to reduce debt and move to its optimal.

Concept Check

In the previous chapter, we examined some of the indirect costs of bankruptcy, including lost sales and tighter credit. What implications, if any, would these costs have on an over-levered firm's decision to reduce debt quickly or gradually?

THE PROCESS OF CHANGE

The process by which firms adjust their leverage will depend on (1) the speed with which they want to change their financing mix, and (2) the availability of new projects that can be financed with the new debt or equity.

Increasing Leverage Quickly

When underlevered firms need to increase leverage quickly, they can do so in a number of ways: borrowing money and buying back stock; replacing equity with debt of equal market value; or selling assets and repurchasing stock.

- Borrowing money and buying back stock (or paying a special dividend) increases leverage because the borrowing increases the debt, whereas the equity repurchase or dividend payment concurrently reduces the equity. A number of companies have used this approach to increase leverage quickly, largely in response to takeover attempts. For example, in 1985, to stave off a hostile takeover, Atlantic Richfield borrowed $4 billion and repurchased stock to increase its leverage from 12% to 34%.

- In a **debt-for-equity swap**, a firm replaces equity with debt of equivalent market value by swapping the two securities. Here, again, the simultaneous increase in debt and the decrease in equity cause the debt ratio to increase substantially. In many cases, as can be seen in Table 19.1, firms offer equity investors a combination of cash and debt in lieu of equity. In 1986, for example, Owens Corning gave its stockholders $52 in cash and debt, with a face value of $35 for each outstanding share, thereby increasing its debt and reducing equity.

- Finally, when firms currently have debt outstanding and want to change their debt ratio, they can do so by *selling a portion of their assets and using the proceeds to repurchase stock*.

Debt-for-Equity Swap: This is a voluntary exchange of outstanding equity for debt of equal market value.

In each of these cases, the firm may be stymied by bond covenants that explicitly prohibit these actions or impose large penalties on the firm. The firm will have to weigh these restrictions against the benefits of the higher leverage and the increased value that flows from it.

In the last few years, several firms have gone through *leveraged recapitalizations*, whereby one or more of the above strategies has been used to increase leverage quickly. Table 19.1 lists some of the firms and the strategies they used.

Table 19.1 **A Selective Sample of Leveraged Recapitalizations**

Company	Date	Trigger for Recap	Strategy Used
CBS Inc.	1985	Hostile takeover bid by Ted Turner	Acquire 21% of common stock.
Caesars World	1987	Hostile bid by Martin Sosnoff	Borrow $1 billion and pay special dividend of $26.25
Carter Hawley Hale	1986	Hostile bid by the Limited	Spin off division and pay special dividend of $325 mil.
Colt Industries	1986		Borrow $1.5 billion, pay a special dividend of $85.
FMC	1986	Potential hostile takeover	Pay special dividend of $80.
GenCorp	1987	Hostile takeover by AFG	Borrow $1.6 billion and buy back stock.
Gillette Corp.	1986	Hostile bid by Revlon	Repurchase 7 million shares in the open market.
Goodyear Tire & Rubber Co.	1986	Hostile bid by James Goldsmith	Sell three units and buy back 20 million shares of stock.
HBO & Co.	1986	Maintain stockholder value	Purchase 26% of the outstanding stock.
Harcourt Brace Jovanovich	1987	Hostile bid by British Painting	Borrow money and pay special dividend.
Holiday Corp.	1986	Hostile takeover bid by Donald Trump	Pay special dividend of $65 per share.
Inco Ltd.	1988	Potential for hostile takeover	Pay $1 billion in special dividends.
Interco Ltd.	1988	Hostile takeover bid by Rales Brothers	Borrow $2.8 billion and pay a special dividend of $14 per share.
Kroger	1988	Hostile takeover bid by Haft Brothers	Pay a special dividend.
Multimedia	1988	LBO proposal from management	Borrow money and buy back stock.
Newmont Mining	1987	Hostile bid by Ivanhoe Partners	Pay a special dividend of $33 per share.
Optical Coating Laboratories	1988		Pay a special dividend of $13 per share.
Owens Corning	1986	Hostile bid by Wickes	Debt-for-Equity swap + Special dividend ($52 + $35 of debt for equity).
Phillips Petroleum	1984	Hostile takeover by Pickens	Double firm's debt and buy back stock.
Quantum Chemical	1988		Pay a special dividend of $50 per share.
Santa Fe Southern Pacific	1987	Potential for hostile takeover	Pay $4 billion to the stockholders.
Shoney's	1988		Special Dividend + Debt-for-Equity swap.
Standard Brand Paints	1987	Hostile bid for Entregrowth	Buy back 53% of the outstanding shares.
Swank Inc.	1987	Hostile takeover	Pay special dividend of $17.
UAL	1987	Potential for hostile takeover	Borrow money and repurchase 63% of outstanding shares.
USG Corp.	1985	Potential for hostile bid from Desert Partners	Special Dividend + Debt-for-Equity swap.
Union Carbide	1985	Hostile bid by GAF Inc.	Special dividend + Debt-for-Equity swap.
Unocal	1985	Hostile bid by T. Boone Pickens	Repurchase 49% of the outstanding shares.

Note, that nearly every one of these restructurings was motivated by a desire to prevent a hostile takeover. Managers seldom initiate large increases in leverage since the leverage puts added pressure on them to perform.

Concept Check

> Closely held firms seldom increase leverage as dramatically as do some of the companies listed in Table 19.1. How would you explain this phenomenon?

IN PRACTICE   CHANGING LEVERAGE QUICKLY: NICHOLS RESEARCH

In 1994, Nichols Research, a firm that provides technical services to the defense industry, had debt outstanding of $6.8 million and market value of equity of $120 million. Based on its EBITDA of $12 million, Nichols had an optimal debt ratio of 30%, which would lower the cost of capital to 12.07% (from the current cost of capital of 13%) and increase the firm value to $146 million (from $126.8 million). There are a number of reasons for arguing that Nichols should increase its leverage quickly:

- Its small size, in conjunction with its low leverage and large cash balance ($25.3 million), makes it a prime target for an acquisition.
- While 17.6% of the shares are held by owners and directors, this amount is unlikely to hold off a hostile acquisition, since institutions own 60% of the outstanding stock.
- The firm has been reporting steadily decreasing returns on its projects, owing to the shrinkage in the defense budget. In 1994 the return on capital was only 10%, which is much lower than the cost of capital.

If Nichols decides to increase leverage, it can do so in a number of ways:

- It can borrow enough money to get to 30% of its overall firm value ($146 million at the optimal debt ratio) and buy back stock. This would require $37 million in new debt.
- It can borrow $37 million and pay a special dividend of that amount.
- It can use its cash balance of $25 million to buy back stock or pay dividends, and increase debt to 30% of the remaining firm value (30% of $121 million).[2] This would require approximately $29.5 million in new debt, which can be used to buy back stock.

Decreasing Leverage Quickly

Firms that have to decrease leverage quickly face a more difficult problem, since the perception that they might not survive affects their capacity to raise new financing. Optimally, such firms would like to issue equity and use it to pay off some of the outstanding debt, but their equity issues might not be well received in the market. Consequently, they have to consider two options—they can either renegotiate debt agreements or sell their assets to pay off the debt.

- When firms *renegotiate debt agreements,* they try to convince some of the lenders to take an equity stake in the firm in lieu of some or all of their debt in the firm. The best bargaining chip the firm possesses is the possibility of default, since lenders faced with default are more likely to agree to these terms. In the late 1980s, for example, many U.S. banks were forced to trade in their Latin American debt-for-equity stakes or receive little or nothing on their loans.

---

[2]We are assuming that the optimal debt ratio will be unaffected by the paying out of the special dividend. It is entirely possible that the paying out of the cash will make the firm riskier (leading to a higher unlevered beta) and lower the optimal debt ratio.

• The firm may choose to *sell assets and use the proceeds to retire some of the outstanding debt.* Many firms that had taken on too much debt in the course of leveraged buyouts in the 1980s and wanted to pay off some of it, adopted this approach.

☐ Concept
Check

> If a firm has to sell some of assets to pay off debt, which assets should be sold off—the best performing or the worst performing? Why?

Increasing Leverage Gradually

Firms that have the luxury of increasing their leverage gradually over time begin by analyzing the availability of good projects that can be financed with the debt. If good projects are available, borrowing the money to take on these projects will provide firms with an added benefit: the firm not only gets the increase in value of moving to the optimal debt ratio, but it also gets the additional increment in value from the positive net present value of new projects.

In the earlier chapters on investment analysis, we defined good projects as those that earn a return greater than the hurdle rate. The return can be measured in either cash-flow terms (as the internal rate of return) or accounting terms (as the return on equity or the return on capital), and must be compared to an appropriate benchmark (cost of equity for equity returns and cost of capital for return on capital).

Firms that have excess debt capacity but do not have good projects to choose from will be better off increasing the debt capacity by repurchasing stock or increasing dividends over time.

Debt Capacity and Acquisitions

It is sometimes argued that firms with excess debt capacity use it to acquire other firms. This makes sense only if the acquisition can be justified on a standalone basis, without the benefit of the added value from moving to the optimal debt ratio. To illustrate, assume that a firm is currently underleveraged but could increase its value by $50 million if its moved to its optimal debt ratio by borrowing $200 million. The firm proceeds to borrow $200 million and buy a target firm worth $175 million; it then argues that it is in fact better off overall because it has a net gain in value of $25 million ($50 million in increased value from moving to the optimal reduced by the overpayment of $25 million on the acquisition). This argument does not hold up, however, because the firm could have increased its value by $50 million if it had borrowed the money and bought back stock. Excess debt capacity cannot be used, therefore, to justify bad investment or acquisition decisions.

IN PRACTICE CHARTING A FRAMEWORK FOR CHANGING LEVERAGE: THE HOME DEPOT

At the end of 1994, the Home Depot had a debt ratio of 0.66%, with $19.5 billion in market value of equity, $127 million in debt, and operating income of $958 million in that year. Table 19.2 summarizes the cost of capital and firm value at different levels of debt from 0% to 90%.

The optimal debt ratio for the Home Depot is 20%, because the cost of capital is minimized and the firm value is maximized at this debt level.

Table 19.2 **DEBT RATIO, WACC, AND FIRM VALUE—THE HOME DEPOT**

Debt Ratio (%)	WACC	Firm Value (%)
0	15.76	$19,566
10	15.28	20,656
20	15.01	21,294
30	15.21	20,805
40	16.33	18,435
50	17.91	15,824
60	18.81	14,629
70	19.71	13,592
80	20.61	12,682
90	21.51	11,878

The Home Depot is not under any immediate pressure to increase its leverage, for its past success and the good reputation of its management provide partial protection against a takeover attempt. Let us assume, however, that the Home Depot decides to increase its leverage over time toward its optimal for two reasons:

1. Its cost of capital is high, and it wants to lower it by using more debt;

2. The optimal debt ratio will probably increase over time, as the firm becomes less risky and the operating cash flows from current operations increase.

The question of how to increase leverage over time can be best answered by looking at the quality of the projects available to the Home Depot in 1994. To make this judgment, we estimate the return on capital earned by the Home Depot in 1994:

$$\text{Return on Capital} = \text{EBIT } (1\text{-tax rate}) / (\text{BV of Debt} + \text{BV of Equity})$$
$$= 958\,(1-.36) / (129 + 3442) = 17.17\%$$

This is higher than the cost of capital of 15.80% that the Home Depot faced in 1994. Assuming that the returns on capital will be higher than the cost of capital in the future, the Home Depot should finance its new projects with debt. Over time, we would expect to see an increase in the debt ratio, although the value of equity will itself increase as earnings are reinvested back in the company. To make forecasts of changes in leverage over time, we made the following assumptions:

- Operating earnings, capital expenditures, and depreciation are expected to grow 23% a year for the next five years (based on analyst estimates of growth).
- The interest rate on new debt is expected to be 8%.
- The dividend payout ratio is expected to be 11% for the next five years.
- The unlevered beta, which is currently close to 1.60, is expected to decline to 1.50 in year 1 and to 1.40 in year 2 and to drop to 1.30 after that.
- The Treasury bond rate is 7%, and the risk premium is assumed to be 5.5%.

The estimated values of debt and equity, over time, are estimated as follows:

$$\text{Equity}_t = \text{Equity}_{t-1}\,(1 + \text{Cost of Equity}_t) - \text{Dividends}_t - \text{Equity Buybacks}_t$$

The rationale is simple: The cost of equity measures the expected return on the stock, inclusive of price appreciation and the dividend yield, and the payment of dividends reduces the value of equity outstanding at the end of the year.[3] The value of debt is estimated by adding the new debt taken on to the debt outstanding at the end of the previous year.

Table 19.3 uses the expected capital expenditures over the next five years, in conjunction with the debt financing, to estimate the debt ratio in each year.

Table 19.3 **ESTIMATED DEBT RATIOS—THE HOME DEPOT**

	Current Year	1	2	3	4	5
Equity	$19,496	$22,495	$25,865	$29,623	$33,788	$38,572
Debt	$129	$710	$1,452	$2,397	$3,604	$5,142
Debt/(Debt+Equity)	0.66%	3.06%	5.31%	7.49%	9.64%	11.76%
Capital Expenditures	$1,100	$1,353	$1,664	$2,047	$2,518	$3,097
− Depreciation	$89	$109	$135	$166	$204	$251
− Net Income[a]	$605	$744	$886	$1,051	$1,245	$1,469
− Dividends	$67	$82	$97	$116	$137	$162
= New Debt	NA	$581	$741	$946	$1,206	$1,539
Beta	1.60	1.53	1.45	1.37	1.39	1.41
Cost of Equity (End of period)	15.80%	15.42%	14.98%	14.52%	14.64%	14.76%
Growth Rate		23.00%	23.00%	23.00%	23.00%	23.00%
Payout Ratio	11%	11%	11%	11%	11%	11%

[a]Net Income$_t$ = Net Income$_{t-1}$ $(1 + g)$ − Interest Rate $(1 - t)$ * (Debt$_t$ − Debt$_{t-1}$)

While the debt ratio increases over time, it is only 11.76% by the end of the fifth year. This is because the market value of equity increases over time, as a result of the expected stock price appreciation. If the Home Depot wants to raise its debt ratio to 20%, it will have to adopt one of two courses:

1. **Increase its dividend payout ratio**   The higher dividend increases the debt ratio in two ways. It increases the need for debt financing in each year, and it reduces the expected price appreciation on the equity. In Table 19.4, for instance, increasing the dividend payout ratio to 35% results in a debt ratio of 14.76% at the end of the fifth year.

2. **Repurchase stock each year**   This affects the debt ratio in much the same way as does increasing dividends, because it increases debt requirements and reduces equity.

 Concept
Check

> What percentage of the outstanding stock would the Home Depot have to buy back each year, in addition to paying out 35% of earnings as dividends, to get to a debt ratio of 20% by the end of the fifth year?

Decreasing Leverage Gradually

The benefits that overlevered firms gain by lowering their debt ratios gradually over time include the residual cash flows that can be used to take on new projects and the increased equity over time, leading to lower debt ratios. For this to work, however, firms must have access to good projects that can be financed either with the **internal equity**

---

[3]The effect of dividends on the market value of equity can best be captured by noting the effect the payment on dividends has on stock prices on the ex-dividend day. Stock prices tend to drop on ex-dividend day by about the same amount as the dividend paid.

Table 19.4 **Estimated Debt Ratio with Higher Dividend Payout Ratio**						
	Current Year	1	2	3	4	5
Equity	$19,496	$22,316	$25,459	$28,933	$32,746	$37,099
Debt	$129	$889	$1,849	$3,061	$4,593	$6,528
Debt/(Debt+Equity)	0.66%	3.83%	6.77%	9.57%	12.30%	14.96%
Capital Expenditures	$1,100	$1,353	$1,664	$2,047	$2,518	$3,097
− Depreciation	$89	$109	$135	$166	$204	$251
− Net Income	$605	$744	$876	$1,029	$1,203	$1,402
± Dividends	$67	$260	$307	$360	$421	$491
= New Debt	$473	$760	$960	$1,213	$1,532	$1,935
Beta	1.60	1.54	1.47	1.39	1.42	1.45
Cost of Equity	15.80%	15.46%	15.06%	14.63%	14.79%	14.96%
Growth Rate		23.00%	23.00%	23.00%	23.00%	23.00%
Payout Ratio	11%	35%	35%	35%	35%	35%

or with new stock issues, leading to higher equity and lower debt ratios. If firms do not have access to good projects, the residual cash flows of the firms will have to be utilized to pay off outstanding debt and lower the debt ratio. It goes without saying that firms should desist from paying dividends or repurchasing stock during the course of this adjustment.

Internal Equity: Internal equity usually is that portion of the earnings that gets reinvested back into the company, that is, the retained earnings.

Hybrid Securities and Changing Financing Mix

In some cases, overlevered firms can gain from having hybrid securities, such as convertible debt, whereby the mix of debt and equity changes over time as the stock price changes. As the firm's fortunes improve, the equity component in convertible debt increases as a proportion of the convertible bond's value, leading to lower debt ratios.

The framework for analyzing optimal capital structure, described in the last few pages, is summarized in Figure 19.1.

IN PRACTICE   A FRAMEWORK FOR CHANGING LEVERAGE: TIME WARNER

In 1994, Time Warner had 379.3 million shares outstanding, trading at $44 per share, and $9.934 billion in outstanding debt, left over from the leveraged acquisition of Time by Warner Communications in 1989. The EBITDA in 1994 was $1.146 billion, and Time Warner had a beta of 1.30. The optimal debt ratio for Time Warner, based on this operating income, is only 10%. Table 19.5 examines the effect on leverage of cutting dividends to zero and using operating cash flows to take on projects and repay debt.

Allowing for a growth rate of 10% in operating income, Time Warner repays $189 million of its outstanding debt in the first year. By the end of the fifth year, the growth in equity and the reduction in debt combine to lower the debt ratio to 21.47%.

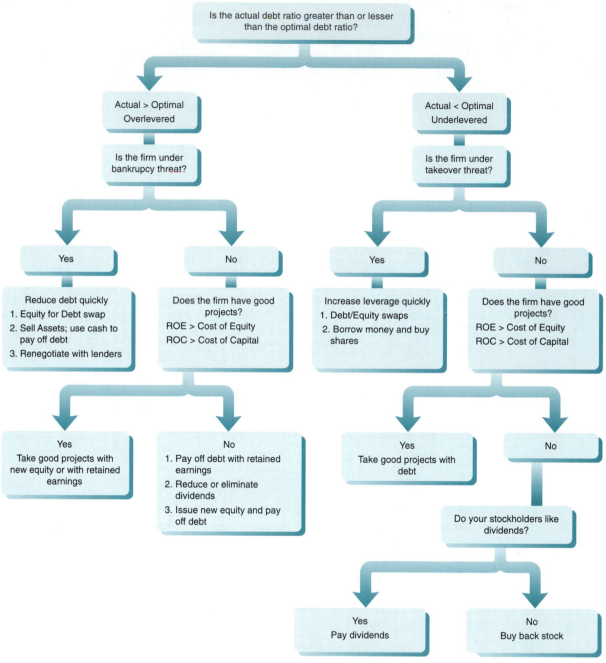

Figure 19.1 A framework for analyzing capital structure

☐ **Concept Check**

Assume that Time Warner plans to invest heavily in its newer multimedia business lines, and that it wants to double its capital expenditures from the levels shown in Table 19.6. Without changing the other assumptions, what effect will this have on leverage over time?

Table 19.5   **Estimated Debt Ratios—Time Warner**

	Current Year	1	2	3	4	5
Equity	$16,689	$19,051	$21,694	$24,651	$27,960	$31,663
Debt	$9,934	$9,745	$9,527	$9,276	$8,988	$8,655
Debt/(Debt + Equity)	37.31%	33.84%	30.52%	27.34%	24.33%	21.47%
Capital Expenditures	$300	$330	$363	$399	$439	$483
− Depreciation	$437	$481	$529	$582	$640	$704
− Net Income	$35	$39	$52	$68	$88	$112
± Dividends	$67	$0	$0	$0	$0	$0
= New Debt	($105)	($189)	($218)	($251)	($289)	($332)
Beta	1.30	1.25	1.21	1.17	1.14	1.11
Cost of Equity	14.15%	13.87%	13.63%	13.42%	13.24%	13.08%
Growth Rate		10.00%	10.00%	10.00%	10.00%	10.00%
Payout Ratio	11%	0%	0%	0%	0%	0%

Security Innovation and Capital Structure Changes

Although the changes in leverage discussed so far in this chapter have been accomplished using traditional securities, such as straight debt and equity, firms that have specific objectives on leverage may find certain products that are designed to meet them. Consider a few examples:

- A firm that intends to raise its debt ratio over time may do so by selling **puts** on its equity. These puts will generate cash flows now and will also provide investors in the stock with the means to ensure themselves against stock price downturns.

Put: This is the right to buy an underlying asset during a specified time period at a price that is fixed at the time the right is issued.

- Another alternative available to a firm that wants to increase leverage over time is a **forward contract** to buy a specified number of shares of equity in the future. These contracts lock the firms into reducing their equity over time and may carry a more positive signal to financial markets than would an announcement of plans to repurchase stock, since firms are not obligated to carry through on these announcements.

Forward Contract: A forward contract is an agreement to buy or sell the underlying asset at a fixed price at a future point in time.

- A firm with high leverage, faced with resistance from financial markets to common stock issues, may consider more inventive ways of raising equity, such as using warrants and **contingent value rights.**

Contingent Value Rights: A contingent value right (CVR) provides the holder with the right to sell a share of stock in the underlying company at a fixed price during the life of the right.

WORKING OUT THE DETAILS

Once a firm has decided to use new financing, either debt or equity, it has to decide on the details of the financing. As we saw in Chapter 15, firms can raise debt and equity in a variety of ways, and they have to make a series of choices on the design of the new financing. In the case of debt, they have to make decisions on the maturity of the debt, any special characteristics (such as fixed versus floating rates, conversion options, and so on) the debt might have, and the currency in which the debt is to be issued. In the case of equity, there are fewer choices, but firms can still raise equity from common stock, warrants or contingent value rights.

In this section, we lay out a sequence of steps that a firm can use to devise an appropriate finance mix. The first step in the analysis is to examine the cash-flow characteristics of the assets or projects that will be financed; the objective is to try and match the cash flows on the liability stream as closely as possible to the cash flows on the asset stream. We then superimpose a series of considerations that may lead the firm to deviate from or modify this financing mix. First, we consider the tax savings that may accrue from using different financing vehicles and weigh the tax benefits against the costs of deviating from the mix. Next, we examine the influence that equity research analysts and ratings agency views have on the choice of financing vehicle; instruments that are looked on favorably by either or, better still, both groups are clearly preferred to those that evoke strong negative responses. We also factor in the difficulty that some firms might have in conveying information to markets; in the presence of asymmetric information, firms may have to make financing choices that do not reflect their asset mix. Finally, we allow for the possibility that firms may want to structure their financing to reduce agency conflicts between stockholders and bondholders.

Step 1: Examine the Cash-Flow Characteristics of Assets

The first, and most important, factor a firm has to consider in the design of the securities it will use to raise funds is the *cash-flow patterns of the assets* that are to be financed with these securities. We argue that firms should begin with the premise that the cash flows on their liability streams should match up with the cash flows on the assets they own.

Why match asset cash flows to cash flows on liabilities? To see why firms should match up cash flows on assets to cash flows on liabilities, let us begin by defining *firm value* as the present value of the cash flows generated by the assets owned by the firm. This firm value will vary over time, not only as a function of firm-specific factors, such as project success, but also as a function of broader macroeconomic variables, such as interest rates, inflation rates, economic cycles, and exchange rates. Figure 19.2 provides the time series of firm value for a hypothetical firm, in which all of the changes in firm value are assumed to occur as a result of changes in macroeconomic variables.

This firm can choose to finance these assets with any financing mix it wants. The value of equity at any point in time is the difference between the value of the firm and the value of outstanding debt. Assume, for instance, that the firm chooses to finance the assets shown in Figure 19.2 using very short-term debt and that this debt is unaffected by changes in macroeconomic variables. Figure 19.3 provides the firm value, debt value, and equity value for the firm over time.

Note that there are periods when the firm value drops below the debt value, which would suggest that the firm is flirting with bankruptcy in those periods. Firms that include this possibility in their financing decision will therefore borrow much less.

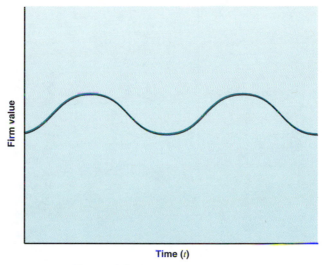

Figure 19.2   Firm value over time

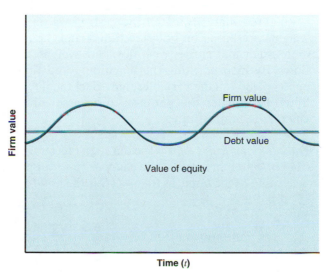

Figure 19.3   Firm value over time with short-term debt

Now consider a firm that finances the assets described in Figure 19.2 with debt that matches up exactly to the assets in terms of cash flows and also in terms of the sensitivity of debt value to changes in macroeconomic variables. Figure 19.4 provides the firm value, debt value, and equity value for this firm.

Because debt value and firm value move together here, the possibility of default is significantly reduced. This, in turn, will allow the firm to carry much more debt, which should provide tax benefits that make the firm more valuable. Thus, matching liability cash flows to asset cash flows allows firms to have higher optimal debt ratios.

Financing maturity   Notwithstanding the discussion above, it is both difficult and expensive to match individual cash flows on assets perfectly with individual cash flows on liabilities, for several reasons. However, firms can often obtain a significant portion of the benefits listed in the previous section by matching the duration of

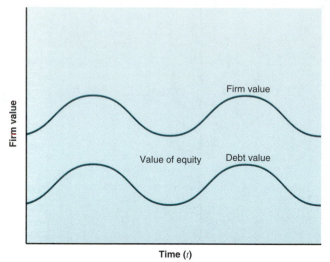

Figure 19.4 Firm value over time with long-term debt

their assets to the duration of their liabilities. The *duration of an asset or a liability* is a weighted maturity of all the cash flows on that asset or liability, whereby the weights are based on both the timing and the magnitude of the cash flows. In general, larger and earlier cash flows are weighted more than smaller and later cash flows. By incorporating the magnitude and timing of all the cash flows, duration encompasses all the variables that affect the interest rate sensitivity of an asset or liability. The higher the duration of an asset or liability, the more sensitive it is to changes in interest rates.

Duration of a firm's debt   The duration of a straight bond or loan issued by a company can be written in terms of the coupons (interest payments) on the bond (loan) and the face value of the bond, as follows (N is the bond maturity):

$$\text{Duration of Bond} = dP/dr = \frac{\left[\sum_{t=1}^{t=N}\dfrac{t*\text{Coupon}_t}{(1+r)^t} + \dfrac{N*\text{Face Value}}{(1+r)^N}\right]}{\left[\sum_{t=1}^{t=N}\dfrac{\text{Coupon}_t}{(1+r)^t} + \dfrac{\text{Face Value}}{(1+r)^N}\right]}$$

Holding other factors constant, we find that the duration of a bond will increase with the maturity of the bond and decrease with the coupon rate on the bond.

Duration of a firm's assets   This measure of duration can be extended to any asset with expected cash flows. Thus the duration of a project or asset can be estimated in terms of its pre-debt operating cash flows:

$$\text{Duration of Project/Asset} = dPV/dr = \frac{\left[\sum_{t=1}^{t=N}\dfrac{t*CF_t}{(1+r)^t} + \dfrac{N*\text{Terminal Value}}{(1+r)^N}\right]}{\left[\sum_{t=1}^{t=N}\dfrac{CF_t}{(1+r)^t} + \dfrac{\text{Terminal Value}}{(1+r)^N}\right]}$$

where

CF_t = After-tax operating cash flow on the project in year t
Terminal Value = Salvage Value at the end of the project lifetime
N = Life of the project

The duration of any asset provides a measure of the interest rate risk embedded in that asset.

One of the limitations of traditional duration analysis is that it keeps cash flows fixed, while interest rates change. On real projects, however, the cash flows will be adversely affected by the increases in interest rates, and the degree of the effect will vary from business to business—more for cyclical firms (automobiles, housing) and less for non-cyclical firms (food processing). Thus the actual duration of most projects will be higher than the estimates obtained by keeping cash flows constant.

One way of estimating duration without depending on the traditional bond duration measures is to use historical data. If the duration is, in fact, the sensitivity of asset values to interest rate changes, and a time series of asset value and interest rate changes is available, a regression of asset value changes on interest rate changes should yield a measure of duration:

$$\Delta \text{ Asset Value}_t = a + b \, \Delta \text{ Interest Rate}_t$$

In this regression, the coefficient b on interest rate changes should be a measure of the duration of the assets. For firms with publicly traded stocks and bonds, the value of assets is the sum of the market values of debt and equity over time. For a private company or for a public company with a short history, the regression can be run, using changes in operating income as the dependent variable:

$$\Delta \text{ Operating Income}_t = a + b \, \Delta \text{ Interest Rate}_t$$

Here again, the coefficient b is a measure of the duration of the assets.

 Concept
Check

> In real projects, analysts often cut the project life off at the end of a specified period and assume a salvage or terminal value. Is this the equivalent of the face value in a bond? Why or why not?

✈ IN PRACTICE   CALCULATING DURATION FOR THE BOEING 777 PROJECT

In this application, we will calculate duration using the traditional measures for the Boeing 777 project. The cash flows for the project are summarized in Table 19.6, together with the present value estimates, calculated using the cost of capital of 12%.

$$\text{Duration of the Project} = \$66,610 \,/\, \$9,220 = 7.22$$

This duration is understated, however, because the project is arbitrarily cut off after 15 years. Using the true life time for the project should yield a higher duration estimate.

Duration and financing choices   Once the duration of the assets is known, the duration of the financing can be set in one of two ways: by matching individual assets and liabilities, or by matching the assets of the firm with its collective liabilities. In the first approach, the cash flows on the financing can be matched up as closely as possible to the individual project being financed. Alternatively, the duration of the financing can be matched up to the duration of the asset it funds. Although this approach provides a precise matching of each asset's characteristics to those of the financing used for it, it has several limitations. First, it is expensive to arrange separate financing for each project, given the fixed costs associated with raising funds. Second, this approach ignores interactions and correlations between projects which might make project-specific financing suboptimal for the firm. Consequently, this approach works only for companies that have very large, independent projects.

	Table 19.6 Calculating a Project's Duration		
Year	Cash Flow	PV of Cash Flow	*t* * PV of Cash Flow
1	$(711.12)	$(634.93)	$(634.93)
2	1,754.92	1,399.01	2,798.02
3	1,867.92	1,329.55	3,988.65
4	1,625.72	1,033.17	4,132.70
5	1,771.84	1,005.39	5,026.95
6	1,465.56	742.50	4,454.99
7	1,666.36	753.78	5,276.44
8	1,246.92	503.61	4,028.88
9	1,971.60	710.98	6,398.81
10	588.10	189.35	1,893.52
11	1,431.76	411.60	4,527.56
12	1,839.88	472.25	5,667.02
13	825.68	189.22	2,459.92
14	640.73	131.11	1,835.48
15	5,384.56	983.74	14,756.08
	Sum =	9,220.33	66,610.10
	Duration =		7.22

❏ Concept
Check

> Drawing on the lessons of diversification from earlier chapters, what are the implications of viewing the firm as holding a portfolio of projects for financing choices?

When it is difficult or costly to pair up financing to the specific projects being financed, the duration of all assets can be estimated (1) by taking a weighted average of the durations of individual assets, or (2) by estimating the duration of all assets from the cumulated operating cash flows to the firm. The duration of liabilities can be estimated collectively as well and matched up as closely as possible to the duration of the assets. This approach saves on transactions cost.

Implications   Based on the relationship between asset duration and the duration of liabilities presented above, several interesting implications emerge:

- Cyclical manufacturing firms are more inclined to use long-term, fixed-rate debt, since their projects are likely to have high duration and to be sensitive to interest rate changes. Thus, if interest rates go up (down), the value of both assets and liabilities will go down (up).

- Real estate firms, whose assets have very long lives and whose largest expected cash flow is the terminal value, are also candidates for using long-term debt to finance their assets.

- Firms that have projects whose cash flows are evenly spread over time, such as retail stores, are more inclined to use shorter term debt, since the duration of their projects is likely to be low.

- Firms that have projects with long gestation periods, whereby the cash flows are low initially but increase over the long term, are more likely to use long-term debt to finance these projects.

The fixed/floating rate choice   In recent years, firms have had far more choices in the design of the interest rate structure of their debt. One of the most common choices firms have to make is whether to make the coupon rate a fixed rate or a floating rate, pegged to an index rate such as the LIBOR. In making this decision, we once again examine the characteristics of the projects being financed with the debt.

Uncertainty about future projects   The assumption that the duration of assets and liabilities can be matched up to arrive at the "right" maturity mix for financing is predicated on the notion that the assets and projects of a firm are well identified and that the interest rate sensitivity of these assets can therefore be estimated easily. For some firms, this may be difficult to do, however. The firm may be in transition (it could be restructuring), or the industry may be changing. In such cases, the firm may use a financing mix that is easy to change (short-term or floating rate loans) until it feels more certain about its future investment plans.

> An Alternative: The presence of derivatives provides an alternative for firms that are faced with this uncertainty. They can use the financing mix that is most appropriate given their current asset mix, and use derivatives to manage the intermediate risk.

Cash flows and inflation   If a firm has assets whose earnings increase as interest rates go up, and decrease as interest rates go down, it should finance those assets with *floating rate debt*. Although few manufacturing projects have these characteristics in low-inflation economies, more do in high-inflation economies, since increases in inflation result in increases in both earnings/revenues and in interest rates.

Floating Rate Debt: The interest rate on floating rate debt varies from period to period and is linked to a specified short-term rate; for instance, many floating rate bonds have coupon rates that are tied to the LIBOR.

Concept Check

The volume of floating rate loans and bonds exploded starting in the late 1970s. How would you relate this growth to the inflation environment of that period? If inflation has indeed become more stable again, what are the prospects for floating rate loans in the future? What other factors may play a role?

Currency risk and financing mix   Many of the observations made about interest rate risk exposure also apply to currency risk exposure. If any of a firm's assets or projects create cash flows that are in a currency other than the one in which the equity is denominated, there is a currency risk. The liabilities of a firm can be issued in these currencies to reduce the currency risk. A firm that expects 20% of its cash flows to be in deutsche marks, for example, would attempt to issue DM-denominated debt in the same proportion to mitigate the currency risk.

   In recent years, firms have used more sophisticated variations on traditional bonds to manage foreign exchange risk. For instance, Philip Morris issued a dual currency bond in 1985—coupon payments were made in Swiss francs, while the principal payment was in U.S. dollars. In 1987, Westinghouse issued **Principal Exchange**

Rate Linked Securities (PERLS), whereby the principal payment was the U.S. dollar value of 70.13 New Zealand dollars. Finally, firms have issued bonds embedded with foreign currency options called Indexed Currency Option Notes (ICON), which combine a fixed rate bullet repayment bond with an option on the foreign currency. This approach is likely to work only for firms that have fairly predictable currency flows, however. For firms that do not, currency derivatives may be a cheaper way to manage currency risk, since the currency exposure changes from period to period.

■ **PERLS:** This is a bond, denominated in the domestic currency, whereby the principal payment at maturity is based on the domestic currency equivalent of a fixed foreign currency amount. For instance, this could be a dollar-denominated bond with the payment at maturity set equal to the dollar value of 1,600 deutsche marks. Thus, if the dollar strengthens against the DM during the life of the bond, the principal payment will decrease.

Other features As we noted in Chapter 15, several special features have been added to corporate bonds. In this section, we examine how the cash flows on assets may help determine whether any of these special features should be included in new debt issued by a firm.

Business risk The most controversial type of risk, in terms of whether and how it should be managed, is *business risk*. Business risk arises from changes in the underlying business in which a firm operates and its exposure to macroeconomic factors. An automobile manufacturing firm, for instance, is exposed to the risk that the economy may go into a recession. Some firms have attempted to add special features to their liabilities to reduce their exposure to business risk:

- Insurance companies have started issuing bonds whose payments can be drastically curtailed if there is a catastrophe that requires payouts by the insurance company. By doing so, they reduce their debt payments in those periods when their overall cash flows are most negative, thereby reducing their likelihood of default.

- Companies in commodity businesses have issued bonds whose principal and interest payments are tied to the price of the commodity. Since the operating cash flows in these firms are also positively correlated with commodity prices, adding this feature to debt decreases the likelihood of default and allows the firm to use more debt. In 1980, for instance, Sunshine Mining issued 15-year silver-linked bond issues, which combined a debt issue with an option on silver prices.

Growth characteristics Firms vary in terms of how much of their value comes from projects or assets already in place and how much comes from future growth. Firms that derive the bulk of their value from future growth use different types of financing and design their financing differently than do those that derive most of their value from assets in place. This is because the current cash flows on "high-growth" firms will be low, relative to the market value. Accordingly, the financing approach used should not create large cash outflows early. It can create substantial cash outflows later, however, reflecting the cash-flow patterns of the firm. In addition, the financing should exploit the value that the perception of high growth adds to securities, and it should put relatively few constraints on investment policies.

Straight bonds do not quite fit the bill because they create large interest payments and do not gain much value from the high-growth perceptions. Furthermore, they are likely to include covenants designed to protect the bondholders, which restrict investment and future financing policy. Convertible bonds, by contrast, create much lower interest payments, impose fewer constraints, and gain value from higher growth perceptions. They might be converted into common stock, but only if the firm is successful.

Convertible Debt: This is debt that can be converted into equity at a rate that is specified as part of the debt agreement (conversion rate).

Step 2: Examine the Tax Implications of the Financing Mix

A firm's financing choices have tax consequences. It is possible, therefore, that the favorable tax treatment of some financing choices may encourage firms to use them more than others, even if it means deviating from the choices that would be dictated by the asset characteristics. Consider the rationale of some companies for their use of **zero-coupon bonds.** Since the IRS allows firms to impute an interest payment on the bonds, the firms using the zeros are able to claim a tax deduction for a noncash expense, decreasing their tax liability in the near periods. Although the imputed interest income to the buyers of these bonds may create a tax liability that affects bond prices and rates, this situation can be avoided by placing these bonds with tax-exempt institutions.

Zero-coupon Bond: A zero-coupon bond pays no coupons during the life of the bond and pays the face value of the bond at maturity; it has a duration equal to its maturity.

The danger of structuring financing with the intention of saving on taxes is that changes in the tax law can very quickly render the benefit moot and leave the firm with a financing mix that is unsuited to its asset mix.

Step 3: Consider How Ratings Agencies and Equity Research Analysts Will React

Firms are rightfully concerned about the views of equity research analysts and ratings agencies on the actions they take, although they often overestimate the influence of both groups. Analysts represent stockholders, and ratings agencies represent bondholders… consequently, they take very different views of the same actions. For instance, analysts may view a stock repurchase by a company with limited project opportunities as a positive action, whereas ratings agencies may view it as a negative action and lower ratings in response. Analysts and ratings agencies also measure the impact of actions using very different criteria. In general, analysts view a firm's actions through the prism of higher earnings per share and by looking at the firm relative to comparable firms, using multiples such as price earnings or price book value ratios. Ratings agencies, on the other hand, measure the effect of actions on the financial ratios, such as debt ratios and coverage ratios, which they then use to assess risk and assign ratings.

Given the weight attached to the views of both these groups, firms sometimes design securities with the intent of satisfying both groups. In some cases, they find ways of raising funds that seem to make both groups happy, at least on the surface. To illustrate, consider the use of leasing, before generally accepted accounting principles required capitalizing of leases. Leasing increased the real leverage of the company and thus the earnings per share, but it did not affect the measured leverage of the company because it was not viewed as debt. To the degree that analysts and ratings agencies rely on quantitative measures and do not properly factor in the effects of these actions, firms can exploit their limitations. In a more recent example, insurance companies in the United States have issued **surplus notes**, which are considered debt for tax purposes and equity under insurance accounting rules. They therefore have the best of both worlds—they can issue debt, while counting it as equity.[4]

Surplus Notes: Surplus notes are notes issued without specific assets as security; the interest payments are made only if earnings exceed a specified level.

When securities are designed in such a way, the real question is whether the markets are fooled and, if so, for how long. A firm that substitutes leases for debt may fool the ratings agency and even the debt markets for some period of time, but it cannot evade the reality that it is much more levered and, hence, much riskier.

Finally, ratings agencies and analysts are only two players in a game that involves far more, including stockholders and bondholders themselves, and the firm's managers. Table 19.7 summarizes the different objectives, criteria, and measurement devices used by each. It is extremely unlikely, given the conflicts in interest between some of these groups, that any one financing action will result in unanimous acceptance.

☐ Concept
Check

> Earlier in this book, we talked about the use of preferred stock. How do accountants and ratings agencies view preferred stock? Could this be a reason why preferred stock is used by firms?

Step 4: Examine the Effects of Asymmetric Information

Firms generally have more information about their future prospects than do financial markets. This **information asymmetry** creates frictions when firms try to raise funds. In particular, firms with good prospects try to distinguish themselves from firms without such prospects by taking actions that are costly and difficult to imitate. Firms also try to reduce the effect of uncertainty in future cash flows by designing their securities to minimize this effect. Firms may therefore issue securities that may not be optimal from the standpoint of matching up to their asset cash flows but are specifically designed to convey information to financial markets and reduce the effects of uncertain cash flows on value.

Information Asymmetry: Information asymmetry arises any time one party to a transaction or agreement has more or better information than the other. Thus managers may know more about their firms than do the firm's stockholders, and stockholders may know more than do bondholders.

A number of researchers have used this information asymmetry argument to draw very different conclusions about the debt structure firms should use. Myers (1977) argued that firms tend to underinvest as a consequence of the asymmetry of information. One proposed solution to the problem is to issue short-term debt, even if the assets

---

[4]In 1994 and 1995, insurance companies issued a total of $6 billion of surplus notes in the private placement market.

Table 19.7 Objective Functions for Different Groups

	Ratings Agencies	Equity Research Analysts	Existing Bondholders	Managers	Stockholders
Objective	Measure risk of default in company's bond issues (existing and new).	Evaluate whether the stock is a good buy for clients (make recommendations).	Ensure that their loans to the firm (or bonds) are protected.	Maximize managerial interests without arousing too much stockholder dissatisfaction.	Maximize stock price.
Measurement device	Financial Ratios measuring —cash-flow-generating capacity —degree of leverage —risk —profitability	* Multiples (PE,PBV) relative to comparable firms * EPS effects * EPS growth	* Financial ratios specified in covenants.	* EPS effects * Earnings growth * Earnings stability * Remuneration systems.	* Discounted Cash-Flow Valuation * Multiples
Questions raised in analysis	* How will this action affect the company's ability to meet its debt payments?	* How will this action affect the company's multiples and its standing relative to comparables?	* How will this action affect the security and safety of the company's existing debt?	* How will this action affect —flexibility? —remuneration? —relationships with large stockholders?	* How will this action affect the stock price?
What makes them happy	1. High coverage ratios 2. Low leverage ratios 3. High profitability ratios	1. Increases in EPS 2. Increases in growth	1. Protection of cash flows and ratings on existing debt (or) 2. Capacity to cash out without loss	1. High flexibility 2. More stability 3. Increase in EPS and growth 4. Higher stock price	1. Higher stock prices

being financed are long-term assets. Flannery (1986) and Kale and Noe (1990) note that, although both short- and long-term debt will be mispriced in the presence of asymmetric information, long-term debt will be mispriced even more. Consequently, they argue that high-quality firms will issue short-term debt, whereas low-quality firms will issue long-term debt.

Goswami, Noe, and Rebello (1995) analyze the design of securities and relate it to uncertainty about future cash flows. They conclude that if the asymmetry of information concerns uncertainty about long-term cash flows, firms should issue coupon-bearing long term debt, with restrictions on dividends. In contrast, firms with uncertainty about near-term cash flows and significant refinancing risk should issue long-term debt, without restrictions on dividend payments. When uncertainty about information is uniformly distributed across time, firms should finance with short-term debt.

Step 5: Consider the Implications of Financing Mix for Agency Costs

The final consideration in designing securities is the provision of features intended to reduce agency conflicts between stockholders and bondholders. As we noted in Chapter 17, differences between bondholders and stockholders on investment, financing, and dividend policy decisions can have an impact on the capital structure either by increasing the costs of borrowing or by increasing the constraints associated with borrowing. In some cases, firms design securities with the specific intent of reducing this conflict and its associated costs:

- We argued earlier that convertible bonds are a good choice for growth companies because of their cash-flow characteristics. It can also be argued that convertible bonds reduce the anxiety bondholders have about equity investors taking on riskier projects and expropriating wealth, by allowing them to become stockholders if the stock price increases enough.

- Many corporate bonds include put options that allow bondholders to put the bonds back at face value if the firm takes a specified action (such as increasing leverage) or if its rating drops. In a variation, in 1988 Manufacturer Hanover issued floating rate, rating-sensitive notes promising bondholders higher coupons if the firm's rating deteriorated over time.

LYONS: Liquid yield option notes are notes whose holders have the right either to put them back to the firm under specified circumstances or to convert them into equity.

- Merrill Lynch introduced **LYONs** (*Liquid Yield Option Notes*), which incorporated put and conversion features to protect against both the risk shifting and claim substitution to which bondholders are exposed.

In Summary

In deciding on the optimal financing mix, firms should begin by examining the characteristics of the assets they own: Are they long term or short term? How sensitive are they to economic conditions and inflation? In what currencies are the cash flows? They should then try to match up the maturity, interest rate and currency mix, and special features on their financing to these characteristics. They can then superimpose tax considerations, the views of analysts and ratings agencies, agency costs, and the effects of asymmetric information to modify this financing mix. Figure 19.5 summarizes the discussion on the preceding pages.

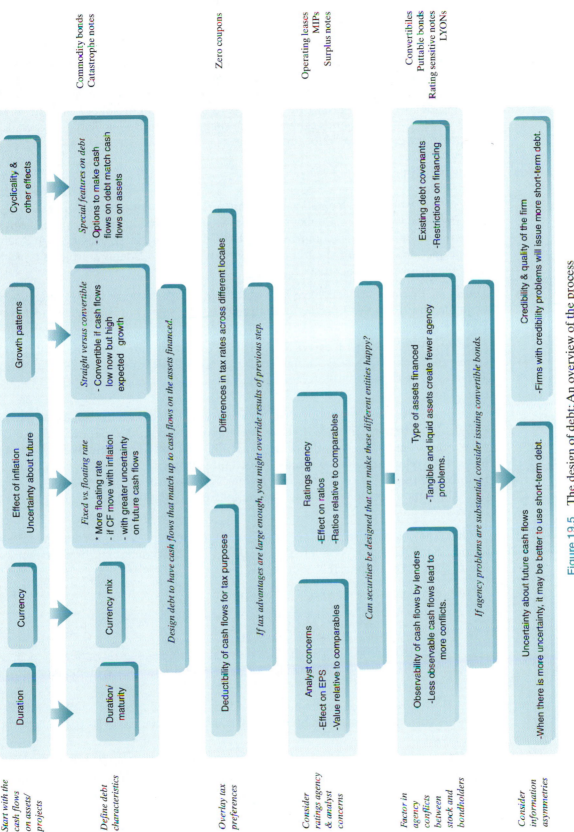

Figure 19.5   The design of debt: An overview of the process

COMING UP WITH THE FINANCING DETAILS: BOEING

In the following extended illustration, we come up with the financing details for Boeing, using two approaches. First, we use a subjective analysis of Boeing's project characteristics to define the appropriate debt mix for the company. Then we use a more quantitative approach for analyzing project characteristics and use it to come up with the financing details for the firm. Both approaches should be considered in light of the analysis done in the previous chapter, which suggested that Boeing had untapped debt potential that could be used for future projects.

Intuitive Approach

In the intuitive approach, we begin with an analysis of the characteristics of a typical project taken on by Boeing and use it to make recommendations for Boeing's new financing. Looking forward, Boeing's projects will primarily be in the aerospace business, since the defense business comprises only 8.6% of the remaining backlog. The Boeing 777 project described in the earlier chapters is typical, and Boeing's projects typically have the following characteristics:

Duration: Boeing's projects have long gestation periods and are very long term. For example, the Boeing 777 project is analyzed over 15 years but is expected to have a 30-year life.

Currency: While Boeing receives 54% of its revenues from overseas, most of its revenues are in dollars, for its foreign contracts are still denominated in dollar terms. There is some exposure to foreign currency risk, however, which is expected to grow over time.

Cash Flows: Boeing's operating cash flows are correlated with the health of the airline business because airlines that are losing money are unlikely to expand or modernize their fleets. The cash flows are generally affected negatively by inflation, for increasing oil prices, in particular, affect the airline business adversely. Finally, Boeing's sales are lumpy; a few large orders, such as SAS's order of 35 planes, comprise the bulk of revenues, making Boeing sensitive to the financial standing of these companies.

Once the characteristics of the projects are known, they can be used as guideposts for putting together a mix of debt that matches up to the asset's cash-flow characteristics. In the case of Boeing, this debt should be

- *Long term,* since the projects are long term.
- *Fixed rate* rather than floating rate debt, for a number of reasons:

a. It increases the duration of the debt.

b. Because cash flows at Boeing are more likely to be adversely affected by inflation than helped by it, it would not be helpful if interest payments moved with inflation.

c. Because Boeing is relatively certain that its future projects will be similar to its current projects, it can feel fairly secure in its analysis of its project characteristics.

- *Be primarily in dollars,* since the operating cash flows are also in dollars.
- *Be linked, if possible, to the health of the airline business*—debt payments should increase when the airline business is doing well and decrease when the airline business is doing badly.

A Quantitative Approach

A quantitative approach estimates Boeing's sensitivity to changes in a number of macroeconomic variables, using two measures: Boeing's firm value (the market value of debt and equity), and its operating income.

Value sensitivity to factors: past data   The value of a firm is the obvious choice when it comes to measuring its sensitivity to changes in interest rates, inflation rates or currency rates, because it reflects the effect of these variables on current and future cash flows as well as the effect on discount rates. It is a viable measurement, however, only if the firm has been publicly traded. In cases in which the firm value is not available, either because the data are missing or the firm has not been listed long enough, the firm values of comparable firms that have been listed for a longer period can be used in the regression. This will provide a measure of the industry characteristics.

We begin by collecting past data on firm value and the macroeconomic variables against which we want to measure its sensitivity. In the case of Boeing, we choose three broad measures (see Table 19.8):

- *Long-term Treasury Bond Rate,* because the sensitivity of firm value to changes in interest rates provides a measure of the duration of the projects. It also provides insight into whether the firm should be using fixed or floating rate debt; a firm whose operating income moves with interest rates should consider using floating rate loans.

- *Nominal GNP,* because the sensitivity of firm value to this variable provides a measure of the firm's cyclicality.

- *Currency Rate,* because the sensitivity of firm value to the currency rate provides a measure of the exposure to currency rate risk and thus helps determine what the currency mix for the debt should be.

This is not intended to be an all-encompassing analysis. An extended analysis might include other variables, such as the inflation rate or industry-specific variables.

Table 19.8   Boeing's Firm Value and Macroeconomic Variables, 1980–1984

Year	Firm Value	Long Bond Rate	Nominal GNP	Weighted Dollar
1980	$4,254	11.90%	2,732	99.37
1981	2,182	14.20	3,053	110.47
1982	3,270	13.80	3,166	123.14
1983	4,254	12.00	3,406	128.65
1984	5,503	12.70	3,772	138.89
1985	8,131	11.40	4,015	125.95
1986	8,179	9.00	4,232	112.89
1987	5,889	9.40	4,524	95.88
1988	9,532	9.70	4,881	95.32
1989	13,959	9.30	5,234	102.26
1990	15,900	9.30	5,514	96.25
1991	17,610	8.80	5,673	98.82
1992	15,391	8.10	6,026	104.58
1993	17,324	7.20	6,348	105.22
1994	18,624	8.00	6,727	98.6

Once these data have been collected, we can then estimate the sensitivity of firm values to changes in the macroeconomic variables by regressing changes in firm value each year against changes in each of the individual variables.

Sensitivity to changes in interest rates   As we discussed earlier, the duration of a firm's projects provides useful information for determining the maturity of its debt. Although bond-based duration measures may provide some answers, they will understate the duration of assets/projects if the cash flows on these assets/projects themselves vary with interest rates. Regressing changes in firm value against changes in interest rates over this period yields the following result:

> Change in Firm Value = 0.13 − 9.95 (Change in Interest Rates)

Based on this regression, the duration of Boeing's projects collectively is about 10 years. In designing its debt, Boeing should try to keep the duration of its bond issues to at least 10 years.

☐ Concept Check

The *R*-squared of this regression is only 13%, and the *t* statistics are marginally significant. What are the implications of these two findings for your conclusions?

Sensitivity to changes in the economy   Is Boeing a cyclical firm? One way of answering this question is to measure the sensitivity of firm value to changes in economic growth. Regressing changes in firm value against changes in the GNP over this period yields the following result:

> Change in Firm Value = 0.14 + 0.67 (GNP Growth)

Boeing is only mildly sensitive to cyclical movements in the economy. This may be because it derives so much of its revenues from overseas sales, and because of the lagged effect of economic downturns on the firm's operating income. (Cancellations in a year may not affect operating income for a couple of years.)

Sensitivity to changes in the dollar   The question of how sensitive Boeing's value is to changes in currency rates can be answered by looking at how the firm value changes as a function of changes in currency rates. Regressing changes in firm value against changes in the dollar over this period yields the following regression:

Change in Firm Value = 0.16 + 0.47 (Change in Dollar)

Boeing's value has not been very sensitive to changes in the dollar over the last 15 years. If this pattern continues, its debt should be primarily dollar debt. If it had been very sensitive to exchange rate changes, or if it expects this pattern to change over time, Boeing might have considered issuing some debt denominated in other currencies to insulate itself against some of the currency risk.

Cash-flow sensitivity to factors: past data   In some cases, it is more reasonable to estimate the sensitivity of operating cash flows directly against changes in interest rates, inflation, and other variables. This will occur if the firm value is not available for a long enough time period, the firm is not a publicly traded firm, or the analyst wants to tie cash flows on the debt directly to operating cash flows rather than to firm value. In fact, given the second reason, it can be argued that both firm value and operating income should be regressed against the relevant variables because each analysis provides valuable information that can be used in designing the financing mix. For Boeing, we repeated the analysis using operating income as the dependent variable, rather than firm value. Figure 19.6 graphs the operating income and firm value at Boeing between 1980 and 1994.

Because the procedure for the analysis is similar, we summarize the conclusions as follows:

- Regressing changes in operating cash flow against changes in interest rates over this period yields the following result:

Change in Operating Income $= 0.09 - 7.42$ (Change in Interest Rates)

Boeing's operating income, like its firm value, has been very sensitive to interest rates, which confirms our conclusion to use long-term debt. It yields a lower estimate of duration than the firm value measure, for two reasons—income

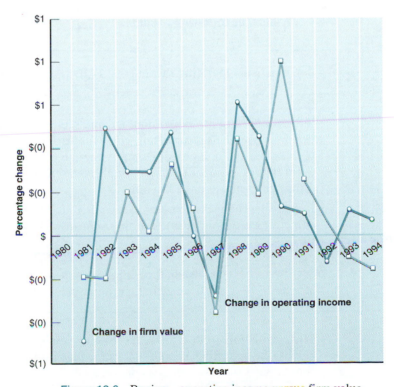

Figure 19.6   Boeing—operating income versus firm value

tends to be smoothed out relative to value, and current operating income does not reflect the effects of changes in interest rates on discount rates and future growth.

- Regressing changes in operating cash flow against changes in GNP over this period yields the following regression:

$$\text{Change in Operating Income} = 0.25 - 1.16 \, (\text{GNP Growth})$$

Boeing's operating income, like its firm value, is not very sensitive to the economic cycle. This may be because of the lagged effect of GNP growth on operating income.

- Regressing changes in operating cash flow against changes in the dollar over this period yields the following regression:

$$\text{Change in Operating Income} = 0.11 - 0.45 \, (\text{Change in Dollar})$$

Boeing's operating income is not very sensitive to changes in the dollar. In fact, the sign of the relationship is different from the firm value/dollar analysis, suggesting again that, at least during the period of this analysis, the firm was not dependent on exchange rates for its success.

- Regressing changes in operating cash flow against changes in inflation over this period yields the following result:

$$\text{Change in Operating Income} = 0.14 + 3.41(\, (\text{Change in Inflation Rate})$$

Surprisingly, Boeing's operating income seems to increase in periods when inflation increases. This is surprising, given the strong negative relationship between interest rates and operating income. Although the relationship is fairly weak, at this point in time, it might consider issuing some floating rate bonds, if more and more of its contracts are linked to inflation.

- Regressing changes in Boeing's operating income against changes in operating income for the airline business in that year results in the following regression:

$$\text{Change in Operating Income} = 0.04 + 0.0002$$
$$(\text{Change in Operating Income: Airlines})$$

The correlation is close to zero. If Boeing's operating income change is regressed against the operating income change for the airline business in the prior year, there is a stronger positive relationship. Overall, Boeing seems to be less dependent on the health of the U.S. airline business than we originally thought.

Overall Recommendations

Based on the analyses of firm value and operating income, our recommendations would essentially match those we would have given using the intuitive approach. However, they would have more depth to them because of the additional information we have acquired from the quantitative analysis:

- The debt issued should be long term and should have a duration of about 10 years.
- The debt should, for the moment, be primarily fixed rate debt.
- The debt should be dollar-denominated, unless Boeing expects to change its mode of payment on contracts and increase its exposure to exchange rate risk.

Although this type of analysis yields interesting results, those results should be taken with a grain of salt. They make sense only if the firm has been in its current business for a long time and expects to remain in it for the foreseeable future. In today's environment, in which firms find their business mixes changing dramatically from period to period as they reorganize, acquire, divest, or restructure, it may be dangerous to base too many conclusions on a historical analysis. In such cases, it might make more sense to look at the characteristics of the industry in which a firm plans to expand, rather than using past earnings or firm value as a basis for the analysis.

CONCLUSION

In this chapter, we have completed our analysis of capital structure by looking at the ways in which firms can go from identifying their optimal debt ratios to actually devising the right financial mix for themselves. In particular, we noted the following:

- Some firms have to change their leverage quickly to respond to external pressure brought on by the likelihood of an acquisition (if a firm is underlevered) or the chance of bankruptcy (if a firm is overlevered). Those firms that want to increase leverage quickly can do so by borrowing money and repurchasing stock, conducting debt-for-equity swaps, or selling assets and paying large special dividends. Those firms that want to decrease leverage quickly can do so by renegotiating their debt agreements to have more of an equity component or by selling assets and paying off debt.
- Some firms have the luxury of moving to their desired leverage gradually over time; they have to decide whether to take on new projects with the financing or to change the financing mix on their existing projects. That decision should be based on the quality of projects; firms with good projects should finance them with new debt, if they want to increase leverage, or with new equity, if they want to decrease leverage.
- Once firms have decided on new financing, they still have to decide on the maturity, interest rate structure, currency, and special features for their financing. In making these decisions, they should first look at the cash-flow characteristics of the assets that will be funded by the new financing and use other factors (such as taxes, the views of analysts and ratings agencies, agency conflicts, and information factors) to modify the financing to meet their specific objectives.

QUESTIONS AND PROBLEMS

1. BMD Inc. is a firm with no debt on its books currently and a market value of equity of $2 billion. Based on its EBITDA of $200 million, it can afford to have a debt ratio of 50%, at which level the firm value should be $300 million higher.

   a. Assuming that the firm plans to increase its leverage instantaneously, what are some of the approaches it could use to get to 50%?

   b. Is there a difference between repurchasing stock and paying a special dividend? Why or why not?

   c. If BMD has a cash balance of $250 million at this time, will it change any of your analysis?

2. MiniSink Inc. is a manufacturing company that has $100 million in debt outstanding and 9 million shares trading at $100 per share. The current beta is 1.10, and the interest rate on the debt is 8%. In the latest year, MiniSink reported a net income of $7.50 per share, and analysts expect earnings growth to be 10% a year for the next five years. The firm faces a tax rate of 40% and pays out 20% of its earnings as dividends (the Treasury bond rate is 7%).

   a. Estimate the debt ratio each year for the next five years, assuming that the firm maintains its current payout ratio.

   b. Estimate the debt ratio each year for the next five years, assuming that the firm doubles its dividends and repurchases 5% of the outstanding stock every year.

3. IOU Inc. has $5 billion in debt outstanding (carrying an interest rate of 9%) and 100 million shares trading at $50 per share. Based on its current EBIT of $500 million, its optimal debt ratio is only 30%. The firm has a beta of 1.20, the tax rate is 40%, and the current Treasury bond rate is 7%. Assuming that the operating income will increase 10% a year for the next five years and that the firm's depreciation and capital expenditures both amount to $100 million annually for each of the five years, estimate the debt ratio for IOU if

   a. It maintains its existing policy of paying $50 million a year in dividends for the next five years.

   b. It eliminates dividends.

4. DGF Corporation has come to you for some advice on how best to increase its leverage over time. In the most recent year, DGF had EBIT of $300 million, owed $1 billion in both book value and market value terms, and had a net worth of $2 billion. (The market value was twice the book value.) It had a beta of 1.30, and the interest rate on its debt

is 8% (the Treasury bond rate is 7%). If it moves to its optimal debt ratio of 40%, the cost of capital is expected to drop by 1%. The tax rate is 40%.

   a. How should the firm move to its optimal? In particular, should it borrow money and take on projects, or should it pay dividends/repurchase stock?

   b. Are there any other considerations that may affect your decision?

5. STL Inc. has asked you for advice on putting together the details of the new debt issues it is planning to make. What information would you need to obtain to provide this advice?

6. Assume now that you have uncovered the following facts about the types of projects STL takes:

   a. The projects are primarily infrastructure projects, requiring large initial investments and long gestation periods.

   b. Most of the new projects will be in emerging markets, and the cash flows are expected to be in the local currencies, when they do occur.

   c. The magnitude of the cash flows will, in large part, depend on how quickly the economies of the emerging markets grow in the long term.

   How would you use this information in the design of the debt?

7. You are attempting to structure a debt issue for Eaton Corporation, a manufacturer of automotive components. You have collected the following information on the market values of debt and equity for the last 10 years:

Year	Market Value of Equity	Debt
1985	1,824.9	436
1986	2,260.6	632
1987	2,389.6	795
1988	1,960.8	655
1989	2,226	836
1990	1,875.9	755
1991	2,009.7	795
1992	2,589.3	833
1993	3,210	649
1994	3,962.7	1053

In addition, you have the following information on the changes in long-term interest rates, inflation rates, GNP, and exchange rates over the same period:

Year	Long Bond Rate (%)	GNP Growth (%)	Weighted Dollar	Inflation Rate (%)
1985	11.40	6.44	125.95	3.50
1986	9.00	5.40	112.89	1.90
1987	9.40	6.90	95.88	3.70
1988	9.70	7.89	95.32	4.10
1989	9.30	7.23	102.26	4.80
1990	9.30	5.35	96.25	5.40
1991	8.80	2.88	98.82	4.20
1992	8.10	6.22	104.58	3.00
1993	7.20	5.34	105.22	3.00
1994	8.00	5.97	98.6	2.60

a. Estimate the duration of this firm's projects. How would you use this information in designing the debt issue?

b. How cyclical is this company? How would that affect your debt issue?

c. Estimate the sensitivity of firm value to exchange rates. How would you use this information in designing the debt issue?

d. How sensitive is firm value to inflation rates? How would you use this information in designing the debt issue?

e. What factors might lead you to override the results of this analysis?

8. Repeat the analysis in Problem 7 for a private firm that has provided you with the following estimates of operating income for the 10 years for which you have the macroeconomic data:

Year	Operating Income
1985	463.05
1986	411.696
1987	483.252
1988	544.633
1989	550.65
1990	454.875
1991	341.481
1992	413.983
1993	567.729
1994	810.968

9. Assuming that you do the regression analysis with both firm value and operating income, what are the reasons for the differences you might find in the results, using each? When would you use one over the other?

10. Pfizer, a major pharmaceutical company, has a debt ratio of 10.30% and is considering increasing its debt ratio to 30%. Its cost of capital is expected to drop from 14.51% to 13.45%. Pfizer had earnings before interest and taxes of $2 billion in 1995 and a book value of capital (debt + equity) of approximately $8 billion. It also faced a tax rate of 40% on its income. The stock in the firm is widely held, but the corporate charter includes significant anti-takeover restrictions.

a. Should Pfizer move to its desired debt ratio quickly or gradually? Explain.

b. Given the choice in part (a), explain how you would move to the optimal.

c. Pfizer is considering using the excess debt capacity for an acquisition. What are some of the concerns it may have?

11. Upjohn, another major pharmaceutical company, is considering increasing its debt ratio from 11% to 40%, which is its optimal debt ratio. Its beta is 1.17, and the current Treasury bond rate is 6.50%. The return on equity was 14.5% in the most recent year, but it is dropping, as health care matures as a business. The company has also been mentioned as a possible takeover target and is widely held.

a. Would you suggest that Upjohn move to the optimal ratio immediately? Explain.

b. How would you recommend that Upjohn increase its debt ratio?

12. U.S. steel companies have generally been considered mature, in terms of growth, and often take on high leverage to finance their plant and equipment. Steel companies in some emerging markets often have high risk and good growth prospects. Would you expect these companies also to have high leverage? Why or why not?

13. You are trying to decide whether the debt structure that Bethlehem Steel has currently is appropriate, given its assets. You regress changes in firm value against changes in interest rates and arrive at the following equation:

$$\text{Change in Firm Value} = 0.20\% - 6.33 \text{ (Change in Interest Rates)}$$

a. If Bethlehem Steel has primarily short-term debt outstanding, with a maturity of one year, would you deem it appropriate?

b. Why might Bethlehem Steel be inclined to use short-term debt to finance longer term assets?

14. Railroad companies in the United States tend to have long-term, fixed rate, dollar-denominated debt. Explain why.

15. The following table summarizes the results of regressing changes in firm value against changes in interest rates for six major footwear companies:

Change in Firm Value = a + b
(Change in Long-Term Interest Rates)

Company	Intercept (a)	Slope Coefficient (b)
LA Gear	−0.07	−4.74
Nike	0.05	−11.03
Stride Rite	0.01	−8.08
Timberland	0.06	−22.50
Reebok	0.04	−4.79
Wolverine	0.06	−2.42

a. How would you use these results to design debt for each of these companies?

b. How would you explain the wide variation across companies? Would you use the average across the companies in any way?

16. You have run a series of regressions of firm value changes at Motorola, the semiconductor company, against changes in a number of macroeconomic variables. The results as follows:

Change in Firm Value = 0.05 − 3.87
(Change in Long-Term Interest Rate)
Change in Firm Value = 0.02 + 5.76
(Change in Real GNP)
Change in Firm Value = 0.04 − 2.59
(Inflation Rate)
Change in Firm Value = 0.05 − 3.40 ($/DM)

a. Based on these regressions, how would you design Motorola's financing?

b. Motorola, like all semiconductor companies, is sensitive to the health of high-technology companies. Is there any special feature you can add to the debt to reflect this dependence?

17. Assume that you are designing the debt that will be issued by Compaq Computer. Knowing what you do about the business—it is high-growth, high-risk, and extremely volatile—what type of debt would you suggest that Compaq use? Why?

18. Heavily regulated companies in the United States, such as power and phone utilities, are governed by regulatory agencies that grant them rate increases based on inflation. They are also restricted in terms of investment policy and cannot diversify into other businesses. What type of debt would you expect these firms to issue? Why?

19. ACM Inc. is a mining company that holds large stakes in copper, zinc, and magnesium mines around the world. Historically, its revenues and earnings have gone up in periods of high inflation and down during periods of deflation or low inflation. What type of debt would you recommend for ACM Inc.? What special features would you consider adding to this debt?

20. In this chapter, we have argued that firms with substantial cash flows in foreign currencies should consider using debt denominated in those currencies. Can you think of good reasons for such firms to continue to issue debt denominated in the local currency and in local markets?

21. A CFO of a small manufacturing firm with long-term assets argues that it is better to use short-term debt because it is cheaper than long-term debt. This in turn, he notes, reduces the cost of capital. Do you agree? Why or why not?

22. GF Technology Inc. is in the business of manufacturing disk drives for computers. While the underlying business is risky, the managers of GF Technology believe that their cash flows are much more stable than perceived by the market, largely because of several long-term contracts the firm has with major computer manufacturers. They are considering the use of convertible bonds to raise funds for the firms. Would you concur? Why or why not?

23. VisiGen Inc. is a biotechnology firm involved in gene therapy. It is trying to raise funds to finance its research and is weighing the pluses and minuses of issuing stock versus warrants. What would your advice be?

PART FOUR

THE DIVIDEND DECISION

Once a firm has chosen the right projects, and adopted the appropriate financing mix for these projects, it must decide how much of the cash generated by these projects, if any, should be returned to the stockholders, and what form this cash return should take. This decision is covered in the next three chapters. In Chapter 20, we examine the most common approach for returning cash to stockholders, which is cash dividends, and we examine the issues that have to be weighed in deciding how much to pay in dividends. In Chapter 21, we develop a framework for analyzing a firm's cash flows and coming up with the appropriate amount to return to its stockholders. Finally, in Chapter 22, we expand our discussion to consider whether the cash should be returned in the form of dividends, equity repurchases, or forward contracts to buy back stock. We also examine alternative approaches to returning assets, rather than cash, back to stockholders.

CHAPTER 20

THE DETERMINANTS OF DIVIDEND POLICY

As a firm starts receiving cash flows from its current operations, it is faced with a decision. Should it reinvest the cash back into the business, or should it pay it out to equity investors? The decision may seem simple enough, but it evokes a surprising amount of controversy. In this chapter, we look at three very different schools of thought on dividend policy. The first argues that dividends do not really matter because they do not affect value. The second vehemently argues that dividends are bad for the average stockholder, because of the tax disadvantage they create, which results in lower value. The third argues that dividends are clearly good because stockholders like them. In this chapter we probe a series of questions to provide the groundwork for analyzing dividend policy:

- What are the ways in which a firm can return cash to its stockholders?
- What are some of the historical patterns that emerge from an examination of dividend policy over time (for U.S. firms)? How different is dividend policy across countries?
- What is the basis for the argument that dividend policy is irrelevant and does not affect value?
- What is the evidence for the argument that dividends create a tax disadvantage?
- What is behind the notion that some stockholders like dividends?
- What do firms actually look at when they set dividend policy?

WAYS OF RETURNING CASH TO STOCKHOLDERS

Dividends have traditionally been considered the primary approach for publicly traded firms to return cash or assets to their stockholders, but they comprise only one of many ways available to the firm to accomplish this objective. In particular, firms can return cash to stockholders through *equity repurchases,* by which the cash is used to buy back outstanding stock in the firm and reduces the number of shares outstanding, or through *forward contracts,* by which the firm commits to buying back its own stock in future periods at a fixed price. In addition, firms can return some of their assets to their stockholders in the form of spin offs and split offs. This chapter focuses on dividends specifically, but the next two chapters examine the other options that are available to firms, and how to choose between paying dividends and alternative approaches.

THE HISTORICAL EVIDENCE ON DIVIDENDS

Several interesting findings emerge from an examination of the dividend policies practiced by firms in the United States in the last 50 years. First, dividends tend to lag behind earnings; that is, increases in earnings are followed by increases in dividends, and decreases in earnings by dividend cuts. Second, firms are typically reluctant to change dividends; this hesitancy is magnified when it comes to cutting dividends making for "sticky" dividend policies. Third, dividends tend to follow a much smoother path than do earnings. Finally, there are distinct differences in dividend policy over the life cycle of a firm, driven by changes in growth rates, cash flows, and project availability.

Dividends Tend to Follow Earnings

Because dividends are paid out of earnings, it should not come as a surprise that earnings and dividends are positively correlated over time. Figure 20.1 shows the movement in both earnings and dividends between 1960 and 1994. This graph reveals that dividend changes tend to lag behind earnings changes over time, and that the dividend series is much smoother than the earnings series.

In the mid-1950s, John Lintner conducted an extensive analysis of how firms set dividends and concluded that firms have three important concerns. First, they set **target dividend payout ratios,** whereby they decide on the fraction of earnings they are willing to pay out as dividends in the long term. Second, they change dividends to match long-term and sustainable shifts in earnings, but they increase dividends only if they feel they can maintain these higher dividends. As a consequence of this concern over having to cut dividends, dividends lag earnings and have a much smoother path. Finally, managers are much more concerned about changes in dividends rather than about levels of dividends.

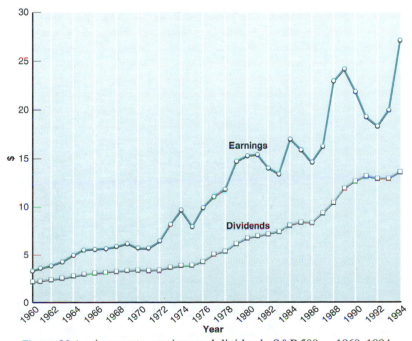

Figure 20.1 Aggregate earnings and dividends: S&P 500 — 1960–1994

Fama and Babiak noted the lagged effect of earnings on dividends, by regressing changes in dividends against changes in earnings in both current and prior periods. They confirmed Lintner's findings that dividend changes tend to follow earnings changes.

Target Dividend Payout Ratio: This is the desired proportion of earnings that a firm wants to pay out in dividends.

Concept Check

What are some of the factors that might determine the extent of the lag between earnings and dividends at a firm?

Dividends Are Sticky

Firms generally do not change their dollar dividends frequently. This reluctance to change dividends, which results in **sticky dividends,** is rooted in several factors. One is the firm's concern about its capability to maintain higher dividends in future periods. Another is the negative market view of dividend decreases and the consequent drop in the stock price. Figure 20.2 provides a summary of the number of firms that increased, decreased, or left their annual dividends unchanged from 1981 to 1990.

Sticky Dividends: This is a reference to the reluctance on the part of firms, empirically, to change dividends from period to period.

As you can see, in most years, the number of firms that do not change their dollar dividends far exceeds the number that do. Among the firms that change dividends, five times as many, on average, increase dividends as decrease them.

Concept Check

The earnings of most cyclical firms decrease during recessions. Should we expect to see most of them cutting dividends as well during these periods? Why or why not?

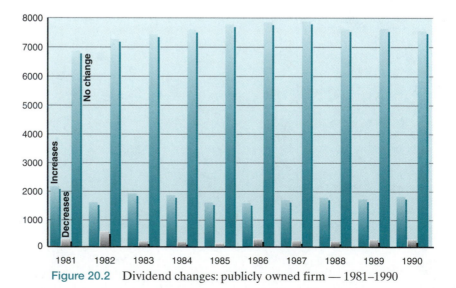

Figure 20.2   Dividend changes: publicly owned firm — 1981–1990

Dividends Follow a Smoother Path than Earnings

As a result of the firms' reluctance to raise dividends until they feel able to maintain them, and to cut dividends unless they absolutely have to, dividends follow a much smoother path than earnings. This stability of dividends is supported by a couple of measures. First, the variability in historical dividends is significantly lower than the variability in historical earnings. Based on annual data on aggregate earnings and dividends from 1960 to 1994, for instance, the standard deviation of dividends is 5.13%, whereas the standard deviation in earnings is 14.09%. Second, the standard deviation in earnings yields across companies is 18.57%, which is significantly higher than the standard deviation of 3.15% in **dividend yields.**

Dividend Yield: This is the dollar dividend per share divided by the current price per share.

A Firm's Dividend Policy Tends to Follow the Life Cycle of the Firm

A firm's life cycle can generally be graphed in terms of investment opportunities and growth. Not surprisingly, firms adopt dividend policies that best fit where they are currently in their life cycles. For instance, high-growth firms with great investment opportunities do not usually pay dividends, whereas stable firms with larger cash flows and fewer projects tend to pay out more of their earnings as dividends. Figure 20.3 graphs the typical path dividend payouts follow over a firm's life cycle.

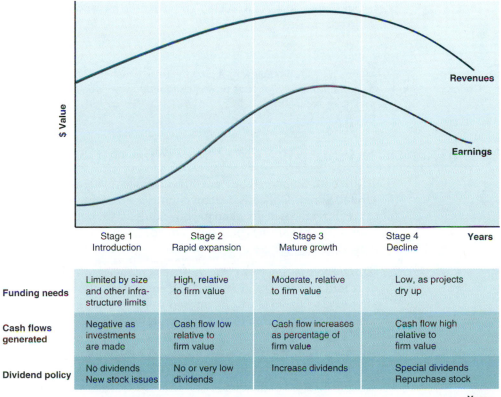

	Stage 1 Introduction	Stage 2 Rapid expansion	Stage 3 Mature growth	Stage 4 Decline	Years
Funding needs	Limited by size and other infra-structure limits	High, relative to firm value	Moderate, relative to firm value	Low, as projects dry up	
Cash flows generated	Negative as investments are made	Cash flow low relative to firm value	Cash flow increases as percentage of firm value	Cash flow high relative to firm value	
Dividend policy	No dividends New stock issues	No or very low dividends	Increase dividends	Special dividends Repurchase stock	

Years

Figure 20.3   Life cycle analysis of dividend policy

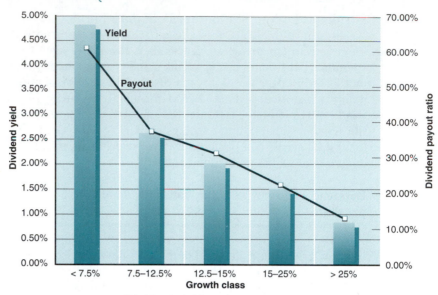

Figure 20.4   Dividend yields and payout ratios: by growth class

This intuitive relationship between dividend policy and growth is reemphasized when payout ratios are correlated with expected growth rates. For instance, looking at all NYSE firms in 1995 and classifying them on the basis of expected growth rates, we estimated the dividend payout ratios and dividend yields by growth class; these are reported in Figure 20.4. As expected growth rates increase, the dividend yields and payout ratios decrease.[1]

□ Concept
Check

Assume that you are following a growth firm in which the growth rates have begun to ease off. If the firm does not start paying dividends, what would you expect to happen to the firm's cash reserves?

DIFFERENCES IN DIVIDEND POLICY ACROSS COUNTRIES

There are both commonalities and differences in dividend policy across countries. As in the United States, dividends in other countries are sticky and follow earnings. However, there are differences in dividend payout ratios across countries. Figure 20.5 summarizes the proportion of earnings paid out in dividends in the G-7 countries in 1982–1984 and again in 1989–1991. These differences can be attributed to a number of factors:

1. *Differences in Stage of Growth:* Just as higher growth companies tend to pay out less in dividends (see Figure 20.3), countries with higher growth pay out less in dividends. For instance, Japan had much higher expected growth in 1982-1984 than the other G-7 countries and paid out a much smaller percentage of its earnings as dividends.

2. *Differences in Tax Treatment:* Unlike the United States, where dividends are double taxed, some of these countries provide at least partial protection against the double taxation of dividends. For instance, Germany taxes corporate retained earnings at a higher rate than corporate dividends.

---

[1]These are growth rates projected by Value Line for firms in October 1995.

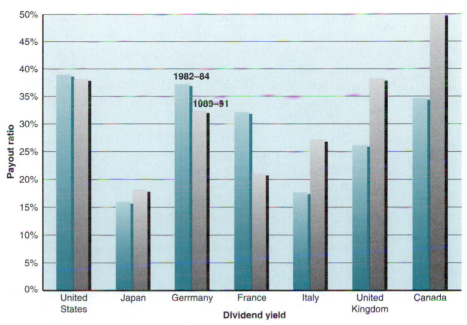

Figure 20.5   Dividend payout ratios in G-7 countries

3. *Differences in Corporate Control:* When there is a separation between ownership and management, as there is in many large publicly traded firms, and stockholders have little control over incumbent managers, the dividends paid by firms will be lower. Managers, left to their own devices, have a much greater incentive to accumulate cash than do stockholders. Not surprisingly, the dividend payout ratios of companies in emerging markets are much lower than the dividend payout ratios in the G-7 countries. The higher growth and relative power of incumbent management in these countries contribute to keeping these payout ratios low .

BACKGROUND ON DIVIDEND PAYMENTS AND POLICY

Firms in the United States generally pay dividends on a quarterly basis, whereas firms in other countries typically pay dividends on a semiannual or annual basis. In this section, we describe the time line associated with the payment of dividends, define different types of dividends, and discuss two widely used measures of dividend policy—the dividend yield and the dividend payout ratio.

The Time Line of Dividends
There are several relevant dates on the time line from the time the board declares the dividend until the dividend is actually paid.

- The first date of note is the *dividend declaration date*—the point at which the board of directors declares the dollar dividend that will be paid for that quarter (or period). This date is important because in announcing its intent to increase, decrease, or maintain dividend, the firms conveys information to financial markets. Thus, if the firm changes its dividends, this is the date on which the market reaction to the change is most likely to occur.

- The next date of note is the **ex-dividend date,** by which time investors have to buy the stock in order to receive the dividend. Because the dividend is not received by investors buying stock after the ex-dividend date, the stock price will generally fall on that day to reflect that loss. The magnitude of the drop, however, will be affected by the tax rates of the marginal investors in the stock.

- The firm paying the dividends closes its books a few days after the ex-dividend date, on the *holder-of-record date*. At the close of business on that day, the company closes its stock transfer books and makes up a list of the shareholders to date. These shareholders will receive the dividends. There should be neither an information nor a price effect on this date.

- The final step involves mailing out the dividend checks on the *payment date*. In most cases, the payment date is two to three weeks after the holder-of-record date. Although stockholders may view this as an important day, there should be no price impact on this day either.

Ex-dividend Date: This is the day by which an investor has to buy stock in order to receive the dividend on the stock.

☐ Concept
   Check

A firm announces an increase in dividends, which is generally considered good news for stock prices. Would you expect stock prices to go up on the ex-dividend day? Why or why not?

Types of Dividends

Dividends can be paid in *cash* or in the form of additional *stock*. Stock dividends increase the number of shares outstanding and generally reduce the price per share; thus, the effect is very similar to a stock split. Dividends can also be *regular dividends,* which are paid at regular intervals (quarterly, semiannual, or annual), or special dividends, which are paid in addition to the regular dividend. Most U.S. firms pay regular dividends every quarter; special dividends are paid at irregular intervals. Finally, firms sometimes pay dividends that are in excess of the retained earnings they show on their books. These are called **liquidating dividends** and are viewed as return on capital rather than ordinary income by the Internal Revenue Service.

Liquidating Dividends: Liquidating dividends are dividends that are larger than the retained earnings on the books.

Measures of Dividend Policy

There are two widely used measures of dividend policy. The first is the *dividend yield,* which relates the dividend paid to the price of the stock:

Dividend Yield = Annual Dividends per share / Price per share

The dividend yield provides a measure of that component of the total return that comes from dividends, with the balance coming from price appreciation.

Expected Return on Stock = Dividend Yield + Price Appreciation

Second, some investors use the dividend yield as a measure of risk and as an investment screen; that is, they invest in stocks with high dividend yields. Studies indicate that stocks with high dividend yields earn excess returns, after adjusting for market performance and risk.

Figure 20.6 tracks dividend yields on stocks listed on the New York Stock Exchange in October 1995. It reveals wide differences across stocks on dividend policy, with a large subset of stocks not paying dividends at all. The median dividend yield of 1.76% and the average dividend yield of 2.11% are low by historical standards, as evidenced by Figure 20.7, which reports average dividend yields by year from 1960 to 1994.

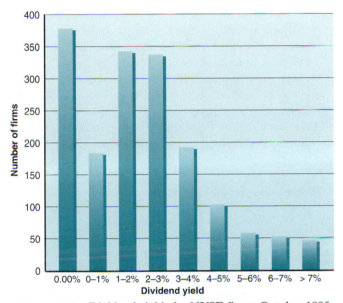

Figure 20.6   Dividend yields for NYSE firms: October 1995

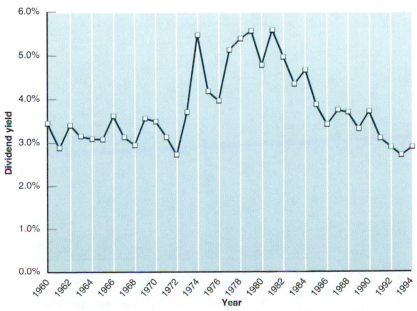

Figure 20.7   Dividend yields on S&P 500 — 1960 – 1994

The second widely used measure of dividend policy is the *dividend payout ratio,* which relates dividends paid to the earnings of the firm.

> Dividend Payout Ratio = Dividends / Earnings

The payout ratio is used in valuation as a way of estimating dividends in future periods, for most analysts estimate growth in earnings rather than dividends. The retention ratio—the proportion of the earnings reinvested back into the firm (Retention Ratio = 1 − Dividend Payout Ratio)—is useful in estimating future growth in earnings. Firms with high retention ratios (low payout ratios) generally have higher growth rates in earnings than do firms with lower retention ratios (higher payout ratios). The dividend payout ratio tends to follow the life cycle of the firm, starting at zero when the firm is in high growth and gradually increasing as the firm matures and its growth prospects decrease. Figure 20.8 graphs the dividend payout ratios of U.S. firms in 1994.

The payout ratios that are greater than 100% represent firms that paid out more than their earnings as dividends. The median dividend payout ratio in 1994 was 24.93%, whereas the average payout ratio was 27.58%.

❑ Concept
Check

How would you explain the behavior of firms that are paying out more than 100% of their earnings as dividends?

WHEN ARE DIVIDENDS IRRELEVANT?

There is a school of thought that argues that what a firm pays in dividends is irrelevant and that stockholders are indifferent about receiving dividends. Like the capital structure irrelevance proposition, the dividend irrelevance argument has its roots in a paper crafted by Miller and Modigliani.

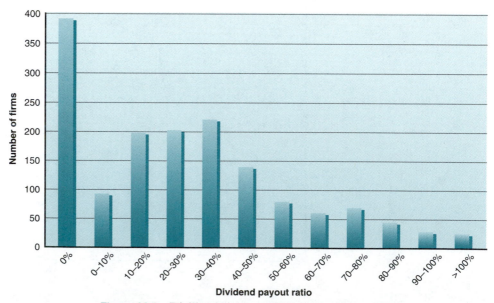

Figure 20.8   Dividend yields on S&P 500 — 1960 – 1994

The Underlying Assumptions

The underlying intuition for the dividend irrelevance proposition is simple. Firms that pay more dividends offer less price appreciation but must provide the same total return to stockholders, given their risk characteristics and the cash flows from their investment decisions. Thus, if there are no taxes, or if dividends and capital gains are taxed at the same rate, investors should be indifferent to receiving their returns in dividends or price appreciation.

For this argument to work, in addition to assuming that there is no tax advantage or disadvantage associated with dividends, we also have to assume the following:

- There are no transactions costs associated with converting price appreciation into cash, by selling stock. If this were *not* true, investors who need cash urgently might prefer to receive dividends.
- Firms that pay too much in dividends can issue stock, again with no flotation or transactions costs, to take on good projects. There is also an implicit assumption that this stock is fairly priced.
- The firm's investment decisions are unaffected by its dividend decisions, and the firm's operating cash flows are the same no matter which dividend policy is adopted.
- Managers of firms that pay too little in dividends do not waste the cash pursuing their own interests (i.e., managers with large free cash flows do not use them to take on bad projects).

Under these assumptions, neither the firms paying the dividends nor the stockholders receiving them will be adversely affected by firms paying either too little or too much in dividends.

☐ Concept
Check

> Assume that a firm that does not pay dividends invests the cash in Treasury bills. Does the fact that the returns earned by these Treasury bills is low make it a bad investment? Why or why not?

A Proof of Dividend Irrelevance

To provide formal proof of irrelevance, assume that LongLast Corporation, an *unlevered* firm manufacturing furniture, has a net operating income after taxes of $100 million, growing at 5% a year, and a cost of capital of 10%. Also assume that this firm has **net capital expenditure** needs (capital expenditures in excess of depreciation) of $50 million, also growing at 5% a year, and that 105 million shares are outstanding. Finally, assume that this firm pays out residual cash flows as dividends each year. The value of LongLast Corporation can be estimated as follows:

$$\text{Free Cash Flow to the Firm} = \text{EBIT} (1 - \text{tax rate}) - \text{Net Capital Expenditures}$$
$$= \$100 \text{ million} - \$50 \text{ million} = \$50 \text{ million}$$
$$\text{Value of the Firm} = \text{Free Cash Flow to Firm} (1 + g) / (\text{WACC} - g)$$
$$= \$50 (1.05) / (.10 - .05) = \$1{,}050 \text{ million}$$
$$\text{Price per share} = \$1{,}050 \text{ million} / 105 \text{ million} = \$10$$

Based on its cash flows, this firm could pay out $50 million in dividends.

$$\text{Dividend per share} = \$50 \text{ million} / 105 \text{ million} = \$0.476$$
$$\text{Total Value per Share} = \$10.00 + \$0.48 = \$10.48$$

■ **Net Capital Expenditures:**   This is the difference between total capital expenditures and depreciation in any period.

To examine how the dividend policy affects firm value, assume that LongLast Corporation is told by an investment consultant that its stockholders would gain if the firm paid out $100 million in dividends, instead of $50 million. It now has to raise $50 million in new financing to cover its net capital expenditure needs. Assume that LongLast Corporation can issue new stock with *no flotation cost* and *no adverse signaling implications* to raise these funds. If it does so, the firm value will remain unchanged, since the value is determined not by the dividend paid but by the cash flows generated on the projects. The stock price will decrease, because there are more shares outstanding, but stockholders will find this loss offset by the increase in dividends per share. In order to estimate the price per share at which the new stock will be issued, note that after the dividend payment, the old stockholders in the firm will own only $1,000 million of the total firm value of $1,050 million.

$$\text{Value of the Firm} = \$1,050 \text{ million}$$
$$\text{Dividends per share} = \$100 \text{ million}/105 \text{ million shares} = \$0.952$$
$$\text{Value of the Firm for existing stockholders after dividend payment} = \$1,000 \text{ million}$$
$$\text{Price per share} = \$1,000 \text{ million} / 105 \text{ million} = \$9.524$$
$$\text{Value accruing to stockholder} = \$9.524 + \$0.952 = \$10.476$$

Another way of seeing this is to divide the stockholders into existing and new stockholders. When dividends are increased by $50 million, and new stock is issued for an equivalent amount, the existing stockholders now own only $1,000 million out of the firm value of $1,050 million, but their loss in firm value is offset by their gain in dividends. In fact, if the operating cash flows are unaffected by dividend policy, we can show that the firm value will be unaffected by dividend policy and that the average stockholder will be indifferent to dividend policy since he or she receives the same total value (price + dividends) under any dividend payment.

To consider an alternative scenario, assume that LongLast Corporation pays out no dividends and retains the residual $50 million as a cash balance. The value of the firm to existing stockholders can then be computed as follows:

$$\text{Value of Firm} = \text{Present Value of After-tax Operating CF} + \text{Cash Balance}$$
$$= \$50 \,(1.05) / (.10 - .05) + \$50 \text{ million} = \$1,100 \text{ million}$$
$$\text{Value per share} = \$1,100 \text{ million} / 105 \text{ million shares} = \$10.476$$

Note that the total value per share is unchanged from the previous two scenarios, as shown in Table 20.1, though all of the value comes from price appreciation.

Table 20.1   VALUE PER SHARE TO EXISTING STOCKHOLDERS FROM DIFFERENT DIVIDEND POLICIES

Value of Firm (Operating CF)	Dividends	Value to Existing Stockholders	Price per Share	Dividends per Share	Total Value per Share
$1,050	$ —	$1,100	$10.48	$ —	$10.48
1,050	10	1,090	10.38	0.10	10.48
1,050	20	1,080	10.29	0.19	10.48
1,050	30	1,070	10.19	0.29	10.48
1,050	40	1,060	10.10	0.38	10.48
1,050	50	1,050	10.00	0.48	10.48
1,050	60	1,040	9.90	0.57	10.48

(continues)

Table 20.1   (<small>CONTINUED</small>)

Value of Firm (Operating CF)	Dividends	Value to Existing Stockholders	Price per Share	Dividends per Share	Total Value per Share
1,050	70	1,030	9.81	0.67	10.48
1,050	80	1,020	9.71	0.76	10.48
1,050	90	1,010	9.62	0.86	10.48
1,050	100	1,000	9.52	0.95	10.48

When LongLast Corporation pays less than $50 million in dividends, the cash accrues in the firm and adds to its value. The increase in the stock price again is offset by the loss of cash flows from dividends.

The irrelevance of dividend policy is grounded on the following assumptions:

- The issue of new stock is assumed to be costless and can therefore cover the cash shortfall created by paying excess dividends.
- It is assumed that firms that face a cash shortfall do not respond by cutting back on projects and thereby affecting future operating cash flows.
- Stockholders are assumed to be indifferent between receiving dividends and price appreciation.
- Any cash remaining in the firm is invested in projects that have zero net present value (such as financial investments) rather than used to take on poor projects.

Implications of Dividend Irrelevance

If dividends are, in fact, irrelevant, firms are spending a great deal of time pondering an issue about which their stockholders are indifferent. A number of strong implications emerge from this proposition. Among them, the value of a firm should not change as its dividend policy changes. This does not imply that the price per share will be unaffected, however, inasmuch as larger dividends should result in lower stock prices and more shares outstanding. In addition, in the long term, there should be no correlation between dividend policy and stock returns. Later in this chapter, we examine some studies that have attempted to examine whether dividend policy is in fact irrelevant in practice.

The assumptions needed to arrive at the dividend irrelevance proposition may seem so onerous that many reject it without testing it. That would be a mistake, however, because the argument does contain a valuable message—namely, a firm that has invested in bad projects cannot hope to resurrect its image with stockholders by offering them higher dividends. In fact, the correlation between dividend policy and total stock returns is weak, as we will see later in this chapter.

THE TAXATION OF DIVIDENDS

The second school of thought on dividends argues that they create a tax disadvantage for the investors who receive them because they are taxed much more heavily than the alternative—capital gains. Carrying this rationale forward, dividend payments should decrease firm value and reduce the returns to stockholders after personal taxes. Consequently, firms will be better off either retaining the money they would have paid out as dividends or repurchasing stock.

Some History on Tax Rates

In the eyes of the Internal Revenue Service, dividends and **capital gains** have always been considered different types of income and, for the most part, are taxed differently. For several decades, until 1986, capital gains in the United States were taxed at a rate that was only 40% of the ordinary tax rate for individuals. Thus, an investor who would have paid a tax rate of 30% on ordinary income would have paid only 12% on capital gains. Under this set-up, the differential advantage of capital gains is clearly a function of the investor's tax rate, with the advantage increasing with the tax rate. In 1979, for example, when the highest marginal tax rate was 70%, some investors were paying 28% on their capital gains (a tax rate differential of 42%). In 1981, a change in the tax law brought the highest marginal tax rate down to 50%, dropping the differential tax advantage to 30%.

Capital Gains (Losses):   This is the portion of the return that an investor earns on an asset that can be attributed to the increase (decrease) in price of that asset.

The Tax Reform Act of 1986 was designed to simplify the tax code. One action it took was to set the same tax rate on dividends and capital gains, capping the highest marginal tax rate at 28%. This simplification did not survive long in practice, however; subsequent changes in the tax law raised the highest marginal tax rate on ordinary income (dividends) to 39.6%, while leaving the capital gains tax rate at 28%.

The tax advantage associated with capital gains for corporations has always been lower than that associated with individuals, even though, for much of the last two decades, the capital gains tax rate has generally been lower than the ordinary tax rate. Obviously, there are no tax differences between dividends and capital gains with pension funds because their income is tax exempt.

In summary, there is a strong factual basis for the argument that historically, in the United States, capital gains have been treated more favorably under tax law than have dividends. The double taxation of dividends—once at the corporate level and once at the investor level—has never been addressed directly in U.S. tax law, but it has been dealt with in other countries in a couple of ways. In some countries, as in Britain, individual investors are allowed a tax credit for the corporate taxes paid on cash flows paid to them as dividends. In other countries, Germany, for example, the portion of the earnings paid out as dividends are taxed at a lower rate than the portion reinvested back into the firm.

The Tax Timing Option

When the 1986 tax law was signed into law, equalizing tax rates on ordinary income and capital gains, some believed that all the tax disadvantages associated with dividends had disappeared. Others noted that, even with the same tax rates, dividends carried a tax disadvantage because the investor had no choice as to when to show the dividend as income; taxes were due when the firm paid out the dividends. In contrast, investors retained discretionary power over when to show and pay taxes on capital gains, because such taxes were not due until the asset was sold. This option allowed investors to reduce the tax liability in one of two ways. First, by taking capital gains in periods when they have low income or capital losses to offset against the gain, investors may be able to reduce the taxes paid. Second, deferring an asset sale until the investor's death may result in tax savings.

Measuring the Dividend Tax Disadvantage

Given the historical evidence that tax rates on dividends have generally been greater than tax rates on capital gains, measuring this tax disadvantage may seem unnecessary. Yet this measurement does provide several pieces of information that may be useful in setting corporate policy. For one thing, it provides the firm with a sense of who its marginal stockholders may be and how they view dividends. Even as individual investors may be bemoaning high dividends, from a tax liability standpoint, pension funds and institutional investors may not have the same misgivings because of their tax-exempt status. This method also gives investors a way of measuring, and sometimes exploiting, differences between their tax rates and those of the marginal investor in the same stock.

Dividends, prices, and ex-dividend days   One of the simplest ways of measuring the tax disadvantage associated with dividends is to measure the price change on the ex-dividend date and compare it to the actual dividend paid. Intuitively, the stock price on the ex-dividend day should drop to reflect the loss in dividends to those buying the stock after that day. It is not clear, however, whether the price drop will be equal to the dividends if dividends and capital gains are taxed at different rates.

To see why, assume that investors in a firm acquired stock at some point in time at a price P and that they are approaching an ex-dividend day, in which the dividend is known to be D. Assume that each investor in this firm can either sell the stock before the ex-dividend day at a price P_B or wait and sell it after the stock goes ex-dividend at a price P_A. Finally, assume that the tax rate on dividends is t_o and that the tax rate on capital gains is t_{cg}. The cash flows the investor will receive from selling *before* the stock goes ex-dividend can be written as

$$CF_B = P_B - (P_B - P)\, t_{cg}$$

The investor receives no dividend. If the sale occurs *after* the ex-dividend day, the cash flow can be written as

$$CF_A = P_A - (P_A - P)\, t_{cg} + D\,(1 - t_o)$$

If the cash flow from selling before the ex-dividend day were greater than the cash flow from selling after, all the investors would sell before, resulting in a drop in the stock price and an unstable market. Similarly, if the cash flows from selling after the ex-dividend day were greater than the cash flows from selling before, everyone would sell after. The result would be a price drop after the ex-dividend day and an unstable market. For this market to be stable, the marginal investors in the stock have to be indifferent between selling before or after the ex-dividend day. This will occur only if the cash flows from selling before are equal to the cash flows from selling after:

$$P_B - (P_B - P)\, t_{cg} = P_A - (P_A - P)\, t_{cg} + D\,(1 - t_o)$$

This can be simplified to yield the following ex-dividend day equality:

$$\frac{P_B - P_A}{D} = \frac{(1 - t_o)}{(1 - t_{cg})}$$

Thus, a necessary condition for the marginal investor to be indifferent between selling before or after the ex-dividend day is that the price drop on the ex-dividend day must reflect the investor's tax differential between dividends and capital gains.

Turning this equation around, it can be argued that by observing a firm's stock price behavior on the ex-dividend day and relating it to the dividends paid by the firm, one can, in the long term, form some conclusions about the tax disadvantage the firm's stockholders attach to dividends. In particular:

If	Tax Treatment of Dividends and Capital Gains
$P_B - P_A = D$	Marginal investor is indifferent between dividends and capital gains.
$P_B - P_A < D$	Marginal investor is taxed more heavily on dividends.
$P_B - P_A > D$	Marginal investor is taxed more heavily on capital gains.

Some obvious measurement and noise problems are associated with this measure, but all the same it does provide some interesting insight into how investors view - dividends.

Ex-dividend day price behavior: the evidence   The earliest study of ex-dividend day price changes was done by Elton and Gruber in 1970. They examined the behavior of stock prices on ex-dividend days for stocks listed on the NYSE between 1966 and 1969. Based on their finding that the price drop was only 78% of the dividends paid, Elton and Gruber concluded that dividends are taxed more heavily than capital gains. They also estimated the price change as a proportion of the dividend paid for firms in different dividend yield classes and reported that price drop is a larger proportion of dividends for firms in the highest dividend yield classes. This, they argued, reflected the fact that investors in these firms are in lower tax brackets. Their conclusions were challenged, however, by those who argue, justifiably, that the investors trading on the stock on ex-dividend days are not the normal investors in the firm. Rather, they are short-term, tax-exempt investors interested in capturing the difference between dividends and the price drops.

In the years since, the highest marginal tax rate on dividends has dropped, especially in the aftermath of the changes to the tax law in 1981 and again in 1986. The composition of investors buying stocks also has changed—a greater proportion of stocks are now held by institutional investors and, in particular, tax-exempt institutional investors. Moreover, as transactions costs have dropped, investors have available to them a number of ways of generating cash from their stockholdings, without dividend payments. Consequently, we would expect the implicit tax differential, reflected in the proportional price drop, to decrease substantially over time.

☐ Concept Check

How would you defend these studies against the criticism that they do not factor in market movements on the ex-dividend days? For instance, the stock price may go up on an ex-dividend day because the market is up strongly, and this may overwhelm the dividend effect.

Dividend capture and arbitrage   If, as these studies suggest, the price drop on the ex-dividend day is less than the dividend to accommodate the tax preferences of the marginal investors, the possibility exists that investors with tax rates different from these marginal investors may be able to make excess returns by trading on or around the ex-dividend day. For example, consider a tax-exempt pension fund that is indifferent between dividends and capital gains. This investor could buy stock before the ex-dividend day (cum-dividend), sell it after it goes ex-dividend, collect the dividend, and wind up with a profit because the dividend exceeds the price drop.

This profit is predicated on several assumptions and may carry some risk. First, the ex-dividend behavior of stock prices measured by these studies looks at the average price drop, relative to dividends, across a large number of stocks and ex-dividend dates spread out over time. On any particular stock, on a specific ex-dividend day, the behavior of the stock price may be very different from these averages. Thus, for **dividend capture** to work, the tax-exempt entity has to be able to diversify its exposure to this risk. Second, certain transactions costs are associated with this strategy that, if large enough, might wipe out the potential gains. This strategy is more likely to work, therefore, for stocks with high dividend yields.

Dividend Capture: This refers to the practice of buying stocks just before ex-dividend dates with the intention of receiving the dividends on these stocks.

 IN PRACTICE   DIVIDEND CAPTURE: TEXAS UTILITIES

To provide an example of dividend capture, consider Texas Utilities, which pays a quarterly dividend of $0.77. Assume that the stock is trading at $35 per share and that tomorrow is an ex-dividend date. Also assume that the price drop on the ex-dividend day is expected to be only 85% of the dividend, based on price behavior on previous ex-dividend days.

Suppose that you are a tax-exempt investor and you carry out the following sequence of actions:

- On the day before the ex-dividend day, you buy 1 million shares at $35 per share.
- At the end of the ex-dividend day, you sell the shares at an expected price of $34.35.

$$\text{Expected Price} = \$35 - \$0.77\,(.85) = \$34.35$$

- You collect the dividend, when paid, of $0.77 per share on 1 million shares.

This strategy will yield the following profit prior to transaction costs:

$$\text{Expected Profit} = \$34.35 \text{ million} + \$0.77 \text{ million} - \$35 \text{ million} = \$0.12 \text{ million}$$

The profits (if any) after transactions costs will represent the net profit from this strategy.

Implications   Dividends have historically been treated less favorably than capital gains by the tax authorities. In the United States, the double taxation of dividends, at least at the level of individual investors, should create a strong disincentive to pay or to increase dividends. Other implications of the tax disadvantage argument include the following:

- Firms with an investor base composed primarily of individuals should have lower dividends than do firms with investor bases predominantly made up of tax-exempt institutions.
- The higher the income level (and hence the tax rates) of the investors holding stock in a firm, the lower the dividend paid out by the firm.
- As the tax disadvantage associated with dividends increases, the aggregate amount paid in dividends decreases. Conversely, if the tax disadvantage associated with dividends decreases, the aggregate amount paid in dividends increases. For instance, the change in the tax law in 1986 should have caused a surge in dividend payments by firms, because it eliminated the distinction between dividends and capital gains.

 Concept Check

Companies generally do not have to pay taxes on 85% of the dividends they receive from other companies, but they have to pay capital gains taxes on all of their gains. What implications does this have for the relative tax advantages of dividends and capital gains?

SOME DUBIOUS REASONS FOR PAYING DIVIDENDS

Notwithstanding the tax disadvantages, firms continue to pay dividends and typically view such payments positively. There are a number of reasons for paying dividends, but only a few of them stand up to rational scrutiny, as we discuss in the following sections.

The Bird-in-the-Hand Fallacy

One rationalization given for why dividends are better than capital gains is that dividends are certain, whereas capital gains are uncertain; risk-averse investors, it is argued, will therefore prefer dividends. This argument is severely flawed, however. The simplest counter-response is to point out that the choice is not between certain dividends today and uncertain capital gains at some unspecified point in the future, but between dividends today and an almost equivalent amount in price appreciation today. This follows from our earlier discussion, where we noted that the stock price dropped by slightly less than the dividend on the ex-dividend day. By paying the dividend, the firm causes its stock price to drop today.

Another response to this argument is that a firm's value is determined by the cash flows from its projects. If a firm increases its dividends, but its investment policy remains unchanged, it will have to replace the dividends with new stock issues. Investors who receive the higher dividend will therefore find themselves losing, in present value terms, an equivalent amount in price appreciation.

Temporary Excess Cash

In some cases, firms are tempted to pay or initiate dividends in years in which their operations generate excess cash. Although it is perfectly legitimate to return excess cash to stockholders, firms should also consider their own long-term investment needs. If the excess cash is a temporary phenomenon, resulting from having an unusually good year or a nonrecurring action (such as the sale of an asset), and the firm expects cash shortfalls in future years, it may be better off retaining the cash to cover some or all of these shortfalls. Another option is to pay the excess cash as a dividend in the current year and issue new stock when the cash shortfall occurs. This is not very practical, for the substantial expense associated with new security issues makes this a costly strategy in the long term. Table 20.2 summarizes the cost of issuing bonds, preferred stock, and common stock, by size of issue.

Table 20.2   ISSUANCE COST FOR SECURITIES

Size of Issue	Bonds	Preferred Stock	Common Stock
		Cost of Issuing Securities	
Under $1 mil	14.0	—	22.0
$1.0–1.9 mil	11.0	—	16.9
$2.0–4.9 mil	4.0	—	12.4
$5.0–$9.9 mil	2.4	2.6	8.1
$10–19.9 mil	1.2	1.8	6.0
$20–49.9 mil	1.0	1.7	4.6
$50 mil and over	0.9	1.6	3.5

This said, it is important to note that some companies do pay dividends and issue stock during the course of the same period, mostly out of a desire to maintain their dividends. Figure 20.9 summarizes new stock issues by firms as a percentage of firm value, classified by their dividend yields.

Although it is not surprising that stocks that pay no dividends are most likely to issue stock, it is surprising that firms in the highest dividend yield class also issue significant proportions of new stock. (Approximately half of all the firms in this class also make new stock issues.) This suggests that many of these firms are paying dividends, on the one hand, and issuing stock, on the other.

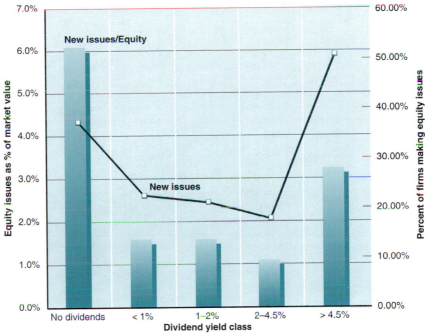

Figure 20.9   Equity issues by dividend class

SOME GOOD REASONS FOR PAYING DIVIDENDS

There are several reasons why firms continue to pay dividends, ranging from investor preferences to clientele effects to information signaling.

Some Investors Like Dividends

Many members of the "dividends are bad" school of thought argue that rational investors should reject dividends because of the tax disadvantage they carry. Whatever one might think of the merits of that argument, some investors do have a strong preference for dividends and view large dividends positively. The most striking empirical evidence for this comes from studies of companies that have two classes of shares: one that pays cash dividends, and another that pays an equivalent amount of stock dividends. Thus, investors are given a choice between dividends and capital gains.

John Long (1978) studied the price differential on Class A and B shares traded on Citizens Utility, an electric utility in the North-East United States. Class B shares paid a cash dividend, whereas Class A shares paid an equivalent stock dividend. Moreover, Class A shares could be converted at little or no cost to Class B shares at the option of its stockholders. Thus, an investor could choose to buy Class B shares to get cash dividends, or Class A shares to get an equivalent capital gain. During the period of this study, the tax advantage was clearly on the side of capital gains; thus, we would expect to find Class B shares selling at a discount on Class A shares. The study found, surprisingly, that the Class B shares sold at a premium over Class A shares. Figure 20.10 summarizes the price differential between the two share classes over the period of the analysis.

We could easily ascribe this phenomenon to irrational investors, but this is not the case. Not all investors like dividends—many see its tax burden as onerous—conversely, many view it positively, for a number of reasons. These investors may not be paying much in taxes and, consequently, do not care about the tax disadvantage associated with dividends. Or, they might need and value the cash flow generated by the dividend payment.

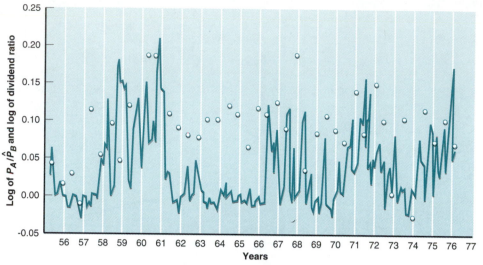

Figure 20.10   Price differential on Citizen's utility stock

Some analysts maintain that the same amount can be raised in cash by selling stock, but the transactions costs and the difficulty of breaking up small holdings and selling unit shares may not make this approach feasible.

Bailey (1988) extended Long's study to examine Canadian utility companies, which also offered dividend and capital gains shares, and had similar findings. Table 20.3 summarizes the price premium at which the dividend shares sold.

Table 20.3   PRICE DIFFERENTIAL BETWEEN CASH
AND STOCK DIVIDEND SHARES

Company	Premium on Cash Dividend Shares over Stock Dividend Shares (%)
Consolidated Bathurst	19.30
Donfasco	13.30
Dome Petroleum	0.30
Imperial Oil	12.10
Newfoundland Light & Power	1.80
Royal Trustco	17.30
Stelco	2.70
TransAlta	1.10
Average	**8.5%**

Note, once again, that, on average, the cash dividend shares sell at a premium of 8.5% over the stock dividend shares. We caution that, although these findings do not indicate that *all* stockholders like dividends, they do indicate that the stockholders in these specific companies liked cash dividends so much that they were willing to overlook the tax disadvantage and pay a premium for shares that offered them.

The Clientele Effect

Stockholders in the companies covered by the studies mentioned in the last section clearly like cash dividends. At the other extreme are companies that pay no dividends, such as Microsoft, and whose stockholders seem perfectly content with that policy. Given the vast diversity of stockholders, it is not surprising that, over time, stockholders tend to invest in firms whose dividend policies match their preferences. Stockholders in high tax brackets, who do not need the cash flow from dividend payments, tend to invest in companies that pay low or no dividends. By contrast, stockholders in low tax brackets, who need the cash from dividend payments, and tax-exempt institutions that need current cash flows will usually invest in companies with high dividends. This clustering of stockholders in companies with dividend policies that match their preferences is called the **clientele effect.**

Dividend Clientele Effect: This refers to the tendency of investors to buy stock in firms that have dividend policies that meet their preferences for high, low, or no dividends.

The existence of a clientele effect is supported by empirical evidence. One study looked at the portfolios of 914 investors to determine whether their portfolio positions were affected by their tax brackets. Not surprisingly, the study found that older and poorer investors were more likely to hold stocks paying high dividends than were younger and wealthier investors.

In another study, dividend yields were regressed against the characteristics of the investor base of a company (including age, income, and differential tax rates), as shown in Table 20.4.

Table 20.4

$$\text{Dividend Yield}_t = a + b\,\beta_t + c\,\text{Age}_t + d\,\text{Income}_t + e\,\text{Differential Tax Rate}_t + \epsilon_t$$

Variable	Coefficient	Implies
Constant	4.22%	
Beta coefficient	−2.145	Higher beta stocks pay lower dividends.
Age/100	3.131	Firms with older investors pay higher dividends.
Income/1000	−3.726	Firms with wealthier investors pay lower dividends.
Differential tax rate	−2.849	If ordinary income is taxed at a higher rate than capital gains, the firm pays less dividends.

Not surprisingly, this study found that safer companies, with older and poorer investors, tended to pay more in dividends than companies with wealthier and younger investors. Overall, dividend yields decreased as the tax disadvantage of dividends increased.

❏ Concept
  Check

> Consider the special case of pension funds, which pay no taxes on dividends or capital gains. What types of stocks are these funds likely to hold and why?

Implications of the clientele effect   The existence of a clientele effect has some important implications. First, it suggests that firms get the investors they deserve, for a firm's dividend policy attracts investors who like it. Second, it means that firms will have a difficult time changing an established dividend policy, even if it makes complete sense to do so. For instance, U.S. telephone companies have traditionally paid high dividends and acquired an investor base that liked these dividends. In the 1990s, many of these firms turned toward multimedia businesses, with much larger reinvestment needs and less stable cash flows. Although the need to cut dividends in the face of the changing business mix might seem obvious, it was nevertheless a hard sell to stockholders, who had become used to the dividends.

The clientele effect also provides an alternative argument for the irrelevance of dividend policy, at least when it comes to valuation. In summary, if investors migrate to firms that pay the dividends that most closely match their needs, it can be argued that the value of any firm should not be determined by dividend policy. Thus, a firm that pays no or low dividends should not be penalized for doing so, because its investors *do not* want dividends. Conversely, a firm that pays high dividends should not have a lower value, since its investors like dividends. This argument assumes that there are enough investors in each dividend clientele to allow firms to be fairly valued, no matter what their dividend policy.

❑ Concept Check

> Over the last 30 years, the proportion of the market value of stocks held by pension funds has increased substantially. What implications does this trend have for dividend policy in the aggregate and why?

Empirical evidence   The question of whether the clientele effect is strong enough to divorce the value of stocks from dividend policy is an empirical one. If the effect is strong enough, the returns on stocks, over long periods, should not be affected by their dividend policies. If there is a tax disadvantage associated with dividends, however, the returns on stocks that pay high dividends should be higher than the returns on stocks that pay low dividends in order to compensate for the tax differences. Finally, if there is an overwhelming preference for dividends, these results should be reversed.

Black and Scholes (1974) examined this question by creating 25 portfolios of NYSE stocks, classifying firms into five quintiles based on dividend yield, and then subdividing each group into five additional groups based on risk (beta), each year for 35 years, from 1931 and 1966. When they regressed total returns on these portfolios against the dividend yields, they found no statistically significant relationship between the two. These findings were contested in a later study by Litzenberger and Ramaswamy (1979), who used updated dividend yields every month and examined whether the total returns in ex-dividend months were correlated with dividend yields. They found a strong *positive* relationship between total returns and dividend yields, supporting the hypothesis that investors are averse to dividends. They also estimated that the implied tax differential between capital gains and dividends was approximately 23%. Miller and Scholes (1981) countered by arguing that this finding was contaminated by the information effects of dividend increases and decreases. In response, they removed from the sample all cases in which the dividends were declared and paid in the same month and concluded that the implied tax differential was only 4%, which was not significantly different from zero.

In the interests of fairness, we point out that most studies of this phenomenon have concluded that total returns and dividend yields are positively correlated. Although many of these studies contend that this is because the implied tax differential between dividends and capital gains is significantly different from zero, there are alternative explanations for the phenomenon. In particular, while one may disagree with Miller and Scholes' conclusions, there is both a theoretical and an empirical basis for their argument that the higher returns on stocks that pay high dividends might have nothing to do with the tax disadvantages associated with dividends but may in fact reflect the price increases associated with unexpected dividend increases.

Information Signaling
Financial markets examine every action a firm takes for implications about future cash flows and firm value. When firms announce changes in dividend policy, they are conveying information to markets, whether or not that is their intent. There are a couple of stories that can be told about what information dividend changes *signal* to financial markets.

Dividends as a positive signal Financial markets tend to view announcements made by firms about their future prospects with a great deal of skepticism mainly because firms routinely make exaggerated claims. At the same time, some firms, with good projects, are undervalued by markets. How do such firms convey information credibly to markets? *Signaling theory* suggests that these firms need to take actions that cannot be easily imitated by firms without good projects. Increasing dividends can be viewed as one such action. By increasing dividends, firms create a cost to themselves, for they commit themselves to paying these dividends in the long term. The fact that they are willing to make this commitment indicates to investors that they believe they have the capacity to generate these cash flows in the long term. This positive signal should therefore lead to a reevaluation of the cash flows and firm values and an increase in the stock price.

Decreasing dividends operates as a negative signal, largely because firms are reluctant to cut dividends. Thus, when firms take this action, markets see it as an indication that these firms are in substantial and long-term financial trouble. Consequently, such actions lead to a drop in stock prices.

The empirical evidence concerning price reactions to dividend increases and decreases is consistent, at least on average, with these stories. Figure 20.11 summarizes the average excess returns around dividend changes for firms.

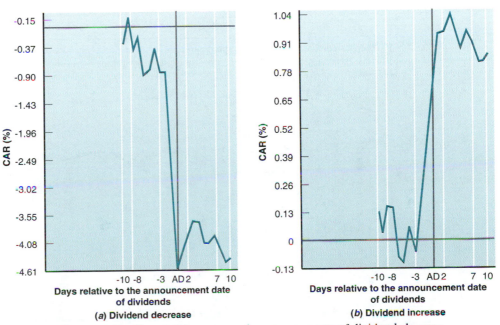

Figure 20.11   Excess returns around announcements of dividend changes

This explanation of why firms increase dividends has to be considered with some caution, however. Although firms with good projects may use dividend increases as a way of conveying information to financial markets, given the substantial tax liability that it may create for stockholders, is it the most efficient way? For smaller firms, which have relatively few signals available to them, the answer might be yes. For larger firms, which have many ways of conveying information to markets, dividend changes might not be the least expensive or the most effective signals. For instance, the information may be more effectively and economically conveyed through an analyst's report on the company.

Dividends as a negative signal An equally plausible story can be told about how an increase in dividends sends a negative signal to financial markets. Consider a firm that has never paid dividends in the past, but has registered extraordinary growth and high returns on its projects. When this firm first starts paying dividends, its stockholders may consider this an indication that the firm's projects are neither as plentiful nor as lucrative as they used to be.

Table 20.5, reproduced from Palepu and Healy (1986), reports the earnings growth around dividend initiations for 151 firms from 1970 to 1979.

Table 20.5 **EARNINGS GROWTH AROUND DIVIDEND INITIATIONS**

Year Relative to Dividend Initiation	Number of Firms	Mean Earnings Growth Rate	Median Earnings Growth Rate
−4	130	14.9%	17.4%
−3	129	−7.1	7.6
−2	128	12.9	10.5
−1	131	42.7[a]	28.0
1	130	55.0[a]	40.2
2	130	22.0[a]	35.9
3	130	35.0[a]	28.2
4	128	3.5	19.5

[a]In their original research they compute earnings performance as earnings changes standardized by stock process. Here they convert these values to earnings growth rates by assuming that the average price earnings ratio for the sample firms is ten.

**Significantly different from zero at the 10% level or lower.

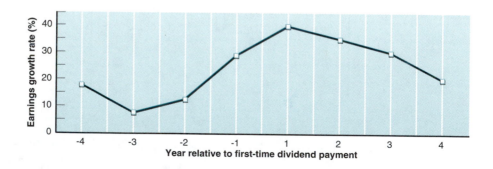

As you can see, the earnings growth rate increases significantly after dividends are initiated, and so dividends may operate as positive signals of future earnings growth even for these firms.

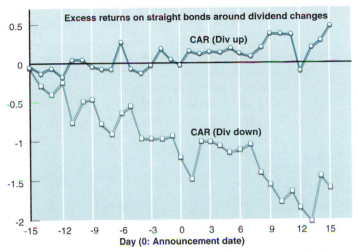

Figure 20.12   Excess returns on straight bonds around dividend changes

STOCKHOLDERS, BONDHOLDERS, AND DIVIDENDS

The question of how much to pay in dividends is intimately connected to the firm's financing decisions—that is, how much debt the firm should carry. In Chapter 19, we examined how firms that want to increase or decrease leverage can do so by changing their dividend policy: increasing dividends increases leverage, and decreasing dividends reduces leverage. In the previous chapters, we also outlined the interests of bondholders in dividend policy. Firms that increase dividends may harm bondholders by increasing their default risk, thus reducing the market value of bonds. Figure 20.12 shows the reaction of bond prices to dividend increases and decreases.

In response to this threat to their interests, bondholders often write in specific covenants into bond agreements on dividend policy, restricting the payment of dividends. These restrictions often play a role in determining a firm's dividend policy.

STOCKHOLDERS, MANAGERS, AND DIVIDENDS

In examining debt policy, we noted that one reason for taking on more debt was to induce managers to be more disciplined in their project choice. Implicit in this free-cash-flow argument is the assumption that cash accumulations, if left to the discretion of the managers of the firm, would be wasted on poor projects. If this is true, we can argue that forcing a firm to make a commitment to pay dividends provides an alternative way of forcing managers to be disciplined in project choice and to reducing the cash that is available for discretionary uses.

If this is the reason why stockholders want managers to make a commitment to paying larger dividends, firms in which there is a clear separation between ownership and management should pay larger dividends than should firms with substantial insider ownership and involvement in managerial decisions.

Survey Results

Given the pros and cons for paying dividends, and the lack of a consensus on the effect of dividends on value, it is worth considering what managers factor in when they make dividend decisions. Baker, Farrely and Edelman (1985) surveyed managers on their views on dividend policy and reported the level of agreement with a series of statements. Table 20.6 summarizes their findings.

Table 20.6 MANAGEMENT BELIEFS ABOUT DIVIDEND POLICY (PERCENTAGE DISTRIBUTION)

Statement of Management Beliefs	Agree	No Opinion	Disagree
1. A firm's dividend payout ratio affects the price of the stock.	61	33	6
2. Dividend payments provide a signaling device of future prospects.	52	41	7
3. The market uses divided announcements as information for assessing firm value.	43	51	6
4. Investors have different perceptions of the relative riskiness of dividends and retained earnings.	56	42	2
5. Investors are basically indifferent with regard to returns from dividends and capital gains.	6	30	64
6. A stockholder is attracted to firms that have dividend policies appropriate to the stockholder's tax environment.	44	49	7
7. Management should be responsive to shareholders' preferences regarding dividends.	41	49	10

This survey clearly shows that, rightly or wrongly, managers believe that their dividend payout ratios affect firm value and operate as signals of future prospects. They also operate under the presumption that investors choose firms with dividend policies that match their preferences and that management should be responsive to their needs.

CONCLUSION

Like investment and financing decisions, dividend decisions involve tradeoffs, although there seems to be little consensus on where the tradeoffs should lead us in terms of the "right" dividend policy. On the one hand, some believe that owing to the tax disadvantages associated with receiving dividends, relative to price appreciation, firms should reduce or even eliminate dividends and consider alternative ways of returning cash to stockholders. On the other hand, many argue that dividend increases operate as positive financial signals and that some investors like dividends, notwithstanding the tax disadvantages. Finally, there is the school of thought that contends that dividend policy should not really affect value, as long as it does not affect the firm's investment policy. This argument maintains that, as long as there are enough investors in each dividend clientele, firms should not be penalized for adopting a particular dividend policy.

In summary, there is some truth to all of these viewpoints, and it may be possible to develop a consensus around the points on which they agree. The reality is that dividend policy requires a tradeoff between the additional tax liability it may create for some investors against the potential signaling and free-cash-flow benefits of making the additional commitment. In some cases, the firm may choose not to increase or initiate dividends because its stockholders are in high tax brackets and are particularly averse to dividends. In other cases, dividend increases may result.

QUESTIONS AND PROBLEMS

1. Based on the empirical evidence that you have been presented with in this chapter, state whether the following statements are true or false.

   a. Firms are reluctant to change dividends.
   True   False

   b. Stock prices generally go up on the ex-dividend date by less than the amount of the dividend.
   True   False

   c. Increasing dividend payments to stockholders generally makes bondholders in the firm better off.
   True   False

2. Dividend policy is often described as "sticky." What is meant by this description? What might explain the sticky nature of dividends?

3. Companies are far more reluctant to cut dividends than to increase them. Why might this be the case? What are the implications for financial markets when firms announce that they will be cutting dividends?

4. Under what assumptions can the Miller–Modigliani argument that dividends are irrelevant be made? What types of firms are most likely to fit these assumptions?

5. Dividends create a tax disadvantage for investors. Is this statement true for all investors and all markets? Under what conditions is it *not* true?

6. A company that historically has had low capital investments and paid out high dividends is entering a new industry, in which capital expenditure requirements are much higher. What should the firm do to its dividends? What practical problems might it run into?

7. "An increase in dividends operates as a positive financial signal." Explain this statement. Is there empirical evidence to support it?

8. Can a dividend increase ever be a negative financial signal? Explain. Is there any evidence to support this hypothesis?

9. If Consolidated Power is priced at $50 with dividend, and its price falls to $46.50 when a dividend of $5 is paid, what is the implied marginal rate of personal taxes for its stockholders? Assume that the tax on capital gains is 40% of the personal income tax.

10. Show that, if companies are excluded from paying taxes on 85% of the dividends they receive from other corporations and if the marginal investor is a corporation, then the ex-dividend day equality becomes

$$\frac{P_B - P_A}{D} = \frac{(1 - .15t_o)}{(1 - t_{cg})}$$

11. You are comparing the dividend policies of three dividend-paying utilities. You have collected the following information on the ex-dividend behavior of these firms.

	NE Gas	SE Bell	Western Electric
Price before	$50	$70	$100
Price after	48	67	95
Dividends/share	4	4	5

If you were a tax-exempt investor, which company would you use to make "dividend arbitrage" profits? How would you go about doing so?

12. Southern Rail has just declared a dividend of $1. The average investor in Southern Rail faces an ordinary tax rate of 50%. Although the capital gains rate is also 50%, it is believed that the investor gets the advantage of deferring this tax until future years. (The effective capital gains rate will therefore be 50% discounted back to the present.) If the price of the stock before the ex-dividend day is $10 and it drops to $9.20 by the end of the ex-dividend day, how many years is the average investor deferring capital gains taxes? (Assume that the opportunity cost used by the investor in evaluating future cash flows is 10%.)

13. LMN Corporation, a real estate corporation, is planning to pay a dividend of $0.50 per share. Most of the investors in LMN Corporation are other corporations, who pay 40% of their ordinary income and 28% of their capital gains as taxes. However, they are allowed to exempt 85% of the dividends they receive from taxes. If the shares are selling at $10 per share, how much would you expect the stock price to drop on the ex-dividend day?

14. UJ Gas is a utility that has followed a policy of increasing dividends every quarter by 5% over dividends in the prior year. The company announces that it will increase quarterly dividends from $1.00 to $1.02 next quarter. What price reaction would you expect to the announcement? Why?

15. Microsoft Corporation, which has had a history of high growth and no dividends, announces that it will start paying dividends next quarter. How would you expect its stock price to react to the announcement? Why?

16. JC Automobiles is a small auto parts manufacturing firm, which has paid $1.00 in annual dividends each year for the last five years. It announces that dividends will increase to $1.25 next year. What would you expect the price reaction to be? Why? If your answer is different from the prior problem, explain the reasons for the difference.

17. Would your answer be different for the previous problem if JC Automobiles were a large firm followed by 35 analysts? Why or why not?

18. WeeMart Corporation, a retailer of children's clothes, announces a cut in dividends following a year in which both revenues and earning dropped significantly. How would you expect its stock price to react? Explain.

19. RJR Nabisco, in response to stockholder pressure in 1996, announced a significant increase in dividends paid to stockholders, financed by the sale of some of its assets. What would you expect the stock price to do? Why?

20. RJR Nabisco also had $10 billion in bonds outstanding at the time of the dividend increase. How would you expect Nabisco's bonds to react to the announcement? Why?

21. A recent innovation in managerial incentive schemes is for the shareholders of a corporation to partially compensate management with stock options. How could such a scheme affect management's decisions concerning optimal dividend policy?

22. If the next tax reform act were to impose a flat tax of 23% on all income, how do you think this would affect corporations' dividend policies? Why?

23. This chapter has demonstrated the consequences of differential taxation of dividends and capital gains: firms have weakened incentives to pay dividends. Why would the U.S. government (acting through the IRS) want these consequences?

CHAPTER 21

A FRAMEWORK FOR ANALYZING DIVIDEND POLICY

In the last chapter, we examined three schools of thought on dividends which came to very different conclusions. Here, we provide a framework that considers points raised by all three schools of thought and provides specific answers to the following questions:

- When should a firm be pressured to increase its payouts to stockholders, and how can such a firm defend itself?

- When should a firm be pressured to reduce its payouts to stockholders, and what are the consequences of excessive dividends?

- What types of firms have the most flexibility in setting dividend policy?

- How should firms measure their dividend policies against comparable firms?

BRINGING IT ALL TOGETHER

Each of the three schools of thought on dividend policy raises some legitimate points. The dividend irrelevancy school emphasizes that the firm's value cannot be changed by dividend decisions and that firms attract stockholders who like their dividend policy. The "dividends are good" school is also grounded on the notion of investor clienteles, but it assumes that stockholders for the most part like dividends and view dividend increases as a positive signal. The "dividends are bad" school is predicated on the tax disadvantages that accrue when dividends are paid.

The Tradeoffs

A firm has to walk a tightrope when it establishes its dividend policy. On the one hand, paying too much in dividends creates several problems: the firm may find itself short of funds for new investments and may have to incur the cost associated with new security issues or capital rationing, and the investors receiving the dividends may face a much larger tax liability. On the other hand, paying too little in dividends can also create problems. For one, the firm will find itself with a cash balance that increases over time, which can lead to investments in "bad" projects, especially when the interests of management in the firm are different from those of the stockholders. In response, some argue for leverage as a way of inducing discipline in the firm. In addition, paying too little in dividends may transfer wealth from stockholders to bondholders, especially if bond prices are set on the assumption that the firm will maintain a reasonable dividend payout.

Determinants of Dividend Policy

Concerning the tradeoff noted above, we would argue that a firm's dividend policy should be determined by the following characteristics.

- *Investment Opportunities:* Other things remaining equal, a firm with more investment opportunities should pay a lower fraction of its earnings as dividends than should a stable firm. As a practical measure, the quality of a firm's projects can be measured by comparing its returns on equity (or capital) to its cost of equity (or capital).

- *Stability in Earnings:* Firms with unstable earnings tend to pay out a much lower fraction of their earnings as dividends because they are concerned about their ability to maintain these dividends. Conversely, firms with stable and predictable earnings typically pay out a much larger proportion of their earnings as dividends.

- *Alternative Sources of Capital:* One of the consequences of paying too high a dividend is that the firm has to raise external financing to cover the shortfall and to take on new projects. To the degree that a firm can do this at low cost, it can afford to pay out a much larger proportion of its earnings as dividends.

- *Degree of Financial Leverage:* Higher financial leverage may reduce dividends for two other reasons, as well. First, as firms borrow more, they are much more likely to face covenants on dividend policy, restricting not only the dollar dividends but also the proportion of earnings that can be paid out as dividends. Second, taking on debt creates a commitment to making interest payments, which reduces the free cash flow available to managers. Because increasing dividends accomplishes the same goal, it can be argued that high financial leverage and high dividends are alternative approaches to keeping managers disciplined

- *Signaling Incentives:* Increases in dividends generally operate as positive signals of future cash flows, resulting in increases in value, whereas cut in dividends operate as negative signals and are associated with negative returns. To the extent that dividends are costly to the firm (by increasing their dependence on external financing) and to its stockholders (by creating a tax liability), it can be argued that alternative signals may be available to the firm which convey the same information at much less cost.

- *Stockholder Characteristics:* A firm whose stockholders like dividends will generally pay a much higher proportion of its earnings as dividends than will one without such stockholders.

A FRAMEWORK FOR ANALYZING DIVIDEND POLICY

In applying a rational framework for analyzing dividend policy, a firm will attempt to answer two questions:

1. How much cash is available to be paid out as dividends, after meeting capital expenditure and working capital needs to sustain future growth, and how much of this cash is paid out to stockholders?

2. How good are the projects that are available to the firm?

In general, firms that have good projects will have much more leeway on dividend policy, since stockholders will expect that the cash accumulated in the firm will be invested in these projects and eventually earn high returns. By contrast, firms that do not have good projects will find themselves under pressure to pay out all of the cash that is available as dividends.

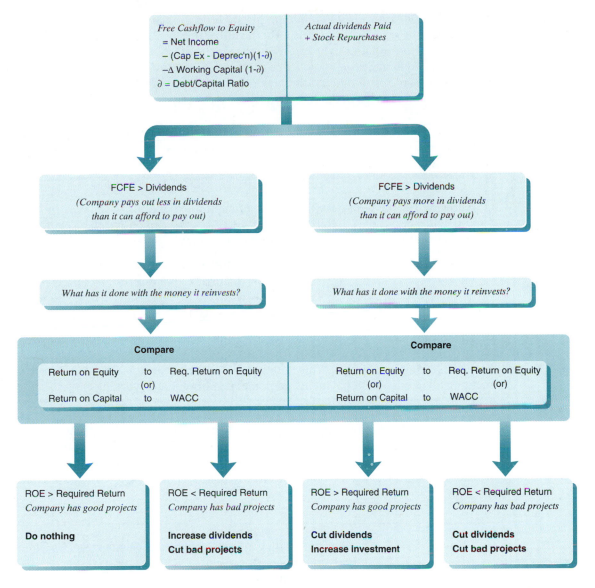

How Much Can a Firm Afford to Pay Out or Return to Its Stockholders?

To estimate how much cash a firm can afford to return to its stockholders, we begin with the net income—the accounting measure of the stockholders earnings during the period—and convert it to a cash flow as follows. First, any capital expenditures are subtracted from the net income, because they represent a cash outflow. Depreciation, on the other hand, is added back in because it is a noncash charge. The difference between capital expenditures and depreciation is referred to as **net capital expenditures** and is usually a function of the growth characteristics of the firm. High-growth firms tend to have high net capital expenditures relative to earnings, whereas low-growth firms have low or no net capital expenditures (because depreciation is offset by capital expenditures). Second, since increases in working capital drain a firm's cash flows, while decreases in working capital increase the cash flows available to equity investors, firms that are growing fast, in industries with high working capital requirements (retailing, for instance) typically have large increases in working capital. Because we are interested in the cash-flow effects, we consider only changes in *noncash working capital* in this analysis. Finally, equity investors also have to consider the effect of changes in the levels of debt on their cash flows. Repaying the principal on existing debt represents a cash outflow, but it may be fully or partially financed by the issue of new debt, which is a cash inflow. Again, netting out the repayment of old debt against the new debt issues provides a measure of the cash-flow effects of changes in debt.

Net Capital Expenditure: This is the difference between capital expenditures and depreciation. It is a measure of the financing needed, from internal or external sources, to meet capital investment needs.

Allowing for the cash-flow effects of net capital expenditures, changes in working capital, and net changes in debt on equity investors, we can define the cash flows left over after these changes as the **free cash flow to equity:**

Free Cash Flow to Equity (FCFE) = Net Income
— (Capital Expenditures − Depreciation)
— (Change in Noncash Working Capital)
+ (New Debt Issued − Debt Repayments)

This is the cash flow available to be paid out as dividends.

Free Cash Flow to Equity: This is the cash flow left over for equity investors after meeting all needs—debt payments, capital expenditures, and working capital.

This calculation can be simplified if we assume that the net capital expenditures and working capital changes are financed using a specified mix of debt and equity.[1] If δ is the proportion of the net capital expenditures and working capital changes that is raised from debt financing, the effect on cash flows to equity of these items can be summarized as follows.

> Equity Cash Flows associated with Capital Expenditure Needs = − (Capital Expenditures − Depreciation) $(1 − \delta)$
> Equity Cash Flows associated with Working Capital Needs
> = − (Δ Working Capital) $(1 − \delta)$

Accordingly, the cash flow available for equity investors after meeting capital expenditure and working capital needs is

Free Cash Flow to Equity = Net Income
— (Capital Expenditures − Depreciation) $(1 − \delta)$
— (Δ Working Capital) $(1 − \delta)$

Assuming that a specified proportion of net capital expenditures and working capital needs will be financed with debt is particularly useful in two cases. First, the target or optimal debt ratio of the firm can be used to forecast the free cash flow to equity that will

---

[1]When we refer to working capital from this point on, we are focusing only on noncash working capital.

be available in future periods. Second, in examining past periods, the firm's average debt ratio over the period can be used to arrive at approximate free cash flows to equity.

IN PRACTICE ESTIMATING FREE CASH FLOWS TO EQUITY—THE HOME DEPOT AND BOEING

In the following analysis, we estimate the free cash flows to equity for the Home Depot and Boeing from 1985 to 1994, using both approaches for estimation.

TABLE 21.1 ESTIMATES OF FCFE FOR THE HOME DEPOT: 1985–1994 (IN MILLIONS)

Year	Net Income	Capital Expenditures	Depreciation	Change in Noncash Working Capital	Net Debt Issued	FCFE
1985	$7.30	$99.77	$5.20	$6.34	$(50.00)	$(143.61)
1986	23.90	52.36	8.70	(15.40)	(83.00)	(87.36)
1987	54.10	89.24	10.65	19.50	(64.60)	(108.59)
1988	76.80	105.12	14.67	32.20	55.20	9.35
1989	112.00	204.97	21.11	131.00	195.40	(7.46)
1990	163.40	400.20	34.36	27.10	227.90	(1.64)
1991	249.20	432.20	52.28	323.10	(260.20)	(714.02)
1992	362.90	432.28	69.54	183.00	573.10	390.26
1993	457.40	900.45	89.84	187.00	(1.70)	(541.91)
1994	604.50	1,101.00	129.60	25.30	141.40	(250.80)
Average	211.15	381.76	43.60	91.91	73.35	(145.58)

As Table 21.1 indicates, the Home Depot had negative free cash flows to equity in 9 out of the 10 years, largely as a consequence of significant capital expenditures. The net debt issued during the period was $73.35 million, and the average net capital expenditure and working capital needs amounted to $430.07 million ($381.76 − $43.60 + $91.91), resulting in a debt ratio of approximately 17%. Using the approximate formulation for FCFE, we find that Table 21.2 yields the following results for FCFE for the same period.

Table 21.2 APPROXIMATE FCFE USING AVERAGE DEBT RATIO

Year	Net Income	Net Capital Expenditures $(1-\delta)$	Change in Noncash WC $(1-\delta)$	FCFE
1985	$7.30	$78.49	$5.26	$(76.46)
1986	23.90	36.24	(12.78)	0.44
1987	54.10	65.23	16.19	(27.31)
1988	76.80	75.07	26.73	(25.00)
1989	112.00	152.60	108.73	(149.33)
1990	163.40	303.65	22.49	(162.74)
1991	249.20	315.33	268.17	(334.31)
1992	362.90	301.07	151.89	(90.06)
1993	457.40	672.81	155.21	(370.62)
1994	604.50	806.26	21.00	(222.76)
Average				(145.81)

δ = Average debt ratio during the period = 17%

Note that the approximate formulation yields the same average FCFE for the period. Because new debt issues are averaged out over the 10 years, this approach also smooths out the FCFE on a year-to-year basis, inasmuch as actual debt issues are generally much more unevenly spread over time.

A similar estimation of FCFE was done for Boeing from 1985 to 1994. The estimates are reported in Table 21.3, based on the approximate formulation.

Table 21.3   **APPROXIMATE FCFE ON BOEING FROM 1985 TO 1994**

Year	Net Income	(Net Capital Expenditures) $(1-\delta)$	Change in Noncash WC $(1-\delta)$	FCFE
1985	$566.00	$156.75	$60.80	$348.45
1986	665.00	315.40	446.50	(96.90)
1987	480.00	222.30	(541.50)	799.20
1988	614.00	116.85	(373.35)	870.50
1989	675.00	698.25	124.45	(147.70)
1990	1,313.00	862.60	(331.55)	781.95
1991	1,567.00	972.80	869.25	(275.05)
1992	1,554.00	1,139.05	(575.70)	990.65
1993	1,244.00	277.40	662.15	304.45
1994	856.00	(329.65)	895.85	289.80
Average	953.40	443.18	123.69	386.54

δ = Average debt ratio during the period = 5%

Unlike the Home Depot, Boeing has positive free cash flows to equity, reflecting its lower net capital expenditure requirements, relative to net income. The differences between Boeing and the Home Depot can be attributed to each firm's position in terms of the growth cycle.

Relationship to dividend payout ratio   The conventional measure of dividend policy—the dividend payout ratio—evaluates dividends as a proportion of earnings. In contrast, our approach estimates dividends as a proportion of the free cash flow to equity:

$$\text{Dividend Payout Ratio} = \text{Dividends} / \text{Earnings}$$
$$\text{Dividend to FCFE Ratio} = \text{Dividends} / \text{FCFE}$$

The ratio of dividends to FCFE provides a measure of how much of the cash that is available to be paid out to stockholders is actually returned to them in the form of dividends. In fact, this definition can be expanded to include equity repurchases:

$$\text{Cash to Stockholders to FCFE Ratio} = (\text{Dividends} + \text{Equity Repurchases}) / \text{FCFE}$$

If this ratio, over time, is equal or close to 1, the firm is paying out all that it can to its stockholders. If it is significantly less than 1, the firm is paying out less than it can afford to and is using the difference to increase its cash balance or to invest in marketable securities. If it is significantly over 1, the firm is paying out more than it can afford and is either drawing on an existing cash balance or issuing new securities.

    IN PRACTICE   COMPARING DIVIDEND PAYOUT RATIOS TO FCFE PAYOUT RATIOS: THE HOME DEPOT AND BOEING

In the following analysis, we compare the dividend payout ratios to the dividends as a percentage of FCFE for the Home Depot and Boeing. Table 21.4 summarizes the Home Depot's dividend payout ratios.

As you can see, the Home Depot paid out only 6.65% of its earnings as dividends over this period. Although this may seem low, the free cash flows to equity were negative over this period,

Table 21.4   THE HOME DEPOT: DIVIDENDS AS PERCENTAGE OF EARNINGS AND FCFE

Year	Net Income	FCFE	Dividends	Payout Ratio (%)	Dividends/FCFE (%)
1985	$ 7.30	$(76.46)	$0.00	0.00	0.00
1986	23.90	0.44	0.00	0.00	0.00
1987	54.10	(27.31)	0.33	0.62	−1.23
1988	76.80	(25.00)	6.78	8.83	−27.12
1989	112.00	(149.33)	6.91	6.17	−4.63
1990	163.40	(162.74)	14.50	8.87	−8.91
1991	249.20	(334.31)	25.33	10.17	−7.58
1992	362.90	(90.06)	35.49	9.78	−39.40
1993	457.40	(370.62)	49.43	10.81	−13.34
1994	604.50	(222.76)	68.01	11.25	−30.53
Average		(145.81)	20.68	6.65	−14.18

suggesting that the Home Depot did not have the cash to pay even these meager dividends. In dollar terms, the Home Depot paid $20.68 million in dividends and generated negative free cash flows to equity of $145.81 million, on average, during this period.

Table 21.5 summarizes dividend payout ratios and FCFE as a percentage of dividends for Boeing from 1985 to 1994.

Table 21.5   BOEING—DIVIDENDS AS PERCENTAGE OF EARNINGS AND FCFE

Year	Net Income	FCFE	Dividends	Dividend Payout Ratio (%)	Dividends/ FCFE (%)
1985	$ 566.00	$348.45	$160.62	28.38	46.10
1986	665.00	(96.90)	184.95	27.81	−190.87
1987	480.00	799.20	212.42	44.25	26.58
1988	614.00	870.50	237.89	38.74	27.33
1989	675.00	(147.70)	269.75	39.96	−182.63
1990	1,313.00	781.95	326.39	24.86	41.74
1991	1,567.00	(275.05)	341.29	21.78	−124.08
1992	1,554.00	990.65	339.42	21.84	34.26
1993	1,244.00	304.45	340.14	27.34	111.72
1994	856.00	289.80	340.88	39.82	117.63
Average	953.40	386.54	275.37	28.88	71.24

[The average payout ratio = Average Dividends/Average Earnings]

During this period, Boeing paid out 28.88% of its earnings as dividends, on average. These dividends amounted to only 71.24% of the cash flows that could have been paid as dividends, however. In dollar terms, Boeing paid out $275.37 million in dividends, on an annual basis, while generating an average of $386.54 million in free cash flows to equity each year.

Why dividends may be less than FCFE   Many firms pay out less in dividends than they have available in free cash flows to equity, for a number of reasons. Although the reasons may vary from firm to firm, they can be categorized as follows:

- The managers of a firm may gain by retaining cash rather than paying it out as a dividend. The desire for empire building may make increasing the size of the firm an objective on its own. Management may also feel the need to build up a cash cushion to tide over periods when earnings may dip. In such periods, the cash cushion may reduce or obscure the earnings drop and may allow managers to remain in control.

- The firm may be unsure about its future financing needs and may choose to retain some cash to take on unexpected projects or meet unanticipated funding needs.

- The firm may have volatile earnings and may retain cash to help smooth out dividends over time.

- Bondholders may impose restrictions on cash payments to stockholders, which may prevent the firm from returning available cash flows to its stockholders.

❏ Concept
Check

What happens to that portion of free cash flow to equity that does not get returned to stockholders as a dividend or in the form of an equity repurchase?

Cross-sectional evidence on dividends and FCFE   The tendency of firms to pay out less in dividends than they have available in free cash flows to equity is brought home when we examine the cross-sectional differences across firms on dividends paid as a percentage of free cash flow to equity. In 1994, for instance, the average dividend to free cash flow to equity ratio across all firms on the NYSE was 61.22%. Figure 21.1 shows the distribution of dividends to FCFE across all firms.

A percentage less than 100% indicates that the firm is paying out less in dividends than it has available in cash flows and that it is generating surplus cash. For those firms that did not make net debt payments (debt payments in excess of new debt issues) during the period, this cash surplus shows up as an increase in the cash balance. A percentage greater than 100% indicates that the firm is paying out more in dividends than it has available in cash flow. These firms have to finance these dividend payments either out of existing cash balances or by making new stock and debt issues.

What Kind of Projects Does the Firm Have?

The alternative to returning cash to stockholders is reinvesting the funds back into the firm. Consequently, a firm's investment opportunities provide another dimension for analyzing dividend policy. Other things remaining equal, a firm with better projects typically has more flexibility in setting dividend policy and defending it against stockholder

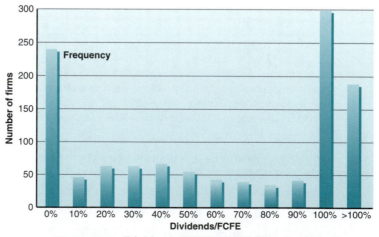

Figure 21.1   Dividends/FCFE: NYSE firms in 1994

demands for more dividends. The question is how do we define a "good" project. Returning to our earlier discussions of investment policy, we see that a good project is one that earns at least the hurdle rate, which is the cost of equity, if cash flows are estimated on an equity basis, or the cost of capital, if cash flows are on a predebt basis.

Conceivably, we could estimate the expected cash flows on every project available to the firm and calculate the internal rates of return or net present value of each project to evaluate project quality. This estimate presents several practical problems however. First, the analyst has to be able to obtain the detailed cash-flow estimates and hurdle rates for all available projects, which can represent a great deal of information. This problem is worse for outside analysts, because much of this information is not public. The second problem is that, even if these cash flows are available for existing projects, they will not be available for projects that will be taken in future years.

An alternative approach to measuring project quality involves using accounting measures of return on past projects. We can assume that these measures are not only good proxies for the cash-flow returns on these projects, but that they are indicative of the project choice available to the firm in both the current and future periods. The accounting measures of return can be compared to the cost of equity (if the measure is the return on equity) or the cost of capital (if the measure is the return on capital), to determine whether the projects are making more than the hurdle rate.

Accounting Measure	Hurdle Rate
Return on Equity$_t$ = Net Income$_t$ / BV of Equity$_{t}-_{t-1}$	Cost of Equity
Return on Capital$_t$ = EBIT$_t$ (1−t) / (BV of Debt$_{t-1}$ + BV of Equity$_{t-1}$)	Cost of Capital

Critics of this approach argue that accounting income is not always a good measure of cash flows. This is undoubtedly true. Nevertheless, there is a high correlation between levels of accounting income and levels of cash flows. Another criticism of this approach is the implicit assumption it makes that the book value of capital is a good measure of the market value of assets in place. Note that the return on the total market value—obtained, for instance, by dividing net income by the market value of equity or the after-tax operating income by the total market value of assets—is not a good measure of the quality of existing projects, because the market value includes a premium for expected growth. Thus, a high-growth firm will have low returns on market value of equity or capital, but this does not mean that the firm's project choices or returns have been substandard.

Relying on past project returns may indeed be dangerous, especially when a firm is making a transition from one stage in its growth cycle to the next, or if it is in the process of restructuring. Under these and other scenarios, it is entirely possible that the expected returns on new projects are very different from past project returns. In such cases, it may be worthwhile to scrutinize past returns for trends that may carry over into the future. The average return on equity or capital for a firm may not reveal these trends very well, because they are slow to reflect the effects of new projects, especially at large firms. An alternative measure, which better captures year-to-year shifts, is the *marginal return on equity or capital,* which is defined as follows:

$$\text{Marginal Return on Equity}_t = (\text{Net Income}_t - \text{Net Income}_{t-1})/ (\text{BV Equity}_{t-1} - \text{BV of Equity}_{t-2})$$

Although the marginal return on equity (capital) and the average return on equity (capital) will move in the same direction, the marginal returns typically change much more than do the average returns, the difference being a function of the size of the firm.

Finally, accounting income and returns may fluctuate from year to year, not only because of changes in project quality, but also because of broader macroeconomic

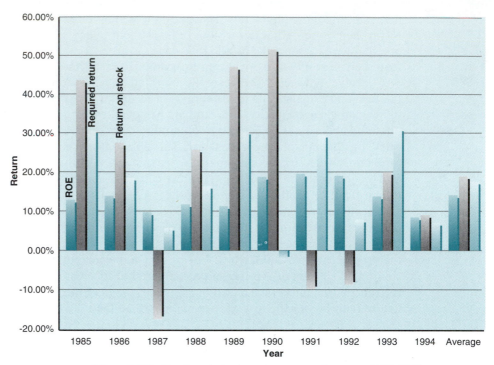

Figure 21.2   Boeing: Actual versus expected return, 1985–1994

factors, such as economic cycles and interest rates. Consequently, the comparisons between accounting returns and hurdle rates should be done across long enough periods, say five to ten years, to average out these other effects.

  IN PRACTICE   EVALUATING PROJECT QUALITY AT BOEING AND THE HOME DEPOT

In the following analysis, we examine both accounting and market measures of return at Boeing and the Home Depot between 1985 and 1994 and compare them to the appropriate hurdle rates to evaluate the quality of the projects taken at each of these firms during the period. We begin with an analysis of Boeing's accounting return on equity, the return from holding the stock, and the required return (given the beta and market performance during each year) from 1985 to 1994, as shown in Figure 21.2.

As you can see, the verdict is mixed. The average return on equity over the entire period is 13.82%, which is lower than the required rate of return of 17.33%, based on Boeing's beta and market returns over the period. The annual return from holding Boeing stock is 18.71%, which is higher than the required return. There is a troubling downward trend in both return on equity and the stock over the last two years; this suggests that the recent performance has not measured up to expectations. Boeing's managers would argue that this is a temporary phase, however, and that returns will improve once the health of the airline industry improves and Boeing is able to deliver on its new jets. They might be right, but stockholders are likely to be skeptical.

Repeating this analysis for the Home Depot during the same time period yields markedly different results. Figure 21.3 summarizes returns on equity, returns on the stock, and the required return at the firm for each year between 1985 and 1994.

During this period, the Home Depot earned more than its required rate of return, both on an accounting basis and in terms of stock price performance. Most of the extraordinary performance occurred in the 1980s, and it can be argued that the increased size of the firm is working against it now. Although stockholders may be willing, at this stage, to accept the firm's contention that it still has great projects, it is going to become increasingly difficult to maintain these returns going forward.

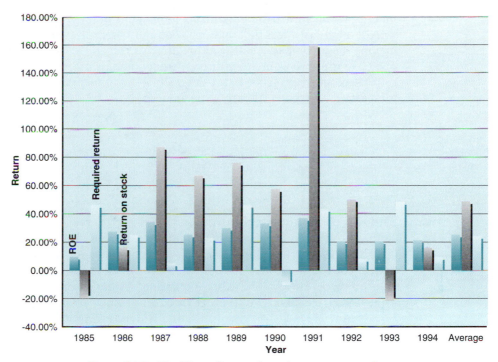

Figure 21.3   The Home Depot: Actual versus expected returns

Dividend Policy, FCFE, and Project Quality: Some Generalizations

Once a firm's capacity to pay dividends and its project quality have been measured, a framework for analyzing dividend policy emerges. Using the first measure, a firm can either be paying out more in dividends than it can afford to (FCFE), or it is paying out less. Using the second measure, a firm can either have good projects (those with returns greater than the hurdle rate) or not. Combining these two measures yields four combinations:

1.   *A firm may have good projects and may be paying out more than its free cash flow to equity as a dividend.* In this case, the firm is losing value on two grounds. First, by paying too much in dividends, it is creating a cash shortfall that has to be met by issuing securities. Second, the cash shortfall often creates capital rationing constraints; as a result, the firm may reject good projects it otherwise would have taken.

2.   *A firm may have good projects and may be paying out less than its free cash flow to equity as a dividend.* Although it will accumulate cash as a consequence, the firm can legitimately argue that it has good projects in which it can invest the cash, although investors may wonder why it did not take the projects in the current period.

3.   *A firm may have poor projects and may be paying out less than its free cash flow to equity as a dividend.* This firm will also accumulate cash, but it will find itself under pressure from stockholders to distribute the cash, because of their concern that the cash will be used to finance poor projects.

4.   *A firm may have poor projects and may be paying out more than its free cash flow to equity as a dividend.* This firm first has to deal with its poor project choices, possibly by cutting back on those that make returns below the hurdle rate. Because the reduced capital expenditure will increase the free cash flow to equity, this may take care of the dividend problem. If it does not, the firm will have to cut dividends as well.

Figure 21.4 illustrates the potential combinations of these possibilities.

Although historical data may provide the basis for estimating the parameters for making these comparisons, the entire analysis can and should be forward looking. The objective is not to estimate return on equity on past projects, but to forecast expected returns on future projects. To the degree that past information is useful in making these forecasts, it is an integral part of the analysis.

In doing this analysis, why does it make sense to look at several years of history rather than just the most current year?

The Effects of Financial Leverage

In the above analysis, we emphasized the interaction of investment and dividend policy. This analysis is further enriched—and complicated—if we bring in the firm's financing decisions as well. In Chapter 19, we noted that one of the ways a firm can increase leverage over time is by increasing dividends or repurchasing stock; at the same time, it can decrease leverage by cutting or not paying dividends. Thus, the question of how much a firm should pay in dividends cannot really be answered without analyzing whether it is under- or overlevered and whether or not it intends to close this leverage gap.

An underlevered firm may be able to pay more than its FCFE as dividend and may do so intentionally to increase its debt ratio. An overlevered firm, on the other hand, may have to pay less than its FCFE as dividends, because of its desire to reduce leverage. In some of the cases described above, leverage can be used to strengthen the suggested recommendations, without even considering it. For instance, an underlevered firm with poor projects and a cash-flow surplus has an added incentive to raise dividends and to reevaluate investment policy, for it will be able to increase its leverage by doing so. In some cases, however, the imperatives of moving to an optimal debt ratio may act as a barrier to carrying out changes in dividend policy. Thus, an overlevered firm with poor projects and a cash-flow surplus may find the cash better spent reducing debt rather than paying out dividends.

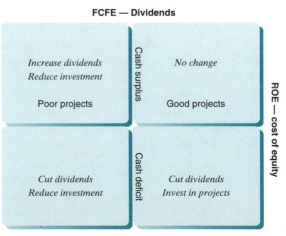

Figure 21.4   Analyzing dividend policy

POOR PROJECTS AND LOW PAYOUT

In this section, we examine the consequences of paying out much less in dividends than a firm has available in cash flows, while facing poor investment opportunities. We also discuss stockholder reaction and management response to the dividend policy.

Consequences of Low Payout

When a firm pays out less than it can afford to in dividends, it accumulates cash. If a firm does not have good projects (now or in the future) in which to invest this cash, it faces several possibilities: In the most benign case, the cash accumulates in the firm and is invested in financial assets. Assuming that these financial assets are fairly priced, these investments are zero net present value projects and should not negatively affect value. However, the firm may find itself the target of an acquisition, financed in part by its large holding of liquid assets.

As the cash in the firm accumulates, the managers may be tempted to take on projects that do not meet their hurdle rate requirements, either to reduce the likelihood of a takeover or to earn higher returns than on financial assets.[2] These actions will clearly lower the value of the firm. Another possibility, and one fraught with even more danger for the firm, is that management may decide to use the cash to finance an acquisition and that such an acquisition will result in a transfer of wealth to the stockholders of the acquired firm. Although managers will argue that such acquisitions make sense from a strategic and synergistic viewpoint, history is replete with cases of firms that used large cash balances, acquired over years of paying low dividends while generating high free cash flows to equity, to finance takeovers that detract from stockholder value.

Stockholder Reaction

Given the range of possible outcomes described above, it is not surprising that the stockholders of firms that pay insufficient dividends and do not have "good" projects put pressure on managers to return more of the cash back to them. In fact, this is the scenario that originally led to the development of the "free cash-flow" hypothesis. Under this hypothesis, which is described more fully in Chapter 16, managers cannot be trusted with large cash flows that they can spend at their discretion. Consequently, it is argued, firms should borrow more and create the commitment to making interest and principal payments, thereby forcing managers to be more disciplined in their investment choices. An alternative to taking on debt is to force firms to disgorge more of these cash flows as dividends.

Management's Defense

Not surprisingly, managers of firms who pay out less in dividends than they can afford to argue that this policy is in the best long-term interests of the firm. They maintain that although the current project returns may be poor, future projects will be both more plentiful and lucrative (in terms of returns). This argument may work initially when presented, but it will become progressively more difficult to sustain if the firm continues to post poor returns on its projects. Managers may also argue that the cash accumulation is needed to meet demands arising from future contingencies. For instance, cyclical firms will often argue that large cash balances are needed to tide them over the next recession.

---

[2]This is especially likely if the cash is invested in Treasury bills or other low-risk, low-return investments. On the surface, it may seem better for the firm to take on risky projects that earn, say, 7%, rather than invest in Treasury bills and make 3%, although this clearly does not make sense after adjusting for the risk.

Again, although there is a kernel of truth to the argument, the "reasonableness" of the cash balance has to be measured against the firm's experience in terms of cash requirements in prior recessions. Finally, in some cases, managers will justify a firm's cash accumulation and low dividend payout based on the behavior of comparable firms. Thus, a firm may argue that it is essentially copying the dividend policy of its closest competitors and that it has to continue to do so to remain competitive. The argument that "every one else does it" cannot be used to justify a bad dividend policy, however.

Although all of these justifications seemingly support stockholder wealth maximization or the best long-term interests of the firm, they may really be just smokescreens designed to hide the fact that this dividend policy may serve managerial rather than stockholder interests. Maintaining large cash balances and low dividends provides incumbent managers with two advantages: they increase the funds that are directly under their control, and thus increase their power to direct future investments, and they increase the margin for safety for these managers, stabilizing earnings and increasing their tenure.

❏ Concept
   Check
> How would this discussion differ if incumbent management were protected from any challenge by stockholders? In general, what are the implications of management protection for dividend policy?

GOOD PROJECTS AND LOW PAYOUT

Although the outcomes for stockholders in firms with poor projects and low dividend payout ratios range from neutral to terrible, the results may be more positive for firms that have a better selection of projects and whose incumbent management has had a history of earning high returns for the stockholders.

Consequences of Low Payout
The immediate consequence of paying out less in dividends than is available in free cash flow to equity is the same for these firms as it is for firms with poor project choice: the cash balance of the firm increases to reflect the cash surplus. The long-term effects of cash accumulation are generally much less negative for these firms, however, for the following reasons:

1. The presence of projects that earn returns greater than the hurdle rate increases the likelihood that the cash will be productively invested in the long term.
2. The high returns earned on internal projects reduces both the pressure and the incentive to invest the cash in poor projects or in acquisitions.
3. Firms that earn high returns on their projects are much less likely to be targets of takeovers, reducing the need to reduce the cash balance quickly.

To summarize, firms that have a history of taking good projects and that expect to continue to have a ready supply of such projects may be able to sustain a policy of retaining cash rather than paying out dividends. In fact, they can actually create value in the long term by using this cash productively.

Stockholder Reaction
Stockholders are much less likely to feel a threat to their wealth in firms that have historically shown good judgment in picking projects. Consequently, they are more likely to acquiesce when managers in those firms withhold cash rather than pay it out. This suggests that, although the free cash-flow hypothesis has a solid basis for arguing that managers can-

not be trusted with large cash balances, it does not apply equally across all firms. The managers of some firms earn the trust of their stockholders because of their capacity to deliver extraordinary returns on both their projects and their stock over long periods of time. These managers will generally have much more flexibility in determining dividend policy.

This discussion helps resolve the tradeoff firms face between satisfying their long-term prospects and paying dividends or repurchasing stock. The notion that greedy stockholders force firms with great projects to return too much cash too quickly is not based in fact. Rather, stockholder pressure for dividends or stock repurchases is greatest in firms whose projects yield marginal or poor return, and least in firms whose projects have high returns.

Management Responses

Managers in firms that have posted stellar records in project and stock returns clearly have a much easier time convincing stockholders of the desirability of withholding cash rather than paying it out. The strongest argument for doing this is that the cash will be used productively in the future and earn above market returns for the stockholders. Not all stockholders will buy this argument, however. Some will argue that future projects may be less attractive than past projects, especially when the industry in which the firm is operating is maturing. For example, many specialty retail firms, such as the Limited, found themselves under pressure to return more cash to stockholders in the early 1990s as margins and growth rates in the business declined.

Thus far, we have assumed that good returns on projects and good returns on stocks go hand in hand. Although this may be true in general, there are some companies that post good records in terms of returns in projects but will find their stock price declining. One explanation for this is that the firm's project returns, though higher than the hurdle rate, were actually lower than expected, resulting in a drop in the stock price. Thus, a firm that reports a return on equity of 22%—much higher than its cost of equity of 15%—may still see its stock price drop if the market expectation was a return on equity of 25%.

❏ Concept
Check

> Assume that you are a stockholder in a firm that has had a good history of project choice but has also accumulated a substantial amount of cash. What are some actions that would lead you to reassess your willingness to allow the firm to retain cash moving forward?

POOR PROJECTS AND HIGH PAYOUT

In many ways, the most troublesome combination of circumstances occurs when firms pay out much more in dividends than they can afford while posting less-than-stellar returns on their projects. These firms have problems with both their investment and their dividend policies, and the dividend problem cannot be solved adequately without addressing the investment problem.

Consequences of High Payout

When a firm pays out more in dividends than it has available in free cash flows to equity, it is creating a cash deficit. The deficit has to be funded by drawing on the firm's cash balance, issuing stock to cover shortfall, or borrowing money to fund its dividends. If the firm uses the first approach, it will reduce equity and raise its debt ratio. The second approach allows the firm to neutralize the drop in equity created by the excess dividends with new stock issues; the downside is the issuance cost of the stock.

The third approach forces the firm to increase its debt while reducing equity, accentuating the increase in the debt ratio.

Because the free cash flows to equity are after capital expenditures, it can be argued that this firm's real problem is not that it pays out too much in dividends, but that it invests too much in bad projects. Cutting back on these projects would therefore increase the free cash flow to equity and eliminate the cash shortfall created by paying too much in dividends.

Stockholder Reaction

The stockholders of a firm that pays much more in dividends than it has available in free cash flow to equity are faced with a quandary: On the one hand, they may want the firm to reduce its dividends to eliminate the need for additional borrowing or equity issues each year. On the other hand, the firm's record in picking projects does not evoke much trust that the management is using funds wisely, and it is entirely possible that the funds saved by not paying the dividends will be used on other poor projects as well. Consequently, these firms will first have to address their investment problems and then cut back on poor projects, which, in turn, will increase the free cash flow to equity. If the cash shortfall persists, the firm should then cut back on dividends.

It is therefore entirely possible, especially if the firm is underleveraged to begin with, that the stockholders will not push for lower dividends but will try to get managers to improve project choice instead. It is also possible that they will push the firm to eliminate enough poor projects so that the free cash flow to equity covers the expected dividend payment.

Management Responses

The managers of firms with poor projects and dividends that exceed free cash flows to equity may contest the notion that they have investment problems rather than dividend problems. They may also disagree that the most efficient way of dealing with these problems is to eliminate some of the capital expenditures. In general, their arguments will mirror those used by any firm with a poor investment track record: the period used to analyze project returns was not representative; it was an industrywide problem that will pass; or the projects have long gestation periods.

Overall, it is unlikely that these managers will convince the stockholders of their good intentions on future projects. Consequently, there will be a strong push toward cutbacks in capital expenditures, especially if the firm is borrowing money to finance the dividends and does not have much excess debt capacity.

❑ Concept
Check

> Assume that you are a stockholder in a firm with a poor track record of investments and high dividends. What questions would you have for the managers of this firm?

GOOD PROJECTS AND HIGH PAYOUT

The costs of trying to maintain unsustainable dividends are most evident in firms that have a selection of good projects to choose from. The cash that is paid out as dividends could well have been used to invest in some of these projects, leading to a much higher return for stockholders and higher stock prices for the firm.

Consequences of High Payout

When a firm pays out more in dividends than it has available in free cash flow to equity, it is creating a cash shortfall. If this firm also has good projects available currently that are not being taken because of capital rationing constraints, it can be argued that the firm is paying a hefty price for its dividend policy. Even if the projects are passed up for other reasons, it can be argued that the cash this firm is paying out as dividends would earn much better returns for it if left to accumulate in the firm.

Dividend payments also create a cash deficit that now has to be met by issuing new securities. On the one hand, issuing new stock carries a potentially large issuance cost, which reduces firm value. On the other hand, if the firm issues new debt, it might become overleveraged, and this may reduce value.

Stockholder Reaction

Rationally, the stockholders' best option in this case is to insist that the firm pay out less in dividends and take on better projects. This may not happen, however, if the firm has paid high dividends for an extended period of time and has acquired stockholders who value high dividends even more than they value the firm's long-term health. Even so, stockholders may be much more amenable to cutting dividends and reinvesting the cash in the firm, if the firm has a ready supply of good projects at hand.

Concept
Check

Companies often start paying dividends because of their desire to attract new investors who will hold only dividend-paying stock. Do you agree with this rationale for paying dividends for a firm that cannot afford these dividends? Why or why not?

Management Responses

The managers of firms that have good projects, while paying out too much in dividends, have to figure out a way to cut dividends and at the same time differentiate themselves from those firms that are cutting dividends owing to declining earnings. The initial suspicion with which markets view dividend cuts can be overcome in part by providing markets with information on project quality at the time of the dividend cut. If the dividends have been paid for a long time, however, the firm may have acquired stockholders who like the high dividends and may not be particularly interested in the projects that the firm has available. If this is the case, the initial reaction to the dividend cut, no matter how carefully packaged, will be negative. However, as disgruntled stockholders sell their holdings, the firm will acquire new stockholders who may be more willing to accept the lower dividends and higher investment policy.

 IN PRACTICE   ANALYZING BOEING'S DIVIDEND POLICY

Using the framework devised above, we are now in a position to analyze Boeing's dividend policy. Earlier, we compared the dividends Boeing paid between 1985 and 1994 to its free cash flows to equity. On average, Boeing paid out 71.24% of its free cash flow to equity as dividends. In 1993 and 1994, however, the dividends paid exceeded the free cash flow to equity, as net income dropped. We then compared Boeing's return on equity and stock to the required rate of return and got at a mixed verdict: on average, between 1985 and 1994, the return on equity has not measured up to the cost of equity, but the returns on the stock have exceeded the cost of equity. In 1993 and 1994, Boeing underperformed its required return on both measures. Finally, in our earlier analysis, we noted that Boeing had excess debt capacity that it could use for project financing or other purposes. Given these statistics, we can make the following recommendations relating to Boeing's dividend policy:

1. The existing dividend payments should be maintained for the next year. If the free cash flows to equity continue to be lower than the dividend payments, the difference should be made up with debt.

2. If net income recovers from 1994 levels to more normal levels (1988–1992 averages, for instance), the firm's dividends will revert to about 70% of the free cash flows to equity. If the firm cannot improve its return on equity substantially, it should attempt to return more cash to its stockholders, in the form of either dividends or equity repurchases.

 IN PRACTICE ANALYZING THE HOME DEPOT'S DIVIDEND POLICY

The Home Depot's dividend policy can also be analyzed using the same framework. First, we noted earlier that the Home Depot paid dividends in eight of the ten years for which we have data, whereas its free cash flows to equity were positive in only one year. In 1994, for instance, the Home Depot paid dividends of $68 million while experiencing negative free cash flows to equity of $222 million. Because growth is dropping off and more cash is being generated from current operations, we can project free cash flows to equity from 1995 to 1999, as shown in Table 21.6. To do so, we assume that net income will grow 14.4% a year, while net capital expenditures and working capital will grow by 6% a year. The working capital in 1994 was $536 million. The debt ratio is assumed to be 20%.

	Growth Rate (%)	1995	1996	1997	1998	1999
Net Income	14.40	$691.55	$791.13	$905.05	$1,035.38	$1,184.48
− (Cap. Exp − Depr) *(1−δ)	6.00	823.75	873.17	925.56	981.10	1,039.96
Δ Working Capital *(1−δ)	6.00	32.18	34.11	36.16	38.33	40.63
= Free CF to Equity		(164.38)	(116.15)	(56.67)	15.96	103.89

Table 21.6 FREE CASH FLOWS TO EQUITY FOR THE HOME DEPOT: 1995–1999

The projected free cash flows to equity are negative from 1995 to 1997 but become positive in 1998. We should also keep in mind that the Home Depot has a fairly strong record of delivering high returns on equity and high stock returns. These returns have declined as the firm has become larger, however. In addition, the firm has a very low debt ratio but can afford to carry more debt.

Based on the negative free cash flows to equity, it would seem reasonable to argue that the Home Depot should cut dividends. This has to be weighed against two other facts, however. First, as the firm's growth opportunities decrease, the free cash flows to equity will become positive. Our projections indicate that this should happen by 1998. Second, the firm has excess debt capacity that can be used to cover the shortfall created by the payment of dividend payments. Given that the announcement of a dividend cut now may send the wrong signal to financial markets, we would recommend that dividends be maintained at their current level and financed with new debt issues (and not new stock issues).

AN ALTERNATIVE APPROACH TO ANALYZING DIVIDEND POLICY

So far, we have examined the dividend policy of a firm by looking at its fundamentals. Many managers would argue that their dividend policies are judged relative to their competitors, however, and many analysts agree. This "comparable firm" approach to analyzing dividend policy can be defined narrowly, by looking at only firms that are similar in size and business mix, for example, or more broadly, by looking at the determinants of dividend policy across all firms.

Using Comparable Firms

In the simplest form of this approach, a firm's dividend yield and payout are compared to its peer group and judged to be adequate, excessive, or inadequate, accordingly. Thus, a utility stock with a dividend yield of 3.5% may be criticized for paying out an inadequate dividend if utility stocks on average pay a much higher dividend, whereas a computer software firm that has a dividend yield of 1.0% may be viewed as paying too high a dividend if software firms on average pay a much lower dividend. Table 21.7 summarizes dividend yield and payout ratios across different industry groups.

Table 21.7 INDUSTRY AVERAGES: END OF 1995		
Industry	**Yield (%)**	**Payout (%)**
Agricultural Products	2.15	30.32
Mining	2.05	43.68
Petroleum Production and Refining	1.58	34.55
Building Contractors and Related Areas	1.33	18.87
Food Production	1.74	27.94
Beverages	1.59	34.65
Tobacco	4.08	61.43
Textile and Clothing Manufacturers	1.67	28.50
Furniture	1.71	28.77
Paper and Plastic Production	2.14	27.53
Publishing	1.78	31.39
Chemicals	1.86	30.98
Pharmaceuticals	2.07	42.11
Consumer Products	1.47	26.74
Autos and Related	2.11	29.39
Miscellaneous Manufacturing	1.98	24.63
Equipment Manufacturing	1.50	22.31
Computers and Office Equipment	1.01	17.72
Consumer Electronics	1.11	17.72
Other Consumer Durables	1.37	24.96
Transportation	1.42	18.75
Telephone Utilities	2.91	51.55
Entertainment (TV and Movies)	1.35	23.14
Electric and Gas Utilities	4.97	64.18
Wholesalers	1.30	21.25
Retailers	1.56	25.44
Restaurants and Eating Places	1.05	22.20
Banks and Financial Service	2.22	30.31
Insurance	1.76	22.94
Real Estate	4.23	47.39
Other Services	1.26	22.65
Computer Software and Services	1.16	20.53
Health Services	1.29	19.38
Average	**1.90**	**30.12**

Comparing a firm's dividend yield and payout to comparable firms may provide some intuitive appeal, but it can be misleading, for a number of reasons. First, it assumes that all firms within the same industry group have the same net capital expenditure and working capital needs, which may not be true, depending on their stage in the life cycles. Second, even if the firms are at the same stage in their life cycles, it is entirely possible that the entire industry is adopting a dividend policy that is unsustainable or sub-optimal.

Concept Check

Assume you are running a firm that has a dividend policy very different from its peer group. How would you defend this policy to investors?

IN PRACTICE Analyzing Boeing and the Home Depot's Dividend Payout Using Comparable Firms

In comparing Boeing's dividend policy to its peer group, we analyze the dividend yields and payout ratios of comparable firms in 1994, as shown in Table 21.8.[3]

Table 21.8 PAYOUT RATIOS AND DIVIDEND YIELDS: AEROSPACE AND DEFENSE FIRMS (PERCENTAGE DISTRIBUTION)

Company	Payout Ratio	Dividend Yield	Expected Growth
Aviall Inc.	8.16	0.45	33
Bombardier	21.92	1.00	20.50
CAE Inc.	36.36	1.78	16.50
GRC Intnl	0.00	0.00	20
Gen'l Dynamics	39.89	2.59	12.50
Hughes Electronic	29.63	2.00	10.50
Litton Industries	0.00	0.00	18
Lockheed Martin	26.09	1.73	12
Loral	17.75	1.07	15
McDonnell Douglas	10.89	0.68	28
Northrop Grumman	32.00	2.67	14.50
Raytheon	25.78	1.76	11
Rockwell Intnl	36.88	2.26	11.50
Thiokol	22.44	1.89	6.50
Average	21.99	1.42	16
Boeing	*39.84*	*1.47*	*9*

As you can see, Boeing had a higher dividend payout ratio and dividend yield than the comparable firms, but it also had a lower expected growth rate. To control for the effect of growth, we regress the dividend measures against expected growth for the subsample, resulting in the following:

$$\text{Dividend Payout Ratio} = 0.395 - 1.06 \text{ (Expected growth rate)} \quad R^2 = 28.72\%$$
$$\text{Dividend Yield} = 0.0278 - 0.08 \text{ (Expected growth rate)} \quad R^2 = 39.97\%$$

Using Boeing's expected growth rate of 9% in these regressions yields the following predicted values for the dividend measures:

$$\text{Predicted Dividend Payout for Boeing} = 0.395 - 1.06 (0.09) = 0.30 \text{ or } 30\%$$
$$\text{Predicted Dividend Yield for Boeing} = 0.0278 - 0.08 (0.09) = 0.0206 \text{ or } 2.06\%$$

When the adjustment is made for growth, Boeing's payout rate is still higher than the predicted value, but its dividend yield is lower than predicted.

[3]The Value Line classification of firms into industry groups was used to put together the comparable firm list.

For the Home Depot, there are far fewer comparable firms in the industry. Table 21.9 summarizes the dividend yields and payout ratios for these firms.

Table 21.9   Payout Ratios and Dividend Yields: Home Improvement Products Retailers (percentage distribution)

Company	Payout Ratio	Dividend Yield	Expected Growth
BMC West	0.00	0.00	15
Grossman's	0.00	0.00	10
Hechinger's	26.67	3.90	2.50
Hughes Supply	10.00	0.88	17
Lowe's Cos	9.47	0.62	20
Wolohan Lumber	25.45	3.08	7
Average	11.93	1.41	11.92
Home Depot	*9.68*	*0.38*	*23*

The Home Depot has a much lower dividend payout ratio and yield than do comparable firms, but a much higher growth rate. Again, the results are ambiguous, since we would expect the higher growth rate to translate into lower dividends. To examine whether the differences can be explained by expected growth, we regress the dividend measures against expected growth, resulting in the following regressions:

$$\text{Dividend Payout Ratio} = 0.256 - 1.15 \text{ (Expected growth rate) } R^2 = 26.31\%$$
$$\text{Dividend Yield} = 0.0374 - 0.20 \text{ (Expected growth rate) } R^2 = 49.54\%$$

Using the Home Depot's expected growth rate of 23% in these regressions yields the following predicted values for the dividend measures.

$$\text{Predicted Dividend Payout for Home Depot} = 0.256 - 1.15 \text{ (0.23)} = -.0085 \text{ or } -.85\%$$
$$\text{Predicted Dividend Yield for Home Depot} = 0.0374 - 0.20 \text{ (0.23)} = -.0086 \text{ or } -.86\%$$

These predicted values suggest that, given its expected growth rate, the Home Depot should not be paying any dividends. This finding is consistent with our earlier analysis that, given the Home Depot's negative free cash flows to equity, it should not be paying a dividend in the first place.

It is important to note, however, that the use of comparable firms is limited by the difficulty in identifying truly comparable firms and in controlling for differences across these firms. The regressions shown above have limited power because of the small number of observations in each case.

Using the Entire Cross Section

The alternative to using only comparable firms in the same industry is to study the entire population of firms and to try to estimate the fundamentals that cause differences in dividend payout across firms. We outlined some of the determinants of dividend policy early in this chapter and suggested some empirical relationships that should hold between dividend payout and proxies for these determinants. In particular, we argued that:

- Dividend payout ratios and earnings variability (or risk) are negatively correlated with each other.
- Dividend payout ratios and project returns (return on equity, return on capital) are negatively correlated with each other.
- Dividend payout ratios and size are positive correlated with each other.

• Dividend payout ratios and debt ratios are negatively correlated with each other.

Using data from 1994, we regressed dividend yields and payout ratios against all of these variables and arrived at the following regression equations:

$$PAYOUT = 0.3789 - 0.2246 \text{ BETA} + 0.0000046 \text{ MKTCAP} + 0.1573 \text{ DBTRATIO} +$$
$$0.0015 \text{ ROE} - 0.30 \text{ NCEX/TA} \qquad R^2 = 13.76\%$$
$$YIELD = 0.0478 - 0.0157 \text{ BETA} - 0.0000008 \text{ MKTCAP} + 0.6797 \text{ DBTRATIO} +$$
$$0.0002 \text{ ROE} - 0.09 \text{ NCEX/TA} \qquad R^2 = 12.88\%$$

where

BETA = Beta of the stock
MKTCAP = Market Value of Equity + Book Value of Debt
DBTRATIO = Book Value of Debt / MKTCAP
ROE = Return on Equity in 1994
NCEX/TA = (Capital Expenditures − Depreciation) / Total Assets

The regression does not have very good explanatory power, however, for it explains only 12% to 13% of the differences in dividend measures. It is also troubling that some of the variables in these regressions have the wrong signs. (The debt ratio, for instance, has a positive instead of a negative coefficient.)

IN PRACTICE ANALYZING BOEING AND THE HOME DEPOT'S DIVIDEND PAYOUT USING THE CROSS SECTION

To illustrate the applicability of the cross-sectional regression in analyzing the dividend policies of the Home Depot and Boeing, we estimate the values of the independent variables in the regressions for the two firms, as shown in Table 21.10.

Table 21.10   **DIVIDEND PAYOUT RATIOS FROM CROSS-SECTIONAL REGRESSIONS**

	The Home Depot	Boeing
ROE	17.60%	8.80%
Beta	1.55	0.95
Market Capitalization	$11,817	$25,796
Net Cap Exp/ Total Assets	30.96%	-2.49%
Debt Ratio	0.96%	10.14%

Substituting into the regression equation for the dividend payout ratio, we predicted the following payout ratios for the two firms:

$$\text{For Boeing} = 0.3789 - 0.2246 (0.95) + 0.0000046 (25,796) + 0.1573 (0.1014) + 0.0015$$
$$(0.088) - 0.30 (-0.0249) = 30.77\%$$
$$\text{For the Home Depot} = 0.3789 - 0.2246 (1.55) + 0.0000046 (11,817) + 0.1573$$
$$(0.0096) + 0.0015 (0.176) - 0.30 (0.3096) = -0.60\%$$

Substituting into the regression equation for the dividend yield, we predict the following dividend yields for the two firms:

$$\text{For Boeing} = 0.0478 - 0.0157 \, (0.95) + 0.0000008 \, (25{,}796) + 0.6797 \, (0.1014) + 0.0002$$
$$(0.088) - 0.09 \, (-0.0249) = 8.34\%$$
$$\text{For the Home Depot} = 0.0478 - 0.0157 \, (1.55) + 0.0000008 \, (11{,}817) + 0.6797$$
$$(0.0096) + 0.0002 \, (0.176) - 0.09 \, (0.3096) = -0.74\%$$

Both measures support our conclusions from the earlier analysis: the Home Depot should not be paying dividends, whereas Boeing should be paying much more in dividends.

CONCLUSION

In this chapter, we expanded on many of the concepts introduced in the previous one and developed a general framework for analyzing dividend policy. Here, we emphasized the link between investment, financing, and dividend policy by noting that firms with a history of taking on good projects and the potential for more good projects in the future acquire much more control over their dividend policy. In particular, they can pay much less in dividends than they have available in cash flows and hold on to the surplus cash, because stockholders trust them to invest the cash wisely. In contrast, stockholders in firms with a history of poor project choice may be much less sanguine about retention of cash, because of the fear that the cash will be invested in poor projects.

Some firms set dividends based on the actions of comparable firms. We examined an analysis based on a narrow definition of comparable firms (firms in the same line of business) and one based on a broader definition. (The determinants of dividend policy were examined in the entire population.)

There is one point worth reemphasizing here. In this chapter, we have developed a framework designed to answer the question of how much cash should be returned to stockholders. Although dividends may be the most widely used approach to returning cash to stockholders, alternatives are available to most firms. Some of these alternatives are examined in the next chapter.

QUESTIONS AND PROBLEMS

1. JLChem Corporation, a chemical manufacturing firm with changing investment opportunities, is considering a major change in dividend policy. It currently has 50 million shares outstanding and pays an annual dividend of $2 per share. The firm's current and projected income statement are provided below (in millions):

	Current	Projected for next year
EBITDA	$1200	$1350
− Depreciation	200	250
EBIT	1000	1100
− Interest Expense	200	200
EBT	800	900
− Taxes	320	360
Net Income	480	540

The firm's current capital expenditure is $500 million. It is considering five projects for the next year:

Project	Investment	Beta	IRR (using cash flows to equity)
A	$190 mil	0.6	12.0%
B	$200 mil	0.8	12.0%
C	$200 mil	1.0	14.5%
D	$200 mil	1.2	15.0%
E	$100 mil	1.5	20.0%

The firm's current beta is 1.0, and the current Treasury bill rate is 5.5%. The firm expects working capital to increase $50 million both this year and next. The firm plans to finance its net capital expenditures and working capital needs with 30% debt.

a. What is the firm's current payout ratio?

b. What proportion of its current free cash flow to equity is it paying out as dividends?

c. What would your projected capital expenditure be for next year? (i.e. which of the five projects would you accept and why?)

d. How much cash will the company have available to pay out as dividends next year? (What is the maximum amount the company should pay out as dividends?)

e. Would you pay out this maximum amount as dividends? Why or why not? What other considerations would you bring to this decision?

f. JKL Corporation currently has a cash balance of $100 million (after paying the current year's dividends). If it pays out $125 million as dividends next year, what will its projected cash balance be at the end of the next year?

2. SASS is a small, closely held corporation that sells statistical software to brokerage houses and investment banks on CD-ROM. SASS will soon buy new, inexpensive "recordable" CD-ROM drives to enable them to produce software for distribution to their customers "in house." This is not only expected to reduce annual production costs by $20,000 per year, but will also enable the company to reduce inventory by $15,000 per year. The new drives will cost $12,000 (including shipping and installation) and will increase next year's depreciation by $2,400 (using MACRS depreciation). SASS finances all net capital expenditures and working capital requirements out of retained earnings and is in the 40% tax bracket.

a. How will the purchase of the new drives affect the company's FCFE for the coming year?

b. How permanent will this effect be?

3. In the problem above, assume that SASS is owned by a husband and wife who currently pay 35% in combined state and federal taxes on personal income. These owners have decided to keep their company focused on the current product line and, hence, will not invest in any future capital expenditures except those needed to replace existing assets (i.e., no new projects).

a. Should they use any increase in FCFE to increase the dividends paid to them by the company?

b. Would your answer change if you learned that the owners intended to sell the business within the next few years?

4. GL Corporation, a retail firm, is making a decision on how much it should pay out to its stockholders. It has $100 million in investable funds. The following information is provided about the firm:

a. It has 100 million shares outstanding, each share selling for $15. The beta of the stock is 1.25, and the T. Bond rate is 8%.

b. The firm has $500 million of debt outstanding. The marginal interest rate on the debt is 12%.

c. The corporation's tax rate is 50%.

e. The firm has the following investment projects:

Project	Investment Requirement	After-Tax Return on capital
A	$15 million	27%
B	10 million	20%
C	25 million	16%
D	20 million	14%
E	30 million	12%

The firm plans to finance all its investment needs at its current debt ratio.

• Should the company return money to its stockholders?

• If so, how much should be returned to stockholders?

5. InTech Corporation, a computer software firm that has never paid dividends before, is considering whether it should start doing so. This firm has a cost of equity of 16% and a cost of debt of 10%. (The tax rate is 40%.) The firm has $100 million in debt outstanding and 50 million shares outstanding, selling for $10 per share. The firm currently has net income of $90 million and depreciation charges of $10 million. It also has projects available as shown below:

The firm plans to finance its future capital investment needs using 20% debt.

a. Which of these projects should the firm accept?

b. How much (if any) should the firm pay out as dividends?

Project	Initial Investment	EBIT	Annual Depreciation	Lifetime	Salvage
1	$10 million	$1 mil	$500,000	5 years	$2.5 mil
2	$40 million	$5 mil	$1 million	10 years	$10 mil
3	$50 million	$5 mil	$1 million	10 years	$10 mil

6. LimeAde Corporation, a large soft drink manufacturing firm, is faced with the decision of how much to pay out as dividends to its stockholders. It expects to have a net income of $1,000 (after depreciation of $500), and it has the following projects:

Project	Initial Investment	Beta	IRR (to equity investors)
A	$500	2.0	21%
B	$600	1.5	20%
C	$500	1.0	12%

The firm's beta is 1.5, and the current T-Bond rate is 9%. The firm plans to finance net capital expenditures (cap ex-depreciation) and working capital with 20% debt. The firm also has current revenues of $5,000, which it expects to grow at 8%. Working capital will be maintained at 25% of revenues. How much should the firm return to its stockholders as a dividend?

7. Triple J is a publicly traded tobacco company that is expecting to experience a 10% annual decrease in revenues, expenses, working capital, and depreciation for each of the next three years. The company paid off all outstanding debt at the beginning of last year and had net income of $48 million in the year just ended. Management has decided to dramatically change the focus of the company to specialize in the telecommunications industry. Toward that end, the managers have decided to forego any additional capital expenditures in the tobacco business for the next three years in order to build a "war chest" to be used to acquire a presence in the target industry. Using the information shown below, determine how large the war chest will be at the end of three years if management keeps the payout ratio at its current level. (You may assume that Triple J will invest any retained earnings in a money market account that will earn 10% per year. Furthermore,

the current balance of the cash account is earmarked for maintaining the existing lines of business, so it shouldn't be included in your calculations.)

8. Is the strategy of Triple J's management described in the last problem in the shareholders' best interests? Why or why not?

9. NoLone Corporation, an all-equity manufacturing firm, has net income of $100 million currently and expects this number to grow at 10% a year for the next three years. The firm's working capital increased by $10 million this year and is expected to increase by the same dollar amount each of the next three years. The depreciation is $50 million and is expected to grow 8% a year for the next three years. Finally, the firm plans to invest $60 million in capital expenditure for each of the next three years. The firm pays 60% of its earnings as dividends each year. RYBR has a cash balance currently of $50. Assuming that the cash does not earn any interest, how much would you expect to have as a cash balance at the end of the third year?

10. Boston Turkey is a publicly traded firm, with the following income statement and balance sheet from its most recent financial year:

INCOME STATEMENT

Revenues	$1,000,000
− Expenses	$400,000
− Depreciation	$100,000
EBIT	$500,000
− Interest Expense	$100,000
Taxable Income	$400,000
− Tax	$160,000
Net Income	$240,000

INCOME STATEMENT FOR YEAR JUST ENDED

Revenues	$500,000,000
− Expenses	$350,000,000
− Depreciation	$70,000,000
EBIT	$80,000,000
− Taxes	$32,000,000
Net Income	$48,000,000
Dividends Paid	$24,000,000

Pertinent Balance Sheet Information
NWC = $70,000,000

BALANCE SHEET

ASSETS		LIABILITIES	
Property, Plant, and Equipment	$1,500,000	Accounts Payable	$500,000
Land and Buildings	$500,000	Long-term Debt	$1,000,000
Current Assets	$1,000,000	Equity (100,000 shares)	$1,500,000
Total	$3,000,000	Total	$3,000,000

Boston Turkey expects its revenues to grow 10% next year and its expenses to remain at 40% of revenues. The depreciation and interest expenses will remain unchanged at $100,000 next year. The working capital, as a percentage of revenue, will also remain unchanged next year.

The managers of Boston Turkey claim to have several projects available to choose from next year, in which they plan to invest the funds from operations, and they suggest that the firm really should not be paying dividends. The projects have the following characteristics:

Project	Equity Investment	Expected Annual CF to Equity	Beta
A	$100,000	12,500	1.00
B	$100,000	14,000	1.50
C	$50,000	8,000	1.80
D	$50,000	12,000	2.00

The Treasury bond rate is 6.25%. The firm plans to finance 40% of its future net capital expenditures (cap ex-depreciation) and working capital needs with debt.

a. How much can the company afford to pay in dividends next year?

b. Now assume that the firm actually pays out $1 per share in dividends next year. The current cash balance of the firm is $150,000. How much will the cash balance of the firm be at the end of next year, after the payment of the dividend?

11. Z-Tec Corporation, a firm providing Internet services, reported net income of $10 million in the most recent year, while making $25 million in capital expenditures (depreciation was $5 million). The firm had no working capital needs and uses no debt.

a. Can the firm afford to pay out dividends right now? Why or why not?

b. Assuming that net income grows 40% a year and that net capital expenditures grow 10% a year, when will the firm be in a position to pay dividends?

12. You are analyzing the dividend policy of Conrail, a major railroad, and you have collected the following information from the last five years:

The average debt ratio during this period was 40%, and the total noncash working capital at the end of 1990 was $10 million.

a. Estimate how much Conrail could have paid in dividends during this period.

b. If the average return on equity during the period was 13.5% and Conrail had a beta of 1.25, what conclusions would you draw about Conrail's dividend policy? (The average Treasury bond rate during the period was 7%, and the average return on the market was 12.5% during the period.)

13. Assume now that you have been asked to forecast cash flows that you will have available to repurchase stock and pay dividends during the next five years for Conrail. In making these forecasts, you can assume the following:

• Net Income is anticipated to grow 10% a year from 1995 levels for the next five years.
• Capital expenditures and depreciation are expected to grow 8% a year from 1995 levels.
• The revenues in 1995 were $3.75 billion and are expected to grow 5% each year for the next five years. The working capital as a percentage of revenues is expected to remain at 1995 levels.
• The proportion of net capital expenditures and depreciation that will be financed with debt will drop to 30%.

a. Estimate how much cash Conrail will have available to pay dividends or repurchase stocks over the next five years.

b. How will the perceived uncertainty associated with these cash flows affect your decision on dividends and equity repurchases?

14. Cracker Barrel, which operates restaurants and gift stores, is reexamining its policy of paying minimal dividends. In 1995, Cracker Barrel reported net income of $66 million; it had capital expenditures of $150 million in that year and claimed depreciation of only $50 million. The working capital in 1995 was $43 million on sales of $783 million. Looking forward, Cracker Barrel expects the following:

Year	Net Income	Capital Expenditure	Depreciation	Noncash Working Capital	Dividends
1991	$240	$314	$307	$35	$70
1992	282	466	295	(110)	80
1993	320	566	284	215	95
1994	375	490	278	175	110
1995	441	494	293	250	124

- Net Income is expected to grow 17% a year for the next five years.

- During the five years, capital expenditures are expected to grow 10% a year, and depreciation is expected to grow 15% a year.

- The working capital as a percentage of revenues is expected to remain at 1995 levels, and revenues are expected to grow 10% a year during the period.

- The company has not used debt to finance its net capital expenditures and does not plan to use any for the next five years.

a. Estimate how much cash Cracker Barrel would have available to pay out to its stockholders over the next five years.

b. How would your answer change if the firm plans to increase its leverage by borrowing 25% of its net capital expenditure and working capital needs?

15. Assume that Cracker Barrel wants to continue with its policy of not paying dividends. You are the CEO of Cracker Barrel and have been confronted by dissident stockholders, demanding to know why you are not paying out your FCFE (estimated in the previous problem) to your stockholders. How would you defend your decision? How receptive will stockholders be to your defense? Would it make any difference that Cracker Barrel has earned a return on equity of 25% over the previous five years, and that its beta is only 1.2? (The T Bond rate was 7%)

16. Manpower Corporation, which provides nongovernment employment services in the United States, reported net income of $128 million in 1995. It had capital expenditures of $50 million and depreciation of $24 million in 1995, and its working capital was $500 million (on revenues of $5 billion). The firm has a debt ratio of 10% and plans to maintain this debt ratio.

a. Estimate how much Manpower Corporation will have available to pay out as dividends next year, if all these items are expected to grow 10%?

b. The current cash balance is $143 million. If Manpower Corporation is expected to pay $12 million in dividends next year and repurchase no stock, estimate the expected cash balance at the end of the next year.

17. How would your answers to the previous problem change if Manpower Corporation plans to pay off its outstanding debt of $100 million next year and become a debt-free company?

18. You are an institutional investor and have collected the following information on five maritime firms in order to assess their dividend policies:

Company	FCFE	Dividends Paid	ROE	Beta
Alexander & Brown	$55	$35	8%	0.80
American President	$60	$12	14.5%	1.30
OMI Corporation	−$15	$5	4.0%	1.25
Overseas Shipholding	$20	$12	1.5%	0.90
Sea Containers	−$5	$8	14%	1.05

The average risk-free rate during the period was 7%, and the average return on the market was 12%.

a. Assess which of these firms you would pressure to pay more in dividends.

b. Which of the firms would you encourage to pay less in dividends?

c. How would you modify this analysis to reflect your expectations about the future of the entire sector?

19. You are analyzing the dividend policy of Black and Decker, a manufacturer of tools and appliances. The following table summarizes the dividend payout ratios, yields, and expected growth rates of other firms in the waste disposal business.

a. Compare Black and Decker's dividend policy to those of its peers, using the average dividend payout ratios and yields.

b. Do the same comparison, controlling for differences in expected growth.

Company	Payout Ratio (%)	Dividend Yield (%)	Exp. Growth (%)
Fedders Corporation	11	1.2	22.0
Maytag Corporation	37	2.8	23.0
National Presto	67	4.9	13.5
Toro Corporation	15	1.5	16.5
Whirlpool Corp.	30	2.5	20.5
Black & Decker	24	1.3	23.0

20. The following regression was run using all NYSE firms in 1995:

$$YIELD = 0.0478 - 0.0157\, BETA - 0.0000008MKTCAP$$
$$MKTCAP + 0.006797\, DBTRATIO + 0.0002\, ROE$$
$$- 0.09\, NCEX/TA \qquad R^2 = 12.88\%$$

where BETA = Beta of the stock
   MKTCAP = Market Value of Equity + Book Value of Debt
   DBTRATIO = Book Value of Debt / MKTCAP
   ROE = Return on Equity in 1994
   NCEX/TA = (Capital Expenditures − Depreciation) / Total Assets

The corresponding values for Black and Decker, in 1995, were as follows:

> Beta = 1.30
> MKTCAP = $5,500 million
> DBTRATIO = 35%
> ROE = 14.5%
> NCEX/TA = 4.00%

Black and Decker had a dividend yield of 1.3% and a dividend payout ratio of 24% in 1995.

a. Estimate the dividend yield for Black & Decker, based on the regression.

b. Why might your answer be different, using this approach, than the answer to the prior question, where you used only the comparable firms?

21. Handy and Harman, a leading fabricator of precious metal alloys, pays out only 23% of its earnings as dividends. The average dividend payout ratio for metal fabricating firms is 45%. The average growth rate in earnings for the entire sector is 10% (Handy and Harman is expected to grow 23%). Should Handy and Harman pay more in dividends just to get closer to the average payout ratio? Why or why not?

22. Is there any situation where a high payout/poor projects combination may actually be to the benefit of the shareholders? (*Hint:* Think about why we have bond covenants.)

CHAPTER 22

RETURNING CASH TO STOCKHOLDERS

In the last two chapters, we established a framework for deciding how much cash a firm should return to its stockholders, while emphasizing that there are several ways besides dividends to accomplish this objective. In this chapter, we explicitly consider some of the alternatives to dividends, such as equity repurchases. We also consider the rationale for the use of stock dividends and attempt to answer the following questions:

- What are the alternatives to paying dividends?
- When should companies repurchase stock rather than pay dividends? When should companies use one of the other alternatives?
- What is the rationale for stock dividends, stock splits, and spinoffs? How are they related to cash dividends?
- Given that changes in dividend policy may have information effects and affect stock prices, how can companies best manage changes in dividends? In particular, how should a firm that plans to cut dividends convey this information to the market?

APPROACHES TO RETURNING CASH TO STOCKHOLDERS (OTHER THAN DIVIDENDS)

In earlier chapters, we noted that dividends represent just one way of returning cash to stockholders. There are other approaches that may provide more attractive options to firms, depending on their stockholder characteristics and their objectives. These include *equity repurchases,* whereby the cash is used to buy back outstanding stock in the firm, reducing the number of shares outstanding; and *forward contracts* to buy equity in future periods, whereby the price at which the shares will be bought back is fixed.

While not strictly representing the return of cash to stockholders, we will also consider four other options: *stock dividends* and *stock splits,* which, though used by many firms to supplement cash dividends, just change the number of shares outstanding, and *spinoffs* and *splitoffs,* which involves the issue of stock that is in only a part of the business and is therefore different from the existing common stock.

EQUITY REPURCHASES

The most widely used alternative to paying dividends is to use the cash to repurchase outstanding stock. Such *equity repurchases* provide some advantages to firms, but they also have some limitations relative to dividends.

The Process of Equity Repurchase

The process of repurchasing equity will depend largely on whether the firm intends to repurchase stock in the open market, at the prevailing market price, or to make a more formal tender offer for its shares. There are three widely used approaches to buying back equity:

- *Repurchase Tender Offers:* In a **repurchase tender offer,** a firm specifies a price at which it will buy back shares, the number of shares it intends to repurchase, and the period of time for which it will keep the offer open, and invites stockholders to submit their shares for the repurchase. In many cases, firms retain the flexibility to withdraw the offer if an insufficient number of shares are submitted or to extend the offer beyond the originally specified time period. This approach is used primarily for large equity repurchases.

Repurchase Tender Offer: This is an offer by a firm to buy back a specified number of shares at a fixed price during the offer period.

- *Open Market Purchases:* In the case of **open market repurchases,** firms buy shares in the market at the prevailing market price. Although firms do not have to disclose publicly their intent to buy back shares in the market, they have to comply with SEC requirements to prevent price manipulation or insider trading. Finally, open market purchases can be spread out over longer time periods than tender offers and are much more widely used for smaller repurchases. In terms of flexibility, an open market repurchase affords the firm more freedom in deciding when to buy back shares and how many shares to repurchase.

Open Market Purchases: This is an offer to buy shares in the market at the prevailing market price.

- *Privately Negotiated Repurchases:* In privately negotiated repurchases, firms buy back shares from a large stockholder in the company at a negotiated price. This method is not as widely used as the first two and may be employed by managers or owners as a way of consolidating control and eliminating a troublesome stockholder.

☐ Concept Check

When making privately negotiated repurchases, would you expect firms to pay a higher or lower price than if they made open market purchases?

The Rationale

In the last decade, more and more firms have used equity repurchases as an alternative to paying dividends. Figure 22.1 summarizes new equity issues and equity repurchases at U.S. corporations between 1981 and 1990.

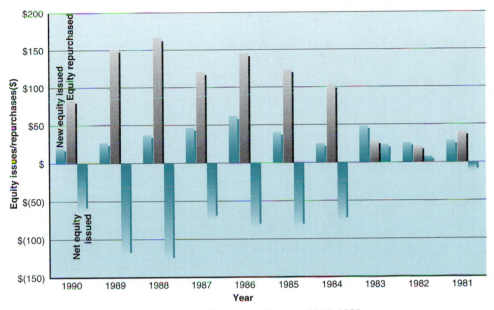

Figure 22.1   Net equity issues—1981–1990

There are several advantages to using equity repurchases as an alternative to dividend payments to return cash to stockholders:

1. Unlike regular dividends, which imply a commitment to continue payment in future periods, equity repurchases are viewed primarily as one-time returns of cash. Consequently, firms with excess cash flows, which are uncertain about their ability to continue generating these cash flows in future periods, should repurchase stocks rather than pay dividends. These firms could choose to pay special dividends instead of repurchasing stock, however, since special dividends also do not imply a commitment to making similar payments in the future.

2. The decision to repurchase stock affords firms much more flexibility to reverse themselves and/ to spread the repurchases over a longer period than does the decision to pay an equivalent special dividend. In fact, there is substantial evidence that many firms that announce ambitious stock repurchase plans do not carry them through to completion.

3. Equity repurchases may offer tax advantages to stockholders, since dividends are taxed at ordinary tax rates, whereas the price appreciation that flows from equity repurchases is taxed at capital gains rate. Furthermore, stockholders have the option not to sell their shares back to the firm and therefore do not have to realize the capital gains in the period of the equity repurchases.

4. Equity repurchases are much more focused in terms of paying out cash only to those stockholders who need it. This benefit flows from the voluntary nature of stock buybacks: those who need the cash can tender their shares back to the firm, whereas those who do not can continue to hold on to them.

5. Equity repurchases may provide a way of increasing insider control in firms, for they reduce the number of shares outstanding. If the insiders do not tender their shares back, they will end up holding a larger proportion of the firm and, consequently, having greater control.

6. Finally, equity repurchases may provide firms with a way of supporting their stock prices when they are under assault. For instance, in the aftermath of the crash of 1987, many firms initiated stock buyback plans to keep stock prices from falling further.

In summary, equity repurchases allow firms to return cash to stockholders and still maintain flexibility in terms of future periods.

What About Reduced Dilution?

Some equity repurchases are motivated by the desire to reduce the number of shares outstanding and therefore increase the earnings per share. This argument is buttressed by assuming that the firm's price/earnings ratio will remain unchanged, leading to a higher price. Although the reduction in the number of shares might increase earnings per share, the effect is usually a consequence of higher leverage and not of the stock buyback per se. In other words, a special dividend of the same amount would have resulted in the same returns to stockholders. Furthermore, the increase in leverage should increase the riskiness of the stock and lower the price/earnings ratio. Whether this will increase or decrease the price per share will depend on whether the firm is moving to its optimal by repurchasing stock, in which case the price will increase, or moving away from it, in which case the price will drop.

To illustrate, assume that an all-equity firm in the specialty retailing business, with 100 shares outstanding, has $100 in earnings after taxes and a market value of $1,500. Assume that this firm borrows $300 and buys back 20 shares, using the funds. As long as the after-tax interest expense on the borrowing is less than $20, this firm will report higher earnings per share after the repurchase. If the firm's tax rate is 50%, for instance, the effect on earnings per share will be as follows:

	Before Repurchase	After Repurchase Interest Expense = $30	After Repurchase Interest Expense = $55
EBIT	$200	$200	$200
− Interest	$0	$30	$55
= Taxable Inc.	$200	$170	$145
− Taxes	$100	$85	$72.50
= Net Income	$100	$85	$72.50
# Shares	100	80	80
EPS	$1.00	$1.0625	$0.91

As you can see, the earnings per share increases when the interest expense is $30 ($15 after taxes) and decreases when the interest expense is $55 ($27.50 after taxes). If we assume that the price/earnings ratio remains at 15, the price per share will change in proportion to the earnings per share. In this case, we should expect to see a drop in the price/earnings ratio, as the increase in leverage will make the firm riskier. Whether the drop will be sufficient to offset or overwhelm the increase in earnings per share will depend on whether the firm has excess debt capacity and whether, by going to 20%, it is moving closer to its optimal debt mix.

❑ Concept
   Check

> In the example above, the earnings per share changed as the firm borrowed money at 10%
> and bought back shares. Under what conditions will EPS go up?

Limitations of Equity Repurchases

Until recently, many critics of dividend policy agreed that equity repurchases were clearly preferable to both regular dividends—because of the tax advantages and the flexibility of the former—and special dividends—because of the tax benefits. There is a downside to this flexibility, however. To the degree that actions taken by firms signal their assurance about future cash flows, it can be argued that a firm that repurchases stock rather than instituting dividends is signaling a greater uncertainty about future cash flows. If this is the case, the increase in value that follows an equity repurchase would be smaller than the increase in value following an equivalent regular dividend payment. If the firm fails to carry out equity repurchase plans to completion, markets will become increasingly skeptical of these plans and respond accordingly.

The Empirical Evidence

Several studies have examined the stock (and bond) price reaction to equity repurchases; most of them indicate a strong positive stock price reaction, with increases ranging from 10% to 20% around the announcements. Furthermore, this increase seems to be permanent rather than transitory, suggesting that the price increase is not just the result of liquidity effects but of something deeper. It is not clear, however, which of the hypotheses best explains these results:

1. The increase in value seems too large to be explained away in terms of the tax benefits of equity repurchase relative to dividends. Because the typical repurchase in this sample involved a buyback of 15% to 20% of the outstanding shares, the tax savings should be roughly 5% to 6%, at the maximum.[1] Unless firms are expected to continue repurchasing large proportions of their equity every year—a very unlikely scenario—it is difficult to arrive at price increases of the magnitude observed in most of these studies.

2. It is also not clear that the price increase can be explained purely in terms of leverage, that is, that these firms were underleveraged to begin with and that buying back stock brings them closer to their optimal debt ratios (and higher firm values). For instance, Vermaelen reports that firms that do not issue debt to repurchase equity actually have higher price increase than firms that do.

3. The final possibility is that the increase in stock prices as a consequence of equity repurchases is the result of the information conveyed to financial markets by such buybacks. In particular, the equity repurchase may be viewed as a signal that the firm believes that its stock is significantly undervalued. Dann and DeAngelo tested this hypothesis by categorizing equity repurchases into privately negotiated buybacks (in which the motivation is usually control) and open market repurchases/tender offers (in which the motivation may include undervaluation), and concluded that stock prices actually declined slightly for the first group. Thus, at least some of the price increase can be attributed to information effects.

[1] A simple approximation of the tax benefit can be estimated by multiplying the equity repurchase proportion by the differential tax rate. Even taking the highest tax differential during the period (about 40%) yields a tax benefit of only 6% on an equity repurchase of 15% of the outstanding equity.

It is unfair to compare the price increase associated with equity repurchases in these studies to the price increases associated with dividend increases noted in the previous chapter, because of the difference in dollar values between the two. Rather, a more appropriate comparison would look at the impact on stock prices of a given dollar change in regular dividends with an equivalent equity repurchase. In that case, we would expect regular dividends to have a much larger impact, because it implies a much larger commitment on the part of the firm.

❑ Concept
Check

> Some stocks, even in the studies noted above, report stock price decreases on the announcement of equity repurchases. How would you explain this?

A Framework for Deciding on Equity Repurchases

Although this signaling argument has some merit, it can be argued that, for most firms, the flexibility and the tax arguments will outweigh this concern. In general, however, the net benefit of equity repurchases, relative to dividends, will depend on the following considerations.

1. *Sustainability and Stability of Excess Cash Flow:* To the degree that both equity repurchases and increased dividends are triggered by excess cash flows, the question of which course of action to take cannot be answered without looking at the sustainability of cash flows. If the excess cash flows are temporary or unstable, firms should repurchase stock; if they are stable and predictable, the signaling argument may tilt firms toward increasing dividends.

2. *Stockholder Tax Preferences:* When capital gains and dividends are taxed at different rates, the tax preferences of the stockholders will determine whether a firm should repurchase stock or pay dividends. If stockholders are taxed at much higher rates on dividends and, consequently, are averse to dividends, the firm will be better off repurchasing stock. If, on the other hand, stockholders prefer dividends, the firm may gain by paying a special dividend.

3. *Predictability of Future Investment Needs:* Firms that are uncertain about the magnitude of future investment opportunities are much more likely to use equity repurchases as a way of returning cash to stockholders.

4. *Undervaluation of the Stock:* An equity repurchase makes even more sense when managers believe or perceive their stock to be undervalued. By buying back the stock, managers can accomplish two objectives. First, if the stock remains undervalued, the remaining stockholders will benefit if managers buy back stock at less than true value. Alternatively, the stock buyback may send a signal to financial markets that the stock is undervalued, and the market will react accordingly by pushing up the price.

IN PRACTICE CHOOSING BETWEEN DIVIDENDS AND EQUITY REPURCHASES—THE GAP

In 1994, the Gap generated free cash flows to equity of $226 million and paid out dividends of only $75 million, resulting in excess cash of $151 million. We would argue that some or all of this excess cash should be used to buy back stock rather than pay dividends, for the following reasons:

1. The earnings and cash flows of specialty retailers are cyclical. If the Gap commits to paying higher regular dividends, it might be unable to maintain those dividends if the economy goes into a recession.

2. The Gap's stockholders have generally bought the stock for price appreciation rather than dividend yield. It is reasonable to assume, therefore, that they would much rather have the option to sell their shares back and make a capital gain, rather than receive a larger dividend (or a special dividend).

3. The Gap's projected expansion overseas creates uncertainty about future investment needs; if overseas expansion goes well, future investment needs will be much higher. This uncertainty tilts the scales in favor of an equity repurchase.

4. The Gap's stock price, like those of other retailers, had dropped significantly between the first quarter of 1994 (when it was at $48 a share) to the first quarter of 1995 (when it was down to $35 a share). The market may well have overreacted to the well-publicized problems faced by specialty retailers.

FORWARD CONTRACTS TO BUY EQUITY

Many firms that announce equity repurchase plans fail to carry these plans to fruition. Although this flexibility in implementation can be viewed as a benefit, it reduces the signaling benefit (and the concurrent price increase) of buying back stock. An alternative strategy, which may preserve the tax advantages of equity repurchases while also increasing the signaling benefit, is to enter into **forward contracts** to acquire stock at a fixed price. Because these contracts are legal commitments, the firm is forced to repurchase the shares at that price. Consequently, the market will likely view the action as a commitment and react accordingly.

Forward Contract: This is a contract to acquire an asset (like stock) at a fixed price at a specified time in the future.

Another advantage of forward contracts is that unlike regular equity repurchases, in which the number of shares that will be bought back in future periods is unknown because the stock price will be different, the number of shares that will be bought back in a forward contract is known because the purchases are at a fixed price. Consequently, the effects of the equity repurchase plans on earnings per share and related multiples can be estimated more precisely.

This certainty comes at a price, however. By agreeing to buy back shares at a fixed price, the firm increases its risk exposure, because it commits to paying this price even if the stock price drops. Although it may gain an offsetting advantage if stock prices go up, the commitment to pay a higher price to buy stocks when stock prices are lower can be a burden, especially if the stock price dropped as a consequence of lower earnings or cash flows.

To summarize, the decision to cement the commitment to buying back stocks by entering into a forward contract will depend, in large part, on whether the signaling benefits are large enough to offset the higher risk and lost flexibility associated with the forward contract. The choice between paying an increased dividend or entering into a

❑ Concept Check

An alternative strategy is to sell puts on the firm's stock, giving holders the option to sell back stock to the firm at a fixed price in the future. How is this different from the forward contract described above?

forward contract involves a tradeoff between the tax savings that may accrue from the forward contract and the increased risk associated with the forward contract.

STOCK DIVIDENDS AND STOCK SPLITS

A **stock dividend** involves issuing to existing stockholders additional shares in the company at no cost. Thus, in a 5% stock dividend, every existing stockholder in the firm receives new shares equivalent to 5% of the number of shares currently owned. Many firms use stock dividends to supplement cash dividends; others view them as an alternative. A *stock split,* in some ways, is just a large stock dividend, for it too increases the number of shares outstanding, but it does so by a much larger factor. Thus, a firm may have a two-for-one stock split, whereby the number of shares in the firm is doubled.

Stock Dividend (Split):   These are additional shares issued at no cost to existing stockholders, in proportion to their current holdings.

The mechanics of a stock split or dividend are simple: the firm issues additional shares in the firm and distributes them to existing stockholders in proportion to their original holdings in the firm. Thus, stock splits and dividends should not alter the proportional ownership of the firm on the part of existing stockholders.

Effect on Value

Because stock dividends and stock splits have no real effect on cash flows but change only the number of shares outstanding, they should not affect the cash flows of the firm, and thus should not increase the value of equity, in the aggregate. Rather, the share price will decline to reflect the increased number of shares. To illustrate, assume that a small manufacturing firm with an aggregate value of equity of $110 million and 10 million shares outstanding declares a 10% stock dividend. The aggregate value of equity will remain $110 million, but the price per share will drop from $11 per share ($110 million/10 million) to $10 per share ($110 million/11 million). Note, however, that the stockholders in this firm are no worse off after the stock dividend, the stock price drop notwithstanding, because they receive a compensatory increase in the number of shares outstanding.

The Rationale

If the effect on stockholder wealth is in fact neutral, why do firms pay stock dividends or announce stock splits in the first place? Some firms view stock dividends as a way of fooling stockholders: Thus, a firm that is in trouble and unable to pay its regular cash dividend may announce that it is "substituting" an equivalent stock dividend. Some stockholders may actually believe that these are substitutes, but it is extremely unlikely that financial markets will not see through this deception. Other firms view stock dividends as a supplement to cash dividends and use them in periods in which they have posted good results. This rationale is more defensible because the announcement of a stock dividend may convey information to financial markets about future prospects. In fact, the use of both stock dividends and stock splits as signals of better cash flows in the future may increase the firm value.

An additional reason given (especially) for stock splits is the desire of some firms to keep their stock prices within a specified trading range. Consequently, if the stock price rises above the range, a stock split may be used to bring the price back down. To illustrate, assume that a firm wants its stock to trade in the $20 to $40 range and that the stock price rises to $45. With a two-for-one stock split, the number of shares will double and the stock price will drop back down to $22.50.

The remaining question is why would a firm have a desired trading range in the first place? Firms that do have a desired range argue that, given restrictions on buying shares in even lots (e.g., 100 shares), a price that is too high reduces the potential market for the stock to wealthier investors and institutional investors. Bringing the price down increases the number of potential buyers for the stock, leading to a higher stock price. Furthermore, there is a control benefit to the stock being more widely held. Both of these arguments are dubious, however. The transactions costs, if one counts the bid-ask spread as one component, actually increases as a percentage of the stock price as the price drops. Thus, the firm may lose more investors than it gains by cutting the price. There is a cost to being widely held, as well, since it increases the gulf between stockholders and managers and leads to higher agency costs.

As noted earlier in Chapter 15, the empirical evidence on stock splits suggests that although the initial price reaction to stock splits is positive, these excess returns are not sustained if the firm cannot maintain or increase its dividends in following periods.

□ Concept
Check

Why would the bid-ask spread increase as a percentage of the stock price when the stock price drops?

DIVESTITURES, SPIN OFFS, SPLIT UPS, AND SPLIT OFFS

Divestitures, spin offs, split ups, and splits offs are other options for returning non-cash assets to stockholders. Consider a company with operations in multiple business lines, some of which are being systematically undervalued; the whole firm is therefore worth less than its parts. This firm has four options:

1. *Divest the undervalued business and pay a liquidating dividend:* One way in which this firm can deal with its predicament is through **divestiture,** which involves selling those parts that are being undervalued by the market for their true market value and then paying out the cash to stockholders in the form of either equity repurchases or dividends.

Divestiture: A divestiture is the sale of a portion or portions of a firm for cash.

2. *Spin off the undervalued businesses:* An alternative is to **spin off** or create a new class of shares in the undervalued business line and to distribute these shares to the existing stockholders. Because the shares are distributed in proportion to the existing share ownership, it does not alter the proportional ownership in the firm.

Spin off: In a spinoff, shares in an asset or assets of a firm are created and distributed to stockholders in proportion to their holdings.

3. *Split up the entire firm:* In a **split up,** the firm splits itself off into different business lines, distributes these shares to the original stockholders in proportion to their original ownership in the firm, and then ceases to exist.

4. *Split off the undervalued business:* A **split off** is similar to a spinoff, insofar as it creates new shares in the undervalued business line. In this case, however, the existing

stockholders are given the option to exchange their parent company stock for these new shares, which changes the proportional ownership in the new structure.

■ **Split off:** In a split off, shares in an asset or assets of a firm are created, and stockholders are given the option to exchange their parent company shares for these new shares.

The Mechanics

In terms of the mechanics, divestitures are the most straightforward to understand. The firm sells the assets to the highest bidder and then uses the cash generated by the sale to pay a special dividend or to buy back stock. In the case of spin offs and split ups, the existing stockholders receive the new shares of stock in proportion to their existing holdings, whereas in the case of split offs, the firm offers stockholders the option to convert their existing shares for the new shares in the subsidiary. The SEC also requires that stock issued in spin offs be registered to prevent abuses of the process.

Spin offs may be taxed as dividends if firms do not meet certain requirements under the tax code, which is designed to ensure that there is a business purpose for the transaction rather than tax avoidance. First, the parent and the subsidiary must be engaged in business for the five years preceding the spin off, and the subsidiary must be at least 80% owned by the parent. Second, the parent has to distribute the shares in the subsidiary without a prearranged plan for these securities to be resold.

The Rationale

Firms may choose to divest or spin off assets for a number of reasons and may choose one approach over the others:

1. *Source of Undervaluation:* The initial rationale for divestitures, spin offs, split offs, and split ups is the perceived undervaluation of some or all of the firm's components. The firm may be undervalued for a number of different reasons, each of which lends itself to a different response.

   - If the poor quality of incumbent management of a division is one of the reasons for the low value assigned to a business, the firm will probably gain the most by selling the business, severing its connection to incumbent management. If, on the other hand, the problem lies in the quality of management at the corporate level, a spin-off may be all that is needed.

   - If there is a broad perception that sections of the business are undervalued because of the pall created by other sections of the business, the appropriate response will be a spinoff, if only one business line is involved, or a splitup, if multiple business lines are involved. For example, consider the pressure brought to bear on the tobacco firms, such as Philip Morris and RJR Nabisco, to spin off their food businesses, because of the perception that the lawsuits overhanging the tobacco businesses were weighing down the values of their food businesses as well. An example of a splitup comes from AT & T and its proposed break up into three business lines, each trading separate shares.

   - If some stockholders believe that a section of the firm is undervalued, a split off may make more sense because it allows these stockholders the option to exchange their shares for the new shares, maximizing the value increment to the firm.

In the case of spinoffs, splitoffs, and splitups, the division or assets can continue to operate relatively smoothly. A sale or breakup of the assets might have a disruptive influence, however, which, in turn, might lower their value.

2. *Tax and Regulatory Concerns:* One or another of these options may provide a tax benefit, making it more favorable. For instance, Marriott spun off its real estate operations into a **REIT** in the late 1980s. One reason for the spin off might have been the perception of undervaluation. An even stronger reason might have been the tax advantages accruing from the REIT status, because REITs do not pay taxes at the entity level. A second concern is that the spun-off entity might be under less regulatory constraints than the parent company. For instance, AT & T may have decided to spin off its nonphone businesses in part because the regulatory burden under which the phone business operated was constraining its other business pursuits as well.

Real Estate Investment Trusts (REITs):   A real estate investment trust is a real estate holding firm with traded securities, which is entitled to special tax treatment in return for restrictions on dividends and investment policy.

3. *Expropriation of Bondholder Wealth:* Some divestitures or spinoffs are motivated by the desire to transfer wealth from bondholders to stockholders. In a divestiture, the sale of an existing asset and the payment of a liquidating dividend clearly leave bondholders worse off. In a spinoff or splitup, the results are more ambiguous, since the spun-off entities often take a share of the debt with them.

☐ Concept
Check

> A badly managed firm is planning to spin off its most profitable businesses and keep the less profitable ones, but it plans to keep the spun-off division under existing management. Will there be an increase in value? Why or why not?

Empirical Evidence

Linn and Rozeff (1984) examined the price reaction to announcements of divestitures by firms and reported an average excess return of 1.45% for 77 divestitures between 1977 and 1982. Their results have been confirmed by a number of other studies of sell-offs. They also note an interesting contrast between firms that announce the sale price and motive for the divestiture at the time of the divestiture and those that do not: in general, markets react much more positively to the first group than to the second, as shown in Table 22.1.

Table 22.1   **MARKET REACTION TO DIVESTITURE ANNOUNCEMENTS**

	Motive Announced	
Price Announced	**Yes**	**No**
Yes	3.92%	2.30%
No	0.70%	0.37%

It appears that financial markets view firms that are evasive about the reasons for and the uses of proceeds from divestitures with skepticism.

Schipper and Smith (1983) examined 93 firms that announced spinoffs between 1963 and 1981 and reported an average excess return of 2.84% in the two days surrounding the announcement. Similar results are reported in Hite and Owens (1983) and Miles and Rosenfeld (1983). Furthermore, there is evidence that the excess returns increase with the magnitude of the spun-off entity. Finally, Schipper and Smith find evidence that the excess returns are greater for firms in which the spinoff is motivated by tax and regulatory concerns.

CHOOSING AMONG THE ALTERNATIVES

As you can see, firms have a variety of options available to them when it comes to returning cash to stockholders. They can pay out the cash as dividends—either regular or special—repurchase stock, enter into forward contracts to buy stock, or spin off businesses and distribute special stock in these businesses to their stockholders. In this section, we will attempt to develop a general framework that brings together all these factors.

The Determinants

The broad determinants of which approach a firm should use to return cash to stockholders include the tax implications of each approach, the effect on a firm's flexibility on future actions, and the signaling benefits (or price effect) that may accrue from each of the actions. In addition, firms often consider how ratings agencies and analysts will view these actions, and the restrictions imposed by existing bond covenants, in making their final decisions.

Information effects and signaling incentives   A clear information effect is associated with each of the actions described above. The signaling benefit from each action will vary, however, depending on the degree of commitment associated with it. Thus, increases in regular dividends convey a larger commitment than do equity repurchases, for example, since regular dividends have to be maintained in future periods. Table 22.2 ranks the actions described above in terms of the commitment associated with each and the associated signaling benefit.

Table 22.2   COMMITMENT AND SIGNALING BENEFIT ASSOCIATED WITH ACTIONS

Action	Commitment	Signaling Benefit
Regular Dividend	To continue payment at the same level in future periods.	High
Special Dividend	None.	None
Equity Repurchase	Generally low, unless the company has a practice of buying back stock. It may, however, operate as a signal that the stock is undervalued currently.	Low-Moderate
Forward Equity Contracts	To buy stock at the forward price.	High
Stock Splits/Dividends	Generally none, but some firms may be expected to maintain the same dollar dividend per share (which would be an increase in dividends).	Low
Spinoffs/Splitups	It may operate as a signal that the business being spun off is undervalued.	Low-Moderate

Stockholder tax preferences   Each of the actions described above has tax consequences, in terms of both the rate at which stockholders will be taxed and the time these taxes are due. These tax consequences will vary across different types of stockholders—individual versus institutional, taxable versus tax-exempt, and wealthy versus poor. Thus, a firm needs to know who its stockholders are in order to choose an optimal approach to returning cash to stockholders. Table 22.3 summarizes the tax consequences of each action for both individual and institutional stockholders.

Table 22.3   TAX CONSEQUENCES OF ACTIONS

Action	Tax Consequences to Individual Investors
Regular Dividend	• Individual investors are taxed at ordinary tax rate.
	• Corporate investors are exempt from paying taxes on 85% of dividends received.
Special Dividend	• Individual investors are taxed at ordinary tax rate.
	• Corporate investors are exempt from paying taxes on 85% of dividends received.
Equity Repurchase	• Both individual and corporate investors are taxed at capital gains tax rate.
Forward Equity Contracts	• Both individual and corporate investors are taxed at capital gains tax rate.
Stock Splits/Stock Dividends	• Generally no tax consequences for investors.
Spinoffs/Splitups	• Not taxable if it fulfills the conditions laid out in the tax law.

Effect on flexibility   Firms value flexibility in making investment, financing, and dividend decisions in the future. To the degree that some of the actions described above reduce flexibility more than others, firms may avoid taking them. The tradeoff, however, is between preserving flexibility and increasing the signaling benefits from a given action. Increasing dividends has a large positive signaling benefit precisely because it requires a commitment on the part of the firm and because its reduces flexibility.

Bond covenants   In some cases, bond covenants may restrict a firm's flexibility in setting or changing dividends. In particular, these covenants may specify that no more than a specified percentage of earnings can be paid out as dividends (to prevent firms from paying out liquidating dividends) and that equity repurchases either have to be approved by bondholders or that the bonds be puttable if the equity repurchase goes through. In fact, bond covenant restrictions on financing policy may also constrain the firm when it comes to deciding how much and how to return cash to stockholders.

In an interesting twist on this same principle, it can be argued that firms that do not use the freedom which covenants grant them to pay dividends may be transferring wealth to bondholders, especially if bond prices are set on the assumption that they will. To illustrate, if the bond covenant restricts dividend payments to 50% of earnings, and bond prices are set on the assumption that they will be set at that level, a firm that pays out only 20% of its earnings as dividends may be enriching the bondholders at the expense of the stockholders.

Ratings agency/analyst views   When the time comes to choose among alternative approaches to returning cash or assets to stockholders, firms often consider the views of investors and equity research analysts, on the one hand, and of rating agencies and other representatives of bondholders, on the other. To the degree that the interests of the groups do not coincide, the firm may have to choose between them. To illustrate, a firm might be under pressure to spin off its most valuable assets if stockholders feel that the value of these assets is being dragged down by a negative perception of the rest of the firm. At the same time, the firms' bondholders may be averse to a spinoff, especially if it reduces their claim on these assets.

❑ Concept
Check

Is it possible that a spinoff will be greeted favorably by both stockholders and bondholders? If yes, explain.

A General Framework
In a general framework, firms will consider *all* of these determinants in deciding how to return cash to stockholders. Based on the above discussion, for instance, we can make the following assumptions:

1. Firms that want to derive the maximum signaling benefit from the return of the cash, and whose stockholders like or are indifferent to cash dividends, will likely increase regular dividends. Firms that want to derive the signaling benefit but whose stockholders are more resistant to dividends might have to enter into forward contracts to repurchase equity.

2. Firms that are unsure about their capacity to keep generating excess cash in future periods are more inclined to use special dividends, if their stockholder base likes dividends, or equity repurchases, if it does not.

3. Firms that do not have excess cash flows in the current period but believe in their capacity to generate higher cash flows in the future may use stock splits and dividends, with the implicit understanding that they will be increasing dividends in future periods.

4. Firms that have assets they believe to be significantly undervalued can sell the assets and return the cash to stockholders (special dividends or equity repurchases) if the assets are liquid and the perceived quality of incumbent management is one of the reasons for the undervaluation. If the assets are not liquid, however, and it is desirable for incumbent management to stay in place, firms should consider spinoffs, whereby existing stockholders get stock in the undervalued assets.

MANAGING CHANGES IN DIVIDEND POLICY

In Chapter 20, we noted that investors tend to buy stocks with dividend policies that meet their specific needs. Thus, investors who want high current cash flows and do not care much about the tax consequences migrate to firms that pay high dividends; those who want price appreciation and are concerned about the tax differential hold stock in firms that pay low or no dividends. One consequence of this clientele effect is that changes in dividends, even if entirely justified by the cash flows, may not be well received by stockholders. In particular, a firm with high dividends which cuts its dividends drastically may find itself facing some very unhappy stockholders. At the other extreme, a firm with a history of not paying dividends which suddenly institutes a large dividend may also find that its stockholders are not pleased.

Is there a way in which firms can announce changes in dividend policy that minimizes the negative fallout that is likely to occur? In this section, we will examine a few case studies of dividend changes and the market reaction to them and draw broader lessons for all firms that may plan to make such changes.

Empirical Evidence

Firms may cut dividends for several reasons; some clearly have negative implications for future cash flows and the current value of the firm, whereas others have more positive implications. In particular, stockholders tend to reduce the value of firms that cut dividends because of poor earnings and cash flows as opposed to, say, a dramatic improvement in project choice. At the same time, financial markets tend to be skeptical of the latter claims, especially if there seems to be contemporaneous evidence of earnings declines. Thus, it is valuable to examine the contemporaneous actions and announcements made by firms that announce dividend cuts to see if the market reaction changes as a consequence.

Woolridge and Ghosh (1985) looked at 408 firms that cut dividends, and the actions taken or information provided by these firms in conjunction with the dividend cuts. In particular, they examined three groups of companies: the first group announced an earnings decline or loss with the dividend cut; the second had made a prior announcement of earnings decline or loss; and the third made a simultaneous announcement of growth opportunities or higher earnings. The results are summarized in Table 22.4.

Table 22.4 **EXCESS RETURNS AROUND DIVIDEND CUT ANNOUNCEMENTS**			
	Periods Around Announcement Date		
Category	**Prior Quarter**	**Announcement Period**	**Quarter After**
Simultaneous Announcement of Earnings Decline/Loss ($N=176$)	−7.23%	−8.17%	+1.80%
Prior Announcement of Earnings Decline or Loss ($N = 208$)	−7.58%	−5.52%	+1.07%
Simultaneous Announcement of Investment or Growth Opportunities ($N=16$)	−7.69%	−5.16%	+8.79%

This study leads us to several interesting conclusions. First, the vast number of firms announcing dividend cuts did so in response to earnings declines (384), rather than in conjunction with investment or growth opportunities (16). The market seems to react negatively to all of them, however, suggesting that it does not attach much credibility to the firm's contentions. The negative reaction to the dividend cut seems to persist in the case of the firms with the earnings declines, whereas it is reversed in the case of the firms with earnings increases or investment opportunities.

Woolridge and Ghosh also found that firms that announced stock dividends or stock repurchases in conjunction with the dividend cuts fared much better than firms that did not. Finally, they noted the tendency across the entire sample for prices to correct themselves, at least partially, in the year following the dividend cut. This suggests that markets tend to overreact to the initial dividend cut and that the price recovery can be attributed to the subsequent correction.

Lessons for Firms

Firms that plan to change dividend policy can draw several lessons these and other studies. First, no matter how good the reasons may be for a firm to cut dividends, it should expect markets to react negatively to the initial announcement of the cut, for two reasons. One is the well-founded skepticism with which markets greet any rationale offered by the firm for dividend cuts. The other is that large dividend changes typically make the existing investor clientele unhappy; although other stockholders may be happy with the new dividend policy, the transition may take a while, during which time stock prices may go down. Second, if a firm has good reasons for cutting dividends, such as an increase in project availability, it will gain at least partial protection by providing information to markets about these projects. Finally, firms that can package dividend cuts with other actions, such as stock repurchases or spinoffs, should do so, because these actions may neutralize at least a portion of the negative reaction to the dividend cuts.

CONCLUSION

Firms can return cash or assets to its stockholders in a number of ways besides paying dividends.

- They can repurchase stock on the open market, in privately negotiated purchases or through tender offers. By doing so, they might be able to reduce the tax liability to their stockholders and solidify control in the firm. The signaling impact of a repurchase may be lower, however, because firms generally do not commit to making repurchases every year. Even firms that announce repurchases often do not carry them through.

- Firms can indicate their commitment to buy back stock by entering into forward contracts to buy stock back at fixed prices in the future. The increased signaling benefit has to be weighed off against the loss of flexibility inherent in the commitment.

- Firms may give their stockholders additional stock through stock dividends and stock splits. Although neither affects the firm's cash flows directly, both might signal higher expected future cash flows to the market, causing stock prices to rise.

- Finally, firms may choose to divest or spin off specific businesses they view to be undervalued. They are more likely to divest if the reason for the undervaluation is the perception of incumbent management and more likely to spin off if the perception is that the market is making a mistake.

QUESTIONS AND PROBLEMS

1. A company that has excess cash on hand is trying to decide whether to pay out the cash as a regular dividend or a special dividend or to repurchase stock with it. What are some of the considerations that would enter into this decision?

2. An equity repurchase will always provide a lesser signaling benefit than will an equivalent dollar increase in regular dividends. Explain this statement. Does it hold true if the comparison is to special dividends?

3. Suppose that a firm's management is anticipating having to make future cuts in dividends when they unexpectedly get awarded a large cash settlement in a court decision. Could the firm conceivably reduce total dividend payments by using the surplus to repurchase shares? If so, would this be the optimal way to use the windfall?

4. In many cases, firms have offered to repurchase shares from one of their shareholders in what is called a "targeted" repurchase. In a targeted repurchase,

only the shareholder named is allowed to tender shares, and the purchase price is often well above the current market price. Such repurchases are generally used to "buy off" someone who has announced the intention to take over the firm. Would such an arrangement benefit or hurt the shareholders who aren't allowed to tender shares? Why?

5. A firm is planning to borrow money to make an equity repurchase to increase its stock price. It is basing its analysis on the fact that there will be fewer shares outstanding after the repurchases, and higher earnings per share.

   a. Will earnings per share always increase after such an action? Explain.

   b. Will the higher earnings per share always translate into a higher stock price? Explain.

   c. Under what conditions will such a transaction lead to a higher price?

6. Stock repurchases can send different signals to the marketplace depending on whether or not management is allowed to tender any shares they own for repurchase. Suppose that JCL Steel has 1 million shares outstanding at a market price of $42 per share. The firm's current debt to capital ratio is 0.5 and interest payments are 10% of debt. JCL has just had a very good year and has $10 million of "extra" cash available. Management owns 5% of outstanding shares, and the firm has just announced that it will reduce debt by $5 million and buy back 100,000 shares at $50 per share. Managers will not be allowed to tender their shares, and earnings before interest and taxes are expected to be $15 million next year.

   a. If the firm's tax rate is 40%, what effect will the combined debt and equity repurchase have on EPS?

   b. Calculate JCL's current P/E ratio and determine the post-split price assuming that the P/E stays the same. Compare it to the $50 tender offer. Do you think management agrees with your assumption? Why or why not?

   c. Could management have caused the stock market to reevaluate its assumption about the "correct" price for JCL stock by buying back the 100,000 shares at the current market price? Why or why not?

   d. Would your answers to (b) and (c) have changed if management had been allowed to tender shares for repurchase?

7. ABT Trucking has excess cash of $300,000 and 100,000 shares outstanding. The firm is contemplating paying this $300,000 out as an extra dividend to

shareholders. Post-dividend, the price is expected to be $27 per share. Alternatively, the company is considering using the excess cash to repurchase 10,000 shares at $30 per share.

   a. If shareholders' ordinary income is taxed at 40% and their capital gains are taxed at 28%, how should the firm disburse the money?

   b. If the shareholders consist mainly of other corporations, how should the firm disburse the money?

8. JR Computers, a firm that manufactures and sells personal computers, is an all-equity firm with 100,000 shares outstanding, $10 million in earnings after taxes, and a market value of $150 million. Assume that this firm borrows $60 million at an interest rate of 8% and buys back 40,000 shares using the funds. If the firm's tax rate is 50%, estimate

   a. The effect on earnings per share of the action.

   b. What the interest rate on the debt would have to be for the earnings per share effect to disappear.

9. Why are forward contracts to buy equity more risky to firms than repurchase agreements? Why might firms choose to use these contracts anyway?

10. JK Tobacco, a diversified firm in food and tobacco is concerned about its stock price, which has dropped almost 25% over the previous two years. The managers of the firm believe that the price drop has occurred because the tobacco division is the target of lawsuits, which may result in a large liability for the firm. What action would you recommend to the firm? What might be some of the barriers to such an action?

11. The stock price of GenChem Corporation, a chemical manufacturing firm with declining earnings, has dropped from $50 to $35 over the course of the last year, largely as a consequence of the market perception that the current management is incompetent. The management is planning to split off the firm into three businesses but plans to continue running all of them. Do you think the splitoff will cause the stock price to increase? Why or why not? What would you recommend?

12. The stock prices of firms generally increase when they announce spinoffs. How would you explain this phenomenon? On which types of firms would you expect spinoffs to have the largest positive impact, and why?

13. The managers of PC Software, an electronics mail-order firm, have seen the stock price of the firm increase over the last year from $25 to $50 and are considering a stock split to bring the stock price down to what they view as a reasonable trading range. By doing so, they hope to make the stock more affordable and to increase their investor base.

a. Would you agree with this rationale for a stock split? Why or why not?

b. How would you expect the stock price to react to the split? Why?

14. First Strike Software, a firm that manufactures software for use by mining companies, has experienced rapid growth in its stock price over the last several years and is now selling at $75 per share. Management is contemplating a three-for-one stock split with the stated intention of "getting the stock price down to a more reasonable level where new individual investors can afford to buy our stock." Management is assuming that the post-split price will be $25 per share, and they feel that the typical small investor will want to invest $5,000 at a time in a stock. In addition, they have obtained the results of a recent Small Investors Association survey which indicates that the "average" brokerage commission schedule is

Fee = $29 + $.025/share (on first 100 shares) +
$.015 (on shares over 100)
+ $15 for odd-lot (i.e., in other than increments of
100 shares) trades

Compare the brokerage commissions paid before and after the stock split by an individual purchasing $5,000 worth of stock. (Round all commissions up to the nearest penny, and round all numbers of shares down.) How much will the typical small investor benefit from this split?

15. In the previous problem, we showed that *new* investors in First Strike will benefit from the stock split. How will *existing* shareholders be affected by the stock split?

16. Why might a firm want to do a "reverse" split (e.g., one-for-two)?

17. WeeKids, a firm that operates play arenas for children, has paid $1 as a dividend per share each year for the last five years. Because of a decline in revenues and increased competition, their earnings have plummeted this year. They substitute a $1 stock dividend for the cash dividend. What would you expect the market reaction to the stock dividend to be? Why?

18. In 1995, the Limited, a specialty retailing firm, announced that it was splitting up its businesses into three separate businesses—the Limited stores forming one business, Victoria's Secret and lingerie becoming the second business, and its other holdings forming the third business. The Limited had been struggling over the previous four years with lackluster sales and operating profits overall, and the market reacted positively to the announcement. What might be some of the explanations for this reaction?

19. JW Bell, a regulated company, also has extensive holdings in nonregulated businesses and reports consolidated income from all segments. There are severe restrictions on investment and financing policy in the regulated component of the business. Can you provide a rationale for spinning off the nonregulated businesses?

20. An article in a business periodical recently argued that the only reason for spinoffs and splitoffs was to make it easier for Wall Street to value firms. Why would a spinoff or a splitoff make it easier to value a firm? Do you agree that this is the only reason for spinoffs and splitoffs? If so, what types of firms would you expect to take these actions?

21. JC Conglo Corporation is a firm that was founded in the 1960s and grew to become a conglomerate through acquisitions. It has substantial corporate costs that get allocated over the different divisions of the firm. Analysts argue that divesting the firm of these divisions will increase value, since the buyer will not have to pay the corporate costs. Under what conditions would spinning off the divisions of the firm add to value of the firm? Conversely, under what conditions would a spinoff have a neutral or negative effect on value?

22. RJR Nabisco, the food and tobacco giant, is waging a battle against dissident stockholders who want it to divest itself of its food division and pay a large dividend to the stockholders. RJR Nabisco offers to spin off the food division, while keeping it under incumbent management. Are stockholders likely to be satisfied? Why or why not?

PART FIVE

VALUATION

In this section, we make the linkage between the corporate financial decisions discussed in the last three sections—investment, financing, and dividend decisions—and the value of the firm. We begin with a discusssion of valuation techniques and models in Chapter 23, with an examination of both discounted cash flow and relative valuation models. We continue with an analysis of the effects of management decisions on value and a discussion of value enhancement strategies in Chapter 24. Finally, in Chapter 25, we examine the value of synergy and control in mergers and report on the empirical evidence on takeovers.

CHAPTER 23

BASICS OF VALUATION

In this chapter, we examine the basic principles of discounted cash-flow valuation and lay the groundwork for linking valuation to the corporate financial decisions discussed thus far. In the process, we attempt to answer the following questions:

- What is the difference between valuing the firm and valuing equity?

- When valuing equity, what is the distinction between the dividend discount model and cash flows to equity model? When will the two models yield similar results? When are the results likely to be different?

- Will firm valuation and equity valuation provide consistent results? When should an analyst use one over the other?

- What are some of the approaches available to estimating expected growth? How is expected growth related to the fundamentals of the firm and to its investment, financing, and dividend policy?

- How sensitive is firm or equity value to changes in assumptions about discount rates and expected growth?

- What are some of the multiples used by analysts to value firms? Why are they so popular? How are they related to discounted cash-flow valuation?

VALUATION APPROACHES

We examine two basic approaches to valuation in this chapter. In the first—discounted cash-flow valuation—the value of any asset is estimated by computing the present value of the expected cash flows on that asset, discounted back at a rate that reflects the riskiness of the cash flows. In a sense, it is a measure of the intrinsic value of an asset. In the second, the value of an asset is computed relative to how similar assets are priced in the marketplace. It is therefore a measure of relative rather than an intrinsic value.

DISCOUNTED CASH-FLOW VALUATION

Intuitively, the value of any asset should be a function of three variables: (1) how much it generates in cash flows; (2) when these cash flows are expected to occur; and (3) the uncertainty associated with these cash flows. Discounted cash-flow valuation brings these three variables together by computing the value of any asset to be the present value of its expected future cash flows:

$$\text{Value} = \sum_{t=1}^{t=n} \frac{CF_t}{(1 + r)^t}$$

where

$$n = \text{Life of the asset}$$
$$CF_t = \text{Cash flow in period } t$$
$$r = \text{Discount rate reflecting the riskiness of the estimated cash flows}$$

The cash flows will vary from asset to asset—dividends for stocks; coupons (interest) and face value for bonds; and after-tax cash flows for real projects. The discount rate is a function of the riskiness of the estimated cash flows—riskier assets carry higher rates; safer projects carry lower rates.

Equity Valuation versus Firm Valuation

One path to discounted cash-flow valuation is to value just the equity stake in the business; a second is to value the entire firm, including equity and any other claim-holders in the firm (bondholders, preferred stockholders, etc.). Although both approaches discount expected cash flows, the relevant cash flows and discount rates are different for each.

The **value of equity** is obtained by discounting expected cash flows to equity—that is, the residual cash flows after meeting all expenses, tax obligations, and interest and principal payments—at the cost of equity—that is, the rate of return required by equity investors in the firm.

$$\text{Value of Equity} = \sum_{t=1}^{t=n} \frac{CF \text{ to Equity}_t}{(1 + k_e)^t}$$

where

$$CF \text{ to Equity}_t = \text{Expected Cash Flow to Equity in period } t$$
$$k_e = \text{Cost of Equity}$$

The dividend discount model is a specialized case of equity valuation, whereby the value of a stock is the present value of expected future dividends.

Value of Equity: This is the value of the equity stake in a business; in the context of a publicly traded firm, it is the value of the common stock, warrants and other equity claims in the firm.

The **value of the firm** is obtained by discounting expected cash flows to the firm, that is, residual cash flows after meeting all operating expenses and taxes, but prior to debt payments—at the weighted average cost of capital—that is, the cost of the different components of financing used by the firm, weighted by their market value proportions.

$$\text{Value of Firm} = \sum_{t=1}^{t=n} \frac{CF \text{ to Firm}_t}{(1 + WACC)_t}$$

where

$$CF \text{ to Firm}_t = \text{Expected Cash Flow to Firm in period } t$$
$$WACC = \text{Weighted Average Cost of Capital}$$

The two approaches use different definitions of cash flow and discount rates, but will yield consistent estimates of value as long as the same set of assumptions is applied for both. It is important to avoid mismatching cash flows and discount rates, since discounting cash flows to equity at the weighted average cost of capital will lead to an upwardly biased estimate of the value of equity, whereas discounting cash flows to the firm at the cost of equity will yield a downward biased estimate of the value of the firm.

Value of Firm: The value of the firm is the value of all investors who have claims on the firm; thus, it includes lenders and bond holders, who have fixed claims, and equity investors, who have residual claims.

□ Concept
Check

> It is often argued that firm valuation is unaffected by financial leverage because the cash flow to the firm is before debt payments. Do you agree? Why or why not?

EQUITY VALUATION MODELS

As noted above, equity valuation models attempt to estimate the value of equity in a firm by discounting cash flows to equity at the rate of return required by equity investors (cost of equity). In this section, we consider two versions of equity valuation models—one narrowly defines cash flows to equity as dividends; the other uses a more expansive definition of cash flows to equity.

Dividend Discount Model

When investors buy stock, they generally expect to get two types of cash flows—dividends during the holding period and an expected price at the end of the holding period. Because this expected price is itself determined by future dividends, the value of a stock is the present value of dividends through perpetuity:

$$\text{Value per share of stock} = \sum_{t=1}^{t=\infty} \frac{DPS_t}{(1 + r)^t}$$

where

$$DPS_t = \text{Expected dividends per share}$$
$$r = \text{Required rate of return on stock}$$

The rationale for the model lies in the present value rule: the value of any asset is the present value of expected future cash flows, discounted at a rate appropriate to the riskiness of the cash flows being discounted.

In the general version of the dividend discount model, we allow for two stages in growth—an initial period of extraordinary growth, followed by stable growth forever:

Extraordinary growth period   Stable growth: g_n forever

Value of the Stock = PV of Dividends during extraordinary phase + PV of terminal price

$$P_0 = \sum_{t=1}^{t=n} \frac{\text{DPS}_t}{(1 + r)^t} + \frac{P_n}{(1 + r)^n} \text{ where } P_n = \frac{\text{DPS}_{n+1}}{(r - g_n)}$$

where

DPS_t = Expected dividends per share in year t
r = Required rate of return for equity investors = Cost of equity
P_n = Price at the end of year n
g_n = Growth rate forever after year n

There are four basic inputs in this model. First, the length of the high-growth period is defined; the longer the high-growth period, the more valuable the stock. Second, the dividends per share each period, during the growth period, is specified; since payout ratios change with growth rates, earnings growth rates and payout ratios may have to be estimated each period for the high-growth period. Third, the rate of return stockholders will demand for holding the stock is estimated, based on the risk and return model used by the analyst. Finally, the terminal price at the end of the high growth period is estimated, using the estimates of stable growth, the dividend payout ratio, and required return after the high growth ends.

Terminal Price: This is the expected price of a stock (or equity) at the end of a specified holding period.

What is a stable growth rate?   It is difficult to talk about extraordinary growth without first defining what we mean by a **stable growth rate.** There are two insights to keep in mind when estimating a "stable" growth rate. First, since this growth rate in the firm's dividends is expected to last forever, the firm's other measures of performance (including earnings) can be expected to grow at the same rate. Consider the long-term consequences of a firm whose earnings grow 6% a year forever, while its dividends grow at 8%. Over time, the dividends will exceed earnings. Similarly, if a firm's earnings grow at a faster rate than its dividends in the long term, the payout ratio will converge toward zero, which is also not a steady state. Thus, although the model's requirement is for the expected growth rate in dividends, if the firm is truly in a steady state, analysts should be able to substitute in the expected growth rate in earnings and get the same result.

Stable Growth Rate: This is a growth rate that a firm can sustain forever in earnings, dividends, and cash flows.

The second issue relates to what growth rate is reasonable as a "stable" growth rate. Again, the assumption that this growth rate will last forever establishes rigorous constraints on "reasonableness." A firm cannot in the long term grow at a rate significantly greater than the growth rate in the economy in which it operates. Thus, a firm that grows at 12% forever in an economy growing at 6% will eventually become larger than the economy. In practical terms, the stable growth rate cannot be larger than the nominal (real) growth rate in the economy in which the firm operates, if the valuation is done in nominal (real) terms. (If the firm's operations are restricted to the domestic arena, this will be the expected growth rate in the domestic economy. For multinationals, the relevant benchmark will be the growth rate in the world economy.) The nominal growth rate in the economy is determined by expected inflation and the real growth rate in GNP. Thus, in 1995 in the United States, the expected nominal growth in the economy, assuming expected inflation[1] in the long term of 3% a year and real growth[2] of 3%, would have been:

$$\text{Expected nominal growth in U.S. economy} = \text{Expected Inflation} + \text{Expected real growth}$$
$$= 3\% + 3\% = 6\%$$

By definition, therefore, a stable firm is one whose growth rate does not exceed 6% by a significant amount. Given the uncertainty associated with estimates of expected inflation and real growth, there can be differences in the benchmark growth rate used by different analysts—analysts with higher expectations of inflation in the long term may project a higher nominal growth rate in the economy.

There is another instance in which an analyst may be able to stray from a strict limit imposed on the "stable growth rate." If a firm is likely to maintain a few years of "above-stable" growth rates, an approximate value for the firm can be obtained by adding a premium to the stable growth rate to reflect the above-average growth in the initial years. Even in this case, the analyst's flexibility is limited. The sensitivity of the model to growth implies that the stable growth rate cannot be more than 1% or 2% above the growth rate in the economy.

Can a stable growth rate be much *lower* than the growth rate in the economy? There are no logical or mathematical limits on the downside. Firms that have a stable growth rate much lower than the growth rate in the economy will become smaller in proportion to the economy over time. Because there is no economic basis for arguing that this *cannot* happen, there is no reason to prevent analysts from using a stable growth rate that is much lower than the nominal growth rate in the economy.

The assumption that the growth rate in dividends has to be constant over time is a difficult assumption to meet, especially given the volatility of earnings. If a firm has an average growth rate that is close to a stable growth rate, the model can be used with little real effect on value. Thus, a cyclical firm that can be expected to have year-to-year swings in growth rates but has an average growth rate of 6% can be assumed to be in stable growth, without a significant loss of generality. This is because since dividends are smoothed even when earnings are volatile, they are less likely to be affected by year-to-year changes in earnings growth. In addition, the mathematical effects of using an average growth rate rather than year-specific growth rates are small.

□ Concept
Check

> An analyst claims that Microsoft, a company with a market value of equity of $80 billion, can grow 15% a year forever, because of its superb management and dominant position in the marketplace. Explain why this is not possible.

Length of the high-growth period   The length of the **high-growth period** is a key input to this valuation model, and it does not lend itself easily to a rigid framework. Let us consider the easy cases first. First, if the firm is growing at a rate close to the stable

---

[1]There is no consensus on the best measure of expected inflation. One simple measure is to use the Treasury bill rate as a predictor of short-term expected inflation. Another is to use surveys of economists on expected inflation. A third approach is to use inflation in the past as a measure of expected inflation in the future. This measure will depend on the length of the historical period. For instance, the average inflation from 1926 to 1990 is approximately 3.25%, but it is much higher (5%) if only the 1981 to 1990 period is used.

[2]The average real growth in the GNP of the United States has averaged between 2% and 3% in the last 30 years. The growth rate in the 1981 to 1990 period is closer to 2%.

growth rate right now, no extraordinary growth is anticipated and it can be assumed that the firm is in stable growth already. Second, if the firm is growing at a rate higher than the stable growth rate, but the higher growth is coming from a single product or service for which the firm has a protected position, the extraordinary growth can be expected to last as long as the protection lasts. Thus, a pharmaceutical firm that is generating high growth because of a single patent protected product, whose patent is expected to expire in four years, can be expected to have a four-year high-growth period.

High-Growth Period: This is a period during which a company's earnings or cash flows are expected to grow at a rate much higher than the overall growth rate of the economy.

In other cases, the estimation is much more difficult. In general, we can make the following assumptions about the length of the high-growth period.

1.   The greater the current growth rate in earnings of a firm, relative to the stable growth rate, the longer the high-growth period, although the growth rate may drop off during the period. Thus, a firm that is growing at 40% currently should have a longer high-growth period than one growing at 14%.

2.   The larger the current size of the firm—both in absolute terms and relative to the market it serves—the shorter the high-growth period. Size remains one of the most potent forces that push firms toward stable growth; the larger a firm, the less likely it is to maintain an above-normal growth rate.

At the risk of sounding arbitrary, we suggest the following guidelines for defining the length of the high growth period as a function of current growth rates:

Current Growth Rate	Length of High-Growth Period
≤ 1% higher than stable growth rate	No high growth
1–10% higher than stable growth rate	5 years
> 10% higher than stable growth rate	10 years

Again, the sensitivity of value to changes in the length of the high-growth period can always be estimated. Although some analysts use growth periods greater than 10 years, the combination of high expected growth and long growth periods creates a potent mix in terms of increasing the size of the firm, in many cases well beyond the realm of reasonableness.

Concept Check   Are there any circumstances under which you would assume that a firm whose earnings are growing 15% a year currently will have no extraordinary growth? Explain.

Required return on stock—discount rates   The dividends and terminal price should be discounted back at a rate that reflects their riskiness to stockholders to arrive at the dividend discount model value. To arrive at this rate, we first have to arrive at a measure of the riskiness, using a risk and return model. If CAPM is used, for instance, the beta of the stock relative to a market index is the measure of risk; if APM is used, the betas of the stock relative to the factors are the measures of risk. We then have to arrive at an expected return based on the risk measure. In CAPM, this requires an estimate for the riskless rate and the risk premium.

Required Return on Equity = Riskless Rate + Beta (Risk Premium)

A similar estimate can be made using APM.

Although the mechanics of estimating required returns have been examined fully in earlier chapters, a couple of points relate specifically to valuation. First, there is a positive correlation between high growth and high risk; high-growth firms tend to have higher betas than do low-growth firms. Building on this point, it is important that, as we change growth rates over time, we also adjust risk accordingly. Thus, when a firm goes from high growth to low growth, the beta needs to be reduced to reflect the lower growth.

❑ Concept
Check

High beta companies can expect their betas to move toward one as they approach stable growth. Explain why. Will the same reasoning apply for high-growth companies that have betas below one (say commodity or mining companies)?

Expected dividends during high-growth period   The first step in estimating expected dividends during the high-growth period is to estimate the expected earnings for each period. This is done using the current earnings and the expected growth rates in earnings, which may either be constant or vary across the high-growth period. These expected earnings are paired with estimated dividend payout ratios in each period, which again may change over the high-growth period. This may seem to be an awkward procedure, since expected dividends could well be estimated using the current dividends and applying a dividend growth rate, but it is used for two reasons. First, most analyst projections for growth are stated in terms of earnings rather than dividends. Second, separating earnings growth from dividend payout provides more flexibility in terms of changing dividend payout ratios as earnings growth rates change. In particular, it allows us to raise dividend payout ratios as earnings growth rates decline.

Estimating earnings growth   The key input in this model is the expected growth rate in earnings. It can be estimated using one of three approaches:

Historical Growth (in Earnings):   This is the growth rate over the past few periods in earnings; it can be calculated either by averaging the year-specific growth rates (arithmetic average) or by estimating the compounded growth rate over the whole period (geometric average).

1. *Historical Growth:*   The growth rate in earnings per share over past periods can be used to estimate future growth. In doing so, we assume that firms whose earnings have grown rapidly in the past will continue to do so in the future. There are two considerations in using this measure. The first is how far back to go; the growth rate will be different for different time periods, but it is important that some consistency be maintained across valuations. The other relates to the measurement of the growth rate itself; because earnings growth compounds over time, the geometric average growth rate in earnings, rather than the arithmetic average, should be used:

$$\text{Geometric average growth rate in earnings} = (\text{EPS}_0 / \text{EPS}_{0-t})^{1/t} - 1$$

2. *Analyst Projections:*   The easiest solution is to use an analyst projection of growth in earnings for the company being valued. For most U.S. companies, such projections are widely available and disseminated by a number of services, including Zacks and I/B/E/S. They are less widely available for non-U.S. companies, because there are far fewer equity research analysts in other markets.

3. *Fundamentals of the firm:*   The most complex—and richest—approach relates expected growth to the fundamentals of the firm. In particular, the expected growth rate should be a function of the proportion of the earnings that are reinvested back into the firm and the returns earned on the projects taken with the money:

$$\text{Expected Growth Rate} = \text{Retention Ratio} * \text{Return on Equity}$$

In Chapter 6, we noted that the return on equity is itself affected by the leverage of the firm, and we expanded it to include this effect:

$$\text{Return on Equity} = \text{ROA} + \text{D/E}\,[\text{ROA} - i\,(1 - t)]$$

where

$$
\begin{aligned}
\text{ROA} &= \text{Return on Assets}^3 = \text{EBIT}\,(1 - t)\,/\,(\text{BV of Debt} + \text{BV of Equity}) \\
\text{D/E} &= \text{Debt / Equity Ratio} \\
i &= \text{Interest rate on Debt} \\
t &= \text{Marginal tax rate}
\end{aligned}
$$

Fundamental Growth Rate: This is the growth rate in earnings estimated from the company's policy on reinvestment and the quality of its projects.

This formulation allows the analyst valuing the firm to bring in the effect of the investment, financing, and dividend decisions of the firm not only in current periods but also in future periods. The return on assets itself is a product of the after-tax operating margin of the firm and the asset turnover ratio:

$$\text{Return on Assets} = \text{After-tax Operating Margin} * \text{Asset Turnover Ratio}$$

where

$$
\begin{aligned}
\text{After-tax Operating Margin} &= \text{EBIT}\,(1 - t) \div \text{Sales} \\
\text{Asset Turnover Ratio} &= \text{Sales}\,/\,(\text{BV of Debt} + \text{BV of Equity})
\end{aligned}
$$

> **Concept Check**
>
> If the historical growth rates, analyst projections, and estimate based on fundamentals are very different from one another, how would you weigh these growth rates?

The earnings growth rate *during the high-growth period* can also take one of many paths, ranging from a constant-growth rate to one that changes each year:

1. *Constant-growth rate during the high-growth period:*   From a purely mechanical standpoint, the simplest assumption is that the earnings growth rate is constant for the high-growth period, after which the growth rate drops to the stable level, as shown in Figure 23.1.

The limitation of this formulation is obvious: it assumes that the growth rate is high during the initial period and is transformed overnight to a lower, stable rate at the end of the period. Although these sudden transformations in growth can happen, it is much

---

[3]Technically, this could be considered a return on capital rather than a return on assets. That might be true, but the formulation takes a different view of assets than the traditional balance sheet. If assets are viewed as fixed assets plus working capital, then adding together the book values of debt, equity, and preferred stock (if any) should provide a measure of these assets.

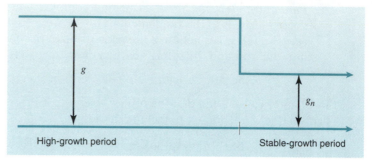

Figure 23.1 Constant-growth rate during high-growth period

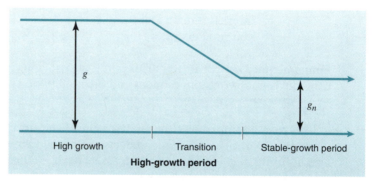

Figure 23.2 High growth followed by transition

more realistic to assume that the shift from high growth to stable growth occurs gradually over time. The assumption that the growth rate drops precipitously from its level in the initial phase to a stable rate also implies that this model is more appropriate for firms with modest growth rates in the initial phase. For instance, it is more reasonable to assume that a firm growing at 12% in the high-growth period will see its growth rate drop to 6%, than it is for a firm growing at 40% in the high-growth period. If we assume that the growth rate and payout ratio are fixed for the high-growth period, the present value of the dividends during the high-growth period can be estimated as follows:

$$P_0 = \frac{DPS_0 * (1 + g) * \left(1 - \frac{(1 + g)^n}{(1 + r)^n}\right)}{r - g}$$

2. *Constant growth for the initial part of the high-growth period, followed by gradual reduction to stable growth:* In this case, the growth rate does not drop precipitously at the end of the high-growth period to the stable rate; rather, it adjusts more gradually to it, as shown in Figure 23.2.

This model allows for growth rates and payout ratios to change at least during the transition period. Thus, it may be more appropriate for firms that are expected to grow at very high rates, say 30% to 40% for the next few years. The present value of dividends during the high-growth phase can then be estimated as follows:

$$P_0 = \underbrace{\sum_{t=1}^{t=n1} \frac{EPS_0 * (1 + g_a)^t * \Pi_a}{(1 + r)^t}}_{\text{High-growth phase}} + \underbrace{\sum_{t=n1+1}^{t=n2} \frac{DPS_t}{(1 + r)^t}}_{\text{Transition}} + \underbrace{\frac{EPS_{n2} * (1 + g_n) * \Pi_n}{(r - g_n)(1 + r)^n}}_{\text{Stable-growth phase}}$$

where

$$
\begin{aligned}
\text{EPS}_t &= \text{Earnings per share in year } t \\
\text{DPS}_t &= \text{Dividends per share in year } t \\
g_a &= \text{Growth rate in high-growth phase (lasts } n1 \text{ periods)} \\
\Pi_a &= \text{Payout ratio in high-growth phase} \\
\Pi_n &= \text{Payout ratio in stable-growth phase} \\
r &= \text{Required rate of return on equity}
\end{aligned}
$$

3. *Growth rates that change every year for the high-growth period:* In the most general formulation, the growth rates and payout ratios can be different in each year of the high-growth period, reflecting changes in investment opportunities and firm size. Under this scenario, the value of a stock is the present value of the dividends each year during the high-growth period added on to the present value of the terminal price at the end of the high-growth period.

☐ Concept
Check

Assume that you are trying to estimate the expected growth rate in earnings for a cyclical firm over the next five years. Given that the earnings growth rate will be affected by future recoveries and recessions, should you try to build expectations of these into the growth rates?

Estimating dividend payout ratios   The other input needed to estimate expected dividends during the high-growth phase is the *dividend payout ratio,* since the expected dividends in period t can be written as

Expected Dividends in period t = Expected Earnings$_t$ * Payout Ratio$_t$

The payout ratio should reflect changes in expected growth. As growth declines, the payout ratio should increase. Figure 23.3 graphs out payout ratio patterns under the two-stage and three-stage earnings growth formulations, and illustrates the linkage between growth rates and payout ratios.

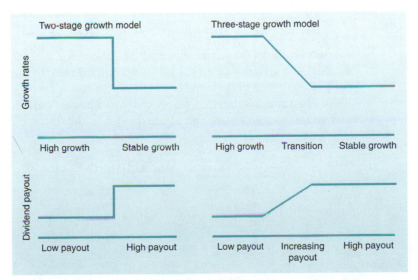

Figure 23.3   Dividend payout ratios and expected growth

> Assume that you are valuing a high-growth firm with low dividend payout using the dividend discount model. If you do not adjust the payout ratio upward when you get to stable growth, what impact will you have on your estimated value?

Estimating terminal price   The *terminal price*—the price at the end of the high-growth period—can be estimated from expected dividends in the first time period following the high-growth period, the required rate of return on the stock in the stable phase, and the expected stable growth rate in dividends as follows:

$$\text{Value of Stock} = \frac{DPS_{n+1}}{r - g_n}$$

where

$$DPS_{n+1} = \text{Expected dividends one year after end of high-growth period}$$
$$r_n = \text{Required rate of return for equity investors in stable phase}$$
$$g_n = \text{Growth rate in dividends forever}$$

As discussed earlier, a stable growth rate is assumed to be fairly close to the growth rate of the economy in which the firm operates. In addition, the payout ratio and risk should reflect the stable growth assumed for the firm, since stable firms pay out more of their earnings as dividends and have lower risk. One way of estimating this new payout ratio is to use the fundamental growth model described in Chapter 4:

$$g = b\,[ROA + D/E\,(ROA - i\,(1 - t)\,)]$$

where

$$b = \text{Retention ratio} = 1 - \text{payout ratio}$$
$$ROA = \text{Return on assets} = [\text{Net Income} + \text{Interest Expense}\,(1 - t)]\,/\,\text{Total Assets}$$
$$D/E = \text{Debt / Equity (in book value terms)}$$
$$i = \text{Interest Expense / Book Value of Debt}$$

Manipulating this growth rate equation yields the payout ratio as a function of the expected growth rate:

$$\text{Payout ratio} = 1 - b = 1 - [g\,/\,(ROA + D/E\,(ROA - i\,(1 - t)))]$$

where the inputs for this equation will be those for the stable growth period. Once estimated, the terminal price has to be discounted back to the present and added back to the present value of dividends.

To illustrate, assume that a firm has the following parameters for the ROA, debt/equity ratios, payout ratios, and interest rates in the initial high-growth phase and in the stable-growth phase:

	Initial Growth Phase	**Stable Period**
ROA	20%	16%
Payout ratio	20%	?
D/E	1.00	1.00
i	10%	8%
Growth rate	?	8%

The tax rate for the firm is 40%.

$$\text{Growth rate in first five years} = (1 - 0.2)\,[.20\ +\ 1\,(.20\ -\ .10*(1 - 0.4))]$$
$$= 27.2\ \%$$
$$\text{Payout ratio after year five} = 1\ -\ [.08\,/\,(.16\ +\ 1\,(.16\ -\ .08*(1 - 0.4)))]$$
$$= 70.59\ \%$$

As the growth rate drops in the stable-growth period, the payout ratio increases from 20% to 70.59%.

Concept Check

In most discounted cash-flow valuations, the bulk of the present value comes from the terminal price. Does this mean that the assumptions made about the high-growth period do not matter very much?

Bringing it all together   Once the expected dividends and the terminal price have been estimated and the discount rate has been obtained from the risk measure for the firm, the present value of the dividends and terminal price is calculated, providing a measure of the value of the stock using the dividend discount model. The cash flows and interactions in the two-stage dividend discount model are represented in Figure 23.4.

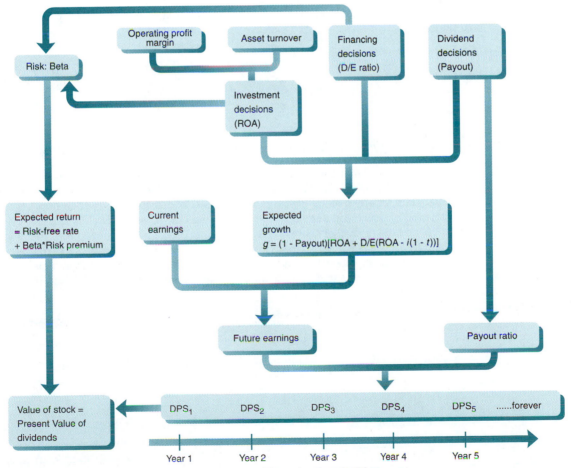

Figure 23.4   The valuation decision

IN PRACTICE VALUING A FIRM IN STABLE GROWTH USING THE DDM: CONSOLIDATED EDISON

Consolidated Edison is the electric utility that supplies power to homes and businesses in New York and its environs. It is a monopoly whose prices and profits are regulated by the state of New York. The firm is in stable growth, based on its size and the area it serves. Its rates are regulated, and it is unlikely that the regulators will allow profits to grow at extraordinary rates. The beta is 0.75 and has been stable over time. In addition, we have the following information.(The T Bond rate is 7.5%)

$$\text{Earnings per share in 1994} = \$3.00$$
$$\text{Dividend Payout Ratio in 1994} = 68.00\%$$
$$\text{Dividends per share in 1994} = \$2.04$$
$$\text{Expected Growth Rate in Earnings and Dividends} = 5\%$$
$$\text{Con Ed Beta} = 0.75$$
$$\text{Cost of Equity} = 7.5\% + 0.75*5.5\% = 11.63\%$$

$$\text{Value of Equity} = \$2.00 * 1.05/(.1163 - .05) = \$32.32$$

Con Ed was trading for $26.75 on the day of this analysis. This valuation would suggest that Con Ed is undervalued, given our estimates of expected growth and risk. It is also possible that the market is right and that we have overestimated the expected growth rate in earnings.

 Concept Check

What would the expected growth rate have to be, in the above formulation, for Con Ed to be correctly valued at $26.75?

IN PRACTICE VALUING A FIRM USING THE TWO-STAGE DDM—AMERICAN EXPRESS

In February 1995, Warren Buffett announced that he was increasing his stake in American Express from 5% to 9.8%, resulting in a surge in the stock price. American Express would be a good candidate for a two-stage dividend discount model, because it has gone through an extended period of depressed earnings (EPS in 1994 was $2.70, while earnings five years earlier was $3.52, and the recovery in earnings is expected to create higher growth over the next five years) and because the firm has a history of paying out what it can afford to in dividends.

In 1994, American Express had earnings per share of $2.70 and paid dividends per share of $0.90. In addition, assume that the following are the estimated inputs for the high-growth and stable-growth periods.

Input	High-Growth Period	Stable-Growth-Period
Length of Period	5 years	Forever, after year 5
Expected Growth Rate	13.04%: From fundmentals (see below)	6%
Beta	1.45	1.10
Cost of Equity	7.5% + 1.45(5.5%)=15.48%	7.50%+1.1(5.5%)=13.55%
Return on Assets	12.50%	12.50%
Debt/Equity Ratio	100%	100%
Dividend Payout Ratio	33.33% (Current)	69.33%: From fundamentals (below)

(continues)

(Continued) Input	High-Growth Period	Stable-Growth Period
Interest Rate on Debt	8.50%	8.50%
Return on Assets	12.50%	12.50%
Debt/Equity Ratio	100%	100%

The corporate tax rate is 36%. The expected growth rate during the high-growth period is estimated to be 13.04%, from the inputs provided above:

$$\begin{aligned} &\text{Expected Growth Rate during high-growth period} \\ &= b\,[\text{ROA} + \text{D/E}\,(\text{ROA} - i\,(1 - t)] \\ &= 0.6667\,(12.50\% + 1\,(12.50\% - 8.50\%\,(1 - .36))) = 13.04\% \end{aligned}$$

The payout ratio for the stable growth period is also estimated from the inputs:

$$\begin{aligned} \text{Stable Period Payout Ratio} &= 1 - g\,/\,[\text{ROA} + \text{D/E}\,(\text{ROA} - i\,(1-t)] \\ &= 1 - .06\,/\,[12.50\% + 1\,(12.50\% - 8.50\%\,(1 - .36))] = 69.33\% \end{aligned}$$

The first component of value is the present value of the expected dividends during the high-growth period. Based on the current earnings ($2.70), the expected growth rate (13.04%), and the expected dividend payout ratio (33.33%), the expected dividends can be computed for each year in the high-growth period, as shown in Table 23.1.

Table 23.1   **EPS, DPS, AND PRESENT VALUE: AMERICAN EXPRESS**

Year	EPS	DPS	Present Value
1	$3.05	$1.02	$0.88
2	$3.45	$1.15	$0.86
3	$3.90	$1.30	$0.84
4	$4.41	$1.47	$0.83
5	$4.98	$1.66	$0.81

$$\begin{aligned} &\text{Cumulative Present Value of Dividends (@15.48\%)} \\ &= \$0.88 + \$0.86 + \$0.84 + \$0.83 + \$0.81 = \$4.22 \end{aligned}$$

The present value of the dividends can also be computed in shorthand using the following computation:

$$\text{PV of Dividends} = \frac{\$0.90 * (1.1304) * \left(1 - \dfrac{(1.1304)^5}{(1.1548)^5}\right)}{.1548 - .1304} = \$4.22$$

The price at the end of the high-growth phase (end of year 5) can be estimated using the constant-growth model:

$$\text{Terminal price} = \text{Expected Dividends per share}_{n+1} / (r - g_n)$$
$$\text{Expected Earnings per share}_6 = \$2.70 * 1.1304^5 * 1.06 = \$5.28$$
$$\text{Expected Dividends per share}_6 = \$5.28 * 0.6933 = \$3.66$$
$$\text{Terminal price} = \$3.66 \div (.1355 - .06) = \$48.51$$

The present value of the terminal price can be then written as

$$\text{PV of Terminal Price} = \frac{\$48.51}{(1.1548)^5} = \$23.62$$

The cumulated present value of dividends and the terminal price can then be calculated as follows:

$$P_0 = \frac{\$0.90 * (1.1304) * \left(1 - \frac{(1.1304)^5}{(1.1548)^5}\right)}{.1548 - .1304} + \frac{\$48.51}{(1.1548)^5} = \$4.22 + \$23.62 = \$27.85$$

American Express was trading at $33.38 in March 1995, at the time of this analysis. The analysis is depicted graphically in Figure 23.5.

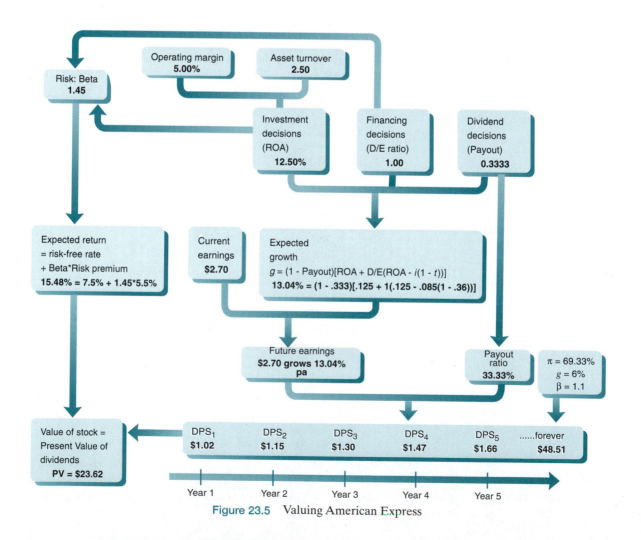

Figure 23.5   Valuing American Express

IN PRACTICE   VALUING A FIRM USING THE THREE-STAGE DDM—THE HOME DEPOT

The Home Depot was one of the great retailing success stories of the 1980s and early 1990s. It posted extraordinary growth both in revenues and profits and reaped its stockholders immense returns. We can use the three-stage dividend discount model because the Home Depot is still in very high growth; analysts project that its earnings per share will grow at 36% a year for the next five years. We can apply the following background information to the analysis:

- *Current Earnings / Dividends*

$$\text{Earnings per share in 1994} = \$1.33$$
$$\text{Dividends per share in 1994} = \$0.16$$

- *Inputs for the High-Growth Period*

$$\text{Length of the high-growth period} = 5 \text{ years}$$
$$\text{Expected growth rate} = 36.00\% \text{ (Based on analyst projections)}$$
$$\text{Beta during high-growth period} = 1.60$$
$$\text{Cost of equity during high-growth period} = 7.5\% + 1.60\,(5.5\%) = 16.30\%$$
$$\text{Dividend payout ratio} = 12.03\% \text{ (based on existing payout ratio)}$$

- *Inputs for the Transition Period*

$$\text{Length of the transition period} = 5 \text{ years}$$
Growth rate in earnings will decline from 36% in year 5 to 6% in year 10 in linear increments.
Payout ratio will increase from 12.03% to 60% over the same period in linear increments.
Beta will drop from 1.60 to 1.00 over the same period in linear increments.

- *Inputs for the Stable Growth*

$$\text{Expected growth rate} = 6\%$$
$$\text{Beta during stable-growth phase} = 1.00 : \text{Cost of Equity}$$
$$= 7.50\% + 1.0\,(5.5\%) = 13.00\%$$
$$\text{Payout ratio} = 60\%$$

In Table 23.2, these inputs are used to estimate expected earnings per share, dividends per share, and costs of equity for both the high-growth and stable periods; the present values are also shown.

Table 23.2   EPS, PAYOUT RATIOS, DPS, AND PRESENT VALUE: THE HOME DEPOT

Period	EPS	Payout Ratio (%)	DPS	Cost of Equity (%)	Present Value
1	$1.81	12.03	$0.22	16.30	$0.19
2	2.46	12.03	0.30	16.30	0.22
3	3.35	12.03	0.40	16.30	0.25
4	4.55	12.03	0.55	16.30	0.30
5	6.19	12.03	0.74	16.30	0.35
6	8.04	21.62	1.74	15.64	0.71
7	9.97	31.22	3.11	14.98	1.10
8	11.77	40.81	4.80	14.32	1.49
9	13.18	50.41	6.64	13.66	1.81
10	13.97	60.00	8.38	13.00	2.02

Note: Since the costs of equity change each year, the present value has to be calculated using the cumulated cost of equity. Thus, in year 7, the present value of dividends is:

$$\text{PV of year 7 dividend} \ = \ \$3.11 \,/[(1.1630)^5 \,(1.1564)\,(1.1498)] \ = \ \$1.10$$

The terminal price at the end of year 10 can be calculated based on the earnings per share in year 11, the stable growth rate of 6%, a cost of equity of 13.00% (based on the beta of 1), and the payout ratio of 60.00%:

$$\text{Terminal price} \ = \ \$13.97 * 1.06 * 0.60 \,/\,(.13 \ - \ .06) \ = \ \$126.96$$

The components of value are as follows:

Present Value of dividends in high-growth phase:	\$1.31
Present Value of dividends in transition phase:	\$7.12
Present Value of terminal price at end of transition:	\$30.57
Value of Home Depot Stock:	\$39.00

Home Depot was trading at \$45 in February 1995.

The high-growth rate embedded in the stock price also implies that the stock price will be sensitive to any information that may reflect on the sustainability of this growth. For instance, Figure 23.6 graphs out the value as a function of the expected growth during the high growth period.

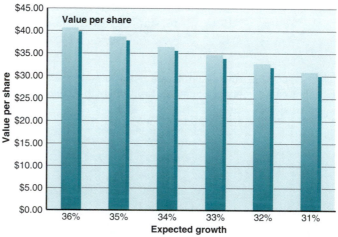

Figure 23.6   The Home Depot: Value vs. expected growth

FCFE Valuation Model

In Chapter 21, while developing a framework for analyzing dividend policy we estimated the free cash flow to equity as the cash flow that the firm can afford to pay out as dividends and contrasted it with the actual dividends. We noted that many firms do not pay out their FCFE as dividends; thus, the dividend discount model may not capture their true capacity to generate cash flows for stockholders. A more appropriate model is the **free cash flow to equity (FCFE) model.**

FCFE Model: This model estimates the value of equity as the present value of the expected free cash flows to equity over time.

Briefly, the FCFE is the residual cash flow left over after meeting interest and principal payments and providing for capital expenditures to maintain existing assets and create new assets for future growth. The free cash flow to equity is measured as follows:

$$\text{FCFE} = \text{Net Income} + \text{Depreciation} - \text{Capital Spending} - \Delta \text{Working Capital} - \text{Principal Repayments} + \text{New Debt Issues}$$

In the special case where the capital expenditures and the working capital are expected to be financed at the target debt ratio δ, and principal repayments are made from new debt issues, the FCFE is measured as follows:

$$\text{FCFE} = \text{Net Income} + (1 - \delta)(\text{Capital Expenditures} - \text{Depreciation}) + (1 - \delta)\Delta \text{Working Capital}$$

In the general version of the FCFE model, we allow for two stages in growth—an initial period of extraordinary growth, followed by stable growth forever.

Extraordinary growth period   Stable growth: g_n forever

Value of the Stock = PV of FCFE during extraordinary phase
+ PV of terminal price

$$P_0 = \sum_{t=1}^{t=n} \frac{\text{FCFE}_t}{(1 + r)^t} + \frac{P_n}{(1 + r)^n} \quad \text{where } P_n = \frac{\text{FCFE}_{n+1}}{(r - g_n)}$$

where

$$
\begin{aligned}
\text{FCFE}_t &= \text{Expected FCFE per share in year } t \\
r &= \text{Required rate of return} \\
P_n &= \text{Price at the end of year } n \\
g_n &= \text{Growth rate forever after year } n
\end{aligned}
$$

Just as in the dividend discount model, there are four basic inputs needed for this model to be usable. First, the *length of the high-growth period* is defined. Second, the *free cash flow to equity* each period during the growth period is specified; this means that net capital expenditures, working capital needs, and the debt-financing mix are all estimated for the high-growth period. Third, the *rate of return* that stockholders will demand for holding the stock is estimated. Finally, the *terminal price at the end of the high-growth period* is estimated, based on the estimates of stable growth, the free cash flows to equity, and required return after the high growth ends.

Of the four inputs, the length of the high-growth period and the rate of return required by stockholders are the same for the dividend discount and FCFE valuation models. The differences in the other two inputs are minor but still worth emphasizing.

Estimating FCFE during the high-growth period As in the dividend discount model, we start with the earnings per share and estimate expected growth in earnings. Thus, the entire discussion about earnings growth in the dividend discount model applies here as well. Once the earnings are estimated, the **net capital expenditures,** working capital needs, and debt-financing needs have to be specified in order to arrive at the FCFE. Just as the dividend payout ratio was adjusted to reflect changes in expected growth, the net

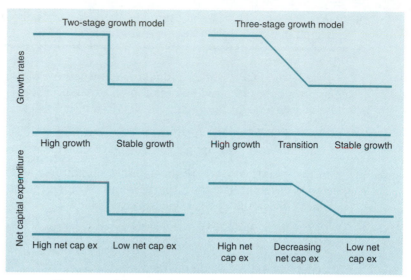

Figure 23.7 Net capital expenditures and expected growth

capital expenditure and working capital needs should change as the growth rate changes. In particular, high-growth companies will have relatively higher net capital expenditures and working capital needs. As the growth rate declines, these requirements should also decline. Figure 23.7 depicts changes in these variables under different earnings growth formulations.

Net Capital Expenditures: This is the difference between capital expenditures and depreciation.

A similar point can be made about leverage. High-growth, high-risk firms generally do not use much leverage to finance investment needs. As the growth tapers off, however, the firm will be much more willing to use debt; thus, debt ratios will likely increase as growth rates drop.

Estimating the terminal price   The terminal price in the FCFE model is also determined by the stable growth rate and the required return. The difference between this model and the dividend discount model lies primarily in the cash flow used to calculate the terminal price: the dividend discount model uses expected dividends in the period after the high-growth period, whereas the FCFE model uses the free cash flow to equity in that period:

$$\text{Value of Stock} = \frac{\text{FCFE}_{n+1}}{r - g_n}$$

In estimating that cash flow, the net capital expenditures and working capital needs should be consistent with the definition of stability. Many analysts assume that stable growth firms have no net capital expenditures.

❑ Concept
Check

Given that we allow for a stable growth rate that includes real growth, do you agree with the practice of assuming that the net capital expenditures will be zero in stable growth? Why or why not? How would you go about estimating net capital expenditures in stable growth?

FCFE valuation versus dividend discount model valuation   The FCFE discounted cash-flow model can be viewed as an alternative to the dividend discount model. Because the two approaches sometimes provide different estimates of value, however, a comparison is in order.

There are two conditions under which the value obtained from using the FCFE in discounted cash-flow valuation will be the same as the value obtained from using the dividend discount model. The first condition is obvious: when the dividends are equal to the FCFE, the value will be the same. The second condition is more subtle: when the FCFE is greater than dividends, but the excess cash (FCFE − Dividends) is invested in projects with net present value of zero, the values will also be similar. For instance, investing in financial assets that are fairly priced should yield a net present value of zero.

More often, the two models will provide different estimates of value. First, when the FCFE is greater than the dividend and the excess cash either earns below-market interest rates or is invested in negative net present value projects, the value from the FCFE model will be greater than the value from the dividend discount model. This is not as unusual as it might seem. There are numerous case studies of firms that, having accumulated large cash balances by paying out low dividends relative to FCFE, chose to use this cash to finance unwise takeovers (the price paid is greater than the value received). Second, the payment of smaller dividends than the firm can afford lowers debt equity ratios; accordingly, the firm may become underleveraged, reducing its value.

When dividends are greater than FCFE, the firm will have to issue either new stock or new debt to pay these dividends. At least three negative consequences for value are possible. One is the flotation cost on these security issues, which can be substantial for equity issues. Second, if the firm borrows the money to pay the dividends, the firm may become overleveraged (relative to the optimal), leading to a loss in value. Finally, paying too much in dividends can lead to capital rationing constraints, whereby good projects are rejected, resulting in a loss of wealth.

When the two models yield different values, two questions remain: (1) What does the difference between the two models tell us? (2) Which of the two models is the appropriate one to use in evaluating the market price?

More often, the value from the FCFE model exceeds the value from the dividend discount model. The difference between the value obtained from the FCFE model and the value obtained from the dividend discount model can be considered one component of the value of controlling a firm—that is, it measures the value of controlling dividend policy. In a hostile takeover, the bidder can expect to control the firm and change the dividend policy (to reflect FCFE), thus capturing the higher FCFE value. In the more infrequent case—the value from the dividend discount model exceeds the value from the FCFE—the difference has less economic meaning but can be considered a warning on the sustainability of expected dividends.

As for the question as to which of the two values is more appropriate for evaluating the market price, the answer lies in the openness of the market for corporate control. If there is a good probability that a firm can be taken over or its management changed, the market price will reflect that likelihood. In that case, the value from the FCFE model would be a more appropriate benchmark. As changes in corporate control become more difficult, either because of a firm's size and/or legal or market restrictions on takeovers, the value from the dividend discount model will provide a more appropriate benchmark for comparison.

 IN PRACTICE   VALUING A FIRM USING STABLE GROWTH—FCFE MODEL: AT&T

Given its large size, it is unlikely that AT&T will be able to grow much faster than the economy in the long term. AT&T also pays out much less in dividends than it generates in FCFE.

> Dividends in 1994 = $1.32/share
> FCFE per share in 1994 = $2.49/share

The leverage is stable, making it a likely candidate for the stable-growth FCFE model. The background information on the firm is as follows:

- Current Information

> Earnings per share = $3.15
> Capital Expenditures per share = $3.15
> Depreciation per share = $2.78
> Change in Working Capital/share = $0.50
> Debt-Financing Ratio = 25%

Earnings, capital expenditures, depreciation, and working capital are all expected to grow 6% a year. The beta for the stock is 0.90, and the Treasury bond rate is 7.50%. The valuation variables are as follows:

- **Cost of Equity** = 7.50% + 0.90 (5.50%) = 12.45%
- **Expected Growth Rate** = 6.00%
- **Base Year FCFE**

> Earnings per share   = $3.15
> − (Capital Expenditures − Depreciation) (1 − Debt Ratio)
> = $(3.15 − $2.78)(1−.25)   = − $0.28
> − (Change in Working Capital) (1 − Debt Ratio)
> = $(0.50 (1−.25)   = − $0.38
> = FCFE   = $2.49

> Value per Share = $2.49 (1.06)/(.1245 − .06) = $41.00

The stock was trading for $51.25 in March 1995. This valuation would suggest that the stock was overvalued at that time, if we accept the assumptions made about expected growth and risk. Alternatively, it can be argued that AT&T still has some extraordinary growth left in it, which will increase the value per share.

 Concept Check

Shortly after this valuation, AT&T announced that it was splitting up into three businesses, each of which would be traded separately, and the market price went up sharply. How would you go about showing that the sum of the parts was greater than the whole?

 IN PRACTICE VALUING A FIRM USING TWO-STAGE GROWTH—FCFE MODEL: AMGEN, INC.

Amgen, a leading biotechnology company, was the rumored target of a takeover attempt in 1995. Although Amgen has had a history of extraordinary growth, its growth is moderating for two reasons: (1) it is becoming a much larger company; and (2) its products are maturing and may face competition soon. Amgen does not pay dividends but has some FCFE. This FCFE is likely to increase as the growth rate moderates and the firm gets larger. Finally, leverage is stable.

The background information on the firm is as follows:

Current Earnings / Capital Expenditures

Earnings per share in 1994 = $3.10
Capital Expenditures in 1994 per share = $1.00
Depreciation per share in 1994 = $0.60

Inputs for the High-Growth Period

Length of high-growth period = 5 years

- Return on Equity = 18.78% (This is much lower than the current return on equity of about 28%; this ROE is going to be difficult to sustain as the firm gets larger.)

- Retention Ratio = 100% (The firm pays no dividends now and is unlikely to do so in the near future because its stockholders are more interested in price appreciation.)

$$\text{Expected Growth Rate} = 1 * 18.78\% = 18.78\%$$

The beta during the high-growth phase is expected to be 1.30.

$$\text{Cost of Equity} = 7.50\% + 1.30\,(5.50\%) = 14.65\%$$

Capital expenditures, depreciation, and revenues are expected to grow at the same rate as earnings (18.78%).

Working capital is expected to be 10% of revenues.

The debt ratio is approximately 18.01%; it is expected to remain unchanged.

Inputs for the Stable Growth

Expected growth rate = 6%
Beta during stable growth phase = 1.10 : Cost of Equity = 7.50% + 1.1 (5.5%) = 13.55%

Capital expenditures are assumed to be offset by depreciation.

Working capital is expected to be 10% of revenues.

The debt ratio is expected to remain at 18.01%.

In estimating the value of the firm,

- The first component of value is the present value of the expected FCFE during the high-growth period, as shown in Table 23.3.

Table 23.3 FCFE OF AMGEN: HIGH-GROWTH PERIOD					
	1	2	3	4	5
Earnings	$3.68	$4.37	$5.19	$6.17	$7.33
− (CapEx-Depreciation)*(1−δ)	0.39	0.46	0.55	0.65	0.78
−Δ Working Capital*(1−δ)	0.38	0.45	0.54	0.64	0.76
Free Cash flow to Equity	2.91	3.46	4.11	4.88	5.79
Present Value (@14.65%)	2.54	2.63	2.72	2.82	2.92

> PV of FCFE during high-growth phase = $2.54 + $2.63 + 2.72 + 2.82 + 2.92 = $13.64

The price at the end of the high-growth phase (end of year 5) can be estimated using the constant-growth model:

$$\text{Terminal price} = \text{Expected FCFE}_{n+1} / (r - g_n)$$
$$\text{Expected Earnings per share}_6 = 7.33 * 1.06 = \$7.77$$
$$\text{Expected FCFE}_6 = \text{EPS}_6 - \Delta \text{Working Capital} (1 - \text{Debt Ratio})$$
$$= \$7.77 - \$0.35 (1 - .1801) = \$7.48$$
$$\text{Terminal price} = \$7.48 / (.1355 - .06) = \$99.07$$

The present value of the terminal price can be then written as

$$\text{PV of Terminal Price} = \frac{\$99.07}{(1.1465)^5} = \$50.01$$

The cumulated present value of dividends and the terminal price can then be calculated as follows:

> PV today = PV of FCFE during high-growth phase + PV of Terminal Price
> = $13.64 + $50.01 = $63.65

Amgen was trading at $60 in March 1995, at the time of this analysis.

Concept Check

> In estimating the terminal value, we assumed that capital expenditures would offset depreciation. What would be the effect on value of assuming that net capital expenditures in year 5 would continue growing at the same rate as earnings?

FCFF Valuation

The free cash flow to the firm (FCFF) is the sum of the cash flows to all claimholders in the firm, including stockholders, bondholders, and preferred stockholders. There are two ways of measuring the free cash flow to the firm. One is to add up the cash flows to the claimholders:

FCFF = Free Cash Flow to Equity
    + Interest Expense (1 − tax rate) + Principal Repayments − New Debt Issues
    + Preferred Dividends

The other involves using earnings before interest payments and taxes (EBIT) as a base for the calculation:

FCFF = EBIT (1 − tax rate) + Depreciation − Capital Expenditure − Δ Working Capital

Both approaches should provide the same estimates of the cash flow.

The differences between FCFF and FCFE arise primarily from cash flows associated with debt—interest payments, principal repayments, and new debt issues—and other non-equity claims, such as preferred dividends.

One widely used measure in valuation is the earnings before interest, taxes, depreciation, and amortization (EBITDA) . The free cash flow to the firm is a closely related concept, but it takes into account the potential tax liability from the earnings as well as capital expenditures and working capital requirements. Another common measure is the **net operating income (NOI)**—the income from operations, prior to taxes and nonoperating expenses. If nonoperating expenses are deducted, the resulting figure is the earnings before interest and taxes (EBIT). Each of these measures is used in valuation models, and each is a variant of the free cash flow to the firm. Each, however, makes some assumptions about the relationship between depreciation and capital expenditures.

Net Operating Income: This is the income from operations prior to taxes, debt payments, and nonoperating expenses.

Concept Check

You are examining a valuation done of a high-growth firm and notice that the after-tax operating income [EBIT $(1 - t)$] is being discounted at the cost of capital to arrive at firm value. What is being assumed about net capital expenditures and working capital, when this is done? Would the fact that this is a high-growth firm make any difference?

Growth in FCFE versus growth in FCFF The primary cause of differences in the growth rates in FCFF and the FCFE is the existence of leverage. Leverage generally increases the growth rate in the FCFE, relative to the growth rate in the FCFF. This can be illustrated using the formulation relating the growth rate to financial fundamentals. The growth rate in earnings per share is defined as

$$g_{EPS} = b \left[ROA + D/E \left(ROA - i \left(1 - t \right) \right) \right]$$

where

g_{EPS} = Growth rate in Earnings per share

b = Retention ratio = $1 -$ Payout ratio

ROA = Return on Assets = (Net Income + Interest Expense $(1 - t)$)/(BV of Debt + BV of Equity)

D/E = Book Value of Debt/Book Value of Equity

i = Interest Expense / Book Value of Debt

As long as the return on assets earned by a firm on its projects exceeds the after-tax interest rate, increasing leverage will increase the growth rate in earnings per share. The cash flow to the firm is a pre-debt cash flow and is not affected by increased leverage. Thus, the growth rate in EBIT, for the same firm, will be a function of just the retention ratio and the return on assets and will generally be lower:

$$g_{EBIT} = b \left(ROA \right)$$

The growth rates in capital expenditures, depreciation, and capital spending will be identical for purposes of calculating the FCFE and FCFF.

Concept Check

Assume that you routinely use the forecasts of earnings growth from analysts to estimate growth in earnings before interest and taxes. What might be some of the perils of this approach? Explain.

The general model   In the general version of the FCFF model, we allow for two stages in growth—an initial period of extraordinary growth, followed by stable growth forever.

Extraordinary growth period	Stable growth: g_n forever

Value of the Stock = PV of FCFF during extraordinary phase + PV of terminal price

$$P_0 = \sum_{t=1}^{t=n} \frac{FCFF_t}{(1 + r)^t} + \frac{P_n}{(1 + r)^n} \text{ where } P_n = \frac{FCFF_{n+1}}{(r - g_n)}$$

where

$$FCFF = \text{Expected FCFF per share in year } t$$
$$r = \text{Weighted Average Cost of Capital}$$
$$P_n = \text{Value of Firm at end of year } n$$
$$g_n = \text{Growth rate forever after year } n$$

Just as in the dividend discount model, there are four basic inputs in this model. First, the *length of the high-growth period* is defined. Second, the *free cash flow to the firm* each period during the growth period is specified; this requires estimating net capital expenditures and working capital needs for the high-growth period. Third, the *cost of capital* that investors demand for holding stock, debt, and other securities is estimated, based on their market value weights. Finally, the *terminal value of the firm at the end of the high-growth period* is estimated, based on the estimates of stable growth, free cash-flows to the firm, and required return after the high growth ends.

The **FCFF model** therefore uses much of the same information needed for the FCFE model, but it differs in certain respects. The free cash flow to the firm is before cash flows to debtholders and is thus based on operating income growth rather than net income growth. In addition, the discount rate is the cost of capital rather than the cost of equity. Finally, the present value of the cash flows provides an estimate of the value of the firm rather than just the equity.

FCFF Model: The FCFF model estimates the value of the firm as the present value of the expected FCFF, discounted back at the cost of capital.

That said, all of the caveats relating to FCFE valuation apply here as well. The assumptions about net capital expenditures and working capital should be consistent with assumptions about growth. The debt ratios matter here, not because they affect the cash flows, but because they help determine the cost of capital and should be changed to reflect the changing characteristics of the firm.

Firm valuation versus equity valuation   Unlike the dividend discount model or the FCFE model, the FCFF model values the firm rather than equity. The value of equity, however, can be extracted from the value of the firm by subtracting out the market value of outstanding debt. Since this model can be viewed as an alternative way of valuing equity, two questions arise: (1) Why value the firm rather than equity? (2) Will the values for equity obtained from the firm valuation approach be consistent with the values obtained from the equity valuation approaches described in the previous chapter?

The advantage of using the firm valuation approach is that cash flows relating to debt do not have to be considered explicitly, since the FCFF is a pre-debt cash flow. By contrast, they have to be taken into account in estimating FCFE. In cases where the leverage is expected to change significantly over time, this can be a significant saving. At the same time, the firm valuation approach requires information about debt ratios and interest rates to estimate the weighted average cost of capital.

The value for equity obtained from the firm valuation and equity valuation approaches will be the same if two conditions are met:

1. *If consistent assumptions are made about growth in the two approaches:* This does not mean that the same growth rate is used in both approaches, and it may require that the growth rates in earnings be adjusted for the effect of leverage. This is especially true for the calculation of the terminal value, whereby a stable growth rate is assumed in both FCFE and FCFF.

2. *If bonds are correctly priced:* The value of equity in the FCFF approach is obtained by subtracting out the market value of the debt from the value of the firm. If the firm's debt is overvalued, the value of equity obtained from the FCFF model will be lower than the value obtained from the equity valuation approaches. Similarly, the value of equity will be higher if the firm's debt is undervalued.

 Concept Check

Assume that you value the equity by first valuing the firm and then subtracting out the outstanding debt. Will this equity value be the same as the value obtained by valuing equity directly? Why or why not?

 IN PRACTICE   VALUING A FIRM USING FCFF MODEL: FEDERATED DEPARTMENT STORES

In 1994, the earnings before interest and taxes at Federated amounted to $531 million, well below EBIT of $628 million in 1988. The earnings are expected to grow at rates slightly above stable levels for the next five years as the firm recovers. In addition, the leverage in 1994 was still significantly above desirable levels, largely as a consequence of the leveraged buyout in the late 1980s. It was anticipated that this debt ratio would be lowered gradually over the next five years to acceptable levels.

We can apply the following background information to value the firm.

<u>Base Year Information</u>

> Earnings before interest and taxes in 1994 = $532 million
> Capital Expenditures in 1994 = $310 million
> Depreciation in 1994 = $207 million
> Revenues in 1994 = $7230 million
> Working Capital as percent of revenues = 25.00%
> Tax rate = 36%

<u>High-Growth Phase</u>

> Length of High-Growth Phase = 5 years
> Expected Growth Rate in FCFF = 8%

Financing Details

- Beta during high-growth phase = 1.25
- Cost of Debt during high-growth phase = 9.50% (pretax)
- Debt Ratio during high-growth phase = 50%

<u>Stable-Growth Phase</u>

$$\text{Expected growth rate in FCFF} = 5\%$$

Financing Details

- Beta during stable-growth phase = 1.00
- Cost of Debt during stable-growth phase = 8.50%
- Debt Ratio during stable-growth phase = 25%

Capital expenditures are offset by depreciation.

Valuation   The forecasted free cash flows to the firm over the next five years are provided in Table 23.4.

Table 23.4   **ESTIMATED FCFF—FEDERATED DEPARTMENT STORES**

	1	2	3	4	5	Terminal year
EBIT	$574.45	$620.41	$670.04	$723.64	$781.54	$820.61
$- t$ (EBIT)	206.80	223.35	241.21	260.51	281.35	295.42
$-$ (Cap Ex $-$ Depreciation)	111.24	120.14	129.75	140.13	151.34	0.00
$-$ Chg Working Capital	144.58	156.15	168.64	182.13	196.70	132.77
= FCFF	101.83	120.77	130.44	140.87	152.15	392.42

Cost of Equity during high-growth phase = 7.5% + 1.25 (5.5%) = 14.38%
Cost of Capital during high-growth phase = 14.38% (0.5) + 9.50% (1−0.36) (0.5) = 10.23%

The free cash flow to the firm in the terminal year is estimated at $392.42 million.

FCFF in terminal year = $EBIT_6$ (1 − t) - (Rev_6 − Rev_5)*Working Capital as % of Revenue
= $820.61 (1−0.36) − $132.77 = $392.42 million
Cost of Equity during stable-growth phase = 7.50% + 1.00 (5.50%) = 13.00%
Cost of Capital in stable-growth phase = 13.00% (0.75) + 8.50% (1−0.36) (0.25) = 11.11%
Terminal value of the firm = $392.42 / (.1111 − .05) = $6,422 million

The value of the firm is the present value of the expected free cash flows to the firm and the present value of the terminal value:

PV of FCFF	$487.17
PV of Terminal Value =	$3,946.93
Value of Firm =	$4,434.11
Value of Debt =	$2,740.58
Value of Equity =	$1,693.52
Value Per Share =	$13.38

Federated Department Stores was trading at $21 per share in March 1995, significantly above the estimated value per share.

 IN PRACTICE VALUING A FIRM WITH THE THREE-STAGE FCFF MODEL: LIN BROADCASTING

LIN Broadcasting was appraised in early 1995 by three investment bankers to determine the appropriate price on a takeover by AT&T. The three appraisals came in at $105 by Morgan Stanley for AT&T, $155 by Lehman Brothers for LIN Broadcasting, and a compromise valuation by Wasserstein Perella of $127.50. LIN Broadcasting is a fast-growing firm in a fast-growing industry segment. Revenues are expected to grow 30% a year for the next few years. The firm has never made a profit after taxes, even though it has posted high growth, because it has had high leverage and nonoperating expenses. Prior to these charges, however, it earned an operating income of $128 million in 1994. Thus, although the FCFE is negative, the FCFF is positive. Finally, the financial leverage is high but can be expected to decline as the industry stabilizes.

The background Information on LIN Broadcasting is as follows:

<u>Current Earnings</u>

EBIT in 1994 = $128.3 million
Capital Expenditures in 1994 = $150.5 million
Depreciation and Amortization in 1994 = $125.1 million
Working Capital was about 10% of revenues in 1994.

<u>Inputs for the High-Growth Period</u>

Length of the High-Growth Period = 5 years
Expected growth rate in Revenues / EBIT = 30.00%

Financing Details

- Beta during High-Growth Period = 1.60
- Cost of Equity during High-Growth Period = 7.5% + 1.60 (5.5%) = 16.30%
- The firm will continue to use debt heavily during this period (Debt Ratio = 60%), at a pretax cost of debt of 10%.

Capital Expenditures and Depreciation are expected to grow at the same rate as revenues and EBIT.

Working Capital will remain at 10% of revenues during this period.

<u>Inputs for the transition period</u>

Weighted Average Cost of Capital = 16.30% (0.40) + 10% (0.64) (0.60) = 10.36%

Length of the transition period = 5 years
Growth rate in EBIT will decline from 30% in year 5 to 5% in year 10 in linear increments.
Capital expenditures will grow 8% a year, and depreciation will grow at 12% a year during the transition period.

Financing Details

- Beta will drop to 1.25 for the entire transition period.
- The debt ratio during this phase will drop to 50%, and the pretax cost of debt will be 9%.

Working Capital will remain at 10% of revenues during the period.

Weighted Average Cost of Capital = 14.38% (0.50) + 9% (0.64) (0.50)= 10.07%

<u>Inputs for the Stable Growth</u>

Expected growth rate in revenues and EBIT= 5%
Capital expenditures and depreciation will grow at the same rate as EBIT.
Beta during stable-growth phase = 1.00 : Cost of Equity = 7.50% + 1.0 (5.5%) = 13%
Debt ratio during stable phase = 40%; pretax cost of debt will be 8.5%.

These inputs are used to estimate free cash flows to the firm, the cost of capital, and the present values during the high-growth and transition period in Table 23.5.

Table 23.5 ESTIMATED FCFF, WACC, AND PRESENT VALUE—LIN BROADCASTING

Period	EBIT (1 − t)	Cap Exp	Depreciation	Chg. WC	FCFF	Debt Ratio (%)	Beta	WACC (%)	Present Value
1	$106.75	$195.65	$162.63	$20.66	$53.07	60.00	1.60	10.36	$48.09
2	138.77	254.35	211.42	26.86	68.99	60.00	1.60	10.36	56.64
3	180.40	330.65	274.84	34.91	89.68	60.00	1.60	10.36	66.72
4	234.52	429.84	357.30	45.39	116.59	60.00	1.60	10.36	78.60
5	304.88	558.80	464.49	59.00	151.57	60.00	1.60	10.36	92.59
6	381.10	603.50	520.23	63.92	233.90	50.00	1.25	10.07	129.81
7	457.31	651.78	582.65	63.92	324.27	50.00	1.25	10.07	163.50
8	525.91	703.92	652.57	57.53	417.03	50.00	1.25	10.07	191.05
9	578.50	760.24	730.88	44.10	505.04	50.00	1.25	10.07	210.20
10	607.43	821.05	818.59	24.26	580.70	50.00	1.25	10.07	219.58

The terminal value at the end of year 10 can be calculated based on the FCFF in year 11, the stable growth rate of 5%, and the cost of capital in the stable-growth phase:

$$\text{FCFF in year 11} = \text{FCFF in year 10} * 1.05 = \$580.70\,(1.05) = \$609.73$$
$$\text{Cost of Capital in stable period} = 13.00\%\,(0.6) + 8.5\%\,(1-.36)\,(0.4) = 9.98\%$$
$$\text{Terminal price} = \$609.73\,/\,(.0998 - .05) = \$12{,}253.55 \text{ million}$$

The components of value are as follows:

Present Value of FCFF in high-growth phase:	$342.64
Present Value of FCFF in transition phase:	$914.15
Present Value of terminal firm value at end of transition:	$4,633.49
Value of LIN Broadcasting:	$5,890.27
Less: Value of Outstanding Debt:	$1,806.60
Value of Equity in LIN Broadcasting:	$4,083.67
Value per share:	$79.29

APPLICABILITY AND LIMITATIONS OF DISCOUNTED CASH-FLOW VALUATION

As we have discussed, discounted cash-flow valuation is based on expected future cash flows and discount rates. Given these informational requirements, this approach is easiest to use for assets (firms) whose cash flows are currently positive and can be estimated with some reliability for future periods, and when a proxy for risk is available to obtain discount rates. The further we get from this idealized setting, the more difficult discounted cash-flow valuation becomes.

Firms in Trouble

A distressed firm generally has negative earnings and cash flows currently and expects to lose money for some time in the future. Estimating future cash flows for these firms is difficult, since there is a strong probability of bankruptcy. Discounted cash-flow valuation does not work very well for firms that have a strong probability of failure, since the approach considers the firm a going concern providing positive cash flows to its investors. Even in the case of firms that are expected to survive, cash flows will have to be estimated until they turn positive, because obtaining a present value of negative cash flows will yield a negative value for equity or the firm.[4]

Cyclical Firms

The earnings and cash flows of cyclical firms tend to follow the economy—rising during economic booms and falling during recessions. If discounted cash-flow valuation is applied to these firms, expected future cash flows are usually smoothed out, unless the analyst wants to undertake the onerous task of predicting the timing and duration of economic recessions and recoveries. Many cyclical firms, in the depths of a recession, look like troubled firms, with negative earnings and cash flows. Estimating future cash flows then becomes entangled with analyst predictions about when the economy will turn and how strong the upturn will be; more optimistic analysts will arrive at higher estimates of value. Although this may be unavoidable, the economic biases of the analyst have to be taken into account before using these valuations.

Firms with Unutilized Assets

Discounted cash-flow valuation reflects the value of all assets that produce cash flows. If a firm has assets that are unutilized (and hence do not produce any cash flows), the value of these assets will not be reflected in the value obtained from discounting expected future cash flows. The same caveat applies, to a lesser degree, to underutilized assets, since their value will be understated in discounted cash-flow valuation. Although this is a problem, it is not insurmountable. The value of these assets can always be obtained externally and added on to the value obtained from discounted cash-flow valuation.[5]

> ❏ Concept Check
>
> It is often standard practice to do a discounted cash-flow valuation using one of the approaches described above and then adding on the cash and marketable securities that a firm may have on its balance sheet. What are the perils with this approach? (Remember that the interest income from the marketable securities is included in the income of the firm.)

Firms with Patents or Product Options

Firms often have unutilized patents or **product options** that do not produce any current cash flows and are not expected to produce cash flows in the near future but, nevertheless, are valuable. For instance, in 1995, Pfizer was one of several pharmaceutical companies with valuable patents in its name, many of which were not expected to generate cash flows for several years to come. If this is the case, the value obtained from discounting expected cash flows to the firm will understate the true value of the firm. Again, the problem can be overcome by valuing these assets in the open market or by using option pricing models and then adding on to the value obtained from discounted cash-flow valuation.

Product Option: A product option gives a firm the exclusive right to produce the product; this may result either from owning the product patent or licensing.

---

[4]The protection of limited liability should ensure that no stock will sell for less than zero. The price of such a stock can never be negative.

[5]If these assets are traded on external markets, the market prices of these assets can be used in the valuation. If not, the cash flows can be projected, assuming full utilization of assets, and the value can be estimated.

Firms in the Process of Restructuring

Firms in the process of restructuring often sell some of their assets, acquire other assets, and change their capital structure and dividend policy. Some of them also change their ownership structure (going from publicly traded to private status) and management compensation schemes. Each of these changes makes estimating future cash flows more difficult and affects the riskiness of the firm. Using historical data for such firms can provide a misleading picture of the firm's value. These firms can be valued, however, even in light of the major changes in investment and financing policy, if future cash flows reflect the expected effects of these changes and the discount rate is adjusted to reflect the new business and financial risk in the firm.

Firms Involved in Acquisitions

At least two specific issues relating to acquisitions need to be considered when using discounted cash-flow valuation models to value target firms. The first is the thorny issue of whether there is synergy in the merger and if its value can be estimated. It can be done, though it does require assumptions about the form the synergy will take and its effect on cash flows. The second, especially in hostile takeovers, is the effect of changing management on cash flows and risk. Again, the effect of the change can and should be incorporated into the estimates of future cash flows and discount rates and, hence, into value.

Private Firms

The biggest problem associated with using discounted cash-flow valuation models to value private firms is the measurement of risk (to use in estimating discount rates), because most risk/return models require that risk parameters be estimated from historical prices on the asset being analyzed. Because securities in private firms are not traded, this is not possible. One solution is to look at the riskiness of comparable firms that are publicly traded. Another is to relate the measure of risk to accounting variables that are available for the private firm.

RELATIVE VALUATION

In relative valuation, the value of an asset is derived from the pricing of "comparable" assets, standardized using a common variable such as earnings, cash flows, book value, or revenues. One illustration of this approach is the use of an industry-average price/earnings ratio to value a firm; the assumption is that the other firms in the industry are comparable to the firm being valued and that the market, on average, prices these firms correctly. Another multiple widely used is the price to book value ratio. In this case, firms selling at a discount on book value, relative to comparable firms, are considered undervalued. The multiple of price to sales can also be used to value firms; the average price/sales ratios of firms with similar characteristics are used for comparison. Although these three multiples are among the most widely used in relative valuation, there are others that play a role in analysis—price to cash flows, price to dividends, and market value to replacement value (Tobin's Q), to name a few.

Ways of Using Multiples

An analyst can come up with the appropriate multiple to use in valuing a firm by using either fundamentals or comparables.

The first approach relates multiples to fundamentals about the firm being valued—specifically, growth rates in earnings and cash flows, payout ratios, and risk. This approach to estimating multiples is equivalent to using discounted cash-flow models, requiring the same information and yielding the same results. Its primary advantage is that it shows the relationship between multiples and firm characteristics and allows us to explore how multiples change as these characteristics change. For instance, what will be the effect of changing profit margins on the price/sales ratio? What will happen to price earnings ratios as growth rates decrease? What is the relationship between price/book value ratios and return on equity?

To relate multiples to fundamentals, consider a simple dividend discount model for a stable-growth firm:

$$\text{Gordon Growth Model: } P_0 = \frac{\text{DPS}_1}{r - g_n}$$

Dividing both sides of this equation by the earnings per share provides us with a formulation for the PE ratio for a stable-growth firm:

$$\frac{P_0}{\text{EPS}_0} = \text{PE} = \frac{\text{Payout Ratio}*(1 + g_n)}{r - g_n}$$

Dividing both sides of the dividend discount model by the book value per share provides us with a formulation for the PBV ratio for a stable-growth firm:

$$\frac{P_0}{\text{BV}_0} = \text{PBV} = \frac{\text{ROE}*\text{Payout Ratio}*(1 + g_n)}{r - g_n}$$

If the return on equity is written in terms of the retention ratio and the expected growth rate, we get the following formulation:

$$\frac{P_0}{\text{BV}_0} = \text{PBV} = \frac{\text{ROE} - g_n}{r - g_n}$$

Finally, dividing both sides of the dividend discount model by the sales per share provides us with a formulation for the PS ratio for a stable-growth firm.

$$\frac{P_0}{\text{Sales}_0} = \text{PS} = \frac{\text{Profit Margin}*\text{Payout Ratio}*(1 + g_n)}{r - g_n}$$

Concept Check

An analyst claims that she uses multiples because she does not like making assumptions about growth, risk, and payout (as is necessary in discounted cash-flow valuation). Respond.

IN PRACTICE ESTIMATING MULTIPLES FROM FUNDAMENTALS—EXXON

Exxon had earnings per share of $3.82 in 1992 and paid out 74% of its earnings as dividends. The growth rate in earnings and dividends, in the long term, is expected to be 6%. The beta for Exxon is 0.75, and the Treasury bond rate is 7%.

$$\text{Current Dividend Payout Ratio} = 74\%$$
$$\text{Expected Growth Rate in Earnings and Dividends} = 6\%$$
$$\text{Cost of Equity} = 7\% + 0.75*5.5\% = 11.13\%$$

$$\text{PE Ratio based on fundamentals} = 0.74 *1.06 / (.1113 -.06) = 15.29$$

Exxon was selling at a PE ratio of 17.02 at the time of this analysis.
Return on Equity = 15%

$$\text{PBV Ratio based on fundamentals} = 0.15 * 0.74 *1.06 / (.1113 -.06) = 2.29$$

Exxon was selling at a P/BV ratio of 2.44 on the day of this analysis.
Net Profit Margin = Net Income÷Revenues = $3.82/$83.06 = 4.7%

$$\text{PS Ratio based on fundamentals} = 0.047 * 0.74 *1.06 / (.1113 -.06) = 0.7187$$

Exxon was selling at a PS ratio of 0.7826 at the time of this analysis.

The second approach estimates multiples for a firm by looking at comparable firms. The key issue in this approach is the definition of a comparable firm. In theory, the analyst should control for all the variables that can influence the multiple. In practice, controlling for these variables may range from the naive (using industry averages) to the sophisticated (multivariate regression models that identify and control for the relevant variables).

IN PRACTICE ESTIMATING MULTIPLES FROM COMPARABLES—BOEING

Table 23.6 compares the multiples for Boeing to other firms in the aerospace/defense industry in 1995.

As you can see, Boeing has a much higher price/earnings and price/sales ratio than comparable firms, but a lower price/book value ratio. It also has lower growth, a lower return on equity, and a lower margin than comparable firms. All these statistics would suggest that Boeing is overvalued, until one considers the possibility that the market is building in the expectation that Boeing's earnings will rebound in future years. Part of the problem with such comparisons is that the multiples and comparables can be manipulated to fit whatever conclusion the analyst is seeking.

Concept Check

When estimating multiples from comparables, what are the implicit assumptions being made about the riskiness of the comparable firms?

Table 23.6   **MULTIPLES FOR BOEING AND COMPARABLE FIRMS**

Company	PE	PBV	PS	Payout Ratio (%)	Beta	Exp. Growth (%)	Margin (%)	ROE (%)	Margin (%)
Aviall Inc.	17.96	0.52	0.20	8.16	1.45	33	1.12	2.88	1.12
Bombardier	21.92	2.88	0.79	21.92	1.00	21	3.60	13.15	3.60
CAE Inc.	20.45	5.63	1.21	36.36	0.55	17	5.91	27.50	5.91
GRC Intnl	42.59	4.30	1.51	0.00	1.05	20	3.54	10.09	3.54
Gen'l Dynamics	15.38	2.32	1.15	39.89	1.10	13	7.49	15.10	7.49
Highes Electronic	14.81	1.84	1.10	29.63	1.00	11	7.45	12.41	7.45
Litton Industries	18.42	2.63	0.58	0.00	1.20	18	3.16	14.25	3.16
Lockheed Martin	15.10	2.64	0.58	26.09	1.25	12	3.81	17.48	3.81
Loral	16.57	2.39	0.76	17.75	0.95	15	4.57	14.44	4.57
McDonnell Douglas	16.04	2.20	0.64	10.89	1.35	28	3.97	13.69	3.97
Northrop Grumman	12.00	2.01	0.44	32.00	1.30	15	3.67	16.78	3.67
Raytheon	14.63	2.28	0.86	25.78	0.80	11	5.86	15.60	5.86
Rockwell Intnl	16.31	2.67	0.77	36.88	0.95	12	4.74	16.35	4.74
Thiokol	11.88	1.62	0.68	22.44	0.95	7	5.76	13.65	5.76
Average	18.15	2.57	0.81	21.99	1.06	16	4.62	14.53	4.62
Boeing	27.09	2.39	1.11	39.84	0.95	9	4	8.82	4.10

APPLICABILITY AND LIMITATIONS OF MULTIPLES

Multiples are simple and easy to relate to. They can be used to obtain estimates of value quickly for firms and assets and are particularly useful when a large number of comparable firms are being traded on financial markets and the market is, on average, pricing these firms correctly.

By the same token, multiples are also easy to misuse and manipulate, especially when comparable firms are used. Given that no two firms are exactly alike in terms of risk and growth, the definition of "comparable" firms is a subjective one. Consequently, a biased analyst can choose a group of comparable firms to confirm his or her biases about a firm's value. Although this potential for bias exists with discounted cash-flow valuation as well, there the analyst is forced to be much more explicit about the assumptions that determine the final value. In the case of multiples, these assumptions are often left unstated.

The other problem with using multiples based on comparable firms is that it builds in errors (overvaluation or undervaluation) that the market might be making in valuing these firms. Thus, if the market has overvalued all computer software firms, for example, using the average PE ratio of these firms to value an initial public offering will lead to an overvaluation of its stock. In contrast, discounted cash-flow valuation is based on firm-specific growth rates and cash flows and is less likely to be influenced by market errors in valuation.

☐ Concept Check

If you were an investment banker pricing an initial public offering, would you value the firm based on comparables or using discounted cash-flow models? Would your answer be different if you were an investor interested in buying this initial public offering as a long-term investment?

CONCLUSION

One basic approach to valuation is discounted cash-flow valuation, whereby the value of any asset is estimated by computing the present value of the expected cash flows on it. This can be done either from the perspective of just the equity investors in the firm, by discounting cash flows to equity—defined strictly as dividends or expansively as free cash flows to equity—at the cost of equity, or from the perspective of all claimholders in the firm, by discounting cash flows to the firm—cash flows prior to debt payments—at the cost of capital. In either case, the actual process of estimation generally requires four inputs—the length of the period for which a firm or asset can be expected to generate growth greater than the stable growth rate (which is constrained to be close to the growth rate of the economy in which the firm operates); the cash flows during the high-growth period; the terminal value at the end of the high-growth period; and a discount rate. The expected growth potential will vary across firms, with some firms already growing at a stable growth rate and others whose growth is expected to last some periods into the future.

The second approach to valuation is relative valuation, whereby the value of any asset is estimated by looking at how "similar" assets are priced in the market. The key steps in this approach are defining "comparable" firms or assets and choosing a standardized measure of value (usually value as a multiple of earnings, cash flows, or book value) to compare the firms. The multiples can also be stated in terms of the same variables—growth, risk, and payout—that determine discounted cash-flow values. Finally, because this approach is based on how comparable assets are priced, it will build in existing market biases—positive or negative—into the valuation.

QUESTIONS AND PROBLEMS

1. Respond true or false to the following statements relating to the dividend discount model.
   a. The dividend discount model cannot be used to value a high-growth company that pays no dividends.
   b. The dividend discount model will undervalue stocks because it is too conservative.
   c. The dividend discount model will find more undervalued stocks when the overall stock market is depressed.
   d. Stocks that are undervalued using the dividend discount model have generally made significant positive excess returns over long periods (five years or more).
   e. Stocks that pay high dividends and have low price/earnings ratios are more likely to be undervalued using the dividend discount model.

2. Ameritech Corporation paid dividends per share of $3.56 in 1992, and dividends are expected to grow 5.5% a year forever. The stock has a beta of 0.90, and the Treasury bond rate is 6.25%.
   a. What is the value per share, using the Gordon Growth Model?

   b. The stock is trading for $80 per share. What would the growth rate in dividends have to be to justify this price?

3. A key input for the Gordon Growth Model is the expected growth rate in dividends over the long term. How, if at all, would you factor in the following considerations in estimating this growth rate?
   a. There is an increase in the inflation rate.
   b. The economy in which the firm operates is growing very rapidly.
   c. The growth potential of the industry in which the firm operates is very high.
   d. The current management of the firm is of very high quality.

4. Newell Corporation, a manufacturer of do-it-yourself hardware and housewares, reported earnings per share of $2.10 in 1993, on which it paid dividends per share of $0.69. Earnings are expected to grow 15% a year from 1994 to 1998, during which period the dividend payout ratio is expected to remain unchanged. After 1998, the earnings growth rate is expected to drop to a stable 6%, and the payout ratio is expected to increase to 65% of earnings. The firm has a beta of

1.40 currently, and it is expected to have a beta of 1.10 after 1998. The Treasury bond rate is 6.25%.

a. What is the expected price of the stock at the end of 1998?

b. What is the value of the stock, using the two-stage dividend discount model?

5. Church & Dwight, a large producer of sodium bicarbonate, reported earnings per share of $1.50 in 1993 and paid dividends per share of $0.42. In 1993, the firm also reported the following:

$$\text{Net Income} = \$30 \text{ million}$$
$$\text{Interest Expense} = \$0.8 \text{ million}$$
$$\text{Book Value of Debt} = \$7.6 \text{ million}$$
$$\text{Book Value of Equity} = \$160 \text{ million}$$

The firm faced a corporate tax rate of 38.5%. The market value debt-to-equity ratio is 5%. The Treasury bond rate is 7%.

The firm expects to maintain these financial fundamentals from 1994 to 1998, at which time it is expected to become a stable firm, with an earnings growth rate of 6%. The firm's financial characteristics will approach industry averages after 1998. The industry averages are as follows:

$$\text{Return on Assets} = 12.5\%$$
$$\text{Debt/Equity Ratio} = 25\%$$
$$\text{Interest Rate on Debt} = 7\%$$

Church & Dwight had a beta of 0.85 in 1993, and the unlevered beta is not expected to change over time.

a. What is the expected growth rate in earnings, based on fundamentals, for the high-growth period (1994 to 1998)?

b. What is the expected payout ratio after 1998?

c. What is the expected beta after 1998?

d. What is the expected price at the end of 1998?

e. What is the value of the stock, using the two-stage dividend discount model?

f. How much of this value can be attributed to extraordinary growth? to stable growth?

6. Medtronic Inc., the world's largest manufacturer of implantable biomedical devices, reported earnings per share in 1993 of $3.95 and paid dividends per share of $0.68. Its earnings are expected to grow 16% from 1994 to 1998, but the growth rate is expected to decline each year after that to a stable growth rate of 6% in 2003. The payout ratio is expected to remain unchanged from 1994 to 1998, after which it will increase each year to reach 60% in steady state. The stock is expected to have a beta of 1.25 from 1994 to 1998, after which the beta will decline each year to

reach 1.00 by the time the firm becomes stable (the Treasury bond rate is 6.25%).

a. Assuming that the growth rate declines linearly (and the payout ratio increases linearly) from 1999 to 2003, estimate the dividends per share each year from 1994 to 2003.

b. Estimate the expected price at the end of 2003.

c. Estimate the value per share, using the three-stage dividend discount model.

7. Kimberly-Clark, a household product manufacturer, reported earnings per share of $3.20 in 1993 and paid dividends per share of $1.70 in that year. The firm reported depreciation of $315 million in 1993 and capital expenditures of $475 million. (There were 160 million shares outstanding, trading at $51 per share.) This ratio of capital expenditures to depreciation is expected to be maintained in the long term. The working capital needs are negligible. Kimberly-Clark had debt outstanding of $1.6 billion and intends to maintain its current financing mix (of debt and equity) to finance future investment needs. The firm is in a steady state, and earnings are expected to grow 7% a year. The stock had a beta of 1.05 (the Treasury bond rate is 6.25%).

a. Estimate the value per share, using the dividend discount model.

b. Estimate the value per share, using the FCFE model.

c. How would you explain the difference between the two models, and which one would you use as your benchmark for comparison to the market price?

8. Ecolab Inc. sells chemicals and systems for cleaning, sanitizing, and maintenance. It reported earnings per share of $2.35 in 1993 and expected earnings growth of 15.5% a year from 1994 to 1998, and 6% a year after that. The capital expenditure per share was $2.25, and depreciation was $1.125 per share in 1993. Both are expected to grow at the same rate as earnings from 1994 to 1998. Working capital is expected to remain at 5% of revenues, and revenues that were $1,000 million in 1993 are expected to increase 6% a year from 1994 to 1998, and 4% a year after that. The firm currently has a debt ratio [D/(D+E)] of 5% but plans to finance future investment needs (including working capital investments) using a debt ratio of 20%. The stock is expected to have a beta of 1.00 for the period of the analysis, and the Treasury bond rate is 6.50%. There are 63 million shares outstanding.

a. Assuming that capital expenditures and depreciation offset each other after 1998, estimate the value per share.

b. Assuming that capital expenditures continue to be 200% of depreciation even after 1998, estimate the value per share.

c. What would the value per share have been if the firm had continued to finance new investments with its old financing mix (5%)? Is it fair to use the same beta for this analysis?

9. Dionex Corporation, a leader in the development and manufacture of ion chromography systems (used to identify contaminants in electronic devices), reported earnings per share of $2.02 in 1993 and paid no dividends. These earnings are expected to grow 14% a year for five years (1994 to 1998) and 7% a year after that. The firm reported depreciation of $2 million in 1993 and capital spending of $4.20 million and had 7 million shares outstanding. The working capital is expected to remain at 50% of revenues, which were $106 million in 1993 and are expected to grow 6% a year from 1994 to 1998 and 4% a year after that. The firm is expected to finance 10% of its capital expenditures and working capital needs with debt. Dionex had a beta of 1.20 in 1993, and this beta is expected to drop to 1.10 after 1998. The Treasury bond rate is 7%.

a. Estimate the expected free cash flow to equity from 1994 to 1998, assuming that capital expenditures and depreciation grow at the same rate as earnings.

b. Estimate the terminal price per share (at the end of 1998). Stable firms in this industry have capital expenditures that are 150% of revenues and maintain working capital at 25% of revenues.

c. Estimate the value per share today, based on the FCFE model.

10. Biomet Inc. designs, manufactures, and markets reconstructive and trauma devices. It reported earnings per share of $0.56 in 1993, on which it paid no dividends. It had revenues per share in 1993 of $2.91. It had capital expenditures of $0.13 per share in 1993 and depreciation in the same year of $0.08 per share. The working capital was 60% of revenues in 1993 and will remain at that level from 1994 to 1998, whereas earnings and revenues are expected to grow 17% a year. The earnings growth rate is expected to decline linearly over the following five years to a rate of 5% in 2003. During the high-growth and transition periods, capital spending and depreciation are expected to grow at the same rate as earnings, but they are expected to offset each other when the firm reaches steady state. Working capital is expected to drop from 60% of revenues during the 1994–1998 period to 30% of revenues after 2003. The firm has no debt currently, but it plans to finance 10% of its net capital investment and working capital requirements with debt.

The stock is expected to have a beta of 1.45 for the high-growth period (1994–1998), and it is expected to decline to 1.10 by the time the firm goes into steady state (in 2003). The Treasury bond rate is 7%.

a. Estimate the value per share, using the FCFE model.

b. Estimate the value per share, assuming that working capital stays at 60% of revenues forever.

c. Estimate the value per share, assuming that the beta remains unchanged at 1.45 forever.

11. Omnicare Inc., which provides pharmacy management and drug therapy to nursing homes, reported earnings per share of $0.85 in 1993 on revenues per share of $12.50. It had negligible capital expenditures, which were covered by depreciation, but had to maintain working capital at 40% of revenues. Revenues and earnings are expected to grow 20% a year from 1994 to 1998, after which the growth rate is expected to decline linearly over three years to 5% in 2001. The firm has a debt ratio of 15%, which it intends to maintain in the future. The stock has a beta of 1.10, which is expected to remain unchanged for the period of the analysis. The Treasury bond rate is 7%.

a. Estimate the value per share, using the free cash flow to equity model.

b. Assume now that you find out that the way that Omnicare is going to create growth is by giving easier credit terms to its clients. How would that affect your estimate of value? (Will it increase or decrease?)

c. How sensitive is your estimate of value to changes in the working capital assumption?

12. Which of the following firms is likely to have a higher value from the dividend discount model, a higher value from the FCFE model, or the same value from both models?

a. A firm that pays out less in dividends than it has available in FCFE but that invests the balance in Treasury bonds.

b. A firm that pays out more in dividends than it has available in FCFE and then issues stock to cover the difference.

c. A firm that pays out, on average, its FCFE as dividends.

d. A firm that pays out less in dividends than it has available in FCFE, but uses the cash at regular intervals to acquire other firms, with the intent of diversifying.

e. A firm that pays out more in dividends than it has available in FCFE, but borrows money to cover the difference (the firm is already over-levered).

13. Union Pacific Railroad reported net income of $770 million in 1993, after interest expenses of $320 million (the corporate tax rate was 36%). It reported depreciation of $960 million in that year, and capital spending was $1.2 billion. The firm also had $4 billion in debt outstanding on the books, rated AA (carrying a yield to maturity of 8%), trading at par (up from $3.8 billion at the end of 1992). The beta of the stock is 1.05, and there were 200 million shares outstanding (trading at $60 per share), with a book value of $5 billion. Union Pacific paid 40% of its earnings as dividends, and working capital requirements are negligible. The Treasury bond rate is 7%.

a. Estimate the free cash flow to the firm in 1993.

b. Estimate the value of the firm at the end of 1993.

c. Estimate the value of equity at the end of 1993 and the value per share, using the FCFF approach.

14. Lockheed Corporation, one of the largest defense contractors in the United States, reported EBITDA of $1,290 million in 1993, prior to interest expenses of $215 million and depreciation charges of $400 million. Capital Expenditures in 1993 amounted to $450 million, and working capital was 7% of revenues (which were $13,500 million). The firm had debt outstanding of $3.068 billion (in book value terms), trading at a market value of $3.2 billion and yielding a pretax interest rate of 8%. There were 62 million shares outstanding, trading at $64 per share, and the most recent beta is 1.10. The tax rate for the firm is 40%. The Treasury bond rate is 7%.

The firm expects revenues, earnings, capital expenditures, and depreciation to grow at 9.5% a year from 1994 to 1998, after which time the growth rate is expected to drop to 4%. (Capital spending will offset depreciation in the steady-state period.) The company also plans to lower its debt/equity ratio to 50% for the steady state (which will result in the pretax interest rate dropping to 7.5%).

a. Estimate the value of the firm.

b. Estimate the value of the equity in the firm and the value per share.

15. In the face of disappointing earnings results and increasingly assertive institutional stockholders, Eastman Kodak considered a major restructuring in 1993. As part of this restructuring, it considered the sale of its health division, which earned $560 million in earnings before interest and taxes in 1993, on revenues of $5.285 billion. The expected growth in earnings was expected to moderate to 6% between 1994 and 1998 and to 4% after that. Capital expenditures in the health division amounted to $420 million in 1993, whereas depreciation was $350 million. Both are expected to grow 4% a year in the long term. Working capital requirements are negligible.

The average beta of firms competing with Eastman Kodak's health division is 1.15. Although Eastman Kodak has a debt ratio [D/(D+E)] of 50%, the health division can sustain a debt ratio [D/(D+E)] of only 20%, which is similar to the average debt ratio of firms competing in the health sector. At this level of debt, the health division can expect to pay 7.5% on its debt, before taxes. The tax rate is 40%, and the Treasury bond rate is 7%.

a. Estimate the cost of capital for the division.

b. Estimate the value of the division.

c. Why might an acquirer pay more than this estimated value?

16. National City Corporation, a bank holding company, reported earnings per share of $2.40 in 1993 and paid dividends per share of $1.06. The earnings had grown 7.5% a year over the prior five years and were expected to grow 6% a year in the long term (starting in 1994). The stock had a beta of 1.05 and traded for 10 times earnings. The Treasury bond rate was 7%.

a. Estimate the P/E ratio for National City Corporation.

b. What long-term growth rate is implied in the firm's current PE ratio?

17. The following were the P/E ratios of firms in the aerospace/defense industry at the end of December 1993, with additional data on expected growth and risk:

Company	P/E Ratio	Expected Growth	Beta	Payout
Boeing	17.3	3.5%	1.10	28%
General Dynamics	15.5	11.5%	1.25	40%
General Motors—Hughes	16.5	13.0%	0.85	41%
Grumman	11.4	10.5%	0.80	37%
Lockheed Corporation	10.2	9.5%	0.85	37%
Logicon	12.4	14.0%	0.85	11%
Loral Corporation	13.3	16.5%	0.75	23%
Martin Marietta	11.0	8.0%	0.85	22%
McDonnell Douglas	22.6	13.0%	1.15	37%
Northrop	9.5	9.0%	1.05	47%
Raytheon	12.1	9.5%	0.75	28%
Rockwell	13.9	11.5%	1.00	38%
Thiokol	8.7	5.5%	0.95	15%
United Industrial	10.4	4.5%	0.70	50%

a. Estimate the average and median P/E ratios. What, if anything, would these averages tell you?

b. An analyst concludes that Thiokol is undervalued because its P/E ratio is lower than the industry average. Under what conditions is this statement true? Would you agree with it here?

c. Using a regression, control for differences across firms on risk, growth, and payout. Specify how you would use this regression to spot under- and overvalued stocks. What are the limitations of this approach?

18. NCH Corporation, which markets cleaning chemicals, insecticides, and other products, paid dividends of $2 per share in 1993 on earnings of $4 per share. The book value of equity per share was $40, and earnings are expected to grow 6% a year in the long term. The stock has a beta of 0.85 and sells for $60 per share. The Treasury bond rate is 7%.

a. Based on these inputs, estimate the price/book value ratio for NCH.

b. How much would the return on equity have to increase to justify the price/book value ratio at which NCH sells for currently?

19. You are trying to estimate a price per share on an initial public offering of a company involved in environmental waste disposal. The company has a book value per share of $20 and earned $3.50 per share in the most recent time period. Although it does not pay dividends, the capital expenditures per share were $2.50 higher than depreciation per share in the most recent period, and the firm uses no debt financing. Analysts project that earnings for the company will grow 25% a year for the next five years. The data on other companies in the environment waste disposal business is shown below:

The average debt/equity ratio of these firms is 20%, and the tax rate is 40%.

a. Estimate the average price/book value ratio for these comparable firms. Would you use this average P/BV ratio to price the initial public offering?

b. What subjective adjustments would you make to the price/book value ratio for this firm and why?

20. Longs Drug, a large U.S. drugstore chain operating primarily in northern California, had sales per share of $122 in 1993, on which it reported earnings per share of $2.45 and paid a dividend per share of $1.12. The company is expected to grow 6% in the long term and has a beta of 0.90. The current Treasury bond rate is 7%.

a. Estimate the appropriate price/sales multiple for Longs Drug.

b. The stock is currently trading for $34 per share. Assuming the growth rate is estimated correctly, what would the profit margin need to be to justify this price per share?

21. You have been asked to assess whether Walgreen Company, a drugstore chain, is correctly priced relative to its competitors in the drugstore industry at the end of 1993. The following are the price/sales ratios, profit margins, and other relative details of the firms in the drugstore industry.

Company	P/S Ratio	Profit Margin (%)	Payout (%)	Expected Growth (%)	Beta
Arbor Drugs	0.42	3.40	18	14.0	1.05
Big B Inc.	0.30	1.90	14	23.5	0.70
Drug Empor.	0.10	0.60	0	27.5	0.90
Fay's Inc.	0.15	1.30	37	11.5	0.90
Genovese	0.18	1.70	26	10.5	0.80
Longs Drug	0.30	2.00	46	6.0	0.90
Perry Drugs	0.12	1.30	0	12.5	1.10
Rite Aid	0.33	3.20	37	10.5	0.90
Walgreen	*0.60*	*2.70*	*31*	*13.5*	*1.15*

Based entirely on a subjective analysis, do you think that Walgreen is overpriced because its price/sales ratio is the highest in the industry? If it is not, how would you rationalize its value?

Company	Price	BV/Share	EPS	DPS	Beta	Expected Growth (%)
Air & Water	$9.60	$8.48	$0.40	$0.00	1.65	10.5
Allwaste	5.40	3.10	0.25	0.00	1.10	18.5
Browning Ferris	29.00	11.50	1.45	0.68	1.25	11.0
Chemical Waste	9.40	3.75	0.45	0.15	1.15	2.5
Groundwater	15.00	14.45	0.65	0.00	1.00	3.0
Intn'l Tech.	3.30	3.35	0.16	0.00	1.10	11.0
Ionics Inc.	48.00	31.00	2.20	0.00	1.00	14.5
Laidlaw Inc.	6.30	5.85	0.40	0.12	1.15	8.5
OHM Corp.	16.00	5.65	0.60	0.00	1.15	9.50
Rollins	5.10	3.65	0.05	0.00	1.30	1.0
Safety-Kleen	14.00	9.25	0.80	0.36	1.15	6.50

Chapter 24

Management Decisions, Corporate Strategy, and Firm Value

The value of a firm is determined, in large part, by the decisions that the management makes—what assets to invest in, how much leverage to take on, and how much to pay out as dividends, to name a few. This chapter examines these issues and attempts to answer the following questions:

- How can the effect of investment, financing, and dividend decisions made by a firm be reflected in its value?
- What is the empirical evidence on the market reaction to changes in investment, financing, and dividend policy?
- What is the effect on value of a corporate restructuring whereby both the asset mix and the financing mix of a firm are changed significantly?
- What are the basic value enhancement strategies available to a firm, and how are they related to our discussion of discounted cash-flow valuation?

Firm Value and Corporate Decisions

Corporate decisions generally fall into one of three categories: asset investments and divestitures, capital structure changes, and dividend policy changes.

Asset Investments and Divestiture

At least two approaches are available for analyzing the effects of asset investments and divestitures. The first views decisions concerning assets from a discounted cash-flow model perspective, as discussed in Chapter 23, and examines the effects of such decisions on firm or equity value. The second decomposes the price/earnings (PE) multiple into current cash-flow and future growth components and relates the quality of available projects to the size of the PE multiple.

DCF framework for analysis Anytime a firm makes new investments or divests itself of existing investments, its value is affected. The simplest approach to analyzing these decisions is the net present value framework, according to which the value of a firm is the sum of the present values of the cash flows from projects in place, as well as the **present value of growth opportunities,** as perceived by the firm's investors:

$$\text{Value of firm} = \sum_{j=1}^{N} \text{PV of Project}_j + \text{NPV of Growth Opportunities}$$

where the firm has N projects in place.

In the context of capital budgeting, taking on a new project with a positive net present value generally increases the value of the firm, whereas accepting a negative net present value project decreases its value.[1] When assets or projects are divested, the effect on value is determined by the difference between the price received for the divested asset and the present value of expected cash flows on the asset. If an asset is divested for more than it is worth (in terms of cash flows), the value of the firm will go up; if it is divested for less than it is worth, the value will go down.

Present Value of Growth Opportunities: This the present value of expected cash flows from projects that will be taken in future periods.

Where to and What to divest?   Firms in trouble are often advised to sell "poor performing" assets and expand or buy "superior performing" assets. The Boston Consulting Group matrix for analyzing a firm's business mix, popularized in the 1970s, classifies businesses on the basis of the growth opportunities and relative market share, as shown in Figure 24.1.

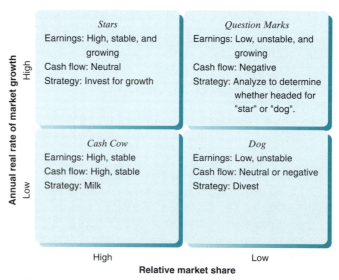

Figure 24.1   BCG matrix for investment opportunities

---

[1]This answer is qualified because of the existence of the additional term that captures the present value of growth opportunities. If by taking the new project, a firm affects investors' perceptions of future growth opportunities, the net effect on value will also include the effect on present value of these changed perceptions.

According to this framework, poorly performing businesses are divested, and the cash from stable cash-producing businesses is invested in high-potential businesses. Although this may make sense intuitively as a good way to run a business, it may not maximize value. In particular, three criticisms have been mounted against this (and similarly motivated) approaches.

1. The businesses that should be divested by the firm should be those in which outsiders have a much higher estimate of value for the assets than the firm, either because they have potential synergy gains or because they are more optimistic about future prospects. These may not be (and are generally unlikely to be) the poorly performing divisions; they may well be the "stars."

2. The firm's new investments should be directed to those projects that provide the highest net present value rather than those that just increase growth and market share.

3. The cash flow from cash cows does not necessarily have to be reinvested in the firm. In some cases, the firm may benefit its stockholders by returning that cash to them in the form of either dividends or stock repurchases.

Concept
Check

> Under what conditions would you advise a firm to divest itself of its worst performing divisions? Would it make any difference if the division were performing poorly because of poor management?

Price/earnings ratios and franchise opportunities   Leibowitz and Kogelman (1992) have developed a slightly different framework for analyzing the effects of investments that earn above-market returns. The value of the equity in a firm is written as the sum of two components—"tangible value," which is the capitalized value of the firm's current earnings stream, and "**franchise value**," which is the capitalized value of the potential projects from which a firm can earn above-market returns. When a firm has no franchise value, the price/earnings ratio is the reciprocal of the cost of equity.

Franchise Value: This is the net present value of future projects that are expected to earn super-normal or above-market returns.

In this framework, the theoretical PE ratio can be expressed as a function of the return on current book value of equity (ROE), the return on future franchise investments (ROFF), and the required rate of return on equity (*r*):

$$PE = \text{Base PE} + (\text{Franchise Factor} * \text{Growth Equivalent})$$
$$= 1/r + [(\text{ROFF} - r)/(\text{ROE}*r) * (\text{PV of Franchise Investments} / \text{BV of Equity})]$$

Thus, a firm that increases its number of franchise investments or improves the potential returns on these investments will be rewarded with an increase in the price/earnings ratio.

 IN PRACTICE   PE RATIOS AND THE FRANCHISE FACTOR—THE HOME DEPOT

Consider a firm like the Home Depot that has a cost of equity of 15%, a book value of equity of $5 billion, and a return on equity of 18%. Assume that the new line of Expo stores that the firm is planning to open is expected to generate significant investment opportunities, that the firm expects to make a return of 25% on these stores, and that the sum of the present value of these investments is expected to be $2 billion. The inputs are as follows:

$$\text{Return on Equity on existing investments} = ROE = 18\%$$
$$\text{Return on Equity on future franchise investments} = ROFF = 25\%$$
$$\text{Required rate of return} = r = 15\%$$
$$\text{Present Value of franchise investments} = \$2 \text{ billion}$$
$$\text{Book Value of Equity} = \$5 \text{ billion}$$

$$\frac{\text{Price}}{\text{Earnings}} = \frac{1}{0.15} + \left(\frac{0.25 - 0.15}{0.18*0.15} * \frac{2000}{5000}\right) = 8.15$$

If the Home Depot improves the return on equity on future investments to 30% and increases the expected present value of franchise investments to $5 billion, the price earnings ratio will increase to reflect these changes:

$$\frac{\text{Price}}{\text{Earnings}} = \frac{1}{0.15} + \left(\frac{0.30 - 0.15}{0.18 * 0.15} * \frac{5000}{5000}\right) = 12.22$$

❑ **Concept Check**

Would it make any difference if the higher return projects in the future were more risky than existing projects? In the Home Depot example, recalculate the price/earnings ratio, assuming that the cost of equity of the new projects will be 18%.

Where do positive net present values come from?   Firms do not have an inexhaustible supply of positive net present value projects. In fact, it can be argued that, in a competitive market, with no barriers to entry, the supply of positive net present value projects in any area will dry up with the entry of new firms into the business. Shapiro (1985) provides a framework for analyzing the sources of positive net present value projects for firms. He suggests that successful firms—those with a continuous stream of good projects—create barriers to entry in a number of ways; they create economies of scale that provide them with cost advantages over their competitors, they differentiate their products through advertising and marketing expertise; they have other cost advantages associated with owning proprietary technology and monopoly control of low-cost raw materials; and they have access to distribution channels not available to new entrants.

Empirical evidence   Although the theory relating investment decisions to firm value is straightforward, the effect of such decisions on market prices is not as clear-cut. Firms generally do not reveal much information about project details or net present value to financial markets at the time of the project announcements. Even if they did so, many believe that financial market participants are myopic and will choose to focus on the near-term impact on earnings and not on the long-term implications for cash flows and value. The empirical evidence, however, suggests otherwise.

McConnell and Muscarella (1985) examined the stock price reaction to 658 announcements of increases and decreases in the dollar value of capital investment. They found that announcements of increases in capital expenditures were associated with positive abnormal returns for the stock and that decreases typically were followed by negative abnormal returns. They also found that stock markets were able to distinguish between value-adding and value-neutral investments. More recently, Woolridge (1992) examined the stock market response to announcements of strategic investment decisions. He evaluated a total of 634 strategic announcements, of which 161 were joint venture formations, 45 were research and development expenditures, 168 were product strategy announcements, and 260 were capital budgeting projects. He found that these announcements, in general, evoked positive responses from financial markets, which he views as evidence that markets are not myopic. Table 24.1 summarizes his results.

Table 24.1	**MARKET REACTION TO INVESTMENT ANNOUNCEMENTS**	
Type of Announcement	**Announcement Day Return (%)**	**Cumulated Market-Adjusted Return (%)**
Joint Venture Formations	0.447	1.412
R & D Expenditures	0.400	1.456
Product Strategies	0.487	−0.350
Capital Expenditures	0.192	1.499

A number of avenues are available for a firm to divest itself of assets. The most obvious is a voluntary sale of the asset, whereby the firm receives cash in return. In contrast, no cash is paid in a **voluntary spin off,** whereby ownership interests in the divested assets are distributed on a pro-rata basis among the shareholders. In a third variation, firms sell stock in a wholly owned subsidiary directly to the public. Table 24.2 provides a summary of studies that have looked at the valuation effects of asset divestitures:

Table 24.2	**MARKET REACTION TO DIVESTITURES AND SPIN OFFS**	
Study	**Type of Divestiture**	**CAR (%)**
Jain (1985)	Asset Divestitures	0.70
Miles & Rosenfeld (1983)	Voluntary Spinoffs	2.50
Schipper & Smith (1983)	Voluntary Spinoffs	2.84
Hite & Owens (1983)	Voluntary Spinoffs	3.30
Schipper & Smith (1986)	Equity Carveouts	1.80
Copeland, Lemgruber & Mayers	Spinoff Announcements	2.49

In general, the reaction to asset divestitures is small but positive, suggesting that these assets are more valuable in the hands of other firms or individuals. The evidence also indicates that the sale of divisions or assets that are not related to the firm's core business is most likely to provide value increments to the firm.

Spin off: A spin off is a proportional distribution of ownership interests in division (or assets) of a firm to existing stockholders.

Concept Check

Under what conditions would you expect the announcement of new investments by a firm to evoke a negative price reaction? How would you reconcile this with the evidence presented above?

Capital Structure Changes

In the most general terms, the decisions firms make on the mix of debt and equity they can use in financing their projects can affect value. From a qualitative standpoint, the tax benefits of borrowing money (interest is tax deductible, whereas dividends are not) must be weighed against the costs of higher leverage (higher bankruptcy costs and agency costs); the net effect (positive or negative) will determine the effect on value.

Cost of capital framework One way of analyzing the effect of capital structure changes is to examine the effect of such changes on the weighted average cost of capital and, consequently, on the value of the firm. As we noted earlier, the value of the firm is the present value of expected cash flows to the firms, discounted at the weighted average cost of capital. When operating cash flows are unaffected by leverage, the value of the firm is maximized when the cost of capital is minimized.

In Chapter 18, we provided an extended application of this approach to finding the optimal capital structure for Boeing in 1990. That year, the earnings before interest and taxes and depreciation (EBITDA) for Boeing were $2.063 billion. The cost of capital and the value of the firm at different levels of debt are reported in Figure 24.2. This analysis suggests that Boeing, which had almost no debt in 1990, would have been able to increase firm value from $16.459 billion to $19.772 billion by moving to its optimal debt ratio of 30%.

Present value of interest tax savings Another approach to evaluating the effects of additional debt on value is to add the present value of interest tax benefits to the value of the unlevered firm:

Value of levered firm = Value of unlevered firm + PV of interest tax benefits

The value of the unlevered firm is obtained by discounting the free cash flow to the firm (FCFF) at the unlevered cost of equity (ρ).

$$\text{Value of unlevered firm} = \text{FCFF}_1 / (\rho - g)$$

where

$$g = \text{Expected growth rate in the free cash flow to the firm}$$

Assuming that debt is perpetual, we can write the value of interest tax benefits in pepetuhitys as a function of the tax rate:[2]

$$\text{Present Value of interest tax benefits} = tD$$

where,

$$t = \text{Tax rate for the firm}$$
$$D = \text{Dollar value of debt taken on by the firm}$$

Bringing the two components together provides the calculation for the value of the firm:

$$\text{Value of levered firm} = \text{FCFF}_1 / (\rho - g) + tD$$

Because bankruptcy or agency costs are not part of the value calculation, the value of a firm can only increase with leverage in this approach.

---

[2]The assumption that debt is perpetual makes the calculation of present value of interest tax benefits much simpler. If r is the interest rate, t is the tax rate, and D is dollar value of debt, the present value of interest tax savings is

$$\text{Present Value of interest tax savings} = rtD/r = tD$$

This assumes that the coupon rate on debt is equal to the market interest rate on the same debt. If the coupon rate (k_c) is *different* from the market interest rate (k_d), the present value of interest tax savings is

$$\text{Present Value of interest tax savings} = k_c tD/k_d$$

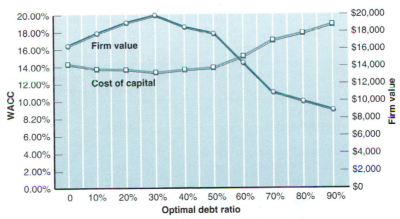

Figure 24.2   WACC and firm value: Boeing

There is an opposing school of thought, emanating from Modigliani and Miller (1958), that argues that capital structure does not impact value. Although the original rationale for this model was based on the absence of taxes, Miller (1977) argues that incorporating corporate and personal taxes into the model yields the same result.

Empirical evidence   A number of studies have looked at the impact of changes in capital structure, either through the issue of new securities or through exchange offers, such as stock repurchases or debt for equity swaps. Smith (1993), in a review article, summarized the results from the numerous studies that examine the valuation effects of these changes. Table 24.3, reproduced from his paper, reports the two-day abnormal returns on common stock around various types of security offerings.

Table 24.3   **MARKET REACTION TO SECURITY ISSUES**

	Type of Issuer	
Type of Security Offering	Industrial (%)	Utility (%)
Common Stock	−3.14	−0.75
Preferred Stock	−0.19	+0.08
Convertible Preferred Stock	−1.44	−1.38
Straight Bonds	−0.26	−0.13
Convertible Bonds	−2.07	n.a.

Although none of the security issues elicits a positive stock price response, the market's response to common stock issues is much more negative than its response to preferred or bond offerings. The surprising finding is that all security issues elicit negative market responses. This does not bode well for a theory of optimal capital structure, for it implies that all such issues move firms away from their optimal.

Smith also summarized the results of numerous studies that looked at exchange offers and other transactions that affect leverage and concluded that transactions that increase leverage generally elicit positive abnormal returns, whereas transactions that reduce leverage usually cause negative abnormal returns. For instance, issuing debt to repurchase equity creates a two-day return, on average, of 21.9%, whereas issuing equity to retire debt results in a two-day abnormal return of −9.9%.

Table 24.4, also reproduced from his paper, provides a summary of academic findings on leverage-changing transactions.

Table 24.4 **MARKET REACTION TO LEVERAGE INDUCING AND DECREASING TRANSACTIONS**

Type of Transaction	Security Issued	Security Retired	Sample Size	Two-day Abnormal Return(%)
Leverage-Increasing Transactions				
Stock Repurchase	Debt	Common	45	21.9
Exchange Offer	Debt	Common	52	14.0
Exchange Offer	Preferred	Common	9	8.3
Exchange Offer	Debt	Preferred	24	2.2
Exchange Offer	Bonds	Preferred	24	2.2
Transactions with no Change in Leverage				
Exchange Offer	Debt	Debt	36	0.6
Security Sale	Debt	Debt	83	0.2
Leverage-Reducing Transactions				
Conversion-forcing call	Common	Convertible	57	−0.4
Conversion-forcing call	Common	Preferred	113	−2.1
Security Sale	Conv.Debt	Conv. Debt	15	−2.4
Exchange Offer	Common	Debt	30	−2.6
Exchange Offer	Preferred	Preferred	9	−7.7
Security Sale	Common	Debt	12	−4.2
Exchange Offer	Common	Debt	20	−9.9

Again, this evidence is difficult to reconcile with a theory of capital structure, unless we assume that firms are generally underleveraged and that increases in leverage are therefore more likely to push a firm toward its optimal.

 Concept Check

> What price reaction would you expect to a firm's announcement that it intends to issue stock and pay down debt? Would you expect the price reaction to be any different if the firm announced that it was using cash reserves (rather than new stock issues) to pay down debt?

Dividend Policy

A simple framework for analyzing changes in dividend policy is to weigh the effects of changing dividend payout—the effects on current dollar dividends received by investors against the effects on expected future growth in earnings and dividends. When dividends are increased, investors receive higher dividends in the initial years at the expense of lower growth in future years. Conversely, when dividends are decreased, investors receive lower cash flows in the initial years but gain from higher growth in future years.

Empirical evidence The market reaction to dividend changes has been analyzed in several studies. Asquith and Mullins (1986) looked at 160 firms that initiated dividends and reported an average abnormal return of 3.7% to the equity investors in these firms.

Aharony and Swary (1980) examined dividend changes and reported positive abnormal returns of 0.9% for dividend increases and negative abnormal returns of −3.6% for dividend decreases in the two days surrounding dividend announcements on common stock investments.

The positive market reaction to dividend increases is supportive of a number of different hypotheses—they result in a transfer of wealth from bondholders to stockholders; they provide a positive signal of future prospects; and stockholders like dividends. All three hypotheses may contribute to the final response.

CORPORATE RESTRUCTURING AND FIRM VALUE

At the most basic level, **corporate restructuring** refers to a collection of actions taken by a firm, usually involving changes in its asset portfolio, its capital structure, and its dividend policy, in conjunction with changes in the ownership structure and management compensation schemes. The framework developed in the prior section can be used to evaluate the effects of such changes on value. This section explores the various facets of restructuring and provides some empirical evidence on the market reaction to corporate restructuring.

Corporate Restructuring: This is a collection of actions taken by a firm which may affect both the asset structure (by adding or divesting assets) and the financing mix (by changing the mix of debt and equity).

Value Consequences of Restructuring

There are several ways of analyzing the consequences of restructuring on value. One approach is to relate growth rates and risk to financial fundamentals and to evaluate the effect of corporate restructuring on these fundamentals. A second approach focuses on economic value added to the firm as a consequence of restructuring.

Effects of corporate decisions on expected growth and risk   Relating expected earnings growth and risk to decisions that the firm takes has its advantages. Changes in financial policy can be translated quickly into changes in the value of equity, through the earnings growth formulation and a discounted cash-flow model. One approach to estimating expected growth in earnings is based on financial fundamentals:

$$g = b\,[(\text{ROA} + \text{D/E}\,(\text{ROA} - i\,(1 - t))]$$

where

$$b = \text{Retention ratio} = 1 - \text{Payout ratio}$$
$$\text{ROA} = (\text{Net Income} + \text{Interest}\,(1 - \text{tax rate}))\,/\,\text{BV of Total Assets}$$
$$= \text{EBIT}\,(1 - t)\,/\,\text{BV of Total Assets}$$
$$\text{D/E} = \text{BV of Debt}\,/\,\text{BV of Equity}$$
$$i = \text{Interest Expense on Debt}\,/\,\text{BV of Debt}$$
$$t = \text{Tax rate on ordinary income}$$

Note that BV of Assets = BV of Debt + BV of Equity.

The effects of corporate decisions on risk and the required rate of return also need to be clarified. The equity beta of a firm can be related to the beta of the underlying business in which it operates and the financial leverage it has taken on:

$$\beta_L = \beta_u\,[1 + (1 - t)\,(\text{D/E})]$$

where

β_L = Levered beta for equity in the firm
β_u = Unlevered beta of the firm; that is the beta of the firm without any debt
t = Tax rate for the firm
D/E = Debt/Equity Ratio

Asset allocation and restructuring When firms take on new investments or divest themselves of existing investments, they affect their expected return on assets—good projects increase the return on assets; bad projects reduce the return; and any investment decision taken by the firm affects its riskiness. The net effect of these changes will determine the effect on value. In general, if the differential between the return on assets and the required rate of return increases as a consequence of the restructuring, the value of the firm increases as well.

Concept
Check

Can you think of scenarios under which a firm increases the return on assets on its existing investments and still loses value?

Financing decisions The simplest way to build in the effects of debt to the dividend discount model is to change the debt equity ratio in the growth rate formula:

$$g = b[ROA + D/E (ROA - i(1 - t))]$$

As the firm borrows more money, the debt/equity ratio and the interest rate i will go up. The new per-share value, after the borrowing, can be calculated based on this growth rate. With the added debt, the equity in the firm will also become more risky, and the new beta of the equity will be

New Beta = {Old Beta/ $(1 + (1 - t)$Old D/E)} * $(1 + (1 - t)$ New D/E ratio)

Dividend decisions Changes in dividend policy can be reflected in the earnings growth rate:

$$g = b[ROA + D/E(ROA - i(1 - t))]$$

In this model, b is the retention ratio (which is zero if the firm pays out all its earnings as dividends, and 1 if it pays out no dividends). By changing the payout ratio, therefore, managers are changing the growth rate. Decreasing dividends will increase the growth rate in earnings but will reduce the dividends per share received each year. In general, firms with very profitable projects (high ROA) can increase value by paying less dividends, and firms with very few profitable projects (low ROA) can increase value by paying more dividends.

An example: Effects of restructuring on expected growth rates and value WR Trible, a manufacturing company that has seen earnings drop over the last few years, is planning a major restructuring, changing both its asset and liability mixes. The current earnings per share for the firm is $2. The effects of the restructuring on the growth rate and the beta are shown below.

The firm is expected to divest itself of its mail-order catalog business, which historically has had lower returns on equity. In addition, the capital budgeting process will be reviewed to improve project choice. This is expected to increase the return on assets from 10% to 16%:

	Before	**Planned Changes**	**After**
ROA	10%	Improve project choice Divest divisions	16%

The firm currently has a debt ratio of 10% of capital and a beta of 0.80. An analysis of the capital structure reveals that the optimal debt ratio for the firm is 50% of capital. The firm plans to borrow and repurchase stock to get to this optimal ratio. The interest rate on debt is expected to increase from 8% to 9%:

D/E	0.11	Increase long-term debt	1.00
Beta	0.80	Leverage increases β	1.23
Interest rate	8.00%		9.00%

The firm currently pays out 50% of its earnings as dividends. It plans to reduce its dividend payout to 25% after the restructuring.

Payout	0.50	Reinvest more in company	0.25
Retention	0.50	" " " "	0.75

The tax rate for the firm is 36%.

Earnings Growth Rate—
first 5 years   5.27%   19.68%
(based on formulation for growth : $g = b\,[\text{ROA} + \text{D/E}\,(\text{ROA} - i\,(1 - t))]$)

The earnings growth rate after 5 years is expected to be 6%, and the dividend payout is expected to be 50% after year 5, whether or not a restructuring occurs. The beta of the stock is expected to be 1.00 in the stable phase, again regardless of the restructuring. The Treasury bond rate is 7%.

Price per share before restructuring =

$$\frac{\$2 * 0.5 * (1.0527) * \left(1 - \dfrac{(1.0527)^5}{(1.114)^5}\right)}{(0.114 - .0527)} + \frac{\$2 * 0.5 * 1.0527^5 * 1.06}{(.125 - .06)(1.114)^5} = \$16.52$$

Price per share after restructuring =

$$\frac{\$2 * 0.25 * (1.1968) * \left(1 - \dfrac{(1.1968)^5}{(1.1374)^5}\right)}{(0.1374 - .1968)} + \frac{\$2 * 0.5 * 1.1968^5 * 1.06}{(.125 - .06)(1.1374)^5} = \$23.95$$

Increase in price because of restructuring = \$23.95 − \$16.52 = \$7.43

Economic value added—a variant on value creation   As firms seek approaches to increase their market value, one concept that has gained favor is **economic value added (EVA),** developed by Stern Stewart & Company of New York. In its simplest form, the economic value added is the difference between the firm's after-tax return on capital and its cost of capital:

EVA = (ROC − WACC) * (Economic Book Value of Assets in place)
   = EBIT (1 − tax rate) − WACC * (Economic Book Value of Assets in place)

where

$$ROC = \text{Return on Capital}$$
$$= \text{EBIT } (1-\text{tax rate}) / \text{Economic Book Value of Assets in place}$$
$$EBIT = \text{Earnings before interest and taxes}$$
$$WACC = \text{Weighted average cost of capital}$$

Assets in place include fixed assets and working capital, and the *economic book value* of assets is the accounting book value adjusted for equity equivalent reserves.[3] A negative EVA indicates that the firm is destroying value, whereas a positive EVA suggests that the firm is creating value.

Economic Value Added (EVA):   This is the difference between the return on capital invested in existing assets and the cost of capital, expressed in dollar (or other currency) terms.

This concept has its genesis in the net present value (NPV) rule in capital budgeting. A "good project" is defined as one in which the after-tax cash flows to the firm, discounted by the weighted average cost of capital, yield a present value that exceeds the initial investment in the project. In general terms, the after-tax cash flow to the firm can be written as

$$\text{After-tax CF to the Firm} = \text{EBIT } (1 - \text{tax rate}) + \text{Depreciation} - \text{Capital Spending}$$

If capital spending is offset by depreciation as is often assumed for firms that are in steady state, and working capital is ignored, this yields the after-tax operating income used in the EVA measure.

This approach is attractive, especially for firms whose substantial assets are tied up in projects, because it simplifies the process of value creation to one or more of a few actions:

1.   Increasing the operating income from assets in place by reducing costs or increasing sales.

2.   Reducing the cost of capital by changing the financing mix.

3.   Reducing the amount of capital tied up in existing projects, without affecting operating income significantly, by reducing working capital investment and selling unutilized or underutilized assets.

In this approach, capital is more efficiently deployed by increasing the amount of capital invested in projects with positive spreads (return on capital exceeds the cost of capital) and withdrawn from projects with negative spreads (return on capital is lower than the cost of capital).

Concept Check

What, if any, is the difference between calculating the net present value of investments in existing assets and the EVA?

Limitations of EVA   The power of EVA derives largely from its simplicity. By reducing the large number of variables and interactions that go into the discounted cash-flow value of a firm to two variables (return on capital and cost of capital) and one interac-

[3]The equity equivalent reserves adjust accounting book value for items such as depreciation and goodwill and are described in detail in Stewart (1991). In reality, the EVA measure should use the market value of assets in place. Because this is difficult to obtain for most firms, the book value of assets is adjusted to provide a proxy for the market value.

tion (the difference between the two variables), EVA has won converts among CEOs who want to increase their stock prices. This simplicity comes at a cost, however, especially for high-growth firms that might view increasing EVA as a mantra for higher stock prices.

To see why, let us return to the basic format described for the dividend discount model earlier in this discussion, where the expected growth was written as a function of the return on assets, the debt/equity ratio, and the retention ratio. Let us then consider two measures of the return on assets: the current returns on assets, which determine the current earnings, and the expected future returns on asset, which determine future growth. Figure 24.3 presents the framework for discounted cash-flow valuation.

By increasing the current return on assets, we will increase the current earnings. If this can be accomplished without affecting the expected future returns on assets, the firm value will generally go up. If, however, the increase in the current return on assets is accomplished by reducing the expected *future* return on assets, the value of the firm may actually decrease.

In practical terms, the current return on assets is derived from assets in place, whereas the expected future return on assets comes from future growth. For firms that derive a significant portion of their value from assets in place, the EVA is an effective

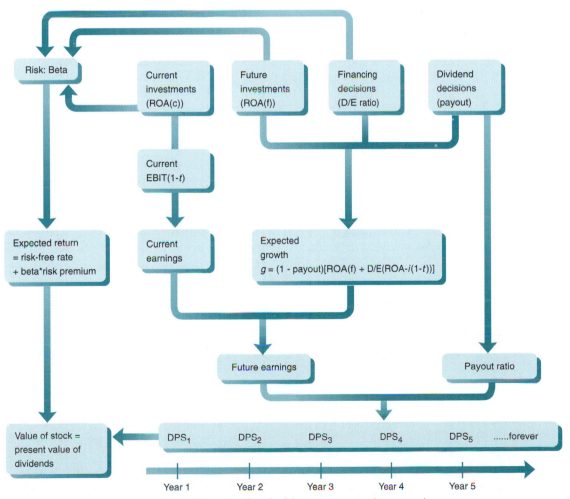

Figure 24.3 The valuation decision: current vs. future projects

proxy for firm value. For firms that obtain a significant portion of their value from future growth, however, there is the risk that the increased return on assets may be obtained by sacrificing future growth opportunities, and thus may lower value. This danger is compounded when managers are reimbursed on the basis of their economic value added. No matter how carefully a firm may define return on assets, there is no substitute for considering the complete picture.

☐ Concept
   Check

> The CEO of a high-growth firm has asked for your advice on whether she should adopt the EVA approach. What issues would you raise with her on the applicability of the approach? If she decides to adopt the approach, what protective mechanisms would you design for her to combat abuse?

CONCLUSION

This chapter illustrates how an understanding of corporate finance leads to better valuation. Every decision made by a firm affects its value. The lessons from this chapter can be summarized as follows:

- When firms make good investment decisions, they increase value; this increase in value can be measured by looking at the net present values of the projects taken. More generally, the quality of a firm's projects is reflected in the multiple of earnings that the market is willing to pay for that firm's stock. Firms that earn high returns on their projects will sell for much higher price earnings multiples. The empirical evidence seems to suggest that markets recognize the value of allocating resources to long-term investments and reward firms that do so.

- When firms change their financing mix, they also change their cost of capital; if they lower their cost of capital, keeping operating cash flows fixed, they will increase their firm value. The empirical evidence seems to suggest that firms that increase leverage are rewarded with higher stock prices.

- Changes in dividend policy can also affect a firm's value because of the effect it can have on investment policy and the signaling implications of dividend changes. In particular, increases in dividends seem to evoke positive market reactions.

The effect of changing investment, financing, and dividend policy can be captured completely in a discounted cash-flow valuation by looking at the impact of these changes on cash flows and discount rates.

QUESTIONS AND PROBLEMS

1. Evaluate, by designating as price up, price down, no effect, or impossible to tell, the effects of the following investment decisions on stock prices:

   a. A stable company with no growth opportunities takes a project with an NPV of $100 million.

   b. A growth company (e.g., Microsoft) takes a project with an NPV of $100 million.

   c. A company takes on a project with an NPV of negative $100 million.

   d. A company announces an acquisition of a target firm for $500 million (the true value of the firm is only $350 million).

   e. A company announces that it will be investing excess cash in Treasury bonds.

2. Answer true or false to the following statements.

a. The value of the equity in a firm will increase as the firm takes on more debt.

b. The value of the firm will increase as it takes on more debt.

c. Debt increases firm value primarily because of the tax benefits it confers on the firm.

d. Debt is always cheaper than equity.

e. At the optimal debt ratio, the value of equity is maximized.

f. At the optimal debt ratio, the value of the firm is maximized.

3. Broderbund Software, a leading developer and publisher of educational software, was trading at $39 in March 1994, and there were 9.50 million shares outstanding. The company had no debt and reported earnings per share of $1.36 in 1993. The company paid no dividends and had a beta of 1.85. The Treasury bond rate is 7.25%.

a. Estimate the proportion of the value attributable to future growth opportunities.

b. Assume that Broderbund takes on a new project that is expected to have an NPV of $10 million. Can you estimate the effect of value of this decision? Why or why not?

c. Would your answer change if Broderbund takes on a new project with an expected NPV of negative $10 million?

4. Novell Inc., which designs and manufactures high-performance local area networks, was trading at $23.75 per share on March 21, 1994. There were 308 million shares outstanding, and the firm had no debt. On March 22, 1994, Novell announced that it planned to acquire WordPerfect Corporation, a private company that produced and sold word processing software, for $1.4 billion. On the announcement, the stock price dropped $3.75 to $20 per share.

a. Estimate the value of equity at Novell, prior to the announcement of the acquisition.

b. Based on the market reaction to the announcement, estimate the value that the market assigned to WordPerfect Corporation.

c. What other rationale could there be for the drop in Novell's stock price on the announcement of the acquisition?

5. Laidlaw Inc., a solid waste disposal company, had a decade of steadily declining return on equity starting in 1984 and continuing through 1993. The return on equity peaked at 16.2% in 1984 and dropped to 8% by 1993. Much of this decline could be attributed to projects that earned substandard returns. In early 1994, the price per share was $6.25, as was the book value per share. The firm paid out 40% of its earnings as dividends in 1993 and had a beta of 1.15. The Treasury bond rate was 7.25%.

As part of a restructuring, the firm expects to choose better projects and improve its return on equity to 12%. The firm is in steady state.

a. Estimate the price/book value ratio, assuming that the firm's return on equity remains at 1993 levels.

b. Estimate the improvement in the price/book value ratio assuming the firm manages to improve its return on equity to 12%.

c. Would it have made any difference if the projects that the firm takes to improve its return on equity were riskier than its past projects?

6. Arkansas Best, a freight system and transportation company, has a beta of 1.10 and a price to book value ratio of 1.3. If the expected growth in earnings in the long term is 5.5%, what would the return on equity on future projects have to be to justify the current price to book value ratio? (Assume that the Treasury bond rate is 7%.)

7. Lotus Development Corporation, a leading manufacturer of personal computer software, reported a return on equity of 14% in 1993 on a book value of equity of $540 million. The stock had a beta of 1.20. (The Treasury bond rate is 7%.) The company was expected, given current trends, to make a return on equity of 13.5% on future projects (which are expected to have a present value of $1 billion).

a. Estimate the price/earnings ratio for Lotus Development Corporation, given these inputs.

b. Estimate the price/earnings ratio for Lotus Development Corporation if it improves its expected return on future projects to 16%.

8. Outback Steakhouse, a firm that operates and licenses casual dining restaurants, had return on equity of 24% in 1996 on a book value of $315 million. It expects to have substantial investment opportunities over the next 10 years, on which it expects to make a return on equity of 28%; the present value of the investments in these investment opportunities is expected to be $1260 million. The beta for the stock is 1.50, and the current Treasury bond rate is 7%.

a. Estimate the appropriate PE ratio for the stock.

b. How much of this PE ratio can be attributed to the "franchise factor"?

c. If the actual PE ratio was 26.8, what would the expected return on equity have to be on the new investment opportunities to break even?

9. Arvin Industries, a major manufacturer of automotive emission and ride control systems, had earnings before interest and taxes of $130 million in 1993 and faced a tax rate of 40%. The firm had depreciation amounting to $76 million and capital spending of $96 million in 1993. There are no anticipated working capital needs.

The firm is in steady state and is expected to grow 6% a year in the long term. The stock was trading at $31 per share in December 1993, and there were 22.2 million shares outstanding. The beta of the stock was 0.90. The debt outstanding was $435 million, and the firm had an A rating (leading to an interest rate on the debt of 8.25%). The Treasury bond rate is 7%.

   a. Estimate the current weighted average cost of capital for Arvin Industries.

   b. Estimate the value of the firm, at its current capital structure.

   c. Assume now that Arvin is planning to issue $100 million of stock and use it to pay down debt. This will raise the rating of the company to AA (leading to a drop in the interest rate paid on the debt to 7.75%). Estimate the new firm value and value of the equity after this transaction.

   d. If there were no default risk and interest tax savings are the only benefit of the borrowing, estimate the value of the firm at the old debt level and the new debt level. (You can assume that all debt is perpetual.)

10. Fairly substantial empirical evidence has accumulated on the effects of changing capital structure. Which of the following statements reflects the findings in these studies?

   a. Firms that borrow money increase their stock prices.

   b. Firm that improve their bond ratings increase their stock prices.

   c. Firms that exchange one security for another increase their stock prices.

   d. Firms that exchange one security for another, and decrease leverage in the process, increase their stock prices.

   e. Firms that exchange one security for another, and increase leverage in the process, increase their stock prices.

11. Long's Drug, a large drugstore chain, paid dividends per share of $1.12 on earnings per share of $2.45 in 1993. The book value of equity in 1993 was $23.80 per share. The stock had a beta of 0.90, and the firm is in its stable growth phase. (The Treasury bond rate is 7%.)

Walgreen Company, another drugstore chain, paid dividends of $0.60 per share on earnings per share of $1.98 in 1993. The book value of equity was $11.55 in 1993. The stock had a beta of 1.15. The firm is in its high-growth phase, which is expected to last five years, after which time the firm will be in its stable-growth phase. (The return on equity is expected to drop to 13% in the stable-growth phase.)

   a. Estimate the value of Long's and Walgreen, based on the current dividend policy.

   b. Estimate the value of Long's and Walgreen if they increase their dividend payout to 60% of earnings.

   c. Estimate the value of Long's and Walgreen if they decrease their dividend payout to 25% of earnings.

   d. What broader lessons would you draw for dividend policy based on this comparison?

12. Black and Decker, a manufacturer of power tools, reported disappointing earnings per share of $0.65 in 1992 and $0.95 in 1993, down from $1.65 in 1988. The stock was trading at $21 per share, and there were 84 million shares outstanding. (The book value of the equity was $1.12 billion at the end of 1993.) The firm had accumulated $2.812 billion in debt (in both book and market value terms) by the end of 1993, on which it was paying almost 10.5% in interest. The high leverage caused the firm's beta to increase to 1.65. The firm is expected to pay out $0.40 per share in dividends in 1993. (The tax rate for the firm is 35%, and the Treasury bond rate is 7%.)

The firm is considering a major restructuring, whereby it will attempt to do the following:

- Improve its pretax return on assets to 1988 levels (which were 16%) by selling some overseas divisions and cutting costs at some domestic divisions.
- Use the cash from the sale of assets (which is expected to be $1 billion) to pay down debt.
- Reduce dividend payout by half.

These changes are expected to affect growth over the next five years, after which time growth is expected to be 6% and the beta is expected to be 1.10, whether or not the firm restructures. (The dividend payout ratio will be adjusted accordingly.)

   a. Estimate the value per share of Black and Decker assuming no restructuring.

   b. Estimate the value per share of Black and Decker assuming that the restructuring goes through.

13. GWT Technology, which provides consulting and on-site remediation services for environmental sites, had earnings per share of $0.50 in 1995. It is consid-

ering a major restructuring, and it expects to make the following changes:

- The return on assets, which was 5% in 1995, is expected to increase to 12.5% as a consequence of divestitures and new acquisitions.
- The debt ratio, which was 15% in 1996, will be raised to 40%; the interest rate on the debt will increase from 7.5% to 8.25%. The corporate tax rate is 40%.
- The firm will lower its dividend payout ratio from 30% to 25%.

The beta for the stock currently is 0.90, and the Treasury bond rate is 7%. The firm is expected to reach steady state in five years and to grow at 6% after that. The dividend payout ratio in steady state will be 60%.

a. Estimate the value of the stock without the restructuring.

b. Estimate the value of the stock with the restructuring.

14. Intermet Corporation, an independent iron foundry organization, reported earnings before interest, taxes, and depreciation of $27 million on revenues of $450 million in 1993. The firm had $86 million in debt outstanding in 1993 (on which it paid 9% interest prior to taxes) and 25 million shares trading at $7.50 per share. The beta of the stock was 1.20. (The Treasury bond rate is 7%.)

As a result of significant cost-cutting actions, Intermet expects to reduce its cost of goods sold (not counting depreciation) to 89% of revenues by the end of 1998 (five years from now). The cost reduction is expected to occur gradually over the next five years. Revenues are expected to grow 6% a year over the same period. Depreciation, which was $26 million in 1993, and capital spending, which was $38 million, are both expected to grow 6% a year from 1994 to 1998. Working capital is expected to remain 7.5% of revenues.

After 1998, the earnings and revenues are expected to grow 5% a year in perpetuity. Capital spending will be offset by depreciation. The debt ratio is expected to remain unchanged, but the pretax cost of debt is expected to drop to 8% by 1998. The tax rate is 40%.

a. Estimate the value of Intermet, as a firm and for the equity, assuming that the cost reductions are effective.

b. Estimate the value of Intermet, as a firm and for the equity, if the cost of goods sold declines to only 91% of revenues by 1998, rather than 89% of revenues.

15. You have been asked to assess the EVA of three airline firms and have collected the following information:

Company	EBIT (1 − t)	Capital Invested	Cost of Capital
AMR	$1.08 billion	$12.5 billion	10.50%
Alaska Air	$60 million	$510 million	11.00%
UAL Corp.	$550 million	$6,000 million	10.25%

a. Estimate the EVA of each of these firms.

b. What does the EVA tell you about the relative financial health of these firms?

c. If you were told that AMR and UAL were already stable-growth firms and that Alaska Air was growing at 15% a year, would it make any difference in your analysis?

16. "Firms that increase their EVA from one year to another should expect to see their market value go up." When is this statement true? When is it false? Explain.

17. Walter Industries, Inc. a holding company with subsidiaries that construct standardized and partially finished shell homes, is currently in the process of coming out of bankruptcy. Estimates for EPS for this year and the next are $.72 and $1.70, respectively, ROA is currently 1.4% and the D/E ratio is 615%. The company currently pays $55 million per quarter in interest and has total debt outstanding of $2788 million. Assume that the company pays no dividends and no taxes. Does the growth rate implied by these earnings figures correspond to one based upon financial fundamentals? Why or why not?

18. Continuing the last question, suppose you were told that Walter's management has recently announced that they have undertaken a massive refinancing effort in order to lower both the level of debt and the average interest rate paid. The new D/E ratio will be 400% and will be 7%. (Dividends and taxes will still be equal to zero.) Additionally, industry forcast for the residential construction industry are improving. Compute the ROA that would be necessary under these circumstances to make the two computations of g agree.

19. Suppose that, in addition to the information you've been provided in the last two questions, you also hear that Walter's managment is considering spinning off their coal mining business, a relatively small subsidiary whose line of business is unrelated to the rest of the company. Will this increase or decrease shareholders' wealth? Why?

20. Bennett Stewart, one of the originators of EVA and a senior partner at New York-based Stern Stewart and Company, tells a story related to him by Roberto Goizetta, the CEO of Coca-Cola: "At one time, Coca-Cola would ship its concentrate to bottlers in stainless steel containers. These containers would sit on the company's balance sheet as an inventory item. If you're concerned with just generating income from the business, it appears to have little in the way of a charge, and thus, it's very attractive for income-oriented companies. But, from the point of view of shareholders, of the investors, the capital side of the stainless steel is costly because it must be financed. Under EVA, that investment on the balance sheet is converted to a charge on the income statement. Operating people discovered that if they were to substitute cardboard containers for stainless steel containers that even though those cardboard containers were consumed more quickly

in the business, they represented a more immediate charge to the earnings becuasue they were eliminated from the balance sheet. The EVA actually increased dramatically as a reult of making a change just like that."

a. Which of the three value-creating actions listed in the book contributed to the increse in EVA.

b. Was this increase a real addition to value, or was it simply an increase "on paper"?

21. Suppose that Congress passes a new tax bill that increases the differential between the capital gains tax rate and that for ordinary income. How will this affect firms' capital structure decisions? More importantly, how will this affect firm value?

CHAPTER 25

ACQUISITIONS AND TAKEOVERS

Firms merge with or acquire other firms for a number of reasons. In the 1960s and 1970s, firms such as Gulf and Western and ITT built themselves into conglomerates by acquiring firms in other lines of business. In the 1980s, firms such as Time, Beatrice, and RJR Nabisco were acquired by other firms, their own management, or wealthy raiders, who saw potential value from restructuring or breaking up these firms. Through time, firms have also acquired or merged with other firms to gain the benefits of synergy, either in the form of higher growth, as in Disney's acquisition of Capital Cities, or lower costs. This chapter examines the motives behind mergers and acquisitions and attempts to answer the following questions:

- How widely used is synergy as a motive for acquisitions? What are the different forms synergy can take? How should synergy be valued?

- Is diversification a good motive for acquisitions?

- What is the value of controlling a firm? How should the value of control be estimated?

- What does the empirical evidence tell us about the prices paid in acquisitions and the motives for such acquisitions?

CLASSIFICATION OF ACQUISITIONS

There are a number of ways in which one firm can acquire another. In a *merger*, the boards of directors of two firms agree to combine and seek stockholder approval for the combination. In most cases, at least 50% of the shareholders of the target and the bidding firm have to agree to the merger. In a *purchase of assets,* one firm acquires the assets of another, although a formal vote by the shareholders of the firm being acquired is still needed. In a **tender offer,** one firm offers to buy the outstanding stock of the other firm at a specific price and communicates this offer in advertisements and mailings to stockholders. By doing so, it bypasses the incumbent management and board of directors of the firm. Consequently, tender offers are used to carry out hostile takeovers.

Tender Offer: This is an offer to buy the existing shares of a company at a specified price, with the intent of taking over the company.

Another difference between mergers and tender offers is that, in a merger, the acquired firm, often ceases to exist as a separate entity after the acquisition. In a tender offer, the acquired firm will continue to exist as long as there are minority stockholders who refuse to tender. From a practical standpoint, however, most tender offers eventually become mergers, if the acquiring firm is successful in gaining control of the target firm.

Motives Behind Acquisitions

A number of motives have been proposed for acquisitions. The simplest rationale is undervaluation—that firms that are undervalued by financial markets, relative to their true value, will be targeted for acquisition by those who recognize this anomaly. Another rationale, used widely to explain the significant premiums paid in most acquisitions, is **synergy,** which refers to the potential additional value from combining two firms, either from operational or financial sources. Yet another explanation is based on a market for corporate control, in which poorly managed firms are taken over and restructured by the new owners, who lay claim to the additional value. Finally, it has been suggested that managerial self-interest and hubris are the primary, though unstated, reasons for many takeovers.

Synergy: This is the increase in value from combining two firms into one entity; that is, it is the difference in value between the combined firm and the sum of the individual firm values.

A Historical Perspective on Mergers and Acquisitions

Merger and takeover activity in the United States has occurred in waves, with different motives behind each wave. The first wave occurred in the early part of this century, when companies like U.S. Steel and Standard Oil were created by acquiring firms within an industry with the explicit objective of dominating these industries and *creating monopolies*. The second wave coincided with the bull market of the 1920s, at which time firms again embarked on acquisitions as a way of extending their reach into *new markets* and expanding market share. During this period, firms like General Foods and Allied Chemical came into being. The third wave occurred in the 1960s and 1970s, when firms such as Gulf and Western focused on acquiring firms in other lines of business with the intent of *diversifying* and forming conglomerates. The fourth wave of acquisitions occurred in the mid-1980s, when firms were acquired primarily with the intent of *restructuring* the firms. In some cases, the acquisitions were financed heavily with debt and were initiated by the managers of the firms being acquired. This wave reached its zenith with the acquisition of RJR Nabisco, but waned toward the end of the decade, as deals became pricier and it became more difficult to find willing lenders.

Interestingly, merger activity seems to increase in years in which the stock market does well, which is counter to what one would expect if the primary motive for acquisitions were undervaluation. Mergers also tend to be concentrated in a few sectors; in the early 1980s, many of the mergers involved oil companies, whereas the focus shifted to food and tobacco companies in the latter half of the decade and shifted again to media and financial service firms in the early 1990s.

Empirical Evidence on Value Effects of Takeovers

Substantial empirical evidence exists concerning the effects of takeovers on the value of both the target and bidder firms. The evidence indicates that the stockholders of target firms are the clear winners in takeovers—they earn significant excess returns not only around the announcement of the acquisitions but also in the weeks leading up to it. Jensen and Ruback (1983) reviewed 13 studies that look at abnormal returns around takeover announcements and reported an average excess return of 30% to target stockholders in successful tender offers and 20% to target stockholders in successful mergers. Jarrell, Brickley, and Netter (1988) reviewed the results of 663 tender offers made between 1962 and 1985 and noted that premiums averaged 19% in the 1960s, 35% in the 1970s, and 30% between 1980 and 1985. Many of the studies report a run-up in the stock price prior to the takeover announcement; this finding suggests either a very perceptive financial market or leaked information about prospective deals.

Some attempts at takeovers fail, either because the bidding firm withdraws the offer or the target firm fights it off. Bradley, Desai, and Kim (1983) analyzed the effects of takeover failures on target firm stockholders and found that, although the initial reaction to the announcement of the failure is negative, albeit statistically insignificant, a substantial number of target firms are taken over within 60 days of the first takeover failing, earning significant abnormal returns (50% to 66%).

The effect of takeover announcements on bidder firm stock prices is not as clear cut. Jensen and Ruback report abnormal returns of 4% for bidding firm stockholders around tender offers and no abnormal returns around mergers. Jarrell, Brickley, and Netter, in their examination of tender offers from 1962 to 1985, note a decline in abnormal returns to bidding firm stockholders from 4.4% in the 1960s to 2% in the 1970s to -1% in the 1980s. Other studies indicate that approximately half of all bidding firms earn negative abnormal returns around the announcement of takeovers; thus, shareholders may be skeptical about the perceived value of the takeover in a significant number of cases.

When an attempt at a takeover fails, Bradley, Desai, and Kim (1983) report negative abnormal returns of 5% to bidding firm stockholders around the announcement of the failure. When the existence of a rival bidder in figured in, the studies indicate significant negative abnormal returns (of approximately 8%) for bidder firm stockholders who lose out to a rival bidder within 180 trading days of the announcement, and no abnormal returns when no rival bidder exists.

☐ Concept Check

The managers of bidding firms whose stock prices go down on acquisitions often argue that this occurs because stockholders do not have as much information as they do about the target firm's finances and its fit with the bidding firm. How would you respond?

VALUING SYNERGY

The most general definition of synergy is a whole that is greater than the sum of its parts. In the context of takeovers, the additional value from synergy can come from a variety of sources, either operational or financial.

Operating Synergy

The key to the existence of synergy is that the target firm controls a specialized resource that becomes more valuable when combined with the bidding firm's resources. The specialized resource will vary depending on the merger. Horizontal mergers occur when two firms in the same line of business merge. In that case, the synergy must come from some form of economies of scale, which reduce costs, or from increased market power, which increases profit margins and sales. Examples include mergers in the financial services sector—Bank of America and Security Pacific, Chase, and Chemical Bank, to name a few. Vertical integration occurs when a firm acquires a supplier of inputs into its production process or a distributor or retailer for the product it produces. The primary source of synergy in this case comes from more complete control of the chain of production. This benefit has to be weighed against the loss of efficiency from having a captive supplier, who does not have any incentive to keep costs low and compete with other suppliers.

Operating Synergy: This is the increase in value that accrues to a combined firm either from economies of scale (lower costs) or increased sales/profits (higher growth).

When a firm with strengths in one functional area acquires another firm with strengths in a different functional area (functional integration), synergy may be gained by exploiting the strengths in these areas. Thus, when a firm with a good distribution network acquires a firm with a promising product line, value is gained by combining these two strengths. The argument is that both firms will be better off after the merger.

Valuing operating synergy Most reasonable observers agree that there is a potential for operating synergy, in one form or the other, in many takeovers. Some disagreement exists, however, over whether synergy can be valued and, if so, how much that value should be. One school of thought argues that synergy is too nebulous to be valued and that any systematic attempt to do so requires so many assumptions that it is pointless. This philosophy, though debatable, implies that a firm should even be willing to pay large premiums for synergy if it cannot attach a value to it.

Although valuing synergy requires assumptions about future cash flows and growth, the lack of precision in the process does not mean that an unbiased estimate of value cannot be made. Thus, we maintain that synergy can be valued by answering two fundamental questions:

1. *What form is the synergy expected to take?* Will it reduce costs as a percentage of sales and increase profit margins (e.g., when there are economies of scale)? Will it increase future growth (e.g., when there is increased market power)?

2. *When can the synergy be expected to start affecting cash flows*—instantaneously or over time?

Once these questions are answered, the value of synergy can be estimated using an extension of discounted cash-flow techniques. First, the firms involved in the merger are valued independently by discounting expected cash flows to each firm at the weighted average cost of capital for that firm. Second, the value of the combined firm, with no synergy, is obtained by adding the values obtained for each firm in the first step. Third, the effects of synergy are built into expected growth rates and cash flows, and the combined firm is revalued with synergy. The difference between the value of the combined firm with synergy and the value of the combined firm without synergy provides a value for synergy.

❏ Concept
Check

"The synergy in a strategic acquisition cannot be valued because the benefits are qualitative and cannot be easily quantified." Respond.

A simple example Consider two small appliance manufacturing firms, Reliable Corporation and SafeTex Corporation, that operate independently and have the following financial characteristics:

Characteristic	Reliable	Safetex
Revenues	$8,000	$4,000
- COGS	6,000	2,400
EBIT	2,000	1,600
Expected growth rate	4%	6%
Cost of Capital	9%	10%

Both firms are in steady state, with capital spending offset by depreciation. No working capital is required, and both firms face a tax rate of 50%. The free cash flow to each firm is then:

Free cash flow to Reliable Corp. = EBIT (1 − tax rate) = 2,000 (1 − 0.5) = 1,000
Free cash flow to Safetex Corp = EBIT (1 − tax rate) = 1,600 (1 − 0.5) = 800

The value of the two firms can be estimated independently:

Value of Reliable Corp. = 1,000 * (1.04)/ (.09 − .04) = $20,800
Value of Safetex Corp. = 800 * 1.06 / (.10−.06) = $21,200

In the absence of synergy, the combined firm value is

Combined firm value with no synergy = $20,800 + $21,200 = $42,000

Assume that combining the firms will create economies of scale in the form of shared distribution and advertising costs, which will reduce the cost of goods sold from 70% of revenues ($8,400/$12,000) to 65% of revenues. The value of this synergy can be estimated by valuing the combined firm, with the lower cost of goods:

	Firm with no synergy	Firm with synergy
Revenues	$12,000	$12,000
COGS	$8,400	$7,800
EBIT	$3,600	$4,200
Growth Rate	5.00%	5.00%
Cost of Capital	9.50%	9.50%
Firm Value	$42,000	$49,000

Value of Synergy = $49,000 − $42,000 = $7,000

Cost of capital for combined firm = 9% [20,800/(20,800+21,200)] + 10% [21,200/(20,800+21,200)] = 9.5%
Expected growth rate = 4% (20,800/(20,800+21,200)) + 6% (20,800/(20,800+21,200)) = 5%

Alternatively, assume that as a consequence of the merger, the combined firm is able to enter new markets and is expected to increase its future growth in revenues from 5% to 6%. Also assume that the cost of goods sold is expected to remain at 70% of revenues. The value of the combined firm can now be estimated as follows:

	Firm with no synergy	Firm with synergy
Revenues	$12,000	$12,000
COGS	$8,400	$8,400
EBIT	$3,600	$3,600

(continues)

(continued)	Firm with no synergy	Firm with synergy
Growth Rate	5.00%	6.00%
Cost of Capital	9.50%	9.50%
Firm Value	$42,000	$54,514

Value of Synergy = $54,514 - $42,000 = $12,514

As this example illustrates, a small change in expected growth can affect the value of the firm dramatically. An increase in perpetuity of 1% in the combined firm's growth rate was sufficient to justify a premium of $12,514 for synergy. This may not seem to be much of a change, but maintaining an increase of 1% in the combined firm's growth year after year becomes more and more difficult with time. The increase in cash flow needed to maintain this higher growth rate rises from $18 in year 1 to $572 in year 15.

 Concept Check

Calculate the value of the synergy in the examples above, assuming that it will take five years for the synergy to be realized in each case.

 IN PRACTICE VALUING SYNERGY: AT&T AND NCR

In 1991, AT&T acquired NCR after a hotly contested takeover for approximately $110 per share. The deal was justified on the basis of the existence of synergy—that is, that acquiring NCR would enable AT&T to enter the personal computer market and increase future growth. The characteristics of the two firms prior to the merger were as follows:

	NCR	AT&T
Current EBIT (1 − tax rate)	$506 million	$4,419 million
Capital Expenditures–Depreciation	$70 million	$0 (offset)
Expected growth rate—next 5 years	8%	6%
Expected growth rate after year 5	5%	5%
Debt /(Debt + Equity)	9%	21%
After-tax cost of debt	6%	5.40%
Beta for equity—next 5 years	1.15	0.95
Beta for equity—after year 5	1.00	1.0

The Treasury bond rate at the time of the merger was 9%. The growth rate of the combined firm is expected to increase from 6.18 % to 7% during the next 5 years, as a consequence of the merger.[1] The growth rate after year 5 is unchanged. The costs of equity and debt of the firms are summarized in Table 25.1.

The costs of capital change as the relative market values of the firm change. Table 25.2 shows the projected cash flows for the two firms operating independently, as well as for the combined firm, without and with synergy.

---

[1]The increase in the growth may seem small. Given that AT&T is a much larger firm than NCR, a small increase in growth translates into significant dollar value for synergy.

Table 25.1 **COSTS OF CAPITAL FOR NCR, AT&T, AND COMBINED FIRM (PERCENTAGE DISTRIBUTION)**

	NCR	AT&T	Combined Firm
Debt (%)	9	21	20
Cost of debt	6.00	5.40	5.42
Equity(%)	91	79	80
Cost of equity	15.33	14.23	14.34
WACC—Year 1	14.52	12.40	12.57
WACC—Year 2	14.52	12.40	12.58
WACC—Year 3	14.52	12.40	12.59
WACC—Year 4	14.52	12.40	12.59
WACC—Year 5	14.52	12.40	12.59
WACC—after year 5	13.31	12.22	12.32

Table 25.2 **PROJECTED CASH FLOWS—NCR, AT&T, AND COMBINED FIRM**

	NCR	AT&T	Combined Firm After Merger		
			Without Synergy	With Synergy	Effect of Synergy
FCFF in year 1	$471	$4,684	$5,155	$5,195	$40
FCFF in year 2	509	4,918	5,427	5,558	132
FCFF in year 3	550	5,164	5,714	5,948	234
FCFF in year 4	594	5,422	6,016	6,364	348
FCFF in year 5	641	5,693	6,334	6,809	475
Terminal Value	8,102	82,756	90,857	97,672	6,815
Present Value	5,949	64,390	70,339	74,895	4,556

Based on the projected increase in the growth rate as a result of synergy, the value of synergy is $4.556 billion. The expected value of NCR to AT&T can be calculated as follows:

$$\text{Value of NCR to AT\&T} = \text{Value of NCR operating independently} + \text{Value of Synergy}$$
$$= \$5.949 \text{ billion} + \$4.556 \text{ billion}$$
$$= \$10.505 \text{ billion}$$
$$\text{Value of Equity in NCR} = \text{Value of firm} - \text{Value of outstanding debt} = \$10,505 - 537$$
$$= \$9,968$$
$$\text{Value per share} = \text{Value of Equity / Number of shares outstanding} = \$9,968 / 70.60$$
$$= \$141.19$$

The premium paid by AT&T is justifiable if the promised synergy benefits materialize. Without the synergy, the equity in NCR would have been valued at $84.26, well below the price paid on the takeover.

❑ Concept Check

In the above analysis, does the fact that AT&T is a much larger firm than NCR affect the estimate of synergy? If so, how? What are the general lessons that can be learned about the value of synergy in mergers of equals (firms of the same size) as opposed to mergers of unequal firms?

Who receives the benefits from synergy?   In general, synergy accrues to the combined firm. Because both the bidding firm and the target firm contribute to the creation of this synergy, the sharing of the benefits of synergy among the two players will depend largely on whether the bidding firm's contribution is unique or easily replaced. If it can be easily replaced, the bulk of the synergy benefits will accrue to the target firm. If it is unique, the benefits will be shared much more equitably.

Bradley, Desai, and Kim (1988) examined an extensive sample of 236 tender offers made between 1963 and 1984 and concluded that the benefits of synergy accrue primarily to the target firms when multiple bidders are involved in the takeover. They estimated the market-adjusted stock returns around the announcement of the takeover for the successful bidder to be 2% in single bidder takeovers and −1.33% in contested takeovers.

Financial Synergy

Synergy can also be created from purely financial factors. We will consider three legitimate sources of **financial synergy** in the following pages—better use for "excess" cash or cash slack, a greater "tax benefit" from accumulated losses or tax deductions, and an increase in debt capacity and therefore firm value. We will begin the discussion, however, with diversification, which, though a widely used rationale for mergers, is not itself a source of increased value.

Financial Synergy: This is the increase in value that accrues to a combined firm from a purely financial effect—lower taxes, higher debt capacity, or better use of idle cash.

Diversification A firm can reduce the variability in its earnings by diversifying into other industries. The benefits of doing so are not obvious, however. Stockholders can diversify at a much lower cost, without having to pay the takeover premiums that firms pay. Furthermore, when a firm diversifies, it takes the choice of which firms to diversify into away from stockholders and puts it in the hands of management.

A takeover motivated solely by diversification considerations has no effect on the combined value of the two firms involved in the takeover. Consider the following example. Dalton Motors, an automobile parts manufacturing firm in a cyclical business, plans to acquire Lube & Auto, an automobile service firm whose business is noncyclical and high growth, solely for the diversification benefit. The characteristics of the two firms are as follows:

	Lube & Auto	Dalton Motors
Current free cash flow to the firm	$100 million	$200 million
Expected growth rate—next 5 years	20%	10%
Expected growth rate—after year 5	6%	6%
Debt /(Debt + Equity)	30%	30%
After-tax cost of debt	6%	5.40%
Beta for equity—next 5 years	1.20	1.00
Beta for equity—after year 5	1.00	1.00

The Treasury bond rate is 7%, and the market premium is 5.5%. The calculations for the weighted average cost of capital and the value of the firms are shown in Table 25.3.

The cost of equity (debt) for the combined firm is obtained by taking the weighted averages of the individual firm's costs of equity (debt); the weights are based on the relative market values of equity (debt) of the two firms. Because these relative market values change over time, the costs of equity and debt for the combined firm also change over time. The value of the combined firm is exactly the same as the sum of the values of the independent firms; thus, there is no value gain from diversification.

	Lube & Auto	Dalton Motor	Lube & Auto + Dalton Motor	Combined Firm
Debt (%)	30%	30%		30%
Cost of debt	6.00%	5.40%		5.65%
Equity(%)	70%	70%		70%
Cost of equity	13.60%	12.50%		12.95%
WACC—Year 1	11.32%	10.37%		10.76%
WACC—Year 2	11.32%	10.37%		10.76%
WACC—Year 3	11.32%	10.37%		10.77%
WACC—Year 4	11.32%	10.37%		10.77%
WACC—Year 5	11.32%	10.37%		10.77%
WACC—after year 5	10.55%	10.37%		10.45%
FCFF in year 1	$120.00	$220.00		$340.00
FCFF in year 2	$144.00	$242.00		$386.00
FCFF in year 3	$172.80	$266.20		$439.00
FCFF in year 4	$207.36	$292.82		$500.18
FCFF in year 5	$248.83	$322.10		$570.93
Terminal Value	$5,796.97	$7,813.00		$13,609.97
Present Value	$4,020.91	$5,760.47	$9,781.38	$9,781.38

Table 25.3 VALUE OF LUBE & AUTO, DALTON MOTORS, AND COMBINED FIRM

This does not imply, however, that the shareholders in the bidding and target firms are indifferent about such takeovers, for the bidding firm pays a significant premium over the market price. To the extent that these firms were correctly valued before the merger (Market Value of Lube & Auto = $4,020.91; Market Value of Dalton Motors = $5,760.47), the payment of a premium over the market price will transfer wealth from the bidding firm to the target firm.

☐ Concept
Check

> Would your analysis have been any different if either Lube & Auto or Dalton Motors had been a private firm? Why or why not?

The absence of added value from this merger may seem puzzling, given that the two firms are in unrelated businesses and thus should gain some diversification benefit. In fact, if the earnings of the two firms are not highly correlated, the variance in earnings of the combined firm should be significantly lower than the variance in earnings of the individual firms operating independently. This reduction in earnings variance does not impact value, however, because it is firm-specific risk, which is assumed to have no effect on expected returns. (The betas, which are measures of market risk, are always the value-weighted averages of the betas of the two merging firms.) But what about the impact of reduced variance on debt capacity? A substantial body of evidence shows that firms with lower variability in earnings can increase debt capacity and thus value. This can be a real benefit of conglomerate mergers, and it is considered separately later in this section.

Cash slack   Managers may reject profitable investment opportunities if they have to raise new capital to finance them. Myers and Majluf (1984) argue that since managers have more information than investors about prospective projects, new stock may have to be issued at less than true value to finance these projects, leading to the rejection of good projects and to capital rationing for some firms. It may therefore make sense for a company with excess cash and no investment opportunities—known as **cash slack**—to take over a cash-poor firm with good investment opportunities, or vice versa. The additional value of combining these two firms lies in the present value of the projects that would not have been taken if they had stayed apart but can now be taken because of the availability of cash.

Cash Slack: This is cash that is in excess of what is needed to finance a firm's existing viable projects; that is, projects that have returns exceeding their hurdle rates.

Concept
Check

In a merger of two firms—one with excess cash/poor projects, and the other with great projects/cash shortages—which firm will get the larger share of the synergy benefits? Explain.

Tax benefits Several tax benefits may accrue from takeovers. First, if one of the firms has tax deductions that it cannot use because it is losing money, whereas the other firm has income on which it pays significant taxes, combining the two firms can result in tax benefits that can be shared by the two firms. The value of this synergy is the present value of the tax savings that accrue because of this merger. In addition, the assets of the firm being taken over may be written up to reflect new market value, in some forms of mergers, leading to higher tax savings from depreciation in future years.

IN PRACTICE TAX BENEFITS OF WRITING UP ASSET VALUES AFTER TAKEOVER: CONGOLEUM, INC.

One of the earliest leveraged buyouts occurred in 1979 involving Congoleum, Inc., a diversified firm in ship building, flooring, and automotive accessories. Congoleum's own management bought out the firm. The favorable treatment that the tax authorities would accord the firm's assets was a major factor behind the takeover. After the takeover—estimated to cost approximately $400 million—the firm would be allowed to write up its assets to reflect their new market values and to claim depreciation on these new values. The firm's tax rate was 48%. The estimated change in depreciation and the present value effect of this depreciation, discounted at the firm's cost of capital of 14.5%, is shown in Table 25.4.

Table 25.4 **DEPRECIATION TAX BENEFITS: BEFORE AND AFTER LBO**

Year	Depreciation Before	Depreciation After	Change in Depreciation	Tax Savings	Present Value
1980	$8.00	$35.51	$27.51	$13.20	$11.53
1981	8.80	36.26	27.46	13.18	10.05
1982	9.68	37.07	27.39	13.15	8.76
1983	10.65	37.95	27.30	13.10	7.62
1984	11.71	21.23	9.52	4.57	2.32
1985	12.65	17.50	4.85	2.33	1.03
1986	13.66	16.00	2.34	1.12	0.43
1987	14.75	14.75	0.00	0.00	0.00
1988	15.94	15.94	0.00	0.00	0.00
1989	17.21	17.21	0.00	0.00	0.00
1980–1989	*$123.05*	*$249.42*	*$126.37*	*$60.66*	*$41.76*

Note that the increase in depreciation is in the first seven years, primarily as a consequence of higher asset values and accelerated depreciation. After year 7, however, the depreciation schedules converge. The present value of the additional tax benefits from the higher depreciation, based on a tax rate of 48%, amounted to $41.76 million, about 10% of the overall price paid on the transaction.

Debt capacity   If the cash flows of the firms are less than perfectly correlated, the cash flow of the combined firm will be less variable than that of the individual firms, resulting in an increase in debt capacity and in the value of the firm. This, however, has to be weighed against the immediate transfer of wealth that occurs to existing bondholders in both firms from the stockholders. The bondholders in the pre-merger firms find themselves lending to a safer firm after the takeover. The coupon rates they are receiving are based on the riskier pre-merger firms, however. If the coupon rates are not renegotiated, the bonds will increase in price, increasing the bondholders' wealth at the expense of the stockholders.

Several models are available for analyzing the benefits of higher debt ratios as a consequence of takeovers. Lewellen (1971) analyzes the benefits in terms of reduced default risk, for the combined firm has less variable cash flows than do the individual firms. His model provides a rationale for an increase in the value of debt after the merger, but at the expense of equity investors. It is not clear, therefore, that the value of the firm will increase after the merger. Stapleton (1985) evaluates the benefits of higher debt capacity after mergers, using the option pricing framework. He shows that the effect of a merger on debt capacity is always positive, even when the earnings of the two firms are perfectly correlated. The debt capacity benefits increase as the earnings of the two firms become less correlated and as investors become more risk averse.

Consider again the merger of Lube & Auto and Dalton Motor, described earlier in the chapter. The value of the combined firm, in that case, was the same as the sum of the values of the independent firms. The fact that the two firms were in different business lines reduced the variance in earnings, but value was not affected, because the capital structure of the firm remained unchanged after the merger, and the costs of equity and debt were the weighted averages of the individual firms' costs.

The reduction in variance in earnings can increase debt capacity, which can increase value. If after the merger of these two firms, the debt capacity for the combined firm were increased from 30% to 40% (leading to an increase in the beta to 1.21 and no change in the cost of debt), the value of the combined firm after the takeover can be estimated as shown in Table 25.5.

Table 25.5   **VALUE OF DEBT CAPACITY—LUBE & AUTO AND DALTON MOTORS**

	Lube & Auto	Dalton Motors	Combined Firm—No New Debt	Combined Firm—Added Debt
Debt (%)	30%	30%	30%	40%
Cost of debt	6.00%	5.40%	5.65%	5.65%
Equity(%)	70%	70%	70%	60%
Cost of equity	13.60%	12.50%	12.95%	13.65%
WACC—Year 1	11.32%	10.37%	10.76%	10.45%
WACC—Year 2	11.32%	10.37%	10.76%	10.45%
WACC—Year 3	11.32%	10.37%	10.77%	10.45%
WACC—Year 4	11.32%	10.37%	10.77%	10.45%
WACC—Year 5	11.32%	10.37%	10.77%	10.45%

(*continues*)

Table 25.5 (*CONTINUED*)

	Lube Auto	Dalton Motors	Combined Firm—No New Debt	Combined Firm—Added Debt
WACC—after year 5	10.55%	10.37%	10.45%	9.76%
FCFF in year 1	$120.00	$220.00	$340.00	$340.00
FCFF in year 2	$144.00	$242.00	$386.00	$386.00
FCFF in year 3	$172.80	$266.20	$439.00	$439.00
FCFF in year 4	$207.36	$292.82	$500.18	$500.18
FCFF in year 5	$248.83	$322.10	$570.93	$570.93
Terminal Value	$5,796.97	$7,813.00	$13,609.97	$16,101.22
Present Value	$4,020.91	$5,760.47	$9,781.38	$11,429.35

As a consequence of the added debt, the value of the firm will increase from $9,781.38 million to $11,429.35 million.

Concept Check

In the example described above, what will happen to stockholder wealth if the merger goes through and the combined firm's debt is kept at pre-merger levels? What will happen to bond prices?

Empirical Evidence on the Value of Synergy

Synergy is a stated motive in many mergers and acquisitions. Bhide (1993) examined the motives behind 77 acquisitions in 1985 and 1986 and reported that operating synergy was the primary motive in one-third of these takeovers. A number of studies examine whether, in fact, synergy exists and, if it does, how much it is worth. If synergy is perceived to exist in a takeover, the value of the combined firm should be greater than the sum of the values of the bidding and target firms operating independently.

$$V(AB) > V(A) + V(B)$$

where

$V(AB)$ = Value of a firm created by combining A and B
$V(A)$ = Value of firm A, operating independently
$V(B)$ = Value of firm B, operating independently

Studies of stock returns around merger announcements generally conclude that the value of the combined firm does increase in most takeovers and that the increase is significant. Bradley, Desai, and Kim (1988) examined a sample of 236 interfirm tender offers between 1963 and 1984 and reported that the combined value of the target and bidder firms increased 7.48% ($117 million in 1984 dollars), on average, on the announcement of the merger. This result has to be read with caution, however, for the increase in the value of the combined firm after a merger is also consistent with a number of other hypotheses explaining acquisitions, including undervaluation and a change in corporate control. It is thus a weak test of the synergy hypothesis.

The existence of synergy generally implies that the combined firm will become more profitable and grow faster after the merger than will the firms operating separately. A stronger test of synergy is to evaluate whether merged firms improve their performance (profitability and growth), *relative to their competitors,* after takeovers. There is little empirical evidence that firms accomplish either objective after mergers. McKinsey and

Co. (1985) examined 58 acquisition programs between 1972 and 1983 for evidence on two questions: (1) Did the return on the amount invested in the acquisitions exceed the cost of capital? (2) Did the acquisitions help the parent companies outperform the competition? They concluded that 28 of the 58 programs failed both tests and that six failed at least one test. Some studies contradict these findings, but they look at all mergers, including those motivated by factors other than synergy.[2] A number of studies have examined whether acquiring related businesses (i.e., synergy-driven acquisitions) provides better returns than acquiring unrelated business (i.e., conglomerate mergers); they have come to conflicting conclusions and have not reached any consensus.[3]

The most damaging evidence on the value of synergy lies in the large number of acquisitions that are reversed within fairly short time periods. Mitchell and Lehn (1990) noted that 20.2% of the acquisitions made between 1982 and 1986 were divested by 1988. Studies that have tracked acquisitions for longer time periods (10 years or more) have found that the divestiture rate of acquisitions rises to almost 50%. Therefore, many firms find that the promised benefits from acquisitions do not materialize in actuality.

 Concept
Check

> "Synergy takes a long time to show up. The reason most studies find no synergy benefits is that they look at short time periods (five years or less) after mergers." Respond.

THE VALUE OF CORPORATE CONTROL

Many hostile takeovers are justified on the basis of the existence of a market for corporate control; that is, investors and firms are willing to pay large premiums over the market price to control the management of firms. This section explores the determinants of the value of corporate control and analyzes related issues, including the value of "restricted voting rights" shares, closely held corporations, and the effects of takeover restrictions.

Determinants of the Value of Corporate Control

The value of wresting control of a firm from incumbent management is inversely proportional to the perceived quality of that management and its capacity to maximize firm value. In general, the value of control will be much greater for a poorly managed firm that operates at below optimum capacity than for a well-managed firm.

The value of controlling a firm comes from changes that can be made to existing management policy which can increase the value of the firm. These changes cover several areas: assets can be acquired or liquidated, the financing mix can be changed and the dividend policy reevaluated; and the firm can be restructured to maximize value. By employing a simple framework, the value of the firm, assuming it is restructured, can be obtained. The value of control can then be written as:

Value of Control = Value of firm, with restructuring − Value of firm, without restructuring

The value of control is negligible for firms that are operating at or close to their optimal value, for a restructuring will yield little additional value. The value of control can

[2]A study by Healy, Palepu, and Ruback (1989) looked at the post-merger performance of 50 large mergers from 1979 to 1983 and concluded that merged firms improved their operating performance (defined as EBITDA/Sales) relative to their industries.
[3]Michel and Shaked (1984) and Duofsky and Varadarajan (1987) found that diversification-driven mergers did better than synergy-driven mergers, in terms of risk-adjusted returns. Varadarajan and Ramanujam (1987) found that synergy-driven mergers did better in terms of return on equity.

be substantial for firms that are operating at well below optimal, because a restructuring can lead to a significant increase in value.

A simple example Nopat Inc. is a specialty retailing firm that is operating at well below potential. Its existing management has taken projects that have, on average, a return on assets of 10%, well below the retail industry average of 16%. The firm has no debt, although its cash flows would support a debt level of 50% of equity (and its rating would be A, with an interest rate of 9%). The firm also pays 60% of its earnings as dividends, although its cash flows would support a dividend payout of only 40%. The current earnings per share is $2, the tax rate for the firm is 40%, and its current beta is 0.8. The Treasury bond rate is 7%. The firm is expected to reach steady state after year 5 and to grow at 6% after that under incumbent management and at 7% with a change in management.

Nopat Inc. can be valued under both incumbent management and with a change in management, as shown in Table 25.6.

Table 25.6 VALUE OF NOPAT INC. WITH INCUMBENT AND NEW MANAGEMENT

	Incumbent Management	New Management
Return on assets	10%	16%
Debt/equity ratio	0%	50 %
Interest rate on debt	NA	9%
Retention ratio	40%	60%
Growth rate—first 5 years	0.4(10%) = 4.00 %	.6(16% + .5 (16%-9%)) = 11.70 %
Growth rate—after year 5	6%	7%
Payout ratio after year 5	60%	60%
Beta of the stock	0.80	1.04
Cost of equity	7% + 0.8 (5.5%) = 11.40%	7% +1.04 (5.5%) = 12.72%
Value of equity per share	$21.60	$25.34

The value of control in this firm is $3.84 per share—the difference between the value of equity per share under incumbent management and the value under new management.

Empirical Evidence on the Market for Corporate Control

The strongest evidence in support of the existence of a market for corporate control lies in the types of firms that are typically acquired in hostile takeovers. The general view that well-managed and well-run firms are being taken over by marauding raiders is incorrect. Research indicates that the typical target firm in a hostile takeover has the following characteristics:

1. It has underperformed other stocks and the overall market, in terms of returns to its stockholders in the years preceding the takeover.
2. It has been less profitable than firms in its peer group in the years preceding the takeover.
3. It has a much lower stockholding by insiders than do firms in its peer groups.

In a comparison of target firms in hostile and friendly takeovers, Bhide (1993) illustrates these differences. His findings are summarized in Figure 25.1.

As you can see, target firms in hostile takeovers, on average, have made a return on equity 2.2% lower than that of other firms in their industry group; they have had

Figure 25.1   Target characteristics—hostile vs. friendly takeovers

returns 4% lower than the market; and they have only 6.5% of their stock held by insiders.

There is also evidence that firms make significant changes in the way they operate after hostile takeovers. In his study, Bhide examined the consequences of hostile takeovers and noted the following changes:

1. Many of the hostile takeovers were followed by an increase in leverage, which resulted in a downgrading of the debt. The leverage was quickly reduced with proceeds from sale of assets, however.

2. There was no significant change in the amount of capital investment in these firms.

3. Almost 60% of the takeovers were followed by significant divestitures, whereby half or more of the firm was divested. The overwhelming majority of the divestitures were of units in business areas unrelated to the company's core business (i.e., they constituted reversal of corporate diversification done in earlier time periods).

4. There were significant management changes in 17 of the 19 hostile takeovers; the entire corporate management team was replaced in seven of the takeovers.

Related Issues

The market for corporate control is a useful framework for examining the efficiency gains from takeovers and their disciplinary effect on management. It is also useful in analyzing a number of related issues.

The valuation effects of restrictions on voting rights   Not uncommonly, shares which have significant restrictions on voting rights trade on exchanges. Although the New York Stock Exchange has generally restricted the issue of shares with differences in voting rights, several firms that trade on other exchanges, both in the United States and Europe, have two or more classes of shares listed at the same time, with significant differences in voting rights.

A **nonvoting share** or a share with significant voting restrictions should sell for a discount on an otherwise similar voting share. In the traditional discounted cash-flow valuation approaches, described earlier in this book, there seems to be no room for considering the effects of such restrictions on value. However, the restructuring framework developed in the prior section and the value of corporate control can be used to shed light on the relative values of voting and nonvoting shares.

Nonvoting share: The owner of a nonvoting share cannot vote on issues normally voted on by stockholders, including elections to boards of directors, changes in the corporate charter, and agreement to merger terms.

Voting rights have value because they give shareholders a say in the management of the firm. To the extent that they can make a difference—by removing incumbent management, forcing management to change policy, or selling to a hostile bidder in a takeover—the price of voting shares will reflect the possibility of a restructuring.[4] Nonvoting shareholders, on the other hand, do not participate in these decisions. If the firm is well run, the potential gain from restructuring is negligible, and the difference in values between voting and nonvoting shares should be as well. If the firm is badly managed, the potential gain from restructuring is significant, and voting shares should sell at a significant premium over nonvoting shares.

□ Concept
Check

> **Under what conditions would you expect voting and nonvoting shares to sell at the same price? Assuming the same dividends on both types of shares, should nonvoting shares ever sell for more than voting shares?**

Empirical evidence   The consensus among researchers who have looked at firms with voting and nonvoting shares is that nonvoting shares sell at a discount, although the discount is fairly small and volatile. Lease, McConnell, and Mikkelson (1983) examined 26 firms that had two classes of common stock outstanding and concluded that the voting shares traded at a premium relative to nonvoting shares.[5] The premium, on average, amounted to 5.44%, and the voting shares sold at a higher price in 88% of the months for which data were available. In four firms that also had voting preferred stock, however, the voting common stock traded at a discount of about 1.17%, relative to nonvoting shares.

A common rationale for having voting shares is to enable insiders in the firm to control the firm, without having to own 51% of the outstanding equity. This is confirmed by DeAngelo and DeAngelo (1985), who examined insider holdings in companies that have dual classes of shares. They found that managers in these companies hold, on average, 59.2% of the high-voting right and 20.8% of the low-voting right. Thus, these managers, who receive only 27.6% of the common stock cash flows, hold an average of 54.8% of the voting rights of the company.

At the same time, the issue of restricted-voting shares has a negative impact on the stock price. A **dual-class recapitalization** refers to the issuance of common stock with different voting rights, often in response to the threat of a hostile takeover, by insiders who want to consolidate their control of the firm. Jarrel and Poulsen (1988) provide evidence on the merits of corporate control by evaluating the effects of dual-class recapitalizations on stockholder wealth. Using a sample of 94 firms that announced dual-class common stock between 1976 and 1987, they found that stock prices reacted negatively to the public announcements of these recapitalizations, as control was reallocated from existing stockholders to incumbent management.

Dual-class Recapitalization: This term refers to the issue of two classes of common stock, one with voting rights and the other without, to replace existing shares.

---

[4]In some cases, the rights of nonvoting stockholders are protected in the specific instance of a takeover by forcing the bidder to buy the nonvoting shares as well.
[5]The two classes of stock received the same dividend.

The effects of takeover restrictions on value   There are two classes of restrictions on takeovers: (1) those imposed by the firm through the use of anti-takeover clauses and amendments in the corporate charter, and (2) those imposed by the state to make takeovers more difficult or even impossible.

In response to the wave of hostile takeovers in the 1980s, a number of firms made changes in their corporate charters in an effort to make takeovers more difficult. A number of reasons were offered for these changes. First, they would release managers from the time-consuming stress of having to deal with hostile takeovers and enable them to spend their time making productive decisions. Second, they would give managers additional tools to extract even more value from hostile bidders in a takeover by increasing their bargaining power. Third, they would enable managers to focus on maximizing "long-term" value as opposed to the "short-term" value maximization supposedly implicit in most takeovers. A range of anti-takeover amendments were offered to this end. Among them were staggered board elections, whereby only a portion of the board could be replaced each year, making it more difficult for a shareholder to gain control; supermajority clauses, whereby more than a majority approval is needed for a merger (typically 70% to 80%); and the barring of two-tier offers.

In theory, these anti-takeover amendments should affect value negatively, because they make takeovers less likely and incumbent management more entrenched. The net effect on value is likely to vary across firms, however. Firms with the most inefficient management are most likely to experience a drop in value upon the passage of these amendments, whereas firms with more efficient management are not likely to show any noticeable change in value.

Empirical evidence   Empirical studies of the announcement effects of the anti-takeover amendments on stock price show a surprising lack of consensus. Linn and McConnell (1983) studied the effects of anti-takeover amendments on the stock price and found positive but insignificant reactions to anti-takeover amendments. DeAngelo and Rice (1983) investigated the same phenomenon and found a negative, albeit insignificant, effect. Dann and DeAngelo (1983) examined standstill agreements and negotiated premium buybacks[6] and reported negative stock price reactions around their announcements, a finding consistent with the loss of shareholder wealth. Dann and DeAngelo (1988) extended their study to anti-takeover measures passed, not in response to a takeover attempt, but *in advance* of a takeover as a defensive measure. They reported a stock price decline of 2.33% around the announcement of these measures.

☐ Concept Check

Examining only anti-takeover amendments that require shareholder approval, identify the types of firms that are most likely to be successful in getting such amendments approved. In particular, do you believe such amendments have a greater chance of success in well-managed or badly managed firms? What relevance does this matter have for the findings mentioned above?

[6]This is a fancy name for *greenmail*, whereby the stake acquired by a raider is bought back by the company at a substantial premium over the price paid. In return, the raider signs a "standstill" agreement not to acquire shares in the company for a specific time period.

Takeover restrictions imposed by the state Many financial markets outside the United States impose significant legal and institutional restrictions on takeover activity. Although few markets forbid takeovers altogether, the cumulated effect of the restrictions in many markets is to make hostile takeovers nearly impossible. Even in the United States, a number of states imposed restrictions on takeovers in the 1980s, in response to the public and political outcry against hostile takeovers. A recent example of state-imposed restrictions is the Pennsylvania law passed in 1990, which contained three provisions to make takeovers more difficult. First, a bidder who crosses ownership thresholds of 20%, 33%, or 50% without management approval must gain the approval of other shareholders to use his or her voting rights. Obtaining this approval is made even more difficult by restricting voting to only those shareholders who have held stock for more than 12 months. Second, the board of directors is allowed to weigh the effect of the takeover on all stakeholders, including customers, employees, and local community groups, in accepting or rejecting a takeover, thus providing members of the board with considerable leeway in rejecting hostile bids. Third, bidders are forced to return any profits made from any sale of stock in the target corporation within 18 months of the takeover attempt, thus increasing the cost of an unsuccessful bid.

Karpoff and Malatesta (1990) examined the consequences of this law and found that the stock prices of Pennsylvania-based firms dropped (after adjusting for market movements), on average, 1.58% on October 13, 1989, the first day a news story was carried on the law. Over the entire period, from the first news story to the introduction of the bill into the Pennsylvania legislature, these firms had a cumulative market-adjusted return of -6.90%.[7]

VALUING LEVERAGED BUYOUTS

There are two important differences between takeovers, in general, and **leveraged buyouts,** in particular. First, most leveraged buyouts in the 1980s were initiated by buyout groups that included existing management, who bought stock from their own stockholders and took their firms private. The second difference lies in the high leverage inherent in leveraged buyouts at the time of the buyout and the rapid changes in leverage across time in these transactions, as assets are sold and debt is repaid. Each of these differences has implications for value and must be incorporated into the valuation framework.

Leveraged Buyout: This is an acquisition financed primarily with debt and often initiated by the management of the firm being bought.

The Value of Going Private
The lure of access to financial markets has induced hundreds of private firms that saw the potential benefits of being publicly traded (including increased access to financial markets, increased liquidity, and a market price for their stock), but no significant costs, to go public. In recent years, however, the managers of many public firms have argued that being a publicly traded firm has significant costs including:

1. The need to keep analysts and stockholders happy, which, in their view, translates into maximizing short-term returns at the expense of long-term value.

---

[7]The controversy provoked by the Pennsylvania anti-takeover law created a strong countermovement among institutional investors, who threatened to sell their holdings in Pennsylvania companies that opted to be covered by the law. Faced with this ultimatum, many Pennsylvania firms chose to opt out of the anti-takeover law.

2. The separation of ownership and management, which can lead to conflicts of interest between stockholders and managers on the best course for the firm to follow and, consequently, suboptimal decisions for the firm.

3. The increased information needs, including the need to provide quarterly financial statements and advance notice of major financing transactions, which can absorb the attention of top management and cost time and money.

Others argue that these costs are overstated and that they are used to provide ex-post rationalization for many leveraged buyouts. The empirical evidence on going-private transactions, however, is clear cut. DeAngelo, DeAngelo, and Rice (1984) report, for example, an average abnormal return of 30% for 81 firms that went private in their sample. Thus, financial markets, at least, seem to believe that some public firms will gain value in going private.

If going private is expected to increase managers' responsiveness to value maximization in the long term—since they are part owners of the firm—the way to incorporate this effect is to build it into the cash flows. The increased efficiency can be expected to show up in the bottom line if it reduces the cost of goods sold and increases operating profit. The emphasis on long-term value should be visible in project choice and should lead to a higher return on assets. This advantage has to be weighed against the capital rationing the firm might face because of limited access to financial markets, which might reduce future growth and profits. The net effect will determine the change in value.

□ Concept Check

> Going private reduces or eliminates one agency conflict—that between stockholders and managers. What effect, if any, does it have on the other agency conflict—between bondholders and equity investors in the firm? Explain.

The Rationale for High Leverage

The second difference between LBOs and other takeovers is the "high leverage" inherent in the LBOs. This high leverage is justified in a number of ways. First, if the target firm has too little debt (relative to its optimal) to begin with, the increase in leverage can be explained partially by the increase in value moving to the optimal provides. The leverage in most leveraged buyouts exceeds the optimal debt ratio, however, which means that some of the debt will have to be paid off quickly in order for the firm to reduce its cost of capital and return to a steady state. A second explanation is provided by Michael Jensen, who argues that managers cannot be trusted to invest free cash flows wisely for their stockholders; they need the discipline of debt payments to maximize cash flows on projects and firm value. This point is made succinctly by Bennett Stewart (1991), who argues that, for management, equity is a pillow whereas debt is a sword. A third rationale is that the high leverage is a temporary phenomenon that disappears once the firm liquidates assets and pays off a significant portion of the debt.

The extremely high leverage associated with leveraged buyouts creates some problems in valuation, however. It significantly increases the riskiness of the cash flows to equity investors in the firm by increasing the fixed payments to debtholders in the firm. Thus, if the cost of equity is used to discount cash flows to equity, it has to be adjusted to reflect the higher financial risk the firm will face after the leveraged buyout. In addition, the expected decrease in this leverage over time, as the firm liquidates assets and pays off debt, implies that the cost of equity will also decrease over time. The discounting has to reflect these changing discount rates.

A leveraged buyout can be analyzed either from the viewpoint of just the equity investors in the deal or as a package of debt and equity. From the equity investors' perspective, the discounting framework is as follows:

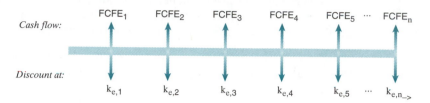

This yields the present value of expected cash flows to equity investors.

If PV of Equity Cash flows   > Equity investment in deal : Deal makes sense to equity.
                    < Equity investment in deal : Deal does not make sense
                                        to equity investors.

Because equity investors provide only a small slice of the financing in a leveraged buyout, it may make more sense to value the entire package of financing for the deal, including both debt and equity. From this standpoint, the discounting framework is as follows:

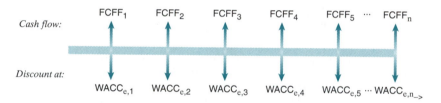

This yields the present value of expected cash flows to the firm.

If PV of Firm Cash flows   > Total cost of deal : Overall deal makes sense.
                              < Total cost of deal: Overall deal does not make sense.

To be viable a leveraged buyout has to pass both tests—it has to make sense overall, and its equity investors need to get more back from the deal than they put in.

 Concept Check

> Is it possible for a deal to make sense from the perspective of equity investors, but not from the perspective of all investors? What has to happen for this to occur?

 IN PRACTICE   VALUING A LEVERAGED BUYOUT: CONGOLEUM INC.[8]

The managers of Congoleum Inc., targeted the firm for a leveraged buyout in 1979. They planned to buy back the stock at $38 per share (it was trading at $24 prior to the takeover) and to finance the acquisition primarily with debt:

Cost of Takeover

Buy back stock: $38 * 12.2 million shares:	$463.60 million
Expenses of takeover:	$7.00 million
Total Cost:	$470.60 million

---

[8]The numbers in this illustration were extracted from the Harvard Business School case on the company. The case is reprinted in Fruhan, Kester, Mason, Piper, and Ruback (1992).

Financing Mix for Takeover

Equity:	$117.30 million
Debt:	$327.10 million
Preferred Stock (@13.5%):	$26.20 million
Total Proceeds	$470.60 million

The debt was composed of three types:

1. Bank debt of $125 million, at a 14% interest rate, to be repaid in annual installments of $16.666 million, starting in 1980.

2. Senior notes of $115 million, at an 11.25% interest rate, to be repaid in equal annual installments of $7.636 million each year from 1981.

3. Subordinated notes of $92 million, at 12.25% interest, to be repaid in equal annual installments of $7.636 million each year from 1989.

The firm also assumed $12.2 million of existing debt, at the advantageous rate of 7.50%; this debt would be repaid in 1982. The net proceeds from the new debt issues is expected to be $314.9 million.

The firm projected operating income (EBIT), capital spending, depreciation, and change in working capital from 1980 to 1984, as shown in Table 25.7 (in millions of dollars):

Table 25.7   EBIT, NET CAP EX, AND CHANGES IN WORKING CAPITAL—CONGOLEUM

Year	EBIT	Capital Spending	Depreciation	Δ Working Capital
Current	$89.80	$6.80	$7.5	$4.0
1980	71.69	15.0	35.51	2.0
1981	90.84	16.2	36.26	14.0
1982	115.73	17.5	37.07	23.3
1983	133.15	18.9	37.95	11.2
1984	137.27	20.4	21.93	12.8

The earnings before interest and taxes are expected to grow 8% after 1984, and the capital spending is expected to be offset by depreciation. The tax rate is 48%.

Congoleum had a beta of 1.25 in 1979, prior to the leveraged buyout. The Treasury bond rate at the time of the leveraged buyout was 9.5%.

Step 1   *Estimate the projected cash flows to the firm and to equity investors in the deal (Table 25.8).*

Table 25.8   PROJECTED CASH FLOWS TO EQUITY AND FIRM: CONGOLEUM

	1980	1981	1982	1983	1984	1985
EBIT	$71.69	$90.84	$115.73	$133.15	$137.27	$148.25
−EBIT (t)	34.41	43.60	55.55	63.91	65.89	71.16
= EBIT (1-t)	37.28	47.24	60.18	69.24	71.38	77.09
+ Depreciation	35.51	36.26	37.07	37.95	21.93	21.62
−Capital Exp.	15.00	16.20	17.50	18.90	20.40	21.62
−Δ WC	2.00	14.00	23.30	11.20	12.80	5.00
= FCFF	55.79	53.30	56.45	77.09	60.11	72.09
−Interest $(1 - t)$	22.32	21.09	19.41	17.74	15.53	13.00
−Principal Repaid	17.14	24.75	24.52	36.75	24.55	20.00
+ New Debt Issues	0.00	0.00	0.00	0.00	0.00	20.00
−Preferred Dividend	3.50	3.50	3.50	3.50	3.50	3.50
= FCFE	12.83	3.96	9.02	19.10	16.53	55.59

The interest expenses and principal repaid were calculated based on the provisions in the debt agreements. All debt repayments after 1984 are assumed to be made from new debt issues (i.e., it is assumed that the firm has reached steady state in terms of its debt ratio).

Step 2   *Estimate debt/equity ratios for future years, based on debt repayments and the estimated value of equity. Recalculate the costs of debt, equity, and capital for future years (Table 25.9).* The value of debt for future years is estimated based on the repayment schedule, and it decreases over time. The value of equity in each of the future years is estimated by discounting the expected cash flows in equity beyond that year at the cost of equity. (Some circular reasoning is involved in this process, for the value of equity is needed to estimate the beta and the cost of equity, and vice versa. It is solved by iterating until the values of equity used in the calculations are consistent.) (Thus, step 3 has to be done before step 2 to arrive at a starting terminal value)

Table 25.9 COST OF CAPITAL—CONGOLEUM	1980	1981	1982	1983	1984	1985
Debt	$327.10	$309.96	$285.17	$260.62	$236.04	$211.45
Equity	$275.39	$319.40	$378.81	$441.91	$504.29	$578.48
Preferred Stock	$26.20	$26.20	$26.20	$26.20	$26.20	$26.20
Debt/Capital	52.03%	47.28%	41.32%	35.76%	30.79%	25.91%
Equity/Capital	43.80%	48.72%	54.89%	60.64%	65.79%	70.88%
Preferred Stock/Capital	4.17%	4.00%	3.80%	3.60%	3.42%	3.21%
Beta	2.02547	1.87988	1.73426	1.62501	1.54349	1.4745
Cost of Equity	20.64%	19.84%	19.04%	18.44%	17.99%	17.61%
After-tax Cost of Debt	6.53%	6.53%	6.53%	6.53%	6.53%	5.00%
Cost of Preferred Stock	13.51%	13.51%	13.51%	13.51%	13.51%	13.51%
Cost of Capital	13.00%	13.29%	13.66%	14.00%	14.31%	14.21%

An alternative approach to estimating equity, which does not require iterations or circular reasoning, is to use the book value of equity rather than the estimated market value in calculating debt equity ratios.[9]

Step 3   *Calculate the terminal values of equity and the firm.* The cash flows to equity and the cost of equity in the terminal year (1985), in conjunction with the expected growth rate of 8%, are used to estimate the terminal value of equity (at the end of 1984):

$$\text{Terminal value of equity (end of 1984)} = \text{FCFE}_{1985}/(k_{e,1985}-.08)$$
$$= \$55.59/(.1761-.08) = \$578.48 \text{ million}$$

The terminal value of the firm at the end of 1984 is estimated by adding in the projected outstanding debt and preferred stock at that time.

$$\text{Terminal value of firm} = \$578.48 + \$211.45 + \$26.20 = \$816.13 \text{ million}$$

---

[9]The book value of equity can be obtained as follows:

$$BV = \text{Equity}_t = \text{BV of Equity}_{t-1} + \text{Net Income}_t$$

It is assumed that no dividends will be paid to equity investors in the initial years of a leveraged buyout.

Step 4 *Calculate the present value of cash flows to equity at the cost of equity and compare to the equity investment in the deal:*

PV of cash flows to equity = $275.39 million of cash flows to equity

= $275.39 million[10]

Equity investment in deal = $117.30 million

The deal makes sense from the viewpoint of equity investors. (The net present value of the deal is $158.09 million.)

Step 5 *Calculate the present value of cash flows to the firm at the cost of capital and compare to the total cost of the deal:*

PV of cash flows to firm = $638.35 million

Total cost of the deal = $470.60 million

The overall deal makes sense. (The net present value of the deal is $167.75 million.)

TAKEOVER VALUATION: BIASES AND COMMON ERRORS

The process of takeover valuation is fraught with potential pitfalls and biases arising from the desire of both the bidder and target firms' management to justify their points of view to their stockholders. The bidder firm aims to convince its stockholders that it is getting a bargain (i.e., that it is paying less than what the target firm is truly worth). In friendly takeovers, the target firm attempts to show its stockholders that the price it is receiving is a fair price (i.e., it is receiving at least what it is worth). In hostile takeovers, a role reversal takes place, with bidding firms trying to convince target firm stockholders that they are not being cheated out of their fair share and target firms arguing otherwise. Along the way, there are a number of common errors and biases that show up in takeover valuation.

Use of Comparables and Multiples

The prices paid in most takeovers are justified using the following sequence of actions. A group of firms comparable to the one being valued is assembled; a multiple is chosen as the basis for valuation; an average multiple is computed for the comparable firms; and subjective adjustments are made to this "average" to arrive at the appropriate multiple that can be used in valuing the target firm. Each of these steps provides an opening for bias to enter into the process. Because no two firms are identical, the choice of comparable firms is a subjective one and can be tailored to justify the conclusion the analyst wants to reach. Similarly, in choosing a multiple, there are a number of possible choices—price earnings ratios, price cash-flow ratios, price book value ratios, and price sales ratios, among others—and the multiple chosen will be the one that best suits the analyst's biases. Finally, once the average multiple is obtained, subjective adjustments can be made to complete the story. In short, a biased analyst can justify any price, using reasonable valuation models.

---

[10]In calculating present value, note that the cost of equity changes each year. Thus, each year's cash flow has to be discounted by the cumulated cost of equity over prior years. The cash flow in 1981 will be discounted back as follows:

PV of CF in 1981 = CF in 1981 $/(1 + k_{e,1980})*(1 + k_{e,1981})$

Similarly, the cash flow in 1982 will be discounted back using the cumulated costs of equity in 1980, 1981, and 1982.

☐ Concept
   Check

"In an acquisition, you have to pay a price comparable to that paid by other acquirers. Therefore, the correct multiple to use will depend on the multiples paid on recent acquisitions." Respond.

Mismatching Cash Flows and Discount Rates

A fundamental principle of valuation is that cash flows should be discounted using a consistent discount rate. Cash flows to equity should be discounted at the cost of equity and cash flows to the firm at the cost of capital; nominal cash flows should be discounted at the nominal discount rate and real cash flows at the real rate; after-tax cash flows at the after-tax discount rate, and pretax cash flows at the pretax rate. The failure to match cash flows with discount rates can lead to significant under- or overvaluation. Some of the more common mismatches include the following.

1. *Using the bidding firm's cost of equity to discount the target firm's cash flows:* If the bidding firm raises the funds for the takeover, it is argued, its cost of equity should be used. This argument fails to take into account the fundamental principle that it is not who raises the money that determines the cost of equity as much as what the money is raised for—the same firm will face a higher cost of equity for funds raised to finance riskier projects and a lower cost of equity to finance safer projects. Thus, the cost of funds raised to finance the acquisition of a target firm will reflect its riskiness; that is, it is the target firm's cost of equity.

2. *Using the cost of capital to discount the cash flows to equity:* If the bidding firm uses a blend of debt and equity to finance the acquisition of a target firm, the argument goes, the cost of capital should be used in discounting the target firm's cash flows to equity (cash flows left over after interest and principal payments). By this reasoning, the value of a share in IBM to an investor will depend on how the investor finances his or her acquisition of the share—increasing if the investor uses margin to buy the stock (since the cost of debt is less than the cost of equity) and decreasing if the investor buys the stock using his or her own cash. The bottom line is that discounting the cash flows to equity at the cost of capital to obtain the value of equity is always wrong and will result in a significant overvaluation of the equity in the target firm.

CONCLUSION

Valuing a firm for a takeover is not an easy task. In addition to all the complexities associated with standard valuation, other roadblocks have to be negotiated before arriving at a final answer. The first is the effect of synergy, assuming it exists and can be described in sufficient detail to be built into the valuation. The second is the impact on value of management changes in the firm; the potential increase in value is much larger for badly managed firms. The third is the effect on value of additional leverage that may be taken on to finance a takeover.

The entire question of valuation in takeovers is framed by the strong biases in the process to justify decisions that have already been made. The use of multiples and comparable firms provides plenty of opportunity for biases to enter the process. The time pressure under which many valuations are performed can also lead to serious errors in analysis. Finally, analysts doing a valuation for a takeover do not have the luxury of drawing on the law of large numbers to bail them out, unlike portfolio managers, who can choose to create portfolios of undervalued firms and hope that, on average, they come out ahead.

QUESTIONS AND PROBLEMS

1. Answer true or false to the following statements.
   a. If there is synergy, the value of the combined firm should be greater than the value of the companies operating independently.
   b. Combining two firms with volatile earnings will increase value because earnings will become more stable after the merger.
   c. When two firms merge and do not use their additional borrowing capacity, there will be a transfer of wealth from stockholders to bondholders.
   d. The empirical evidence suggests that merger gains are often overstated and fail to materialize in practice.
   e. Firms generally become more profitable after mergers, relative to other firms in the industry.

2. Answer true or false to the following questions.
   a. The value of control is greater for a badly managed firm than for a well-managed one.
   b. Shares with restricted voting rights should sell for as much as shares with no voting right restrictions, if no one is attempting to take over the firm.
   c. The empirical evidence suggests that the passage of anti-takeover amendments by a firm reduces its stock price.
   d. Takeover restrictions passed by the state should not affect stock prices since all firms will be covered by these restrictions.
   e. Hostile takeovers are bad for the economy because firms reduce investment, increase debt, and sell assets after these takeovers.

3. There is a common sentiment that mergers occur most frequently in an industry when that industry is undergoing rapid change. Given that many of the mergers in the early 1980s involved oil and tobacco companies, and that many recent mergers have involved media and financial service firms, does this sentiment seem to hold true? Explain your answer.

4. Mergers are often classified by whether they involve firms in entirely different industries (a *conglomerate merger*), firms that directly compete in the same industry (a *horizontal merger*), or firms where one firm acquires one of its suppliers or customers (a *vertical merger*). Would operating synergy usually be created in each type of merger? If so, how much (relative to the other types of mergers)?

5. Which of the three types of mergers is most likely to spark government intervention or regulation, and why?

6. American automobile manufacturers have recently "partnered" with Japanese manufacturers by investing heavily in each other. Though these partnerships only rarely take the form of a true merger, what type of operational synergy might be created?

7. American Hostels, a national hotel chain, is considering making a tender offer for Southern Inns, a smaller company. American anticipates that the acquisition would create synergy with a present value of $55 million. American calculates that Southern has a value of $370 million while operating independently and that the value of Southern's outstanding debt is $120 million. If Southern has 5 million shares outstanding, what is the maximum price per share that American should offer?

8. In the question above, assume that the value of $370 million for Southern while operating independently reflects the value *under current management* and that American's managers feel that they can increase the value of Southern to $500 million if they manage it. (This increase in value would be in addition to the synergy noted above). How much should American be willing to pay for Southern's stock?

9. In addition to the information in the last two problems, assume that American has already managed to acquire 4.95% of the outstanding shares of Southern and that the current price per share is $60. Assume that American can sell their current interest at the $60 per share price. How much should they be willing to pay for the remaining shares? Explain your answer.

10. If one firm buys another firm, the acquisition may be either taxable or nontaxable. Generally, if shareholders of the target firm receive cash in return for their shares (as is typical in a tender offer), the IRS will consider the shareholders to have realized capital losses or gains. Alternatively, if shareholders of the target firm receive shares in the acquiring firm (as is typical in many mergers), the IRS does not consider losses or gains to have been realized, and therefore imposes no taxes on the transaction. How will this affect the acquiring firm's decision as far as whether to offer cash or stock?

11. Assume that you own 100 shares of Sciatic, a small software development firm. When you read the *Wall Street Journal* this morning, Sciatic's shares were selling at $50. There are 10,000 shares outstanding, with most of those being held by small investors such as yourself. On the way to work, you hear on the radio that a group of outside investors have managed to acquire 20% of the firm and are attempting a hostile takeover. They are offering $75

a share for any and all outstanding shares. The analyst on the radio goes on to state that, due to the bidder's expertise at managing similar companies, the equity in the firm is expected to be worth $1 million if their bid is successful. Assume that there will be no tax effects if you sell your shares.

a. Should you sell your shares to the bidder?

b. What will happen if everyone makes the same sell/keep decision you do?

c. What does this imply about the bid price of successful takeover attempts?

12. The following are the details of two potential merger candidates, Northrop and Grumman, in 1993:

	Northrop	Grumman
Revenues	$4,400.00	$3,125.00
Cost of Goods Sold (w/o Depreciation) as % of Revenue	87.50%	89.00%
Depreciation	$200.00	$74.00
Tax Rate	35.00%	35.00%
Working Capital	10% of Revenue	10% of Revenue
Market Value of Equity	$2,000.00	$1,300.00
Outstanding Debt	$160.00	$250.00

Both firms are in steady state and are expected to grow 5% a year in the long term. Capital spending is expected to be offset by depreciation. The beta for both firms is 1, and both firms are rated BBB, with an interest rate on their debt of 8.5%. (The Treasury bond rate is 7%.)

As a result of the merger, the combined firm is expected to have a cost of goods sold of only 86% of total revenues. The combined firm does not plan to borrow additional debt.

a. Estimate the value of Grumman, operating independently.

b. Estimate the value of Northrop, operating independently.

c. Estimate the value of the combined firm, with no synergy.

d. Estimate the value of the combined firm, with synergy.

e. How much is the operating synergy worth?

13. In the Grumman–Northrop example described in question 12, the combined firm did not take on additional debt after the acquisition. Assume that, as a result of the merger, the firm's optimal debt ratio increases to 20% of total capital from current levels. (At that level of debt, the combined firm will have an A rating, with an interest rate on its debt of 8%.)

If it does not increase debt, the combined firm's rating will be A+ (with an interest rate of 7.75%).

a. Estimate the value of the combined firm if it stays at its existing debt ratio.

b. Estimate the value of the combined firm if it moves to its optimal debt ratio.

c. Who gains this additional value if the firm moves to the optimal debt ratio?

14. In April 1994, Novell, Inc. announced its plan to acquire WordPerfect Corporation for $1.4 billion. At the time of the acquisition, the relevant information on the two companies was as follows:

	Novell	WordPerfect
Revenues	$1,200.00	$600.00
Cost of Goods Sold (w/o Depreciation) as % of Revenue	57.00%	75.00%
Depreciation	$42.00	$25.00
Tax Rate	35.00%	35.00%
Capital Spending	$75.00	$40.00
Working Capital (as % of Revenue)	40.00%	30.00%
Beta	1.45	1.25
Expected Growth Rate in Revenues/ EBIT	25.00%	15.00%
Expected Period of High Growth	10 years	10 years
Growth rate After High-Growth Period	6.00%	6.00%
Beta After High-Growth Period	1.10	1.10

Capital spending will be offset by depreciation after the high-growth period. Neither firm has any debt outstanding. The Treasury bond rate is 7%.

a. Estimate the value of Novell, operating independently.

b. Estimate the value of WordPerfect, operating independently.

c. Estimate the value of the combined firm, with no synergy.

d. As a result of the merger, the combined firm is expected to grow 24% a year for the high-growth period. Estimate the value of the combined firm with the higher growth.

e. What is the synergy worth? What is the maximum price Novell can pay for WordPerfect?

15. Assume, in the Novell–WordPerfect merger described in question 14, that it will take five years for the firms to work through their differences and start realizing their synergy benefits. What is the synergy worth, under these circumstances?

a. In January, 1996, Novell Inc. announced plans to sell several of its word processing and spreadsheet software divisions, including WordPerfect, to Corel. Corel would give Novell 9.95 million shares of Corel common stock, and $10.75 million in cash for the divisions. Corel would also license a number of Novell technologies, and would pay a minimum of $70 million in royalties over the next five years. The total value of the deal was estimated at approximately $185 million. Novell had obviously found WordPerfect to be worth less than it thought. Look back at the Novell-WordPerfect merger described above and discuss which of the figures given may have led to such an extreme overvaluation of the worth of WordPerfect by Novell.

16. In 1996, Aetna, a leading player in health insurance, announced its intentions to acquire U.S. Healthcare, the nation's largest HMO, and provided synergy as a rationale. On the announcement of the merger, Aetna's stock price, which was $57, dropped by $2.50, while U.S. Healthcare's stock price surged from $31 to $37.50. Aetna had 400 million shares, and U.S. Healthcare had 50 million shares outstanding at the time of the announcement.

  a. Estimate the value that financial markets are attaching to synergy, if any, on this merger.

  b. How would you reconcile the market reaction to the rationale presented by management for the acquisition?

17. IH Corporation, a farm equipment manufacturer, has accumulated almost $2 billion in losses over the last seven years of operations and is in danger of not being able to carry forward these losses. EG Corporation, an extremely profitable financial service firm, which had $3 billion in taxable income in its most recent year, is considering acquiring IH Corporation. The tax authorities will allow EG Corporation to offset its taxable income with the carried-forward losses. The tax rate for EG Corporation is 40%, and the cost of capital is 12%.

  a. Estimate the value of the tax savings that will occur as a consequence of the merger.

  b. What is the value of the tax savings, if the tax authorities allow EG Corporation to spread the carried-forward losses over four years—that is, allow $200 million of the carried-forward losses to offset income each year for the next four years?

18. In the acquisition described in question 17 above between EG and IH Corporations, which firm's stockholders would you expect to claim the larger portion of the synergy tax benefits? Explain.

19. You are considering a takeover of PMT Corporation, a firm that has significantly underperformed its peer group over the last five years, and you wish to estimate the value of control. The data on PMT Corporation, the peer group, and the best managed firm in the group are as follows.

	PMT Corp.	Peer Group	Best Managed
Return on Assets (After-tax)	8.00%	12.00%	18.00%
Dividend Payout Ratio	50.00%	30.00%	20.00%
Debt/Equity Ratio	10.00%	50.00%	50.00%
Interest Rate on Debt	7.50%	8.00%	8.00%
Beta	Not Available	1.30	1.30

PMT Corporation reported earnings per share of $2.50 in the most recent time period and is expected to reach stable growth in five years, after which the growth rate is expected to be 6% for all firms in this group. The beta during the stable growth period is expected to be 1 for all firms. There are 100 million shares outstanding, and the Treasury bond rate is 7%. (The tax rate is 40% for all firms.)

  a. Value the equity in PMT Corporation, assuming that the current management continues in place.

  b. Value the equity in PMT Corporation, assuming that it improves its performance to peer group levels.

  c. Value the equity in PMT Corporation, assuming that it improves its performance to the level of the best managed firm in the group.

20. The managers of PMT Corporation are considering adopting an amendment to the corporate charter requiring a super-majority clause to replace the board of directors. They have hired you as a consultant and have asked for your advice on the effect such an amendment will have on their stock price and the likelihood that stockholders will acquiesce to the amendment.

  a. What would you advise management to do, in terms of the charter amendment?

  b. Would your advice be any different if you were a major stockholder in the firm?

21. You are attempting to do a leveraged buyout of Boston Turkey but have run into some roadblocks. You have some partially completed projected cash-flow statements and need help to complete them.

Year	1	2	3
Revenues	$1,100,000	$1,210,000	$1,331,000
(Less) Expenses	$440,000	$484,000	$532,400

Year	1	2	3
(Less) Deprec'n	$100,000	$110,000	$121,000
= EBIT	$560,000	$616,000	$677,600
(Less) Interest	$360,000	$324,000	$288,000
Taxable Income	$200,000	$292,000	$389,600
(Less) Tax	$80,000	$116,800	$155,840
= Net Income	$120,000	$175,200	$233,760

Year	4	5	Term. Year
Revenues	$1,464,100	$1,610,510	$1,707,141
(Less) Expenses	$585,640	$644,204	$682,856
(Less) Deprec'n	$133,100	$146,410	$155,195
= EBIT	$745,360	$819,896	$869,090
(Less) Interest	$252,000	$216,000	$180,000
Taxable Income	$493,360	$603,896	$689,090
(Less) Tax	$197,344	$241,558	$275,636
= Net Income	$296,016	$362,338	$413,454

The capital expenditures are expected to be $120,000 next year and to grow at the same rate as revenues for the rest of the period. Working capital will be kept at 20% of revenues. (Revenues this year were $1 million.)

The leveraged buyout will be financed with a mix of $1 million of equity and $3 million of debt (at an interest rate of 12%). Part of the debt will be repaid by the end of year 5, and the debt remaining at the end of year 5 will remain on the books permanently.

   a. Estimate the cash flows to equity and the firm for the next *five years*.

b. The cost of equity in year 1 has been computed. Compute the cost of equity each year for the rest of the period (use book value of equity for the calculation).

Item	1
Equity	1 million
Debt	3 million
Debt/Equity Ratio	3
Beta	2.58
Cost of Equity	24.90%

c. Compute the terminal value of the firm and of the equity alone.

d. Evaluate whether the leveraged buyout makes sense from the viewpoint of equity investors and the viewpoint of the entire deal.

22. J & L Chemical is a profitable chemical manufacturing firm. The business is highly cyclical, however, and the profits of the firm have been volatile. The management of the firm is considering acquiring a food processing firm to reduce the earnings volatility and its exposure to economic cycles.

a. Would such an action be in the best interests of its stockholders? Explain.

b. Would your analysis be any different if it were a private firm? Explain.

c. Is there any condition under which you would argue for such an acquisition for a publicly traded firm?

PART SIX

OTHER TOOLS AND TECHNIQUES

This final section looks at a diverse set of topics. Chapter 26 looks at the additional issues, such as currency and political risk, that arise as a consequence of investing in foreign markets. Chapters 27 and 28 develop the basics of option pricing and applications of option pricing models in corporate finance, including the options to expand and delay projects in investment analysis and the value of flexibility in financing decisions. Chapter 29 examines whether and how firms should manage risk, and Chapter 30 expands on the use of corporate financial models for small and private companies.

CHAPTER 26

INTERNATIONAL FINANCE

The principles of corporate finance do not change just because a project is a "foreign project" or because the financing for the project is in a different currency. A good project is always one that earns a return greater than the hurdle rate; using debt makes sense only if the firm has excess debt capacity, and dividends should be paid only if there are surplus cash flows. Certain issues relating to investment, financing, and dividend decisions are specific to nondomestic projects, however. In particular, we examine the following questions in this chapter:

• What are the determinants of changes in currency rates? How can they be used in forecasting expected cash flows in another currency and converting these cash flows into the domestic currency?

• Should investment analysis of foreign projects be done in the local currency or in the firm's domestic currency?

• Is the risk that arises from currency rate changes firm specific or market risk? Should firms adjust their hurdle rates to reflect this risk?

• What political and regulatory risk is associated with nondomestic projects, and how is this risk built into the analysis?

• When raising funds for nondomestic projects, what are the determinants of the details of this financing?

WHY CURRENCY RATES MOVE

One source of risk unique to international projects is **exchange rate risk**. A company may find its cash flows augmented or depleted by movements in exchange rates over time.

Exchange Rate Risk: This is the uncertainty created in expected cash flows in a domestic currency, as a result of unanticipated changes in currency rates.

Spot Rates and Forward Rates

Before we examine the theories on why exchange rates move over time, it is important that we define a few terms. The **spot rate** for a currency is the current rate at which that currency can be converted into another one. For example, a spot rate of $0.65 per deutsche mark (DM) indicates that one deutsche mark can be converted into $0.65 in the marketplace today. In the case of most currencies today, these spot rates are set by financial markets and are determined by demand and supply; thus, they are **floating rates**. The spot rates for some currencies, however, are set by the governments, these rates are known as **fixed rates**. If governments err in setting these rates, as they tend to do, they must either lower or raise these rates to realistic levels, thereby producing currency devaluations and revalutions.

Spot Rate: This is the current rate at which one currency can be converted into another one.

Floating and Fixed Exchange Rates: Floating exchanges rates are set by demand and supply, whereas fixed exchange rates are set by governments.

Frequently, firms or individuals enter into contracts to exchange currencies at a future date at rates that are set at the time of the contracts. These contracts are called **forward contracts**; the prices set in these contracts are called **forward prices**. **Futures contracts** represent a variant on forward contracts; the key distinctions are that futures contracts are standardized in terms of units and delivery dates, and that the parties to the contract are forced to settle their differences each day, rather than waiting for the final expiration date. Because they are traded on exchanges, the futures' price is determined by demand and supply, but should be closely related to the forwards' price.

Forward Contract (Price):   This is a contract to buy or sell a currency at a fixed price (called the forward price) some time in the future.

Finally, exchange rates can be stated in terms of either the number of units of domestic currency that can be received for a unit of the foreign currency, or vice versa. For instance, the exchange rate between dollars and deutsche marks can be stated either in U.S. terms ($0.65 per DM) or European terms (1.54 DM per $).

Purchasing Power Parity

Purchasing Power Parity (PPP):   Purchasing power parity posits that exchange rates should be set so that the same basket of goods will sell at the same price in different countries.

Purchasing power parity is founded on the common-sense principle that differences in inflation rates in two economies will cause the exchange rates between these economies to change. To be more specific, if one country experiences higher inflation than another, the currency of the first country will lose value relative to the second. This relationship, in turn, is built on the premise that a specific basket of goods should sell for the same price across different countries. Thus, if a bottle of wine costs $10 in the United States, it should cost the same in France, if the price in French francs is converted into dollars. If this were not true, economists argue, the possibility of arbitrage would exist, whereby some people would buy the good in the country in which it is cheaper and sell it in the country in which it is more expensive. More formally, if i_d is the inflation rate in the domestic currency and i_f is the inflation rate in the foreign currency, the change in exchange rates from one period to another can be written as follows:

$$\Delta \text{ Exchange Rate}_{d/f} = \frac{E(\text{SpotRate})_{d,f}}{\text{Spot Rate}_{d,f}} = \frac{(1 + i_d)}{(1 + i_f)}$$

where

Exchange Rate$_{d/f}$ = Number of units of the domestic currency for a unit of foreign currency

To provide a simple example, assume that the domestic inflation rate is 10% and the foreign inflation rate is 5%. It will take approximately 5% more of the domestic currency to buy a unit of the foreign currency next period.[1] In other words, the domestic currency will depreciate each period at a rate approximately equal to the difference between the domestic inflation rate and the foreign inflation rate if the domestic rate is higher, and appreciate at that rate if it is lower.

Purchasing power parity has often been criticized for its unrealistic assumption that goods can move freely (with no tariffs and costs) across borders, keeping exchange rates in line with inflation rates. Although this criticism is valid, the power of the argument holds over longer periods, even without this assumption. Thus, although exchange rates may not move as purchasing power parity suggests they should over short periods and for small differences in inflation rates, they clearly do move as predicted over longer periods and for larger differences in inflation rates.

❑ Concept
Check

Some currencies, such as the Mexican peso, the Brazilian real, and the Russian ruble, have depreciated dramatically over the last few years against the U.S. dollar. To what would you attribute this depreciation?

Fisher Equation: This equation sets the nominal interest rate equal to the sum of the expected inflation rate and expected real interest rate.

Fisher Effect

One of the fundamental propositions governing the behavior of interest rates over time is the **Fisher Equation,** which equates the nominal interest rate (R) to the sum of expected inflation rate (i) and the real rate (r).[2]

$$\text{Nominal Interest Rate} = R = i + r$$

Ideally, this equation should apply to both domestic and foreign markets:

$$\text{Nominal Interest Rate in Domestic Currency} = R_d = i_d + r_d$$
$$\text{Nominal Interest Rate in Foreign Currency} = R_f = i_f + r_f$$

It can be argued that real rates have to be equal across countries to prevent the flight of capital to those countries with higher real rates. If one makes this assumption, the purchasing power parity theorem can be modified in terms of nominal interest rates, rather than inflation. Formally, the expected change in exchange rates over a period can be written as follows:

[1]This is an approximate answer. The correct depreciation rate is 4.76% ($1.10/1.05 - 1 = .0476$).

[2]To be more precise, it equates $(1 + R) = (1 + i)(1 + r)$.

$$\Delta \text{ Exchange Rate}_{d/f} = \frac{\text{E(SpotRate)}_{d,f}}{\text{Spot Rate}_{d,f}} = \frac{(1 + R_d)}{(1 + R_f)}$$

This is called the **International Fisher effect**. Thus, countries with high nominal interest rates can expect their currency to depreciate over time, because these rates are indicative of high inflation.

International Fisher Effect: The international Fisher effect posits that the currency of a country with high interest rates will depreciate over time, relative to currencies of countries with low interest rates.

Studies that have looked at the relationship between changes in exchange rates and nominal interest rates over time are generally supportive of this proposition.

Critics of this proposition provide what they claim is counterevidence. When countries raise their interest rates, their currencies generally strengthen rather than weaken, which is at odds with this theory. They fail to take into account, however, that these increases in nominal rates may also be increases in real rates, which encourage the flow of capital to those countries and strengthens their currency. It is only when real rates are held constant across countries, which is much more feasible with longer time horizons, that we should expect to see the international Fisher effect.

Concept Check

Central to the international Fisher effect is the argument that capital flows across countries will equalize real rates. What might impede this process? What are the consequences for the international Fisher effect?

Interest Rate Parity

Although the international Fisher effect relates the expected change in the spot rate to the interest rate differential, the **interest rate parity** relates the same differential to the forward rate. In particular, the forward rate for a currency can be written as follows:

$$\frac{\text{Forward Rate}_{d,f}}{\text{Spot Rate}_{d,f}} = \frac{(1 + R_d)}{(1 + R_f)}$$

where Forward Rate$_{d,f}$ is the number of units of the domestic currency that will be received for a unit of the foreign currency in a forward contract, and Spot Rate$_{d,f}$ is the number of units of the domestic currency that will be received for a unit of the same foreign currency in a spot contract. It follows that if the domestic interest rate is higher than the interest rate in another country, the forward rate against that country's currency will be higher than the spot rate. Thus, if the domestic interest rate is 10% and the foreign rate is 5%, the forward contract will provide approximately 5% more of the domestic currency for every unit of the foreign currency than will the spot contract.

Interest Rate Parity: Interest rate parity posits that the forward rate between two currencies will be equal to the spot rate, adjusted for the interest rate differential between the currencies.

Interest rate parity has a much stronger relationship with exchange rate changes than either purchasing power parity or the international Fisher effect, especially over short periods, because deviations from it can be taken advantage of in financial markets; expected spot rates are not traded, whereas futures contracts are.

Arbitrage and interest rate parity: an illustration Assume that the one-year interest rate in the United States is 5% and that the one-year interest rate in Germany is 4%. Furthermore, assume that the spot exchange rate is $0.65 per deutsche mark. The one-year forward rate, based on interest rate parity, should be as follows.

$$\frac{\text{Forward Rate}_{d,f}}{\$0.65} = \frac{(1.05)}{(1.04)}$$

resulting in a forward rate of $0.65625 per deutsche mark. We will now illustrate the arbitrage that will be feasible if the forward rate deviates from this equilibrium price.

Forward rate > $0.65625 Assume that the forward rate is $0.67 per deutsche mark. The sequence of actions needed for the arbitrage is shown in Table 26.1.

Table 26.1 **ARBITRAGE ACTIONS WHEN FORWARD RATE IS TOO HIGH**

Action	Cash Flow
Now	
1. Sell a forward contract at $0.67 per deutsche mark.	$0.00
2. Borrow the spot rate in the U.S. domestic markets (@5%).	+ $0.65
3. Convert the dollars into deutsche marks at spot rate.	− $0.65/+ 1 DM
4. Invest deutsche marks in the German market (@ 4%).	− 1 DM
Net Cash Flow Now	$0.00
At the End of Year	
1. Collect on deutsche mark investment.	1.04 DM
2. Convert into dollars at forward rate.	− 1.04 DM to + $0.6968
3. Repay dollar borrowing with interest.	− $0.6825
Net Cash Flow	+ $0.0143

This arbitrage results in a riskless profit of $0.0143, with no initial investment. The process of this arbitrage will push forward rates down toward the equilibrium price.

Forward rate < $0.65625 Assume that the forward rate is $0.64 per deutsche mark. The sequence of actions that would be needed for the arbitrage is shown in Table 26.2.

Table 26.2 **ARBITRAGE ACTIONS IF FORWARD RATE IS TOO LOW**

Action	Cash Flow
Now	
1. Buy a forward contract at $0.64 per deutsche mark.	$0.00
2. Borrow the spot rate in the German market (@4%).	+ 1 DM
3. Convert the deutsche marks into dollars at spot rate.	− 1 DM/$0.65
4. Invest dollars in the U.S. market (@ 5%).	− $0.65
Net Cash Flow Now	$0.00

(continues)

(*continued*)	Action	Cash Flow
At the End of Year		
1. Collect on dollar investment.		$0.6825
2. Convert into dollars at forward rate.($0.64/DM)		− $0.6825/+1.0664 DM
3. Repay DM borrowing with interest.		− 1.04 DM
	Net Cash Flow	+ 0.0264 DM

This arbitrage results in a riskless profit of 0.0264 DM, with no initial investment. The process of this arbitrage will push forward rates up toward the equilibrium price.

Concept Check

> How will the arbitrage be affected if the arbitrageur can only lend at a rate lower than the risk-free rate and borrow at a rate that is higher? What are the implications for the arbitrage price?

Forward Rates and Expected Spot Rates

Taken together, the international Fisher effect and the interest rate parity theorem suggest that, in equilibrium, the forward rate should be equal to the expected spot rate:

$$\text{Forward Rate}_{d,f} = E\,(\text{Spot Rate}_{d,f})$$

The empirical evidence on this equation is mixed, however. Some earlier studies concluded that the forward rate was in fact an unbiased predictor of the spot rate and that there was no evidence of a risk premium. More recent studies find evidence of a risk premium, however, albeit one that changes signs from positive in some periods (with forward rates being less than expected spot rates) and negative in others.

Other Factors

All of the parity conditions laid out above for the relationship between current spot rates and expected spot rates are long-term conditions. In the short term, however, exchange rates may deviate from "equilibrium" levels for a number of reasons. One cause for such deviation is *speculation*. In the last few years, there have been several cases in which foreign exchange traders have speculated against a weak currency, driving it down, in many cases, well below equilibrium levels. In 1990 and 1991, for instance, foreign exchange traders in Europe sold the French franc and the British pound, while buying the deutsche mark; in the process, they weakened the Franc and the pound and made enormous profits. The sheer volume of the speculative trading often made it extremely risky for anyone to take short-term counter-positions, based on fundamentals. Counter to speculation is *intervention*, whereby central banks intervene and buy or sell their own currencies to maintain their value. In some cases, this intervention is in response to speculation and is designed to keep the currency from falling below what the central bank views as a "fair" level. In other cases, it is designed to move the exchange rate to what the central bank considers a "fairer"' level. Finally, central banks may attempt to set exchange rates at unrealistic levels for political or economic reasons; examples are concerted attempts to drive a currency's value down (below "fair market" levels) to help a country's exporters gain an advantage in foreign markets. Many Asian countries that are dependent on exports, such as Malaysia, Thailand, and Taiwan, have been accused of doing this from time to time.

We would argue that any attempt to drive currency rates away from their equilibrium values is unlikely to succeed in the long term. A firm with a long-term project in France should not worry about changes in the French franc which are based on factors other than fundamentals. These changes are likely to be transitory and are unlikely to affect the long-term prospects for the company.

EXCHANGE RATE RISK

It should be clear from the preceding section that exchange rates do move over time and that some of the change is unanticipated and has nothing to do with fundamentals. As a consequence, three questions arise:

1. What are the types of risk to which a firm may be exposed as a result of changing exchange rates?
2. To what other types of risk may a firm be exposed, as a consequence of its international operations?
3. Should firms try to manage or minimize these risks?

Decomposing Exchange Rate Risk

When a firm owns assets or has projects that create cash flows in a foreign currency, changes in exchange rates can affect the values of these assets and projects. Exchange rate risk is viewed and measured very differently by accountants and financial economists: accounting rules are designed to measure the effect of exchange rate changes on current income and the book values of assets and liabilities on the balance sheet, whereas economists are much more interested in the effects of exchange rate changes on future cash flows and the resultant effect on the value of the firm.

Translation exposure   From an accounting standpoint, the risk of changing exchange rates is captured in what is called **translation exposure,** which is the effect of these changes on the current income statement and the balance sheet. In making translations of foreign operations from the foreign to the domestic currency, two issues need to be addressed. The first relates to whether all financial statement items that are in a foreign currency should be translated at either the current exchange rate or the rate that prevailed at the time of the transaction. The second is whether the profit or loss that is created when the exchange rate adjustment is made should be treated as a profit or loss in the current period or deferred until a future period.

Translation Exposure: This is the effect of changing exchange rates on the current income statement and balance sheet of a company.

The accounting standards in the United States apply different rules for translation, depending on whether the foreign entity is a self-contained unit, in which case the **functional currency** is the foreign currency, or a direct extension of the parent company, in which case the functional currency is the U.S. dollar. For the first group, FASB 52 requires that all of an entity's assets and liabilities be converted into the parent's currency at the prevailing exchange rate. The increase or decrease in equity that occurs as a consequence of this translation is captured as an unrealized foreign exchange gain or loss and will not affect the income statement until the underlying assets and liabilities are sold or liquidated. For the second group, only the monetary assets and liabilities have to be converted, based on the prevailing exchange rate, and the net income is adjusted for unrealized translations gains or losses.

Functional currency: This is the currency in which all assets are denominated and income is measured.

Translation exposure matters from the narrow standpoint of affecting reported earnings and balance sheet values. The more important question, however, is whether investors view these translation changes as important in determining firm value or whether they view them as risk that will average out across companies and across time. The answers to these questions are mixed. In fact, several studies suggest that earnings effects caused by exchange rate changes do not influence the stock prices of firms. These findings add credence to the belief that investors view translation risk as diversifiable and do not demand a premium for it.

☐ Concept
  Check

> You have just reported a significant drop in earnings per share this quarter because of a shift in exchange rates, and your stock price does not drop. Is this evidence of an irrational market? How would you explain this phenomenon?

Economic exposure   While translation exposure is focused on the effects of exchange rate changes on financial statements, **economic exposure** attempts to look deeper at the effects of such changes on firm value. These changes, in turn, can be broken down into two types. *Transactions exposure* looks at the effects of exchange rate changes on transactions and projects that have already been entered into and that are denominated in a foreign currency. *Operating exposure* measures the effects of exchange rate changes on expected future cash flows and discount rates and, thus, on total value.

Economic Exposure: This is the effect of changes in exchange rates on the value of a firm.

Shapiro (1990) presents a time pattern for economic exposure, in which he notes that firms are exposed to exchange rate changes at every stage in the process, from developing new products for sale abroad to entering into contracts to sell these products to waiting for payment on these products. To illustrate, a weakening of the U.S. dollar will increase the competition among firms that depend on export markets and increase their expected growth rates and value, while hurting those firms that need imports as inputs to their production process.

Political and Regulatory Risk

Firms that operate in politically stable domestic markets often fear overseas expansion, because of the increased political risk that may be associated with operating in a politically less stable environment. The political risk can take many forms, ranging from bloody revolutions (e.g., the existing government is overthrown) to more limited changes (e.g., the basic laws and regulations are rewritten as a consequence of a political shift). The effects on the firm can also extend from expropriation, whereby the firm's assets are seized with no compensation, to a reduction in expected cash flows as a result of changing laws.

Certain factors help determine a country's political risk. A history of peaceful transition in power, a well-established system of laws whereby contracts are enforced, and continuity in laws and policy all seem to decrease a country's risk, although it can be

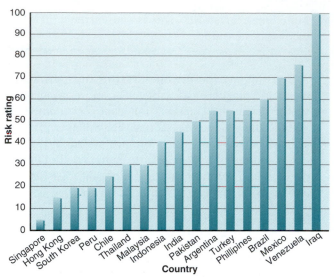

Figure 26.1   Country risk measures - *The Economist*, 12/94

argued that the difference between the more stable economies, such as the United States, and less stable ones, such as some of the emerging markets such as Brazil and Indonesia, is merely one of degree. Although the existence of political risk cannot be disputed, the measurement of political risk is still extremely subjective. *The Economist*, a respected international newsmagazine, does provide quarterly measures of political risk by country; its estimates for September 1995 are summarized in Figure 26.1.

Another risk firms face when they venture out of their domestic markets is the risk of operating in unfamiliar terrain, with different regulations and cultures. If ignored, these differences can end up costing the firm.

❑ Concept
   Check

> Suppose you have a choice between investing in a democracy, in which political power can shift quickly from one political party to another, with unpredictable effects on policy, and a dictatorship, in which the existing regime promises you stable policy. Which one has more political risk? Which one would you choose? Why?

Managing Exchange Rate and Other Risk

As the preceding section illustrates, exchange rate changes affect not only current income but also the value of the firm. In addition, a firm may be exposed to political and regulatory risk as it takes on projects in other countries. The followup questions then become:

1. Should firms try to manage or minimize their exposure to exchange rate, political, and other risk?

2. If they decide to do so, what products are available to help them hedge this risk?

Any time a firm enters into a transaction that exposes it to cash flows in a foreign currency, it is exposed to exchange rate risk. If the firm ventures into other countries, it creates additional political and regulatory risk for itself. The manager can leave the firm exposed to these risks and assume that the stockholders in the firm will be able to diversify away the risk, or the manager can hedge the risk, using a variety of financial instruments. This choice cannot be made without considering the following factors.

1. *Stockholder Composition*   For stockholders to be able to diversify away the foreign exchange risk that flows through to firms, they must be internationally diversified. Thus, an investor who holds Siemens and GE in the same portfolio may not be affected much by movements in the $/DM exchange rate, because of offsetting effects on his or her investments. If a firm's stockholders fit this profile, hedging exchange rate risk becomes much less of a priority. If, on the other hand, the stockholders in a firm are not internationally diversified, a much better argument can be made for diversifying exchange rate risk.

2. *Diversification Across Countries*   Some companies accomplish a diversification of a different kind, because they have economic exposures in many currencies. To illustrate, Citibank, with operations in more than 90 countries, is less likely to be concerned about hedging the exchange rate risk than, say, WalMart, whose only international investments are in Mexico.

3. *Cost of Hedging Risk*   Hedging foreign exchange risk exposure is cheaper in some currencies than in others and for shorter periods than for longer ones. Other things remaining equal, the greater the cost of hedging risk, the less likely firms will be to hedge. In terms of the types of exposure described above, firms are much more inclined to hedge translation and other short-term exchange rate risk exposure, because of the low cost of hedging. They are less inclined to hedge long-term exchange rate risk exposure and political risk, because the hedges are more difficult and much more expensive to acquire.

In summary, firms with limited foreign operations primarily domestic investors and short-term transactions exposures are likely to gain the most by hedging. Firms with far-flung foreign operations, internationally diversified investors, and long-term exchange rate risk exposures or political risk exposure should be much more cautious about hedging that risk.

In closing, it is worth pointing out that firms will always be exposed to the expected changes in exchange rates; it is only the *unexpected* component of the changes that is being hedged away. To illustrate, if the Home Depot opens a store in Mexico, and the expected annual inflation rate is 40% higher in Mexico than in the United States, the firm should expect the peso to depreciate about 40% a year. The *actual* exchange rate change may be very different for a number of reasons, however; among other factors, there may be political upheaval, and the actual inflation rate differential may turn out to be much higher or lower than the anticipated 40%. It is this component of the exchange rate change that can be hedged using forward, futures, or options contracts.

❑ Concept
Check

> Assume that you are advising the managers of a large publicly traded firm, in which the managers own a substantial chunk of the outstanding stock. Should this firm hedge exchange rate risk? Why or why not?

Hedging exchange rate and political risk   Firms can hedge exchange rate risk using money markets to borrow or lend in a foreign currency. For instance, a firm that has an obligation to pay 100 million DM in six months can buy a sufficient quantity of deutsche marks today and invest them at the German risk-free rate, thus eliminating its exposure to exchange rate risk. In recent years, a variety of financial instruments have also been offered to financial managers who are interested in hedging exchange rate risk, at least on transactions. The most widely used are the forward contracts, which we described earlier in this chapter. Firms can essentially enter into contracts that fix the exchange rate at which future cash flows will be converted into the domestic currency, eliminating the exchange rate risk component. For firms that do not want to pay the extra cost associated with tailoring a contract to meet their specific needs, an alternative is to use traded futures contracts to accomplish the same purpose. Although the hedge may be less than perfect in this case, it may still eliminate most of the exchange rate risk in a transaction. Finally, firms can use currency options to hedge risk—put options if they expect to get paid in a foreign currency, or call options if they expect to pay cash flows in a foreign currency.

Giddy (1983) suggests a simple rule that can be used to determine whether companies should use options or forward contracts to hedge risk. If the currency flow is known, Giddy argues, forward contracts provide much more complete protection and should therefore be used. If the currency flow is unknown, options should be used, since a matching forward contract cannot be created.

Although these approaches work well at hedging transactions and translation risk exposure, they generally do not do as well in hedging economic exposure. In those cases, firms either have to diversify across foreign markets, like Citicorp, or pass the risk through to their stockholders and hope that they can diversify the risk away.

A variety of financial instruments are available to help companies hedge foreign exchange risk, but far fewer choices are available to those firms that want to protect themselves against political risk. Insurance contracts can be bought for specific contingencies, such as a foreign government pulling out of an agreed-to transaction or the nationalization of a subsidiary, but these contracts tend to be expensive and imperfect in their protection. Here, again, firms will be better off diversifying across multiple markets and allowing investors to diversify away the political and other risks.

 IN PRACTICE   HEDGING TRANSACTIONS EXPOSURE AT BOEING

In December 1995, Boeing announced that Singapore Airlines had agreed to purchase 70 Boeing 777 planes between 1997 and 2004, at a total cost of Singapore $16.5 billion. Assume that the expected cash inflow will be in Singapore dollars and that the amounts are as shown in Table 26.3.

Table 26.3 EXPECTED CASH FLOWS FOR SINGAPORE AIRLINES CONTRACT	
Year	**Expected Inflow (Sing $)**
1997	1.5 billion
1998	3.0 billion
1999	2.5 billion
2000	3.5 billion
2001	3.0 billion
2002	3.0 billion

[The cash inflows are expected to be at the end of each year.]

Consider the expected cash inflow of $1.5 billion in 1997. There are several ways in which Boeing can insulate itself against unanticipated changes in the exchange rate between U.S. and Singapore dollars.

Approach 1: Money market approach   Assume that the two-year riskless interest rate in Singapore is 6.0% and that Boeing is able to lend at this rate. Boeing can do the following to hedge its risk:

Step 1: Calculate the present value of the expected cash inflow, using the two-year riskless rate in Singapore:

$$\text{Present Value of Expected Cash Inflow} = \text{S\$1.5 billion} / 1.06^2 = \text{S\$1.335 billion}$$

Step 2: Borrow S\$1.335 billion at the risk-free rate for two years and convert into U.S. dollars at the spot exchange rate.

Step 3: At the end of the second year, receive the cash inflow of S\$1.5 billion and use it to pay off the loan, with interest.

For this transaction to work, the following conditions need to hold:

1. The expected cash flow has to be guaranteed. In this case, because Singapore Airlines is partially owned by the Singapore government, this is not an unreasonable assumption.
2. The fact that the cash flow is guaranteed should enable Boeing to borrow at close to the risk-free rate, using the expected cash flow as security.
3. The currency has to be freely convertible into the domestic currency.

Approach 2: Use of forward contracts Boeing can also hedge its risk by using forward contracts. In this case, for instance, Boeing can sell a forward contract; that is, it can enter into a contract to sell S\$1.5 billion in two years at the forward rate. The forward rate will depend on the interest rate differential between the United States and Singapore. In December 1995, for instance, the two-year rate in Singapore was 6%, whereas in the United States it was 5%; the spot rate was U.S. \$0.70 per Singapore dollar.

$$\text{Forward Rate}_{\text{us\$,S\$}} \text{in year } t = \text{Spot Rate} \frac{(1 + \text{R}_d)^t}{(1 + \text{R}_f)^t}$$

$$= \$0.70 \frac{(1.05)^2}{(1.06)^2} = 0.6869$$

Boeing would therefore enter into a contract to sell S\$1.5 billion at US\$ 0.6869 per Singapore dollar in two years. It would then have guaranteed proceeds, in U.S. dollars, of the following:

$$\text{Expected Proceeds in two years} = \text{S\$1.5 billion} * 0.6869 = \$1.03035 \text{ billion}$$

This process can be repeated with all the other cash flows as well.

Approach 3: Purchase of a put contract Boeing can also buy a put contract, giving it the right to sell \$1.5 billion Singapore dollars in two years at a guaranteed price. The put contract will provide a floor price (which will be the strike price), but Boeing will have to pay for it up front. For instance, assume that Boeing wants to lock in the current spot rate of \$0.70 per Singapore dollar as the floor price and that a two-year put contract trades at \$0.02 cents per Singapore dollar. The steps involved are as follows:

Step 1: Buy two-year put contracts for \$1.5 billion Singapore dollars at \$0.02 cents per Singapore dollar. The cost of the put contract will then be \$30 million.

Step 2: At expiration, check the spot exchange rate. If the exchange rate is greater than \$0.70 per Singapore dollar, allow the option to expire unexercised. If it is less than the strike price (\$0.70), then exercise the option.

A put option is clearly a more expensive way of reducing exchange rate risk, because it allows the firm to profit on the upside, if the Singapore dollar strengthens more than expected, while protecting it on the downside, if it weakens.

❑ Concept
Check

Assume that you are worried about risk in the above transaction, but that you believe there is still a much greater chance that the Singapore dollar will strengthen rather than weaken. Would you use the forward contract or the put option? Why?

INVESTMENT ANALYSIS OF FOREIGN PROJECTS

Regardless of whether the project is domestic or foreign, the decision of whether or not to take a new project remains grounded in the expected cash flows and hurdle rates for that project. That said, there are unique issues that are associated with analyzing projects with cash flows in currencies other than the firm's domestic currency and that are based in a different country.

Estimating Cash Flows

In the earlier chapters on capital budgeting, we considered several examples of project analyses in which we estimated the cash flows and returns on projects over their lifetime. The process of estimating cash flows in non-domestic currencies for projects follows many of the same steps, but the analyst has to answer two key questions during the estimation process. The first relates to the currency in which the analysis is to be done; the cash flows can be estimated in either the domestic or the foreign currency. If the cash flows are to be estimated in the domestic currency, the exchange rate has to be forecast for future years and used to convert the expected cash flows. The second question relates to how the cash flows should be adjusted to reflect political risk and other constraints that are associated with operations in a different country. For instance, some countries have strict restrictions on cash withdrawals from projects taken within their jurisdiction; such restrictions have to be built into the cash-flow estimates on the project.

Exchange rate forecasts   From a purely mechanical standpoint, the only additional input needed for the estimation of cash flows of foreign projects is the expected exchange rate. In making these estimates, firms should draw heavily on the purchasing power and interest rate parity theorems outlined earlier in the chapter, where we noted the relationship among exchange rate changes over time, differences in inflation, and differences in interest rates. Three basic approaches can be used to obtain these exchange rate estimates for future periods:

1. If forward or futures contracts are traded, and forward (or futures) rates are available for the life of the project, the forward rates can be used as predictors of the expected spot rates. This is, by far, the most straightforward approach, because it requires no estimation on the part of the firm. The key problem, however, is that even when futures contracts are traded, they are available for shorter time periods, say, up to two or three years, whereas typical projects have much longer lifetimes.

2. When futures rates are not available for longer time horizons, the international Fisher effect can be used to estimate expected spot rates in the future. This, of course, requires the existence of long-term bond markets in both economies, where interest rates can be observed and used in the estimation.

3. When long-term interest rates are not available in one of the two countries, the final option is to draw on purchasing power parity. This requires estimating expected inflation rates in both countries for long periods and then using these rates to arrive at expected spot rates. Consequently, it is inherently more time consuming and noisy than the first two approaches.

Some firms use forecasting services to obtain exchange rate forecasts. Several studies have compared the forecasts from these services to those obtained from the parity theorems; they conclude that there is no evidence that the services outperform simple mechanical forecasts, especially in the long term.

A simple solution to this estimation problem may be to estimate all cash flows in the foreign currency, but, as we will see in the next section, the expected change in exchange rates will then have to be reflected in the discount rate.

IN PRACTICE   ESTIMATING CASH FLOWS ON THE HOME DEPOT STORE IN MEXICO

Assume that the Home Depot is considering opening a megastore in Mexico City, selling home improvement products. Table 26.4 provides estimates of the expected cash flows in Mexican pesos for the 10-year time horizon of the project.

Table 26.4   **ESTIMATED CASH FLOW FROM THE HOME DEPOT STORE IN MEXICO**

Year	Expected ATCF (in millions of pesos)
0	−1000
1	200
2	300
3	425
4	600
5	800
6	1,150
7	1,550
8	2,000
9	2,500
10	3,125

The current spot rate is $0.13 per peso.

Step 1:   Forecast exchange rates for the next 10 years, using the international Fisher effect. To do so, assume that the spot interest rate in Mexico is 35%, while the spot interest rate in the United States is 5%. For simplicity, assume that these rates apply for all 10 years.[3]

$$\text{Expected Exchange Rate in } t \text{ years} = \text{Spot Rate}\frac{(1 + R_d)^t}{(1 + R_f)^t}$$

$$\text{Expected Exchange Rate in 1 year} = \$0.13\frac{(1.05)}{(1.35)} = \$.1011111$$

The expected spot rates are then estimated for the remaining periods.

Step 2:   Convert the expected cash flows from pesos to U.S. dollars using the expected exchange rate, as shown in Table 26.5.

Although these cash flows do not themselves tell us whether this store is a "good" investment for the Home Depot, they will provide us with such an answer once we compare the returns provided by these cash flows against an appropriate "hurdle rate."

---

[3]In reality, the spot interest rates will have to be obtained for each period separately and the expected exchange rates estimated from these.

	Table 26.5 FORECASTED ATCF IN PESOS AND DOLLARS: HOME DEPOT STORE		
Year	Expected ATCF (in millions of pesos)	Exchange Rate	Expected ATCF (millions of $)
0	−1,000	0.13	$(130.00)
1	200	0.101111111	20.22
2	300	0.078641975	23.59
3	425	0.061165981	26.00
4	600	0.047573541	28.54
5	800	0.037001643	29.60
6	1,150	0.028779055	33.10
7	1,550	0.02238371	34.69
8	2,000	0.017409552	34.82
9	2,500	0.013540763	33.85
10	3,125	0.010531704	32.91

Adjusting cash flows for constraints   The normal assumption in estimating project cash flows is that the after-tax cash flow can be withdrawn by the firm and used elsewhere, presumably where returns are higher. Although this assumption is generally justified in regular projects, it may not hold in countries that *restrict cash withdrawals* from projects; the parent company might be forced either to leave the cash idle in the foreign currency or to invest it back into that country. This may not be an onerous assumption when numerous projects with excess returns are available in that country. It may end up costing the company, however, if it is forced to keep the proceeds in substandard projects until it can remit the cash. In such cases, only that portion of the cash that can be remitted each period should be considered in the capital budgeting analysis. Because the remaining cash earns below-market returns, this will make the project much less attractive.

The second factor to consider in estimating cash flows is *taxes*. The parent firm may find itself facing different tax obligations in the foreign country, and, domestically, depending on how much of the cash it chooses to transfer from the subsidiary to itself and how it does so. For instance, a U.S. firm that has a subsidiary in France will pay French taxes on the income the subsidiary makes. It may also have to pay domestic taxes if it remits the cash in the form of a dividend from the subsidiary to the parent. Depending on the tax rates in the two locales, and the laws on offsetting taxes paid in a foreign locale, the after-tax cash flows will vary as a function of the firm's remittance policy.

 IN PRACTICE ESTIMATING CASH FLOWS WITH TAXES AND REMITTANCE CONSTRAINTS: THE HOME DEPOT

Consider the above example of an investment by the Home Depot in Mexico. Assume that Mexico restricts companies from remitting any of the funds for the first five years of a project; after the five-year period, remittances are unrestricted. Furthermore, assume that the cash flows in the first five years will have to be invested at the below-market rate of 25% (the riskless rate is 35%). The effects on the project cash flows are shown in Table 26.6.

	Table 26.6 ATCF WITH REMITTANCE RESTRICTIONS: THE HOME DEPOT			
Year	Expected ATCF (in pesos)	ATCF—Remittance Restrictions	Exchange Rate	Expected ATCF ($)
0	−1,000	−1,000	0.13	$(130.00)
1	200	0	0.101111111	—

(continues)

| | Expected ATCF | ATCF—Remittance | | Expected |
| (continued) | (in pesos) | Restrictions | | ATCF ($) |
Year			Exchange Rate	
2	300	0	0.078641975	—
3	425	0	0.061165981	—
4	600	0	0.047573541	—
5	800	0	0.037001643	—
6	1,150	5260.351563	0.028779055	151.39
7	1,550	1,550	0.02238371	34.69
8	2,000	2,000	0.017409552	34.82
9	2,500	2,500	0.013540763	33.85
10	3,125	3,125	0.010531704	32.91

Although the net present values have not yet been computed, the net present value of this project will be lower because the unremitted cash flows are invested at below-market rates. This may mean that a project that is acceptable without remittance restrictions may become unacceptable with such restrictions.

Concept Check

In the above example, assume that you are allowed to keep unremitted cash in government securities, earning the riskless rate. Will your net present value still be affected negatively by the cash-flow restrictions?

Estimating Discount Rates

The other input needed for analyzing foreign projects is the hurdle rate. As with the cash flows, the basic principles continue to apply: If the cash flows being discounted are cash flows to the firm, the appropriate discount rate is the cost of capital, whereas if they are cash flows to equity, the appropriate discount rate is the cost of equity. Two additional factors have to be considered in estimating hurdle rates for foreign projects:

1. In what currency should the discount rates be estimated? In other words, which risk-free rate (domestic or foreign) and risk premium should be used to arrive at the cost of equity, and which borrowing rate (domestic or foreign) should be used for the cost of debt?

2. Should there be any adjustment to the cost of equity and the cost of capital, upward or downward, to reflect differences in risk between domestic and foreign projects?

The answer to the first question is straightforward: the rules of consistency that require us to match cash flows to discount rates require us also to match the currency in which the cash flows are estimated to the discount rate used; that is, if the cash flows are estimated in the domestic currency, the discount rate also has to be measured using domestic units, whereas if the cash flows are estimated in the foreign currency, the discount rate also has to be estimated using the risk-free rate and risk premium in that currency. Done right, these discount rates will reflect the differences in nominal rates in the two countries.

The answer to the second question is more difficult to come by. On the one hand, some analysts argue that taking a project in another country allows the company to diversify across economies and thus reduce risk, suggesting that the discount rate (in domestic unit terms) should be lower for foreign projects. This argument is based on the assumption that investors in the firm's stock cannot accomplish this diversification themselves. On the other hand, there are those who advocate the use of a higher discount rate to reflect the additional risks associated with taking on projects in other countries. In particular, they note that foreign projects expose firms to exchange rate and political risk. Here, again, the assumption is that investors cannot accomplish the diversification themselves.

Overall, the question of whether or not discount rates should be different for foreign projects cannot be answered without looking at the stockholders in the firm and the availability of instruments to hedge risk. If stockholders are well diversified internationally and firms can hedge risk at low cost, it can be argued that exchange rate risk should not affect discount rates. Because financial instruments to hedge exchange rate risk are more easily accessible than are those that hedge political risk, the former should be much less likely to affect discount rates than the latter.

If we decide that a risk premium should be attached to discount rates to reflect the political or other risk that cannot easily be diversified away, the magnitude of the premium has to be estimated. These premiums can be estimated in two ways, though neither is perfect. The first approach is to use the historical premiums earned by stocks in that country, relative to domestic stocks, and to assume that this premium will continue to be a reasonable proxy for future premiums. The problem with this approach is that there is not much reliable historical data in many markets outside of the United States, and the numbers that come out of short time periods can be misleading. The second approach is to use the country bond ratings assigned by ratings agencies (Figure 26.2) as a way of estimating their political risk. Because ratings are linked to default spreads, these spreads can be used as a proxy for the risk premium for investing in real projects in a country. To illustrate, assume that the Home Depot is considering a project in Mexico, that Mexico has a BBB rating from the agencies, and that BBB bonds in the United States carry a default spread of 1.5% over the Treasury bond rate. This spread can be added on to the company's dollar cost of capital to reflect the additional risk associated with investing in Mexico. Thus, if the cost of capital for U.S. stores is 12.5%, the cost of capital for Mexican stores will be 14%.

Country Bond Rating: This is default risk rating assigned to a country's obligations by a rating agency such as Standard and Poor's.

IN PRACTICE   ESTIMATING AND USING DISCOUNT RATES FOR THE HOME DEPOT PROJECT IN MEXICO

Based on the reasoning in the preceding section, assume that the Home Depot decides to use a dollar cost of capital of 14% for its Mexican stores. The net present value of the project can be computed as shown in Table 26.7.

This project has a positive net present value.

The same analysis could have been done in Mexican peso terms. The cost of capital in peso terms is as follows:

$$\text{Cost of Capital in peso terms} = (1 + \text{Cost of Capital (\$)})$$
$$* \text{Expected appreciation in \$/Peso}$$
$$= 1.14 * (1.35/1.05) - 1 = 46.57\%$$

The present value can then be computed as shown in Table 26.8.

The net present value of 124.23 million pesos can be converted at the current exchange rate of $0.13 per peso to yield the same net present value as that obtained using the dollar cash flows and the dollar cost of capital.

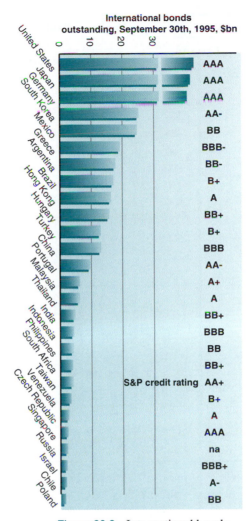

Figure 26.2   International bonds

Year	Expected ATCF (in pesos)	Exchange Rate	Expected ATCF ($)	PV in Dollars (@ 14%)
0	−1,000	0.13	(130.00)	(130.00)
1	200	0.101111111	20.22	17.74
2	300	0.078641975	23.59	18.15
3	425	0.061165981	26.00	17.55
4	600	0.047573541	28.54	16.90
5	800	0.037001643	29.60	15.37
6	1,150	0.028779055	33.10	15.08
7	1,550	0.02238371	34.69	13.87
8	2,000	0.017409552	34.82	12.21
9	2,500	0.013540763	33.85	10.41
10	3,125	0.010531704	32.91	8.88
			NPV =	$16.15

Table 26.7   PRESENT VALUE IN DOLLARS OF THE HOME DEPOT MEXICO STORE

Table 26.8 **PRESENT VALUE IN PESOS—THE HOME DEPOT MEXICO STORE**

Year	Expected ATCF (in pesos)	Exchange Rate	Expected ATCF ($)	PV in Pesos
0	−1,000	0.13	(130.00)	−1,000
1	200	0.101111111	20.22	136.4522417
2	300	0.078641975	23.59	139.644107
3	425	0.061165981	26.00	134.9711561
4	600	0.047573541	28.54	130.0031775
5	800	0.037001643	29.60	118.2615
6	1,150	0.028779055	33.10	115.9850238
7	1,550	0.02238371	34.69	106.6562851
8	2,000	0.017409552	34.82	93.89347867
9	2,500	0.013540763	33.85	80.07484779
10	3,125	0.010531704	32.91	68.28995304
			NPV =	124.2317706

$$\text{NPV in \$ terms} = \text{NPV in peso terms} * \text{Current \$/peso rate}$$
$$= 124.2317706 * 0.13 = \$16.15 \text{ million}$$

 Concept Check

Using these discount rates, estimate the net present value of this project with the remittance restrictions. How would you explain the difference?

THE FINANCIAL MIX FOR FOREIGN PROJECTS

In Chapters 15 through 19, we looked at a series of questions relating to the optimal mix of debt and equity for projects. Much of that discussion is still relevant when considering foreign projects, but here we will concentrate on those factors that might affect the optimal financing mix for these projects.

The Choices

When firms decide to go outside their domestic markets to raise capital, to finance either international or domestic operations, they open up new financing options, some of which may provide opportunities to save on costs. They include the following:

1. Firms can have their equity listed and traded on the exchanges of other countries. By doing so, they may be able to expand the potential market for their stock, but they will have to meet the security listing requirements of the foreign market. Several leading U.S. companies (including Ford, GM, GE, and IBM) have their stock listed on the London and Tokyo exchanges. Similarly, many companies from outside the United States, such as Glaxo Wellcome, Daimler Benz, and Toyota, have their stock listed and traded on the U.S. exchanges, where they are called **American Depository Receipts (ADRs).**

American Depository Receipt (ADR): This is the stock of a foreign company that is denominated in dollars and traded on a U.S. stock exchange.

2. Firms that have access to foreign markets often have a choice when it comes to short-term borrowing. They can borrow either domestically or in an overseas market. Firms in the United States, for instance, can borrow short term in dollars on the Eurodollar market, sometimes at rates that are lower than those on domestic borrowing, largely as a consequence of differences in regulation and taxes across the markets.

3. *Firms also expand their long-term borrowing options because they can issue* **Eurobonds**—*bonds denominated in one currency and traded simultaneously on several European bond markets.* These bonds are not subject to the same restrictions as domestic offerings. Thus, large firms with access to multiple markets may be able to raise funds at a lower rate.

Eurobonds: These are corporate bonds that are denominated in one currency (say DM) and traded on several European markets.

4. *An alternative to Eurobonds is* **foreign bonds**, *whereby a company issues bonds in a market other than its own and generally in the foreign currency.* Thus, Ford can issue bonds denominated in deutsche marks, in Germany or denominated in pounds in the United Kingdom. These bonds generally have nicknames that are suggestive of the country in which they are listed—Samurai bonds for Japan; Bulldog bonds for the United Kingdom; and Yankee bonds for the United States.

Foreign Bonds: These are bonds issued by a company in a market other than its own, generally in the foreign currency.

The availability of these choices is likely to reduce the ultimate costs that firms pay for raising funds.

Concept Check

Under what conditions might a firm get better terms issuing foreign bonds? Alternatively, under what conditions should a firm stick with domestic bonds?

The Optimal Financing Mix

What does venturing into foreign markets do to the optimal debt ratio for a company? Looking back at the tradeoffs we made to arrive at the optimal debt ratio, we noted that adding debt provided significant tax benefits, which were related to the tax rate and exposed the firm to bankruptcy risk, which, in turn, was related to the variability of its cash flows. When a firm takes on foreign projects, it affects many, if not all, of the variables in this tradeoff:

1. *The tax rate for earnings generated on overseas projects may be very different from the tax rate for earnings on domestic projects.* Although the tax offset available to most firms for the overseas taxes they pay provides partial protection against double taxation, firms will still have to pay more in taxes if the overseas tax rate is higher. Furthermore, if firms are allowed to deduct interest expenses against income, they might be tempted to shift more of their debt to the high tax rate locales, in order to maximize their tax benefits.

2. *As firms diversify across countries, they might affect the variability of their earnings; diversification will generally reduce the volatility, whereas the exchange rate risk will increase it.* If they are able to hedge the latter at little cost, using forwards and futures, the firms might be able to increase their debt capacity.

3. *Firms that have access to capital in multiple markets may be able to monitor these markets and may find some bargains, in terms of lower borrowing rates.* These benefits have to be balanced against the regulatory constraints involved in entering some of these markets and against any differences in reputations across borders. Thus, Siemens might be able to borrow at a lower rate in Germany, because of its name recognition and higher profile in that country than in the United States.

Generally speaking, we should expect to see optimal debt ratios increase with international diversification. We should also observe a greater willingness to use foreign currency debt, partly to match up to the cash flows on the projects being financed and partly to take advantage of differences in tax rates across countries.

VALUATION

The final issue we will examine in this chapter is the effect of a firm's international operations on its value. Because valuation can be considered an extension of capital budgeting, many of the same principles apply. The expected cash flows to a firm have to be estimated in the domestic currency, which requires that the cash flows from foreign operations be forecast first and then converted using expected exchange rates. Because the total cash flows from foreign operations can be viewed as the cash flows from a portfolio of foreign projects, one advantage analysts have while doing valuation, as opposed to a single capital budgeting project, is that forecast errors in exchange rates may average out, especially if the firm has projects in a large number of countries. The discount rate used to obtain the present value can be adjusted for diversification benefits (which will push it down) and for exchange rate and political risk (which will push it up), taking into account the magnitude of the foreign operations relative to firm value.

To illustrate, the valuation of Boeing in Chapter 23 was based on estimated cash flows in dollar terms and a dollar discount rate. In reality, more than 50% of Boeing's revenues in future years will come from sales overseas, which will expose Boeing to exchange rate and also political risk in foreign countries and provide international diversification benefits. The expected growth rate in Boeing's earnings and the discount rates used should reflect these effects. As exchange rates move from period to period, the actual earnings may deviate from the expected earnings, even if all the other assumptions hold; these deviations should partially average out over the long time horizon that is used in valuation. If stockholders are well diversified internationally, they will not demand an extra premium for this risk, and discount rates will not need to be adjusted. Alternatively, if stockholders are not well diversified, and they perceive the exchange rate risk as a market risk, the discount rate can be adjusted upward to reflect the additional exchange rate risk. In the case of Boeing, we would argue that the first view is the more realistic one, for it has always depended on overseas sales and is substantially held by institutions. Consequently, we would make no adjustment to the discount rate in doing the valuation.

There is some evidence that there is still a "home bias" in the portfolios held by individuals, whereby domestic holdings in portfolios exceed what they should be, given that a truly diversified investor will hold investments from around the world, in proportion to their market value. As long as this home bias exists, a risk premium will probably be associated with overseas expansion and the exchange rate risk that accrues to firms.

CONCLUSION

As the international operations of firms expand, it is worth remembering that the principles of corporate finance continue to hold. In this chapter, we made the following points:

- Exchange rates will move over time, partly because of shifts in fundamentals, such as interest rates and inflation rates, and partly because of other factors, such as speculation, and central bank intervention.

- When exchange rates move, firms that are exposed to cash flows in foreign currencies will be affected, creating additional variability in the cash flows. Although firms can hedge some or all of this variability, they should do so only if the cost of hedging is low and their stockholders are not internationally diversified.

- When it comes to hedging exchange rate risk, firms have a variety of choices, ranging from traded securities, such as futures and options, to lending and borrowing in the money market.

- In analyzing foreign projects, firms have to forecast exchange rates and convert future cash flows into the domestic currency. The net present value can then be computed using a discount rate that may have an added premium for the political and other risk associated with the foreign investment.

- When firms venture out of their own borders, they expand their choices in terms of financing and may alter their optimal debt ratios, partly because of the effect foreign investments have on tax rates and partly because of the effects on cash-flow variability of international diversification.

QUESTIONS AND PROBLEMS

1. The dollar/peso rate is $0.13 per peso right now. The expected inflation rate in the United States is 3%, whereas the corresponding inflation rate in Mexico is 35%.

   a. Estimate the expected spot rate one year from now.

   b. If expected inflation rates remain unchanged, estimate the expected spot rate two years from now.

   c. Now assume that the expected inflation rate in the second year will drop to 20% in Mexico, while remaining at 3% in the United States. Estimate the expected spot rate two years from now.

2. The following table is extracted from *The Economist* and summarizes actual inflation rates and changes in currency rates over the last year. Using these data, test the purchasing power parity proposition. What would you conclude?

Currency	Inflation Rate (%)	Change in $ versus Currency (%)
China	12.10	3.35
Indonesia	20.60	4.96
Malaysia	10.10	2.39
Singapore	1.30	−4.08
South Korea	2.40	−3.39
Japan	2.00	−2.96
Taiwan	2.90	0.41

Currency	Inflation Rate (%)	Change in $ versus Currency (%)
Thailand	6.60	2.10
Philippines	11.00	8.71
India	10.10	11.90
United States	2.80	

3. The U.S. dollar is trading at $0.85 per Swiss franc. The one-year interest rate in the United States is 5%, whereas the one-year rate in Switzerland is 3.50%.

   a. Estimate the forward rate in $/Swiss franc.

   b. Assume that the actual one-year forward rate is $0.84 per Swiss franc. How would you take advantage of this misplacing?

4. The U.S. dollar is trading at $1.56 per British pound, and the one-year forward rate is $1.55 per British pound. If the one-year interest rate in the United States is 5%, estimate the one-year interest rate in Britain.

5. The following table lists exchange rates for the U.S. dollar against six major currencies, and the one-year

Currency	Exchange Rate $/ Unit of Currency	One-year Interest Rate (%)
Canada	$0.73	5.57
France	0.21	5.50
Germany	0.71	3.95

Currency	Exchange Rate $/ Unit of Currency	One-year Interest Rate (%)
Italy	0.06	10.75
Japan	0.99	2.35
UK	1.56	6.69
United States	1.00	5.00

interest rates prevailing in December 1995.

   a. Estimate the expected spot exchange rates one year from now, based on these data.

   b. Why might the actual exchange rates deviate from these expected rates?

6. You are estimating cash flows for a store that the Limited plans to open in Germany. The expected cash flows have been projected in deutsche marks for this store and are summarized below:

Year	Cash Flows in DM
0	−15,000
1	1,350
2	1,485
3	1,634
4	1,797
5	1,977
6	2,174
7	2,392
8	2,631
9	2,894
10	3,183

The current exchange rate is $0.65 per DM, and the interest rate in the United States is 5%; it is 4% in Germany. (You can assume that these are the spot rates for 1- to 10-year bonds.)

   a. Estimate the expected cash flows in U.S. dollars.

   b. Assume that the Limited uses a cost of capital of 12% for U.S. stores. Would you adjust this for the German store. Why or why not?

   c. Calculate the net present value of the store, in dollar terms.

   d. Calculate the net present value of the store, in DM terms.

7. In estimating discount rates for foreign projects, firms should weigh the exchange rate and political risk associated with these projects against the diversification benefits that may accrue from these projects. Comment.

8. A small private firm and a large publicly traded firm with institutional stockholders are both considering expanding their operations in China. Would you expect them to view the expansion risk similarly? If so, why? If not, why not? How would these differences be reflected in investment analysis?

9. Sprint is considering a major investment in China, and it has estimated its cash flows in Chinese yuan for the life of the project, as shown in the following table.

Year	CF in Chinese Yuan
0	(1,600)
1	(800)
2	(1,000)
3	150
4	300
5	500
6	650
7	800
8	900
9	1,000
10	1,100
11	1,210
12	1,331
13	1,464
14	1,611
15	1,772

The current exchange rate is 8.5 Chinese yuan for every U.S. dollar. In the absence of an active bond market, Sprint is forced to rely on purchasing power parity to estimate expected exchange rates. The expected inflation rate is 3% in the United States and 12% in China.

   a. Estimate the cash flows in U.S. dollars.

   b. Sprint has a cost of capital of 10% for U.S. projects. China is rated BBB by the ratings agencies, and BBB rated bonds trade at a premium of 1.5% above the U.S. Treasury bond rate currently. What would you use as the discount rate for the Chinese project?

   c. Estimate the net present value of the project.

   d. An analyst who looks at your analysis argues that it should be done entirely in the foreign currency rather than in U.S. dollars. How would you respond?

10. Both companies and individuals may be subject to exchange rate risk; companies because they may buy resources, sell products, or manufacture goods in a foreign country, and individuals because they may buy goods produced in a foreign country or because they may work for a company subject to exchange rate risk. To understand the risks they face, consider the following

questions:

a. What is meant by a "weak dollar"?

b. Who is hurt by a weak dollar?

c. Who benefits from a weak dollar?

11. In 1995, Bililly & Co., a major manufacturer of pharmaceuticals, reported much higher earnings in 1995 than in 1994. Most of the increase was due to an increase in revenue from foreign sales. The dollar had been steadily weakening against all other foreign currencies throughout 1995. Should Bililly's stock react to the higher earnings?

12. If the inflation rate in Japan is expected to be greater than the inflation in the United States for an indefinite period and the real interest rates in each country are equal, what would happen to the spot rate for dollars per yen over time?

13. A trade deficit occurs when a country imports more goods than it exports. In return, the exporting country acquires a large amount of the importing country's currency. What is likely to be the effect on the exchange rate between the two countries' currencies? Explain.

14. Futures contracts are traded on organized exchanges, and the exchange itself guarantees the performance of the parties involved. Forward contracts are traded over-the-counter (OTC), and no such guarantee is made. Does this difference imply that forward and futures contracts will have differ-

ent risks? Explain.

15. Futures and forward contracts also differ in that parties to a futures contract are forced to settle their differences ("marked to market") every day while forward contracts are settled only at termination. Does this difference also imply that forward and futures contracts will have different risks? Explain.

16. If the current spot rate for dollars per DM is $.65/DM, what is the current spot rate for DM per dollar?

17. If the current spot rate for dollars per DM is $.65/DM and the current spot rate for pounds per DM is £.43/DM, what should be the current spot rate for dollars per pound?

18. Continuing the previous problem, assume that the actual spot rate for dollars per pound is $1.55/£. If your wealth is currently in dollars, how would you take advantage of this mispricing? How much would you earn per dollar invested?

19. The Japanese yen is trading at ¥105.61 per US dollar, and the forward rate is ¥106.5 per dollar. The one-year interest rate in Japan is 7% and the one-year interest rate in Germany is 7.25%. If you can currently receive 1.5285 DM per US dollar, what is the exchange rate expected to be one year from now?

CHAPTER 27

OPTION PRICING THEORY

Options are derivative securities; that is, they are securities that derive their value from an underlying asset. Although traded options are of comparatively recent origin, option-like securities have existed for a very long time. In this chapter, we look at a number of questions relating to the determinants of option value:

- What are the characteristics of call or put options?
- What are the determinants of option value?
- What are the basic option pricing models, and on what assumptions are they built? In particular, what is a replicating portfolio and how can it help in pricing options?

The technology available for valuing options has expanded dramatically in the last 25 years, especially since the development of the basic option pricing model by Black and Scholes. Their model, though setting the general framework for valuing options, has been modified to work in a variety of settings. An alternative model for option pricing, the binomial model, provides more insight into the determinants of option value.

WHAT IS AN OPTION?

An option provides the holder with the right to buy or sell a specified quantity of an *underlying asset* at a fixed price (called a *strike price* or an *exercise price*) at or before the expiration date of the option. Because it is a right and not an obligation, the holder can choose not to exercise the right and allow the option to expire. There are two types of options *call options* and *put options*.

Call Options

A **call option** gives the buyer of the option the right to buy the underlying asset at a fixed price, called the **strike** or **exercise price,** at any time prior to the expiration date of the option; the buyer pays a price for this right. If at expiration the value of the asset is less than the strike price, the option is not exercised and expires worthless. If, on the other hand, the value of the asset is greater than the strike price, the option is exercised—the buyer of the option buys the stock at the exercise price, and the difference between the asset value and the exercise price comprises the gross profit on the investment. The net profit on the investment is the difference between the gross profit and the price paid for the call initially. Table 27.1 summarizes the transactions involved in a call option.

Call Option: A call option gives its holder the right to buy the underlying asset at a fixed price any time before the expiration of the option.

Strike Price: This is the price at which the holder of a call (put) option can buy (sell) the underlying asset any time before expiration.

Table 27.1 A SUMMARY OF TRANSACTIONS IN A CALL OPTION		
	Now	**At Expiration**
Buyer of call	Pays the call price and gets the right to exercise	If asset value (S) > Strike price (K) buyer exercises Gross profit = $S - K$ Net profit = $S - K$ - Call price
Seller of call	Receives the call price and agrees to deliver the asset at the exercise price if the buyer demands it anytime before expiration.	If asset value < strike price buyer does not exercise Buyer's Loss = Call price Seller's gain = Call price

A **payoff diagram** illustrates the cash payoff on an option at expiration. For a call, the net payoff is negative (and equal to the price paid for the call) if the value of the underlying asset is less than the strike price. If the price of the underlying asset exceeds the strike price, the gross payoff is the difference between the value of the underlying asset and the strike price, and the net payoff is the difference between the gross payoff and the price of the call. This is illustrated in Figure 27.1.

Payoff Diagram: A payoff diagram shows the cash flows on a call or put option as a function of the price of the underlying asset at expiration.

Put Options

A **put option** gives the buyer of the option the right to sell the underlying asset at a fixed price, again called the strike or exercise price, at any time prior to the expiration

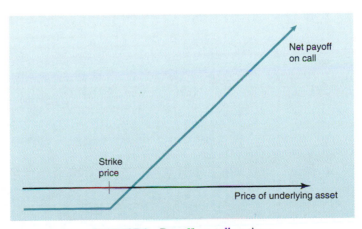

Figure 27.1   Payoff on call options

date of the option. The buyer pays a price for this right. If the price of the underlying asset is greater than the strike price, the option will not be exercised and will expire worthless. If, on the other hand, the price of the underlying asset is less than the strike price, the owner of the put option will exercise the option and sell the asset at the strike price, claiming the difference between the strike price and the market value of the asset as the gross profit. Again, netting out the initial cost paid for the put yields the net profit from the transaction. Table 27.2 summarizes the transactions involved in a put.

Table 27.2 A SUMMARY OF TRANSACTIONS IN AN PUT OPTION		
	Now	**At Maturity**
Buyer of put	Pays the put price and gets the right to exercise	If asset value(S) < strike price (K) buyer exercises Gross profit = $K - S$ Net profit = $K - S -$ Put price
Seller of put	Receives the put price and agrees to buy the asset at the exercise price if the buyer demands it	If asset value > strike price buyer does not exercise Buyer's Loss = Put price Seller's gain = Put price

Put Option: A put option gives its holder the right to sell the underlying asset at a fixed price any time before the expiration of the option.

A payoff diagram   A put has a negative net payoff if the value of the underlying asset exceeds the strike price, and it has a gross payoff equal to the difference between the strike price and the value of the underlying asset if the asset value is less than the strike price. This is depicted in Figure 27.2.

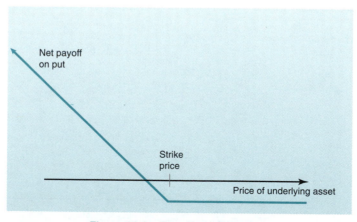

Figure 27.2   Payoff on put option

DETERMINANTS OF OPTION VALUE

The value of an option is determined by a number of variables relating to the underlying asset and financial markets.

Variables Relating to the Underlying Asset

Current value of the underlying asset   Options are assets that derive value from an underlying asset. Consequently, changes in the value of the underlying asset affect the value of the options on that asset. Because calls provide the right to buy the underlying asset at a fixed price, an increase in the value of the asset will increase the value of the calls. Puts, on the other hand, become less valuable as the value of the asset increases.

Variance in value of the underlying asset   The buyer of an option acquires the right to buy or sell the underlying asset at a fixed price. The higher the variance in the value of the underlying asset, the greater the value of the option. This is true for both calls and puts. Although it may seem counterintuitive that an increase in a risk measure (variance) should increase value, options are different from other securities for buyers of options can never lose more than the price they pay for them. In fact, they have the potential to earn significant returns from large price movements.

Dividends paid on the underlying asset   The value of the underlying asset can be expected to decrease if dividend payments are made on the asset during the life of the option. Consequently, the value of a call on the asset is a *decreasing* function of the size of expected dividend payments, and the value of a put is an *increasing* function of expected dividend payments.

☐ Concept
Check

> In Chapter 20, on dividends, we noted that stock prices tend to increase when dividends increase and drop when dividends decrease. How would you reconcile that conclusion with the above statement that the value of the underlying asset generally decreases more with higher dividends?

Variables Relating to the Option Characteristics

Strike price of option   A key characteristic used to describe an option is the strike price. In the case of calls, where the holder acquires the right to buy at a fixed price, the value of the call will decline as the strike price increases. In the case of puts, where the holder has the right to sell at a fixed price, the value will increase as the strike price increases.

Time to expiration on option   Both calls and puts become more valuable as the time to expiration increases. This is because the longer time to expiration provides more time for the value of the underlying asset to move, increasing the value of both types of options. In addition, in the case of a call, where the buyer has to pay a fixed price at expiration, the present value of this fixed price decreases as the life of the option increases, increasing the value of the call. In the case of a put, the present value of the expected proceeds from the sale of the asset at the exercise price at expiration decreases as the time to expiration is extended.

Variables Relating to Financial Markets

Riskless interest rate corresponding to life of option   Because the buyer of an option pays the price of the option up front, an opportunity cost is involved. This cost will depend on the level of interest rates and the time to expiration on the option. The riskless interest rate also enters into the valuation of options when the present value of the exercise price is calculated, for the exercise price does not have to be paid (received) until expiration on calls (puts). Increases in the interest rate will increase the value of calls and reduce the value of puts.

American versus European Options: Variables Relating to Early Exercise

A primary distinction between American and European options is that American options can be exercised at any time prior to its expiration, whereas European options can be exercised only at expiration. The possibility of early exercise makes American options more valuable than otherwise similar European options; it also makes them more difficult to value. There is one compensating factor that enables American options to be valued using models designed for the European options. In most cases, the time premium associated with the remaining life of an option makes early exercise suboptimal.

Although early exercise is not optimal generally, there are at least two exceptions to this rule. One is a case where the underlying asset pays large dividends, thus reducing the value of the asset and any call options on that asset. In this case, call options may be exercised just before an ex-dividend date, if the time premium on the options is less than the expected decline in asset value as a consequence of the dividend payment. The other exception arises when an investor holds both the underlying asset and **deep in-the-money puts** on that asset at a time when interest rates are high. In this case, the time premium on the put may be less than the potential gain from exercising the put early and earning interest on the exercise price.

In-the-money put (call):   An in-the-money put (call) is one whereby the strike price is higher (lower) than the stock price right now; in other words, there would be a positive cash flow from immediate exercise. A *deep in-the-money* call or put is one whereby the difference between the strike price and the stock price is large.

A Summary of the Determinants of Option Value

Table 27.3 summarizes the variables and their predicted effects on call and put prices.

Table 27.3 SUMMARY OF VARIABLES AFFECTING CALL AND PUT PRICES

Factor	Effect on	
	Call Value	Put Value
Increase in underlying asset's value	Increases	Decreases
Increase in strike price	Decreases	Increases
Increase in variance of underlying asset	Increases	Increases
Increase in time to expiration	Increases	Increases
Increase in interest rates	Increases	Decreases
Increase in dividends paid	Decreases	Increases

OPTION PRICING MODELS

Option pricing theory has made vast strides since 1972, when Black and Scholes published their path-breaking paper providing a model for valuing dividend-protected European options. Black and Scholes used a **replicating portfolio**—a portfolio composed of the underlying asset and the risk-free asset that had the same cash flows as the option being valued—to come up with their final formulation. Although their derivation is mathematically complicated, there is a simpler binomial model for valuing options that draws on the same logic.

Replicating Portfolio: A replicating portfolio is a portfolio composed of the underlying asset and a riskless asset, which generates the same cash flow as a specified call or put option.

The Binomial Model

The *binomial option pricing model* is based on a simple formulation for the asset price process in which the asset, in any time period, can move to one of two possible prices. The general formulation of a stock price process that follows the binomial is shown in Figure 27.3. In this figure, S is the current stock price; the price moves up to Su with probability p and down to Sd with probability $1 - p$ in any time period.

Creating a replicating portfolio   The objective in creating a replicating portfolio is to use a combination of risk-free borrowing/lending and the underlying asset to create the same cash flows as the option being valued. The principles of arbitrage apply here, and the value of the option must be equal to the value of the replicating portfolio. In the case of the general formulation above, where stock prices can either move up to Su or down to Sd in any time period, the replicating portfolio for a call with strike price K will involve borrowing $\$B$ and acquiring Δ of the underlying asset, where:

$$\Delta = \text{Number of units of the underlying asset bought} = (C_u - C_d)/(Su - Sd)$$

where

C_u = Value of the call if the stock price is Su
C_d = Value of the call if the stock price is Sd

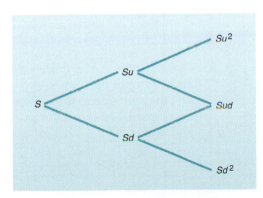

Figure 27.3 Binomial price path

In a multiperiod binomial process, the valuation has to proceed iteratively—that is, starting with the last time period and moving backward in time until the current point in time. The portfolios replicating the option are created at each step and valued, providing the values for the option in that time period. The final output from the binomial option pricing model is a statement of the value of the option in terms of the replicating portfolio, composed of Δ shares (option delta) of the underlying asset and risk-free borrowing/lending.

Value of the call = Current value of underlying asset * Option Delta − Borrowing needed to replicate the option

---

The determinants of value   The binomial model provides insight into the determinants of option value. The value of an option is determined not by the *expected* price of the asset but by its *current* price, which, of course, reflects expectations about the future. This is a direct consequence of arbitrage. If the option value deviates from the value of the replicating portfolio, investors can create an arbitrage position, that is, one that requires no investment, involves no risk, and delivers positive returns. The option value increases as the time to expiration is extended, as the price movements (*u* and *d*) increase, and as the interest rate increases.

The Black-Scholes Model

Although the binomial model provides an intuitive feel for the determinants of option value, it requires a large number of inputs, in terms of expected future prices at each node. The Black-Scholes model is not an entirely different model; rather, it is one limiting case of the binomial, but it reduces the informational requirements substantially.

The binomial model is a discrete-time model for asset price movements, including a time interval (*t*) between price movements. As the time interval is shortened, the limiting distribution, as $t \to 0$, can take one of two forms. If as $t \to 0$, price changes become smaller, the limiting distribution is the normal distribution and the price process is a continuous one. If as $t \to 0$, price changes remain large, the limiting distribution is the Poisson distribution—that is, a distribution that allows for price jumps. The Black-Scholes model applies when the limiting distribution is the normal distribution, and it explicitly assumes that the price process is continuous and that there are no jumps in asset prices.[1]

The model   The version of the model presented by Black and Scholes was designed to value European options, which were dividend-protected. Thus, neither the possibility of early exercise nor the payment of dividends affects the value of options in this model.

The value of a call option in the Black-Scholes model can be written as a function of the following variables:

S = Current value of the underlying asset
K = Strike price of the option
t = Life to expiration of the option
r = Riskless interest rate corresponding to the life of the option
σ^2 = Variance in the ln (value) of the underlying asset

---

[1]Stock prices cannot drop below zero because of the limited liability of stockholders in publicly listed firms. Hence, stock prices, by themselves, cannot be normally distributed, because a normal distribution requires some probability of negative values. The distribution of stock prices is assumed to follow a log-normal distribution in the Black-Scholes model. This is why the variance used in this model is the variance in the log of stock prices.

The model itself can be written as

$$\text{Value of call} = S\,N\,(d_1) - K\,e^{-rt}\,N(d_2)$$

where

$$d_1 = \frac{\ln\left(\dfrac{S}{K}\right) + (r + \dfrac{\sigma^2}{2})t}{\sigma\sqrt{t}}$$

$$d_2 = d_1 - \sigma\sqrt{t}$$

The process of valuation of options using the Black-Scholes model involves the following steps:

Step 1:   The inputs to the Black-Scholes are used to estimate d_1 and d_2, which are standardized normal varibles.

Step 2:   The cumulative normal distribution functions, $N(d_1)$ and $N(d_2)$, corresponding to these standardized normal variables are estimated.

Step 3:   The present value of the exercise price is estimated, using the continuous time version of the present value formulation:

$$\text{Present value of exercise price} = K\,e^{-rt}$$

Step 4:   The value of the call is estimated from the Black-Scholes model.

The determinants of value   The determinants of value in the Black-Scholes model are the same as those in the binomial—the current value of the stock price, the variability in stock prices, the time to expiration on the option, the strike price, and the riskless interest rate. The principle of replicating portfolios that is used in binomial valuation also underlies the Black-Scholes model. Table 27.4 provides the replicating portfolios for calls and puts, using the binomial and the Black-Scholes models.

Table 27.4   REPLICATING PORTFOLIO FOR CALL AND PUT OPTIONS WITH MODELS

Option Position	Replicating Portfolio	
	With Binomial	**With Black-Scholes**
Buy Call Option	Borrow $B	Borrow $K\,e^{-rt}\,N\,(d_2)$
	Buy Δ shares of stock	Buy $N(d_1)$ shares of stock
Sell Call Option	Lend $B	Lend $K\,e^{-rt}\,N\,(d_2)$
	Sell short Δ shares	Sell short $N(d_1)$ shares
Buy Put Option	Lend B'	Lend $K\,e^{-rt}\,(1 - N\,(d_2))$
	Sell short Δ' shares	Sell short $(1 - N\,(d_1))$ shares
Sell Put Option	Borrow $B	Borrow $K\,e^{-rt}\,(1 - N\,(d_2))$
	Buy Δ' shares	Buy $(1 - N(\,(d_1))$ shares

where B, B', Δ and Δ' are estimated from the binomial process.

Model Limitations and Fixes

The version of the Black-Scholes model presented here does not take into account the possibility of early exercise or the payment of dividends, both of which impact the value of options. Furthermore, adjustments exist which, though not perfect, provide partial corrections to value.

Dividends   The payment of dividends reduces the stock price. Consequently, call options will become less valuable and put options more valuable as dividend payments increase. There are two possible adjustments for dividends, one for short-term options and the other for long-term options.

Short-term options   When options have only a short time to expiration (less than one year), the present value of the expected dividends during the life of the option can be estimated and subtracted from the current value of the asset to obtain a "dividend-adjusted value," which can be used as the input for S in the Black-Scholes model:

$$\text{Adjusted Stock Price} = S' = S - \Sigma \frac{\text{Div}_t}{(1 + r)^t}$$

$$\text{Value of call} = S' N(d_1) - K e^{-rt} N(d_2)$$

where

$$d_1 = \frac{\ln\left(\dfrac{S'}{K}\right) + (r + \dfrac{\sigma^2}{2})t}{\sigma\sqrt{t}}$$

$$d_2 = d_1 - \sigma\sqrt{t}$$

To illustrate, consider a call option on IBM with a strike price of $45 and four months to expiration. The stock is trading at $50. Using past stock prices, we can estimate the variance in the log of stock prices for IBM at 0.06. There is one dividend, amounting to $0.56, which is expected to be paid in two months. The riskless rate is 3%.

Present value of expected dividend = $0.56 / 1.03$^{2/12}$ = $0.5572
Dividend-adjusted stock price = $50 − $0.56 = $49.44
Strike Price = $45   Time to expiration = 4 months = 4/12
Variance in log(stock prices) = 0.06   Riskless rate = 3%

The value from the Black-Scholes is

$d_1 = 0.8072$ $N(d_1) = 0.7901$
$d_2 = 0.6658$ $N(d_2) = 0.7472$
Value of Call = $49.44 (0.7901) − $45 \exp^{-(0.03)(4/12)} (0.7472) = $5.78

A Note on Estimating the Inputs to the Black-Scholes Model

The Black-Scholes model requires inputs that are consistent on time measurement. As presented here, all the inputs have to be annualized. The variance, estimated from ln(asset prices), can be annualized easily because variances are linear in time if the serial correlation is zero. Thus, if monthly (weekly) prices are used to estimate variance, the variance is annualized by multiplying by 12 (52).

Long-term options   The present value approach to dealing with dividends becomes tedious and difficult to apply to long-term options. If the dividend yield (y = dividends/

current value of the asset) of the underlying asset is expected to remain unchanged during the life of the option, the Black-Scholes model can be modified to take dividends into account.

$$C = S e^{-yt} N(d_1) - K e^{-rt} N(d_2)$$

where

$$d_1 = \frac{\ln\left(\frac{S}{K}\right) + (r - y + \frac{\sigma^2}{2})t}{\sigma\sqrt{t}}$$

$$d_2 = d_1 - \sigma\sqrt{t}$$

From an intuitive standpoint, the adjustments have two effects. First, the value of the asset is discounted back to the present at the dividend yield to take into account the expected drop in value from dividend payments. Second, the interest rate is offset by the dividend yield to reflect the lower carrying cost from holding the stock (in the replicating portfolio).

Primes and scores are securities traded on the American Stock Exchange. A **score** entitles the holder to all price appreciation on an underlying traded stock over the life of the score, whereas the **prime** entitles the holder to all dividends (and the stock price, capped at the current level). Thus, the score is a long-term call option on the underlying stock.

Primes and Scores: A score is a security that entitles its holder to all price appreciation on an underlying traded stock over the life of the score. A prime entitles its holder to all dividends over the same period.

Consider primes and scores on IBM with a five-year lifetime. The current price of the stock is $50, and the stock is expected to maintain its current dividend yield (current yield = $2.26/$50 = 4.52%). The five-year bond rate is 5.5%. The inputs to the Black-Scholes model are

S = Current asset value = $50   Time to expiration = 5 years
K = Strike price = $50   Variance in log(stock prices) = 0.06
Riskless rate = 5.5%   Dividend yield = 4.52%

The value from the Black-Scholes model is

$d_1 = 0.3633$ $\qquad\qquad\qquad\qquad N(d^1) = 0.6418$
$d_2 = -.1844$ $\qquad\qquad\qquad\qquad N(d2) = 0.4268$
Value of Score = $50 \exp^{-(0.0452)(5)} (0.6418) - $50 \exp^{-(0.055)(5)} (0.4268) = \$9.39$

Since the holder of the prime is entitled to all cash flows other than the price appreciation, the value of a prime can be estimated as follows:

Value of Prime = Value of Stock − Value of Score = $50 − $9.39 = $40.61

Early exercise   There are two basic approaches for dealing with the possibility of early exercise. One values the option to each ex-dividend day and chooses the maximum of the estimated call values; the other uses a modified version of the binomial model to consider the possibility of early exercise.

Approach 1: Pseudo-American valuation

Step 1: Define when dividends will be paid and how much the dividends will be.

Step 2: Value the call option to each ex-dividend date using the dividend-adjusted approach described above, whereby the stock price is reduced by the present value of expected dividends .

Step 3: Choose the maximum of the call values estimated for each ex-dividend day.

To illustrate, consider an option with a strike price of $35 on a stock trading at $40. The variance in the log(stock prices) is 0.05, and the riskless rate is 4%. The option has a remaining life of eight months, and three dividends are expected during this period:

Expected Dividend	Ex-Dividend Day
$0.80	In 1 month
$0.80	In 4 months
$0.80	In 7 months

The call option is first valued to just before the first ex-dividend date:

$$S = \$40 \qquad K = \$35 \qquad t = 1/12 \quad \sigma^2 = 0.05 \qquad r = 0.04$$

The value from the Black-Scholes model is

$$\text{Value of Call} = \$5.132$$

The call option is then valued to before the second ex-dividend date:

$$\text{Adjusted Stock Price} = \$40 - \$0.80/1.04^{1/12} = \$39.20$$
$$K = \$35 \qquad t = 4/12 \qquad \sigma^2 = 0.05 \qquad r = 0.04$$

The value of the call based on these parameters is

$$\text{Value of call} = \$5.07$$

The call option is then valued to before the third ex-dividend date:

$$\text{Adjusted Stock Price} = \$40 - \$0.80/1.04^{1/12} - \$0.80/1.04^{4/12} = \$38.41$$
$$K = \$35 \qquad t = 7/12 \qquad \sigma^2 = 0.05 \qquad r = 0.04$$

The value of the call based on these parameters is

$$\text{Value of Call} = \$5.128$$

The call option is then valued to expiration:

$$\text{Adjusted Stock Price} = \$40 - \$0.80/1.04^{1/12} - \$0.80/1.04^{4/12} - \$0.80/1.04^{7/12} = \$37.63$$
$$K = \$35 \qquad t = 8/12 \qquad \sigma^2 = 0.05 \qquad r = 0.04$$

The value of the call based on these parameters is

$$\text{Value of Call} = \$4.76$$
$$\text{Pseudo-American value of the call} = \text{Maximum } (\$5.132, \$5.07, \$5.128, \$4.76) = \$5.132$$

Approach 2: Using the binomial

Step 1: If the variance in log(stock prices) has been estimated for the Black-Scholes, convert these into inputs for the binomial model:

$$u = \text{Exp} \left[(r - \sigma^2/2)(T/m) + \sqrt{(\sigma^2 T/m)} \right]$$
$$d = \text{Exp} \left[(r - \sigma^2/2)(T/m) - \sqrt{(\sigma^2 T/m)} \right]$$

where u and d are the up and down movements per unit time for the binomial, T is the life of the option, and m is the number of periods within that lifetime.

Step 2: Specify the period in which the dividends will be paid and make the assumption that the price will drop by the amount of the dividend in that period.

Step 3: Value the call at each node of the tree, allowing for the possibility of early exercise just before ex-dividend dates. There will be early exercise if the remaining time premium on the option is less than the expected drop in option value as a consequence of the dividend payment.

Step 4: Value the call at time 0, using the standard binomial approach.

The impact of exercise on the value of the underlying asset   The derivation of the Black-Scholes model is based on the assumption that exercising an option does not affect the value of the underlying asset. This may be true for listed options on stocks, but it is not true for some types of options. For instance, the exercise of warrants increases the number of shares outstanding and brings fresh cash into the firm, both of which will affect the stock price.[2] The expected negative impact (dilution) of exercise will decrease the value of warrants compared to otherwise similar call options. We will look at the adjustment for dilution that has to be made for warrants in the next chapter.

Valuing puts   The value of a put is related to the value of a call with the same strike price and the same expiration date through an arbitrage relationship that specifies that

$$C - P = S - K e^{-rt}$$

where C is the value of the call and P is the value of the put (with the same life and exercise price).

This arbitrage relationship can be derived fairly easily and is called *put-call parity*. To see why put-call parity holds, consider creating the following portfolio:

a. Sell a call and buy a put with exercise price K.

b. Buy the stock at current stock price S.

The payoff from this position is riskless and always yields K at expiration (t). To see this, assume that the stock price at expiration is $S*$:

Position	Payoffs at t if $S*>K$	Payoffs at t if $S*>K$
Sell call	$-(S*-K)$	0
Buy put	0	$K - S*$
Buy stock	$S*$	$S*$
Total	K	K

Because this position always yields K risklessly, its value must be equal to the present value of K at the riskless rate ($K e^{-rt}$).

$$S + P - C = K e^{-rt}$$
$$C - P = S - K e^{-rt}$$

This relationship can be used to value puts. Substituting the Black-Scholes formulation for the value of an equivalent call,

$$\text{Value of put} = S e^{-yt} (N(d_1) - 1) - K e^{-rt} (N(d_2) - 1)$$

[2]Warrants are call options issued by firms, either as part of management compensation contracts or as a way of raising equity.

where

$$d_1 = \frac{\ln\left(\dfrac{S}{K}\right) + (r - y + \dfrac{\sigma^2}{2})t}{\sigma\sqrt{t}}$$

$$d_2 = d_1 - \sigma\sqrt{t}$$

CONCLUSION

An option is an asset with payoffs that are contingent on the value of an underlying asset. A call option provides its holder with the right to buy the underlying asset at a fixed price, whereas a put option provides its holder with the right to sell at a fixed price, any time before the expiration of the option. The value of an option is determined by six variables: (1) the current value of the underlying asset; (2) the variance in this value; (3) the strike price of the option; (4) the life of the option; (5) the riskless interest rate; and (6) the expected dividends on the asset. Both the binomial and the Black-Scholes models are used to value options by creating replicating portfolios, composed of the underlying asset and riskless lending or borrowing. These models can be used to value assets that have option-like characteristics.

QUESTIONS AND PROBLEMS

1. Answer true or false to the following questions.

    a. An option with less time to expiration will sell at a higher price than an option with more time to expiration. (Assume that the options are on the same stock and have the same strike price.)

    b. An option on a stock with higher variance will sell at a higher price than a similar option on a stock with lower variance.

    c. An option can never sell for less than you can make by exercising the option.

    d. A call option is always more valuable than a put option with the same strike price (with the same expiration on the same stock).

    e. The payment of a dividend renders call options less valuable and put options more valuable.

    f. A call option with a higher strike price can never sell for more than a call option with a lower strike price and the same expiration date.

    g. Listed options will never be exercised early on a stock on which dividends are not paid.

    h. As an option approaches expiration, its value will go down if the stock price does not change. (Assume that interest rates and the stock price variance do not change and dividends are not paid on the stock.)

    i. The likelihood of early exercise on an option (on a stock that pays a dividend) increases as the time to expiration on the option decreases.

    j. If a company's beta goes up, the options on the company's stock will become more valuable.

2. The following is the binomial path for an underlying asset whose price currently is $50:

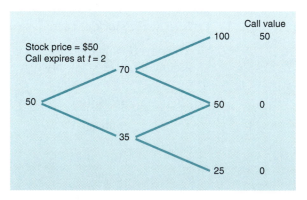

Stock price = $50
Call expires at $t = 2$

    The riskless interest rate is 10%.

    a. Estimate the current value of a call with a strike price of 60 expiring at $t=2$.

    b. Estimate the current value of a put with a strike price of 60 expiring at $t=2$.

    c. Explain how you would replicate a call with a strike price of 60 at $t=0$ and at $t=1$.

    d. Explain how you would replicate a put with a strike price of 60 at $t=0$ and at $t=1$.

3. The following are prices of options traded on Microsoft Corporation, which pays no dividends.

	Call		Put	
	K=85	K=90	K=85	K=90
1-month	2.75	1.00	4.50	7.50
3-month	4.00	2.75	5.75	9.00
6-month	7.75	6.00	8.00	12.00

The stock is trading at $83, and the annualized riskless rate is 3.8%. The standard deviation in log stock prices (based on historical data) is 30%.

a. Estimate the value of a three-month call, with a strike price of 85.

b. Using the inputs from the Black-Scholes model, specify how you would replicate this call.

c. What is the implied standard deviation in this call?

d. Assume now that you buy a call with a strike price of 85 and sell a call with a strike price of 90. Draw the payoff diagram on this position.

e. Using put-call parity, estimate the value of a three-month put with a strike price of 85.

4. You are trying to value three-month call and put options on Merck, with a strike price of 30. The stock is trading at $28.75 and expects to pay a quarterly dividend per share of $0.28 in two months. The annualized riskless interest rate is 3.6%, and the standard deviation in log stock prices is 20%.

a. Estimate the value of the call and put options, using the Black-Scholes model.

b. What effect does the expected dividend payment have on call values? on put values? Why?

5. There is the possibility that the options on Merck, described in question 4, could be exercised early.

a. Use the pseudo-American call option technique to determine whether this will affect the value of the call.

b. Why does the possibility of early exercise exist? What types of options are most likely to be exercised early?

6. You have been provided the following information on a three-month call:

$$S = 95 \quad K = 90 \quad t = 0.25 \quad r = 0.04$$
$$N(d_1) = 0.5750 \quad N(d_2) = 0.4500$$

a. If you wanted to replicate buying this call, how much money would you need to borrow?

b. If you wanted to replicate buying this call, how many shares of stock would you need to buy?

7. Go Video, a manufacturer of video recorders, was trading at $4 per share in May 1994. There were 11 million shares outstanding. At the same time, the company had 550,000 one-year warrants outstanding, with a strike price of $4.25. The stock has had a standard deviation (in log stock prices) of 60%. The stock does not pay a dividend. The riskless rate is 5%.

a. Estimate the value of the warrants, ignoring dilution.

b. Why does dilution reduce the value of the warrants?

8. You are trying to value a long-term call option on the NYSE Composite Index, expiring in five years, with a strike price of 275. The index is currently at 250, and the annualized standard deviation in stock prices is 15%. The average dividend yield on the index is 3% and is expected to remain unchanged over the next five years. The five-year Treasury bond rate is 5%.

a. Estimate the value of the long-term call option.

b. Estimate the value of a put option, with the same parameters.

c. What are the implicit assumptions you are making when you use the Black-Scholes model to value this option? Which of these assumptions are likely to be violated? What are the consequences for your valuation?

9. A new security on AT&T will entitle the investor to all dividends on AT&T over the next three years, limit upside potential to 20%, but also provide downside protection below 10%. AT&T stock is trading at $50, and three-year call and put options are traded on the exchange at the following prices:

	Call Options		Put Options	
K	1-year	3-year	1-year	3-year
45	$8.69	$13.34	$1.99	$3.55
50	$5.86	$10.89	$3.92	$5.40
55	$3.78	$8.82	$6.59	$7.63
60	$2.35	$7.11	$9.92	$10.23

How much would you be willing to pay for this security?

10. If one values an option using the Black-Scholes formula, does the option value increase or decrease as volatility increases? Why?

11. Suppose you purchased 100 shares of IBM six months ago at $80/share. The stock is currently selling at $100 a share, and you'd like to "lock in" your profits. However, you suspect that the stock is going to rise even more. Describe how you could use a put or call option to insure against a price decline.

12. If you value equal-lived calls and puts on the same stock when K = S, the call will always be worth more than the put. Why?

13. "To really make money speculating in options, you have to take opposite positions (i.e., buy one and sell the other) in calls and puts on a stock!" Evaluate this statement.

14. Everything else held equal, an option's value will decrease as it gets closer to expiration. Why?

15. If a call is exercised, the IRS considers the buyer to have bought the stock for a total cost equal to the exercise price plus the premium paid for the option itself. If a call expires unexercised, the IRS allows the buyer to claim a capital loss equal to the premium paid for the option. Given these tax considerations, is it possible that an option holder might find it profitable to exercise an out-of-the-money call?

16. A straddle involves buying a put and a call with the same strike price. Draw the payoff diagram associated with a straddle and discuss when this strategy will make or lose money. When would you use this strategy?

17. You are considering purchasing a call on First Strike Software, a small software development company. The current stock price is $20, the strike price is $25, the variance in stock prices is 20%, and the risk free rate is 6.25%. If the dividend yield is 4% and the call will have one year to expiration, how much should you pay?

18. You think that Webscape, a small manufacturer of World Wide Web browsing software currently selling at $61 per share, is overvalued. You estimate that the correct value of the stock is $24 per share, and you think that the market will come to agree with your assessment within the next 6 months. Webscape doesn't pay dividends, the volatility in stock prices is 15%, and the current risk-free rate is 6.25%. If you decide to use a put option with a strike price equal to the current market price to profit on this opportunity, how much do you expect to make on a per share basis?

19. Suppose that, in addition to buying a put to take advantage of the anticipated decline in Webscape's stock price as described above, you also decide to partially finance this strategy by selling a call with a strike price equal to the current market price. Now what would your expected per-share profit be? Does selling the call increase or decrease the risk of this strategy to you?

CHAPTER 28

APPLICATIONS OF OPTION PRICING THEORY IN CORPORATE FINANCE

Option pricing theory has a wide range of applications in corporate finance, involving everything from basic capital budgeting to valuation. When firms consider projects, often they also have to consider the opportunities that these projects may create in the future in terms of opening up new markets or expanding existing ones; thus, options are embedded in these projects. When firms consider financing choices, they have to examine the consequences of such choices for their flexibility, which can be viewed as the option to take on projects in the future. When firms are valued, the product patents they own, which are options on these products, have to be valued as well. In this chapter, we look at a series of these applications. In particular, we focus on the following:

- What are the options embedded in capital budgeting projects? How can these options be valued using option pricing models, and how can these values be used in conjunction with traditional capital budgeting analysis?

- How can option pricing be used in the context of valuation?

- How can option pricing theory be used to illustrate the conflicts between stockholders and bondholders? How is it useful in designing and valuing securities?

A FEW CAVEATS ON APPLYING OPTION PRICING MODELS

The option pricing models described in the preceding chapter can be used to value any asset that has the characteristics of an option, with some caveats. In this section, we apply option pricing theory in a variety of contexts. In many of the cases described below, the options being valued are not on financially traded assets (such as stocks or commodities) but are **real options** (such as those on projects or natural resources reserves). We begin by offering a few caveats on the application of option pricing models to these cases and suggesting some adjustments that might need to be made to these models.

Real Option: A real option is an option on a non-traded asset, such as an investment project or a gold mine.

The Underlying Asset Is Not Traded

Option pricing theory, as presented in both the binomial and the Black-Scholes models, is built on the premise that a replicating portfolio can be created using the underlying asset and riskless lending and borrowing. Although this is a perfectly justifiable assumption in the context of listed options on traded stocks, it becomes less defensible when the underlying asset is not traded and arbitrage is therefore not feasible. Because the options presented in this section are on assets that are not traded, the values from option pricing models have to be interpreted with caution.

The Price of the Asset Follows a Continuous Process

As we mentioned in Chapter 27, the Black-Scholes option pricing model is derived under the assumption that the underlying asset's price process is continuous (i.e., there are no price jumps). If this assumption is violated, as it is with most real options, the model will underestimate the value of deep out-of-the-money options. One solution is to use higher variance estimates to value deep out-of-the-money options and lower variance estimates for at-the-money or in-the-money options. Another solution is to use an option pricing model that explicitly allows for price jumps, although the inputs to these models are often difficult to estimate.[1]

The Variance Is Known and Does Not Change over the Life of the Option

Option pricing models assume that the variance is known and does not change over the option lifetime; this assumption is not unreasonable *when applied to listed short-term options on traded stocks.* When option pricing theory is applied to long-term real options, however, problems arise with this assumption, for the variance is unlikely to remain constant over extended periods of time and may in fact be difficult to estimate in the first place. Again, modified versions of the option pricing model exist that allow for changing variances, but they require that the process by which variance changes be modeled explicitly.

Exercise Is Instantaneous

The option pricing models are based on the premise that the exercise of an option is instantaneous. This assumption may be difficult to justify with real options, however; exercise may require building a plant or constructing an oil rig, for example, actions that do not occur in an instant. The fact that exercise takes time also implies that the true life of a real option is often less than the stated life. Thus, although a firm may own the rights to an oil reserve for the next 10 years, the fact that it takes several years to extract the oil reduces the life of the natural resource option the firm owns.

OPTIONS IN CAPITAL BUDGETING

In Chapters 7 and 8, we examined the process of analyzing a project and deciding whether or not to accept it. In particular, we noted that a project should be accepted *only if the returns on the project exceed the hurdle rate.* In the context of cash flows and discount rates, this translates into projects with positive net present values. The limitation with traditional investment analysis, which analyzes projects on the basis of expected cash flows and discount rates, is that it fails to consider fully the myriad options that are usually associated with many projects.

In this section, we analyze three options that are embedded in capital budgeting projects: the option to delay a project, especially when the firm has exclusive rights to the project; the option to expand a project to cover new products or markets some time in the future; and the option to abandon a project if the cash flows do not measure up to expectations.

---

[1]Jump process models that incorporate the Poisson process require inputs on the probability of price jumps, the average magnitude, and the variance, all of which can be estimated but with a significant amount of noise.

The Option to Delay a Project

Projects are typically analyzed based on their expected cash flows and discount rates at the time of the analysis. The net present value computed on that basis is a measure of its value and acceptability at that time. Expected cash flows and discount rates change over time, however, as does the net present value. Thus, a project that has a negative net present value now may have a positive net present value in the future. In a competitive environment, in which individual firms have no special advantages over their competitors in taking projects, this may not seem significant. In an environment in which a project can be taken by only one firm (because of legal restrictions or other barriers to entry to competitors), however, the changes in the project's value over time give it the characteristics of a call option.

In the abstract, assume that a project requires an initial investment of X (in real dollars) and that the present value of expected cash inflows computed right now is PV. The net present value of this project is the difference between the two:

$$NPV = PV - X$$

Now assume that the firm has exclusive rights to this project for the next n years and that the present value of the cash inflows may change over that time because of changes in either the cash flows or the discount rate. Thus, the project may have a negative net present value right now, but it may still be a good project if the firm waits. Defining V as the present value of the cash flows, we can summarize the firm's decision rule on this project as follows:

If
$V > X$ Project has positive net present value.
$V < X$ Project has negative net present value.

This relationship can be presented in a payoff diagram of cash flows on this project, as shown in Figure 28.1, assuming that the firm holds out until the end of the period for which it has exclusive rights to the project.

Note that this payoff diagram is that of a call option—the underlying asset is the project; the strike price of the option is the investment needed to take the project; and the life of the option is the period for which the firm has rights to the project. The present value of the cash flows on this project and the expected variance in this present value represent the value and variance of the underlying asset.

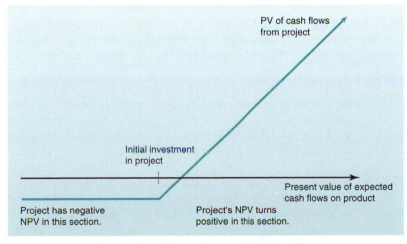

Figure 28.1   The option to delay a project

Obtaining the inputs for option valuation   On the surface, the inputs needed to apply option pricing theory to valuing the option to delay are the same as those needed for any application: the value of the underlying asset; the variance in the value; the time to expiration on the option; the strike price; the riskless rate and the equivalent of the dividend yield. Estimating these inputs for a project option valuation can be difficult, however.

Value of the underlying asset   In the case of project options, the underlying asset is the project itself. The current value of this asset is the present value of expected cash flows from initiating the project now, which can be obtained by performing a standard capital budgeting analysis. There is likely to be a substantial amount of noise in the cash-flow estimates and the present value, however. Rather than being considered as a problem, this uncertainty should be viewed as the reason why the project delay option has value. If the expected cash flows on the project were known with certainty and were not expected to change, there would be no need to adopt an option pricing framework, for there would be no value to the option.

Variance in the value of the asset   As noted in the prior section, considerable uncertainty is likely to be associated with the cash-flow estimates and the present value that measures the value of the asset now, partly because the potential market size for the product may be unknown, and partly because technological shifts can change the cost structure and profitability of the product. The variance in the present value of cash flows from the project can be estimated in one of three ways. One is, if similar projects have been introduced in the past, the variance in the cash flows from those projects can be used as an estimate. A second is if probabilities can be assigned to various market scenarios, cash flows can be estimated under each scenario, and the variance can be estimated across present values. A third is to use the average variance in firm value for the industry to which the firm belongs. Table 28.1 summarizes average variances in 1994.

   The value of the option is derived largely from the variance in cash flows—the higher the variance, the higher the value of the project delay option. Thus, the value of an option to do a project in a stable business will be less than the value of one in an environment in which technology, competition, and markets are all changing rapidly.

Exercise price on option   A project delay option is exercised when the firm owning the rights to the project decides to invest in it. The cost of making this investment is equivalent to the exercise price of the option. The underlying assumption is that this cost remains constant (in present value dollars) and that any uncertainty associated with the project is reflected in the present value of cash flows.

Expiration of the option and the riskless rate   The project delay option expires when the rights to the project lapse; investments made after the project rights expire are assumed to deliver a net present value of zero as competition drives returns down to the required rate. The riskless rate to use in pricing the option should be the rate that corresponds to the expiration of the option.

Dividend yield   Delay in taking a project, once the net present value turns positive, involves some cost. Because the project rights expire after a fixed period, and excess profits (which are the source of positive present value) are assumed to disappear after that time as new competitors emerge, each year of delay translates into one less year of

Table 28.1 EQUITY AND FIRM VALUE STANDARD DEVIATIONS (SD) BY INDUSTRY (PERCENTAGE DISTRIBUTION)

SIC Code	Industry	Debt Ratio	σ: Equity	σ: Firm
1	Agricultural—Crops	33.24	29.75	20.94
2	Agricultural—Livestock	35.32	49.52	33.09
7	Agricultural Services	26.93	31.78	24.04
8	Forestry	46.58	21.12	13.24
10	Fishing, Hunting, and Trapping	20.75	43.12	34.75
11	Metal Mining	26.93	43.24	32.38
12	Coal Mining	62.39	36.39	16.40
13	Oil and Gas Extraction	30.83	46.29	32.92
14	Mining of Nonmetals	25.06	31.21	24.14
15	Building Contractors	37.73	64.09	41.02
16	Heavy Construction	14.88	46.09	39.63
17	Construction—Special Trade	25.01	39.64	30.45
20	Food and Kindred Products	24.91	29.22	22.69
21	Tobacco Products	45.70	34.31	20.26
22	Textile Mill Products	37.68	48.26	31.23
23	Apparel and Other Finished Products	21.10	51.85	41.48
24	Lumber and Wood Products	24.54	61.23	46.88
25	Furniture and Fixtures	20.02	36.68	29.90
26	Paper and Allied Products	34.26	33.14	22.89
27	Printing and Publishing	20.01	36.47	29.73
28	Chemicals and Allied Products	14.40	37.37	32.38
29	Petroleum Refining	42.23	28.54	18.02
30	Rubber and Plastic Products	23.86	37.36	29.13
31	Leather and Leather Products	19.81	38.41	31.36
32	Stone, Clay, Glass, and Concrete	34.94	49.70	33.38
33	Primary Metal Industries	36.97	38.74	25.60
34	Fabricated Metal Products	31.25	39.90	28.37
35	Industrial and Commercial Machinery	19.73	49.62	40.37
36	Electronic and Electrical Equipment	12.45	48.62	42.89
37	Transportation Equipment	31.56	41.15	29.11
38	Measuring, Analyzing and Controlling Instruments	12.88	49.17	43.17
39	Miscellaneous Manufacturing	16.72	44.77	37.74
40	Railroad Transportation	40.93	26.19	16.96
41	Suburban Transit and Highway Transportation	42.89	22.19	14.36
42	Motor Freight Transportation	32.91	56.42	38.81
44	Water Transportation	48.34	36.11	20.40
45	Air Transportation	48.81	41.72	23.07
47	Transportation Services	34.31	47.83	32.45
48	Communications	26.36	40.19	30.36
49	Electric, Gas and Sanitary Services	48.24	22.55	13.70

(*continues*)

Table 28.1   (Continued)

SIC Code	Industry	Debt Ratio	σ: Equity	σ: Firm
50	Wholesale trade—Durable goods	23.03	52.81	41.28
51	Wholesale trade—Nondurable goods	26.22	43.52	32.86
52	Building Materials, Hardware, and Garden Dealers	37.73	45.31	29.39
53	General Mechandise	40.93	35.76	22.50
54	Food Stores	35.02	31.64	21.70
55	Auto Dealers and Gas Service Stations	26.07	47.64	35.96
56	Apparel and Accessory Stores	23.69	45.70	35.54
57	Home Furniture, Furnishings, and Equipment Stores	27.18	43.66	32.58
58	Eating and Drinking Establishments	22.18	48.20	38.12
59	Miscellaneous Retail	18.91	47.99	39.43
60	Depository Institutions	26.93	57.73	42.94
61	Nondepository Institutions	12.44	34.35	30.41
62	Security and Commodity Brokers, Dealers	8.90	42.86	39.28
63	Insurance Carriers	10.58	34.56	31.18
64	Insurance Agents, Brokers, and Services	11.65	27.12	24.28
65	Real Estate	43.42	50.88	30.17
67	Holding and Other Investment Services	31.10	33.06	23.75
70	Hotels, Rooming Houses, and Lodging Places	44.27	50.96	29.81
72	Personal Services	21.57	35.12	28.16
73	Business Schools	9.54	50.03	45.50
75	Auto Repair, Services, and Parking	37.89	32.69	21.57
76	Miscellaneous Repair Services	76.22	35.14	12.64
78	Motion Pictures	24.61	60.26	46.10
79	Amusement and Recreation Services	32.52	43.16	30.10
80	Health Services	20.51	58.89	47.37
82	Educational Services	15.10	50.79	43.53
87	Engineering, Accounting, Research Services	18.52	45.68	37.72
89	Services not listed elsewhere	32.77	36.54	25.58

Variances by Bond Rating Class

Bond Rating	Annualized σ	Correlation with Stock Returns
AAA	5.50	10
AA	6.00	10
A	6.50	10
BBB	7.00	15
BB	8.50	15
B	9.50	20
CCC	12.00	25
CC	13.50	30
C	15.00	40

value-creating cash flows.[2] If the cash flows are evenly distributed over time and the projected life of the project is *n* years, the cost of delay can be written as

$$\text{Annual cost of delay} = \frac{1}{n}$$

Thus, if the project rights are for 20 years, the annual cost of delay works out to 5% a year.

Concept Check

In a normal option, it almost never pays to exercise early. Why, in the case of a project option, might this not hold true?

Valuing the option to delay a project: an illustration   Assume that a pharmaceutical company has been approached by an entrepreneur who has patented a new drug to treat ulcers. The entrepreneur has obtained FDA approval and has the patent rights for the next 20 years. Although the drug shows promise, it is still very expensive to manufacture and has a relatively small market. Assume that the initial investment to produce the drug is $500 million and that the present value of the cash flows from introducing the drug now is only $350 million. The technology and the market are volatile, and the annualized variance in the present value, estimated from a simulation, is 0.05.[3]

The net present value of introducing the drug is negative, but the rights to this drug may still be valuable because of the variance in the present value of the cash flow. In other words, this drug may not only be viable but also extremely profitable a year or two from now. To value this right, we first define the inputs to the option pricing model:

Value of the underlying asset (S) = PV of cash flows from project if introduced now
= $350 million
Strike price (K) = Initial Investment needed to introduce the product = $500 million
Variance in underlying asset's value (σ^2) = 0.05
Time to expiration = Life of the patent (t) = 20 years
Dividend yield = 1/Life of the patent = y = 1/20 = 0.05

Assume that the 20-year riskless rate (r) is 7%. The value of the option can be estimated as follows:

Call Value = $350 \exp^{(-0.05)(20)} (0.7065) - 500 \exp^{(-0.07)(20)} (0.3240) = \$51.02$ million

Thus, this ulcer drug, which has a negative net present value if introduced now, is still valuable to its owner.

Concept Check

If you were negotiating for the pharmaceutical company, would you offer to pay $51.02 million for the rights to this drug? Why or why not? If you were negotiating for the entrepreneur, would you demand this price? Why or why not?

[2]A value-creating cash flow is one that adds to the net present value because it earns a return in excess of the required return for investments of equivalent risk.
[3]See Chapter 11 on dealing with uncertainty in capital budgeting for a discussion of simulations.

Practical considerations   Clearly, that the option to delay is embedded in many projects, but several problems are associated with the use of option pricing models to value these options. First, *the underlying asset in this option, which is the project, is not traded, making it difficult to estimate its value and variance.* We would argue that the value can be estimated from the expected cash flows and the discount rate for the project, albeit with error. The variance is more difficult to estimate, however, because we are attempting the estimate a variance in project value over time. We have suggested three ways of estimating this variance—from similar projects, simulations, and by looking at the variances of firms involved in the same business. Thus, the stock price variance of publicly traded biotechnology firms may be used as a proxy for the variance of a biotechnology project's cash flows.

Second, the *behavior of prices over time may not conform to the price path assumed by the option pricing models.* In particular, the assumption that value follows a diffusion process and that the variance in value remains unchanged over time may be difficult to justify in the context of a project. For instance, a sudden technological change may dramatically change the value of a project, either positively or negatively.

Third, *there may be no specific period for which the firm has rights to the project.* Unlike the example above, in which the firm had exclusive rights to the project for 20 years, often the firm's rights are less clearly defined, both in terms of exclusivity and time. For instance, a firm may have significant advantages over its competitors, which may, in turn, provide it with the virtually exclusive rights to a project for a period of time. The rights are not legal restrictions, however, and could erode faster than expected. In such cases, the expected life of the project itself is only an estimate.

❑ Concept Check

Why is it so important that the firm have rights to the project in order to apply the option pricing approach to valuing the option to delay?

Implications of viewing the right to delay a project as an option   Several interesting implications emerge from the analysis of the option to delay a project as an option. First, a project may have a negative net present value based on expected cash flows currently, but it may still be a "valuable" project because of the option characteristics. Thus, a negative net present value should encourage a firm to reject a project but, it should not lead it to conclude that the rights to this project are worthless. Second, a project may have a positive net present value but still not be accepted right away because the firm may gain by waiting and accepting the project in a future period, for the same reasons that investors do not always exercise an option just because it is in the money; this is more likely to happen if the firm has the rights to the project for a long time and the variance in project inflows is high. To illustrate, assume that a firm has the patent rights to produce a new type of disk drive for computer systems and that building a new plant will yield a positive net present value right now. If the technology for manufacturing the disk drive is in flux, however, the firm may delay taking the project in the hopes that the improved technology will increase the expected cash flows and, consequently, the value of the project.

Valuing a patent   A **product patent** provides a firm with the right to develop and market a product. The firm will do so only if the present value of the expected cash flows from the product sales exceed the cost of development, as shown in Figure 28.2. If this

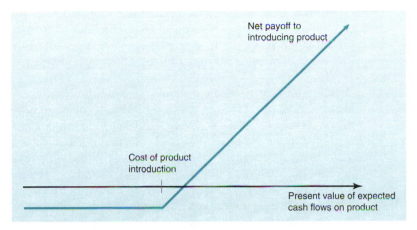

Figure 28.2 Payoff to introducing product

does not occur, the firm can shelve the patent and not incur any further costs. If I is the present value of the costs of developing the product, and V is the present value of the expected cash flows from development, the payoffs from owning a product patent can be written as

$$\text{Payoff from owning a product patent} = V - I \quad \text{if } V > I$$
$$= 0 \quad \text{if } V \leq I$$

Thus, a product patent can be viewed as a call option, whereby the product itself is the underlying asset.

Product Patent: A product patent gives its owner the exclusive right to produce and market the product in question for a specified period of time.

Assume that a pharmaceutical firm has the patent rights, for the next 20 years, to a drug that requires an initial investment of $1.5 billion to develop and a present value, right now, of cash inflows of only $1 billion. The drug is very expensive to produce now, but the technology is rapidly evolving, and there is a possibility that this project will become valuable in the future. Assume that a simulation of the project under a variety of technological and competitive scenarios yields a variance in the present value of inflows of 0.03. The current riskless 20-year bond rate is 10%.

The inputs to the option pricing model are as follows:

Value of the underlying asset = Present value of inflows (current) = $1,000 million
Exercise price = Present value of cost of developing product = $1,500 million
Time to expiration = Life of the patent = 20 years
Variance in value of underlying asset = Variance in PV of inflows = 0.03
Riskless rate = 10%
Cost of delay $(y) = 1/20 = 5\%$

Based on these inputs, the Black-Scholes model provides the following value for the call:

$$d_1 = 1.1548 \qquad\qquad N(d_1) = 0.8759$$
$$d_2 = 0.3802 \qquad\qquad N(d_2) = 0.6481$$

$$\text{Call Value} = 1{,}000 \, \exp^{(-0.05)(20)} (0.8759) - 1{,}500 \, \exp^{(-0.10)(20)} (0.6481) = \$190.66 \text{ million}$$

Therefore, even though this product has a negative net present value currently, it is a valuable product when viewed as an option. This value can then be added to the value of the other assets the firm possesses, providing a useful framework for incorporating the value of product options and patents into an analysis.

Valuing natural resource options   In a natural resource investment, the underlying asset is the natural resource, and the value of the asset is based on the estimated quantity and the price of the resource. Thus, in a gold mine, for example, the underlying asset is the value of the estimated gold reserves in the mine, based on the current price of gold. In most such investments, a cost is associated with developing the resource; the difference between the value of the asset extracted and the cost of the development is the profit to the owner of the resource (see Figure 28.3). Defining the cost of development as X and the estimated value of the resource as V, we can write the potential payoffs on a natural resource as follows:

$$\text{Payoff on natural resource investment} = V - X \qquad \text{if } V > X$$
$$= 0 \qquad \text{if } V \le X$$

Thus, the investment in a natural resource option has a payoff function similar to a call option.

To value a natural resource investment as an option, we need to make assumptions about a number of variables:

1. Available reserves of the resource: Because this is not known with certainty at the outset, it has to be estimated. In an oil tract, for instance, geologists can provide reasonably accurate estimates of the quantity of oil available in the tract.

2. Estimated cost of developing the resource: The estimated development cost is the exercise price of the option. Again, a combination of knowledge about past costs and the specifics of the investment has to be used to derive a reasonable measure of development cost.

3. Time to expiration of the option: The life of a natural resource option can be defined in one of two ways. First, if the ownership of the investment has to be Xrelinquished at the end of a fixed period of time, that will be the life of the option. In many offshore oil leases, for instance, the oil tracts are leased to the oil company for five to

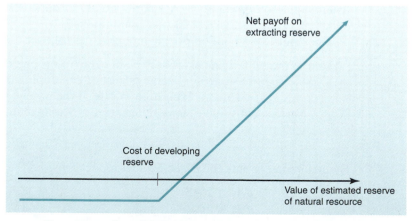

Figure 28.3   Payoff from developing natural resource reserves

ten years. The second approach is based on the inventory of the resource and the capacity output rate, as well as estimates of the number of years it would take to exhaust the inventory. Thus, a gold mine with a mine inventory of 3 million ounces and a capacity output rate of 150,000 ounces a year will be exhausted in 20 years, which is defined as the life of the natural resource option.

4. *Variance in value of the underlying asset:* The variance in the value of the underlying asset is determined by variability in the price of the resource and variability in the estimate of available reserves. In the special case whereby the quantity of the reserve is known with certainty, the variance in the underlying asset's value will depend entirely on the variance in the price of the natural resource.

5. *Dividend yield:* Just as dividends reduce the value of a stock and produce a cash flow to stockholders, production on an annual basis depletes the value of the underlying natural resource asset and provides a cash flow on the asset. The net production revenue as a percentage of the market value of the reserve is the equivalent of the dividend yield and is treated the same way in calculating option values.

An important issue in using option pricing models to value natural resource options is the effect of **development lags** on the value of these options. Because the resources cannot be extracted instantaneously, a time lag has to be allowed for between the decision to extract the resources and the actual extraction. A simple adjustment for this lag is to take the present value of developed reserve based on the length of the lag. If there is a one-year lag in development, the current value of the developed reserve will be discounted back one year at the "cash flow/asset value" ratio (dividend yield).

Development Lag: This is the time between the decision to extract a natural resource and the actual extraction.

Valuing an oil reserve[4] Consider an offshore oil property with an estimated oil reserve of 50 million barrels of oil; the present value of the development cost is $12 per barrel, and the development lag is two years. The firm has the rights to exploit this reserve for the next 20 years, and the marginal value per barrel of oil is $12 per barrel currently (price per barrel − marginal cost per barrel). Once developed, the net production revenue each year will be 5% of the value of the reserves. The riskless rate is 8%, and the variance in ln(oil prices) is 0.03.

Given this information, the inputs to the Black-Scholes can be estimated as follows:

Current value of the asset = S = Value of the developed reserve discounted back the length of the development lag at the dividend yield = $12 * 50 /(1.05)^2 = $470.12 million.

(If development is started today, the oil will not be available for sale until two years from now. The estimated opportunity cost of this delay is the lost production revenue over the delay period—hence, the discounting of the reserve back at the dividend yield.)

Exercise price = Present value of development cost = $12 * 50 = $600 million
Time to expiration on the option = 20 years
Variance in the value of the underlying asset = 0.03
Riskless rate = 8%
Dividend yield = Net production revenue / Value of reserve = 5%

---

[4]The following is a simplified version of the illustration provided by Siegel, Smith and Paddock to value an offshore oil property.

Based on these inputs, the Black-Scholes model provides the following value for the call:

$$d_1 = 1.0359 \qquad N(d_1) = 0.8498$$
$$d_2 = 0.2613 \qquad N(d_2) = 0.6030$$

Call Value $= 470.12 \exp^{(-0.05)(20)} (0.8470) - 600 \exp^{(-0.08)(20)} (0.5088) = \$74.55$ million

This oil reserve, though not viable at current prices, is still a valuable property because of its potential to create value if oil prices go up.

☐ Concept
Check

Assume that oil prices increase by \$5 per barrel today and drop back by \$5 tomorrow. Will these changes affect the value of the oil reserve? If so, why? If not, why not?

The Option to Expand a Project

In some cases, firms take projects in order to take on other projects or to enter other markets in the future. In such cases, it can be argued that the initial projects are options allowing the firm to take other projects, and the firm should therefore be willing to pay a price for such options. A firm may accept a negative net present value on the initial project because of the possibility of high positive net present values on future projects.

To examine this option using the same framework developed earlier, assume that the present value of the expected cash flows from entering the new market or taking the new project is V, and that the total investment needed to enter this market or take this project is X. Furthermore, assume that the firm has a fixed time horizon, at the end of which it has to make the final decision on whether or not to take advantage of this opportunity. Finally, assume that the firm cannot move forward on this opportunity if it does not take the initial project. This scenario implies the option payoffs shown in Figure 28.4. As you can see, at the expiration of the fixed time horizon, the firm will enter the new market or take the new project if the present value of the expected cash flows at that point in time exceeds the cost of entering the market.

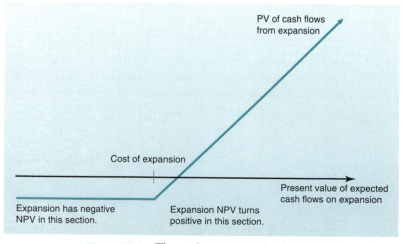

Figure 28.4   The option to expand a project

IN PRACTICE   VALUING AN OPTION TO EXPAND: THE HOME DEPOT

Assume that the Home Depot is considering opening a small store in France. The store will cost 100 million FF to build, and the present value of the expected cash flows from the store is 80 million FF. Thus, by itself, the store has a negative NPV of 20 million FF.

Assume, however, that by opening this store, the Home Depot acquires the option to expand into a much larger store anytime over the next five years. The cost of expansion will be 200 million FF, and it will be undertaken only if the present value of the expected cash flows exceeds 200 million FF. At the moment, the present value of the expected cash flows from the expansion is believed to be only 150 million FF. (If the present value were higher, the Home Depot would have opened the larger store right away.) The Home Depot still does not know much about the market for home improvement products in France, and there is considerable uncertainty about this estimate. The variance is 0.08.

The value of the option to expand can now be estimated by defining the inputs to the option pricing model as follows:

$$\text{Value of the underlying asset } (S) = \text{PV of cash flows from expansion, if done now}$$
$$= 150 \text{ million FF}$$
$$\text{Strike price } (K) = \text{Cost of Expansion} = 200 \text{ million FF}$$
$$\text{Variance in underlying asset's value} = 0.08$$
$$\text{Time to expiration} = \text{Period for which expansion option applies} = 5 \text{ years}$$

There is no cost of delay.

Assume that the five-year riskless rate is 6%. The value of the option can be estimated as follows:

$$\text{Call Value} = 150 \, (0.6314) - 200 \, \exp^{(-0.06)(5)} \, (0.3833) = 37.91 \text{ million FF}$$

This value can be added on to the net present value of the original project under consideration

$$\text{NPV of store} = 80 \text{ million FF} - 100 \text{ million FF} = -20 \text{ million}$$
$$\text{Value of option to expand} = 37.91 \text{ million FF}$$
$$\text{NPV of store with option to expand} = -20 \text{ million} + 37.91 \text{ million} = 17.91 \text{ mil FF}$$

The Home Depot should open the smaller store, even though it has a negative net present value, because as a consequence, it acquires an option of much greater value.

Practical considerations   The practical considerations associated with estimating the value of the option to expand are similar to those associated with valuing the option to delay. In most cases, firms with options to expand have no specific time horizon by which they have to make an expansion decision, making these open-ended options, or, at best, options with arbitrary lives. Even in those cases in which a life can be estimated for the option, neither the size nor the potential market for the product may be known, and estimating either can be problematic. To illustrate, consider the Home Depot example discussed above. Although we adopted a period of five years, at the end of which the Home Depot has to decide one way or another on its future expansion in France, it is entirely possible that this time frame is not specified at the time the store is opened. Futhermore, we have assumed that both the cost and the present value of expansion are known initially. In reality, the firm may not have good estimates for either before opening the first store, because it does not have much information on the underlying market.

 Concept
Check

Firms that require their initial ventures in new markets to carry their own weight (i.e., have positive net present values) are much less likely to enter these markets. Comment.

Implications   Firms implicitly use the option to expand as a way to rationalize taking projects that may have negative net present value but provide significant opportunities to tap into new markets or sell new products. Although the option pricing approach adds rigor to this argument by estimating the value of this option, it also provides insight into those occasions when it is most valuable. In general, the option to expand is more valuable for more volatile businesses with higher returns on projects (such as biotechnology or computer software) than for stable businesses with lower returns (such as housing, utilities, or automobile production).

It can also be argued that research and development (R&D) provides one immediate application for this methodology. Firms that expend large resources on research and development argue that they do so because it provides them with new products for the future. In recent years, however, more firms have stopped accepting this explanation at face value as a rationale for spending more money on R&D and have started demanding better returns from their investments.

Research, development, and test market expenses   Firms that spend considerable amounts of money on research and development or test marketing are often stymied when they try to evaluate these expenses, because the payoffs are often in terms of future projects. At the same time, after the money has been spent, the products or projects may not turn out to be viable; consequently, the expenditure is treated as a sunk cost. In fact, it can be argued that R&D has the characteristics of a call option—the amount spent on the R&D is the cost of the call option, and the projects or products that might emerge from the research provide the options. If these products are viable (i.e., the present value of the cash inflows exceeds the needed investment), the payoff is the difference between the two; if not, the project will not be accepted, and the payoff is zero.

Several logical implications emerge from this view of R&D. First, research expenditures should provide much higher value for firms that are in volatile technologies or businesses, because the variance in product or project cash flows is positively correlated with the value of the call option. Thus, Minnesota Mining and Manufacturing (3M), which expends a substantial amount on R&D on basic office products, such as the Post-it pad, generally receives less value for its research than does Intel, whose research primarily concerns semiconductor chips. Second, the value of research and the optimal amount to be spent on research will change over time as businesses mature. The best example is the pharmaceutical industry. Pharmaceutical companies spent most of the 1980s investing substantial amounts in research and earning high returns on new products, as the health care business expanded. In the 1990s, however, as health care costs started leveling off and the business matured, many of these companies found that they were not getting the same payoffs on research and started cutting back.

❏ Concept Check

This approach presupposes that the research is applied and directed toward finding commercial products. Would the same arguments apply for basic research, such as the research done on basic theory at universities and some research institutions like Bell Labs? Why or why not?

The Option to Abandon a Project

The final option to consider here is the option to abandon a project when its cash flows do not measure up to expectations. In our discussion of decision trees in

Chapter 11, we noted that having the option to abandon will generally increase the value of a project and make it more acceptable. To illustrate the option to abandon, assume that V is the remaining value on a project if it continues to the end of its life, and L is the liquidation or abandonment value for the same project at the same point in time. If the project has a life of n years, the value of continuing the project can be compared to the liquidation (abandonment) value—if it is higher, the project should be continued; if it is lower, the holder of the abandonment option could consider abandoning the project:

$$\text{Payoff from owning an abandonment option} = 0 \quad \text{if } V > L$$
$$= L \quad \text{if } V \le L$$

These payoffs are graphed in Figure 28.5, as a function of the expected project value. Unlike the prior two cases, the option to abandon takes on the characteristics of a put option.

To illustrate, assume that a firm is considering taking a 10-year project that requires an initial investment of $100 million in a real estate partnership, and where the present value of expected cash flows is $110 million. Although the net present value of $10 million is small, assume that the firm has the option to abandon this project anytime (by selling its share back to the other partners) in the next 10 years; if abandoned, the net salvage value of the project is $50 million. The variance in the present value of the cash flows from being in the partnership is 0.06.

The value of the abandonment option can be estimated by determining the characteristics of the put option:

$$\text{Value of the underlying asset } (S) = \text{PV of cash flows from project}$$
$$= \$110 \text{ million}$$
$$\text{Strike price } (K) = \text{Salvage value from abandonment} = \$50 \text{ million}$$
$$\text{Variance in underlying asset's value} = 0.06$$
$$\text{Time to expiration} = \text{Life of the project} = 10 \text{ years}$$
$$\text{Dividend yield} = 1/\text{Life of the project} = 1/10 = 0.10 \text{ (we are assuming that the}$$
$$\text{project's present value will drop by roughly } 1/n \text{ each year into the project)}$$

Assume that the 10-year riskless rate is 7%. The value of the put option can be estimated as follows:

$$\text{Call Value} = 110 \exp^{(-.10)(10)} (0.8455) - 50 \exp^{(-0.07)(10)} (0.5961) = \$19.41 \text{ million}$$
$$\text{Put Value} = \$19.41 - 110 \exp^{(-.10)(10)} + 50 \exp^{(-0.07)(10)} = \$3.77 \text{ million}$$

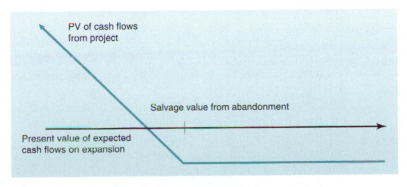

Figure 28.5 The option to abandon a project

The value of this abandonment option has to be added on to the net present value of the project of $10 million, yielding a total net present value with the abandonment option of $13.57 million. Note, however, that abandonment becomes a more and more attractive option as the remaining project life decreases, since the present value of the remaining cash flows will decrease.

Practical considerations   In the above analysis, we assumed, rather unrealistically, that the abandonment value was clearly specified up front and that it did not change during the life of the project. This may be true in some very specific cases, in which an abandonment option is built into the contract. More often, however, the firm has the option to abandon, and the salvage value from doing so can be estimated with noise up front. Furthermore, the abandonment value may change over the life of the project, making it difficult to apply traditional option pricing techniques. Finally, it is entirely possible that abandoning a project may not bring in a liquidation value but may create costs instead; a manufacturing firm may have to pay severance to its workers, for instance. In such cases, it would not make sense to abandon, unless the cash flows on the project are even more negative.

Implications   The fact that the option to abandon has value provides a rationale for firms to build the flexibility to scale back or terminate projects if they do not measure up to expectations. Firms can do this in a number of ways. The first, and most direct way, is to build in the option contractually with those parties that are involved in the project. Thus, contracts with suppliers may be written on an annual basis rather than long term, and employees may be hired on a temporary basis rather than permanently. The physical plant used for a project may be leased on a short-term basis rather than bought, and the financial investment may be made in stages rather than as an initial lump sum. Building in this flexibility carries a cost, but the gains may be much larger, especially in volatile businesses.

VALUING EQUITY AS AN OPTION

As described in earlier chapters, discounted cash-flow valuation provides an estimate of the value of the equity or the firm based on forecasted cash flows and the present value of these cash flows, at the appropriate discount rate. *Multiples,* on the other hand, value equity by looking at comparable firms and adjusting for differences among them. Here, we offer an alternative view of the determinants of equity value.

Limited Liability: The principle of limited liability restricts the losses of an investor who is protected by it to his or her investment in an asset.

The General Framework

The equity in a firm is a residual claim; that is, equity holders lay claim to all cash flows left over after other financial claimholders (debt, preferred stock, etc.) have been satisfied. If a firm is liquidated, the same principle applies—equity investors receive whatever is left over in the firm after all outstanding debts and other financial claims are paid off. The principle of **limited liability** protects equity investors in publicly traded firms if the value of the firm is less than the value of the outstanding debt, however, and they cannot lose more than their investment in the firm. The payoff to equity investors on liquidation can therefore be written as

$$\text{Payoff to equity on liquidation} = V - D \quad \text{if } V > D$$
$$= 0 \qquad \text{if } V \leq D$$

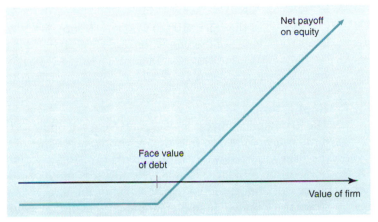

Figure 28.6 Payoff on equity as option on a firm

where

V = Value of the firm

D = Face value of the outstanding debt and other external claims

A call option, with a strike price of K, on an asset with a current value of S, has the following payoffs:

$$\text{Payoff on exercise} = S - K \quad \text{if } S > K$$
$$= 0 \qquad \text{if } S \leq K$$

Equity can thus be viewed as a call option for the firm; exercising the option requires that the firm be liquidated and the face value of the debt (which corresponds to the exercise price) paid off, as shown in Figure 28.6.

If the debt in the firm is a single issue of zero-coupon bonds with a fixed lifetime, and the firm can be liquidated by equity investors at any time prior, the life of equity as a call option corresponds to the life of the bonds.

Application to Valuation: A Simple Example

Assume that you have a firm whose assets are currently valued at $100 million; the standard deviation in this asset value is 40%. Also assume that the face value of debt is $80 million. (It is zero-coupon debt with 10 years left to maturity.) If the 10-year Treasury bond rate is 10%, how much is the equity worth? What should the interest rate on debt be?

At the outset, the information provided may seem inadequate to answer these questions. The use of the option pricing approach provides a solution, however. The parameters of equity as a call option are as follows:

Value of the underlying asset = S = Value of the firm = $100 million
Exercise price = K = Face value of outstanding debt = $80 million
Life of the option = t = Life of zero-coupon debt = 10 years
Variance in the value of the underlying asset = σ^2 = Variance in firm value = 0.16
Riskless rate = r = Treasury bond rate corresponding to option life = 10%

Based on these inputs, the Black-Scholes model provides the following value for the call:

$$d_1 = 1.5994 \qquad N(d_1) = 0.9451$$
$$d_2 = 0.3345 \qquad N(d_2) = 0.6310$$

$$\text{Value of the call} = 100\,(0.9451) - 80\,\exp^{(-0.10)(10)}\,(0.6310) = \$75.94 \text{ million}$$
$$\text{Value of the outstanding debt} = \$100 - \$75.94 = \$24.06 \text{ million}$$
$$\text{Interest rate on debt} = (\$80\,/\,\$24.06)^{1/10} - 1 = 12.77\%$$

Implications

The first implication of viewing equity as a call option is that equity will have value, even if the value of the firm falls well below the face value of the outstanding debt. Although the firm will be viewed as troubled by investors, accountants, and analysts, its equity is not worthless. In fact, just as deep out-of-the-money traded options command value because of the possibility that the value of the underlying asset may increase above the strike price in the remaining lifetime of the option, equity commands value because of the time premium on the option (the time until the bonds mature and come due) and the possibility that the value of the assets may increase above the face value of the bonds before they come due.

Returning to the preceding example, assume that the value of the firm is only $50 million, well below the face value of the outstanding debt ($80 million). Assume that all the other inputs remain unchanged. The parameters of equity as a call option are as follows:

$$\text{Value of the underlying asset} = S = \text{Value of the firm} = \$50 \text{ million}$$
$$\text{Exercise price} = K = \text{Face value of outstanding debt} = \$80 \text{ million}$$
$$\text{Life of the option} = t = \text{Life of zero-coupon debt} = 10 \text{ years}$$
$$\text{Variance in the value of the underlying asset} = \sigma^2 = \text{Variance in firm value} = 0.16$$
$$\text{Riskless rate} = r = \text{Treasury bond rate corresponding to option life} = 10\%$$

Based on these inputs, the Black-Scholes model provides the following values for the call:

$$d_1 = 1.0515 \qquad N(d_1) = 0.8534$$
$$d_2 = -0.2135 \qquad N(d_2) = 0.4155$$

$$\text{Value of the call} = 50\,(0.8534) - 80\,\exp^{(-0.10)(10)}\,(0.4155) = \$30.44 \text{ million}$$
$$\text{Value of the bond} = \$50 - \$30.44 = \$19.56 \text{ million}$$

As you can see, the equity in this firm still has substantial value, because of the option characteristics of equity. This might explain why stock in firms that are in Chapter 11 and essentially bankrupt still has value.

Obtaining Option Pricing Inputs—Some Real-World Problems

The examples used thus far to illustrate the use of option pricing theory to value equity have made some simplifying assumptions. Among them are the following:

1. There are only two claimholders in the firm—debt and equity.
2. There is only one issue of debt outstanding, and it can be retired at face value.
3. The debt has a zero coupon and no special features (convertibility, put clauses, etc.)
4. The value of the firm and the variance in that value can be estimated.

Each of these assumptions is made for a reason. First, by restricting the claimholders to two, the problem is made more tractable; introducing other claimholders, such as preferred stock, makes it more difficult, though not impossible, to arrive at a result. Second, by assuming only one zero-coupon debt issue that can be retired at face value anytime prior to maturity, the features of the debt are made to correspond closely to the features of the strike price on a standard option. Third, if the debt is coupon debt, or if more than one debt issue is outstanding, the equity investors can be forced to exercise (liquidate the firm) at these earlier coupon dates if they do not have the cash flows to meet their coupon obligations. Finally, knowing the value of the firm and the variance in that value makes the option pricing possible, but it also raises an interesting question about the usefulness of option pricing in the valuation context. If the bonds of the firm are publicly traded, the market value of the debt can be subtracted from the value of the firm to obtain the value of equity much more directly.

The option pricing approach does have its advantages, however. Specifically, when the debt of a firm *is not* publicly traded, option pricing theory can provide an estimate of value for the equity in the firm. Even when the debt is publicly traded, the bonds may not be correctly valued, and the option pricing framework can be useful in evaluating the values of debt and equity. Finally, relating the values of debt and equity to the variance in firm value provides some insight into the redistributive effects of actions taken by the firm.

Application to Valuation
Because most firms do not fall into the neat framework developed above (having only one zero-coupon bond outstanding), some compromises have to be made to use this model in valuation.

Value of the firm   The value of the firm can be obtained in one of two ways. In the first, the market values of outstanding debt and equity are cumulated, assuming that all debt and equity are traded, to obtain firm value. The option pricing model then reallocates the firm value between debt and equity. In the second, the market values of the assets of the firm are estimated, either by discounting expected cash flows at the weighted average cost of capital or by using prices from a market that exists for these assets.

Variance in firm value   The variance in firm value can be obtained directly if both stocks and bonds in the firm trade in the marketplace. Defining σ_e^2 as the variance in the stock price, and σ_d^2 as the variance in the bond price, w_e as the market-value weight of equity, and w_d as the market-value weight of debt, we can write the variance in firm value as[5]

$$\sigma_2 \text{firm} = w_e^2\,\sigma_e^2 + w_d^2\,\sigma_d^2 + 2\,w_e\,w_d\,\rho_{ed}\,\sigma_e\,\sigma_d$$

where ρ_{ed} is the correlation between the stock and the bond prices.

When the bonds of the firm are not traded, the variance of similarly rated bonds is used as the estimate of σ_d^2 and the correlation between similarly rated bonds and the firm's stock is used as the estimate of ρ_{ed}. The bottom panel in Table 28.1 provides measures of standard deviation and correlation for bonds in different ratings classes.

Maturity of the debt   Most firms have more than one debt issue on their books, and much of the debt comes with coupons. Because the option pricing model allows for only one input for the time to expiration, these multiple bond issues and coupon payments have to be compressed into one measure; that is, these multiple issues have to be converted into one equivalent zero-coupon bond. One solution, which takes into account both the coupon payments and the maturity of the bonds, is to estimate the duration of each debt issue and

---

[5] This is an extension of the variance formula for a two-asset portfolio.

calculate a face-value-weighted average of the durations of the different issues. This value-weighted duration is then used as a measure of the time to expiration of the option.

IN PRACTICE   VALUING EQUITY AS AN OPTION—WANG LABS

Wang Labs was in trouble in March 1993. The firm was officially in Chapter 11 and had debt outstanding, with a face value of $529.40 million. The weighted average duration of this debt was 5.1 years, and the weighted average maturity of the debt was 8.7 years. The value of the firm estimated using projected cash flows to the firm, discounted at the weighted average cost of capital, was $410 million.

	1993	1994	1995	1996	1997
Revenues	$1,300	$1,010	$1,067	$1,121	$1,177
− COGS	1,000	658	705	741	778
− SG & A	750	279	267	269	282
EBIT	(450)	73	95	111	117
− EBIT* t	(162)	26	34	40	42
EBIT (1 − t)	(288)	47	61	71	75
Terminal value					$794

The weighted average cost of capital is 10%, and the cash flows to the firm are expected to stay constant after 1997. There are no working capital requirements, and capital expenditures are offset by depreciation.

$$\text{Present Value of FCFF at WACC} = \$410 \text{ million.}$$

The stock has been traded on the NYSE, and the variance based on monthly prices between 1987 and 1991 is 0.0262. Wang Lab bonds that are due in 2008 have been traded from 1987 to 1991, and the variance in monthly prices for these bonds is 0.0126. The correlation between stock price and bond price changes has been 0.27. The proportion of debt in the capital structure during the priod (1987–1991) was 86.1%.
The stock and bond price variances are first annualized:

Annualized variance in stock price = $0.0262 * 12 = 0.3144$ Standard deviation = 0.5607
Annualized variance in bond price = $0.0126 * 12 = 0.1512$ Standard deviation = 0.3896

Annualized variance in firm value

$$= (0.139)^2 (0.3144) + (0.861)^2 (0.1512) + 2 (0.139) (0.861)(0.27)(0.5607)(0.3896)$$
$$= 0.1323$$

The five-year bond rate (corresponding to the weighted average duration of 5.1 years) is 6%.
The parameters of equity as a call option are as follows:

Value of the underlying asset = S = Value of the firm = $410 million
Exercise price = K = Face value of outstanding debt = $529.4 million
Life of the option = t = Weighted average duration of debt = 5.1 years
Variance in the value of the underlying asset = σ^2 = Variance in firm value = 0.1323
Riskless rate = r = Treasury bond rate corresponding to option life = 6%

Based on these inputs, the Black-Scholes model provides the following value for the call:

$$d_1 = 0.4721 \qquad N(d_1) = 0.6816$$
$$d_2 = -0.3493 \qquad N(d_2) = 0.3632$$

Value of the call = $410 (0.6816) − 529.4 \exp^{(-0.06)(5.1)} (0.3632) = \$137.87$ million

Wang's equity was trading at $85 million in March 1993.

VALUING OPTIONS IN CAPITAL STRUCTURE AND DIVIDEND POLICY DECISIONS

Option pricing theory can be applied to capital structure decisions in a number of ways: by illustrating the conflict between stockholders and bondholders when it comes to investment analysis and conglomerate mergers; for designing and evaluating debt, equity, and hybrid securities; for examining the value of flexibility, which is often cited by firms that choose not to use excess debt capacity and pay out what they can in dividends.

The Conflict Between Bondholders and Stockholders

You will recall that stockholders and bondholders have different objective functions, and this can lead to agency problems, whereby stockholders expropriate wealth from bondholders. The conflict can manifest itself in a number of ways. For instance, stockholders have an incentive to take riskier projects than bondholders and to pay out more in dividends than bondholders would like. The conflict between bondholders and stockholders can be illustrated dramatically by using the option pricing methodology developed in the previous section.

Taking on risky projects   Because equity is a call option on the value of the firm, other things remaining equal, an increase in the variance in the firm value will lead to an increase in the value of equity. It is therefore conceivable that stockholders can take risky projects with negative net present values, which, while making them better off, may make the bondholders and the firm less valuable. To illustrate, consider the example on page 759 relating to a firm with a value of assets of $100 million, a face value of zero-coupon 10-year debt of $80 million, and a standard deviation in the value of the firm of 40%. The equity and debt in this firm are valued as follows:

Value of Equity = $75.94 million
Value of Debt = $24.06 million
Value of Firm = $100 million

Now assume that the stockholders have the opportunity to take a project with a negative net present value of -$2 million; the project is a very risky one that will push up the standard deviation in firm value to 50%. The equity as a call option can then be valued using the following inputs:

Value of the underlying asset = S = Value of the firm = $100 million − $2 million = $98 million (the value of the firm is lowered because of the negative net present value project.)

Exercise price = K = Face value of outstanding debt = $80 million
Life of the option = t = Life of zero-coupon debt = 10 years
Variance in the value of the underlying asset = σ^2 = Variance in firm value = 0.25
Riskless rate = r = Treasury bond rate corresponding to option life = 10%

Based on these inputs, the Black-Scholes model provides the following value for the equity and debt in this firm.

Value of Equity = $77.71
Value of Debt = $20.29
Value of Firm = $98.00

The value of equity rises from $75.94 million to $77.71 million, even though the firm value declines by $2 million. The increase in equity value comes at the expense of bondholders, who find their wealth decline from $24.06 million to $20.19 million.

Conglomerate mergers   Bondholders and stockholders may also experience conflict in the case of **conglomerate mergers,** whereby the variance in earnings and cash flows of the combined firm can be expected to decline because the merging firms have earning streams that are not perfectly correlated. In these mergers, the value of the combined equity in the firm will decrease after the merger because of the decline in variance; consequently, bondholders will gain. Stockholders can reclaim some or all of this lost wealth by utilizing their higher debt capacity and issuing new debt.

Conglomerate Merger: This is a merger motivated entirely by diversification; a firm in one line of business merges with a firm in a different line of business.

To illustrate, suppose you are provided with the following information on two firms, Lube and Auto (a car service) and Gianni Cosmetics (a cosmetics manufacturer), that hope to merge.

	Lube and Auto	Gianni Cosmetics
Value of the firm	$100 million	$150 million
Face value of debt	$80 million	$50 million (zero-coupon debt)
Maturity of debt	10 years	10 years
Std. dev. in firm value	40%	50%
Correlation between firm cash flows	0.4	

The 10-year bond rate is 10%.

The variance in the value of the firm after the acquisition can be calculated as follows (with the weights based upon firm values):

$$\text{Variance in combined firm value} = w_1^2\,\sigma_1^2 + w_2^2\,\sigma_2^2 + 2\,w_1\,w_2\,\rho_{12}\,\sigma_1\,\sigma_2$$
$$= (0.4)^2\,(0.16) + (0.6)^2\,(0.25) + 2\,(0.4)\,(0.6)\,(0.4)\,(0.4)\,(0.5)$$
$$= 0.154$$

The values of equity and debt in the individual firms and the combined firm can then be estimated using the option pricing model:

	Lube and Auto	Gianni	Combined firm
Value of equity in the firm	$75.94	$134.47	$207.43
Value of debt in the firm	$24.06	$15.53	$42.57
Value of the firm	$100.00	$150.00	$250.00

The combined value of the equity prior to the merger is $210.41 million; it declines to $207.43 million after that. The wealth of the bondholders increases by an equal amount. Thus, there is a transfer of wealth from stockholders to bondholders as a consequence of the merger. Conglomerate mergers that are not followed by increases in leverage are likely to cause this type of redistribution of wealth across claimholders in the firm.

Security Design and Valuation
Option pricing theory is particularly valuable for firms attempting to design securities that include option features. In the earlier section on capital structure, we noted several securities, both debt and equity, that have these features.

Warrants   A warrant is a call option issued by a firm to raise funds. The proceeds from the warrant issue go to the firm, and the firm issues the stock, if needed, to cover the warrant exercise. Accordingly, warrants have to be valued differently from other call options, since the derivation of the Black-Scholes model is based on the assumption that exercising an option does not affect the value of the underlying asset. This may be true for listed options on stocks, but it is not true for warrants. Rather, the exercise of warrants increases the number of shares outstanding and brings fresh cash into the firm, both of which will affect the stock price.[6] The expected negative impact (dilution) of exercise makes warrants less valuable than otherwise similar call options. The adjustment for dilution in the Black-Scholes to the stock price involves three steps:

Step 1   The stock price is adjusted for the expected dilution from warrant exercise.

$$\text{Dilution-adjusted } S = (S\, n_s + W\, n_w) / (n_s + n_w)$$

where

S = Current value of the stock n_w = Number of warrants outstanding
W = Market value of warrants outstanding n_s = Number of shares outstanding

When the warrants are exercised, the number of shares outstanding will increase, reducing the stock price. The numerator reflects the market value of equity, including both stocks and warrants outstanding.

Step 2   The variance used in the option pricing formula is the variance in the value of the equity in the company (i.e., the value of stocks plus warrants).

Step 3   Once the call is valued using the option pricing model, the option value is adjusted to reflect dilution:

$$\text{Dilution-adjusted value} = \text{Call Value from model} * n_s / (n_w + n_s)$$

 IN PRACTICE   VALUING A WARRANT ON SIEMENS

In July 1993, Siemens had 3 million warrants outstanding that expire in five years (in 1998), with an exercise price of 693 DM. There were 55.80 million shares outstanding in the company, and the stock was trading at 657.50 DM at that time, with a dividend yield of 1.98%. The five-year bond rate in Germany was 5.88%. The annualized variance in the value of equity for Siemens was 13.89%.
The inputs to the warrant valuation model are as follows:

$$S = (55.80 * 657.50 \text{ DM} + 3.0 * W)/(55.80 + 3.0)$$
$$K = \text{Exercise price on warrant} = 693 \text{ DM}$$
$$t = \text{Time to expiration on warrant} = 5 \text{ years}$$
$$r = \text{Riskless rate corresponding to life of option} = 5.88\%$$
$$\sigma^2 = \text{Variance in value of stock} = 0.1389$$
$$y = \text{Dividend yield on stock} = 1.98\%$$

The results of the Black-Scholes valuation of this option are

$$d_1 = 0.5438 \qquad N(d_1) = 0.7067$$
$$d_2 = -0.2896 \qquad N(d_2) = 0.3861$$

$$\text{Value of Warrant} = [657.50 \exp^{-(0.0198)\,(5)} (0.7067) - 693 \exp^{-(0.0588)(5)} (0.3861)]$$
$$* (55.80/58.80) = 195.81 \text{ DM}$$

The warrants were trading at 120.5 DM in July 1993.

Contingent Value Rights   **Contingent value rights** are put options sold by firms to either raise funds for projects or to signal their financial strength to markets. More specifically, firms that believe they are undervalued might try to signal this undervaluation by issuing puts to stockholders. In recent years, a number of firms that intend to repurchase stock have also sold puts both to support their stock price and to signal their intention to carry through on their repurchase plans.

---

[6]Warrants are call options issued by firms, either as part of management compensation contracts or to raise equity.

■ **Contingent value rights (CVR):** A contingent value right is a security issued by a firm, entitling its holder to sell the firm's stock back to the firm at a specified exercise price.

Convertible bonds A convertible bond is a bond that can be converted into a predetermined number of shares, at the option of the bondholder. It generally does not pay to convert at the time of the bond issue, but conversion becomes a more attractive option as stock prices increase. Firms generally add conversions options to bonds to lower the interest rate paid on the bonds.

❑ Concept
Check

When a firm issues puts, what effect does that issue have on the beta of the stock? Explain.

Determinants of value The conversion option is a call option on the underlying stock; its value is therefore determined by the variables that affect call option values—the underlying stock price, the conversion ratio (which determines the strike price), the life of the convertible bond, the variance in the stock price, and the level of interest rates. The payoff diagrams on a call option and on the conversion option in a convertible bond are illustrated in Figure 28.7.

Like a call option, the value of the conversion option will increase with the price of the underlying stock, the variance of the stock, and the life of the conversion option, and will decrease with the exercise price (determined by the conversion option). The effects of increased risk in the firm can cut both ways in a convertible bond—it decreases the value of the straight bond portion, while increasing the value of the conversion option. These offsetting effects generally mean that convertible bonds will be less exposed to changes in the firm's risk than other types of securities.

Option pricing models can be used to value the conversion option, with three caveats: (1) conversion options are *long term,* making the assumptions about constant variance and constant dividend yields much shakier; (2) conversion options result in *stock dilution*; and (3) conversion options are often *exercised before expiration,* making it dangerous to use European option pricing models. These problems can be partially alleviated by using a binomial option pricing model, allowing for shifts in variance and early exercise and factoring in the dilution effect.

The value of a convertible bond is also affected by a feature that allows for the adjustment of the conversion ratio (and price) if the firm issues new stock below the conversion price or has a stock split or dividend. In some cases, the conversion price has to

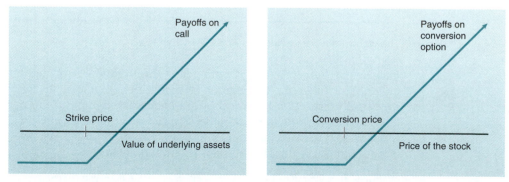

Figure 28.7 Call option and conversion option: comparing payoffs

be lowered to the price at which new stock is issued. This rule is designed to protect the convertible bondholder from misappropriation by the firm.

Concept Check

Firms often use convertible bonds because they are cheaper than straight bonds. Do you agree with this statement? Under what conditions are convertible bonds cheaper than straight bonds?

IN PRACTICE   VALUING A CONVERSION OPTION / CONVERTIBLE BOND: GENERAL SIGNAL

In December 1994, General Signal had convertible bonds outstanding with the following features:

- The bonds matured in June 2002. There were 100,000 shares outstanding.
- The bonds had a face value of $1,000 and were convertible into 25.32 shares per bond until June 2002.
- The coupon rate on the bond was set at 5.75%.
- The company was rated A−. Straight bonds of similar rating and similar maturity were yielding 9.00%.
- The stock price in December 1994 was $32.50. The volatility (standard deviation in log stock prices) based on historical data was 50.00%.
- There were 47.35 million shares outstanding. Exercising the convertible bonds will create 2.532 million additional shares (100,000 * 25.32 shares).

The two components of the convertible bond can be valued as follows.

1. Straight Bond Component: If this bond had been a straight bond, with a coupon rate of 5.75% and a yield to maturity of 9.00% (based on the bond rating), the value of this straight bond would have been

$$\text{PV of bond} = \sum_{t=1}^{t=15} \frac{28.75}{(1.045)^t} + \frac{1,000}{(1.09)^{7.5}} = \$832.73$$

This is based on semiannual coupon payments (of $28.75 for semiannual periods).

2. Valuing the Conversion Option: The value of the conversion option is estimated using the Black-Scholes model, with the following parameters for the conversion option:

Number of calls/bond = 25.32
Stock price = $32.50   Strike price = $1000/25.32 = $39.49
Time to expiration = 7.5 years   Standard deviation in stock prices (ln) = 0.5
Riskless rate = 7.75% (Rate on 7.5 year Treasury bond)
Dividend yield on stock = 3.00%

Allowing for the dilution inherent in the exercise (see section on warrant pricing for details on the valuation correction):

Value of one call = $12.85
Value of the conversion option = $12.85 * 25.32 = $325.43

3. Value of Convertible Bond: The value of the convertible bond is the sum of the straight bond and conversion option components:

Value of convertible bond = Value of straight bond + Value of conversion option
= $832.73 + $325.43 = $1158.16

This valuation is based on the assumption that the conversion option is unconstrained and the bonds are not callable. The effects of introducing these changes into the analysis are examined in the following sections.

The effect of forced conversion Companies that issue convertible bonds sometimes have the right to force conversion if the stock price rises to a specified level. This right to force conversion caps the profit that can be made on the conversion option and, hence, reduces its value. Figure 28.8 illustrates the effect of **forced conversion** on the expected payoffs.

Forced Conversion: In a forced conversion, a firm has the right to force convertible bondholders to convert their bonds into stock if the stock price rises above a specified level.

The value of a capped call, with an exercise price of K_1 and a cap of K_2, can be calculated as follows:

$$\text{Value of capped call } (K_1, K_2) = \text{Value of call } (K_1) - \text{Value of call } (K_2)$$

This is because the cash flows on a capped call can be replicated by buying the call with a strike price of K_1 and selling the call with a strike price of K_2. This approach can be used to estimate the effects of forced conversion on the value of the option.

Callable bonds The issuer of a **callable bond** preserves the right to call back the bond and pay a fixed price (generally at a premium over the par value) for it. Thus, if interest rates decline (bond prices rise) after the initial issue, the firm can repay the bonds at the fixed price rather than the market value. Adding the call option to a bond generally makes it less attractive to buyers, since it reduces the potential upside on the bond. As interest rates go down, and the bond price increases, the bonds are more likely to be called back.

Capped Call: A capped call limits the payoff on a call by forcing conversion or capping the profits at a fixed maximum price.

Callable Bonds: A callable bond can be called back by the issuing company at face value or a fixed call price.

The distinction between a straight bond and a callable bond is illustrated in Figure 28.9. The difference on the upside between straight and callable bonds is illustrated in

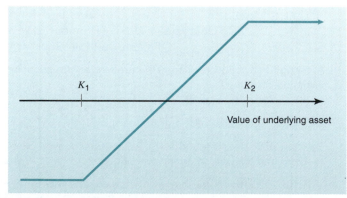

Figure 28.8 Value of a capped call

this figure: as interest rates decline, the values of the two bonds diverge, whereas they converge as interest rates increase.

Most callable bonds share several common features. Most come with an initial period of **call protection,** during which the bonds cannot be called back. Such bonds are called *deferred callable bonds.* The call price on most callable bonds is set at an initial level above par value plus one annual coupon payment, but declines as time passes and approaches the par value.

Call Protection: A call protected bond is one that cannot be called back during the period in which has the protection.

Valuing the callability option   The issuer's right to call back a bond if interest rates drop (or bond prices rise) to an attractive level is a call option on the bond and can be valued as such. The payoffs on a callable bond are shown in Figure 28.10.

As you can see, the value of the callable feature on a callable bond increases as interest rates decline and as the volatility of interest rates increases.

Since the callable feature is held by the issuer of the bond, the value of a callable bond can be written as follows:

Value of Callable Bond = Value of Straight Bond − Value of Call Feature in Bond

A callable bond should therefore sell for less than an otherwise similar straight bond.

Traditional analysis   The traditional approach to analyzing callable bonds is to estimate **yields to call** as well as **yields to maturity.** The yield to call is based on the assumption that the bond will be called at the first call date, whereas the yield to maturity assumes holding the bond until maturity. The two yields are compared, and the investor chooses the lower of the two as a measure of the expected return on the bond. This approach can also be extended to calculate the yield to all possible call dates; the

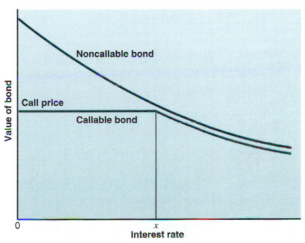

Figure 28.9   Straight versus callable bonds

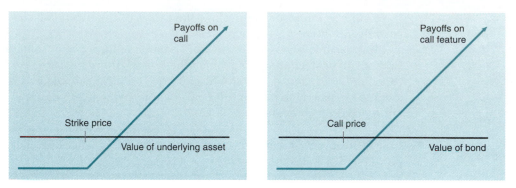

Figure 28.10   Payoffs on call feature on bond to seller of bond

lowest of these yields is chosen as the expected yield on the callable bond. This yield is called the **yield to worst.**

Yields to Call, Maturity, and Worst: The yield to maturity is the internal rate of return on a bond calculated assuming that the bond is held until maturity. The yield to call is the internal rate of return if the bond is held until the first call date. The yield to worst is the lowest of the yields to call dates.

Although this approach may give the investor some sense of the potential downside from the callability of the bond, it suffers from all the standard problems of the "yield to maturity" calculation. First, it assumes that the investor can reinvest all coupons until the bond is called at the yield to call; this is not a realistic assumption since calls are much more likely if interest rates go down. Second, it does not examine the rate at which the proceeds from the called bond can be reinvested by the investor. Third, it assumes that the bond will be called on the call date, which takes away the option characteristics of the call feature.

Consider a corporate bond with 20 years to maturity and a 12% coupon rate that is callable in two years at 105% of the face value. The bond is trading at 98 currently. The yields to maturity and the yields to call on the corporate bond are as follows:

$$\text{Yield to Maturity} \sum_{t=1}^{t=40} \frac{60.00}{(1 + r/2)^t} + \frac{1,000}{(1 + r)^{20}} = \$980: \text{Solve for } r$$

The yield to maturity is approximately 12.26%.

The yield to call can be similarly calculated:

$$\text{Yield to Call} \sum_{t=1}^{t=4} \frac{60.00}{(1 + r/2)^t} + \frac{1,050}{(1 + r/2)^4} = \$980: \text{Solve for } r$$

The yield to call is approximately 15.43%.

Determinants of value—option pricing approach   The call feature in a callable bond can be valued using option pricing models—it is a series of call options on the underlying bond, and its value is determined by the level and volatility of interest rates. The standard option pricing models need to be modified before they can be applied in this context.

Once the call feature is valued as a series of options, the yield on a callable bond can be adjusted for the option features; the difference between this adjusted yield and treasuries of equivalent maturity is called the **option-adjusted spread.** This approach is a more realistic way of considering the effects of the call feature on expected yields than the traditional yield to call approach.

Option-Adjusted Spread: The option-adjusted spread is the difference between the yield to maturity of a bond, adjusted for its call option features, and the yield to maturity on treasuries of equivalent maturity.

To illustrate, consider a 17-year callable bond with a coupon rate of 12%. How would you value the straight bond, the call feature on the straight bond, and the value of the callable bond as a function of the yield on the bond? The actual option valuation shown in Table 28.2 was done using a binomial option pricing model, an interest rate volatility of 12%, and a short-term interest rate of 6%.

Table 28.2   VALUE OF CALL FEATURE AS A FUNCTION OF YIELD

Yield (%)	Value of Straight Bond ($)	Value of Call Feature ($)	Value of Callable Bond ($)
20.51	60	0.00	60.00
19.55	63	0.00	63.00
18.66	66	0.00	66.00
17.59	70	0.00	70.00
16.63	74	0.00	74.00
15.54	79	0.02	78.98
14.56	84	0.06	83.94
13.51	90	0.22	89.78
12.57	96	0.67	95.33
11.46	104	2.11	101.89
10.59	111	4.60	106.40
9.59	120	9.80	110.20
8.60	130	17.81	112.19
7.73	140	27.21	112.79

Although the value of the straight bond increases as the yield drops, the callable bond's value stops increasing because the call feature becomes more and more valuable as the yield decreases. In fact, the value of the callable bond is maximized at $112.94.

Value of flexibility   When making financial decisions, managers consider the effects such decisions will have on their capacity to take new projects or meet unanticipated contingencies in future periods. Practically, this translates into firms maintaining excess debt capacity or larger cash balances than are warranted by current needs, to meet unexpected future requirements. While maintaining this financing flexibility has value to firms, it also has a cost; the large cash balances earn low returns and excess debt capacity implies that the firm is giving up some value and has a higher cost of capital.

The value of flexibility can be analyzed using the option pricing framework; a firm maintains large cash balances and excess debt capacity in order to have the option to take projects that might arise in the future. The value of this option will depend upon two key variables:

1. *Quality of the Firm's Projects*: It is the excess return that the firm earns on its projects that provides the value to flexibility. Other things remaining equal, firms operating in businesses where projects earn substantially higher returns than their hurdle rates should value flexibility more than those that operate in stable businesses where excess returns are small.

2. *Uncertainty about Future Projects*: If flexibility is viewed as an option, its value will increase when there is greater uncertainty about future projects; thus, firms with predictable capital expenditures should value flexibility less than those with high variability in capital expenditures.

This option framework would imply that firms such as Microsoft and Compaq, which earn large excess returns on their projects and face more uncertainty about future investment needs, can justify holding large cash balances and excess debt capacity, whereas a firm such as Chrysler, with much smaller excess returns and more predictable investment needs, should hold a much smaller cash balance and less excess debt capacity. In fact, the value of flexibility can be calculated as a percentage of firm value, with the following inputs for the option pricing model.

S = Annual Net Capital Expenditures as percent of Firm Value (1 + Excess Return)

K = Annual Net Capital Expenditures as percent of Firm Value

t = 1 year (To provide an annual estimate)

σ^2 = Variance in ln(Net Capital Expenditures)

y = Annual Cost of Holding Cash or Maintaining Excess Debt Capacity as % of Firm Value

To illustrate, assume that a firm which earns 18% on its projects has a cost of capital of 13%, and that net capital expenditures are 10% of firm value; the variance in ln(net capital expenditures) is 0.04. Also assume that the firm could have a cost of capital of 12% if it used its excess debt capacity. The value of flexibility as a percentage of firm value can be estimated as follows:

S = 10% (1.05) = 10.50%   [Excess Return = 18% − 13% = 5%]
K = 10%
t = 1 year
σ^2 = 0.04
y = 13% − 12% = 1%

Based on these inputs and a riskless rate of 5%, the annual value of flexibility is 1.31% of firm value.

CONCLUSION

Option pricing theory has a wide range of applications in corporate finance, many of which we have explored in this chapter. We began the chapter with a discussion of some of the measurement issues that make the pricing of real options more difficult than the pricing of options on financial assets. We then considered three options embedded in investment projects: the option to delay a project, the option to expand a project and the option to abandon a project. In all of these cases, the underlying asset was the project, and the options added value to the project. We then posed the argument that equity could be viewed as a call option on the firm and that equity would have value even when the firm value was less than the outstanding claims on it. Furthermore, viewing equity as an option allows us to consider the conflict between stockholders and bondholders much more clearly and provides us with insights on why conglomerates may make stockholders worse off, while making bondholders better off. Finally, we used option pricing theory to examine the value of flexibility in a firm.

QUESTIONS AND PROBLEMS

1. Options and futures contracts are both called derivative securities, and they're often mentioned in the same breath. What is the primary difference between the two?

2. The previous chapter showed that the time premium associated with the remaining life of an American call option usually makes early exercise sub-optimal. This implies that we may price most American calls as European calls because we can safely make the assumption that the right to exercise early is worth zero. (More succinctly, this is usually phrased as "American calls are worth more alive than dead.") Should we make the same assumption concerning callable bonds? Why or why not?

3. How do warrants and convertible bonds differ, and what does this difference imply about the strike prices of each?

4. You have been asked to value a 10-year convertible bond with the following features:

   Current rating of company issuing bond = BBB
   Current interest rate on 10-year BBB straight bonds
   = 12%
   Coupon rate on 10-year convertible bond = 8%

   The convertible bond can be converted into 40 shares of stock at $25. The current stock price is $20, and the company pays an annual dividend of $1 per share. The standard deviation of the stock is 10%, and the 10-year Treasury bond rate is 10%.

   a. What is the conversion option worth?

   b. What is the value of the straight bond portion of the convertible bond?

5. You are considering purchasing a callable bond that has 20 years to maturity and an 11.5% coupon rate that is callable (effective immediately) at 95% of face value. If similar non-callable bonds have a yield to maturity of 12% and the bond is currently selling for $900, what is the call option worth to the company?

6. A company is considering delaying a project that has annual after-tax cash flows of $25 million but that costs $300 million to take. (The life of the project is 20 years, and the cost of capital is 16%.) A simulation of the cash flows leads you to conclude that the standard deviation in the present value of cash inflows is 20%. If you can acquire the rights to the project for the next 10 years, what are the inputs for the option pricing model? (The six-month Treasury

bill rate is 8%, the 10-year bond-rate is 12%, and the 20-year bond rate is 14%.)

7. You are valuing the compensation package of an executive for your company. He has been guaranteed $500,000 next year, and he will also receive $10,000 for every dollar above $50 the stock price rises over the next year. The bonus package will be capped off at $250,000 (i.e., the executive will receive no additional bonuses if the stock price exceeds $75). The current stock price is $45. This company has only put options traded on it on the options exchange. The prices of the traded put options are provided below:

Strike price	3 month	6 month	1 year
45	1.00	2.25	3.00
50	7.00	9.00	12.00
75	30.25	30.50	31.00

The riskless interest rate is 10%. Value this package.

8. You have been approached by a real estate conglomerate with a deal: You can buy 100,000 square feet of space in a mall at $50/square foot. Over the next 10 years, you expect to make an after-tax cash inflow of $500,000 a year. At the end of 10 years, you expect to be able to sell the space back at $5 million to other investors.

   a. From a standard capital budgeting analysis, would you take this project if your discount rate were 15%?

   b. Assume that, as an inducement, the promoters offer to give you the option to buy another 100,000 square feet at today's price anytime over the next five years. The five-year bond rate is 6%, and the prices per square foot for the last six years have been as follows:

Year	Price/Square Foot
−6	$20
−5	$30
−4	$55
−3	$70
−2	$55
−1	$50

What is the value of this option?

9. Designate the following statements as true or false:

   a. Equity can be viewed as an option because equity investors have limited liability (limited to their equity investment in the firm).

b. Equity investors will sometimes take bad projects (with negative net present value) because they can add to the value of the firm.

c. Taking on a good project (with positive NPV)—which is less risky than the average risk of the firm—can negatively impact equity investors.

d. The value of equity in a firm is an increasing function of the duration of the debt in the firm (i.e., equity will be more valuable in a firm with longer-term debt than an otherwise similar firm with short-term debt).

e. In a merger in which two risky firms merge and do not borrow more money, equity can become less valuable because existing debt will become less risky.

10. XYZ Corporation has $500 million in zero-coupon debt outstanding, due in five years. The firm had earnings before interest and taxes of $40 million in the most recent year (the tax rate is 40%). These earnings are expected to grow 5% a year in perpetuity, and the firm paid no dividends. The firm had a cost of equity of 12% and a cost of capital of 10%. The annualized standard deviation in firm values of comparable firms is 12.5%. The five-year bond rate is 5%.

a. Estimate the value of the firm.

b. Estimate the value of equity, using an option pricing model.

c. Estimate the market value of debt and the appropriate interest rate on the debt.

11. One way to express the value of the firm in the previous problem is by using call options. To do so, we would depict ownership positions of the bondholders and equity holders as:

Equity holders	Bondholders
1. Equity holders own a call option on the firm with an exercise price of $500 million.	1. Bondholders own the firm.
	2. Bondholders have sold a call on the firm with an exercise price of $500 million to the equity holders.

How would you describe their ownership positions in terms of put contracts?

12. McCaw Cellular Communications reported earnings before interest and taxes of $850 million in 1993, and had a depreciation allowance of $400 million in that year (which was offset by capital spending of an equivalent amount). The earnings before interest and taxes are expected to grow 20% a year for the next five years and 5% a year after that. The

cost of capital is 10%. The firm has $10 billion in debt outstanding with the following characteristics:

Duration	Debt
1 year	$2 billion
2 years	$4 billion
5 years	$4 billion

The annualized standard deviation in the firm's stock price is 35%, whereas the annualized standard deviation in the traded bonds is 15%. The correlation between stock and bond prices has been 0.5. The firm has a debt/equity ratio of 50%, and the after-tax cost of debt is 6%. (The beta of the stock is 1.50; the 30-year Treasury bond rate is 7%.) The three-year bond rate is 5%.

a. Estimate the value of the firm.

b. Estimate the value of the equity.

c. The stock was trading at $60, and there were 210 million shares outstanding in January 1994. Estimate the implied standard deviation in firm value.

d. Estimate the market value of the debt.

13. You are examining the financial viability of investing in some abandoned copper mines in Chile, which still have significant copper deposits. A geology survey suggests that there might still be 10 million pounds of copper in the mines and that the cost of opening up the mines will be $3 million (in present value dollars). The capacity output rate is 400,000 pounds a year, and the price of copper is expected to increase 4% a year. The Chilean government is willing to grant a 25-year lease on the mine. The average production cost is expected to be 40 cents a pound, and the current price per pound of copper is 85 cents. (The production cost is expected to grow 3% a year, once initiated.) The annualized standard deviation in copper prices is 25%, and the 25-year bond rate is 7%.

a. Estimate the value of the mine using traditional capital budgeting techniques.

b. Estimate the value of the mine based on an option pricing model.

c. How would you explain the difference between the two values?

14. You have been asked to analyze the value of an oil company with substantial oil reserves. The estimated reserves amount to 10 million barrels, and the estimated present value of the development cost for each barrel is $12. The current price of oil is $20 per barrel, and the average production cost is estimated to be $6 per barrel. The company has the rights to these reserves for the next 20 years, and the 20-year bond rate is 7%. The company also proposes to extract 4% of its reserves each year to meet cash-flow needs. The annualized standard deviation in the price of the oil is 20%. What is the value of this oil company?

15. You are analyzing a capital budgeting project that is expected to have a PV of cash inflows of $250 million and will cost $200 million (in present value dollars) initially. A simulation of the project cash flows yields a variance in present value of cash inflows of 0.04. You have to pay $12.5 million a year to retain the project rights for the next five years. The five-year Treasury bond rate is 8%.

   a. What is the value of the project, based on traditional NPV?

   b. What is the value of the project as an option?

   c. Why are the two values different? What factor (or factors) determine the magnitude of this difference?

16. Cyclops, Inc., a high-technology company specializing in state-of-the-art visual technology, is considering going public. The company has no revenues or profits yet on its products, but it has a 10-year patent to a product that will enable contact lens users to obtain maintenance-free lens that will last for years. Although the product is technically viable, it is exorbitantly expensive to manufacture, and its immediate potential market will be relatively small. (A cash-flow analysis of the project suggests that the present value of the cash inflows on the project, if adopted now, would be $250 million, whereas the cost of the project would be $500 million.) The technology is evolving rapidly, and a simulation of alternative scenarios yields a wide range of present values, with an annualized standard deviation of 60%. To move toward this adoption, the company will have to continue to invest $10 million a year in research. The 10-year bond rate is 6%.

   a. Estimate the value of this company.

   b. How sensitive is this value estimate to the variance in project cash flows? What broader lessons would you draw from this analysis?

17. Answer true or false to the following statements:

   a. The right to pursue a project will not be valuable if there is a great deal of uncertainty about the viability of the project.

   b. A project can be viewed as an option only if there are some barriers to entry which prevent competitors from replicating it.

   c. A company that has valuable patents that do not yet generate cash flows and earnings will be undervalued using traditional discounted cash-flow valuation.

   d. A company should take on a project as soon as it becomes financially viable (i.e., when its NPV exceeds zero).

   e. The value of a project will increase as the volatility of the industry and the technology underlying the project increase.

18. FSS, Inc. has 5 million warrants outstanding that expire in three years. The current stock price is $45, and the warrants have a strike price of $57. There are 95 million shares outstanding in the company, the stock's dividend yield is 3.25%, the three-year T-bond rate is 7.23%, and the annualized variance in the value of FSS' equity is 12%. How much is each warrant worth?

19. You are analyzing a convertible bond with a face value of $1,000 and an annual coupon of 4%, which is convertible into 30 shares of stock anytime over the next 20 years. The current stock price is $27, and the convertible is trading at $1,177. Estimate the following:

   a. The conversion ratio and conversion price.

   b. The conversion premium.

   c. If the interest rate on straight bonds issued by the same company is 8%, estimate the value of the conversion option.

20. ITC Corporation has convertible bonds outstanding with the following features:

   • The bonds mature in 15 years; there are 100,000 bonds outstanding.

   • Each bond can be converted into 50 shares of stock anytime until expiration.

   • The coupon rate on the bond is 5%; straight bonds issued by the company are yielding 10%.

   • The current stock price is $15 per share, and the standard deviation in ln (stock prices) is 40%.

   • There are 20 million shares outstanding.

   a. Value the conversion option.

   b. Estimate the value of the straight bond portion.

   c. If these bonds were issued at par, who would be gaining? Who would be losing?

   d. What impact would forced conversion have on the value of this convertible bond?

21. A company has two issues of bonds outstanding; they both have the same maturities and coupon rates, but differ in one respect—the first issue (Issue A) is callable, whereas the second is not. Respond true or false to the following statements:

   a. The callable bonds will trade for a higher price than the noncallable bonds.

   b. The callable bonds have a shorter duration than the noncallable bonds.

   c. The callable bonds will have a higher yield than the noncallable bonds.

   d. The callable bonds will be more sensitive to interest rate changes than the noncallable bonds.

CHAPTER 29

RISK MANAGEMENT

In this chapter, we return to a topic we addressed earlier in the book—the measurement and management of risk. Firms are clearly exposed to a number of different sources of risk; some try to manage their risk exposures aggressively. Here, we examine the sources of risk, the various risk management products that are available, and the question of whether or not companies should manage risk, by answering the following questions:

- What are the different types of risk to which a firm is exposed, and how can they be categorized?

- How can a firm's risk exposure best be measured?

- What types of risk should a firm try to manage, and what is the payoff to active risk management?

- What are the different risk management products available, and how can a firm choose among them?

DEFINING AND CATEGORIZING A FIRM'S RISK EXPOSURE

Firms are exposed to a variety of risks, some of which are specific to the firm and others which are marketwide. Some can be hedged at low cost, whereas other risk is either expensive or impossible to hedge. In this section, we return to a theme we introduced earlier in this book on the categorization of risk, as a prelude to examining whether and how a company should manage risk.

Firm-Specific versus Market Risk

A fundamental feature of all the models for risk and return presented earlier in this book is the distinction between firm-specific and market risk. You will recall that *firm-specific risk* refers to risk that is isolated to a particular firm, group of firms, or an industry, which can be reduced, if not eliminated, by holding a well-diversified portfolio. *Market risk* is risk that is spread across firms and cannot be diversified away by holding such a portfolio.

Building on this distinction, the standard risk models conclude that firm-specific risk will not be rewarded and that only market risk is reflected in expected returns. If a particular risk is indeed firm-specific, firms that expend time and resources eliminating it may be doing their stockholders a disservice, because they (the stockholders) could have eliminated it themselves, at very little cost. To illustrate, consider the conglomerate mergers of the 1960s and 1970s; these acquisitions were driven by the stated motive of diversifying across industries. Although these acquisitions reduced exposure to industry risk, they did so at enormous cost (in the form of premiums in the acquisitions), whereas stockholders could have accomplished the same objective simply by holding mutual funds. When we are dealing with market risk, the call becomes more dicey. If a risk management product reduces market risk without reducing cash flows, it will clearly increase firm value. If, as is more likely, it reduces both market risk and cash flows, however, the net effect can be positive, negative, or neutral, depending on the change in each.

In Chapter 11, we noted how difficult it is in practice to distinguish between firm-specific and market risk; several types of risk fall in a "gray area" between the two. In Chapter 26, for instance, we pointed out that some firms consider exchange rate risk to be firm-specific risk, whereas others classify it as market risk. Part of the reason for this confusion is that different firms have different investor clienteles. Widely held firms whose investors are well diversified may categorize more risks as firm specific, whereas firms for whom a significant portion of the stock is held by an undiversified investor may look at many of the same risks as market risks.

□ Concept
Check

> Assume that you are looking at a firm whose CEO has his entire wealth invested in the firm and owns 20% of the outstanding stock. Will some of the risk the CEO views as market risk be viewed as firm specific by institutional investors in the firm? What kind of conflicts would you expect to arise as a consequence?

Continuous versus Event Risk

Another useful distinction to make when considering risk is to differentiate between risk that is continuous and risk that is tied to the occurrence of a specific event. For instance, interest rate risk is continuous, for interest rates can change by infinitesimal amounts, whereas the exposure of an insurance company to claims from a major earthquake in Southern California is event risk. The approaches available for managing risk are different for these two types. In the case of **continuous risk,** firms can avail themselves of futures, forward contracts, or options, whereas insurance products are usually more effective hedges against **event risk.**

Continuous Risk: This is risk arising from a source or factor that can change continuously; for example, interest rates and inflation.

Event Risk: This is the risk created by a specific event—for example, an earthquake, fire, or judgment in a lawsuit.

Event risk generally has a much larger impact on a firm's cash flows and value than does continuous risk. Consequently, investors perceive event risk as much riskier to the firm than equivalent continuous risk. In the early 1990s, for instance, tobacco firms were faced with the possibility of lawsuits potentially amounting to billions of dollars in damages. Even though the probability of these damages being awarded might have been low, the sheer size of the damages depressed tobacco companies' stock and bond prices for much of the period.

MEASURING RISK EXPOSURE

Once the sources of risk to a firm have been identified and classified into firm specific or market risk, the firm's exposure to these sources of risk can be measured. Theoretically, **risk exposure** can be measured at two levels. At the first level, the exposure of a firm's cash flows to changes in the specified variables (such as exchange rates or interest rates) are measured, providing a measure of both firm-specific and market risk, since cash flows are affected by both. At the second level, the exposures of firm or equity value to changes in the same variables are estimated; over extended periods, this provides a measure of market risk only.

Risk Exposure: This is a measure of how much the cash flows and value of a firm are affected by a specific risk source.

Within both approaches, the analysis can be done either at the level of equity investors or from the perspective of all investors in the firm. Thus, the exposure of cash flows to risk factors can be examined using either cash flows to equity or cash flows to the firm. If accounting measures are used, the analysis can be done using either net income or operating income. The exposure of value to the same risk factors can be estimated using either the value of equity or total firm value. To see why the risk exposure of the firm may be different from that of its equity investors, note the following:

Value of Equity = Value of the Firm − Value of Non-equity Claims

If debt is the only nonequity claim, the value of equity is the difference between the value of the firm and the value of the outstanding debt. The risk exposure of equity will be equal to that of the firm in only one case: when the risk exposure of debt is equal to the risk exposure of the firm. To illustrate, consider the exposure of a firm to interest rate risk, which can be measured through duration. The duration of the equity will be equal to the duration of the firm only if the debt has the same duration as the firm. In every other case, the duration of the equity will be different from that of the firm.

Knowing the differences between the duration of equity and that of the firm might help point out problems in the debt design and suggest ways in which the firm can alter the debt. For instance, a firm that has financed long-term projects with short-term debt will find the duration of its equity to be significantly higher than that of the firm. It can reduce this mismatch by issuing more long-term debt. More importantly, this information provides the basis for risk management—firms can hedge their risk at the equity level without having to eliminate firm risk.

❏ Concept Check

> Assume that a firm with cash flows that are negatively correlated with the level of interest rates uses floating rate debt to finance assets. Will the duration of the equity be greater or less than the duration of the firm? Explain.

Measurement Devices

The next issue to address is which measurement device should be used in estimating risk exposure. Many firms approach this issue subjectively, by examining the type of business in which they are operating and postulating the effects of changes in macroeconomic variables on their cash flows and value. Other approaches are available however, that provide not only a sense of the relationship but also quantitative measures of it. These approaches include Monte Carlo simulations, analytical measures, and regressions using historical data.

Monte Carlo simulations   In a **Monte Carlo simulation,** the firm's cash flows or values are analyzed as a function of changes in specific macroeconomic variables, such as interest rates, exchange rates, and inflation rates. The steps involved in such a simulation are as follows:

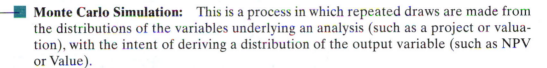

Monte Carlo Simulation: This is a process in which repeated draws are made from the distributions of the variables underlying an analysis (such as a project or valuation), with the intent of deriving a distribution of the output variable (such as NPV or Value).

Step 1:   Model the firm's cash flows or value as a function of the macroeconomic variables being analyzed. This can be done analytically, through a discounted cash-flow model or with the help of historical data.

Step 2:   Specify a distribution for each of the macroeconomic variables. For instance, for interest rates, provide a distribution for the level of rates in a future period, based on historical experience.

Step 3:   Draw one outcome from each macroeconomic distribution and calculate the firm's cash flows and value, given that outcome.

Step 4:   Repeat the process numerous times, obtaining cash flows and values each time.

Step 5:   Examine how value changes as a function of changes in the specified macroeconomic variable.

 IN PRACTICE   ESTIMATING RISK EXPOSURE AT MERCK

The following illustration draws on an article by Lewent and Kearny, explaining how Merck approached the measurement of exchange rate risk exposure in 1987. The authors were interested in measuring Merck's exposure to exchange rate risk, and they approached the question using a Monte Carlo simulation:

Step 1:   Using a mixture of historical data, fundamentals, and outside forecasts, Lewent and Kearny arrived at a range of possible values for both the DM and the Japanese yen. In the case of both currencies, they concluded that the upper limit on absolute changes from year to year was 20%, and they developed a distribution for each currency for the next five years. In doing so, they assigned probabilities for changes from period to period, assuming that there was some mean reversion in the process (i.e., that if the dollar strengthened by 20% in one year, the probability of doing so the next year would be lower). The ranges they assigned to the currencies are shown in Figure 29.1.

Step 2:   Lewent and Kearny estimated the effect of the exchange rate changes on the projected net income in their strategic plan. Based on their modeling of the relationship between net income and the exchange rates, they estimated the effects of a strengthening, weakening, and neutral dollar on net income, as shown in Figure 29.2.

They also translated the effect of exchange rate changes into a cumulative effect on net income, which they used as a basis for measuring Merck's exchange rate risk over multiple periods. Lewent and Kearney then proceeded to consider whether and how the exchange rate risk should be hedged. We will return to that discussion later in this chapter.

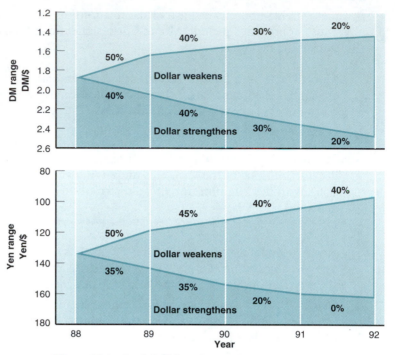

Figure 29.1   Probabilities of currency rate movements

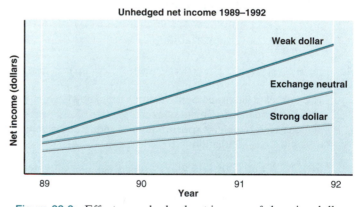

Figure 29.2   Effect on unhedged net income of changing dollar

Analytical measures   The second approach to estimating risk exposure is analytical. If firm value or cash flows can be modeled as a function of a macroeconomic variable, it is possible to estimate the sensitivity directly from the model. This can be illustrated best using duration, which has historically been used as a measure of interest rate risk for bonds. The derivation of the duration equation starts by specifying bond price as a function of interest rates.

$$\text{PV of Bond} = \sum_{t=1}^{t=N} \frac{\text{Coupon}_t}{(1 + r)^t} + \frac{\text{Face Value}}{(1 + r)^N}$$

Differentiating the bond price with respect to interest rate should provide a formal measure of bond price sensitivity to interest rate changes:

$$\text{Duration of Bond} = dP/dr = \frac{\left[\sum_{t=1}^{t=N}\dfrac{t * \text{Coupon}_t}{(1 + r)^t} + \dfrac{N * \text{Face Value}}{(1 + r)^N}\right]}{\left[\sum_{t=1}^{t=N}\dfrac{\text{Coupon}_t}{(1 + r)^t} + \dfrac{\text{Face Value}}{(1 + r)^N}\right]}$$

The bond price differential, *dP/dr,* is called the *duration of the bond*; it measures the interest rate sensitivity of the bond.

This analysis is straightforward for a bond because the cash flows on the bond do not vary with interest rates. With regard to firm value, however, the modeling becomes more involved because the cash flows of the firm may vary with interest rates, accentuating the effect of interest rate changes. To illustrate, assume that the value of the firm was written as a function of interest rates:

$$\text{Value of Firm} = \sum_{t=1}^{t=\infty}\frac{CF \text{ to Firm}(r)_t}{(1 + \text{WACC}(r))^t}$$

where

$$CF \text{ to Firm}(r)_t = \text{Cash flow to the firm in period } t, \text{ as a function of } r$$
$$\text{WACC}(r) = \text{Cost of capital as a function of } r$$

If the cash flows and the cost of capital can be modeled as a function of interest rates, it is possible that a measure similar to duration can be estimated for firm value.

□ Concept Check

> Would you expect the duration of firm value as defined above to be greater than or less than the conventional estimate of duration, which keeps cash flows constant? Explain.

Regressions using historical data   The third approach to measuring risk exposure draws on historical data on firm value, cash flows, and macroeconomic variables. It is the same approach we developed in Chapter 19 to lay the groundwork for the design of debt. Here, past changes in firm value or cash flows are regressed against past changes in a macroeconomic variable to obtain a measure of the sensitivity to that variable. Thus, the sensitivity of firm value to long-term interest rates is estimated as follows:

$$\Delta \text{ Firm Value}_t = a + b \Delta \text{ Interest Rate}_t$$

where

$$\Delta \text{ Firm Value}_t = \text{Percentage change in firm value in period } t$$
$$\Delta \text{ Interest Rate}_t = \text{Change in long-term interest rate in period } t[1]$$

The slope coefficient in the regression, *b,* becomes a measure of the exposure of firm value to changes in long-term rates. This analysis can be repeated using equity value and cash flows.

When examining several macroeconomic variables, this analysis can be done either one variable at a time, if the objective is to isolate its effect, or together, in a multiple regression, to capture the cumulative effect of all of the variables. Thus, a firm that is

---

[1] In theory, this change should be a percentage change in $(1 + r)$ to make it comparable to the traditional duration measures. Thus, an increase in rates from 8% to 9% will result in $(1 + r)$ going from 1.08 to 1.09, producing a percentage change of 0.926%. As a rough approximation, the change in rates, which is 1%, can be used without altering the results substantially.

interested in evaluating the exposure of its cash flows to change in interest rates, exchange rates, and inflation can do the following:

$$\Delta\,CF_t = a + b\,\Delta\,\text{Interest Rate}_t + c\,\Delta\,\text{Exchange Rate}_t + d\,\Delta\,\text{Inflation Rate}_t$$

where

$$\Delta\,CF_t = \text{Change in cash flow in period } t$$

The coefficients on each of the macroeconomic variables become measures of the firm's cash-flow exposure to each.

The availability of historical data makes this approach easy to use, but there are some caveats. First, the regressions often provide very noisy estimates of the exposures. For instance, regressing firm value against long-term rates for Boeing using historical data for the last 15 years provides a duration estimate of 9.94 years, but the standard error of 7.13 on the regression provides a range from 2.81 years to 17.07 years for the duration.[2] Second, even if the regressions are estimated precisely, the underlying assumption is that past patterns will continue into the future. Although this may be acceptable for firms that expect to retain the same business mix in the future as they had during the regression, it becomes less defensible when firms change business mixes over the period. Third, statistical problems are associated with the regressions, especially with several independent variables. In the regression shown above, changes in interest rates, for instance, are likely to be correlated with changes in inflation rates, resulting in larger standard errors and noisier estimates.[3]

Despite these problems, the regression methodology has some value. Regression estimates can be used in conjunction with the subjective understanding of the firm's business and the other approaches listed above to measure risk exposure. Regression estimates can also be obtained for a number of firms within a peer group to arrive at average estimates by industry. These estimates are likely to be less noisy than those for any individual firm. Moreover, when it comes to firm or equity value, at least, the data can be sliced finer, at monthly or even weekly intervals, to arrive at better estimates of risk exposures.

☐ Concept
Check

> Why might the average estimates obtained across firms within an industry be more reliable estimates of risk exposure than those obtained directly from the firm?

IN PRACTICE ESTIMATING RISK EXPOSURE FOR THE HOME DEPOT

In the following example, we estimate the risk exposure of the Home Depot equity investors to interest rate risk, exchange rate risk, economic risk, and inflation risk. Table 29.1 provides annual data on stock prices and macroeconomic variables from 1983 to 1995.

To measure risk exposure, we first compute the percentage changes in these variables on a year-to-year basis as shown in Table 29.2. [For interest rates and inflation rates, the percentage changes in (1+rate) are computed. Thus, if interest rates drop from 8% to 7%, as they did in 1995, the percentage change is computed to be 1.07/1.08-1].

[2]This range is estimated by using a confidence level of 67%. The range become even larger for higher confidence intervals.

[3]In a multiple regression, the independent variables should be uncorrelated with one other. When this is not true, multicollinearity is said to exist.

Table 29.1   **STOCK PRICE, INTEREST RATES, INFLATION RATES, AND EXCHANGE RATES: THE HOME DEPOT**

Year	Stock Price ($)	Interest Rate (%)	Inflation Rate (%)	Exchange Rate
1983	2.59	12.00	3.20	128.65
1984	1.75	12.70	4.30	138.89
1985	1.23	11.40	3.50	125.95
1986	1.77	9.00	1.90	112.89
1987	2.78	9.40	3.70	95.88
1988	4.69	9.70	4.10	95.32
1989	8.17	9.30	4.80	102.26
1990	12.88	9.30	5.40	96.25
1991	33.66	8.80	4.20	98.82
1992	50.63	8.10	3.00	104.58
1993	39.50	7.20	3.00	105.22
1994	46.00	8.00	2.60	98.6
1995	47.75	7.00	2.80	102.3

Table 29.2   **CHANGES IN VARIABLES: THE HOME DEPOT**

Year	Change in Stock Price (%)	Change in Interest Rates (%)	Change in Inflation Rate (%)	Change in Weighted Dollar (%)
1984	−32.43	0.63	1.07	7.96
1985	−29.71	−1.15	−0.77	−9.32
1986	43.90	−2.15	−1.55	−10.37
1987	57.06	0.37	1.77	−15.07
1988	68.71	0.27	0.39	−0.58
1989	74.20	−0.36	0.67	7.28
1990	57.65	0.00	0.57	−5.88
1991	161.34	−0.46	−1.14	2.67
1992	50.42	−0.64	−1.15	5.83
1993	−21.98	−0.83	0.00	0.61
1994	16.46	0.75	−0.39	−6.29
1995	3.80	−0.93	0.19	3.75

The risk exposures are computed in two ways. In the first, the changes in stock prices are regressed against each of the variables separately:

$$\text{Change in Stock Price} = 0.39 \quad + 3.06 \text{ Change in Interest Rates}$$
$$(0.17) \qquad (20.69)$$

$$\text{Change in Stock Price} = 0.37 \quad - 9.36 \text{ Change in Inflation Rates}$$
$$(0.16) \qquad (17.14)$$

$$\text{Change in Stock Price} = 0.38 \quad + 0.34 \text{ Change in Weighted Dollar}$$
$$(0.17) \qquad (2.28)$$

The standard errors are reported in parentheses. The alternative approach to dealing with risk is to throw all of the variables into the same regression and estimate risk exposures:

$$
\begin{aligned}
\text{Change in Stock Price} = 0.44 \quad & + 18.18 \text{ Change in Interest Rates} \\
(0.22) \quad & (30.05) \\
& - 19.40 \text{ Change in Inflation Rate} \\
& (25.04) \\
& + 0.06 \text{ Change in Weighted Dollar} \\
& (2.50)
\end{aligned}
$$

Based on these regressions, we conclude that the Home Depot's equity investors were positively impacted by interest rate increases during the period, negatively affected by increases in inflation, and unaffected by changes in the dollar. None of the regressions provides significant coefficients, however, which could be used to argue that the Home Depot is not exposed to much risk on any of these fronts. Using quarterly or monthly data may provide us with more robust conclusions, however.

THE PAYOFFS TO RISK MANAGEMENT

Once risk has been identified and measured, the next question is whether or not firms should try to manage risk, which often involves the use of derivatives or insurance.

The Effect on Value
You will recall that the value of a firm is the present value of the expected cash flows, discounted back at a rate that reflects both the riskiness of the underlying business and the financing mix used by the firm. In other words, firm value is driven by two inputs—expected cash flows and discount rates. Thus, for risk management to affect value it has to impact either one or both of these variables. The possible scenarios are simplified in Table 29.3.

Table 29.3   POSSIBLE EFFECTS OF RISK MANAGEMENT ON VALUE

Effect on Cash Flow	Effect on Discount Rate	Effect on Value
Unaffected	Unaffected	None
Decrease	Unaffected	Decrease
Unaffected	Decrease	Increase
Decrease	Decrease	Depends on net effect

The scenarios under which risk management has a *negative* or *neutral* effect on value are fairly easy to document.

- If a firm spends money, thus reducing cash flows, to eliminate firm-specific risk that does not affect discount rates, the effect on value will be negative.
- If a firm is able to hedge a firm-specific risk costlessly, neither cash flows nor discount rates will be affected; consequently, there will be no change in value.

Implicit in both of these scenarios is the assumption that there are no positive feedback effects from reducing the firm-specific risk. In particular, we are assuming that reducing firm-specific risk will not alter the expected cash flows from existing projects, future investment decisions, or the optimal financing mix (and cost of capital) for the firm. Also implicit is the assumption that the typical investor in the firm is well diversified and thus does not care about the firm-specific risk. To the extent that any or all of these assumptions are violated, risk management may *increase* firm value.

Potential Value Gains

The value gains from risk management come from many areas, including tax savings, default risk/debt capacity, investment policy, dividend policy, perceived risk, and undiversified investors.

Tax savings All valuation is done on an after-tax basis. Thus, any effect that risk management has on the expected taxes paid over time will affect the expected after-tax cash flows and, through them, the value. If tax rates are linear and losses can be offset against income in other years, risk management should not affect the tax savings. When tax rates increase with income or there are restrictions on the carry-forward or -back of tax losses, however, risk management can increase tax savings and value.

To illustrate, assume that a firm faces a tax rate of 35% for income below $1 billion but has to pay a super-normal profit tax of 50% on income above $1 billion. Also assume that this firm is sensitive to exchange rate changes and that its unhedged taxable income and tax liability are as follows over time:

Year	Taxable Income (in billions)	Taxes
1	0.5	0.175
2	1.5	0.6
3	0.7	0.245
4	1.7	0.7
5	1	0.35

Now assume that the firm uses risk management to smooth out its income over time. The taxable income and taxes under this scenario are reported in Table 29.4, along with nominal and present value of the taxes (using a cost of capital of 12.5%) over the five years.

Table 29.4 TAXES ON INCOME WITH AND WITHOUT HEDGE				
Year	Taxable Income	Taxes	Taxable Income with Hedge	Taxes with Hedge
1	$0.5000	$0.1750	$0.9000	$0.3150
2	1.5000	0.6000	1.1000	0.4000
3	0.7000	0.2450	1.2000	0.4500
4	1.7000	0.7000	1.2000	0.4500
5	1.0000	0.3500	1.0000	0.3500
Nominal	5.4000	2.0700	5.4000	1.9650
PV		1.4329		1.3873

As you can see, risk management does not alter the nominal taxable income over time, but it does result in tax savings, both in nominal and present value terms.

Concept
Check

In the example above, we assumed that income could be smoothed at no cost. Assuming that there is a cost to smoothing, how much should this firm be willing to pay (in present value terms) for the smoothing?

Effects on Default Risk/ Debt Capacity   The cost of capital that is used to discount the cash flows of a firm is generally a function of its debt ratio. In Chapter 18, we noted that there is an optimal debt ratio for most firms, at which the cost of capital is minimized. The optimal debt ratio is determined by many variables, but the variability in operating income is one of the most important. Firms with volatile operating income will be less inclined to borrow, because they have a much greater chance of bankruptcy and face much higher costs of borrowing. If the volatility in operating income is caused by risk factors against which a firm can hedge, such as short-term exchange rate movements, risk management may reduce income volatility and increase the optimal debt ratio, which will lower the cost of capital and increase the firm value.

The benefits of risk management from the perspective of default risk can be presented in another way: when outlining the costs of bankruptcy, we noted that the indirect costs of bankruptcy, arising from the perception of customers and suppliers that a firm is in trouble, are usually much greater than the direct costs. In such cases, reducing income volatility using risk management techniques will reduce these indirect costs and increase firm value.

IN PRACTICE: DEFAULT RISK, DEBT CAPACITY, AND RISK MANAGEMENT

FOP Inc. is a consumer products company with extensive operations in other countries and, consequently, a high exposure to foreign exchange risk. In 1995, FOP reported EBITDA of $584 million and had an optimal debt ratio of 40%, based on the minimization of cost of capital. Figure 29.3 graphs the firm's value and cost of capital against debt ratios.

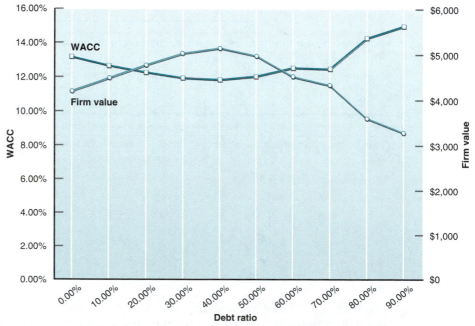

Figure 29.3   FOP Inc: WACC and firm value and debt ratios

As you can see, the firm value is maximized at $5.14 billion, at 40% debt. It uses no debt currently and has a firm value of $4.2 billion, because managers were concerned about the volatility in operating income.

Assume that half of the volatility in operating income comes from exchange rate risk and that managers will be willing to move to the optimal debt ratio if the exchange rate risk is eliminated. The increase in value associated with risk management can then be estimated as follows:

Value of the firm at current debt ratio of 0% = $4.2 billion
Value of the firm at optimal debt ratio of 30% = $5.14 billion
Increase in value from going to the optimal = $0.94 billion

FOP Inc. will gain from risk management, even if hedging the risk is expensive, because of the significant value gain it will experience from exploiting excess debt capacity.

Effects on investment policy   Ideally, in a frictionless world with no agency costs and efficient markets, managers would make investment decisions based purely on their merit and would raise funds from financial markets to finance good projects. In reality, investment decisions are made under a variety of constraints. First, managers are often more risk averse than their stockholders when it comes to taking projects, because bankruptcy might have much more serious consequences for them. Second, bondholders may write covenants into bond agreements to restrict investment policy, because of their concerns about risk shifting. Third, financial markets may not appraise investment projects fairly; thus, firms that need external financing for good projects may end up not taking the projects at all.

Risk management may help ease all of these constraints. Managers may be much more willing to take on projects in countries with volatile currencies if they know that they can hedge some or all of the exchange rate risk away. Bondholders may be more willing to ease investment constraints if the firm uses risk management products to eliminate some of the volatility in projects, and firms with volatile income may be able to access external financing much more easily if they can smooth income using risk management techniques.

> **Concept Check**
>
> Why might other stakeholders in the firm (such as managers and bondholders) view bankruptcy risk differently from stockholders?

To illustrate, consider CTS Inc., an apparel retail firm with a competent, though conservative, management team. The managers operate under the constraint that the standard deviation of operating income should not exceed 30%, on an annual basis. (Beyond this level, the bankruptcy risk is assumed to increase significantly.)

CTS Inc. is offered the opportunity to expand into the Mexican market, but this venture will increase the variance of the operating income to 35%, which is above the self-imposed constraint. Some of the increase is associated with the greater growth and risk in these markets, but some of it reflects the high exchange rate risk associated with the peso.

Assuming that the exchange rate risk can be eliminated and that doing so reduces the variance in operating income to below 30%, CTS Inc. can now expand into the Mexican market without violating its risk constraints.

> **Concept Check**
>
> In the example above, the constraints on variability and risk are largely self imposed. Would your analysis have been any different if the constraints had been imposed by an external entity (say, bondholders)?

Effects on dividend policy In our discussion of dividend policy in Chapters 20 and 21, we noted that firms often hold back on cash that could be paid to stockholders because of their concerns about varying income over time and their desire to maintain stable dividends. This cash retention, in turn, may adversely affect firm value if it is invested in substandard projects or used for acquisitions. Risk management may provide managers with the tools to smooth income over time, enabling them to be less conservative in their dividend policy. If retaining less cash translates into taking fewer poor projects over time, firm value will be increased.

Effects on perceived risk Occasionally, firms may find that markets perceive them to be much more risky than they really are. If the source of the misperception is a risk source that can be hedged, the firm may gain by eliminating it. For instance, assume that you are the manager of a firm that has very stable real growth but whose sales are primarily overseas. The earnings of this firm may shift considerably from period to period, depending on exchange rate changes. If markets focus on this variability and penalize the firm disproportionately, the firm may be better off using some of its resources to hedge away this risk.

Benefits for undiversified investors Thus far, we have focused on the potential benefits of risk management to well-diversified investors in the firm. Additional benefits that accrue to investors who are *not* well diversified. In some cases, these investors are also significant stakeholders and top managers in the firm. They are affected by risk that would be classified as firm-specific, because they are not well diversified, and any actions taken by the firm to reduce this risk will be viewed positively. This benefit is magnified for private firms, particularly those owned by one or a few investors.

This discussion can be expanded to include a firm's employees who do not own a financial stake in the firm but still have a considerable amount of their human capital invested in the firm. If the firm has volatile income, which creates default risk, these employees may demand higher compensation to work for the firm. One benefit of risk management might be to ease the concerns these employees have about risk; consequently, the firm saves on the compensation it would have had to pay to retain these employees.

Propositions About Risk Management
We can posit some simple, but powerful, propositions about risk management:

> **Proposition 1:** If risk can be hedged at negligible cost—through operational decisions, financial decisions, or with derivatives—it should be. At worst, hedging risk will have no effect on value; at best, it will provide positive feedback effects that will increase value.
>
> **Proposition 2:** When risk can be hedged at a cost, it makes sense to hedge the risk only if the benefits that arise from the hedging—such as reduced taxes, increased debt capacity, or better investment decisions—exceed the cost.

Corollary 1: Closely held or private firms typically gain more from risk hedging than do firms that are widely held, with well-diversified investors.

Corollary 2: Firms that experience significant agency problems between managers and stockholders, and stockholders and bondholders, are likely to gain more from risk hedging than are firms that do not suffer from such problems, and will find their investment choices expanded the most by using risk management products.

Corollary 3: Firms that are most exposed to indirect bankruptcy costs will also gain the most from risk management products. In Chapter 17, we noted that firms that manufacture tangible goods with long lives or provide long-term service and warranties are more exposed to indirect bankruptcy costs. The use of the risk management products will reduce the expected bankruptcy cost and increase the optimal debt ratio.

❏ Concept
Check

> Small, privately run firms should not use risk management products, because such products will be much more costly for them than for large multinational firms. Comment.

CHOOSING AMONG RISK MANAGEMENT PRODUCTS

Once a firm has measured its risk exposure and decided to hedge away the risk, it has to decide on the exact mechanism for risk reduction. In recent years, a number of new products have been created expressly for the purpose of risk management. We will look at the forces behind the evolution of these new products and the choices firms have when it comes to risk management.

The Choices
When firms decide to manage risk, they have a variety of choices. They can use futures contracts, forward contracts, options, and swaps to manage interest rates, exchange rate, and commodity price risk; and insurance products to manage event risk. The first group—derivatives such as futures, forwards, options, and swaps—has seen a surge in usage in the last two decades on the part of U.S. companies. The second group is made up of the more traditional insurance products that companies have used for a much longer period of time to protect against specific types of risk.

Swap: A swap is an exchange on one set of cash flows (such as those on a floating rate loan) for another of equivalent market value (such as those on a fixed rate loan).

Futures, Forwards, Options, and Swaps   The most widely used derivative products in risk management are futures, forwards, options, and swaps. Although there are fundamental differences among these products, the basic building blocks for all of them are relatively simple. Let us begin with the simplest—the forward contract. A forward contract is an agreement to buy a specified asset at a fixed price in the future, and so the payoff diagram is as shown in Figure 29.4. If the actual price at the time the forward contract expires is greater than the forward price, the buyer of the contract makes a gain equal to the difference; if the actual price is lower, the buyer makes a loss. Because forward contracts are between private parties, however, the possibility always exists that the losing party may default on the agreement.

The payoff diagram on a *futures contract* is similar to that of a forward contract, with three major differences. First, because futures contracts are traded on exchanges, they are much more liquid and there is no default or credit risk. This condition has to be offset against the fact that futures contracts are standardized and cannot be adapted to

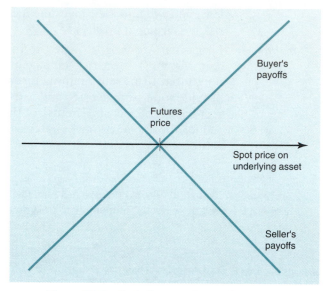

Figure 29.4 Cash flows on forward contract

meet the firm's precise needs. Second, futures contracts require both parties (buyer and seller) to settle differences on a daily basis rather than waiting for expiration. Thus, if a firm buys a futures contract on oil, and oil prices go down, the firm is obligated to pay the seller of the contract the difference. By settling futures contracts at the end of every day, they are converted into a sequence of one-day forward contracts. Third, when a futures contract is bought or sold, the parties are required to put up a percentage of the price of the contract as a "margin." This operates as a performance bond, ensuring that there is no default risk.

A *swap contract* is a contract to exchange one set of cash flows for another one of equivalent value. For instance, in a fixed-for-floating swap, a firm with an obligation to pay fixed cash flows may convert that obligation into cash flows tied to an interest rate that changes from period to period, as shown in Figure 29.5.

Note that a swap can be decomposed into a portfolio of forward contracts. For instance, in the above example, the party in this swap contract has agreed to sell a fixed rate cash flow for an amount specified at the initiation of the swap contract. Although forward contracts are completely exposed to credit risk, and futures contracts are almost completely protected, swap contracts maintain some credit risk. The risk, however, is less than that in a forward contract because of the shortening of the performance period. In the above example, when the fixed rate loan is swapped for a floating rate loan, with rates reset every six months, the performance period becomes six months, because the parties will settle the differences at that interval.

Options differ from futures and forward contracts in their payoff profiles, which limit losses to the buyers to the prices paid for the options. A call option gives buyers the rights to buy a specified asset at a fixed price anytime before expiration, whereas a put option gives buyers the right to *sell* a specified asset at a fixed price. Figure 29.6 illustrates both payoff diagrams. We examined the pricing of call and put options in detail in Chapter 27. Although the payoff diagrams for options look very different from those for futures and forwards, an option can always be created by combining a forward contract with a risk-free security. This insight was used to create the replicating portfolios that underlie option pricing models.

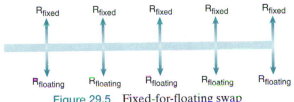

Figure 29.5   Fixed-for-floating swap

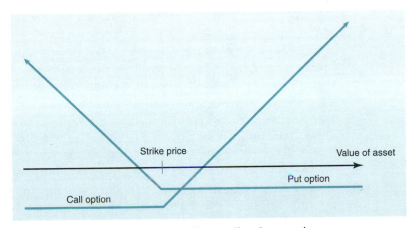

Figure 29.6   Payoffs on call and put options

Insurance products   The alternative route to risk management is to buy insurance to cover specific event risk. Just as a homeowner buys insurance on his or her house to protect against the eventuality of fire or other damage, companies buy insurance to protect their assets against possible loss. In fact, it can be argued that, in spite of the attention given to the use of derivatives in risk management, traditional insurance remains the primary vehicle.

Insurance does not eliminate risk; rather, it shifts it from the firm buying the insurance to the insurance firm selling it. Smith and Mayers argue that this risk shifting may provide a benefit to both sides, for a number of reasons. First, the insurance company may be able to create a portfolio of assets, thereby gaining diversification benefits that the firm itself cannot obtain. Second, the insurance company might acquire the expertise to evaluate risk and process claims more efficiently as a consequence of its repeated exposure to that risk. Third, insurance companies might provide other services, such as inspection and safety services, that benefit both sides. Although a third party could arguably provide the same service, the insurance company has an incentive to ensure the quality of the service.

Choosing among products   Once firms have decided to hedge or manage a specific risk, they have to pick among competing products to achieve this objective. To make this choice, let us review their costs and benefits:

- *Forward contracts* provide the most complete risk hedging because they can be designed to a firm's specific needs, but only if the firm knows its future cash-flow needs. The customized design may result in a higher transaction cost for the firm, however, especially if the scale of the cash flows is small, and forward contracts may expose both parties to credit risk.

- *Futures contracts* provide a cheaper alternative to forward contracts, insofar as they are traded on the exchanges and do not have be customized. They also eliminate credit risk, but they require margins and cash flows on a daily basis. Finally, they may not provide complete protection against risk because they are standardized.

- Unlike futures and forward contracts, which hedge both downside and upside risk, *option contracts* provide protection against only downside risk, while preserving upside potential. This benefit has to be weighed against the cost of buying the options, however, which will vary with the amount of protection desired.

- *Swap contracts*, especially in conjunction with forward or option contracts, can provide customized solutions for firms that are exposed to risk, but have very specific views about future price movements. For instance, a firm that believes that interest rates will either fall dramatically or increase marginally in the next period can use swaps and options to create payoffs that match these expectations.

- In combating event risk, a firm can either *self-insure* or use a *third-party insurance* product. Self-insurance makes sense if the firm can achieve the benefits of risk pooling on its own, does not need the services or support offered by insurance companies, and can provide the insurance more economically than the third party.

As with everything else in corporate finance, firms have to make tradeoffs. The objective, after all, is not complete protection against risk, but as much protection as makes sense, given the marginal benefits and costs of acquiring the protection.

 IN PRACTICE: EXTENDING THE RISK MANAGEMENT DECISION—MERCK

Extending the example introduced earlier in the chapter, Lewent and Kearny followed up their measurement of exchange rate risk exposure for Merck with decisions on whether this risk should be managed and, if so, what instruments to use to do so.

To make the argument that exchange rate risk should be managed, Lewent and Kearny looked at three external factors:

1. *Stock prices and exchange rate volatility:* Lewent and Kearny found no evidence that the stock price was negatively affected by earnings variations caused by exchange rate volatility; analysts following the stock also seemed to believe that exchange rate effects were, at best, second-order effects.

2. *Investor clienteles:* They considered two groups—those who viewed Merck as a foreign exchange play and did not want it to hedge its risk, and those who wanted a pure play on the health care business and wanted risk hedged. They decided that it would be inappropriate to give too much weight to any specific type of investor.

3. *Dividend policy:* From the perspective of maintaining dividends, Kearny and Lewent noted that exchange rate changes may undercut Merck's policy of increasing dividends. Thus, managing exchange rate risk may enable Merck to maintain and grow dividends as planned.

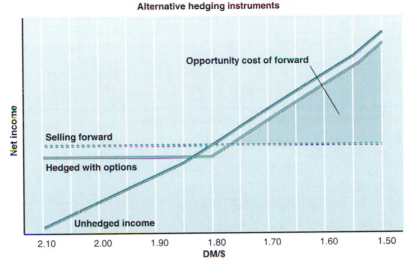

Figure 29.7   Opportunity cost of using a forward

Looking at internal factors, Kearny and Lewent were concerned about exchange rate movements undercutting Merck's ability to maintain and increase its R&D.

Overall, Kearny and Lewent concluded that managing exchange rate risk was important, given the dividend policy and internal concerns stated above. They then compared forwards and options as alternative approaches to managing exchange rate risk and noted that the tradeoff was between the higher cost of the option, up front, versus its ability to allow Merck to share in the upside if exchange rates moved in their favor. Figure 29.7 illustrates the opportunity cost of using a forward as opposed to an option.

Given the possibility of exchange rate movements in both directions, and Merck's desire to maintain a share of the upside if exchange rates weakened, Kearny and Lewent concluded that options should be used to manage exchange rate risk. They also made the following recommendations:

- Hedge risk on a multiyear basis rather than on a year-to-year basis, based on their assumption that there was mean reversion in exchange rates.

- Do not use options that are too far out-of-the-money, because they will be less effective in insuring against adverse exchange rate movements.

- Hedge on a partial basis and self-hedge for the remainder.

RISK MANAGEMENT IN PRACTICE

A number of surveys have examined the state of risk management in U.S. companies. The first was done by Booth, Smith and Stolz on financial institutions in 1982. In 1985, Block and Gallagher surveyed the Fortune 500 companies on their use of interest rate risk products. In 1989, Davis surveyed financial executives on their use of risk management products, and Miller did the same with subscribers to Business International Publications. The results of these surveys are summarized in Table 29.5.

The findings are summarized in Rawls and Smithson as follows:

- Most firms view risk management as an important function, though they seldom make formal statements about their objectives in risk management.

- Most firms use risk management, albeit selectively, to reduce risk. One of the reasons given for risk management is to secure a competitive advantage; that is, export firms want to lock in exchange rates when the dollar is low to provide them with a cost advantage for the future.

Table 29.5   RESULTS OF RISK MANAGEMENT SURVEYS

	DAVIS (1989) 255 Members of FEI		MILLAR (1989) 173 Subscribers of Business International Pubs.	BOOTH/SMITH/STOLTZ (1984) 238 Financial Institutions	BLOCK/GALLAGHER (1986) 193 of Fotune 500
1a. Rank Risk Management versus other financial objectives					
• Minimize Borrowing Cost	1 (100)				
• Maintain/Improve Credits	2 (61)		▶ 1 (100)		
• Maintain Financial Risk	3 (56)		2 (52)		
• Broaden Funding Sources	4 (37)		3 (16)		
1b. How is the Risk Management function organized?					
• Percent of firms where treasury is profit center	▼	7%	3%	16%	
• Percent of firms having risk management policy statement	15%	13%	20%	46%	
2. Goals for Risk Management					
• Eliminate All Risk	2%	7%	58%	59%	▶
• Eliminate Risk Selectivity	31%	34%	52%	52%	67%
• Allow Profits			8%	16%	
• Actively Seeks Profits			5%	7%	1%
• Seek Competitive Advantage			29%	25%	32%
• Tax/Reg./Acctg. Arbitrage			0%	4%	
• Do Not Manage Risk	46%	22%	16%	1%	
3. What exposures does the firm manage?/How does the firm measure its exposure?					
• Gap / Duration / Simulation — Translation			26%	39%	
Transaction (Firm Com.)			14%	79%	
Transaction (Within 1 yr.)			52%	62%	
Transaction (Beyond 1 yr.)				16%	
Contingent Exposure				15%	
Competitive Exposure				15%	
4. What Risk Management Instruments has the firm used?					
• Forwards		45%	35%	99%	
• Futures	8%	14%	25%	20%	17%
• Swaps	24%	9%	68%	64%	▶
• Options	24%	9%	43%	48%	19%

▶ **Combined**   ▦ **Interest Rates   FX Rates**

• Many of the firms use simulations, rather than duration measures, to measure and manage interest rate risk exposure. In the case of exchange rate risk, the focus is on hedging transactions risk exposure.

• The most widely used risk management product is the foreign exchange forward contract; futures contracts are relatively unused.

Rawls and Smithson followed up to examine whether firms were communicating their risk management policies to their stockholders; they concluded that they were not. Of the 20 annual reports that Rawls and Smithson examined, only seven mentioned risk management. Given that stockholders need this information in order to decide on additional risk hedging, it can be argued that firms still have a long way to go before they can claim to be reporting their risk management activities.

These surveys also examined some of the primary problems associated with risk management; the results are summarized in Rawls and Smithson (Table 29.6).

Table 29.6   RANK OF DIFFICULTIES WITH IMPLEMENTATION OF RISK MANAGEMENT

Rank of Difficulties With Implementing Risk Management (Relative Ranks)	DAVIS (1989) 255 members of F.E.I.	BOOTH/SMITH/STOLTZ (1984) 238 Financial Institutions	BLOCK/GALLAGHER (1986) 193 of Fortune 500
Resistance by Senior Mgmt. or Board of Directors			
	4 (23)	2	2 (78)
Lack of Knowledge			
	2 (88)	1	3 (69)
Accounting/Legal Difficulties			
	5 (20)	2	5 (38)
Cost (Upfront fees or Foregone Gains)			
	3 (45)	—	1 (100)
No Suitable Instrument			
	1 (100)	—	4 (44)

Although many firms mentioned top management resistance and lack of knowledge as primary problems, the accounting treatment of risk management products also created problems for firms that have used them. Even accountants admit that accounting standards have lagged behind the development of new risk management products and that many of these products are either not dealt with at all or are treated inconsistently.

CONCLUSION

Firms deal with risk as part of their day-to-day operations. Some risk is specific to the firm or the industry in which it operates, whereas other risk is marketwide. There are four basic steps in managing this risk:

1. The first step in risk management is to identify the risks to which a firm is exposed and to classify this risk into that which investors in the firm can diversify away by holding a well-diversified portfolio and that which they cannot.

2. Once the risk has been identified, firms have to measure their exposure to this risk using one of several approaches: through simulations (the effects of changing the risk variable are calculated for cash flows and value), analytically (cash flows and value are modeled as a function of the risk variable, and the risk measure is derived from the model), or through regressions (historical data are used to measure the relationship between the risk variables and cash flows or value).

3. After the risk exposure has been measured, the firm must decide whether to manage or hedge this risk. For risk management to change value, it has to affect either expected cash flows or discount rates, and the effect on value can be positive, neutral, or even negative. Risk management can have a positive effect on value by increasing tax savings, reducing default risk and its associated costs, and changing investment decisions. This effect has to be weighed against the costs of hedging the risk; if the benefits exceed the costs, risk management increases firm value.

4. Once firms have decided to hedge risk, they have a variety of choices. For firms with specific risk and cash-flow exposures to risk, such as a known future cash inflow or outflow in a foreign currency, and a desire to hedge this risk, forward contracts provide the most complete protection. For firms that are willing to settle for less than a perfect hedge, standardized futures contracts trading on the exchanges may provide sufficient protection. Finally, for firms that have specific views on the future, options and swaps enable downside risk to be hedged while preserving upside potential.

QUESTIONS AND PROBLEMS

1. What will be the duration of a zero-coupon bond? Why?

2. Interest rate swaps are usually based on the T-bond rate or on the London Interbank Offered Rate (LIBOR). These two rates are not perfectly correlated with one another. Discuss what this implies about companies' preferences for swaps based on one rate versus the other.

3. One of the newest innovations in derivative securities has been the swaption, an option that offers the buyer the opportunity, but not the obligation, to enter into a swap with a counterparty using a fixed set of terms. Why would a company use a swaption instead of a swap?

4. What feature of swaps would tend to make them less risky than an equivalent loan?

5. In addition to currency and interests rate swaps, companies seem to participate in what may be called "quality swaps." In a quality swap, a company with a good credit record who can borrow at attractive rates may swap interest rate payments with another company who can't borrow anywhere near as cheaply. Many researchers have claimed that this is a sign of market inefficiency, saying that an efficient market would have realized that the good-quality firm was going to turn around and pass its interest payment obligations off to the low-quality borrower and, so realizing, would have set the interest rate to that required of the low-quality firm. Can you think of another explanation that does not require an inefficient market?

6. You have been asked to analyze the risk profile of a retail firm that sells home improvement products, primarily in the United States, Mexico, and Canada.
   a. List the different types of risk that this firm must face.
   b. Categorize this risk as either firm-specific or market risk. In making this categorization, what are you assuming about stockholders in the retail firm?

7. A firm argues for an acquisition on the grounds that the action will reduce the variability in future earnings and that lower risk leads to higher value. How would you respond?

8. What are the conditions under which risk management has no effect on value? To which types of firms are these conditions most likely to apply?

9. Firms wishing to hedge both interest rate risk and exchange rate risk may use what is called a fixed-floating currency swap where one party sends fixed payments in 1 currency and the other party sends floating payments in another currency. However, finding a counterparty with these types of swaps can be rather difficult. Is there any other way to do this using swaps?

10. Firms should not diversify firm-specific risk because investors can do so themselves. Comment.

11. Assume that you have a five-year maturity, 10% annual coupon bond selling at par. Using duration, what is the approximate bond price change if interest rates increase by 2 percent?

12. Calculate the exact percentage change in the bond's price from the previous problem by manually figuring the new price and then the percentage change. Does this agree with the answer we got using the duration formula? Why or why not?

13. One way to adjust the duration formula for bonds to get greater precision is to add a convexity factor, CX, which is equal to 10^8*(the price change from a one-basis-point rise in yield + the price change from a one-basis-point decrease in yield). The new, adjusted formula for duration then implies that

$$\frac{\Delta P}{P} = D \frac{\Delta r}{1 + r} + \frac{1}{2} CX (\Delta r)^2$$

Calculate the predicted change in price for the bond in the previous problem using this formula and compare it to the actual change in price.

14. All three of the previous problems have shown that even after adjusting duration for the presence of

convexity in the yield curve we still only have an approximation of the percentage change in price. Why don't we just go ahead and use the exact change?

15. You have been asked to measure the exposure of a firm to interest rate risk and have been provided with the results of a simulation. The results summarize firm value as a function of the level of interest rates, as shown in the table below:

Level of Interest Rates (%)	Probability of Occurrence (%)	Firm Value ($)
3	5	$28,571
4	10	22,222
5	20	18,182
6	30	15,385
7	15	13,333
8	10	11,765
9	5	10,526
10	3	9,524
11	2	8,696

a. How would you use these results to measure the firm's exposure to interest rate risk?

b. What are some of the concerns you might have in using the results of this simulation?

16. You have been asked to measure the exposure of the same firm to interest rate risk, this time using historical data. You have been given information on operating income and interest rates for the last 15 years for this firm:

a. Estimate the sensitivity of the firm to operating income.

Year	Operating Income ($)	Long Bond Rate (%)
1980	150	11.90
1981	130	14.20
1982	138	13.80
1983	165	12.00
1984	155	12.70
1985	180	11.40
1986	220	9.00
1987	205	9.40
1988	200	9.70
1989	210	9.30
1990	215	9.30
1991	230	8.80
1992	270	8.10
1993	315	7.20
1994	300	8.00

b. Name some concerns you might have about using this regression to measure risk.

17. The following table provides stock prices for Ford Automobile Company for 15 years, in conjunction with data on interest rates, exchange rates, and inflation rates.

Year	Stock Price ($)	Interest Rate (%)	Inflation Rate (%)	Exchange Rate
1980	2.22	11.90	13.50	99.37
1981	1.82	14.20	10.30	110.47
1982	4.31	13.80	6.10	123.14
1983	7.06	12.00	3.20	128.65
1984	7.57	12.70	4.30	138.89
1985	9.66	11.40	3.50	125.95
1986	14.06	9.00	1.90	112.89
1987	18.82	9.40	3.70	95.88
1988	25.25	9.70	4.10	95.32
1989	21.75	9.30	4.80	102.26
1990	13.32	9.30	5.40	96.25
1991	14.06	8.80	4.20	98.82
1992	21.44	8.10	3.00	104.58
1993	32.25	7.20	3.00	105.22
1994	27.88	8.00	2.60	98.6
1995	28.88	7.00	2.80	102.3

a. Estimate the exposure of Ford's equity to each of these risk sources individually (in simple regressions) and collectively (in a multiple regression).

b. Why might the exposure of Ford's equity be different from that of the overall firm?

18. A firm whose assets have a long duration (i.e., there is a strong negative impact on the value when interest rates increase) decides to issue debt to finance these assets.

a. What would happen to the duration of equity, relative to asset duration, if the firm decided to issue floating rate debt to finance these assets?

b. Under what conditions will the duration of equity be equal to the duration of the assets?

19. A firm with significant exchange rate risk exposure is trying to decide whether to use forward, futures, or option contracts to hedge this risk.

a. If the firm knows with certainty the cash flows on which it has exchange rate risk exposure, what instrument will provide the most complete protection against the exchange rate risk?

b. Assume that the firm wants to hedge its downside risk without giving up all of its upside potential from exchange rate changes. What product would you recommend?

CHAPTER 30

CORPORATE FINANCE FOR PRIVATELY HELD FIRMS

A great deal of the discussion and many of the examples in this book relate to publicly traded firms. In reality, however, most businesses are much smaller than the typical companies used to illustrate the concepts in this book, and many of these businesses are either closely held or privately owned. In this chapter, we aim to expand our discussion to show that the principles of corporate finance continue to hold, no matter how small a business might be or how concentrated its holdings are. In particular, we will attempt to answer the following questions:

- How is risk measured for private firms? Do the traditional risk and return models, which assume that the average investor is diversified, have to be modified for private firms?

- In analyzing projects, what are some of the special considerations that might come into play for private firms?

- In making decisions on capital structure, what constraints might a private firm face in developing and moving to an optimal capital structure?

- In deciding how much cash an owner can take out of a private business, how relevant is the discussion of dividend policy as it relates to a large public firm?

- In valuing a private business, what factors need to be considered? What, if any, should be the discount for the absence of liquidity in valuation?

PRIVATE VERSUS PUBLICLY TRADED BUSINESSES

Let us begin by categorizing private and publicly traded businesses. A *private business* is one in which the equity in the business is not traded on financial markets; in general, neither is the debt. In a publicly traded firm, by contrast, at least a portion of the firm's equity is traded in financial markets. Private and public firms differ in many ways, creating implications for corporate finance:

- While publicly traded entities are usually organized as corporations, which have limited liability and are taxed on their income, private businesses can take a number of different forms. Most small private businesses are either sole proprietorships or partnerships. As they increase in size, some take on the corporate form.[1] In some

---

[1]Many private businesses are organized as subchapter S corporations, which preserve the corporate structure, while passing income through to the owners of the corporation.

of these forms, the owner has unlimited liability for debt taken on by the business; in all of them, income flows through the entity to the owner, who is taxed at the individual tax rate.

- Publicly traded firms operate under much more stringent accounting standards and information disclosure requirements than do private firms.
- The public trading of stock in a firm creates a database of historical stock prices, which can be used to estimate risk parameters, design debt, and measure risk exposure. The absence of such trading on private firms creates an information gap that makes it difficult to apply some of the models we have developed in this book.
- In general, private firms tend to be smaller than publicly traded firms.
- Ownership and the management are much more likely to be separated in publicly traded firms, whereas the owners are usually the top managers in private firms.
- The owners of private firms tend to invest the bulk of their wealth in these firms, whereas the stockholders of publicly traded firms are much more likely to be diversified investors, institutional or otherwise.

Although the distinction made between private and publicly traded firms in this section is absolute, it may serve us better to think of this distinction on a continuum, with some firms falling closer to one extreme—large, publicly traded firms with dispersed and diversified stockholders—and other firms to the other extreme—small, privately run businesses whose owners run the business and invest their entire wealth in it.

As you can see in Figure 30.1, along this continuum there are some publicly traded firms that, by virtue of their small size and closely held stock, have more in common with private firms than they do with large publicly traded ones. Similarly, some very large private firms, with professional managers and corporate structures, act and operate more like their publicly traded counterparts. Thus, much of our discussion, though couched in terms of private firms, also applies to those firms that fall close to them along the continuum.

INVESTMENT ANALYSIS

Investment analysis, as we have emphasized throughout this book, is built around two elements—*expected cash flows* and *hurdle rates*. Although these inputs have to be estimated for all firms—small or large, private or public—it is entirely possible that a small, private firm and a large publicly traded firm can look at the same project and arrive at very different estimates of cash flows and discount rates. In this section, we examine the reasons for these differences and the overall implications for investment decisions.

Estimating Cash Flows

When analyzing a project, the incremental after-tax cash flows are estimated and used to decide whether the project should be accepted or rejected. There are several reasons why the cash flows on the same project may vary, depending on the firm considering the project.

Large, publicly Large private Small, closely held Small, private
traded firms businesses publicly traded firms business
with dispersed
stockholders

Figure 30.1   The continuum from private to publicly traded firms

Taxes The taxes due on the cash flows generated by a project will vary, depending on the tax status of the business. Even among corporations, the tax rate can vary, depending on the income generated and the existence of tax loss carry-forwards and other tax deductions. Thus, a small firm may face a lower marginal tax rate than a larger one, and a firm with tax loss carry-forwards may pay less in taxes than one without.

When a private firm is considering the same project, the tax differences can be even larger. Private businesses that are organized as partnerships or **subchapter S corporations** are not taxed at the entity level; rather, the income flows through to the partners or owners, who are taxed at their individual tax rates. Furthermore, the laws governing depreciation, tax credits, and loss carry-forwards for private businesses can be very different from those governing large publicly traded firms.

Subchapter S Corporation: This is a corporate form that is adopted by some private firms, in which the income is taxed not at the entity level but at the level of the owners of the corporation.

When analyzing projects for private businesses, therefore, it is important that the cash flows be computed after taxes, and that these taxes include those paid by individuals on income that flows through to them from the entity. Thus, it would be a mistake for a partnership not to calculate after-tax cash flows just because the entity does not pay taxes; the cash flows would have to be computed after taxes are computed at the partner level. When different partners face different tax rates, an average tax rate, weighted by the estimated share held by each partner, should be computed and used.

☐ Concept Check

Publicly traded firms will pay much more in taxes than will sole proprietorships on the same earnings, because the income is taxed twice for these firms, once at the entity level and once at the level of the investor. Do you agree? Explain.

Operating expenses *Operating expenses* are those expenses incurred to create the revenues on a project. They include expenses, such as material and labor, that go into cost of goods sold, and should be considered similarly by small, private businesses and large publicly traded companies. They also include management expenses; these are typically clear cut in publicly traded firms, which generally use professional managers who are compensated for their management activities explicitly, but they may not be as obvious in small, private businesses. In the latter case, the owners who also operate as managers may not distinguish between a management salary and a return on investment, because both are taxed at the individual tax rate.

There are two solutions to this problem. The first is to compute an opportunity cost for the owner's time, based on the compensation he or she would have earned *at the next best alternative investment*. Thus, an investment banker who quits his job to run his own business can charge a cost equivalent to what he would have made at his investment banking job. The limitation of this approach is that it charges this opportunity cost for all activities in which the owner engages and does not distinguish between activities that can be done by others at much lower cost, and more important activities. The second solution is more flexible; it involves assigning a cost to each activity in which the owner is involved, based on how much it would cost to hire a *third party to provide the service*. Thus, if the owner spends three hours a week on accounting tasks, the cost of hiring an accounting agency to provide the same service will be the assigned cost.

Operating efficiency   The cash flows on a project are a function of how efficiently the firm is managed. On the one hand, larger firms, which are publicly traded, should enjoy economies of scales and thus have lower expenses for a given level of revenues. These economies of scale show up in a number of different ways—suppliers provide better credit terms, fixed costs per unit are lower, and some services can be shared across projects. On the other hand, publicly traded firms may not have the same incentives to be efficient, because the management and the ownership of the firm are separated. The owner/managers of private firms, by contrast, should be much more concerned about being efficient, since they gain directly from any increases in the bottom line.

 IN PRACTICE   Estimating Cash Flows for a Private Firm: T.E. Lowe

T.E. Lowe is a general store in a small town in New Jersey, owned by Al and Zina Jones. The store has been profitable, and the owners are considering expanding. The facts on the expansion are as follows:

- The expansion will require an initial construction and remodeling expense of $150,000 and will increase the store size by 15%. Of this investment, $50,000 can be depreciated straight line over the next five years.

- This expansion is expected to increase the annual revenues from $1 million to $1.10 million. The store has an average gross profit margin, prior to depreciation, of 40%.

- Both revenues and expenses are expected to grow 4% a year, for the next five years.

- The Joneses pay approximately 40% of their income as taxes.

- As a result of the expansion, Al Jones expects to spend 10 hours more a month on inventory stocking, and Zina Jones expects to spend an additional five hours more a month on paperwork.

- The inventory is usually maintained at 20% of revenues.

- The Joneses expect to stay in business for five more years, after which they hope to sell the store at an expected price of 1.5 times the revenues.

The cash flows from the expansion can be estimated as follows.

Initial investment   Initially, the Joneses will have to pay construction and remodeling cost of $150,000. Inventory will increase from $200,000 to $220,000 to reflect the expected growth in revenues. This increase in working capital of $20,000 will be part of the initial investment.

Annual after-tax cash flows for next five years   Ignoring the owners' time for the moment, revenues will increase as a consequence of the expansion. After factoring in the cost of goods sold, which is 60% of revenues, and the depreciation, which is $10,000 a year, the incremental taxable income can be computed as shown in Table 30.1. From this taxable income, the Joneses will be paying 40% as taxes. In addition, the inventory will increase as revenues increase each year.

Factoring in owners' time   Assume that it will cost $25/hour to get an experienced hand to manage the inventory and $15/hour to hire a good salesperson. The cost of the owners' time can then be estimated on an annual basis as follows:

$$\text{Cost of Additional Time Spent on Inventory} = 10 \times 12 \times \$25 = \$3,000$$
$$\text{Cost of Additional Time Spent on Sales} = 5 \times 12 \times \$15 = \$900$$
$$\text{After-tax Cost of Imputed Salaries} = \$3,900\,(\,1 - 0.4\,) = 2,340$$

Table 30.1   ESTIMATED ATCF ON STORE EXPANSION

Year	1	2	3	4	5
Revenues	$100,000	$104,000	$108,160	$112,486.4	$116,985.9
− COGS	60,000	62,400	64,896	67,491.8	70,191.5
Gross Profit	40,000	41,600	43,264	44,994.6	46,794.3
− Depreciation	10,000	10,000	10,000	10,000	10,000
Taxable Income	30,000	31,600	33,264	34,995	36,794
Taxes	12,000	12,640	13,306	13,998	14,718
Net Income	18,000	18,960	19,958	20,997	22,077
+ Depreciation	10,000	10,000	10,000	10,000	10,000
− Δ W Cap.	800	832	865	900	936
AT Cash Flow	27,200	28,128	29,093	30,097	31,141

When these costs are factored in, the after-tax cash flows can be estimated, as shown in Table 30.2.

Table 30.2   EFFECT OF IMPUTED SALARY ON ATCF

Year	1	2	3	4	5
ATCF	$27,200	$28,128	$29,093	$30,097	$31,141
−Imputed Salary	2,340	2,434	2,531	2,632	2,737
ATCF w/ Change	24,860	25,694	26,562	27,465	28,403

Estimating the incremental salvage value   At the end of five years, the expected price at which the store can be sold will be higher because of the higher revenues. To calculate the additional sales price as a consequence of the expansion, consider the salvage value with and without the expansion:

Salvage value without the expansion = Revenue in year 5 * 1.5
= $1,000,000 (1.04^5) * 1.5 = $1,824,979
Salvage value with the expansion = Revenue in year 5 * 1.5
= $1,100,000 (1.04^5) * 1.5 = $2,007,477
Increase in salvage value as a result of the expansion = $2,007,477 − $1,824,979
= $182,498

Summarizing the cash flows on the expansion   Summarizing the cash flows from the initial investment to the incremental salvage value, we arrive at the following:

Year	Initial Investment	ATCF	Salvage Value
0	$(170,000)		
1		$24,860	
2		25,694	
3		26,562	
4		27,465	
5		28,403	$182,498

□ Concept
Check

> Assume that, in doing this analysis, the cost of owners' time had been ignored. What are the consequences for investment decisions made by private firms?

Estimating Discount Rates

Although cash flows comprise one-half of investment analysis, discount rates comprise the other. In the earlier sections on investment analysis, we argued that the discount rate on a project should reflect both the riskiness of the project and the financing mix (debt and equity) used for the project. We measured risk using models that defined risk from the perspective of a well-diversified investor. In the capital asset pricing model, this is measured with the market beta; in the arbitrage pricing model, with the multiple factor betas.

This argument becomes much more tenuous when analyzing private or closely held firms. In particular, the owners of these firms often have the bulk of or even their entire wealth tied up in their businesses. They are therefore exposed to *all* risk and not just the nondiversifiable risk. We can argue that the use of traditional risk and return models in these firms will result in understated discount rates and that a premium must be added to reflect diversifiable risk.

Even if we concede that the traditional risk and return models should be used to estimate a base discount rate and that a premium should then be added to estimate the appropriate rate for a small, private firm, we are left with two measurement issues:

1. Given that risk parameters in most risk and return models are estimated using historical market prices, how can they be estimated for private firms, which are not traded?

2. Once the risk parameters have been estimated and used to arrive at a discount rate, how should a premium be estimated for the diversifiable risk?

We analyzed the first of these questions in detail in Chapter 12, where we argued that the risk parameters for private firms could be estimated using publicly traded firms that are in the same line of business or by using accounting earnings as a proxy for market value. When it comes to the second question, however, we are in uncharted territory, since none of the widely used risk and return models measures and rewards diversifiable risk. There are at least two ways of estimating this premium, however—using total betas or historical data.

Total beta   A variant of the capital asset pricing model can be used, in which betas are estimated using the total variance instead of just the systematic variance:

$$\text{Market Beta} = \frac{\text{Market Covariance}}{\text{Average Market Variance}} = \frac{\sigma_{j,m}}{\sigma_m^2}$$

$$\text{Total Beta} = \frac{\text{Total Variance}}{\text{Systematic Variance}} \beta = \frac{1}{R^2}\beta$$

where σ_j is the standard deviation in the stock returns, and σ_m is the standard deviation in market returns. In other words, the **total beta** assumes that *all* risk, rather than just market risk, has to be considered in setting discount rates for a private firm. To illustrate, consider the risk parameters estimated for Boeing and the Home Depot, using the systematic risk and then the total risk.

Total Beta: This is a beta estimated using the total variance of the firm, rather than just the market portion of the variance.

	Market Beta	R-squared	Total Beta
Boeing	1.39	33.76%	4.12
Home Depot	1.60	31.75%	5.04

The total betas, by definition, will always be larger than the market betas because they factor in diversifiable risk.

How can this approach help to estimate the beta for a private firm? After all, the stock in such a firm is not traded, and neither the market nor the systematic variance can be estimated for such a firm. The answer lies in using comparable firms. Table 30.3

Table 30.3 **MARKET AND TOTAL BETAS BY INDUSTRY**

Industry	CAPM beta	R-squared	Total Beta
Agricultural Products	0.74	25%	2.96
Mining	0.64	30%	2.13
Petroleum Production & Refining	0.59	20%	2.95
Building Contractors & Related Areas	1.08	40%	2.70
Food Production	0.85	30%	2.83
Beverages	0.95	35%	2.71
Tobacco	1.11	40%	2.78
Textile & Clothing Manufacturers	0.98	40%	2.45
Furniture	0.93	35%	2.66
Paper & Plastic Production	1.03	35%	2.94
Publishing	0.99	30%	3.30
Chemicals	1.34	45%	2.98
Pharmaceuticals	1.36	40%	3.40
Consumer Products	1.06	40%	2.65
Autos & Related	0.99	40%	2.48
Miscellaneous Manufacturing	1.07	30%	3.57
Equipment Manufacturing	1.02	35%	2.91
Computers & Office Equipment	1.27	20%	6.35
Consumer Electronics	1.26	25%	5.04
Other Consumer Durables	1.08	35%	3.09
Transportation	1.10	45%	2.44
Telephone Utilities	1.20	50%	2.40
Entertainment (TV & Movies)	1.25	30%	4.17
Electric & Gas Utilities	0.58	50%	1.16
Wholesalers	1.08	40%	2.70
Discount Retailers	0.89	37%	2.40
Retailers	1.19	40%	2.98
Restaurants & Eating Places	1.20	35%	3.43
Banks & Financial Service	1.23	45%	2.73
Insurance	0.85	45%	1.89
Real Estate	0.69	35%	1.97
Other Services	1.05	30%	3.50
Computer Software & Services	1.33	25%	5.32
Health Services	1.32	40%	3.30
AVERAGE	1.03	36%	3.04

CHAPTER 30 CORPORATE FINANCE FOR PRIVATELY HELD FIRMS   **805**

reports average market betas and total betas by industry sector. Using this approach, we can argue that a private firm in any sector can use the total beta to arrive at a measure of expected return.

To illustrate, assume that you are trying to estimate the discount rate for T.E. Lowe's expansion project. From Table 30.3, it is clear that discount retail firms have an average market beta of 0.89, and an average total beta of 2.40. Using the total beta to estimate the cost of equity, and allowing for a risk-free rate of 6% and a risk premium of 5.5%, we arrive at the following figure:

$$\text{Cost of Equity using total beta} = 6\% + 2.40\,(5.5\%) = 19.2\%$$

This is much higher than the cost of equity that is estimated using the market beta.

$$\text{Cost of Equity using CAPM beta} = 6\% + 0.89\,(5.5\%) = 10.9\%$$

While T.E. Lowe will use the first figure, a large, publicly traded retail firm will use the second, lower cost of equity.

Historical data   Consider again how we estimated risk premiums for publicly traded firms. We looked at the historical premiums earned by stocks over bonds and bills and used these as measures of the average premium. It is possible that a variant of this approach can be used for small, private firms. While these firms are not traded, venture capital funds that invest in these companies report either total returns by period or trade in financial markets. The average premium earned by such funds over similar funds that invest in publicly traded companies can be used as a measure of the premium for the private firm. In doing so, however, we should note that these funds, if diversified across industry groups, will end up reducing their exposure to diversifiable risk, although the firms in which they are invested are exposed to this risk.

To illustrate, assume that you have been asked to estimate the cost of equity for HiSoft Inc., a small privately run software firm. Assume, further, that over the last 10 years, venture capital firms specializing in technology have made 15% more than the S&P 500. If we assume that the risk-free rate is 6% and that the market (S&P 500) will continue to make a premium of 5.5% over the risk-free rate, the cost of equity for HiSoft Inc. can be estimated as follows:

$$\text{Cost of Equity} = \text{Risk-free Rate} + \text{Market Risk Premium} + \text{Venture Capital Premium}$$

$$= 6\% + 5.5\% + 15\% = 26.5\%$$

> **Concept Check**
>
> What are we assuming about the historical premiums earned by venture capital firms when we use this approach? What are the limitations of this approach?

Completing the Analysis

Once cash flows and discount rates have been estimated, private firms are in nearly the same position as publicly traded firms; they have to decide whether to accept or reject projects. In making these judgments, other factors may come into play. For instance, capital rationing constraints are likely to be much more stringent for small, private firms that have no access to capital markets than for publicly traded firms. Consequently, the small, private firms are more likely to use internal rates of return or profitability indices than net present values to rank projects and decide in which to invest.

To illustrate, let us once return again to the store expansion. The cash flows from the expansion are reproduced in Table 30.4.

Table 30.4 ESTIMATED CASH FLOWS AND SALVAGE VALUE FROM STORE EXPANSION

Year	Initial Investment	ATCF	Salvage Value
0	$(170,000)		
1		$24,860	
2		25,694	
3		26,562	
4		27,465	
5		28,403	$182,498

Earlier, we estimated the cost of equity appropriate for T.E. Lowe as 19.2%, based on the firm's total risk, rather than the market risk. The internal rate of return of the expansion can be estimated from the cash flows; the net present value profile for the project is reproduced in Figure 30.2.

As you can see, the internal rate of return of 16.55% is lower than the estimated cost of equity of 19.2%, which suggests that the store should not expand. Interestingly, a larger publicly traded retail firm, with its lower cost of equity, would have found this to be an acceptable project.

❏ Concept
Check

> Assume now that the owners of the store argue that they are making only 5% on their savings in the bank and note that the internal rate of return on the expansion exceeds this return. How would you counter their argument?

Implications

To summarize, the discount rate used on a project will generally be much higher if the decision maker is a small, private business, reflecting the premium demanded for diversifiable risk. The cash flows on a project, on the other hand, may be higher or lower

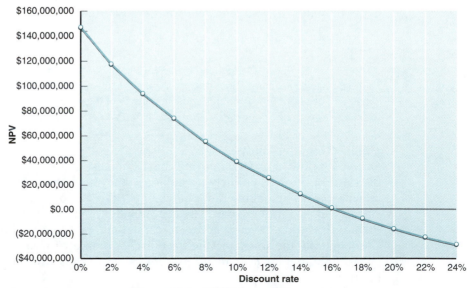

Figure 30.2 NPV of expansion project

for a private firm, depending on the tax effects and whether or not the increased efficiency associated with the firm's owners being managers is offset by the economies of scale enjoyed by larger publicly traded firms. The bottom line, then, is that two firms, one private and the other public, may look at the same project and come to very different conclusions.

If the cash flows on a project are similar, private firms are likely to reject projects they would deem acceptable if they were publicly traded, had access to capital markets, and were less concerned about diversifiable risk. Because value is lost as a consequence, we propose the following:

- When a publicly traded firm acquires a private firm, one of the sources of synergy in the acquisition is the removal or the loosening of the investment constraints under which the private firm operates. The greater the constraints, the greater the potential gains from the acquisition.

- As the cost of "foregone projects" increases, firms will be much more likely to attempt to go public. By doing so, they relieve the constraints and increase their value.

On the other hand, if the cash-flow gains that result when owner/managers run the project exceed the negative effect of higher discount rates, a project may have a higher net present value to a private firm than to a larger, publicly traded firm. This helps explain why publicly traded firms go private (as is the case in many leveraged buyouts) or why firms stay private when they have the option of going public.

To illustrate, assume that CVS, a large publicly traded retail firm, is considering buying T.E. Lowe from its current owners. Assume that the store is valued at $1.5 million, based on current cash flows (without the expansion). CVS can afford to pay a premium over this value, reflecting the fact that the expansion—which the current owners found to be not viable, given the discount rate—is economically attractive. In fact, the net present value of the cash flows on the expansion can be estimated using CVS's discount rate, which is assumed to be 10.90%. This net present value of $33,061 can be viewed as the premium CVS can pay over and above the estimated value.

☐ Concept
   Check

In an acquisition such as this one, what factors will determine how the synergy gains will be shared between the buyer of the business and the seller?

CAPITAL STRUCTURE DECISIONS

In Chapters 15 through 19, we examined the question of whether firms should use debt or equity by evaluating the tradeoff from using debt. On the one hand, debt provides tax benefits that equity does not and forces managers to be more disciplined in their choice of projects. On the other hand, debt increases expected bankruptcy costs, reduces the capacity of the firm to react to contingencies, and creates conflicts between lenders and equity investors. Although both private and publicly traded firms face the same tradeoffs, the magnitude of the costs and the benefits may vary across the two groups.

Default Risk

Firms that borrow money increase their exposure to default risk. The expected bankruptcy cost is a function of both the probability of bankruptcy and the explicit and implicit costs of bankruptcy. However, private firms may find themselves exposed to more of both components of the bankruptcy costs than public firms, for the following reasons:

- The existence of limited liability protects equity investors in publicly traded firms and restricts their losses to their investment in these firms. In the case of private firms, the owner's personal assets may be exposed to loss if the firm defaults on its debt.
- The implicit costs of bankruptcy refer to the lost sales and higher costs that arise when the firm is perceived to be in financial trouble. Smaller firms, which have fewer assets, are much more exposed to these costs than larger firms.
- Finally, larger firms have generally enjoyed far more leeway in renegotiating debt when they get into financial trouble than have smaller firms, increasing the probability of default for the smaller firms.

Other things remaining equal, private firms are typically less likely to borrow as a consequence of higher bankruptcy costs.

Concept Check

> What, if any, implication does the fact that many private businesses have unlimited liability have for the agency problems between stockholders and bondholders? What are the consequences for capital structure decisions?

Tax Benefits

Interest expense is tax deductible, whereas cash flows to equity investors are taxed. To the extent that the tax rates for publicly traded firms are different from the tax rates on private businesses, the tax benefits of debt may be different for the two groups.

Agency Costs

Taking on debt has implications for two agency conflicts. In terms of the relationship between equity investors and managers, it acts as a disciplining force on managers when there is a separation of management and ownership. This positive effect has to be weighed against the potential agency problems that arise between stockholders and bondholders when firms borrow money. Bondholders, who are concerned about the capacity of stockholders to shift risk, make cash withdrawals from the firm and take on additional debt, put restrictive covenants into bond agreements, and reduce the firm's flexibility to make investment, financing, and dividend decisions.

It can be argued that private firms gain less from the "discipline" debt induces, since the owners of these firms are often the top managers as well, and that they lose more from the exposure to the bondholder–stockholder conflict, since bond agreements are generally more restrictive for small, private firms than for larger publicly traded ones.

Value of Flexibility

Finally, borrowing reduces a firm's capacity to be flexible in meeting unforeseen contingencies. The need for this flexibility increases as a firm's access to financing markets decreases. In other words, firms that can raise large amounts of external financing are much less likely to worry about maintaining excess debt capacity and large cash balances. Private firms have limited access to new financing, however. When private firms want to raise equity financing, they are restricted to the owner's assets or to venture capital. When they want to raise debt, they are often restricted to bank debt. This restriction, in turn, increases the value of maintaining flexibility; consequently, private firms are more likely to fight to preserve excess debt capacity.

Implications for the Use of Debt

To summarize, a comparison of the costs and benefits of debt for private and public firms yields the following conclusions:

- Taking on debt increases default risk and expected bankruptcy cost much more substantially for small, private firms than for larger, publicly traded firms, partly because the owners of the private firm are exposed much more frequently to unlimited liability, and partly because the perception of financial trouble can be much more damaging to small, private firms.

- Taking on debt yields a much smaller advantage in terms of disciplining decision makers in the case of privately run firms, since there is no separation of ownership and management.

- Taking on debt generally exposes small, private firms to far more restrictive bond covenants and higher agency costs than it does large, publicly traded firms.

- The loss of flexibility associated with using excess debt capacity is likely to weigh much more heavily on small, private firms than large, publicly traded firms, owing to the small firm's lack of access to public markets.

Barring the scenario in which the individual tax rate is substantially higher than the corporate tax rate and the tax benefits of debt are therefore substantially larger for small, private firms, all of the factors mentioned above would result in much lower debt ratios at small private firms.

 Concept Check

There is empirical evidence to indicate that closely held or family-run publicly traded firms are less levered than other publicly traded firms. How would you explain this?

DIVIDEND POLICY

In our discussion of dividend policy for large publicly traded firms, we noted that the payment of dividends exposes these firms to double taxation—once at the corporate level and once at the level of the individual. We also argued that firms often pay dividends to signal their financial health to markets, and we emphasized the role of investor clienteles in determining the appropriate dividend policy for a firm. None of these points has any relevance for a private firm, however. Because income from these firms flows through to the owner anyway, there is no additional tax implication of the owner taking more cash out of the business; that is, paying a higher dividend. Furthermore, there are no financial markets to impress, and the only investor clients that matter are the firm's owners.

Given these facts, dividend policy analysis for a small, private firm boils down to a very simple question: How much of a firm's cash flows should be reinvested back in the firm, and how much should be taken out for personal consumption? The answer to this question lies partly in the quality of projects that the firm has and partly in the cash needs of the owner(s). Other things remaining equal, owners of firms with high-return projects should reinvest more of their cash back into the business, especially given their lack of access to financial markets; the greater the current need for cash by the owner, the more cash should be taken out of the business. This tradeoff between growth and the owner's current needs for cash will determine how much cash the owner takes out of the business.

VALUATION

You will recall that the value of an asset is the present value of the expected cash flows on that asset, discounted at a rate that reflects the riskiness of the cash flows. That said, there are some differences between valuing private and publicly traded businesses. In this section, we will first focus on the differences in cash flows and discount rates and then examine two issues that are particularly relevant for private businesses—the effect of the illiquidity on value, and the effect of a personal component to the business.

Estimating Cash Flows

Estimating both current cash flows and expected future growth rates is much more difficult to do for private firms than for publicly traded firms. In calculating current cash flows, for instance, it is often difficult to draw a distinction between management compensation and return on capital in private firms, for owners often also operate as managers. Thus, an owner-manager who draws a low salary while owning the firm may demand and deserve a much higher remuneration packet when the firm becomes public. The absence of the strict informational requirements that apply to publicly traded firms also makes the financial statements of private firms less reliable.

In estimating future growth for publicly traded firms, analysts can draw on a rich information set—a long history of earnings and projections of future growth from other analysts. Substantially less information is available for private firms, however. Past history is often unreliable, and there are few or no "outside" projections of growth rates. Consequently, estimates of future growth for private firms are likely to exhibit much more error.

Although no simple solution exists for this information problem, we have to accept the fact that values estimated for private firms will generally be much more noisy than those estimated for publicly traded firms.

❏ Concept Check

> An analyst contends that private firms are impossible to value because of the dearth of historical information. How would you respond?

Estimating Discount Rates

As we emphasized in the section on investment analysis, models of risk and return used in estimating discount rates—including the capital asset pricing model and the arbitrage pricing model—use parameters estimated from past prices or returns. These traditional estimation procedures cannot be used for firms that are not traded or have been traded for only a short time period. The techniques suggested in the section on investment analysis, such as using publicly traded firms that are in the same business as the private firms, or estimating accounting betas, can also be used in the context of valuation to estimate discount rates.

In investment analysis, we added a premium to this discount rate to reflect the fact that the owners of private firms are exposed to diversifiable risk. In valuation, we would argue against making such an adjustment, because a business should be valued from the perspective of the bidder who would assign the highest value to it. In other words, the owner of a private business should value the business on the assumption that there are diverisified buyers out there who are concerned only about the nondiversifiable risk. If such buyers do not materialize, the owner might have to accept a lower value, but to concede this discount up front would be a mistake.

❏ Concept
Check

Assume that you do build in a diversifiable risk premium to your discount rate. What would the effect be on valuation? If you sold a private business at this value to a diversified investor, who gets the synergy premium?

Valuing a Baseball Franchise

Major league baseball came to a grinding halt in September 1994, as owners and players disagreed about whether player salaries were getting out of control. Owners argued that they were and that most teams were losing money, although they refused to share their financial statements. The players argued that the teams were in fact making money but using creative bookkeeping to report losses.[2]

While the owners and the players wrangled over the state of finances in the game, the Baltimore Orioles were sold for $173 million to a new owner, Peter Angelenos, after having been bought by Edward Bennett Williams for $12 million 20 years earlier. In 1992, Bob Lurie managed to get $100 million from local interests for the financially troubled San Francisco Giants and actually turned down an offer for $115 million to move the team to Tampa/St. Petersburg. Of course, these transactions do not imply that these franchises were worth this much in terms of revenue-generating power, since there are substantial side benefits to owning a sports franchise, especially for a publicity-seeking owner.[3]

In the following analysis, we attempt to value three baseball franchises as of September 1994, before the players' strike, and then consider the implications for value of these same franchises six months later.

Cash flows

Revenues A major league baseball franchise has several sources of revenues, although the magnitude of the revenue is affected by the revenue-sharing arrangement within the league. The two leagues that comprise major league baseball—the National League and the American League—each have very different revenue-sharing arrangements. We will consider one National League team—the Pittsburgh Pirates—and two American League teams—the New York Yankees and the Baltimore Orioles—in our analysis. Sources of revenue for the teams include the following:

1. Home game receipts: The first, and most obvious, source of revenues for a major league team are the receipts at the 81 home games it plays as part of a regular baseball season. In the American League, the home team and the visiting team split gate receipts on an 80–20 basis, whereas the National League allows home teams to keep approximately 95% of the home gate receipts. Luxury box receipts are kept by the home team.

2. Road game receipts: National League teams get to keep most of their home game receipts, but they receive relatively small amounts (about 43 cents a ticket, or 5% of gate receipts) from the 81 road games they play. The American League teams, by contrast, get to keep more 20% of their road game revenues.

3. Concessions and parking: The sales from concession stands selling souvenirs, food, soft drinks, and beer are a source of profit to the team, either directly or through the sale

---

[2]Roger Noll, a Stanford economist, argued that a number of team owners were intermingling expenses from other businesses they owned with their baseball franchises and were paying exorbitant salaries to themselves and their kin from the franchises.

[3]See George Steinbrenner . . . Need I say more!

of the concession rights to outsiders. Because fans need to be in attendance for these sales to occur, these revenues are correlated with the home game attendance and receipts.

4. *National TV revenues:* Major league baseball has contracts with national networks, allowing them to carry some of the regular season games, the playoffs, and the World Series. These revenues are shared equally among the different franchises. One criticism mounted against major league baseball in 1994 was that it had allowed a lucrative contract for $1 billion with CBS to expire and had replaced it with one with ABC, NBC, and ESPN for about half the amount, dropping each team's share from $14 million in 1993 to about $7.5 million in 1994.

5. *Local TV revenues:* Local television revenues are determined by the size of the local media market. The New York Yankees, playing in the largest media market in the nation, for example, signed a contract with MSG Network for $486 million over 12 years. The Seattle Mariners, on the other hand, signed a three-year contract in 1994 with KIRO-TV for $7 million. Under the revenue-sharing arrangement, about 25% of cable revenues have to be shared with the rest of the league, while local broadcast TV revenues belong entirely to the home team.[4]

6. *National licensing:* Major league ball clubs also receive revenues from the national licensing of the club's name, which can be very large for well known franchises, like the Yankees and Dodgers, and smaller for lesser known franchises, like the Mariners.

7. *Stadium advertising:* The billboards and giant television screens in most stadiums provide an avenue for advertisers to get their messages out to fans; the revenues from such advertising accrue to the club.

8. *Other revenues:* This category covers all other sources of revenues. For instance, the Baltimore Orioles, in their new stadium (built by the city), received almost $5.374 million in revenues from club seats and private suites and $3.633 million in unidentified "other" revenues.

Table 30.5 provides estimates for each of these categories for the Pittsburgh Pirates, Baltimore Orioles, and New York Yankees in 1993.

Table 30.5   ESTIMATED REVENUES FROM BASEBALL

	Pittsburgh Pirates	Baltimore Orioles	New York Yankees
Net Home Game Receipts	$15,116,398	$29,596,120	$26,000,000
Road Receipts	806,586	4,556,488	5,000,000
Concessions and Parking	2,209,391	13,367,911	15,000,000
National TV Revenues	12,500,000	12,500,000	12,500,000
Local TV Revenues	7,500,000	14,183,000	44,000,000
National Licensing	4,162,747	3,050,949	6,000,000
Stadium Advertising	100,000	4,391,383	5,500,000
Other Revenues	1,000,000	9,200,000	6,000,000
Total Revenues	**43,395,122**	**90,845,851**	**120,000,000**

As you can see, the lucrative television contract signed by the New York Yankees gives them the edge in terms of revenues over the other two teams.

---

[4]The Yankees, for instance, did not sign a single contract with MSG Network. Instead, they signed several contracts that pay the team unusually large fees for rights to videos, film libraries, and other services, so that they could shield the revenues from revenue sharing.

Expenses   The primary expenditure incurred by baseball teams is the cost of player salaries and other related expenses (including the cost of operating the minor league teams). These expenses vary from team to team and from year to year. In addition, expenses are associated with contractual obligations when players are released. Other categories of expenditures include the following:

- A fairly large cost is associated with both team operations (travel, lodging, etc.) and stadium operations.
- Some teams pay to rent their stadiums from the cities in which they play. For teams that own their own stadiums, there might be a depreciation or amortization charge if the stadium was built recently.
- The most troublesome category is the general administrative cost, since many team owners have been accused of nepotism in hiring; specifically, relatives have been hired on the teams' playrolls at inflated salaries. Ideally, these salaries should be treated as dividends to the owner rather than expenditures.

Table 30.6 summarizes the expenses faced by the Pittsburgh Pirates, Baltimore Orioles, and New York Yankees in 1993.

Table 30.6 ESTIMATED EXPENSES FROM BASEBALL	Pittsburgh Pirates	Baltimore Orioles	New York Yankees
Player Salaries	$26,188,403	$27,771,482	$45,000,000
Team Operating Expenses	6,239,025	3,803,907	6,000,000
Player Development	9,163,095	8,768,399	12,000,000
Stadium and Game Operations	4,370,986	3,269,790	5,000,000
Other Player Costs	1,991,000	4,795,751	5,500,000
General and Administrative Costs	5,267,617	7,921,151	9,000,000
Broadcasting	1,250,000	—	—
Rent and Amortization	—	6,252,151	—
Total Operating Expenses	**54,470,126**	**62,582,631**	**82,500,000**

Discount rates   We will estimate the beta of a firm that derives much of its revenues from baseball—Topps—in our valuation of baseball franchises. Topps, which manufactures Bazooka Bubble Gum and baseball cards, is publicly traded on the New York Stock Exchange and had an estimated beta of 1.10 in 1994.[5] This beta yields a cost of equity of

$$\text{Cost of Equity} = 8.00\% + 1.1\,(5.5\%) = 14.05\%$$

The financial leverage used varies substantially from team to team. Allowing for a mix of 75% equity and 25% debt in the financing, and a pretax cost of debt of 9%, the cost of capital can be estimated as follows: (The tax rate was 44%).

$$\text{Cost of Capital} = 14.05\%\,(0.75) + 9\%\,(1\text{-}0.44)\,(0.25) = 11.80\%$$

Valuation   The operating after-tax cash flows to owning the three teams highlighted above can be estimated as shown in Table 30.7.

[5]This beta was estimated based on 60 months of price data, using the S&P 500 index.

Table 30.7 ESTIMATED EBIT FROM BASEBALL FRANCHISES			
	Pittsburgh Pirates	**Baltimore Orioles**	**New York Yankees**
Total Revenues	$43,395,122	$90,845,851	$120,000,000
Total Operating Expenses	54,470,126	62,582,631	82,500,000
EBIT	(11,075,004)	28,263,220	37,500,000
Taxes (at 44%)	(4,873,002)	12,435,817	16,500,000
EBIT (1-tax rate)	(6,202,002)	15,827,403	21,000,000

The Pittsburgh Pirates have negative earnings before interest and taxes, partly as a result of losing key players to the free agent market after 1992. If we use the average revenues from 1990 to 1992 instead of the current year numbers, the after-tax operating income for the Pirates is closer to $5 million. (This is a normalized operating income.)

Allowing for a growth of 3% in the long term in these after-tax operating incomes, and factoring in the cost of capital of 11.80%, we find that the values of the three teams are as follows:

Value of the Pittsburgh Pirates = $5,000,000 * 1.03 / (.1180 − .03) = $58.5 million
Value of the Baltimore Orioles = $15,827,403 * 1.03 / (.1180 − .03) = $185.3 million
Value of the New York Yankees = $21,000,000 * 1.03 / (.1180 − .03) = $245.8 million

Analyzing the Effect of Illiquidity on Value

Private businesses cannot be bought and sold as easily as publicly traded securities. This lack of liquidity, or *illiquidity,* makes these investments less attractive, and, therefore, less valuable, than otherwise similar investments that are more liquid.

Determinants of the liquidity discount   The size of the liquidity discount assigned to a business or an asset will depend on a number of factors, including the following:

- *Type of assets owned by the firm*: Even if a business is not liquid, its assets may be. The more liquid the assets, the lower the liquidity discount assigned in valuing that firm or its securities. Thus, a business whose assets are primarily made up of cash and marketable securities will have less of a liquidity discount than one that is primarily made up of plant and equipment.
- *Size of the business*: Businesses can bypass the absence of liquidity by borrowing on their assets. From a practical standpoint, this method is more feasible for larger businesses than for smaller ones. Consequently, the larger the firm, the smaller the size of the liquidity discount.
- *Health of the business*: Building on the notion that businesses can borrow on their assets and bypass the lack of liquidity, it is clear that the owners of healthy businesses, which make substantial profits, suffer less of a liquidity problem than do

 Concept Check

An argument can be made that all investments, whether private or public, trade at a liquidity discount, and that the only difference is the magnitude of the discount. In the case of publicly traded firms, this discount takes the form of the bid-ask spread (i.e., the difference between the price at which you can buy a security and the price at which you can sell it). Do you agree?

owners of troubled businesses. Healthier businesses should therefore sell at smaller discounts than troubled ones.

- *Cash-flow generating capacity*: Businesses that generate substantial cash flow should have smaller liquidity discounts than businesses that do not have that capacity to generate cash flows.

Empirical evidence   **Restricted securities** are securities issued by a company, but not registered with the SEC, that can be sold through private placements to investors but cannot be resold in the open market, except under provisions of SEC's rule 144. Furthermore, they cannot be sold for a two-year holding period, and only limited amounts can be sold after that. Studies of these securities going back to 1966 have provided several consistent findings.

Restricted Securities: These are securities issued by a publicly listed company that can be sold in private placements to investors who are restricted from selling these securities; they do not have to be registered with the SEC.

Restricted securities trade at significant discounts on publicly traded shares in the same company. Maher (1975) examined restricted stock purchases made by four mutual funds between 1969 and 1973 and concluded that they traded an average discount of 35.43% on publicly traded stock in the same companies. Using data from 1970, Moroney (1971) reported a mean discount of 35% for acquisitions of 146 restricted stock issues by 10 investment companies. In a more recent study of this phenomenon, Silber (1991) found that the median discount for restricted stock was 33.75%. Silber reported that the discounts tended to be smaller for larger and more diversified companies and larger for companies in trouble. He developed the following relationship between the size of the discount and the characteristics of the firm issuing the registered stock:

$$LN(RPRS) = 4.33 + 0.036\ LN(REV) - 0.142\ LN(RBRT) + 0.174\ DERN + 0.332\ DCUST$$

where

RPRS = Relative price of restricted stock (to publicly traded stock)
REV = Revenues of the private firm (in millions of dollars)
RBRT = Restricted Block relative to Total Common Stock in %
DERN = 1 if earnings are positive; 0 if earnings are negative
DCUST = 1 if there is a customer relationship with the investor; 0 otherwise

From concept to practice   Two basic approaches can be used to estimate the **liquidity discount** for a private business:

- *Approach 1*: Based on past studies, use the average liquidity discount of 30% for private firms. Adjust subjectively for size (decrease the discount for larger firms).
- *Approach 2*: Using the empirical evidence developed from studying registered shares, estimate the discount as a function of its determinants—the size of the firm, the stability of cash flows, the type of assets, and cash-flow-generating capacity.

Liquidity Discount: This is the discount applied to the estimated value for an asset to reflect the lack of liquidity on the asset.

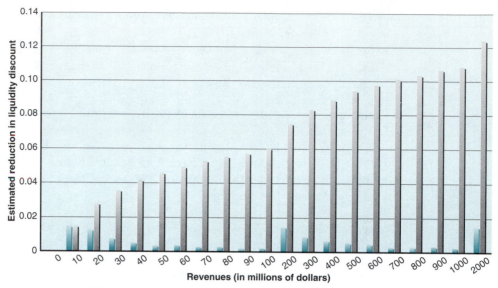

Figure 30.3   Effects of increasing revenues on liquidity discounts: estimated from Silber regression

The Silber study suggests the relationship between the amount of revenues and the liquidity discount pictured in Figure 30.3.

Thus, if an analyst has to estimate the liquidity discount for a private business with revenues of $120 million, this graph could be used to arrive at an estimate.

> Liquidity Discount for small firm with negligible revenues = 30%
> Liquidity Discount for this business = 30% − 6% = 24%

The 6% comes from Figure 30.3; it is the reduction in liquidity discount as a function of the revenues.

Valuing Businesses with a Personal Component

Many businesses derive a significant portion of their value from a "**key person,**" often the owner, and may be worth much less if run by someone else. In these cases, it is important to build in the consequences of losing this key person to the valuation. It is also important to factor in to the analysis the additional risk associated with the dependence on an individual.

Key Person: The key person in a firm valuation is a person whose presence provides a significant portion of the value of the firm.

Valuing a restaurant—Lutece   Lutece is a renowned restaurant located at 249 East 50th Street in Manhattan. In 1994, Lutece was sold by its owner/chef Andre Soltner to Ark Restaurants, a publicly traded restaurant chain, for an undisclosed amount. The *New York Times,* blanching as a result of the sale ran the headline, "Lutece, a Dining Landmark, Is Sold to a Chain Operator." The headline was then followed by an article detailing the surprise marriage of the classic French restaurant to Ark, a company largely known for operating "theme" concept restaurants. Bryan Miller, the *Times'* former restaurant reviewer and writer of the piece, likened the addition of Lutece to Ark's portfolio to "hanging a Van Gogh in a community art exhibit."

Lutece was founded in 1961 by Andre Soltner and quickly acquired a reputation for serving food of exceptional quality. It has received a five-star rating from Mobil for 24 consecutive years and is one of five New York city restaurants that gets a four-star rating (the highest) from the *New York Times*. In a sign of slippage, however, its ranking in the Zagat Survey of New York City restaurants dropped to eighth from its position at or near the top for much of the 1970s and 1980s.

Estimating cash flows   The following are background characteristics of Lutece:

- The restaurant seats up to 92 diners. It has one seating for lunch and two seatings for dinner. It fills in 70% of its seats at lunchtime, and 80% of its seats at dinner.
- The restaurant stays open 340 days every year; it is closed the remaining 25 days.
- The average price of a lunch is $30; the average price of a dinner is $66. Approximately one-third of this cost is for liquor.
- The restaurant employs 42 employees. The cost of food is approximately 30% of the price of the meal, and the payroll amounts to $800,000 a year.
- The annual rent for the space used by Lutece is $600,000.

Table 30.8 provides an estimation of the after-tax operating cash flows for Lutece in 1994.

Table 30.8   ESTIMATED AFTER-TAX OPERATING INCOME FROM LUTECE

	Assumption	Base Year
Revenues		
Lunch	(70% occupancy; $30 per person)	$656,880
Dinner	(80% occupancy; $66 per person)	1,651,584
Total		2,308,464
Expenses		
Food	(30% of revenues)	692,539
Staff	($800,000 for staff expenses)	800,000
Rent		600,000
Total		2,092,539
EBIT		215,925
Taxes	(Assumed tax rate of 40%)	86,370
EBIT (1− t)		129,555

These cash flows are expected to grow 6% a year for three years and 3% a year after that. Table 30.9 summarizes the expected cash flows over the next three years.

Table 30.9   ESTIMATED OPERATING INCOME IN FUTURE YEARS

	Base Year	1	2	3
Revenues	$2,308,464	$2,446,972	$2,593,790	$2,749,418
Expenses	2,092,539	2,218,092	2,351,177	2,492,248
EBIT	215,925	228,880	242,613	257,170
Taxes	86,370	91,552	97,045	102,868
EBIT (1–t)	129,555	137,328	145,568	154,302

Estimating discount rates   The acquirer, Ark Restaurants, has a relatively low beta (0.70) and gets only about 10% of its financing needs from debt. Assuming that the underlying risk in investing in Lutece is similar, the cost of equity can be estimated as follows:

$$\text{Cost of Equity} = 8\% + 0.7\,(5.5\%) = 11.85\%$$

(This assumes that the long-term Treasury bond rate is 8%.)

If Ark Restaurants can borrow money at 9% and faces a 40% tax rate, the cost of capital can be calculated as follows:

$$\text{Cost of Capital} = 11.85\%\,(.90) + 9\%\,(1-0.4)\,(.10) = 11.20\%$$

Estimating value   The value of Lutece can be estimated by discounting the cash flows at the weighted average cost of capital. Allowing for a growth rate of 6% over the next three years and 3% after that, the value of the restaurant can be estimated as follows:

Value at the end of the high growth period

$$\begin{aligned}
&= EBIT_4\,(1-t)/(1+g_4)/(WACC - g_4)\\
&= \$154{,}302\,(1.03)\,/(.112-.03)\\
&= \$1{,}938{,}184
\end{aligned}$$

$$\begin{aligned}
\text{Value of Lutece} &= \$137{,}328/1.112 + \$145{,}568/1.112^2 + (\$154{,}302+\$1{,}938{,}184)/1.112^3\\
&= \$1{,}762{,}985
\end{aligned}$$

Valuing the key man   There is no argument that some of Lutece's value derives from Andre Soltner's presence as chef. It would be worth examining how much this value would change if he were to be replaced by somebody else. The simplest way to evaluate this effect is to

• Estimate the effect on occupancy of replacing Mr. Soltner with another chef, and, through this, the effect on cash flows; to the extent that occupancy and cash flows decline, the value of the restaurant will decline.
• Calculate the value of the restaurant based on the discounted cash flows.

In extreme cases, where the entire value of an enterprise depends on one person, the value can drop essentially to zero if the key person were to leave or die. In less extreme cases, the value of the key person can be estimated to be the difference between the values of the enterprise with and without that person in place.[6]

---

[6]Consider the value of David Letterman to CBS. One estimate in the *New York Times* claimed that 20% of the profits at CBS could be traced to the success of David Letterman's show. If this is true, CBS may be getting an incredible bargain, even at $5 million a year.

CONCLUSION

Private businesses operate under far more constraints than do publicly traded firms. They have less access to capital, and their owners are more exposed to risk that would be diversified away by a stockholder in a publicly traded firm. They also operate under different accounting and tax rules than do publicly traded firms. These differences have consequences for investment, financing, and dividend policy.

- In investment analysis, the tighter capital rationing constraints in conjunction with the higher discount rates that private firms may use to reflect diversifiable risk will lead them to reject some projects that publicly traded firms will take. This tendency has to be weighed against any efficiency gains that arise because owners operate as managers in private firms, and thus have a greater incentive to maximize returns and value.

- In financing policy, private firms are typically exposed to greater bankruptcy costs—explicit and implicit—and stricter bond covenants, when they borrow. This tendency, in turn, will operate as an incentive to keep debt much lower at private firms than at otherwise similar publicly traded firms.

- In dividend policy, private firms are much less likely to be driven by tax considerations (since income flows through to the owners and gets taxed anyway) and signaling implications (since the equity is not traded). Therefore, deciding how much to reinvest back into the business becomes a tradeoff between higher growth, on the one hand, and current cash needs, on the other.

- Private firms should be valued in much the same way as publicly traded firms, with two adjustments. The first is a discount reflecting the lack of liquidity associated with owning a private business. The second is an adjustment reflecting the personal component in the business—that is, the value of a "key person" in the business.

QUESTIONS AND PROBLEMS

1. The owner of a small, closely-held corporation anticipates doubling his sales during the next year and has decided to double his fixed asset investment to support the expected new sales. The company is currently financed solely with equity, but he plans on taking out a personal loan to finance the expansion. If the firm currently has assets of $1 million and he plans to take out a $500,000 personal loan, what will the new equity ratio (E/A) of the company be?

2. A friend of yours works for a small, private corporation and has just been promoted. She is now eligible to participate in an employee stock purchase program wherein the company will match any stock purchase she makes in the company dollar-for-dollar up to a maximum of $5,000 per year. So, for example, if she buys $1,000 of the firm's stock, the firm will also give her another $1,000 worth of stock. Disregard transactions costs and assume that she "vests" immediately (i.e., she can leave and take the stock she purchased and the stock the company purchased anytime she wants). Should she participate in the stock plan? What are the benefits and disadvantages?

3. "Section 179 expensing" refers to a provision in the Tax Code which permits firms to expense (rather than depreciate) up to $17,500 worth of capital equipment. Discuss how this benefits small firms, contrasting the selection of projects that large firms would potentially invest in with the group that small firms might invest in.

4. From a taxation viewpoint, why would small firms generally be more inclined to lease equipment instead of buy?

5. Privately held firms typically raise debt by taking out a bank loan while large publicly owned firms often make use of bond issues. Explain how differential public disclosure requirements for these two type of firms can drive this choice of financing source.

6. Joe Drain runs a successful plumbing service in a wealthy suburb. He is considering expanding his operations into the next town. The details on the expansion are as follows:

- Three plumbing vans, at the cost of $20,000 a van, and equipment costing $40,000 will have to be acquired for the expanded operations. The initial investment can be depreciated straight line over five years to a salvage value of $25,000.

- The expansion will require hiring three new plumbers, each of whom will be paid $30,000 a year.
- A small office will be rented at a cost of $15,000 a year.
- The revenue from the expanded operation is expected to be $200,000 each year for the next five years. Operating expenses, including insurance, are expected to amount to $20,000 a year.
- Joe Drain's tax rate is 40%.
- There are three publicly traded firms that run plumbing and drainage services. Their average beta is 1.05, and the R-squared is 40%. (T Bond rate is 7%.)

Based on this information, answer the following questions.

a. Estimate the cash flows on this expansion, assuming that the operation will fold after five years.

b. Estimate an appropriate discount rate for the project.

c. Should Joe Drain go through with this expansion?

7. A publicly traded firm and a private firm are looking at the same project. Assuming that they have the same expectations of revenue on this project, answer the following questions:

a. Under what conditions will the publicly traded firm assign a higher value to the project?

b. Under what conditions will the private firm assign a higher value to the project?

8. Conglom, Inc. is a large publicly traded firm that creates growth by acquiring small, successful private businesses. What are the necessary conditions for this strategy to be successful? What are some of the dangers of adopting this strategy?

9. You have just completed a traditional capital structure analysis for LoCap, Inc, a privately run business. Based on its cash flows and an analysis of its cost of capital at different levels of debt, you conclude that the optimal debt ratio for the firm is 40%. The firm has no debt, and the owner insists that any leverage is dangerous.

a. Do you agree with him?

b. If you do not agree, would you suggest moving to the optimal debt ratio? Why or why not?

10. You have been asked to value Barrista Espresso, a chain of espresso coffee shops that have opened on the east coast of the United States. You have collected the following information:

- The company had earnings before interest and taxes of $10.50 million in the most recent year. However,

the founders of the company had never charged themselves a salary, which would have amounted to $1 million, based on comparable companies.

- The tax rate is 36%.
- The capital expenditures in the most recent year amounted to $4.5 million, whereas depreciation was only $1 million.
- Working capital is expected to remain at 10% of revenues.
- Earnings, revenues, and net capital expenditures are expected to grow 30% a year for five years and 6% after that forever.
- There are three comparable companies, which are publicly traded:

	Beta	D/E	k_d
Starbucks:	1.74	9.53%	9.00%
Au Bon Pain:	1.21	31.43%	8.50%
Sbarro:	1.12	0.00%	NA

Barrista Espresso is expected to maintain a debt ratio of 12% and face a cost of debt of 8.75%. (Revenues were $30 million.) (T Bond rate is 7%.)

a. Estimate the value of Barrista Espresso, as a firm.

b. Estimate the value of equity in Barrista Espresso.

c. Would your valuation be any different if you were valuing the company for an initial public offering rather than a private valuation? Explain.

11. What are some of the determinants of the size of the liquidity discount? Answer true or false to the following statements:

a. There should be no liquidity discount attached to the value, if the valuation is being done for an initial public offering.

b. The liquidity discount should be larger for a high-growth firm with no current cash flows than for a stable firm with positive cash flows.

c. The liquidity discount will become smaller for firms when they start losing money.

d. The size of the liquidity discount will depend partly on the buyer's characteristics.

12. Using discounted cash-flow models, you have valued a business at $250 million, for a private sale. The business, which does make money, had revenues of $200 million in the most recent year. How much of a liquidity discount would you apply to this firm

a. based on the Silber regression?

b. based on correcting the average discount (25%) for the size of the firm?

13. You are trying to value a bed-and-breakfast business in Vermont for its owner, based on the following information:

- The business had pretax operating income of $100,000 in the most recent year. This income has grown 5% a year for the last three years and is expected to continue growing at that rate for the foreseeable future.

- About 40% of this operating income can be attributed to the fact that the owner is a master chef. He does not plan to stay on if the business is sold.

- The business is financed equally with debt and equity. The pretax cost of borrowing is 8.00%. The beta for publicly traded firms in the hospitality business is 1.10. The Treasury bond rate is 7.00%.

- The capital maintenance expenditure, net of depreciation, was $10,000 in the most recent year, and it is expected to grow at the same rate as operating income.

- The business is expected to have an operating life of 10 years, after which time the building will be sold at an anticipated price of $1.5 million, net of capital gains taxes.

- The tax rate is 40%.

a. Value the business, for sale.

b. How much would the value change if the owner offered to stay on for the next three years?

CHAPTER 31

A FINAL REVIEW

Having gone through an extended discourse of the different components of corporate finance, we are now in a position to summarize our conclusions. In this chapter, we review the basic principles developed throughout this book. We also apply these principles to an extended example, which we then use to develop the linkages between the various components of corporate finance.

THE PRINCIPLES OF CORPORATE FINANCE

We began this book by noting that any decision that has a financial component is a corporate finance decision. We then classified corporate finance decisions into three groups—investment decisions, financing decisions, and dividend decisions. In this section, we review some of the general principles we have developed in each category.

The Objective Function

Even before we started looking at the optimal ways of picking and financing projects, we established an *objective function*. In corporate finance, the objective in decision making is assumed to be the maximization of the firm value and, in specific cases, the maximization of the stock price. Although this objective function provides a strong and measurable focus for corporate financial decisions, it does have some serious problems. First, managers, who are the decision makers in the firm, may focus on their own interests and not act in the best interests of stockholders. Second, the stockholders may enrich themselves at the expense of bondholders, even if it means making decisions that are not in the best interests of the entire firm. Third, the price of the stock may not reflect the long-term value of the firm, but may instead reflect short-sighted market assessments and poor information. Finally, extensive social costs may be created as a consequence of stock price or firm value maximization.

Despite these problems, we continue to argue for firm value maximization, for two reasons. First, the *alternative* objective functions, such as maximizing market share or earnings, are even more flawed than value maximization. Second, the excesses of value maximization are self correcting. If managers pursue their interests at the expense of stockholder interests much too vigorously, stockholders will act to rein them in through proxy battles and hostile takeovers. If stockholders take advantage of bondholders, the bondholders will write in more restrictive covenants into bond agreements. If markets become much too short term and inefficient, long-term investors will step in to exploit these inefficiencies. Finally, if the social costs become excessive, governments will act to restrict and regulate social concerns.

> Proposition 1:   The objective in corporate financial decision making is the maximization of firm value.

Investment Analysis

The first, and arguably most important, set of corporate finance decisions are investment decisions—that is, decisions about whether and where to allocate their resources. To summarize, we argued that firms should not invest in projects that make returns that are lower than a hurdle rate that reflects the riskiness of the projects. Although returns on projects can be calculated using accounting earnings and accounting measures of investment (book value), we argue that a measure of return that is based on the level and timing of cash flows is more accurate.

> Proposition 2:   Returns computed based on cash flows provide a more accurate measure of a project's returns than do those based upon accounting income.

> Proposition 3:   A good measure of project return will factor in the timing of the cash flows; earlier cash flows are weighed more heavily than later cash flows.

To estimate the appropriate hurdle rate, we start off with the basic proposition that riskier projects should have higher hurdle rates. The capital asset pricing model and the arbitrage pricing model, the two basic models for risk that we introduced in this book, clarify this relationship explicitly as follows:

1. They assume that the variability in returns on an investment is the measure of its overall risk.
2. Of this risk, they assume that only the portion that cannot be eliminated by an investor holding a well-diversified portfolio will be rewarded.
3. The nondiversifiable risk of any investment can be measured using either a beta measured relative to a market portfolio (in the CAPM) or multiple betas measured relative to macroeconomic factors (in the arbitrage pricing model).
4. The expected return on an investment is a linear function of its beta (in the CAPM) or betas (in the arbitrage pricing mode).

> Proposition 4:   The hurdle rate on an investment is a function of the nondiversifiable risk inherent in that investment, which is measured by the beta or betas of the investment; the higher the beta(s), the higher the hurdle rate.

We then defined two types of hurdle rates—a *cost of equity,* which is a function of the risk faced by equity investors, and a *cost of capital,* which is a weighted average of the costs of all the different types of financing a firm might use. When analyzing investments, it is important to choose the right hurdle rate for the given cash flow.

> **Proposition 5:**   If the cash flows on an investment are cash flows to equity investors (i.e., cash flows left over after debt payments), the appropriate hurdle rate is the cost of equity. If the cash flows are prior to debt payments (i.e., cash flows to the firm), the appropriate hurdle rate is the cost of capital.

Once the returns and the appropriate hurdle rates are computed, several investment decision rules are available to help the firm decide to accept or reject projects. The only decision rules that are based on cash flows and factor in the time value of money are the *net present value* and *internal rate of return* rules. The net present value is conceptually a more robust rule, but the internal rate of return may be more attractive to companies with capital rationing constraints.

Overall, firms that make good investment decisions (i.e., take positive net present value projects) will increase in value, whereas those that take on projects that earn less than the hurdle rate (negative net present value projects) will drop in value. It is worth noting, however, that good projects are the result of good strategic decisions and the firm's capacity to create differential advantages over their competitors.

Capital Structure

When firms borrow money, they weigh the advantages of debt—interest is tax deductible, and debt imposes discipline on errant management—against the costs of debt—increased risk of bankruptcy and increased constraints and restrictions. When the agency problems in a firm (between stockholders and managers and stockholders and bondholders) are negligible, there are no default risks or taxes, the financing decision becomes irrelevant to firm value. Under most other scenarios, the value of the firm will be a function of its financial leverage.

To examine the optimal debt ratio for a firm, we start with the proposition that the value of a firm is the present value of the expected cash flows to the firm, discounted back at the cost of capital. If the cash flows are kept constant, the value of the firm will be maximized when the cost of capital is minimized. Thus, the optimal debt ratio becomes that ratio at which the cost of capital is minimized; or the debt ratio at which the value of the firm is maximized is its optimal debt ratio.

> **Proposition 6:**   The optimal debt ratio for a firm is the ratio at which the value of the firm is maximized. When operating cash flows are unaffected by leverage, minimizing the cost of capital will maximize firm value.

When firms operate at debt ratios that are significantly different from their optimal, they are forsaking some firm value. At one extreme, firms that are significantly underlevered may be open to hostile acquisition bids; the firm will have to increase its leverage or it will be taken over. At the other extreme, firms that are significantly overlevered run the risk of bankruptcy. In either case, if firms have time to change their leverage, they can adjust their financing mixes gradually over time to move to their optimal ratios by financing new projects predominantly with debt (if they want to increase leverage) or with equity (if they want to decrease leverage).

> **Proposition 7:**   Firms that operate at debt ratios that are significantly different from their optimal debt ratios are imposing a cost on their stockholders, in terms of lost value.

As a final step in this process, we examine the forces that make up the design of the firm's financing—its duration (short or long term), currency, and any special features it might have. We argue that firms should try to match up the characteristics of their financing as closely as possible to the characteristics of the assets being financed; by doing so, they increase their capacity to carry debt and thereby increase their value. In some cases, however, firms deviate from this rule in order to take advantage of tax benefits or to cater to the desires of equity research analysts and ratings agencies. Furthermore, firms may use debt that does not meet their specific asset needs in order to reduce potential agency problems between stockholders and bondholders. For instance, firms that believe they are being underrated by bondholders may use short-term debt to finance long-term assets.

> **Proposition 8:**   By matching the characteristics of its financing to its assets, a firm reduces default risk, increases debt capacity, and increases value. Conversely, firms that mismatch their assets and liabilities reduce debt capacity and have an adverse impact on value, unless they are more than compensated by higher tax benefits or reduced agency costs.

Dividend Policy

Once a firm has made the right investment decisions and chosen the optimal financial mix, it has to figure out what to do with the cash flows generated by these projects. Ideally, this should be a very simple decision. A firm should take the cash flows that are left over after meeting operating expenses and taxes, finance all projects that are viable, and return the balance to the stockholders. In the real world, however, this decision is complicated by a number of factors. First, dividend payments generally have adverse tax consequences for some individual investors. If enough of such investors hold the stock, it may make sense for a firm with leftover cash to look for ways to return this cash (for instance, through equity repurchases) without creating high tax liabilities. Second, firms that institute specific dividend policies tend to attract investors that like these dividend policies. Thus, firms that pay high dividends attract investors who like dividends, and firms that do not pay dividends accumulate investors who like price appreciation. The bottom line is that dividends are generally not changed often and, given the existence of stockholder clienteles, should not be changed frequently. Third, dividend changes, when announced, affect stock prices, for higher dividends are viewed as a signal of good future prospects. Finally, in addition to affecting stockholders, the dividend policy decision also affects bondholders. Dividend payments take cash from within the company, where it could have been used to pay off debt, and pays it out to stockholders.

In our analysis of dividend policy, we first examine the relationship between dividends that are paid and dividends that a firm *could have* paid—the cash flows left over after meeting all debt payments, as well as capital expenditures and working capital needs. This cash flow is defined as the free cash flow to equity. Many firms pay out much less in dividends than they can afford to, given their free cash flows to equity. Such firms accumulate significant cash balances and face pressure from stockholders to return more cash, especially if their track record in picking the right projects is poor. Firms that pay out more in dividends than they have available in free cash flows to equity will experience stress either on their current cash balance or on their capacity to raise external financing to make these dividend payments.

> **Proposition 9:**   Firms that have a history of superior project returns typically enjoy the greatest flexibility when it comes to setting dividend policy. Conversely, firms that have posted substandard project returns are much more likely to face pressure from their stockholders to return more cash.

Linkage to Value
Given the central role that value plays in the corporate financial objective function, the last step in this process is to link up the firm's corporate financial decisions to its value. We do so using the traditional *discounted cash-flow model.* Changes in investment policy, financing policy, and dividend policy affect current cash flows, expected growth, and risk. Once the effects of a decision are measured in terms of cash flows and discount rates, its effect on value can be computed.

> **Proposition 10:**   Firms that want to increase their value can do so by taking actions that result in higher expected cash flows (by increasing current cash flows or expected future growth), lower discount rates (by reducing nondiversifiable risk or by changing financing mixes), or both.

The Big Picture
To summarize, we can apply the lessons noted above to come up with a "big picture" that clarifies all the linkages. The big picture from Chapter 1 is reproduced here in Figure 31.1.

Although the linkages were not explained in Chapter 1, they should be clear now. In the real world of taxes, default risk, and agency problems, investment decisions affect financing decisions, and vice versa, and dividend decisions affect financing decisions, and vice versa.

A COMPREHENSIVE CORPORATE FINANCIAL ANALYSIS

As a final step in this process, let us consider the steps involved in a comprehensive corporate financial analysis, in which we analyze a firm's risk profile and tie it into investment, financing, and dividend policy.

Step 1: Establish the Firm's Risk Profile
Risk is fundamental to almost everything we do in corporate finance. We begin with an estimate of a firm's risk, using either the CAPM (in which case, the market beta is estimated) or the APM (multiple betas are estimated). The regressions that provide these beta estimates also provide us with information about the firm's past performance and the sources of risk (market versus firm specific). Regressions provide noisy estimates of risk parameters; thus, it makes sense to look at whether these parameters are reasonable, given both the firm's financing decisions and its underlying business risk.

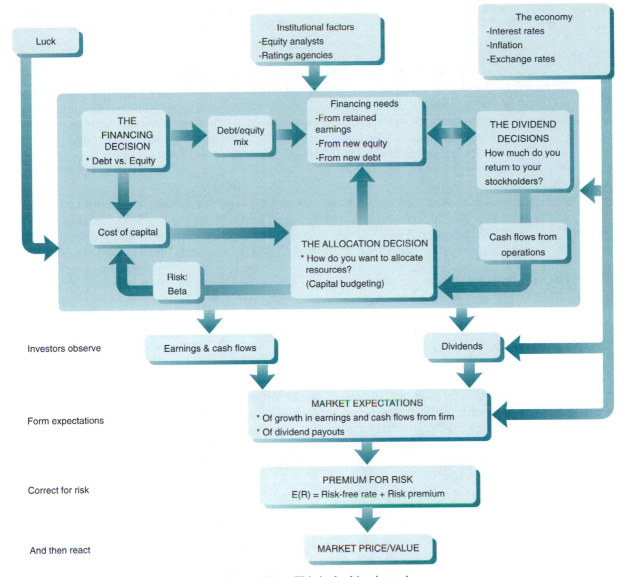

Figure 31.1   This is the big picture!

Step 2: Estimate the Firm's Cost of Equity and Capital

By themselves, the estimated risk parameters are useful only insofar as they help us estimate expected returns for the overall equity in the firm; these expected returns are measures of the costs of equity. Computing the market value weighted average of the costs of equity and debt gives us the cost of capital. Although either the cost of equity or the cost of capital can be used in capital budgeting, the cash flows on the projects have to be matched up to the appropriate discount rate—cash flows to equity are discounted at the cost of equity, and cash flows to the firm at the cost of capital.

Step 3: Use the Costs of Financing to Assess Investment Projects

In assessing investment projects, we begin by estimating the cash flows that will be generated by these projects and then assess whether the returns on these projects exceed the hurdle rate, which can be either the cost of equity or the cost of capital, depending on whether cash flows are after or before debt payments. If the project risk is different from that for the rest of the firm, its cost of equity should be assessed separately.

Step 4: Evaluate the Firm's Optimal Financing Mix

In the special case where the firm's cash flows are unaffected by leverage, the optimal financing mix of debt and equity for a firm is the one at which the cost of capital is minimized; more typically, it is the debt ratio at which firm value is maximized. Once a firm's optimal financing mix has been identified and implemented, both its cost of equity and cost of capital will have to be reestimated and used to reassess old projects as well as new ventures.

Step 5: Assess the Firm's Capacity to Pay More or Less in Dividends

A firm's dividend policy can be examined for the most part by analyzing whether the firm is paying out more or less in dividends than it can afford and by examining the quality of projects available to the firm. If firms that have a history of poor projects hold back cash that they could have paid in dividends, stockholder concerns about wasting this money will put pressure on the company to pay out more. If firms with great project prospects and limited access to capital markets pay out too much in dividends, they may face capital rationing constraints that will result in lost value to stockholders. Any change in dividend policy has to factor in stockholder preferences and the signaling effects that may accrue.

Step 6: Value the Firm

In this final part of the analysis, we tie in the risk parameters estimated in the first step with the cash flows generated as a result of both current projects and expected future growth. The value that emerges as a consequence of discounting cash flows to equity at the cost of equity is a measure of the value of equity of the firm; if cash flows to the firm are discounted at the cost of capital, it is a measure of the value of the firm itself.

As a final analysis, it is worth reestimating value, including the changes that emerge from the investment, financing, and dividend decisions. This value is a "restructured value" and should be significantly higher than the status quo valuation.

AN EXTENDED EXAMPLE: HERSHEY FOODS

In 1994, Hershey Foods, the largest U.S. producer of chocolate and confectionery products, reported revenues of $3.6 billion and net income of $264.4 million. In the following analysis, we will take an extended look at the company's finances in December 1994.

Step 1: Estimate and Analyze the Risk Parameters for Hershey Foods

We begin by estimating the CAPM risk parameters for Hershey Foods and examining its past performance as an investment. To do so, we collected monthly return data on Hershey from January 1990 to November 1994 and correlated them with the returns on the S&P 500 over the same period. Figure 31.2 summarizes both return series.

Beta To estimate the market beta to use in the CAPM, we regressed returns on Hershey against the S&P 500 to arrive at the following:

$$R_{\text{hershey}} = 0.33\% + 1.01\, R_{\text{S\&P 500}} \qquad R^2 = 36.66\%$$

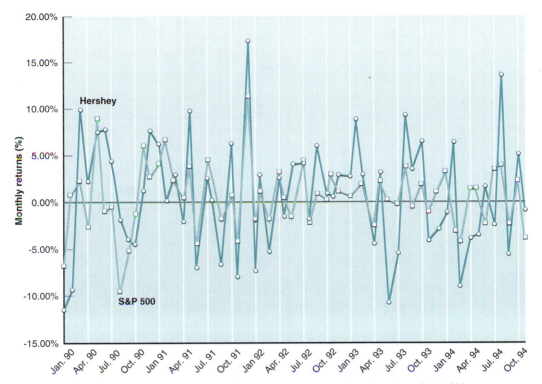

Figure 31.2   Returns from January 1990–1994: Hershey Foods vs. S&P 500

The slope coefficient from the regression, which is 1.01, is the regression estimate of the beta. This is fairly close to the estimates of beta obtained from services such as Value Line (0.95) and S&P (1.00).

Stock price performance   Hershey's performance as a stock can be analyzed by comparing the intercept to that based on the CAPM, which is $R_f(1 - \beta)$.

$$\text{Intercept based on CAPM} = 0.565\% \; (1 - 1.01) = -0.01\%$$
$$\text{Excess Return} = 0.33\% - (-0.01\%) = 0.34\%$$

The monthly risk-free rate during the period (1990-94) was 0.565%. Based on this analysis, we conclude that, after adjusting for risk, Hershey Foods outperformed the market by 0.34% on a monthly basis from January 1990 to November 1994. Annualized, this works out to an excess return of 4.17% over the period.

More on Hershey's risk characteristics   The R-squared of the regression is 36.66%, suggesting that the market risk, which is nondiversifiable, accounts for 36.66% of Hershey's risk, while the remaining 63.34% comes from firm-specific sources. This may not matter much to a well-diversified investor holding stock in Hershey Foods, but it has relevance for both investors who may not be well diversified and for managers at the firm.

The effects of leverage on Hershey's beta   We noted earlier that increasing leverage increases the equity beta for a stock. In particular, the beta for a stock can be written as a linear function of its debt/equity ratio:

$$\beta_{\text{levered}} = \beta_{\text{unlevered}} \left[1 + (1 - \text{tax rate}) \, (\text{Debt/Equity}) \right]$$

where the debt/equity ratio is defined in market value terms. The beta from the regression for Hershey is 1.01. At the time of this analysis, we estimated the market value of equity for Hershey, using the market price of $47.25 as of December 1994, and the number of shares outstanding (85 million):

$$\text{Market Value of Equity} = \$47.25 * 85 \text{ million} = \$4.016 \text{ billion}$$

In December 1994, Hershey had $662 million in debt outstanding, none of which was publicly traded, and paid an interest expense of $30.2 million on this debt that year. Based on its bond rating of AA, the market interest rate on this debt in December 1994 was 8.70%. Given that Hershey's debt had an average maturity of 10 years, the market value of debt can be estimated as follows:

$$\text{Market Value of Debt} = \text{Interest Expenses} * (\text{PVA}, 10 \text{ years}, 8.70\%) + \text{Face Value}/1.087^{10} = \$30.2 \text{ mil} (\text{PVA},10\%,8.70\%) + \$662.6/1.087^{10} = \$484 \text{ million}$$

Given the market value of equity ($4.016 billion) and the market value of debt ($484 million), we can estimate the market value debt/equity ratio for December 1994:

$$\text{Debt/Equity Ratio} = \text{Market Value of Debt}/\text{Market Value of Equity}$$
$$= \$484/\$4,016 = 12.05\%$$

Assuming that Hershey's debt/equity ratio during the period of the regression was similar, the effect of leverage on the firm's beta can be estimated by first calculating the unlevered beta: (The marginal corporate tax rate between 1990 & 1994 was 34%.)

$$\text{Unlevered Beta} = 1.01/(1+(1 - 0.34)(.1205)) = 0.94$$

We can then break down the actual beta (1.01) into that portion that can be attributed to leverage and that which is attributed to the underlying business risk:

$$\text{Total Risk} = \text{Business Risk} + \text{Financial Risk}$$
$$1.01 = 0.94 \qquad + 0.07$$

Step 2: Compute the Cost of Equity and Capital
The next step in the process is to use the risk parameters estimated for debt and equity to compute the costs of debt and equity, and to use these costs to estimate a cost of capital.

Estimating the cost of equity   The beta estimated from the regression can be used to estimate the cost of equity for Hershey Foods. The long-term Treasury bond rate in December 1994 was 8.00%, and the 5.5% historical premium earned by stocks over bonds can be used to estimate the cost of equity:

$$\text{Cost of Equity} = 8.00\% + 1.01\,(5.5\%) = 13.56\%$$

The long-term Treasury bond rate and premium are used to arrive at the cost of equity, because the cost of equity is used to analyze long-term projects.

Estimating the cost of debt   The cost of debt is the market interest rate at which Hershey can borrow. It is clearly affected by both Hershey's rating (AA) and the long-term Treasury bond rate at the time of this analysis (8.00%). Allowing for a premium of 0.70% for the rating, and a corporate tax rate of 36%, we find that this works out to a cost of debt of (The corporate tax rate increased to 36% at the end of 1994.)

$$\text{Pretax Cost of Debt} = \text{Treasury Bond Rate} + \text{Default Premium} = 8.70\%$$
$$\text{After-tax Cost of Debt} = 8.70\%\,(1 - 0.36) = 5.57\%$$

Estimating the market value weights of debt and equity   In the previous section, we estimated the market values of equity and debt as $4.016 billion and $484 million, respectively. The debt and equity proportions in capital can then be computed as follows:

$$\text{Equity Weight} = 4016/(4016 + 484) = 89.24\%$$
$$\text{Debt Weight} = 484/(4016 + 484) = 10.76\%$$

Estimating the cost of capital   The costs of financing and the relative proportions of debt and equity can be used to compute the cost of capital for Hershey in December 1994.

$$\text{WACC} = 13.56\%\,(89.24\%) + 5.57\%\,(10.76\%) = 12.70\%$$

Step 3: Investment Analyses at Hershey Foods

In this section, we consider how the costs of equity and capital estimated above enter into investment analyses, by examining two hypothetical projects. Before we begin, it is important to note that the cost of equity is much higher than the cost of capital, but both can be used as discount rates in investment analysis. The basic rule enunciated earlier holds: if the cash flow being discounted is a cash flow to equity investors, the appropriate discount rate is the cost of equity; if the cash flows being discounted are cash flows prior to debt payments, the appropriate discount rate is the cost of capital. Table 31.1 summarizes the appropriate use of each in the context of investment analysis.

Table 31.1   DISCOUNT RATES AND CASH FLOWS IN INVESTMENT ANALYSIS

Cash Flow	Discount Rate	NPV
Free Cash Flow to Firm = EBIT (1 − tax rate) + Depreciation − Capital Reinvestment Needs − Change in Working Capital	WACC (12.70%)	NPV = PV of FCFF − Total Initial Investment If NPV > 0: Accept If NPV < 0: Reject
Free Cash Flow to Equity = Free Cash Flow to Firm − Interest Expenses (1 − t) − Principal Repayments + New Debt Issues	Cost of Equity (13.56%)	NPV = PV of FCFE − Equity in Initial Investment

---

An investment project with risk similar to Hershey's underlying business   Hershey Foods is considering introducing a new brand of candy, which will require an initial investment of $100 million in plant and equipment. It is planning to finance this project using $14.83 million in debt and $85.17 million in equity. The debt will carry an interest rate of 8.70% and will be repaid in a balloon payment at the end of 10 years. The project is expected to generate $25 million in earnings before interest and taxes each year for the next 10 years. The depreciation is expected to be $10 million each year for the next 10 years. Working capital will increase $2 million each year for the next 10 years and will be salvaged at the end of the project life. The tax rate is 36%.

The cash flows on the project can be estimated, on both an equity and firm basis, as shown in Table 31.2.

Table 31.2   CASH FLOWS ON PROJECT OF SIMILAR RISK

Initial Investment	Free Cash Flow to Firm		Free Cash Flow to Equity	
Plant & Equip. = $100.00m	EBIT (1 − t) = 25(.64)= $16m		FCFF	= $24m
− Debt Issued = $14.83m	+ Depreciation	= $10m	− Int Exp (1 − t) = $0.83m	
Equity Invest. = $85.17m	− Cap Ex	= $0m	FCFE	= $23.17m
	− Δ Work. Cap.	= $2m		
	FCFF	= $24m		

Salvage Value of Working Capital = $20 million

The net present values can then be estimated on both a firm and an equity basis. The net present value is computed first on a firm basis:

$$
\begin{aligned}
&\text{NPV (using firm cash flows)}\\
&= \text{FCFF (PVA,WACC,10 years)} - \text{Total Investment}\\
&\quad + \text{Salvage of Working Capital}/(1+\text{WACC})^{10}\\
&= \$24 \text{ (PVA, 12.70\%,10 years)} - \$100 \text{ million}\\
&\quad + \$20 \text{ million}/1.127^{10} = \$37.86 \text{ million}
\end{aligned}
$$

The net present value is also estimated on an equity basis:

> NPV (using cash flows to equity)
> $= \text{FCFE (PVA}, k_e, 10 \text{ years}) - \text{Equity Investment} + \text{Salvage of WC}/(1+k_e)^{10} - \text{Principal Repaid}/(1+k_e)^{10}$
> $= \$23.17 \text{ (PVA, } 13.56\%, 10 \text{ years}) - \$85.17 \text{ million} + \$20 \text{ million}/1.1356^{10} - \$14.83 \text{ million}/1.1356^{10} = \$39.26 \text{ million}$

This project has a positive net present value and should be accepted.

An investment project with risk different from Hershey's underlying business
Hershey's is considering introducing a mail-order and computerized shopping service that will sell candy, flowers, and other gift items. This project is expected to have a different risk profile from the rest of Hershey Foods, but a number of publicly traded firms are in the same line of business, as shown in Table 31.3.

Table 31.3   BETAS OF COMPARABLE FIRMS

Firm	Beta	D/E Ratio
Home Shopping Network	1.25	9.88%
Land's End	1.00	9.68%
Lillian Vernon	1.15	3.80%
Spiegel	1.70	64.49%
Average	1.275	21.96%

Unlevered Beta for Mail-order/Catalog Firms $= 1.275/(1+0.64*0.2196) = 1.12$
Levered Beta based on Hershey's D/E ratio (12.05%) $= 1.12 (1+0.64*.1205) = 1.21$
Cost of Equity for this project $= 8.00\% + 1.21 (5.5\%) = 14.66\%$
Cost of Capital for this project $= 14.66\% (.8924) + 5.57\% (.1076) = 13.68\%$

Although the net present of this project can be estimated using these discount rates, a short cut can be used to estimate whether or not the project is acceptable. If this project requires the same initial investment as the previous project and produces identical cash flows, the accounting returns on this project can be computed as follows:

Expected return on equity on the project

> Expected Net Income on Project $= \$15.47$ million
> Book Value of Equity Investment in Project $= \$85.17$ million
> Return on Equity $= \$15.47$ million$/\$85.17$ million $= 18.16\%$

The return on equity is greater than the cost of equity of 14.66%, which suggests that this project should be accepted.

Expected return on assets on the project

Expected EBIT$(1 - t) = \$16$ million
Book Value of Total Investment in Project $= \$100$ million
Return on Capital $= \$16$ million$/\$100$ million $= 16\%$

The return on capital on this project is greater than the cost of capital (13.68%), which also suggests that this project is acceptable.

Although accounting returns do not provide as accurate a measure as cash flows, they do provide an approximate measure of return, which is generally correlated with the cash-flow returns.

Step 4: Evaluate Hershey's Optimal Financing Mix

Let us first consider where Hershey Foods stands in terms of debt capacity, from the viewpoint of the costs and benefits of borrowing, as shown in Table 31.4.

Table 31.4 COSTS AND BENEFITS OF BORROWING—HERSHEY	
Cost/Benefit	**Hershey Standing**
Benefits	
1. Tax Benefits	• Hershey's has no special tax factors to consider. It does not have any tax loss carry-forwards, and it receives benefits comparable to those of most U.S. corporations.
2. Discipline of Debt	• Hershey's is not a closely held company, and there is a separation of ownership and management. The management of the company owns less than 2% of the outstanding stock; therefore, there should be some benefit from borrowing.
Costs	
1. Bankruptcy Costs	• Hershey's has a substantial and stable cash flow from operations. It is not a cyclical firm and has a low probability of bankruptcy.
	• The implicit cost of bankruptcy is low, since customers (who buy Hershey's products) are not particularly sensitive to default risk.
2. Agency Costs	• Hershey's assets are tangible (plant and equipment) and produce cash flows quickly. The potential for risk shifting is fairly small within Hershey's existing businesses.
3. Financial Flexibility	• Hershey's is in a stable and fairly predictable business; the need for flexibility is small.

From this perspective, Hershey Foods should gain from borrowing.

The cost of capital for Hershey Foods computed in the earlier sections is based on the actual debt ratio of 10.76%. Figure 31.3 summarizes Hershey's cost of capital as a function of debt ratios, ranging from 0% to 90%; the objective is to find the debt ratio at which the cost of capital is minimized.

The optimal debt ratio for Hershey, when the cost of capital is minimized and the value of the firm is maximized, is 40%. Table 31.5 summarizes the costs of equity, debt, and capital at both the current and the optimal debt ratios.

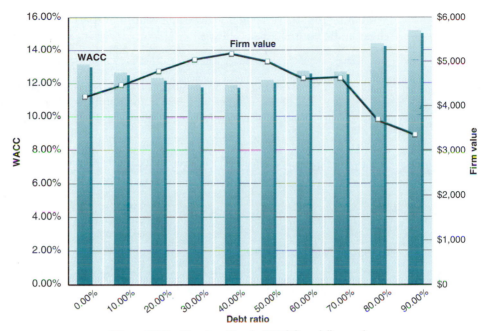

Figure 31.3   Hershey Foods: WACC and firm value

	Current	Optimal
Table 31.5 **Costs of debt, equity and capital—Hershey Foods**		
Beta	1.01	1.34
Cost of Equity	13.56%	15.36%
Equity/(Debt + Equity)	89.24%	60.00%
Bond Rating	AA	BB
After-tax Cost of Debt	5.57%	6.72%
Debt/(Debt + Equity)	10.76%	40.00%
Cost of Capital	12.70%	11.90%

Thus, if Hershey moves to a 40% debt ratio, the cost of capital will drop from 12.70% to 11.90%, although the beta will increase and the bond rating will drop. The firm value will increase as a consequence, as the firm saves on annual financing costs:

Current Firm Value = MV of Debt + MV of Equity = 484 + $4,016 = $4,500 million
Savings each year from reduced WACC = (.127−.119) (4,500) = $36 million

Assuming that these savings do not increase over time, and last in perpetuity, the present value of the savings can be computed as follows:

PV of Savings = $36 million/.119 = $302 million
PV of Savings per share = $302 million/ 85 million = $3.55
Price per share after the change = $47.25 + $3.55 = $50.80

Assuming that these savings grow 6% a year in perpetuity, the present value of the savings can be computed as follows:

$$PV \text{ of Savings} = \$36 \text{ million} * 1.06 / (.119 - .06) = \$646.78 \text{ million}$$
$$PV \text{ of Savings per share} = \$646.78 \text{ million}/85 \text{ million} = \$7.61$$
$$\text{Price per share after the change} = \$47.25 + \$7.61 = \$54.86$$

If, in fact, Hershey introduces a rating constraint of BBB, the optimal debt ratio will be lower, and, consequently, the firm value will be slightly lower.

	Constrained Optimal	Unconstrained Optimal
Debt Ratio	30.00%	40.00%
WACC at Optimal	12.02%	11.90%
Firm Value at Optimal	$5,032	$5,147

The cost of introducing a rating constraint can be estimated as the difference between the constrained and unconstrained optimals.

As a final step, we examine what kind of debt Hershey should introduce by looking at the sensitivity of firm value to changes in interest rates, inflation rates, the economy, and the weighted dollar. The regressions are summarized below:

$$\text{Change in Firm Value} = 0.08 - 7.42 \text{ Change in Long-Term Rate}$$
$$\text{Change in Firm Value} = 0.14 - 1.16 \text{ Change in GNP}$$
$$\text{Change in Firm Value} = 0.11 - 0.45 \text{ Change in Weighted Dollar}$$
$$\text{Change in Firm Value} = 0.14 + 3.41 \text{ Change in Inflation Rate}$$

Based on these regressions, Hershey Foods should be using long-term debt, with a duration of approximately 7.42 years. The firm is not particularly cyclical (as evidenced by the regression against GNP) or exposed to currency risk (as evidenced by the regression against the dollar). Its value seems to be positively correlated with inflation, which would present an argument for floating rate loans.

Step 5: Evaluate Hershey's Dividend Policy

To evaluate Hershey's dividend policy, we first examine how much cash Hershey had available to pay in dividends between 1985 and 1994 by estimating the free cash flows to equity each year:

$$\text{Free Cash Flow to Equity} = \text{Net Income} - (\text{Capital Expenditures} - \text{Depreciation})$$
$$(1 - \text{Debt Ratio}) - \text{Change in Working Capital} (1 - \text{Debt Ratio})$$

The free cash flows to equity and dividends are reported each year from 1985 to 1994 in Figure 31.4.

In all but three years, the dividends paid were less than the free cash flows to equity. In fact, on average, the dividends were 65% of the estimated free cash flows to equity over the period. The net effect was an increase in Hershey's cash balance over the period.

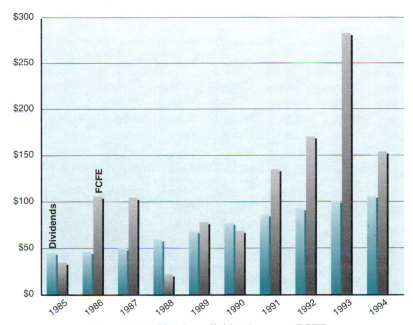

Figure 31.4   Hershey: dividends versus FCFE

The other half of the analysis examines the project choices Hershey made over the period by comparing the return on equity to the cost of equity. In addition, the average and marginal returns on equity can be estimated:

Average Return on Equity = Net Income / BV of Equity
Marginal Return on Equity = Δ Net Income / Δ Book Value of Equity

The average return on equity measures the returns earned by Hershey on all its projects, old and new, whereas the marginal return on equity measures the returns on the new projects taken in each year. Two propositions emerge from these measures.

Proposition 1:   For large firms, small changes in the average return on equity arise from large changes in the marginal return on equity.

Proposition 2:   For large firms, the marginal return on equity is a much better leading indicator of project quality than is average return on equity.

Figure 31.5 summarizes average and marginal returns on equity at Hershey Foods from 1985 to 1994.

Although the return on equity has been relatively stable at around 15%, the marginal return on equity has been declining over the last four years.

Our analysis suggests two facts. First, Hershey is not paying out as much in dividends as it is capable of doing. Second, the quality of Hershey's projects is declining; in fact, it has dropped below the cost of equity in 1994. Based on these two facts, we believe that Hershey should be looking for ways to return more cash to its stockholders.

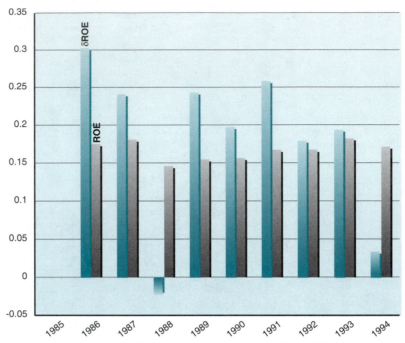

Figure 31.5 Hershey Foods: marginal ROE vs. ROE

Step 6: Estimate the Value of Hershey's Stock

Finally, we estimate the value of Hershey stock, using both the dividend discount and free cash flows to equity models. In doing so, we make the following assumptions:

- The earnings per share in 1994 is $3.05; the return on assets in that year is 13.70%; and the debt/equity ratio is 12.70%.

- The high-growth period is expected to last five years, during which time the growth rate is determined by fundamentals to be 8.92%; the growth rate after that is expected to be 6%.

- The dividend payout ratio is expected to be 40% for the high-growth period and 59.64% after that.

- The beta for the stock is expected to be 1.01 forever; the long-term bond rate at the time of this valuation is 8%.

- The capital expenditures in 1994 is $2.10, whereas the depreciation is $1.41; both are expected to grow at the same rate as earnings for the high-growth period and offset each other after that.

- The working capital, which was 3.84% of revenues in 1994, is expected to remain at that level in perpetuity.

Using these assumptions, we first estimate the earnings per share, dividends per share, and the terminal price based on the dividend discount model, as shown in Table 31.6.

$$\text{Present Value of Dividends} = \$26.11$$

Similar estimates are made for the free cash flows to equity (FCFE) and terminal price, as shown in Table 31.7.

$$\text{Present Value of FCFE} = \$44.03$$

Table 31.6   ESTIMATED EARNINGS PER SHARE
AND DIVIDENDS PER SHARE: HERSHEY FOODS

Year	EPS	DPS	TERM. PR.
1	$3.32	$1.33	
2	$3.62	$1.45	
3	$3.94	$1.58	
4	$4.29	$1.72	
5	$4.68	$1.87	$39.12

Table 31.7   ESTIMATED FCFE—HERSHEY FOODS

Year	EPS	Deprec'n	Capital Exp.	(Cex-Dep)(1−¶)	WC-Ch(1−¶)	FCFE/sh	Term. Val.
1	$3.32	$1.54	$2.29	$0.67	$0.13	$2.52	
2	3.62	1.67	2.49	0.73	0.14	2.75	
3	3.94	1.82	2.71	0.79	0.16	2.99	
4	4.29	1.99	2.96	0.86	0.17	3.26	
5	4.68	2.16	3.22	0.94	0.18	3.55	$63.81

Figure 31.6 summarizes the inputs driving this base-case valuation. As a final check on this process, the FCFE value was reestimated, with the following changes:

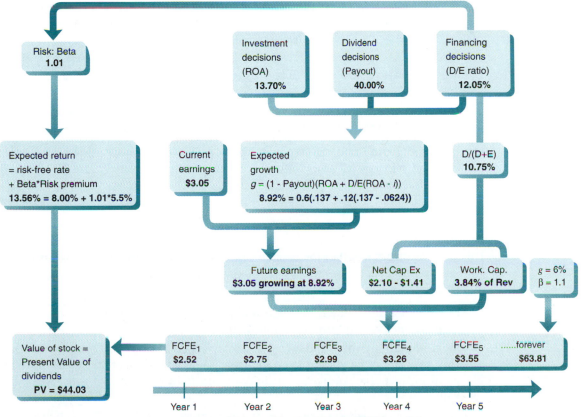

Figure 31.6   Valuing Hershey Foods: FCFE model

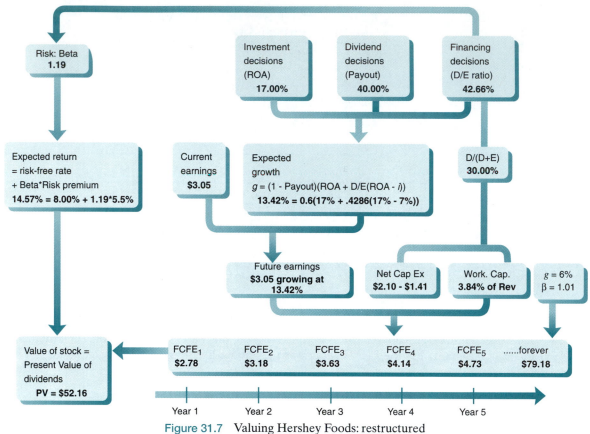

Figure 31.7   Valuing Hershey Foods: restructured

- The debt ratio was raised to 30%, in keeping with our finding that the firm has excess debt capacity.
- It was assumed that Hershey would sell its lower-return pasta division to a competitor and, in the process, raise its return on assets to 17%.

The expected growth rate will be much higher as a consequence, although the cost of equity will also increase. The net effect is positive, as illustrated in Figure 31.7, since the value per share increases to $52.16.

CONCLUSION

This chapter brings together the concepts developed throughout this book into a comprehensive whole. In the process, we reemphasized many of the points we made earlier. In particular,

- Maximizing firm value is the central objective that drives much of the theory and many of the prescriptions in corporate finance.
- Decisions about where and how much to invest determine, in large part, whether a firm will in fact be able to keep increasing its value; firms that consistently take good projects (i.e., projects that make more than their hurdle rate) will add to value.
- While, under certain circumstances, the way projects are financed may be irrelevant to firm value, more often, the financing mix used for projects does affect firm value.

- Firms have to look at their cash-generating capacity and the quality of their projects before setting dividend policy; once established, a given dividend policy will attract an investor clientele that likes it, making it more difficult to change.
- The value of a firm is the end product of its investment, financing, and dividend decisions. Conversely, any changes in these decisions will affect firm value.

QUESTIONS AND PROBLEMS

1. The management of TractTech Corporation, a farm-equipment manufacturing firm that is under siege from stockholders, argues that it has done a good job of increasing the earnings of the firm over its tenure. The dissident stockholders argue that the stock price over the period has decreased substantially.

   a. How would you reconcile increasing earnings and a decreasing stock price, if markets are efficient?

   b. Under what conditions should the management be held accountable for this stock price decrease?

2. You have been asked for some advice on investment policy by Celentano Corporation, a leading manufacturer of pasta. The company has historically maintained a hurdle rate of 20%, which was set by looking at the returns on equity made by companies in the peer group. Consequently, it has rejected any projects that have made a return on equity less than this hurdle rate.

   a. Do you agree with the way in which this company has set its hurdle rate? If not, why not?

   b. Assume that the average unlevered beta for comparable firms is 0.80 and that Celentano has no debt. If the current Treasury bond rate is 6%, what would you estimate the hurdle rate to be?

   c. What is the cost to Celentano of maintaining the current hurdle rate?

3. Biogene Corporation, a pharmaceutical company, has traditionally estimated its cost of equity using the beta from the CAPM. Its current beta is 1.10, and its debt to capital ratio is 25%. Based on its default risk, Biogene can borrow at 1% above the current Treasury bond rate of 6%. The corporate tax rate is 36%.

   a. Estimate the cost of equity and capital for Biogene Corporation.

   b. Assume that you are analyzing a project in the same line of business as Biogene Corporation. Would you accept the project if it has an internal rate of return of 12.5%, based on predebt cash flows and total investment?

   c. Would your answer change if the firm were considering a project in a much riskier line of business? (The average beta of comparable firms is 1.80.)

4. NewCap Corporation, a news media company, is reexamining its policy of financing its projects entirely with equity. An analysis of its cost of capital suggests that the cost of capital will be 1.50% lower than the current one if the firm moves to a 30% debt ratio. (The current beta of the firm is 0.90, and the current Treasury bond rate is 7%.) The current earnings before interest and taxes is $100 million, and net capital expenditures are zero; the earnings are expected to grow 5% a year forever. Tax rate = 40%)

   a. Estimate the value of the firm under the current debt ratio.

   b. Estimate the value of the firm under the optimal debt ratio.

   c. What concerns might you have in moving to the optimal? How would you alleviate these concerns?

5. OverCap Inc., a food processing firm, is still recovering from a leveraged recapitalization, which increased its debt ratio to 70% of capital. Based on its cash flows, its optimal debt ratio is 40%. The firm is considering whether it should sell assets and reduce its debt ratio immediately.

   a. Under what conditions should it do so?

   b. Under what conditions would you recommend lowering the debt ratio gradually instead?

6. DivPoor Corporation, a specialty retailing firm, has traditionally followed a policy of not paying out dividends. The return on equity on its projects is 15%, but the marginal return on equity in the last three years has been below 12%.

   a. If the beta for the stock is 1.15 and the Treasury bond rate is 6%, would you advise the firm to continue to withhold the cash?

   b. If not, how would you recommend returning the cash?

7. You are trying to value Morgan Technology, a manufacturer of computer monitors, using the dividend

discount model. You have collected the following information on the firm:

- The company has earnings per share currently of $2 and pays 20% of its earnings as dividends. Its book value of equity per share is $10, and it is trading at 2.5 times the book value.

- The firm has no leverage currently and is expected to maintain this policy for the high-growth phase, which is expected to last three years. During the high-growth phase, the beta is expected to be 1.5.

- After three years, the firm is expected to reach stable growth, and earnings are expected to grow 6% a year. The fundamentals are expected to approach industry averages for return on assets (where the average is 14%), leverage (where the industry average debt/equity ratio is 25%), and unlevered beta (where the industry average unlevered beta is 0.8). (Interest rate on debt is 8%.) (Tax rate is 40%.)

The long-term Treasury bond rate is 6%.

a. Estimate the expected growth rate during the high-growth period.

b. Estimate the terminal value per share at the end of the high-growth period.

c. Estimate the value per share using the dividend discount model.

d. What would happen to this value if the return on assets during the high-growth period were increased by 4%?

e. What would happen to this value if the debt/equity ratio were increased to 25% immediately, rather than after three years?

f. What would happen to this value if the dividends paid during the first three years were 40% of earnings?

8. Agency problems between the shareholders and the managers of a firm often interfere with the primary stated goal of financial decision making, the maximization of firm value. Explain how managerial incentive schemes can be constructed to mitigate this agency problem.

9. Why is net income not an appropriate measure of the cash flows from a firm?

10. Both the Capital Asset Pricing Model and the Arbitrage Pricing Theory assume that only non-dversifiable risk will be rewarded. Under what circumstances will this assumption not hold true?

11. What are the costs associated with underutilizing debt? With over utilizing debt?

12. Discuss how default risk is affected if a firm chooses to fund long-term projects with short-term debt.

13. When is it appropriate to use historic returns to calculate a firm's beta, and when is it not?

14. Suppose that congress passes a new tax bill that decreases the difference between the capital gains tax rate and that for ordinary income. How will this affect firms' capital structure decisions?

SOLUTIONS TO ODD-NUMBERED QUESTIONS AND PROBLEMS

Note: Use 5½% premium for all relevant solutions.

CHAPTER 2

2-1 **e.** to maximize firm value/stock prices.

2-3 *Annual Meeting:* Stockholders may not show up at annual meetings or be provided with enough information to have effective oversight over incumbent management. In addition, the corporate charter is often tilted to provide incumbent managers with the advantage, if there is a context at the annual meeting.

Board of Directors: Directors are often chosen by the incumbent managers (rather than by stockholders), own few shares and lack the expertise/information to ask tough questions of incumbent managers.

2-5 The fact that markets are volatile, by itself, does not imply that they are not efficient. If the underlying value of the investments traded in the market is changing a lot from period to period, prices should be volatile. Even if the underlying value is not moving as much as prices are, the fact that markets make mistakes (which is what the noise is) does not imply that the prices are not unbiased estimates of value.

2-7 This strategy is likely to work if higher market share leads to higher profits and cash flows in the long term. If, on the other hand, the higher market share is obtained by cutting prices and sacrificing long-term profitability, the strategy is unlikely to work.

CHAPTER 3

3-1 **a.** $192,772
    b. $31,373

3-3 $1,468

3-5 **a.** $6.58 million
    b. $6.04 million

3-7 $22.71

3-9 12.79%

3-11 $17,738.11

3-13 $311.22 million.

3-15 **a.**

Year	Nominal	PV
0	$5.50	$5.50
1	$4.00	$3.74
2	$4.00	$3.49
3	$4.00	$3.27
4	$4.00	$3.05
5	$7.00	$4.99
	$28.50	$24.04 million

b. The sign-up bonus has to be reduced by $3.73 million and the final year's cash flow has to be increased by $5.23 million to arrive at a contract with a nominal value of $30 million and a present value of $24.04 million.

3-17 **a.** $1,755.14
    b. $1,609.25
    c. yes
    d. 9.17%

3-19 **a.** $10.43
    b. $0.83

3-21 $876.05

CHAPTER 4

4-1 $1,000,000

4-3 **a. and b.**

	1992	1993	% Change
Revenues	$10,000.00	$10,100.00	1.00%
−Labor	$4,000.00	$2,500.00	−37.50%
−Material	$2,000.00	$2,010.00	0.50%
−Depreciation	$1,000.00	$1,300.00	30.00%
−Operating Expenses	$500.00	$450.00	−10.00%

	1992	1993	% Change
EBIT	$2,500.00	$3,840.00	53.60%
−Interest Expenses	$500.00	$520.00	4.00%
Taxable Income	$2,000.00	$3,320.00	66.00%
−Tax	$700.00	$1,261.60	80.23%
Net Income	$1,300.00	$2,058.40	58.34%
# Shares	1500	1500	0.00%
EPS	$0.87	$1.37	58.34%

c. The growth rate in earnings per share is being driven by the increase in operating income.

4-5 $10 million

4-7 $16.5 million

4-9 The firm should be able to pay out $40 million in dividends. If it does pay out only $10 million each year for the next four years, the net accumulation of cash will equal $120 million.

4-11 $250 million

4-13 1.724

4-15

Current Liabilities =	$333.33
Debt =	$1,272.76
Equity =	$593.91
Fixed Assets =	$1,800.00
Accounts Receivable =	$200.00
Inventory =	$0

4-17 $5 million

4-19 1.40

CHAPTER 5

5-1 I would prefer to invest in A. It has the highest expected return and the lowest standard deviation.

5-3 **a.** Expected Return = 15.00%
Standard Deviation = 30.92%

   b. It would depend upon my risk aversion. It is possible that I would invest in individual securities if I were extremely risk averse (A) and risk loving (B).

5-5 **a.** 0.00

   b. Weight on A = 0.50
Weight on B = 0.50

   c. 10%

5-7 15%

5-9 2.25%

5-11 No. The fund actually underperformed by –0.80%

5-13 **a.** 71.43% (only one solution)

5-15 **a.** 12.85%

   b. 3.93%

CHAPTER 6

6-1 **a.** 13.88%

   b. 11.63%

   c. I would use the expected return of 11.63% as the cost of equity.

6-3 **a.** 15.75%

   b. The cost of equity will rise by 1.1%.

   c. All of the risk can be attributed to business risk.

6-5 **a.** 13.20%

   b. $54.10

   c. –7.00%

   d. –3.70%

   e. 0.923

6-7 **a.** 1.43

   b. 1.86

6-9 **a.**

Firm	Operating Leverage
PharmaCorp	0.93
SynerCorp	1.28
BioMed	1.57
Safemed	1.90

   b. Firms with high operating leverage also have high betas.

6-11 The beta reflects market risk and is estimated relative to a stock index. To the extent that commodity prices and stock prices are not highly positively correlated the low betas reflect the low market risk inherent in these stocks. I would expect these firms to have substantial firm-specific risk.

6-13 **a.** 8.53%

   b. 95%

   c. 1.13

6-15 **a.** 18.83%

   b. Yes, it would change to 15.48%.

   c. 3.49%
3.91%

   d. 1.89

6-17 **a.** 1.01

Year	Beta
1	1.41
2	1.27

6-19 **a.** 1.13

   b. The firms might not be directly comparable in terms of business mix. Furthermore, the risk of a firm may be affected by its size; if the private firm is much smaller, this beta might not adequately reflect its risk. Finally, this beta reflects only market risk; the private firm may care about firm-specific risk as well.

6-21 **a.** 1.08

   b. 1.02

6-23 **a.** 1.29

   b. 0.25 – 1.25

   c. The regression estimate is very noisy. It is entirely possible that both of these estimates are from the same distribution; I would trust the "comparable firm" estimate more.

CHAPTER 7

7-1 31.68%

7-3 16.67%

7-5 **1.** earning growth rate = 0
2. dividend payout ratio = 100%

7-7 **a.** 5 years
b. 7.02 years

7-9 **1.** −338,448.05
2. −668,282.46
The firms should reject the project.

7-11 An increase of $2/share

7-13 **a.** 7.10%
b. No.
c. Negative.

7-15 Yield to Maturity.

CHAPTER 8

8-1 **a.** $2.71 million
Nominal Value of Tax Savings = $4.8 million
b. $4.29 million
Nominal Value of Tax Savings = $4.8 million
c. Because it provides more tax benefits earlier in the process.

8-3 In Problem 8-1, if salvage value is ignored, PV of Tax Savings from Ignoring Salvage = $0.49 mil.
In Problem 8-2, if salvage value is ignored, Present value of Tax Savings from Ignoring Salvage = $0.71 mil.

8-5 **a.** $2.9 million
b. $0.72 million
c. $2.96 million
d. $1 million

8-7 $45,084.35

8-9 $301,126

8-11 **a.**

Year	ATCF
1	$48,020
2	78,063
3	112,843
4	153,012
5	212,461

b. Yes

8-13 **a.** There is no cost the first three years. The after-tax salary paid in last two years is an opportunity cost = $62,589
b. $54,126
c. $6,823
d. $184,000
e. $73,967

8-15 **a.** In year 5.
b. You will lose less cutting back on old products. $41.02 million
c. $15.28 million

8-17 **a.** $26.45 million
b. 50.09%

CHAPTER 9

9-1 **a.** I would accept Projects B, C, D, E, G, and H. since they have the highest PI.
b. $45 million

9-3 Choose option b (gas heating system).

9-5 I would choose 1-year subscription-lowest EAC

9-7 $184,118

9-9 The EAC declines as you increase the lifetime; it becomes lower than 1029.45 at 14 years.

9-11 Pick project C; Highest annualized NPV

9-13 More than $40,000.

9-15 **a.** Projects II, IV, and V.
b. Project I, II and IV
c. The differences arise because of the reinvestment rate assumptions; with the IRR, intermediate cash flows are reinvested at the IRR; with the PI, cash flows are reinvested at the cost of capital.

9-17 Yes.

CHAPTER 10

10-1 a. NPV = $4,311,500
IRR = 50.51%

b.

Sales/Sq Foot	NPV	IRR
$100	−$3.199 million	NA
$200	−$1.321 million	0%
$300	$555,897	19.19%
$400	$2.433 million	35.36%
$500	$4.31 million	50.51%

Variable Cost%	NPV	IRR
40%	$4,311 mil	50.51%
50%	$2.746 mil	37.93%
60%	$1.181 mil	24.77%
70%	−$.383 mil	10.24%

c. Financial breakeven = $270/sq./ foot

Accounting breakeven = $200/sq. foot

10-3 a. I would draw from these distributions to do my simulations.

b. Over a large number of simulations, I would expect the average NPV to converge to the base case (−$1.745 million) and the average IRR to also converge on the base case (7.55%).

c. I would look at the distribution of NPV and IRR across the simulations.

10-5 a.

	NPV	Probability
Better ▸$40 for 5 years $49.42		0.15

Full Intro
$(50)

Regional Intro
Succeeds ($20) Succeeds (75%)

| As well as ▸$20 for 5 years $(7.54) | | 0.15 |

Test
Marketing
($5)

Worse than ▸ $5 for 5 years $(50.26)   0.15

Fails

Fails (25%)

$(23.18)   0.15

Stop after test
marketing

$(5.00)   0.4

b. $(6.74)

c. The option to abandon has no value here, since the project cash flows are always positive.

10-7 a. NPV = $13,452,323
IRR = 36.67%

b.

# of Units Sold	NPV	IRR
25,000	$799,559	13.60%
50,000	$5,017,147	21.70%
75,000	$9,234,735	29.35%
100,000	$13,452,323	36.67%
125,000	$17,669,911	43.73%

c. 20,261

Accounting Breakeven = 0 (Profits are positive with just advertising revenues)

10-9 a.

Build Plant ($50,000,000) :$10 million each year for 10 years **$1,445,671**

($10,000,000) ─

Abandon Plant

($10,000,000)

NPV of Project = 0.6 * $1,445,671 + 0.4 * ($10,000,000) = ($3,132,597)

b. No. I would not do the test market, since the expected present value of the project does not cover the test market cost.

c. The solution is not sensitive to the number of years you stay in business, as long as the working capital is fully salvageable.

10-11 a. Yes.
b. $778,000

10-13 Annual Cash Flow needed to make NPV positive in 2 years = $10,000,000 (APV,14%,2) = $6,072,897

Number of Subscribers needed for 2-year life to have positive NPV = $6,072,897/$6 = 1012125

b. Approximately 25 years.

10-15 a. 82,121

b. If I was uncertain about the life, I would have to calculate this breakeven for each life

time (2 years, 3 years, 4 years, etc.) and then look at an expected value for the breakeven.

CHAPTER 11

11-1 a. This is project-specific risk that should be diversified across projects. It should not be factored into investment analysis.

b. This is firm-specific risk that should be diversifiable across investments. It should not be factored into investment analysis.

c. This is firm-specific risk that should be diversifiable. It should be factored into investment analysis.

11-3 a. 17.50%

b. In the previous section, I assumed that the stockholders in the firm would not care about exchange rate risk since they can diversify it away themselves. If the stock-holders in the Limited were not capable

11-5 a. 1.00

b. Beta = 1.60
Cost of Capital = 10.03%

11-7 a. 13.09%

b. No. I did not charge a premium for currency risk, sine Hershey is a widely held stock with institutional investors who are capable of handling exchange rate risk on their own.

d. This is firm-specific risk that should not affect investment analysis.

e. This is market risk; it should be considered while estimating discount rates and value.

f. This is market risk and should be considered while doing investment analysis.

g. This is market risk, and it should be reflected in the discount rate.

of being well diversified (e.g, the stock might be closely held), I would have added a premium to the estimated cost of equity to reflect exchange rate and politi-cal risk.

c. I did not charge a premium for the underly-ing economic risk in the Malaysian economy (by using a higher risk premium), but I did not explicitly charge a premium for the political risk.

d. If Hershey had been privately held, I would have charged premiums for both currency and political risk.

11-9

Year	OF	PV at 16.08%	Cert. Eq. CF	PV at 7%
0	$(10,000,000)	$(10,000,000)	$(10,000,000)	$(10,000,000)
1	$3,500,000	$3,015,162	$3,226,223	$3,015,162
2	$4,000,000	$2,968,556	$3,398,699	$2,968,556
3	$4,500,000	$2,877,003	$3,524,452	$2,877,003
4	$5,000,000	$2,753,851	$3,609,737	$2,753,851
5	$5,000,000	$2,372,373	$3,327,376	$2,372,373
		$3,986,945		$3,986,945

11-11 a. 10.91%

b. I would not charge a higher cost of capi-tal for the New York City City store, because estimation risk is firm-specific risk and should not be built into the dis-count rate.

11-13 a. 11.32%

b. 9.67%

c. 10.50%

11-15 a. If debt is allocated on the basis of the rela-tive market values of the divisions, the costs of capital will be the same as those calcu-lated in problem 13.

b. Cost of Capital for tobacco division = 10.82%
Cost of Capital for food division = 10.58%

CHAPTER 12

12-1 Most utilities in the United States are regulated to prevent them from reaping the spoils of their

monopolistic position—higher prices and higher profits. If the regulations were removed, and they continued to be natural monopolies, they would increase their excess returns.

12-3 As a private firm, you might be run more efficiently than your competitors and have lower overhead expenses. You might also have the capacity to be more flexible than your competition. Your competitors, on the other hand, may have better access to funds and be less exposed to the kinds of firm-specific risk that you have to worry about.

12-5 **a.** Patents provide explicit protection against competition, allowing the firms that possess them to charge higher prices and earn higher returns.

b. If patent protection were weakened, I would expect excess returns in the pharmaceutical industry to drop.

c. If there is no patent protection, pharmaceutical firms will have to compete like all other consumer product firms—with advertising to create brand name, by reducing costs and establishing a cost advantage, or by offering products that are tailored to market segments that are not being served. Firms with low cost structures and good marketing teams are likely to be winners.

12-7 **a.** Given that the personal computer market is an intensely competitive one, with several large players, I would recommend a niche computer that would take advantage of her technical expertise and her capacity to keep overhead costs down.

b. She would need to convert her technical expertise—say, in graphics design—to produce a computer that served professional graphics designers better than the existing products. Furthermore, she would need to team up with a production specialist who can then produce these computers at low cost.

c. A sophisticated niche offering, priced with higher margins, provides the best opportunity for a small firm with technical expertise.

12-9 **a.** McDonald's was the first fast-food chain. It offered a standardized menu at low prices at all its locations. As the first entrant to do this successfully with independent franchises, it reaped enormous gains.

b. McDonald's clearly has unparalleled brand name recognition, especially overseas. I would foresee it taking advantage of this to grow internationally.

12-11 **a.** 13.45%
b. 5.34%
c. No.

12-13 **a.** The software firm did better than its required rate of return, whereas the auto firm lagged its required return.

b. The software firm did better than its peer group, as did the auto firm.

c. The software firm did less well than the market expected it to, whereas the auto firm did better.

12-15 **a.**

Firm	Differential
Chrysler	−0.60%
Ford	1.95%
GM	−2.83%

b. I would conclude that Ford picked the best projects and GM the worst.

c. The return on equity is a flawed measure because its focuses on accounting income instead of cash flows and also reflects all projects taken by the company, rather than just the most recent ones. Furthermore, the book value of equity can be affected by actions such as buybacks.

12-17 **a.** ($267.28)
b. $(1,733.3)
c. Yes. I would continue the project because the PV of continuing > Salvage Value.

12-19 No. It only implies that in those businesses where larger firms have cost advantages over smaller firms, they may be able to establish a differential advantage on this basis. It is also possible that economies of scale level off once a firm reaches a certain size, and that size may actually create diseconomies beyond that level.

12-21 If Japanese firms had lower labor costs—leading to higher cash flows—and lower costs of capital—leading to lower discount rates, it is possible that the same project could have a positive NPV for Japanese firms and a negative one for U.S. firms.

CHAPTER 13

13-1 **a.** Net income will drop by $300,000 = $500,000 (1 − .4)
There will be no effect on the balance sheet.

b. Capitalized Value of Lease = $1,895,393
Depreciation each year = $379,079

Interest Expense in year 1 = $189,539
In year 1, Net Income will be reduced by $341,171.
There will be a liability of $1,895,393 on the balance sheet.

13-3 **a.** Quickshop = 0   LoMart = 0.33

b. If operating leases are capitalized/: Quickshop = 36.61% LoMart = 33.33%

13-5 **a.**
b.

Year	Lease Payment	Interest (1 − t)	Depreciation (t)	Principal Pmt.	Year	ATCF	Differential CF	Interest
1	$(1,050,000)	$700,000	$240,000	$627,454	1	$(1,157,454)	$457,453.95	$1,000,000.00
2	$(1,050,000)	$656,078	$240,000	$690,199	2	$(1,176,278)	$476,277.57	$937,254.61
3	$(1,050,000)	$607,764	$240,000	$759,219	3	$(1,196,984)	$496,983.55	$868,234.67
4	$(1,050,000)	$554,619	$240,000	$835,141	4	$(1,219,760)	$519,760.13	$792,312.74
5	$(1,050,000)	$496,159	$240,000	$918,655	5	$(1,244,814)	$544,814.36	$708,798.62
6	$(1,050,000)	$431,853	$240,000	$1,010,521	6	$(1,272,374)	$572,374.02	$616,933.09
7	$(1,050,000)	$361,117	$240,000	$1,111,573	7	$(1,302,690)	$602,689.65	$515,881.00
8	$(1,050,000)	$283,307	$240,000	$1,222,730	8	$(1,336,037)	$636,036.84	$404,723.71
9	$(1,050,000)	$197,715	$240,000	$1,345,003	9	$(1,372,719)	$672,718.74	$282,450.69
10	$(1,050,000)	$103,565	$240,000	$1,479,504	10	$(1,413,069)	$713,068.84	$147,950.36

After-tax   **Borrow and Buy Option**

c. NPV of Leasing = −$7,374,761
NPV of Buying = −$7,789,293

d. $414,532

13-7 **a.** $748,497
b. $1,387,049

13-9 **a.** $1,689.92
b. Debt Ratio without Capitalized Lease payments = 0%

c. Debt Ratio with Capitalized Lease Payments = 40.32%

13-11 **a.** Buy
b. Lease.

13-13 Sell and lease back

13-15 **a.** Yes.
b. No. It is still better to lease rather than buy.

CHAPTER 14

14-1 **a.** 1.81
b. 0.39
c. Accounts Receivable Turnover = 2.52
Inventory Turnover Ratio = 10.25
d. 139.54

14-3 **a.** $17.70
b. $54.20
If these savings grow 6% a year forever, PV of Savings = $1,149

14-5 $16.14 million

14-7 **a.** Permanent Current Assets = 10% of Revenues in first three quartersSeasonal Current Assets = 10% of Additional Revenue in Fourth Quarter=Transitionary Component of Current Assets = Difference between actual current assets and forecasted current assets
b. I would finance the permanent portion of working capital using current liabilities and

long-term financing, the seasonal component with current liabilities and short-term financing.

14-9 **a.** $204,124
b. $235,702

14-11 $7.69 million

14-13 $191,279. The firm will need much more of a cash cushion if there is variability in cash usage.

14-15 **a.** Initial Inv = $3.5 million; ATCF in year 1 = $1.40 million.
b. $16.50 million

14-17 **a.** $1.08
b. $0.85

14-19 2 days.

14-21 Yes.

14-23 **a.** First loan = 10.38%
Second loan = 9.98%
b. The discount loan.

CHAPTER 15

15-1 Income bonds do share some characteristics with preferred stock. The primary difference is that interest paid on income bonds is tax deductible while preferred dividends are not. Income bondholders also have prior claims on the assets, if the firm goes bankrupt. In calculating cost of capital, the primary difference again will be that the cost of income bonds will be lower, because of the tax savings.

15-3 This security looks like preferred stock.

15-5 42.24%

15-7　**a.** You should consider the reputation of the investment banker. A more reputable investment banker may be able to attract wary investors into the offering. If you are a high-technology or biotechnology firm, where technical knowledge may be essential in the valuation process, you should pick an investment banker with some experience with similar issues.

　b. 40% of the firm

　c. 44.44%

15-9 This statement is not true. First, on a market value basis, U.S. firms are not more heavily dependent on debt than firms in other countries. Second, equity includes not just external equity (which U.S. firms are reluctant to use) but internal equity. When the fact that U.S. firms have more internal equity to invest is considered than firms in faster growth economies, the debt ratios do not look as high.

15-11　**d.** Possibly since (the underpricing is greatest for small stocks with significant uncertainty) and (it might operate as a promotion).

15-13 Not necessarily. I would value the conversion option before I concluded that convertible debt was cheaper.

15-15 While venture capitalists may demand a disproportionate share of the ownership, this may reflect the higher risk that they face. Furthermore, many of these firms would not have been able to raise needed funds if venture capitalists had been unwilling to step in and provide it.

15-17 I do not think so. The fixed claims that preferred stockholders have make them more like debt. If the preferred stock is cumulative, I would treat it more like debt.

CHAPTER 16

16-1 If the firm does not have an immediate need for the cash, I would suggest waiting until January to take advantage of the January effect (small firms earn a substantial premium over large firms). I would be less inclined to suggest this if the firm has to make the issue in June, since the waiting period will be much longer.

16-3 I would not. There is no evidence that forecasting services are effective at forecasting interest rates or stock prices.

16-5 I would advise that the firm reveal the information immediately and preempt the analysts. By doing so, it may be able to put its best spin on the story and minimize the negative market reaction.

16-7 The fact that the stock price declines on the announcement of the rights offering suggests that markets are reacting to the fact that the firm is making an equity issue. This is consistent with the evidence. I would try to package this announcement with news about what the funds from the equity issue will be used for—new projects or investments.

Note that the actual rights issue will cause the stock price to drop, but for a different reason. The rights issue will generally be at a much lower price than the current stock price.

16-9 It may be pulling off a coup in the short term, especially relative to the ratings agencies and some analysts. Markets are unlikely to be fooled very long. In fact, I would expect markets to treat these securities as debt and assess risk accordingly.

16-11 I would expect the stock price to go up. Both stock splits and dividend increases have generally been viewed as positive signals by financial markets, leading to stock price increases.

16-13 I would not follow her advice. The empirical evidence suggests that price momentum in financial markets is very weak, especially in the short term.

16-15 The fact that revenues/earnings occur in the summer months does not mean that stock prices will also peak in those months. In fact, what happens to stock prices during those months will depend in large part on whether or not the sales in those months exceed expectations.

CHAPTER 17

17-1　**a.** $1.26 million

　b. $14 million

　c. $8.09 million

　d. If savings are permanent = $18 million
　　　If savings are for 10 years = $8.85 million

17-3　**a.** $1.8 billion

　b. Yes. The net operating loss will mean that this tax savings will not occur for a while.

17-5　**a.** Moderate.

　b. Moderate to high.

c. Low.
d. Low.
e. Highest.

17-7 That is not true. Due to the agency conflicts between stockholders and bondholders, bondholders charge higher interest rates or write in much stronger covenants, either of which impose real costs on the firm.

17-9 That is not true. There is a cost to maintaining flexibility—opportunity costs associated with maintaining excess debt capacity and large cash balances. These costs may outweigh the benefits for some firms, especially those with mediocre investment prospects.

17-11 a. The past policy of not using debt can be justified by noting that returns on projects were high (increasing the need for flexibility) and that earnings in the future were likely to be volatile (because of the growth).
b. Given that returns on projects are declining, I would argue for a greater use for debt.

17-13 Bond covenants have a real cost to firms because they reduce their flexibility. These covenants might prevent firms from taking good projects (if the covenants restrict investment policy), repurchasing stock, or taking fresh debt for new projects.

17-15 a. An electric utility is regulated (reducing agency costs) has stable and predictable cash flows (reducing bankruptcy needs) and knows its future investment needs with some precision (reducing the need for flexibility). All of these factors will increase its capacity to carry debt.
b. Yes. Both the "regulation" and the "monopoly characteristics" reduce the agency costs and bankruptcy costs, increasing debt capacity.

17-17 I would expect the debt ratios of large firms to increase because governments will then bear a portion of the bankruptcy costs.

17-19 I would expect strong firms to issue straight debt and financially weak firms to issue preferred or convertible preferred.

17-21 The fact that the stock price goes to zero in a bankruptcy is not caused by the bankruptcy but by the actions that the firm has taken in the years prior that reduced cash flows and value. In other words, it is not caused by the bankruptcy and should not be viewed as cost occurring as a consequence of it.

17-23 It is in the interests of incumbent managers to keep leverage low. By doing so they minimize the chances that the firm will go bankrupt (which might affect their personal value) substantially and they also reduce the oversight that might come with higher debt ratios. Thus, you would expect firms to be underlevered if stockholders do not have much power.

CHAPTER 18

18-1 a. Book Value Debt/Equity Ratio = 100%
Debt/Equity Ratio in market value terms = 50%
b. Book Value Debt/(Debt + Equity) = 50%
Market Value Debt/(Debt + Equity) = 33.33%

c. 7.20%
d. 14.60%
e. 12.13%

18-3 1.

Option	Cost of Equity	2. Option	Cost of Debt	3. Option	Cost of Capital
1	13.58%	1	6.60%	1	12.59%
2	16.12%	2	7.80%	2	11.96%
3	28.31%	3	10.80%	3	13.72%

4.

	ΔFirm Value	New Firm Value	Debt	Equity	Stock Price
Option 1	($216)	$5,784	$1,000	$4,784	$75.68
Option 2	$86	$6,086	$3,000	$3,086	$81.72
Option 3	($693)	$5,307	$5,000	$307	$66.14

5. Option 2.
6. If Rubbermaid's income is more volatile, the firm should be more cautious in adding debt.
7. If the new debt or equity is used to take projects, the analysis would change for three reasons:

a. the projects may have a different risk profile than the firm's risk profile.
b. the NPV of the projects has to be added to the value change calculated.
c. the firm value itself will increase as the new debt and equity is issued.

8. I would factor in the firm's need for flexibility into the analysis—the greater the need for flexibility the less likely it is that I would add on debt. Further, I would look at how responsive managers are to stockholders; if they are not, I would be more likely to add debt.

9. The higher rating in Option 1 lowers the cost of debt, but it is accomplished by replacing debt with more expensive equity.

18-5 **1.** Yes.
2. WACC without the $100 million = 13.30%
WACC with the $100 million = 13.14%

18-11 **a.** 12.66%
b. 12.06%
c. $1.24
d. 41.93%

18-13 **a, b and c.**

Debt Ratio	D/E Ratio	Beta	Cost of Equity	Interest Rate	ROE	ROE-COE
0%	0.00%	0.68	10.76%	6.70%	18.29%	7.53%
10%	11.11%	0.73	11.03%	7.00%	19.81%	8.78%
20%	25.00%	0.79	11.37%	7.50%	21.64%	10.27%
30%	42.86%	0.87	11.81%	8.00%	23.90%	12.09%
40%	66.67%	0.98	12.39%	8.50%	26.79%	14.40%
50%	100.00%	1.13	13.21%	9.00%	30.72%	17.52%
60%	150.00%	1.35	14.43%	10.00%	35.97%	21.54%
70%	233.33%	1.72	16.47%	11.00%	44.27%	27.81%
80%	400.00%	2.46	20.54%	12.00%	60.23%	39.69%
90%	900.00%	4.68	32.76%	15.00%	95.12%	62.35%

d. Value of the firm might not be maximized at 90% debt, because the focus of this approach is to maximize equity value. To the degree that this can be accomplished by expropriating wealth from bondholders, this may not maximize firm value. It is also based upon the presumption that the ROA will be unaffected by the change in rating that accompany the higher debt ratio.

18-15 **a.** $700 million
b. 11.99%
c. $12.49%

18-17 **a.** $2,111 million
b. $2,214.41 million

18-19 **a.** Because Reebok has a high EBIT relative to firm value. If one adds back depreciation to this return, it is quite clear that at existing levels, Reebok has substantial cash flows to meet any debt payments, which in turn is pushing up the optimal debt ratio.
b. My primary concern with moving towards this optimal would lie in whether these operating cash flows are sustainable, given the volatility of the product market that Reebok serves.

3. $50.85
4. No. It is not a desirable project. Project has negative NPV.
5. This is now an acceptable project.

18-7 **a.** 50%
b. $22.55

18-9 **a.** 13.16%
b. 10% (pre-tax)
6% (after-tax)
c. 11.97%
d. 22.40%
e. 29.63%
f. 13.52%

18-21 **a.** 53.94%
b. 9.56%
c. Cost of Capital = 9.41%
New Value of Firm = $5,651
d. Assuming that the 1995 operating income is depressed would lead us to conclude that the true optional debt ratio would be higher than 30%.

18-23 **a.** $28,439
b. $34,443
c. If NYNEX Plans to enter the entertainment business, which is riskier and more profitable, it might have to user a lower optimal debt ratio to reflect the business risk.

18-25 It is true that the return on equity can be increased by borrowing money, since the after-tax cost of debt is likely to be lower than the return on assets (which is currently equal to the return on equity) of 12.75%. Borrowing money will also increase the cost of equity, however. The net effect will determine whether leverage will increase firm value. If the business risk of the firm is high (a high unlevered beta), then the increase in the cost of equity may exceed the increase in return on equity.

CHAPTER 19

19-1 a. **1.** It can borrow $1.15 billion and buy back stock.

2. It can borrow $1.15 billion and pay special dividends.

3. It can borrow more than $1.15 billion and take projects over time, in which case its optimal dollar debt will be higher.

b. From the viewpoint of the effect on equity, there is no difference between repurchasing

stock and paying a special dividend. There may be a tax difference to the recipient, since dividends and capital gains are taxed differently.

c. If BMD has a cash balance of $250 million, it can use this cash to buy back stock. BMD, therefore, needs to borrow only $1.025 billion to get 50%.

19-3 a. If the existing policy of paying $50 million in dividends is continued.

	Current	1	2	3	4	5
Debt	$5,000.00	$5,000.00	$5,000.00	$5,000.00	$5,000.00	$5,000.00
Equity	$5,000.00	$5,630.00	$6,330.09	$7,108.06	$7,972.58	$8,933.28
D/(D+E)	50.00%	47.04%	44.13%	41.29%	38.54%	35.89%
D/E	100.00%	88.81%	78.99%	70.34%	62.71%	55.97%
Dividends	$50.00	$50.00	$50.00	$50.00	$50.00	$50.00
Beta	1.20	1.15	1.11	1.07	1.03	1.00
Expected Return	13.60%	13.32%	13.08%	12.87%	12.68%	12.51%
Dividend Yield	1.00%	0.89%	0.79%	0.70%	0.63%	0.56%
Exp. Price App.	12.60%	12.43%	12.29%	12.16%	12.05%	11.95%

b. If the existing policy of paying $50 million in dividends is continued

	Current	1	2	3	4	5
Debt	$5,000.00	$5,000.00	$5,000.00	$5,000.00	$5,000.00	$5,000.00
Equity	$5,000.00	$5,680.00	$6,435.65	$7,275.37	$8,208.50	$9,245.45
D/(D+E)	50.00%	46.82%	43.72%	40.73%	37.85%	35.10%
D/E	100.00%	88.03%	77.69%	68.73%	60.91%	54.08%
Dividends	$ -	$ -	$ -	$ -	$ -	$ -
Beta	1.20	1.15	1.10	1.06	1.02	0.99
Expected Return	13.60%	13.30%	13.05%	12.83%	12.63%	12.46%
Dividend Yield	0.00%	0.00%	0.00%	0.00%	0.00%	0.00%
Exp. Price App	13.60%	13.30%	13.05%	12.83%	12.63%	12.46%

19-5 1. Are the projects short term or long term?
2. What is the pattern of cash flows on these projects?
3. Are these cash flows stable or volatile?
4. In what currency will these cash flows be?
5. What other factors (economy, industry-specific facts) affect cash flows?

19-7 a. 6.5 years
b. Change in Firm Value = 0.38 − 4.68 (GNP Growth). The t statistic on the slope coefficient is 1.15. While the regression suggests that the firm is countercyclical, the t statistic is not statistically significant.
c. The firm's value is unaffected by changes in exchange rates.
d. Change in Firm Value = 0.10 − 6.84 (Change in Inflation Rate).
Again, although the results suggest that the

firm's value is negatively affected by inflation, the t statistic is only 1.30.

e. On all of these regressions, there is considerable noise in the estimates. If the results from these regressions deviate significantly from industry averages, I would use the industry averages. In addition, if I knew that the firm was planning to enter into new businesses, I would factor these into my analysis.

19-9 When the regression analysis is done with both operating income and firm value as dependent variables, there might be different results from each because:

a. Operating income might be smoothed out, whereas firm value is not.

b. Firm value reflects changes not only in operating income but also in discount rates and expected future growth.

I would be more inclined to use firm value to measure duration and sensitivity to economic factors. I would use operating income to examine sensitivity to inflation, especially if floating rate debt is to be issued.

19-11 a. Since Upjohn is a potential takeover target, I would suggest moving to the optimal debt ratio quickly.

b. While the current return on equity is greater than the current cost of equity, the decline in the return on equity would suggest a greater emphasis on stock buybacks and dividends.

19-13 a. Given that firm value is negatively affected by changes in interest rates, and that the regression suggests that the duration of the debt should be 6.33 years, I would argue that Bethlehem Steel should have debt with a maturity greater than a year.

b. It might make sense, however, for Bethlehem Steel to use short-term debt to finance long-term projects, if

1. they believe that they are much less risky than the market assesses them to be (bond ratings, betas . . .)

2. they anticipate changing their business mix in the near future and entering different businesses.

3. they believe that they can forecast changes in the term structure better than other market participants

19-15 a. It can be argued that the slope coefficient is a measure of the duration of the assets owned by these firms; hence, it can determine the duration of the debt.

b. The slope coefficients are estimated with substantial noise; I would use the average across all six firms as my measure of duration for each of them.

19-17 I would argue for the issuance of convertible debt. This would allow for a low coupon rate and would ensure that the value of the debt will increase if the firm is doing well.

19-19 Given that cash flows move with inflation, I would use floating rate debt. One feature that ACM might consider adding on to its debt is a call option on a commodity—such as copper, zinc, or magnesium—that the company produces. This will reduce the interest rate that ACM will have to pay on the debt and tie cash flows on it much more directly to commodity prices.

19-21 I disagree. By using short-term debt to finance long-term projects, the CFO is exposing the firm to refinancing risk. If we factor in both this risk and the expected rates at which future debt will be raised (from the forward rates in the term structure), the expected cost on short-term debt, in the long term, should be equal to the expected cost of using long-term debt.

19-23 The decision on whether to use equity or warrants will depend upon the market's perception of the firm's volatility. If the market is overestimating the riskiness/volatility of the firm, issuing warrants may be preferable to issuing equity. If, on the other hand, it is underestimating the riskiness/volatility of the firm, issuing equity may be preferable.

CHAPTER 20

20-1 a. True
b. True
c. False

20-3 Cutting dividends may send a very negative signal to markets. When firms announce that they will be cutting dividends, markets assume the worst, that is, that the firm is in serious financial trouble, and the company's stock price usually drops sharply.

20-5 No. It does not apply to tax-exempt investors or to corporations.

20-7 An increase in dividends suggests to markets that the firm has the confidence that its future cash flows will be high enough to continue making these dividend payments. This confidence is the positive signal that might lead markets to increase their assessment of the firm's value. The

empirical evidence is supportive, with stock prices increasing on dividend increases.

20-9 41.67%

20-11 As a tax-exempt investor, you make returns based upon the difference between the price drop and the dividend. Consequently, you will make excess returns on the first two stocks. On both an absolute and percentage basis, NE Gas is your best bet.

20-13 $0.65

20-15 The stock price may react negatively. The dividend may signal that Microsoft's project choice is becoming less attractive, and this will have negative consequences for future growth and project returns. In addition, stockholders in Microsoft are likely to be oriented to capital gains and may not like the dividends.

20-17 The price reaction will be more muted. Since the 35 analysts following the firm are likely to dig up any "positive" information about the company, the dividend increase at the margin conveys less information than it would for a smaller firm.

20-19 I would expect the stock price reaction to be positive. The fact that RJR Nabisco was under stockholder pressure to begin with suggests that their assets were making below-market returns. Selling such assets would therefore be a positive action; returning the cash to stockholders would add to this reaction because it eliminates the chance that this cash will be invested in other poor projects.

20-21 It will motivate the managers to increase stock price as quickly as possible. To do so, they may seek to influence the board of directors to delay "regular" dividend increases or to forego a special dividend. To the extent that such actions may not be in the best interests of the firm's current clientele of shareholders, the resulting price increase may actually not be to the shareholders' best interests.

20-23 One of the major criticisms of the U.S. capital markets in recent years has been that U.S. investors are very short-term oriented, requiring firms to concentrate on similarly short-termed projects.

CHAPTER 21

21-1
  a. 20.83%
  b. FCFE 42.55%
  c. Accept projects A, C and E. The total investment is $ 490 million.
  d. Estimation of FCFE next year $337 million
  e. No, because of my concerns that I would not be able to maintain these dividends. I would also hold back some cash for future projects if I feel that investment needs could vary substantially over time.
  f. The cash balance will increase by $212 million.

21-3
  a. No.
  b. Yes. In this case, it's probably better to pay out higher dividends prior to the sale of the company.

21-5
  a. Project B.
  b. $66 million

21-7 $340.732 million

21-9 $160.95 million

21-11
  a. No, because its FCFE is negative (−10 million)
  b. By year 4.

21-13
  a.

Year	FCFE
1996	$324.39
1997	$360.31
1998	$400.08
1999	$444.12
2000	$492.86

  b. It will make me more conservative in paying out the entire amount in FCFE in the year in which I make it.

21-15 I would defend my decision by noting that I have a track record of great projects and that I am retaining the cash for future projects. My track record will probably make me credible, at least as long as I can keep my return on equity above my cost of equity.

21-17 The company will have a negative FCFE, since it will have to generate enough cash flows to make the principal payment of $100 million. If the company pays a dividend of $12 million, the cash balance will decrease by approximately $50 million.

21-19
  a. Black and Decker pays less in dividends than the average company in the sector.
  b. Black and Decker also has higher growth than the average company in the sector. Black & Decker's predicted payout ratio = 21.30%
Black & Decker's predicted dividend yield = 1.71%

21-21 No. I would expect, given the higher growth rate, that Handy and Harman will pay less in dividends than the average firm in the sector. The higher growth creates a greater reinvestment need.

CHAPTER 22

22-1 *Signaling effects:* A regular dividend should send out a stronger positive signal than either a special dividend or a stock buyback.

Tax Effects: A stock buyback may have less negative tax consequences for some investors in the stock than dividends.

Sustainability: A regular dividend presumes that the firm will have similar cash flows in the future to sustain the dividend.

22-3 Yes. The surplus could be used to buy back shares and reduce the number of shares outstanding. Then, the company can maintain its dividends per share and still lower total dividend payments. If the firm does not have attractive projects, this may be the optimal way to use the windfall.

22-5 **a.** No. The earnings per share will increase only if the return on assets exceeds the after-tax cost of borrowing.

b. No. The risk will increase as leverage increases and the stock price may go down even with higher EPS.

c. If the increase in earnings per share more than offsets the higher risk from increased leverage, the price will go up.

22-7 **a.** The firm should buy back shares. The net taxes paid, even by investors who sell, will be at the capital gains rate.

b. Corporations are exempt from having to pay taxes on 70% of the dividends they receive from other corporations. This may make dividends more attractive to them, relative to stock buybacks.

22-9 Forward contracts to buy equity are riskier than announcements of buybacks because they represent legal obligations to buy stock at a stated price. The firm does not have the option to back down.

22-11 No. The splitoff will not solve the problem because incumbent management (which is the problem) is still running the firm. I would recommend breaking up the firm and selling its component parts to outsiders, or a splitoff where incumbent management explicitly disavows control in the splitoff entities.

22-13 No. Given the preponderance of investment that is institutional investment and the fact that the price is only $50 (rather than $400 or $500), I do not believe that this action is going to increase the investor base for the company. While I would expect an initial positive reaction to the split, this increase will be sustained only if the firm follows up with positive news that confirms the signal sent by the split—that is, that higher earnings and stock prices will follow.

22-15 Existing stockholders will benefit in one of two ways. If they choose to sell their shares, they will also face lower commissions post-split. If they choose to keep their stock, they will benefit because the company will be able to raise new equity capital at a slightly lower rate than before (since the company can now offer a slightly lower premium for compensating new investors for transaction costs).

22-17 I would expect the stock price reaction to be negative. A stock dividend is a cosmetic event with no cash flows associated with it and cannot replace a cash dividend.

22-19 Spinning of the nonregulated businesses may relieve them of the burden of having to worry about the consequences of their actions for the regulated parent company. It will also allow them to set dividend and financing policy which is more consistent with their own interests.

22-21 The spin-off will add to the value of the firm only if the corporate costs are excessive or unnecessary and thus can be reduced or eliminated without hurting the divisional profitability. If, on the other hand, the corporate costs represent costs that would now have to be borne by the independent divisions, the spin-off should not increase value.

CHAPTER 23

23-1 **a.** False.
b. False.
c. False.
d. True.
e. True.

23-3 **a.** There will be an increase in the stable growth rate; the discount rate will also go up.

b. The stable growth rate will be higher, if the economy is growing faster.

c. The stable growth rate will not be affected, but the high growth period for this company will be longer.

d. Again the stable growth rate will be unaffected, but the high growth period and growth rate will be higher.

23-5 **a.** 13.5%
b. 58.76%

c. 0.95
d. $28.25
e. $18.47

Year	EPS	DPS	
1994	$1.70	$0.48	
1995	$1.93	$0.54	
1996	$2.19	$0.61	
1997	$2.49	$0.70	
1998	$2.83	$0.79	$28.25

Cost of Equity = 7% + 0.85 * 5.5% = 11.68%
PV of Dividends and Terminal Price (@ 11.68%) = $18.47

f. Value of Extraordinary Growth = $3.47
Value of Stable Growth = $7.79

23-7 **a.** $36.20
b. $50.20

c. The FCFE is greater than the dividends paid. The higher value from the model reflects the additional value from the cash accumulated in the firm. I would use the FCFE model, because it is a more realistic model.

23-9 a.

Year	FCFE
1	$1.57
2	$1.82
3	$2.11
4	$2.45
5	$2.83
6	$3.71

b. $61.32

c. $39.61

23-11 a. $13.14

b. It is impossible to say. Easier credit increases working capital needs (draining cash flows). It also, however, increases revenues. The net effect can be positive or negative.

c. WC as % of Revenue   Value Per Share

60%	$8.62
50%	$10.88
40%	$13.14
30%	$15.40
20%	$17.66

23-13 a. $734.80 million

b. $16,853 million

c. Value of Equity = $12,853 million
Value Per Share = $64.27 million

23-15 a. 11.56%

b. FCFE Terminal Value

$266	
$283	
$302	
$321	
$342	
$364	$5,014

$4,062 million

c. There might be potential for synergy, with an acquirer with related businesses. The health division at Kodak might also be mismanaged, creating the potential for additional value from better management.

23-17 a. Average = 13.2   Median = 12.25
[If firms are homogeneous, the average is a measure of market valuation]

b. This statement is likely to be true only if:

  1. Thiokol has the same growth prospects and risk profile of the typical firm in the industry. It also generates cash flows for disbursement as dividends which are similar to the typical firm in the industry.

  2. Thiokol has higher growth potential and/or lower risk than the typical firm in the industry.

c. The regression of P/E ratios on fundamentals yields the following:

$$P/E = -2.33 + 35.74 \text{ Growth Rate} + 11.97 \text{ Beta} + 2.90 \text{ Payout Ratio}$$
$$R2 = 0.4068$$

The following table provides predicted P/E ratios for the firms in the group:

	Actual P/E	Predicted P/E	Difference
Boeing	17.3	12.9	4.4
General Dynamics	15.5	17.9	−2.4
GM-Hughes	16.5	13.68	2.82
Grumman	11.4	12.07	-0.67
Lockheed Corp	10.2	12.31	−2.11
Logicon	12.4	13.17	-0.77
Loral Corporation	13.3	13.21	0.09
Martin Marietta	11	11.34	−0.34
McDonnell Douglas	22.6	17.15	5.45
Northrop	9.5	14.82	−5.32
Raytheon	12.1	10.85	1.25
Rockwell	13.9	14.85	−0.95
Thiokol	8.7	11.44	−2.74
United Industrial	10.4	9.11	1.29

Again, negative numbers indicate that the stock is undervalued. The problem with a regression like this one is that it has relatively few observations and is likely to be thrown off by a few extreme observations.

23-19 a. No. The average price/book value ratio of these firms is 1.66, based on the following:

  1. These firms have, on average, a lower growth rate than the firm being valued.

  2. The firm being valued has more free cash flows available for paying dividends than the average firm in the sector.

  3. The firm is unlevered. It should therefore have a lower beta.

b. On all three counts, a higher price/book value ratio should be used for this company.

23-21 No. One would explain its high price to sales ratio by pointing to the combination of a high profit margin and a moderate growth rate. Based on the regression, the predicted PS ratio would be 0.4955.

CHAPTER 24

24-1 a. Price up.
 b. Impossible to tell.
 c. Price down.
 d. Price down.
 e. No effect.

24-3 a. $31.20
 b. No. The value of Broderbund owes a great deal to the expected positive NPV of future projects. Hence, when Broderbund takes on a positive NPV project, it may be in line with market expectations and not affect the price.
 c. Yes. Here the price will drop.

24-5 a. 0.36
 b. 0.75
 c. Yes. Taking on riskier projects would have pushed up the beta of the firm, reducing the benefit of the higher ROE.

24-7 a. 7.26
 b. 9.96

24-9 a. 9.24%
 b. $1898 million
 c. New Firm Value = $1775 million
 New Equity Value = $1440 million
 d. Value of Firm at Old Debt Level = $1518
 Value of Firm at New Debt Level = $1478

24-11 a. *Long's Drug Store* = $18.59
 Walgreen = $17.33
 b. Long's = $19.54
 Walgreen = $16.46
 c. Long's = $15.60
 Walgreen = $17.33
 d. Companies that have good projects (high ROE) will generally gain by cutting back dividends, whereas companies with mediocre projects will gain by increasing them.

24-13 a. $4.22
 b. $4.98

24-15

Firm	EVA
AMR	$(233) billion
Alaska Air	$4 million
UAL	$(65) million

 b. The firms with positive EVA would be considered healthy. To the extent that EVA is negative for AMR and UAL, they are not creating value for their stockholders. Alaska Air, on the other hand, created value for their stockholders.
 c. The EVA provides a measure of the efficiency of use of existing assets. To the extent that Alaska Air has more growth expected, I would need to consider the quality of these projects as well.

24-17 So price should be equal to $12 * 2.18 = $26.16 It does not.[-Provide narrative reason why]

24-19 Walter's current management probably has a lot of experience in their core business and relatively little experience running a coal-mining company. To the extent that other parties will be better suited to manage the coal company once it's been spun off, shareholders will probably see their wealth increase.

24-21 Investors will be less likely to desire dividends over capital gains, so firms will tend to retain more earnings. Long-term, this will result in a gradual decrease in D/E ratios. Since firms will be financing a greater portion of their capital needs with equity instead of debt, and since equity tends to be more expensive than debt, the required rates of return (WACCs) for the firms will increase. Since ROCs will stay the same, EVAs (and share prices) will decrease.

CHAPTER 25

25-1 a. True.
 b. False.
 c. True.
 d. True.
 e. False.

25-3 Yes. The early 1980s were a period of rapid change for oil companies as we were just recovering from the effects of the oil embargo in the late 1970s. Similarly, changing societal views on smoking were rapidly changing the market for tobacco products in the late 1980s. Finally, rapid technological changes and a general tendency toward deregulation have affected both the media and financial services sectors in the first half of the 1990s.

25-5 Horizontal mergers. The accompanying increases in market power in such mergers are contrary to the government's stated desire to foster competitiveness.

25-7 $61 per share

25-9 $88.41.
 If American owns 4.95% of the outstanding shares (or 247,500 shares), then they need to buy the remaining 4,752,500 shares. The equity will be worth $435 million. However, American is now faced with the mutually exclusive choices of buying the remaining shares or selling their current stake. The best way to handle this is to realize that there is an opportunity cost to not selling the current stake, so the net

value of the remaining equity to American will be $420,147,000.

25-11 a. You will only sell your shares if you feel the takeover attempt will fail. If the attempt succeeds, each share will be worth $100, so you won't be willing to sell for $75. If it fails, each share will only be worth the current market price of $50.

b. This implies that tender offers will only succeed if everyone thinks they'll fail . . . but if everyone thinks they'll fail, then they'll succeed . . . but everyone should realize they'll succeed and, hence, hang on to their shares, etc. . . See the problem?

c. The underlying reason for the paradox above is that the bid price is lower than the post-takeover value per share. Normally, successful bid must be set *above* the expected value per share, so that shareholders who sell profit more than shareholders who don't. That way, enough shareholders will tender their shares. In fact, all shareholders will want to tender their shares, but in order for the bidders to make money on the deal, they also set a restriction on how many shares they will buy.

25-13 a. $7,540

b. $7,897

c. The equity investors should gain the additional value of $357 million.

25-15 $382.33 million

25-17 a. $714 million

b. $607.47 million

25-19 a. $12.65

b. $25.18

c. $41.94

25-21 a.

Year	FCFE	FCFF
1	($20,000)	$296,000
2	($168,800)	$325,600
3	($114,640)	$358,160
4	($57,224)	$393,976
5	$3,774	$433,374

b.

Year	Cost of Equity
2	23.11%
3	21.41%
4	19.95%
5	18.78%
6	17.85%

c. Terminal Value of Equity = $3,060,662
Terminal Value of Firm = $4,560,662

d. The deal does not make sense from the viewpoint of equity investors. Overall, the deal does not make sense.

CHAPTER 26

26-1 a. 0.09918519

b. 0.07567462

c. 0.08513395

26-3 a. 0.86231884

b. I would sell the forward contract and borrow Swiss francs.

26-5

Country	Expected Spot Exchange Rate
Canada	$0.7261
France	$0.2090
Germany	$0.7172
Italy	$0.0569
Japan	$1.0156
UK	$1.5353
United States 1 0.05	

b. The inflation rates may be different from anticipated. There might also be trading noise and speculation that causes the actual exchange rates to vary from expected rates.

26-7 Yes. It does not mean, however, that they should demand a premium for these risks. It is possible that this risk, if allowed to flow through to the firm's investors, may be diversifiable risk. It should then not affect discount rates or project choice. Alternatively, if the investors are unable to diversify this risk, the exchange rate and political risk should be factored into the analysis.

26-9 a.

Year	CF ($)
0	$(188.24)
1	$(86.55)
2	$(99.50)
3	$13.73
4	$25.25
5	$38.69
6	$46.26
7	$52.36
8	$54.17
9	$55.35
10	$56.00
11	$56.65
12	$57.30
13	$57.97
14	$58.66
15	$59.34

b. Cost of capital of 11.5% (in dollar terms).

c. $(115.30)

d. It should not matter. If the discount rate is also in Yuan, the net present value should be the same.

26-11 No.

26-13 The importing country's currency is likely to weaken against the exporting country's currency. The exporting country will wind up with a large supply of capital, so the cost of capital (the interest rate) will go down. Similarly, the importing country will have a decrease in supply of capital, driving interest rates up. In terms of the formula for the international Fisher effect, the numerator will increase while the denominator decreases, resulting in an increase in the amount of domestic currency necessary to purchase one unit of the foreign currency.

26-15 Yes. The daily mark-to-market feature of futures means that the counterparty at a disadvantage is more likely to pay up (because he gains the chance to gain back his losses if spot prices reverse, paying a relatively small amount to do so). Counterparties to forwards, on the other hand, have more incentive to default when they're "losers" because there's no remaining length of the contract for them to lose (forwards only settle up at maturity) and because the loser has to pay up the losses in one large lump sum.

26-17 $1.538/£

26-19 DM 1.54499/$

CHAPTER 27

27-1
a. False.
b. True.
c. True.
d. False.
e. True.
f. True.
g. False.
h. True.
i. True.
j. False.

27-3
a. $4.42
b. Buy 0.4919 Shares of Stock (this is N(d1) from the model) and borrow $K e^{-rt} N(d2) = 85 \exp^{-(0.038)(0.25)} (0.4324) = \$36.40$
c. 0.2739
d.

e. $5.62

27-5
a. First value the three-month call, as above: Value of Call = $0.64

Then, value a call to the first (and only) dividend payment: Value of Call = $0.51

Since the value of the three-month call is higher, there is no anticipated exercise.

b. If the dividend payment is large enough, it may pay to exercise the call just before the ex-dividend day (before the stock price drops) rather than wait until expiration. This early exercise is more likely for call options: (a) the larger the dividend on the stock, and (b) the closer the option is to expiration.

27-7
a. $0.93 (without dilution adjustment)
$0.80 (without dilution adjustment)

b. Dilution increases the number of shares outstanding. For any given value of equity, each share is worth less.

27-9 $51.20

27-11 A put option with a strike price of $100 (the current market price) would insure you against price declines. If the stock price does drop below $100, you exercise the put, getting $100 per share. If the share price climbs above $100, you let the put expire unexercised.

27-13 This statement is arguably true. Suppose you expect the price of a particular stock to go up. You could simply buy calls in the stock and then wait for the increase, but doing so would require a cash outlay today to purchase the calls in return for the expectation of a cash inflow in the future. If you really think that the stock is going to go up, you might as well show the courage of your convictions by partially financing purchase of the calls by selling puts. Note, however, that doing so exposes you to much more risk; if all you own is the call and the stock price goes down, you're simply out the price you paid for the call, but if you have sold a put and prices go down then you're out not only the call price but also the difference between the strike price on the puts and the new (lower) market price.

27-15 Yes. If the exercise date is early enough in the next tax year that there is very small chance that the stock price will go back up, the option holder might choose to exercise early if getting the tax shelter of the loss on the purchase today has a greater PV than getting a tax shelter from the unexercised option on next year's taxes.

27-17 $2.01

27-19 Using the same inputs to call formula as in the previous problem, the call will have a theoretical price of $7.52. You will then expect to make ($61−$24) − $5.65 + $7.52 = $38.87

per share. This does, however, increase your risk substantially. If the price goes up you will have to buy shares at S > $61 and sell them at $61, so you will lose money.

CHAPTER 28

28-1 A futures contract imposes an obligation on both the buyer and the seller of the contract to carry out the contract. An options contract provides the buyer with a right, which he or she can choose to exercise.

28-3 The conversion option in a convertible bond is linked to the underlying bond, that is, if the con-

28-5 $62.38

28-7 $36,200

28-9 **a.** True.

b. False.

c. True.

version option is exercised the underlying bond ceases to exist. In contrast, a warrant is a self-standing security. Exercising a warrant does not affect any other security.

28-11

Equity holders	Bondholders
1. Equity holders own the firm.	**1.** Bondholders are owed $500 million in interest and principal.
2. Equity holders owe $500 million in interest and principal to bondholders.	**2.** Bondholders have sold a put option on the firm with an exercise price of $500 million to the equity holders to the equity holders.
3. Equity holders own a put option on the firm with an exercise price of $500 million.	

28-13 **a.** $309,755

b. $828,674

c. The latter considers the option characteristics of owning the mine, that is, that copper prices may go up, and is higher.

28-15 **a.** $50 million

b. $68.68

c. The latter captures the value of delaying the project. The difference between the two values will increase as the variance in the project cash flows increases.

28-17 **a.** False.

b. True.

c. False.

d. False.

e. True.

28-19 **a.** Conversion Ratio = 30 shares/bond
Conversion Price = $27

b. Conversion Premium = $367

c. $607.27

28-21 **a.** False.

b. True.

c. True.

d. False.

CHAPTER 29

29-1 The duration of a zero-coupon bond will always be equal to it's maturity. With a zero-coupon bond, all cash flows come at the same horizon (the maturity date) so the weighted average is equal to the maturity.

29-3 A swaption would allow the company to enter into the swap agreement if the unfavorable events occurred (e.g., if the exchange rates changed to their disadvantage) but would also allow them the flexibility of foregoing the swap

if favorable exchange rates or interest rates came about.

29-5 It is possible that the high-quality firm might have more information about the low-quality firm than the market does.

29-7 The risk that will be diversified in an acquisition is firm-specific risk. Stockholders can do it themselves without having to pay the premium that the firm has to.

29-9   Yes. Enter into a fixed-fixed swap with a foreign counterparty and an interest rate swap with a domestic counterparty. Then give the domestic counterparty the payments from the foreign counterparty.

29-11   −7.58%

29-13   −$71.90. This is much closer to the exact change of −7.21% noted in the previous problem.

29-15   **a.**   I would estimate the effect of interest rate changes (risk) on firm value. This will give me a measure of the need for risk management.

  b.   Simulations are dependent upon the underlying models used to arrive at the results. In particular, the relationship between interest rates and value in this case are determined by the valuation model used. In addition, the probability distribution for interest rate changes is based upon past data. Flaws in either of these assumptions may cause the results of the simulation to be skewed.

29-17   **a.**   The results of the regression are as follows:% Change in Stock Prices = 0.20 − 15.99 (Change in Long Bond Rate):Very negatively affected by increases in interest rates.

% Change in Stock Prices = 0.16 − 13.42 (Change in Inflation Rate): negatively affected by higher inflation.

% Change in Stock Prices = 0.25+0.89 (Change in Exchange Rate): Exchange rates do not seem to impact stock prices much.

  b.   The exposure of Ford's equity to these risk sources might be different from the exposure of Ford as a firm to the same risk sources because the exposure of Ford's debt to these same sources may be different from that of its equity. (The only condition under which the equity and firm exposures will be similar is if the value of debt moves with the value of the firm.

29-19   **a.**   Forward contracts provide the most complete protection because they can be tailored to a firm's precise needs.

  b.   Option contracts provide downside protection while preserving upside potential. They are also more expensive.

CHAPTER 30

30-1   It will still be I.

30-3   There are conceivably projects where depreciating the required capital equipment would result in a "reject" decision while expensing it would yield an "accept" decision. Let's call them "marginal" projects. A large company will undoubtedly take advantage of the exclusion just as a small company will, but it will most likely use this on the capital investment required for one of its "big" projects, not a marginal project. Even if it does invest in marginal projects, it will only find it wealth-enhancing to invest in a limited number of them (i.e., the number it can invest in before the exclusion runs out). Effectively, this exclusion serves to "reserve" the marginal projects for small firms, so that they have a group of projects that they can invest in which are "protected" from competition from large firms.

30-5   Publicly traded firms are required to publicly disclose their financial statements. Since they have to do so whether or not they issue bonds, the associated costs are "sunk" costs and shouldn't figure into the cost of issuing bonds. Private firms, on the other hand, are not required to publicly release their financial statements, so the cost of doing so in order to sell bonds is sizable. On the other hand, if a private firm borrows money

from a bank, it doesn't face these sizable costs associated with public disclosure.

30-7   **a.**   The publicly traded firm will assign a higher value to the project if it treats a substantial portion of the risk in the project as diversifiable (to its investors) and thus ignores it in analysis.

  b.   The private firm will assign a higher value to the project if the bulk of the risk on the project is market risk (and affect both the private and public firms) and the private firm is more efficient, leading to lower costs and higher operating profits.

30-9   **a.**   No. All debt is not dangerous; if the firm has enough cash flows to make debt payments comfortably even in the event of a downturn, the firm may gain from borrowing money and using these funds for projects.

  b.   I would not however recommend moving all the way to the optimal. Private firms are more exposed to bankruptcy risk, agency costs (which will show up as stricter covenants), and they do need flexibility more than large publicly traded firms since they cannot access financial markets. For all these reasons, they might want to borrow less than the optimal.

30-11 **a.** True.
b. True.
c. False.
d. True.

30-13 **a.** $841,137
b. $904,878

CHAPTER 31

31-1 **a.** The stock price is determined by expectations. If the earnings did not increase as much as expected, the stock price can go down.
b. If the management is responsible for the reduction in earnings growth—it should be held accountable for the price drop.

31-3 **a.** Cost of Equity = 12.05%
Cost of Capital = 10.16%
b. Yes.
c. Yes. I would now reject the project.

31-5 **a.** If it is under bankruptcy threat, it should try to reduce its debt ratio quickly.
b. If the firm is not under bankruptcy threat and if the default risk does not affect operations, it can afford to pay down the debt gradually.

31-7 **a.** 16%
b. $41.30
c. $28.93
d. The value would go up. The expected growth rate would be 19.2% during the high growth period.
e. Both the expected growth rate and the beta will increase during the high growth period.
f. Expected growth rate and terminal price would be lower.

31-9 Net income will not be an appropriate measure of cash flows to the firm when
a. there is leverage; net income is an equity measure
b. there are net capital expenditures, which reduce cash flows
c. there are working capital investments to be made.

31-11 If debt is underutilized, the cost of capital will be higher than it should be and the firm value will be lower. From a practical standpoint, this firm may also have trouble raising funds to finance projects because of its dependence on internal equity. (Firms are reluctant to use new stock issues.) If debt is overutilized, the firm runs the risk of bankruptcy and its associated costs.

31-13 When the firm has not changed substantially—either in terms of business or financial risk—during the course of the period of the regression, historical data can be used to estimate betas. It is not appropriate if it has changed its business or financial mix during the period.

Index